HUMAN RESOURCE MANAGEMENT

Visit the *Human Resource Management*, eighth edition, Companion Website at **www.pearsoned.co.uk/torrington** to find valuable **student** learning material including:

- Brand new video case studies featuring a range of well-known organisations.
- Over 250 multiple choice questions to test your understanding with Grade Tracker function to test your learning and monitor your progress.
- Extra assignments and exercises.
- Extensive links to valuable resources on the web.
- Flashcards to help you learn and revise.
- An online glossary to explain key terms.

Eighth Edition

HUMAN RESOURCE MANAGEMENT

Derek Torrington

Laura Hall

Stephen Taylor

Carol Atkinson

Financial Times Prentice Hall is an imprint of

Harlow, England • London • New York • Boston • San Francisco • Toronto
Sydney • Tokyo • Singapore • Hong Kong • Seoul • Taipei • New Delhi
Cape Town • Madrid • Mexico City • Amsterdam • Munich • Paris • Milan

Pearson Education Limited
Edinburgh Gate
Harlow
Essex CM20 2JE
England

and Associated Companies throughout the world

Visit us on the World Wide Web at:
www.pearsoned.co.uk

First published in Great Britain under the Prentice Hall Europe imprint in 1987
Second edition published in 1991
Third edition published 1995
Fourth edition published 1998
Fifth edition published 2002
Sixth edition published 2005
Seventh edition published 2008
Eighth edition published 2011

ISBN: 978-0-273-73232-7

British Library Cataloguing-in-Publication Data
A catalogue record for this book is available from the British Library

Library of Congress Cataloging-in-Publication Data
Human resource management / Derek Torrington . . . [et al.]. – 8th ed.
p. cm.
Rev. ed. of: Human resource management / Derek Torrington, Laura Hall, Stephen Taylor. 7th ed. 2008.
Includes bibliographical references and index.
ISBN 978-0-273-73232-7
1. Personnel management. I. Torrington, Derek, 1931- Human resource management.
HF5549.T675 2011
658.3–dc22

2010036348

10 9 8 7 6 5 4 3 2 1
15 14 13 12 11

Typeset in 10/12.5pt Sabon by 35
Printed and bound by Rotolito

Brief contents

Supporting resources

Visit **www.pearsoned.co.uk/torrington** to find valuable online resources:

Companion Website for students:

- Brand new video case studies featuring a range of well-known organisations.
- Over 250 multiple choice questions to test your understanding with Grade Tracker function to test your learning and monitor your progress.
- Extra assignments and exercises.
- Extensive links to valuable resources on the web.
- Flashcards to help you learn and revise.
- An online glossary to explain key terms.

For instructors:

- Complete, downloadable Instructor's Manual.
- Over 1,000 PowerPoint slides that can be downloaded and used for presentations.
- Testbank of question material.

Also: The Companion Website provides the following features:

- Search tool to help locate specific items of content.
- E-mail results and profile tools to send results of quizzes to instructors.
- Online help and support to assist with website usage and troubleshooting.

For more information please contact your local Pearson Education sales representative or visit **www.pearsoned.co.uk/torrington**.

Pearson Custom publishing

Our Custom publishing programme allows academics to pick and choose content from one or more Pearson Education texts for their course and combine it into a definitive course text.

Here are some common examples of Custom solutions which have helped over 500 courses across Europe:

- Different chapters from across our publishing imprints combined into one book
- Lecturer's own material combined together with textbook chapters or published in a separate booklet
- Third party cases and articles that you are keen for your students to read as part of the course
- Or any combination of the above

The Pearson Education Custom text published for your course is professionally produced and bound- just as you would expect from a normal Pearson Education text. You can even choose your own cover design and add your university logo. Since many of our titles have online resources accompanying them we can even build a Custom website that matches your course text.

Whatever your choice, our dedicated Editorial and Production teams will work with you throughout the process, right until you receive a copy of your Custom text.

Some lecturers teaching *Human Resource Management* have found that the flexibility of Custom publishing has allowed them to include additional material on certain aspects of their course.

To give you an idea of combinations which have proved popular, here is a list of subject areas in which Pearson Education publish one or more key texts that could provide extra chapters to match the emphasis of your course:

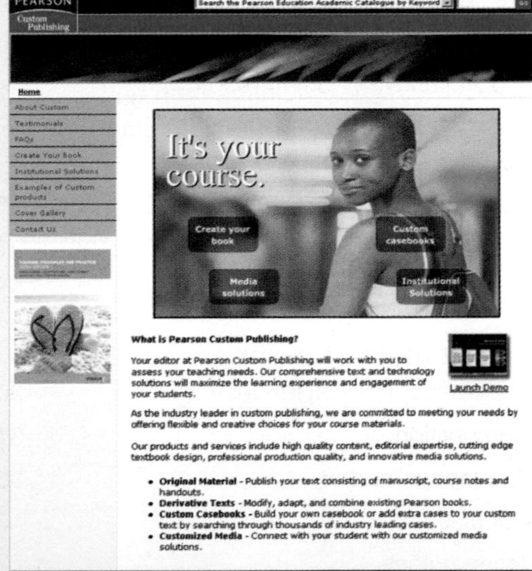

- Human Resource Management
- Employment/Industrial Relations
- Human Resource Development
- Human Resource Strategy
- Organisational Behaviour
- Leadership and Change Management
- Management Skills

For more details on any of these books or to browse other material from our entire portfolio, please visit: **www.pearsoned.co.uk**

If, once you have had time to review this title, you feel Custom publishing might benefit you and your course, please do get in contact. However minor, or major the change – we can help you out.

You can contact us at: **www.pearsoncustom.co.uk**
or via your local representative at: **www.pearsoned.co.uk/replocator**

Contents

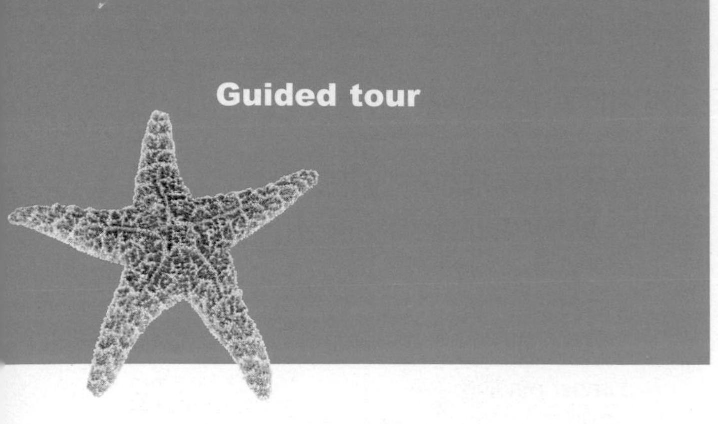

Guided tour

CHAPTER 7

RECRUITMENT

THE OBJECTIVES OF THIS CHAPTER ARE TO:

1 Identify alternative courses of action to take when an employee leaves an organisation
2 Explain the role played by job descriptions, person specifications and competencies in the recruitment process
3 Compare and contrast the major alternative recruitment methods
4 Assess developments in recruitment advertising and online recruitment
5 Explore the concept of employer branding
6 Clarify the need for control and evaluation procedures in recruitment
7 Assess different approaches to shortlisting

Learning objectives enable you to focus on what you should have learnt by the end of the chapter.

Chapter 7 Recruitment

of talented applicants. Making out that the experience of working in a role is more interesting or exciting than it really is may be ultimately counterproductive because it raises unrealistic expectations which can damage the psychological contract established with the organisation. This can lead to demotivation and, perhaps, an early resignation. You will find further information and discussion exercises about realistic recruitment in Case 7.1 on our companion website **www.pearsoned.co.uk/torrington.**

DETERMINING THE VACANCY

The first questions to be answered in recruitment are: Is there a vacancy? Is it to be filled by a newly recruited employee? Potential vacancies occur either through someone leaving, as a result of expansion or organisational change requiring new skills. When a person leaves, there is no more than a prima facie case for filling the vacancy thus caused. There may be other ways of filling the gap. Vacancies caused by expansion may be real or imagined. The desperately pressing need of an executive for an assistant may be a plea more for recognition than for assistance. The creation of a new post to deal with a specialist activity may be more appropriately handled by contracting that activity out to a supplier. Recruiting a new employee may be the most obvious tactic when a vacancy occurs, but it is not necessarily the most appropriate. This is clearly the case in periods of economic turmoil, when many employers may wish to think more creatively about how to deal with a vacancy. Listed below are some of the options, several of which we discuss in Chapter 4:

- Reorganise the work
- Use overtime
- Mechanise the work
- Stagger the hours
- Make the job part time
- Subcontract the work
- Use an agency

ACTIVITY 7.1

Can you think of further ways of avoiding filling a vacancy by recruiting a new employee? What are the advantages and disadvantages of the methods you have thought of? For what types of job with which you are familiar would each of your methods, and those listed above, be most appropriate?

If your decision is that you are going to recruit, there are four questions to determine the vacancy:

1 What does the job consist of?
2 In what way is it to be different from the job done by the previous incumbent?
3 What are the aspects of the job that specify the type of candidate?
4 What are the key aspects of the job that the ideal candidate wants to know before deciding to apply?

159

Activity boxes allow you to review and apply your learning at regular intervals throughout the text.

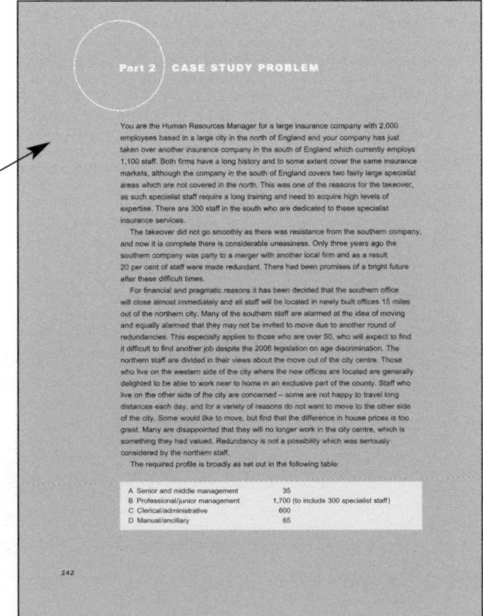

Part 2 CASE STUDY PROBLEM

You are the Human Resources Manager for a large insurance company with 2,000 employees based in a large city in the north of England and your company has just taken over another insurance company in the south of England which currently employs 1,100 staff. Both firms have a long history and to some extent cover the same insurance markets, although the company in the south of England covers two fairly large specialist areas which are not covered in the north. This was one of the reasons for the takeover, as such specialist staff require a long training and need to acquire high levels of expertise. There are 300 staff in the south who are dedicated to these specialist insurance services.

The takeover did not go smoothly as there was resistance from the southern company, and now it is complete there is considerable uneasiness. Only three years ago the southern company was party to a merger with another local firm and as a result 20 per cent of staff were made redundant. There had been promises of a bright future after these difficult times.

For financial and pragmatic reasons it has been decided that the southern office will close almost immediately and all staff will be located in newly built offices 15 miles out of the northern city. Many of the southern staff are alarmed at the idea of moving and equally alarmed that they may not be invited to move due to another round of redundancies. This especially applies to those who are over 50, who will expect to find it difficult to find another job despite the 2006 legislation on age discrimination. The northern staff are divided in their views about the move out of the city centre. Those who live on the western side of the city where the new offices are located are generally delighted to be able to work near to home in an exclusive part of the county. Staff who live on the other side of the city are concerned – some are not happy to travel long distances each day, and for a variety of reasons do not want to move to the other side of the city. Some would like to move, but find that the difference in house prices is too great. Many are disappointed that they will no longer work in the city centre, which is something they had valued. Redundancy is not a possibility which was seriously considered by the northern staff.

The required profile is broadly as set out in the following table:

A Senior and middle management	35
B Professional/junior management	1,700 (to include 300 specialist staff)
C Clerical/administrative	600
D Manual/ancillary	65

242

Case study problems at the end of each part help consolidate your learning of major themes by applying them to real-life examples.

Follow the **Web icon** in the margin of the text to find a range of resources on the website **(www.pearsoned.co.uk/torrington)** which will help you to check your understanding of key topics.

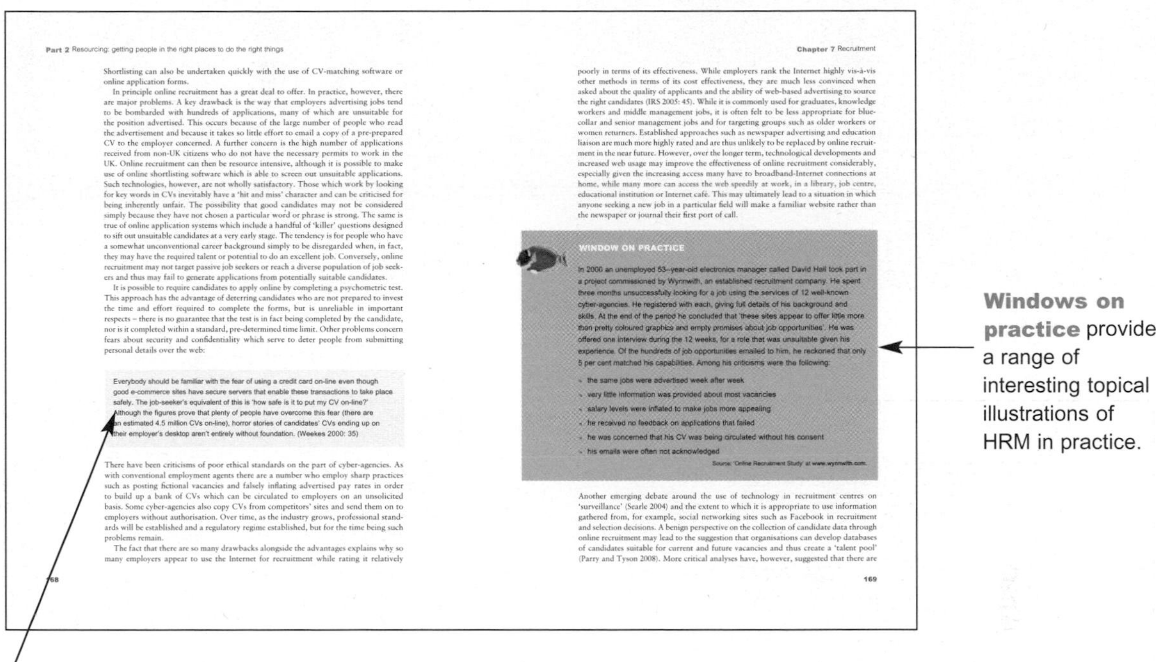

Windows on practice provide a range of interesting topical illustrations of HRM in practice.

The book is full of **quotes** which relate to the chapter and help to contextualise your learning.

Each chapter comes with a comprehensive list of **References** to help you take your learning further.

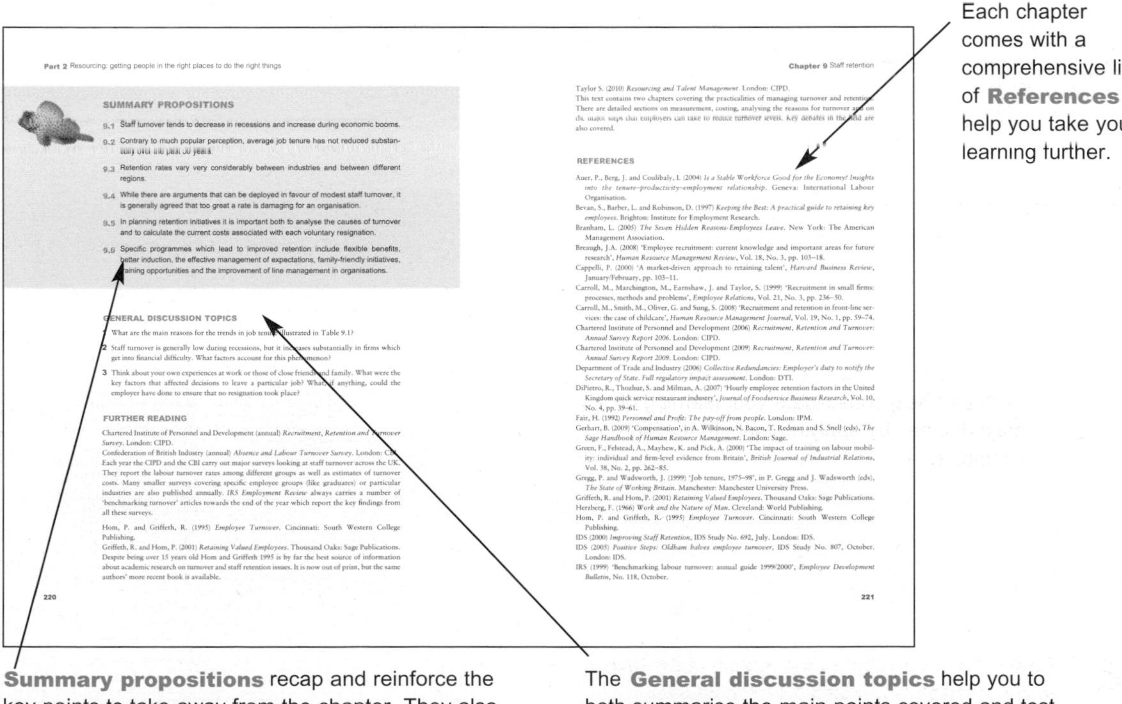

Summary propositions recap and reinforce the key points to take away from the chapter. They also provide a useful revision tool.

The **General discussion topics** help you to both summarise the main points covered and test your understanding of them.

Preface

This book has been through many editions in 30 years, and it has steadily evolved in line with the development of the personnel/HR function and the changing mix of students studying the subject. Since the last edition the world has undergone a major recession, triggered by a banking crisis unprecedented in modern times. This has created great uncertainty about how HRM will be changed and a series of spurious new solutions.

In preparing for this edition the authors have spent endless hours in analysing trends, reviewing the changes and examining all the novelties before discussing these among ourselves to formulate the changes needed to ensure that the book continues to reflect the reality of working life as it is evolving rather than speculating about what might be. We also have to ensure that the book makes sense to readers in different parts of the world and to those with differing experience (or without experience) of employment.

The result of this is to maintain the central parts of the book as before, although with considerable reworking and updating of individual chapters. The main changes are:

a Part 1 has been expanded from four chapters to six in order to enlarge our review of the main current changes in the context within which HRM operates.

b The first chapter in each of Parts 2–6 in recent editions has been entitled 'The strategic aspects of . . .' (resourcing, pay, etc.). We have now removed those chapters so that strategic aspects are continually treated as part of all the more specific activities covered.

c Part 7, previously called 'Emerging issues' has been re-titled 'Contemporary issues' as so many of the topics seem to be constant or re-emerging!

d Skills, that were previously set at the end of each Part, have now been collected together in Part 8 and expanded beyond the original group of face-to-face skills.

e A new chapter, 'Organisation design and flexibility', has been added to Part 1. The topic of organisational design was a regular feature of the book until being dropped – with some misgivings – for the sixth and seventh editions because a number of our reviewers said it was taught by different subject groupings in their departments. The Chartered Institute of Personnel and Development (CIPD) is reflecting a revival of interest in the subject in conjunction with the issue of flexibility.

Part of the book's strategy has always been to keep it as an authored rather than edited text. We hope this maintains a reasonable level of consistency across all chapters in terms of ideas, understanding, integration of the material and of style. To ensure effective coverage of the rapidly expanding and diversifying field of contemporary HRM, we asked Carol Atkinson to join all our discussions for the last edition and she now joins us as a full member of the author team.

There is a range of assessment material and illustrations, as well as several design features to assist readers further in using and learning from the text; these include:

a Integrated **Window on practice boxes** provide a range of illustrative material throughout the text, including examples of real company practice, survey results, anecdotes and quotations, and court cases.

b Integrated **Activity boxes** encourage readers to review and critically apply their understanding at regular intervals throughout the text, either by responding to a question or by undertaking a small practical assignment, individually or as part of a group. In recognition that this text is used on both professional and academic courses, most of the exercises reflect the fact that many students will have little or no business experience. Others may appear to exclude students who are not in employment by asking readers to consider an aspect in their own organisation; however, the organisation could be a college or university, the students' union, a political body or sports team.

c **Discussion topics**: at the end of each chapter there are two or three short questions intended for general discussion in a tutorial or study group.

e **Case study problems**: at the end of each Part we have included one short case study with several questions to enable readers to review, link and apply their understanding of the previous chapters to a business scenario.

f **Web links** are given as appropriate at various points in the text. These are either to the text's companion website, where there is a great deal of further material, or to other websites containing useful information relating to the topics covered.

g **Annotated readings** for each chapter suggest further relevant readings, with guidance on their value.

h Each Part of the text includes **a brief introduction** to its scope and purpose.

i **Chapter objectives** to open and **Summary propositions** to conclude each chapter set up the readers' expectations and review their understanding progressively.

j There are full **References** at the end of each chapter to aid further exploration of the chapter material, as required.

l **Website**: **www.pearsoned.co.uk/torrington** has more material, including further case studies or exercises for each chapter and support for both tutor and student.

m **Glossary.** The book closes with a short glossary of terms taken selectively from the text.

n **The honeycomb.** As a way of expressing the essential unity and interdependence of the disparate elements of HRM, we use the image of the honeycomb, made up of six-sided cells adjoining each other in a hive. These represent the six major parts of the HR contribution embedded in the hive of the employing organisation around the central core of contemporary issues. That is as far as our metaphor reaches; there are no references to pollen, or fertilisation or honey, and certainly none to queens or drones. The intellectual flaw is that there is no place for a skills cell, which is inappropriately outside but see how we deal with that when you get to Part VIII.

Figure P.1 The honeycomb of HRM

Acknowledgements

We are grateful to the following for permission to reproduce copyright material:

Figures

Figure 2.2 from *Labour Force Survey*, www.statisticsgov.uk, Crown Copyright material is reproduced with the permission of the Controller, Office of Public Sector Information (OPSI); Figure 3.2 from *Strategic Human Resource Management*, John Wiley & Sons, Inc. (Fombrun, C., Tichy, N.M. and Devanna, M.A. 1984), p. 41, reproduced with permission of John Wiley & Sons, Inc.; Figures 4.1 and 4.2 from *Smart Working: The impact of work organisation and job design*, CIPD (2008), with the permission of the publisher, the Chartered Institute of Personnel and Development, London (www.cipd.co.uk); Figure 4.3 from 'Manpower strategies for flexible organisations', *Personnel Management*, August (Atkinson, J. 1984); Figure 5.1 from 'The fall and rise of strategic planning', *Harvard Business Review* (Mintzberg, H. 1994); Figure 7.2 from 'Research on employee recruitment: so many studies, so many remaining questions', *Journal of Management*, Vol. 26, No. 3 (Breaugh, J. and Starke, M. 2000), reprinted by permission of Sage Publications; Figure 9.1 from *Personnel and Profit: The pay-off from people*, IPM (Fair, H. 1992), p. 41; Figure 11.1 from 'Front-line managers as agents in the HRM performance causal chain: theory, analysis and evidence', *Human Resource Management Journal*, Vol. 17, No. 1, pp. 3–20 (Purcell, J. and Hutchinson, S. 2007), reproduced with permission of Wiley-Blackwell; Figure 11.2 from *Understanding the People Performance Link: Unlocking the black box*, Research Report, CIPD (Purcell, J., Kinnie, N., Hutchinson, S., Rayton, B. and Swart, J. 2003), with the permission of the publisher, the Chartered Institute of Personnel and Development, London (www.cipd.co.uk); Figure 11.3 from 'Employees and high-performance work systems: testing inside the black box', *British Journal of Industrial Relations*, Vol. 38, No. 4, p. 506 (Ramsay, H., Scholarios, D. and Harley, B. 2000), reproduced with permission of Wiley-Blackwell; Figure 12.1 from *Performance Management in Action: Current trends and practice*, CIPD (2009), with the permission of the publisher, the Chartered Institute of Personnel and Development, London, (www.cipd.co.uk); Figure 14.1 from *Managing Employee Absenteeism*, American Psychological Association (Rhodes, S. and Steers, R. 1990); Figure 15.1 from *Leaning into the Future: Changing the way people change organizations*, Nicholas Brealey Publications (Binney, G. and Williams, C. 1995), p. 317; Figure 16.2 from 'Measuring organisational learning capability among the workforce', *International Journal of Manpower*, Vol. 28, No. 3/4, p. 227 (Chiva, R., Alegre, J. and Lapiedra, R. 2007), © Emerald Group Publishing Limited, all rights reserved; Figure 19.1 from *Managing Human Resources: Personnel management in transition*, 4th edn, Blackwell (Bach, S. (ed.) 2005), p. 401, Figure 15.1.

Tables

Table 2.1 from the Office for National Statistics, Crown Copyright material is reproduced with the permission of the Controller, Office of Public Sector Information (OPSI); Tables 2.2 and 2.3 from *Labour Force Survey Statistics*, www.statistics.gov.uk, Crown Copyright material is reproduced with the permission of the Controller, Office of Public Sector Information (OPSI); Table 3.1 from 'Linking competitive strategies with human resource management practices', *Academy of Management Executive*, No. 3, August (Schuler, R.S. and Jackson, S.E. 1987), Academy of Management; Table 4.1 from 'Organisational learning and organisational design', *The Learning Organization*, Vol. 13, No. 1, pp. 25–48 (Curado, C. 2006), © Emerald Group Publishing Limited, all rights reserved; Table 7.2 from Labour Market Trends (2002) *Labour Market Spotlight*, August, Crown Copyright material is reproduced with the permission of the Controller, Office of Public Sector Information (OPSI); Table 8.1 from *Recruitment, Retention and Turnover: Annual Survey Report 2009*, with the permission of the publisher, the Chartered Institute of Personnel and Development, London (www.cipd.co.uk); Table 13.3 from 'Leadership that gets results', *Harvard Business Review*, March–April, pp. 80 and 82–3 (Goleman, D. 2000); Table 30.1 from *What's Happening with Wellbeing at Work?*, CIPD (2007), with the permission of the publisher, the Chartered Institute of Personnel and Development, London (www.cipd.co.uk).

In some instances we have been unable to trace the owners of copyright material, and we would appreciate any information that would enable us to do so.

HUMAN RESOURCE MANAGEMENT IN CHANGING TIMES

Peter Drucker was one of the giants in the development of management thinking. Some observers even gave him credit as being the man who invented management, and he was one of the most influential thinkers in the field throughout the last half of the twentieth century. In 1954 he described human resource management, or personnel management as it was then known, as a glorified filing job made up of bits and pieces without a clear identity and purpose. This stigma hung round personnel and HR until quite recently. For this reason we are keen to demonstrate the interconnectedness of the discipline to which we are introducing you. We choose the metaphor of the honeycomb, a tight structure of contiguous cells of activity with a shared purpose. In HR training and development is not a distinct activity from employee relations and performance management; reward is not to be considered separately from selection, retention, diversity and health and well-being.

Part 1 puts in place the totality of HRM in two ways. First comes the nature of HRM itself and the context within which it has to operate: it is a specialism which is everywhere and in everything. Second, we introduce two of the methods which HR uses and needs to understand in all of its dealings within the business of which it is a part. 'Organisation' is a term often used to describe the entity within which people are employed, but its other meaning is the process of making the right things happen. Readers will remember the disastrous earthquake in Haiti at the beginning of 2010. For the first week afterwards there was intense interest and worldwide concern. Public donations poured in, rescue teams and equipment were mustered and there was a universal will to help, but there was no viable organisation on the ground. Growing resources, personnel and motivation were mired in chaos. Only as a form of organisation was gradually developed did things begin to improve. HR people need to understand the differing nature of organisational entities and the organising processes that are needed within them. The other method is planning, which will be the next phase of making things happen by calculating demand and supply, and how gaps may be filled. The final chapter is putting in place an international perspective for HR, so that our understanding and activity are not limited to the parochial or national, but think internationally or even globally.

Part 1 closes with a short case study to get you talking and thinking.

CHAPTER 1

THE NATURE OF HUMAN RESOURCE MANAGEMENT

THE OBJECTIVES OF THIS CHAPTER ARE TO:

1. Define the term 'human resource management'
2. Explain the different ways in which the term 'human resource management' is used
3. Set out the main objectives of the human resource function
4. Review the historical evolution of the modern HR function
5. Introduce some key current debates in HRM
6. Explain the philosophy of HRM that is adopted in this book

Human resource management (HRM) is the basis of all management activity, but it is not the basis of all business activity. A business may depend fundamentally on having a unique product, like the Dyson vacuum cleaner, or on obtaining the necessary funding, like the London bid to stage the Olympic Games, or on identifying a previously unnoticed market niche, like Saga Services. The basis of management is always the same: getting the people of the business to make things happen in a productive way, so that the business prospers and the people thrive.

All organisations have to draw on a range of resources to function and to achieve their objectives. They need access to capital to finance their operations, land and premises to operate from, energy, equipment and raw materials in order to manufacture a product or deliver a service. They also require access to some form of distribution network so that they can publicise, sell or dispense their goods and services. In addition, human resources are required in order to provide organisations with know-how, ideas and manpower. In a competitive market economy the effectiveness and efficiency with which an organisation manages its relationship with the suppliers of all these kinds of resources determines its success. And the scarcer the resource and the more critical it is to a particular organisation's operations, the greater the skill, time and effort needed in order to manage the relationship.

There was a time when most people employed by organisations were required simply to provide manual labour. Relatively little skill, experience or intelligence was needed to do the jobs. The requisite training was cheap and speedy to provide, and payment methods unsophisticated. Finding people to do the work was rarely a problem and there were no restrictions of significance when it came to firing those who were not satisfactory or who displeased managers in some other way. This remains the situation in some industries and in some parts of the world, but in industrialised countries such as the UK it is now increasingly rare. Instead we have a situation in which the majority of jobs require their holders to have mastered some form of specialised skill, or at the very least to possess attributes which others do not share to the same extent (National Statistics 2006: 7). The demand for higher-level skills has grown particularly quickly, there being a need for many more people to fill professional and managerial jobs than was the case 20 years ago. Moreover, almost all informed commentators believe that these established trends will accelerate in the future.

Just as the workforce has changed, so have the methods used to manage its members. The more specialised their roles, the harder it has become to find individuals with the right skills, qualifications, attributes and experience to undertake them. It has also become harder to keep people once they are employed because competitors are always keen to secure the services of the most talented people by offering them a better deal. Employing organisations have had to acquire a capacity for developing people effectively, together with increasingly sophisticated approaches to recruitment, selection, retention, employee relations and performance management. Further sophistication is required thanks to the substantial body of employment regulation that now governs the management of the employment relationship in countries like the UK.

These developments have led to the evolution of a more complex HRM function, charged with overseeing all aspects of managing the relationship between an organisation and its people in a professional and productive manner. The management of people, however, can never be a responsibility shouldered by specialists alone. It is an area of management activity that all managers must share if it is to be carried out effectively and contribute to the achievement of competitive advantage.

In this chapter we introduce HRM by setting out its purpose and showing how the effective management of people helps organisations to achieve their objectives. We go on to examine the historical development of HR work and speculate on how this may evolve further in the future. The next part of the chapter introduces thinking about the extent and nature of the link between HR activities and organisational effectiveness and performance. Finally, we introduce some of the major current issues and debates in HR which we will be revisiting in several later chapters.

WINDOW ON PRACTICE

In 2008, twenty-five years after it was first planned, Terminal 5 at Heathrow airport in London finally opened its doors to passengers. The total cost of the building was £4.3 billion. The new terminal was exclusively for the use of British Airways who had been planning for several years to move all its existing operations from the various other terminals at Heathrow into Terminal 5 and had gone so far as to contribute £330 million to its flamboyant interior design. The day before the opening an article in the *Financial Times* reported executives' concerns that the look of the place would raise expectations too high, but that it was 'beyond imagination to contemplate failure' (Blitz 2008). Yet spectacular failure was what followed.

In the first few days of operation over 300 flights scheduled to depart from Terminal 5 were cancelled, very long queues formed at check-in and transfer desks, while some 28,000 passengers found themselves separated from their luggage. The immediate cost to British Airways was £16 million, but the long-term direct costs were authoritatively estimated to be around £150 million (BBC 2008a) and there were vast further losses resulting from a deterioration in the airline's already poor brand image.

And why did this debacle happen? It appears that the major reason was simply extraordinarily poor management of people. The major immediate problem arose because the staff were not properly trained to use the equipment at Terminal 5 and were unprepared when it came to solving the technical 'glitches' that quickly appeared once the baggage handling machinery started operating. In addition long delays were caused on the first day as a result of staff being unable to find the staff car park or get through security screening on schedule. Later on, as flights began to arrive, staff simply failed to 'remove luggage quickly enough at the final unloading stage' (BBC 2008b).

Matters were not helped by the persistence over a long period of very poor employment relationships at British Airways. Done and Willman (2008) reported that the failure of the airline to solve this fundamental problem was the real underlying cause of the Terminal 5 debacle. An unnamed Heathrow executive said that they had all been expecting an outbreak of 'fuck 'em disease' as the new terminal opened and some staff simply decided 'not to work very hard'. British Airways' staff were committed neither to the success of the operation nor to their employer. Goodwill was in short supply, leading staff to be intransigent and uncooperative when effort, positive enthusiasm and flexibility were what was required.

DEFINING HUMAN RESOURCE MANAGEMENT

The term 'human resource management' is not easy to define. This is because it is commonly used in two different ways. On the one hand it is used generically to describe the body of management activities covered in books such as this. Used in this way HRM is really no more than a more modern and supposedly imposing name for what was long labelled 'personnel management'. On the other hand, the term is equally widely used to denote a particular approach to the management of people which is clearly distinct from 'personnel management'. Used in this way 'HRM' signifies more than an updating of the label; it also suggests a distinctive philosophy towards carrying out people-oriented organisational activities: one which is held to serve the modern business more effectively than 'traditional' personnel management. We explore the substance of these two meanings of human resource management in the following paragraphs, referring to the first as 'HRM mark 1' and the second as 'HRM mark 2'.

HRM mark 1: the generic term

The role of the human resource functions is explained by identifying the key **objectives** to be achieved. Four objectives form the foundation of all HR activity.

Staffing objectives

Human resource managers are first concerned with ensuring that the business is appropriately staffed and thus able to draw on the human resources it needs. This involves designing organisation structures, identifying under what type of contract different groups of employees (or subcontractors) will work, before recruiting, selecting and developing the people required to fill the roles: the right people, with the right skills to provide their services when needed. There is a need to compete effectively in the employment market by recruiting and retaining the best, affordable workforce that is available. This involves developing employment packages that are sufficiently attractive to maintain the required employee skills levels and, where necessary, disposing of those judged no longer to have a role to play in the organisation. The tighter a key employment market becomes, the harder it is to find and then to hold on to the people an organisation needs in order to compete effectively. In such circumstances increased attention has to be given to developing competitive pay packages, to the provision of valued training and development opportunities and to ensuring that the experience of working in the organisation is, as far as is possible, rewarding and fulfilling. Recent years have seen organisations take a more strategic approach, at least in their rhetoric, towards the meeting of staffing objectives. They are, for example, increasingly seeking to differentiate and position themselves in their labour markets vis-à-vis competitors by managing their reputations as employers, by engaging in **employer branding** exercises and by seeking to be recognised as 'employers of choice'.

Performance objectives

Once the required workforce is in place, human resource managers seek to ensure that people are well motivated and committed so as to maximise their performance in their different roles. Training and development has a role to play, as do reward systems to maximise effort and focus attention on performance targets. In many organisations, particularly where trade unions play a significant role, human resource managers negotiate improved performance with the workforce. The achievement of performance objectives also requires HR specialists to assist in disciplining employees effectively and equitably where individual conduct and/or performance standards are unsatisfactory. Welfare functions can also assist performance by providing constructive assistance to people whose performance has fallen short of their potential because of illness or difficult personal circumstances. Last but not least, there is the range of employee involvement initiatives to raise levels of commitment and to engage employees in developing new ideas. It is increasingly recognised that a key determinant of superior competitive performance is a propensity on the part of an organisation's employees to demonstrate **discretionary effort**. Essentially this means that they choose to go further in the service of their employer than is strictly required in their contracts of employment, working longer hours perhaps, working with greater enthusiasm or taking the initiative to improve systems and relationships. Willingness to engage in such behaviour cannot be forced by managers. But they can help to create an environment in which it is more likely to occur. A term that is currently very fashionable in HR circles is '**employee engagement**', an idea which encapsulates what is required if organisations are successfully to enhance individual performance. Engaged employees know what is expected of them, have a sense of ownership of their work, are satisfied (hopefully very satisfied) with their jobs and, as a result, prepared to contribute positively both with their effort and their ideas.

Change-management objectives

A third set of core objectives in nearly every business relates to the role played by the HR function in effectively managing change. Frequently change does not come along in readily defined episodes precipitated by some external factor. Instead it is endemic and well-nigh continuous, generated as much by a continual need to innovate as from definable environmental pressures. Change comes in different forms. Sometimes it is merely structural, requiring reorganisation of activities or the introduction of new people into particular roles. At other times cultural change is sought in order to alter attitudes, philosophies or long-present organisational norms. In any of these scenarios the HR function can play a central role. Key activities include the recruitment and/or development of people with the necessary leadership skills to drive the change process, the employment of change agents to encourage acceptance of change and the construction of reward systems which underpin the change process. Timely and effective employee involvement is also crucial because 'people support what they help to create'. However, it must also be remembered that change, particularly when imposed without genuine employee involvement, is also a major potential source of conflict in organisations. This can be minimised if plenty of time is available, but a degree of conflict is inevitable where groups of staff lose out in some way as a result of change. The effective management of conflict and its avoidance through careful management of expectations and involvement in decision making are thus also significant features of an effective HR manager's role.

Administration objectives

The fourth type of objective is less directly related to achieving competitive advantage, but is focused on underpinning the achievement of the other forms of objective. In part it is simply carried out in order to facilitate an organisation's smooth running. Hence there is a need to maintain accurate and comprehensive data on individual employees, a record of their achievement in terms of performance, their attendance and training records, their terms and conditions of employment and their personal details. However, there is also a legal aspect to much administrative activity, meaning that it is done because the business is required by law to comply. Of particular significance is the requirement that payment is administered professionally and lawfully, with itemised monthly pay statements being provided for all employees. There is the need to make arrangements for the deduction of taxation and national insurance, for the payment of pension fund contributions and to be on top of the complexities associated with Statutory Sick Pay and Statutory Maternity Pay, as well as maternity and paternity leave. Additional legal requirements relate to the monitoring of health and safety systems and the issuing of contracts to new employees. Accurate record keeping is also central to ensuring compliance with a variety of other legal obligations such as the National Minimum Wage and the Working Time Regulations. HR professionals often downgrade the significance of effective administration, seeking instead to gain for themselves a more glamorous (and usually more highly paid) role formulating policy and strategy. This is a short-sighted attitude. Achieving excellence (i.e. professionalism and cost effectiveness) in the delivery of the basic administrative tasks is important as an aim in itself because it can provide a source of competitive advantage vis-à-vis other organisations that struggle administratively. Moreover, as Stevens (2005: 137) demonstrates, sound administration in HR matters is important to achieve if 'potential legislative risks' are to be minimised. It also helps the HR function in an organisation to gain and maintain the credibility and respect that are required in order to influence other managers in the organisation. In this respect it can be persuasively argued that efficient administration is a prerequisite if the HR function is to make a really significant contribution in the three other areas outlined above.

ACTIVITY 1.1

Each of the four types of HR objective is important and necessary for organisations in different ways. However, at certain times one or more can assume greater importance than the others. Can you identify types of situations in which each could become the most significant or urgent?

HRM mark 2: a distinctive approach to the management of people

The second meaning commonly accorded to the term 'human resource management' denotes a particular way of carrying out the range of activities discussed above. Under this definition, a 'human resource management approach' is something qualitatively different from a 'personnel management approach'. Commentators disagree, however, about how fundamental a shift is signified by a movement from personnel management to human resource management. For some, particularly those whose focus of interest is on the management of collective relationships at work, the rise of HRM in the last two decades of the twentieth century represented something new and very different from the dominant personnel management approach in earlier years. A particular theme in their work is the contention that personnel management is essentially *workforce centred*, while HRM is *resource centred*. Personnel specialists direct their efforts mainly at the organisation's employees; finding and training them, arranging for them to be paid, explaining management's expectations, justifying management's actions, satisfying employees' work-related needs, dealing with their problems and seeking to modify management action that could produce an unwelcome employee response. The people who work in the organisation are the starting point, and they are a resource that is relatively inflexible in comparison with other resources, like cash and materials. Although indisputably a management function, personnel management is not totally identified with management interests. Just as sales representatives have to understand and articulate the aspirations of the customers, personnel managers seek to understand and articulate the aspirations and views of the workforce. There is always some degree of being in between management and the employees, mediating the needs of each to the other.

HRM, by contrast, is directed mainly at management needs for human resources (not necessarily employees) to be provided and deployed. Demand rather than supply is the focus of the activity. There is greater emphasis on planning, monitoring and control, rather than mediation. Problem solving is undertaken with other members of management on human resource issues rather than directly with employees or their representatives. It is totally identified with management interests, being a general management activity, and is relatively distant from the workforce as a whole. David Guest (1987) emphasises the differences between the two approaches in his model illustrating 'stereotypes of personnel management and human resource management' (*see* Table 1.1).

An alternative point of view, while recognising the differences, downplays the significance of a break between personnel and human resources management. Such a conclusion is readily reached when the focus of analysis is on what HR/personnel managers actually do, rather than on the more profound developments in the specific field of collective employee relations. Legge (1989 and 1995) concludes that there is very little difference in fact between the two, but that there are some differences that are important; first, that human resource management concentrates more on what is done to managers

Table 1.1 Personnel versus HRM

	Personnel management	Human resource management
Time and planning perspective	Short term, reactive, ad hoc, marginal	Long term, proactive, strategic, integrated
Psychological contract	Compliance	Commitment
Control systems	External controls	Self-control
Employee relations perspective	Pluralist, collective, low trust	Unitarist, individual, high trust
Preferred structures/ systems	Bureaucratic/mechanistic, centralised, formal defined roles	Organic, devolved, flexible roles
Roles	Specialist/professional	Largely integrated into line management
Evaluation criteria	Cost minimisation	Maximum utilisation (human asset accounting)

than on what is done by managers to other employees; second, that there is a more proactive role for line managers; and third, that there is a top management responsibility for managing culture – all factors to which we return later in the book. From this perspective, human resource management can simply be seen as the most recent mutation in a long line of developments that have characterised personnel management practice as it evolved during the last century. Below we identify four distinct stages in the historical development of the personnel management function. HRM, as described above, is a fifth. On the companion website there is a journalist's view of contemporary HRM to which we have added some discussion questions.

The evolution of personnel and HR management

Theme 1: social justice

The origins of personnel management lie in the nineteenth century, deriving from the work of social reformers such as Lord Shaftesbury and Robert Owen. Their criticisms of the free enterprise system and the hardship created by the exploitation of workers by factory owners enabled the first personnel managers to be appointed and provided the first frame of reference in which they worked: to ameliorate the lot of the workers. Such concerns are not obsolete. There are still regular reports of employees being exploited by employers flouting the law, and the problem of organisational distance between decision makers and those putting decisions into practice remains a source of alienation from work.

In the late nineteenth and early twentieth centuries some of the larger employers with a paternalist outlook began to appoint welfare officers to manage a series of new initiatives designed to make life less harsh for their employees. Prominent examples were the progressive schemes of unemployment benefit, sick pay and subsidised housing provided by the Quaker family firms of Cadbury and Rowntree, and the Lever Brothers' soap business. While the motives were ostensibly charitable, there was and remains a business as well as an ethical case for paying serious attention to the welfare of employees. This is based on the contention that it improves commitment on the part of staff and leads potential employees to compare the organisation favourably vis-à-vis competitors. The result is higher productivity, a longer-serving workforce and a bigger pool of applicants for each job. It has also been argued that a commitment to welfare reduces the scope for the development of adversarial industrial relations. The more conspicuous welfare initiatives promoted by employers today include employee assistance schemes, childcare facilities and health-screening programmes.

Theme 2: humane bureaucracy

The second phase marked the beginnings of a move away from a sole focus on welfare towards the meeting of various other organisational objectives. Personnel managers began to gain responsibilities in the areas of staffing, training and organisation design. Influenced by social scientists such as F.W. Taylor (1856–1915) and Henri Fayol (1841–1925) personnel specialists started to look at management and administrative processes analytically, working out how organisational structures could be designed and labour deployed so as to maximise efficiency. The humane bureaucracy stage in the development of personnel thinking was also influenced by the Human Relations School, which sought to ameliorate the potential for industrial conflict and dehumanisation present in too rigid an application of these scientific management approaches. Following the ideas of thinkers such as Elton Mayo (1880–1949), the fostering of social relationships in the workplace and employee morale thus became equally important objectives for personnel professionals seeking to raise productivity levels.

Theme 3: negotiated consent

Personnel managers next added expertise in bargaining to their repertoire of skills. In the period of full employment following the Second World War labour became a scarce resource. This led to a growth in trade union membership and to what Allan Flanders, the leading industrial relations analyst of the 1960s, called 'the challenge from below'. Personnel specialists managed the new collective institutions such as joint consultation committees, joint production committees and suggestion schemes set up in order to accommodate the new realities. In the industries that were nationalised in the 1940s, employers were placed under a statutory duty to negotiate with unions representing employees. To help achieve this, the government encouraged the appointment of personnel officers and set up the first specialist courses for them in the universities. A personnel management advisory service was also set up at the Ministry of Labour, which still survives as the first A in ACAS (the Advisory, Conciliation and Arbitration Service).

Theme 4: organisation

The late 1960s saw a switch in focus among personnel specialists, away from dealing principally with the rank-and-file employee on behalf of management, towards dealing with management itself and the integration of managerial activity. This phase was characterised by the development of career paths and of opportunities within organisations for personal growth. This too remains a concern of personnel specialists today, with a significant portion of time and resources being devoted to the recruitment, development and retention of an elite core of people with specialist expertise on whom the business depends for its future. Personnel specialists developed techniques of manpower or workforce planning. This is basically a quantitative activity, boosted by the advent of information technology, which involves forecasting the likely need for employees with different skills in the future.

Theme 5: human resource management

The term 'human resource management' dates from the early 1980s when courses with that name began to be offered as part of MBA programmes at leading American business schools. It is unclear who coined the term, but the notion that employees should properly be regarded as 'human resources' dates from at least ten years earlier. Terms such as 'human resource utilisation', 'human resource development' and even 'human capital', which we tend to think of as more recent additions to the management vocabulary, were widely used among sociologists in the early 1970s (*see* Harbison 1972). The term 'human resources' was originally coined to distinguish people and their potential contribution from 'natural resources'.

By the late 1980s Human Resource Management was a very widely used term, swiftly replaced the term 'personnel management' in many organisations and quickly came to be associated with the distinct approach to the management of people in organisations that started to evolve at that time. The big change that was occurring across most of the developed world was the decline of trade union influence in organisations and alongside that, the breaking down of established national collective bargaining systems. These had previously covered most industries and the great majority of employees. They ensured that pay and other terms and conditions of employment were the same throughout a whole industry in each country, meaning that these were not issues about which local managers could make decisions. With the decentralisation of bargaining and the rise in many industries of non-union firms, managers in the private sector found themselves free and able to develop their own, local policies and practices. Some chose to adopt a macho approach, particularly during recessionary periods when employees were in no position to resist the introduction of efficiency and cost-saving measures, leaner organisational structures and downsized workplaces. Others sought to enhance their profitability and competitiveness by seeking to gain employee commitment and by investing in their people. Either way it was not long before organisations began to take an explicitly strategic approach to the management of human resources, setting objectives and seeking in a more proactive way to achieve these. As time went by the same kind of approach was increasingly used in the public sector too, so that by the turn of the millennium it was the norm for organisations to employ human resource managers, officers and assistants whose aim was to add value by carrying out the four areas of activity we set out above in as efficient and effective manner as possible. The objective, quite explicitly, was to make a major contribution to the achievement and maintenance of competitive advantage.

Theme 6: A 'new HR'?

Some writers and commentators have recently begun to argue that we are now witnessing the beginning of a new sixth stage in the evolution of personnel/HR work. While there is by no means a clear consensus about this point of view, it is notable that leading thinkers have identified a group of trends which they believe to be sufficiently dissimilar, as a bundle, from established practices to justify, at the very least, a distinct title. Bach (2005: 28–9) uses the term 'the new HR' to describe 'a different trajectory' which he believes is now clearly discernible. Others have started using the term HR 2.0, likening recent developments to a new and improved edition of a software package. A number of themes are identified including a global perspective and a strong tendency for issues relating to legal compliance to move up the HR management agenda and to occupy management time. Bach also sees as significant the increased prevalence of multi-employer networks which he calls 'permeable organizations'. Here, instead of employees having a single, readily defined employer, there may be a number of different employers, or at least more than one organisation which exercises a degree of authority over their work. Such is the case when organisational boundaries become blurred as they have a tendency to in the case of public-private partnerships, agency working, situations where work is outsourced by one organisation to another, joint ventures, franchises and where strong supply chains are established consisting of smaller organisations which are wholly or very heavily reliant on the custom of a single large client corporation.

In each of these cases 'the new HR' amounts to a change of emphasis in response to significant long-term trends in the business environment. It is therefore legitimate to question the extent to which it really represents anything genuinely 'new' as far as HR practice is concerned. However, in addition, Bach and others draw attention to another development which can be seen as more novel and which does genuinely represent 'a different trajectory'. This is best summarised as an approach to the employment relationship which views employees and potential employees very much as individuals or at least small groups rather than as a single group and which seeks to engage them emotionally. It is associated with a move away from an expectation that staff will demonstrate commitment to a set of corporate values which are determined by senior management and towards a philosophy which is far more customer focused. Customers are defined explicitly as the ultimate employers and staff are empowered to act in such a way as to meet their requirements. This involves encouraging employees to empathise with customers, recruiting, selecting and appraising them according to their capacity to do so. In turn, and this is what makes 'the new HR' different from established HRM, managers are starting to refer to the staff and line managers whom they 'serve' as their 'internal customers', a client group which they aim to satisfy and which they survey regularly as a means of establishing to what extent they are achieving this aim. Another term that is becoming very much more commonly used in HR is 'strategic business partner'. The image conjured up here is of the HR manager as internal consultant, assisting clients in the achievement of their objectives and expecting to be judged on results.

The practice of viewing staff as internal customers goes further still in some organisations with the use of HR practices that borrow explicitly from the toolkit of marketing specialists. We see this in the widespread interest in employer branding exercises (*see* Chapter 7) where an organisation markets itself in quite sophisticated ways, not to customers and potential customers, but to employees and potential employees.

Gratton (2004) shows how highly successful companies such as Tesco go further still in categorising job applicants and existing staff into distinct categories which summarise their principal aspirations as far as their work is concerned in much the same way that organisations seek to identify distinct market segments to use when developing, designing, packaging and marketing products and services. Such approaches aim to provide an 'employment proposition' which it is hoped will attract the right candidates, allow the appointment of highly effective performers, motivate them to provide excellent levels of service and subsequently retain them for a longer period of time. Lepak and Snell (2007) also note a move in HR away from 'the management of jobs' and towards 'the management of people', which includes the development of employment strategies that differ for different groups of employees. Importantly this approach recognises the capacity that most people have to become emotionally engaged in their work, with their customers, with their colleagues and hence (if to a lesser extent) with their organisations. The employment relationship is not just a transactional one in which money is earned in exchange for carrying out a set of duties competently, but also a relational one which involves emotional attachments. The 'new HR' understands this and seeks to manage people accordingly.

Cardy *et al.* (2007) are also keen to advocate the repositioning of the HR function as one which is focused on providing services to 'internal customers' with the aim of satisfying them. Like Gratton they argue in favour of a degree of segmentation. They also take the concept of 'customer equity' long used by marketing analysts and apply it to the employment relationship, developing the notion of 'employee equity'. The argument they advance is complex, but at base they advocate thinking about employment from the perspective of the employee and take steps which serve to:

- increase the value employees perceive that they derive from the relationship (value equity)
- improve the reputation of the organisation as an employer (brand equity)
- establish and maintain high levels of loyalty with employees (retention equity).

Saunders and Hunter (2009) adopt the same philosophy, but focus on the practicalities of transforming a traditionally focused HR function into one which sees managers and employees at all levels as customers whom the function needs to satisfy if it is to achieve its wider, longer-term objectives.

What we appear to be seeing here is a re-positioning of HR thinking and activity. The aim is the same, namely to help the organisation achieve its objectives, but the means are different. Instead of simply devising and then operationalising HR strategies and policies which suit the short-term, current financial needs of the organisation, there is an increased recognition that this cannot be done successfully over the longer term without the active engagement and support of people. In a world where many are employed because of their knowledge, in which skills that employers seek are often scarce and in which employees enjoy substantial protection from the law, there are major limits imposed on the extent of management's freedom to manage people at will. The most successful organisations are thus those which are best able to recruit good people, retain them and motivate them. This means looking after their interests and involving them as far as is possible in decision making – often using technologies that enable collaborative decision making. Hence we see the evolution of thinking based around internal customers, collaboration, partnership and employee engagement which are characteristic of the new HR trajectory.

ACTIVITY 1.2

Lynda Gratton (2004) reports that Tesco uses the following five 'identities' to categorise its staff. The way that they are managed and the reward packages that are available to them can thus be tailored so as to be more appropriate to the needs and aspirations of each individual:

- work–life balancers
- want it all
- pleasure seekers
- live to work
- work to live

Which of these categories best describes you as far as your present employment is concerned? What about friends and members of your family? Choose any two of the categories and think about in what ways it would make sense to manage people in each group differently from one another.

DELIVERING HRM OBJECTIVES

The larger the organisation, the more scope there is to employ people to specialise in particular areas of HRM. Some, for example, employ employee relations specialists to look after the collective relationship between management and employees. Where there is a strong tradition of collective bargaining, the role is focused on the achievement of satisfactory outcomes from ongoing negotiations. Increasingly, however, employee relations specialists are required to provide advice about legal developments, to manage consultation arrangements and to preside over employee involvement initiatives.

Another common area of specialisation is in the field of training and development. Although much of this is now undertaken by external providers, there is still a role for in-house trainers, particularly in management development. Increasingly the term 'consultant' is used instead of 'officer' or 'manager' to describe the training specialist's role, indicating a shift towards a situation in which line managers determine the training *they* want rather than the training section providing a standardised portfolio of courses. The other major specialist roles are in the fields of recruitment and selection, health, safety and welfare, compensation and benefits and human resource planning.

In addition to the people who have specialist roles there are many other people who are employed as human resources or personnel generalists. Working alone or in small teams, they carry out the range of HR activities and seek to achieve all the objectives outlined above. In larger businesses generalists either look after all personnel matters in a particular division or are employed at a senior level to develop policy and take responsibility for HR issues across the organisation as a whole. In more junior roles, human resource administrators and assistants undertake many of the administrative tasks mentioned earlier. It is increasingly common for organisations to separate the people responsible for undertaking routine administration and even basic advice from those employed to manage case work, to develop policies and to manage the strategic aspects of the HR role. In some cases the administrative work is outsourced to specialist providers, while in others a **shared services model** has been established whereby a centralised administrative function is distinguished from decentralised teams of HR advisers working as part of management teams in different divisions. Figure 1.1 summarises the roles and objectives of HRM.

Most HR practitioners working at a senior level are now professionally qualified, having secured membership of the Chartered Institute of Personnel and Development (CIPD). The wide range of elective subjects which can now be chosen by those seeking qualification through the Institute's examinations has made it as relevant to those seeking a specialist career as to those who prefer to remain in generalist roles. However, many smaller businesses do not need, or cannot afford, HR managers at all. They may use consultants or the advisory services of university departments. They may use their bank's computer to process the payroll, but there is still a human resource dimension to their managers' activities.

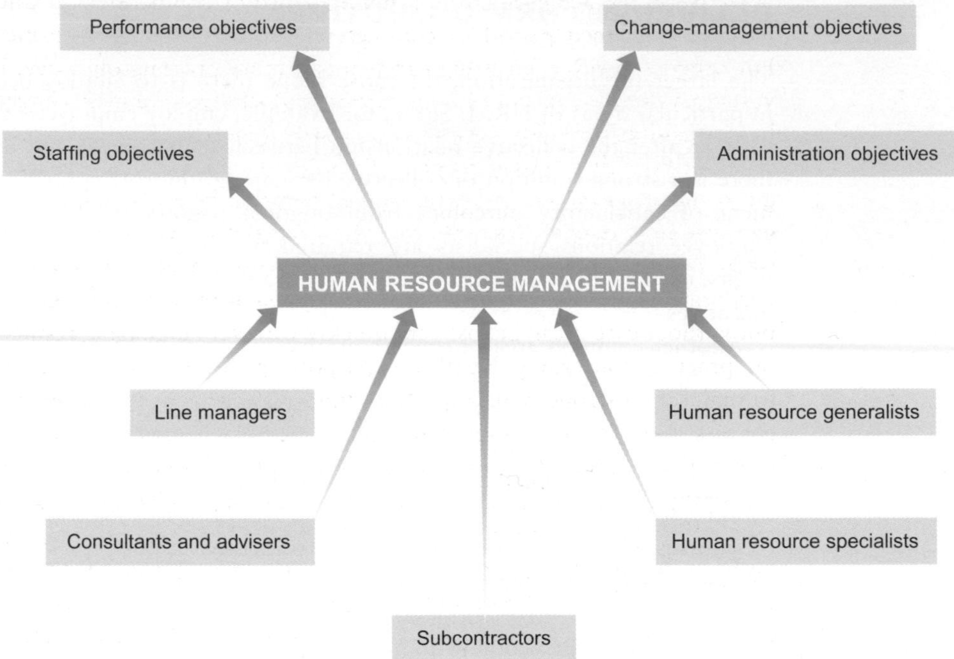

Figure 1.1 HRM roles and objectives

ACTIVITY 1.3

Which of the various HR roles described above would you be most interested in undertaking? The generalist role, a specialist role or perhaps that of a consultant or subcontractor?

What are the main reasons for your choice?

HRM AND THE ACHIEVEMENT OF ORGANISATIONAL EFFECTIVENESS

As Storey *et al.* (2009: 4) point out, unless HR activity can be shown to add value to an organisation, there would be no point in devoting time and resources to it except insofar as is necessary 'to comply with prevailing employment laws or to meet minimum operational requirements in hiring, firing, labour deployment and the like'. So for the past decade and a half the theme which has dominated the HR research agenda has been the study of links between HR practices and organisational effectiveness. Throughout the book we make reference to this research in the context of different HR activities, but it is helpful briefly to set out at the start how what happens in the field of HR impacts on an organisation's ability to meet its objectives.

What those objectives are will vary depending on the type of organisation and its situation. For most businesses operating in the private sector the overriding long-term objective is the achievement and maintenance of competitive advantage, by which is meant a sustained period of commercial success vis-à-vis its principal competitors. For others, however, ensuring survival is a more pressing objective. In the public and voluntary sectors notions of competition and survival are increasingly present too, but here organisational effectiveness is primarily defined in terms of meeting a service need as cost efficiently as possible and to the highest achievable standard of quality. Meeting government-set targets is central to the operation of many public sector organisations, as is the requirement to ensure that the expectations of users are met as far as is possible. For all sizeable organisations there is also a need to foster a positive long-term corporate reputation. Developing such a reputation can take many years to achieve, but without care it can be lost very quickly with very damaging results (*see* the Window on practice concerning Heathrow Airport, p. 5). In particular, organisations need to maintain a strong reputation for sound management in the financial markets. This enables them to raise money with relative ease when they need to and also helps to ensure that managers of investment funds and financial advisers see it or its shares as a desirable place to put their clients' money. The maintenance of a positive reputation in the media is also an important objective as this helps to maintain and grow the customer base. In this context corporate ethics and social responsibility are increasingly significant because they are becoming more prominent factors in determining the purchasing decisions of consumers. The HR function should play a significant role in helping to achieve each of these dimensions of organisational effectiveness.

The contribution of the HR function to *gaining* competitive advantage involves achieving the fundamental aims of an organisation in the field of people management more effectively and efficiently than competitor organisations. These aims were discussed above – mobilising a workforce, maximising its performance, managing change effectively and striving to achieve excellence in administration.

The contribution of the HR function to *maintaining* competitive advantage involves recognising the significance of the organisation's people as an effective barrier preventing would-be rivals from expanding their markets into territory that your organisation holds. The term human capital is more and more used in this context to signify that the combined knowledge and experience of an organisation's staff is a highly significant source of competitive advantage largely because it is difficult for competitors to replicate easily. Attracting, engaging, rewarding, developing and retaining people effectively is thus vital. Failing to do so enables accumulated human capital to leak away into the hands of competitors, reducing the effectiveness of commercial defences and making it harder to maintain competitive advantage.

Fostering a positive reputation among would-be investors, financial advisers and financial journalists is also an aspect of organisational effectiveness to which the HR function makes a significant contribution. Key here is the need to reassure those whose job is to assess the long-term financial viability of the organisation that it is competently managed and is well placed to meet the challenges that lie ahead in both the short and the longer term. The ability to attract and retain a strong management team is central to achieving this aspect of organisational effectiveness as is the ability of the organisation to plan for the future by having in place effective succession planning arrangements and robust systems for the development of the skills and knowledge that will be key in the future. Above all financial markets need to be assured that the organisation is stable and is thus a safe repository for investors' funds. The work of Stevens and his colleagues (2005) is helpful in this context. They conceive of the whole HR contribution in terms of the management of risk, the aim being to ensure that an organisation 'balances the maximisation of opportunities and the minimisation of risks'.

Finally, the HR function also plays a central role in building an organisation's reputation as an ethically or socially responsible organisation. This happens in two distinct ways. The first involves fostering an understanding of and commitment to ethical conduct on the part of managers and staff. It is achieved by paying attention to these objectives in recruitment campaigns, in the criteria adopted for the selection of new employees and the promotion of staff, in the methods used to develop people and in performance management processes. The second relates to the manner in which people are managed. A poor ethical reputation can be gained simply because an organisation becomes known for treating its staff poorly. In recent years well-known brands of fast food chains in the UK have suffered because of their use of zero-hours contracts, while several large multinationals have had their reputations stained by stories in the media about the conditions under which their employees in developing countries are required to work.

CONTEMPORARY DEBATES IN HRM

The world in which HR managers exist and with which they interact is continually changing, generating new issues and conundrums to consider. While in most cases managers have a fair degree of choice about how to deal with new ideas and new sets of circumstances, the choices themselves are often difficult. Our final task in this opening chapter is to introduce readers to a number of these issues in general terms. All raise themes to which we will return at various stages later in the book.

In one way or another all the major debates that occupy HR professionals, analysts and commentators concern the appropriate response to the major trends that are evolving in our business environment. But people differ in their analysis of the extent and nature of these developments and this colours their ideas about whether or not radical change in the way that people are managed is or is not appropriate. Here we can usefully distinguish between three separate fields of debate.

The first is concerned with understanding and conceptualising the nature of current responses. How are organisations dealing with the issues that they face in terms of the management of their people? Are they developing new approaches that differ fundamentally from those that have been established for some time or are we witnessing a more steady, considered evolution of practice?

The second field of debate concerns what HR managers *should* be doing. Are new or radical changes in policy and practice necessary? Or is the correct response to environmental developments the further refinement of more familiar approaches? Further debate concerns the extent to which the answer to these questions is broadly the same for all employing organisations or whether it differs quite profoundly from industry to industry or firm to firm.

A third debate is oriented towards longer-term future developments. Many believe and have argued persuasively that we are currently witnessing changes in our business environment which are as fundamental and significant as those which accompanied the Industrial Revolution 200 years ago. They further argue that the world of work which will emerge in future decades will be wholly different in major respects from that we currently inhabit. It follows that those organisations which 'see the future' most clearly and change accordingly stand to gain most. But are these predictions really accurate? Could the analysis on which they are built be faulty in key respects?

Of course it is also possible to ask rather different kinds of questions about the HR practices that are being, will be or should be developed, which in turn lead us to engage in various types of debate. Some, for example, focus exclusively on the requirements of the organisation and the search for competitive advantage. What can the HR function do which will maximise organisational growth, effectiveness and efficiency? However, many also like to think more broadly and to concern themselves with the impact of employment practice on the workforce and on society in more general terms. Hence we also engage in debates that are essentially ethical in nature or which have a prominent moral, sociological or political dimension.

In Chapter 2 we will review some of the major long-term contemporary developments in our business environment and reflect on how these have in the past and are likely in the future to influence HRM practice and to determine what HR managers make their priorities. Our aim here is to introduce three debates which are currently prominent in HRM and to which we will return on a number of occasions in different guises later in the book. They are among the most prominent in each of the categories set out above: what is happening, what should be happening and what will happen?

The evolving psychological contract

According to many, one consequence of evolving environmental pressures is a significant and fundamental change in what has become known as 'the psychological contract'. This refers to the expectations that employees have about the role that they play and to what the employer is prepared to give them in return. Whereas a legal contract of employment sets out terms and conditions of employment, remuneration arrangements and the basic rules which are to govern the employment relationship, the psychological contract concerns broad expectations about what each party thinks it will gain from the relationship. By its nature the psychological contract is not a written document. Rather, it exists entirely within people's heads. But this has not prevented researchers from seeking to pin it down and to track the extent to which we are witnessing ongoing change in established psychological contracts.

While people disagree about the extent to which this change has in fact occurred, there is general agreement about the phenomenon itself and the notion that an 'old' psychological contract to which generations of employees have become accustomed is being superseded to some extent by a 'new' psychological contract which reflects the needs of the present business environment. From the employee perspective we can sum up the old psychological contract as follows:

> I will work hard for and act with loyalty towards my employer. In return I expect to be retained as an employee provided I do not act against the interests of the organisation. I also expect to be given opportunities for development and promotion should circumstances make this possible.

By contrast, the new psychological contract takes the following form:

Table 1.2 Comparing transactional and relational contracts

Transactional contract might contain	Relational contract might contain
Employer: Pay Performance-based pay Having a job	Employer: Job security Career prospects Training and development
Employee: Long hours Multiskilled Willing to change	Employee: Loyalty Conformity

I will bring to my work effort and creativity. In return I expect a salary that is appropriate to my contribution and market worth. While our relationship may be short term, I will remain for as long as I receive the developmental opportunities I need to build my career.

A switch from the 'old' approach to the 'new' involves employers giving less job security and receiving less loyalty from employees in return. Instead, employees are given developmental opportunities and are expected to give the employer flexibility. The whole perception of the employment relationship on both sides is thus radically different.

Another way of conceptualising changing psychological contracts is to see them as becoming more transactional and less relational in nature. The difference between these two types of deal is shown in Table 1.2.

The big question is how far has a change of this nature actually occurred? Are we really witnessing a slow decline in the old psychological contract, characterised by many as 'relational' in nature and its replacement by the new more transactional version, or have reports of its death been exaggerated? Moreover, if changes of this type are occurring are they being pushed through by managers with or without agreement? Are old psychological contracts being 'breached' in order to replace them with new ones, or is this a process that employees as well as organisations see some benefit in accepting?

On this issue there is a great deal of disagreement. Many researchers claim to have found evidence of substantial change in many industries across the developed world, particularly as regards reduced employee loyalty (e.g. Coyle-Shapiro and Kessler 2000, Maguire 2002, Schalk and Freese 2007, Bickle and Witzki 2008). Yet others, notably Guest and Conway in their many studies conducted in the UK on behalf of the CIPD, have found relatively little evidence of any change in the state of the psychological contract. Their findings (e.g. Guest and Conway 2000 and 2001, CIPD 2005) suggest that while some change has occurred in the public sector, perceptions closer to the 'old' psychological contract remain a great deal more common than those associated with the 'new' approach.

It is difficult to reach firm conclusions about why these very marked differences of opinion exist. It is possible that the old psychological contract remains intact for most people, but that a significant minority, particularly managers and some public sector workers, have had to adjust to profound change. It is also possible that organisations have tried to move away from the old approach towards the new one, but have found it difficult to take their employees with them and have thus sought other methods of increasing their competitiveness. A third possibility, suggested by Atkinson (2004), is that the differences in the conclusions people reach about this issue derive from the methodologies they adopt when studying it. She argues that large-scale studies which involve sending questionnaires to employees have tended to report little change in the state of the psychological contract, while smaller-scale studies based on interviews with managers and trade union officials tend to report the opposite.

ACTIVITY 1.4

How would you characterise your current psychological contract at work? To what extent and in what ways does it differ from psychological contracts you have experienced in previous jobs or from those of your friends and family?

Best practice versus best fit

The debate between best practice and best fit is an interesting one of general significance which has consequences across the field of HRM. As well as being a managerial issue it concerns one of the most significant academic controversies in the HR field of recent years (Kaufman 2010). At root it is about whether or not there is an identifiable 'best way' of carrying out HR activities which is universally applicable. It is best understood as a debate between two schools of thought, although in practice it is quite possible to take a central position which sees validity in both the basic positions.

Adherents of a best practice perspective argue that there are certain HR practices and approaches to their operation which will invariably help an organisation in achieving competitive advantage. There is therefore a clear link between HR activity and business performance, but the effect will only be maximised if the 'right' HR policies are pursued. A great deal of evidence has been published, using various methodologies, which appears to back up the best practice case. The major early contributions drew on US-based and UK-based data (e.g. Pfeffer 1994; Huselid 1995; Wood and Albanese 1995; Delery and Doty 1996; Fernie and Metcalf 1996; Patterson *et al.* 1998; Guest and Conway 2000), in recent years the same kind of research has been carried out in other countries too. Gill and Meyer (2008), for example, found support for the assertion that best practice is associated with superior business performance in a study of 179 Australian workplaces, Gooderham *et al.* (2008) finding some support for the theory in their study of 3,821 firms based across the European Union.

While there are differences of opinion on questions of detail, all strongly suggest that the same basic bundle of human resource practices or general human resource management orientation tends to enhance business performance in all organisations irrespective of the particular product market strategy being pursued. According to David Guest this occurs through a variety of mechanisms:

> human resource practices exercise their positive impact (i) by ensuring and enhancing the competence of employees, (ii) by tapping their motivation and commitment, and (iii) by designing work to encourage the fullest contribution from employees. Borrowing from elements of expectancy theory (Vroom 1964, Lawler 1971), the model implies that all three elements should be present to ensure the best outcome. Positive employee behaviour should in turn impact upon establishment level outcomes such as low absence, quit rates and wastage, as well as high quality and productivity. (Guest 2000: 2)

The main elements of the 'best practice bundle' that these and other writers identify are those which have long been considered as examples of good practice in the HRM field. They include the use of more advanced selection methods, a serious commitment to employee involvement, substantial investment in training and development, the use of individualised reward systems and harmonised terms and conditions of employment as between different groups of employees.

The alternative 'best fit' school also identifies a link between human resource management practice and the achievement of competitive advantage. Here, however, there is no belief in the existence of universal solutions. Instead, all is contingent on the particular circumstances of each organisation. What is needed is HR policies and practices which 'fit' and are thus appropriate to the situation of individual employers. What is appropriate (or 'best') for one will not necessarily be right for another. Key variables include the size of the establishment, the dominant product market strategy being pursued and the nature of the labour markets in which the organisation competes. It is thus argued that a small organisation which principally achieves competitive advantage through innovation and which competes in very tight labour markets should have in place rather different HR policies than those of a large firm which produces low-cost goods and faces no difficulty in attracting staff. In order to maximise competitive advantage, the first requires informality combined with sophisticated human resource practices, while the latter needs more bureaucratic systems combined with a 'low cost – no frills' set of HR practices.

The best fit or contingency perspective originated in the work of Joan Woodward and her colleagues at Imperial College in the 1950s. In recent years it has been developed and applied to contemporary conditions by academics such as Randall Schuler and Susan Jackson, John Purcell and Ed Lawler. In addition, a number of influential models have been produced which seek to categorise organisational contingencies and suggest what mix of HR practices is appropriate in each case. Examples are those of Miles and Snow (1978), Fombrun *et al.* (1984) and Sisson and Storey (2000) – a number of which we look at in more detail in Chapter 3. Here too recent contributions have come from many different countries, contingency theories of HRM finding strong support from researchers working in China (Chow *et al.* 2008), Taiwan (Wang and Shyu 2008) and Japan (Takeuchi 2009).

To a great extent the jury is still out on these questions. Interestingly, however, some subfields in HRM are dominated by best practice thinking, while others broadly accept best fit assumptions. A good example of the former is employee selection (*see* Chapter 8), where for decades researchers have debated which of the various selection methods that can be used (interviews, psychometric tests, assessment centres, etc.) is 'best' in terms of its predictive validity. An example of the latter is the field of reward management (*see* Part 6) where no single best approach has yet to be identified, it being generally accepted that different situations require different types of reward package to be provided. When it comes to research on the HR function as a whole proponents of both the 'best practice' and 'best fit' perspectives can draw on bodies of empirical evidence to back up their respective positions and so the debate continues. A significant departure from both best fit and best practice thinking is represented by an approach to HR strategy making which is 'resource based'. This is fundamentally different in that it starts with an analysis of the attributes of a workforce, particularly those which account for superior performance in comparison with the competition. The focus is thus on existing human resources rather than on the business strategy or on adopting an HR formula that has worked well for other organisations. You will read more about this type of analysis and its impact in Chapter 3.

The future of work

Debates about what will happen in the future are inevitably speculative, but a great deal of attention and government research funding has recently been devoted to this issue. It matters from a public policy point of view because judgements about employers' human resource needs in the future must determine decisions about education and training now. Government actions in the fields of economic policy, employment legislation and immigration are also affected.

A good starting point is the work of influential writers such as Charles Handy (1994 and 2001), Jeremy Rifkin (1995), Susan Greenfield (2003), Richard Watson (2008), Peter Capelli (2008) and Richard Donkin (2010). In different ways they have argued that increasing competitive intensity and globalisation is leading to the emergence of a world of work which is very different in many respects from that which most in western industrialised countries currently experience. Both the type of work we do and the nature of our contractual arrangements will, it is argued, change profoundly as we complete our journey out of the industrial era and into a new post-industrial age.

The first consequence will be a marked shift towards what is described as knowledge work. In the future, it is claimed, most people will be employed, in one way or another, to carry out tasks which involve the generation, interpretation, processing or application of knowledge. Automation and the availability of cheaper labour in developing countries will see further declines in much manufacturing activity, requiring the western economies to create wealth from the exploitation of scientific and technological advances. It follows that many more people will be employed for their specialist knowledge and that far fewer routine jobs will exist than is currently the case. Demand for professional and technical people will increase, while demand for manual and lower-skilled workers will decrease. It also means that competitive advantage from an employer's perspective will derive from the capacity to create and deploy knowledge more effectively than others can.

The second major claim that is made is that the 'job' as we have come to know it will become rarer and rarer. In the future many fewer people will occupy defined jobs in organisations. Instead we will tend increasingly to work on a self-employed basis carrying out specific, time-limited projects for organisations. This is inevitable, so the argument goes, in a highly volatile business climate – what Watson (2008: 270) describes as 'a bonfire of the certainties'. Organisations simply will not be able to offer long-term guarantees of work and so will be forced to stop offering contracts of employment in the way that they currently do. The future is therefore bleak for people who want job security, but bright for those who are happy working for many employers and periodically re-educating themselves for a new type of career. In many respects these arguments are persuasive. They are based on a rational analysis of likely developments in the business environment as globalisation and technological advances further evolve. They remain, however, highly controversial and are increasingly subject to challenge by researchers who argue that change on this kind of scale is not currently happening and will not happen in the near future. A prominent critic of the views expressed by the predictors of radical change is Peter Nolan (*see* Nolan 2001 and Nolan and Wood 2003), who argues that the case is often overstated to a considerable degree:

> Change is evident, to be sure, but the shifts in the patterns and rhythms of work are not linear, pre-determined by technology or, as some writers have uncritically assumed, driven by universal trends in market globalisation. (Nolan and Wood 2003: 165)

Instead, according to Nolan and his colleagues, we are witnessing the resolute continuation of established approaches and some reversal of trends that began to develop in the 1980s and 1990s but which have since petered out. Job tenure in the UK, for example, has risen significantly in recent years while the proportion of people employed on fixed-term contracts and a self-employed basis has either fallen or remained broadly stable. While we are seeing a growth in the proportion of people employed in professional and scientific roles, the proportion of people employed in relatively low-skilled jobs in the service sector is also growing quickly.

Moynagh and Worsley (2005: 93–100) also argue that a future in which jobs as we know them become much less common is highly unlikely; indeed they argue that for many people long-term employment, even life-time employment with one organisation, is likely to continue. Their reasons are as follows:

- employees will want stable employment for financial reasons
- stable employment will aid the accumulation of knowledge
- organisations will want to hang on to key staff
- managing change will be easier with a stable workforce.

As a result they conclude that 'the open-ended permanent contract appears set to remain the norm for most employees' and that 'change will occur more in the content of jobs than in the frequency of movement between jobs'.

Critics of Handy and the other futurologists have thus identified a gap between a rhetoric which emphasises fundamental change and a reality which gives little support to the view that we are in the process of shaping a 'new world of work'. These different conceptions of the future may well derive from a preference for a focus on different types of environmental development. A reading of the major contemporary product market trends can easily lead to predictions of radical change. The twin forces of technological advance and globalisation do indeed point to a transformation of many aspects of our lives. But trends in employment are equally determined by developments in the labour market and regulatory environments. These suggest a strong preference on the part of both employees and law makers for a continuation of traditional approaches towards employment.

A PHILOSOPHY OF HUMAN RESOURCE MANAGEMENT

The philosophy of human resource management that is the basis of this book has been only slightly modified since it was first put forward in 1979 (Torrington and Chapman 1979: 4). Despite all the changes in the labour market and in the government approach to the economy, this seems to be the most realistic and constructive approach, based on the earlier ideas of Enid Mumford (1972) and McCarthy and Ellis (1973). The original was:

> Personnel management is most realistically seen as a series of activities enabling working man and his employing organisation to reach agreement about the nature and objectives of the employment relationship between them, and then to fulfil those agreements. (Torrington and Chapman 1979: 4)

Our definition for the fifth, sixth and seventh editions was:

> Human resource management is a series of activities which: first enables working people and the organisation which uses their skills to agree about the objectives and nature of their working relationship and, secondly, ensures that the agreement is fulfilled. (Torrington *et al.* 2008: 14)

This remains our philosophy. Only by satisfying the needs of the individual contributor will the business obtain the commitment to organisational objectives that is needed for organisational success, and only by contributing to organisational success will individuals be able to satisfy their personal employment needs. It is when employer and employee – or business and supplier of skills – accept that mutuality and reciprocal dependence that human resource management is exciting, centre stage and productive of business success. Where the employer is concerned with employees only as factors of production, personnel management is boring and a cost that will always be trimmed. Where employees have no trust in their employer and adopt an entirely instrumental orientation to their work, they will be fed up and will make ineffectual the work of any HR function.

SUMMARY PROPOSITIONS

1.1 Human resource management is fundamental to all management activity.

1.2 It is possible to identify two distinct definitions of the term 'human resource management'. The first describes a body of management activities, while the second signifies a particular approach to carrying out those activities.

1.3 Human resource managers are concerned with meeting four distinct sets of organisational objective: staffing, performance, change management and administration.

1.4 HRM activities are carried out in various ways through various forms of organisational structure. In some larger organisations HR generalists work alongside specialists in particular HR disciplines.

1.5 Human resource management can be characterised as one of the more recent in a series of incarnations that personnel practitioners have developed since the origins of the profession over 100 years ago.

1.6 The HRM function contributes to the achievement of different dimensions of organisational effectiveness. Prominent are the gaining and maintaining of competitive advantage, the fostering of a positive standing in financial markets and the development of a reputation for corporate social responsibility.

1.7 Three of the most prominent current debates focus on the nature of the psychological contract, the relative wisdom of the 'best fit' and 'best practice' approaches and predictions about the future of work.

1.8 The philosophy of human resource management in this book is that it is a series of activities which: first, enables working people and the business which uses their skills to agree about the nature and objectives of their working relationship; and, second, ensures that the agreement is fulfilled.

GENERAL DISCUSSION TOPICS

1 How far do you think it is possible to agree with both the 'best fit' and 'best practice' perspectives on HRM? In what ways are they compatible with each other?

2 What are the major advantages and disadvantages associated with HR managers seeing employees as 'internal customers' who need to be satisfied?

3 How far do you agree with the view that an HR function which achieves administrative excellence adds value to an organisation just as much as one which focuses on improving its employees' performance?

FURTHER READING

British Journal of Industrial Relations (Vol. 41, No. 2).
The special edition, published in June 2003, was devoted to research on and debates about the future of work. Many leading writers in the field contributed articles which set out the findings from a major national research project that has involved 22 universities.

Legge, K. (1995) *Human Resource Management: Rhetorics and Realities*. London: Macmillan.
This seminal book provides a rigorous discussion of the differences between personnel management and HRM, as well as introducing and considering a series of other debates about the nature of HRM and its purpose for organisations.

Withers, M., Williamson, M. and Reddington, M. (2010) *Transforming HR: Creating Value through People*, 2nd edn. London: Butterworth Heinemann/Elsevier.
A very accessible book which develops many of the themes we have introduced in this chapter, going on to explore the particular contribution the HR function can make in the contemporary business environment.

REFERENCES

Atkinson, C. (2004) 'Why methods matter: researching the psychological contract', *Human Resources and Employment Review*, Vol. 2, No. 2, pp. 111–16.

Bach, S. (2005) 'Personnel Management in Transition', in S. Bach (ed.), *Managing Human Resources: Personnel management in transition*, 4th edn. Oxford: Blackwell.

BBC (2008a) 'BA's terminal losses top £16 million', BBC News Website, 3 April.

BBC (2008b) 'What did go wrong at Terminal 5?', BBC News Website, 30 March.

Bickle, G. and Witzki, A. (2008) 'New psychological contracts in the world of work: economic citizens or victims of the market?', *Society and Business Review*, Vol. 3, No. 2, pp. 149–61.

Blitz, R. (2008) 'The trouble with great expectations', *Financial Times*, 26 March.

Capelli, P. (2008) 'Introduction', in P. Capelli (ed.), *Employment Relationships: New models of white collar work*. Cambridge: Cambridge University Press.

Cardy, R., Miller, J. and Ellis, A. (2007) 'Employee equity: Toward a person-based approach to HRM', *Human Resource Management Review*, Vol. 17, pp. 140–51.

Chow, I., Huang, J.C. and Liu, S. (2008) 'Strategic HRM in China: Configurations and competitive advantage', *Human Resource Management*, Vol. 47, No. 4, pp. 687–706.

CIPD (2005) *Managing Change: The role of the psychological contract*. London: Chartered Institute of Personnel & Development.

Coyle-Shapiro, J. and Kessler, I. (2000) 'Consequences of the psychological contract for the employment relationship: a large-scale survey', *Journal of Management Studies*, Vol. 37, No. 7.

Delery, J. and Doty, D.H. (1996) 'Modes of theorising in strategic human resource management: tests of universalistic, contingency and configurational performance predictions', *Academy of Management Journal*, Vol. 39, No. 4, pp. 802–35.

Done, K. and Willman, J. (2008) 'Goodwill of staff is often in short supply', *Financial Times*, 5 April.

Donkin, R. (2010) *The Future of Work*. Basingstoke: Palgrave.

Fernie, S. and Metcalf, D. (1996) 'Participation, Contingent Pay, Representation and Workplace Performance: Evidence from Great Britain', *Discussion Paper 232*, Centre for Economic Performance, London School of Economics.

Fombrun, C., Tichy, N.M. and Devanna, M.A. (1984) *Strategic Human Resource Management*. New York: Wiley.

Gill, C. and Meyer, D. (2008) 'High and low road approaches to the management of human resources: An examination of the relationship between business strategy, human resource management and high performance work practices', *International Journal of Employment Studies*, Vol. 16, No. 2, pp. 67–112.

Gooderham, P., Parry, E. and Ringdal, K. (2008) 'The impact of bundles of strategic human resource management practices on the performance of European firms', *International Journal of Human Resource Management*, Vol. 19, No. 11, pp. 2041–56.

Gratton, L. (2004) *The Democratic Enterprise: Liberating your business with freedom, flexibility and commitment*. Harlow: Pearson Education.

Greenfield, S. (2003) *Tomorrow's People*. London: Penguin/Allen Lane.

Guest, D.E. (1987) 'Human resource management and industrial relations', *Journal of Management Studies*, Vol. 24, No. 5, pp. 503–21.

Guest, D.E. (2000) 'Human resource management, employee well-being and organisational performance', Paper given at the CIPD Professional Standards Conference, University of Warwick.

Guest, D.E. (2001) 'Human resource management: when research confronts theory', *International Journal of Human Resource Management*, Vol. 12, No. 7, pp. 1092–106.

Guest, D.E. and Conway, N. (2000) *The Psychological Contract in the Public Sector*. London: CIPD.

Guest, D.E. and Conway, N. (2001) *Public and Private Sector Perceptions on the Psychological Contract*. London: CIPD.

Handy, C. (1994) *The Empty Raincoat: Making sense of the future*. London: Hutchinson.

Handy, C. (2001) *The Elephant and the Flea: Looking backwards to the future*. London: Hutchinson.

Harbison, F. (1972) 'Human resources as the wealth of nations', in I. Berg (ed.), *Human Resources and Economic Welfare*. New York: Columbia University Press.

Huselid, M. (1995) 'The impact of human resource management practices on turnover, productivity and corporate financial performance', *Academy of Management Journal*, Vol. 38, No. 3.

Kaufman, B. (2010) 'SHRM in the post-Huselid era: Why it is fundamentally misspecified', *Industrial Relations*, Vol. 49, No. 2, pp. 286–313.

Lawler, E.E. (1971) *Pay and Organizational Effectiveness. A psychological view*. New York: McGraw-Hill.

Legge, K. (1989) 'Human resource management: a critical analysis', in J. Storey (ed.), *New Perspectives on Human Resource Management*. London: Routledge.

Legge, K. (1995) *Human Resource Management: Rhetorics and realities*. London: Macmillan.

Lepak, D. and Snell, S.A. (2007) 'Employment sub-systems and the HR architecture', in P. Boxall, J. Purcell and P. Wright (eds), *The Oxford Handbook of Human Resource Management*. Oxford: Oxford University Press.

Maguire, H. (2002) 'Psychological contracts: are they still relevant?', *Career Development International*, Vol. 7, No. 3, pp. 167–80.

McCarthy, W.E.J. and Ellis, N.D. (1973) *Management by Agreement*. London: Hutchinson.

Miles, R.E. and Snow, C.C. (1978) *Organisational Strategy, Strategy and Process*. New York: McGraw-Hill.

Moynagh, M. and Worsley, R. (2005) *Working in the Twenty-first century*. Leeds: ESRC.

Mumford, E. (1972) 'Job satisfaction: a method of analysis', *Personnel Review*, Vol. 1, No. 3, pp. 48–57.

Nolan, P. (2001) 'Shaping things to come', *People Management*, 27 December, pp. 30–1.

Nolan, P. and Wood, S. (2003) 'Mapping the future of work', *British Journal of Industrial Relations*, Vol. 41, No. 2, pp. 165–74.

Patterson, M.G., West, M.A., Lawthom, R. and Nickell, S. (1998) *Impact of People Management Practices on Business Performance*. Issues in People Management No. 22. London: IPD.

Pfeffer, J. (1994) *Competitive Advantage Through People*. Boston: Harvard Business School Press.

Rifkin, J. (1995) *The End of Work: The decline of the global labour force and the dawn of the post market era*. New York: Putnam.

Saunders, J. and Hunter, I. (2009) *Service Led Design: Planning the new HR function*. London: Gower Publishing.

Schalk, R. and Freese, C. (2007) 'The impact of organizational changes on the psychological contract', in K. Isaksson, C. Hogstedt, C. Eriksson and T. Theorell (eds), *Health Effects of the New Labour Market*. New York: Springer.

Sisson, K. and Storey, J. (2000) *The Realities of Human Resource Management: Managing the employment relationship*. Buckingham: Open University Press.

Stevens, J. (ed.) (2005) *Managing Risk: The human resources contribution*. London: LexisNexis Butterworths.

Storey, J., Ulrich, D. and Wright, P. (2009) 'Introduction', in J. Storey, D. Ulrich and P. Wright (eds), *The Routledge Companion to Strategic Human Resource Management*. London: Routledge.

Takeuchi, N. (2009) 'How Japanese manufacturing firms align their human policies with business strategies: testing a contingency performance prediction in a Japanese context', *International Journal of Human Resource Management*, Vol. 20, No. 1, pp. 34–56.

Torrington, D.P. and Chapman, J.B. (1979) *Personnel Management*. Hemel Hempstead: Prentice Hall.

Torrington, D.P., Hall, L.A. and Taylor, S. (2008) *Human Resource Management*, 6th edn. Harlow: FT/Prentice Hall.

Vroom, V.H. (1964) *Work and Motivation*. New York: Wiley.

Wang, D.S. and Shyu, C.L. (2008) 'Will the strategic fit between business and HRM strategy influence HRM effectiveness and organizational performance?', *International Journal of Manpower*, Vol. 29, No. 2, pp. 92–110.

Watson, R. (2008) *Future Files: The five trends that will shape the next fifty years*. London: Nicholas Brealey Publishing.

Withers, M., Williamson, M. and Reddington, M. (2010) *Transforming HR: Creating value through people*, 2nd edn. London: Butterworth Heinemann/Elsevier.

Wood, S. and Albanese, M. (1995) 'Can we speak of high commitment management on the shop floor?', *Journal of Management Studies*, Vol. 32, No. 2, pp. 215–47.

An extensive range of additional materials, including multiple choice questions, answers to questions and links to useful websites can be found on the Human Resource Management companion website at **www.pearsoned.co.uk/torrington**.

THE CONTEXT OF HUMAN RESOURCE MANAGEMENT

THE OBJECTIVES OF THIS CHAPTER ARE TO:

1. Set out the major contemporary trends in the business environment which have significance for HR practice
2. Discuss the sources of increased competitive intensity and the organisational consequences from an HRM perspective
3. Explain the significance of demographic trends for future labour market conditions and the extent of diversity among the working population
4. Explore patterns in demand for and supply of labour, skills levels and skills shortages in the UK
5. Describe the development of employment regulation and speculate on its likely future direction
6. Debate the reasons for trade union decline and prospects for a revival in trade union membership
7. Introduce the rise of ethical consumerism and ethical investment and its potential significance for HRM practice

Over the past twenty years the world of work in countries such as the UK has changed in important ways. In some industries and professions profound adjustments have occurred leading many commentators to argue that we have experienced a second industrial revolution, every bit as significant in its long-term impact as the first one was in the late eighteenth and nineteenth centuries. Elsewhere significant changes have occurred, but of a less profound nature and over a longer timescale. As far as the workplace is concerned, it is thus fair to conclude that the British workplace has experienced a mixture of evolution and revolution. The same is true of the HR function and of the HR agenda in organisations. Major change has occurred and continues to occur, but over a long period of time in response to developments in the business environment. The big unknown question is whether these long-term trends will continue in the same broad direction, and if so, what will continuation mean for the way that organisations recruit, retain and motivate people in the future?

At the time of writing (spring 2010) the economies of most western industrialised countries appear to be emerging from a period of severe recession. Recovery, however, is unsteady and it is not clear whether or not we will see a return to the established pre-recession trend of solid, steady growth. We cannot yet be certain that the recent economic downturn will have been a relatively short interruption to the established pattern of growth which will soon resume, or whether it marks a turning point, signalling the start of a new era of persistently low growth and higher unemployment. Either is a possible outcome. However, for the purposes of this chapter, when thinking about the future, we will assume a continuation of the most established, better-entrenched trends, focusing on those with particular significance for contemporary HRM practice. We concentrate on those developments that have had the most strategic importance rather than on those that are largely operational in their impact. Our focus will be on developments in the labour market, on regulation, on trade unions and on the rise of greater ethical awareness. We start with what is probably the most important single trend of recent years, namely the increase in the amount and level of competition facing most organisations.

COMPETITION

There are no internationally recognised indices or generally recognised methods for tracking the growth of competitive pressures in a particular industry over time. Competitive pressures can be as fierce in a market dominated by three or four major international players as it is in industries characterised by many thousands of smaller businesses fighting to maintain a small market share. Instead economists tend to rely on a range of diverse proxy-measures, none of which by themselves prove that we are experiencing considerably greater competitive intensity, but which taken together strongly suggest that we are. Hence over time there have been strong trends towards greater concentration of market power in the hands of larger organisations (Mahajan 2006), much greater levels of import penetration into UK markets from overseas producers (Wadhwani 1999) and a reduction in the amount of time in which any one organisation is able to achieve and maintain market dominance in an industry (Thomas and D'Aveni 2004). In some industries competition has become so intense that they are characterised by economists as being 'hyper-competitive' in nature (Sparrow 2003).

The trend has three principal causes, although the extent to which each has a significance in particular industries varies. Across much of the manufacturing sector, agriculture and the extractive industries, globalisation is the key source of additional competition. National markets are increasingly being subsumed into single international markets with many more players and far less predictability. Hence, for example, the UK steel industry has been transformed over 30 years from one which mainly produced steel for consumption in the UK to one which sells its products all over the world and competes fiercely with overseas providers. In 1970 only 5 per cent of steel used in the UK was imported, by 2006 over half came from overseas.

In other industries technology is the main driver of increased competition. Technological advances both create greater opportunities, but also drive competitive intensity by requiring organisations to keep ahead of their rivals all the time. This is the case across the IT, telecommunications, pharmaceuticals, science-based industries and hi-tech manufacturing sectors, a result being a progressive lowering of prices for consumers. A good example is broadcasting, where thanks to technological developments, the number of TV channels widely available to UK consumers increased from one in 1950 to five in 2000 and now numbers hundreds.

The third major cause is government policy which has increasingly favoured the creation of competitive markets in sectors which were previously regulated or even nationalised. Governments see the promotion of competition as a means of improving efficiency and quality of services, at the same time driving wealth creation and innovation in the economy. Foreign exchange controls have been removed, as have many tariff barriers, making international trade easier and cheaper. The presence of a European single market is the most prominent example of government acting so as to encourage competition across national borders. The EU, as is the case with other international institutions such as the World Trade Organisation, acts as forum for discussion and agreement about other regulations, many of which in recent years have been designed explicitly to free up markets to greater competition by removing barriers and protectionist rules. A good example here is the growth of competition in the airline industry as international agreements restricting the number of airlines which could operate each major route have been removed, allowing considerable increases in competition.

A fourth driver of increased competitive intensity has emerged in consequence of the first three. Greater competition has empowered consumers and this in turn has both raised expectations in terms of service levels and made us less loyal to particular products or brands. We are now much more likely to take our business elsewhere, if we are unhappy with the service we are getting or with goods we have been supplied with. We seek value for money and take steps to compare prices and quality before deciding what to buy. We do this simply because we have more opportunity to exercise choice. In this way the presence of more competition serves in itself to drive greater competitive intensity. Nowhere is this more true than in business-to-business transactions, where organisations have to bid against one another to secure contracts and also negotiate prices with suppliers.

These established trends will continue. Technology continues to advance at a fast rate, itself helping to make global economic activity easier and cheaper. Meanwhile governments show no sign of reversing their preference for deregulation, privatisation and marketisation. Consumers show no sign at all of losing their appetite for choice and the ability to shop around for the best value.

What are the implications for employment practices and for the human resource management agenda? The following are some of the most important: flexibility, cost control and an increasing need to demonstrate the worth of the HR function to an organisation.

Flexibility

Competition leads to increased volatility and unpredictability in an organisation's trading environment. The greater the degree of competitive intensity the more fleet of foot an organisation is required to be. Changes have to be made more quickly and more regularly, resources being switched from one activity to another in order that opportunities may be seized when they occur. Established sources of competitive advantage may cease to add value, while new potential sources must be exploited. This means that once valued skills can quickly become obsolete, leading to redundancies and to a requirement for staff to develop new skills. It also requires organisations to be in a position to deploy people opportunistically so that there are sufficient people with the right qualifications in a position to provide a new service, develop a new product or meet increased demand for new lines.

We can thus anticipate that flexibility is likely to move further up the HR management agenda in the decades ahead. There will be a greater level of 'churn' as people leave and join organisations with somewhat greater frequency, a great deal more multiskilling on the part of non-specialists and greater investment in employee development so that an organisation is able both to recruit and to retain good people, while also maximising its capacity for flexibility.

Cost control

Another inevitable consequence of increased competitive intensity, particularly for UK organisations which are obliged to compete with rivals in developing countries with much lower cost bases, is a continual need to reduce expenditure and to keep a lid on costs. From an HR perspective this inevitably means that less money is available for pay rises or enhanced benefit packages. This poses a major problem in an era of tightening labour markets because it means that an organisation's capacity to buy its way out of a skills shortage is severely limited. A premium is therefore placed on the capacity to recruit and retain effectively at relatively low cost. Over time this is leading to a shift in traditional approaches to rewarding employees, making much more use of the approaches associated with 'total reward' thinking we outline in Chapter 23. We are likely in the future to see greater focus being placed on relational rewards, creating jobs which are as 'rewarding' as possible in the widest sense of the word, but which are less costly. This is a lot harder to achieve in practice than giving people pay rises, requiring more sophisticated interpersonal skills, the possession on the part of managers of a good deal of emotional intelligence and creative thinking about the management of the employment relationship. Methods will have to be found and introduced which have the effect of making people feel more valued, just as positively motivated and generally highly satisfied with their work, but which do not involve paying them more money.

Evaluating the HR contribution

The third major implication of increased competition from an HRM point of view is increased pressure for the function itself to demonstrate its own worth in terms of valued added and costs controlled. This is already an issue that is moving up organisational agendas and is one we explore in Chapters 28 and 29. In the future we can expect to see more examples of HR accounting measures being developed and used, more quantative targets being set for HR specialists to meet, more benchmarking of HR performance against that of competitors and pressure to organise the HR function in such a way as to secure greater value for money. It is likely that this will involve greater use of information technology as activities that can be are automated and/or transferred online to organisational intranets. In many cases this will reduce the requirement for people to undertake HR roles which are essentially administrative in nature (e.g. payroll officers) or which can be carried out by IT applications (e.g. many training roles). Outsourcing of HR activity to specialist suppliers, at present relatively rare and generally restricted to defined areas of HR activity such as training and payroll administration, will also increase as organisations find that they can buy in services that are of higher quality than those provided in-house, but less expensive too.

Internationalisation

Since 1950 world output has increased six-fold while world trade has increased twenty-fold. As a result the proportion of goods and services which are exported and consumed in countries other than that in which they originate has increased very markedly indeed. This globalisation of economic activity is not just a major cause of greater competitive intensity. The process works in the other direction too, as organisations act more internationally in order to help them survive and thrive in a more competitive environment. As the proportion of goods and services traded internationally has grown, organisations have responded by forming strategic alliances across national boundaries, by merging to give themselves a greater international market presence and by outsourcing aspects of their production processes to overseas suppliers or subsidiaries as a means of cutting costs. UK employees are thus now much more likely than they were 20 years ago to be employed by international corporations, many of which are owned by parent companies based overseas. At the same time larger UK companies have acquired assets in other countries. Indeed the UK economy is one of the most internationally focused, having embraced globalisation more enthusiastically than most. UK companies are among the biggest foreign investors in the world. After US companies, UK companies are the second biggest international investors. They also invest more in the USA than those of any other country. In total 15 per cent of all foreign direct investment is accounted for by UK-based organisations, while 11 per cent of all international investment comes into the UK. This represents a quarter of all foreign direct investment into the European Union. When it is considered that the UK economy in terms of its size represents just 5 per cent of the world economy, it can be seen just how very internationally focused the economy has become.

There are major consequences for all organisational functions. For the HR function internationalisation has created a need to understand and operate within international cultural and institutional constraints. It has also required the recruitment of people in one country to work on a long-term basis as expatriates in other countries. Increasingly HR managers in the UK are required to report to corporate managers based elsewhere and vice versa, while new forms of organisation structure have had to be developed to enable corporations to operate effectively across international borders. We will return to these issues in Chapter 6.

ACTIVITY 2.1

Aside from the need to become more flexible, pressure to reduce costs, internationalisation and a need for the HR function in organisations to justify its existence, what other people management consequences flow from increasing competitive intensity between organisations?

THE LABOUR MARKET

In February 2010 the Office for National Statistics reported that 28.9 million people of working age in the UK were employed, the number being classed as economically active being rather higher at 31.4 million. This is rather lower than at the equivalent point in 2009 due to the impact of recession, but it is a great deal higher than the figure reported in 1971 when the government first started collecting statistics on this measure. Table 2.1 shows how the number of people who are employed or otherwise recorded as being economically active has increased steadily over the past 40 years by around a fifth. This substantial increase in demand for labour reflects economic growth and population growth over this period, but it is nonetheless remarkable when it is considered that the growth has occurred despite three major economic recessions, the introduction of transformational labour-saving technologies, and the exporting overseas of many jobs formerly based in the UK. Major industrial restructuring has occurred, yet the demand for labour over the long term has increased steadily.

Another way of tracking growth in demand for labour involves looking at the total number of jobs. This is a rather higher figure because it includes jobs held by people who are not classed as being of working age (e.g. people over state retirement age) and also takes account of those who have two or more part-time jobs. As can be seen in Figure 2.1, the number of jobs in 2010 was estimated to be 30.9 million. This is lower than the peak reached in 2007, but still much higher than a decade ago and some five million higher than was the case in the 1970s. We can therefore conclude that the long-term trend is strongly towards increased demand for people and that in the long term there will be continued higher demand.

Table 2.1 The labour market, 1971–2010

	EMPLOYED	ECONOMICALLY ACTIVE
1971	24.6 million	25.6 million
1976	24.8 million	26.1 million
1981	24.7 million	27.0 million
1986	24.7 million	27.8 million
1991	26.7 million	28.9 million
1996	26.0 million	28.4 million
2001	27.6 million	29.1 million
2006	28.7 million	30.3 million
2009	29.3 million	31.5 million
2010	28.9 million	31.4 million

Source: Office for National Statistics.

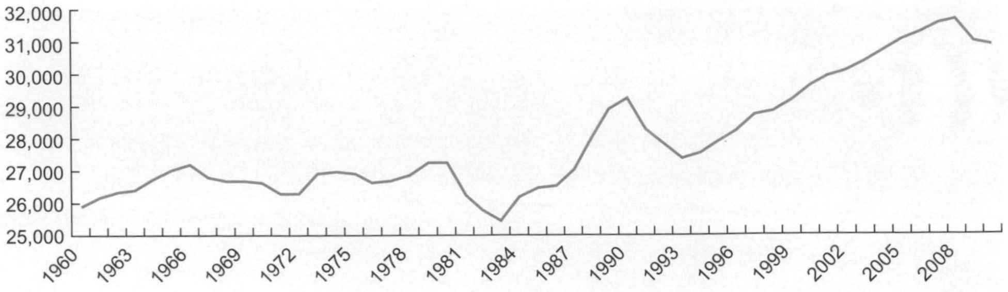

Figure 2.1
Jobs in the UK
Source: Compiled from Office for National Statistics data.

But what sort of skills will employers be looking for? Long-term trends here paint a clear picture too. The official method used to classify occupations in the UK was changed in 1999, so it is not possible to make a precise comparison of today's figures with those produced by government statisticians before then. Nonetheless an obvious long-term pattern can be seen in the two sets of statistics presented in Tables 2.2 and 2.3. These show a pronounced switch occurring over a long period of time, and continuing strongly in more recent years, away from skilled, semi-skilled and unskilled manual work towards jobs which require higher-level and more specialised skills. The major growth areas have long been in the professional, technical and managerial occupations, but there has also been a considerable increase in service-sector jobs which require the job-holder to deal directly with customers. These changes reflect the shift that has occurred over recent decades away from an economy with a sizeable manufacturing sector, towards one which is dominated to a far greater degree by the private and public services sectors.

Table 2.2
Changes in occupations, 1951–1999

Occupation	% in 1951	% in 1999
Higher professionals	1.9	6.4
Lower professionals	4.7	14.9
Employers and proprietors	5.0	3.4
Managers and administrators	5.5	15.7
Clerks	10.7	14.9
Foremen, supervisors and inspectors	2.6	3.1
Skilled manual	24.9	12.7
Semi-skilled manual	31.5	23.0
Unskilled manual	13.1	5.9

Source: Labour Force Survey statistics accessed at www.statistics.gov.uk.

Table 2.3
Changes in occupations, 2001–2008

Occupation	% in 2001	% in 2008
Managers and senior officials	12.9	15.2
Professional occupations	11.7	12.9
Associate professional and technical occupations	13.2	14.6
Administrative and secretarial	14.9	12.6
Skilled trades	9.5	8.2
Personal services	7.5	8.6
Sales and customer services	8.6	8.5
Process, plant and machine operatives	8.7	6.9
Elementary occupations	13.2	12.4

Source: Labour Force Survey statistics accessed at www.statistics.gov.uk.

ACTIVITY 2.2

Why do you think countries such as the UK have seen so great a transformation in their industrial structure since the 1970s. Why are there so many fewer manufacturing jobs and so many more jobs in the service sector? Why are organisations so much more likely to employ small numbers of people than was the case 50 years ago?

One of the most vigorously contested debates among labour market economists concerns the nature of the skills that employers will be looking for in the future, a debate that has very important implications for government education policy, which, as a result, is itself controversial (see Grugulis *et al.* 2004). In recent years a highly influential group has argued that in the future economies such as that of the UK will see a speeding up of the trends identified above. Influenced by figures such as Manuel Castells of Berkeley University in California, it has become common for policymakers to believe that a 'new economy' is rapidly developing which will increasingly be dominated by companies which are 'knowledge intensive' in nature. According to this 'upskilling thesis', lower-skilled jobs will be rarer and rarer in industrialised countries. Because they can be done far more cheaply in developing economies, they will increasingly be exported overseas. It follows that governments such as that of the UK should prepare the workforce as best they can for the challenges of a 'high-skill, high-wage economy' in which those who do not have a relevant higher education are going to struggle to make a living.

Critics of Castells tend to look to the writings of a very different American academic guru figure – Harry Braverman. His theories derive from a Marxian perspective as well as from observations of the activities of corporations in the 1960s and 1970s. This contrasting 'deskilling thesis' argues that businesses competing in capitalist economies will always look for ways of cutting their labour costs, and that they do this in part by continually reducing the level of skills required by the people they employ. It follows that, far from leading to a demand for higher-level skills and knowledge, the advent of an economy based on information and communication technologies will *over time* reduce such demand.

Both schools draw on widely documented trends to back up their positions. The up-skillers draw attention to the fact that the major growth areas in labour demand are in the higher-skilled occupational categories. Demand for graduates is increasing, demand for lower-skilled people is less strong, and is decreasing in some industries. They also draw attention to the emergence of skills shortages in many industries as employers find it steadily harder to recruit people with the abilities and experience they need.

By contrast, the down-skillers draw attention to the growth of call-centre-type operations which use technology to reduce the amount of knowledge and expertise required by customer services staff, and to the increasing use of bureaucratic systems which reduce the number of situations in which people have a discretion to make decisions. They also point to the strong growth in industries such as retailing and hotels which are characterised by employment of people who need only to have low-level skills and who are relatively lowly paid. They thus forecast a situation in which the workforce is heavily overqualified and in which graduates are increasingly employed in jobs for which no degree is necessary. They also argue that many of the 'skills' that employers say are in short supply are not in fact 'skills' at all, but are merely 'attributes' or 'characteristics'. The target here is an evolving business language that refers to 'communication skills', 'interpersonal skills', 'teamworking skills', 'problem-solving skills' and 'customer-handling skills'. These, it is argued, have nothing whatever to do with a knowledge-based economy and cannot be gained through formal education.

But who is right? The answer is profoundly important from a public policy point of view because decisions have to be taken today in order to ensure that the labour force is appropriately qualified to meet the needs of the economy in future decades. The answer is just as significant for organisations, not least because if it is the case that the current labour force is seriously under-skilled vis-à-vis future requirements, much of the onus for addressing the evolving 'gap' will fall on employers. Such a situation will also mean that the 'tight' labour market conditions which characterised many labour markets in the early years of the twenty-first century will return and get tighter still, placing effective recruitment and retention back at the top of the HR agenda.

The most authoritative current predictions are probably those contained in the *Leitch Review of Skills* (2006) and in its associated documentation (see www.hm-treasury.gov.uk). Lord Sandy Leitch, a leading figure in the UK's financial services sector, was commissioned by the government to carry out a wide-ranging review of the country's skills base and of future skills gaps in 2004. His final report was published late in 2006 along with much of the research evidence he drew on in reaching his conclusions. Of particular relevance to the debate we are considering here is the report written by Rachel Beaven and her colleagues from the Warwick Institute of Employment Research and Cambridge Econometrics looking at alternative skills scenarios for the UK economy through until 2020 (Beaven *et al.* 2005).

Leitch comes down strongly on the side of the up-skilling side of our debate. His view is that there will continue to be substantial growth in the number of jobs in the UK. He states that 'demand for skills will grow inexorably' as technology advances and globalisation of the world economy continues (Leitch 2006: 1). However, he also concludes that the existing skills base is far from 'world class' and that the UK is not nearly sufficiently well placed if it is to seize the opportunities presented, lift productivity levels and maintain its position as a leading international economy.

Beaven *et al.* (2005: 37) conclude that the number of jobs in the UK will grow to 30.1 million by 2020 (i.e. a growth of over 2.3 million), but that we will at the same time see considerable further falls in the number of people employed in unskilled occupations (down by 845,000), many skilled trades (down by 301,000) and in the number of administrative and secretarial jobs (down by 357,000). So much of the overall increase, and more besides, will be accounted for by the higher-skilled, higher-paid occupations. They estimate that demand for managers will grow by 889,000 and for professional and technical people by 1.65 million. The other major growth areas will be in occupations in the sales, customer services and personal services areas (up by 1.2 million by 2020). Importantly, this increased demand for labour will coincide with a period in which the size of the working population is projected to fall as the large cohort of people born between 1945 and 1964 – the 'baby-boom generation' – retire. Because there are many hundreds of thousands fewer UK-born individuals in succeeding cohorts, the actual number of new managers, professionals and service-sector workers that will need to be recruited in order to meet projected levels of demand will be up to eight times greater.

Meeting this demand, according to the Leitch Report, is going to require a very substantial lifting of the existing UK skills base. He concludes that the UK is not currently well placed to achieve this, and more importantly, that in significant respects major competitor nations are a good deal better placed. Over a third of adults in the UK do not 'hold the equivalent of a basic school-leaving qualification', 'almost half have difficulty with numbers' and 'one seventh are not functionally literate'.

We can thus conclude by asserting with some confidence that the long-term trend towards higher-skilled, professional occupations and away from unskilled and lower-skilled jobs will continue for the foreseeable future. Moreover, it is clear from Lord Leitch's conclusions that meeting the demand for these jobs is going to be difficult without major investment in adult education and training on the part of both the government and employers. Encouraging the immigration of skilled workers from overseas will contribute to reducing skills gaps somewhat, but it will not help those whose existing levels of attainment and skill are at too low a level to enable them to find long-term employment in an economy based on higher-level skills and expertise.

From the point of view of employing organisations the future is most likely to involve a substantial further tightening of skilled labour market, lifting still further the advantages that will accrue to those who are best placed to recruit and then to retain the limited numbers of people who will have the most sought-after skills, knowledge and experience. The likelihood is therefore that the approaches described in this chapter, such as employer branding, overseas recruitment and effective retention strategies will play an increasingly central role in organisations' HRM activities.

On the other hand, the outlook for lower-skilled and unskilled workers appears bleak. Even more than is already the case these groups are likely to have difficulty finding and securing jobs. There are going to be more people than there are employment opportunities. So these labour markets will loosen, employers strengthening their power at the expense of the workforce.

ACTIVITY 2.3

Assuming that Lord Leitch's predictions are broadly correct, what other HRM activities are likely to become increasingly important over the next 20 years in addition to those focused on improving the effectiveness of recruitment and retention practices in organisations?

Longer-term demographic trends also point to growing skills shortages and tightening labour markets. This is because the total number of people of working age is projected to decline somewhat. This is a result of the structure of the UK's population which is illustrated clearly in Figure 2.2. In the middle of the diagram you see a bulge, representing the generation born between 1945 and 1964. This cohort is often referred to as that of the 'baby boomers' because of the high birth rates that occurred at that time. It is largely because of the size of this generation, as well as the increased propensity of women to work for longer periods of their lifetimes, that the supply of labour has

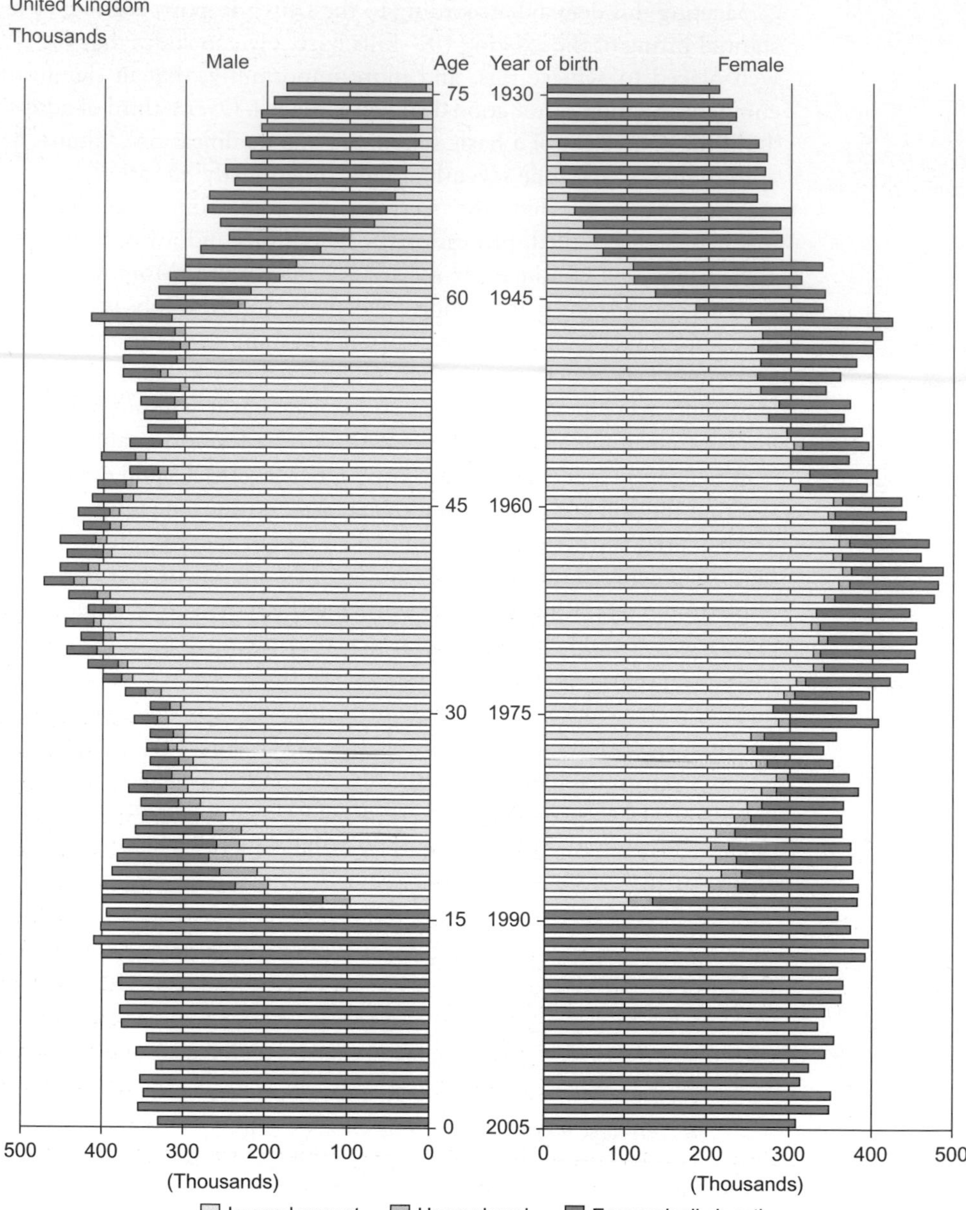

Figure 2.2 Population structure: by age, sex and economic activity, autumn 2005[1]

1 Not seasonally adjusted.
Source: Labour Force Survey.

been able to keep pace with the growing demand for labour in the economy over recent decades. This situation, however, has already begun to change as the big baby-boom generation has started to retire. The cohort of people coming up behind the baby boomers (born between 1965 and 1985), as you can see from Figure 2.2 and Table 2.4, is considerably smaller in number, meaning that there are hundreds of thousands fewer people aged between 25 and 45 than there are between 45 and 65. After 2010, when the first baby boomers reach 65 there will be a steady growth in the mismatch between the supply of labour, which will decrease, and the demand for labour, which we expect will continue to increase.

Table 2.4 Total births, 1945–2010

	Total births (millions)	Average per year
1945–1964	17.6	880,000
1965–1984	16.1	803,000
1985–2004	14.8	738,000

ACTIVITY 2.4

Why do you think that people, on average, choose to have fewer children than they did a generation ago? Can anything be done to reverse the trend? How far should governments see it as their role to encourage more births?

On the face of it, therefore, demographic trends also point to a tightening of labour markets as employers compete with one another to recruit and retain a diminishing working population. However, matters are not as simple as they may appear. First, it must be remembered that over 20 per cent of the working age population (almost eight million people) who are of working age are not working or seeking work at any one time. These principally comprise students in full-time education, people with long-term health problems, people who have taken early retirement and people who are devoting their time to bringing up children or caring for other adults. If just a quarter of the people in this 'economically inactive' category were to find employment, even if on a part-time basis, it would substantially reduce the extent to which the labour market is going to tighten in coming decades. Second, it must be remembered that the size of the working population will increase somewhat between 2010 and 2020 as a result of the raising of the female state pension age from 60 to 65, and thereafter as the state pension age is raised to 66 for men from 2016 and again for men and women to 67 in 2034 and 68 in 2044. On the other side of the equation, however, is the substantial increase in the proportion of young people who the government plans should attend university and the impact on the size of the working population arising from increasing the age at which young people can leave full-time education to 18.

A further factor to take into account is immigration. In recent years the number of overseas migrants coming to the UK to work has greatly exceeded the number of existing UK residents leaving to emigrate overseas. Precise numbers are difficult to establish because so many of the new arrivals since 2004 originate in the Eastern European countries which gained accession to the European Union in May 2004. There is a requirement for migrant workers from these countries to register with the government, but there is no penalty exacted on those who fail to do so, no requirement for self-employed people to register and no means of knowing how many of those who have registered have stayed in the UK to work on a temporary basis before returning home. Estimates of the overall figures are thus unreliable. The government's official statistics estimate current levels of net immigration to be running at around 150,000 a year, but other figures issued by government departments suggest that this is an underestimate. For example,

Table 2.5 UK population projections to 2031

	2006	2011	2016	2021	2026	2031
						thousands
United Kingdom	60,587	62,761	64,975	67,191	69,260	71,100
England	50,763	52,706	54,724	56,757	58,682	60,432
Wales	2,966	3,038	3,113	3,186	3,248	3,296
Scotland	5,117	5,206	5,270	5,326	5,363	5,374
Northern Ireland	1,742	1,812	1,868	1,922	1,966	1,999

in the year to April 2007 as many as 713,000 new national insurance numbers were issued to employees from overseas who had secured jobs in the UK (Taylor 2007). This is equivalent to almost 2.5 per cent of the total working population being added in one year alone.

If current patterns of immigration and emigration continue in the future the UK's population will increase dramatically, meaning that many concerns about an inadequate supply of labour can cease. This is the case, not least because the average age of people coming into the UK from overseas to settle is much lower than that of existing UK residents who leave to settle abroad. Table 2.5 shows population projections assuming a continuation of current trends. But it is reasonable to question the extent to which the absorption of such a vast number of people would ever be politically possible given the implications there would be for demand on housing, roads and public services. Moreover, the government has introduced new immigration rules which aim to reduce the numbers of immigrants substantially. It is also reasonable to question for how long the current interest in migrating to the UK from overseas can continue.

Looking forward, two major practical implications arise as a result of these demographic trends which are likely to become increasingly significant as far as the management of people is concerned. First, organisations are going to find it increasingly difficult to fill more highly skilled and specialised roles, at least from traditional sources. Second, we can be certain that we are therefore going to see much greater ethnic and cultural diversity in the make-up of our workforce.

WINDOW ON PRACTICE

In 2006 the Confederation of British Industry (CBI) published a survey of employers which revealed a lack of basic educational skills among new recruits. According to respondents the big problem in the UK is a lack of basic numerical skills among school leavers, but good reading and writing skills are also in short supply. The problem extends to graduate recruits too. The survey suggests that 23 per cent of employers are unhappy with levels of literacy among their graduates and that 13 per cent are concerned about numeracy levels. The response, according to the CBI, is for one in three employers to provide remedial tuition in reading, writing and arithmetic.

Source: Green 2006.

Tighter labour markets

Labour markets are already much tighter in the UK than they were ten or twenty years ago. According to successive annual surveys carried out by the Chartered Institute of Personnel and Development (CIPD 2002–9), a good majority of employers are now regularly experiencing difficulties recruiting the people they need. Moreover, the position has not changed hugely as a result of the recent recession, as Table 2.6 indicates.

The key reasons for recruitment difficulties according to the survey respondents are a lack of specialist skills in the labour market, a tendency for qualified job applicants to ask for more money than can be afforded and a lack of sufficient experience on the part of people applying for jobs.

A snapshot survey by the Learning and Skills Council (2006) shows that the problem extends to small and medium-sized businesses too as these findings indicate:

- 17 per cent of organisations in their sample had vacancies at the time the survey was conducted – a total of 571,000.
- 7 per cent of organisations had vacancies at that time which they classed as 'hard to fill'.
- 25 per cent of vacancies are considered by employers to be in areas where there are skills shortages (i.e. around 150,000 at any one time).
- 16 per cent of organisations claim that there are 'skills gaps' among their existing staff.
- 6 per cent of all staff are described by employers as not being proficient in their jobs due to skills gaps (that is 1.3 million employees in England).

From a human resource management point of view the likely outcome over the coming decades is one in which the art of recruiting and retaining people in a tight labour market returns to the top of the HR agenda. Competence in this area, more than any other, will make the difference between an HRM function which is successful and one that is not. It will be necessary for organisations to work hard at developing and retaining positive reputations as employers, to differentiate their offerings as employers from those of their competitors through employer branding exercises and to take a flexible approach to staffing their organisations. Where wage budgets are under pressure, it will be necessary for all managers to develop strong interpersonal skills, to demonstrate emotional intelligence and to see themselves as team leaders more than as supervisors. Effective management development programmes will thus be more necessary than is currently the case, while employee development more generally will assume greater significance as a key method of attracting and retaining people. Another area of HR activity that is likely to assume particular importance is the capacity to design organisations and to allocate activities across teams in such a way as to minimise the reliance on the hard-to-recruit groups.

Table 2.6 Employers experiencing recruitment problems

Year	%	Year	%
2002:	77%	2006:	82%
2003:	93%	2007:	84%
2004:	85%	2008:	86%
2005:	85%	2009:	81%

Managing a diverse team

Over the course of the past decade we have seen an increase of 70 per cent in the number of people working in the UK who originate elsewhere (Caldwell 2007). While the pace of growth may well decline, there is no question that the numbers will further increase in the years to come, not least because employers will increasingly seek comparatively rare skills overseas. In London and in some other urban centres many organisations already operate with a workforce which is highly diverse in terms of its national origin. The extent to which this happens is likely to increase much further in the coming decades. It means that gaining an understanding of cultural differences in terms of workplace expectations will need to widen beyond the ranks of expatriate workers to encompass a far wider group of managers and employees. Organisations which are able to achieve this most successfully stand to benefit greatly from the development of a good reputation in overseas labour markets and among communities of people who have migrated to the UK from the same countries and regions. Moreover, they stand to gain from enhanced performance on the part of their overseas recruits.

It is partly a question of being culturally sensitive in a general sense. Not only do organisations which are serious about diversity need to eliminate unfairness or discrimination, they need to be seen to be doing so and hence perceived by their employees, all the time, as acting entirely equitably. The other requirement is the development on the part of managers and colleagues who originate in the UK of a full understanding of the way in which workplaces are culturally different in many overseas countries and hence that recruits coming to the UK from abroad have different expectations and different behavioural norms that need to be respected and taken into account. Laroche and Rutherford (2007) give many good examples in their book. Examples are as follows:

- In the UK when we select people for jobs we focus primarily on the skills and experience that are necessary to do the particular job well. The better matched the skills and the more relevant the experience, the better the chances that a candidate will be offered the job. For candidates from elsewhere in the world, particularly for people from Southern Asia and the Middle East such an approach is alien. They are used to a business culture in which educational qualifications are far more significant, the most successful job applicants being those with the highest degrees from the most prestigious institutions. Moreover, a broad range of experience is seen as being more important than experience that is focused narrowly in one area. As a result CVs sent by people from these countries are typically very different from those that UK-based applicants would draw up. They will also tend to stress different kinds of qualities when interviewed.
- Interpersonal behaviour in UK workplaces appears cold and unfriendly to people from other parts of the world. We tend to like to maintain a substantial 'personal space' around us which, when it is 'invaded' by someone else, makes us feel uncomfortable. Touching extends just to formal handshaking and, occasionally, perhaps a brief congratulatory pat on the back or upper arm. We rarely display emotion at work, and tend to regard such displays with suspicion, regarding the person concerned as lacking in their capacity to make cool, detached judgements. The situation in many overseas countries is very different. Personal space is much smaller, handshakes last for longer. touching is common, even senior managers display plenty of emotion and people regularly kiss and hug one another at work.

- Business cultures in UK workplaces are a great deal less hierarchical than is the case in most other countries. Managers are not, on the whole, autocratic in their approach. They consult widely before making decisions, tend to have reasonably open and genuine relationships with those they manage and will often actively encourage critical scrutiny of their thinking. Delegation of authority for decision making is the norm, senior managers often not expecting to be informed about everything that is going on in their divisions. The situation in many other countries, including European countries, is wholly different. Hierarchy is more important, questioning the boss unacceptable and consultation far rarer. Managers expect to be informed about what is happening and delegate decision making to a far lesser extent.

ACTIVITY 2.5

According to the demographers at the United Nations several European countries are going to see substantial falls in their populations over the next 40 years due to low fertility rates. It is estimated that the German population will fall from 83 million to 79 million by 2050, and the Italian population from 58 million to 51 million. In Russia the projected fall is from 143 million to 112 million. By contrast the British and French populations are projected to increase modestly during this period, while in Turkey the population will increase hugely from 77 million today to 101 million in 2050.

What do you think are the main long-term implications for organisations in these different European countries? What will the effect be on the labour market? What will be the effect on the capacity of public sector organisations to deliver vital public services?

REGULATION

The third major long-term trend which has had a major impact on the way organisations manage people in recent decades has been the very substantial increase in the extent of employment legislation. We will discuss the practical impact of this important trend in Chapters 10 and 20, but it is necessary to explain its broad significance at this stage.

In 1954 the eminent legal scholar Professor Otto Khan-Freund (1954: 44) correctly stated that:

> There is, perhaps, no major country in the world in which the law has played a less significant role in the shaping of industrial relations than in Great Britain and in which the law and legal profession have less to do with labour relations.

This situation has now wholly changed. Over the past 40 years the UK has moved from having some of the most lightly regulated labour markets in the world to sharing, along with the other EU member states, a very highly regulated system. It is reasonable to characterise this change as comprising a regulatory revolution, so great has been the transformation in the amount of regulation to which the employment relationship has become subject and its day-to-day impact on management practice.

While some areas of employment law are a great deal more employer friendly than others, the overall impact has been to restrict the freedom of managers to run their organisations in ways that they might otherwise wish to. The law now gives very important rights to employees and to people working under other forms of contract. There is, for example, a large body of anti-discrimination law protecting people from adverse treatment at the hands of their employers, either directly or indirectly, on the following grounds:

- sex
- marital status
- race
- ethnicity
- national origin
- disability
- age
- sexual orientation
- religion or belief
- fixed-term status
- part-time status
- trade union membership
- non-trade union membership
- trade union activity
- ex-offenders with spent convictions

In addition, new EU regulations extending a measure of protection to agency workers will bc introduced from 2011.

Aside from discrimination law we now also have well-established law which restricts the freedom of employers to dismiss employees. Unless the reason is lawful and the manner in which the matter is handled is considered reasonable, an employment tribunal can require the employer either to re-employ or compensate the employee who has been unfairly dismissed. Other major areas of employment law cover health and safety at work, working time, wage levels, deductions from wages, data protection, the rights of employees when their organisation changes hands, severance payments and whistle-blowing. In addition, there is a huge and growing body of family-friendly employment regulation giving minimum periods of leave and payments to mothers and fathers of new babies, adoptive parents, parents of children and those who have caring responsibilities for adults.

However, it is also reasonable to assert that this regulatory revolution has now nearly run its course and that we are unlikely to witness in future years a continuation in this field of the established pace of change. There is no question that the existing body of employment law will be further adjusted from time to time to improve the extent to which it meets the legislators' aims. For example, we can anticipate reform of equal pay law and greater clarity being established over which groups of atypical workers are and are not covered by different areas of employment law. There are also good reasons for anticipating a greater degree of pan-EU harmonisation of employment regulation in the future, involving perhaps dismissal law, as further attempts are made to 'level the playing field' in a bid to enhance free, fair and open competition across the Union. However, measures of this kind will on the whole amount to fine-tuning of existing employment rights rather than major extensions along the lines we have witnessed since the 1970s.

However, this does not mean that the impact of regulation on organisations will lessen, nor that HR managers will have to pay less attention to developments in the regulatory sphere. Instead, there are good grounds for arguing that future years will see a shift away from direct regulation of the labour market towards other forms of regulation which have the capacity to have just as significant an impact.

This process has already begun, as government ministers are increasingly looking to employers to assist them in meeting objectives across a wide range of policy areas. We can expect to see this trend increasing because many of the changes governments are seeking to effect can only realistically be achieved with the active cooperation of employers. Moreover, in some cases, policy objectives require quite major changes in our accustomed behaviour, making them something of a 'hard sell' at the ballot box. Because employer organisations do not have votes, there is reason to expect that the lion's share of the changes will be obtained from *forcing* them to adjust their methods, governments being happy merely to *persuade* the populace as a whole of the need to change. There are numerous examples regularly reported including a potential role for employers in helping the government reach its targets for reducing obesity, encouraging employers to sponsor academy schools and the achievement of the ambitious pension-savings agenda we discuss in Chapter 25. Other major examples include the following:

- lifting skills levels among the adult population
- the welfare-to-work agenda
- reducing carbon emissions
- meeting sustainability and waste-reduction targets

ACTIVITY 2.6

To what extent do you think the government will be successful in persuading employers to devote time and resources to helping to increase skills and attainment levels among the UK population? What grounds are there for anticipating a degree of resistance on the part of employers?

TRADE UNIONS

The most significant and fundamental recent trend in UK employee relations has been the substantial decline in the number of people joining trade unions and taking part in trade union activity. In the UK membership levels reached a historic peak in 1979, when it was recorded that over 13 million people (58 per cent of all employees) were members of listed trade union organisations. In almost every year since then the number has declined as people have let their membership lapse, older members have retired and younger people have not replaced them. By 2008 membership among employees stood at 7.2 million and represented just 24.9 per cent of the working population (DBERR 2009: 8). The rate of decline has reduced somewhat in recent years, some unions reporting modest increases in their membership levels, but trade union density (i.e. the percentage of employees in membership) has fallen year on year for all but two of the past 30 years. By 2004 49 per cent of UK workplaces employing over 25 people stated that they employed no union members at all (Kersley *et al.* 2006: 110), while in hundreds of thousands more unions have no influence of any significance. For most employees, therefore, the norm is now to work in a non-union workplace.

The reasons for the decline in unionisation have long been debated by academic researchers and by the trade unions themselves. The issue remains the subject of considerable controversy and has by no means been settled. Despite the publication of a huge amount of evidence on the possible antecedents, no genuine consensus has been established. As a result, there is also little agreement about what the trade unions can now do, if indeed there is anything they can do, to arrest the decline in their membership levels and embark on a successful process of renewal.

Trade union leaders have tended in the past to place the blame for their decline on the actions of governments, particularly those of the conservative administrations of 1979–1997 when union density fell fastest (Bryson 2007: 183). During the 1980s a series of hostile employment Acts passed on to the statute books which did not help the union cause and were intended to reduce their power. The only serious full-frontal legal attack on the ability of unions to recruit members came in the form of regulations which made it impossible to sustain closed-shop agreements whereby membership of a specific trade union was a necessary precondition of employment in certain workplaces. This represented a major reform, affecting over five million employees who worked in closed shops (Dunn and Gennard 1984). Other legislative changes are often cited as having had a powerful, if less direct, impact. For example, a series of measures (still on the statute book) made it harder than it had been for unions to organise strikes and other forms of industrial action. Secondary action (sometimes known as sympathy action) was effectively outlawed, while secret ballots of union members and week-long cooling-off periods started to be required ahead of any action. These measures had the effect of reducing the influence of trade unions, and hence can be claimed to have made people less likely to see a point in becoming members. The same kind of effect is said to have followed the privatisation of state-run corporations and the decentralising of collective bargaining in the public sector.

As an explanation for much of the union decline, however, this argument lacks credibility when subjected to scrutiny. First and foremost it ignores the fact that substantial declines in union membership were a feature of the employee relations scene in the vast majority of industrialised countries in the 1980s and 1990s, including those which had governments that were favourable to their cause (Vissa 2002). Indeed the decline was a good deal steeper and faster in several other major OECD countries including Australia, Austria, France, New Zealand and the USA where unions lost more than half their members in the last quarter of the twentieth century (Blanchflower 2007: 3). Second, it is notable that the decline in union membership in the UK continued after 1997 with the election of the Blair government which swiftly introduced measures designed to enhance the position of trade unions in the workplace (e.g. compulsory recognition laws and the right for all to be represented by a union official at serious grievance and disciplinary hearings).

A second commonly advanced explanation is the impact of industrial restructuring. According to this point of view unions declined simply because the type of workplaces in which they have historically been recognised and have been able to attract large numbers of members have also declined in number. In their place types of workplace which have not traditionally been unionised have become much more numerous. Established industries in which union membership is the norm have declined (e.g. mining, shipbuilding, heavy manufacturing industry). The jobs that have been lost have been replaced by those in the service sector in which union membership is a great deal rarer (e.g. call centres, hospitality, tourism, retailing). The size of the average workplace has declined too, and this has had an adverse impact on the propensity of employees to join a union. There are far fewer large factories employing thousands on assembly lines than there used to be, and many more small-scale office and hi-tech manufacturing operations. Management styles in small workplaces, even when part of a much larger group, inevitably tend to be more ad hoc and personal. Grievances, disputes and requests for a pay rise are thus discussed and settled in face-to-face meetings or informally between people who know each other well, without the need to involve a trade union.

This explanation carries more weight, but there are problems with it. Metcalf (2005), for example, argues that only a small proportion of the total loss of members in the last 30 years can be ascribed to industrial restructuring. He points out that union density in manufacturing is actually relatively low (27 per cent or so), so the loss of jobs in that sector can have had only a relatively marginal effect. Moreover, we have seen considerable growth since 1997 in the number of public sector jobs – a sector in which union density is particularly high (64 per cent). He is also keen to slay the myth that a major reason for union decline is the increase in the proportion of jobs held by women. Contrary to popular perception women are just as likely to join unions as men are where a union organises and since 2003 more union members have been female than male.

In recent years a third explanation has achieved greater recognition and acceptance (*see* Metcalf 2005 and Bryson 2007). It is simply argued that people have become less interested in joining unions, see no real point in doing so and do not believe that they will gain by joining. Metcalf focuses in particular on the reduction in what is known as the 'union wage premium', by which is meant the additional amount of money earned by union members when compared with non-union members. In the 1980s this stood at 10 per cent, giving people a clear incentive to join unions and take part in their activities. The premium fell to 5 per cent by 2004 and, according to Bryson (2007: 197) has now dropped to 'a statistically non-significant three percent'. More generally, Bryson (2007: 190) presents evidence that people do not have great faith in unions to make a real difference to their working lives. In non-union workplaces 66 per cent believe that having a union would 'make no difference', while a further 14 per cent assert that unions would make matters worse. The view is more favourable in unionised workplaces, but even here over 40 per cent of employees do not think that the presence of a union has any positive impact. These surveys do not demonstrate that people are actively hostile to unions or to the prospect of joining, rather the picture that emerges is one of widespread indifference and lack of interest. There is a sense that unions are no longer seen as being of relevance to working life as they were in the past.

Part of the explanation may lie in the development in recent years of tight labour market conditions making it relatively easy for people who are dissatisfied with their jobs to secure alternative employment. In particular, the proliferation of small workplaces in the private services sector means that alternative employment is readily available for suitably qualified people. When receptionists, shop workers, sales executives, call-centre staff or IT people are dissatisfied with their work, their workplace or their managers, they can simply look for another job and resign. They do not need to move house to find work and are unlikely, in the present economic climate, to suffer any decline in income. Their jobs thus matter less to them than was the case in the days of the steel town, the mining village or the city suburb in which one big employer provided the lion's share of all employment. In short, there is now less need to join a union because there are other ways of resolving problems at work and relieving discontent.

Another interesting possible explanation for the lack of interest in union membership could be the rise more generally in society of a greater sense of individualism. This trend is difficult to quantify or measure in any clear, objective way, but it is widely recognised by leading sociologists as being the most significant single contemporary social trend (*see* Giddens 2006 and Puttnam 2001). Could it simply be that as time passes people are generally becoming less community focused in their orientation, less concerned with notions of solidarity or collective action and more concerned with forging their own individual identities and their own economic destinies? Evidence in support of this idea is provided by the statistics on union density among different age groups (DBERR 2009). Membership is far higher among older people than younger colleagues, suggesting that a significant shift in attitudes has occurred across the generations. Union density among over-fifties is 38 per cent, while among 35–49-year-old it is 33 per cent. Among the 25–34-year-old age group it falls to 22 per cent, while only 9 per cent of those aged 16 to 24 are members.

It is difficult to reach any firm, definitive conclusions about the causes of trade union decline. In practice it is likely that all the above explanations are to some extent 'factors' which help explain what has happened. Whatever the precise cause there is no question that the future outlook for trade unions in the present economic and political climate looks bleak. The question of whether continued trade union decline is inevitable has been considered by many and, as with most debates about the future, this one is characterised by diverse views. From a trade union perspective there are grounds for pessimism, despite years of new initiatives aimed at recruiting new members in the private sector. Not only has the proportion of younger people who choose to join unions declined dramatically, but we continue to see the fastest growth rates in industries which have not traditionally been unionised. With the exception of some jobs in the public sector, the fastest-growing professions are all ones that have very low rates of union density (e.g. technicians, consultants, software engineers, nursery nurses, hairdressers and beauticians). These factors lead Metcalf (2005) to calculate that 'long run union density will be around 20 per cent, implying a rate of 12 per cent in the private sector'.

The alternative view rests first of all on the observation that trade unions have been through periods of decay before and have later recovered. Kelly (1998) shows how union membership declined steeply during the 1920s and early 1930s, density falling as low as 22 per cent in 1933, only to recover again afterwards. His theory of 'long waves' in industrial relations leads him to conclude that workers will only ever put up with so much 'exploitation and domination' by employers, before beginning to unite to fight back. Others take heart from research which shows that many employees in the non-union sectors (including young people) are neither strongly opposed to unions, nor unwilling to countenance joining a union in the future. Fifty per cent of those asked in a poll in 2001 said that they would be either 'very likely' or 'fairly likely' to join if one were available at their workplace (Charlwood 2003: 52), while positive attitudes to unions appear to be just as common among non-members as they are among members (Prowse and Prowse 2006). These figures suggest that unions could create a renaissance for themselves if they could find more effective ways of organising and marketing themselves in the private services sector, and in garnering greater positive enthusiasm for their activities among an indifferent public.

ACTIVITY 2.7

What do you think are the main advantages and disadvantages for HR managers when trade unions decline in organisations where they previously had high levels of membership and considerable influence?

ETHICAL AWARENESS

Another long-term social trend of potential significance for HRM practice is the steady growth in ethical awareness on the part of consumers and investors in the UK. Starting from quite a low base this growth has begun to reach levels at which it is having a serious impact both on policy making generally in organisations and on reputation management in particular.

The Internet, and particularly the growth of social networking applications, is playing a key role in raising ethical awareness because it allows campaigning groups with an interest in ethical and wider political issues to address their audiences directly without the need to have their message 'filtered' by mainstream media organisations such as newspapers, radio stations and TV networks. This makes it easier for unethical activity on the part of corporations to be publicised and spread very rapidly across the whole world. Indeed, so rapidly can such a message be spread that it is already widely disseminated nowadays before the corporation is able to rebut in the mainstream media or indeed to threaten a libel action.

Each year since 2000 the Co-operative Bank has published its 'Ethical Consumerism Report'. This tracks the growth of ethical consumerism in the UK, as well as ethical behaviour more generally. It demonstrates substantial year-on-year increases over the past decade in the proportion of the UK population who claim to have acted ethically in one of the ways listed in Table 2.7 'at least once' during the year in question.

These reports also track year-on-year growth in purchases of organic, Fairtrade and ecologically sustainable products, the extent of charitable donations, ethical consumer boycotts, the use of public/private transport and usage of ethical banking and investment products. Current annual growth rates in most of the categories are between 13 per cent and 18 per cent. In 2008 particularly big increases were recorded (vis-à-vis 2007) in

Table 2.7 Consumers' ethical behaviour

	1999	2009
Recycling	73%	96%
Supporting local shops/suppliers	61%	87%
Avoided a product/service due to ethical reputation	44%	64%
Chose a product/service due to ethical reputation	51%	60%
Bought primarily for ethical reasons	29%	52%
Felt guilty about an unethical purchase	17%	43%
Sought information on a company's reputation	24%	38%
Actively campaigned on environmental/social issues	15%	26%

the purchase of fairtrade items (up 61 per cent), energy-efficient light bulbs (up 58 per cent), rechargeable batteries (up 79 per cent) and green cars (up 132 per cent). The markets for ethical products remain relatively small, but the direction of travel is very much in their favour.

Like ethical consumerism, ethical investment or 'socially responsible investment' as it is more commonly called, has grown substantially in recent years. As yet it remains very much a niche market, but one which is by no means insubstantial. Kurtz (2008) estimates that around 10 per cent of 'assets under management' in both the USA and Europe 'is now invested according to some type of social constraint'. As a result, the significance of ethical investment funds in financial markets is increasing markedly. Moreover, there are good grounds for anticipating much greater growth in the future. This is because financial analysts and journalists are increasingly accepting the view that socially responsible organisations are more likely to give them a superior return on their investment than rivals that have a less ethical reputation. Kiernan (2005) argues that this change in attitudes among the investment community is largely occurring as a result of industrial restructuring and the impact of globalisation on western economies. He argues that the knowledge economy is developing and interest is growing among would-be investors in digging deeper into a company's activities than a simple analysis of its financial performance, and that this includes corporate ethics alongside other considerations:

> As we move deeper and deeper into the era of knowledge value and intangibles, conventional balance sheets and profit and loss statements are capturing and reflecting less and less of a company's true value, investment risk and competitive potential. What is needed instead is a new, more dynamic, 'iceberg balance sheet' approach, one that focuses investor and senior management attention where it properly belongs, on the roughly 80 per cent of companies' true value that can not be explained by traditional, accounting-driven securities analysis: in short, one that provides a focus on leading indicators of performance, not trailing ones. (Kiernan 2007: 16–18)

Much of the contemporary corporate social responsibility agenda has little to do with HRM. The emphasis tends to be on green issues of various kinds, on charitable activities, on maintaining high standards of corporate governance, on animal testing, embryo research and on sourcing supplies which are themselves produced ethically.

However, employment matters have a place at this table and always have had, particularly in respect of working conditions in developing countries. For well over a decade now campaigns to persuade people to boycott products manufactured in sweatshops or using child labour have met with considerable success in several countries. Several large corporations, including Nike and Reebok, have been targeted by such campaigns and have had to adjust their practices in response.

In the future there are good reasons to expect that organisations stand to gain a good deal more than they currently do by developing and maintaining a reputation for ethical HR practice. This is likely to happen if the extent of ethical awareness continues to grow and more purchasing and investment decisions are influenced by an assessment of a corporation's ethics. The main reason is that in such an environment organisations will increasingly seek to compete for business in part by deliberately fostering for themselves an ethical image. 'We are socially responsible' will thus be a message that advertisers will increasingly seek to get over and, crucially, to associate with high-value brands. While pursuing such a strategy will pay dividends in an increasingly ethically aware market place, it also carries considerable risks if the corporation is caught failing to live up to the image it has created for itself. Negative stories in the media concerning the way in which employees are treated in a company will have the capacity to do great damage to a corporate reputation and seriously to contaminate a hard-won positive brand image. The growth of new media and their global reach merely serve to increase the potential damage.

It follows that many organisations in the future will have to take greater care than they currently do to develop and then to maintain a reputation as good, fair employers. This is particularly true of corporations whose survival depends on sales of goods and services to a mass consumer market, but also on those dependent on attracting investment from the market. Another group of employers which may find the business case for adopting ethical HR practices becomes increasingly compelling in the future are those who have a particular interest in recruiting people who have a choice about where they work. Increased ethical awareness among younger people may well mean that those which have a poor reputation as employers fail to attract the best minds even if those individuals are treated well.

WINDOW ON PRACTICE

In recent years the Honda Formula 1 racing team has taken a number of steps aimed at improving its 'green credentials'. These have led to the organisation being awarded ISO 14001 accreditation which rewards environmental initiatives. Not all the steps taken are directly related to HRM, but many are and those that are not nonetheless help to enhance the attractiveness of the Honda brand in its key labour markets. The major initiatives are as follows:

- replacing sponsors' logos on the cars with pictures of the earth taken from space
- introducing an environmental awareness training programme for staff
- encouraging staff to monitor their use of energy at home
- actively seeking feedback and ideas for new initiatives from staff
- removing personal waste bins next to desks and installing recycling bins for collective use in their place
- encouraging staff to switch to environmentally friendly cars
- encouraging homeworking to reduce commuting

Source: Cotton 2008.

SUMMARY PROPOSITIONS

2.1 The most important recent trend in the HR business environment is the growth in competitive intensity organisations face in most industries. This has meant that organisations face less predictable trading conditions and hence a need for greater flexibility in their staffing practices.

2.2 There is a clear long-term trend towards increased demand for labour in the UK economy. This has occurred despite three international recessions, the introduction of major new labour-saving technologies, the exporting of thousands of jobs overseas and the wholesale restructuring of UK industry. It is thus likely to continue in the future.

2.3 It is likely that labour markets will tighten in the future due to a fall in the size of the UK-born working population, reduced levels of immigration and substantially increased demand for higher, more specialised skills on the part of employers.

2.4 Over recent decades we have seen a revolution in the extent and nature of employment regulation in the UK. However, the current regulatory agenda as far as employment relationships are concerned has now mostly run its course. In the future regulatory pressure on employers will instead shift to facilitating government aims in other areas of policy.

2.5 Consumers and investors are becoming increasingly ethically aware. Over time this trend will have an impact on HR practice, making it necessary for organisations to treat their employees well and be seen to be doing so.

GENERAL DISCUSSION TOPICS

1 What are the major trends in your own organisation's demand for skills. To what extent do you foresee these being harder to source in the future and why?

2 What purpose does a study of current demographic trends serve from the point of view of the HR function in organisations?

3 Why do you think consumers and investors have become so much more aware of ethical issues and prepared to act on their ethical beliefs since 2000?

FURTHER READING

The government's Office for National Statistics has an excellent website which can be used to gain access to a large range of authoritative articles and statistics concerning demographic trends and the demand and supply of skills in the UK. You will find summaries of the most recent trends in their annual publications *Social Trends* and *Labour Market Review*.

An article by Katherine Kent (2009) entitled 'Employment: Changes over 30 years' can be downloaded from the National Statistics website. It summarises all the major measures and presents a clear picture of key contemporary developments in the labour market.

The Evolution of the Modern Workplace edited by William Brown and his colleagues (Brown *et al.* 2009) draws on data from successive Workplace Employment Relations Surveys to provide an authoritative and wide-ranging account of the major trends and their impact.

REFERENCES

Barratt, C. (2009) *Trade Union Membership 2008*. London: Department for Business, Enterprise and Regulatory Reform/National Statistics.

Beaven, R., Bosworth, D., Lewney, R. and Wilson, R. (2005) *Alternative Skills Scenarios to 2020 for the UK Economy*. Cambridge: Cambridge Econometrics.

Blanchflower, D.G. (2007) 'International patterns of union membership', *British Journal of Industrial Relations*, Vol. 45, No. 1, pp. 1–28.

Brown, W., Bryson, A., Forth, J. and Whitfield, K. (2009) *The Evolution of the Modern Workplace*. Cambridge: Cambridge University Press.

Bryson, A. (2007) 'New Labour, New Unions?', *British Social Attitudes Survey: The twenty-third report*. London: National Centre for Social Research.

Caldwell, C. (2007) 'No easy answers on immigration', *Financial Times*, 19 October.

Charlwood, A. (2003) 'Willingness to unionize amongst non-union workers', in H. Gospel and S. Wood (eds), *Representing Workers: Union recognition and membership in Britain*. London: Routledge.

Chartered Institute of Personnel and Development (2002–2009) *Recruitment, Retention and Turnover: Annual survey report 2007*. London: CIPD.

Cotton, C. (2008) 'Go the Green Mile', *People Management Guide to the Reward and Benefits Market*, January, pp. 8–9.

Davidson, J.D. and Rees-Mogg, W. (1997) *The Sovereign Individual: The coming economic revolution. How to survive and prosper in it*. Basingstoke: Macmillan.

Dunn, S. and Gennard, J. (1984) *The Closed Shop in British Industry*. London: Macmillan.

Giddens, A. (2006) *Sociology*, 5th edn. London: Polity Press.

Green, M. (2006) 'Employers alarmed at skills shortage', *Financial Times*, 21 August.

Grugulis, I., Warhurst, C. and Keep, E. (2004) 'What's happening to "Skill"', in C. Warhurst, I. Grugulis and E. Keep (eds), *The Skills That Matter*. Basingstoke: Palgrave.

Kelly, J. (1998) *Rethinking Industrial Relations: Mobilization, collectivism and long waves*. London: Routledge.

Kent, K. (2009) 'Employment: changes over 30 years', *Economic and Labour Market Review*, Vol. 3, No. 2, pp. 30–6.

Kersley, B., Alpin, C., Forth, J., Bryson, A., Bewley, H., Dix, G. and Oxenbridge, S. (2006) *Inside the Workplace: Findings from the 2004 Workplace Employment Relations Survey*. Abingdon: Routledge.

Khan-Freund, O. (1954) 'Legal framework', in A. Flanders and H. Clegg (eds), *The System of Industrial Relations in Great Britain*. Oxford: Blackwell.

Kiernan, M. (2007) 'Capturing next generation alphadrivers', in UNEP Finance Initiative, *The Working Capital Report*. UNEPFI, pp. 16–18.

Kurtz, L. (2008) 'Socially responsible investment and shareholder activism', in A. Crane, A. McWilliams, D. Matten, J. Moon and D. Siegel (eds), *The Oxford Handbook of Corporate Social Responsibility*. Oxford: Oxford University Press.

Laroche, L. and Rutherford, D. (2007) *Recruiting, Retaining and Promoting Culturally Different Employees*. New York: Butterworth Heinemann.

Learning and Skills Council (2006) *National Employers Skills Survey 2005: Key findings*. London: LSC (available online).

Leitch, S. (2006) *Prosperity for all in the Global Economy: World-class skills. The Final Report of the Leitch Review of Skills*. London: HM Treasury.

Mahajan, S. (2006) 'Concentration ratios for business by industry in 2004', *Economic Trends*, 635. October. London: Office for National Statistics.

Metcalf, D. (2005) 'Trade unions: resurgence or perdition? An economic analysis', in S. Fernie and D. Metcalf (eds), *Trade Unions: Resurgence or Demise?*. London: Routledge.

Prowse, P.J. and Prowse, J.M. (2006) 'Are non-union workers different to their union colleagues? Evidence from the public services', *Industrial Relations Journal*, Vol. 37, No. 3, pp. 222–41.

Puttnam, R. (2001) *Bowling Alone*. New York: Simon & Schuster.

Sparrow, P.L. (2003) 'The future of work?', in D. Holman, T. Wall, C. Clegg, P. Sparrow and A. Howard (eds), *The New Workplace: A guide to the human impact of modern working practices*. Chichester: Wiley.

Taylor, A. (2007) 'UK immigration may be close to peak', *Financial Times*, 24 July.

Thomas, L.G. and D'Aveni, R.A. (2004) 'The rise of hypercompetition from 1950 to 2002: evidence of increasing industry destabilization and temporary competitive advantage'. Working Paper. Copenhagen Business School.

Vissa, J. (2002) 'Why fewer workers join unions in Europe: a social custom explanation of membership trends', *British Journal of Industrial Relations*, Vol. 40, No. 3, pp. 403–30.

Wadhawani, S. (1999) 'Is Inflation Dead?'. Lecture delivered at the National Council of Applied Research, New Delhi, India, 17 December.

CHAPTER 3

STRATEGIC HUMAN RESOURCE MANAGEMENT

THE OBJECTIVES OF THIS CHAPTER ARE TO:

1. Clarify the use of the terms strategic human resource management and human resource strategy, and arrive at workable definitions of each
2. Explain the feasibility and nature of the link between business strategy and HR strategy
3. Evaluate three theoretical perspectives on the nature of HR strategy and show how each expresses a different view on how the contribution of people to the organisation might be understood and enhanced

There is a strong lobby propounding the view that human resources are a critical, if not *the* source of, competitive advantage for the business, rather than, say, access to capital or use of technology (*see*, for example, Salaman *et al.* 2005). It is therefore logical to suggest that attention needs to be paid to the nature of this resource and its management as this will impact on human resource behaviour and performance and consequently the performance of the organisation. Indeed Boxall and Purcell (2008: 55) argue that

> effective human resource strategy is a necessary, though not a sufficient condition, of firm viability.

It is not, therefore, surprising that the rhetoric of strategic human resource management has been readily adopted, especially as a strategic approach is considered to be one of the characteristics of HRM as opposed to personnel management, which is seen as operational. In the most recent Workplace Employment Relations Survey (WERS) it was found that 87 per cent of workplaces with a strategic plan included some issues relating to employment relations (broadly defined) (Kersley *et al.* 2006).

STRATEGIC HUMAN RESOURCE MANAGEMENT AND HUMAN RESOURCE STRATEGY

Our understanding of HR strategy has changed considerably since strategy first became the subject of great attention. We have moved from viewing strategy as a physical document to seeing it as an incremental process, affected by political influences and generating learning. Tyson's (1995) definition of human resource strategy is a useful starting point, although somewhat limited, as will be seen from our later discussion:

> the intentions of the corporation both explicit and covert, toward the management of its employees, expressed through philosophies, policies and practices.

This definition is helpful because research on human resource strategy in the early 1980s tended to focus on seeking an HR strategy document in order to determine whether there was a strategic approach to HR and what that approach was. This was rather like searching for the Holy Grail. Not surprisingly few complete HR strategies were found and HR specialists berated themselves for having failed in this critical area. Gradually the thinking changed to encompass a view that HR strategy need not be written on a piece of paper, or need not, indeed, be explicit, as the Tyson quotation illustrates. The Cranet Survey of International Strategic HR found that 39 per cent of UK companies do not have a written HR strategy (Guthridge and Lawson 2008).

ACTIVITY 3.1

Using an organisation with which you are familiar:

1. Identify the explicit intentions of the organisation towards the management of its people in terms of overall philosophy, policies and practices.
2. Assess the extent to which you consider these intentions to be implemented in practice, giving evidence to support your judgement.
3. How can you explain any mismatch between explicit intentions and actual practice?

Further developments in thinking began to accept the idea that strategies are neither finished, nor complete, but rather incremental and piecemeal. There is compelling evidence to suggest that strategic HR tends to be issue based rather than the formulation of a complete and integrated strategy. Strategic thinking, strategic decision making and a strategic orientation were gradually understood as much more realistic expectations.

In parallel with this thinking there were developments in the general strategy literature which viewed strategy as a process which was not necessarily rational and top down, but a political and evolutionary process (*see*, for example, Mintzberg 1994). Mintzberg argues that strategy is 'formed' rather than 'formulated' and that any intended strategy is changed by events, opportunities, the actions of employees and so on – so that the realised strategy is different from the initial vision. Strategy, Mintzberg argues, can only be identified in retrospect and, as Boxall and Purcell (2008) suggest, is best seen in the ultimate behaviour of the organisation. Wrapped up in this view is also the idea that strategy is not necessarily determined by top management alone but can be influenced 'bottom up', as ideas are tried and tested in one part of the organisation and gradually adopted in a wholesale manner if they are seen to be applicable and successful. In tracing back strategy to its roots Storey (2007), for example, notes that there are likely to be instances of incremental learning and false leads. This is not to say that producing a strategy is an unhelpful act, and indeed research carried out by PricewaterhouseCoopers indicated that those organisations with a written HR strategy generated 35 per cent greater revenues per employee than those without (Higginbottom 2002).

This leads on to the concept of strategy as learning both in content and in process, which is supported by the notion of strategy as a process of change. Literature draws out the need to sense changes in the environment, develop a resultant strategy and turn this strategy into action. While the HR function has often found itself excluded from the strategy formation process, HR strategy has more often been seen in terms of the implementation of organisational strategies. However, implementation of HR strategy has been weak, at best. Among the qualities of the most successful organisations is the ability to turn strategy into action quickly (Ulrich 1998), in other words to implement the chosen strategy, and this continues to be a challenge according to Kaplan and Norton (2005) who found that 95 per cent of employees did not know or did not understand their company's strategy. A lack of attention to the implementation of HR strategy has been identified (Skinner and Mabey 1997), and the information that does exist suggests that this has been a problematic area. However, frameworks such as the

HR scorecard (Becker *et al.* 2001), and others, are aimed, at least in part, at facilitating the management and implementation of HR architecture ('the sum of the HR function, the broader HR system, and the resulting employee behaviors', p. 1) as a strategic asset, and we look at this in more detail in Chapter 29.

One organisation where the HR function has had a major role to play in the successful implementation of HR strategy is Kwik-Fit Financial Services. The overriding strategic purpose was to make the organisation 'a fantastic place to work' and this led to initiatives focusing on improving the working environment and encouraging employees to bring their whole selves to work (Griffiths 2006). There are further details in a case study on the website **www.pearsoned.co.uk/torrington**.

WINDOW ON PRACTICE

Implementing Strategy at Fujitsu

Fujitsu Services, which designs, builds and operates IT systems and services, was formed in 2002 when the Japanese IT group acquired ICL. Three years after this a need was identified to ensure all employees were working towards the same goal and communicating clearly. To meet this strategic need a programme called 'Reputation' was designed with the aim of aligning all employees (senior managers, on-call engineers, service desk teleworkers) operating out of more than 20 countries, to the same values and customer brand so that customers received a consistent experience.

The Reputation model was introduced into small group sessions cascading through the organisation with 'Reputation champions' initially leading the programme. These champions trained 2,000 managers to deliver the programme to their teams.

The values chosen to reflect the company brand were: realism, straight-talking and tenacious. These were important as historically Fujitsu had been known for over-promising and under-performing. Both the HR and marketing functions promoted the programme aiming to ensure the internal (staff) and external (customers) coherence of the brand.

Staff were helped to understand how their behaviour affected colleagues, customers and the business overall, and a shared vocabulary has been developed. All staff were encouraged to regard themselves as key players, and always 'put their best face forward'. The sessions were also designed to open lines of communication and engage staff in debates about the business in groups with a mix of staff level and from a range of departments. This was intended to help people recognise that their goals were the same. Employee contributions were viewed as key and the programme intended to be interactive, not top-down.

Fujitsu aimed to embed their values across the business: for example when HR policies are designed these are tested against the values, with the idea of ensuring a consistent experience. Cohesive working is the ultimate aim of the programme.

Source: Chubb, L. (2008) 'Build a better brand', *People Management*, Vol. 14, No. 15, pp. 24–5, 24 July.

THE LINK BETWEEN BUSINESS AND HR STRATEGY

The nature, desirability and feasibility of the link between business strategy and HR strategy is a consistent theme which runs through the strategy literature, although, as we shall discuss later, some theories suggest that implementing 'best practice' in HRM is even more important than this. Figure 3.1 is a simple model that is useful in visualising different ways in which this relationship may be played out and has relevance for the newer conceptions of strategy based on the resource-based view of the firm, as well as earlier conceptions.

In the *separation model* (A) there is no relationship at all, if indeed organisational and human resource strategy *does* exist in an explicit form in the organisation. This is a typical picture of 20 years ago, but it still exists today, particularly in smaller organisations.

The *fit model* (B) represents a growing recognition of the importance of people in the achievement of organisational strategy. Employees are seen as key in the implementation of the declared organisational strategy, and HR strategy is designed to fit with this. Some of the early formal models of HR strategy, particularly that proposed by Fombrun *et al.* (1984), concentrate on how the HR strategy can be designed to ensure a close fit, and the same approach is used in the Schuler and Jackson example in Table 3.1.

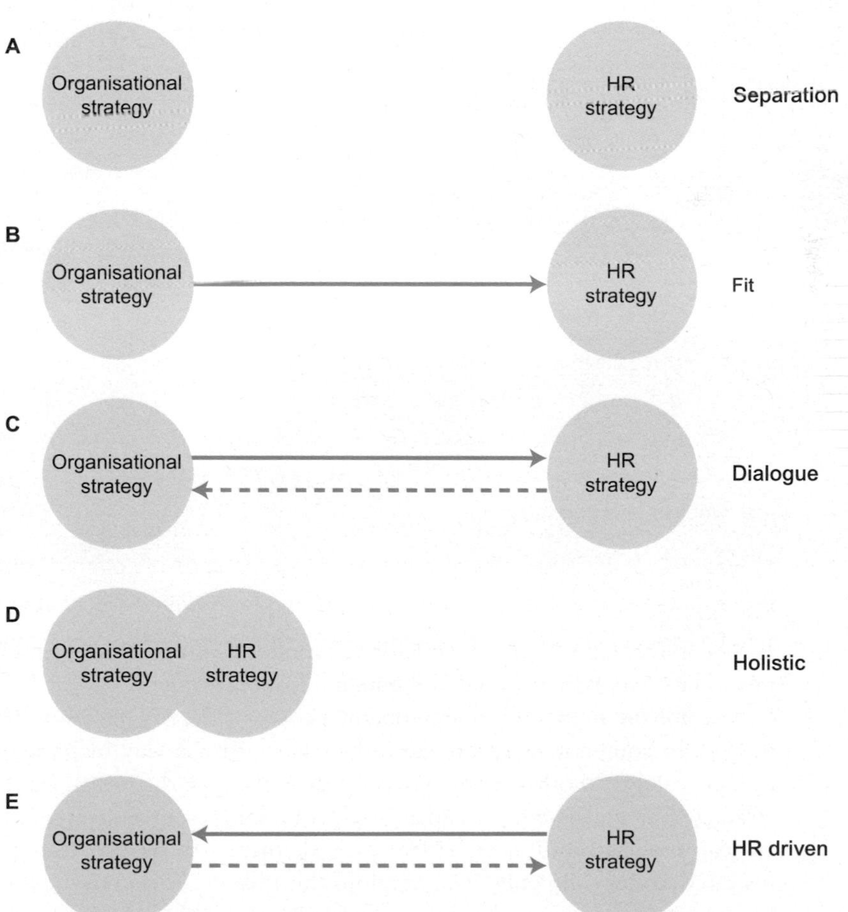

Figure 3.1 Potential relationships between organisational strategy and HR strategy

This whole approach depends on a view of strategy formulation as a logical rational process, which remains a widely held view. The relationship in the fit model is exemplified by organisations which cascade their business objectives down from the senior management team through functions, through departments, through teams and so on. Functions, for example, have to propose a functional strategy which enables the organisational strategy to be achieved. Departments have to propose a strategy which enables the functional strategy to be achieved, and so on. In this way the HR function (as with any other) is required to respond to organisational strategy by defining a strategy which meets organisational demands.

The *dialogue model* (C) takes the relationship one step further, as it recognises the need for two-way communication and some debate. What is demanded in the organisation's strategy may not be viewed as feasible and alternative possibilities need to be reviewed. The debate, however, is often limited, as shown in the example in the Window on practice which follows.

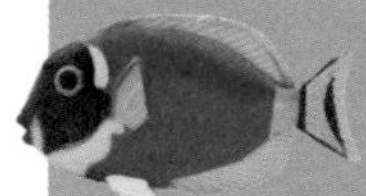

WINDOW ON PRACTICE

In one large multinational organisation an objectives-setting cascade was put in place. This cascade allowed for a dialogue between the planned organisation strategy and the response of each function. In the organisation strategy there was some emphasis on people growth and development and job fulfilment. The HR Department's response included among other things an emphasis on line management involvement in these areas, which would be supported by consultancy help from the HR Department.

The top management team replied to this by asking the HR Department to add a strategic objective about employee welfare and support. The HR Department strongly argued that this was a line management responsibility, along with coaching, development and so on. The HR Function saw its customers as the managers of the organisation, not the employees. The result of the debate was that the HR Function added the strategic objective about employee welfare.

Although the approach in this case appeared two-way, the stronger of the parties was the management team, and they were determined that their vision was the one that would be implemented!

The holistic model and the HR-driven model (D and E) show a much closer involvement between organisational and human resource strategy.

The *holistic model* (D) represents the people of the organisation being recognised as the key to competitive advantage rather than just the way of implementing organisational strategy. In other words HR strategy is not just the means for achieving business strategy (the ends), but an end in itself. Human resource strategy therefore becomes critical and, as Baird *et al.* (1983) argued, there can be no strategy without human resource strategy. Boxall (1996) develops this idea in relation to the resource-based firm, and argues convincingly that business strategy can usefully be interpreted as more broad than a competitive strategy (or positioning in the marketplace). In this case business strategy can encompass a variety of other strategies including HRM, and he describes these strategies as the pieces of a jigsaw. This suggests mutual development and some form of integration, rather than a slavish response to a predetermined business strategy, for example the integration of HR and marketing strategies so that the customer brand and the employer brand are aligned, and Simmons (2009) gives an example of this in relation to corporate social responsibility.

The *HR-driven model* (E) offers a more extreme form, which places human resource strategy in prime position. The argument here is that if people are the key to competitive advantage, then we need to build on our people strengths. Logically, then, as the potential of our employees will undoubtedly affect the achievement of any planned strategy, it would be sensible to take account of this in developing our strategic direction. Butler (1988/89) identifies this model as a shift from human resources as the implementers of strategy to human resources as a driving force in the formulation of the strategy. Again this model is a reflection of a resource-based strategic HRM perspective, and sits well with the increasing attention being given to the notion of 'human capital' where it is the collective nature and quality of the people in the organisation which provide the potential for future competitive advantage (*see*, for example, Lengnick-Hall and Lengnick-Hall 2003).

ACTIVITY 3.2

1 Which of these approaches to human resource strategy most closely fits your organisation? (If you are a full-time student read one or two relevant cases in *People Management* and interpret these as 'your organisation'.)

2 Why did you come to this conclusion?

3 What are the advantages and disadvantages of the approach used?

THEORETICAL PERSPECTIVES OF STRATEGIC HUMAN RESOURCE MANAGEMENT

Three theoretical approaches to strategic HRM can be identified. The first is founded on the concept that there is 'one best way' of managing human resources in order to improve business performance. The second focuses on the need to align employment policies and practice with the requirements of business strategy in order that the latter will be achieved and the business will be successful. This second approach is based on the assumption that different types of HR strategies will be suitable for different types of business strategies. Third, a more recent approach to strategic HRM is derived from the resource-based view of the firm, and the perceived value of human capital. This view focuses on the quality of the human resources available to the organisation and their ability to learn and adapt more quickly than their competitors. Supporters of this perspective challenge the need to secure a mechanistic fit with business strategy and focus instead on long-term sustainability and survival of the organisation via the pool of human capital.

Universalist approach

The perspective of the universalist approach is derived from the conception of human resource management as 'best practice', as we discussed in Chapter 1. In other words it is based on the premise that one model of labour management – a high-commitment model – is related to high organisational performance in all contexts, irrespective of the particular competitive strategy of the organisation. An expression of this approach can be seen in Guest's theory of HRM (Guest 1989), which is a prescriptive model based on four HR policy goals: strategic integration, commitment, flexibility and quality. These policy goals are related to HRM policies which, as long as the whole set are achieved, are expected to produce desirable organisational outcomes such as high job performance, problem solving, change, innovation and cost effectiveness; and low employee turnover, absence and grievances.

Other examples come from researchers aiming to demonstrate positive relationships between specific HR practices and indicators of organisational performance, for example MacDuffie (1995). They carried out large-scale statistical research projects resulting in the identification of bundles of HR practices which they argued relate to higher organisational performance when used in combination. As Godard (2004: 349) points out, this 'high performance paradigm has been promoted as "best practice" both for employers, in that it yields higher performance than traditional employment relations practices, and for employees, in that it focuses on motivation and development. Perhaps the best-known proponent of this perspective is Pfeffer (1998) who claims that the appropriate bundle of HR practices which will result in higher performance is: emphasising employment security; recruiting the right people; extensive use of self-managed teams and decentralisation; high wages solidly linked to organisational performance; high spending on training; reducing status differentials; and sharing of information. He suggests that these practices applied in total will benefit all organisations. However, as Lepak and Shaw (2008) point out, Pfeffer's elaboration is based more on interpretation than solid empirical evidence. We consider this perspective in more depth in Chapter 11.

While there is some support for this perspective, there remains some debate as to which particular bundle of human resource practices will stimulate high commitment, as different researchers appear to have found different contradictory bundles. In addition there are contradictions within some of the models, for example in Guest's model between flexibility and commitment. The universalist approach is also unitarist, being based on the assumption that all managers have to do is to apply a certain set of practices and higher performance will result as workers will comply with whatever is required of them without questioning whether it is to their advantage to do so. These models provide some clarity which is attractive but this is where the problems also lie, as managing people is far more complex than suggested in the model, and in most studies little account appears to be taken of context. Because the prescriptive approach brings with it a set of values, it suggests that there is only one best way and this is it. Finally, Storey (2007) argues that such universalist approaches do not represent a *strategic choice*, being a representation of HRM in its generic sense, as a strategic choice is a differentiator. He argues that, in the early years of HRM, universalist approaches could be construed as strategic as few organisations had adopted them; however, as HRM has become mainstream it could be argued this no longer applies.

ACTIVITY 3.3

To what extent could or should an organisation apply best practice to some groups of employees and not others?

Use an organisation which you know well and identify whether this is happening, and evaluate the benefits and disadvantages of this approach.

Fit or contingency approach

The fit or contingency approach is based on two critical forms of fit. The first is external fit (sometimes referred to as vertical integration) – that HR strategy fits with the demands of business strategy; the second is internal fit (sometimes referred to as horizontal integration) – that all HR policies and activities fit together so that they make a coherent whole, are mutually reinforcing and are applied consistently. While external fit is most commonly interpreted as fit with business strategy, Lepak and Shaw (2008) remind us that HR strategy must also fit with, for example, the technology and industry sector, and they consider fit with workforce trends and worker values as emerging factors in respect of fit.

One of the foundations of the fit approach is found in Fombrun *et al.* (1984), who proposed a basic framework for strategic HRM, demonstrating, within the firm, how human resource management and organisation structure (which interact) are derived from the firm's mission and strategy management, with all in turn being influenced by political, economic and cultural forces in the external context. This exemplifies how the *fit model* (B) is used (*see* Figure 3.1). Figure 3.2 shows how activities *within* human resource management can be unified and designed in order to support the organisation's strategy.

The strength of this model is that it provides a simple framework to show how selection, appraisal, development and reward can be mutually geared to produce the required type of employee performance. For example, if an organisation required cooperative team behaviour with mutual sharing of information and support, the broad implications for managing employees would be:

- **Selection**: successful experience of teamwork and sociable, cooperative personality; rather than an independent thinker who likes working alone.
- **Appraisal**: based on contribution to the team, and support of others; rather than individual outstanding performance.
- **Reward**: based on team performance and contribution; rather than individual performance and individual effort.

There is little doubt that this type of internal fit is valuable. However, questions have been raised over the model's simplistic response to organisation strategy. The question

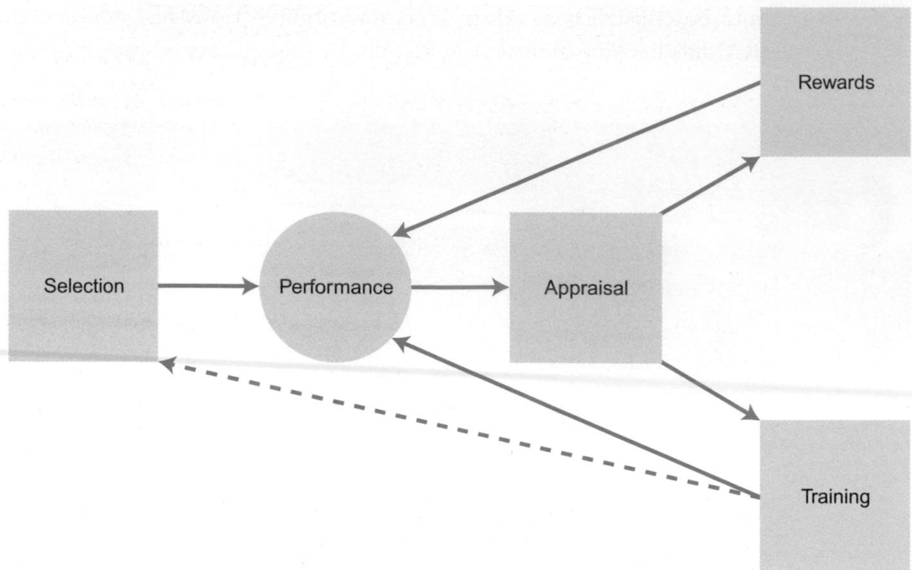

Figure 3.2 The human resource cycle
Source: C. Fombrun, N.M. Tichy and M.A. Devanna (1984) *Strategic Human Resource Management*, p. 41. New York: John Wiley and Sons, Inc. © John Wiley and Sons Inc., 1984. Reprinted by permission of John Wiley and Sons, Inc.

'what if it is not possible to produce a human resource response that enables the required employee behaviour and performance?' is never addressed. So, for example, the distance between now and future performance requirements, the strengths, weaknesses and potential of the workforce, the motivation of the workforce and employee relations issues are not considered.

This model has been criticised because of its dependence on a rational strategy formulation rather than on an emergent strategy formation approach; and because of the nature of the one-way relationship with organisational strategy. It has also been criticised owing to its unitarist assumptions, as no recognition is made for employee interests and their choice of whether or not to change their behaviour.

Taking this model and the notion of fit one step further, human resource strategy has been conceived in terms of generating specific employee behaviours. In the ideal form of this there would be analysis of the types of employee behaviour required to fulfil a predetermined business strategy, and then an identification of human resource policies and practices which would bring about and reinforce this behaviour. In a step change from previous thinking Schuler and Jackson (1987) produce an excellent example of this concept. They used the three generic business strategies defined by Porter (1980) and for each identified employee role behaviour and HRM policies required. Their conclusions are shown in Table 3.1. Sanz-Valle *et al.* (1999) found some partial support for the Schuler and Jackson model in terms of the link between business strategy and HR practices, but they did not investigate the implications of this link for organisational performance.

Similar analyses can be found for other approaches to business strategy, for example in relation to the Boston matrix (Purcell 1992) and the developmental stage of the organisation (Kochan and Barocci 1985). Some human resource strategies describe the behaviour of all employees, but others have concentrated on the behaviour of chief executives and senior managers; Miles and Snow (1984), for example, align appropriate managerial characteristics to three generic strategies of prospector, defender and analyser. The types of strategies described above are generic, and there is more concentration

Strategy	Employee role behaviour	HRM policies
1 Innovation	A high degree of creative behaviour	Jobs that require close interaction and coordination among groups of individuals
	Longer-term focus	Performance appraisals that are more likely to reflect longer-term and group-based achievements
	A relatively high level of cooperative, interdependent behaviour	Jobs that allow employees to develop skills that can be used in other positions in the firm
		Compensation systems that emphasise internal equity rather than external or market-based equity
	A moderate degree of concern for quality	Pay rates that tend to be low, but that allow employees to be stockholders and have more freedom to choose the mix of components that make up their pay package
	A moderate concern for quantity; an equal degree of concern for process and results	Broad career paths to reinforce the development of a broad range of skills
	A greater degree of risk taking; a higher tolerance of ambiguity and unpredictability	
2 Quality enhancement	Relatively repetitive and predictable behaviours	Relatively fixed and explicit job descriptions
	A more long-term or intermediate focus	High levels of employee participation in decisions relevant to immediate work conditions and the job itself
	A moderate amount of cooperative, interdependent behaviour	A mix of individual and group criteria for performance appraisal that is mostly short term and results orientated
	A high concern for quality	A relatively egalitarian treatment of employees and some guarantees of employment security
	A modest concern for quantity of output	Extensive and continuous training and development of employees
	High concern for process: low risk-taking activity; commitment to the goals of the organisation	
3 Cost reduction	Relatively repetitive and predictable behaviour	Relatively fixed and explicit job descriptions that allow little room for ambiguity
	A rather short-term focus	Narrowly designed jobs and narrowly defined career paths that encourage specialisation, expertise and efficiency
	Primarily autonomous or individual activity	Short-term results-orientated performance appraisals
	Moderate concern for quality	Close monitoring of market pay levels for use in making compensation decisions
	High concern for quantity of output	Minimal levels of employee training and development
	Primary concern for results; low risk-taking activity; relatively high degree of comfort with stability	

Table 3.1 Business strategies, and associated employee role behaviour and HRM policies

Source: R.S. Schuler and S.E. Jackson (1987) 'Linking competitive strategies with human resource management practices', *Academy of Management Executive*, No. 3, August. Reproduced with permission of the Academy of Management.

in some organisations on tailoring the approach to the particular needs of the specific organisation.

Many human resource strategies aim not just to target behaviour, but through behaviour change to effect a movement in the culture of the organisation. The target is, therefore, to change the common view of 'the way we do things around here' and to attempt to manipulate the beliefs and values of employees. There is much debate as to whether this is achievable.

We have previously recounted some of the concerns expressed about Fombrun *et al.*'s specific model; however, there is further criticism of the fit or matching perspective as a whole. Grundy (1998) claims that the idea of fit seems naive and simplistic. Ogbonna and Whipp (1999) argue that much literature assumes that fit can be targeted, observed and measured and there is an underlying assumption of stability. Given that most companies may have to change radically in response to the environment, any degree of fit previously achieved will be disturbed. Thus they contend that fit is a theoretical ideal which can rarely be achieved in practice. Boxall (1996) criticises the typologies of competitive advantage that are used, arguing that there is evidence that high-performing firms are good 'all rounders' and questioning a number of elements: the fact that strategy is a given and no account is taken of how it is formed or by whom; the assumption that employees will behave as requested; and the aim for consistency, as it has been shown that firms use different strategies for different sections of their workforce.

However, in spite of the criticisms of this perspective, it is still employed in both the academic and practitioner literature – *see*, for example, Holbeche's (2008) book entitled *Aligning Human Resources and Business Strategy*.

A further form of fit which we have not mentioned so far is cultural fit, and the Window on practice below demonstrates this aspect.

WINDOW ON PRACTICE

The influence of national culture on human resource management strategies

Fields and his colleagues (2006) investigated whether, under similar conditions, organisations in different cultural contexts would strategically respond in a different manner. They compared US organisations with Hong Kong Chinese organisations and studied their strategic approach in conditions of uncertainty in the supply of qualified labour. They studied three aspects of HR relevant to this situation:

- training and development
- monitoring and assessment of employee performance, and
- staffing through an internal labour market

They found, as they expected, that in these conditions the Hong Kong Chinese companies increased their use of these three HRM strategies, but that the US companies decreased their use. They explain these different strategic approaches by reference to the cultural context.

You may wish to look ahead to the work of Hofstede, which we present in Chapter 6, before reading on.

Training and development (TD)

They suggest that more TD would be positively viewed by the more collective Chinese culture as a symbol that the organisation is fulfilling its moral obligation to employees, as a way to increase the value of each individual to the collective organisation, and as a reward. Each of these would be valued by Chinese employees, and would encourage them to remain with the organisation. Alternatively in the more individualistic US culture managers would be reluctant to invest in TD when labour supply is scarce as employees may take advantage of this and use it to find a better job elsewhere.

Emphasis on performance assessment (PA)

They suggest that in the Chinese culture, with greater power distance, greater PA may be viewed by employees as a positive symbol that managers are interested in them, and may act as a reminder of the employees' moral association with the organisation – thus encouraging employees to stay. Alternatively in the US culture with lower power distance, more PA would be viewed negatively. It may be seen as emphasising the difference between managers and employees, and as a way of tightening up the employment relationship, both of which may lead employees to seek employment elsewhere.

Internal labour market (IL)

Greater use of the IL might be viewed in a collectivist culture by the Chinese employees as evidence that they are valued by the organisation and thus it may encourage retention. Alternatively in an individualistic culture employees may view this unfavourably as evidence of a subjective rather than objective (based on merit) approach to promotion, and managers may view it as a means by which employees can barter for better rewards in a tight labour market.

Source: Adapted from Fields, D., Chan, A., Aktar, S. and Blum, T. (2006) 'Human resource management strategies under uncertainty', *Cross Cultural Management: An International Journal*, Vol. 13, No. 2, pp. 171–86.

Resource-based approach

The resource-based view of the firm (Barney 1991) has stimulated attempts to create a resource-based model of strategic HRM (Boxall 1996). The resource-based view of the firm is concerned with the relationships between internal resources (of which human resources is one), strategy and firm performance. It focuses on the promotion of sustained competitive advantage through the development of human capital rather than merely aligning human resources to current strategic goals. Human resources can provide competitive advantage for the business, as long as they are unique and competing organisations cannot copy or substitute for them. The focus is not just on the behaviour of the human resources (as with the fit approach), but on the skills, knowledge, attitudes and competencies which underpin this, and which have a more sustained impact on long-term survival than current behaviour (although this is still regarded as important). Briggs and Keogh (1999) maintain that business excellence is not just about 'best practice' or 'leapfrogging the competition', but about the intellectual capital and business intelligence to anticipate the future, today.

Barney states that in order for a resource to result in sustained competitive advantage it must meet four criteria, and Wright *et al.* (1994) demonstrate how human resources meet these. First, the resource must be *valuable*. Wright and his colleagues argue that this is the case where demand for labour is heterogeneous, and where the supply of labour is also heterogeneous – in other words where different firms require different competencies from each other and for different roles in the organisation, and where the supply of potential labour comprises individuals with different competencies. On this basis value is created by matching an individual's competencies with the requirements of the firm and/or the job, as individuals will make a variable contribution, and one cannot be substituted easily for another.

The second criterion, *rarity*, is related to the first. An assumption is made that the most important competence for employees is cognitive ability due to future needs for adaptability and flexibility. On the basis that cognitive ability is normally distributed in the population, those with high levels of this ability will be rare. The talent pool is not unlimited and many employers are currently experiencing difficulties in finding the talent that they require.

Third, resources need to be *inimitable*. Wright *et al.* argue that this quality applies to the human resource as competitors will find it difficult to identify the exact source of competitive advantage from within the firm's human resource pool. Also competitors will not be able to duplicate exactly the resource in question, as they will be unable to copy the unique historical conditions of the first firm. This history is important as it will affect the behaviour of the human resource pool via the development of unique norms and cultures. Thus even if a competing firm recruited a group of individuals from a competitor they would still not be able to produce the same outcomes in the new firm as the context would be different. Two factors make this unique history difficult to copy. The first is causal ambiguity – in other words it is impossible to separate out the exact causes of performance, as the sum is always more than the parts; and, second, social complexity – that the complex of relationships and networks developed over time which have an impact on performance is difficult to dissect.

Finally, resources need to be *non-substitutable*. Wright and his co-authors argue that although in the short term it may be possible to substitute human resources with others, for example technological ones, in the long term the human resource is different as it does not become obsolete (like technology) and can be transferred across other products, markets and technologies.

Wright *et al.* noted that attention has often been devoted to leaders and top management in the context of a resource-based approach, and indeed Boxall (1996) contends that this approach provides the theoretical base on which to concentrate in the renewal and development of the critical resource of leaders in the organisation. However, Wright

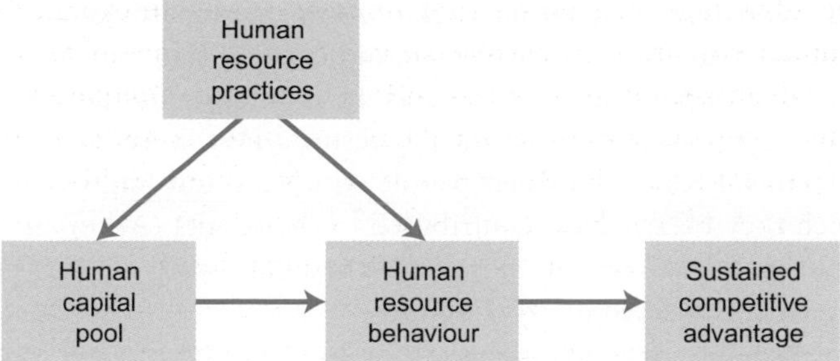

Figure 3.3 A model of human resources as a source of sustained competitive advantage
Source: P. Wright, G. McMahon and A. McWilliams (1994) 'Human resources and sustained competitive advantage: a resource-based perspective', *International Journal of Human Resource Management*, Vol. 5, No. 2, p. 318. Reproduced with the permission of Taylor and Francis Ltd. *See* www.tandf.co.uk/journals.

and his co-authors view all human resources in the organisation as the pool of capital. This sits well with the view of strategy as evolutionary and strategy being influenced from the bottom up as well as from the top down. Also it is likely that top managers are more easily identified for their contribution to the organisation and hence are more likely to be mobile, therefore, than other employees who may not be so easily identified. However, different segments of the human resource are viewed differently by organisations in terms of their contribution to competitive advantage, so for some organisations the relevant pool of human capital may not be the total pool of employees.

Whereas fit models focus on the means of competitive advantage (HR practices) the resource-based view focuses on the source (the human capital). Wright *et al.* argue that while the practices are important they are not the source of competitive advantage as they can be replicated elsewhere, and they will produce different results in different places because of the differential human capital in different places. The relationship between human capital, human resource practices and competitive advantage is shown in Figure 3.3.

Boxall (1996) argues that this theoretical perspective provides a conceptual base for asserting that human resources are a source of competitive advantage, and as such valued as generating strategic capability. Thus there is a case for viewing HR strategy as something more than a reactive matching process. Indeed Wright *et al.* argue that it provides the case for HR to be involved in the formulation of strategy rather than just its implementation. They suggest that it provides a grounding for asserting that not every strategy is universally implementable, and that alternatives may have to be sought or the human capital pool developed further, via human resource practices, where this is possible.

The importance of this perspective is underlined by the current emphasis on a firm's intangible assets. Numerous studies have shown that a firm's market value (the sum of the value of the shares) is not fully explained by its current financial results (*see*, for example, Ulrich and Smallwood 2002) or its tangible assets and the focus has moved to a firm's intangible assets such as intellectual capital and customer relationships – all of which are derived from human capital (*see*, for example, Schmidt and Lines 2002). This emphasis has resulted in a great deal of attention being paid to the evaluation of human capital through measuring, reporting and managing it, and we discuss this in more detail in Chapter 29. Human capital is loaned: 'human capital is not owned by the organization, but secured through the employment relationship' (Scarborough 2003a: 2) and because this is so, the strategy for the management of people is also critical.

The perceived importance of people as an intangible asset is demonstrated in the action of Barclays Group who on their Investor's Day were keen to demonstrate not only their financial results but their people strategies and improvements in staff satisfaction which they believe have contributed to the results (Arkin and Allen 2002). The Barclays approach is covered in more detail in a case study on this book's companion website **www.pearsoned.co.uk/torrington**.

This approach has great advantages from an HR point of view. People in the organisation become the focus, their contribution is monitored and made more explicit, the way people are managed can be seen to add value and money spent on people can be seen as an investment rather than a cost. Some firms are using the balanced scorecard to demonstrate the contribution that human capital makes to firm performance, such as Aviva, and Scarborough (2003b) argues that this builds a bridge between the role of the HR function and the strategy of the firm. However, there are inbuilt barriers in the language of the resource-based view. One is the reference to people as 'human capital' which some consider to be unnecessarily instrumental. Another is the focus on 'firms' and 'competitive advantage' which makes it harder to see the relevance of this perspective for organisations in the public sector. There is also the issue of what is being measured and who decides this. The risk is that too much time is spent measuring and that not everything that is measured is of critical value to the organisation. So far, such measures appear very varied, although different firms will, of course, need to measure different things. Measures often appear to be taken without a coherent framework, as appears to be the case in the results documented by Scarborough and Elias (2002) for their ten case study organisations. The balanced scorecard and the HR scorecard, however, appear to be useful mechanisms in this respect. The evaluation of human capital is considered in greater depth in Chapter 29.

Why does the theory matter?

It is tempting to think of these theories of strategic HRM as competing with each other. In other words one is right and the others are wrong. If this were the case HR managers/directors and board members would need only to work out which is the 'right' theory and apply that. This is, of course, a gross oversimplification, as each theory can be interpreted and applied in different ways, and each has advantages and disadvantages. It could be argued that different theories apply in different sectors or competitive contexts. For example Guest (2001) suggests that there is the possibility that a 'high performance/high commitment' approach might always be most appropriate in manufacturing, whereas strategic choice (which could be interpreted as choice to fit with business strategy) might be more realistic in the services sector. This could be taken one step further to suggest that different theories apply to different groups in the workforce. Indeed Storey (2007), on the basis of work in the public and private sector suggests that there is value in HR directors crafting their strategy via four simultaneous pathways: best practice; best fit; building on and exploiting the people resource base (the three theoretical approaches we have discussed); and responding to an analysis of trends and demographics.

Consequently, these three theories do not necessarily represent simple alternatives. It is also likely that some board directors and even HR managers are not familiar with any of these theories. In spite of that, organisations, through their culture, and individuals within organisations operate on the basis of a set of assumptions, and these assumptions are often implicit. Assumptions about the nature and role of human resource strategy, whether explicit or implicit, will have an influence on what organisations actually do. Assumptions will limit what are seen as legitimate choices.

Understanding these theories enables HR managers, board members, consultants and the like to interpret the current position of HR strategy in the organisation, confront current assumptions and challenge current thinking and potentially open up a new range of possibilities.

This chapter forms the underpinning for the other strategic issues later in the book and links with key material in Chapter 5 on HR planning, Chapter 15 on Organisational change and development, Chapter 28 on The changing HR function and Chapter 29 on IT and human capital measurement.

SUMMARY PROPOSITIONS

2.1 It is more helpful to focus on the concept of strategic HRM than on HRM strategy as the former directs us to consider strategic thinking and a strategic orientation, rather than a 'strategy' which is written down and exists as a physical entity.

2.2 The nature of the link between business strategy and HR strategy is critical and can be played out in a variety of ways.

2.3 Three theoretical perspectives on strategic HR management can be identified: universalist/best practice; contingency/fit; and the resource-based/human capital view.

GENERAL DISCUSSION TOPICS

1 Is it feasible to link business strategy with the management of people in organisations?

2 Human resource strategies can be stimulating to produce and satisfying to display, but how can we make sure that they are implemented?

FURTHER READING

Millmore, M., Lewis, P., Saunders, M., Thornhill, A. and Morrow, T. (2007) *Strategic Human Resource Management: Contemporary issues*. London: Prentice Hall/Financial Times.

This text provides a good overview of different perspectives on HR strategy and chapters dedicated to strategic approaches in specific areas such as recruitment and selection, performance management, development, reward, diversity management and managing the employment relationship.

Salaman, G., Storey, J. and Billsberry, J. (2005) *Strategic Human Resource Management: Theory and practice. A reader*. London: The Open University in association with Sage.

This is an excellent source book bringing together a variety of perspectives and divided into four sections: strategic human resource management and knowledge; strategic human resource management and business performance; the emergence of new organisational forms and relationships and strategic human resource management in practice. Each chapter is an article previously published, and is either produced in full or summarised. This means that some work is older than others, but the choice of chapters means that key and influential strategic works (for example Wright *et al.* 2001 referred to in this chapter) are grouped together.

WEB LINK

www.cranet.org

REFERENCES

Arkin, A. and Allen, R. (2002) 'Satisfaction guaranteed', *People Management*, Vol. 8, No. 21, pp. 40–2.

Baird, L., Meshoulam, I. and DeGive, G. (1983) 'Meshing human resources planning with strategic business planning: a model approach', *Personnel*, Vol. 60, Part 5, pp. 14–25.

Barney, J. (1991) 'Firm resources and sustained competitive advantage', *Journal of Management*, Vol. 17, No. 1, pp. 99–120.

Becker, B., Huselid, M. and Ulrich, D. (2001) *The HR Scorecard: Linking people, strategy and performance*. Boston: Harvard Business School Press.

Boxall, P.F. (1996) 'The strategic HRM debate and the resource-based view of the firm', *Human Resource Management Journal*, Vol. 6, No. 3, pp. 59–75.

Boxall, P. and Purcell, J. (2008) *Strategy and Human Resource Management*. Basingstoke: Palgrave Macmillan.

Briggs, S. and Keogh, W. (1999) 'Integrating human resource strategy and strategic planning to achieve business excellence', *Total Quality Management*, July, p. 447.

Butler, J. (1988) 'Human resource management as a driving force in business strategy', *Journal of General Management*, Vol. 13, No. 4, pp. 88–102.

Chubb, L. (2008) 'Build a better brand', *People Management*, Vol. 14, No. 15, pp. 24–5.

Fields, D., Chan, A., Aktar, S. and Blum, T. (2006) 'Human resource management strategies under uncertainty', *Cross Cultural Management: An International Journal*, Vol. 13, No. 2, pp. 171–86.

Fombrun, C., Tichy, N.M. and Devanna, M.A. (1984) *Strategic Human Resource Management*. New York: John Wiley and Sons.

Godard, J. (2004) 'A critical assessment of the high-performance paradigm', *British Journal of Industrial Relations*, Vol. 42, No. 2, pp. 349–78.

Griffiths, J. (2006) 'Keep-fit scheme', *People Management*, Vol. 12, No. 7, pp. 18–19.

Grundy, T. (1998) 'How are corporate strategy and human resources strategy linked?', *Journal of General Management*, Vol. 23, No. 3, pp. 49–72.

Guest, D. (1987) 'Human resource management and industrial relations', *Journal of Management Studies*, Vol. 24, No. 5, pp. 503–21.

Guest, D. (1989) 'Personnel and HRM: Can you tell the difference?', *Personnel Management*, January, pp. 48–51.

Guest, D. (2001) 'Human resource management: when research confronts theory', *International Journal of Human Resource Management*, Vol. 12, No. 7, pp. 1092–106.

Guthridge, M. and Lawson, E. (2008) 'Divide and survive', *People Management*, Vol. 14, No. 19, pp. 40–4.

Higginbottom, K. (2002) 'Profits rise with a written HR strategy', *People Management*, Vol. 8, No. 25, p. 9.

Holbeche, L. (2008) *Aligning Human Resources and Business Strategy*. Oxford: Butterworth-Heinemann. © Roffey Park Management Institute.

Kaplan, R. and Norton, D. (2005) 'The office of strategy management', *Harvard Business Review*, Vol. 83, No. 10, pp. 73–80.

Kersley, B., Alpin, C., Forth, J., Bryson, A., Bewley, H., Dix, G. and Oxenbridge, S. (2006) *Inside the Workplace: Findings from the 2004 Workplace Employment Relations Survey*. London: Routledge.

Kochan, T.A. and Barocci, T.A. (1985) *Human Resource Management and Industrial Relations: Text, readings and cases*. Boston: Little Brown.

Lengnick-Hall, M. and Lengnick-Hall, C. (2003) *Human Resource Management in the Knowledge Economy*. San Francisco: Berrett-Koehler Inc.

Lepak, D. and Shaw, J. (2008) 'Strategic HRM in North America: looking to the future', *The International Journal of Human Resource Management*, Vol. 19, No. 8, pp. 1486–99.

MacDuffie, J. (1995) 'Human resource bundles and manufacturing performance: organizational logic and flexible production systems in the world auto industry', *Industrial and Labor Relations Review*, Vol. 48, No. 2, pp. 197–221.

Miles, R.E. and Snow, C.C. (1984) 'Organisation strategy, structure and process', *Academy of Management Review*, Vol. 2, pp. 546–62.

Mintzberg, H. (1994) 'The fall and rise of strategic planning', *Harvard Business Review*, January–February, pp. 107–14.

Ogbonna, E. and Whipp, R. (1999) 'Strategy, culture and HRM: evidence from the UK food retailing sector', *Human Resource Management Journal*, Vol. 9, No. 4, pp. 75–90.

Pfeffer, J. (1998) *The Human Equation*. Boston: Harvard Business School Press.

Porter, M. (1980) *Competitive Strategy*. New York: Free Press.

Purcell, J. (1992) 'The impact of corporate strategy on human resource management', in G. Salaman *et al.* (eds), *Human Resource Strategies*. London: Sage Publications.

Salaman, G., Storey, J. and Billsberry, J. (2005) 'Strategic human resource management: defining the field', in G. Salaman, J. Storey and J. Billsberry (eds), *Strategic Human Resource Management: Theory and practice. A reader*. London: Sage/Open University.

Sanz-Valle, R., Sabater-Sánchez, R. and Aragón-Sánchez, A. (1999) 'Human resource management and business strategy links: an empirical study', *International Journal of Human Resource Management*, Vol. 10, No. 4, pp. 655–71.

Scarborough, H. (2003a) *Human Capital: External reporting framework*. London: CIPD.

Scarborough, H. (2003b) 'Recipe for success', *People Management*, Vol. 9, No. 2, pp. 32–5.

Scarborough, H. and Elias, J. (2002) *Evaluating Human Capital: Research report*. London: CIPD.

Schmidt, J. and Lines, S. (2002) 'A measure of success', *People Management*, Vol. 8, No. 9, pp. 32–4.

Schuler, R.S. and Jackson, S.E. (1987) 'Linking competitive strategies with human resource management practices', *Academy of Management Executive*, Vol. 1, No. 3, pp. 207–19.

Simmons, J. (2009) 'Both sides now: aligning internal and external brands for a socially responsible era', *Marketing Intelligence and Planning*, Vol. 27, No. 5, pp. 38–41.

Skinner, D. and Mabey, C. (1997) 'Managers' perceptions of strategic HR change', *Personnel Review*, Vol. 26, No. 6, pp. 467–84.

Storey, J. (2007) 'What is strategic HRM', in J. Storey (ed.), *Human Resource Management: A critical text*. London: Thompson Learning.

Tyson, S. (1995) *Human Resource Strategy*. London: Pitman.

Ulrich, D. (1998) 'A new mandate for human resources', *Harvard Business Review*, January–February, pp. 125–34.

Ulrich, D. and Smallwood, N. (2002) 'Seven up', *People Management*, Vol. 8, No. 10, pp. 42–4.

Wright, P., McMahon, G. and McWilliams, A. (1994) 'Human resources and sustained competitive advantage: a resource-based perspective', *International Journal of Human Resource Management*, Vol. 5, No. 2, May, pp. 301–26.

Wright, P., Dunford, B. and Snell, S. (2001) 'Human resources and the resource-based view of the firm', *Journal of Management*, Vol. 27, pp. 701–21.

An extensive range of additional materials, including multiple choice questions, answers to questions and links to useful websites can be found on the Human Resource Management companion website at **www.pearsoned.co.uk/torrington**.

CHAPTER 4

ORGANISATION DESIGN AND FLEXIBILITY

THE OBJECTIVES OF THIS CHAPTER ARE TO:

1. Explain the principles of organisation design
2. Outline the most common types of organisational structure
3. Explain the principles of job design and describe its relationship to organisational performance
4. Discuss the reasons for and types of organisational flexibility
5. Explain forms of employee flexibility and discuss the extent to which they are implemented in practice

ORGANISATION DESIGN

Organisational design relates to the shaping of an organisation to ensure efficient delivery of its activity. Organisation design activities therefore focus on:

> Finding the most appropriate structures, relationships between departments and sections, and allocation of work activities, including definition of duties and role responsibilities. (CIPD Professional Map 2009)

We discuss all of these elements in this chapter, focusing particularly on organisational structures and individual job design.

Organisational design requires that choices be made on a number of issues and that these choices are consistent with contextual factors, such as the organisation's strategy and its environment (Burton and Obel 2004). Three key issues are **high** versus **low formality**, **differentiation** versus **integration** and **decentralisation** versus **centralisation**. We consider these below.

High versus **low formality** refers to the extent to which an organisation has formal procedures. Typically small firms are relatively informal, low employee numbers meaning that face-to-face communication is usually possible in order to discuss and agree a way forward. As organisations grow, however, procedures are normally established which guide action to ensure consistency across a range of situations and people. It is important to ensure that procedures are supportive and enabling of action, rather than constraining and dis-empowering as can be the case when organisations become very large and develop a plethora of inflexible procedures.

Differentiation requires specialisation of effort to ensure that an individual job or task is undertaken effectively, while **integration** is coordinating the output of the individual people so that the whole task is completed satisfactorily. Organising individual jobs varies according to the degree of predictability in what has to be done, so that organising manufacturing jobs or a call centre tends to emphasise strict obedience to the rules, clearly defined tasks and much specialisation. Jobs which have constantly fresh problems and unpredictable requirements, like marketing and social work, produce frequent redefinition of job boundaries, a tendency to flexible networks of working relationships rather than a clear hierarchy and a greater degree of individual autonomy. The integrating process will be influenced by the amount of differentiation. The greater the differentiation, the harder the task of coordination.

Centralisation/decentralisation refers to the extent to which certain aspects of authority and decision making are held at the top of the organisation, as opposed to being devolved down to local level. Historically organisations have tended to favour centralisation, although the past couple of decades have seen greater decentralisation in the form, for example, of strategic business units. Here, the management of a particular unit is given an agreed budget and an agreed set of targets for the forthcoming period. Thereafter it has the freedom to manage itself as it sees fit provided that it first submits regular reports and, second, meets the targets and complies with the budget expectations. Decentralisation is thought to make decision making and responding to local needs and customers easier and quicker to achieve.

Table 4.1 Organisation design choices

Mechanistic design	High formalisation	Extensive use of written procedures High degree of task specialisation Strict performance control
	Low integration	Little use of liaison processes Little use of liaison structures
	High centralisation	Little delegation of decision-making authority
Organic design	Low formalisation	Little use of written procedures Low degree of task specialisation Relaxed performance control
	High integration	Extensive use of liaison processes Extensive use of liaison structures
	Low centralisation	Extensive delegation of decision-making authority

Source: Curado 2006: 38.

Using these three elements gives a range of design choices, often classified using systems metaphors (Eriksen 2005). Burns and Stalker (1961), for example, outline the classical distinction between organic and mechanistic designs. Organic systems are frequently described as loosely coupled systems where there is little formalisation, where complex integrating mechanisms are used, and decision making is delegated. In contrast, mechanistic organisations are highly formalised and centralised, and tend to use less complex integration mechanisms (Curado 2006). These design choices are presented in Table 4.1.

While organisations have long reflected upon design choices, these have been made increasingly complex by a range of contemporary concerns. Information technology advances have led to new ways of managing and communicating, styles of management have shifted from command and control to supporting and facilitating, and demographic changes have led to a more diverse workforce incorporating, for example, far greater numbers of women. These developments have led to a number of changes to organisational structures and job design which we consider in the chapter. One of the most important changes to arise has been that of workforce flexibility. Indeed, the CIPD (2008b) report on job design suggests that delivering working-time flexibility is the most important aspect of organisation design. Globalisation of markets has led to ever greater product market competition and an increased need to gain competitive advantage. In striving for this, employers have provided less secure jobs, using 'flexible' workers in order to keep costs down and to retain or increase market share. Developments in technology enable a greater control of workflow, requiring flexible working hours to extend capital utilisation. The change in the economic base whereby there are more service industries with an emphasis on knowledge and knowledge workers has also influenced flexibility, as jobs in a knowledge-based economy tend to be more flexible than industrial jobs, with more varied working hours. Allied to this has been a perceived need for '24/7' service availability, leading to a dramatic move away from the standard working time model of 9–5 Monday to Friday and to employers demanding a far more flexible approach to work organisation.

The demand for flexibility, however, has not all been from employers. It has coincided with changes that have created a greater supply of labour at non-standard times. One of the primary drivers of this has been the increased labour force participation of women, particularly women in the childbearing years, which has led to a greater requirement for flexible working arrangements in order to accommodate child care responsibilities. There has also been an increase in single parent families and dual career couples, meaning that a growing proportion of the workforce has to reconcile both work and non-work commitments. This augments the supply of labour at non-standard times, such as nights and weekends. A further demographic influence is the ageing population of western countries, with employees demanding flexibility to deal with both child care and elder care responsibilities. Pension concerns (*see* Chapter 25) may also force workers to remain in the workforce longer than previously anticipated and research has shown that older workers frequently aspire to work flexibly in the later stages of their careers (CIPD 2005). Flexibility for both organisational and employee benefit is thus a significant contemporary issue in organisation and job design and we discuss this in detail later in this chapter.

ACTIVITY 4.1

Thinking of an organisation with which you are familiar, how would you describe it in terms of the three key elements of organisation design:

- To what extent are differentiation and integration evident?
- Are procedures predominantly formal or informal?
- What is the degree of centralisation versus decentralisation?

ORGANISATION STRUCTURES

As our discussion above suggests, there is no single ideal organisational form:

> organizations are as different and varied as the nations and societies of the world. They have differing cultures – sets of values and norms and beliefs – reflected in different structures and systems. (Handy 1993: 180)

Organisational structures reflect the decisions made by organisations about issues of formalisation, differentiation and centralisation (Table 4.1) and are based around hierarchy:

> The hierarchy is the chain of command, the pyramid of authority that narrows at the top . . . if we eliminate all the paraphernalia of rank and authority in large organizations, we don't really know what we would end up with. There are no clear examples of large human organizations that operate without a formal hierarchy . . . some form of hierarchy is necessary for organizing a complex set of people and resources. (Leavitt *et al.* 1973: 31–2)

Hierarchy creates a predictable **system** of roles and jobs. It enables us to understand how to get things done and how matters will be handled. Hierarchy also distributes **power**, rations power and ensures that people accept the power of others in the system. Holders of specified roles or jobs are empowered to make certain decisions and to control the behaviour of other people: power is distributed and rationed. Traditionally, large organisations have had **tall** hierarchies (i.e. many levels in them) with **narrow** spans of control (each person being responsible for the supervision of only a small number of people). Since the 1980s, however, there has been a trend to much **flatter** hierarchies with much **wider** spans of control. This trend has been termed **delayering** and is the process of taking out layers of management in the hierarchy in order to speed response times and make the operation more efficient.

WINDOW ON PRACTICE

Delayering in large organisations

From the mid-1980s onwards many organisations which had traditionally had tall hierarchies set about the process of delayering. This was common practice in financial services organisations such as large banks (*see*, for example, Atkinson 2002) and in some newly privatised industries such as BT (*see*, for example, Newell and Dopson 1996). The logic behind this restructuring process was to make organisations more flexible and responsive to increasingly dynamic and competitive market conditions by devolving decision-making responsibilities to those closest to the customer. In removing layers of middle management which had come to be seen as blockages to change and responsiveness, organisations sought to improve the efficiency and effectiveness of their operations.

While the theory behind delayering was sound, its implementation was in many instances problematic. As is often the case with change programmes, senior management gave insufficient consideration to people aspects of delayering. There is a large body of research from this period which identifies the negative impact on the morale and motivation of those remaining in delayered organisations. Those left behind were said to suffer from 'survivor syndrome', characterised by mourning for lost colleagues, fearing for their own future job security and suffering work intensification as they struggled to cope with often increased workloads with fewer staff. In the face of these conditions, the hoped-for efficiency gains were rarely achieved.

While a huge variety of organisational structures is possible, most can be categorised into one of three broad types: entrepreneurial, bureaucratic and matrix.

The entrepreneurial form

The entrepreneurial form relies on central power and can be described as primarily organic. It is like the spider's web, with one person or group so dominant that all power stems from the centre, all decisions are made by and all behaviour reflects expectations of the centre. There are few collective decisions, much reliance on individuals, and with actions requiring the approval of key figures. This form is frequently found in businesses where decisions must be made quickly and with flair and judgement rather than careful deliberation. Newspaper editing has an entrepreneurial form of organisation and most of the performing arts have strong centralised direction.

This is the form of most small and growing businesses as they owe their existence to the expertise or initiative of one or two people, and it is only by reflecting accurately that originality that the business can survive. As the business expands this type of structure can become unwieldy because too many peripheral decisions cannot be made without approval from the centre, which then becomes overloaded. It is also difficult to maintain if the spider leaves the centre of the web, as a successor may not have the same degree of dominance. In some instances the problem of increasing size has been dealt with by maintaining entrepreneurial structure at the core of the enterprise and giving considerable independence to satellite organisations, provided that overall performance targets are met.

An extreme example is the organisation of the entourage surrounding a celebrity. An entertainer of international reputation may employ dozens or hundreds of people, but the sole purpose of their employment is to sustain and extend the reputation of the spider at the centre of their web. If that person dies the whole surrounding organisation rapidly unravels, having lost its reason for existence. Less unusual examples are in financial services, where a fund manager's team may collapse if that person leaves, or in a school, where the tone of all that is done is largely determined by the head teacher.

The bureaucratic form

The bureaucratic form emphasises the distribution rather than centralisation of power and responsibility: it has a more extended and complex hierarchy and is primarily mechanistic in structure. It has been the conventional means of enabling an organisation to grow beyond the entrepreneurial form to establish an existence that is not dependent on a single person or group of founders. Disney is a classic example of a business, originally totally dependent on the flair of its founder, developed, expanded and diversified despite the demise of Walt Disney. Because the emphasis is on role rather than flair, operational processes become more predictable and consistent, with procedure and committee replacing individual judgement. Responsibility is devolved through the structure; this is a method of organisation well suited to stable situations, making possible economies of scale and the benefits of specialisation. There is seldom the flexibility to deal with a volatile environment and there is also a tendency to be self-sufficient:

> The problem is that rules are inflexible instruments of administration which enshrine experience of past rather than present conditions, which cannot be readily adapted to suit individual needs, and which can become barriers behind which it is tempting for the administrator to hide. (Child 1984: 8)

Bureaucracy has been the standard form of structure for large organisations at least since the building of the Egyptian pyramids and remains the dominant form today. It has, however, come under criticism more recently because of its inappropriateness in times of change and a tendency to frustrate personal initiative. 'Bureaucracy' is definitely a dirty word, so companies work hard at overcoming its drawbacks.

The matrix form

The matrix form emphasises the coordination of expertise into project-oriented groups of people with individual responsibility. It has been developed to counter some of the difficulties of the entrepreneurial and bureaucratic forms and tries to combine the strengths of both organic and mechanistic approaches. It was first developed in the United States during the 1960s as a means of satisfying the government on the progress of orders placed with contractors for the supply of defence material. Checking on progress proved very difficult with a bureaucracy, so it was made a condition of contracts that the contractor should appoint a project manager with responsibility for meeting the delivery commitments and keeping the project within budget. In this way the government was able to deal with a single representative rather than with a number of people with only partial responsibility. The contractors then had to realign their organisation so that the project manager could actually exercise the degree of control necessary to make the responsibility effective. They did this either by appointing a project manager with considerable status and power, or by creating product teams with specialists seconded from each functional area. The first method leaves the weight of authority with the functional hierarchy, while the project managers have a mainly coordinating, progress-chasing role as lone specialists. The second method shifts power towards the project managers, who then have their own teams of experts, with the functional areas being seen as a resource rather than the centre of action and decision.

Matrix is the form that appeals to many managers because it is theoretically based on expertise and provides scope for people at relatively humble levels of the business to deploy their skills and carry responsibility. It has, however, recently lost favour because it can generate expensive support systems for project managers needing additional secretaries, assistants and all the panoply of office, as well as the unwieldy administration referred to above.

This threefold classification is a means of analysis rather than a description of three distinct types of organisation with any undertaking being clearly one of the three. Bureaucracies will typically have matrix features at some points and few entrepreneurial structures are quite as 'pure' as implied here. Most large organisations could have one form dominant in one section of the business and another form dominant elsewhere. Large banks, for example, are bureaucratic in their retailing operations as consistency is of paramount importance and any changes need to be put into operation simultaneously by a large number of people while being comprehensible to a large number of customers. The same banks will, however, tend to an entrepreneurial emphasis in their merchant banking activities and in currency dealings.

The organisation of individual departments

The overall structure of the organisation is important, but the organisation of individual jobs and their interconnection within individual departments is equally important. 'Department' designates a distinct area, division or branch of an enterprise over which a manager has authority for the performance of specified activities. Two key aspects of design are to establish its purpose and activities. The **purpose** of creating a department may be a basic organistional objective, such as manufacture, or customer care, or maintenance, or it may be to make things run more smoothly. A common example is a systems department to interface between the people in the business and the information technology that processes data. Those who understand the electronic gadgetry are grouped together because of a skill they have in common. A countervailing argument is that it is better for skills to be dispersed. Matrix patterns of organisation go part of the way towards this. Once a skill-based department is established there are the risks of it being separated from the mainstream, aloof and having problems of communication. An alternative to organisation on the basis of skills in common is to group people in departments on the basis of frequent contact. The obvious example is the grouping of secretaries, personal assistants and data-input personnel. If they are all together in a secretarial services department there are the benefits of flexibility, shared facilities – from dictionaries to photocopiers – specialised supervision and general economies of scale. On the other hand, if they are located individually with the people with whom they work, there are the advantages of easy access for receiving instructions, providing information, and a wider range of duties.

Once the purpose of the department has been decided, the next step is to decide on the **activities** it is to undertake: what tasks will it undertake and what responsibilities will it have? Establishing these parameters will lead to the next step of design: what types of people are needed in the department, with what types of expertise and what will they do? We go on now to consider these questions in the section on job design.

ACTIVITY 4.2

What experience have you, or someone you know, had of organisational re-structuring? What happened? To what extent did the re-structuring achieve its aims?

JOB DESIGN

Job design is the process of putting together a range of tasks, duties and responsibilities to create a composite for individuals to undertake in their work and to regard as their own. It is crucial: not only is it the basis of individual satisfaction and achievement at work, it is necessary to get the job done efficiently, economically, reliably and safely. As long as there have been organisations, there has been debate on the best way to design the jobs within them and for much of this time the interest in job design has centred round attempts to improve employee satisfaction with the working situation. The focus has changed from designing jobs which ensure employee compliance, to designing those which generate employee commitment. In this way, job design is seen to be integral to efforts to harness employee efforts to improve organisational performance. The evolution of thinking in job design is encapsulated well by a diagram drawn from a recent CIPD report (Figure 4.1).

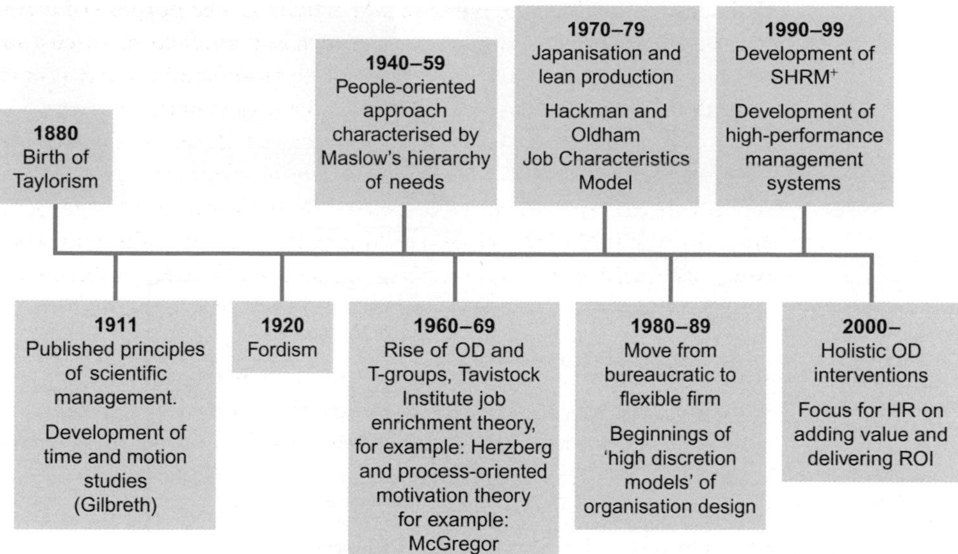

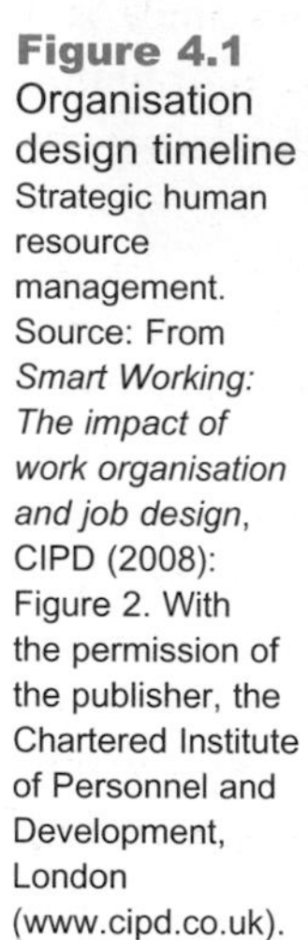
Figure 4.1 Organisation design timeline
Strategic human resource management.
Source: From *Smart Working: The impact of work organisation and job design*, CIPD (2008): Figure 2. With the permission of the publisher, the Chartered Institute of Personnel and Development, London (www.cipd.co.uk).

The first attempts at job design were influenced by F.W. Taylor and the scientific school of management. This approach was founded on the division of labour into simple jobs and rigid allocations of individuals to narrowly defined tasks. Concerns centred around efficiency, time and motion studies, for example, ensuring tasks were structured in a way that allowed workers to conduct them in the most efficient manner. This led to highly specialised jobs, workers at Ford's factories on assembly lines each carrying out, for example, very narrow specified elements of the construction of a motor car. Scientific management was premised upon the idea of 'man as machine', that is rational, unemotional and focused upon economic concerns. Incentives, such as bonuses, were designed to meet the extrinsic motivations of employees. Jobs were, however, routine, repetitive and monotonous, leading to boredom and industrial unrest among workers.

The recognition that workers had needs beyond economic ones led, from the 1940s on, to worker motivation being a key concern within job design. Abraham Maslow, for example, suggested that there was a hierarchy of needs within workers and that job design should meet a range of needs, such as social, rather than simply focusing on economic concerns. In the period 1940–60, a range of motivational theories influenced job design. We do not have the space here to provide a comprehensive review of motivation theory and suggest the reader refers to an organisational behaviour text for further information. We do intend, however, to focus in some detail on one of the most influential pieces of research on job design, Hackman and Oldham's (1976) Job Characteristics Model (JCM, Figure 4.2). Despite first appearing in the 1970s, it has resonance and influence to this day (*see*, for example, Wood and Wall 2007).

The JCM specifies certain aspects which must be designed into a job in order to ensure the positive outcomes of meaningful work, responsibility and knowledge. Achieving these will lead to high internal motivation and links to enhanced individual and organisational performance.

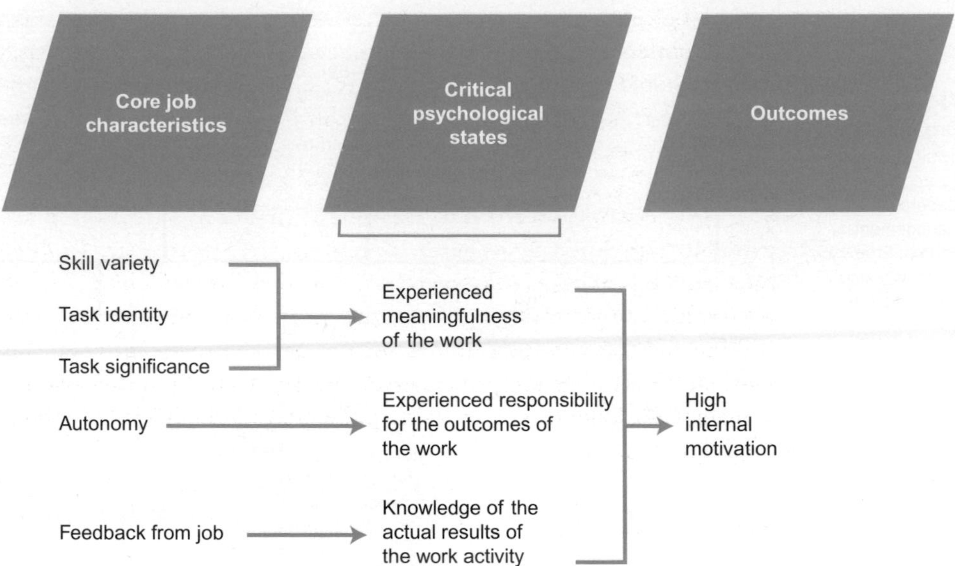

Figure 4.2 Hackman and Oldham's Job Characteristics Model (1976)
Source: From *Smart Working: The impact of work organisation and job design*, CIPD (2008): Figure 3. With the permission of the publisher, the Chartered Institute of Personnel and Development, London (www.cipd.co.uk).

Skill variety

Skill variety is the extent to which the tasks in a job require a range of skills and abilities. Jobs designed in accordance with scientific management principles were highly specialised, requiring a narrow range of skills and abilities, and the negative outcomes arising from the boredom and monotony created by this became evident. The JCM suggested that jobs should require workers to use a wide range of skills and abilities and led to a focus on **job enrichment**, the process of incorporating more skills and abilities into jobs. Wood and Wall (2009) make a case for the continuing importance of job enrichment in job design, arguing that it has been overlooked in the drive for high performance work systems (*see* Chapter 11) and that it should continue to be a key element within human resource management endeavour.

Task identity

Task identity refers to the degree to which a job provides the opportunity to undertake a whole and identifiable piece of work. Completing such a piece of work is critical to positive psychological outcomes, the negative impact of not doing this again being apparent from, for example, the alienation caused by working on an assembly line. Car manufacturers such as Volvo have over the years experimented with principles such as autonomous work teams, where a team is tasked with the construction of an entire car, rather than individuals being tasked with specified elements of it, in order to provide this task identity. While such experiments have not been unproblematic, they are an attempt to design jobs so as to provide workers with meaningful work.

Task significance

Task significance is the extent to which a job has an impact, whether on the organisation, its employees or customers. The more impact a job is seen to have, the better the psychological outcomes for the worker. A key aspect of job design is thus that workers should understand the contribution made by their job to the organisational endeavour. An oft quoted example in this respect is the hospital cleaner who sees his/her job not as cleaning but helping to deliver high quality patient care. When conceptualised in this way, the cleaner's job takes on a high level of task significance.

Together, skill variety, task identity and task significance comprise the 'meaningfulness' of the work undertaken. Job design should aim to achieve all three in order to promote motivation in workers and thus higher performance. While some organisations have worked to design jobs to achieve this, there are still many contemporary organisations which adopt somewhat Taylorist principles. One only has to think of the level of routine and specialisation in jobs such as call centre operatives or fast food restaurant workers to see that the principles of the JCM are by no means universally adopted. This may go some way to explaining the typically high level of labour turnover in such organisations.

Autonomy

Autonomy describes the extent to which the individual undertaking the job has the discretion to make decisions about how it is done, including scheduling the work and deciding upon the procedures used to carry it out. Autonomy creates the positive outcome of responsibility, which again influences motivation. The flattening organisational structures discussed earlier in this chapter have led, since the mid-1990s, to an organisational preoccupation with worker autonomy in the guise of 'empowerment' (*see*, for example, Cooney 2004). Empowerment devolves responsibility to workers and removes the need for close supervision control, impossible given the removal or reduction of middle managers in many organisations. Working-time flexibility, which we discuss below, can also create more worker autonomy (Hall and Atkinson 2006). More recently, the concern to create worker autonomy has been reflected in high performance work organisation designs focusing on employee involvement mechanisms (*see* Chapter 19 for further information on these).

Feedback

Feedback is about receiving direct and clear information about levels of performance. This leads to worker knowledge which again, according to the JCM, leads to higher motivation. It is this need for feedback which underpins many contemporary performance management systems (*see* Chapter 12).

The JCM thus led to a paradigm shift in which jobs were designed which required a range of skills and abilities, provided greater freedom to workers, who often worked in autonomous teams, and adopted flexible working practices. Its principles impacted on models of the flexible firm in the 1980s, high performance work systems in the 1990s and through to organisational development approaches of this century. Job design is, however, still dependent on individual characteristics; some workers will, for example, be more receptive to being stretched and challenged than others. Morgeson and Humphrey (2006) also argue that its effectiveness will depend on organisational context, as we see in the Window on practice below which considers role redesign for midwives in the NHS.

WINDOW ON PRACTICE

The redesign of midwives' roles

A central premise of the NHS HRM strategies is the need to redesign workforce roles and develop new ones, while at the same time expanding the scope of jobs so that staff can take on new responsibilities and skills. The effect of this for midwives was to design 'extended' roles, expanded to include work traditionally performed by doctors, with some aspects of their previous role being delegated to maternity support workers. Midwives felt, however, that the extended roles often prevented them from providing individualised woman-centred care, as they spent time going from one woman to another performing repetitive technical tasks. Work was often described as a 'production line' and a case of 'get them in, get them delivered, and ship them out'. They also felt that there was greater ambiguity in their role and that its extension reduced autonomy and recognition, de-skilling them as they became reliant on technology rather than expertise. In order to undertake the extended roles, the delivery of care, where midwives obtain the greatest job satisfaction and their highest intrinsic motivation, was delegated to maternity support workers. The professional boundaries of midwifery and their traditional social and emotional skills are thus being eroded or replaced as they take on more technical roles previously undertaken by doctors and reluctantly relinquish their traditional social and caring roles to maternity support workers.

Critics of the NHS HRM policies suggest that role redesign, rather than improving work satisfaction, is being used to reduce labour costs, de-skill staff and promote greater flexibility of labour. The demotivational effects of this upon midwives raises questions about government assumptions that NHS role redesign will improve midwives' productivity.

Source: Adapted from Prowse, J. and Prowse, P. (2008) 'Role redesign in the National Health Service: the effects on midwives' work and professional boundaries', *Work, Employment and Society*, Vol. 22, No. 4, pp. 695–712.

ACTIVITY 4.3

Thinking of a job you have held, or one you have observed (for example, your interactions with workers in fast-food restaurants) analyse it in terms of the Job Characteristics Model. To what extent does it offer:

- Skill variety
- Task identity
- Task significance
- Autonomy
- Feedback?

What are the implications of your analysis for worker motivation and performance?

ORGANISATIONAL FLEXIBILITY

A crucial aspect of organisation and job design is the extent to which it affords flexibility to the organisation. Such flexibility has increased significantly since the mid-1980s, with many employees experiencing significant change in their traditional working patterns. Atkinson (1984), for example, suggested a 'flexible firm' model that explains employer behaviour in terms of work organisation and flexibility. However, tight labour markets in the period 1997–2007 have increasingly required employers to accommodate employee demands for flexibility in order to recruit and retain scarce labour.

It is often argued that employer and employee needs in flexible working practices are complementary and that the practices adopted have benefits for both parties. There are tensions, however, between employer and employee needs. Practices presented as beneficial to employees are, in fact, often detrimental to them. For example, despite meeting the needs of some employees for flexibility, part-time work is often insecure and low paid. Nevertheless, it can be argued that the meeting of employee need is dependent upon whether the employee has access to a contract of choice. We present below flexible working practices that are typically considered to be demand led, adopting Atkinson's (1984) model of the flexible firm. While this model is much criticised, it remains one of the most comprehensive treatments of organisational flexibility.

Model of the 'flexible firm'

Atkinson (1984) describes how firms may develop flexibility in their approach to employment, as shown in Figure 4.3. The model comprises forms of flexibility including numerical, temporal and functional and we consider these below.

Numerical flexibility

Numerical flexibility allows the organisation to respond quickly to the environment in terms of the numbers of people employed. Some traditional full-time, permanent posts are replaced by short-term contract staff, staff with rolling contracts, outworkers and so on. This enables the organisation to reduce or expand the workforce quickly and cheaply.

The flexible firm in this analysis has various ways of meeting the need for human resources. First are core employees, who form the primary labour market. They are highly regarded by the employer, well paid and involved in those activities that are unique to the firm or give it a distinctive character. These employees have improved career prospects and offer the type of flexibility to the employer that is so prized in the skilled professional with wide experience and adaptability.

There are then two peripheral groups: first, those who have skills that are needed but not specific to the particular firm, like typing and word processing. The strategy for these posts is to rely on the external labour market to a much greater extent, to specify a narrow range of tasks without career prospects, so that the employee has a job but not a career. Some employees may be able to transfer to core posts, but generally limited scope is likely to maintain a fairly high turnover, so that adjustments to the vagaries of the product market are eased.

The second peripheral group is made up of those enjoying even less security, as they have contracts of employment that are limited, either to a short-term or a part-time attachment. There may also be a few job sharers, although job sharing is not widely

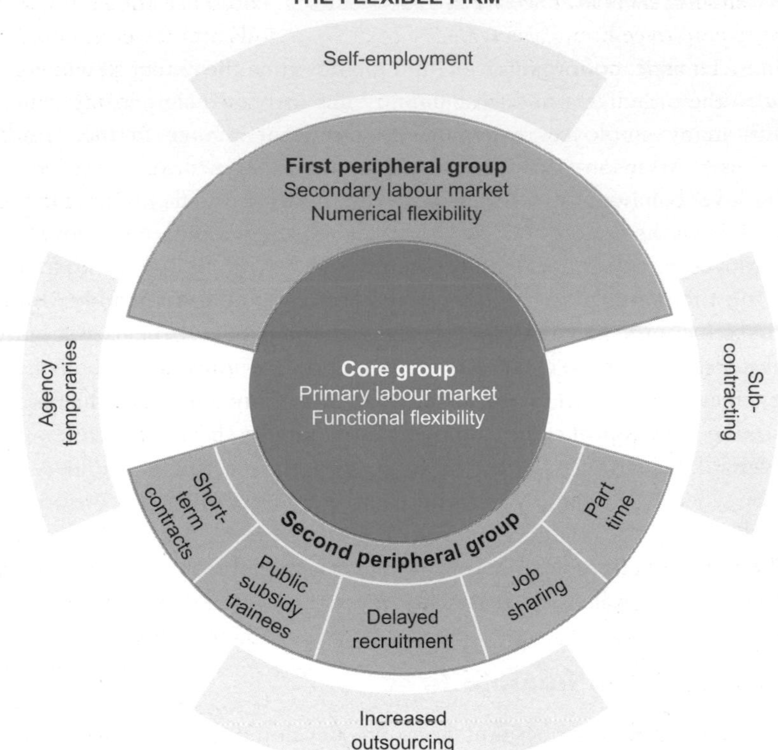

Figure 4.3 Atkinson's model of the flexible firm
Source: J. Atkinson (1984) 'Manpower strategies for flexible organisation', *Personnel Management*, August. Used with the permission of the author.

practised. An alternative or additional means towards this flexibility is to contract out the work that has to be done, either by employing temporary personnel from agencies or by outsourcing the entire operation, adjusting the organisation boundary, redefining what is to be done in-house and what is to be contracted out to various suppliers.

An interesting development in the use of numerical flexibility has emerged in the recession which started in 2008. A significant number of firms, including professional ones such as management consultancies, have been reluctant to make staff redundant, remembering the staff shortages in periods of economic growth which followed the large-scale redundancy programmes in previous recessions. There has been widespread use of numerical flexibility in maintaining employment, some workers, for example, working enforced three- or four-day weeks. Annual hours systems have been used by car manufacturers, many of whom ceased production for two or three months, paying workers and allowing them to bank the hours for use at times when demand and thus production levels increased. In this way, organisations have been able to maintain employment of skilled workers through recession in anticipation of more buoyant economic times ahead.

Temporal flexibility

Temporal flexibility concerns varying the pattern of hours worked in order to respond to business demands and employee needs. Moves away from the 9–5, five-day week include the use of annual hours contracts, increased use of part-time work, job sharing and flexible working hours. For example, an organisation subject to peaks and troughs of demand, such as an ice cream manufacturer, could use annual hours contracts so that more employee hours are available at peak periods and fewer are used when business is slow. Flexible hours systems can benefit the employer by providing employee cover outside the 9–5 day and over lunchtimes, and can also provide employee benefits by allowing personal demands to be fitted more easily around work demands.

Research evidence suggests increasing use of temporal flexibility. Longer opening hours in retailing and the growth of the leisure sector means that many more people now work in the evening (17 per cent) and at night (6 per cent) than used to be the case. The proportion of jobs that are part time also continues to rise, albeit at a slower rate than in the 1970s and 1980s, while the length of the working week for higher-paid full-time workers has increased by three hours on average during the past decade. There has also been some growth in the use of annual hours, but these arrangements have not become as widespread as was predicted a decade ago. Only 6 per cent of employers have chosen to adopt this approach for some of their staff (Kersley *et al.* 2006).

Functional flexibility

The term 'functional flexibility' refers to a process in which employees gain the capacity to undertake a variety of tasks rather than specialising in just one area. Advocates of such approaches have been influenced by studies of Japanese employment practices as well as by criticisms of monotonous assembly-line work. Horizontal flexibility involves each individual employee becoming multiskilled so that he or she can be deployed as and where required at any time. Vertical flexibility entails gaining the capacity to undertake work previously carried out by colleagues higher up or lower down the organisational hierarchy.

The primary purpose of functional flexibility initiatives is to deploy human resources more efficiently. It should mean that employees are kept busy throughout their working day and that absence is more easily covered than in a workplace with rigidly defined demarcation between jobs. A further efficiency gain comes from employees being more stretched, fulfilled and thus productive than in a workplace with narrowly defined jobs. Despite its potential advantages research suggests that employers in the UK have been less successful than competitors elsewhere in Europe at developing functional flexibility. According to Blyton (1998), this is primarily because of a reluctance to invest in the training necessary to support these new forms of working. By contrast, Reilly (2001) points to employee resistance and the increased likelihood of errors occurring when functional flexibility programmes are introduced. It could also simply be a reflection of increased specialisation as jobs become more technically complex relying to a greater extent on specific expert knowledge. Either way the Workplace Employment Relations Survey (2004), shows a decline in formal multiskilling programmes during recent years. In 2004 only 19 per cent of workplaces reported that at least three-fifths of their core employees were trained to do more than one job, compared with 29 per cent in 1998 (Kersley *et al.* 2006: 92).

Case 4.1 on this book's companion website, **www.pearsoned.co.uk/torrington** explores flexible working strategies further.

Network organisations

As we noted above, Atkinson's model of the flexible firm is much criticised but has no clear successor. The network organisation (Powell 1990) has, however, received increasing interest in the debate on organisational flexibility in recent years. Network organisations describe long-term contractual arrangements between supplier and client organisations which involve a co-production process. For example, the outsourcing of cleaning or information technology operations to an external supplier. In this way, an organisation can gain numerical and functional flexibility by establishing relationships with other organisations, rather than through its own labour management strategies, as advocated in Atkinson's model of the flexible firm. Functional flexibility is achieved through agreements with specialist suppliers or producers while numerical flexibility is delivered through outsourcing and the use of temporary agency labour. These inter-organisational relationships are often referred to as strategic alliances, joint ventures, partnerships or subcontracting. They are ongoing relationships which can lead to the blurring of organisational boundaries such that it can be difficult for the worker to know who (s)he is working for. We look at a public sector example of a network organisation in the Window on practice below.

WINDOW ON PRACTICE

Public Private Partnerships

Hebson *et al.* (2003) investigated public private partnerships (PPP) in which the traditional delivery of public services on the basis of procedural, bureaucratic principles is replaced by the specification of highly detailed performance contracts agreed between purchaser and supplier. The employment relationship – as experienced by public services workers – becomes caught in this contractual relationship, with the potential for tension and change especially magnified where the public sector acts as purchaser and the private sector acts as supplier as in PPP. The article draws on two detailed case studies of PPPs in health and local government services.

PPPs tend to be characterised by transfers of large numbers of public sector workers and by strong inter-organisational differences in the management of work and employment. Where an employer is locked into a tightly specified performance contract with a client organisation, this will have a direct bearing on its approach to managing employment. Consequently, the assumption that workers forge an unproblematic association with a single employer is especially misplaced in those situations where the employer, as supplier, must respond to the changing demands of the client organisation; moreover, notions of commitment become blurred where, as is often the case with PPPs, activities are carried out on the site of the client organisation and workers from the supplier organisation work alongside others employed by the client organisation. Thus new contracting principles redraw the boundaries of the employment contract by introducing a direct (albeit sometimes complex) connection between the form of relationship among organisations (such as a legal contract or an informal agreement, for example) and the employment relationship between employer and employee within each organisation.

The authors suggest that, while the traditional model of delivering high-quality services at a relatively low cost arguably relied on a shared public sector ethos among managers and workers, the new model is likely to be associated with deteriorating quality of services provision, increasing costs and more explicit reliance on managerial prerogative. They identify cost cutting and work intensification associated with PPPs and suggest that the future is likely to be marked by increased instability, reduced job security and de-motivation.

Source: Adapted from: Hebson, G., Grimshaw, D. and Marchington, M. (2003) 'PPPs and the changing public sector ethos: case-study evidence from the health and local authority sectors', *Work Employment and Society*, Vol. 17, No. 3, pp. 481–501.

Debates about flexibility

The growth in flexible working practices combined with their promotion by governments since the 1990s has led to the development of robust debates about their desirability and usage in practice. As much controversy has centred on the Atkinson model of the flexible firm as on the rather different elements that go to make it up. There has been a continuing debate, for example, about whether the model of core and periphery is a description of trends or a prescription for the future. Two streams of research have flowed from these interpretations. The first concerns the extent to which the model has been adopted in practice, the second focuses on the advantages and disadvantages of the model as a blueprint for the future organisation of work.

Evidence on the first of these questions is patchy. There is no question that rhetoric about flexibility and the language of flexibility is increasingly used. The flexible firm model appears to be something that managers aspire to adopt, but the extent to which they have actually adopted it is questionable. While some evidence suggests that there has been a steady increase in part-time work across Europe, findings from the 'Future of Work Programme' in the UK (funded by the Economic and Social Research Council (ESRC)) have challenged the degree of change that has actually occurred. Nolan and Wood (2003) have found that traditional working patterns, premised upon full-time permanent employment, remain dominant. Further, in many organisations the drive for economies of scale means that far from becoming more flexible, organisations are just as likely to introduce bureaucratic systems and standardised practices in response to competitive pressures. And yet we also have seen for a long period now increased use of part-time workers, consultants, subcontractors, agency workers and of moves towards multiskilling. Karen Legge's (1995) conclusion that flexibility is used in a pragmatic and opportunistic way rather than as a strategic HRM initiative thus seems to hold true today.

The desirability of flexibility is debatable. The theoretical advantage for organisations is that flexibility enables them to deploy employee time and effort more efficiently so that staff are only at work when they need to be and are wholly focused on achieving organisational objectives throughout that time. However, the extent to which this is achieved in practice is not clear. Many writers equate the term 'flexibility' with 'insecurity' and argue that the consequences for organisations in terms of staff commitment and willingness to work beyond contract are damaging, staff turnover is likely to increase and recruiting talented people will be harder too. It is questionable that the flexible firm model, at least as far as the 'peripheral' workforce is concerned, is compatible with best practice approaches to HRM which seek to increase employees' commitment. This is equally the case for the network organisation where terms and conditions for those providing numerical flexibility are still typically inferior to those providing functional flexibility. Another view, however, is that soft HRM adopting high-commitment HRM practices can adopt functional flexibility through practices such as flexible job design, cross-training, use of teams and work groups and job rotation and enlargement. Lepak and Snell (1999) go further in arguing that soft and hard approaches may not be mutually exclusive and that the ability to manage different forms of flexibility may give an organisation sustainable competitive advantage, one that draws on robust HR policies.

Further critiques come, however, from Sisson and Storey (2000: 83) who make the observation that too much 'hollowing out' can impair organisational learning and lead to the loss of expertise, a loss from which it is difficult to recover. These unintended consequences, it is argued, can worsen rather than improve an organisation's competitive position. Others (*see* Heery and Salmon 2000; Burchell *et al.* 1999) see too much flexibility as having damaging longer-term economic consequences. For example, it can lead to a reduced willingness by employers to invest in training, the absence of which creates skills shortages that hold back economic development. It can also lead to a situation in which managers exploit the vulnerability of peripheral workers by intensifying their work to an unacceptable degree. Finally, it can be argued that in dividing people into 'core' and 'peripheral' groups, flexible firms perpetuate inequality in society more generally and that this leads to poverty, crime, family breakdown and political alienation. Fudge and Owens (2007) label the new types of work 'precarious' and point to the fact that in most cases it is carried out by women who are much less likely than men to enjoy the benefits associated with long-term, full-time, stable, pensionable employment associated with an income which is sufficient to sustain a household.

ACTIVITY 4.4

What evidence do you see of numerical and functional flexibility in the organisation you work for, or one with which you are familiar?

To what extent do you think these forms of flexibility benefit:

- The employer?
- The employees?

EMPLOYEE FLEXIBILITY

In this section, we consider employee flexibility, often termed work-life integration (WLI), and explore the mechanisms by which this might be achieved. A number of high-profile organisations now seek to position themselves as 'employers of choice' by adopting such WLI policies and it is increasingly suggested that WLI is high up the agenda of many

Table 4.2 Options for achieving work-life integration

Part-time	Term-time working	Unpaid leave
Flexitime	Job share	Unpaid sabbaticals
Compressed week	Self-rostering	Work from home
Annual hours	Shift swapping	Informal flexibility

organisations, both in the UK and internationally. Certainly the latest WERS survey (Kersley *et al.* 2006) noted that increasing availability of flexible working options was found compared with the previous 1998 survey. However, the availability of practices says little about their uptake and we outline below the 'rhetoric versus reality' of WLI in UK organisations.

WLI options focus on three different types of work flexibility. First, there is flexibility in terms of the number of hours worked; second, the exact timing of those hours; and, third, the location at which the work is carried out. Clearly some options may reflect all three types of flexibility. While UK legislation only addresses the need of parents and other carers (*see* Chapter 20), there is a strong lobby for flexible work options to be potentially available for all employees. There are many possible options, and clearly not all of these are appropriate for all jobs or employees, and employers will need to be convinced of their business benefits. In addition, flexibility will mean different things to different people, depending on their age, life circumstances, values, interests, personality and so on. At present flexible options which require reduction in hours, rather than rearrangement of hours, are predominantly taken up by women (Atkinson and Hall 2009). Part-time working remains the most available and most popular (*see*, for example, CIPD 2005; Kersley *et al.* 2006). There are, however, a number of other possibilities. We outline these in Table 4.2 and refer the reader to specific texts on WLI for further detail (*see*, for example, Stredwick and Ellis 2005).

An interesting contribution is made by Strachan and Burgess (1998) who suggest that, in addition to the commonly accepted practices outlined in Table 4.2, employers should also provide practices to ensure both income and job security. They argue that employment that does not generate enough income to support a family cannot be described as 'family friendly' and casual employees, who often remain outside the organisation's internal labour market, may be denied WLI benefits. We return to this argument in the 'rhetoric versus reality' section below, noting for now the problems that may arise for employers providing WLI practices while also seeking other forms of flexibility from employees.

Benefits of work-life integration

As we note in Chapter 20, there is limited regulation of WLI in the UK, the government adopting a 'business case' approach to it. This approach suggests that the benefits that flow from adopting WLI practices are greater than the costs associated with them, thus encouraging employers to offer such practices. We consider in this section the benefits that are said to accrue from WLI practices that underpin this 'business case'.

WLI practices have been shown in some instances to raise morale, increase levels of job satisfaction and reduce absence, especially unplanned absence. IDS (2006) reported that flexible working has a positive impact on retention, recruitment and absenteeism and Perry-Smith and Blum (2000) found that bundles of work-life balance policies were related to higher organisational performance. In our own research we found that informal flexibility was highly valued and associated with employee discretionary effort in terms of supporting colleagues, and patients where appropriate, and being available and flexible to cover emergencies (Hall and Atkinson 2006). Employees appreciated the flexibility they were given and therefore wanted to give something back, recognising the need for 'give and take'.

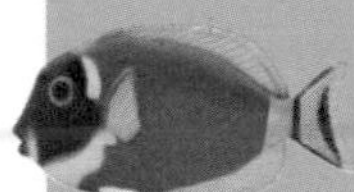

WINDOW ON PRACTICE

Benefits Experienced

Scott (2007) reports on the Britannia Building Society, which found that absence and employee turnover have both reduced as a result of its flexible working policy. Absence dropped from 3.06 per cent in 2004 to 2.35 per cent in 2006 and turnover from 18.94 per cent in 2004 to 12.6 per cent in 2006. While they had adopted flexible working before 2004 it was ad hoc and inconsistent so improvements were made by getting board commitment, engaging people across in the business in focus groups and including the input of representatives into a new HR policy on flexible working. Britannia also claims that there is a direct link with customer satisfaction.

Phillips (2007) reports on Ellis Fairbank, Recruitment Consultants, who state that flexible working for all staff has increased productivity and helped to attract top talent. They also found lower absence, reduced employee turnover and raised morale. The consultancy specified the availability of flexible working in their advertising campaign to attract staff.

Such advertising is a surprisingly underused practice. The CIPD (2005) in their survey found that only 36 per cent of respondent employers to their survey used flexible working in their recruitment advertising compared with 74 per cent who communicate this information in staff handbooks.

Sources: Summarised from Scott, A. (2007) 'Flexible Working cuts absence', *People Management*, Vol. 13, No. 6, p. 15, 22 March; and from Phillips, L. (2007) 'Add muscle with flexible work', *People Management*, Vol. 13, No. 5, p. 10, 8 March.

In a baseline study covering employers and employees, conducted by the Institute for Employment Research at the University of Warwick and IFF Research Ltd (Hogarth *et al.* 2001), 91 per cent of employers and 96 per cent of employees felt that people work better when they can balance their work with other aspects of their lives. Employers can also find that such policies meet business needs for flexibility and are a way of addressing diversity issues.

Take-up of WLI options

So far the demand for flexible work options is much greater than the take-up, and this has been referred to as the 'take-up gap'. Hogarth *et al.* (2001) report that 47 per cent of employees not currently using flexitime would like to do so, and 35 per cent would like a compressed week. The desire for working different or more flexible hours is a significant determinant of employees moving jobs either within or between employers (Boheim and Taylor 2004) to achieve the flexibility they desire, and the researchers also point to rigidities in the British labour market, which does not offer enough jobs with flexible hours. Some WLI strategies cost the organisation money and financial limits are set for such practices to be viable. The Automobile Association (AA) experienced difficulties in setting up teleworking at home. The productivity of home-workers was greater than that of site-based staff, but in order to offset the cost of technology and infrastructure such workers had to be more than 1.5 times as productive as site staff. To gain such productivity tight management and measurement of home-based teleworkers is necessary (Bibby 2002).

Policies and some line managers may limit access to work-life integration to certain groups, which is clearly evidenced in the latest WERS survey (Kersley *et al.* 2006). There is also evidence that some employers do not take a strategic approach to work-life integration, but use it in a fire-fighting manner, to deal with situations when they reach breaking point (for example in a case study of a Further Education college, *see* Glynn *et al.* 2002). While organisations can sometimes easily provide reduced hours work for, say, administrative and sales staff, it is much more difficult to do this with professional staff. Anecdotal evidence suggests that many professionals moving from full- to part-time work find that they are really expected to do a full-time job in part-time hours and with part-time pay. Edwards and Robinson (2004) found that the lack of a strategic approach to reducing hours for nurses resulted in an unsatisfactory situation for both part-timers and full-timers alike.

There is some evidence that flexibility requests for child-care reasons are dealt with more favourably than requests on any other basis. The association that WLI practices have with women bringing up children creates two problems. The first is that WLI becomes a 'women's issue' (Atkinson and Hall 2009), as something done for women with children who are not interested in real careers. The second is that this causes alienation from the rest of the workforce who are not allowed these special privileges. In particular, working part time has been a popular option in combining work and other commitments, and yet there is considerable evidence that this limits career development (*see*, for example, MacDermid *et al.* 2001).

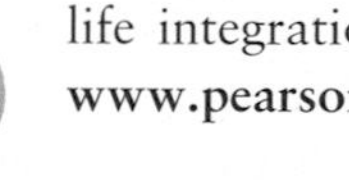

There is some evidence that the public sector makes much better provision for work-life integration than the private sector. Case 4.2 on this book's companion website, **www.pearsoned.co.uk/torrington** explores this further.

ACTIVITY 4.5

Discuss the following statement. To what extent do you agree or disagree with it, and why?

'Employees should be equally entitled to WLI options, as long as business needs are met. It doesn't matter whether the reason is child-care, the desire to engage in sports activities, do extra gardening, or just loll around on the sofa watching television.'

Managers are also a barrier: the Work Foundation found that managers were the main barrier to introducing and implementing work-life integration policies (CIPD 2003). While it is clear to those at a senior level in an organisation that WLI practices can be of value, it is line managers who have the unenviable task of reconciling performance and flexibility, especially where flexible working for some may mean higher workloads for others. There is a pressure on line managers to be fair and their decisions about who can work flexibly and in what way are under scrutiny and may result in a backlash. Managing workers who are not visible (working at home for example) is a particular concern for line managers. Felstead *et al.* (2003) report the fear that working at home is a 'slacker's charter', but they also found that home-workers themselves had fears about not being able to easily demonstrate their honesty, reliability and productivity. Some managed this by working more hours than they should in order to demonstrate greater output. To counteract this fear, managers in Felstead's study introduced new surveillance devices, set output targets and brought management into the home via home visits. Managers also felt that home-working represented a potential threat to the integration of teams and the acceptance of corporate culture, and that it impeded the transmission of tacit knowledge. Overall, managing working-time flexibility has emerged as a challenge in the past few years and line managers are likely to need much more support and encouragement in order to do this effectively.

Employee role and WLI

WLI is not available to most employees. Felstead *et al.* (2003) reveal that the option to work at home is usually the privilege of the highly educated and/or people at the top of the organisational hierarchy. People in these jobs, they suggest, have considerably more influence over the work processes they are engaged in. They also report that although more women than men work at home, there are more men who have the choice to work at home. Nolan and Wood (2003) also note that WLI is not for the lower paid. They report that 5 per cent of such employees hold more than one job, and usually work in low-paid, low-status jobs in catering and personal services. A similar scene is painted by Polly Toynbee (2003). She also reports that many of these low-paid workers work for agencies and are thereby distanced from the ultimate 'employer'. In these circumstances WLI policies are unlikely to be available in any case, nor even if working only for one employer: Toynbee reports a hospital porter saying, 'you can't survive, not with a family, unless you do the long, long hours, unless you both work all the hours there are' (p. 59). Felstead *et al.* (2002) highlight an assumption in the WLI literature, which portrays working at home as always a 'good thing'. They argue that what is important is the *option* to work at home, as some people work at home doing low-paid unsatisfying jobs with no choice of work location, such conditions not necessarily being conducive to WLI. This reinforces the need outlined by Strachan and Burgess (1998), cited above, for policies of income and employment security to be included with WLI practices if more sophisticated policies are to be considered to be effective.

Rhetoric or reality?

Although a number of blue chip organisations actively publicise their WLI practices, we suggest that problems of implementation, line manager resistance and the restriction of such practices to certain groups mean that WLI is still an aspiration rather than a reality for many employees. White *et al.* (2003), for example, argue that they are enjoyed by only a small proportion of the workforce, and in any case only have a small effect on the problem. They argue for more fundamental changes in working practices with safeguards to protect WLI, such as giving teams themselves the responsibility for addressing these issues when setting output targets for themselves. We suggest that work continues to be organised in a way that predominantly meets the needs of employers, the 'business case' for WLI integration often failing to initiate sufficient action to offer genuine WLI to the majority of employees.

SUMMARY PROPOSITIONS

4.1 Organisation design requires that choices are made in terms of formality, differentiation and centralisation of operations. Increasingly, flexibility is also central to organisation design.

4.2 While an infinite range of organisational structures is possible, most can be described as entrepreneurial, bureaucratic or matrix in form. In practice, many organisations combine all three types of structure to varying degrees.

4.3 Hackman and Oldham's model of job design, the Job Characteristics Model (JCM), led to a paradigm shift in job design. Its influences continue to this day and lead to the design of jobs incorporating skill variety, task identity, task significance, autonomy and feedback.

4.4 Organisations increasingly require employees to be flexible in their working patterns. Models such as Atkinson's flexible firm and Powell's network organisation attempt to describe/prescribe mechanisms of organisational flexibility.

4.5 Tight labour markets in recent decades have required organisations to respond to employee demands for flexibility. A large number of work-life integration (WLI) practices now exist, although in reality large numbers of employees do not have access to them.

GENERAL DISCUSSION TOPICS

1 Flatter organisational structures which decentralise decision making and empower employees will almost always be more efficient than highly centralised organisations with tall hierarchies.

2 If the principles of job design that are required to make jobs motivating and lead to high employee performance have been recognised since the mid-1970s, why do so many contemporary organisations continue to design jobs along Tayloristic principles?

3 Flexibility in working time is nearly always for organisational benefit. In practice, few employees actually benefit from working-time flexibility.

FURTHER READING

Kalleberg, A. (2001) 'Organising flexibility: the flexible firm in a new century', *British Journal of Industrial Relations*, Vol. 39, No. 4, pp. 479–504.
Kalleberg presents a thoughtful and comprehensive literature review on and critique of the flexible firm. Alternatives to this, including network organisations, are discussed.

Stredwick, J. and Ellis, S. (2005) *Flexible Working*, 2nd edn. London: CIPD.
This book presents detailed information on both organisational and employee flexibility. There is detailed discussion on WLI practices and how to implement these effectively.

Wood, S. and Wall, T. (2007) 'Work enrichment and employee voice in human resource management: performance studies', *International Journal of Human Resource Management*, Vol. 18, No. 7, pp. 1335–72.
The authors argue that diminishing importance has been given over recent decades to work enrichment, and to a lesser extent to employee voice, in conceptions of high-performance management. They review high-performance organisation literature and consider the place of job enrichment within this. They suggest that the emphasis within this is on practices that create the flexible employee and agile organisation and not on the enriched employee or healthy organisation. They argue for a greater emphasis upon job enrichment and employee voice as forms of involvement in order to create high-performing organisations.

REFERENCES

Atkinson, C. (2002) 'Career management and the changing psychological contract', *Career Development International*, Vol. 7, No. 1, pp. 14–23.

Atkinson, C. and Hall, L. (2009) 'The role of gender in varying forms of flexible working', *Gender, Work and Organisation*, Vol. 16, No. 6, pp. 650–66.

Atkinson, J. (1984) 'Manpower strategies for flexible organisations', *Personnel Management*, August.

Bibby, A. (2002) 'Home start', *People Management*, Vol. 8, No. 1, pp. 36–7.

Blyton, P. (1998) 'Flexibility', in M. Poole and M. Warner (eds), *The IEBM Handbook of Human Resource Management*. London: Thomson.

Boheim, R. and Taylor, M. (2004) 'Actual and preferred working hours', *British Journal of Industrial Relations*, Vol. 42, No. 1, pp. 149–66.

Burchell, B.J., Day, D., Hudson, M., Ladipo, D., Mankelow, R., Nolan, J., Reed, H., Wichert, I. and Wilkinson, F. (1999) *Job Insecurity and Work Intensification: Flexibility and the changing boundaries of work*. London: Joseph Rowntree Foundation.

Burns, T. and Stalker, G. (1961) *The Management of Innovation*. London: Tavistock.

Burton, R. and Obel, B. (2004) *Strategic Organizational Diagnosis and Design: The dynamics of fit*, 3rd edn. Dordrecht: Kluwer Academic Publishers.

Child, J. (1984) *Organisation*. London: Harper & Row.

CIPD (2003) 'Managers obstruct flexibility', *People Management*, Vol. 9, No. 18, p. 9.

CIPD (2005) *Flexible Working: Impact and implementation. An employer survey*. London: CIPD.

CIPD (2008a) *Smart Working: The impact of work organisation and job design*. London: CIPD.

CIPD (2008b) *Smart Working: How smart is UK PLC?* London: CIPD.

CIPD Professional Map (2009) http://www.cipd.co.uk/hr-profession-map/professional-areas/organisation-design-detailed-information (accessed 14 January 2010).

Cooney, R. (2004) 'Empowered self-management and the design of work teams', *Personnel Review*, Vol. 33, No. 6, pp. 677–92.

Curado, C. (2006) 'Organisational learning and organisational design', *The Learning Organisation*, Vol. 13, No. 1, pp. 25–48.

Edwards, C. and Robinson, O. (2004) 'Evaluating the business case for part-time working amongst qualified nurses', *British Journal of Industrial Relations*, Vol. 42, No. 1, pp. 167–83.

Eriksen, J. (2005) 'The influences of organizational design on strategy and performance: the case of exploration and exploitation', paper presented at the *Workshop on Organizational Design, EIASM*, Brussels, 7–8 March.

Felstead, A., Jewson, N. and Walters, S. (2003) 'Managerial control of employees working at home', *British Journal of Industrial Relations*, Vol. 41, No. 2, pp. 241–64.

Felstead, A., Jewson, N., Phizacklea, A. and Walters, S. (2002) 'The option of working at home: another privilege for the favoured few', *New Technology, Work and Employment*, Vol. 17, No. 3, pp. 204–23.

Fudge, J. and Owens, R. (2007) 'Precarious work, women and the new economy: the challenge to legal norms', in J. Fudge and R. Owens (eds), *Precarious Work, Women and the New Economy*. Oxford: Hart Publishing.

Glynn, C., Steinberg, I. and McCartney, C. (2002) *Work–Life Balance: The role of the manager*. Horsham: Roffey Park Institute.

Hall, L. and Atkinson, C. (2006) 'Improving working lives: flexible working and the role of employee control', *Employee Relations*, Vol. 28, No. 4, pp. 374–86.

Handy, C.B. (1993) *Understanding Organizations*, 4th edn. Harmondsworth: Penguin.

Hebson, G., Grimshaw, D. and Marchington, M. (2003) 'PPPs and the changing public sector ethos: case-study evidence from the health and local authority sectors', *Work Employment and Society*, Vol. 17, No. 3, pp. 481–501.

Heery, E. and Salamon, J. (eds) (2000) *The Insecure Workforce*. London: Routledge.

Hogarth, T., Hasluck, C., Pierre, G. with Winterbotham, M. and Vivian, D. (2001) *Work–Life Balance 2000: Results from the baseline study*. Research Report 249, London: DfEE.

IDS (2006) *Flexitime Schemes*, IDS Studies, No. 822. London: IDS.

Kalleberg, A. (2001) 'Organising flexibility: the flexible firm in a new century', *British Journal of Industrial Relations*, Vol. 39, No. 4, pp. 479–504.

Kersley, B., Alpin, C., Forth, J., Bryson, A., Bewley, H., Dix, G. and Oxenbridge, S. (2006) *Inside the Workplace: Findings from the 2004 Workplace Employment Relations Survey*. London: Routledge.

Leavitt, H.J., Dill, W.R. and Eyrig, H.B. (1973) *The Organizational World*. New York: Harcourt, Brace Jovanovich.

Legge, K. (1995) *Human Resource Management: Rhetoric and realities*. Basingstoke: Macmillan.

Lepak, D.P. and Snell, S.A. (1999) 'The human resource architect: toward a theory of human capital allocation and development', *Academy of Management Review*, Vol. 24, No. 1, pp. 31–48.

MacDermid, S., Lee, M., Buck, M. and Williams, M. (2001) 'Alternative work arrangements among professionals and managers', *Journal of Management Development*, Vol. 20, No. 4, pp. 305–17.

Morgeson, F. and Humphrey, S. (2006) 'The work design questionnaire (WDQ): developing and validating a measure for assessing job design and the nature of work', *Journal of Applied Psychology*, Vol. 91, No. 6, pp. 1321–39.

Newell, H. and Dopson, S. (1996) 'Muddle in the middle: organisation re-structuring and management careers', *Personnel Review*, Vol. 25, No. 4, pp. 4–20.

Nolan, P. and Wood, S. (2003) 'Mapping the future of work', *British Journal of Industrial Relations*, Vol. 41, No. 2, pp. 165–74.

Perry-Smith, J. and Blum, T. (2000) 'Work–family human resource bundles and perceived organizational performance', *Academy of Management Journal*, Vol. 43, pp. 1107–17.

Powell, W. (1990) 'Neither market nor hierarchy: network forms of organization', *Research in Organisational Behaviour*, Vol. 12, pp. 295–336.

Prowse, J. and Prowse, P. (2008) 'Role redesign in the National Health Service: the effects on midwives' work and professional boundaries', *Work, Employment and Society*, Vol. 22, No. 4, pp. 695–712.

Reilly, P. (2001) *Flexibility at Work*. Aldershot: Gower.

Sisson, K. and Storey, J. (2000) *The Realities of Human Resource Management: Managing the employment relationship*. Buckingham: Open University Press.

Strachan, G. and Burgess, J. (1998) 'The "family-friendly" workplace', *International Journal of Manpower*, Vol. 19, No. 4, pp. 250–65.

Stredwick, J. and Ellis, S. (2005) *Flexible Working*, 2nd edn. London: CIPD.

Toynbee, P. (2003) *Hard Work: Life in low-pay Britain*. London: Bloomsbury.

White, M., Hill, S., McGovern, P., Mills, C. and Smeaton, D. (2003) '"High performance" management practices, working hours and work–life balance', *British Journal of Industrial Relations*, Vol. 41, No. 2, June, pp. 175–95.

Wood, S. and Wall, T. (2007) 'Work enrichment and employee voice in human resource management: performance studies', *International Journal of Human Resource Management*, Vol. 18, No. 7, pp. 1335–72.

An extensive range of additional materials, including multiple choice questions, answers to questions and links to useful websites can be found on the Human Resource Management companion website at **www.pearsoned.co.uk/torrington**.

WORKFORCE PLANNING

THE OBJECTIVES OF THIS CHAPTER ARE TO:

1. Discuss the contribution and feasibility of workforce planning
2. Explore the scope of workforce planning
3. Explain an integrated workforce planning framework

Workforce planning has experienced a chequered history. In the 1960s and 1970s it was heralded as a critical tool for business success, as planning to get the right people in the right place at the right time was seen to be essential to achieving rapid growth. In the 1980s and 1990s planning was viewed as a suitable tool for managing downsizing and redundancies. Some question whether planning continues to be meaningful in an era of rapid and discontinuous change, while others suggest that it is even more important:

> the need for strategic workforce planning and execution of workforce plans has never been greater as organisations . . . operate in more turbulent environments and confront the key challenges of competing for key skills and talents and of containing payroll costs (Lavelle 2007: 371)

and it is a key role in supporting strategic HRM (Boxall and Purcell 2003). Yet it is unappreciated and underused or neglected (*see*, for example, Guthridge and Lawson 2008); and Peter Reilly, Director of the Institute of Employment Studies, suggests that employers struggle with planning at the best of times, but ignore it when downsizing (Arkin 2008).

THE CONTRIBUTION AND FEASIBILITY OF HR PLANNING

A useful starting point is to consider the different contributions that strategy and planning make to the organisation. A common view has been that they are virtually one and the same – hence the term 'strategic planning'. Henry Mintzberg (1994: 108) distinguished between *strategic thinking*, which is about synthesis, intuition and creativity to produce a not too precisely articulated vision of direction, and *strategic planning*, which is about collecting the relevant information to stimulate the visioning process and also programming the vision into what needs to be done to get there. It is helpful to look at human resource planning in the same way, and this is demonstrated in Figure 5.1. In more detail he suggests:

- **Planning as strategic programming** – planning cannot generate strategies, but it can make them operational by clarifying them; working out the consequences of them; and identifying what must be done to achieve each strategy.
- **Planning as tools to communicate and control** – planning can ensure coordination and encourage everyone to pull in the same direction; planners can assist in finding successful experimental strategies which may be operating in just a small part of the organisation.
- **Planners as analysts** – planners need to analyse hard data, both external and internal, which managers can then use in the strategy development process.

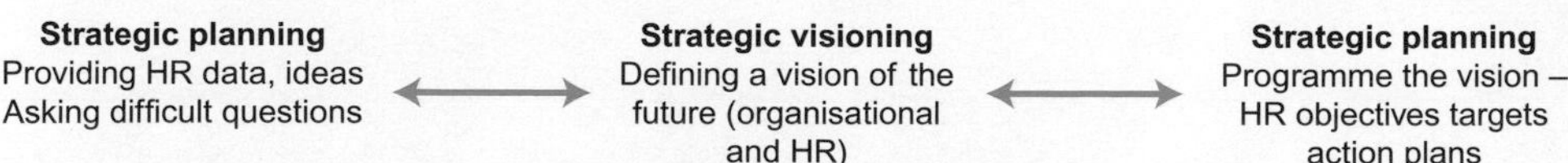

Figure 5.1 Human resource strategic visioning and strategic planning
Source: After Mintzberg 1994.

- **Planners as catalysts** – raising difficult questions and challenging the conventional wisdom which may stimulate managers into thinking in more creative ways.

Organisational and human resource planners make an essential contribution to strategic visioning. Sisson and Storey (2000) identify HR planning as 'one of the basic building blocks of a more strategic approach'. There are four specific ways in which HR planning is critical to strategy, as it can identify:

- *capability gaps* – lack of sufficient skills, people or knowledge in the business which will prevent the strategy being implemented successfully;
- *capability surpluses* – providing scope for efficiencies and new opportunities or ventures to capitalise on the skills, people and knowledge that are currently underused, in order to influence or shape the strategy;
- *poor workforce utilisation* – suggesting inappropriate human resource practices that need to be altered;
- *talent pool development* – to ensure a ready internal supply of employees capable of promotion, and especially a leadership pipeline.

If you turn back to Chapter 3 and look again at the resource-based view of the firm you will see how these four aspects are crucial to sustaining competitive advantage through making the most of human resources.

Our environment of rapid and discontinuous change makes any planning difficult, and workforce planning is especially difficult as people have free will, unlike other resources, such as finance or technology. Longer-term planning is also important and yet more difficult, as, for example, Guthridge and Lawson (2008) maintain that quarterly business reporting encourages businesses to focus on short-term planning. A survey by the Adecco Institute found acceptance of the need for long-term planning and yet the average planning horizon of HR specialists was 1.1 years (Chubb 2008). The contribution and implementation of workforce planning is likely to be enhanced if:

- plans are viewed as flexible and reviewed regularly, rather than being seen as an end point in the process;
- stakeholders, including all levels of manager and employee, are involved in the process. Surveys and focus groups are possible mechanisms, in addition to line manager representatives on the HR planning team;
- planning is owned and driven by senior managers rather than HR specialists, who need to facilitate the process;
- plans are linked to business and HR strategy;
- plans are user friendly and not overly complex;
- it is recognised that while a comprehensive plan may be ideal, sometimes it may only be feasible to plan on an issue-by-issue basis, or by different workforce specialisms or segments (see Lavelle 2007 for a good example of segmentation).

WINDOW ON PRACTICE

Workforce Planning and the NHS

Workforce planning is considered to be a top priority for the NHS as an appropriate and competent workforce is required to provide successful service delivery and quality, and to this end a rapid review of workforce planning was commissioned by the House of Commons Health Committee's Workforce Review Team to identify the nature of workforce planning; to provide examples of best practice; and identify the current effectiveness of UK health sector workforce planning. The work was carried out by the Institute for Employment Research at Warwick University.

The review team found that:

- workforce planning is not a homogeneous activity and can be carried out at different levels, for example organisational or national
- traditional healthcare workforce planning has focused on supply and demand for specific occupations, in other words it is segmented
- this approach can result in professional silos and an integrated approach, planning for the system as a whole would add value, as covering all staff groups simultaneously is essential to address skill mix and substitution issues
- data availability and lack of resources to build sophisticated models restricts planning activity
- planning for internal labour markets, that is the movement between posts within the organisation, is also important
- it is important to plan for demographic factors both in terms of healthcare need and in terms of workforce supply
- given the importance of quality in a healthcare setting productivity improvement can be expressed as higher quality from the same inputs (i.e. workforce)
- there is a general lack of published work on good practices in workforce planning, and no examples of fully integrated workforce planning models were found
- workforce planning time horizons are generally longer in the public than the private sector and succession planning remains important in larger hierarchical public bodies
- 'workforce planning requires accurate data, modelling, continuous and iterative planning, specialist skills, scenario building and stakeholder involvement' (p. 117)
- workforce planning is essential for the NHS as a long lead time is required for training; wage adjustments are influenced by market forces; patient needs must be met; and taxpayers' money should not be wasted by training too many staff.

Source: Curson, J., Dell, M., Wilson, R., Bosworth, D. and Baldauf, B. (2010) 'Who does workforce planning well?: Workforce Rapid Review Team Summary', *International Journal of Health Care Quality Assurance*, Vol. 23, No. 1, pp. 110–19.

While this example relates specifically to the NHS, it is also typical of other parts of the public sector such as social care.

THE SCOPE OF WORKFORCE PLANNING

Traditionally workforce planning, generally termed manpower planning, was concerned with the numbers of employees and the levels and types of skill in the organisation. A typical model of traditional workforce planning is shown in Figure 5.2. In this model the emphasis is on balancing the projected demand for and supply of labour, in order to have the right number of the right employees in the right place at the right time. The demand for people is influenced by corporate strategies and objectives, the environment and the way that staff are utilised within the business. The supply of people is projected from current employees (via calculations about expected leavers, retirements, promotions, etc.) and from the availability of the required skills in the labour market. Anticipated demand and supply are then reconciled by considering a range of options, and plans to achieve a feasible balance are designed.

As the world has moved on this model has been viewed as too narrow, being heavily reliant on calculations of employee numbers or potential employee numbers. It has also been criticised for giving insufficient attention to skills (Taylor 2008). In addition there has been an increasing recognition of the need to plan, not just for hard numbers, but for the **softer** issues of employee behaviour, organisation culture and systems; these issues have been identified as having a key impact on business success in the current environment.

Increasingly there is a need for organisations to integrate the process of planning for numbers and skills of employees; employee behaviour and organisational culture; organisation design and the make-up of individual jobs; and formal and informal systems. These aspects are all critical in terms of programming and achieving the vision or the strategic choice. Each of these aspects interrelates with the others. However, reality has always been recognised as being a long way from identified best practice. Undoubtedly

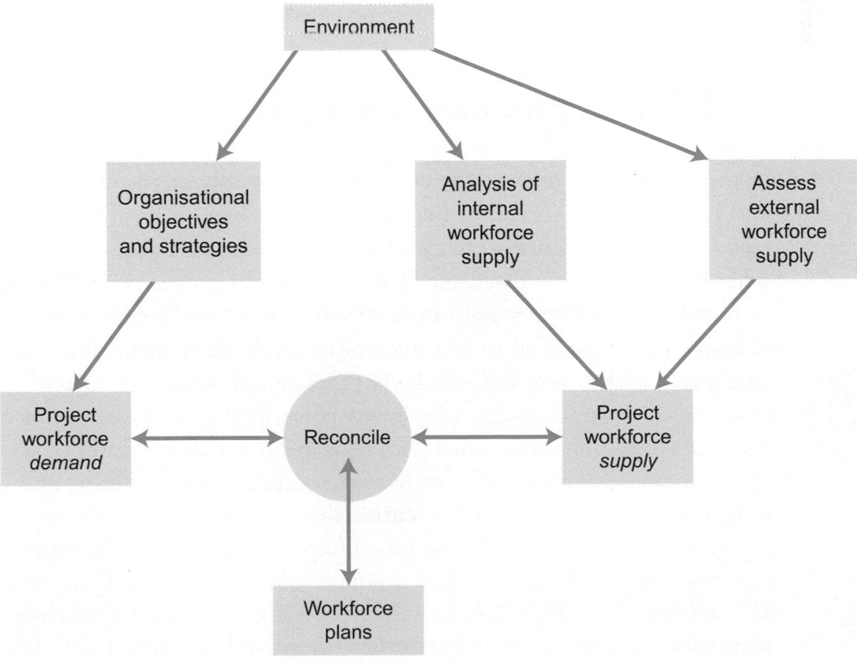

Figure 5.2 A model of traditional workforce planning

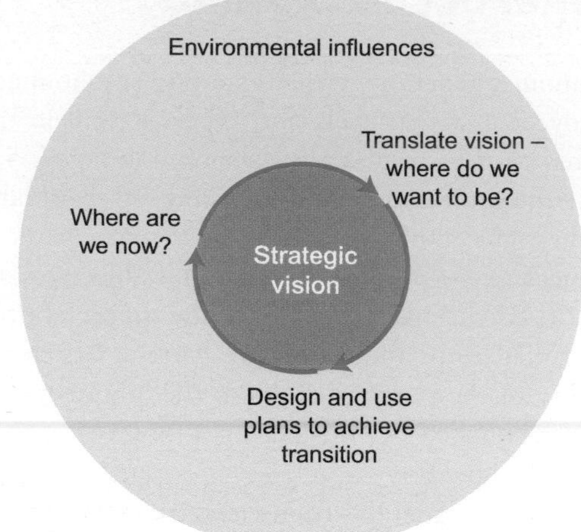

Figure 5.3 Integrated workforce planning framework

different organisations will place different emphases on each of these factors, and may well plan each separately or plan some and not others.

The framework we shall use in this chapter attempts to bring *all* aspects of workforce planning together, incorporating the more traditional approach, but going beyond this to include behaviour, culture, systems and so on. Our framework identifies 'where we want to be', translated from responses to the strategic vision; 'where we are now'; and 'what we need to do to make the transition' – all operating within the organisation's environment. The framework is shown in diagrammatic form in Figure 5.3. An alternative framework to use may be the HR scorecard (*see* Becker *et al.* 2001). Chapter 29 provides more details.

We shall now look in more depth at each of these four areas. The steps are presented in a logical sequence. In practice, however, they may run in parallel, and/or in an informal fashion, and each area may well be revisited a number of times.

ANALYSING THE ENVIRONMENT

In this chapter we refer to the environment broadly as the context of the organisation, and this is clearly critical in the impact that it has on both organisational and human resource strategy. Much strategy is based on a response to the environment – for example, what our customers now want or what competitors are now offering – or in anticipation of what customers will want or what they can be persuaded to want. In human resource terms we need to identify, for example, how difficult or easy it will be to find employees with scarce skills and what these employees will expect from an employer so that we can attract them. (*See* **www.pearsoned.co.uk/torrington** WP Exercise, 5.1, note 1.) We shall be concerned with legislation which will limit or widen the conditions of employment that we offer, with what competitors are offering and with what training schemes are available locally or nationally.

Data on relevant trends can be collected from current literature, company annual reports, conferences/courses and contacts and networking. Over recent years considerable attention has been given to the need for companies to benchmark their activities, processes and outcomes against other 'successful' organisations. However, much care

Trend area	Possible sources
Social	Census information CIPD journals News media *Social Trends* *General Household Survey* *Employment Gazette* Local papers
Demographics	*Labour Market Quarterly* Census information *Employment Gazette* Local council, Learning and Skills Councils
Political and legislative	News media *Proceedings of European Parliament* *Proceedings of British Parliament* *Hansard* *Industrial Relations Review and Report* *Industrial Law Journal* *IDS Brief*
Industrial and technological	*Employment Digest* Journals specifically for the industry *Financial Times* Employers' association Trade association
Competitors	Annual reports Talk to them!

Table 5.1 Sources of information on environment trends

needs to be taken to select the most appropriate benchmarks, and Denrell (2005) warns of how misleading it can be to look only at successful organisations, and recommends that unsuccessful organisations should be similarly explored. Looking at successes only may lead to the assumption that certain practices they use are critical to that success, and yet unsuccessful organisations may use similar practices. The key is understanding the context and considering the full picture of how organisations are differentiated. Table 5.1 gives examples of the many possible sources for each major area.

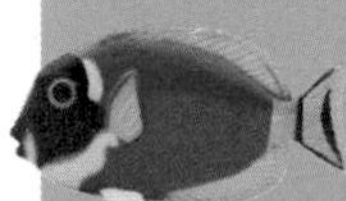

WINDOW ON PRACTICE

Analysing the Environment at Queensland University of Technology Library in Australia

Stokker and Hallam (2009) identify change as the main driver for the Library's engagement with workforce planning. They believed environmental scanning was a key part of the process to explore trends impacting on libraries, the context, and trends within libraries. The scanning was carried out over 12 months and involved adding relevant document and literature and inviting guest specialist speakers to address library staff. All library staff were involved in the scanning process and

five key areas were investigated, each led by a member of the senior library team. The five areas were:

- Higher education sector/government policy
- Teaching and learning
- Client service
- Research
- Information resources and scholarly information

Initial findings were then developed in more detail. For example several trends emerged that would impact on the faculty liaison service such as the university's desire to gain a higher research profile by increasing the number of researchers and research students. This led to the development of three workforce planning strategies for the faculty liaison service: methods to allow librarians to specialise in research support or academic skills support; a review of the job classification scheme allowing librarians to progress further in recognition of their specialist work; and the design of a development programme to allow liaison librarians to acquire new skills and knowledge.

In addition to staff involvement in environmental scanning they were also represented in the workforce planning party and planning strategies were built using consultation. These methods were used to encourage staff ownership and engagement.

Source: Stokker, J. and Hallam, G. (2009) 'The right person, in the right job, with the right skills at the right time: A workforce-planning model that goes beyond metrics', *Library Management*, Vol. 15, No. 89, pp. 561–71.

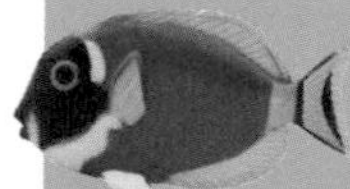

WINDOW ON PRACTICE

The impact of demographics, legislation and pension reforms

Demographics, legislation and pension reforms have come together to create a very different environment for organisations than the one that existed towards the end of the last century. The number of younger people in the population is reducing in proportion to the number of older people, as birth rates are lower in the UK than previously (although they are now beginning to increase) and people are living longer. These changes have an impact on many organisations. For example, skills loss and shortages will require organisational planners to devise novel solutions. Currently EU workers (especially from Poland and Eastern Europe) are being recruited in the UK to compensate for skills shortages.

At a national level the Employment Equality (Age) Regulations came into force in 2006, introducing a default retirement age (DFA) of 65, preventing organisations from requiring people to retire earlier (without a legitimate business aim for doing so). Employees will have the right to request to work beyond 65. Prior to this, organisations could choose to have a much earlier retirement age, and in the 1980s and 1990s early retirement was widely used and viewed as a favourable means to downsize the organisation. Additional changes relating to pensions also form part of the context. The age at which individuals may claim their state pension is currently 65 for men and 60 for women (although these ages are gradually being equalised at 65), and state retirement age will rise further in the future, so that by 2046 both men and women will not reach state pension age until aged 68, in order to cope with the impact of the demographic changes. Furthermore changes in occupational pension schemes are resulting in less well-funded occupational pensions and the need for many employees to work longer to build up a better pension.

Given this environment one of the approaches organisations may need to employ is to delay retirement age even further (beyond 68), to encourage employees to stay on so that vital skills are retained for longer, or alternatively adopt a flexible retirement age rather than a mandatory age (employees being protected until they are 65 in any case). Firms are encouraged to plan ahead to defuse the 'demographic time bomb' (Chubb 2008).

Once one has acquired and constantly updated data on the environment, a common method of analysis is to produce a map of the environment, represented as a wheel. The map represents a time in the future, say three years away. In the centre of the wheel can be written the core purpose of the organisation as it relates to people, or potential future strategies or goals. Each spoke of the wheel can then be filled in to represent a factor of the external environment, for example, potential employees, a specific local competitor, competitors generally, regulatory bodies, customers, government. From all the spokes the six or seven regarded as most important need to be selected.

These can then be worked on further by asking what demands each will make of the organisation, and how the organisation will need to respond in order to achieve its goals. From these responses can be derived the implications for human resource activities. For example, the demands of potential employees may be predicted as:

- We need a career, not just a job.
- We need flexibility to help with childrearing.
- We want to be treated as people and not as machines.
- We need a picture of what the organisation has in store for us.
- We want to be better trained.

And so on.

Managers then consider what the organisation would need to offer to meet these needs in order to meet a declared organisational goal or strategy. It is a good way of

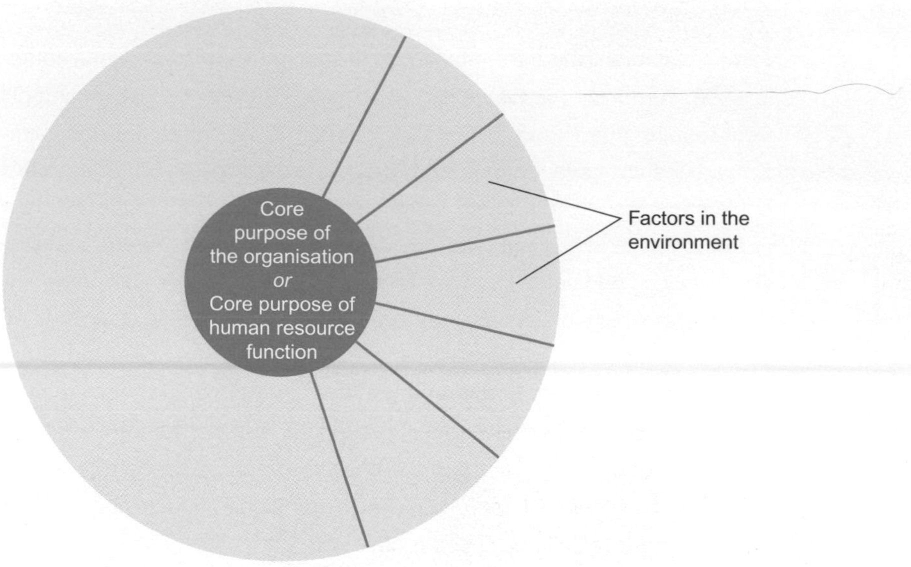

Individual factors in the environment

Demands from the factor	*Responses from the organisation*

Figure 5.4
Mapping the environment

identifying human resource issues that need to be addressed. The analysis can also be fed back into identifying and clarifying the future vision or goals in human resource terms. Figure 5.4 gives an outline for the whole process. (For a worked example *see* **www.pearsoned.co.uk/torrington** WP Exercise, 5.1, note 2.)

ACTIVITY 5.1

Draw a map of the external environment, for any organisation in which you are involved, for three to five years ahead. Individually, or as a group, brainstorm all the spokes in the wheel and select the six most important ones. Draw up a demands and responses list for each. Write a summary (one side of A4) of what you think your organisation's priorities should be in the people area over the next three to five years.

Table 5.2 The beginnings of a human resource implications checklist

Corporate goal	Human resource implications in respect of:	Methods of achieving this
	New tasks? For whom? What competencies needed? Relative importance of team/individual behaviour Deleted tasks? How will managers need to manage?	

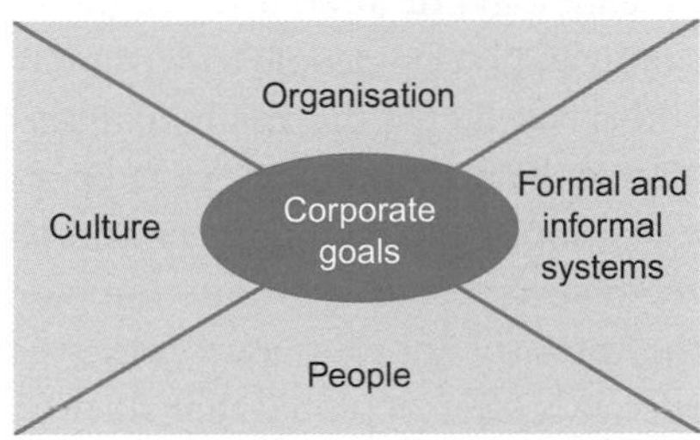

Figure 5.5 Strategic brainstorming exercise

Managers write a corporate goal in the centre and brainstorm changes that need to take place in each of the four areas, one area at a time

FORECASTING FUTURE HUMAN RESOURCE NEEDS

Organisation, behaviour and culture

There is little specific literature on the methods used to translate the strategic objectives of the organisation and environmental influences into qualitative or soft human resource goals. In general terms, they can be summed up as the use of managerial judgement. Brainstorming, combined with the use of structured checklists or matrices, can encourage a more thorough analysis. Organisation-change literature and corporate planning literature are helpful as sources of ideas in this area. Three simple techniques are a human resource implications checklist (*see* Table 5.2), a strategic brainstorming exercise (Figure 5.5) and a behavioural expectation chart (*see* **www.pearsoned.co.uk/torrington** HRP Exercise, 5.1, note 3). The HR scorecard may be a useful tool for this aspect of planning, and the use of **scenarios** may also be helpful (*see*, for example, Boxall and Purcell 2003; Turner 2002). Scenarios and contingency planning can be used to provide a picture of alternative organisational futures and alternative HR responses to these.

Employee numbers and skills (demand forecasting)

There is far more literature in the more traditional area of forecasting employee number demand based on the organisation's strategic objectives. Both objective and subjective approaches can be employed. Objective methods include statistical and work-study approaches.

Statistical models generally relate employee number demand to specific organisational circumstances and activities. Models can take account of determining factors, such as production, sales, passenger miles, level of service. A simple model might relate people demand to production, using a constant relationship, without making any assumptions about economies of scale. In this model if output is to be doubled, then employees would also need to be doubled. (*See* **www.pearsoned.co.uk/torrington** HRP Exercise, 5.1, note 4.)

More complicated equations can be formulated which describe the way that a combination of independent factors is expected to affect the dependent employee demand. By inserting new values for the independent factors, such as new projected sales figures, we can work out the demand for employees from the equation. The equations can also be represented as graphs, making the relationships clear to see. These models can be adapted to take account of projected changes in utilisation, owing to factors such as the introduction of new technology, or alternative organisational forms, such as high-performance teams, or simply expecting people to work harder and for longer hours.

The work-study method is based on a thorough analysis of the tasks to be done, and the time each takes. From this the person-hours needed per unit of output can be calculated, and standards are developed for the numbers and levels of employees required. These are most useful when one is studying production work. They need to be checked regularly to make sure they are still appropriate. Work study is usually classified as an objective measure; however, it is often accepted that since the development of standards and the grouping of tasks is partly dependent on human judgement, it could be considered as a subjective method.

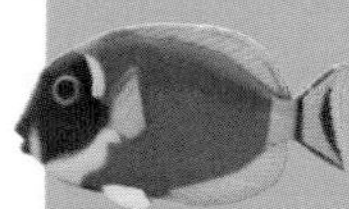

WINDOW ON PRACTICE

The postman's lot

Measuring workload has changed at Royal Mail. Roy Mayall (2009) who has been a postman for many years explains in this short book how volume of mail was previously measured by the weight of the grey boxes that mail is delivered in to the sorting offices. More recently he says it is done by averages, and it was agreed in consultation with the union that the average figure of letters in a box was estimated at 208. Subsequently Mayall reports that this estimate was changed to 150, and when a colleague did a one-man experiment counting the letters over a two-week period he found the average to be 267. Mayall recognises that this figure is neither representative nor scientific but the story does show how apparently objective figures can be subjective.

Source: Mayall, R. (2009) *Dear Granny Smith: A letter from your postman*. London: Short Books.

The most common subjective method of demand forecasting is managerial judgement (sometimes referred to as managerial opinion or the inductive method), and this can also include the judgements of other operational and technical staff, as well as all levels of managers. This method relies on managers' estimates of workforce demand based on past experience and on corporate plans. Managerial judgements can be collected from

Table 5.3 A range of methods to change employee utilisation

- Introducing new materials or equipment, particularly new technology
- Introducing changes in work organisation, such as:
  - quality circles
  - job rotation
  - job enlargement
  - job enrichment
  - autonomous work groups
  - high-performance teams
  - participation
  - empowerment
- Organisation development
- Introducing changes in organisation structure, such as:
  - centralisation/decentralisation
  - new departmental boundaries
  - relocation of parts of the organisation
  - flexible project, matrix and network structures
- Introducing productivity schemes, bonus schemes or other incentive schemes
- Encouraging greater staff flexibility, multiskilling and work interchangeability
- Altering times and periods of work
- Training and appraisal of staff
- Developing managers and use of performance management

the 'bottom up' with lower-level managers providing estimates to go up the hierarchy for discussion and redrafting. Alternatively, a 'top-down' approach can be used with estimates made by the highest level of management to go down the hierarchy for discussion and redrafting. When this method is used it is difficult to cope with changes that are very different from past experiences. It is also less precise than statistical methods, but it is more comprehensive. Managerial judgement is a simple method, which can be applied fairly quickly and is not restricted by lack of data, particularly historical data, as are statistical techniques. However, managerial judgement is important even when statistical techniques are used. (*See* **www.pearsoned.co.uk/torrington** WP Exercise, 5.1, note 5.)

A specialised procedure for the collection of managerial opinions is based on the idea of the oracle at Delphi. A group of managers anonymously and independently answer questions about anticipated human resource demand. A compilation of the answers is fed back to each individual, and the process is repeated until all the answers converge.

The way that human resources are utilised will change the number of employees required and the necessary skills needed. There are many ways to change how employees are used, and these are shown in Table 5.3. Some methods are interrelated or overlap and would therefore be used in combination. (*See* **www.pearsoned.co.uk/torrington** HRP Exercise, 5.1, note 6.) Interconnections between most of these areas and soft human resources planning are also apparent.

ANALYSING THE CURRENT SITUATION AND PROJECTING FORWARD

Organisation, behaviour and culture

It is in this area that more choice of techniques is available, and the possibilities include the use of questionnaires to staff (*see* **www.pearsoned.co.uk/torrington** HRP Exercise, 5.1, note 7), interviews with staff and managerial judgement. Focus groups are an increasingly popular technique where, preferably, the chief executive meets with, say,

20 representative staff from each department to discuss their views of the strengths and weaknesses of the organisation, and what can be done to improve. These approaches can be used to provide information on, for example:

- Employee engagement
- Motivation of employees
- Job satisfaction
- Organisational culture
- The way that people are managed
- Attitude to minority groups and equality of opportunity
- Commitment to the organisation and reasons for this
- Clarity of business objectives
- Goal-focused and other behaviour
- Organisational issues and problems
- What can be done to improve
- Organisational strengths to build on

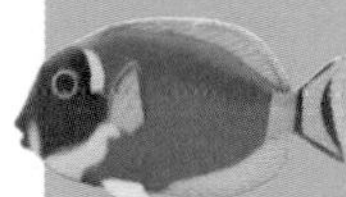

WINDOW ON PRACTICE

Jennifer Hadley is the Chief Executive of Dynamo Castings, a long-established organisation which had experienced rapid growth and healthy profits until the past three years. Around 800 staff were employed mostly in production, but significant numbers were also employed in marketing/sales and research/development. Poor performance over the last three years was largely the result of the competition who were able to deliver a quality product more quickly and at a competitive price. Dynamo retained the edge in developing new designs, but this consumed a high level of resources and was a lengthy process from research to eventual production. Most employees had been with the company for a large part of their working lives and the culture was still appropriate to the times of high profit where life had been fairly easy and laid back. Messages about difficult times, belt tightening and higher productivity with fewer people had been filtered down to employees, who did not change their behaviour but did feel threatened.

It was with some trepidation that Jennifer decided to meet personally with a cross-section of each department to talk through company and departmental issues. The first meeting was with research/development. As expected, the meeting began with a flood of concerns about job security. No promises could be given. However, the mid-point of the meeting was quite fruitful, and the following points, among others, became clear:

- development time could be reduced from two years to one if some production staff were involved in the development process from the very beginning;

- many development staff felt their career prospects were very limited and a number expressed the wish to be able to move into marketing. They felt this would also be an advantage when new products were marketed;
- staff felt fairly paid and would be prepared to forgo salary rises for a year or two if this would mean job security; they liked working for Dynamo and didn't want to move;
- staff were aware of the difficult position the company was in but they really didn't know what to do to make it any better;
- development staff wanted to know why Dynamo didn't collaborate with Castem Ltd on areas of mutual interest (Jennifer didn't know the answer to this one).

The meeting gave Jennifer not only a better understanding of what employees felt, but also some good ideas to explore. Departmental staff knew their problems had not been wiped away, but did feel that Jennifer had at least taken the trouble to listen to them.

Turnover figures, performance data, recruitment and promotion trends and characteristics of employees may also shed some light on these issues.

Data relating to current formal and informal systems, together with data on the structure of the organisation, also need to be collected, and the effectiveness, efficiency and other implications of these need to be carefully considered. Most data will be collected from within the organisation, but data may also be collected from significant others, such as customers, who may be part of the environment.

Current and projected employee numbers and skills (employee supply)

Current employee supply can be analysed in both individual and overall statistical terms. To gain an overview of current supply the following factors may be analysed either singly or in combination: number of employees classified by function, department, occupation, job title, competencies, skills, qualifications, training, age, length of service, performance assessment results. (*See* **www.pearsoned.co.uk/torrington** HRP Exercise, 5.1, note 8.)

Forecasting employee supply is concerned with predicting how the current supply of employees will change, primarily how many will leave, be internally promoted or transferred. These changes are forecast by analysing what has happened in the past, in terms of staff retention and/or movement, and projecting this into the future to see what would happen if the same trends continued. The impact of changing circumstances would also need to be taken into account when projecting analyses forward. Bell (1989) provides an extremely thorough coverage of possible analyses, on which this section is based. Behavioural aspects are also important, such as investigating the reasons why staff leave, the criteria that affect promotions and transfers and changes in working conditions and in HR policy. Analyses fall broadly into two categories: analyses of staff leaving, and analyses of internal movements.

Analyses of staff leaving the organisation

Annual labour turnover index

The annual labour turnover index is sometimes called the percentage wastage rate, or the conventional turnover index. This is the simplest formula for wastage and looks at the number of staff leaving during the year as a percentage of the total number employed who could have left.

$$\frac{\text{Leavers in year}}{\text{Average number of staff in post during year}} \times 100 = \text{percentage wastage rate}$$

(*See* **www.pearsoned.co.uk/torrington** HRP Exercise, 5.1, note 9.)

This measure has been criticised because it gives only a limited amount of information. If, for example, there were 25 leavers over the year, it would not be possible to determine whether 25 different jobs had been left by 25 different people, or whether 25 different people had tried and left the same job. Length of service is not taken into account with this measure, yet length of service has been shown to have a considerable influence on leaving patterns, such as the high number of leavers at the time of induction.

Stability index

The stability index is based on the number of staff who could have stayed throughout the period. Usually, staff with a full year's service are expressed as a percentage of staff in post one year ago.

$$\frac{\text{Number of staff with one year's service at date}}{\text{Number of staff employed exactly one year before}} \times 100 = \text{per cent stability}$$

(*See* **www.pearsoned.co.uk/torrington** HRP Exercise, 5.1, note 10.)

This index, however, ignores joiners throughout the year and takes little account of length of service.

Cohort analysis

A cohort is defined as a homogeneous group of people. Cohort analysis tracks what happens as some people leave a group of people with very similar characteristics who all joined the organisation at the same time. Graduates are an appropriate group for this type of analysis. A graph showing what happens to the group can be in the form of a survival curve or a log-normal wastage curve, which can be plotted as a straight line and can be used to make predictions. The disadvantage of this method of analysis is that it cannot be used for groups other than the specific group for which it was originally prepared. The information has also to be collected over a long time period, which produces problems of availability and reliability of data.

Half-life

The half-life is a figure expressing the time taken for half the cohort to leave the organisation. The figure does not give as much information as a survival curve, but it is useful as a summary and as a method of comparing different groups.

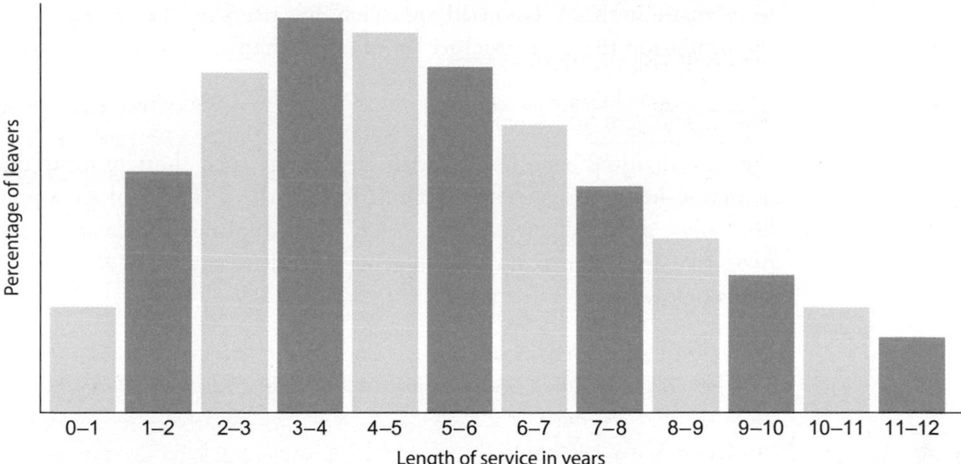

Figure 5.6 Census analysis: percentage of leavers with differing lengths of service

Census method

The census method is an analysis of leavers over a reasonably short period of time – often over a year. The length of completed service of leavers is summarised by using a histogram, as shown in Figure 5.6. (*See* **www.pearsoned.co.uk/torrington** HRP Exercise, 5.1, note 11.)

Retention profile

Staff retained, that is those who remain with the organisation, are allocated to groups depending on the year they joined. The number in each year group is translated into a percentage of the total number of individuals who joined during that year.

Age and retirement profile

Analyses by staff group, whether by seniority or specialism, of potential retirements over the next three to five years can provide an age and retirement profile.

We move now to methods of analysing internal movements. These focus on either overall analyses of movement patterns in the organisation or talent planning, which has a more individual emphasis.

Analyses of internal movements

Movement patterns

Age and length of service distributions can be helpful to indicate an overall pattern of problems that may arise in the future, such as promotion blocks. They need to be used in conjunction with an analysis of previous promotion patterns in the organisation. (*See* **www.pearsoned.co.uk/torrington** HRP Exercise, 5.1, note 12.) An alternative is a stocks and flows analysis of the whole organisation or a part of it, such as a department. The model is constructed to show the hierarchy of positions and the numbers employed in each. Numbers moving between positions, and in and out of the organisation over any time period, can be displayed. The model displays visually promotion and lateral move channels in operation, and shows what happens in reality to enable comparison to be made with the espoused approach, but users need to recognise, and work within, the limitation that the structure of jobs will change more rapidly than in the past.

Talent analysis and succession

On an individual basis many organisations pay special attention to analysing the talent available in the organisation to ensure that there is a pool to supply succession into key roles, especially leadership roles. Such analyses increasingly involve a range of proactive approaches to talent in general, and we say more about this in the section on plans below.

ACTIVITY 5.2

1. Why do employees leave organisations?
2. What are the determinants of promotion in your organisation? Are they made explicit? Do staff understand what the determinants are?
3. What would be your criteria for promotion in your organisation?

RECONCILIATION, DECISIONS AND PLANS

We have already said that, in reality, there is a process of continuous feedback between the different stages of human resource planning activities, as they are all interdependent. On the soft side (organisation, behaviour and culture) there is a dynamic relationship between the future vision, environmental trends and the current position. Key factors to take into account during reconciliation and deciding on action plans are the acceptability of the plans to both senior managers and other employees, the priority of each plan, key players who will need to be influenced and the factors that will encourage or be a barrier to successful implementation.

On the hard side, feasibility may centre on the situation where the supply forecast is less than the demand forecast. Here, the possibilities are to:

- alter the demand forecast by considering changes in the utilisation of employees (such as training and productivity deals, or high-performance teams and work intensification): by using different employees with higher skills; employing staff with insufficient skills and training them immediately; or outsourcing the work;
- alter the supply forecast by, say, reducing staff turnover, delaying retirement, or widening the supply pool by including EU nationals;
- change the company objectives, as lack of human resources will prevent them from being achieved in any case. Realistic objectives need to be based on the resources that are, and are forecast to be, available either internally or externally.

When the demand forecast is less than the internal supply forecast in some areas, the possibilities are to:

- consider and calculate the costs of overemployment over various timespans;
- consider the methods and cost of keeping staff but temporarily reducing their drain on company finances (for example by unpaid sabbaticals; reduced working hours); or losing staff;
- consider changes in utilisation: work out the feasibility and costs of retraining, redeployment and so on;
- consider whether it is possible for the company objectives to be changed. Could the company diversify, move into new markets, etc.?

We have also noted the interrelationship between the soft and the hard aspects of planning. For example, the creation of high-performance teams may have implications for different staffing numbers, a different distribution of skills, alternative approaches to reward and a different management style. The relocation of a supplier's staff on to the premises of the company that they supply, in order to get really close to this customer, could have implications for relocation, recruitment, skills required and culture encouraged. Emphasis on engagement and organisational learning may have implications for turnover and absence levels, training and development provision, culture encouraged and approach to reward.

Once all alternatives have been considered and feasible solutions decided, specific action plans can be designed covering all appropriate areas of HRM activity. While these have been grouped in separate sections, below, there is clearly potential overlap between the groups.

Human resource supply plans

Plans may need to be made concerning the timing and approach to recruitment or downsizing. For example, it may have been decided that in order to recruit sufficient staff, a public relations campaign is needed to promote the employer brand. Promotion, succession, transfer and redeployment and redundancy plans are also relevant here. Plans for the retention of those aged over 50 and flexible retirement plans are a key theme at present and we consider some examples of these in Chapter 21 on Equal opportunities and diversity. Further information on strategic and operational planning for downsizing can be found in Torrington *et al.* (2009).

WINDOW ON PRACTICE

A planned approach to downsizing

The recent recession has created a challenge in how to emerge in a healthy and strong position, unlike in the previous recession where unplanned and unthought-through downsizing meant that there was insufficient talent in many organisations to take advantage of the the upturn. Evidence suggests that organisations are taking a more planful approach this time.

For example the law firm Norton Rose has asked some of its graduate trainees who have been offered places but not yet started work if they would be prepared to defer their appointment until business picks up again. They were offered £10,000 if they accepted this option and used their time constructively such as doing voluntary work or learning a language. They are also using a redundancy avoidance plan in order to retain key workers by asking them to voluntarily change their terms and conditions for a year giving Norton Rose the chance to agree unpaid sabbaticals and reduced working hours. (Phillips 2009)

KPMG has asked employees to voluntarily work a four day week, if required or take a sabbatical at 30 per cent pay for between four and twelve weeks. It is proposed that these temporary changes to employment contracts last 18 months, that the maximum salary loss in any year be limited to 20 per cent and full benefits be paid throughout. (*People Management* 2009)

Source: Phillips, L. (2009) '"Slash graduate recruitment at your peril": firms advised to plan for the future', *People Management*, p. 8, 9 April; *People Management* (2009) 'KPMG asks staff to accept temporary flexible contracts if the need arises', *People Management*, Vol. 15, No. 3, p. 8, 29 January.

Talent plans

Increasingly there is the need to focus on plans for the attraction, development and retention of the talent pool. We review this in much more detail in Chapter 26. The concentration is now on the need to build and develop a pool of talent, without a clear view of how the talent will be used in the future, unlike earlier succession planning where individuals were groomed in advance to take on a specific role. Developing a talent pool is a more dynamic approach and fits well with the resource-based view of the firm. While the link to business strategy is emphasised, there is more recognition of individual aspirations and a greater opportunity for people to put themselves forward to be considered for the talent pool. Developing talent at different leadership levels in the organisation is considered important, and current debates focus on the definition of talent in terms of what it means and to whom it applies. Warren (2006) discusses the issue of inclusivity and whether organisations should focus on an elite of high-performing, high-potential individuals, or whether inclusivity should be more broadly defined. Much greater consideration is given to the required balance between internal talent development and external talent. Simms (2003) provides an interesting debate on these issues, which is provided as Case study 5.2 at **www.pearsoned.co.uk/torrington.**

Organisation and structure plans

Organisation and structure plans may concern departmental existence, remit and structure and the relationships between departments. They may also be concerned with the layers of hierarchy within departments and the level at which tasks are done, and the organisational groups within which they are done. For more details of structural issues see Chapter 4. Changes to organisation and structure will usually result in changes in employee utilisation.

Employee utilisation plans

Any changes in utilisation that affect human resource demand will need to be planned. Some changes will result in a sudden difference in the tasks that employees do and the numbers needed; others will result in a gradual movement over time. Other plans may involve the distribution of hours worked, for example the use of annual hours contracts; or the use of functional flexibility where employees develop and use a wider range of skills. There are implications for communications plans as the employees involved will need to be consulted about the changes and be prepared and trained for what will happen. There will be interconnections with supply plans here: for example, if fewer employees will be needed, what criteria will be used to determine who should be made redundant and who should be redeployed and retrained, and in which areas?

Learning and development plans

There will be development implications from both the human resource supply and the utilisation plans. The timing of development can be a critical aspect. For example, training for specific new technology skills loses most of its impact if it is done six months before the equipment arrives. If the organisation wishes to increase recruitment by promoting the excellent development that it provides for employees, then clear programmes of what will be offered need to be finalised and resourced so that these can then be used to entice candidates into the organisation. If the organisation is stressing customer service or total quality, then appropriate development will need to be carried out to enable employees to achieve this. Decisions whether to buy in talent and skills or develop them internally will affect the emphasis on and approach to development.

Performance management and engagement plans

These plans may include the development or renewal of a performance management system; and ensuring that employees are assessed on objectives or criteria that are key to organisational success, and which may then be linked to reward. They may also include setting performance and quality standards; culture change programmes aimed at encouraging specified behaviour and performance; or empowerment or career support to improve engagement and motivation.

Reward plans

It is often said that what gets rewarded gets done, and it is key that rewards reflect what the organisation sees as important. For example, if quantity of output is most important for production workers, bonuses may relate to number of items produced. If quality is most important, then bonuses may reflect reject rate, or customer complaint rate. If managers are only rewarded for meeting their individual objectives there may be problems if the organisation is heavily dependent on teamwork. If individuals are rewarded for short-term gains rather than the achievement of objectives relating to longer-term sustainability, then as evidence from the banking crisis demonstrates individuals will work to achieve short-term gains at the expense of long-term sustainability.

Employee relations plans

These plans may involve unions, employee representatives or all employees. They would include any matters which need to be negotiated or areas where there is the opportunity for employee involvement and participation.

Communications plans

The way that planned changes are communicated to employees is critical. Plans need to include not only methods for informing employees about what managers expect of them, but also methods to enable employees to express their concerns and needs for successful implementation. Communications plans will also be important if, for example, managers wish to generate greater employee commitment by keeping employees better informed about the progress of the organisation.

Once the plans have been made and put into action, the planning process still continues. It is important that the plans be monitored to see if they are being achieved and if they are producing the expected results, and pick up any unanticipated consequences. Plans will also need to be reconsidered on a continuing basis in order to cope with changing circumstances.

SUMMARY PROPOSITIONS

5.1 Even in a context of rapid and discontinuous change workforce planning still has a valuable contribution to make, but as human resource planning deals with people, planners need to plan for what is acceptable as well as what is feasible.

5.2 The scope of workforce planning covers not only numbers of people and skills, but also structure, culture, systems and behaviour.

5.3 An integrated framework which attempts to cover all aspects of workforce planning involves:

- analysing the external environment and business strategy;
- analysing where do we want to be? (forecasting HR requirements);
- analysing where are we now? (defining the current HR position and projecting this forward);
- comparing the two and forming plans to bridge the gap.

5.4 Workforce planning is a continuous process rather than a one-off activity.

GENERAL DISCUSSION TOPICS

1 Discuss the proposition that traditional (numbers) workforce planning is only of interest to organisations in periods of growth when unemployment levels are low.

2 'It is worthwhile planning even if you have no strategy.' For what reasons might you agree or disagree with this statement?

WEB LINKS

www.healthcareworkforce.nhs.uk

www.creatingpeopleadvantage.com

www.adeccoinstitute.com

FURTHER READING

Day, G. and Schoemaker, P. (2005) 'Scanning the periphery', *Harvard Business Review*, November, pp. 135–48.
This article underlines the organisational importance of keeping a constant eye on peripheral features in an organisation's environment as well as its direct and close competitors. Examples are included of challenges different organisations have faced and there are practical suggestions about how organisations could improve their scanning of the peripheral environment. Included is a self-assessment tool to identify the need for an organisation to have peripheral vision, and to assess its capability for peripheral vision. The capability part encompasses an assessment of leadership orientation, knowledge management systems, strategy-making processes, organisational structure and incentives, and culture (values, beliefs and behaviours).

Pfeffer, J. and Sutton, R. (2006) 'The real brain teaser', *People Management*, Vol. 12, No. 8, pp. 28–30.
This article challenges the notion that identifying talent within organisations is unproblematic. The authors demonstrate how performance varies over time, that talent is determined by the standards of performance accepted at the time it is identified, and that talent is as much a product of effort training and environment as it is of innate ability. Thus talent can easily be missed.

McNeilly, M. (2002) 'Gathering information for strategic decisions', *Strategy and Leadership*, Vol. 30, No. 5, pp. 29–34.
Focuses on information gathering, making strategic decisions and taking action, and provides some useful tools for each of these three stages. Some interesting suggestions for making strategic decisions include scenario planning and acting out scenarios in advance.

Turner, P. (2002) *Strategic Human Resource Forecasting*. London: CIPD.
An excellent and detailed text which covers issues involved in forecasting, strategy and planning and the HR role in this. Turner includes a wide range of aspects of HR from employee numbers to employee relations and organisation design.

REFERENCES

Arkin, A. (2008) 'Down but not out', *People Management*, Vol. 14, No. 13, pp. 18–23.

Becker, B., Huselid, M. and Ulrich, D. (2001) *The HR Scorecard: Linking people, strategy and performance*. Boston: Harvard Business School Press.

Bell, D.J. (1989) *Planning Corporate Manpower*. London: Longman.

Boxall, P. and Purcell, J. (2003) *Strategy and Human Resource Management*. Basingstoke: Palgrave, Macmillan.

Chubb, L. (2008) 'Plan ahead to defuse the "demographic timebomb"', *People Management*, Vol. 14, No. 9, p. 7.

Curson, J., Dell, M., Wilson, R., Bosworth, D. and Baldauf, B. (2010) 'Who does workforce planning well? Workforce rapid review team summary', *International Journal of Health Care Quality Assurance*, Vol. 23, No. 1, pp. 110–19.

Denrell, J. (2005) 'Selection bias and the perils of benchmarking', *Harvard Business Review*, 20 April, pp. 114–19.

Felsted, A. and Taylor, A. (2006) 'Aviva says job cuts will save £250m annually', *Financial Times*, 14 September.

Guthridge, M. and Lawson, E. (2008) 'Divide and survive', *People Management*, Vol. 14, No. 19, pp. 40–4.

Lavelle, J. (2007) 'On workforce architecture, employment relationships and lifecycles: expanding the purview of workforce planning and management', *Public Personnel Management*, Vol. 36, No. 4, pp. 371–84.

Mayall, R. (2009) *Dear Granny Smith: A letter from your postman*. London: Short Books.

Michaels, E., Handfield-Jones, H. and Axelrod, B. (2001) *The War for Talent*. Harvard: McKinsey and Company Incorporated/Harvard Business School Publishing.

Mintzberg, H. (1994) 'The fall and rise of strategic planning', *Harvard Business Review*, January/February, pp. 107–14.

People Management (2009) 'KPMG asks staff to accept temporary flexible contracts if the need arises', *People Management*, Vol. 15, No. 3, p. 8.

Phillips, L. (2009) '"Slash graduate recruitment at your peril": firms advised to plan for the future', *People Management*, p. 8.

Simms, J. (2003) 'The generation game', *People Management*, Vol. 9, No. 9, pp. 26–31.

Sisson, K. and Storey, J. (2000) *The Realities of Human Resource Management*. Buckingham: Open University Press.

Stokker, J. and Hallam, G. (2009) 'The right person, in the right job, with the right skills at the right time: a workforce-planning model that goes beyond metrics', *Library Management*, Vol. 15, No. 89, pp. 561–71.

Taylor, S. (2008) *Employee Resourcing*. London: IPD.

Torrington, D., Hall, L., Taylor, S. and Atkinson, C. (2009) *Fundamentals of Human Resource Management*. Harlow: Pearson Education.

Turner, P. (2002) 'How to do HR forecasting and planning', *People Management*, Vol. 8, No. 6, pp. 48–9.

Warren, C. (2006) 'Curtain call', *People Management*, Vol. 12, No. 6, pp. 24–9.

An extensive range of additional materials, including multiple choice questions, answers to questions and links to useful websites can be found on the Human Resource Management companion website at **www.pearsoned.co.uk/torrington**.

THE INTERNATIONAL DIMENSION

THE OBJECTIVES OF THIS CHAPTER ARE TO:

1. Provide an overview of research and practice in international human resource management
2. Explore the major dimensions of cultural difference between workplaces based in different countries
3. Assess how institutional differences help account for differences in HRM practice across national borders
4. Explain how international HRM practice varies from nationally based HRM practice
5. Review aspects of communication and coordination in international organisations
6. Discuss the major steps necessary to ensure the successful deployment of expatriate staff.

In Chapter 2 we explained how the globalisation of economic activity over recent decades and, in particular, its acceleration in the last 20 years have had a huge impact on the context in which HRM activity now takes place. Most organisations in the private sector are now obliged to compete, either directly or indirectly, with others based overseas. This is vastly increasing the extent of competition, is making the business environment more volatile and is thus a key driver behind many of the contemporary developments in HRM practice which we introduce in this book. Globalisation is also providing both the rationale and the opportunity for organisations which once restricted their activity to a national market to expand overseas and become multinational corporations (MNCs) with interests in several countries and an international workforce to manage. There are now more than 60,000 multinational companies, between them accounting for around a third of all international exports and 10 per cent of international economic activity (Cooke 2007: 489–90). Estimates of the number of people employed directly in MNCs vary considerably, but it is probably in the region of 100 million people worldwide (*see* Marginson and Meardi 2009). Public sector organisations are also affected by globalisation, being required to benchmark their performance against other equivalent bodies overseas and to take on approaches that have been found to work well in other countries. Labour markets are becoming increasingly international as organisations seek to source elsewhere key skills that are in short supply at home. In recent years, for example, the National Health Service, has recruited heavily from overseas countries. While the numbers have reduced somewhat since 2007, at their peak between 2000 and 2006 well over 10,000 nurses a year were registering in the UK having trained in other countries. This represented more than half of all new nurses recruited (Buchan and Seccombe 2009: 11–13).

Unsurprisingly as globalisation has picked up pace, international HRM has become one of the most widely researched and written about fields of study. Numerous books and articles have been published over the past 20 years examining all aspects of practice in international organisations, a number of fascinating debates evolving about what is happening, what should happen and about the longer-term direction of travel. In one short chapter we can only begin to introduce this subject, so we will focus on two or three key issues that have generated the most interest to date. We start by introducing some studies in the field of comparative HRM, exploring why it is that the way people are managed, and expect to be managed, varies so much from country to country. We go on to discuss key issues in the management of people in international corporations, focusing in particular on communication and coordination difficulties. Finally we introduce some specific issues that arise in connection with the employment of expatriate staff.

WINDOW ON PRACTICE

Helen Deresky (2008: 5) reproduces a whimsical description of globalisation 'from an unknown source', relating to the death of Princess Diana in Paris:

> Princess Diana was an English princess
> With an Egyptian boyfriend

Who crashed in a French tunnel,
Driving in a German car with a Dutch engine,
Driven by a Belgian who was drunk on Scotch whisky,
Followed closely by Italian paparazzi,
On Japanese motorcycles.
She was treated by an American doctor,
Using Brazilian medicines.
This is sent to you by an American Indian,
Using Bill Gates's technology.
You are probably reading this on your computer
That uses Taiwanese chips
And a Korean monitor,
Assembled by Bangladeshi workers in a Singapore plant,
Transported by Indian lorry drivers,
Unloaded by Sicilian longshoremen
And trucked to you by Mexican immigrants.

CULTURAL VARIATIONS

The history of the European Union's attempt to establish a supranational institution is one of constant, but reluctant recognition of the stubbornness of national differences and the accentuation of regional differences among, for instance, the Basques, the Flemish and the Scottish. The cultural diversity and intensity of feeling on national issues in a close-knit and economically developed region like western Europe indicates the significance of cultural difference on a global scale. Nationality is important in HRM because of its effect on human behaviour and the consequent constraints on management action.

Some things that initially appear specific to a particular national culture turn out to be understood and welcomed in almost all cultures. Westernisation and globalisation are prime targets for international terrorism because of the cultural vales that are seen to undermine the social cohesion of other cultures, as well as the apparent reluctance of western governments to change their colonial assumptions and their interference in the internal affairs of other countries. Despite that widespread hostility Italian pizza has been adopted in most countries of the world, and the expansion has been largely brought about by Pizza Hut, which is owned by Pepsi-Cola, an American company known for a drink that has also gone to every corner of the globe. Who would have expected that Muscovites would daily queue up outside the largest McDonald's in the world until it was overtaken by the branch in Beijing? Few brands are more obviously global than Microsoft.

Newspapers and magazines in social democracies and socialist republics frequently devote more space in a year to the British Royal Family than to any other topic, despite the fact that the institution is utterly British and theoretically alien to their political systems. Countless millions every day follow the fortunes of some very ordinary people in the Australian suburb of Ramsey Street, and even more watch association football. The wide international acceptability of these things could suggest that we are all members of the global village with converging tastes and values. Yet certain facets of national culture remain deeply rooted and have a way of undermining that argument.

> It is difficult to prove that any given language determines management behaviour in specific ways. Nevertheless, it seems incontestable that the French have developed their language as a precision tool for analysis and conceptualisation; that the Japanese use their language as an emollient for creating an atmosphere conducive to harmonious interaction; and that the Americans use their version of English as a store of snappy neologisms to excite, distract and motivate. (Holden 1992)

In recent years a number of extensive, questionnaire-based studies have been carried out among employees and managers working in different countries, the results subsequently being 'mapped'. The dominant features of business cultures across the globe have thus been categorised into readily understood types which demonstrate how they differ one from another. The best known studies are those by:

- Kluckohn (1954)
- Strodtbeck (1961)
- Hofstede (1980, 1991 and 2001)
- Hall and Hall (1990)
- Trompenaars (1993)
- Lewis (1996)
- House *et al.* (2004)

Inevitably the mapping process oversimplifies matters to a considerable extent, downplaying the extent of cultural variation between organisations, generations and regions within countries, as well as changes over time, while emphasising cultural differences between countries. However, because the researchers have all, without exception, found that work cultures vary much more between countries than within national boundaries, these studies can claim to be both valid and useful.

While it may be simplistic, there is a great deal of truth in the finding across all these studies that the UK's dominant workplace culture is one in which organisations tend to have less formal hierarchical structures than elsewhere, much more decentralisation of authority, a relatively relaxed view of change and a preference for keeping emotions hidden. The observation is useful, particularly as the basis for making broad international comparisons, but it must also be recognised that there are also plenty of organisations, communities and individuals who do not share these cultural norms, so care has to be taken not to simply 'read off' a set of national characteristics from the published typologies and assume it applies everywhere, equally within any single country.

Despite being subjected to a great deal of criticism over the years, Gert Hofstede's work in this field remains by far the most widely quoted and cited, making it a truly seminal contribution to the study of HRM. Hofstede's studies remain unrivalled in terms of their scale and scope, comprising the analysis of detailed questionnaires issued to many thousands of IBM employees in 70 different countries over a long period. The studies have led to the publication of several detailed books, including a number of editions of *Culture's Consequences: International Differences in Work-Related Values* which was originally published in 1980 but has been updated on several occasions since. Hofstede's organisation also runs a most interesting website which explains his work and from which all manner of charts can be downloaded which show how different countries 'score' on all his dimensions (**www.geert-hofstede.com**).

Hofstede defines national culture as 'the collective mental programming which distinguishes one nation from another'. He originally identified four dimensions that allow different national characteristics to be classified or mapped. These are as follows:

1 **Individualism** is the extent to which people expect to look after themselves and their family only. The opposite is collectivism which has a tight social framework and in which people expect to have a wider social responsibility to discharge because others in the group will support them. Those of a collectivist persuasion believe they owe absolute loyalty to their group.
2 **Power distance** measures the extent to which the less powerful members of the society accept the unequal distribution of power. In organisations this is the degree of centralisation of authority and the exercise of autocratic leadership.
3 **Uncertainty avoidance.** The future is always unknown, but some societies socialise their members to accept this and take risks, while members of other societies have been socialised to be made anxious about this and seek to compensate through the security of law, religion or technology.
4 **Masculinity.** The division of roles between the sexes varies from one society to another. Where men are assertive and have dominant roles these values permeate the whole of society and the organisations that make them up, so there is an emphasis on showing off, performing, making money and achieving something visible. Where there is a larger role for women, who are more service oriented with caring roles, the values move towards concern for the environment and the quality of life, putting the quality of relationships before the making of money.

Hofstede found some clear cultural differences between nationalities and from this he concluded that countries emphasising large power distance and strong uncertainty avoidance were likely to produce forms of organisation that relied heavily on hierarchy and clear orders from superiors: **a pyramid of people.** In countries where there is small power distance and strong uncertainty avoidance there would be an implicit form of organisation that relied on rules, procedures and clear structure: **a well-oiled machine.** The implicit model of organisation in countries with small power distance and weak uncertainty avoidance was a reliance on ad hoc solutions to problems as they arose, as many of the problems could be boiled down to human relations difficulties: **a village market.** The picture is completed by the fourth group of countries where there is large power distance and weak uncertainty avoidance, where problems are resolved by constantly referring to the boss who is like a father to an extended family, so there is concentration of authority without structuring of activities. The implicit model of organisation here is: **the family.** Table 6.1 shows which countries are in the different segments.

Pyramid of people	Well-oiled machine	Village market	Family
Arab-speaking	Austria	Australia	East Africa
Argentina	Costa Rica	Britain	Hong Kong
Belgium	Finland	Canada	Indonesia
Brazil	Germany	Denmark	India
Chile	Israel	Ireland	Jamaica
Colombia	Switzerland	Netherlands	Malaysia
Ecuador		New Zealand	Philippines
France		Norway	Singapore
Greece		South Africa	West Africa
Guatemala		Sweden	
Iran		United States	
Italy			
Japan			
Korea			
Mexico			
Pakistan			
Panama			
Peru			
Portugal			
Salvador			
Spain			
Taiwan			
Thailand			
Turkey			
Uruguay			
Venezuela			
Yugoslavia			

Table 6.1

Note: Hofstede's study was carried out in the countries where IBM employees were based in sufficient numbers in 1971. That is why not all countries are included here.

The implicit form of organisation for Britain is a village market, for France it is a pyramid of people, for Germany it is a well-oiled machine and for Hong Kong it is a family. If we can understand the organisational realities and detail in those four countries, then this can provide clues about how to cope in Denmark, Ecuador, Austria or Indonesia because they each share the implicit organisational form and implicit organisational culture of one of the original four.

ACTIVITY 6.1

Identify your country and its type from those shown in Table 6.1. If it is not there, pick one with which you are familiar.

1. Do you agree with Hofstede's description of the type of organisation that is implicit?
2. Think of examples of that implicit type of organisation that affects HR activities.

Understanding cultural differences is not quite as easy as the task in Activity 6.1 might imply, because the clusters show only relative similarities and, inevitably, other studies do not entirely agree with Hofstede (for example, Ronen and Shenkar 1985), but there is sufficient agreement for us to regard the four-way classification as useful, if not completely reliable.

Hofstede later produced (2001) a refinement of the uncertainty avoidance dimension: 'Confucian dynamism', or long-term versus short-term orientation. Later he used the term 'time orientation' instead. Management researchers are typically from Western Europe or the United States, with all the cultural bias that such an orientation involves. Working with the Canadian Michael Bond, Hofstede used a Chinese value survey technique in a fresh study and uncovered the cultural variable of long-term orientation that none of the original, western questions had reached. The highest scoring countries on this dimension were China, Hong Kong, Taiwan, Japan and South Korea. Singapore was placed ninth. Hofstede argues that countries in the West have derived their culture largely from the three religions of Judaism, Christianity or Islam, all of which are centred on the assertion of a truth that is accessible to true believers, whereas none of the religions of the East are based on the assertion that there is a truth that a human community can embrace. The 'Confucian' values found attached to this long-term orientation included perseverance, clearly maintained status differentials, thrift and having a sense of shame. In many ways these values are valuable for business growth, as they put social value on entrepreneurial initiative, support the entrepreneur by the willing compliance of others seeking a place in the system, encourage saving and investment and put pressure on those who do not meet obligations.

Hofstede's work is interesting in that it demonstrates that cultures (or collective mental programming) among a national people remain strikingly and persistently divergent despite convergence in areas such as technology and economic systems. Hence he found huge differences in culture between the OECD countries – i.e. the most industrially advanced countries – indicating that economic development does not have a major impact on culture. On uncertainty avoidance, for example, among OECD countries Greece is five times higher than Denmark. On the masculinity index Japan is 18 times higher than Sweden and Norway.

From a strategic perspective cultural diversity has many implications for human resource management. Hodgetts and Luthans (2000: 36) selected some of these where the culture of a society can directly affect management approaches.

1 **The centralisation of decision making.** In some societies (especially the pyramid of people type) all important decisions are taken by a small number of managers in senior positions. In other societies (like the village markets) decision making is more decentralised. In a joint venture between two dissimilar societies, not only will these differences of approach need to be recognised, but management systems will have to enable members of the two cultures to understand each other and work together.

2 **Rewards and competition.** The level of financial rewards between countries can be a problem, when those in country A appear to receive much more money than those in country B for doing the same job, but a more subtle difference is the way in which rewards are disbursed. In some instances there is a culture favouring individual recognition, while elsewhere there is a convention of group rewards. Similarly some societies encourage competition rather than cooperation, and in others the reverse applies.

3 **Risk.** As Hofstede demonstrated in his first study, attitudes towards taking risks are a clear discriminator between cultures, with marked variations of uncertainty avoidance.
4 **Formality.** The well-oiled machine cultures place great emphasis on clear procedures and strict rules, while pyramid of people cultures emphasise clear hierarchies and observance of rank. This contrasts strongly with the village market type societies where relationships are more informal and ad hoc action more likely.
5 **Organisational loyalty.** In Japan there tends to be a strong sense of loyalty to one's employer, while in Britain and the United States there is a growing sense of identification with one's occupational group, rather than with a particular employer. The long-standing importance of professional bodies and the declining long-term reliability of corporations to look after one's career development have increased this loyalty to one's occupation rather than to one's employer.
6 **Short- or long-term orientation.** Hofstede's identification of an eastern predilection for the long term is beginning to influence strategic decisions on where to locate those organisational activities for which long-term thinking is particularly appropriate.

INSTITUTIONAL VARIATIONS

The work of Hofstede and others who have carried out similar studies emphasises cultural differences between countries, the implication being that different approaches to the management if people are required in each place if an organisation is to maximise its ability to recruit, retain, engage and motivate its staff. In recent years, however, studies have been published which question this point of view. There is general agreement that HR systems and policies do vary from country to country, but the extent to which this is due to cultural differences is disputed. Instead it is strongly argued that institutional differences offer a better explanation (Whitley 1999, Edwards and Rees 2006, Wright and Van de Voorde 2009). This conclusion has been reached from a reading of many studies looking at how HR practices vary across different locations within the same multinational company. A widely advanced view is that the following factors have a major influence on how HR is practised on a day-to-day basis:

- local laws
- enforcement mechanisms/agencies
- government and local government policies
- collective bargaining structures
- labour market institutions
- national training systems
- pension arrangements
- social security systems

Moreover, it is further argued and that over time these become so well embedded as to become management norms in the countries concerned:

> In the local context, the labour laws and regulations restrict the range of possible HRM practices, local managers have taken-for-granted views about good management practices that influence the policies and practices that they suggest for the subsidiary, strong professional norms may exist, and processes of institutionalization might also take place among MNCs in the focal country. (Bjorkman 2006: 465)

While there is now a degree of international convergence as far as employment law is concerned thanks to the efforts of bodies such as the International Labour Organisation and the European Union (EU), national systems remain very different from one another. Even within the EU where so many employment law principles apply in all member states, considerable differences persist. Dismissal law, for example, the most fundamental of all employment rights which we discuss in Chapter 10, is completely different in different countries. In the UK many are excluded from bringing unfair dismissal cases at all, while those who can are unlikely to win much by way of damages unless they are older workers with many years' service and would have difficulty finding alternative employment. In many other EU countries a suspected unfair dismissal can give rise to criminal proceedings, the case being brought not by the aggrieved employee, but by a local labour inspectorate. Damages are also far higher in many jurisdictions, fines also being levied by way of punishment. The most restrictive regime of all operates in Holland where no lawful dismissal can take place without it first being approved by the relevant local district labour office. The approval process can take several weeks, during which time the employee has to be paid. In the United States, by contrast, in most states there is no unfair dismissal law at all, the longstanding doctrine of 'employment at will' being adhered to which allows employees to be dismissed lawfully 'for good reason, bad reason or no reason at all'.

The presence in law of such different approaches to dismissal inevitably has a profound effect on the way that people are managed and their expectations about work. Employees in the USA have far less job security than their counterparts in the UK, and much, much less than those working in the Netherlands. This means that managers enjoy greater power in the USA, while employees know that they can be fired at any time irrespective of their conduct or performance. On the one hand this makes it easier for managers to impose their will and force through change, but it also means that particular efforts have to be put into gaining employee commitment and engendering a sense of joint purpose. In the Netherlands, managerial power is heavily circumscribed as far as dismissal is concerned, ruling out a highly autocratic approach and meaning that change has to be negotiated to a greater extent. The position in the UK lies somewhere in between. So here we have three countries with markedly different approaches to dismissal leading to diverse HR practices. Yet all three fall within the 'Village market' category in Hofstede's model, being similar in terms of their cultural norms.

The debate about which factors, cultural or institutional, best explain differences between the dominant approaches to HR practised across borders is ultimately of little practical relevance. Both play a part to a greater or lesser extent in different types of situation. De Cieri (2007: 519–20) demonstrates this by looking at recruitment and selection practices. These, she argues, in part vary from country to country because of cultural differences. In Anglo-Saxon cultures selection processes tend to be competitive and objective, the aim being to secure the services of the person who is likely to perform best in the job. Elsewhere in the world where personal networks and relationships play a stronger role in the business culture and where power distance (as defined by Hofstede) is great it is the norm for employees to be appointed through family or clan connections, on personal recommendation, or on occasion because a bribe of some kind has been paid. These are cultural explanations for the differences. But there are also institutional explanations. In countries such as the UK and the USA discrimination law serves to deter employers from selection on anything other than objective grounds. De Cieri goes on to give other examples of HRM practices in which both institutional and cultural factors play a role in shaping international divergence, exploring performance appraisal and diversity management in particular.

ACTIVITY 6.2

What other examples of HR practices or established employment norms can you think of which differ from country to country? How far are these explained by cultural or by institutional differences, or is there some other explanation?

HRM IN INTERNATIONAL ORGANISATIONS

In terms of its aims and objectives IHRM (i.e. HRM in an international organisation) is no different from HRM in an organisation based in one country. The purpose is to mobilise an appropriately qualified workforce, and subsequently to retain it, motivate it and develop it. IHRM, however, is more complex and necessarily has a rather different emphasis:

- IHRM involves working with an organisational structure that is more complex
- there are a greater number of more diverse stakeholder groups to take account of
- there is greater involvement in people's private/family lives because of the expatriation element
- diversity is necessary in terms of management style
- there are greater numbers of external influences and risks to understand and manage

IHRM is also harder because of the communication difficulties that arise due to distance and language differences as well as cultural and institutional traditions and assumptions such as those we discussed above. This makes effective knowledge management and change management harder to achieve in particular. International HR managers thus need to have a somewhat different skill set from domestically-focused HR managers and tend to develop careers exclusively in international organisations.

A particular issue of significance for international organisations concerns the design of internal structures and reporting lines. While these are always complex issues for large organisations, they are made a great deal more involved when geographically diverse workforces are involved. The major alternatives are as follows:

- by product group
- by organisational function
- by geographic region
- matrix structures

In the latter case individuals may report to two or three different people for different purposes, a direct line manager based in the same geographic location, a regional manager working in the same specialist area of activity but based in another country and others with responsibility for particular projects and initiatives being run internationally from a corporate headquarters based elsewhere.

Linked to the question of the overall structure is the issue of who should manage plants or other units located in countries other than that of the corporate HQ. Most international companies are firmly rooted in a home country and wish to appoint home country nationals in sufficient numbers around global operations as a means of exercising financial control. However, in a truly global organisation, where the original location of the corporate HQ is irrelevant to staffing policy, and perhaps where ownership is no longer concentrated in one country, the nationality of each unit manager is less of an issue. This is also true of many international organisations that are not commercial (e.g. the EU, the United Nations and its associated bodies). Here corporate culture tends to supersede separate national cultures, and it becomes possible simply to promote people to new positions in different countries on the basis of individual merit. Deresky (2008: 343–6) identifies the following three approaches.

The **ethnocentric approach** is to fill key overseas positions with people from headquarters. This is typical of businesses that are at the internalisation stage of expansion and retain a strong, centralised structure. The people appointed have a full understanding of the company ethos, products and technology, and may be essential where there is a shortage of appropriately skilled and experienced local personnel. This approach, however, denies promotion opportunities to local managers and prevents the business from making use of its full overseas staff potential.

The **polycentric approach** employs local managers to fill key positions in their own countries. This has the obvious advantage that they are familiar with the culture, language and ways of doing business in their own country and probably already have many useful contacts as a basis of their essential network. Once this step is taken there is the potential problem of maintaining effective coordination across the business as a whole. The benefits of strong centralisation are lost. The US company, for instance, that has Americans in all its local CEO positions has people with a common national culture and background, as well as familiarity with the company's products and procedures. If that company opts instead to appoint CEOs who are from the local country, there is no longer the same degree of what can be taken for granted in shared values, attitudes and understanding. Will the CEO in Taiwan have the same understanding of the business use of bribes (or 'sweeteners', 'gifts in appreciation', 'special fees' and so on) as the CEO in Kuwait, in Detroit or in Stockholm? If polycentric staffing becomes widespread will the social understanding and cultural awareness at headquarters become increasingly less effective in relation to the subsidiaries?

The **global** approach is one where the most appropriate person for a particular job is recruited from anywhere in the group, or even outside, so that the entire management cadre gradually becomes internationalised with a shared global view as well as local understanding. This usually works only in a mature and very large business with a great deal of international experience.

Communication

Communicating across geographical, ethnic and national boundaries is a major challenge for HR people. Brandt and Hulbert (1976) studied organisational feedback in a number of multinational companies that had their headquarters in Europe, Japan and the United States. They found that the American organisations had many more feedback reports and meetings between headquarters and subsidiaries than their European or Japanese counterparts. In contrast, Pascale (1978) found that Japanese managers in Japan used face-to-face contacts more than American managers as well as more upwards and lateral communication. Japanese managers in America used communication in the same way as Americans.

There are various ways in which expectation determines communication content and all can impair the accuracy of message transmission. Such problems are compounded by geographical distance, cultural differences and subtleties of language.

Cognitive dissonance does more than lead to misunderstanding; it can also distort or inhibit action. Not only do recipients of information find it difficult to understand, remember and take action, they will also grapple with the dissonance that the problematical new information presents. One of the ways in which they do this is to distort the message so that what they actually hear is what they expect to hear and can easily understand rather than the difficult, challenging information that is being put to them.

There are frequent problems with language. In Shell International there used to be a term to describe the purpose of certain types of meeting as 'flocking', which is a wonderfully precise term to express the nature and purpose of those particular gatherings that take place, yet French and German people have great difficulty in understanding the nuances of the term, because neither language has an equivalent that distinguishes between, for example, flocking and herding.

The problem of jargon is where a word or a phrase has a specialised meaning that is immediately understandable by those in the know, but meaningless or misleading to those who do not share the specialised knowledge. The Maslow hierarchy of human needs is by now quite well known in management circles. On one occasion a lecturer was describing the ideas that were implicit in this notion and was surprised some months later in an examination script to see that one of the students had heard not 'hierarchy' but 'high Iraqui'. The unfamiliarity of the word 'hierarchy' had been completely misinterpreted by that particular student, who had imposed her own meaning on the words because of the need to make sense of what she heard. Professor Eugene McKenna relates how he was lecturing on the same subject of motivation, describing job enlargement and job enrichment. After the lecture a puzzled student asked him, 'what exactly was the job in Richmond?'

A quite different aspect of communication for HR people in international business is disseminating information and messages within the organisation. They need to develop corporate culture and a sense of collaboration across national boundaries in order to integrate the different units in the business. They need to ensure that members of different units understand, for instance, why a company has been acquired in South America, even though it seems to threaten the livelihood of some parts of the parent organisation. Comprehensive communication can raise awareness of the wider market and the opportunities that are waiting to be grasped.

There is a need for constant communication throughout the business to disseminate information and to sustain changing values. The organisation must operate holistically. It is not the sum of its parts: the whole exists in every part, as in the human body. If you are ill a doctor can obtain information about your illness from any part of you. A sample of your blood or the taking of your temperature is just as good wherever it comes from. If you are to be protected against cholera, which attacks the intestines, you have an injection in your arm. If you are about to be shot in the chest, your entire body will shiver in fear.

When a company is operating internationally, one logical main channel for communication could be the work-flow pattern. If a washing machine is produced by manufacturing electronic components in California, sub-assemblies and wiring harnesses in Korea and final assembly in Scotland, there is an easy sequence to follow. Job instructions, guidance notes, queries, telephone calls, specifications, requisitions, authorisations, order forms are some of the many ways in which groups of people communicate with those before and after them in the work flow, or critically adjacent to the process, like the HR people. Among the most effective international communicators are airlines, as their entire business is moving not only customers but also staff constantly across national boundaries to different organisational outposts of the business: the business activity creates the communications. All international businesses require centralised, coordinated communications to create common purpose and to share ideas and benefits, but those that do not have a natural work-flow link across national boundaries will have a greater need in this respect.

The communications management challenge for HRM is at two extremes. At one is the personal behaviour and skill of individual people in making themselves understood, persuading others to do things, negotiating agreements with people from different cultural backgrounds, overcoming language barriers, appreciating different frames of reference and developing heightened sensitivity to varying behavioural norms and conventions. Communication is an individual activity, reflecting personal style and the HRM requirement is for cultural awareness and perhaps language training. In this type of communication the manager is a skilled solo performer. The other extreme is impersonal and systemic, more concerned with channels of communication than with individual behaviour, and more concerned with systematic distribution of carefully chosen information and the organisation of communications opportunities. In this type of communication the manager metaphorically writes the score and then conducts the orchestra.

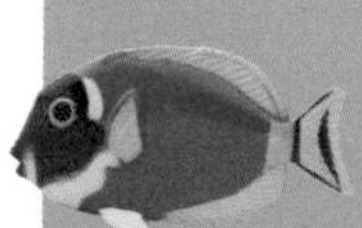

WINDOW ON PRACTICE

An expression that is often repeated in the French workplace is 'Pourquoi le faire simple si l'on peut le faire complique?' (why make something simple if one can make it complicated?). This slightly ironic comment encapsulates the French practice of opting for elaborate and time-consuming work systems rather than less complicated alternatives.

A similar point of view was expressed by Ann Moran who was involved in a merger between a British company and a French one. She describes some of the cultural differences and their impact:

the effort needed to communicate has doubled. The French expect a response from the person to whom a communication was sent and not from a delegated person. To reply otherwise is taken as a slight.

More upward and more complicated communications are needed whilst keeping [within] the formal hierarchical framework that is normal in French companies. Open questioning of superiors by the French is not common.

In meetings French colleagues do not feel constrained to follow the agenda and sometimes walk out of the meeting for a private discussion.

Source: Moran 1994: 112–13.

Coordination

Managers working internationally give themselves major problems of coordination by adopting measures that they see as necessary for business success. On the one hand they have to encourage diversity of local action, so that what is done fits local circumstances. On the other hand their global thinking requires careful coordination as the way to synergy, so that the global business does more and better together than it could possibly achieve as a number of independent units.

Bartlett and Goshal (1989) described three conventional approaches to coordination that were used, stemming from the nationality of the parent company, the Japanese, the American and the European.

Japanese centralisation

The typical Japanese approach is for a strong headquarters group to retain for themselves all major decisions and frequently intervene in the affairs of overseas subsidiaries. This appears to stem from their difficulty in dealing with foreigners:

> a major strategic challenge for Japanese firms is to accept that non-Japanese must somehow be given more direct responsibility and opportunity for promotion within the company at local level . . . there has to be letting-go from the centre. But this is no easy thing. For companies must overcome severe impediments associated with wariness, distrust and lack of knowledge about the world beyond Japan.
> (Holden 1994: 127)

American formalisation

The American approach is described as formalisation. Power is vested not in headquarters or in the managers of local companies, but in formal systems, policies and standards, so that it is the systems that drive the business. Many American businesses went international at the time when the use of control systems was being rapidly developed to cope with the large size of the businesses. The idea of delegation and holding others accountable by means of extensive computerised information systems seemed eminently suitable for operating the increasing number of overseas units, especially when in view of the apparent unpopularity of overseas postings among American managers (e.g. Tung and Miller 1990).

European socialisation

In European companies the approach to coordination is described as socialisation. There has been a reliance on key, highly skilled and trusted individuals. These people were carefully selected and developed a detailed understanding of the company's objectives and methods. Their personal development included the establishment of close working relationships and mutual understanding with colleagues. Once groomed these key decision makers were despatched to manage the subsidiaries, so that the headquarters and the subsidiaries were both strengthened.

> because it relies on shared values and objectives, it represents a more robust and flexible means of co-ordination. Decisions reached by negotiations between knowledgeable groups with common objectives should be much better than those made by superior authority or by standard policy. (Bartlett and Ghoshal 1989: 163)

These three different approaches worked best for companies headquartered in those three regions of the globe. As the world becomes smaller and companies become more diverse with subsidiaries that are fully mature, more sophisticated methods are needed: companies are not international, but global. The influence of the parent company's national culture remains strong, but a cosmopolitan tendency is gradually blurring some of the traditional boundaries.

Any management will benefit from considering additional methods of coordination. Some of our suggestions will fit well with their current practice, adding to their strength; others will not yet seem suitable, others will not seem suitable at all. The first suggestion is summed up by using the word *evangelisation*, to describe winning the acceptance throughout the business of a common mission and a shared purpose. The need to win hearts and minds has been a thread in management thinking for many years, but it is particularly significant in the international or global business because of the number of barriers to be overcome in coordination, especially the barriers of language, culture, national boundaries and parochial self-interest.

Coordination by evangelisation works through **shared belief**. The beliefs may be interpreted in different ways and may produce varied behaviours, but there is the attempt to spread relatively simple doctrines to which members of the business subscribe and through which they are energised. It is now commonplace for companies to have mission statements, which come close to being unifying articles of faith.

Evangelisation also works through **parables.** We all love a good story and we learn from the message that the stories convey. Ed Schein (2004: 237–42) identified 'stories and legends' as one of the key mechanisms for articulating and reinforcing the organisation's culture. A corporate magazine or intranet can partly serve the purpose of circulating the good news about heroic deeds in all parts of the company network. Better are the word of mouth exchanges and accounts of personal experience. Those who visit another country have to be fully exploited when they return. Returning expatriates have stories to tell to all members of the company to which they are coming back, not just to the senior managers conducting the debriefing. Occasional visitors to other branches of the business also need to be encouraged to tell their stories. They return with important technical understandings that need to be shared, but they also return with an awareness of the visited company which can contribute to the bonding between units.

Evangelisation can use **apostles**, ambassadors sent out to preach the faith. These are those management role holders who are constantly on the move. Because of their frequent movement they know the worldwide organisation well and can describe one component to another, explaining company policy, justifying particular decisions and countering parochial thinking. They can also move ideas around ('In Seoul they are wondering about . . . what do think?') and help in the development of individual networks ('Try getting in touch with Oscar Jennings in Pittsburgh . . . he had similar problems a few weeks ago'). At times of crisis, apostles are likely to be especially busy, countering rumour and strengthening resolve. In mature companies apostles will have home bases in different regions, just as expatriates will move in various directions and not simply from the centre out, but before the business reaches maturity it will probably be important that most of the apostles come from headquarters and have personally met, and can tell stories about, the founder.

Coordination can also be improved by the development and promulgation of *standards and norms*. Many British companies have sought the accreditation of BS 5750, the British Standard for quality, others claim to be equal opportunity employers. Global companies will wish to set standards for many aspects of their operation. Cynthia Haddock (1994) describes how Shell develops and maintains standards relating to alcohol and drug abuse. If standards are adopted throughout a global company, they become a form of coordination. Furthermore it is not necessary for all of them to be developed at the centre. Decentralised standard formulation can enable different parts of the global business to take a lead as a preliminary to universal adoption of the standard they have formulated: an excellent method of integration.

There is obvious scope for coordination through *systems*. Many global businesses are dominated by a single system, which reaches every part of the business. Any international airline has a ticketing and booking system which links thousands of computer terminals in order to operate the airline. The system is only useful if it provides the global link, and provision of the systems link constantly reinforces with all personnel the interrelationship of the activities in all countries where the airline operates. Although that is a specialised example, all businesses have systems and they can be developed to avoid duplication and overlap, so that, for example, in one country a team develops a spare part retrieval system that is quickly adopted for use throughout the business, while in another country they concentrate on an aspect of accounting procedures or systematic advice on training opportunities.

A similar approach is to concentrate *capability* by encouraging the development of particular expertise in different locations, but for group-wide application and exploitation. Bartlett and Ghoshal (1989: 106) offer the intriguing example of how Teletext was developed by Philips. Because of an interest from the BBC, the British Philips subsidiary began work on the possibility of transmitting text and simple diagrams through a domestic television set. Within Philips generally it was regarded as 'a typical British toy – quite fancy but not very useful'. Despite little encouragement and sales that were initially disappointing, the British persisted. Ten years after starting work, there were three million Teletext receivers in use in Britain and Philips had established a world lead in a product for which there was initially only a British market.

Harmonisation

Across all decision making in IHRM, however organisations are structured, however good the communication systems and however well coordinated they are, there runs an ever-present and highly significant tension. This relates to the degree of harmonisation and centralisation that is possible or desirable.

Organisations want to develop strong corporate cultures and take active steps to manage culture and cultural change in order to achieve this. In nationally based corporations shaping corporate culture is straightforward provided it runs with the grain of the national culture. However, when a strong centralised corporate identity is imposed on an international company, inevitably it will run against the grain of some national cultures. The same is true of HR policies and practices. What works well in one national culture will jar in another leading to demotivation, reduced performance, lower levels of trust and recruitment/retention problems.

In-depth knowledge of local labour market conditions, expectations and attitudes is the only means of judging where to strike a balance between centralisation and diversity. A long-held mantra which sums up the best approach to take is simple:

> Think global, act local.

This means developing HR strategies for the whole global operation, but implementing them differently so as to take account of local cultural and institutional differences.

ACTIVITY 6.3

1. Think of where you work, or where you have worked, and identify three activities where global thinking needs to influence local action. What are the local people management implications of this?
2. In the same situation what aspects of local action influence, or should influence, global thinking?

MANAGING EXPATRIATES

A feature of HRM in international organisations which makes it different from HRM in a nationally based organisation is the need, on a regular basis, to post people overseas. International organisations need to have on their payroll substantial numbers of people who originate in one country, often where corporate HQ is located, but work elsewhere in an international operation. Overseas employees can be divided into a number of distinct categories:

- Engineers are staff who regularly spend short periods of a week or two overseas, often working on specific projects such as setting up new production processes.
- Cosmopolitans are a small elite group who are familiar with different countries and are comfortable dealing with different cultural contexts all the time. They travel from location to location throughout their working year, spending little more than a week or two in each country before moving on.
- Occasional parachutists are firmly based in one country, but their work takes them from time to time to sites based in other countries for a few days at a time.
- Expatriates are staff whose normal place of work is in one country, but who are sent on secondment for a period of two or three years to work overseas, usually in a relatively senior position, before returning home to their original workplace.

The management of all these groups requires some specialist knowledge and experience if it is to be carried out well, but it is expatriates who pose the biggest challenge. Unlike cosmopolitans they are not used to living overseas and will often find it hard to adjust, particularly when they take their families overseas with them. But unlike the engineers and occasional parachutists their role is long term and for the duration of their period working abroad they form an integral part of the overseas operation they are being sent to manage or work in. They also expect to be repatriated and anticipate that they will benefit from their overseas experience by gaining promotion to a more senior post.

The great majority of expatriates are men, usually married men, leading to the 'army wife' syndrome. Whether male or female the expatriate's spouse is nearly always placed in a position of total or partial dependency by corporate expatriation: one career is subordinated to another. This dependency is not only economic, it affects the social position and status that a couple have while overseas. For expatriate wives with a professional career in suspension, this can require considerable ingenuity to adapt. Because of the demands that expatriation makes on both individuals and families, it thus has to be managed carefully and thoroughly.

WINDOW ON PRACTICE

Susan Harris was an expatriate wife and mother in Malaysia, who had readily suspended a career in management consultancy so that her husband could take the career opportunity that three years in Miri on the island of Borneo offered. Provided with a house and servants on the shores of the South China Sea under perpetual sunshine in Kuala Lumpur, she dealt with the problem of enforced idleness by working voluntarily as a tutor with students taking management qualifications, at the same time as improving her own qualifications through distance learning.

Helga Nordstrom finished her executive career in the same company with a posting in Singapore, accompanied by her recently retired husband, who improved his golf handicap, became stage manager of a local amateur dramatic society and wrote a book about the Swedish history of neutrality.

Selection for expatriation

The possibility of an extended overseas assignment can come as a shock, which may or may not be welcome, presenting all the problems of considering the potential career handicap of turning down the opportunity and the potential domestic problems of accepting it. Employers seldom have the luxury of a large number of appropriately qualified people readily available to fill any vacancy, but the most satisfactory general approach to selection for expatriation is through the combination of performance management and career planning.

A feature of annual appraisal can be a discussion of whether people are interested in working overseas at all, the degree of technical expertise and managerial experience they possess and the domestic/social constraints that would affect the timing of such a move. That can then be developed by identifying timings that would be appropriate for such a move, preferred locations and even some language training. As with all career management initiatives, this sets up expectations of the future that the management may not be able to deliver because of changes in business activity, but it provides a cadre of people who would welcome an overseas move.

The particular location is the next most important determinant in matching the person to the job. Among the most important issues are:

1. **Culture**. How different from home is the culture of the country – religion, the social position of women, the degree of political stability/instability, personal security and petty crime, local press and television, cable television, availability of foreign newspapers, health hazards?
2. **Economic development**. How well developed is the economy of the country – standard/cost of living, availability of familiar foods and domestic equipment, transport, post and telephone, local poverty, health and education facilities, availability of international schools?
3. **Geographical location**. How far away is it and where is it – climate, in a cosmopolitan city or more remote, the importance/unimportance of language proficiency, the size of the local expatriate community, employment prospects of spouse?
4. **The job**. What has to be done and what is the situation, the nature of the organisation, proportion of expatriates, technical, commercial and managerial demands of the job, staffing and support, the extent of role in managing local nationals?

The most important aspect of selection is making sure that the potential appointee and members of the family have a full understanding of what will be involved. It is essential, however, that those proceeding on an overseas posting should be appropriate for it. If there is not an appropriate person in the organisation, then recruitment from outside is preferable to assigning someone about whose suitability there are doubts. There is no profile of the ideal expatriate, but here are some selection issues arranged under the four headings used already:

1 **Culture**. How well prepared is the expatriate family for an unfamiliar culture? In many ways the developed countries of Western Europe present fewer problems than those of further afield, but English is spoken more widely in Singapore than, for instance, in France. Malaysia is a multi-ethnic society, but with a Muslim majority in the population. The Muslim dominance of life in most Middle East countries has profound implications for expatriates, requiring a degree of puritanism that will be unfamiliar and a social role for women that is quite unlike that which western women experience. In the developing countries of the East there may be superb hotels, but little else to do in the evening. Manila and Bangkok have plenty of after-dark facilities for men on their own, but little for couples and even less for women on their own. Whatever the culture is, open-mindedness and tolerance are essential qualities for the expatriates to develop.
2 **Economic development**. Several Eastern countries now enjoy a standard of living and material convenience that matches or surpasses that of fortunate people in the West, so that the expatriate will find excellent systems of transportation, postal and telecommunication systems that will be similar to those of the home country. Elsewhere the situation will be very different and everyday life will require a great deal more adjustment once one is outside the air-conditioned cocoon of the multinational company's offices. Medical and dental facilities may be sparse and few expatriate families can avoid being affected by the conditions of those among whom they live. Not only may they be distressed by the living conditions they see in most parts of the Indian sub-continent and Africa, for instance, they will also have to contend with very high urban crime rates in some places.
3 **Geographical location**. This is a further twist to the economic development question. The heat and humidity of tropical climates is supportable when moving from air-conditioned home, via air-conditioned car to air-conditioned office or shopping mall. Those moving to more remote areas have greater problems in coping with the climate and the relative isolation, so they need to be emotionally self-sufficient and not too dependent on outside stimulation. The distance from home is another determinant of personal suitability to the posting. The Parisian working in Brussels could easily contemplate weekly commuting: the native of Brussels working in Madagascar could not. There will be a smaller expatriate community in most Italian cities than in Hong Kong, so that the expatriate family may have to work harder at establishing social contacts, and will therefore require considerable social skills and self-confidence. The geographical location will also determine the importance of local language proficiency for all members of the expatriate family.
4 **The job**. In a global business questions about the job may initially seem unproblematic. Many expatriates are simply moving to exercise their well-developed company expertise in a different location. The situation will, however, always be different no matter how similar the conventions and procedures. The various demands of the job need to be thoroughly considered, especially what may be involved in managing local nationals, where the subtleties of response to leadership and expectations of authority will probably still baffle the expatriate when finally on the way home from the tour of duty.

Preparing for expatriation

> While 89 per cent of companies formally assess a candidate's job skills prior to a foreign posting, less than half go through the same process for cultural suitability. Even fewer gauge whether the family will cope. (*Financial Times*, 5 March 2001)

If there is the relative luxury of a 12-month period of preparation, language training can make real progress. This comes to life most effectively when there is a strong flavour of cultural orientation and familiarisation as well, so that two of the basic requirements of preparation are dealt with simultaneously. The nature of the language training provided is usually slightly different for the expatriate employee and for the expatriate spouse. The employee will concentrate on technical and business terms, while the spouse concentrates on what will be useful in everyday matters like shopping and trying to get the washing machine repaired, or in local social contacts.

More general aspects of cultural familiarisation can be achieved by various means, often depending on the individual. Some will read avariciously, both travel books and the range of novels that have been written about most parts of the world. Others prefer film and video. Can there be any better preparation for Australian suburban life than watching several episodes of *Neighbours*?

Some companies use returned expatriates to write and present case histories about the country, with the obvious advantages that the potential expatriate can discuss with someone face to face their personal experiences in a situation which they are about to encounter. It should also be automatic for the potential expatriate to meet socially with any nationals from the country of expatriation who may be visiting the host company during the pre-departure stage.

The success of an overseas assignment will be enhanced by some previous experience overseas and some experience of the location, but brief business trips scarcely qualify as previous experience. A holiday could be better, as people on holiday usually go at least partly to see the country and the people. Much better is a visit before the move, which is made to prepare for the move. By this method it is possible to deal with such crucial issues as housing. Nothing reassures one about impending relocation so much as knowing where one is going to live. If there are children, arrangements for their schooling can also be made.

Arrangements for responsibilities in the home country during a posting abroad can be extensive. There may be children remaining in boarding schools, or elderly relatives to be catered for and pets to worry about, as well as renting the family home and many more. There may be a need for some company help, especially with financial and similar arrangements.

Travel arrangements themselves are relatively straightforward, but still have to be organised. There may be a need for family visas and one or more work permits, removal of household effects as well as personal baggage, health checks and whatever inoculations and medication are required.

Repatriation

Coming back from an overseas assignment seldom receives the attention it needs. It is not expected to be problematic and therefore receives little attention: all the problems are expected to be related to getting out and getting settled. Why should there be problems about coming home?

> The long-term implications of ineffective repatriation practices are clear: few good managers will be willing to take international assignments because they see what happened to their colleagues . . . the only people willing to take on foreign assignments in the future will be those who have not been able to succeed on the home front. (Deresky 2008: 370)

The first potential problem is the nature of the overseas experience. If it has been thoroughly satisfactory for all members of the family, with an enhanced lifestyle, plenty of career development and scope for the employee, plenty of money and an exciting experience for the family in an agreeable climate, then there may not be much initial enthusiasm for returning home, so that it will be like coming back from an extended holiday, with all the reluctance about leaving good friends and stimulating experiences to return to dreary old Barnstaple or Dusseldorf or Des Moines.

On the other hand if the overseas experience has been difficult, with a loss of social life, disagreeable climate, frustrations and disappointment at work and all sorts of petty inconveniences, then the prospect of returning home can become an obsession, with the days ticked off on the calendar and a great build-up of anticipation. When the day of return to hearth and home at last comes, Barnstaple (or Dusseldorf or Des Moines) may soon seem just a little ordinary compared with the wonderful picture that had been built up in expectation.

The second major problem is the career situation of the returning expatriate. Virtually all repatriated personnel experience some personal difficulty in reintegrating on return. There may be loss of status, loss of autonomy, lack of career direction and lack of recognition of the value of overseas experience. It may not be considered a management responsibility to fuss over a manager's personal readjustment, but an American study (Adler 1991: 238) showed that the effectiveness of expatriates took between six and 12 months to return to an acceptable level on repatriation, so there are some hard-headed reasons for taking it seriously.

ACTIVITY 6.4

Expatriate assignments frequently end in failure, in that the posting is not completed or fails to meet its initial objectives. Briscoe *et al.* (2009: 179) identify three types of expatriate failure:

- dropout (the expatriate returns home early)
- brownout (the expatriate performs poorly while overseas)
- turnover upon repatriation (the expatriate resigns shortly after returning home)

What different factors do you think contribute to each of these three types of failure? What steps can IHRM specialists take to reduce the likelihood of them happening?

SUMMARY PROPOSITIONS

6.1 The rise and proliferation of multinational organisations is both a consequence and cause of globalisation.

6.2 Understanding cultural diversity is crucial to managing an international organisation effectively. Work by Hofstede has identified four distinguishing factors of national culture: individualism, power distance, uncertainty avoidance and masculinity. He later added a fifth: Confucian dynamism or time orientation.

6.3 Institutional variation is another major determinant of differences between the prevalent approaches to HRM found in different countries.

6.4 Problems of communication in any international business are made more difficult by different frames of reference, stereotyping, cognitive dissonance and language.

6.5 Traditional forms of coordination can be roughly stereotyped as Japanese centralisation, American formalisation or European socialisation. More particular forms of coordination include evangelisation, standards and norms, systems and locating capability.

6.6 In order to maximise the likelihood that an expatriate posting will be successful, particular care must be taken when selecting, preparing and the repatriating expatriate staff.

GENERAL DISCUSSION TOPICS

1 Towards the end of the chapter different stereotypes of international employees were suggested. In terms of the employment and management do you think that distinguishing between the 'engineer' and the 'occasional parachutist' is helpful, or are they basically the same?

2 Multinational companies tend to be unpopular with social activists, who mount demonstrations against their apparent greed and serious impact on some of the societies in which they operate. What are the arguments for and against this point of view?

3 Can an HRM manager from one culture carry out a line management role working in a different culture?

FURTHER READING

Sparrow, p. (ed.) (2009) *Handbook of International Human Resource Management*. Chichester: Wiley.
Stahl, G. and Bjorkman, I. (eds) (2006) *Handbook of Research in International Human Resource Management*. Cheltenham: Edward Elgar.
Numerous books and articles are published each year about the different aspects of HRM introduced in this chapter. These recent edited volumes contain articles by academic researchers and cover the field effectively.

Steers, R., Sanchez-Runde, C. and Nardon, L. (2010) *Management Across Cultures*. Cambridge: Cambridge University Press.
This work introduces and discusses communications and cultural issues.

REFERENCES

Adler, N.J. (1991) *International Dimensions of Organizational Behavior*. Boston: PWS-Kent.

Bartlett, C.A. and Ghoshal, S. (1989) *Managing Across Borders*. London: Random House.

Bjorkman, I. (2006) 'International human resource management research and institutional theory', in G. Stahl and I. Bjorkman (eds), *Handbook of Research in International Human Resource Management*. Cheltenham: Edward Elgar.

Buchan, J. and Seccombe, I. (2009) *Difficult Times, Difficult Choices. The UK nursing labour market review 2009*. London: Royal College of Nursing.

Brandt, W.K. and Hulbert, J.M. (1976) 'Patterns of communication in the multinational company', *Journal of International Business Studies*, September, pp. 57–64.

Briscoe, D., Schuler, R. and Claus, L. (2009) *International Human Resource Management: Policies and practices for multinational enterprises*, 3rd edn. New York: Routledge.

Cooke, W.N. (2007) 'Multinational companies and global human resource strategy', in P. Boxall, J. Purcell and P. Wright (eds), *The Oxford Handbook of Human Resource Management*. Oxford: Oxford University Press.

De Cieri, H. (2007) 'Transnational firms and cultural diversity', in P. Boxall, J. Purcell and P. Wright (eds), *The Oxford Handbook of Human Resource Management*. Oxford: Oxford University Press.

Deresky, H. (2008) *International Management*, 6th edn. Upper Saddle River: Pearson Education.

Edwards, T. and Rees, C. (2006) *International Human Resource Management: Globalisation, national systems and multinational companies*. London: FT/Prentice Hall.

Haddock, C. (1994) 'How Shell's organisation and HR practices help it to be both global and local', in D.P. Torrington (ed.), *International Human Resource Management*. London: Prentice Hall International.

Hall, E. and Hall, M. (1990) *Understanding Cultural Differences*. Yarmouth: Intercultural Press.

Hodgetts, R.M. and Luthans, F. (2000) *International Management*. New York: McGraw-Hill.

Hofstede, G. (1980) *Culture's Consequences: International differences in work-related values*. Beverly Hills: Sage Publications.

Hofstede, G. (1991) *Cultures and Organizations: Software of the mind*. London: McGraw-Hill.

Hofstede, G. (2001) *Culture's Consequences: Comparing values, behaviors, institutions, and organizations across nations*. Thousand Oaks: Sage Publications.

Holden, N.J. (1992) 'Management language and Euro-communications: 1992 and beyond', in M. Berry (ed.), *Cross-Cultural Communication in Europe*, Proceedings of Conference on Cross-Cultural Communication, Helsinki. Turku: Institute for European Studies.

Holden, N.J. (1994) 'NEC: International HRM with Vision', in D.P. Torrington (ed.), *International Human Resource Management*. London: Prentice Hall International.

House, R., Hanges, P., Javidan, M., Dorfman, P. and Gupta, V. (2004) *Culture, Leadership and Organisations: The GLOBE study of 62 societies*. Thousand Oaks: Sage Publications.

Kluckhohn, C. (1954) *Culture and Behaviour*. New York: Free Press.

Lewis, R.D. (1996) *When Cultures Collide: Managing successfully across cultures*. London: Nicholas Brealey.

Marginson, P. and Meardi, G. (2009) 'Multinational companies and collective bargaining: Employment profile of MNCs'. European Industrial Relations Observatory On-line.

Moran, A. (1994) 'Ferranti-Thomson Sonar Systems: An Anglo-French venture in high tech collaboration', in D.P. Torrington (ed.), *International Human Resource Management*. London: Prentice Hall International.

Pascale, R.T. (1978) 'Communication and decision making across cultures: Japanese and American comparisons', *Administrative Science Quarterly*, March, pp. 91–110.

Ronen, S. and Shenkar, O. (1985) 'Clustering countries on attitudinal dimensions: a review and synthesis', *Academy of Management Review*, Vol. 10, No. 3, pp. 435–54.

Schein, E.H. (2004) *Organizational Culture and Leadership*. San Francisco: Jossey-Bass.

Steers, R., Sanchez-Runde, C. and Nardon, L. (2010) *Management Across Cultures*. Cambridge: Cambridge University Press.

Strodtbeck, K. (1961) *Variations in Value Orientations*. Westport: Greenwood.

Trompenaars, F. (1993) *Riding the Waves of Culture: Understanding cultural diversity in global business*. London: McGraw-Hill.

Tung, R.L. and Miller, E.L. (1990) 'Managing in the twenty-first century: the need for global orientation', *Management International Review*, Vol. 30, 1990/1991, pp. 5–18.

Whitley, R. (1999) *Divergent Capitalisms: The social structuring and change of national business systems*. Oxford: Oxford University Press.

Wright, P. and Van de Voorde, K. (2009) 'Multilevel issues in IHRM: mean differences, explained variance and moderated relationships', in P. Sparrow (ed.), *Handbook of International Human Resource Management*. Chichester: Wiley.

Part 1 CASE STUDY PROBLEM

You have just been appointed to replace the HR Director in an organisation where members of the Board felt that HR practice had become over-preoccupied with fashionable ideas and was not meeting the needs of the business and the people who worked there. They have asked you to:

1. Review the ways in which human resource management is being conducted across the entire business, within the line as well as by the HR specialists.
2. Identify aspects of best practice that are currently being employed by leading-edge HR practitioners in other organisations and which would be relevant to your situation.
3. Recommend steps to be taken as a preliminary to a possible expansion overseas, setting up small manufacturing plants in the Republic of Ireland and somewhere in South East Asia.
4. Draft proposals for a programme of strategic initiatives to enhance HRM throughout the business.

On investigation you find:

1. A scheme of employee involvement in management decision making has foundered because of resistance from two unions with members in the organisation, whose representatives were excluded from discussions about the proposals; and by reservations held by a number of senior managers, who felt that the scheme had not been properly thought through and that it was too radical a development.
2. The concept of performance management has been introduced at the same time as moves to empower line managers. Many line managers feel that empowerment means no more than taking the blame for things that go wrong, and many of their subordinates feel that they are now cut off from the centralised, expert services of the HR function.
3. Members of the HR function say that they have lost credibility and job satisfaction by a series of grandiose schemes that were not fully developed and which could not be fully implemented in a short time.
4. Reporting to you are three people:
   - Charles is long-serving Training Officer, whose opening comment to you was, 'In training I try to see it as establishing a learning community that is separate from the hurly burly of commercial operations'.
   - Henry is Employee Relations Manager, currently on holiday.
   - Susan is Personnel Manager, a recent appointee of your predecessor with the task of coordinating and developing the HR operation. Your first conversation with her

begins with her saying, 'I hope you don't mind if I speak frankly, but I am totally frustrated. Catherine (your predecessor) was off the wall. It was all about changing everything, but she had no grasp of the practicalities of running a business and knew nothing of HR. They hired her because she had a PhD in marketing, but she was hopeless. Charles lives in another world. He used to run the apprentice school in a large engineering company and was probably brilliant dealing with young lads, but simply cannot adjust.

'Henry is all right – up to a point. He certainly has his finger on the pulse about what is going on on the shop floor, but he has problems with women in positions of authority. He copes with me but Catherine was another matter. She insisted on an employee involvement scheme that was radical to an extreme, and she refused any consultation with the unions. Henry did not simply disagree with her scheme (quite rightly in my view) but it also confirmed his prejudice about women.'

Required

Produce outline proposals for the Board to consider, setting out what you would do in the first six months and in the following 12 months to deal with this situation and what you expect to achieve in that time. Include any resource implications of your proposals. *Keep whatever you prepare for this exercise, as we come back to it later in the book.*

Locate the organisation in a real context, either in a company or other organisation with which you are familiar or in a particular industry that interests you.

RESOURCING: GETTING PEOPLE IN THE RIGHT PLACES TO DO THE RIGHT THINGS

In this part of the book, we deal with the resourcing aspects of HRM, how to get the right people in the right places and how to keep them. In particular circumstances, we may also need to understand how to end the contract legally and effectively. The first major activity of the human resource specialist is to find and bring in the people that the business needs for its success. These people may not be employees; they may be consultants or subcontractors. They may be temporary, full time, part time or occasional, and the working relationship between the business and its people is the contract, which sums up the features of that relationship so that both parties know where they stand. Nearly always there is a face-to-face meeting between the parties to agree terms before the relationship begins. The process of 'coming to terms' is one of mutual assessment. Many prospective employees reject a prospective employer by deciding not to apply for a post, or by discontinuing their application. Employers usually choose between many, and often feel there are too few applicants. Once recruited, people have to be retained within the business by a series of strategies that sustain their interest and motivation as well as keeping the focus of their activities within an evolving organisation and a changing business context. Contracts end as well as begin, and we have to be sure that the arrangements to end the contract are as sound as those for it to start.

The whole resourcing process is symbolised by the mutual assessment that takes place in the selection interview: 'Is this person right for us?' and 'Is this job and situation right for me?' The answers to those questions have major implications for both parties. The uncertainty about whether or not the right answers are found at the interview is why we have to examine resourcing so closely. At the end of Part 2 you will find a case study which will help you to put these ideas into context and explore them more thoroughly.

RECRUITMENT

THE OBJECTIVES OF THIS CHAPTER ARE TO:

1. Identify alternative courses of action to take when an employee leaves an organisation
2. Explain the role played by job descriptions, person specifications and competencies in the recruitment process
3. Compare and contrast the major alternative recruitment methods
4. Assess developments in recruitment advertising and online recruitment
5. Explore the concept of employer branding
6. Clarify the need for control and evaluation procedures in recruitment
7. Assess different approaches to shortlisting

Recruitment 'includes those practices and activities carried out by the organization with the primary purpose of identifying and attracting potential employees' (Breaugh and Starke 2000: 45). There is always a need for replacement employees and those with new skills that business growth or change make necessary. In 2006, the Institute for Employment Research estimated that UK employers would create an additional 1.3 million jobs before 2014. While economic forecasts have altered radically in the intervening period, skills shortages persist in certain sectors despite overall recruitment demand declining. It is clear that effective recruitment remains a central HR objective whether labour markets are tight or slack. Recruitment is also an area in which there are important social and legal implications, but perhaps most important is the significant part played in the lives of individual men and women by their personal experience of recruitment and the failure to be recruited. Virtually everyone reading these pages will know how significant those experiences have been in their own lives.

WINDOW ON PRACTICE

On graduating from university, Howard was employed as a management trainee by a large bank and was soon assigned to taking part in interviews of prospective graduate recruits, which he found interesting and a boost to his ego. After two years in the bank a programme of reorganisation led to Howard being out of a job. It was seven months before he was employed again and he had undergone many disappointments and frustrations. His new post was again in recruitment and he wrote himself a short homily on a postcard which he kept propped up on his desk. It said:

When you turn someone down, remember:
First, what the experience of rejection can do to a person.
Second, that the rejected person may be a customer.
Third, you may want to recruit that person later.

Over three million people are recruited by employers in the UK each year. It can be a costly and difficult process, with nearly three-quarters of employers experiencing difficulties recruiting for specialist skills (CIPD 2009). In such circumstances the employer needs to 'sell' its jobs to potential employees so as to ensure that it can generate an adequate pool of applicants, but even then for some groups of staff it can be difficult to find people who are both willing and able to fill the vacancies that are available. Even where it is easier to attract applicants, it is still an expensive business with an average cost of £4,000 per employee, rising to £6,125 when the associated labour turnover costs are included (CIPD 2009). However, as Barber (1998) points out, it is important that employers do not consider the recruitment process to be finished at the point at which a pool of applications has been received. It continues during the shortlisting and interviewing stages and is only complete when an offer is made and accepted. Until that time there is an ongoing need to ensure that a favourable impression of the organisation as an employer is maintained in the minds of those whose services it wishes to secure. That said, it is also important to avoid overselling a job in a bid to secure the services of talented applicants. Making out that the experience of working in a role is more interesting or exciting than it really is may be ultimately counterproductive because it raises unrealistic expectations which can damage the psychological contract established with the organisation. This can lead to demotivation and, perhaps, an early resignation. You will find further information and discussion exercises about realistic recruitment in Case 7.1 on our companion website **www.pearsoned.co.uk/torrington.**

DETERMINING THE VACANCY

The first questions to be answered in recruitment are: Is there a vacancy? Is it to be filled by a newly recruited employee? Potential vacancies occur either through someone leaving, as a result of expansion or organisational change requiring new skills. When a person leaves, there is no more than a prima facie case for filling the vacancy thus caused. There may be other ways of filling the gap. Vacancies caused by expansion may be real or imagined. The desperately pressing need of an executive for an assistant may be a plea more for recognition than for assistance. The creation of a new post to deal with a specialist activity may be more appropriately handled by contracting that activity out to a supplier. Recruiting a new employee may be the most obvious tactic when a vacancy occurs, but it is not necessarily the most appropriate. This is clearly the case in periods of economic turmoil, when many employers may wish to think more creatively about how to deal with a vacancy. Listed below are some of the options, several of which we discuss in Chapter 4:

- Reorganise the work
- Use overtime
- Mechanise the work
- Stagger the hours
- Make the job part time
- Subcontract the work
- Use an agency

ACTIVITY 7.1

Can you think of further ways of avoiding filling a vacancy by recruiting a new employee? What are the advantages and disadvantages of the methods you have thought of? For what types of job with which you are familiar would each of your methods, and those listed above, be most appropriate?

If your decision is that you are going to recruit, there are four questions to determine the vacancy:

1. What does the job consist of?
2. In what way is it to be different from the job done by the previous incumbent?
3. What are the aspects of the job that specify the type of candidate?
4. What are the key aspects of the job that the ideal candidate wants to know before deciding to apply?

The conventional HR approach to these questions is to produce job descriptions and personnel specifications. Methods of doing this are well established. Good accounts are provided by Pearn and Kandola (1988), Brannick and Levine (2002) and IRS (2003). The approach involves breaking the job down into its component parts, working out what its chief objectives will be and then recording this on paper. A person specification listing the key attributes required to undertake the role can then be derived from the job description and used in recruiting the new person. An example of a job description is given in Figure 7.1.

Job title: SENIOR SALES ASSISTANT

Context
The job is in one of the 13 high-technology shops owned by 'Computext'
Location: Leeds
Supervised by, and reports directly to, the Shop Manager
Responsible for one direct subordinate: Sales Assistant

Job summary
To assist and advise customers in the selection of computer hardware and software, and to arrange delivery and finance where appropriate.
Objective is to sell as much as possible, and to ensure that customers and potential customers see 'Computext' staff as helpful and efficient.

Job content
Most frequent duties in order of importance

1 Advise customers about hardware and software.
2 Demonstrate the equipment and software.
3 Organise delivery of equipment by liaising with distribution department.
4 Answer all after-sales queries from customers.
5 Contact customers two weeks after delivery to see if they need help.
6 Advise customers about the variety of payment methods.
7 Develop and keep up to date a computerised stock control system.

Occasional duties in order of importance

1 Arrange for faulty equipment to be replaced.
2 Monitor performance of junior sales assistant as defined in job description.
3 Advise and guide, train and assess junior sales assistant where necessary.

Working conditions
Pleasant, 'business-like' environment in new purpose-built shop premises in the city centre. There are two other members of staff and regular contact is also required with the Delivery Department and Head Office. Salary is £18,000 p.a. plus a twice yearly bonus, depending on sales. Five weeks' holiday per year plus statutory holidays. A six-day week is worked.

Other information
There is the eventual possibility of promotion to shop manager in another location depending on performance and opportunities.

Performance standards
There are two critically important areas:

1 Sales volume. Minimum sales to the value of £700,000 over each six-month accounting period.
2 Relations with customers:
   - Customers' queries answered immediately.
   - Customers always given a demonstration when they request one.
   - Delivery times arranged to meet both customer's and delivery department's needs.
   - Complaints investigated immediately.
   - Customers assured that problem will be resolved as soon as possible.
   - Customers never blamed.
   - Problems that cannot be dealt with referred immediately to Manager.

Figure 7.1 Job description for a senior sales assistant

An alternative approach which allows for more flexibility is to dispense with the job description and to draw up a person specification using other criteria. One way of achieving this is to focus on the characteristics or competences of current job holders who are judged to be excellent performers. Instead of asking 'What attributes are necessary to undertake this role?' this second method involves asking 'What attributes are shared by the people who have performed best in the role?' According to some (for example Whiddett and Kandola 2000), the disadvantage of the latter approach is that it tends to produce employees who are very similar to one another and who address problems with the same basic mindset (corporate clones). This has also led to the suggestion that competency-based approaches can present a barrier to achieving an organisation's equality and diversity objectives (Kirton and Healy 2009). Where innovation and creativity are required, it is helpful to recruit people with more diverse characteristics, and the use of competencies may constrain this.

INTERNAL RECRUITMENT

Vacancies, of course, are often filled internally, creating what are referred to as 'internal labour markets'. Sometimes organisations advertise all vacancies publicly as a matter of course and consider internal candidates along with anyone from outside the organisation who applies. This approach is generally considered to constitute good practice, especially in respect of equality of opportunity and diversity, and is widely used in the UK public sector. However, many organisations prefer to invite applications from internal candidates *before* they look to external labour markets for new staff (Newell and Shackleton 2000; CIPD 2009). There are considerable advantages for the employer: it is much less expensive with no need for job advertisements or recruitment agencies. Instead a message can simply be placed in a company newsletter or posted on its intranet or staff noticeboards. Further cost savings and efficiency gains can be made because internal recruits are typically able to take up new posts much more quickly than people being brought in from outside. Even if they have to work some notice in their current positions, they are often able to take on some of their new responsibilities or undergo relevant training at the same time. The other advantage stems from the fact that internal candidates, as a rule, are more knowledgeable than new starters coming in from other organisations about what exactly the job involves. They are also more familiar with the organisation's culture, rules and geography, and so take less time to settle into their new jobs and to begin working at full capacity.

Giving preference to internal recruits, particularly for promotions, has the great advantage of providing existing employees with an incentive to work hard, demonstrate their commitment and stay with the organisation when they might otherwise consider looking for alternative employment. The practice sends a strong signal from management that existing employees are valued and that attractive career development opportunities are available to them. Failing to recruit internally may thus serve to put off good candidates with potential from applying for the more junior positions in an organisation.

The main disadvantage of only advertising posts internally is that a limited field of candidates are considered. While it may mean that someone who 'fits in well' is recruited, it may also mean that the best available candidate is not even considered. Over the long term the organisation can thus end up being less well served than it would have been had internal candidates been required to compete with outside people for their posts. For this reason internal recruitment sits uneasily with a commitment to equal opportunities and to the creation of a diverse workforce. Talented candidates from under-represented groups are not appointed because they never get to know about the vacancies that the organisation has.

It is also important to note that the management of internal recruitment practices is difficult to carry out effectively. Research carried out by the Institute of Employment Studies (2002) shows that serious problems often occur when internal candidates fail to be selected. This is because they tend to enter the selection process with higher expectations of being offered the position than is the case with external candidates. Bitterness, antipathy and low morale are thus likely to follow. Moreover, failed internal candidates are considerably more likely to pursue claims of unfair discrimination following a selection process than external candidates. For these reasons it is essential that great care is taken when managing internal recruitment to ensure that the approach taken is both fair and seen to be fair. Giving honest, full, accurate and constructive feedback to failed candidates is an essential part of the process.

METHODS OF RECRUITMENT

Once an employer has decided that external recruitment is necessary, a cost-effective and appropriate method of recruitment must be selected. There are a number of distinct approaches to choose from, each of which is more or less appropriate in different circumstances. As a result most employers use a wide variety of different recruitment methods at different times. In many situations there is also a good case for using different methods in combination when looking to fill the same vacancy. Table 7.1 sets out the usage of different methods reported in a recent CIPD survey of 755 UK employers (CIPD 2009).

It is interesting to compare the figures in Table 7.1 with those reported in surveys of how people actually find their jobs in practice. These repeatedly show that informal methods (such as word of mouth and making unsolicited applications) are as common as, if not more common than, formal methods such as recruitment advertising, especially in sectors such as retail and hospitality (Warhurst and Nickson 2007). In 2002, the Labour

Table 7.1 Usage of various methods of recruitment by 755 employers in 2009

Method	Usage
Corporate website	78%
Recruitment agencies	76%
Local newspaper advertisements	70%
Specialist journals and trade press	55%
Employee referral scheme	46%
Job Centre Plus	43%
Education liaison	34%
National newspaper advertisements	31%
Search consultants	31%
Commercial job boards	29%
Apprenticeships	25%
Secondments	23%
Social networking sites, e.g. LinkedIn	7%

Source: Table compiled from data in CIPD (2009) *Recruitment, Retention and Turnover: Annual Survey Report*. London: CIPD.

Table 7.2 Methods of obtaining a job

	Men	Women
Hearing from someone who worked there	30%	25%
Reply to an advertisement	25%	31%
Direct application	14%	17%
Private employment agency	10%	10%
Job centre	9%	8%
Other	12%	9%

Source: *Labour Market Trends* (2002) 'Labour market spotlight', August.

Force Survey asked over a million people how they had obtained their current job. The results are shown in Table 7.2.

THE RECRUITMENT METHODS COMPARED

All the various methods of recruitment have benefits and drawbacks, and the choice of a method has to be made in relation to the particular vacancy and the type of labour market in which the job falls. A general review of advantages and drawbacks is given in Table 7.3.

ACTIVITY 7.2

We have seen the significance of informal methods of recruitment whereby new employees come as a result of hearing about a vacancy from friends, or putting their names down for consideration when a vacancy occurs. Employees starting employment in this way present the employer with certain advantages as they come knowing that they were not wooed by the employer: the initiative was theirs. Also they will probably have some contacts in the company already who will help them to settle and cope with the induction crisis. What are the drawbacks of this type of arrangement?

RECRUITMENT ADVERTISING

In order to assist them in drafting advertisements and placing them in suitable media, many employers deal with a recruitment advertising agency. Such agencies provide expert advice on where to place advertisements and how they should be worded and will design them attractively to achieve maximum impact. Large organisations often subcontract all their advertising work to an agency operating on the basis of a service-level agreement.

Recruitment advertising companies (as opposed to headhunters and recruitment consultants) are often inexpensive because the agency derives much of its income from the commission paid by the journals on the value of the advertising space sold, the bigger agencies being able to negotiate substantial discounts because of the amount of business they place with the newspapers and trade journals. A portion of this saving is then passed

Table 7.3 Advantages and drawbacks of traditional methods of recruitment

Job centres		
Advantages:	(a)	Applicants can be selected from nationwide sources with convenient, local availability of computer-based data.
	(b)	Socially responsible and secure.
	(c)	Can produce applicants very quickly.
	(d)	Free service for employers.
Drawbacks:	(a)	Registers are mainly of the unemployed rather than of the employed seeking a change.
	(b)	Produces people for interview who are not genuinely interested in undertaking the job.
Commercial employment agencies and recruitment consultancies		
Advantages:	(a)	Established as the normal method for filling certain vacancies, e.g. secretaries in London.
	(b)	Little administrative chore for the employer.
Drawbacks:	(a)	Can produce staff who are likely to stay only a short time.
	(b)	Widely distrusted by employers.
	(c)	Can be very expensive.
Management selection consultants		
Advantages:	(a)	Opportunity to elicit applicants anonymously.
	(b)	Opportunity to use expertise of consultant in an area where employer will not be regularly in the market.
Drawbacks:	(a)	Internal applicants may feel, or be, excluded.
	(b)	Cost.
Executive search consultants ('headhunters')		
Advantages:	(a)	Known individuals can be approached directly.
	(b)	Useful if employer has no previous experience in specialist field.
	(c)	Recruiting from, or for, an overseas location.
Drawbacks:	(a)	Cost.
	(b)	Potential candidates outside the headhunter's network are excluded.
	(c)	Recruits remain on the consultant's list and can be hunted again.
Visiting universities		
Advantages:	(a)	The main source of new graduates from universities.
	(b)	Rated by students as the most popular method.
Drawbacks:	(a)	Need to differentiate presentations from those of other employers.
	(b)	Time taken to visit a number of universities (i.e. labour intensive).
Schools and the Careers Service		
Advantages:	(a)	Can produce a regular annual flow of interested enquirers.
	(b)	Very appropriate for the recruitment of school-leavers, who seldom look further than the immediate locality for their first employment.
Drawbacks:	(a)	Schools and the advisers are more interested in occupations than organisations.
	(b)	Taps into a limited potential applicant pool.

on to the employer so that it can easily be cheaper *and* a great deal more effective to work with an agent providing this kind of service. The HR manager placing, say, £50,000 of business annually with an agency will appreciate that the agency's income from that will be between £5,000 and £7,500, and will expect a good standard of service. The important questions relate to the experience of the agency in dealing with recruitment, as compared with other types of advertising, the quality of the advice they can offer about media choice and the quality of response that their advertisements produce.

In choosing where to place a recruitment advertisement the aim is to attract as many people as possible with the required skills and qualifications and to reach people who are either actively looking for a new job or thinking about doing so. The need is therefore to place the advertisement where job seekers who are qualified to take on the role are most likely to look. Except in very tight labour markets, where large numbers of staff are required at the same time, there is no point in placing a recruitment advertisement outside a newspaper's or journal's recruitment pages. In some situations, newspaper readership figures are helpful when deciding where to advertise. An example would be where there are two or more established trade journals or local newspapers competing with one another, both of which carry numerous recruitment advertisements. Otherwise readership figures are unimportant because people tend to buy different newspapers when job searching than they do the rest of the time. It is often more helpful to look at the share of different recruitment advertising markets achieved by the various publications, as this gives an indication of where particular types of job are mostly advertised. For example, in the UK in recent years the *Guardian* newspaper has gained and sustained a substantial share of national recruitment advertising for jobs in the media, education and the public sector. For the more senior private sector jobs, however, the established market leaders are the *Daily Telegraph*, the *Sunday Times* and the *Financial Times*. While recruitment advertising agents are well placed to advise on these issues, it is straightforward to get hold of information about rates charged by different publications and their respective market shares. Good starting points are the websites of British Rate and Data (**www.brad.co.uk**), which carries up-to-date information about thousands of publications, and the National Readership Survey (**www.nrs.co.uk**) which provides details of readership levels among different population groups. Table 7.4 reviews the advantages and drawbacks of various methods of job advertising.

Drafting the advertisement

The decision on what to include in a recruitment advertisement is important because of the high cost of space and the need to attract attention; both factors will encourage the use of the fewest number of words. Where agencies are used they will be able to advise on this, as they will on the way the advertisement should be worded, but the following is a short checklist of items that must be included.

- Name and brief details of employing organisation
- Job role and duties
- Training to be provided
- Key points of the personnel specification or competency profile
- Salary
- Instructions about how to apply

Many employers are reluctant to declare the salary that will accompany the advertised post. Sometimes this is reasonable as the salary scales are well known and inflexible, as in much public sector employment. Elsewhere the reluctance is due either to the fact that the employer has a general secrecy policy about salaries and does not want to publicise

Table 7.4 The advantages and drawbacks of various methods of job advertising

Internal advertisement		
Advantages:	(a)	Maximum information to all employees, who might then act as recruiters.
	(b)	Opportunity for all internal candidates to apply.
	(c)	If an internal candidate is appointed, there is a shorter induction period.
	(d)	Speed.
	(e)	Cost.
Drawbacks:	(a)	Limit to number of applicants.
	(b)	Internal candidates not matched against those from outside.
	(c)	May be unlawful if indirect discrimination. (*See* Chapter 21.)
Vacancy lists outside premises		
Advantage:	(a)	Economical way of advertising, particularly if premises are near a busy thoroughfare.
Drawbacks:	(a)	Vacancy list likely to be seen by few people.
	(b)	Usually possible to put only barest information, like the job title, or even just 'Vacancies'.
Advertising in the national press		
Advantages:	(a)	Advertisement reaches large numbers.
	(b)	Some national newspapers are the accepted medium for search by those seeking particular posts.
Drawbacks:	(a)	Cost.
	(b)	Much of the cost 'wasted' in reaching inappropriate people.
Advertising in the local press		
Advantages:	(a)	Recruitment advertisements more likely to be read by those seeking local employment.
	(b)	Little 'wasted' circulation.
Drawback:	(a)	Local newspapers appear not to be used by professional and technical people seeking vacancies.
Advertising in the technical press		
Advantage:	(a)	Reaches a specific population with minimum waste.
Drawbacks:	(a)	Relatively infrequent publication may require advertising copy six weeks before appearance of advertisement.
	(b)	Inappropriate when a non-specialist is needed, or where the specialism has a choice of professional publications.
Internet		
Advantages:	(a)	Information about a vacancy reaches many people.
	(b)	Inexpensive once a website has been constructed.
	(c)	Speed with which applications are sent in.
	(d)	Facilitates online shortlisting.
Drawbacks:	(a)	Can produce thousands of unsuitable applications.
	(b)	Worries about confidentiality may deter good applications.

the salary of a position to be filled for fear of dissatisfying holders of other posts, or to the fact that the employer does not know what to offer and is waiting to see 'what the mail brings'. All research evidence, however, suggests that a good indication of the salary is essential if the employer is to attract a useful number of appropriate replies (*see* Barber 1998: 42–3).

ACTIVITY 7.3

Table 7.5 contains phrases about the value in pay terms of 12 different jobs. Try putting them in rank order of actual cash value to the recipient. Then ask a friend to do the same thing and compare your lists.

Table 7.5 Phrases from a quality newspaper about salary

1	*c.*£60,000 + bonus + car + benefits
2	from *c.*£35k
3	£30,000–£40,000 + substantial bonus + car
4	You will already be on a basic annual salary of not less than £40,000
5	Six-figure remuneration + profit share + benefits
6	*c.*£60,000 package
7	Attractive package
8	Substantial package
9	£50,000 OTE, plus car and substantial benefits
10	£ excellent + benefits
11	£ Neg.
12	*c.*£60k package + banking benefits

ONLINE RECRUITMENT

The use of the Internet for recruitment purposes is one of the most striking recent developments in the field, but its practical significance remains a question of debate. Initially, it was predicted that it would revolutionise the recruitment industry and that most of us would find out about jobs online. It now appears that these predictions greatly overstated the influence of the Internet. A recent review of the use and success of online recruitment methods in the UK (Parry and Tyson 2008) draws the conclusion that, while the use of online recruitment methods is now widespread among many organisations, its use has not dominated the recruitment market in the way predicted.

Online recruitment can draw on either corporate or commercial websites, the former being by far the more popular (see Table 7.1). Corporate websites, i.e. the employer's own website, advertise jobs alongside information about the products and services offered by the organisation. Commercial websites, provided by cyber-agencies, combine the roles traditionally played by both newspapers and employment agents. They advertise the job and undertake shortlisting before they send on a selection of suitable CVs to the employer.

For employers the principal attraction of online recruitment is that it allows jobs to be advertised inexpensively to a potential audience of millions. According to Frankland (2000) the cost of setting up a good website is roughly equivalent to that associated with advertising a single high-profile job in a national newspaper. Huge savings can also be made by dispensing with the need to print glossy recruitment brochures and other documents to send to potential candidates. It is also a method that is easy for both candidates and employer to use. The other big advantage is speed. People can respond within seconds of reading about an opportunity by emailing their CV to the employer.

Shortlisting can also be undertaken quickly with the use of CV-matching software or online application forms.

In principle online recruitment has a great deal to offer. In practice, however, there are major problems. A key drawback is the way that employers advertising jobs tend to be bombarded with hundreds of applications, many of which are unsuitable for the position advertised. This occurs because of the large number of people who read the advertisement and because it takes so little effort to email a copy of a pre-prepared CV to the employer concerned. A further concern is the high number of applications received from non-UK citizens who do not have the necessary permits to work in the UK. Online recruitment can then be resource intensive, although it is possible to make use of online shortlisting software which is able to screen out unsuitable applications. Such technologies, however, are not wholly satisfactory. Those which work by looking for key words in CVs inevitably have a 'hit and miss' character and can be criticised for being inherently unfair. The possibility that good candidates may not be considered simply because they have not chosen a particular word or phrase is strong. The same is true of online application systems which include a handful of 'killer' questions designed to sift out unsuitable candidates at a very early stage. The tendency is for people who have a somewhat unconventional career background simply to be disregarded when, in fact, they may have the required talent or potential to do an excellent job. Conversely, online recruitment may not target passive job seekers or reach a diverse population of job seekers and thus may fail to generate applications from potentially suitable candidates.

It is possible to require candidates to apply online by completing a psychometric test. This approach has the advantage of deterring candidates who are not prepared to invest the time and effort required to complete the forms, but is unreliable in important respects – there is no guarantee that the test is in fact being completed by the candidate, nor is it completed within a standard, pre-determined time limit. Other problems concern fears about security and confidentiality which serve to deter people from submitting personal details over the web:

> Everybody should be familiar with the fear of using a credit card on-line even though good e-commerce sites have secure servers that enable these transactions to take place safely. The job-seeker's equivalent of this is 'how safe is it to put my CV on-line?' Although the figures prove that plenty of people have overcome this fear (there are an estimated 4.5 million CVs on-line), horror stories of candidates' CVs ending up on their employer's desktop aren't entirely without foundation. (Weekes 2000: 35)

There have been criticisms of poor ethical standards on the part of cyber-agencies. As with conventional employment agents there are a number who employ sharp practices such as posting fictional vacancies and falsely inflating advertised pay rates in order to build up a bank of CVs which can be circulated to employers on an unsolicited basis. Some cyber-agencies also copy CVs from competitors' sites and send them on to employers without authorisation. Over time, as the industry grows, professional standards will be established and a regulatory regime established, but for the time being such problems remain.

The fact that there are so many drawbacks alongside the advantages explains why so many employers appear to use the Internet for recruitment while rating it relatively poorly in terms of its effectiveness. While employers rank the Internet highly vis-à-vis other methods in terms of its cost effectiveness, they are much less convinced when asked about the quality of applicants and the ability of web-based advertising to source the right candidates (IRS 2005: 45). While it is commonly used for graduates, knowledge workers and middle management jobs, it is often felt to be less appropriate for blue-collar and senior management jobs and for targeting groups such as older workers or women returners. Established approaches such as newspaper advertising and education liaison are much more highly rated and are thus unlikely to be replaced by online recruitment in the near future. However, over the longer term, technological developments and increased web usage may improve the effectiveness of online recruitment considerably, especially given the increasing access many have to broadband-Internet connections at home, while many more can access the web speedily at work, in a library, job centre, educational institution or Internet café. This may ultimately lead to a situation in which anyone seeking a new job in a particular field will make a familiar website rather than the newspaper or journal their first port of call.

WINDOW ON PRACTICE

In 2000 an unemployed 53–year-old electronics manager called David Hall took part in a project commissioned by Wynnwith, an established recruitment company. He spent three months unsuccessfully looking for a job using the services of 12 well-known cyber-agencies. He registered with each, giving full details of his background and skills. At the end of the period he concluded that 'these sites appear to offer little more than pretty coloured graphics and empty promises about job opportunities'. He was offered one interview during the 12 weeks, for a role that was unsuitable given his experience. Of the hundreds of job opportunities emailed to him, he reckoned that only 5 per cent matched his capabilities. Among his criticisms were the following:

- the same jobs were advertised week after week
- very little information was provided about most vacancies
- salary levels were inflated to make jobs more appealing
- he received no feedback on applications that failed
- he was concerned that his CV was being circulated without his consent
- his emails were often not acknowledged

Source: 'Online Recruitment Study' at **www.wynnwith.com.**

Another emerging debate around the use of technology in recruitment centres on 'surveillance' (Searle 2004) and the extent to which it is appropriate to use information gathered from, for example, social networking sites such as Facebook in recruitment and selection decisions. A benign perspective on the collection of candidate data through online recruitment may lead to the suggestion that organisations can develop databases of candidates suitable for current and future vacancies and thus create a 'talent pool' (Parry and Tyson 2008). More critical analyses have, however, suggested that there are issues of concern around privacy and equity and that information can be used in unintended ways (Searle 2004). There has also been a flurry of interest around using Web 2.0 technologies for recruitment. As with other online recruitment methods, the initial importance attached to these has not borne fruit, with relatively few employers using platforms such as Twitter or Secondlife for recruitment purposes (*People Management* 2009). There have, however, been a number of well-publicised cases surrounding information made available on, for example, Facebook to influence recruitment decisions in a way detrimental to candidates. This is an area in which practice precedes research and in which there are doubtless still many debates to be had on appropriate uses of such technologies.

EMPLOYER BRANDING

In recent years, considerable interest has developed in employer branding, which advocates competing for staff by borrowing techniques long used in marketing goods and services to potential customers. In particular, many organisations have sought to position themselves as 'employers of choice' in their labour markets with a view to attracting stronger applications from potential employees. Those who have succeeded have often found that their recruitment costs fall as a result because they get so many more unsolicited applications.

Central to these approaches is the development over time of a positive **'brand image'** of the organisation as an employer, so that potential employees come to regard working there as highly desirable. This approach has been used to positive effect by a number of public sector employers offering jobs that are presented as intrinsically rewarding rather than highly remunerated when recruiting, for example, teachers, social workers and police officers. It is also used in the voluntary sector to appeal to potential employees whose values match those of the organisation (Nickson *et al.* 2008). However, developing a good brand image is an easier task for larger companies with household names than for those which are smaller or highly specialised, but the possibility of developing and sustaining a reputation as a good employer is something from which all organisations stand to benefit.

The key, as when branding consumer products, is to build on any aspect of the working experience that is different from that offered by other organisations competing in the same broad applicant pool. It may be relatively high pay or a generous benefits package, it may be flexible working, or a friendly and informal atmosphere, strong career development potential or job security. This is then developed as a 'unique selling proposition' and forms the basis of the employer branding exercise. The best way of finding out what is distinctive and positive about working in your organisation is to carry out some form of staff attitude survey. Employer branding exercises simply amount to a waste of time and money when they are not rooted in the actual lived experience of employees because people are attracted to the organisation on false premises. As with claims made for products that do not live up to their billing, the employees gained are not subsequently retained, and resources are wasted recruiting people who resign quickly after starting.

Once the unique selling propositions have been identified they can be used to inform all forms of communication that the organisation engages in with potential and actual applicants. The aim must be to repeat the message again and again in advertisements, in recruitment literature, on Internet sites and at careers fairs. It is also important that existing employees are made aware of their employer's brand proposition, both as it forms the basis of their own psychological contract with the organisation and because so much recruitment is carried out informally through word of mouth. Provided the message is accurate and provided it is communicated effectively over time, the result will be a 'leveraging of the brand' as more and more people in the labour market begin to associate the message with the employer.

While branding emerged initially as a response to the difficulties of recruiting in tight labour markets, it has been suggested recently that it also has an important role to play during recessions when labour markets are slacker. We reflect some of the key messages from a recent *People Management* (2009) guide in the Window on practice that follows.

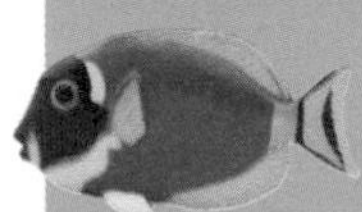

WINDOW ON PRACTICE

An employer brand that fails to live up to its messages will be found out quickly – particularly in a downturn when trust is at a premium. Difficult economic times can test a brand's values and responses such as dismissing employees by text or imposing pay cuts without consultation can destroy employer brand equity overnight. This is likely to have implications both for current employees and for the organisation's ability to recruit in the future. Companies need to maintain communications with potential employees even though they may not be in a position to recruit immediately in order to maintain a positive image for when it is required. For example, KPMG, despite having filled all its graduate vacancies in 2009, is taking great pains to keep applicants up to date about posts to be filled, how the situation is changing and inviting them to register on the website if they want to stay in touch with the firm about future vacancies. In this way, it hopes to stay ahead in the 'war for talent' in times of greater prosperity.

Source: *People Management* 2009.

CONTROL AND EVALUATION

The HR manager needs to monitor the effectiveness of advertising and all other methods of recruitment, first, to ensure value for money and, second, to ensure that the pool of applicants produced by the various methods is suitable. Breaugh and Starke (2000) present a model of the organisational recruitment process which outlines a number of possible recruitment objectives and their links to successful recruitment outcomes. This is reproduced as Figure 7.2.

This is potentially a useful model in helping organisations to decide which objectives to adopt; they must then ensure that they have robust processes for collecting data to evaluate the extent to which relevant objectives have been achieved. There is also a good case for monitoring to ensure equality of opportunity is apparent across the recruitment process, in terms, for example, of gender, ethnic origin, reviewing those who are successful at each stage of the process and taking remedial action where an imbalance becomes apparent.

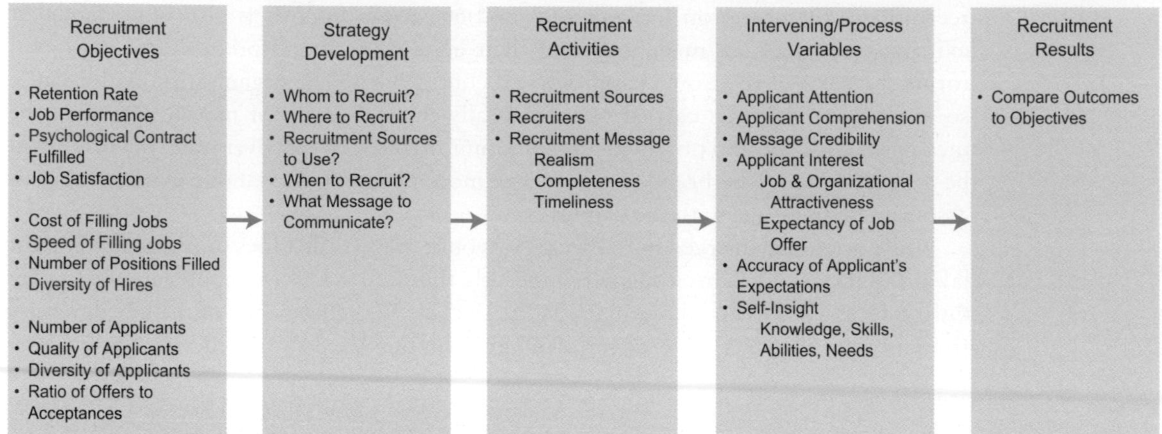

Figure 7.2 A model of the organisational recruitment process
Source: J. Breaugh and M. Starke (2000) 'Research on employee recruitment: so many studies, so many remaining questions', *Journal of Management*, Vol. 26, No. 3, pp. 405–34.

There needs, however, to be more information than this in order to get to the more intangible questions, such as 'Did the best candidate not even apply?' The most important source of information about the quality of the recruitment process is the people involved in it. Do telephonists and receptionists know how to handle the tentative employment enquiry? What did they hear from applicants in the original enquiries that showed the nature of their reaction to the advertisement? Is it made simple for enquirers to check key points by telephone or personal visit? Is there an unnecessary emphasis on written applications before anything at all can be done? Useful information can also be obtained from both successful and unsuccessful applicants. Those who have been successful will obviously believe that recruitment was well done, while the unsuccessful may have good reason to believe that it was flawed. However, those who are unsuccessful sometimes ask for feedback on the reasons. If a recruiter is able to give this, it is also a simple extension of this process to ask the applicant for comment on the recruitment process.

CORRESPONDENCE

If an organisation is to maximise its chances of recruiting the best people to the jobs it advertises it must ensure that all subsequent communication with those who express an interest is carried out professionally. The same is true of casual enquirers and those who find out about possible vacancies informally through word of mouth. Failing to make a positive impression may well result in good candidates losing interest or developing a preference for a rival organisation which takes greater care to project itself effectively in its labour markets. This is known as the 'social process' model of recruitment (Nickson *et al.* 2008) and supports the focus on employer branding and the formation of the psychological contract during recruitment: the recruitment process is two way, with candidates making decisions about prospective employers as well as vice versa and it is important to create a positive impression with potential employees. Providing information to would-be candidates who express an interest is the first step. This is often seen as unnecessary and costly, but it should be seen as the organisation's opportunity to sell itself as an employer to its potential applicant pool. The following are commonly provided:

- a copy of the relevant job description and personnel specification;
- a copy of the advertisement for reference purposes;
- a copy of any general recruitment brochure produced by the organisation;
- the staff handbook or details of a collective agreement;
- details of any occupational pension arrangements;
- general information about the organisation (e.g. a mission statement, annual report or publicity brochures).

It is also essential to have some method of tracking recruitment, either manually or by computer, so that an immediate and helpful response can be given to applicants enquiring about the stage their application has reached. Moreover, it is necessary to ensure that all applicants are informed about the outcome of their application. This will reduce the number of enquiries that have to be handled, but it is also an important aspect of public relations, as the organisation dealing with job applicants may also be dealing with prospective customers. Many people have the experience of applying for a post and then not hearing anything at all. Particularly when the application is unsolicited, HR managers may feel that there is no obligation to reply, but this could be bad business as well as disconcerting for the applicant. Standard letters ('I regret to inform you that there were many applications and yours was not successful . . .') are better than nothing, but letters containing actual information ('out of the 72 applications, we included yours in our first shortlist of 15, but not in our final shortlist of eight') are better. Best of all are the letters that make practical suggestions, such as applying again in six months' time, asking if the applicant would like to be considered for another post elsewhere in the organisation, or pointing out the difficulty of applying for a post that calls for greater experience or qualifications than the applicant at that stage is able to present.

ACTIVITY 7.4

Recruiters are interested in the job to be done, so that they concentrate on how the vacancy fits into the overall structure of the organisation and on the type of person to be sought. Applicants are interested in the work to be done, as they want to know what they will be doing and what the work will offer to them. Think of your own job and list both types of feature.

The job to be done:	The work that is offered:
1	1
2	2
3	3
4	4
5	5

How does your listing of features in the second list alter the wording of advertisements and other employment documentation?

SHORTLISTING

Shortlisting of candidates can be difficult in some instances because of small numbers of applicants and in other instances because of extremely large numbers of applicants. Such difficulties can arise unintentionally when there is inadequate specification of the criteria required or intentionally in large-scale recruitment exercises such as those associated with an annual intake of graduates.

In such circumstances it is tempting for the HR department to use some form of arbitrary method to reduce the numbers to a more manageable level. Examples include screening people out because of their handwriting style or because their work history is perceived as being unconventional in some way. No doubt there are other whimsical criteria adopted by managers appalled at making sense of 100 or so application forms and assorted curricula vitae. Apart from those that are unlawful, these criteria are grossly unfair to applicants if not mentioned in the advertisement, and are a thoroughly unsatisfactory way of recruiting the most appropriate person.

It is far more satisfactory to have in place a fair and objective system for shortlisting candidates which produces the best group of alternative candidates to move forward to the interview stage. This can be achieved in one of three basic ways – which can be used separately or in combination. The first involves using a panel of managers to undertake shortlisting, reducing the likelihood that individual prejudices will influence the process. A number of distinct stages can be identified:

- **Stage 1:** Panel members agree essential criteria for those to be placed on the shortlist.
- **Stage 2:** Using those criteria, selectors individually produce personal lists of, say, ten candidates. An operating principle throughout is to concentrate on who can be included rather than who can be excluded, so that the process is positive, looking for strengths rather than shortcomings.
- **Stage 3:** Selectors reveal their lists and find their consensus. If stages 1 and 2 have been done properly the degree of consensus should be quite high and probably sufficient to constitute a shortlist for interview. If it is still not clear, they continue to:
- **Stage 4:** Discuss those candidates preferred by some but not all in order to clarify and reduce the areas of disagreement. A possible tactic is to classify candidates as 'strong', 'possible' or 'maverick'.
- **Stage 5:** Selectors produce a final shortlist by discussion, guarding against including compromise candidates: not strong, but offensive to no one.

The second approach involves employing a scoring system as advocated by Roberts (1997) and Wood and Payne (1998). As with the panel method, the key shortlisting criteria are defined at the start of the process (e.g. three years' management experience, a degree in a certain discipline, current salary in the range of £20,000–£30,000, evidence of an ability to drive change, etc.). The shortlister then scores each CV or application form received against these criteria awarding an A grade (or high mark) where clear evidence is provided that the candidate matches the criteria, a B grade where there is some evidence or where the candidate partially meets the criteria and a C grade where no convincing evidence is provided. Where a structured application form has been completed by the candidates, this process can be undertaken quickly (two or three minutes per application) because a candidate can be screened out whenever, for example, more than one C grade has been awarded.

The third approach involves making use of the software systems on the market which shortlist candidates electronically. The different types of system and some of the drawbacks were described above in the section on online recruitment. Despite the problems, such systems can be useful where the criteria are very clearly and tightly defined, and where an online application form is completed which makes use of multiple-choice answers. Such forms can be scored speedily and objectively, the candidate being given feedback on whether or not they have been successful. Only those who make the 'right' choices when completing the online questionnaire are then invited to participate in the next stage of the recruitment process.

SUMMARY PROPOSITIONS

7.1 Alternatives to filling a vacancy include reorganising the work; using overtime; mechanising the work; staggering the hours; making the job part time; subcontracting the work; using an employment agency.

7.2 Recent trends indicate a greater use by employers of recruitment agencies and executive consultants, open days, recruitment fairs, etc.

7.3 Advertising agencies and specialist publications provide a wealth of information to ensure that advertisements reach the appropriate readership.

7.4 Online recruitment provides great potential advantages for employers but is not seen as being especially effective at present.

7.5 Employer branding involves actively selling the experience of working for an organisation by focusing on what makes the experience both positive and distinctive.

7.6 Increasing the amount of information provided to potential applicants reduces the number of inappropriate applications.

7.7 Care with shortlisting increases the chances of being fair to all applicants and lessens the likelihood of calling inappropriate people for interview.

GENERAL DISCUSSION TOPICS

1 What are the advantages and disadvantages of online recruitment from an employer's point of view?

2 What steps could an organisation take to maintain its employer brand in times of recession when recruitment is limited?

3 Can you improve on the suggestions for shortlisting that the chapter contains?

FURTHER READING

Barber, A.E. (1998) *Recruiting Employees: Individual and organizational perspectives*. Thousand Oaks: Sage Publications.

Parry, E. and Tyson, S. (2008) 'An analysis of the use and success of online recruitment methods in the UK', *Human Resource Management Journal*, Vol. 18, No. 3, pp. 257–74.

Taylor, S. and Collins, C. (2000) 'Organizational recruitment: enhancing the intersection of research and practice', in C. Cooper and E. Locke (eds), *Industrial and Organizational Psychology*. Oxford: Blackwell.

Academic research on recruitment as opposed to selection processes is relatively undeveloped and there remain many central issues that have not been rigorously studied. In the USA the gap has been filled to some extent in recent years. The best summary and critique of this work is provided by Barber (1998). Taylor and Collins (2000) provide a shorter treatment with an additional practical focus. Parry and Tyson (2008) present a detailed review on the progress and limitations of online recruitment in recent years in the UK.

Chartered Institute of Personnel and Development (CIPD).

CIPD commissions a large survey each year on recruitment and selection issues which tracks all the major trends and provides authoritative evidence about employer practices. The institute's journal, *People Management*, also publishes a very useful supplement each July reviewing developments in the recruitment industry.

Edwards, M. (2005) 'Employer and employee branding: HR or PR?', in S. Bach (ed.), *Managing Human Resources: Personnel management in transition*. Oxford: Blackwell.

This is one of the first serious analyses of academic thinking on the emerging concept of employer branding.

REFERENCES

Barber, A.E. (1998) *Recruiting Employees: Individual and organizational perspectives*. Thousand Oaks: Sage Publications.

Brannick, M.T. and Levine, E.L. (2002) *Job Analysis: Methods, research and applications for human resource management in the new millennium*. Thousand Oaks: Sage Publications.

Breaugh, J. and Starke, M. (2000) 'Research on employee recruitment: so many studies, so many remaining questions', *Journal of Management*, Vol. 26, No. 3, pp. 405–34.

Chartered Institute of Personnel and Development (2009) *Recruitment, Retention and Turnover: Annual Survey Report 2009*. London: CIPD.

Edwards, M. (2005) 'Employer and employee branding: HR or PR?', in S. Bach (ed.), *Managing Human Resources: Personnel management in transition*. Oxford: Blackwell.

Frankland, G. (2000) 'If you build it, they will come', *People Management*, 16 March, p. 45.

Hirsh, W., Pollard, E. and Tamkin, P. (2002) *Free, Fair and Efficient? Open internal job advertising* (W. Hirsh, E. Pollard and P. Tamkin). Brighton: IES.

Institute for Employment Research (2006) *Working Futures 2004–2014: National Report*. Warwick: Institute for Employment Research.

IRS (2003) 'Job descriptions and person specifications', *IRS Employment Review*, No. 776, 23 May.

IRS (2005) 'Online recruitment in the UK: 10 years older and wiser', *IRS Employment Review*, No. 822, pp. 42–8.

Kirton, G. and Healy, G. (2009) 'Using competency-based assessment centres to select judges: implications for equality and diversity', *Human Resource Management Journal*, Vol. 19, No. 3, pp. 302–18.

Labour Market Trends (2002) 'Labour market spotlight', August.

Newell, S. and Shackleton, V. (2000) 'Recruitment and selection', in S. Bach and K. Sisson (eds), *Personnel Management: A comprehensive guide to theory and practice*. Oxford: Blackwell.

Nickson, D., Warhurst, C., Dutton. E. and Hurrell, S. (2008) 'A job to believe in: recruitment in the Scottish voluntary sector', *Human Resource Management Journal*, Vol. 18, No. 1, pp. 20–35.

Parry, E. and Tyson, S. (2008) 'An analysis of the use and success of online recruitment methods in the UK', *Human Resource Management Journal*, Vol. 18, No. 3, pp. 257–74.

Pearn, M. and Kandola, R. (1988) *Job Analysis: A practical guide for managers*. London: IPM.

People Management (2009) *PM Guide . . . to recruitment marketing*. London: People Management.

Roberts, G. (1997) *Recruitment and Selection*. London: IPD.

Searle, R. (2004) 'New technology: the potential impact of surveillance techniques in recruitment practices', *Personnel Review*, Vol. 35, No. 3, pp. 336–51.

Warhurst, C. and Nickson, D. (2007) 'Employee experience of aesthetic labour in retail and hospitality', *Work, Employment and Society*, Vol. 21, No. 103, pp. 103–20.

Weekes, S. (2000) 'Hire on the wire', *Personnel Today*, 2 May, pp. 31–5.

Whiddett, S. and Kandola, B. (2000) 'Fit for the job?', *People Management*, 25 May, pp. 30–4.

Wood, R. and Payne, T. (1998) *Competency-based Recruitment and Selection: A practical guide*. Chichester: Wiley.

An extensive range of additional materials, including multiple choice questions, answers to questions and links to useful websites can be found on the Human Resource Management Companion Website at **www.pearsoned.co.uk/torrington.**

SELECTION METHODS AND DECISIONS

THE OBJECTIVES OF THIS CHAPTER ARE TO:

1. Explain the importance of viewing selection as a two-way process
2. Examine the development and use of selection criteria
3. Evaluate the range of selection methods that are available (interviewing will be dealt with in detail in Part 8, Selected HR skills) and consider the criteria for choosing different methods
4. Review approaches to selection decision making
5. Explain how selection procedures can be validated

While the search for the perfect method of selection continues, in its absence HR and line managers continue to use a variety of imperfect methods to aid the task of predicting which applicant will be most successful in meeting the demands of the job, and/or be the best fit with the work group and culture of the organisation. Selection is increasingly important as more attention is paid to the costs of poor selection, including poor performance, additional training, demotivation of others, high levels of absence, and so on, in addition to the £4,000 the CIPD (2009) found to be the average cost of filling a vacancy. This context has promoted greater attention to the applicant's perspective and increasing use of technology in selection. In addition, equal opportunities legislation has underlined the importance of using well-validated selection procedures, so that the selection process discriminates fairly, and not unfairly, between applicants. Chapter 21 deals with issues of equality of opportunity.

SELECTION AS A TWO-WAY PROCESS

The various stages of the selection process provide information for decisions by both the employer and the potential employee. While employment decisions have long been regarded as a management prerogative, it is acknowledged that selection is increasingly being viewed as a two-way or 'social' process. Lievens *et al.* (2002) suggest that labour market shortages have promoted a concern for the organisation's image and the treatment of applicants during the recruitment and selection process. As we noted in the previous chapter, specialist skills remain in scarce supply even in slacker labour markets and organisations continue to focus on managing their 'employer brand'. This means that a wholesale return to the days of the exercise of management prerogative is unlikely and that, in the selection process, we must be concerned not only with the job to be done, but also with the work and the organisational context that is offered.

Throughout the selection process applicants choose between organisations by evaluating the developing relationship between themselves and the prospective employer. This takes place in the correspondence from potential employers; in their experience of the selection methods used by the employer; and in the information they gain at interview. Applicants will decide not to pursue some applications. Either they will have accepted another offer, or they will find something in their dealings with the organisation that discourages them and they withdraw. When large numbers of candidates withdraw it may be because the information provided by the organisation was sufficiently detailed, accurate and realistic for them to be able to make a wise decision that they were not suited to the organisation and that time would be wasted by continuing. On the other hand, it might be that potentially admirable recruits were lost because of the way in which information was presented, lack of information, or the interpretation that was put on the 'flavour' of the correspondence.

The frame of reference for the applicant is so different from that of the manager in the organisation that the difference is frequently forgotten. The majority of applicants vest a significant amount of time and energy in the submission of an application. The fact that the consideration of this is but one element of a demanding job for the recipient is incomprehensible to some and unacceptable to many. The psychological contract of a potential employee begins to be formed at this stage and this fact should not be overlooked: timely responses are the first element of this process. If candidates are selected for interview they will also be influenced by recruiter behaviour in deciding whether to accept a job offer, if one is made. Papadopoulou *et al.* (1996), for example, demonstrated that candidates were influenced by the recruiter's ability to supply adequate and accurate information, as this is what they had expected from the interview. In addition they were influenced by the way the recruiter managed the interaction, as well as the content, so the recruiter's control of the interaction, their listening ability and in particular their ability/willingness to allow the candidate to present themselves effectively are all important.

Some of the points that seem to be useful about interacting with the candidate are:

1 Reply, meaningfully and quickly. Web-based selection can speed things up considerably, and we look at this in more detail later in the chapter.
2 Conduct correspondence in terms of what the applicants want to know. How long will they have to wait for an answer? If you ask them in for interview or assessment centre, how long will it take, what will it involve, do you defray expenses, can they park their car, how do they find you, etc.?
3 Interviewers should be trained to ensure that they have not only full knowledge of the relevant information, but also the skills to manage the interaction effectively.

SELECTION CRITERIA

Selection criteria need to be explicitly defined in order to choose the most appropriate selection procedure and approach, make credible selection decisions and validate the selection process. Selection criteria are typically presented in the form of a person specification representing the ideal candidate, and cover such areas as skills, experience, qualifications, education, personal attributes, special attributes, interests and motivation (IRS 2003). Although the IRS found that person specifications were used by three-quarters of the organisations in their study, Lievens *et al.* (2002) challenge the use of traditional person specifications as jobs become less defined and constantly change. Three perspectives can be used to determine selection criteria – job fit, team/functional fit (*see*, for example, Werbel and Johnson 2001) and organisational fit. There has recently been an increasing emphasis on team and organisational fit, which has been supported by greater use of competencies in selection. We discuss individual job fit and competencies below.

Individual job criteria

Individual job criteria contained in job descriptions and person specifications are derived from the process of job analysis. Although it is reasonably easy to specify the factors that should influence the personnel specification, the process by which the specification is formed is more difficult to describe. Van Zwanenberg and Wilkinson (1993) offer a dual perspective. They describe 'job first – person later' and 'person first – job later' approaches. The first starts with analysing the task to be done, presenting this in the form of a job description and from this deriving the personal qualities and attributes or competencies that are necessary to do the task. The difficulty here is in the translation process and the constant change of job demands and tasks. The alternative approach suggested by van Zwanenberg and Wilkinson starts with identifying which individuals are successful in a certain job and then describing their characteristics.

Branine (2008) suggests that person- rather than job-related approaches are now more common.

Competency-based criteria

In addition to, or sometimes instead of, a person specification, many organisations are developing a competency profile as a means of setting the criteria against which to select. Competencies have been defined as underlying characteristics of a person which result in effective or superior performance; they include personal skills, knowledge, motives, traits, self-image and social role (*see* Chapter 18 for further details). Organisations design competency frameworks which they draw on for a number of purposes, including selecting applicants who have the desired competencies in, for example, communication, team working and planning and organising. Woodruffe (2000) and Whiddett and Hollyforde (2003) are useful practical sources of information on how to use competencies in the selection process.

Until recently organisational criteria involving competencies were rarely made explicit and they were often used at an intuitive level. However, Townley (1991) argues that organisations are increasingly likely to focus on more general attitudes and values than narrow task-based criteria. The aim is to promote objective selection criteria, although Kirton and Healey (2009) warn that these still require human interpretations so may be less objective than suggested. Barclay (1999) explains how fit with the organisation is often expressed in terms of personality, attitudes, flexibility, commitment and goals, rather than the ability to do the specific job for which the person is being recruited. In many organisations, for example call centres, such selection approaches have led to a much greater emphasis on these competencies than on the education or experience typically demanded by the use of person specifications. Such organisational criteria are also important where jobs are ill defined and constantly changing. It should be noted, however, that using competencies as the only selection criterion is considered to be limiting and unhelpful (*see*, for example, Brittain and Ryder (1999) and Whiddett and Kandola (2000)). Critiques of selection based on competency have also included the danger of 'cloning', that is selecting very similar types for an organisation and thus limiting diversity, and that competencies are backward looking, focusing on what has previously made the organisation successful rather than the competencies that it may need for future success. We present a discussion of this in the Window on practice below.

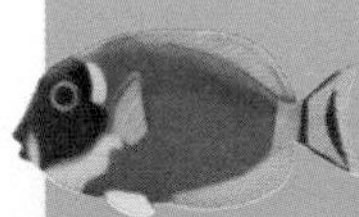

WINDOW ON PRACTICE

Why firms need 20:20 vision when selecting talent

Organisations devote a great deal of time to analysing their competencies and using them as the backbone for people management processes. However, for the selection of future talent there is always the niggling doubt that competencies might refer so much to the present – or indeed the past – that the people chosen will suffer from built-in obsolescence.

This is hardly a novel criticism, and to some extent it can be answered by focusing research on future competencies. Unfortunately, formal methods of analysing competencies do not cope well with a future orientation. It's hard to imagine asking about hypothetical critical incidents in five or ten years' time, or making detailed comparisons between future high and low performers. Even if this problem could be overcome, there is something illogical about using the same competency framework both to manage today's performance and to bring in the leaders who will mature over the next 15 years. To identify tomorrow's leaders, we need to address the requirements of the future and focus on choosing people with the potential to meet those requirements, and then develop them to realise their potential.

So far, so obvious, but if it is so obvious why do so many companies take the opposite approach? Why do they analyse competencies for today or even tomorrow and simply trust they will still be valid in 2020? The difficulty most organisations have is that they don't have much clue, let alone any certainty, about what the year 2020 might bring or require.

However hard it may be, it is worth spending time thinking about the future requirements of the organisation and determining what the indicators of excellence might be in a future leader. At the same time, it is important to acknowledge uncertainty and build this into the way we choose future leaders, perhaps by selecting for flexibility but also by selecting an array of talent rather than a narrow blueprint.

Source: *People Management*, 4 May 2006, p. 48.

Next steps in selection criteria?

As we discussed above, both person specifications and competency approaches have their critics. The search continues for criteria that will improve the process of selecting potential employees and in the following Window on practice we outline O2's approach to this, one which aims to select employees on the basis of performance.

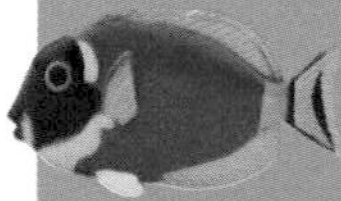

WINDOW ON PRACTICE

Performance-based selection at O2

Mobile phone firm O2 is planning to roll out performance-based selection following successful pilots in one of its call centres and its retail division. Selection is focused on a performance profile, rather than a traditional competency profile, and involves an evaluation interview that focuses on between four and six accomplishments in a candidate's career and what O2 describes as a 'talent assessment matrix' to rate skills and behaviours required to be successful in a specified role.

Having selected over 500 new employees using this method, O2 suggests that candidates are of a noticeably higher standard than those selected using competency-based methods and that it has been easier to identify less suitable candidates. It is also suggested that the process makes for a more effective interview, with 'more meaningful dialogue' and it being easier to assess motivation and willingness to work.

While a significant investment has been required in helping managers to develop the new styles of questioning required, O2 suggests that this approach is the next generation of selection method, incorporating performance management and selection techniques. Potential candidates gain an insight into the objectives for the role and the organisation is better placed to assess their likelihood of achieving these objectives.

Source: Summarised from Philips, L. (2007) 'O2 hires on performance', *People Management*, 23 August.

ACTIVITY 8.1

Write a person specification for your job (or one with which you are familiar). Now write a list of the competencies required to undertake the same role. Which do you think will be more helpful in the selection process and why?

CHOOSING SELECTION METHODS

There are a range of selection methods which we outline below and it is unusual for one selection method to be used alone. A combination of two or more methods is generally used, and the choice of these is dependent upon a number of factors:

1 **Selection criteria for the post to be filled.** For example, group selection methods and assessment centre activities would be most useful for certain types of job, such as managerial, professional, supervisory and those who will be part of self-managing teams.
2 **Acceptability and appropriateness of the methods.** For the candidates involved, or likely to be involved, in the selection. The use, for example, of intelligence tests may be seen as insulting to applicants already occupying senior posts.
3 **Abilities of the staff involved in the selection process.** This applies particularly in the use of tests and assessment centres. Only those staff who are appropriately qualified by academic qualification and/or attendance on a recognised course may administer psychological tests.
4 **Administrative ease.** For administrative purposes it may be much simpler, say, to arrange one or two individual interviews for a prospective candidate than to organise

a panel consisting of four members, all needing to make themselves available at the same time. Web-based testing may save much administrative time, particularly when there are large numbers of candidates.

5 **Time factors.** Sometimes a position needs to be filled very quickly, and time may be saved by using telephone or video-based interviews, or organising individual interviews rather than group selection methods, which would mean waiting for a day when all candidates are available.

6 **Accuracy.** Accuracy in selection generally increases in relation to the number of appropriate selection methods used (*see*, for example, IRS 2002a).

7 **Cost.** Tests may cost a lot to set up but once the initial outlay has been made they are reasonably cheap to administer. Assessment centres involve an even greater outlay and continue to be fairly expensive to administer. Interviews, on the other hand, cost only a moderate amount to set up in terms of interviewer training and are fairly cheap to administer. For the costlier methods great care needs to be taken in deciding whether the improvement in selection decision making justifies such costs.

SELECTION METHODS

We present below recent CIPD research which outlines the most frequently used selection methods (Table 8.1). It is interesting to note, given our above discussion on competencies as selection criteria, that competency-based interviewing is the most frequently used selection method in this survey. In discussing recruitment (Chapter 7), we considered the shortlisting process and the sifting of applications. We go on here to look in more detail at selection methods, many of which may be used at different stages in the selection process.

The 'classic trio', application forms, interviews and references, are traditional methods of selection. We consider these first, other than for face-to-face interviews which we consider in depth in Part 8. We then move on to consider more advanced methods of selection, such as testing and assessment centres.

Table 8.1 Methods used to select applicants (%)

Method	%
Competency-based interviews	69
Interviews following contents of a CV/application form (that is, biographical)	68
Structured interviews (panel)	59
Tests for specific skills	50
General ability tests	44
Literacy and/or numeracy tests	39
Telephone interviews	38
Personality/aptitude questionnaires	35
Assessment centres	35
Group exercises (for example role-playing)	26
Pre-interview referencing	19
Online tests (selection)	17
Other	6
Base: 754	

Source: From *Recruitment, Retention and Turnover: Annual Survey Report 2009*, CIPD (2009), Table 10. With the permission of the publisher, the Chartered Institute of Personnel and Development, London (www.cipd.co.uk).

The classic trio

Application forms

Application forms are generally used as a straightforward way of giving a standardised synopsis of the applicant's history. This helps applicants present their case by providing them with a predetermined structure, it speeds the sorting and shortlisting or sifting of applications either by hand or electronically and it guides the interviewers, with each piece of information on the form being taken and developed in the interview, as well as providing the starting point for employee records. While there is heavy use of CVs for managerial and professional posts, many organisations, especially in the public sector, require both – off-putting to the applicant but helpful to the organisation in eliciting comparable data from all applicants. Application forms are increasingly available electronically; this not only speeds up the process but also enables 'key word' searches of the data on the forms (for alternative ways in which this may be carried out *see* Mohamed *et al.* (2001)), but there are questions about the legality of this method when used alone.

Application forms can also be used to collect biodata. Biodata have been defined by Anderson and Shackleton (1990) as 'historical and verifiable pieces of information about an individual in a selection context usually reported on application forms'. Biodata are perhaps of most use for large organisations filling fairly large numbers of posts for which they receive extremely large numbers of applications. This method is an attempt to relate the characteristics of applicants to characteristics of a large sample of successful job holders. The obvious drawbacks of this procedure are, first, the time that is involved and the size of sample needed, so that it is only feasible where there are many job holders in a particular type of position. Second, it lacks face validity for applicants who might find it difficult to believe that success in a position correlates with being, for example, the first born in one's family. Such methods are not currently well used and Taylor (2008) notes their controversial nature and perceived unfairness. In addition, the 1998 Data Protection Act prohibits the use of an automated selection process (which biodata invariably are) as the *only* process used at any stage in the procedure. Despite this, Breaugh (2009) presents a review of biodata research and suggests that, as a selection method, it is one of the best predictors of employee performance and turnover and argues for its increased usage.

Despite their widespread use, there remain concerns about the reliability of application forms and CVs and this issue is dealt with in Case study 8.1 at **www.pearsoned.co.uk/torrington.**

Telephone interviewing

Telephone interviews can be used if speed is particularly important, and if geographical distance is an issue, as interviews with appropriate candidates can be arranged immediately. CIPD (2009) reports that 38 per cent of organisations use this method of selection, often as one of a combination of screening tools, as well as a test of telephone manner, where required. There is evidence that telephone interviews are best used as a part of a structured selection procedure, rather than alone – generally in terms of pre-selection for a face-to-face interview (Murphy 2005). However, they may also have an important role when selecting for jobs in which telephone manner is critical such as call centre and contact centre staff. There may be problems such as lack of non-verbal information, and difficulties getting hold of the applicant. However, positive aspects have been reported, such as concentration on content rather than the person. From an applicant perspective telephone interviews can be daunting, if they have no experience of them, and Murphy (2005) refers to and replicates checklists for organisations and candidates in the most effective use of such interviews.

References

One way of informing the judgement of managers who have to make employment offers to selected individuals is the use of references. Candidates provide the names of previous employers or others with appropriate credentials and then prospective employers request them to provide information. Reference checking is increasing as organisations react to scandals in the media and aim to protect themselves from rogue applicants (IRS 2002b). There are two types: the factual check and the character reference.

The factual check

The factual check is fairly straightforward as it is no more than a confirmation of facts that the candidate has presented. It will normally follow the employment interview and decision to offer a post. It simply confirms that the facts are accurate. The knowledge that such a check will be made – or may be made – will help focus the mind of candidates so that they resist the temptation to embroider their story.

The character reference

The character reference is a very different matter. Here the prospective employer asks for an opinion about the candidate before the interview so that the information gained can be used in the decision-making phases. The logic of this strategy is impeccable: who knows the working performance of the candidate better than the previous employer? The wisdom of the strategy is less sound, as it depends on the writers of references being excellent judges of working performance, faultless communicators and – most difficult of all – disinterested. The potential inaccuracies of decisions influenced by character references begin when the candidate decides who to cite. The candidate will have some freedom of choice and will clearly choose someone from whom he/she expects favourable comment.

Advanced methods of selection

We turn now to consider some more advanced methods of selection and issues surrounding their usage.

Self-assessment and peer assessment

There is increasing interest in providing more information to applicants concerning the job. This may involve a video, an informal discussion with job holders or further information sent with the application form. This is often termed giving the prospective candidate a 'realistic job preview' (Wanous 1992), enabling them to assess their own suitability to a much greater extent and some organisations have taken the opportunity to provide a self-selection questionnaire on the company website. Another way of achieving this is by asking the candidates to do some form of pre-work. This may also involve asking them questions regarding their previous work experiences which would relate to the job for which they are applying.

WINDOW ON PRACTICE

Job experience day at Pret à Manger

Pret à Manger has reduced staff turnover from 130 per cent (not high for the industry) to 98 per cent. They put this down to the use of a job experience day, which candidates have to do after an initial interview, but before they are granted a further competency-based interview.

Applicants do a day's work for which they are paid and they receive guidance and mentoring from an existing team member who is assigned to them for the day. But the aim is to enable applicants to work across a wide range of tasks with a wide range of team members. During the day the candidate also has an interview with the shop manager.

Team members who would be the applicant's future colleagues assess the applicant on competencies relevant to the job and then vote at the end of the day as to whether they would employ the applicant. The manager does not get a vote but can lobby for or against any candidate.

The success rate for the day is around 50 per cent. Pret à Manger has found this a good way of sifting large numbers of applicants and at the same time developing team commitment to new recruits.

Source: Summarised from L. Carrington (2002) 'At the cutting edge', *People Management*, Vol. 8, No. 10, 16 May, pp. 30–1.

Testing

The use of tests in selection is surrounded by strong feelings for and against. Those in favour of testing in general point to the unreliability of the interview as a predictor of performance and the greater potential accuracy and objectivity of test data. Tests can be seen as giving credibility to selection decisions. Those against them either dislike the objectivity that testing implies or have difficulty in incorporating test evidence into the rest of the evidence that is collected. Questions have been raised as to the relevance of the tests to the job applied for and the possibility of unfair discrimination and bias. Also, some candidates feel that they can improve their prospects by a good interview performance and that the degree to which they are in control of their own destiny is being reduced by a dispassionate routine.

Tests remain heavily used, and the key issue debated currently is the extent to which tests should be administered over the web. CIPD (2009) found 44 per cent of organisations using general ability tests, 39 per cent of organisations using literacy/numeracy tests and 35 per cent using personality tests and Murphy (2006) in an IRS survey also found extensive usage. Testing is more likely to be used for management, professional and graduate jobs – although as testing on the web becomes more common it is likely to be used for a wider range of jobs.

Tests are chosen on the basis that test scores relate to, or correlate with, subsequent job performance, so that a high test score would predict high job performance and a low test score would predict low job performance.

Critical features of test use

Validity

Different types of validity can be applied to psychological tests. Personnel managers are most concerned with predictive validity, which is the extent to which the test can predict subsequent job performance. Predictive validity is measured by relating the test scores to measures of future performance, such as error rate, production rate, appraisal scores, absence rate or whatever criteria are important to the organisation. Sometimes performance is defined as the level of the organisation to which the individual has been promoted – so the criteria here are organisational rather than job specific. If test scores relate highly to future performance, however defined, then the test is a good predictor. Lockyer and Scholarios (2004), for example, suggest that ability tests and work sample tests have high predictive validity for manual workers.

Reliability

The reliability of a test is the degree to which the test measures consistently whatever it does measure. If a test is highly reliable, then it is possible to put greater weight on the scores that individuals receive on the test. However, a highly reliable test is of no value in the employment situation unless it also has high validity.

Use and interpretation

Tests need to be used and interpreted by trained or qualified testers. Test results, especially personality tests, require very careful interpretation as some aspects of personality will be measured that are irrelevant to the job. The British Psychological Society (BPS) can provide a certificate of competence for occupational testing at levels A and B. Both the BPS and CIPD have produced codes of practice for occupational test use. It is recommended that tests are not used in a judgemental, final way, but to stimulate discussion with the candidate based on the test results and that feedback is given to candidates. In addition it is recommended in the CIPD code that test data alone should not be used to make a selection decision (which could contravene the 1998 Data Protection Act), but should always be used as part of a wider process where inferences from test results can be backed up by information from other sources. Norm tables and the edition date of a test are also important features to check. For example Ceci and Williams (2000) warn that intelligence is a relative concept and that the norm tables change over time – so using an old test with old norm tables may be misleading.

Problems with using tests

A number of problems can be incurred when using tests.

1. In the last section we commented that a test score that was highly related to performance criteria has good validity. The relationship between test scores and performance criteria is usually expressed as a correlation coefficient (r). If $r = 1$ then test scores and performance would be perfectly related; if $r = 0$ there is no relationship whatsoever. A correlation coefficient of $r = 0.4$ is comparatively good in the testing world and this level of relationship between test scores and performance is generally seen as acceptable. Tests are, therefore, not outstanding predictors of future performance.
2. Validation procedures are very time consuming, but are essential to the effective use of tests. There are concerns that with the growth of web testing, new types of tests, such as emotional intelligence tests, are being developed without sufficient validation (Tulip 2002).
3. The criteria that are used to define good job performance in developing the test are often inadequate. They are subjective and may account to some extent for the mediocre correlations between test results and job performance.
4. Tests are often job specific. If the job for which the test is used changes, then the test can no longer be assumed to relate to job performance in the same way. Also, personality tests only measure how individuals see themselves at a certain time and cannot therefore be reliably reused at a later time.
5. Tests may not be fair as there may be a social, sexual or racial bias in the questions and scoring system. People from some cultures may, for example, be unused to 'working against the clock'.
6. Increasingly organisations are using competencies as a tool to identify and develop the characteristics of high performance. However, it can be difficult to relate competencies to psychological tests (Fletcher 1996).

WINDOW ON PRACTICE

Ensuring tests are 'fair and reasonable' and free from ethnic or sexual bias

Indirect discrimination would result when a test unfairly and unjustifiably disadvantages one race or sex compared with another, and test results need to be monitored to show that this is not happening. Organisations need to be able to demonstrate that the test has been developed or tailored and assessed in relation to the job content and person specification. Alternative means of taking the test also need to be developed when the use of tests would disadvantage a disabled person.

Source: Summarised from M. Palmer (2002) 'Very testing testing', *People Management*, Vol. 8, No. 1, 10 January, pp. 18–19.

ACTIVITY 8.2

In what ways could you measure job performance for the following?

- A data input clerk
- A mobile plumber
- A call centre operator
- A supervisor

Types of test for occupational use

Aptitude tests

People differ in their performance of tasks, and tests of aptitude (or ability) measure an individual's potential to develop in either specific or general terms. This is in contrast to attainment tests, which measure the skills an individual has already acquired. When considering the results from aptitude tests it is important to remember that a simple relationship does not exist between a high level of aptitude and a high level of job performance, as other factors, such as motivation, also contribute to job performance.

Aptitude tests can be grouped into two categories: those measuring general mental ability or general intelligence, and those measuring specific abilities or aptitudes.

General intelligence tests

Intelligence tests, sometimes called mental ability tests, are designed to give an indication of overall mental capacity. A variety of questions are included in such tests, including vocabulary, analogies, similarities, opposites, arithmetic, number extension and general information. Ability to score highly on such tests correlates with the capacity to retain new knowledge, to pass examinations and to succeed at work. However, the intelligence test used would still need to be carefully validated in terms of the job for which the candidate was applying. And Ceci and Williams (2000) note that intelligence is to some extent determined by the context – so an individual's test score may not reflect capacity to act intelligently. Indeed practical intelligence, associated with success in organisations, may be different from the nature of intelligence as measured by tests (Williams and Sternberg 2001). Examples of general intelligence tests are found in IDS (2004).

Special aptitude tests

There are special tests that measure specific abilities or aptitudes, such as spatial abilities, perceptual abilities, verbal ability, numerical ability, motor ability (manual dexterity) and so on. An example of a special abilities test is the Critical Reasoning Test developed by Smith and Whetton (*see* IDS 2004).

Trainability tests

Trainability tests are used to measure a potential employee's ability to be trained, usually for craft-type work. The test consists of the applicants doing a practical task that they have not done before, after having been shown or 'trained' how to do it. The test measures how well they respond to the 'training' and how their performance on the task improves. Because it is performance at a task that is being measured, these tests are sometimes confused with attainment tests; however, they are more concerned with potential ability to do the task and response to training.

Attainment tests

Whereas aptitude tests measure an individual's potential, attainment or achievement tests measure skills that have already been acquired. There is much less resistance to such tests of skills. Few candidates for a secretarial/administrative post would refuse to take a keyboard speed test, or a test on 'Word', 'PowerPoint' or 'Excel' software before interview. The candidates are sufficiently confident of their skills to welcome the opportunity to display them and be approved. Furthermore, they know what they are doing and will know whether they have done well or badly. They are in control, whereas they feel that the tester is in control of intelligence and personality tests as the candidates do not understand the evaluation rationale. Attainment tests are often devised by the employer.

Personality tests

The debate still rages about the importance of personality for success in some jobs and organisations. The need for personality assessment may be high but there is even more resistance to tests of personality than to tests of aptitude, partly because of the reluctance to see personality as in any way measurable. There is much evidence to suggest that personality is also context dependent, and Iles and Salaman (1995) also argue that personality changes over time. Both of these factors further complicate the issue. Personality tests are mainly used for management, professional and graduate jobs, although there is evidence of their use when high-performance teams are developed.

Theories of human personality vary as much as theories of human intelligence. Jung, Eysenck and Cattell, among others, have all proposed different sets of factors/traits which can be assessed to describe personality. Based on research to date, Robertson (2001) argues that it is now possible to state that there are five basic building blocks of personality: extroversion/introversion; emotional stability; agreeableness; conscientiousness and openness to new experiences. Myers–Briggs is a well used personality test; for details *see* McHenry (2002).

It is dangerous to assume that there is a standard profile of 'the ideal employee' (although this may fit nicely with theories of culture change) or the ideal personality for a particular job, as the same objectives may be satisfactorily achieved in different ways by different people. Another problem with the use of personality tests is that they rely on an individual's willingness to be honest, as the socially acceptable answer or the one best in terms of the job are seemingly easy to pick out, although 'lie detector' questions are usually built in. Ipsative tests (as opposed to normative tests)* seek to avoid the social desirability problem by using a different test structure – but other problems arise from this approach. Heggestad *et al.* (2006) suggest that in their pure form ipsative tests are inappropriate for selection and that in their partial form they might be just as susceptible to faking as normative tests.

WINDOW ON PRACTICE

A different type of personality test: Waves

Smethurst (2006) reports on a new type of test which has been developed by Saville Consulting. There are two key differences between this and previous personality tests. The first is that both normative and ipsative questions are used, and the second is that talent and motivation are assessed together in a single test rather than in separate questionnaires.

Source: Summarised from S. Smethurst (2006) 'The window test', *People Management*, Vol. 12, No. 2, 26 January, pp. 28–30.

Dalen *et al.* (2001) showed that tests are manipulable but not sufficiently for the candidate to match an ideal profile, and that such manipulation would be exposed by detection measures within the test. There is a further problem that some traits measured by the test will not be relevant in terms of performance on the job. Currently there is an increasing interest in aesthetic issues in selection, for example, the attitudes and appearance of potential employees (Warhurst and Nixon 2007) and it is difficult to see how tests will be used to measure these attributes.

WINDOW ON PRACTICE

Online testing: the case for and against

CIPD (2009) reports that 17 per cent of respondents to its survey used online tests and there is much interest in developing this area. Tests can be used in one of three different ways:

- uncontrolled – anyone can register to use them on the open Internet;
- controlled – candidates need first to be registered by the organisation using the test, and their identity must be checked;
- supervised – as above, and a qualified tester from the organisation also logs on and ensures that time limits and other requirements are met.

* Ipsative tests require the candidate to make a *choice*, usually between two statements or adjectives, rather than allowing the candidate to answer, for example, 'true' or 'false' or give a rating of 'to what extent' they agree an item applies to themselves, as in a normative test.

For:

- Cheaper in the long run
- Immediate analysis
- Immediate feedback to candidate
- Can be used for wider range of (lower-paid) jobs
- Speeds processes and helps to retain potential candidates
- Good for company image
- Can use a wider range of different tests – e.g. video scenarios, followed by 'what would you do next?'
- Can be convenient for applicants

Against:

- Worries over confidentiality and security of personal data
- Appears cold and impersonal
- Open to misuse – who is actually completing the test?
- Can encourage the rapid development of new tests which are not properly validated

Group selection methods and assessment centres

Group methods

The use of group tasks to select candidates is not new – the method dates back to the Second World War – but such measures have gained greater attention through their use in assessment centres. Plumbley (1985) describes the purpose of group selection methods as being to provide evidence about the candidate's ability to:

- get on with others;
- influence others and the way they do this;
- express themselves verbally;
- think clearly and logically;
- argue from past experience and apply themselves to a new problem;
- identify the type of role they play in group situations.

These features are difficult on the whole to identify using other selection methods and one of the particular advantages of group selection methods is that they provide the selector with examples of behaviour on which to select. When future job performance is being considered it is behaviour in the job that is critical, and so selection using group methods can provide direct information on which to select rather than indirect verbal information or test results. The increasing use of competencies and behavioural indicators, as a way to specify selection criteria, ties in well with the use of group methods.

There is a range of group exercises that can be used including informal discussion of a given topic, role plays and groups who must organise themselves to solve a problem within time limits which may take the form of a competitive business game, case study or physical activity.

Group selection methods are most suitable for management, graduate and sometimes supervisory posts. One of the difficulties with group selection methods is that it can be difficult to assess an individual's contribution, and some people may be unwilling to take part.

ACTIVITY 8.3

To what extent does a person's behaviour on these group selection tasks accurately reflect behaviour on the job? Why?

Assessment centres

Assessment centres incorporate multiple selection techniques, and the group selection methods outlined above form a major element, together with other work-simulation exercises such as in-basket tasks, psychological tests, a variety of interviews and presentations. Assessment centres are used to assess, in depth, a group of broadly similar applicants, using a set of competencies required for the post on offer and a series of behavioural statements which indicate how these competencies are played out in practice. Even assuming that the competencies for the job in question have already been identified, assessment centres require a lengthy design process to select the appropriate activities so that every competency will be measured via more than one task. Assessment centres have been proven to be one of the most effective ways of selecting candidates – this is probably due, as Suff (2005) notes, to the use of multiple measures, multiple assessors and predetermined assessment criteria.

A matrix is usually developed to show how the required competencies and the activities link together. In terms of running the centre sufficient well-trained assessors will be needed, usually based on the ratio of one assessor for two candidates to ensure that the assessor can observe each candidate sufficiently carefully. Lists of competencies and associated behaviours will need to be drawn up as checklists and a careful plan will need to be made of how each candidate will move around the different activities – an example of which is found in Table 8.2. Clearly candidates will need to be very well briefed both before and at the start of the centre.

At the end of the procedure the assessors have to come to an agreement on a cumulative rating for each individual, related to job requirements, taking into account all the selection activities. The procedure as a whole can then be validated against job performance rather than each separate activity. The predictive validities from such procedures are not very consistent, but there is a high 'face validity' – a feeling that this is a fairer way of selecting people. Reliability can also be improved by the quality of assessor training, careful briefing of assessors and a predetermined structured approach to marking. The chief disadvantage of these selection methods is that they are a costly and time-consuming procedure, for both the organisation and the candidates. The time commitment is extended by the need to give some feedback to candidates who have been through such a long procedure which involves psychological assessment – although feedback is still not always provided for candidates. There is evidence of increasing use of assessment

Day One Times	Activity	Who is involved
9.30–10.00	Introduction to centre	All
10.00–10.45	General discussion – given topics	All
10.45–11.15	Coffee	
11.15–12.00	General intelligence test	All
12.00–12.30	One-to-one interviews (30 mins each)	Candidates A, B, C
12.30–1.30	Lunch	
1.30–2.00	One-to-one interviews (30 mins each)	Candidates B, E, C
2.00–2.45	Spatial reasoning test	All
2.45–3.15	Coffee	
3.15–4.00	Personality test	All
4.00–4.30	One-to-one interviews (30 mins each)	Candidates C, F, D
Day Two Times	**Activity**	**Who is involved**
9.30–10.15	Verbal reasoning test	All
10.15–10.45	One-to-one interviews (30 mins each)	Candidates D, A, F
10.45–11.15	Coffee	
11.15–12.00	Critical thinking test	All
12.00–12.30	One-to-one interviews (30 mins each)	Candidates E, B, A
12.30–1.30	Lunch	
1.30–3.00	In-tray exercise	All
3.00–3.30	Coffee	
3.30–4.00	One-to-one interviews (30 mins each)	Candidates F, D, E

Note: Based on six candidates (A, B, C, D, E, F) and three assessors.

Table 8.2 An example of the scheduling of events – based on an assessment centre for a professional post (central government)

centres and CIPD (2009) reports that 35 per cent of organisations in its survey used such centres for selection. Some organisations have been improving their centres (*see* IRS 2002b) by making the activities more connected or by using longer simulations or scenarios which are a reflection of real-life experience on the job, and are carrying out testing separately from the centre. Some are assessing candidates against the values of the company rather than a specific job, in view of the rapid change in the nature of jobs, and others, such as Britvic, are running a series of assessment centres which candidates must attend, rather than only one. A helpful text relating competency profiles and assessment centre activities is Woodruffe (2000), and IDS (2005) provides examples of different company experiences.

Work sampling/portfolios

Work sampling of potential candidates for permanent jobs can take place by assessing candidates' work in temporary posts or on government training schemes in the same organisation. For some jobs, such as photographers and artists, a sample of work in the form of a portfolio is expected to be presented at the time of interview. It has been suggested that managers and professionals should also be developing portfolios of their work experiences and achievements as one way of enhancing their employability.

Other methods

A number of other less conventional methods such as physiognomy, phrenology, body language, palmistry, graphology and astrology have been suggested as possible selection methods. While these are fascinating to read about there is little evidence to suggest that they could be used effectively. Thatcher (1997) suggests that the use of graphology is around 10 per cent in Holland and Germany and that it is regularly used in France; in the UK he found 9 per cent of small firms (with fewer than 100 employees), 1 per cent of medium-sized firms (100–499 employees) and 5 per cent of larger firms used graphology as a selection method. In 1990 Fowler suggested that the extent of use of graphology is much higher in the UK than reported figures indicate, as there is some reluctance on the part of organisations to admit that they are using graphology for selection purposes. There are also concerns about the quality of graphologists – who can indeed set themselves up with no training whatsoever. The two main bodies in this field in the UK are the British Institute of Graphology and the International Graphology Association and both these organisations require members to gain qualifications before they can practise.

WINDOW ON PRACTICE

It is interesting to contrast different approaches to selection in different countries. Bulois and Shackleton (1996) note that interviews are the cornerstone of selection activity in both Britain and France, but that they are consciously used in different ways. In Britain they argue that interviews are increasingly structured and criterion referenced, whereas in France the approach tends to be deliberately unstructured and informal. They note that in France the premise is that 'the more at ease the candidates are, the higher the quality of their answer', whereas in Britain they characterise the premise as 'the more information you get about an individual, the better you know him/her and the more valid and reliable your judgement is' (p. 129). Tixier (1996), in a survey covering the EU (but excluding France), Switzerland, Sweden and Austria, found that structured interviews were favoured in the UK, Scandinavia, Germany and Austria. This contrasted with Italy, Portugal, Luxembourg and Switzerland where unstructured styles were preferred.

Bulois and Shackleton identify selectors in Britain as being more aware of the limitations of interviews and as attempting to reduce the subjectivity by also carrying out assessment centres and psychological tests; whereas in France these methods were identified as unnatural, tedious and frustrating. Interviews are much more likely to be supplemented by handwriting analysis in France – both methods being identified as valuable, flexible and cheap sources of information. Shackleton and Newell (1991) report that handwriting analysis was used in 77 per cent of the organisations that they surveyed in France compared with 2.6 per cent of the organisations they surveyed in the UK.

Both culture and employment legislation clearly have an influence on the selection methods adopted in any country and the way in which they are used.

ACTIVITY 8.4

Design an assessment centre for the anti-rape detective job as described in Case 8.1 on the companion website **www.pearsoned.co.uk/torrington**.

FINAL SELECTION DECISION MAKING

The selection decision involves measuring the candidates individually against the selection criteria defined, often in the person or competency specification, and not against each other. A useful tool to achieve this is the matrix in Table 8.3. This is a good method of ensuring that every candidate is assessed against each selection criterion and in each box in the matrix the key details can be completed. The box can be used whether a single selection method was used or multiple methods. If multiple methods were used and contradictory information is found against any criterion, this can be noted in the decision-making process.

When more than one selector is involved there is some debate about how to gather and use the information and about the judgement of each selector. One way is for each selector to assess the information collected separately, and then for all selectors to meet to discuss assessments. When this approach is used, there may be some very different assessments, especially if the interview was the only selection method used. Much heated and time-consuming debate can be generated, but the most useful aspect of this process is sharing the information in everyone's matrix to understand how judgements have been formed. This approach is also helpful in training interviewers.

An alternative approach is to fill in only one matrix, with all selectors contributing. This may be quicker, but the drawback is that the quietest member may be the one who has all the critical pieces of information. There is a risk that not all the information available may be contributed to the debate in progress. Iles (1992), referring to assessment centre decisions, suggests that the debate itself may not add to the quality of the decision, and that taking the results from each selector and combining them is just as effective.

Table 8.3

Selection criteria	Candidate 1	Candidate 2	Candidate 3	Candidate 4
Criterion a				
Criterion b				
Criterion c				
Criterion d				
Criterion e				
General comments				

VALIDATION OF SELECTION PROCEDURES

We have already mentioned how test scores may be validated against eventual job performance for each individual in order to discover whether the test score is a good predictor of success in the job. In this way we can decide whether the test should be used as part of the selection procedure in future. The same idea can be applied to the use of other individual or combined selection methods. Yet, despite the cost involved in selecting potential employees, few firms formally evaluate the success of their selection methods. Some guidelines on the evaluation process are outline in the Window on practice below.

WINDOW ON PRACTICE

How to . . . evaluate your selection process

There are several benefits of formally evaluating your selection process:

- identifying those aspects of the process that are working well and that are able to predict high levels of performance in post;
- finding aspects that are less useful and could be tweaked or removed;
- assessing return on investment (ROI) in your selection process, helping you to base the business case for your strategy on objective data.

What follows is a step-by-step guide to evaluating your selection process.

1 Pick a role

Ideally, this will be a role with at least a dozen of your current staff in the same post. The fewer the staff, the less statistically robust the evaluation will be.

2 Obtain selection data

Enter assessment ratings from your selection process in a spreadsheet, with a single person in each row and ratings for each competency assessed using each assessment method in columns.

If you assessed 'customer focus', 'commitment to excellence' and 'strategic thinking' by, say, interview and psychometric test, your first column would contain the rating for 'customer focus' assessed during the interview.

The second column would contain the rating for 'commitment to excellence' from the interview. The third column would contain the rating for 'strategic thinking' from interview. The fourth column would contain the rating for 'customer focus' assessed via the psychometric test, the fifth for 'commitment to excellence' via psychometrics, and so on.

3 Obtain staff performance data

The simplest way of obtaining this information is to ask line managers to rate each employee's performance using either a single criterion (say, job performance) or a range of criteria perhaps related to your target competencies (such as customer service or achieving results).

A behaviourally anchored rating scale should be produced for each measure of performance to make sure line manager ratings are as accurate as possible. You then include the performance ratings as further columns in your spreadsheet.

4 Carry out simple analysis

You now need to calculate correlations (the statistical relationship) between each element of your selection process and the performance data you have collected. Although you can buy specialist statistical software for this purpose, most standard spreadsheet packages, such as Microsoft Excel, are more than capable of carrying out correlations at the touch of a button.

Once you have this information, you will know how well your existing selection process is likely to predict future performance in post, and you will be able to carry out ROI calculations.

5 Compute the ROI

Typically, ROI calculates the improvement that is made by using new selection procedures over older ones.

To compute ROI, we need to make a number of assumptions. For example, we should assume that the value to the organisation of an employee producing excellent performance is 40 per cent greater than the value of an average performer.

We also need to include a figure that shows us the improvement in validity of a new assessment method over an existing one (in this context, 'validity' means how well an assessment method predicts performance or behaviour). For example, we may find that the correlation (expressed as a value between zero and one) between a rating on a psychometric test or interview and a line manager rating is now 0.35, and previously was 0.25. We have therefore increased our predictive validity by 0.1. We now have the figures we need to calculate ROI.

For example, say there is one post to fill with five remaining candidates. Tests cost £50 per candidate, the annual salary is £40,000 and the estimated tenure of the recruit is five years. Forgive the calculations, but this, as they say, allows you to put your money where your mouth is.

The first stage of the calculation is to multiply salary (for argument's sake, £40,000) by the increase in validity (0.1) by the increased value of excellent performers (£40,000 × 0.1 × 40 per cent = £1,600).

The second stage is to multiply this figure by the number of recruits to be selected for the post and their likely tenure (£1,600 × one recruit × five years = £8,000).

The final stage is to divide this figure (£8,000) by the cost, which in this case may be £50 per candidate multiplied by five candidates (£250). So the final figure is 8,000/250, or £32.

This is the benefit/cost ratio or, put simply, the return is 32 times the investment. To sound even more impressive, it can be expressed as a percentage return on investment by multiplying by 100: 3,200 per cent.

→

6 Apply the findings

It is, of course, important to interpret what you have found in the context of the organisation. For example, you may be surprised to find that your best sales staff are more people oriented than task oriented and are more amiable than they are assertive. This makes sense in low-pressure sales environments where building client relationships is key to success.

Use your findings to make improvements to your existing selection process and also to tailor development for your existing staff. In the example above, you may want to consider training your sales staff to be more people oriented and amiable in their approach, and ensure that you look for these behaviours at point of selection.

Source: *People Management*, 10 January 2008, p. 42.

ACTIVITY 8.5

How would you validate the selection process for the anti-rape detective job as described in Case 8.1 on the companion website **www.pearsoned.co.uk/torrington**?

SUMMARY PROPOSITIONS

8.1 Selection is a two-way process. The potential employer and the potential employee both make selection decisions.

8.2 A combination of selection methods is usually chosen, based upon the job, appropriateness, acceptability, time, administrative ease, cost, accuracy and the abilities of the selection staff.

8.3 The most well-used selection methods are application forms, interviews (including those conducted by video and telephone), tests, group selection procedures, assessment centres and references. There is increasing use of online selection methods.

8.4 A procedure for selection decision making needs to be agreed which can integrate all the selection information available.

8.5 Selection methods should be validated. A simple system is better than no system at all.

GENERAL DISCUSSION TOPICS

1 It could be argued that the selection process identifies candidates who are competent in the selection process rather than candidates who are most competent to perform the job on offer. Discuss this in relation to all forms of selection.

2 'It is unethical and bad for business to make candidates undergo a selection assessment centre without providing detailed feedback and support.' Discuss.

FURTHER READING

Human Resource Management Review, Vol. 19, No. 3, September 2009, 'Employee Selection at the Beginning of the 21st Century' Special Issue.
This is a special edition on selection and presents an up-to-date review of research on important selection topics, such as the legal environment in which employee selection occurs, how selection issues should be considered in the context of international and cultural issues, and how the central focus during the selection process may be on other factors than job relatedness.

International Journal of Selection and Assessment, Vol. 11, No. 2/3, June/September 2003.
This is a special edition of the journal and it is devoted to the role of technology in shaping the future of staffing and assessment. Contains some highly relevant articles, including, for example, using technology in the recruiting, screening and selection process; applicant and recruiter reactions to technology; Internet-based personality testing and privacy in Internet-based selection systems.

IRS (2002) 'Of good character: supplying references and providing access', *Employment Review*, No. 754, 24 June, pp. 34–6.
Second of a two-part series on references – this one concentrating on providing references and employee access to references about them. Useful to read this in conjunction with No. 752, 27 May, entitled 'The check's in the post' which focuses on the legal position and on the content and nature of references.

Murphy, N. (2006) 'Voyages of discovery: carrying out checks on job applicants', *IRS Employment Review*, No. 850, 7 July, pp. 42–8.
This article reports the results of a survey into employer practices to check the background details of applicants, and is much broader than seeking references from previous employers. It covers the type of information that is checked on, together with the mechanisms used.

REFERENCES

Anderson, N. and Shackleton, V. (1990) 'Staff selection decision making into the 1990s', *Management Decision*, Vol. 28, No. 1, pp. 5–8.

Barclay, J. (1999) 'Employee Selection: a question of structure', *Personnel Review*, Vol. 28, No. 1/2, pp. 134–51.

Branine, M. (2008) 'Graduate recruitment and selection in the UK', *Career Development International*, Vol. 13, No. 6, pp. 497–513.

Breaugh, J. (2009) 'The use of biodata for employee selection: past research and future directions', *Human Resource Management Review*, Vol. 19, pp. 219–31.

Brittain, S. and Ryder, P. (1999) 'Get complex', *People Management*, 25 November, pp. 48–51.

Bulois, N. and Shackleton, V. (1996) 'A qualitative study of recruitment and selection in France and Britain: the attitudes of recruiters in multinationals', in I. Beardwell (chair), *Contemporary Developments in Human Resource Management*. Paris: Editions ESKA, pp. 125–35.

Carrington, L. (2002) 'At the cutting edge', *People Management*, Vol. 8, No. 10, pp. 30–1.

Ceci, S. and Williams, W. (2000) 'Smart bomb', *People Management*, 24 August, pp. 32–6.

Chartered Institute of Personnel and Development (2009) *Recruitment, Retention and Turnover: Annual Survey Report 2009*. London: CIPD.

Dalen, L., Stanton, N. and Roberts, A. (2001) 'Faking personality questionnaires in selection', *Journal of Management Development*, Vol. 20, No. 8, pp. 729–41.

Fletcher, C. (1996) 'Mix and match fails to work on competencies', *People Management*, Vol. 2, No. 18, pp. 53–4.

Fowler, A. (1990) 'The writing on the wall', *Local Government Chronicle*, 26 January, pp. 20–8.

Heggestad, E., Morrison, M., Reeve, C. and McCloy, R.A. (2006) 'Forced-choice assessments of personality for selection: evaluating issues of normative assessment and faking resistance', *Journal of Applied Psychology*, Vol. 91, No. 1, pp. 9–24.

Iles, P. (1992) 'Centres of excellence? Assessment and development centres, managerial competence and human resource strategies', *British Journal of Management*, Vol. 3, pp. 79–90.

Iles, P. and Salaman, G. (1995) 'Recruitment, selection and assessment', in J. Storey (ed.), *Human Resource Management: A critical text*. London: Routledge.

Incomes Data Services (2004) *IDS Study Plus: Psychological tests*, IDS Study No. 770, Spring. London: IDS.

Incomes Data Services (2005) *Assessment Centres*, IDS Study No. 800, June. London: IDS.

IRS (2002a) 'Psychometrics: the next generation', *Employment Review*, No. 744, pp. 36–40.

IRS (2002b) 'The check's in the post', *Employment Review*, No. 752, pp. 34–42.

IRS (2003) 'Setting the tone: job descriptions and person specifications', *Employment Review*, No. 776, pp. 42–8.

Kirton, G. and Healey, G. (2009) 'Using competency-based assessment centres to select judges: implications for diversity and equality', *Human Resource Management Journal*, Vol. 19, No. 3, pp. 302–18.

Lievens, F., van Dam, K. and Anderson, N. (2002) 'Recent trends and challenges in personnel selection', *Personnel Review*, Vol. 31, No. 5, pp. 580–601.

Lockyer, C. and Scholaris, D. (2004) 'Selecting hotel staff: why best practice does not always work', *International Journal of Contemporary Hospitality Management*, Vol. 16, No. 2, pp. 125–35.

McHenry, R. (2002) 'The Myers–Briggs response', *People Management*, Vol. 8, No. 24, p. 34.

Mohamed, A., Orife, J. and Wibowo, K. (2001) 'The legality of a key word search as a personnel selection tool', *Personnel Review*, Vol. 24, No. 5, pp. 516–22.

Murphy, N. (2005) 'Got your number: using telephone interviewing', *IRS Employment Review*, No. 832, pp. 43–5.

Murphy, N. (2006) 'Testing the waters: employers' use of selection assessments', *IRS Employment Review*, No. 852, pp. 42–8.

Palmer, M. (2002) 'Very testing testing', *People Management*, Vol. 8, No. 1, pp. 18–19.

Papadopoulou, A., Ineson, E. and Williams, D. (1996) 'The graduate management trainee pre-selection interview', *Personnel Review*, Vol. 25, No. 4, pp. 21–37.

Philips, L. (2007) 'O2 hires on performance', *People Management*, 23 August, p. 10.

Plumbley, P.R. (1985) *Recruitment and Selection*, 4th edn. London: Institute of Personnel Management.

Robertson, I. (2001) 'Undue diligence', *People Management*, Vol. 7, No. 23, pp. 42–3.

Shackleton, V. and Newell, S. (1991) 'Management selection: a comparative survey of methods used in top British and French companies', *Journal of Occupational Psychology*, Vol. 64, pp. 23–36.

Smethurst, S. (2006) 'The window test', *People Management*, Vol. 12, No. 2, pp. 28–30.

Suff, R. (2005) 'Centres of attention', *IRS Employment Review*, No. 816, pp. 42–8.

Taylor, S. (2008) *Employee Resourcing*. London: IPD.

Thatcher, M. (1997) 'A test of character', *People Management*, 15 May.

Tixier, M. (1996) 'Employers' recruitment tools across Europe', *Employed Relations*, Vol. 18, No. 6, pp. 67–78.

Townley, B. (1991) 'Selection and appraisal: reconstituting social relations?', in J. Storey (ed.), *New Perspectives in Human Resource Management*. London: Routledge.

Tulip, S. (2002) 'Personality trait secrets', *People Management*, Vol. 8, No. 17, pp. 34–8.

van Zwanenberg, N. and Wilkinson, L.J. (1993) 'The person specification: a problem masquerading as a solution?', *Personnel Review*, Vol. 22, No. 7, pp. 54–65.

Wanous, J.P. (1992) *Organisational Entry: Recruitment, selection, orientation and socialisation of newcomers*. Reading: Addison-Wesley.

Warhurst, C. and Nickson, D. (2007) 'Employee experience of aesthetic labour in retail and hospitality', *Work, Employment and Society*, Vol. 21, No. 103, pp. 103–20.

Werbel, J. and Johnson, D. (2001) 'The use of person–group fit for employment selection: a missing link in person–environment fit', *Human Resource Management*, Vol. 40, No. 3, pp. 227–40.

Whiddett, S. and Hollyforde, S. (2003) *The Competencies Handbook*. London: IPD.

Whiddett, S. and Kandola, B. (2000) 'Fit for the job?', *People Management*, 25 May.

Wilkinson, L.J. and van Zwanenberg, N. (1994) 'Development of a person specification system for managerial jobs', *Personnel Review*, Vol. 23, No. 1, pp. 25–36.

Williams, W. and Sternberg, R. (2001) *Success for Managers*. London: Lawrence Erlbaum Associates.

Woodruffe, C. (2000) *Development and Assessment Centres: Identifying and assessing competence*, 3rd edn. London: IPD.

An extensive range of additional materials, including multiple choice questions, answers to questions and links to useful websites can be found on the Human Resource Management companion website at **www.pearsoned.co.uk/torrington**.

STAFF RETENTION

THE OBJECTIVES OF THIS CHAPTER ARE TO:

1. Examine recent trends in job tenure and turnover in the UK
2. Assess the arguments for and against investing resources in staff turnover reduction programmes
3. Outline the main reasons for voluntary resignations
4. Set out how staff turnover can be costed
5. Explore some approaches which improve staff retention rates

The previous two chapters focused on the processes used to mobilise a workforce: activities which are often expensive and time consuming. It is estimated that the costs associated with recruiting and training a new employee average between half and one and a half times the annual salary for the post in question, depending on the approaches used (Branham 2005: 3). In this chapter we consider the most important way in which human resource managers seek to reduce the time and money spent on these activities, namely by trying to ensure that people choose not to leave an organisation voluntarily in the first place.

The extent of interest in employee retention issues varies over time as labour markets become successively tighter and looser depending on economic conditions. Until recessionary conditions developed in 2008 unemployment had been low for over a decade, making it harder to recruit staff with the necessary skills and attitudes. During this period employee retention moved to the top of the HRM agenda, leading to the publication of several new books and articles exploring how organisations can ensure that they have the best chance of retaining the people they employ (e.g. Williams 2000, Cappelli 2000 and Larkan 2006). Some focused on retaining people generally, while others developed the view that organisations should concentrate primarily on retaining their best performers. These authors tended to use the term 'the war for talent' to illustrate the significance and difficulty faced by those competing for the services of individuals who have the capacity to make a real difference to an organisation's competitive position. After 2008, as in previous recessions, employee retention became less significant for many organisations. Keeping people was not the problem they faced, instead it was how to downsize workforces in the most effective and efficient manner. It also fell down the agenda because fewer people leave their employers voluntarily during periods of recession, there being a shortage of alternative employment opportunities open to them. As the economy recovers and job prospects improve, however, we can anticipate a return to a situation in which employers face problems retaining good people in tight labour markets. Moreover, as always happens after lengthy periods of recession, staff turnover reaches its highest levels in the immediate aftermath. High rates of 'pent-up turnover' take employers by surprise as large numbers of staff who have had to remain in jobs in which they were not entirely happy take the first opportunity available to them to switch employment. For this reason wise employers retain an interest in employee retention even when the skills they seek are in relatively plentiful supply. This helps to reduce the extent of any race to the exit doors when unemployment falls and wars for talent resume.

ACTIVITY 9.1

Employee retention becomes an important item on the HRM agenda when organisations are faced with skills shortages. When labour is in reasonably good supply leavers can easily be replaced by new starters. Aside from working harder at retaining staff, what alternative approaches could be adopted to help staff an organisation when the skills it requires are in short supply?

TURNOVER RATES AND TRENDS

In recent years there has been a mismatch between the rhetoric about job tenure and the reality. Some consultants, academics and management gurus continue to make much mileage out of the claim that 'there are no longer any jobs for life', suggesting that the length of time we spend working for organisations has fallen substantially in recent years. In fact this is a misleading claim. All the available evidence strongly suggests that job tenure has been broadly stable for several decades. OECD statistics show that the average length of time that *permanent employees remain in a job* remained steady at or around eight years from 1992 until 2002 (Auer *et al.* 2004: 3), while Labour Force Survey data confirm that long periods of job tenure remain the norm for a substantial portion of the working population (*see* Table 9.1). People tend to move from employer to employer early on in their careers, often staying in one employment for just a few months. But once they find a job (or an employer) that they like, the tendency is to remain for several years. 'Jobs for life' have, in truth, always been a relative rarity, but the evidence suggests that long-term tenure remains a reality for many employees. Over a third of UK employees have already been in their current jobs for over eight years.

The overall figures mask substantial differences between tenure and turnover rates in different industries. Studies undertaken annually by the Chartered Institute of Personnel and Development persistently show retailing and catering to be the sectors with the highest turnover levels, with rates averaging over 40 per cent in recent years. By contrast the most stable workforces are to be found in the public services, where reported annual turnover rates are only 11 or 12 per cent (CIPD 2009: 26). Rates also vary from region to region and over time, being highest when and where average pay levels are highest and unemployment is low, and between different professions. As a rule, the more highly paid a person is, the less likely that person is to switch jobs, but there remain some highly paid professions such as sales where turnover is always high. It is also interesting to observe how much more inclined younger workers are to switch jobs than their older colleagues. Macaulay (2003) calculated what proportion of employees had completed more than a year's service with their employer. For the over-50s the figure was 86 per cent, for the 18–24 age group it was only 51 per cent.

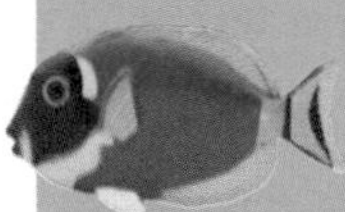

WINDOW ON PRACTICE

The length of time that employees remain in their jobs, or at least with the same employers, varies considerably from country to country. Auer *et al.* (2006) analysed the proportion of staff who had less than a year's service in the OECD countries and the proportion who had completed more than ten years' service. The country with the most shorter-term employees is the USA, where 24.5 per cent have less than a year's service, while only 26.2 per cent have been with their employers for more than ten years. At the other end of the scale is Greece, where only 9.8 per cent have less than a year's service and as many as 52 per cent have over ten years' service. High rates of job stability are also common in Italy, Belgium and Portugal. By contrast relatively low stability rates are found in the UK, Denmark and Ireland.

Table 9.1 Job tenure in the UK among permanent employees

Length of service	Percentage of the workforce
1 month–2 years:	27
2–5 years:	24
5–8 years:	13
8–12 years:	9
Over 12 years:	24

Source: Adapted from DTI 2006: 4.

ACTIVITY 9.2

Why do you think staff turnover rates are so much higher in some industries than others? Make a list of the different factors you consider may account for variations.

THE IMPACT OF STAFF TURNOVER

There is some debate about the level which staff turnover rates have to reach in order to inflict measurable damage on an employer. The answer varies from organisation to organisation. In some industries it is possible to sustain highly successful businesses with turnover rates that would make it impossible to function in other sectors. Some chains of fast-food restaurants, for example, are widely reported as managing with turnover rates in excess of 300 per cent. This means that the average tenure for each employee is only four months (Ritzer 1996: 130; Cappelli 2000: 106). DiPietro *et al.* (2007) cite statistics from the USA that show staff turnover rates in the restaurant industry generally to be 104 per cent, an average figure that is kept so high because of poor retention rates in the low-paying, fast-food sector. Yet the companies concerned are some of the most successful in the world. By contrast, in a professional services organisation, where the personal relationships established between employees and clients are central to ongoing success, a turnover rate in excess of 10 per cent is likely to cause damage to the business.

There are sound arguments that can be made in favour of a certain amount of staff turnover. First, it is fair to say that organisations need to be rejuvenated with 'fresh blood' from time to time if they are to avoid becoming stale and stunted. This is particularly true at senior levels, where new leadership is often required periodically to drive change forward. More generally, however, new faces bring new ideas and experiences which help make organisations more dynamic. Second, it is possible to argue that a degree of turnover helps managers to keep firmer control over labour costs than would otherwise be the case. This is particularly true of organisations which are subject to regular and unpredictable changes in business levels. When income falls it is possible to hold back from replacing leavers until such time as it begins to pick up again. In this way organisations are able to minimise staffing budgets while maintaining profit levels during leaner periods. Redundancy bills are also lower in organisations with relatively high staff turnover because they are able to use natural wastage as the main means of reducing their workforce before compulsory lay-offs are needed. Third, it can be plausibly argued that some employee turnover is 'functional' rather than 'dysfunctional' because it results in the loss of poor performers and their replacement with more effective employees.

The arguments against staff turnover are equally persuasive. First are the sheer costs associated with replacing people who have left, ranging from the cost of placing a recruitment advertisement, through the time spent administering and conducting the selection process, to expenses required in inducting and training new employees. On top of these there are less easily measurable losses sustained as a result of poorer performance on the part of less experienced employees. For larger organisations employing specialist recruiters these costs can add up to millions of pounds a year, with substantial dividends to be claimed from a reduction in staff turnover levels by a few percentage points. The second major argument in favour of improving staff retention results from a straightforward recognition that people who leave represent a lost resource in whom the organisation has invested time and money. The damage is all the greater when good people, trained and developed at the organisation's expense, subsequently choose to work for competitors. Finally, it is argued that high turnover rates are symptomatic of a poorly managed organisation. They suggest that people are dissatisfied with their jobs or with their employer and would prefer to work elsewhere. These moves thus send a negative message to customers and help create a poor image in the labour market, making it progressively harder for the organisation affected to recruit good performers in the future. We may thus conclude that the case for seeking to reduce staff turnover varies from organisation to organisation. Where replacement employees are in plentiful supply, where new starters can be trained quickly and where business levels are subject to regular fluctuation it is possible to manage effectively with a relatively high level of turnover. Indeed, it may make good business sense to do so if the expenditure required to increase employee retention is greater than the savings that would be gained as a result. In other situations the case for taking action on turnover rates is persuasive, particularly where substantial investment in training is required before new starters are able to operate at maximum effectiveness. Companies which achieve turnover rates below their industry average are thus likely to enjoy greater competitive advantage than those with relatively high rates.

TURNOVER ANALYSIS AND COSTING

There is little that an organisation can do to manage turnover unless there is an understanding of the reasons for it. Information about these reasons is notoriously difficult to collect. Most commentators recommend exit interviews (that is, interviews with leavers about their reasons for resigning), but the problem here is whether the individual will feel able to tell the truth, and this will depend on the culture of the organisation, the specific reasons for leaving and the support that the individual will need from the organisation in the future in the form of references. Despite their disadvantages, exit interviews may be helpful if handled sensitively and confidentially – perhaps by the HR department rather than the line manager. You will find further information and discussion exercises about them on our companion website **www.pearsoned.co.uk/torrington**. In addition, analyses of turnover rates between different departments and different job groups may well shed some light on causes of turnover. Attitude surveys can also provide relevant information.

WINDOW ON PRACTICE

It is very easy for an organisation to get itself into a vicious circle of turnover if it does not act to stem a retention problem. Modest turnover rates can rapidly increase as the pressures on remaining staff become greater, leading to serious operational difficulties. As soon as more than one or two people leave an established team, more is demanded of those left to carry the burden. First, there may be a sizeable time gap between leavers resigning and new starters coming into post. Then there is the period when the new people are learning their jobs, taking more time to accomplish tasks and needing assistance from more established employees. The problem can be compounded with additional pressure being placed on managers and HR specialists faced with the need to recruit people quickly, leading to the selection of people who are not wholly suited to the jobs in question. The result is greater turnover as people respond by looking for less pressured job opportunities elsewhere.

Problems of this kind were faced by the Japanese engineering company, Makita. It addressed the issue by increasing its induction programme from half a day to four weeks and by taking a good deal more care over its recruitment and selection processes. The result was a reduction in turnover levels from 97 per cent in 1997 to 38 per cent in 1999.

Source: IDS (2000) *Improving Staff Retention*, IDS Study 692, July, pp. 14–17.

People leave jobs for a variety of different reasons, many of which are wholly outside the power of the organisation to influence. One very common reason for leaving, for example, is retirement. It can be brought forward or pushed back for a few years, but ultimately it affects everyone. In many cases people leave for a mixture of reasons, certain factors weighing more highly in their minds than others. The following is one approach to categorising the main reasons people have for voluntarily leaving a job, each requiring a different kind of response from the organisation.

Outside factors

Outside factors relate to situations in which someone leaves for reasons that are largely unrelated to their work. The most common instances involve people moving away when a spouse or partner is relocated. Others include the wish to fulfil a long-term ambition to travel, pressures associated with juggling the needs of work and family and illness. To an extent such turnover is unavoidable, although it is possible to reduce it somewhat through the provision of career breaks, forms of flexible working and/or child-care facilities.

Functional turnover

The functional turnover category includes all resignations which are welcomed by both employer and employee alike. The major examples are those which stem from an individual's poor work performance or failure to fit in comfortably with an organisational or departmental culture. While such resignations are less damaging than others from an organisation's point of view they should still be regarded as lost opportunities and as an unnecessary cost. The main solution to the reduction of functional turnover lies in improving recruitment and selection procedures so that fewer people in the category are appointed in the first place. However, some poorly engineered change management schemes are also sometimes to blame, especially where they result in new work pressures or workplace ethics.

Push factors

With push factors the problem is dissatisfaction with work or the organisation, leading to unwanted turnover. A wide range of issues can be cited to explain such resignations. Insufficient development opportunities, boredom, ineffective supervision, poor levels of employee involvement and straightforward personality clashes are the most common precipitating factors. Organisations can readily address all of these issues. The main reason that so many fail to do so is the absence of mechanisms for picking up signs of dissatisfaction. If there is no opportunity to voice concerns, employees who are unhappy will inevitably start looking elsewhere.

Pull factors

The opposite side of the coin is the attraction of rival employers. Salary levels are often a factor here, employees leaving in order to improve their living standards. In addition there are broader notions of career development, the wish to move into new areas of work for which there are better opportunities elsewhere, the chance to work with particular people, and more practical issues such as commuting time. For the employer losing people as a result of such factors there are two main lines of attack. First, there is a need to be aware of what other employers are offering and to ensure that as far as possible this is matched – or at least that a broadly comparable package of pay and opportunities is offered. The second requirement involves trying to ensure that employees appreciate what they are currently being given. The emphasis here is on effective communication of any 'unique selling points' and of the extent to which opportunities comparable to those offered elsewhere are given.

What are the most common reasons?

UK-based studies focusing on people's reasons for leaving organisations are few and far between, but those that have been published tend to emphasise that a mix of different factors apply and that these vary from industry to industry (e.g. DiPietro *et al.* 2007; Carroll *et al.* 2008). Taylor and his colleagues interviewed 200 people who had recently changed employers about why they left their last jobs. They found a mix of factors at work in most cases but concluded that push factors were a great deal more prevalent than pull factors as causes of voluntary resignations (Taylor 2002). Very few people appear to leave jobs in which they are broadly happy in search of something even better. Instead the picture is overwhelmingly one in which dissatisfied employees seek alternatives because they no longer enjoy working for their current employer.

Interestingly this study found relatively few examples of people leaving for financial reasons. Indeed more of the interviewees took pay cuts in order to move from one job to another than said that a pay rise was their principal reason for switching employers.

Other factors played a much bigger role:

- dissatisfaction with the conditions of work, especially hours;
- a perception that they were not being given sufficient career development opportunities;
- a bad relationship with their immediate supervisor.

This third factor was by far the most commonly mentioned in the interviews, lending support to the often-stated point that people leave their managers and not their organisations.

Branham (2005), drawing on research undertaken by the Saratoga Institute, reached similar conclusions. His seven 'hidden reasons employees leave' are as follows:

- the job or workplace not living up to expectations;
- a mismatch between the person and the job;
- too little coaching and feedback;
- too few growth and advancement opportunities;
- feeling devalued and unrecognised;
- stress from overwork and work-life imbalance;
- loss of trust and confidence in senior leaders.

Samuel and Chipunza (2009) looked at why long-serving staff had remained in their jobs, rather than focusing on why leavers had left. Their study took place in four large South African organisations, two in the private sector and two in the public sector. They found that the four key factors that served to retain staff were:

- training and development;
- challenging and interesting work;
- freedom for innovative thinking;
- job security.

It would follow logically that organisations that do not provide these to their people will lose staff to competitors who can.

ACTIVITY 9.3

Think about jobs that you or members of your family have left in recent years. What were the key factors that led to the decision to leave? Was there one major factor or did several act together in combination?

Costing

When deciding what kind of measures to put in place in order to improve staff retention generally or the retention of particular individuals, organisations need to balance the costs involved against those that are incurred as a direct result of voluntary resignations. Although it is difficult to cost turnover accurately, it is possible to reach a fair estimate by taking into account the range of expenses involved in replacing one individual with another. Once a figure has been calculated for a job, it is relatively straightforward to compute the savings to be gained from a given percentage reduction in annual turnover rates. Figure 9.1 shows the approach to turnover costing recommended by Hugo Fair (1992).

Costing turnover each year permits organisations to state with some confidence how much money is being saved as a result of ongoing staff turnover reduction programmes. It can also be used as a means of persuading finance directors of the case for investing money in initiatives which can be shown to improve retention. An example of an organisation which has done this is Positive Steps Oldham, a not-for-profit company set up when two local careers service organisations merged (*see* IDS 2005). The new organisation employs 205 people and at the time it was formed had an overall staff turnover rate of 38 per cent. Over a three-year period, as a result of various targeted initiatives, turnover

Enter number of employees	______	(a),
Enter average weekly wage	£ ______	(b),
Multiply (a) × (b)	£ ______	(c),
Multiply (c) × 52	£ ______	(d) = *Total paybill*
Enter current turnover rate	______ %	(e),
Multiply (e) × (a)	______	(f) = *Staff loss p.a.*
Enter average number of days to replace	______	(g),
Multiplier rate for overtime/temps.	______	(h),
Multiply (b) × (h)	£ ______	(i),
Multiply (f) × (g) × [(i)/5]	£ ______	(j) = Immediate cover costs
Preparation and interview time per applicant (days)	______	(k),
Shortlisted applicants per position	______	(l),
Enter average manager weekly wage	£ ______	(m),
Multiply (f) × (k) × (l) × [(m)/5]	£ ______	(n) = Interview time costs
Enter average recruitment fees	______ %	(o),
Multiply (d) × (e) × (o)	£ ______	(p) = Recruitment fee costs
Length of induction training (days)	______	(q),
Frequency of this training (p.a.)	______	(r),
Multiply [(b)/5] × (q) × [(f) + (r)]	£ ______	(s) = Induction training cost
Duration of learning curve (months)	______	(t),
Enter non-productive element	______ %	(u),
Multiply (d) × (e) × [(t)/12] × (u)	£ ______	(v) = Non-productive costs
Multiply (t) × (u) (months)	£ ______	(w),
Multiply (d) × (e) × (h) × [(w)/12]	£ ______	(x) = Continuing cover costs
Multiply (g) × [(b)/5] × (f)	£ ______	(y) = Salary savings
Add (j) + (n) + (p) + (s) + (v) + (x) − (y)	£ ______	(z) = *Turnover cost p.a.*
Potential cost saving		
Enter expected turnover reduction	______ %	(1),
Multiply (z) × [(1)/(e)]	£ ______	(2) = Labour turnover savings
Enter reduction in replacement time	______ %	(3),
Multiply (j) × (3)	£ ______	(4) = Added cover savings
Add (2) + (4)	£ ______	(5) = *Total savings p.a.*

Figure 9.1 A sample form for costing labour turnover

Source: H. Fair (1992) *Personnel and Profit: The pay-off from people*, p. 41. London: IPM. Used with permission of CIPD Publications.

fell to a much more healthy 14 per cent. Not only did this make the organisation much more effective, it also substantially reduced overheads. The company model for calculating turnover costs includes direct and indirect costs along the lines put forward by Fair in Figure 9.1. At Positive Steps Oldham it was estimated that around £20,000 a year was saved by reducing turnover by more than half.

STAFF RETENTION STRATEGIES

The straightforward answer to the question of how best to retain staff is to provide them with a better deal, in the broadest sense, than they perceive they could get by working for alternative employers. Terms and conditions play a significant role, but other factors are often more important. For example, there is a need to provide jobs which are satisfying, along with career development opportunities, as much autonomy as is practicable and, above all, competent line management. Indeed, at one level, most of the practices of effective human resource management described in this book can play a part in reducing turnover. Organisations which make use of them will enjoy lower rates than competitors who do not. Below we look at six measures that have been shown to have a positive effect on employee retention, focusing particularly on those practices which are not covered in any great depth elsewhere in the book.

Pay

There is some debate in the retention literature about the extent to which raising pay levels reduces staff turnover. On the one hand there is evidence to show that, on average, employers who offer the most attractive reward packages have lower attrition rates than those who pay poorly (Gerhart 2009: 215–16), an assumption which leads many organisations to use pay rates as their prime weapon in retaining staff (White 2009: 35–9). On the other, there is evidence which suggests that pay is a good deal less important than other factors in a decision to quit one's job (Bevan *et al.* 1997; Taylor 2002). The consensus among researchers specialising in retention issues is that pay has a role to play as a satisfier, but that it will not usually have an effect when other factors are pushing an individual towards quitting. Raising pay levels may thus result in greater job satisfaction where people are already happy with their work, but it will not deter unhappy employees from leaving. Sturges and Guest (1999), in their study of leaving decisions in the field of graduate employment, summed up their findings as follows:

> As far as they are concerned, while challenging work will compensate for pay, pay will never compensate for having to do boring, unstimulating work. (Sturges and Guest 1999: 19)

Recent research findings thus appear to confirm the views expressed by Herzberg (1966) that pay is a 'hygiene factor' rather than a motivator. This means that it can be a cause of dissatisfaction at work, but not of positive job satisfaction. People may be motivated to leave an employer who is perceived as paying badly, but once they are satisfied with their pay additional increases have little effect.

The other problem with the use of pay increases to retain staff is that it is an approach that is very easily matched by competitors. This is particularly true of 'golden handcuff' arrangements which seek to tie senior staff to an organisation for a number of years by paying substantial bonuses at a defined future date. As Cappelli (2000: 106) argues, in a buoyant job market, recruiters simply 'unlock the handcuffs' by offering equivalent signing-on bonuses to people they wish to employ.

It is important that employees do not perceive their employers to be treating them inequitably. Provided pay levels are not considerably lower than those paid by an organisation's labour market competitors, other factors will usually be more important contributors towards high turnover levels. Where the salaries that are paid are already broadly competitive, little purpose is served by increasing them further. The organisation may well make itself more attractive in recruitment terms, but the effect on staff retention will be limited. Moreover, of course, wage costs will increase.

There is potentially more to be gained from enhancing benefits packages, because these are less easily imitated or matched by competitors. Where particular benefits, such as staff discounts, holiday entitlements or private healthcare schemes, are appreciated by staff, they are more likely to have a positive effect on staff turnover than simply paying higher base wages. Potentially the same is true of pension schemes, which are associated with relatively high levels of staff retention. However, the research evidence suggests that except for older employees who have completed many years of service, most pension schemes are not sufficiently valued by staff to cause them to stay in a job with which they are dissatisfied (Taylor 2009). Arguably, the best way of using benefits to keep a lid on staff turnover is to move towards flexible schemes such as those discussed in Chapter 25. An employer which allows individual employees to choose how they make up their own remuneration package will generally be more attractive than one which only offers a 'one size fits all' set of benefits.

While pay rates and benefit packages may play a relatively marginal role in the retention of good people, reward in the broader sense plays a more significant role. If employees do not find their work to be 'rewarding' in the broadest sense of the word, they will be much more likely to start looking for alternative jobs. Providing more rewarding work is a good deal harder for managers to achieve because different people find different aspects of their work to be rewarding. There is thus a need to understand what makes people tick and to manage them as individuals accordingly. Getting this right is difficult, but achieving it is worthwhile from the point of view of retaining people. It is far harder for would-be competitors to imitate the effective motivation of an individual than it is for them to increase the salary that a person is paid.

ACTIVITY 9.4

The case for arguing that pay rates have a relatively minor role to play in explaining individual resignations rests partly on the assumption that other elements of the employment relationship are more important. It is argued that people will 'trade in' high pay in order to secure other perceived benefits and that consequently low-paying employers can retain staff effectively.

What other factors do you think employees consider to be more important than pay? What role can the HRM function play in helping to develop these?

Managing expectations

For some years research evidence has strongly suggested that employers benefit from ensuring that potential employees gain a 'realistic job preview' before they take up a job offer. The purpose is to make sure that new staff enter an organisation with their eyes wide open and do not find that the job fails to meet their expectations. A major cause of job dissatisfaction, and hence of high staff turnover, is the experience of having one's high hopes of new employment dashed by the realisation that it is not going to be as enjoyable or stimulating as anticipated.

Several researchers have drawn attention to the importance of these processes in reducing high turnover during the early months of employment (e.g. Wanous 1992: 53–87; Breaugh 2008: 105–8). The need is to strike a balance at the recruitment stage between sending out messages which are entirely positive and sending out those which are realistic. In other words, it is important not to mislead candidates about the nature of the work that they will be doing.

Realistic job previews are most important when candidates, for whatever reason, cannot know a great deal about the job for which they are applying. This may be because of limited past experience or it may because the job is relatively unusual and not based in a type of workplace with which job applicants are familiar. An example quoted by Carroll *et al.* (1999: 246) concerns work in nursing homes, which seems to attract people looking to undertake a caring role but who are unfamiliar with the less attractive hours, working conditions and job duties associated with the care assistant's role. The realistic job preview is highly appropriate in such a situation as a means of avoiding recruiting people who subsequently leave within a few weeks.

The importance of unmet expectations as an explanation for staff turnover is also stressed by Sturges and Guest (1999: 16 and 31) in their work on the retention of newly recruited graduates. Here the problem is one of employers overselling graduate careers when competing with others to secure the services of the brightest young people:

> False impressions are given and a positive spin put on answers to questions so as to deter able applicants from taking up alternative offers. As a result, graduates start work confident in the belief that their days will be filled with interesting work, that they will be treated fairly and objectively in terms of performance assessment, that their career development will be fostered judiciously, and that their working lives will in some way be 'fun' and 'exciting'. That is fine if it really can be guaranteed. Unfortunately such is often not the case, and unsurprisingly it leads to early dissatisfaction and higher turnover rates than are desirable. (Jenner and Taylor 2000: 155)

A solution, apart from the introduction of more honest recruitment literature, is to provide periods of work experience for students before they graduate. A summer spent working somewhere is the best possible way of finding out exactly what a particular job or workplace is really like. The same argument can be deployed in support of work experience for young people who are about to leave school in order to enter the job market.

Induction

Another process often credited with the reduction of turnover early in the employment relationship is the presence of effective and timely induction. It is very easy to overlook in the rush to get people into key posts quickly and it is often carried out badly, but it is essential if avoidable early turnover is to be kept to a minimum. Gregg and Wadsworth (1999: 111) show in their analysis of 870,000 workers starting new jobs in 1992 that as many as 17 per cent had left within three months and 42 per cent within 12 months. No doubt a good number of these departures were due either to poorly managed expectations or to ineffective inductions.

Induction has a number of distinct purposes, all of which are concerned with preparing new employees to work as effectively as possible and as soon as is possible in their new jobs. First, it plays an important part in helping new starters to adjust emotionally to the new workplace. It gives an opportunity to ensure that they understand where things are, who to ask when unsure about what to do and how their role fits into the organisation generally. Second, induction provides a forum in which basic information about the organisation can be transmitted. This may include material about the organisation's purpose, its mission statement and the key issues it faces. More generally a corporate induction provides a suitable occasion to talk about health and safety regulations, fire evacuation procedures and organisational policies concerning matters like the use of telephones for private purposes. Third, induction processes can be used to convey to new starters important cultural messages about what the organisation expects and what employees can expect in return. It thus potentially forms an important stage in the establishment of the psychological contract, leaving new employees clear about what they need to do to advance their own prospects in the organisation. All these matters will be picked up by new starters anyway in their first months of employment, but incorporating them into a formal induction programme ensures that they are brought up to speed a good deal more quickly, and that they are less likely to leave at an early date.

There is no 'right' length for an induction programme. In some jobs it can be accomplished effectively in a few days, for others there is a need for some form of input over a number of weeks. What is important is that individuals are properly introduced both to the organisation and to their particular role within it. These introductions are usually best handled by different people. Organisational induction, because it is given to all new starters, is normally handled centrally by the HR department and takes place in a single place over one or two days. Job-based induction takes longer, will be overseen by the individual's own line manager and will usually involve shadowing colleagues. The former largely takes the form of a presentation, while the latter involves the use of a wider variety of training methods.

Rankin (2006) demonstrates that employers in the UK rarely evaluate their induction programmes in terms of the impact they are having. Employees are asked from time to time to rate specific induction courses, but it is rare for more sophisticated analysis to be carried out. As a result the programmes themselves are not always designed very effectively. They reflect what managers think new employees need in their first weeks of work and not what employees may actually need. They also tend to be standardised across organisations, little thought being given to the particular requirements of different employee groups (Wolff 2009). Given these findings it is fair to conclude that there is room for a good deal of improvement in this area of HR work and that improved employee retention may well be a result.

WINDOW ON PRACTICE

IRS (2000: 11) describes an original approach taken to the induction of staff at a large Novotel Hotel in London. Unusually for the hotel industry the induction programme here lasts for three weeks. It includes some job shadowing of experienced staff, but also consists of several days spent in a training room learning about the hotel's main services and learning how to deal with difficult customers. A variety of training techniques are used including quizzes, games, discussion forums and role-play exercises. The management saw their retention rates increase by 12 per cent after the introduction of the new programme.

Family-friendly HR practices

Labour Force Survey statistics show that between 5 per cent and 10 per cent of employees leave their jobs for 'family or personal reasons' (IRS 1999: 6), while Hom and Griffeth (1995: 252) quote American research indicating that 33 per cent of women quit jobs to devote more time to their families – a response given by only 1 per cent of men. UK employers believe that 21 per cent of their leavers resign 'to have children or look after them', a further 7 per cent leaving to look after other family members (CIPD 2009: 31). Official statistics also show that average job tenure among women with children in the UK is over a year shorter than that of women without children and almost two years shorter than that of men. Taken together these statistics suggest that one of the more significant reasons for voluntary resignations from jobs is the inability to juggle the demands of a job with those of the family. They indicate that there is a good business case, particularly where staff retention is high on the agenda, for considering ways in which employment can be made more family friendly.

As a result of legislation under the Working Time Regulations 1998, the Employment Relations Act 1999, the Employment Act 2002 and the Work and Families Act 2006, UK employers are now obliged by law to provide the following as a minimum floor of rights:

- nine months' paid leave for all employees paid according to a formula set out in the regulations;
- an additional three months' unpaid maternity leave for employees;
- reasonable paid time off for pregnant employees to attend ante-natal clinics;
- specific health and safety measures for workers who are pregnant or have recently given birth;
- four weeks' paid holiday each year in addition to eight bank holidays;
- a total of three months' unpaid parental leave for mothers and fathers on the birth or adoption of a child;
- reasonable unpaid time off for employees to deal with family emergencies such as the sickness of a child or dependent relative;

- consideration of reasonable requests by parents of young children and with caring responsibilities for adults to work flexibly;
- two weeks' paid paternity leave for new fathers.

Many employers, however, have decided to go a good deal further down this road than is required by law. The most common example is the provision of more paid maternity leave and the right, where possible, for mothers to return to work on a part-time or job-share basis if they so wish. Crèche provision is common in larger workplaces, while others offer child-care vouchers instead. Career breaks are offered by many public sector employers, allowing people to take a few months off without pay and subsequently to return to a similar job with the same organisation. Flexitime systems such as those described in Chapter 5 are also useful to people with families and may thus serve as a retention tool in some cases. There is also growing interest in 'elder care' arrangements aimed specifically at providing assistance to those seeking to combine work with responsibility for the care of elderly relatives. An example in the UK is the 'granny crèche' established by Peugeot for employees at its plant in Coventry.

Providing flexible working opportunities of these kinds is a very good way of retaining staff, particularly when organisations do more than their competitors. This is because juggling family and work responsibilities is a big issue in many employees' lives and because evidence suggests that it is thus hugely appreciated by them (Di Petro *et al.* 2007).

Training and development

There are two widely expressed, but wholly opposed, perspectives on the link between training interventions and employee turnover. On the one hand is the argument that training opportunities enhance commitment to an employer on the part of individual employees, making them less likely to leave voluntarily than they would if no training were offered. The alternative view holds that training makes people more employable and hence more likely to leave in order to develop their careers elsewhere. The view is thus put that money spent on training is money wasted because it ultimately benefits other employers.

Green *et al.* (2000: 267–72) report research on perceptions of 1,539 employees on different kinds of training. They found that the overall effect is neutral, 19 per cent of employees saying that training was 'more likely to make them actively look for another job' and 18 per cent saying it was less likely to do so. However, they also found the type of training and the source of sponsorship to be a significant variable. Training which is paid for by the employer is a good deal less likely to raise job mobility than that paid for by the employee or the government. Firm-specific training is also shown in the study to be associated with lower turnover than training which leads to the acquisition of transferable skills. The point is made, however, that whatever the form of training an employer can develop a workforce which is both 'capable and committed' by combining training interventions with other forms of retention initiative.

The most expensive types of training intervention involve long-term courses of study such as an MBA, CIPD or accountancy qualification. In financing such courses, employers are sending a very clear signal to the employees concerned that their contribution is valued and that they can look forward to substantial career advancement if they opt to stay. The fact that leaving will also mean an end to the funding for the course, and in some cases a requirement to pay back a sum equivalent to the fees, provides more direct incentives to remain with the sponsoring employer.

Improving the quality of line management

If it is the case that many, if not most, voluntary resignations are explained by dissatisfaction on the part of employees with their supervisors, it follows that the most effective means of reducing staff turnover in organisations is to improve the performance of line managers. Too often, it appears, people are promoted into supervisory positions without adequate experience or training. Organisations seem to assume that their managers are capable supervisors, without recognising that the role is difficult and does not usually come naturally to people. Hence it is common to find managers who are 'quick to criticise but slow to praise', who are too tied up in their own work to show an interest in their subordinates and who prefer to impose their own solutions without first taking account of their staff's views. The solution is to take action on various fronts to improve the effectiveness of supervisors:

- select people for line management roles following an assessment of their supervisory capabilities;
- ensure that all newly appointed line managers are trained in the art of effective supervision;
- regularly appraise line managers on their supervisory skills.

This really amounts to little more than common sense, but such approaches are the exception to the rule in most UK organisations.

WINDOW ON PRACTICE

In 2009 the Chartered Institute of Personnel and Development's annual survey on recruitment and retention matters asked employers to state what steps they were currently taking to address staff retention. The range of initiatives was extensive and broadly appropriate given what the research evidence tells us are the principal reasons for voluntary resignations. The top ten initiatives were as follows:

10) better promotion of the employer brand (21%)
9) offering coaching and mentoring (24%)
8) improving work-life balance (31%)
7) improving benefits (32%)
6) improving employee involvement (35%)
5) improving line management HR skills (39%)
4) increasing pay (42%)
3) improving selection techniques (42%)
2) improving induction processes (45%)
1) increasing learning and development opportunities (47%)

SUMMARY PROPOSITIONS

9.1 Staff turnover tends to decrease in recessions and increase during economic booms.

9.2 Contrary to much popular perception, average job tenure has not reduced substantially over the past 30 years.

9.3 Retention rates vary very considerably between industries and between different regions.

9.4 While there are arguments that can be deployed in favour of modest staff turnover, it is generally agreed that too great a rate is damaging for an organisation.

9.5 In planning retention initiatives it is important both to analyse the causes of turnover and to calculate the current costs associated with each voluntary resignation.

9.6 Specific programmes which lead to improved retention include flexible benefits, better induction, the effective management of expectations, family-friendly initiatives, training opportunities and the improvement of line management in organisations.

GENERAL DISCUSSION TOPICS

1. What are the main reasons for the trends in job tenure illustrated in Table 9.1?
2. Staff turnover is generally low during recessions, but it increases substantially in firms which get into financial difficulty. What factors account for this phenomenon?
3. Think about your own experiences at work or those of close friends and family. What were the key factors that affected decisions to leave a particular job? What, if anything, could the employer have done to ensure that no resignation took place?

FURTHER READING

Chartered Institute of Personnel and Development (annual) *Recruitment, Retention and Turnover Survey*. London: CIPD.

Confederation of British Industry (annual) *Absence and Labour Turnover Survey*. London: CBI.

Each year the CIPD and the CBI carry out major surveys looking at staff turnover across the UK. They report the labour turnover rates among different groups as well as estimates of turnover costs. Many smaller surveys covering specific employee groups (like graduates) or particular industries are also published annually. *IRS Employment Review* always carries a number of 'benchmarking turnover' articles towards the end of the year which report the key findings from all these surveys.

Hom, P. and Griffeth, R. (1995) *Employee Turnover*. Cincinnati: South Western College Publishing.

Griffeth, R. and Hom, P. (2001) *Retaining Valued Employees*. Thousand Oaks: Sage Publications.

Despite being over 15 years old Hom and Griffeth 1995 is by far the best source of information about academic research on turnover and staff retention issues. It is now out of print, but the same authors' more recent book is available.

Taylor S. (2010) *Resourcing and Talent Management*. London: CIPD.
This text contains two chapters covering the practicalities of managing turnover and retention. There are detailed sections on measurement, costing, analysing the reasons for turnover and on the major steps that employers can take to reduce turnover levels. Key debates in the field are also covered.

REFERENCES

Auer, P., Berg, J. and Coulibaly, I. (2004) *Is a Stable Workforce Good for the Economy? Insights into the tenure–productivity–employment relationship*. Geneva: International Labour Organisation.

Bevan, S., Barber, L. and Robinson, D. (1997) *Keeping the Best: A practical guide to retaining key employees*. Brighton: Institute for Employment Research.

Branham, L. (2005) *The Seven Hidden Reasons Employees Leave*. New York: The American Management Association.

Breaugh, J.A. (2008) 'Employee recruitment: current knowledge and important areas for future research', *Human Resource Management Review*, Vol. 18, No. 3, pp. 103–18.

Cappelli, P. (2000) 'A market-driven approach to retaining talent', *Harvard Business Review*, January/February, pp. 103–11.

Carroll, M., Marchington, M., Earnshaw, J. and Taylor, S. (1999) 'Recruitment in small firms: processes, methods and problems', *Employee Relations*, Vol. 21, No. 3, pp. 236–50.

Carroll, M., Smith, M., Oliver, G. and Sung, S. (2008) 'Recruitment and retention in front-line services: the case of childcare', *Human Resource Management Journal*, Vol. 19, No. 1, pp. 59–74.

Chartered Institute of Personnel and Development (2006) *Recruitment, Retention and Turnover: Annual Survey Report 2006*. London: CIPD.

Chartered Institute of Personnel and Development (2009) *Recruitment, Retention and Turnover: Annual Survey Report 2009*. London: CIPD.

Department of Trade and Industry (2006) *Collective Redundancies: Employer's duty to notify the Secretary of State. Full regulatory impact assessment*. London: DTI.

DiPietro, R., Thozhur, S. and Milman, A. (2007) 'Hourly employee retention factors in the United Kingdom quick service restaurant industry', *Journal of Foodservice Business Research*, Vol. 10, No. 4, pp. 39–61.

Fair, H. (1992) *Personnel and Profit: The pay-off from people*. London: IPM.

Gerhart, B. (2009) 'Compensation', in A. Wilkinson, N. Bacon, T. Redman and S. Snell (eds), *The Sage Handbook of Human Resource Management*. London: Sage.

Green, F., Felstead, A., Mayhew, K. and Pick, A. (2000) 'The impact of training on labour mobility: individual and firm-level evidence from Britain', *British Journal of Industrial Relations*, Vol. 38, No. 2, pp. 262–85.

Gregg, P. and Wadsworth, J. (1999) 'Job tenure, 1975–98', in P. Gregg and J. Wadsworth (eds), *The State of Working Britain*. Manchester: Manchester University Press.

Griffeth, R. and Hom, P. (2001) *Retaining Valued Employees*. Thousand Oaks: Sage Publications.

Herzberg, F. (1966) *Work and the Nature of Man*. Cleveland: World Publishing.

Hom, P. and Griffeth, R. (1995) *Employee Turnover*. Cincinnati: South Western College Publishing.

IDS (2000) *Improving Staff Retention*, IDS Study No. 692, July. London: IDS.

IDS (2005) *Positive Steps: Oldham halves employee turnover*, IDS Study No. 807, October. London: IDS.

IRS (1999) 'Benchmarking labour turnover: annual guide 1999/2000', *Employee Development Bulletin*, No. 118, October.

IRS (2000) 'Improving retention and performance through induction', *Employee Development Bulletin*, No. 130, pp. 10–16.

Jenner, S. and Taylor, S. (2000) *Recruiting, Developing and Retaining Graduate Talent*. London: Financial Times/Prentice Hall.

Labour Market Trends (2001) 'Length of time continuously employed by occupation and industry', *Labour Market Trends*, February. London: ONS.

Lambert, S. (2000) 'Added benefits: the link between work-life benefits and organizational citizen behavior', *Academy of Management Journal*, Vol. 43, No. 5, pp. 801–15.

Larkan, K. (2006) *The Talent War: How to find and retain the best people for your company*. New York: Marshall Cavendish.

Macaulay, C. (2003) 'Job mobility and job tenure in the UK', *Labour Market Trends*, November. London: ONS.

Rankin, N. (2006) 'Welcome stranger: employers' induction arrangements today', *IRS Employment Review*, No. 849, June, pp. 38–48.

Ritzer, G. (1996) *The Macdonaldisation of Society: An investigation into the changing character of contemporary social life*, revised edn. Thousand Oaks: Pine Forge.

Samuel, M. and Chipunza, C. (2009) 'Employee retention and turnover: using motivational variables as a panacea', *African Journal of Business and Management*, Vol. 3, No. 8, pp. 410–15.

Sturges, J. and Guest, D. (1999) *Shall I Stay or Should I Go?* Warwick: Association of Graduate Recruiters.

Taylor, S. (2002) *The Employee Retention Handbook*. London: CIPD.

Taylor, S. (2009) 'Occupational pensions' pay', in G. White and J. Druker (eds), *Reward Management: A critical text*, 2nd edn. London: Routledge.

Taylor, S. (2010) *Resourcing and Talent Management*. London, CIPD.

Wanous, J.P. (1992) *Recruitment, Selection, Orientation and Socialization of Newcomers*. Reading: Addison Wesley.

White, G. (2009) 'Determining pay', in G. White and J. Druker (eds), *Reward Management: A critical text*, 2nd edn. London: Routledge.

Williams, M. (2000) *The War for Talent*. London: CIPD.

Wolff, C. (2009) 'Employee induction: the 2009 IRS survey', *IRS Employment Review*, No. 918, March.

An extensive range of additional materials, including multiple choice questions, answers to questions and links to useful websites can be found on the Human Resource Management companion website at **www.pearsoned.co.uk/torrington**.

CHAPTER 10

ENDING THE CONTRACT

THE OBJECTIVES OF THIS CHAPTER ARE TO:

1 Outline the framework in which the law of unfair dismissal operates

2 Set out the major reasons for which an employer can and cannot lawfully dismiss employees

3 Explain the concept of 'reasonableness' in unfair dismissal cases and its significance

4 Review the law on dismissals on grounds of capability, misconduct and redundancy

5 Describe the operation of the law of constructive dismissal and the law of wrongful dismissal

In the previous chapter we looked at situations in which employees decide to end their contracts of employment by giving their employers notice. Here we focus on circumstances when the contract is brought to an end by the employer through a dismissal of one kind or another, something that around one and a half million employees experience in the UK each year (Fitzner 2006). In some cases employees are happy to leave (or at least not unhappy) such as when they are retiring or when they are due to receive a large redundancy payment. In others their dismissal is neither unexpected nor even unwelcome, such as when a fixed-term contract comes to an end. A good proportion of dismissals are thus entirely uncontentious. However, when people who have been dismissed are unhappy and perceive either that the manner of the dismissal or the reason for it was unlawful they can take their case to an Employment Tribunal. In practice, around one in seven of all dismissed workers who qualify do bring such claims (Knight and Latreille 2000), leaving the Employment Tribunal Service (ETS) to deal with 40,000–50,000 cases each year (ETS 2009). If someone wins his or her case he or she may ask to be reinstated, but will usually settle for a compensation payment. The size of such awards is not generally substantial (around £8,000 on average), but occasionally people are awarded larger sums. Whatever the final outcome there are often additional legal costs for the employer to bear, not to mention the loss of a great deal of management time. An organisation's reputation as a good employer can also be damaged by adverse publicity arising from such cases. Employers generally take careful account of the requirements of the law when dismissing employees. The alternative is to run the risk of being summoned to an employment tribunal and possibly losing the case or being required to reach a financial settlement with the ex-employee that is large enough to deter further legal action. To a great extent the law therefore effectively determines practice in the field of dismissal.

In the UK there are three forms of dismissal claim that can be brought to a tribunal. Rights associated with the law of wrongful dismissal are the longest established. A person who claims wrongful dismissal complains that the way that he or she was dismissed breached the terms of his or her contract of employment. Constructive dismissal occurs when someone feels forced to resign as a direct result of the employer's actions. In this area the law aims to deter employers from seeking to avoid dismissing people by pushing them into resignation. The third category, unfair dismissal, is by far the most common. It is best defined as a dismissal which falls short of the expectations of the law as laid down in the Employment Rights Act 1996. You will find some practical case study exercises relating to unfair dismissal law on our companion website **www.pearsoned.co.uk/torrington**.

UNFAIR DISMISSAL

The law of unfair dismissal dates from 1971, since when it has been amended a number of times. Although additions and the outcomes of leading cases have made it more complex than it was originally, the basic principles have stood the test of time and remain in place. In most circumstances the right to bring a claim of unfair dismissal applies to employees who have completed a year's continuous service with their employer on the date their contract was terminated. This allows the employer a period of 12 months to assess whether or not an individual employee is suitable before the freedom to dismiss is restricted. The one-year restriction on qualification applies except where the reason for the dismissal is one of those listed below which are classed as 'automatically unfair' or 'inadmissible'. A further requirement is that the claim form is lodged at the tribunal office before three months have elapsed from the date of dismissal. Unless there are circumstances justifying the failure to submit a claim before the deadline, claims received after three months are ruled out of time.

Until recently people who were over the age of 65 or 'the normal retiring age' in a particular employment had no right to bring an unfair dismissal case to an employment tribunal. This restriction was removed as part of the introduction of age discrimination law in 2006. At the time of writing (March 2010), however, it remains lawful for an employer to retire people mandatorily at the age of 65 provided a prescribed procedure is followed.

Before a case comes to tribunal, officers of the Advisory, Conciliation and Arbitration Service (ACAS) will often try to help the parties reach a settlement. The papers of all cases lodged with the employment tribunals' offices are sent to ACAS with a view to conciliation taking place ahead of a tribunal hearing. As a result the majority of cases either get settled or are withdrawn without the need for the parties to attend a full hearing. ACAS also offers an alternative arbitration method of resolving unfair dismissal claims. Where both sides agree they can opt to have their case heard outside of the judicial system by ACAS officials whose aim is to conciliate a mutually acceptable settlement. If none can be agreed the arbitrator makes a binding judgment, but only after trying hard to settle the case satisfactorily. This alternative system has not been taken up by many. Employers and employees, so it seems, prefer to have their cases settled in court by a panel led by an Employment Judge.

When faced with a claim of unfair dismissal, and where it is not disputed that a dismissal took place, an employment tribunal asks two separate questions:

1 Was the reason for the dismissal one which is classed by the law as legitimate?

2 Did the employer act reasonably in carrying out the dismissal?

Where the answer to the first question is 'no', there is no need to ask the second because the dismissed employee will already have won his or her case. Interestingly the burden of proof shifts as the tribunal moves from considering the first to the second question. It is for the employer to satisfy the tribunal that it dismissed the employee for a legitimate reason. The burden of proof then becomes neutral when the question of reasonableness is addressed.

ACTIVITY 10.1

Consider the working activities of some of your colleagues (and perhaps your own working activities). What examples are there of behaviour that you feel justify dismissal? Make a list of your ideas and check them when you have finished this chapter and see how many might be classified by a tribunal as unfair dismissals.

Automatically unfair reasons

Certain reasons for dismissal are declared in law to be inadmissible or automatically unfair. Where the tribunal finds that one of these was the principal reason for the dismissal, they find in favour of the claimant (i.e. the ex-employee) whatever the circumstances of the case. In practice, therefore, there is no defence that an employer can make to explain its actions that will be acceptable to the tribunal. Moreover, the one-year service requirement does not apply so all employees can bring cases from the first day of employment. Some of the automatically unfair reasons relate to other areas of employment law such as non-discrimination, working time and the minimum wage, which are discussed in more detail in Chapter 20. In 2010 the list of automatically unfair reasons for dismissal was as follows:

- Dismissal for a reason relating to pregnancy or maternity.
- Dismissal for a health and safety reason (e.g. refusing to work in unsafe conditions).
- Dismissal because of a spent conviction.
- Dismissal for refusing to work on a Sunday (retail and betting-shop workers only).
- Dismissal for a trade union reason.
- Dismissal for taking official industrial action (during the first 12 weeks of the action).
- Dismissal in contravention of the part-time workers or fixed-term employees regulations.
- Dismissal for undertaking duties as an occupational pension fund trustee, employee representative, member of a European Works Council or in connection with jury service.
- Dismissal for asserting a statutory right (including rights exercised under the Employment Rights Act, as well as those connected with the Working Time Regulations, the National Minimum Wage Regulations, the Public Interest Disclosure Act and the Information and Consultation of Employees Regulations; the right to request flexible working, the right to time off for dependants, the right to adoptive, parental or paternity leave, the right to be accompanied at disciplinary and grievance hearings and the claiming of working tax credits).

Potentially fair reasons

From an employer's perspective it is important to be able to satisfy the tribunal that the true reason for the dismissal was one of those reasons classed as potentially fair in unfair dismissal law. Only once this has been achieved can the second question (the issue of reasonableness) be addressed. The potentially fair grounds for dismissal are as follows:

- Lack of capability or qualifications: if an employee lacks the skill, aptitude or physical health to carry out the job, then there is a potentially fair ground for dismissal.
- Misconduct: this category covers the range of behaviours that we examine in considering the grievance and discipline processes: disobedience, absence, insubordination and criminal acts. It can also include taking industrial action.
- Redundancy: where an employee's job ceases to exist, it is potentially fair to dismiss the employee for redundancy.
- Statutory bar: when employees cannot continue to discharge their duties without breaking the law, they can be fairly dismissed. Most cases of this kind follow disqualification of drivers following convictions for speeding, driving while under the influence of alcohol or drugs, or dangerous driving. Other common cases involve foreign nationals whose work permits have been terminated.
- Some other substantial reason: this most intangible category is introduced in order to cater for genuinely fair dismissals for reasons so diverse that they could not realistically be listed. Examples have been security of commercial information (where an

employee's husband set up a rival company) or employee refusal to accept altered working conditions.

- Dismissals arising from official industrial action after 12 weeks have passed.
- Dismissals that occur on the transfer of an undertaking where a valid ETO (economic, technological or organisational) reason applies.
- Mandatory retirements which follow the completion of the procedures set out in the Employment Equality (Age) Regulations 2006 (*see* Chapter 20).

Determining reasonableness

Having decided that potentially fair grounds for the dismissal exist, the tribunal then proceeds to consider whether the dismissal is fair in the circumstances. The test used by the tribunal in reaching decisions about the fairness of a dismissal is that of the reasonable employer. Tribunal members are not required to judge cases on the basis of what they would have done in the circumstances or what the best employers would have done. Instead they have to ask themselves whether what the employer did in the circumstances of the time fell within a possible band of reasonable responses. In practice this means that the employer wins the case if it can show that the decision to dismiss was one that a reasonable employer *might* conceivably have taken.

In assessing reasonableness tribunals always take a particular interest in the procedure that was used. They are also keen to satisfy themselves that the employer has acted broadly consistently in its treatment of different employees and that it has taken into account any mitigating circumstances that might have explained a deterioration in an employee's conduct or performance. In addition, they are required to have regard to the size and resources of the employer concerned. Higher standards are thus expected of a large PLC or a public sector body with a well-staffed HR department than of a small owner-managed business employing a handful of people. The former, for example, might be expected to wait for several months before dismissing someone on grounds of ill health, while a small business could justify dismissing after a few weeks because of the operational difficulties the absence was causing.

The significance attached to procedure has varied over the years. Until 1987 employers were able to argue successfully that although the procedure used was deficient in some respects, the outcome was not affected. This changed following the judgment of the House of Lords in the case of *Polkey* v. *AE Dayton Services* (1987). Henceforth, until the introduction of new regulations in 2004, tribunals were obliged to find dismissals unfair where the employer had not completed a proper procedure before making the final decision to dismiss. Since 2009, when the 2004 regulations were repealed, the law has returned to the position set out in the *Polkey* ruling. Any major procedural deficiency will render a dismissal unfair in law, whatever the outcome might have been had these procedures been followed. Employers are thus obliged to follow any procedures they have themselves devised in addition to the minimum standard set out by ACAS in its code of practice.

In this book we have separated the consideration of discipline from the consideration of dismissal in order to concentrate on the practical aspects of discipline (putting things right) rather than the negative aspects (getting rid of the problem). The two cannot, however, be separated in practice and the question of dismissal needs to be reviewed in the light of the material in Chapter 22.

WINDOW ON PRACTICE

The case of *Kulkarni* v. *Milton Keynes Hospital NHS Foundation Trust* (2009) concerned a part-qualified doctor who was disciplined after a patient complained that he had placed his stethoscope inside her underwear without first getting her consent. Because the outcome of the case could, if it went against the claimant, have led to a situation in which he could not practise as a doctor in the UK, he asked his employer if he might be permitted legal representation at the disciplinary hearing. The request was turned down.

The outcome of this case, which went in favour of Dr Kulkarni, hinged on the detail of his contract and of the Trust's policies. However, in passing judgment the Court of Appeal made some clear points about how employers should deal with requests such as Dr Kulkarni's in the future.

Unusually we see here the application in a UK employment case of principles derived from the European Convention on Human Rights. The Court of Appeal made reference to a Belgian case that was decided in the European Court of Human Rights in 1982 in making its judgment.

Article 6 of the Convention concerns the right to a fair trial. The judgment confirms that the right to legal representation does not apply in a conventional disciplinary hearing which may lead to the loss of a job. However, where the potential outcome would be *in effect* the loss of a career (i.e. the loss of a right to practise as a member of a profession), then Article 6 can apply.

In another case (*R (on the application of G)* v. *Governors of X School* (2009)) a male music teacher was alleged to have kissed a 15-year-old boy. Here too the High Court found that legal representation should have been available to the claimant at all stages in the disciplinary process because the outcome could have been a ban from working in any educational institution, and hence the loss of his career and not just his job.

Lack of capability

A common reason for dismissal is poor performance on the part of an employee. The law permits dismissals for this reason. It also allows employers to determine for themselves what constitutes an acceptable level of performance in a job, provided of course that a broadly consistent approach is followed for all employees. However, such dismissals are only considered to be reasonable (and hence fair in law) if the employee concerned has both been formally warned about his or her poor performance at least once and been given a reasonable opportunity to improve. Formality in this context means that a formal hearing has been held at which the employee has been entitled to be represented and after which there has been a right of appeal to a more senior manager.

The employer will always need to demonstrate the employee's unsuitability to the satisfaction of the tribunal by producing evidence of that unsuitability. This evidence must not be undermined by, for instance, giving the employee a glowing testimonial at the time of dismissal or by the presence of positive appraisal reports on the individual's personal file. Lack of skill or aptitude is a fair ground when the lack can be demonstrated and where the employer has not contributed to it by, for instance, ignoring it for a long period. Redeployment to a more suitable job is also an option employers are expected to consider before taking the decision to dismiss.

The requirement on employers to warn an employee formally that his or her performance is unsatisfactory at a meeting at which the employee has the opportunity to answer back, and the subsequent requirement to give the employee concerned support during a reasonable period in which he or she has an opportunity to improve, means that dismissals on grounds of poor performance can take several weeks or months to carry through. Moreover, during this time relationships can become very strained because formal action has been taken and a formal warning given. For these reasons managers often seek to avoid dismissing in line with the expectations of the law, instead seeking to dress up poor performance dismissals as redundancies or cases of gross misconduct. However, employment tribunals are very aware of this tendency and always find dismissals that occur in such circumstances to be unfair.

Another aspect of employee capability is health. It is potentially fair to dismiss someone on the grounds of ill health which renders the employee incapable of discharging the contract of employment. Even the most distressing dismissal can be legally admissible, provided that it is not too hasty and that there is consideration of alternative employment. Employers are expected, however, to take account of any medical advice available to them before dismissing someone on the grounds of ill health. Companies with occupational health services are well placed to obtain detailed medical reports to help in such judgements but the decision to terminate someone's employment is ultimately for the manager to take and, if necessary, to justify at a tribunal. Medical evidence will be sought and has to be carefully considered but dismissal remains an employer's decision taken on managerial grounds, not a medical decision.

Normally, absences through sickness have to be frequent or prolonged in order for dismissal on the grounds of such absence to be judged fair, although absence which seriously interferes with the running of a business may be judged fair even if it is neither frequent nor prolonged. In all cases the employee must be consulted and effectively warned before being dismissed. In the leading case of *Egg Stores* v. *Leibovici* (1977) the EAT set out nine questions that have to be asked to determine the potential fairness of dismissing someone after long-term sickness:

> (a) how long has the employment lasted; (b) how long had it been expected the employment would continue; (c) what is the nature of the job; (d) what was the nature, effect and length of the illness; (e) what is the need of the employer for the work to be done, and to engage a replacement to do it; (f) if the employer takes no action, will he incur obligations in respect of redundancy payments or compensation for unfair dismissal; (g) are wages continuing to be paid; (h) why has the employer dismissed (or failed to do so); and (i) in all the circumstances, could a reasonable employer have been expected to wait any longer?

A different situation is where an employee is frequently absent for short spells. Here too it is potentially reasonable to dismiss, but only after proper consideration of the illnesses and after warning the employee of the consequences if the attendance record does not improve. Each case has to be decided on its own merits. Medical evidence must be sought and a judgment reached about how likely it is that high levels of absence will continue in the future. The fact that an employee is wholly fit at the time of his or her dismissal does not mean that it is necessarily unfair. What matters is the overall attendance record and its impact on the organisation.

In another leading case, that of *International Sports Ltd* v. *Thomson* (1980), the employer dismissed an employee who had been frequently absent with a series of minor ailments ranging from althrugia of one knee, anxiety and nerves to bronchitis, cystitis, dizzy spells, dyspepsia and flatulence. All of these were covered by medical notes. (While pondering the medical note for flatulence, you will be interested to know that althrugia is water on the knee.) The employer issued a series of warnings and the company dismissed the employee after consulting its medical adviser, who saw no reason to examine the employee as the illnesses had no connecting medical theme and were not chronic. The Employment Appeals Tribunal held that this dismissal was fair because proper warning had been given and because the attendance record was deemed so poor as not to be acceptable to a reasonable employer. This position was confirmed by the Court of Appeal in *Wilson* v. *The Post Office* (2000) where it was held to be quite acceptable, in principle, for an employer to dismiss someone simply because of a poor absence record.

The law on ill-health dismissals was affected in important ways by the passing of the Disability Discrimination Act 1995. In Chapter 20 we look at this important piece of legislation in detail. Here it is simply necessary to state that dismissing someone who is disabled according to the definition given in the Act, without first considering whether adjustments to working practices or the working environment would allow that person to continue working, is unlawful. Reasonable adjustments might well include tolerance of a relatively high level of absence, especially where the employer is large enough to be able to cope perfectly well in the circumstances. Employers are well advised to pay particular attention to disability discrimination issues when dismissing people on the grounds of ill health because the level of compensation that can be awarded by tribunals in such cases is considerably higher than it is for unfair dismissal. In practice we now have a situation in which two bodies of law (unfair dismissal and disability discrimination) cover ill-health dismissals. Care needs to be taken to adhere to the requirements of both.

ACTIVITY 10.2

Some American companies evaluate the individual performance of all their employees each year and use the scores to rank everyone in a particular department or division. They then fire the bottom 10 per cent as a matter of policy. Can you explain why such an approach would be unlawful in the UK? Should it be made lawful or remain unlawful?

Misconduct

The law expects employers to make a distinction between two classes of misconduct when dismissing employees or considering doing so. Misconduct is defined as a breach of the employers' rules.

1. **Gross misconduct.** This occurs when an employee commits an offence which is sufficiently serious to justify summary dismissal. To qualify, the employee must have acted in such a way as to have breached either an express term of his or her contract or one of the common law duties owed by an employee to an employer (see Chapter 20). In practice this means that the employee's actions must be 'intolerable' for any reasonable employer to put up with.
2. **Ordinary misconduct.** This involves lesser transgressions, such as minor breaches of rules and relatively insignificant acts of disobedience, insubordination, lateness, forgetfulness or rudeness. In such cases the employer is deemed by the courts to be acting unreasonably if it dismisses as a result of a first offence. The dismissal would only be fair if, having been formally warned at least once, the employee failed to improve his/her conduct.

Employers have a wide degree of discretion when it comes to deciding what exactly does and does not constitute gross misconduct, and this will vary from workplace to workplace. For example, a distinction can be made between uttering an obscene swear word in front of colleagues (ordinary misconduct) and swearing obscenely to a customer (gross misconduct). While much depends on the circumstances, the tribunals also look carefully at an employer's established policies on matters of conduct.

Where the disciplinary rules spell out clearly the type of conduct that will warrant dismissal then a dismissal for this reason may be fair. Conversely, if the rules are silent or ambiguous as to whether particular conduct warrants dismissal, a dismissal for a first offence may be unfair. It is important, therefore, for employers to set out in writing what standards of conduct they expect, to make clear what will be regarded as 'sackable misconduct' and to ensure that everyone is aware of these rules.

The second key principle in misconduct cases concerns procedure. Whether the individual is dismissed summarily for gross misconduct or after a number of warnings for ordinary misconduct, the tribunals look to see if a reasonable procedure has been used and satisfy themselves that the employer has followed any of its own procedures which go beyond the minimum standard set out in the ACAS code of practice. They thus ask questions such as the following:

- Was the accusation thoroughly, promptly and properly investigated by managers before the decision was made to dismiss or issue a formal warning?
- Was a formal hearing held at which the accused employee was given the opportunity to state his/her case and challenge evidence brought forward by managers?
- Was the employee concerned permitted to be represented at the hearing by a colleague or trade union representative?
- Was the employee treated consistently when compared with other employees who had committed similar acts of misconduct in the past?

Only if the answers to all these questions is 'yes' will a tribunal find a dismissal fair. They do not, however, expect employers to adhere to very high standards of evidence gathering such as those employed by the police in criminal investigations. Here, as throughout employment law, the requirement is for the employer to act reasonably in all the circumstances, conforming to the principles of natural justice and doing what it thought to be right at the time, given the available facts.

WINDOW ON PRACTICE

In recent years employment tribunals have had to come to grips with a new type of dismissal case, situations in which people are dismissed for downloading and storing pornographic images from the Internet. Tribunals have had to consider whether or not such actions constitute gross misconduct (leading to summary dismissal without notice), or whether they should be considered as ordinary misconduct, in which case summary dismissal for a first offence would be regarded as being unfair.

Cases have been decided in different ways depending on the clarity of established rules and procedural matters. In *Parr* v. *Derwentside District Council* (1998), Mr Parr was summarily dismissed having been caught by his employers accessing pornography from his computer while at work. He claimed that he had visited the site concerned by accident, had got himself stuck in it and had subsequently 'revisited it only because he was disturbed by the prospect that entry could easily be made by children'. His claim for unfair dismissal failed because the employers had used a fair procedure and because they were able to show that Mr Parr had broken established codes of conduct.

By contrast, in *Dunn* v. *IBM UK Ltd* (1998), a summary dismissal occurring in similar circumstances was found to fall outside the 'band of reasonable responses'. In this case the employers were found not to have investigated the matter properly and not to have convened a fair disciplinary hearing, the whole matter having been handled far too hastily. Moreover, there was no company policy on Internet usage for Mr Dunn to have broken and he was unaware that he had done anything that would be construed as gross misconduct. He won his case, but had his compensation reduced by 50 per cent on the grounds that he was partly responsible for his own dismissal.

In a third case, *Humphries* v. *VH Barnett & Co* (1998), a tribunal stated that in normal circumstances the act of accessing pornography from the Internet while at work should not be construed as gross misconduct unless such a policy was made clear to employees and established as a workplace rule. However, in this case, the tribunal decided that the pictures downloaded were so obscene that Mr Humphries could be legitimately treated as having committed an act of gross misconduct.

Source: IDS (1999), 'Downloading pornography', *IDS Brief 637*, May.

Redundancy

Dismissal for redundancy is protected by compensation for unfair redundancy, compensation for genuine redundancy and the right to consultation before the redundancy takes place:

> An employee who is dismissed shall be taken to be dismissed by reason of redundancy if the dismissal is attributable wholly or mainly to:
>
> the fact that his employer has ceased, or intends to cease, to carry on the business for the purposes of which the employee was employed by him, or has ceased, or intends to cease, to carry on that business in the place where the employee was so employed,

> or
>
> the fact that the requirements of that business for employees to carry out work of a particular kind, or for employees to carry out work of a particular kind in the place where he was so employed, have ceased or are expected to cease or diminish. (Employment Rights Act 1996, s.139(1))

Apart from certain specialised groups of employees, anyone who has been continuously employed for two years or more is guaranteed a compensation payment from an employer, if dismissed for redundancy. The compensation is assessed on a sliding scale relating to length of service, age and rate of pay per week. If the employer wishes to escape the obligation to compensate, then it is necessary to show that the reason for dismissal was something other than redundancy. The inclusion of age in the criteria for calculating redundancy payments has remained, despite the introduction of age discrimination law in 2006.

Although the legal rights relating to redundancy have not altered for 35 years, there have been persistent problems of interpretation, different courts reaching different decisions when faced with similar sets of circumstances (*see* IRS 2000). In 1999 the House of Lords provided some long-needed clarification of key issues in the case of *Murray et al.* v. *Foyle Meats Ltd*, where it was decided that tribunals should look at the actual facts of someone's working situation rather than at their written contractual terms when deciding whether or not their jobs were redundant. In so doing it confirmed that the practice of 'bumping', where the employer dismisses a person whose job is remaining in order to retain the services of another employee whose job is disappearing, is acceptable under the statutory definition. The questions laid out by the Employment Appeals Tribunal (EAT) in *Safeway* v. *Burrell* (1997) are thus now confirmed as those that tribunals should ask when considering these cases:

- Has the employee been dismissed?
- Has there been an actual or prospective cessation or diminution in the requirements for employees to carry out work of a particular kind?
- Is the dismissal wholly or mainly attributable to the state of affairs?

The employer has to consult with the individual employee before dismissal takes place, but there is also a separate legal obligation to consult with recognised trade unions or some other body of employee representatives where no union is recognised. If 20 or more employees are to be made redundant, then the employer must give written notice of intention to any recognised unions concerned and the Department for Business, Enterprise and Regulatory Reform (DBERR) at least 30 days before the first dismissal. If it is proposed to make more than 100 employees redundant within a three-month period, then 90 days' advance notice must be given. Having done this, the employer has a legal duty to consult on the redundancies. There is no obligation to negotiate with employees, merely to explain, listen to comments and reply with reasons. Employees also have the right to reasonable time off with pay during their redundancy notice so that they can seek other work.

One of the most difficult aspects of redundancy for the employer is the selection of who should go. The traditional approach provides that people should leave on a last-in-first-out basis, or LIFO, as this provides a rough-and-ready justice with which it is difficult to argue from the point of view of consistency. It frees the employer from any obligation to choose on grounds of merit and is also inexpensive as the people who leave are those entitled to the least compensation. It is, however, questionable whether a pure LIFO-based system could be justified under age discrimination law as the approach is clearly detrimental to younger staff. In *Rolls Royce* v. *Unite* (2009) the High Court ruled that a system which included length of service alongside other factors was justifiable in law when it had been agreed with a recognised trade union, but as yet (i.e. March 2010) there has been do definitive ruling on the general question of whether or not a system that is based entirely on the LIFO principle can be justified.

In any event employers have tended to prefer other selection schemes in recent years. The preference nowadays is for one of two alternative types of approach.

- A matrix-type system in which a mix of criteria are used to score employees. Typically these include factors such as performance, qualifications, competence, future potential and attendance records.
- A selection-based system in which a new post-redundancy organisation structure is drawn up. Employees are then invited to apply for the jobs that will remain.

Increasingly, employers are trying to avoid enforced redundancy by a range of strategies, such as not replacing people who leave, early retirement and voluntary redundancy. It is also much more common than was the case in the past for employees to agree to work shorter hours or to take pay cuts as part of a deal to minimise redundancies or even avoid them altogether. Employers are also tending to make the management of redundancy more palatable by appointing specialist redundancy counsellors or outplacement consultants to advise people who are at risk of redundancy about how to secure new jobs or access training. Contrary to some popular perception there is no legal requirement to offer such services or to ask for volunteers before carrying through a programme of compulsory redundancies.

WINDOW ON PRACTICE

Mr Kirker, a man with a visual impairment, was selected for redundancy by managers at British Sugar PLC. The selection criteria included assessments of competence and potential, on both of which measures he scored poorly because of his disability. He took his case to an employment tribunal and won. It was ruled that in dismissing him, the employer had unlawfully discriminated on grounds of disability. Had it not been for the visual impairment, he would have been retained.

There are no limits on the amount of compensation that can be awarded in disability discrimination cases, so the tribunal can make an award based on their estimate of the true level of financial loss suffered by the individual concerned. In Mr Kirker's case the figure was £103,146. British Sugar subsequently lost an appeal to the Employment Appeal Tribunal.

Source: *British Sugar* v. *Kirker* [1998] IRLR 624.

Some other substantial reason

As the law of unfair dismissal has evolved since 1971 one of the most controversial areas has been the category of potentially fair dismissals known as 'some other substantial reason'. Many commentators see this as a catch-all or dustbin category which enables employers to dismiss virtually anyone provided a satisfactory business case can be made. All manner of cases have been successfully defended under this heading including the following: dismissals resulting from personality clashes, pressure to dismiss from subordinates or customers, disclosure of damaging information, the dismissal of a man whose wife worked for a rival firm, and the dismissal of a landlord's wife following her husband's dismissal on grounds of capability.

The majority of cases brought under this heading, however, result from business reorganisations where there is no redundancy. These often occur when the employer seeks to alter terms and conditions of employment and cannot secure the employee's agreement. Such circumstances can result in the dismissal of the employee together with an offer of re-employment on new contractual terms. Such dismissals are judged fair provided a sound business reason exists to justify the changes envisaged. It will usually be necessary to consult prior to the reorganisation but the tribunal will not base its judgment on whether the employee acted reasonably in refusing new terms and conditions. The test laid down in *Hollister* v. *The National Farmers' Union* (1979) by the Court of Appeal merely requires the employer to demonstrate that the change would bring clear organisational advantage.

Written statement of reasons

The Employment Rights Act 1996 (s.92) gives employees the right to obtain from their employer a written statement of the reasons for their dismissal if they are dismissed after completing a year's continuous service. If asked, the employer must provide the statement within 14 days. If it is not provided, the employee can complain to an employment tribunal that the statement has been refused and the tribunal will award the employee two weeks' pay if they find the complaint justified. The same right applies where a fixed-term contract of more than a year's duration is not renewed after having expired. The employee can also complain, and receive the same award, if the employer's reasons are untrue or inadequate, provided that the tribunal agrees.

Such an award is in addition to anything the tribunal may decide about the unfairness of the dismissal, if the employee complains about that. The main purpose of this provision is to enable the employee to test whether there is a reasonable case for an unfair dismissal complaint or not. Although the statement is admissible as evidence in tribunal proceedings, the tribunal will not necessarily be bound by what the statement contains. If the tribunal members were to decide that the reasons for dismissal were other than stated, then the management case would be jeopardised.

CONSTRUCTIVE DISMISSAL

When the conduct of the employer causes an employee to resign, the ex-employee may still be able to claim dismissal on the grounds that the behaviour of the employer constituted a repudiation of the contract, leaving the employee with no alternative but to resign. The employee may then be able to claim that the dismissal was unfair. It is not sufficient for the employer simply to be awkward or whimsical; the employer's conduct must amount to a significant breach, going to the root of the contract, such as physical assault, demotion, reduction in pay, change in location of work or significant change in duties. The breach must, however, be significant, so that a slight lateness in paying wages would not involve a breach, neither would a temporary change in place of work.

Some of the more interesting constructive dismissal cases concern claims that implied terms of contract have been breached, such as the employer's duty to maintain safe systems of working or a relationship of mutual trust and confidence.

WINDOW ON PRACTICE

A former manager of an off-licence called Mrs Gullyes won a case of constructive dismissal. She argued successfully that her employer had breached an implied term of her contract and that this had led directly to her resignation.

At the time of her resignation, Mrs Gullyes had been employed as a branch manager for four years – a job she carried out with conspicuous success. As a result she had been promoted into a manager's role in a larger branch with severe staffing problems. She accepted the new post with some reluctance after agreeing with the company that she could transfer again if things did not work out.

She found the new job hard from the start, finding herself working 76 hours a week and gaining insufficient help from other members of staff. After a few months she went away on holiday, returning to find that two of her staff had been transferred to other branches in her absence. At this point she requested a transfer herself and was refused. She resigned and brought a claim of constructive dismissal.

Mrs Gullyes won her case by arguing that the company had breached its common law duty to provide adequate support to her in the new job. The case was appealed to the EAT, where she won again.

Whitbread PLC/Thresher v. *Gullyes* (1994).

Constructive dismissal, like unfair dismissal, dates from 1971. It too only applies to employees who have completed a year's continuous service. The cases are harder for employees to win and easier for employers to defend because of the need to establish that a dismissal has taken place, before issues of reasonableness in the circumstances are addressed. The burden of proof is on the employee to show that he/she was forced into resigning as a result of a repudiatory breach on the part of the employer.

COMPENSATION FOR DISMISSAL

Having found in favour of the applicant in cases of unfair or constructive dismissal, the tribunal can make two types of decision: either they can order that the ex-employee be re-employed or they can award some financial compensation from the ex-employer for the loss that the employee has suffered. Originally it was intended that re-employment should be the main remedy, although this was not previously available under earlier legislation. In practice, however, the vast majority of ex-employees (over 98 per cent) want compensation.

Tribunals will not order re-employment unless the dismissed employee wants it and it is considered reasonable for the employer to take the individual back. Tribunals can choose between reinstatement or re-engagement. In reinstatement the old job is given back to the employee under the same terms and conditions, plus any increments, etc., to which the individual would have become entitled had the dismissal not occurred, plus any arrears of payment that would have been received. The situation is just as it would have been, including all rights deriving from length of service, if the dismissal had not taken place. The alternative of re-engagement will be that the employee is employed afresh in a job comparable to the last one (usually in a different department), but without continuity of employment. No employer can ever be required to reinstate or re-engage. Even if a tribunal considers that it would be practicable and just in a particular case, the employer can refuse and opt instead to pay a higher level of compensation. In practice it is increasingly rare for re-employment orders to be made, compensation being awarded instead in the vast majority of cases.

Tribunals currently calculate the level of awards under three headings. First is the basic award which is based on the employee's age and length of service. It is calculated in the same way as statutory redundancy payments, and like them has not been changed following the introduction of age discrimination law:

- half a week's pay for every year of service below the age of 22;
- one week's pay for every year of service between the ages of 22 and 41;
- one and a half weeks' pay for every year of service over the age of 41.

The basic award is limited, however, because tribunals can only take into account a maximum of 20 years' service when calculating the figure to be awarded. A maximum weekly salary figure is also imposed by the Treasury. This was £380 in 2010. The maximum basic award that can be ordered is therefore £11,400. In many cases, of course, where the employee has only a few years' service the figure will be far lower. In addition a tribunal can also order compensation under the following headings:

- Compensatory awards take account of loss of earnings, pension rights, future earnings loss, etc. The maximum level in 2010 was £65,300.
- Additional awards are used when an employer fails to comply with an order of reinstatement or re-engagement. The maximum award is 52 weeks' pay, but also subject to a £380 per week cap.

A tribunal can reduce the total level of compensation if it judges the individual concerned to have contributed to his or her own dismissal. For example, a dismissal on grounds of poor work performance may be found unfair because no procedure was followed and consequently no warnings given. This does not automatically entitle the ex-employee concerned to compensation based on the above formulae. If the tribunal judges the ex-employee to have been 60 per cent responsible for his or her own dismissal the compensation will be reduced by 60 per cent. Reductions are also made when the employer has failed to follow procedures fully, but in which the outcome would not have differed had it done so. If the tribunal concludes that the employee would have been made redundant or dismissed in any event they reduce compensation accordingly.

Further reductions are made if an ex-employee is judged not to have taken reasonable steps to mitigate his or her loss by applying for new jobs while waiting for the case to come to court.

ACTIVITY 10.3

In what circumstances do you think a dismissed employee might welcome reinstatement or re-engagement, and in what circumstances might the employer welcome it?

WRONGFUL DISMISSAL

In addition to the body of legislation defining unfair and constructive dismissal there is a long-standing common law right to damages for an employee who has been dismissed wrongfully.

Cases of wrongful dismissal are taken to employment tribunals where the claim is for less than £25,000; otherwise they are taken to the county court. These cases are concerned solely with alleged breaches of contract. Employees can thus only bring cases of wrongful dismissal against their employers when they believe their dismissal to have been unlawful according to the terms of their contract of employment. Wrongful dismissal can, therefore, be used when the employer has not given proper notice or if the dismissal is in breach of any clause or agreement incorporated into the contract. This remains a form of remedy that very few people use, but it could be useful to employees who do not have sufficient length of service to claim unfair dismissal and whose contracts include the right to a full disciplinary procedure. There may also be cases where a very highly paid employee might get higher damages in an ordinary court than the maximum that the tribunal can award.

WINDOW ON PRACTICE

In order to bring a claim of unfair dismissal ex-employees must have been employed continuously for at least 12 months by the organisation concerned when they are dismissed. As a result it is common for employers to dismiss people after 11 months' service in the belief that they will never have to justify their actions in court. However, such approaches can backfire, as was shown in the case of *Raspin* v. *United News* (1999). Here the applicant brought a case of wrongful dismissal, basing the claim on the presence in the contract of employment of a disciplinary procedure. The Employment Appeals Tribunal decided that had the employer fulfilled its contractual duties and dismissed the employee using the procedure, the date of the dismissal would have occurred after 12 months' service had been completed. In assessing compensation the matter was thus treated as if it was an unfair dismissal claim.

NOTICE

An employee qualifies for notice of dismissal on completion of four weeks of employment with an employer. At that time the employee is entitled to receive one week's notice. This remains constant until the employee has completed two years' service, after which it increases to two weeks' notice, thereafter increasing on the basis of one week's notice per additional year of service up to a maximum of 12 weeks for 12 years' unbroken service with that employer. These are minimum statutory periods. If the employer includes longer periods of notice in the contract, which is quite common with senior employees, then it is bound by the longer period.

The employee is required to give one week's notice after completing four weeks' service and this period does not increase as a statutory obligation. If an employee accepts a contract in which the period of notice to be given is longer, then that is binding, but the employer may have problems of enforcement if an employee is not willing to continue in employment for the longer period.

Neither party can withdraw notice unilaterally. The withdrawal will be effective only if the other party agrees. Therefore, if an employer gives notice to an employee and wishes later to withdraw it, this can be done only if the employee agrees to the contract of employment remaining in existence. Equally, employees cannot change their minds about resigning unless the employer agrees. Notice exists when a date has been specified. The statement 'We're going to wind up the business, so you will have to find another job' is not notice: it is a warning of intention.

SUMMARY PROPOSITIONS

10.1 Of the many dismissals that take place in a year, a minority are reported to tribunals and a small minority are found in favour of the ex-employee.

10.2 The main grounds on which an employee can be dismissed without the likelihood of an unfair dismissal claim are lack of capability, misconduct, redundancy, statutory bar, some other substantial reason and fair mandatory retirement.

10.3 If an employee is dismissed on one of the above grounds, the dismissal must still be procedurally acceptable and fair in the circumstances.

10.4 An employee who resigns as a result of unreasonable behaviour by the employer can claim constructive dismissal and, if successful, have his or her case treated as if he or she had in fact been dismissed.

10.5 Employers must give minimum notice periods, in most cases amounting to a week for every year of service, when terminating employees' contracts.

GENERAL DISCUSSION TOPICS

1 If you were dismissed in circumstances that you regarded as legally unfair, would you prefer to seek satisfaction through ACAS conciliation or through a tribunal hearing? Why?

2 In some countries a dismissal cannot be made until *after* a tribunal hearing, so that its 'fairness' is decided before it takes effect. What do you see as the benefits and drawbacks of that system?

3 What changes would you make in the criteria for dismissal on the grounds of misconduct?

FURTHER READING

Collins, H. (2004) *Nine Proposals for the Reform of the Law on Unfair Dismissal*. London: Institute of Employment Rights.

Davies, A.C.L. (2009) *Perspectives on Employment Law*, 2nd edn. Cambridge: Cambridge University Press.

Dickens, L., Jones, M., Weekes, B. and Hant, M. (1985) *Dismissed: A study of unfair dismissal and the industrial tribunal system*. Oxford: Blackwell.

These three publications provide thought-provoking introductions to the major debates about the law of unfair dismissal and how it might be reformed.

Rojot, J. (2001) 'Security of employment and employability', in R. Blanpain and C. Engels (eds), *Comparative Labour Law and Industrial Relations in Industrialized Market Economies*. The Hague: Kluwer.

There is a huge variety of different laws regulating dismissal in different countries. In the USA most states retain the doctrine of 'employment at will', placing no general statutory restrictions on the right of an employer to dismiss. In the Netherlands, by contrast, employers cannot generally dismiss without first getting the approval of a government officer. A good account of the various systems in use around the globe is provided by Rojot (2001).

IDS (2005) *Unfair Dismissal*. London: Incomes Data Services.

Yew, J. (2005) *Dismissals: Law and practice*. London: The Law Society.

These are the two most comprehensive and current guides to the law of unfair dismissal. Both review the leading cases and deal with all the practical aspects of dismissing people lawfully.

REFERENCES

Collins, H. (2004) *Nine Proposals for the Reform of the Law on Unfair Dismissal*. London: Institute of Employment Rights.

Davies, A.C.L. (2009) *Perspectives on Employment Law*, 2nd edn. Cambridge: Cambridge University Press.

Employment Tribunal Service (2009) *Annual Report*. London: HMSO.

Fitzner, G. (2006) *How Have Employees Fared? Recent UK Trends*. Employment Relations Research Series 56. London: DBERR.

IDS (1999) 'Downloading pornography', *IDS Brief 637*, May.

IDS (2005) *Unfair Dismissal*. London: Incomes Data Services.

IRS (2000) 'The (re)definition of redundancy', *Industrial Relations Law Bulletin*, No. 633, January.

Knight, K.G. and Latreille, P.L. (2000) 'Discipline, dismissals and complaints to employment tribunals', *British Journal of Industrial Relations*, Vol. 38, No. 4, p. 533.

Rojot, J. (2001) 'Security of employment and employability', in R. Blanpain and C. Engels (eds), *Comparative Labour Law and Industrial Relations in Industrialized Market Economies*. The Hague: Kluwer.

Yew, J. (2005) *Dismissals: Law and practice*. London: The Law Society.

LEGAL CASES

British Sugar v. *Kirker* [1998] IRLR 624.
Dunn v. *IBM UK Ltd* (1998) *IDS Brief* 637, May 1999.
Egg Stores v. *Leibovici* [1977] ICR 260.
Hollister v. *The National Farmers' Union* [1979] ICR 542.
Humphries v. *VH Barnett & Co* (1998) *IDS Brief* 637, May 1999.
International Sports Ltd v. *Thomson* [1980] IRLR 340.
Kulkarni v. *Milton Keynes Hospital NHS Foundation Trust* [2009] IRLR 829.
Murray et al. v. *Foyle Meats Ltd* [1999] IRLR 562.
Parr v. *Derwentside District Council* (1998) *IDS Brief* 637, May 1999.
Polkey v. *AE Dayton Services* [1987] ICR 142.
R (on the application of G) v. *Governors of X School* [2009] IRLR 434.
Raspin v. *United News* [1999] IRLR 9.
Rolls Royce v. *Unite* [2009] IRLR 49.
Safeway v. *Burrell* [1997] IRLR 200.
Whitbread PLC/Thresher v. *Gullyes* [1994] EAT 478/92.
Wilson v. *The Post Office* [2000] IRLR 834.

An extensive range of additional materials, including multiple choice questions, answers to questions and links to useful websites can be found on the Human Resource Management companion website at **www.pearsoned.co.uk/torrington**.

Part 2 CASE STUDY PROBLEM

You are the Human Resources Manager for a large insurance company with 2,000 employees based in a large city in the north of England and your company has just taken over another insurance company in the south of England which currently employs 1,100 staff. Both firms have a long history and to some extent cover the same insurance markets, although the company in the south of England covers two fairly large specialist areas which are not covered in the north. This was one of the reasons for the takeover, as such specialist staff require a long training and need to acquire high levels of expertise. There are 300 staff in the south who are dedicated to these specialist insurance services.

The takeover did not go smoothly as there was resistance from the southern company, and now it is complete there is considerable uneasiness. Only three years ago the southern company was party to a merger with another local firm and as a result 20 per cent of staff were made redundant. There had been promises of a bright future after these difficult times.

For financial and pragmatic reasons it has been decided that the southern office will close almost immediately and all staff will be located in newly built offices 15 miles out of the northern city. Many of the southern staff are alarmed at the idea of moving and equally alarmed that they may not be invited to move due to another round of redundancies. This especially applies to those who are over 50, who will expect to find it difficult to find another job despite the 2006 legislation on age discrimination. The northern staff are divided in their views about the move out of the city centre. Those who live on the western side of the city where the new offices are located are generally delighted to be able to work near to home in an exclusive part of the county. Staff who live on the other side of the city are concerned – some are not happy to travel long distances each day, and for a variety of reasons do not want to move to the other side of the city. Some would like to move, but find that the difference in house prices is too great. Many are disappointed that they will no longer work in the city centre, which is something they had valued. Redundancy is not a possibility which was seriously considered by the northern staff.

The required profile is broadly as set out in the following table:

A Senior and middle management	35
B Professional/junior management	1,700 (to include 300 specialist staff)
C Clerical/administrative	600
D Manual/ancillary	65

Current Staffing	Northern	Southern	Total
A	30	20	50
B	1,400	700	2,100
(there are no specialist professional staff in the north and 300 in the south)			
C	540	370	910
D	30	10	40

In terms of staffing demand it has been estimated that a total staffing of 2,400 is required for the next three-year period with hopes of some increase after this period, based on growth.

The reduction in the number of professional/junior management staff required reflects a general reduction of all types of professional staff due to the economies of scale and more sophisticated IT use. The only professional staff group to increase in size is the IT group.

The reduction in clerical/administrative staff is due largely to the use of more sophisticated IT systems.

The increase in the number of manual/ancillary staff is due to the move to a much larger site with substantial grounds, including a range of on-site facilities due to a non-city-centre location.

You are informed that staffing levels and the move should be complete in six months' time and that, as HR Manager, you are to have a high-profile role. You have initially been asked for a recommended strategy and plan to achieve the target resourcing figures with the least possible disruption and damage to morale.

Required

1. What information would you gather before putting your proposal together?
2. What issues would you address in the proposal?
3. What options are there for achieving the target, what impact might each have, and which would you recommend and why?

PART 3

PERFORMANCE: SUCCESS THROUGH INDIVIDUAL AND COLLECTIVE ACHIEVEMENT

It is no good having all the right people all in the right places if they are not delivering the goods. This part of the book starts with consideration of the broad relationship between HR practice and organisational performance. We then consider more specifically how to manage individual employee performance. It has been suggested that there has been a general change of emphasis in attitude to the contract between the parties, away from a contract *of employment* towards a contract *for performance*. We all have to perform effectively. A large part of achieving effective performance is getting the organisational processes right, but within the organisational framework there are the teams, groups and individuals who do the work. Also within that framework we have to understand what it is that motivates people to perform and deploy leadership skills that match those motivations. A key feature is the nature of leadership and how it is carried out effectively, especially in situations requiring change.

Performance management is an idea that has been developed to coordinate several features, especially targets, training, appraisal and payment, in order to deliver effectiveness. Also included here is the management of absence or of attendance. What is needed is not just managing processes which encourage people to attend but also dealing with the problem of people being absent. These are separate issues, not simply alternative ways of wording the problem.

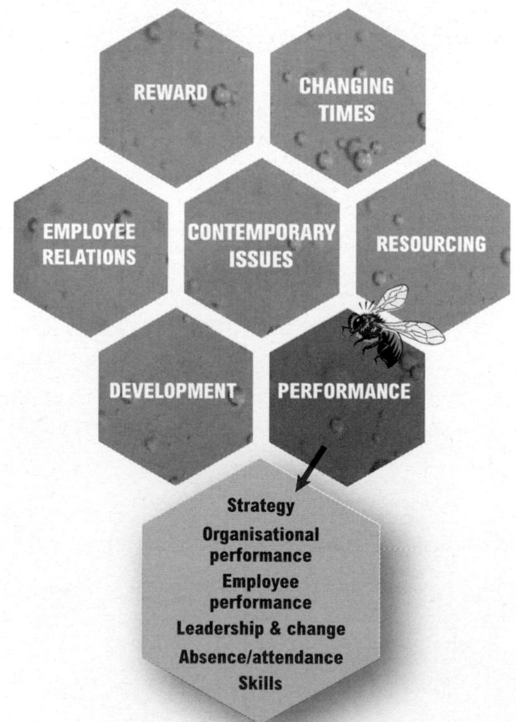

CHAPTER 11

HRM, EMPLOYEE ENGAGEMENT AND ORGANISATIONAL PERFORMANCE

THE OBJECTIVES OF THIS CHAPTER ARE TO:

1. Explain the background to HR/performance research
2. Define and explain high performance work systems (HPWS)
3. Outline the role of employee attitudes within HPWS
4. Consider employee responses to HR practices
5. Discuss the role of line manager in HPWS
6. Define and explain employee engagement
7. Outline critiques of HPWS

HR AND HIGH PERFORMANCE WORKING

Since the early 1990s, a stream of publications has sought to demonstrate the 'added value' of HR activities in enhancing organisational performance and contributing to the bottom line. This contribution is linked to progressive HR practices, such as sophisticated recruitment, selection, training and development, which create sustainable competitive advantage for the organisation through its people. Such practices promote investment in and development of employees as the organisation's 'human capital' producing gains for both employer and employees. The employer benefits from enhanced organisational performance, employees receive training and development, career development, high levels of pay and the satisfactions of delivering good performance that is recognised. This approach has been termed **high performance working**. Organisations compete primarily on quality and take a 'high road' approach to HR, ensuring they have a highly skilled and well-managed cadre of staff. The prominence, perhaps even dominance, of high performance working within HR is reflected in the launch, in late 2008, by the Chartered Institute of Personnel and Development (CIPD) of its flagship project, 'Shaping the Future', undertaking an in-depth exploration of high performance working. High performance working is not, however, without is critics, some arguing that it creates work intensification for employees, others that it is unlikely to work in particular industrial sectors. In this chapter, we review developments in this field and assess the current position.

HIGH PERFORMANCE WORK SYSTEMS

Efforts to show how HR practices lead to improved organisational performance drew initially on large-scale statistical studies to demonstrate that HR practices had a positive impact on employee performance and resultant business performance (*see*, for example, Delery and Doty 1996; MacDuffie 1995; Huselid 1995). Huselid, for example, evaluated the links between progressive HR practices and organisational performance using a sample of nearly 1,000 firms. His findings suggested clear statistical relationships between these practices and employee outcomes such as reduced labour turnover and productivity and long- and short-term firm measures of corporate financial performance.

Such studies are thus widely considered to have demonstrated a link between HR practices and organisational performance. It is also generally agreed that grouping HR practices into 'bundles' in what has become known as a **high performance work system** (**HPWS**, Boxall and Macky 2009) is performance enhancing. Such practices generally devolve a degree of control to employees, through, for example, involvement programmes, team-based work, enhanced training and development, and introduce a range of progressive methods which benefit employees, for example, gain sharing and high-wage reward systems (Ramsay *et al.* 2000). The focus on using bundles is explained by the complementarities thesis (Macky and Boxall 2007) which suggests that the effect of combining a number of HR practices is greater than the effect of using them independently: combinations produce synergy. The performance-enhancing effect of these bundles is explained by Cooke (2001) in what has become known as the 'AMO' model, that is, ability, motivation and opportunity. In effect, a high performance work system built upon progressive HR practices develops employees' skills and competencies (their capability), increases their motivation and supports employees in making use of their knowledge and skills. This then leads on to enhanced individual and organisational performance.

The construction of HPWS and their positive effects was clearly well received by HR practitioners seeking to demonstrate the value of their role. The research and theory on HPWS is not, however, unproblematic. One key issue is the direction of causality between HR practices and performance. In other words, do HPWS lead to high performance or do highly performing organisations invest in HPWS? This has been the focus of a number of studies. Guest *et al.* (2003), for example, explored the relationship between HRM and performance in 366 UK companies using objective and subjective performance measures and cross-sectional and longitudinal data. Their study confirmed the association between HRM and performance but failed to show that HRM *causes* higher performance. This is an issue that continues to vex both academics and practitioners.

A further issue of debate has been the bundle of HR practices that should be incorporated within a HPWS. Research has focused on defining a system of work practices that leads to superior organisational performance, but the practices included have varied widely by study. Paauwe and Boselie (2005) suggest that the top four practices to be included are training and development, contingent pay and reward schemes, performance management (including appraisal) and sophisticated recruitment and selection. Definitive agreement on the contents of a HPWS is lacking however. This is further complicated by debates about whether there is one bundle of practices that will be effective in all organisations, or whether the bundle of practices will be contingent upon organisation conditions. This has led to different conceptualisations of HR strategy which we discuss in Chapter 3.

In the Window on Practice below, we outline what Pfeffer (1998) argues to be an effective bundle of HR practices, one which he suggests will be effective in all organisations. We also use Pffefer's work in relation to HR strategy in Chapter 3.

WINDOW ON PRACTICE

In his book, *The Human Equation: Building Profits by Putting People First*, Pfeffer (1998) suggests that the following seven HR practices comprise the 'bundle' of practices that will drive high employee and organisation performance.

1 **Employment security and internal labour markets**. Organisations should commit to provide secure jobs for employees wherever possible and employees should trust that the organisation would provide continuing employment for them. Further, systems of career development and progression should be made available to employees in an internal labour market.

2 **Selective hiring and sophisticated selection**. Organisations should use structured and 'best practice' methods of selection to ensure that employees brought into the organisation have the necessary and skills and are a good organisational 'fit'.

3 **Extensive training, learning and development**. A 'human capital' or 'soft' approach to employees should be adopted in which employees are viewed as assets to be invested in and developed rather than costs to be minimised. Returns on training and development costs will be accrued through improved performance and decreased employee turnover.

4 **Employee involvement.** Mechanisms should be adopted that allow employees to voice their opinions and influence decision making within the organisation, critically at the level of the jobs they do and preferably at a wider organisational level.

5 **Self-managed teams/team working.** Employees should be grouped into teams with a high degree of autonomy in deciding how to manage the tasks to be undertaken. Such autonomy will again have positive outcomes in terms of performance gains.

6 **High compensation contingent on performance.** Compensation should be set at a high level and employees must demonstrate high levels of achievement against, for example, objectives or targets to receive full compensation. Bonuses or performance-related pay may be examples of effective HR practices.

7 **Reduction of status differentials/harmonisation.** Terms and conditions should similarly be applied to all employee groups. Pensions, for example, should not be made available to one employee group but not another.

Pfeffer argues that this bundle of progressive HR practices will be synergistic and will produce high performance gains.

Source: Pfeffer, J. (1998) *The Human Equation: Building Profits by Putting People First*. Boston: Harvard Business School Press.

ACTIVITY 11.1

What is your view on the HR practices in Pffefer's bundle? Do you think they are likely to improve performance? How similar are they to the practices of an organisation with which you are familiar? Are there any practices missing in your view?

Case 11.1 on this book's Companion Website, **www.pearsoned.co.uk/torrington**, explores HPWS strategies further.

THE 'BLACK BOX' OF THE HRM/PERFORMANCE LINK

In the past decade, the focus has shifted from seeking to identify the bundles of HR practices within a HPWS to seeking to explain *how* HR practices lead to enhanced performance. This has become known as unlocking the 'black box' of the HRM/performance link (Purcell *et al.* 2003). Purcell's work has led to the argument that HR practices improve performance through the influence they have upon employee attitudes. HR practices are thus at the beginning of a causal chain which seeks to influence attitudes, behaviour and then outcomes such as performance (Figure 11.1).

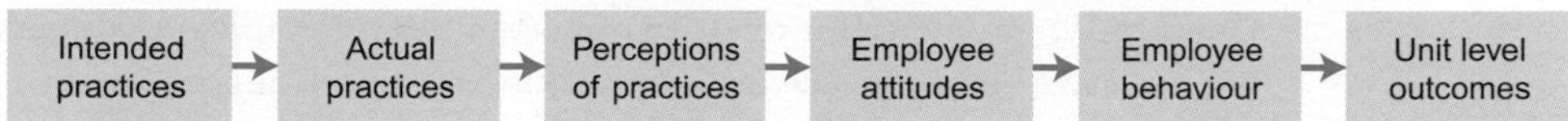

Figure 11.1 The people management–performance causal chain
Source: Purcell and Hutchinson 2007, p. 7, Fig. 1.

In academic terms, employee attitudes are described as being the mediating variables between practice and improved performance. Clearly if attitudes are the crux of how to influence performance, it is important to understand which employee attitudes HR practices should seek to influence. There is currently a great deal of debate around this and we outline below a number of attitudes that are suggested to be within the 'black box' of the HRM/performance link.

Commitment

Initial theorising around employee attitudes focused on the concept of commitment, reflected in the widespread use of the terms 'high commitment work practices' and 'high commitment management' and their linkage with high performance. Detailed considerations of commitment suggest that it has three components, continuance, normative and affective (Allen and Meyer 1990). It is, however, the latter two components that HR practices primarily seek to influence: that is, normative commitment, the employee's feelings of obligation to remain with the organisation and affective commitment, the employee's emotional attachment to, identification with and involvement in the organisation (Allen and Meyer 1990). Indeed, commitment was for a period considered to be the ultimate aim of HRM. For example:

> The concept of organizational commitment lies at the heart of any analysis of HRM. Indeed the whole rationale for introducing HRM policies is to increase levels of commitment so that other positive outcomes can ensue. (Guest 1998: 42)

Gaining employee commitment, winning the battle for their hearts and minds, was thus the holy grail of HRM. It was argued that affective commitment from employees would lead to discretionary behaviour, employees going above and beyond what was required of them to deliver their best, and thus improve performance. Further, normative commitment would reduce labour turnover and absence costs.

More recently, however, many researchers have suggested that the importance of commitment has been overplayed and, even, that there is not a great deal of evidence to link high commitment and high levels of organisational performance (Benkhoff 1997). This has led to consideration of other mechanisms through which to influence employee behaviour.

Involvement

Employee involvement has more recently emerged within the HPWS debate as a key mechanism through which to enhance performance, leading to the use of such terms as 'high involvement management'. We discuss employee involvement in detail in

Chapter 19, but in brief it refers to opportunities for employees to make decisions, take the initiative and influence decision making, certainly at the level of their own job and potentially at the level of the organisation. It is argued that involvement enhances work motivation and job satisfaction, and these can in turn enhance individual and collective performance (Wood and Wall 2007). There has thus been a strong focus on the role of involvement in driving high performance.

Other employee attitudes

In recent years, however, there has been a questioning of the dominance of commitment and involvement within HPWS. It has been argued that other attitudes such as job satisfaction, motivation and trust are also important in encouraging employees to engage in discretionary behaviour (Macky and Boxall 2007). In our own work, we have argued that employee attitudes such as happiness are also important in affecting behaviour and performance. Happiness has long been neglected in HR literature following unsuccessful attempts to link happiness via job satisfaction to improved performance. It has re-emerged, however, in the positive psychology movement, which refocuses the attention of psychologists on what makes people happy as opposed to the historical trend of investigating what makes people unhappy. Conceptualising happiness as well-being, rather than job satisfaction, has led psychologists to argue once again for a link between this attitude and performance. This theorising is beginning to make its way into the HR literature, Peccei (2004), for example, investigating the extent to which HR practices influence well-being and potentially performance. Our own research certainly supports this line of argument and there is much work to be done in the area of employee attitudes and which HR practices influence them and to what extent.

ACTIVITY 11.2

1 Which attitudes do you believe to be important in generating outcomes such as improved performance, reduced turnover and absence?

2 To what extent do you think HR practices can influence these?

EMPLOYEE PERSPECTIVE ON THE HR/PERFORMANCE LINK

There has been an increasing recognition that much of the research on HR practices and their impact on performance has focused on managerial perspectives of organisational outcomes and that employee reactions and attitudes to HRM have been neglected. This is despite Kinnie *et al.* (2005: 11) arguing that:

> the fulcrum of the HRM-performance causal chain is the employees' reactions to HR practices as experienced by them.

Most studies have focused on managers' views, they being regarded as the sole representative on organisational opinion as to how HR practice influences performance. Latterly, however, there has more been research which focuses on the employee perspective on this issue. We outline our own research, which is in this tradition, in the Window on practice below.

WINDOW ON PRACTICE

We conducted research into the HR practice of flexible working, now considered to be a key element of a bundle of performance-enhancing HR practices, in an NHS Acute Trust. We interviewed employees and asked for their views on flexible working, the reasons for its implementation, its impact on themselves and its outcomes. A key benefit of our qualitative approach to data collection, which did not predetermine categories of employee response, was that it allowed employees to frame explanations in their own words and identify issues that were important to them in their working lives rather than issues that researchers had decided were important. An interesting outcome of this approach was that employees identified the role of flexible working in making them happy and suggested that such happiness encouraged them to display discretionary behaviour and enhanced performance outcomes. Happiness emerged as an important employee attitude and, it is interesting to note, the employees in our study made no mention of attitudes such as commitment or trust.

Source: Atkinson, C. and Hall, L. (2009) 'Happiness and HPWS in the NHS', paper presented at Performance and Reward Conference, Manchester Metropolitan University, April 2009.

While our findings are preliminary, they support the growing body of research on employee perspectives on the HR/performance link which suggests that focusing on managerial perceptions alone may provide only limited insight. Understanding of employee perspectives on HR practices is vital in designing effective HPWS.

THE ROLE OF THE LINE MANAGER

It is increasingly being suggested that another issue that is fundamental in the HR/performance link is the role of line managers. The tendency to decentralise HR over the past two decades (*see* Chapter 28) has meant that HR practices are typically enacted by line managers. They thus have a crucial but often overlooked role in turning HR practice into reality. Purcell and Hutchinson's (2007) work demonstrates the importance of line managers and their need for well-designed HR practices to use in their people management activities. Line managers are the key to HR effectiveness: good practices are rendered inadequate by poor management behaviour and poor practices made better by good management behaviour. The centrality of line managers to HR practices driving performance is demonstrated in Figure 11.2.

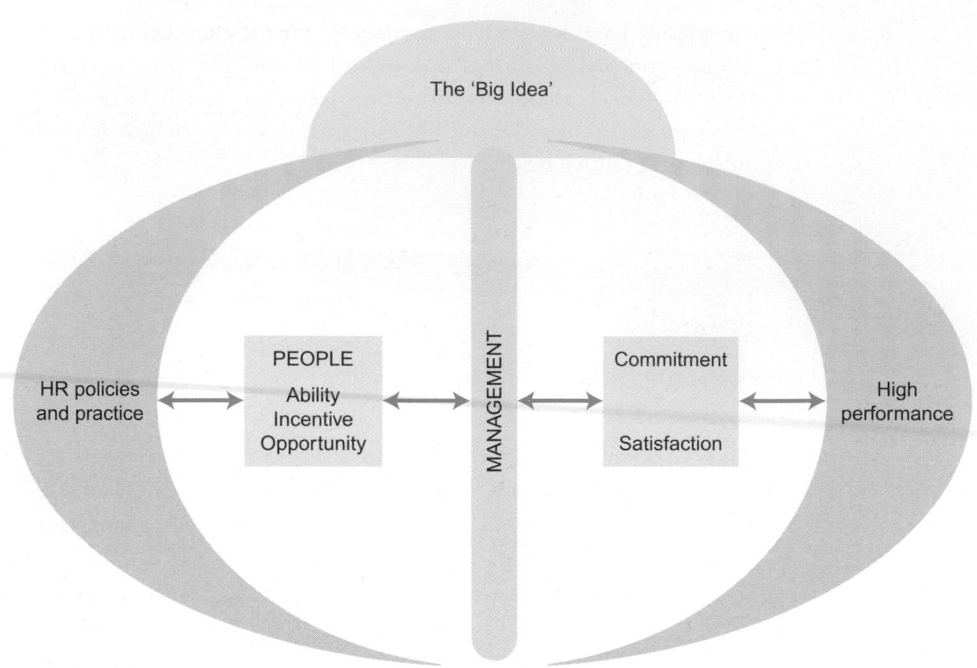

Figure 11.2 'High performance' model of HR practices and business performance
Source: Adapted from *Understanding the People–Performance Link: Unlocking the black box*, Research Report, CIPD (Purcell, J., Kinnie, N., Hutchinson, S., Rayton, B. and Swart, J., 2003). With the permission of the publisher, the Chartered Institute of Personnel and Development, London (www.cipd.co.uk).

Others have also linked strength of leadership to the key attitude of employee commitment. A study reported in *People Management* (2009) confirms this, outlining the necessary management behaviours as communicating, making it clear what is expected; listening, valuing and involving the team; being supportive; being target focused; having clear strategic vision; showing active interest in others; having good leadership skills and being respected. The implications of the line manager role are drawn out in the Window on practice below.

WINDOW ON PRACTICE

Until recently, research examining the link between HRM and organisational performance has ignored the part played by front-line managers (team leaders or supervisors) in delivering HR practices. This is curious given the increasing role of line managers in HRM and the mounting evidence of a gap between espoused and enacted HR policies as a result of line managers' difficulty with implementation. The HR practices applied may be quite different in content and style from what was intended, but it is these that staff react to. Line managers therefore play a mediating role between employees and HR practices, and it is the relationship between individuals and line managers (sometimes referred to as 'leader member exchange') that can be key in determining attitudes and behaviour.

Perceptions of leadership management behaviour are significant in explaining employee commitment, job autonomy, job challenge and sense of achievement.

Similarly, satisfaction with HR policies has an impact on the same employee outcomes. But, significantly, the effect of good management leadership behaviour and satisfying HR policies – as perceived by the employee – has a greater influence on these outcomes than either does by itself.

The implications are clear. To make an impact on the bottom line, HR needs to improve the people management provided by front-line managers; to clarify their role and provide support in areas such as involvement, training, coaching and development. Also important is the relationship between front-line managers and their own managers, as line managers' own levels of commitment and job satisfaction are significantly influenced by the quality of this relationship.

Source: Adapted from Hutchinson, S. (2005) 'The role of front-line managers in delivering HR practices', *People Management*, 13 October, p. 50.

As the Window on practice suggests, if HR practice really is to enhance organisational performance, the role of line manager is crucial and must not be overlooked. This has significant implications in terms of their training and preparation to deal with HR matters.

ACTIVITY 11.3

1 Think of your own experiences of HR practices, for example, pay or training. What impact have the actions of your line manager had in these experiences?

2 To what extent would you agree that line managers are vital in effectively implementing HR practices?

EMPLOYEE ENGAGEMENT

Employee engagement is a term that is widely used and 'engaging employees' is popularly considered to transform employee productivity and profitability. It has, not surprisingly, attracted a great deal of attention. In 2009, the Department for Business, Innovation and Skills commissioned a report, *Engaging for Success*, widely referred to as the McLeod Report; the CIPD has produced numerous reports on engagement and has termed one of its 'professional areas' engagement in its new HR professional map (CIPD 2009); and there are a plethora of HR consultancies suggesting that their services can create employees who are engaged and will enhance organisational performance. Many are clearly convinced of the benefits of employee engagement. Yet it is an area in which practice runs ahead of research and many academics are more sceptical about the benefits or existence of engagement. They suggest that engagement is a fad with little basis in theory and research and that it is simply a re-labelling of well-established constructs such as commitment and job satisfaction. Its prominence within the field of HR means, however, that it cannot be ignored and we include it here as it seems to us that, should engagement be a discrete concept in its own right, it fits within the HR/performance debate.

There is no widely accepted definition of engagement, possibly because of a lack of academic research into the concept. The CIPD define it thus:

> a combination of commitment to the organisation and its values plus a willingness to help out colleagues. (Organisational citizenship, CIPD 2009: 9)

Engagement thus has both attitudinal and behavioural components (e.g. commitment and focused effort: Macey and Schneider 2008), supporting our position that it fits within the debates covered in this chapter. It is the attitudinal and behavioural combination which leads to the argument that engagement creates workers who are passionate about their roles and perform to high levels. It is perhaps this focus on enhancing performance, coupled with research which shows that only around a third of UK employees are actually engaged with their employers, that has created such interest from government, professional bodies and consultancies.

Employee voice and involvement have a key role in creating engaged employees. The three main drivers of engagement are having opportunities to feed your views upwards, feeling well informed about what is happening in the organisation and thinking that your manager is committed to your organisation (CIPD 2009). Other studies support this, emphasising the importance of involvement in decision making and the opportunity to voice opinion (*see* Chapter 19 for fuller discussion of employee involvement). Delivering involvement requires real and sustained understanding and buy-in from senior management, the need for all managers to receive effective training in engagement and people skills and for organisational values to be practised as espoused. We present in the Window on practice below Sainsbury's approach to employee engagement.

WINDOW ON PRACTICE

Engagement at Sainsbury's

I think most companies would recognise that in order to improve performance you need motivated people. But you need to define what 'engagement' means for your organisation.

For us, colleague engagement doesn't start and finish at the checkout. We have 150,000 people working with us, and we will only achieve our goal if everyone pulls together.

In 2005, we developed a sales-led recovery programme, Making Sainsbury's Great Again, that refocused on the core elements of our brand: great food at fair prices delivered by great colleagues. A cornerstone of this was the creation of a new goal and values. We also wanted to give colleagues back a voice through listening to their opinions and ideas and demonstrating that we believed their contribution made a difference.

Colleague Councils exist in every Sainsbury's location, giving people a chance to voice their opinions on everything from facilities to charity fundraising. In August 2004 we launched our 'Tell Justin' scheme. This has received over 27,000 suggestions from colleagues, many of which have been adopted. We also organised 'The Big Pitch' which encouraged colleagues to put forward ideas to improve the business. Nearly 600 took part, with 12 selected to present their ideas to a judging panel led by chief executive Justin King.

The results of our opinion surveys clearly show the impact engagement has in relation to business performance. Our ten highest performing stores on engagement outperform on sales, service, availability and absence, while those with the lowest engagement scores remain below target on the same measures.

Increasingly, we are learning that it's not only what we do internally that influences engagement. Over the past two years we have focused on community initiatives and found these also made a difference.

Source: *People Management* (2009) 'Employee Branding', 5 November, p. 18.

As we noted above, employee engagement is often poor, standing at around only a third of UK employees with high engagement levels. This is often due to lack of senior management engagement, poor or inconsistent management at all levels and poor communications and involvement processes. A long hours culture and poor work-life balance can also damage engagement. There thus seems to be significant opportunity for enhancing both engagement and performance through improved management and HR practice.

Case 11.2 on this book's Companion Website, **www.pearsoned.co.uk/torrington**, explores employee engagement further.

CRITIQUES OF HPWS

We have thus far considered HPWS from the perspective that, if implemented successfully, benefits will accrue to both employer and employees. There is another school of thought within the HPWS debate, however, that suggests that such systems in fact are often detrimental to employees. Ramsey *et al.* (2000) present a detailed argument to this effect, drawing on labour process theory. They acknowledge that HPWS can lead to performance gains for organisations but suggest that these arise from work intensification for employees. Progressive HR practices, far from providing high pay, training and influence for employees, lead to increased responsibility, insecurity and job strain and force employees to work harder in a manner that is detrimental to them (Figure 11.3).

Ramsay *et al.* (2000) test both the labour process model and a more traditional HPWS model using data from the Workplace Employee Relations Survey (WERS) (Kersley *et al.* 2006). While they find little empirical support for either model, they argue that drawing on labour process theory, which considers how managers minimise the gap between average and maximum labour power by finding ways to make employees work longer and/or harder, delivers a sound explanation for how HPWS drive enhanced performance.

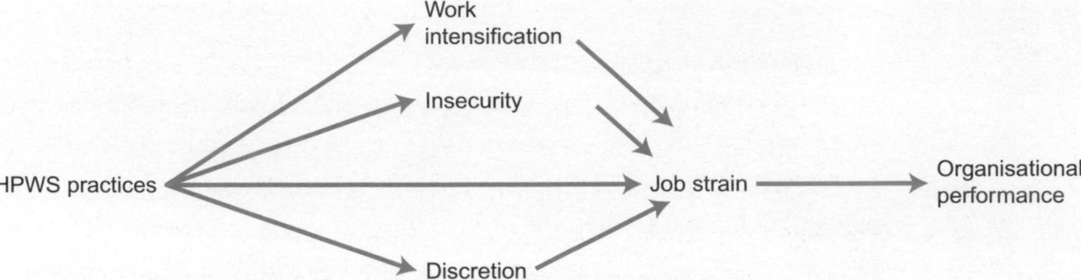

Figure 11.3 Labour process (LP) model
Source: Ramsay *et al.* (2000: 506, Fig. (c)).

There a number of other studies that also develop the argument that HPWS create work intensification for employees (*see*, for example, White *et al.* 2003). If this is so, they may be a short-term means to improved performance, rather than the long-term sustainable approach to competitive advantage that they are claimed to be. We present in the Window on practice below an article questioning HPWS theory and arguing the case for good practice in people management.

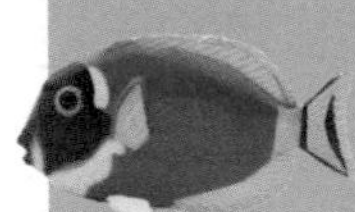

WINDOW ON PRACTICE

Give employees a voice and they do not talk about 'performance' or 'best practice HRM'. Instead they will tell you how the three Rs of respect and recognition from managers, and good relationships at work can affect their motivation and generate long-term commitment. These were by far the most important motivational factors to emerge from a four-year research project. The results suggest that, rather than strive for best practice HRM, organisations should pay more attention to 'good personnel management'.

An association between HRM practices and the competitive advantage of firms has been well established. But the precise mechanism of this causal chain is rarely specified, and frequently based on assumptions about employee outcomes of commitment, motivation and increased competence. As a result, a 'black box' has been created, with organisations left wondering how it works. In the absence of that knowledge, they are prescribed a make-believe scenario whereby they borrow Dorothy's ruby slippers from *The Wizard of Oz* (the appropriate bundle of HR practices), click them together three times and then arrive at their destination (high organisational performance with happy workers). Although Dorothy was content not to question this method and had blind faith in the wizard, corporate managers and academics with organisational performance at stake generally want to know more before 'clicking'.

When employees were given the chance to speak their minds, as opposed to completing a questionnaire, a very different picture of their motivation and commitment emerged.

First, respondents stated clearly: 'You don't work in a factory to get job satisfaction.' They were there, they said, because they would not be able to get the same pay and job security elsewhere with the skills they had. They also confided that they were under increasing amounts of job strain, that there was 'more on us now' and that management was always 'on our backs'.

To relieve the monotony and boredom of life on the line, employees played the management's game. On one line, for instance, they went along with the practice of taking turns to be line leader, even though this clearly resulted in increased stress and work intensification. The findings tend to support the theory that increases in organisational performance are the result of managerial control, work intensification and stress, rather than 'soft' HR, which promotes motivation and commitment.

However, when questioned more deeply about their motivation, employees did stress the positive impact of relationships, both with management and fellow workers, and the importance of respect and recognition. Working on the line and therefore being able to experience these processes made it apparent that, although HRM and high-performance work practices could be mutually reinforcing, HR practices were not the vehicle that drove the three Rs. Rather, it is the other way round: when managers fulfil the three Rs, they encourage motivation and the employees' willingness to 'play the HR game'. What matters to employees is not necessarily best practice, but simply good practice. Without recognition, respect and relationships, the outcomes of HRM practices are hindered. It is therefore essential that these foundations are maintained and developed throughout the organisation.

Source: Adapted from Pass, S. (2005) 'On the line', *People Management*, 15 September, p. 38.

Other critiques include the role of employee volition (*see*, for example, McBride 2008). This centres on the argument that workers are not as acquiescent as current HPWS theory implies, that is, they may resist rather than comply with managers' attempts to implement progressive HR practices. Even where this is not so, McBride goes on to argue that the culture and history of employment relationships in certain industrial sectors, for example shipbuilding, are such that HPWS are simply inappropriate. Perhaps most worryingly of all, for HR practitioners, are the analyses of, for example, the WERS (Kersley *et al.* 2006) that suggest that, for most UK workers, progressive HR practice is rare. This would suggest that HPWS do not really exist for most employees and that debates as to how HR practice can improve organisational performance are falling on deaf management ears.

ACTIVITY 11.4

1. Think about the HR practices that you have experienced. To what extent have these been of benefit to you?
2. Drawing on this, are you more likely to support the argument that HPWS are beneficial to employees or the argument that they merely create work intensification?

SUMMARY PROPOSITIONS

11.1 High performance working derives from the enactment of progressive HR practices, such as sophisticated recruitment and selection practices and training and development, which creates sustainable competitive advantage for an organisation through its people.

11.2 High performance work systems (HPWS) define bundles of HR practices that work synergistically to create enhanced performance. There is, however, no agreement as to which practices should be in the bundle.

11.3 Employee attitudes are generally accepted to mediate the impact of HR practice on performance within the 'black box' of the HR performance link. Commitment and involvement are two key employee attitudes.

11.4 It is important to understand employee perspectives on HR practices in order to design HPWS that effectively enhance performance.

11.5 Line managers are the key to HR effectiveness: good practices are rendered inadequate by poor management behaviour and poor practices made better by good management behaviour.

11.6 Employee engagement is popularly considered to transform employee productivity and profitability. There is a great deal of interest in engagement from government and practitioners, although it is an area in which practice runs ahead of research and theory.

11.7 Critiques of HPWS suggest that increased performance arises out of work intensification for all employees; that employees may not simply passively accept organisational HR practice; and that, in certain sectors, HPWS may not be appropriate or effective.

GENERAL DISCUSSION TOPICS

1 There is evidence that many employees do not have access to progressive HR practices in their workplaces. To what extent do you think that HPWS can be said to exist in contemporary organisations?

2 Research into HPWS has typically focused on organisational perspectives. What difference to the understanding of effective HR practice do you think the inclusion of the employee perspective will bring?

3 Drawing on labour process theory suggests that HPWS create work intensification for employees. To what extent do you accept this? To what extent can HPWS then be said to create sustainable competitive advantage for organisations?

FURTHER READING

Boxall, P. and Macky, K. (2009) 'Research and theory on high-performance work systems: progressing the high-involvement stream', *Human Resource Management Journal*, Vol. 19, No. 1, pp. 3–23.

This wide-ranging and informative article both provides a comprehensive review of the field of HPWS literature and considers issues such as work intensification and the need to explore employee perspectives on HPWS.

Marchington, M. and Zagelmeyer, S. (2005) 'Foreword: linking HRM and performance: a never-ending search?', *Human Resource Management Journal*, Vol. 15, No. 4, pp. 3–8.

This article introduces a special issue of the journal that deals with HRM and performance. The foreword outlines a number of key issues, such as the contents of the 'bundle' of HR practices required and the need to consider worker perspectives on HR. It discusses some key issues in an accessible way and introduces the other articles in the journal, all of which deal with the HR/performance link. The special issue will give readers a broad insight into work in the field.

McLeod, D. and Clarke, N. (2009) *Engaging for Success*. London: Department for Business, Innovation and Skills.

This is a government-commissioned report which gives a resounding, if somewhat uncritical, endorsement to the notion of employee engagement and its performance-enhancing outcomes. It is a useful introduction to the issue, considering how to promote engagement and what the barriers to engagement may be. It also presents a number of case studies on organisational practice that may be of interest to practitioner readers.

REFERENCES

Allen, J. and Meyer, N. (1990) 'The measurement and antecedents of affective, continuance and normative commitment', *Journal of Occupational Psychology*, Vol. 63, No. 1, pp. 1–18.

Appelbaum, E. and Berg, P. (2001) 'High performance work systems and labor market structures', in P. Berg and A. Kalleberg (eds), *Sourcebook of Labor Markets*. New York: Kluwer Academic/Plenum Publishers.

Benkhoff, B. (1997) 'Ignoring commitment is costly: new approaches establish the missing link between commitment and performance', *Human Relations*, Vol. 50, No. 6, pp. 701–26.

Boxall, P. and Macky, K. (2009) 'Research and theory on high-performance work systems: progressing the high-involvement stream', *Human Resource Management Journal*, Vol. 19, No. 1, pp. 3–23.

CIPD (2009) *Employee Engagement in Context*. London: CIPD.

Cooke, F. (2001) 'Human resource strategy to improve organizational performance: a route for firms in Britain?', *International Journal of Management Reviews*, Vol. 3, No. 4, pp. 321–39.

Delery, J. and Doty, D. (1996) 'Modes of theorizing in strategic human resource management: tests of universalistic, contingency and configurational performance predictions', *Academy of Management Journal*, Vol. 39, No. 4, pp. 802–35.

Guest, D. (1998) 'Beyond HRM: commitment and the contract culture', in P. Sparrow and M. Marchington (eds), *Human Resource Management: The new agenda*. London: Financial Times/Pitman Publishing.

Guest, D. and Conway, N. (2004) *Employee Well-being and the Psychological Contract: A report for the CIPD*. London: CIPD.

Guest, D., Michie, J., Conway, N. and Sheehan, M. (2003) 'Human resource management and corporate performance in the UK', *British Journal of Industrial Relations*, Vol. 41, pp. 291–314.

Huselid, M. (1995) 'The impact of human resource management practices on turnover, productivity and corporate financial performance', *Academy of Management Journal*, Vol. 38, No. 3, pp. 635–73.

Hutchinson, S. (2005) 'The role of front-line managers in delivering HR practices', *People Management*, 13 October, p. 50.

Kersley, B., Alpin, C., Forth, J., Bryson, A., Bewley, H., Dix, G. and Oxenbridge, S. (2006) *Inside the Workplace: Findings from the 2004 Workplace Employment Relations Survey*. Abingdon: Routledge.

Kinnie, N., Hutchinson, S., Purcell, J., Rayton, B. and Swart, J. (2005) 'Satisfaction with HR practices and commitment to the organization: why one size does not fit all', *Human Resource Management Journal*, Vol. 15, No. 4, pp. 9–29.

MacDuffie, J. (1995) 'Human resource bundles and manufacturing performance: organizational logic and flexible production systems in the world auto industry', *Industrial and Labor Relations Review*, Vol. 48, No. 2, pp. 197–221.

Macey, W. and Schneider, B. (2008) 'The meaning of employee engagement', *Industrial and Organizational Psychology*, Vol. 1, pp. 3–30.

Macky, K. and Boxall, P. (2007) 'The relationship between "high performance work practices" and employee attitudes: an investigation of additive and interaction effects', *International Journal of Human Resource Management*, Vol. 18, No. 4, pp. 537–67.

McBride, J. (2008) 'The limits of high performance work systems in unionised craft-based work settings', *New Technology Work and Employment*, Vol. 23, No. 3, pp. 213–28.

McLeod, D. and Clarke, N. (2009) *Engaging for Success*. London: Department for Business, Innovation and Skills.

Paauwe, J. and Boselie, P. (2005) 'Human resource function competencies in European companies', *Personnel Review*, Vol. 34, No. 5, pp. 550–66.

Pass, S. (2005) 'On the Line', *People Management*, 15 September, p. 38.

Peccei, R. (2004) 'Human resource management and the search for the happy workplace', Inaugural Address to the Erasmus Research Institute of Management, Erasmus University, Rotterdam, 15 January.

People Management (2009) 'Employee Branding', 5 November, p. 18.

Pfeffer, J. (1998) *The Human Equation: Building profits by putting people first*. Boston: Harvard Business School Press.

Purcell, J., Kinnie, N., Hutchinson, S., Rayton, B. and Swart, J. (2003) *Understanding the People Performance Link: Unlocking the black box*. Research Report. London: CIPD.

Purcell, J. and Hutchinson, S. (2007) 'Front-line managers as agents in the HRM performance causal chain: theory, analysis and evidence', *Human Resource Management Journal*, Vol. 17, No. 1, pp. 3–20.

Ramsay, H., Scholarios, D. and Harley, B. (2000) 'Employees and high-performance work systems: testing inside the black box', *British Journal of Industrial Relations*, Vol. 38, No. 4, pp. 501–31.

White, M., Hill, S., McGovern, P., Mills, C. and Smeaton, D. (2003) 'High-performance management practices, working hours and work–life balance', *British Journal of Industrial Relations*, Vol. 41, No. 2, pp. 175–95.

Wood, S. and Wall, T. (2007) 'Work enrichment and employee voice in human resource management–performance studies', *International Journal of Human Resource Management*, Vol. 18, No. 7, pp. 1335–72.

CHAPTER 12

EMPLOYEE PERFORMANCE MANAGEMENT

THE OBJECTIVES OF THIS CHAPTER ARE TO:

1. Clarify the nature and purpose of performance management and performance appraisal
2. Explain the stages of a typical performance management system
3. Review how team performance and individual performance management can be integrated
4. Review the implementation of performance management systems
5. Explore the contribution of 360-degree/multi-rater feedback

Managing individual performance in organisations has traditionally centred on assessing performance and allocating reward, with effective performance seen as the result of the interaction between individual ability and motivation.

Increasingly, it is recognised that planning and enabling performance have a critical effect on individual performance, with performance goals and standards, appropriate resources, guidance and support from the individual's manager all being central.

The words 'performance management' are sometimes used to imply organisational targets, frameworks like the balanced scorecard, measurements and metrics, with individual measures derived from these. This meaning of performance management has been described by Houldsworth (2004) as a harder 'performance improvement' approach compared with the softer developmental and motivational approaches to aligning the individual and the organisation, which she suggests equates to good management practice. We adopt this as a very helpful distinction and in this chapter focus on the softer approach to employees and teams, covering aspects of the organisational measurement approach in Chapter 29 on Information Technology and human capital measurement.

PERFORMANCE MANAGEMENT AND PERFORMANCE APPRAISAL

Appraisal systems

Traditionally performance appraisal systems have provided a formalised process to review employee performance. They are centrally designed, usually by the HR function, requiring each line manager to appraise the performance of his/her staff, usually each year. This normally requires the manager and employee to take part in a performance review meeting. Elaborate forms are often completed as a record of the process, but these are not living documents, they are generally stored in the archives of the HR department, and the issue of performance is often neglected until the next round of performance review meetings.

What is being appraised varies and might cover personality, behaviour or job performance, with measures being either quantitive or qualitative. Qualitative appraisal is often an unstructured narrative on the general performance of the appraisee, although some guidance might be given about the areas on which the appraiser should comment. The problem with qualitative appraisals is that they may leave important areas unappraised, and that they are not suitable for comparison purposes.

Coates (1994) argues that what is actually measured in performance appraisal is the extent to which the individual conforms to the organisation. Some traditional appraisal was based on measures of personality traits that were felt to be important to the job. These included traits such as resourcefulness, enthusiasm, drive, application and other traits such as intelligence. One difficulty with these is that everyone defines them differently. Raters, therefore, are often unsure of what they are rating, leaving more scope for bias and prejudice. Another problem is that since the same scales are often used for many different jobs, traits that are irrelevant to an appraisee's job may still be measured.

Other approaches link ratings to behaviour and performance on the job. So performance may be reviewed against key aspects of the job or major headings on the job description. Behaviourally anchored rating scales (BARS) and behavioural observation scales (BOS) are specific methods of linking ratings with behaviour at work, although evidence suggests that these are not widely used (Williams 2002).

Another method of making appraisal more objective is to use the process to set job objectives over the coming year and, a year later, to measure the extent to which these objectives have been met. The extent to which the appraisee is involved in setting these objectives varies considerably. When a competency profile has been identified for a particular job, it is then possible to use this in the appraisal of performance. Many appraisal systems combine competency assessment with assessment against objectives or job accountabilities. IRS (2005b) report that 89 per cent of their respondents that used appraisals measured employees against objectives or goals, with 56 per cent measuring against competencies and 53 per cent measuring against pre-set performance standards, as might be used in a harder approach to performance improvement.

Lastly, performance may be appraised by collecting primary data via various forms of electronic surveillance system. There are increasing examples of how activity rates of computer operators can be recorded and analysed, and how the calls made by telephone sales staff can be overheard and analysed. On another level some companies test the performance of their sales staff by sending in assessors acting in the role of customer, often termed 'mystery shoppers'.

In a survey (IRS 2005a) 146 of the 154 respondents used appraisal, and of the 146 respondents, of mixed size, but mainly large companies, 91 per cent appraised all employees. But while performance appraisal has gradually been applied to wider groups of employees, beyond managers and professionals, there are also concerns that appraisal systems are treated as an administrative exercise, are ineffective and do little to improve performance of employees in the future. Despite this, the Department of Health has designed an employee-led performance management system, as outlined in the Window on practice below.

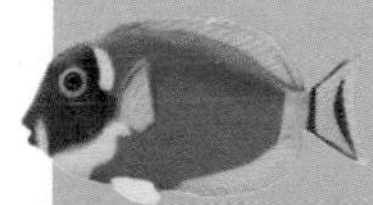

WINDOW ON PRACTICE

The Department of Health (DoH) has launched an employee-led performance management system in a bid to improve the organisation's effectiveness and capability. The new system is part of its total performance management (TPM) strategy, which aims to look at the performance of the department itself in leading the country's health and social care system.

The TPM strategy brings together a business improvement model, which was initially based on the NHS Modernisation Agency's 'ten high-impact changes' strategy, a performance scorecard framework to 'capture the contribution of the department to the wider health and social care system', and the employee-led performance management system. This system comprises the following four 'building blocks': employee competency, which is based on the 'Professional skills for government' framework; effective objective-setting; performance development; and staff well-being and motivation.

It is the department's focus on this fourth area that makes the approach different, according to the head of organisation development and change at the DoH, Bill Phillips. 'Traditional performance reviews have focused on competency and performance only,' he explained. 'But these have failed to address morale, motivation or the employees' sense of identity.' By designing its performance management system to be employee led, the DoH was signalling a departure from the civil service's traditional top-down, paternalistic approach, Phillips said.

Employees will now arrange two formal reviews with their line managers every year. These will be timed to fit in with the DoH's business planning cycle in order to maintain the connection between the organisation's objectives and what its staff are doing. All 2,245 employees in the department will have a half-day learning session and a formal introduction to the process before embarking upon it.

Source: Adapted from *People Management*, 4 May 2006, p. 14.

A further problem with performance management systems is the lack of clarity of purpose. The Employment Studies Institute (IRS 2001) suggests that appraisal is a victim of its own expectations, in that it is expected to deliver in too many areas. Systems may focus on development, identifying future potential, reward, identifying poor performers, or motivation. In systems where appraisal results were linked to reward the manager was placed in the position of an assessor or judge. Alternatively some systems focused on support or development, particularly in the public sector. These provided a better opportunity for managers to give constructive feedback, for employees to be open about difficulties, and for planning to improve future performance. Many systems try to encompass both approaches; for example in the IRS survey (IRS 2005b) 92 per cent of companies used appraisal to determine training and development needs (mainly formally), and 65 per cent used the system either formally or informally to determine pay, with 43 per cent using it formally or informally to determine bonuses. However, as these approaches conflict, the results are Typically unsatisfactory.

WINDOW ON PRACTICE

Applicability of appraisal in different cultural settings

The way that an appraisal process is used may be affected by the cultural context in which it takes place. For example, Varma *et al.* (2005) compare the use of performance appraisal in manufacturing organisations in the USA and India using statistical analysis. They found that interpersonal affect (the like-dislike relationship between supervisor and subordinate) appeared to have no impact in performance appraisal rating given in the USA but that in India supervisors inflated the rating of low performers. They suggest that this may be due to local cultural norms and a collectivist Indian culture as opposed to an individualistic US culture, and a greater concern in India for positive relationships.

Another example is an event experienced by one of the present authors when running a course on Performance Appraisal in the Czech Republic some time after the Velvet Revolution. Managers on the course said that the use of performance appraisal would be entirely unacceptable at that time as workers would associate it with what had gone before under the communist regime. Apparently every year a list of workers was published in order of the highest to the lowest performer. While this list was claimed to represent work performance the managers said that in reality it represented degrees of allegiance to the communist party and was nothing to do with work performance.

The effectiveness of appraisal systems hinges on a range of different factors. Research by Longenecker (1997) in the USA sheds some light on this. In a large-scale survey and focus groups he found that the three most common reasons for failure of an appraisal system were: unclear performance criteria or an ineffective rating instrument (83 per cent); poor working relationships with the boss (79 per cent); and that the appraiser lacked information on the manager's actual performance (75 per cent). Other problems were a lack of ongoing performance feedback (67 per cent) and a lack of focus on management development/improvement (50 per cent). Smaller numbers identified problems with the process, such as lack of appraisal skills (33 per cent) and the review process lacking structure or substance (29 per cent).

Ownership of the system is also important. If it is designed and imposed by the HR function there may be little ownership of the system by line managers. Similarly, if paperwork has to be returned to the HR function it may well be seen as a form-filling exercise for someone else's benefit and with no practical value to performance within the job. There is an increasing literature indicating that appraisal can have serious negative consequences for the employee and IRS (2005b) found that while 40 per cent of respondents in their survey reported no negative consequences, 30 per cent had negative impacts for the organisation, the individual or a relationship, and were able to explain specific incidents where this had happened. Political manipulation of the appraisal process is increasingly being recognised as problematic.

More fundamentally the problem with appraisal not only relates to poor design or implementation, but is rooted deeply in the basic reaction of organisational members to such a concept. There is an increasing body of critical literature addressing the role and theory of appraisal. These debates centre on the underlying reasons for appraisal (*see*, for example, Barlow 1989; Townley 1989, 1993; Newton and Findlay 1996) and the social construction of appraisal (*see*, for example, Grint 1993). This literature throws some light on the use and effectiveness of performance appraisal in organisations.

Performance management systems

While many appraisal systems are still in existence and continue to be updated, performance management systems are increasingly seen as the way to manage employee performance, and have incorporated the appraisal/review process into this. In Part 8, Selected HR skills, we consider the performance appraisal interview in the context of either an appraisal or a performance management system. Clark (2005: 318) provides a useful definition of performance management, stating that the essence of it is:

> Establishing a framework in which performance by human resources can be directed, monitored, motivated and refined, and that the links in the cycle can be audited.

CIPD (2005) reports that 87 per cent of the organisations it surveyed operated a formal process to measure manager performance. Of these 37 per cent were new systems, demonstrating the increasing focus on the issue of performance. Systems are typically closely tied into the objectives of the organisation, so that the resulting performance is more likely to meet organisational needs. CIPD (2009) reports that a number of elements comprise a performance management system (Figure 12.1).

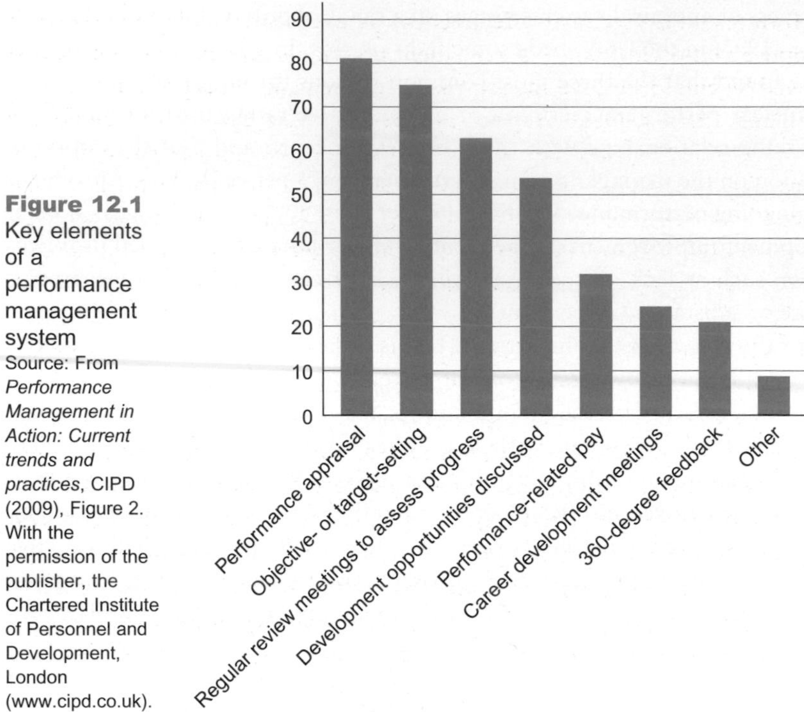

Figure 12.1 Key elements of a performance management system
Source: From *Performance Management in Action: Current trends and practices*, CIPD (2009), Figure 2. With the permission of the publisher, the Chartered Institute of Personnel and Development, London (www.cipd.co.uk).

Performance appraisal or review is almost always a key part of the system, but is integrated with *performance planning*, which links an individual's objectives to business objectives to ensure that employee effort is directed towards organisational priorities: support for *performance delivery* (via development plans, coaching and ongoing review) to enable employee effort to be successful, and that performance is *assessed* and successful performance *rewarded and reinforced*.

The conceptual foundation of performance management relies on a view that performance is more than ability and motivation. It is argued that clarity of goals is key in enabling the employee to understand what is expected and the order of priorities. In addition goals themselves are seen to provide motivation, and this is based on goal-setting theory originally developed by Locke in 1968 and further developed with practical applicability (Locke and Latham 1990). Research to date suggests that for goals to be motivating they must be sufficiently specific, challenging but not impossible and set participatively. Also the person appraised needs feedback on future progress.

The other theoretical base of performance management is expectancy theory, which states that individuals will be motivated to act provided they expect to be able to achieve the goals set, believe that achieving the goals will lead to other rewards and believe that the rewards on offer are valued (Vroom 1964). Given such an emphasis on a link into the organisation's objectives it is somewhat disappointing that Bevan and Thompson (1992) found no correlation between the existence of a performance management system and organisational performance in the private sector. Similarly, Armstrong and Baron (1998a) report from their survey that no such correlation was found. CIPD (2005) reports, however, that 61 per cent of organisations surveyed regarded their systems as effective to some degree and Houldsworth (2003), using the Henley and Hay Group survey of top FTSE companies and public sector respondents, reports that 68 per cent of organisations rated their performance management effectiveness as excellent. While Houldsworth *et al.* (2005) propose that performance management practice is now more sophisticated and better received by employees, we suggest that it still remains an act of faith.

Some performance management systems are development driven and some are reward driven. CIPD (2005) found that 35 per cent of survey respondents reported a link with reward. A view is emerging of performance management which centres on 'dialogue', 'shared understanding', 'agreement' and 'mutual commitment', rather than rating for pay purposes. To this end organisations are increasingly suggesting that employees take more ownership of performance management (*see* Scott 2006 for a good example) and become involved in collecting self-assessment evidence throughout the year (IDS 2005). While these characteristics may feature in more sophisticated systems, Houldsworth (2003) reports that 77 per cent of organisations link performance assessments with pay, and it appears that many organisations are trying to achieve both development and reward outcomes. She also contrasts systems driven by either performance development or performance measurement, finding that the real experience of developmental performance management is that it is motivational, encourages time spent with the line manager, encourages two-way communication and is an opportunity to align roles and training with business needs. Alternatively, where there is a measurement focus, performance management is seen as judgemental, a chance to assess and get rid of employees, emphasises control and getting more out of staff, raises false expectations and is a way to manage the salaries bill. (*See* Table 12.1.)

Table 12.1 Characteristics of performance management systems

- Top-down link between business objectives and individual objectives (compared with performance appraisal where there may be no objectives, or objectives not explicitly linked to business objectives)
- Line manager driven and owned (rather than being owned by the HR function, as typically with performance appraisal)
- A living document where performance and development plans, support and ongoing review are documented as work progresses, and prior to annual review (rather than an archived document retrieved at appraisal time to compare achievement with intentions)
- Performance is rewarded and reinforced

ACTIVITY 12.1

Think of the performance appraisal or performance management system at your place of work.

- To what extent does it focus on development and to what extent does it focus on reward?
- How, and how well, are each of these purposes achieved? Explain why this is.
- What would you do to improve the system, and what impacts would these actions have?

STAGES IN A PERFORMANCE MANAGEMENT SYSTEM

Figure 12.2 shows a typical performance management system, including both development and reward aspects, the main stages of which are discussed below.

Business mission, values, objectives and competencies

There is an assumption that before it is able to plan and manage individual performance the organisation will have made significant steps in identifying the performance required of the organisation as a whole. In most cases this will involve a mission statement so that performance is seen within the context of an overriding theme. In addition many organisations will identify the strategic business objectives that are required within the current business context to be competitive and that align with the organisation's mission statement.

Many organisations will also identify core values of the business and the key competencies required. Each of these has a potential role in managing individual performance. Organisational objectives are particularly important, as it is common for such objectives to be cascaded down the organisation in order to ensure that individual objectives contribute to their achievement (for an example of an objective-setting cascade, *see* Figure 12.3).

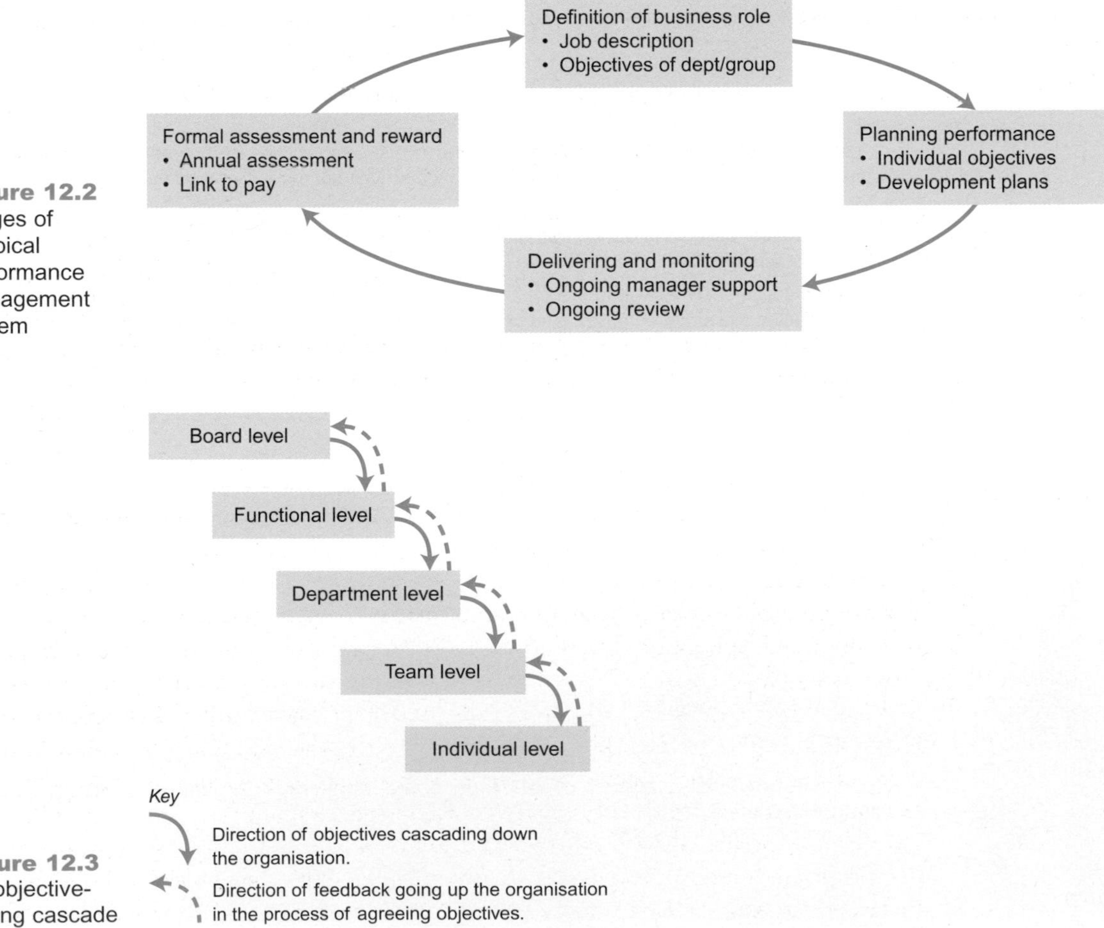

Figure 12.2 Stages of a typical performance management system

Figure 12.3 An objective-setting cascade

Planning performance: a shared view of expected performance

Individual objectives derived from team objectives and an agreed job description can be jointly devised by manager and employee. These objectives are outcome/results oriented rather than task oriented, are tightly defined and include measures to be assessed. The objectives are designed to stretch the individual, and offer potential development as well as meeting business needs. It is helpful to both the organisation and the individual if objectives are prioritised. Many organisations use the 'SMART' acronym for describing individual objectives or targets:

- Specific
- Measurable
- Appropriate
- Relevant
- Timed

It is clearly easier for some parts of the organisation than others to set targets. There is often a tendency for those in technical jobs, such as computer systems development, to identify purely technical targets, reflecting the heavy task emphasis they see in their jobs. Moving staff to a different view of how their personal objectives contribute to team and organisational objectives is an important part of the performance management process. An objective for a team leader in systems development could be:

> To complete development interviews with all team members by end of July 2010 (written March 2010).

Clearly, the timescale for each objective will need to reflect the content of the objective and not timescales set into the performance management system. As objectives are met, managers and their staff need to have a brief review meeting to look at progress in all objectives and decide what other objectives should be added, changed or deleted. Five or six ongoing objectives are generally sufficient for one individual to work on at any time. A mix of objectives about new developments and changes as well as routine aspects of the job is generally considered to be appropriate.

The critical point about a *shared* view of performance suggests that handing out a job description or list of objectives to the employee is not adequate. Performance expectations need to be understood and, where possible, to involve a contribution from the employee. For example, although key accountabilities may be fixed by the manager, they will need to be discussed. Specific objectives allow for and benefit from a greater degree of employee input as employees will have a valid view of barriers to overcome, the effort involved and feasibility. Expressing objectives as a 'what' statement rather than a 'how' statement gives employees the power to decide the appropriate approach once they begin to work on the issue. Incorporating employee input and using 'what' statements are likely to generate a higher degree of employee ownership and commitment. However, difficulties have been experienced with purely 'what' objectives as there may be appropriate and inappropriate ways of achieving an objective. For example, a manager with an objective to ensure that another department agrees to a plan of action could achieve this in different ways. The manager may pressure susceptible members of the other department and force agreement through without listening to the other department's perspective. This may alienate the other department and damage future good relations. Alternatively the manager could adopt a collaborative approach so that the needs of both departments are met, providing a sound basis for future cooperation between the departments. More sophisticated systems now incorporate the 'how' as well (*see* IDS 2003).

Planning the support, development and resources necessary for employees to achieve their objectives is imperative. Without this support it is unlikely that even the most determined employees will achieve the performance required.

Concerns have been expressed over restricting the objectives to those which specify output targets, and there is now evidence of increasing use of input targets, such as developing a critical competency which is valued by the organisation and relevant to the achievement of objectives.

WINDOW ON PRACTICE

Leadership competencies in performance management

People managers at Microsoft are scored in a 'leadership league' to underline the drive for performance management, according to one of the company's HR business partners. As the software industry has become more complex and competitive, the company decided to develop its culture and leadership competency is a very important part of the evolved culture. A spokesman said:

'If a manager does not achieve excellence goals and good employee feedback, even if their business results are exceptional, they will not receive "execution excellence",' she said. 'This is part of Microsoft's performance review and is tied to salary increases and bonuses, so it's a real driver.'

The league rating is partly based on the employee survey, which asked staff to rate how their manager interacted with the rest of business. League scores are based on the competencies in Microsoft's People Scorecard, which gives a performance snapshot and includes the employee feedback.

Source: *People Management* online version, 18 November 2009.

Williams (2002) argues that as individuals cannot always control their results it is important to have behavioural targets as well as output targets. It is also recommended that there is a personal development plan which would again underpin the achievement of objectives.

Delivering and monitoring performance

While the employee is working to achieve the performance agreed, the manager retains a key enabling role. Organising the resources and off-job training is clearly essential. So too is being accessible. There may well be unforeseen barriers to the agreed performance which the manager needs to deal with, and sometimes the situation will demand that the expected performance needs to be revised. The employee may want to sound out possible courses of action with the manager before proceeding, or may require further information. Sharing 'inside' information that will affect the employee's performance is often a key need, although it is also something that managers find difficult, especially with sensitive information. Managers can identify information sources and other people who may be helpful.

Ongoing **coaching** during the task is especially important as managers guide employees through discussion and by constructive feedback. They can refer to practical job experiences to develop the critical skills and competencies that the employee needs, and can provide job-related opportunities for practice. Managers can identify potential role models to employees, help to explain how high achievers perform so well, and oil the organisational wheels.

ACTIVITY 12.2

Think of any organisation in which you have had some involvement:

- How has individual performance been supported?
- How effective was/is this?
- How would you improve the way in which performance was/is supported?

Employees carry out ongoing reviews to plan their work and priorities and also to advise the manager well in advance if the agreed performance will not be delivered by the agreed dates. Joint employee/manager review ensures that information is shared. For example, a manager needs to be kept up to date on employee progress, while the employee needs to be kept up to date on organisational changes that have an impact on the agreed objectives. Both need to share perceptions of how the other is doing in their role, and what they could do that would be more helpful.

These reviews are normally informal, although a few notes may be taken of progress made and actions agreed. They need not be part of any formal system and therefore can take place when the job or the individuals involved demand, and not according to a pre-set schedule. The review is to facilitate future employee performance, providing an opportunity for the manager to confirm that the employee is 'on the right track', redirecting him or her if necessary. They thus provide a forum for employee reward in terms of recognition of progress. A 'well done' or an objective signed off as completed can enhance the motivation to perform well in the future. During this period evidence collection is also important. In the Scottish Prison Service (IDS 2003) line managers maintain a performance monitoring log of their team members' positive and negative behaviours in order to provide regular feedback and to embed the practice of ongoing assessment. Employees are expected to build up a portfolio of evidence of their performance over the period to increase the objectivity of reviews and to provide an audit trail to back up any assessment ratings. It is also during this part of the cycle that employees in many organisations can collect 360-degree feedback to be used developmentally and as part of an evidence base.

Formal performance review/assessment

Regular formal reviews are needed to concentrate on developmental issues and to motivate the employee. Also, an annual review and assessment is needed, of the extent to which objectives have been met – and this may well affect pay received. In many organisations, for example Microsoft and AstraZeneca, employees are now invited to prepare an initial draft of achievement against objectives (IDS 2003). Some organisations continue to have overall assessment ratings which have to conform to a forced distribution, requiring each team/department to have, say, 10 per cent of employees on the top point, 20 per cent on the next point, and so on, so that each individual is assessed relative to others rather than being given an absolute rating. These systems are not popular and Roberts (2004) reports how staff walked out in a part of the Civil Service over relative assessment; AstraZeneca does not encourage its managers to give an overall rating to staff at all as its research suggested that this was demotivating (IDS 2003). Research by the Institute for Employment Studies (IRS 2001) found that review was only seen as fair if the targets set were seen as reasonable, managers were seen to be objective and judgements were consistent across the organisation.

Some organisations encourage employees to give upward feedback to their managers at this point in the cycle. For further details of this stage in the process *see* Part 8, Selected HR skills.

Reward

Many systems still include a link with pay, but difficulties may be experienced, for example, the merit element of pay may be too small to motivate staff. Armstrong and Baron (1998a) report that staff almost universally dislike the link with pay, and a manager in one of their case study companies reported that 'the whole process is an absolute nightmare' (p. 172). Clark (2005) provides a good discussion of the problems with the pay link and we include a detailed discussion of performance related pay in Chapter 23.

There are other forms of reward than monetary and the Institute for Employment Studies (IRS 2001) found that there was more satisfaction with the system where promotion and development, rather than money, were used as rewards for good performance.

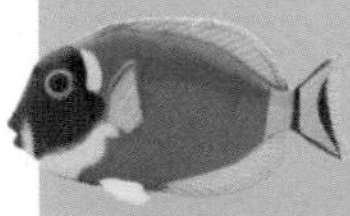

WINDOW ON PRACTICE

Performance management at Orange

To meet a very competitive environment and the convergence of a number of businesses Orange recognised that it needed to make its performance management process more robust. There were a number of concerns with the existing system including the five-point ratings scale; executives feeling that HR owned the process; employees feeling that objective setting often did not support the business; and some feelings of lack of support and direction.

The new system has five core principles:

- one clear cascade process for objectives
- reward should stay linked to performance
- a balance between 'what' and 'how' objectives
- process needs to be owned by the business
- performance should be clearly and consistently differentiated across the ratings

The design of the system was led by senior representatives of the core businesses and a decision was made to keep the best parts of the current system and incorporate 'snippets of good stuff' from elsewhere, rather than looking for a 'best practice' model used elsewhere to implement.

The five-point ratings scale was kept but the labels attached to each point were changed to demonstrate that the mid-point was a good place to be (which was used previously when employees had met their objectives and were doing a good job, and which had caused disagreements). The new scale ranged from 'unacceptable' (one); 'getting there' (two); 'great stuff' (three, the mid-point); 'excellent' (four) to 'exceptional' (five). The distribution curve used to ensure consistent ratings was abandoned in favour of 'calibration' which takes place at various levels and involves managers sharing the ratings they have given to those who report directly to them with other managers at their level, providing justification for their ratings and being prepared to explore and discuss their views. Objective setting is now linked into the balanced scorecard approach they have adopted, with Vice Presidents' objectives being set at the same time (and published on the intranet) and cascaded down the organisation. Objectives are weighted to ensure prioritisation, and staff must have two or three behavioural ('how' or input) objectives. Orange has a profit-sharing scheme for non-managers called 'success share', and now performance ratings are used to determine the proportion received by each individual. For managers the bonus scheme has altered, giving senior managers more flexibility to allocate rewards for each point on the five-point scale, without having to manipulate ratings.

Source: Summarised from R. Johnson (2006) 'Orange Blossoms', *People Management*, Vol. 12, No. 21, 26 October, pp. 56–60.

INDIVIDUAL VERSUS TEAM PERFORMANCE MANAGEMENT

There is one key aspect of employee performance management which we have yet to touch upon and that is how organisations can use performance management to support team performance as well as individual performance. Despite the claimed importance of team working, only 6 per cent of organisations in a recent survey operated a team appraisal system (CIPD 2005). Supporting team and individual performance is a critical balancing act in most cases as, if managers and employees are not mindful in their objective setting, development, review and reward process, there can be conflicts built into performance management activity causing employees' pursuit of individual objectives to damage the performance of the team they are in and vice versa. The complications that can arise and the way they are best dealt with will depend very much on the type of team(s) to which the employee belongs and the individual circumstances. Below we consider different types of team situation and the challenges these bring for performance management, and how both individual performance and team performance can best be enhanced at the same time.

It is generally agreed that teamworking has increased but this may take many forms. First, let us look at the situation where an employee has a base role in a departmental team, such as the 'training team', 'contracts team', 'schools marketing team', for example, reflecting where that person is placed in the organisation and who that person's line manager is. If this is the only team to which the employee belongs then it is highly likely that he or she will agree individual performance management objectives with the team leader which relate to the employee's role in the achievement of the team's objectives. One of those individual objectives may of course focus on collegiality or support to other members of the functional team.

However many employees will at the same time be members of other teams, perhaps ongoing cross-functional teams or time-limited cross-functional problem-solving teams. The objectives for this cross-functional team may be owned elsewhere in the organisation. One danger in such a situation is that if the employee does not have at least one objective relating to his or her role in this second team then this aspect of his or her job may suffer as effort is prioritised on areas that relate purely to his or her home team. This will be especially so if any kind of reward is attached to achievement of objectives. So neglect of a part of the employee's job relating to the second team is the first potential problem. The remedy to this is fairly straightforward, but easily overlooked. An objective relating to the contribution the employee makes to the second team needs to be included (an input objective), or alternatively an objective relating to the achievement of one or more objectives of the second team (an output objective). An example of the first may concern the team role the employee is required to play in that second team, perhaps focusing on strengthening it, if it is not well developed, or may concern the skills that are needed in that team given its stage of development, or may concern the extent to which the employee is collaborative in his or her work with the team. An example of the second may concern, say, the team delivering on a target date, to the standard agreed, or other output targets it has agreed.

The second potential problem is that the employee's individual objectives may actually conflict with the objectives of the second team of which he or she is a part. This conflict may be political in nature, where the home team leader agrees an objective with an individual that he or she should influence the second team to, for example, plan in a certain amount of training, before the roll-out of a new IT system. However, if roll-out is to commence on the target date agreed by the second team, fitting in this training may be extremely difficult, if not impossible. The employee in this situation may not be able to win, either he or she fails to achieve his or her individual objective or the second team of which he or she is a part fails to achieve one of its objectives.

Van Vijfeijken *et al.* (2006) provide another example of potential conflict in relation to the operation of management teams, where the employee (this time a departmental head) has individual objectives relating to the achievement of the department's objectives, but is also part of the organisation's management team which has its own set of objectives. The researchers identified potential conflicts between the individual objectives of different department heads in the management team, and also between any individual head's goals and the team goals. An example here might be that a department head of marketing has an objective relating to cost reductions in their department, whereas a management team goal may concern an extensive marketing campaign to launch a new product. There is a great deal written about how such management teams need to distance themselves from their department (*see*, for example, Garratt 1990) and operate in the interests of the organisation as a whole. This is clearly difficult if the department head has individual objectives relating to the department, which will drive monetary or other rewards. Such contradictions need to be openly aired at an early stage, but this is often not the case, due to lack of awareness, inertia or politicking.

We turn now to consider permanent self-managed teams or the like. Often in such teams all performance management objectives are team based, with the whole team needing to pull together to achieve these objectives effectively. In such teams there may in addition be individual input objectives such as skills development. These teams are more likely to fit the classical definition of a team. Moxon (1993) defines a team as having a common purpose; agreed norms and values which regulate behaviour; members with interdependent functions; and a recognition of team identity. Katzenbach and Smith (1993) and Katzenbach (1997) have also described the differences that they see between teams and work groups, and identify teams as comprising individuals with complementary skills, shared leadership roles, mutual accountability and a specific team purpose, among other attributes. In organisations this dedication only happens when individuals are fully committed to the team's goals. This commitment derives from an involvement in defining how the goals will be met and having the power to make decisions within teams rather than being dependent on the agreement of external management. These are particularly characteristics of self-managing teams.

The problems most likely to occur with team objectives in this setting are peer pressure and social loafing (*see*, for example, Clark 2005). Peer pressure can be experienced by an individual, such as, for example, the pressure not to take time off work when feeling ill, as this may damage achievement of objectives; or pressure to work faster, make fewer mistakes and so on. This pressure is likely to be much greater when rewards are attached to the achievement of team objectives. Individuals will vary in the competitiveness and in the value they place on monetary rewards and this may cause a pressure for all. Social loafing occurs in a situation where one or more team members rely on the others to put in extra effort to achieve objectives, to cover for their own lack of effort. It works when some members are known to be conscientious or competitive or to care deeply about the rewards available, and there are others who are likely to be less concerned and who know the conscientious team members will make sure by their own efforts that the objectives are achieved.

IMPLEMENTATION AND CRITIQUE OF PERFORMANCE MANAGEMENT

Performance management needs to be line driven rather than HR driven, and therefore mechanisms need to be found to make this happen. The incorporation of line managers alongside HR managers in a working party to develop the system is clearly important as it not only takes account of the needs of the line in the system design, but also demonstrates that the system is line led. CIPD (2005) reports that 75 per cent of managers suggest that they own and operate the performance management process. Training in the introduction and use of the system is also ideally line led, and Fletcher and Williams (1992) give us an excellent example of an organisation where line managers were trained as 'performance management coaches' who were involved in departmental training and support for the new system. However, some researchers have found that line managers are the weak link in the system (*see*, for example, Hendry *et al.* 1997). The Department of Trade and Industry (DTI) (*see* IRS 2001) notes that any system is only as good as the people who operationalise it. See Case 12.1 at this book's companion website, **www.pearsoned.co.uk/torrington** which deals with the introduction of a performance management system.

WINDOW ON PRACTICE

Fletcher and Williams (1992) report on a scheme that was introduced by training a series of nominated line manager coaches from each department of an organisation. They had then to take the message back to their colleagues and train them, tailoring the material to their department (Personnel/Training providing the back-up documentation). These were serving line managers who had to give up their time to do the job. Many of them were high-flyers, and they have been important opinion leaders and influencers – though they themselves had to be convinced first. Their bosses could refuse to nominate high-quality staff for this role if they wished, but they would subsequently be answerable to the Chief Executive. This approach was taken because it fits with the philosophy of performance management (i.e. high line-management participation), and because it was probably the only way to train all the departmental managers in the timescale envisaged.

Source: Summarised from C. Fletcher and R. Williams (1992) *Performance Management in the UK: Organisational Experience*. London: IPM, p. 133.

Redman *et al.* (2000) found incomplete take-up of performance management, with some aspects being adopted and not others. They noted that there was a general lack of integration of activities. This is rather unfortunate as one of the key advantages of performance management is the capacity for integration of activities concerned with the management of individual performance. However, Hendry *et al.* (1997) reported the comments of Phil Wills from GrandMet, that there is still little understanding of what an integrated approach to performance management means and Williams (2002) suggests that there is still confusion over the nature of performance management.

Performance management seems to suffer from the same problems as traditional appraisal systems. Armstrong and Baron (1998a) report, for example, that over half the respondents to their survey feel that managers give their best ratings to people that they like (p. 202), and over half the managers surveyed felt that they had not received sufficient training in performance management processes (p. 203). They also report

(1998b) that the use of ratings was consistently derided by staff and seen as subjective and inconsistent. Performance ratings can be seen as demotivating, and forced distributions are felt to be particularly unfair. Yet Houldsworth (2003) found 44 per cent of the Henley and Hay Group survey sample adopted forced distributions.

In terms of individual objective setting linked to organisational performance objectives, there are problems when strategy is unclear and when it evolves. Rose (2000) also reports a range of problems, particularly the fact that SMART targets can be problematic if they are not constantly reviewed and updated, although this is a time-consuming process. Pre-set objectives can be a constraining factor in such a rapidly changing business context, and they remind us of the trap of setting measurable targets, precisely because they are measurable and satisfy the system, rather than because they are most important to the organisation. He argues that a broader approach which assesses the employee's accomplishments as a whole and the contribution to the organisation is more helpful than concentrating on pre-set objectives. Williams (2002) also notes that there is more to performance than task performance, such as volunteering and helping others. He refers to this as contextual performance; it is sometimes referred to as collegiate behaviour.

A further concern with SMART targets is that they inevitably have a short-term focus, yet what is most important to the organisation is developments which are complex and longer term, which are very difficult to pin down to short-term targets (*see*, for example, Hendry *et al.* 1997). In this context systems which also focus on the development of competencies will add greater value in the longer term. Armstrong and Baron (1998b) do note that a more rounded view of performance is gradually being adopted, which involves the 'how' as well as the 'what', and inputs such as the development of competencies. There is, however, a long way to go adequately to describe performance and define what is really required for organisational success.

For an in-depth example of performance management in the Scottish Prison Service *see* Case 12.2 at this book's companion website, **www.pearsoned.co.uk/torrington**.

360-DEGREE FEEDBACK

The term 360-degree feedback, a very specific term used to refer to multi-rater feedback, is increasingly being used within performance management systems and as a separate development activity.

The nature of 360-degree feedback

This approach to feedback refers to the use of the whole range of sources from which feedback can be collected about any individual. Thus feedback is collected from every angle on the way that the individual carries out his or her job: from immediate line manager; peers; subordinates; more senior managers; internal customers; external customers; and from individuals themselves. It is argued that this breadth provides better feedback than relying on the line manager alone, who will only be able to observe the individual in a limited range of situations, and Atwater and his colleagues (2002) suggest that 360-degree feedback provides a better way to capture the complexities of performance. Individuals, it is argued, will find feedback from peers and subordinates compelling and more valid (*see*, for example, Borman 1997 and Atwater *et al.* 2001).

Such all-round feedback enables the individual to understand how he or she may be seen differently (or similarly) by different organisational groups, and how this may contrast with the individual's own views of his or her strengths and weaknesses. This provides powerful information for the development of self-awareness.

WINDOW ON PRACTICE

Johnson (2001) reports on the merger between two pharmaceuticals companies – UniChem from the UK and Alliance Sante from France to form Alliance UniChem. In an attempt to focus managers from diverse cultures on a single vision the HR department concentrated on all aspects of performance management, in particular 360-degree feedback which was felt to be a pragmatic and practical tool. Four key values were identified: excellence, service, innovation and partnership, and competencies were drawn up to reflect these. The process had to be introduced very sensitively as 360-degree feedback was virtually unheard of in three countries covered by the company – Italy, Spain and Portugal, and in France it was seen very much as an American tool and regarded with considerable suspicion.

The most senior managers went through the process first, and it was then piloted in different countries. The tool was developed to be used in five different languages, and the customised package adopted came with development activities for each competency, and coaching sessions to ensure that feedback was not interpreted without analysis and support. The whole process formed part of a self-development programme.

Source: Summarised from R. Johnson (2001) 'Doubled entente', *People Management*, Vol. 7, No. 9, 3 May, pp. 38–9.

ACTIVITY 12.3

1 Think of your current or previous role, in paid employment or any other capacity, and:
- identify one or two critical incidents (such as making a presentation or attending an important meeting for the first time);
- identify a longer-term activity you have been involved in (such as a project group or working party).

2 For both of these, identify who could have provided you with constructive feedback, and why, and what specific questions you would have asked of them.

3 Now think ahead. What plans can you make to incorporate feedback into an up-coming one-off or longer-term activity?

Feedback is based on a survey approach which involves the use of a carefully constructed questionnaire that is used with all the contributors of feedback. This questionnaire may be bought off the peg, providing a well-tested tool, or may be developed internally, providing a tool which is more precisely matched to the needs of the organisation. Whichever form is used, the essence is that it is based on behavioural competencies (for a more detailed explanation of these *see* Chapter 18), and their associated behaviours. Contributors will be asked to score, on a given scale, the extent to which the individual displays these behaviours. Using a well-designed questionnaire, distributed to a sufficient number of contributors and employing appropriate sophisticated analysis, for example specifically designed computer packages which are set up to detect and moderate collusion and bias on behalf of the contributors, should provide reliable and valid data for the individual. The feedback is usually presented to the individual in the form of graphs or bar charts showing comparative scores from different feedback groups, such as peers, subordinates, customers, where the average will be provided for each group, and single scores from line manager and self. In most cases the individual will have been able to choose the composition of the contributors in each group, for example which seven subordinates, out of a team of ten, will be asked to complete the feedback questionnaire. But beyond this the feedback will be anonymous as only averages for each group of contributors will be reported back, except for the line manager's score. The feedback will need to be interpreted by an internal or external facilitator, and done via a face-to-face meeting. It is generally recommended that the individual will need some training in the nature of the system and how to receive feedback, and the contributors will need some training on how to provide feedback. The principle behind the idea of feedback is that individuals can then use this information to change their behaviours and to improve performance, by setting and meeting development goals and an action plan.

Benefits may include a stronger ownership of development goals, a climate of constructive feedback, improved communication over time and an organisation which is more capable of change as continuous feedback and improvement have become part of the way people work. A brief guide to 360-degree feedback is provided by Goodge and Watts (2000)

Difficulties and dilemmas

As with all processes and systems there needs to be clarity about the purpose. Most authors distinguish between developmental uses, which they identify as fairly safe and a good way of introducing such a system, and other uses, such as to determine pay awards. There seems to be an almost universal view that using these data for pay purposes is not advisable, and in the literature from the United States there is clearly a concern about the legal ramifications of doing this. Ward (1995) provides a useful framework for considering the different applications of this type of feedback, and reviews in some detail other applications such as using 360-degree feedback as part of a training course to focus attention for each individual on what he or she needs to get out of the course. Other applications he suggests include using 360-degree feedback as an approach to team building, as a method of performance appraisal/management, for organisation development purposes and to evaluate training and development. Edwards and Ewen (1996) suggest that it can be used for nearly all HR systems, using selection, training and development, recognition and the allocation of job assignments as examples.

Most approaches to 360-degree feedback require rater confidentiality as well as clarity of purpose, and this can be difficult to maintain with a small team, so raters may feel uncomfortable about being open and honest. In their research Pillutla and Ronson (2006) demonstrate how peer evaluations may be biased and warn against recruitment, reward and promotion decisions being made on this basis. The dangers of collusion and bias need to be eliminated, and it is suggested that the appropriate software systems can achieve this, but they are of course expensive, as are well-validated off-the-peg systems.

Follow-up is critical and if the experience of 360-degree feedback is not built on via the construction of development goals and the support and resources to fulfil these, the process may be viewed negatively and may be demotivating. There is an assumption that the provision of such feedback will motivate the individuals receiving it to develop and improve their performance, but Morgan and Cannan (2005) found very mixed results in their Civil Service research. One-third of their respondents were not motivated to act on the feedback and in this case felt that the 360-degree process was an isolated act with lack of follow-up, depending heavily on the proactivity of the individuals involved, with little support.

London *et al.* (1997) report concerns about the way systems are implemented, and that nearly one-third of respondents they surveyed experienced negative effects. Atwater and his colleagues (2002) found some negative reactions such as reduced effort, dissatisfaction with peers who provided the feedback and a lower commitment to colleagues. Fletcher and Baldry (2001) note that there are contradictions in the results from 360-degree feedback so far, and they suggest that further research is needed on how feedback affects self-esteem, motivation, satisfaction and commitment. The DTI (2001) suggested that sufficient resources need to be devoted to planning a system and that it should be piloted before general use. Clearly, 360-degree feedback needs to be handled carefully and sensitively and in the context of an appropriate organisational climate so that it is not experienced as a threat. Atwater *et al.* (2002) suggest that to counteract any negative effects it is important to prepare people for making their own ratings and on how they can provide honest and constructive feedback to others, ensure confidentiality and anonymity of raters, make sure the feedback is used developmentally and owned by the person being rated (for example that person may be the only one to receive the report), provide post-feedback coaching and encouragement and encourage people to follow up the feedback they have received.

SUMMARY PROPOSITIONS

12.1 Employee performance management systems incorporate appraisal activity, but include other aspects such as a link to organisational objectives, an emphasis on ongoing review, motivation, coaching and support, and reinforcement/reward for performance achieved.

12.2 There is a conflict in many appraisal and performance management systems as managers frequently have a dual role as assessor and developer.

12.3 Current trends in sophisticated appraisal activity include greater employee ownership, emphasis on the 'how' as well as the 'what', emphasis on evidence collection from both manager and employee, and upward feedback to the line manager as well as downward feedback to the employee.

12.4 Most employee performance management systems focus on the individual, but there is a need to ensure that team contributions are not neglected and more importantly that team and individual goals do not conflict.

12.5 360-degree feedback is increasingly being used to provide individuals with a basis for changing behaviour and improving performance. It is important to use this process developmentally rather than linking it directly to pay awards.

GENERAL DISCUSSION TOPICS

1. In what ways is the concept of performance management different from the way in which management has been traditionally practised? What are the advantages and disadvantages for employees and employers?
2. 360-degree feedback may have many advantages, but there is the argument that it can never really work because of the built-in biases, such as marking a boss well because you're due for a pay rise; marking yourself low so that you can be happily surprised by others' evaluations; marking peers down to make oneself look better. Discuss as many built-in biases as you can think of, and suggest how they might be tackled and whether substantive improvements could be made.

FURTHER READING

CIPD (2009) *Performance Management in Action: Current trends and practice*. London: CIPD.
A recent report that provides up-to-date information on this topic, reflecting organisational practice at a time of economic recession. Discusses the changing context both economically and in relation to issues such as the role of line manager and the need to consider online systems.

Cunneen, P. (2006) 'How to improve performance management', *People Management*, Vol. 12, No. 1, pp. 42–3.
Rao, A. (2007) 'Effectiveness of performance management systems: an empirical study in Indian companies', *International Journal of Human Resource Management*, Vol. 18, No. 10, pp. 1812–40.
The first article provides some brief and well-focused guidance for implementing a performance management system. The second considers the effectiveness of such systems, integrating consideration of cultural issues within the Indian context.

Kuvaas, B. (2006) 'Performance appraisal satisfaction and employee outcomes: mediating and moderating roles of work motivation', *International Journal of Human Resource Management*, Vol. 17, No. 3, pp. 504–22.
Poon, J. (2004) 'Effects of performance appraisal politics on job satisfaction and turnover intention', *Personnel Review*, Vol. 33, No. 3, pp. 322–34.
These articles reflect a stream of research looking at the outcomes of appraisal from the employee perspective, in particular focusing on job satisfaction, intention to quit and commitment. Comparing both articles provides an interesting country comparison, with savings banks being investigated in Norway by Kuvaas and a cross-sector study of part-time MBA students in Malaysia being carried out by Poon.

Nurse, L. (2005) 'Performance appraisal, employee development and organizational justice: exploring the linkages', *International Journal of Human Resource Management*, Vol. 16, No. 7, pp. 1176–94.

An interesting article which explores different ways in which performance appraisal (PA) contributes to organisational justice, which is a topic of increasing interest. Nurse identifies the way that PA contributes to procedural justice (fairness of the process by which PA decisions are made); distributive justice (fairness of the outcomes and rewards from PA) and interactional justice. The research was carried out with a cross-section of organisations in Barbados.

REFERENCES

Armstrong, M. and Baron, A. (1998a) *Performance Management: The new realities*. London: IPD.

Armstrong, M. and Baron, A. (1998b) 'Out of the tick box', *People Management*, 23 July, pp. 38–41.

Atwater, L., Waldman, D. and Brett, J. (2002) 'Understanding and optimising multi-source feedback', *Human Resource Management*, Vol. 41, No. 2, pp. 193–208.

Audit Commission (2002) *Performance Breakthrough: Improving performance in public sector organizations*. London: The Audit Commission.

Barlow, G. (1989) 'Deficiencies and the perpetuation of power: latent functions in management appraisal', *Journal of Management Studies*, Vol. 26, No. 5, pp. 499–518.

Bevan, S. and Thompson, M. (1992) 'An overview of policy and practice', *Personnel Management in the UK: An anaylsis of the issues*. London: IPM.

Borman, W. (1997) '360° ratings: an analysis of assumptions and a research agenda for evaluating their validity', *Human Resource Management Review*, Vol. 7, pp. 247–68.

Brown, M. and Heywood, J. (2005) 'Performance appraisal systems: determinants and change', *British Journal of Industrial Relations*, Vol. 43, No. 4, pp. 659–79.

CIPD (2005) *Performance Management*. London: CIPD.

CIPD (2009) *Performance Management in Action: Current trends and practice*. London: CIPD.

Clark, G. (2005) 'Performance management strategies', in G. Salaman, J. Storey and J. Billsberry (eds), *Strategic Human Resource Management: Theory and practice*. London: The Open University in association with Sage.

Coates, G. (1994) 'Performance appraisal as icon: Oscar-winning performance or dressing to impress?', *International Journal of Human Resource Management*, Vol. 5, No. 1, pp. 167–91.

Cook, S. and Macauley, S. (1997) 'How colleagues and customers can help improve team performance', *Team Performance Management*, Vol. 3, No. 1, pp. 12–17.

Edwards, M.R. and Ewen, A.J. (1996) *360 Degree Feedback*. New York: Amacom, American Management Association.

Egan, G. (1995) 'A clear path of peak performance', *People Management*, 18 May, pp. 34–7.

Farrell, C. (2001) *360 Degree Feedback: Best practice guidelines*. London: DTI.

Fletcher, C. and Baldry, C. (2001) 'Multi-source feedback systems: a research perspective', in I. Robertson and C. Cooper (eds), *Personnel Psychology and HRM*. Chichester: John Wiley & Sons Ltd.

Fletcher, C. and Williams, R. (1992) *Performance Management in the UK: Organisational experience*. London: IPM.

Garratt, B. (1990) *Creating a Learning Organisation*. Hemel Hempstead: Director Books.

Goodge, P. and Watts, P. (2000) 'How to manage 360° feedback', *People Management*, 17 February, pp. 50–2.

Grint, K. (1993) 'What's wrong with performance appraisals? A critique and a suggestion', *Human Resource Management Journal*, Vol. 3, No. 3, pp. 61–77.

Hendry, C., Bradley, P. and Perkins, S. (1997) 'Missed a motivator?', *People Management*, 15 May, pp. 20–5.

Hendry, C., Woodward, S., Bradley, P. and Perkins, S. (2000) 'Performance and rewards: cleaning out the stables', *Human Resource Management Journal*, Vol. 10, No. 3, pp. 46–62.

Hogetts, R.M., Luthans, F. and Slocum, J. (1999) 'Strategy and HRM initiatives for the '00s: environment redefining roles and boundaries, linking competencies and resources', *Organizational Dynamics*, Vol. 28, No. 2, pp. 7–21.

Houldsworth, E. (2003) 'Managing individual performance', paper presented to the CIPD National Conference, Harrogate, 22–24 November.

Houldsworth, E. (2004) 'Managing performance', in D. Rees and R. McBain (eds), *People Management: Challenges and opportunities*. Basingstoke: Macmillan.

Houldsworth, E., Jirasinghe, D. and Everall, K. (2005) 'How can HR get the measure of performance management?', *People Management*, Vol. 11, No. 16, p. 48.

Hurley, S. (1998) 'Application of team-based 360° feedback systems', *Team Performance Management*, Vol. 4, No. 5, pp. 202–10.

IDS (2003) *IDS Studies: Performance Management*, No. 748, April. London: IDS.

IDS (2005) *IDS Studies: Performance Management*, No. 796, April. London: IDS.

IRS (2001) 'Performance appraisal must try harder', *IRS Employment Trends*, No. 724, March, pp. 2–3.

IRS (2005a) 'Appraisals (1): not living up to expectations', *IRS Employment Review*, No. 828, 29 July, pp. 9–15.

IRS (2005b) 'Appraisals (2): learning from practice and experience', *IRS Employment Review*, No. 829, 12 August, pp. 13–17.

Johnson, R. (2001) 'Doubled entente', *People Management*, Vol. 7, No. 9, pp. 38–9.

Johnson, R. (2006) 'Orange Blossoms', *People Management*, Vol. 12, No. 21, pp. 56–60.

Katzenbach, J.R. (1997) 'The myth of the top management team', *Harvard Business Review*, November–December, pp. 82–91.

Katzenbach, J.R. and Smith, D.K. (1993) 'The discipline of teams', *Harvard Business Review*, Vol. 71, No. 2, pp. 111–20.

Locke, E. (1968) 'Towards a theory of task performance and incentives', *Organisational Behaviour and Human Performance*, Vol. 3, No. 2, pp. 157–89.

Locke, E. and Latham, G. (1990) *A Theory of Goal Setting and Task Performance*. Englewood Cliffs: Prentice-Hall.

London, M., Smither, J. and Adsit, D. (1997) 'Accountability: the Achilles' heel of multi-source feedback', *Group and Organizational Dynamics*, Vol. 22, No. 2, pp. 162–84.

Longenecker, C. (1997) 'Why managerial performance appraisals are ineffective: causes and lessons', *Career Development International*, Vol. 2, No. 5, pp. 212–18.

Mabey, C. and Salaman, G. (1995) *Strategic Human Resource Management*. Oxford: Blackwell.

Morgan, A. and Cannan, K. (2005) '360 degree feedback: a critical enquiry', *Personnel Review*, Vol. 34, No. 6, pp. 663–80.

Moxon, P. (1993) *Building a Better Team*. Aldershot: Gower in association with ITD.

Newton, T. and Findlay, P. (1996) 'Playing God? The performance of appraisal', *Human Resource Management Journal*, Vol. 6, No. 3, pp. 42–58.

Pillutla, M. and Ronson, S. (2006) 'Survival of the similar', *People Management*, Vol. 12, No. 6, pp. 36–7.

Redman, T., Snape, E., Thompson, D. and Ka-Ching Yan, F. (2000) 'Performance appraisal in the National Health Service: a Trust Hospital study', *Human Resource Management Journal*, Vol. 10, No. 1, pp. 1–16.

Roberts, Z. (2004) 'Q&A: "We must move on"', *People Management*, Vol. 10, No. 10, pp. 16–17.

Rose, M. (2000) 'Target practice', *People Management*, 23 November, pp. 44–5.

Scott, A. (2006) 'Intensive care', *People Management*, Vol. 12, No. 9, pp. 14–15.

Storr, F. (2000) 'This is not a circular', *People Management*, 11 May, pp. 38–40.

Townley, B. (1989) 'Selection and appraisal: reconstituting social relations', in J. Storey (ed.), *New Perspectives on Human Resource Management*. London: Routledge.

Townley, B. (1993) 'Performance appraisal and the emergence of management', *Journal of Management Studies*, Vol. 30, No. 2, pp. 27–44.

Varma, A., Pichler, S. and Srinivas, E. (2005) 'The role of interpersonal affect in performance appraisal: evidence from two samples – the US and India', *International Journal of Human Resource Management*, Vol. 16, No. 11, pp. 2029–44.

van Vijfeijken, H., Kleingeld, A., van Tuijl, H. and Algera, J. (2006) 'Interdependence and fit in team performance management', *Personnel Review*, Vol. 35, No. 1, pp. 98–117.

Vroom, V. (1964) *Work and Motivation*. Chichester: John Wiley & Sons Ltd.

Ward, P. (1995) 'A 360 degree turn for the better', *People Management*, 9 February, p. 24.

Williams, R. (2002) *Managing Employee Performance*. London: Thompson Learning.

An extensive range of additional materials, including multiple choice questions, answers to questions and links to useful websites can be found on the Human Resource Management companion website at **www.pearsoned.co.uk/torrington**.

CHAPTER 13

LEADERSHIP

THE OBJECTIVES OF THIS CHAPTER ARE TO:

1. Introduce a working definition which reflects the general nature of leadership
2. Examine the trait approach to leadership
3. Examine the style (behavioural) and contingency approaches to leadership
4. Explore the nature of heroic and post-heroic leadership
5. Discuss the emergence of the concept of followership

Leadership is one of the most loaded and misunderstood words in management. Individual managers are often seduced by concepts of leadership that show them to be knights in shining armour with superhuman qualities and (this is the really dangerous bit) adoring followers. The followers rarely have that view of their managers. We must not, however, underestimate the importance of leadership. There are indeed sometimes needs for individual leaders who have outstanding personal qualities and who achieve extraordinary change in their business. Sometimes more subtle leadership qualities are more important, and there are infinitely more roles which call on different and more modest leadership skills, which can be learned and which are equally important, even if they do not merit shining armour and a white charger.

Understanding leadership was well developed in the second half of the twentieth century and it is this work which is the basis of our understanding and analysis today. The one major addition of recent years has been an appreciation of the impact of the changing circumstances of contemporary business and the role of women. All of the twentieth-century studies and theories were based on two complementary assumptions; first, the business norm was of large, stable organisations steadily getting bigger; second, management was almost exclusively a male activity, with male norms. This led to explanations and suggestions based on those two givens. We now see a weakening of both assumptions. Effective businesses are not necessarily large, growing organisations and there are many more women in the workforce and in management positions within it. Although charismatic leaders (a predominantly male concept) are still needed in some situations, empowering leaders are increasingly required. We have also seen an increasing interest in the concept of followership and its impact on leadership effectiveness. We chart the development of leadership theories and their implications throughout this chapter.

LEADERSHIP AND MANAGEMENT

Northouse (2006) suggests that there are four components that characterise leadership: that leadership is a process; it involves influence; it occurs within a group context; and it involves goal attainment. This corresponds with Shackleton's (1995) definition, which we shall use as a working definition for the remainder of the chapter:

> Leadership is the process in which an individual influences other group members towards the attainment of group or organizational goals. (Shackleton 1995: 2)

This definition is useful as it leaves open the question of whether leadership is exercised in a commanding or a facilitative manner. It does suggest, however, that the leader in some way motivates others to act in such a way as to achieve group goals.

The definition also makes no assumptions about who the leader is; it may or may not be the nominal head of the group. Managers, therefore, may or may not be leaders, and leaders may or may not be managers. Some authors distinguish very clearly between the nature of management and the nature of leadership but this draws on a particular perspective, that of the transformational leader, and we will consider this in the section on whether the organisation needs heroes. This is a school of thought that concentrates on the one leader at the top of the organisation, which is very different from organisations and individuals who use the terms manager and leader interchangeably with nothing more than a vague notion that managers should be leaders. Indeed, any individual may act as a manager one day and a leader the next, depending on the situation. In addition we should not assume that leadership is always a downwards process, as sometimes employees and managers lead upwards (Hollington 2006).

The flow of articles on leadership continues unabated, but it would be a mistake to think that there is an ultimate truth to be discovered; rather, there is a range of perspectives from which we can try to make sense of leadership and motivation. Grint (1997: 3) puts it well when he comments that

> What counts as leadership appears to change quite radically across time and space.

In the following three sections we will look at three questions which underlie virtually all the work on leadership. First, what are the traits of a leader, or an effective leader? Second, what is the 'best' leadership style or behaviour? Third, if different styles are appropriate at different times, what factors influence the desired style?

WHAT ARE THE TRAITS OF LEADERS AND EFFECTIVE LEADERS?

Trait approaches, which were the earliest to be employed, seek to identify the traits of leaders – in other words what characterises leaders as opposed to those who are not leaders. These approaches rest on the assumption that some people were born to lead due to their personal qualities, while others are not. It suggests that leadership is only available to the chosen few and not accessible to all. These approaches have been discredited for this very reason and because there has been little consistency in the lists of traits that research has uncovered. However, this perspective is frequently resurrected (*see*, for example, Fache 2009).

Kilpatrick and Locke (1991), in a meta-analysis, did seem to find some consistency around the following traits: drive to achieve; the motivation to lead; honesty and integrity; self-confidence, including the ability to withstand setbacks, standing firm and being emotionally resilient; cognitive ability; and knowledge of the business. They also note the importance of managing the perceptions of others in relation to these characteristics. Northouse (2006) provides a useful historical comparison of the lists of traits uncovered in other studies. Perhaps the most well-known expression of the trait approach is the work relating to charismatic leadership. House (1976), for example, describes charismatic leaders as being dominant, having a strong desire to influence, being self-confident and having a strong sense of their own moral values. We will pick up on this concept of leadership in the later section on heroes.

In a slightly different vein Goleman (1998) carried out a meta-analysis of leadership competency frameworks in 188 different companies. These frameworks represented the competencies related to outstanding leadership performance. Goleman analysed the competencies into three groups: technical, cognitive and emotional, and found that, in terms of the ratios between the groups, emotional competencies 'proved to be twice as important as the others'. Goleman goes on to describe five components of emotional intelligence:

- **Self-awareness:** this he defines as a deep understanding of one's strengths, weaknesses, needs, values and goals. Self-aware managers are aware of their own limitations.
- **Self-regulation:** the control of feelings, the ability to channel them in constructive ways. The ability to feel comfortable with ambiguity and not panic.
- **Motivation:** the desire to achieve beyond expectations, being driven by internal rather than external factors, and to be involved in a continuous striving for improvement.
- **Empathy:** considering employees' feelings alongside other factors when decision making.
- **Social skill:** friendliness with a purpose, being good at finding common ground and building rapport. Individuals with this competency are good persuaders, collaborative managers and natural networkers.

Goleman's research is slightly different from previous work on the trait approach, as here we are considering what makes an effective leader rather than what makes a leader (irrespective of whether they are effective or not). It is also different in that Goleman refers to competencies rather than traits. There is a further discussion of competencies in Chapter 18; it is sufficient for now to say that competencies include a combination of traits and abilities, among other things. There is some debate over whether competencies can be developed in people. The general feeling is that some can and some cannot. Goleman maintains that the five aspects of emotional intelligence can be learned and provides an example in his article of one such individual. In spite of his argument we feel that it is still a matter for debate, and as many of the terms used by Goleman are similar to those of the previous trait models of leadership, we have categorised his model as an extension of the trait perspective. To some extent his work sits between the trait approach and the style approach which follows. It is interesting that a number of researchers and writers are recognising that there is some value in considering a mix of personality characteristics and behaviours, and in particular Higgs (2003) links this approach to emotional intelligence.

Rajan and van Eupen (1997) also consider that leaders are strong in emotional intelligence, and that this involves the traits of self-awareness, zeal, resilience and the ability to read emotions in others. They argue that these traits are particularly important in the development and deployment of people skills. Heifetz and Laurie (1997) similarly identify that in order for leaders to regulate emotional distress in the organisation, which is inevitable in change situations, the leader has to have 'the emotional capacity to tolerate uncertainty, frustration and pain' (p. 128). Along the same lines Goffee (2002) identifies that inspirational leaders need to understand and admit their own weaknesses (within reason); sense the needs of situations; have empathy and self-awareness.

ACTIVITY 13.1

Think of different leaders you have encountered – in particular those that were especially effective or ineffective:

1 What differences can you identify in terms of their traits (personal characteristics)?

2 What differences can you identify in terms of their behaviour?

3 Are the trait and behaviour lists connected in any way? If so how?

4 Which of these two approaches – trait or behaviour – do you find more useful in helping you to understand the nature of effective leadership?

WHAT IS THE 'BEST WAY TO LEAD'? LEADERSHIP STYLES AND BEHAVIOURS

Dissatisfaction with research on leadership that saw leadership as a set of permanent personal characteristics that describe the leader led to further studies that emphasised the nature of the leadership process – the interaction between leader and follower – aiming to understand how the leaders *behave* rather than what they *are*. The first such studies sought to find the 'best' leadership style; from this perspective leadership comprises an ideal set of behaviours that can be learned. Fulop *et al.* (1999) suggest that Douglas McGregor's (1960) work, *The Human Side of Enterprise*, can be understood from this perspective. McGregor argued that American corporations managed their employees as if they were work shy, and needed constant direction, monitoring and control (theory 'x'), rather than as if they were responsible individuals who were willing and able to take on responsibility and organise their own work (theory 'y'). McGregor argued that the underlying assumptions of the manager determined the way he or she managed the employees and this in turn determined how the employees would react. Thus if employees were managed as if they operated on theory 'x' then they would act in a theory 'x' manner; conversely if employees were managed as if they operated on theory 'y' then they would respond as theory 'y' employees would respond. The message was that management style should reinforce theory 'y' and thus employees would take on responsibility, be motivated by what they were doing and work hard. Although the original book was written 50 years ago, this approach is being revisited (*see*, for example, Heil *et al.* 2000) and it fits well with the empowering or post-heroic approach to leadership that we discuss later in the chapter. Another piece of research from the style approach is that by Blake and Mouton (1964), who developed the famous 'Managerial Grid'. The grid is based on two aspects of leadership behaviour. One is concern for production, that is, task-oriented behaviours such as clarifying roles, scheduling work, measuring outputs; the second is concern for people, that is, people-centred behaviour such as building trust, camaraderie, a friendly atmosphere. These two dimensions are at the heart of many models of leadership and have been recently explored by Cowsgill and

Table 13.1 Blake and Mouton's four leadership styles

High concern for people Low concern for production **Country Club management**	High concern for people High concern for production **Team management**
Low concern for people Low concern for production **Impoverished management**	Low concern for people High concern for production **Authority-compliance management**

Source: Adapted from R.R. Blake and J.S. Mouton (1964) *The Managerial Grid*. Houston, Texas: Gulf Publishing

Grint (2008) who seek to develop the task/relationship dichotomy by suggesting that senior managers who seek to satisfy the demands of both their superiors and subordinates will be the most successful leaders.

Blake and Mouton proposed that individual leaders could be measured on a nine-point scale in each of these two aspects, and by combining them in grid form they identified the four leadership styles presented in Table 13.1.

Such studies, which are well substantiated by evidence, suggest that leadership is accessible for all people and that it is more a matter of learning leadership behaviour than of personality characteristics. Many leadership development courses have therefore been based around this model. However, as Northouse (2006) argues, there is an assumption in the model that the team management style (high concern for people and high concern for production; sometimes termed 9,9 management) is the ideal style; and yet this claim is not substantiated by the research. This approach also fails to take account of the characteristics of the situation and the nature of the followers.

WINDOW ON PRACTICE

A large organisation adopted the Managerial Grid as the framework for its leadership development programme. The programme was generally well accepted and successful application of the team management style was seen to be connected to future promotions. Most managers, on leaving the programme, set out to display 9,9 leadership behaviours. However, this had unexpected and undesirable consequences. Not only were team members daunted by their managers suddenly displaying a different style, but sometimes the 9,9 style was not appropriate in the circumstances in which it was used. The organisation eventually discontinued the programme due to the damage that it was causing.

Much of the recent work on the notion of transformational/heroic leadership, and empowering/post-heroic leadership, similarly assumes that what is being discussed is the one best way for a leader to lead, and we return to this leadership debate later on.

DO LEADERS NEED DIFFERENT STYLES FOR DIFFERENT SITUATIONS?

WINDOW ON PRACTICE

Goffee and Jones (2006) highlight the situational nature of leadership by using examples of key figures. They identify how Winston Churchill was an inspirational wartime leader but when this time and place were gone his 'bulldog' style was not well suited to leading the reconstruction of post-war Britain. As an alternative they name Nelson Mandela who is someone who could offer leadership across a wide range of contexts, adjusting from leading whilst in a prison cell on Robben Island to leading from Union House in Pretoria when he was released and was elected President of South Africa.

Source: Goffee, R. and Jones, G. (2006) 'The Lizard Kings', *People Management*, Vol. 12, No. 2, 26 January, pp. 32–4.

A variety of models, sometimes termed contingency models, have been developed to address the importance of context in terms of the leadership process, and as a consequence these models become more complex. Many, however, retain the concepts of production-centred and people-centred behaviour as ways of describing leadership behaviour, but use them in a different way. Hersey and Blanchard (1988) developed a model which identified that the appropriate leadership style in a situation should be dependent on their diagnosis of the 'readiness', that is, developmental level or maturity, of their followers. The model is sometimes referred to as 'situational leadership', and works on the premise that leaders can 'adapt their leadership style to meet the demands of their environment' (Hersey and Blanchard 1988: 169). Readiness of followers is defined in terms of ability and willingness. Level of ability includes the experience, knowledge and skills that an individual possesses in relation to the particular task at hand; and level of willingness encompasses the extent to which the individual has the motivation and commitment, or the self-confidence, to carry out the task. Having diagnosed the developmental level of the followers, Hersey and Blanchard suggest, the leader then adapts his or her behaviour to fit. They identify two dimensions of leader behaviour: task behaviour, which is sometimes termed 'directive'; and relationship behaviour, which is sometimes termed 'supportive'. Task behaviour refers to the extent to which leaders spell out what has to be done. This includes 'telling people what to do, how to do it, when to do it, where to do it, and who is to do it' (Hersey 1985: 19). On the other hand, relationship behaviour is defined as 'the extent to which the leader engages in two-way or multi-way communication. The behaviours include listening, facilitating and supporting behaviours' (ibid.). The extent to which the leader emphasises each of these two types of behaviour results in the usual two-by-two matrix. The four resulting styles are identified, as shown in Table 13.2.

There is an assumption that the development path for any individual and required behaviour for the leader is to work through boxes 1, 2, 3 and then 4 in the matrix.

Table 13.2 Hersey and Blanchard's four styles of leadership

High relationship behaviour Low task behaviour Followers are able, but unwilling or insecure **Supportive (participating) style (3)**	High relationship behaviour High task behaviour Followers are unable, but willing or confident **Coaching (selling) style (2)**
Low relationship behaviour Low task behaviour Followers are both able and willing or confident **Delegation style (4)**	Low relationship behaviour High task behaviour Followers are unable and unwilling or insecure **Directing (telling) style (1)**

Source: Adapted from P. Hersey and K.H. Blanchard (1988) *Management of Organizational Behavior: Utilizing Human Resources*, 5th edn. Englewood Cliffs, NJ: Prentice-Hall International. © Copyright material, adapted and reprinted with the permission of Center for Leadership Studies, Escondido, CA92025.

Hersey and Blanchard produced questionnaires to help managers diagnose the readiness of their followers.

Other well-known contingency models include Fielder's (1967) contingency model where leadership behaviour is matched to three factors in the situation: the nature of the relationship between the leader and members, the extent to which tasks are highly structured and the position power of the leader. The appropriate leader behaviour (that is, whether it should be task oriented or relationship oriented) depends on the combination of these three aspects in any situation. Fielder's model is considered to be well supported by the evidence. The research was based on the relationship between style and performance in existing organisations in different contexts. For a very useful comparison of contingency models *see* Fulop *et al.* (1999). An important contextual issue is that of nationality and culture. In the Window on practice below, we discuss how leadership styles varied in a study of American and Japanese expatriate managers.

WINDOW ON PRACTICE

Yooyanyong and Muenjohn (2010) report that strong competition in international markets has increased the demand for expatriate managers and that the leadership style of these managers is a key factor in their success. They compared the leadership styles of American and Japanese managers and found significant differences in terms of decision making, visionary ability, training succession and supervising. The authors conclude that national culture and background are likely to have influenced the leadership styles displayed. For example, Japan has a collectivist culture as compared to America's individualistic culture which is likely to influence decision-making styles.

Source: Adapted from: Yooyanyong, P. and Muenjohn, N. (2010) 'Leadership Styles of Expatriate Managers: a comparison between American and Japanese expatriates', *The Journal of American Academy of Business*, Vol. 15, No. 2, pp. 161–7.

Such differences are indicative of the complexities of determining appropriate leadership styles contingent upon the organisational and national context. Goleman (2000) makes a further contribution to this debate in identifying six leadership styles.

Table 13.3 Six leadership styles reported by Goleman

Coercive style	Leader demands immediate compliance
Authoritative style	Leader mobilises people towards a vision
Affiliative style	Leader creates emotional bonds and harmony
Democratic style	Leader uses participation to build consensus
Pacesetting style	Leader expects excellence and self-direction from followers
Coaching style	Leader develops people for the future

Source: Reprinted by permission of *Harvard Business Review.* Adapted from 'Leadership that gets results', by D. Goleman, March–April, pp. 80 and 82–3.

Goleman (2000) reports the results of some research carried out by Hay/McBer who sampled almost 20 per cent of a database of 20,000 executives. The results were analysed to identify six different leadership styles, which are shown in Table 13.3, but most importantly Goleman reports that 'leaders with the best results do not rely on only one leadership style' (p. 78).

Goleman goes on to consider the appropriate context and impact of each style, and argues that the more styles the leader uses the better. We have already reported Goleman's work on emotional intelligence, and he links this with the six styles by suggesting that leaders need to understand how the styles relate back to the different competencies of emotional intelligence so that they can identify where they need to focus their leadership development.

ACTIVITY 13.2

For each of Goleman's six styles think of a leader with whom you have worked, or of whom you know. For each of these individuals write a list of the behaviours that they use. Then consider the impact that these behaviours have on followers.

Do the behaviours have the same impact on all followers? If not, why not?

In a less mechanistic vein Goffee and Jones (2006) suggest that what works for one leader will not necessarily work for another. While adaptability of styles to suit different contexts is key, aspiring leaders need to discover what it is about themselves that they can mobilise in a leadership situation. Given this perspective leadership appears very personal and is influenced by psychosocial perspectives and our sense of self (Ford 2010).

One of the differences between the contingency models we have just discussed and the 'best' style models is the implications for development. The Blake and Mouton model suggests leaders can be developed to lead in the one best way. The Hersey and Blanchard model, and most other contingency models, stress the flexibility of the leader – to learn to lead differently with different employees depending on their needs; hence the leader should learn many styles and learn to diagnose the needs of their employees. Fielder's model, however, emphasises matching the leader to the context (a selection decision), rather than developing leaders in the context. An interesting recent contribution to this field comes from Hannah *et al.* (2009) who acknowledge its high degree of complexity and present an overarching model which seeks to integrate a substantial number of the factors discussed above. Time will tell whether this model will withstand empirical testing and criticism and come to provide a robust mechanism for guiding leadership theory and practice.

DO WE REALLY NEED HEROES?

A different approach to understanding leadership is transformational leadership, which focuses on the leader's role at a strategic level, so there is a concentration on the one leader at the top of the organisaton. There is a wide range of literature in this vein, most of it written in the 1980s. Since that time the academic literature may have moved on but the image of the transformational leader still remains widely attractive. While this is a different approach it links back to our original three questions about leadership. Transformational leadership shows elements of the trait approach, as leaders are seen to 'have' charisma, which sets them apart as extraordinary and exceptional, and they are also seen to use a set of 'ideal' behaviours, with the assumption in many studies that this is the 'best' approach. A recent analysis of leadership advertisements demonstrates the extent to which notions of transformational leadership now dominate conceptualisations of leadership (den Hartog *et al.* 2007).

The leader is usually characterised as a hero, although Steyrer (1998) proposes that there are other charismatic types such as the father figure, the saviour and the king. Such leaders appear to know exactly what they are doing and how to 'save' the organisation from its present predicament (and consequently such leadership is found more often when organisations are in trouble). Leaders involve followers by generating a high level of commitment, partly due to such leaders focusing on the needs of followers and expressing their vision in such a way that it satisfies these needs. They communicate high expectations to followers and also the firm belief that followers will be able to achieve these goals. In this way the leader promotes self-confidence in the followers and they are motivated to achieve more than they ordinarily expect to achieve. In terms of behaviours, perhaps the most important is the vision of the future that the leader offers and that he or she communicates this and dramatises this to the followers. Such leaders are able to help the followers make sense of what is going on and why as well as what needs to be done in the future. It is from this perspective that the distinction between management and leadership is often made. Bennis and Nanus (1985), for example, suggest leadership is path finding while management is path following; and that leadership is about doing the right thing whereas management is about doing things right. Kotter (1990) identified leaders as establishing a direction (whereas managers plan and budget); leaders align people with the vision (whereas managers organise things); leaders motivate and inspire (whereas managers control and solve problems); and leaders encourage change (whereas managers encourage order and predictability). Other writers analysing leadership from this perspective include Tichy and Devanna (1986) and Bass (1985), and there is a wide research base to support the findings. The approach does have a great strength in taking followers' needs into account and seeking to promote their self-confidence and potential, and the idea of the knight in shining armour is very attractive and potentially exciting – Tichy and Devanna, for example, present the process of such leadership as a three-act drama. However, in spite of the emphasis on process there is also an emphasis on leadership characteristics which harks back to the trait approach to leadership, which has been characterised as elitist.

Maybe we should ask whether organisations really require such leaders or, indeed, whether such transcendental, all-powerful leaders can really exist (Ford 2010). A very different conception of leadership is now offered as an alternative, partly a reaction to the previous approach, and partly a response to a changing environment. This is termed empowering or post-heroic leadership, and could be described as the currently favoured ideal way to lead.

WINDOW ON PRACTICE

Goffee and Jones (2006) provide an excellent example of leadership by someone lower down in the organisation. They met Marcia, who was a cleaning supervisor in a large New York office block. She had the ability to read people from different cultures, and although often brash was able to use humour to great effect, not tolerating slovenly cleaning. She managed in unpromising circumstances to forge a high-performing team as members knew she demanded that the job be done well but at the same time she cared about them.

Source: Goffee, R. and Jones, G. (2006) 'The Lizard Kings', *People Management*, Vol. 12, No. 2, 26 January, pp. 32–4.

Fulop *et al.* (1999) identify factors in a rapidly changing turbulent environment which by the 1990s diluted the appropriateness of concentrating on the one leader at the top of the organisation. These factors include: globalisation making centralisation more difficult; technology enabling better sharing of information; and change being seen as a responsibility of all levels of the organisation – not just the top. They also note a dissatisfaction with corporate failures, identify few transformational leaders as positive role models, suggest that such a model of male authoritarian leadership is less relevant, and in particular that the macho leader with all the answers does not necessarily fit well with the encouragement of creativity and innovation. In addition they suggest that increasing teamwork and an increasing emphasis on knowledge workers mean that employees will be less responsive now to a transformational leader. The emphasis has therefore moved away from understanding the traits and style of the one leader at the top of the organisation who knows how to solve all the organisation's problems, to how empowering or post-heroic leaders can facilitate many members of the organisation in taking on leadership roles. In this context Applebaum *et al.* (2003) comment that female leadership styles are more effective in today's team-based consensually driven organisations. Many commentators speak of leaders with integrity and humility, the ability to select good people and to remove barriers so they can fulfil their potential and perform (*see*, for example, Collins 2003; Alimo-Metcalfe and Alban-Metcalfe 2002).

The leader becomes a developer who can help others identify problems as opportunities for learning, and who can harness the collective intelligence of the organisation, and Fulop *et al.* (1999) note that this means in practice that they encourage the development of a learning organisation. Senge (1990), who is a protagonist of the learning organisation (*see* Chapter 16 for further details), sees the leader's new roles in encouraging a learning organisation as designer, teacher and steward, rather than a traditional charismatic decision maker. He suggests that leaders should *design* the organisation in terms of vision, purpose, core values and the structures by which these ideas can be translated into business decisions. However, he also suggests that the leader should involve people at all levels in this design task. It is the role of the leader not to identify the right strategy, but to encourage strategic thinking in the organisation, and to design effective learning processes to make this happen. The leader's role as a *teacher* is not to teach people the correct view of reality, but to help employees gain more insight into the current reality. The leader therefore coaches, guides and facilitates. As a *steward* the leader acts as a servant in taking responsibility for the impact of his or her leadership on others, and in the sense that he or she overrides his or her own self-interest by personal commitment to the organisation's larger mission. To play this role effectively, Senge suggests, the leader will need many new skills, in particular vision-making skills – a never-ending sharing of ideas and asking for feedback. Skills that will encourage employees to express and test their views of the world are also key. These involve actively seeking others' views, experimenting, encouraging enquiry and distinguishing 'the way things are done' from 'the way we think things are done'. We explore this leader-servant relationship in the Window on practice below.

WINDOW ON PRACTICE

The world, it seems, is crying out for a different style of leader: the type who is not motivated by self-interest and the pursuit of power and 'servant-leadership', an idea dreamt up 40 years ago by the American management development guru Robert Greenleaf, but was based on a much older tradition of service, offers a viable alternative. Great leaders are motivated by the desire to serve others and the best test of the servant-leader is whether those who are served grow as people. Do they, while being served, become healthier, wiser, freer, more autonomous, more likely themselves to become servants? There are ten characteristics of a servant leader:

1. **Listening.** Seeks to identify the will of a group and helps to clarify that will.
2. **Empathy.** Strives to understand and empathise with others.
3. **Healing.** Has the potential for healing, or helping to 'make whole', oneself and others.
4. **Awareness.** Understands issues involving ethics and values; can view most situations from a more integrated, holistic position.
5. **Persuasion.** Seeks to convince others, rather than to coerce compliance. This aspect offers one of the clearest distinctions between the traditional authoritarian model and that of servant-leadership.
6. **Conceptualisation.** Demonstrates the ability to look at a problem (or an organisation) from a conceptualising perspective, meaning that he or she must think beyond day-to-day realities.

7 **Foresight.** Displays the ability to predict the likely outcome of a situation.

8 **Stewardship.** Greenleaf's view of all institutions was one in which chief executives, staff and trustees all played significant roles in holding their institutions in trust for the greater good of society.

9 **Commitment to the growth of people.** Is deeply committed to the growth of each individual within his or her institution.

10 **Building community.** Seeks to identify some means for building a community among those who work within a given institution.

Arkin argues that leaders adopting these characteristics might be what is required to lead organisations out of troubled times.

Source: Adapted from: Arkin, A. (2009) 'Back Seat Drivers', *People Management*, 7 May, p. 26.

This changing perspective on leadership is further demonstrated by an increasing interest in **authentic leadership**. Wong and Cummings (2009) argue that authentic leadership is at the heart of effective leadership because of its emphasis on honesty, integrity and high ethical standards. Authentic leadership focuses on relationship building with followers and in this way raises the profile of followership, an emergent theme with leadership theory which we discuss below. This focus on authenticity is perhaps an outcome of the economic uncertainties starting in 2007 in which trust in those leading in government and institutions was severely damaged. Authenticity certainly became a widely used term late in the decade to describe the behaviour required of politicians and leaders: followers want leaders who mean what they say and live what they believe (Deegan 2009).

Aligned to authentic leadership, the notion of **ethical leadership** is also becoming popular. Neubert *et al.* (2009) suggest that leaders can become 'agents of virtue', positively influencing the ethical climate within an organisation. They suggest that this can have positive outcomes such as increased job satisfaction and improved organisational commitment. In this way, positive ethical leadership behaviours can have desirable impacts on organisational performance. Ethical leadership also makes prominent the role of followers and **respectful leadership** follows in this vein (Quaquebeke and Eckloff 2010). Both authentic and ethical leaders allow employees to identify and solve problems themselves and learn to take responsibility. The role of the leader is to develop collective self-confidence. As Grint (1997: 13) puts it, 'the apparent devolvement (or desertion – depending on your perspective) of responsibility has become the new standard in contemporary models of leadership'. For further discussion on the devolution of responsibility *see* Case 13.1 on this book's companion website **www.pearsoned.co.uk/torrington**.

These visions of leadership are very attractive but they do require a dramatic change in thinking for both leaders and followers. For leaders there is the risk of giving away power, learning to trust employees, developing new skills, developing a different perspective of their role and overriding self-interest. For followers there is the challenge of taking responsibility – which some may welcome, but others shun. Yet, if sustained competitive advantage is based on human capital and collective intelligence, these perspectives would seem to have much to offer.

While empowering/authentic/ethical leaders have been shown to fit with the current climate we may sometimes need heroic leaders. Kets de Vries (2003) makes the point that heroic leadership will never die as change makes people anxious and we need heroic leaders to calm them down, but since no one can live up to the expectations of heroic leaders, they will eventually become a disappointment. We conclude with the thought that there is no one best way – different leaders and different leader behaviours are needed at different times. For an example of a mixed approach to leadership *see* Case 13.2 on the companion website, **www.pearsoned.co.uk/torrington**, about Tim Smith of the Eden Project.

FOLLOWERSHIP

Much of the research on leadership takes a rather managerialist approach: that is, it assumes that leadership is a 'good thing' if only the right way of doing it can be found. Increasingly, however, more critical perspectives on leadership can be found which question the whole premise of leadership (see, Ford *et al.*, 2008 for an example of this trend). One aspect of critical perspectives is to suggest that followers are important, but largely neglected, in treatments of leadership. Followers are clearly critical if leaders are to lead, but little thought has been given to them other than as a recipient of the leader's actions. There are a number of studies which have started to develop thinking in terms of followership, for example, Rigio *et al.* (2008) have presented an edited collection of papers from a 1996 conference on followership. Jackson and Parry's (2008) work suggests ways of thinking that will support the examination of followers, for example, social identity theories. These are early days for the study of followers but those who are engaging in this research have gone so far as to suggest that including the study of followers in leadership theory may call into question much of the existing theory. We give an example of this in the Window on practice that follows which explores followership using a metaphor from Greek mythology, that of Odysseus leading his followers home from war.

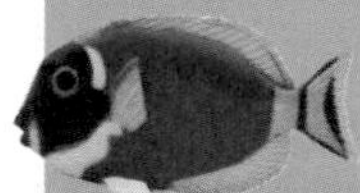

WINDOW ON PRACTICE

The story starts at the end of the Trojan war, when Odysseus sets out to return to his home in Ithaca. He leads several ships of soldiers who, we may presume, are similarly keen to return home. They are not to know that it is only Odysseus who will set foot once again on Ithaca, for the many adventures they will meet along the way will result in their decimation. Many men are lost in a battle at their first port of call, the island of the Cicones. The survivors return to their ships and make land next at the island of the Lotus-eaters. The small scouting party ate the lotus and decided they wished to stay, indulging in a life of intoxicated wonder. We can only imagine their feelings after they have been dragged back to the ship and prevented from swimming back to the island. That the crew has been banned from eating is a presaging of later prohibitions: should they drink wine they will be turned to swine, and should they listen to music they will go mad. Only Odysseus, the boss, the leader, is allowed such luxuries.

On the travellers go, to the island of the Cyclops. They come across a cave and feast on some of the sheep they find there. Polyphemus, a one-eyed giant, returns to the cave and imprisons them. The men, having eaten, are punished by themselves being eaten – Polyphemus chooses two each day for his dinner. Odysseus, of course, is not one of these, and it is his cleverness, Homer tells us, that saves the skins of himself and his crew who, after Odysseus has blinded Polyphemus, are smuggled out tied to the stomachs of sheep. At Telepylos most of the remaining men are eaten, speared or stoned by giants. Only the members of crew on the ship with Odysseus are saved, but they are soon to arrive at Aeaea, where the enchantress Circe gives the scouting party wine that turns them into swine. We see again how Odysseus's crew are denied the pleasures of the flesh, here wine, that Odysseus is able to indulge in. He spends a year as Circe's lover while his followers wait around. On they eventually go, and the next thing they are to be denied is listening to the unbearably beautiful (albeit deadly) voices of the Sirens. Odysseus, of course, can listen as he has his men deafen themselves by stopping their ears with beeswax. At Scylla and Charybdis, six men have to be eaten by the six-headed monster, the Scylla, in order that the rest can make their way through. They, however, are all to perish at the next island, Helios, and Odysseus was left to his own devices.

Leadership contains, in this earliest recounting, a promise to followers of only horror, failure, betrayal, disappointment and denial. We are told that followers are incapable of agency unless organised by a leader, but is it not the case that without his crew Odysseus literally could not have sailed between the Greek islands? Without his crew Odysseus is revealed to be incapable. We can imagine one of his crew telling his story:

> The crew had waited interminably for Odysseus to continue the journey home to Ithaca, but Odysseus was bewitched on this enchanted island until one day we saw our chance. Circe was away. The lads begged me to go to Odysseus and to tempt him with thoughts of his home, his wife and son, so that he would agree we could leave that fated island and return to Ithaca. He eventually gave in, but blow me down if he did not find another reason for delay, and another, and another. And all along the way he was enjoying himself, while our number of men dwindled until only a few of us now remain. I have a foreboding about the future. I fear none of us will return to Ithaca.

Source: Adapted from: Ford, J. and Harding, N. (2009) 'Telling an untold story: on being a follower rather than a leader', EGOS Colloquium 2009, Barcelona.

This alternative telling of Odysseus's tale presents a very different perspective from the heroic one that has been perpetuated across the centuries. This may have resonance for many who, since 2007, have lost their jobs in, for example, the banking sector and faced economic hardship while those leading them into that position have benefited from large pay-offs and enormous pensions. It may now be that the time is right for a more detailed examination of the flipside of leadership: followership.

ACTIVITY 13.3

Thinking of your own experiences of being led (at work, school or other settings), what consideration was there of the role of followers? How could including their perspective have changed events?

SUMMARY PROPOSITIONS

13.1 Leadership is a process where one person influences a group of others to achieve group or organisational goals – leadership is thus about motivation.

13.2 The trait model of leadership, although often discredited, continues to play a part in our understanding of leadership.

13.3 Behavioural models are more helpful than earlier models as they concentrate on what leaders do rather than on what they are.

13.4 Some behavioural models offer a 'one best way' of leadership, but more sophisticated models take account of contingency factors such as maturity of followers and the nature of the task.

13.5 Models of transformational leadership treat the leader as a hero who can (single-handedly) turn the organisation around and deliver it from a crisis.

13.6 Empowering and post-heroic leadership models conceptualise the leader as teacher and facilitator, who involves many in the leadership task.

13.7 There is an increasing interest in authentic and ethical leadership as an appropriate response to leading in turbulent economic times.

13.8 Critical perspectives on leadership argue for the surfacing of the role of followers and suggest that this may call into question much current leadership theory.

GENERAL DISCUSSION TOPICS

1 Do we need leaders at all? Discuss what alternatives there might be.

2 Consider the four types of charismatic leader identified by Steyrer (1998): hero, father figure, missionary and saviour. Discuss the ways in which the types of leader are similar or different.

3 In what way do you think that including the perspective of followers in the study of leadership will contribute to theory?

FURTHER READING

IDS (2003) *IDS Studies: Leadership Development*, No. 753. London: Incomes Data Services.
A useful book outlining the work of five case study organisations, in terms of their conception of leadership, what prompted their leadership development programmes and an outline of the programmes themselves. The case organisations are the Dixons group, the Inland Revenue, Novartis Pharmaceuticals, Portsmouth City Council and Skipton Building Society.

Goffee, R. and Jones, G. (2006) *Why Should Anyone be Led by You?* Boston: Harvard Business School Press.
Goffee, R. and Jones, G. (2006) 'This time it's personal', *People Management*, Vol. 12, No. 21, pp. 28–33.
Goffee and Jones combine sound concepts and practical advice on leadership, in the thought-promoting book and article. They identify the context where the hierarchy is long enough to get things done, and that the challenge facing many leaders is to enable highly talented followers to perform to their best. They recognise that leadership, as well as being non-hierarchical, is situational and relational. In meeting the leadership challenge, they suggest, leaders need to know themselves and show who they are to a sufficient extent; they need to be prepared to take personal risks; they need to be sensitive to context and re-write this; they need to be authentic, but conform sufficiently; and they need to manage the social distance between themselves and their followers.

Rigio, R., Chaleff, I. and Lipman-Blumen, J. (eds) (2008) *The Art of Followership: How great followers create great leaders and organizations*. San Francisco: Jossey-Bass.
This book developed out of a series of papers presented at a conference on followership. The editors argue that a new subfield within leadership, that of followership, is emerging. The book seeks to define followership, set out what constitutes effective followership and consider the drawbacks and pitfalls of followership. It also discusses future research and practice in followership. It is a comprehensive treatment of this recent stream of research.

REFERENCES

Alimo-Metcalfe, B. and Alban-Metcalfe, J. (2002) 'The great and the good', *People Management*, Vol. 8, No. 1, pp. 32–4.

Applebaum, S., Audet, L. and Miller, J. (2003) 'Gender and leadership? Leadership and gender? A journey through the landscape of theories', *Leadership and Organisation*, Vol. 24, No. 1, pp. 43–51.

Arkin, A. (1997) 'The secret of his success', *People Management*, 23 October, pp. 27–8.

Arkin, A. (2009) 'Back seat drivers', *People Management*, 7 May, p. 26.

Bass, B.M. (1985) 'Leadership: good, better, best', *Organisational Dynamics*, Winter, pp. 26–40.

Beckhard, R. (1992) 'A model for the executive management of organizational change', in G. Salaman (ed.), *Human Resource Strategies*. London: Sage.

Bennis, W.G. and Nanus, B. (1985) *Leaders: The strategies for taking charge*. New York: Harper and Row.

Binney, G. and Williams, C. (2005) 'The myth of managing change', in G. Salaman, J. Storey and J. Billsberry (eds), *Strategic Human Resource Management: Theory and practice. A reader*. London: Sage.

Blake, R.R. and Mouton, J.S. (1964) *The Managerial Grid*. Houston, Texas: Gulf Publishing.

Buchanan, D. and Huczynski, A. (1997) *Organisational Behaviour*. London: Prentice Hall.

Collins, J. (2003) 'From good to great', presentation to the CIPD National Conference, Harrogate, 22–24 November.

Cowsgill, R. and Grint, K. (2008) 'Leadership, task and relationship: Orpheus, Prometheus and Janus', *Human Resource Management Journal*, Vol. 18, No. 2, pp. 188–95.

Deegan, D. (2009) 'The changing face of leadership: past, present and future,' www.trainingjournal.com, December.

Den Hartog, D., Caley, C. and Dewe, P. (2007) 'Recruiting leaders: an analysis of leadership advertisements', *Human Resource Management Journal*, Vol. 17, No. 1, pp. 58–75.

Edwards, C. (2006) 'On being gregarious', *People Management*, Vol. 12, No. 8, pp. 32–4.

Eriksson, C. (2004) 'The effects of change programmes on employee emotions', *Personnel Review*, Vol. 33, No. 1, pp. 110–26.

Fache, D. (2009) 'Are great leaders born or are they made?', *Frontiers of Health Service Management*, Vol. 26, No. 2, pp. 27–30.

Fielder, F.E. (1967) *A Theory of Leadership Effectiveness*. New York: McGraw-Hill.

Ford, J. (2010) 'Studying leadership critically: a psychosocial lens on leadership identities', *Leadership*, Vol. 6, No. 1, pp. 1–19.

Ford, J. and Harding, N. (2009) 'Telling an untold story: on being a follower rather than a leader', EGOS Colloquium 2009, Barcelona.

Ford, J., Harding, N. and Learmonth, M. (2008) *Leadership as Identity: Constructions and deconstructions*. London: Palgrave Macmillan.

Fulop, L. and Linstead, S. (1999) *Management: A critical text*. South Yarra: Macmillan Business.

Fulop, L., Linstead, S. and Dunford, R. (1999) 'Leading and managing', in L. Fulop and S. Linstead (eds), *Management: A critical text*. South Yarra: Macmillan Business.

Goffee, R. (2002) 'Send out the right signals', *People Management*, Vol. 8, No. 21, pp. 32–8.

Goffee, R. and Jones, G. (2006) 'The Lizard Kings', *People Management*, Vol. 12, No. 2, 26 January, pp. 32–4.

Goleman, D. (1998) 'What makes . . . a leader?', *Harvard Business Review*, November–December, pp. 93–102.

Goleman, D. (2000) 'Leadership that gets results', *Harvard Business Review*, March–April, pp. 78–90.

Greenhalgh, L. (2001) 'Managers Face up to the new era', *Mastering Management*, Series 23. London: Financial Times.

Grint, K. (1997) 'Introduction', in K. Grint (ed.), *Leadership*. Oxford: Oxford University Press.

Hannah, S., Woodfolk, R. and Lord, R. (2009) 'Leadership self-structure: a framework for positive leadership', *Journal of Organizational Behavior*, Vol. 30, pp. 269–90.

Hayes, J. (2007) *The Theory and Practice of Change Management*, 2nd edn. Basingstoke: Palgrave Macmillan.

Heifetz, R. and Laurie, D. (1997) 'The work of leadership', *Harvard Business Review*, January–February, pp. 124–34.

Heil, G., Bennis, W. and Stephens, D.C. (2000) *Douglas McGregor, Revisited: Managing the human side of the enterprise*. New York: Wiley.

Hersey, P. (1985) *Situational Selling*. Escondido: Center for Leadership Studies.

Hersey, P. and Blanchard, K.H. (1988) *Management of Organizational Behavior: Utilizing Human Resources*, 5th edn. Englewood Cliffs: Prentice-Hall International.

Higgs, M. (2003) 'How can we make sense of leadership in the 21st century?', *Leadership and Organisation Development Journal*, Vol. 24, No. 5, pp. 273–84.

Hollington, S. (2006) 'How to lead your boss', *People Management*, Vol. 12, No. 24, pp. 44–5.

Hollyforde, S. and Whiddett, S. (2002) *The Motivation Handbook*. London: CIPD.

Hope, K. (2006) 'Lessons learnt', *People Management*, Vol. 12, No. 6, pp. 30–1.

House, R. (1976) 'A 1976 theory of charismatic leadership', in J. Hunt and L. Larson (eds), *Leadership: The cutting edge*. Carbondale: Southern Illinois University Press.

Jackson, B. and Parry, K. (2008) *A Very Short, Fairly Interesting and Reasonably Cheap Book about Studying Leadership*. London: Sage.

Kakabadse, A., Myers, A., McMahon, T. and Spony, G. (1997) 'Top management styles in Europe: implications for business and cross-national teams', in K. Grint (ed.), *Leadership*. Oxford: Oxford University Press.

Kanter, R.M. (1983) *The Change Masters*. New York: Simon and Schuster.

Kets de Vries, M. (2003) 'The dark side of leadership', *Business Strategy Review*, Vol. 14, No. 3, pp. 25–8.

Kilpatrick, S. and Locke, E. (1991) 'Leadership: do traits matter?', *Academy of Management Executive*, Vol. 5, No. 2, pp. 48–60.

Kotter, J. (1990) *A Force for Change: How leadership differs from management*. New York: Free Press.

Kubler-Ross, E. (1997) *On Death and Dying*. Washington DC: Touchstone.

McClelland, D.C. (1971) *Motivational Trends in Society*. Morristown: General Learning Press.

McGregor, D. (1960) *The Human Side of Enterprise*. New York: McGraw-Hill.

Mullins, L. (1999) *Management and Organisational Behaviour*, 5th edn. Harlow: Financial Times/Pitman Publishing.

Neubert, N., Carlson, D., Kacmar, K., Roberts, J. and Chonko, L. (2009) 'The virtuous influence of ethical leadership behavior: evidence from the field', *The Journal of Business Ethics*, Vol. 90, pp. 157–70.

Northouse, P. (2006) *Leadership: Theory and practice*, 4th edn. California: Sage Publications.

Quaquebeke, N. and Eckloff, T. (2010) 'Defining respectful leadership: what it is, how it can be measured, and another glimpse at what it is related to', *Journal of Business Ethics*, Vol. 91, pp. 343–58.

Rajan, A. and van Eupen, P. (1997) 'Take it from the top', *People Management*, 23 October, pp. 26–9.

Rigio, R., Chaleff, I. and Lipman-Blumen, J. (eds) (2008) *The Art of Followership: How great followers create great leaders and organizations*. San Francisco: Jossey-Bass.

Senge, P. (1990) *The Fifth Discipline: The art and practice of the learning organisation*. London: Century Business, Random House.

Shackleton, V. (1995) *Business Leadership*. London: Routledge.

Steyrer, J. (1998) 'Charisma and the archetypes of leadership', *Organisation Studies*, Vol. 19, No. 5, pp. 807–28.

Tichy, N. and Devanna, M. (1986) *The Transformational Leader*. New York: Wiley.

Vroom, V. (1964) *Work and Motivation*. Chichester: John Wiley.

Walmsley, H. (1999) 'A suitable ploy', *People Management*, 8 April, pp. 48–50.

Walton, J. (1999) *Strategic Human Resource Development*. Harlow: Financial Times/Prentice Hall.

Williams, M. (2000) *The War for Talent: Getting the best from the best*. London: CIPD.

Wong, C. and Cummings, G. (2009) 'The influence of authentic leadership behaviours on trust and work outcomes of health care staff', *Journal of Leadership Studies*, Vol. 3, No. 2, pp. 6–23.

Worrall, L. and Cooper, C. (2006) 'Short changed', *People Management*, Vol. 12, No. 13, 29 June, pp. 36–8.

Yooyanyong, P. and Muenjohn, N. (2010) 'Leadership styles of expatriate managers: a comparison between American and Japanese expatriates', *The Journal of American Academy of Business*, Vol. 15, No. 2, pp. 161–7.

An extensive range of additional materials, including multiple choice questions, answers to questions and links to useful websites can be found on the Human Resource Management companion website at **www.pearsoned.co.uk/torrington**.

CHAPTER 14

MANAGING ATTENDANCE AND ABSENCE

THE OBJECTIVES OF THIS CHAPTER ARE TO:

1. Review the national context on employee absence
2. Identify the impact of absence on the organisation
3. Explore the process of absence from work and absence causation
4. Discuss methods by which long- and short-term absence can be minimised

Our understanding of the importance of attendance at the workplace and the problem of absence is linked to the changes in working practices over the past 200 years

> industrial revolutions which transformed the economies of nations that had hitherto known only agriculture and handicrafts, aided by simple machines, brought new dangers and difficulties into society. (Neal and Robertson 1968: 9)

The standard workplace became the factory, with the central discipline of machinery powered from a single source, first water and later other forms of energy, and for reasons connected to supply of fuel, raw materials and transport. The underlying principle was that work had to be centralised to be efficient, and that principle has continued, regardless of the nature of the work being done. The modern 'factory' may be a merchant bank in London, a restaurant in Paris, an automobile plant in Chicago, a hospital in Cape Town, a film studio in Bollywood or a hotel in Bangkok, but the workers have to be there, usually in large numbers. There may be moves towards home-working, decentralisation and subcontracting, but the traditional reasons of power, raw materials and transport have been replaced by specialisation and the concomitant need for intense communication, social interaction and proximity to the supply chain, facilities and resources. If employees need to be brought together for these newer reasons, they obviously need to be there at roughly the same time. People have to attend work in a specific place and at a specified time for a specified period. Attendance is key; absence is a problem.

Attendance and absence are relatively easy to monitor in the sense of a common culture and rules, deviation from which is obvious and manageable. Absence has always been a matter of concern to all employers, and methods for reducing it have frequently focused on disciplinary or punitive measures. Recently absence has been framed in a more positive discourse, and the focus is now on what can be done to promote attendance, as well as the rehabilitation of employees with long-term absence.

THE NATIONAL CONTEXT

Absence may be short-term or long-term, authorised or unauthorised, due to sickness, holiday, maternity/paternity, parenting, the performance of public duty, company business, public holiday and so on. CIPD carries out an annual survey of the level of absence omitting holidays and company business. In 2009 it found an average of 7.4 days per employee per year, down from 8.0 days per employee in 2008 (CIPD 2009). The average level of absence varies according to employment sector, from 9.7 days per employee in the public sector, 9.4 days in the not-for-profit sector (the only area to show an increase since the previous year), 6.5 days in manufacturing and production, and 6.4 days in private sector services. CIPD is not the only organisation conducting such surveys and the results reported are broadly similar. It seems as if the increased attention paid in recent years by companies to health, well-being and absence monitoring has so far had little effect. Even worldwide recession and economic crisis has not brought numbers down much. Bevan of the Work Foundation (Silcox 2006) concluded that absence has remained broadly at the same level for the past 30 years with small fluctuations due to unemployment and the wider economic cycle.

WINDOW ON PRACTICE

Comparative absence figures

Lokke and her colleagues (2007) used data from the European Employee Index. The data were collected from employees, randomly selected, in 2004. Days absence per employee in 2004 were as follows: Denmark 2.8; Norway 3.5; Sweden 3.9; Finland 4.6. In each country absence in the public sector was higher than in the private sector, except for Sweden where there were no differences.

It is interesting to compare these figures with British data for the same year where the CBI reports 6.8 working days lost per employee (CBI/AXA 2005) and the CIPD reports 8.4 (CIPD 2005). The differences might be explained, however, by the choice of respondents, as the British surveys collect data from managers in organisations about their employees, rather than directly from employees themselves. In addition the TUC (2005) reports European comparisons based on figures produced by the University of Surrey. These indicate that short-term absence in Britain is lower than in any other country, apart from Denmark; and that long-term absence is lower than others except for Ireland, Austria and Germany.

There is a clear message that comparative figures are difficult to produce as so much depends on sources and methods.

Sources: Lokke, A., Eskildsen, J. and Jensen, T. (2007) 'Absenteeism in the Nordic Countries', *Employee Relations*, Vol. 29, No. 1, pp. 16–29.
TUC (2005) *Countering an Urban Legend: Sicknote Britain?* TUC: London.
CBI/AXA (2005) *Who Cares Wins: Absence and labour turnover 2005.* CBI/AXA: London.
CIPD (2005) *Absence Management: A survey of policy and practice.* CIPD: London.

In terms of the patterns of absence most surveys report that absence is higher in larger than in smaller organisations and public sector absence is usually found to be higher than that in the private sector: for example in 2006 the CIPD (CIPD 2006) found the public sector absence rate to be 4.3 per cent. Reviewing the Labour Force Survey, the General Household Survey and employer surveys, Barham and Leonard (2002) found that absence does tend to be concentrated in some groups of people rather than others: in addition to higher rates in the public sector they found higher rates for women, full-time workers and those aged under 30. They also found differences by occupational group, with managers, professionals and administrative professionals having lower levels than other groups. The CBI found that sickness absence was higher among manual workers, and this to some extent must reflect the nature of job demands. The CIPD (2006) found that absence levels were highest in the food, drink and tobacco sector, local and central government and the health sectors; and lowest in media and publishing, the voluntary sector, and the hotel, restaurant and leisure sector. The relative positions of these sectors on measures of absence change to some extent each year.

The CBI reports that absence costs the UK economy around £13 billion per year and it constantly asserts that around 13 per cent of all absence is not genuine, while unions point to the efforts that workers often make to attend work even when ill (*see*, for example, TUC 2005). Big sporting events, such as the World Cup, often attract attention in terms of their impact on absence levels, but organisations can use these events to their advantage given some thought. Smethurst (2006) reports on how Prudential and Egg responded to the World Cup by offering more flexible working over the period, with incentive schemes and themed competitions to incorporate interest in the event.

At a national level the government has an interest in reducing absence and loss of employment due to sickness. Roberts (2003) reports that while there were 1.46 million people claiming unemployment pay, there were 2.7 million people out of work claiming long-term sickness and disability benefits. Roberts goes on to explain how this situation has stimulated a focus on how society manages long-term sickness and rehabilitation. The government has an interest in reducing NHS costs and invalidity benefit costs, and the Department for Work and Pensions has arranged a two-year series of job rehabilitation pilot studies. The pilots will test three different approaches, healthcare interventions, workplace interventions and combined interventions, and the aim is to learn which approaches are most successful.

WINDOW ON PRACTICE

International approaches to long-term absence

James and his colleagues (2002) explain how different countries have enacted legislation in respect of sickness absence. For example, in Sweden employers must ensure that they have assessed rehabilitation needs at an early stage, and are then obliged to put any relevant rehabilitation measures in place. In the Netherlands employers must submit a report on any employee who is unable to work within 13 weeks of the start of the absence. They are required to submit this to a social security agency and must produce a 'work resumption plan'. In New South Wales, Australia, where workers have been absent for 12 weeks employers must establish a work rehabilitation programme, and if there are more than 20 people employed, they must appoint a rehabilitation coordinator and prepare plans for return to work.

Source: Summarised from P. James, I. Cunningham and P. Dibben (2002) 'Absence management and the issues of job retention and return to work', *Human Resource Management Journal*, Vol. 12, No. 2, pp. 82–94.

THE ORGANISATIONAL CONTEXT

Barham and Leonard (2002) question the accuracy of data in absence surveys. They argue that given the low response rates to such surveys, there is no evidence to suggest that the survey findings are representative of the whole population. In addition the CIPD found that much management absence is not recorded. It is likely that respondents are those with better absence information. On this basis they argue that absence costs to the organisation are underestimated.

The CIPD found that over 90 per cent of organisations in its survey considered absence to be a significant cost to the organisation, but less that half monitored this cost. The average cost was reported to be £598 per year per employee. Barham and Leonard

(2002) suggest that estimating the costs of absence is complicated, and that the estimate needs to include not only the direct costs (i.e. paying salary and benefits for a worker who is not there), but also indirect costs such as organising replacement staff, overall reductions in productivity and administrative costs. Bevan (2002), reporting research from the Employment Studies Institute, suggests that there are virtually no robust data on direct and indirect costs of absence and that most employers underestimate the true costs of sickness absence, particularly in respect of long-term sickness. Costing currently does not distinguish between short-term and long-term sickness. Using case study research Bevan reports that long-term sickness costs account for between 30 per cent and 70 per cent of absence costs. He goes on to argue, on the basis of this research, that even the most sophisticated companies are not well equipped to calculate such costs.

Statutory Sick Pay (SSP) changes in 1994 have given absence costs a higher profile as the burden has been passed to the employer, although there were compensatory mechanisms in place; direct costs to the employer are higher and are more prominent.

Traditionally employers have concentrated on short-term absence, and while long-term absence accounts for only around 20 per cent of absence incidents it can represent more than 40 per cent of total working time lost, according to the CBI, although figures do vary. CIPD (2006) found that long-term absence was most significant in the public sector where it accounts for 25 per cent of absence, compared with 17 per cent in manufacturing, 16 per cent in not-for-profit organisations and 12 per cent in private services. Reducing such absence is increasingly seen as having the potential to create significant costs savings. Cost is not the only factor in influencing organisations to attend to long-term absence, and we have already mentioned government interest in this. In addition, the Disability Discrimination Act 1995 requires employers to provide reasonable adjustments to enable disabled workers to continue in employment, and the term 'disabled' extends to those suffering from long-term ill health. It has been argued that employers have a more explicit duty of care to their employees due to UK and EU legislation, and there is a growing concern for the well-being of employees, partly due to fear of litigation.

In summary, the evidence suggests that absence levels in the UK are decreasing to a small extent, but that there is insufficient evidence as yet to conclude how UK absence rates compare with the rest of Europe. Long-term sickness generates proportionately greater costs and problems than short-term sickness and it is appropriate that the focus on this has increased significantly in recent years.

PROCESS AND CAUSES OF ABSENCE

The CIPD found the most frequently stated causes of absence are minor illness for short-term absence and back pain and minor illness (for manual workers) and stress and minor illness (for non-manual workers). For long-term illness the most frequent causes for manual workers are back pain and musculo-skeletal injuries; and for non-manual workers stress remains the greatest, and an increasing cause. The increase in stress as a cause may well be partly due to the fact that this is now a more legitimate reason for non-attendance than previously. Case 14.1 on this book's companion website at **www.pearsoned.co.uk/torrington** focuses on stress as a reason for absence. It is important to bear in mind that recorded causes of absence in organisations will be those causes which employees perceive the organisation to view as legitimate.

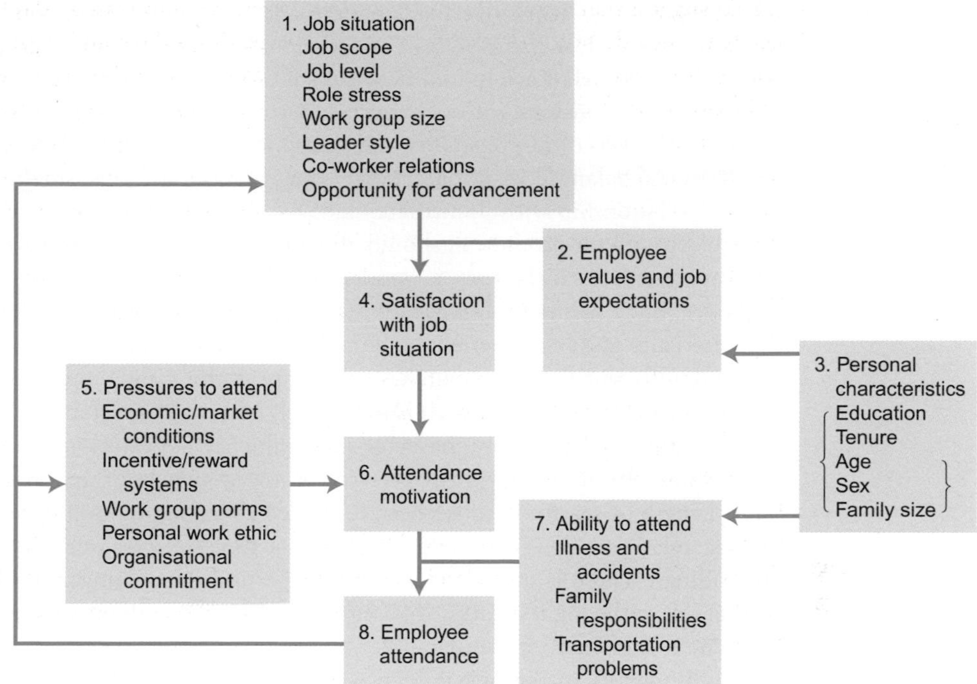

Figure 14.1 The Rhodes and Steers process model of attendance
Source: S. Rhodes and R. Steers (1990) *Managing Employee Absenteeism*, Reading: Addison Wesley.

The causes of absence are complex and interrelated and a process approach is generally agreed to be the most useful way of understanding absence behaviour, although there are criticisms that such models are not supported by the evidence. One of the most widely quoted models is from Rhodes and Steers (1990) and in our view this is the most useful of the process models. For an alternative model *see* Nicholson (1977).

The Rhodes and Steers model (*see* Figure 14.1) not only includes content information on the causes of absence but also incorporates a range of interdependent processes. In essence the model focuses on attendance motivation and the ability to attend in terms of resulting attendance behaviour.

Rhodes and Steers suggest that *attendance motivation* is directly affected by two factors: *satisfaction with the job* and *pressure to attend*. Pressure to attend may result from such factors as market conditions. Examples include the likelihood that there will be redundancies at the individual's workplace and how easy it would be to get another job; incentives to attend, such as attendance bonuses; work-group norms on what is acceptable in the work group and the effects of absence on other group members; personal work ethic producing internal pressure to attend based on beliefs about what is right; and commitment to the organisation through an identification with the beliefs and values of the organisation and an intention to remain with the organisation. On this basis threat of redundancies, attendance bonuses, team structures where team members have to cover the workload of an absent member, a personal ethic about the need to attend work wherever possible, and feelings of loyalty to the organisation should all promote the motivation to attend.

Rhodes and Steers suggest that satisfaction with the job is determined by the *job situation* and moderated by *employee values and job expectations*. Factors in the job situation are identified as job scope and level of responsibility and decision making;

role stress such as work overload, underload, difficult working conditions or hours; work-group size; leadership style of an individual's immediate manager, particularly the openness of the relationship and how easy it is to discuss and solve problems jointly; strength of relationships with co-workers; and the opportunity for promotion. On this basis higher levels of responsibility and the opportunity to make decisions in relation to job demands, balanced workload and good working conditions, small work group size, an open relationship with immediate manager, good relationships with colleagues and the opportunity for promotion should all improve attendance motivation.

However, job satisfaction is moderated by the values and expectations of the employee. Such values and expectations are shaped by both personality and personal characteristics and life experiences, but can also change during the course of one's life. The extent to which the job matches up to expectations and values will have a bearing on job satisfaction; a close match is more likely to lead to satisfaction than a mismatch.

Personality and personal characteristics influence expectations and values and job satisfaction. We have previously referred to the influence of age and sex on absence rates. Length of service has also been identified as having an influence. However, none of these relationships is clear-cut, and different pieces of research often produce different findings. There is most evidence for suggesting that younger workers and female workers have the highest rates of absence, and it is argued that younger workers value free time to a greater extent than older workers.

This brings us to the last influence on attendance, which is the *ability to attend*. This influence is interposed between attendance motivation and actual attendance. For example an employee could be highly motivated to attend, but may have insurmountable transportation difficulties, family or domestic responsibilities, or may be genuinely ill. In these cases motivation to attend does not result in attendance.

MANAGING FOR ATTENDANCE

The complex interrelationship of the causes of absence needs to be taken into account in its management. Many organisations have introduced policies for managing absence that focus on minimising short-term rather than long-term absence. The role of sickness in long-term absence has been given little priority in the past, as has the issue that short-term absence, if badly handled, can lead to long-term absence. Typically long-term absence and short-term absence require different approaches. Attendance management policies need to take into account causes of absence, which may be identified by patterns of absence and by enabling individuals to be open about why they are not at work. Measures range from proactive methods intended to reduce the risk of ill health; measures intended to reduce spells of absence and those intended to reduce the length of absence. Typically there is a mix of processes both to discourage absence and positively to encourage attendance, but these work differently with those on long- and short-term sickness absence.

Whatever approach is chosen, there is a great need for consistency in the construction and implementation of absence management policies and procedures, not only in terms of ensuring fairness and as a support for any disciplinary action taken, but also in terms of providing employees with clear expectations about how absence will be tackled, and promoting an attendance culture. While different approaches work in different sectors and with different types of staff, there is a strong argument that the policies themselves need to be consistent in any organisation, to encourage employee acceptance and line manager support. For example Dunn and Wilkinson (2002) report the difficulties that a line manager in a production company experienced due to the fact that manufacturing staff were subject to more stringent absence procedures than other staff in the company.

Lack of consistency in implementation also weakens any policy and procedures. The role of the line manager is key and there is much emphasis on giving the line manager ownership of absence and attendance issues, with support from HR. Whatever policies and procedures are set up it is critical that the line manager feels ownership of these and applies them in practice. James and his colleagues (2002) found that two-thirds of their interviewees in a long-term absence management study noted that there were problems in the way that line managers carried out their responsibilities. Managers frequently did not follow the guidelines in matters such as ongoing contact with absent employees, and consequently HR did not know what was going on and often had to step in and manage cases. James and his colleagues found that managers' behaviour resulted from time pressures, lack of awareness of what the procedure was and lack of training.

WINDOW ON PRACTICE

Managing absence at HBOS

Mary McFadzean (2003) reports on a pilot project at HBOS which encouraged HR to look at absence from a different perspective. The project was intended to test two theories: first, that much absence had non-medical causes and therefore could be tackled by HR and, second, that absence could be reduced without buying in any extra resources.

To introduce the project workshops were held with HR members and best practice guidelines were made available, HR advisers were then encouraged to go out and talk to managers about absence. The best practice model included an emphasis on finding the underlying cause of absence in terms of social or work-related issues, based on the belief that such issues are the root cause of much absence, and if not dealt with they will gradually produce medical symptoms. The skill was therefore in getting beyond the symptoms on the medical note to understand the underlying cause of absence. Once the underlying cause was understood then temporary or permanent changes could be made to help, such as reducing targets, hours and responsibilities or changing work patterns.

HBOS promoted an absence champion network in its first-tier approach which would adopt the best practice principles provided by HR, and would receive up-to-date information on absence and target cases for intervention (over 20 days' absence for long-term absence and four periods in a year for short-term absence). HR received consistent management information, and progress was monitored in all cases.
A health provider network was also set up, as a second-tier approach (for long-term absence), to target high-risk areas and the two top causes of absence. Individuals were referred after ten days' absence in these cases, and the health provider network

included a psychologist and a physiotherapist. Treatment was considered justified if there was deemed to be an 80 per cent chance of return to work. HBOS feels that rehabilitation back into work needs to become part of the business culture.

The project was only carried out in some areas and performance was measured against control groups. HBOS saved 21,000 days over the six-month period (6,000 headcount) and £880,000. Short-term absence was reduced by 35 per cent, but there was no impact on long-term absence, which continues to creep up.

Source: Summarised from M. McFazdean (2003) 'Managing Absence', paper presented at the CIPD National Conference, Harrogate, 22–24 October.

It has been found that some measures to manage absence actually increase absence, so monitoring any new policies and procedures is critical. In terms of implementing a new absence strategy, the advice given by Huczynski and Fitzpatrick (1989) still holds good. The ALIEDIM process they suggest comprises the following stages:

- Assess the absence problem
- Locate the absence problem
- Identify and prioritise absence causes
- Evaluate the current absence control methods
- Design the absence control programme
- Implement the absence control programme
- Monitor the effectiveness of the absence control programme

The mix of policies and methods chosen will be specific to the needs of the individual organisation, and Case 14.2 on the book's companion website, **www.pearsoned.co.uk/torrington**, explains the mix chosen by Newry and Mourne Police Unit in Ireland. Below are some of the most frequently used approaches to managing absence. Some are most appropriate for short-term absence, and some better suited to long-term absence, others meet the needs of both.

Accurate records

Managing absence is almost impossible without an accurate picture of current absence levels and patterns, which requires identification of areas of high absence and the most common reasons for absence in the organisation. The CIPD (2006) found that 60 per cent of those organisations reporting a reduction in absence said that this was due to improved monitoring. However, such data collection is more often reported in the public sector and manufacturing industry than in the rest of the private sector. The HSE (Silcox 2005a) in a bid to aid employers has produced a new computerised absence recording and management tool, SART, which it hopes will also encourage employers to record such data in a more consistent manner. Prior to its review of absence Carlsberg-Tetley (IDS 2001) did not have an accurate picture of sickness absence. Although some records were kept, absence was inconsistently measured and recorded, so there was no reliable information about level of absence and patterns. This was their first task in tackling absence. They decided to adopt the 'Bradford factor' method for scoring absence where both frequency of absence spells and absence duration are used but with the weight being given to the former. The Bradford factor formula, devised by Bradford University, is shown in Figure 14.2. For further information on statistics see IDS (2005a).

Absence score = (spells of absence × spells of absence) × duration of absence

Figure 14.2 The Bradford factor formula for scoring absence
Note: The score is usually calculated over a year.

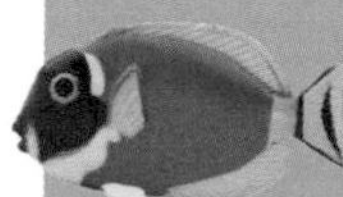

WINDOW ON PRACTICE

Absence data at Brakes

AHP (Active Health Partners) who manage absence and attendance for Brakes receive weekly updates from the payroll in order to update their absence data and produce reports. These reports are available to managers and include:

- details of who is absent and their expected return
- individual data for each employee including: days lost; absence rate; longest absence spell; number of absence spells; any Monday and Friday absences
- department breakdowns
- details relating to those employees most frequently absent
- reasons for absence overall
- trend reports
- number of accidents

This information is regularly discussed, typically weekly at the conference call between all managers in a region.

Source: IDS (2005b) 'Brakes', *Absence Management*, No. 801, November. London: IDS.

Absence reports are frequently produced by HR and sent to line managers – and such reports will often include details of employees where trigger points have been hit and where intervention is required by the line manager. However, Dunn and Wilkinson (2002) found that the attention line managers gave to these reports varied, and some managers never even looked at the reports, because they did not agree that this was the best way to manage staff. As one manager commented, 'I know my staff well enough not to need these reports . . . at the end of the day it all comes down to good management and knowing your staff'. Some managers argued that the reports were of little use because the employees they managed often worked long hours (beyond contract) and came in at weekends. It was felt that to punish such employees, who were clearly committed to the company, because they had reached certain absence levels was unreasonable, and would be counter-productive.

Absence review and trigger points

In order to focus attention on those with less satisfactory absence records many organisations identify trigger points in terms of absence spells or length, or Bradford factor scores which indicate that action is needed when an individual's absence record hits the trigger. Such policies for reviewing absence appear to be critical in absence reduction, and the CIPD (2006) reports that 67 per cent of organisations reporting a decrease in absence levels put this down to tightened policies for reviewing absence. The HBOS Window on practice above describes the trigger points that HBOS uses. However, such trigger points may be well known to employees, and Connex (IDS 2001) found that some employees were able to manipulate the system and regularly have absence levels just below the trigger point. To overcome this some organisations have a rolling year, rather than, say, a calendar year or a financial year, against which absence levels are assessed – on the grounds that it will be much more difficult for employees to keep track of their absence levels and manipulate the system. In fact Dunn and Wilkinson (2002) found organisations where the trigger system was avoided because it was felt that it would encourage employees to take off time until they were just under the trigger limit.

Some organisations have absence review groups, such as the absence champion network at HBOS, and the safety, health and absence unit at HM Customs and Excise (IDS 2001). While the role of these groups varies, they are frequently used to review all absences and identify those who have hit trigger points which will then require intervention, such as an absence review meeting with the employee.

Absence targets and benchmarking

Many organisations have absence targets phrased in terms of a reduction on current absence levels or a lower absence level to attain. However, the CIPD (2006) found that although 80 per cent of the organisations it surveyed believed that absence levels could be reduced, less than half of these had set targets for this, and only around 37 per cent benchmarked their absence levels against other organisations. An alternative approach, used by some organisations, is to give managers absence targets for their group, and tie this into their performance review and performance payments. This is the approach used in Connex (IDS 2001). Such overall and local targets need to be carefully used, however, so as not to give the impression to employees that absence is not allowed.

ACTIVITY 14.1

We have noted that some organisations link improvements in absence levels in their departments to managers' performance assessments and performance-related pay.

1 What are the potential advantages of this approach?

2 What are the potential problems?

3 How else might managers be encouraged to treat absence levels as a key priority?

Training and support for line managers

Most organisations recognise that line managers play a key role in making absence procedures work and in reducing absence levels, and training is usually available when a new absence system is introduced. Connex (IDS 2001) has introduced a creative form of training. The company takes managers to an employment tribunal to view an absence-related case so that managers will understand the consequences of not dealing fairly and consistently with employees when they have to deal with similar situations at work. HM Customs and Excise (IDS 2001) uses training videos showing role plays of return to work interviews (*see* below). These demonstrate that such a meeting is not about accusation or recrimination. The idea is that managers watch the video with their team of supervisory staff and then discuss the issues that arise.

However, there is evidence that further training is needed. Both James *et al.* (2002) and Dunn and Wilkinson (2002) found managers who could not understand how 'sickness' could be managed, were scared of dealing with the situation and were embarrassed about asking personal questions about an employee's state of health.

Absence notification procedures

Many organisations specify that when employees phone in as absent they must phone themselves, rather than asking another person to phone on their behalf. Many also specify that the employee must speak to their direct line manager or nominated representative. This means that such a telephone conversation can be the first stage of the absence management process. The conversation is welfare based and the intention is that the manager is able to ask about the nature of the problem and the anticipated date of return to work. Brakes (IDS 2005b), interestingly, outsources potential absence reporting calls to a nurse helpline. The nurse gives confidential advice on how to manage symptoms but makes no recommendation about whether the individual should attend work or not. The nurse does, however, make a record of the call and notifies the appropriate line manager and also informs the line manager when the individual is ready to return to work. Apparently managers appreciate the removal of this burden and concentrate their attention on those employees whose absence level has reached a trigger point.

Some organisations, such as First Direct (IDS 2001), make every effort to offer alternative work. For example, a telephone operator who cannot do telephone work with a sore throat may be able to do other work, and managers are asked to bear this in mind when employees phone in sick and to try to encourage the employees to come in, where appropriate, to carry out other tasks. This telephone conversation is also seen as an important tool in reducing the length of the absence.

Better understanding of the causes of absence

Understanding absence requires sound data. Three measures are commonly used. The **absence rate** is the number of days of absence, when attendance would be expected, of all employees. The **absence percentage rate** is the absence rate divided by the total number of actual working days for all employees over the year, multiplied by 100. This simple percentage is widely used to compare absence level with national data and with data of other organisations in the same sector.

The **absence frequency rate** is the number of spells of absence over the period, usually a year. Comparing this and the absence percentage rate gives a key snapshot of the absence situation in the organisation. As well as making external comparisons, the same types of analysis can be used to compare departments, work groups, occupations, grades and so on.

Analysis of absence data may help employers develop absence management methods relevant to the most frequent causes. However, as we have said, the reasons employees give for absence will be those that the organisation considers legitimate, and further investigation may be necessary.

Organisations can encourage individuals to be open about the real cause for their absence, for example a minor illness may be used as an excuse to cover for caring responsibilities, a stressful working environment or alcohol or drug problems. However, this is easier said than done. The London Borough of Brent (IRS 2002b) has decided that the next stage in its efforts to tackle long-term absence is to try to unpick the causes of such absence. The employer has a feeling that the explanation may be partly related to issues of stress and the nature and organisation of the work. Helping employees to feel they can trust the employer sufficiently to admit the real cause of absence means that absence can then effectively be tackled by providing the appropriate form of support. Another key tool is risk assessment, so, for example, some organisations will assess the risk of back pain or stress and then training can be provided to meet identified needs. The CIPD (2006) found that organisations used risk assessments, training, staff surveys, policy development, flexible working, employee assistance programmes, focus groups and changes in work organisation as methods to identify and reduce stress. The HSE encourages the use of focus groups for stress identification and management and more details and examples can be found in Silcox (2005b).

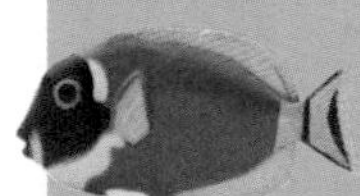

WINDOW ON PRACTICE

Risk assessments for stress

Stress accounts for a large proportion of sickness absence in the NHS, and researchers from the Institute of Work, Health and Organisations at Nottingham University studied five groups of hospital staff working under pressure: nurses, healthcare assistants, technical and professional staff, catering staff and clerical/reception staff. The aim was to measure and tackle stress at work. The intervention began with risk assessment, and a well-being questionnaire was used to gather employee feelings about tiredness and exhaustion. Employees were asked to identify not only causes of stress but also changes to management practice which would provide a solution. One of the examples provided is the catering team who identified causes as peak-time high workloads, poorly maintained equipment and inadequate training. Resultant interventions included regular equipment maintenance, additional peak-time staff and regular team briefings.

Source: Summarised from HSE (2002b) *Interventions to control stress at work in hospital staff*, HSE Contract Research Paper No. 435. London: HSE.

Ongoing contact during absence

Maintaining contact during absence is considered by many as a way of reducing the length of absence, demonstrating that there is continuing interest in the employee's welfare, so maintaining employee motivation. In some cases it is the line manager who will keep in touch, and in others, such as Walter Holland and Son (IDS 2001), there are liaison officers who fulfil this role. Contact may be by telephone, and with longer periods of absence may involve home visits. A useful summary of a wide range of methods of keeping in touch with employees who are off sick is in Silcox (2005c). The Employers Organisation for Local Government (EO) (HSE 2002a) suggests that more effort should be made to keep in touch with employees after operations, partly to keep them up to date, but also to see if it is possible for them to come back to work on light duties or on a part-time basis. In working out its policy of visits, Bracknell Forest Council (IRS 2002a) pays due attention to the requirements of the Human Rights Act 1998. The council recommends one visit per month in working hours and considers this is reasonable in terms of the need to demonstrate 'respect for private and family life', and the wish to avoid putting pressure on employees to return to work too early.

Return to work interviews and formal absence reviews

Return to work interviews are used increasingly as a key part of attendance procedures. CIPD (2006) reports that these were used by 81 per cent of organisations in 2006 compared with 57 per cent in 2000. CIPD also reports that these interviews are regarded as the most effective way of managing short-term absence. For some organisations these interviews are mandatory, even following a single day's absence, but there is frequently some flexibility about the nature of the interview depending on the circumstances. The general purpose of such interviews is to: welcome the employee back and update them on recent events; check that the employee is well enough to resume normal duties and whether any further organisational support is needed; reinforce the fact that the employee has been missed and that attendance is a high priority in the organisation; and review the employee's absence record. Dunn and Wilkinson (2002) found managers in their research who said that there was not time to concentrate on return to work interviews, as the practicalities of getting the job done were more critical. They also found a view among line managers that they were just so glad to get the employee back that they did not want to 'rock the boat'. Where formal absence reviews are held these need to be handled with sensitivity and tact, and care needs to be taken so that the interview does not become recriminatory or accusatory.

Use of disciplinary procedures

If someone is genuinely ill and unable to work, disciplinary action whether threatened or real is unlikely to bring about a return to work. There are, however, situations in which people who are too ill to work have to be dismissed. Never a pleasant task, it often falls to the HR manager to carry it out. The key is to make sure that the dismissal is carried out in a legally sound manner. This issue is covered in greater detail in Chapters 10 and 25, so it is only necessary here to summarise the main points:

1. Dismissing someone who is unable to work because of ill health is potentially fair under unfair dismissal law.

2 It is necessary to warn the individual concerned that he or she may be dismissed if he or she does not return to work and to consult with the individual ahead of time to establish whether a return in the foreseeable future is feasible.

3 It is necessary to act on whatever medical advice is available.

4 In larger organisations, except where a person's job is very specialised or senior, it is normally considered reasonable to refrain from dismissing a sick employee for at least six months.

5 In any case no dismissal should occur if the employee falls under the definition of 'disabled' as set out in the Disability Discrimination Act 1995. In these cases an employee should only be dismissed once the employer is wholly satisfied that no reasonable adjustments could be made to accommodate the needs of the sick employee so as to allow him or her to return to work.

Where someone is persistently absent for short periods of time, the course of action taken will depend on whether there is a genuine underlying medical condition which explains most of the absences. If there is such a condition, the matter should be handled in the same way as cases of long-term absence due to ill health outlined above. If not, then it is feasible for the employer to take a tougher line and to threaten disciplinary action at an earlier stage. It is quite acceptable in law to dismiss someone whose absence record is unacceptably high, provided the individual has been warned ahead of time and given a fair opportunity to improve his or her attendance. It is also necessary to treat different employees in a consistent fashion. Taking disciplinary action in the form of issuing a formal warning is therefore credible and likely to be successful.

Absence levels and performance assessments

Some organisations include the review of attendance levels as a measure of performance in annual assessments. Dunn and Wilkinson (2002) found that in the three retail companies in their case sample, employees were assessed via a separate rating category on their absence levels. Employees with unacceptable absence levels would not be put forward for transfers or promotion. At HBOS (IDS 2005a) line managers have a key performance objective relating to employee absence, reflecting their enhanced roles in managing absence.

Attendance bonus and rewards

Some organisations pay bonuses direct to employees on the basis of their attendance records. For example in Richmondshire District Council (Silcox 2005d) staff receive an additional day's leave for 100 per cent attendance in the previous year. When this bonus and other absence management measures were employed, absence was reduced from ten days to eight days in the first year. The council argues not only that this is a cost saving, but that an anticipated day's holiday is much easier to manage than an unanticipated day's sickness absence. Connex (IDS 2001) will pay a quarterly attendance bonus of £155 at the end of each 13-week period for full attendance and an additional lump sum of £515 if an employee has had no sickness absence during a full calendar year. In addition Connex sends out letters commending employees for improving their absence record. The company considers that its absence scheme is a success as 80 per cent of eligible employees now qualify for payments. However, some managers do not support attendance bonuses as they feel that employees are already paid to turn up, and they are effectively being paid twice. Connex also found managers who felt that attendance bonuses were a signal to employees that managers cannot control the work environment themselves and that they have relinquished all responsibility for managing absence. On the other hand, Dunn and Wilkinson (2002) found that managers felt attendance bonuses were unfair as they penalised those employees who were genuinely ill. A further problem is that such rewards may encourage employees to come into work when they are genuinely ill which is not good for either the individual or the organisation. Such rewards therefore remain controversial.

ACTIVITY 14.2

In terms of your own organisation consider the approaches by which sickness absence is minimised in terms of proactive ill-health prevention methods, discouragement of sickness absence, and encouragement of attendance:

1 Where is the emphasis in terms of approach?
2 Why do you think this is so?
3 Is this the most appropriate approach? Why?
4 To what extent are different employee groups treated differently?
5 Why do you think this is so?
6 Is this the most appropriate approach? Why?

Occupational health support, health promotion and well-being

A number of organisations carry out pre-employment screening to identify any potential health problems at this stage. Others screen employees for general fitness and for potential job hazards, such as working with radiation, or VDUs. General screening may involve heart checks, blood tests, eye tests, well-woman/man clinics, ergonomics and physiotherapy, and discussions about weight and lifestyle, such as smoking, drinking and fitness levels. The value of such screening is that problems can be identified at an early stage so that the impact on sickness absence will be minimised. In some organisations positive encouragement will be given to employees to follow healthy lifestyles, such as healthy eating, giving up smoking, taking up exercise routines. Increasing numbers of employers offer exercise classes and/or an on-site gym, or alternatively pay for gym membership. Healthier canteen menus are appearing, as well as healthier snacks in some vending machines. However, the CIPD (2006) found that barriers to such well-being initiatives were lack of resources, lack of senior management buy-in, and lack of employee buy-in, especially in manufacturing and production. The government has provided some funding (together with other organisations) for nine health promotion projects in England, and a good example of one of these is the 'Be Active 4 Life' Programme at Exeter City Council which will be evaluated soon after the time of writing by a team from Loughborough University. Details of this project and the eight others are provided by Silcox (2005e).

For long-term absence the CIPD (2006) reported that the involvement of occupational health professionals was seen to be the most effective management tool, although HSE (2002c) shows that only one in seven workers has the benefit of comprehensive occupational health support. However, such support does not have to be in-house and can be purchased: this is the course followed by the London Borough of Brent (IRS 2002b).

Physiotherapists, counsellors and psychologists are often employed, and the occupational health role may include remedial fitness training and exercise therapy for those recovering from an illness. Stress counselling is increasingly being provided and if this is offered as part of an employee assistance programme can reduce the liability in stress-related personal injury cases. Also training in stress management may be offered.

James and his colleagues (2002) found that the role of occupational health workers was ambiguous and problematic. Their respondents suggested that while occupational health professionals worked on behalf of the employer, they tended to see themselves as representing employee interests. They also found that employees were very sceptical about visiting occupational health workers as they saw it as the first step in the termination of their employment.

Changes to work and work organisation

Many employers appear to offer flexible working hours, part-time work and working from home. Employers also sometimes consider offering light duties or redeployment. However, James and his colleagues (2002) found that operational factors often limited what was possible. In the three manufacturing organisations they visited it was not always feasible to offer light duties or make adjustments to the workplace. They also found that other departments were reluctant to accept someone who was being redeployed after sickness, partly because they felt the employee might have lost the work habit, and also because there might be problems with pay if the levels of the old and new job differed. They also noted that there might be no budget to pay for adaptations to equipment or to purchase further equipment.

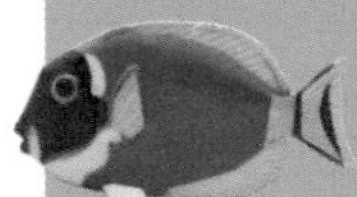

WINDOW ON PRACTICE

Flexible working cuts sickness absence

People Management reports that the London Borough of Merton has halved its sickness absence rate and improved productivity by introducing flexible working as part of a work-life balance pilot project. The flexible patterns of work involved a compressed working week, working from home, career breaks, job sharing and special leave including compassionate leave. Keith Davis, the Assistant Chief Executive, explained that the management style had to change from managing attendance to managing output, and significant training was required. The council plans to roll out the scheme over the entire council.

Source: Summarised from *People Management* (2002) 'Flexible working cuts sickness absence', Vol. 8, No. 1, 10 January, p. 13.

Practical support

There are many ways in which the employer can provide practical support to minimise sickness absence. Many organisations have experienced frustrations while employees are on waiting lists for diagnostic procedures and operations. In order to speed up medical treatment that employees need some organisations are prepared to pay the medical costs for employees where there is a financial case to do this, for example the Corporation of London (Silcox 2005f). Training in areas such as stress management and time management may help employees minimise feelings of stress, childcare support may simplify childcare arrangements, and phased return to work after a long-term absence is also a useful strategy. For more details on phased return to work and some examples *see* Silcox (2005g).

SUMMARY PROPOSITIONS

14.1 Employee absence continues to be a major problem for both the country and business in terms of direct costs and lost performance.

14.2 The most often reported cause of short-term absence is minor illness; however, back pain for manual workers and stress for non-manual workers are the leading causes of long-term absence.

14.3 It is important to understand the true nature of the causation of absence, as remedies can only be developed with this knowledge. Absence can result from a complex interrelationship of factors.

14.4 Typical attendance management policies include absence monitoring and reporting, absence review and trigger points, training and support for line managers, absence notification procedures, better understanding of the causes of absence, risk assessments, ongoing contact during absence, return to work interviews and absence review interviews, use of disciplinary procedure, absence-influenced performance assessments, absence bonus and rewards, occupational health support, changes to work and work organisation, and practical support. The mix of policies and processes used needs to be tailored to the needs of the organisation.

GENERAL DISCUSSION TOPICS

1 'If we gave employees longer holidays and more flexibility in the hours that they worked it would reduce the conflict between personal responsibilities/interests and work responsibilities. This reduction in conflict would reduce unplanned absence from work.' To what extent do you agree with this statement and why?

2 To what extent do you consider that absence statistics underestimate the extent of absence in the UK, and why?

3 It could be argued that encouraging employees to engage in exercise and keep fit will improve their work motivation and sense of well-being, and that this would reduce absence. To what extent do you agree with this notion?

FURTHER READING

Evans, A. and Walters, M. (2003) *From Absence to Attendance*, 2nd edn. London: CIPD.
A thorough text which covers absence measuring and monitoring; understanding the causes of absence; absence management policies; the disciplinary and legal framework of absence management; and developing and implementing absence management strategies.

James, P., Cunningham, I. and Dibben, P. (2006) 'Job retention and return to work of ill and injured workers: towards an understanding of the organizational dynamics', *Employee Relations*, Vol. 28, No. 3, pp. 290–303.
This paper proposes a conceptual framework of policies and practices appropriate to the effective management of long-term ill and injured workers and makes some assessment of UK current practices in relations to this framework.

Johns, G. (2001) 'Contemporary research on absence from work: correlates, causes and consequences', in I. Robertson and C. Cooper (eds), *Personnel Psychology and HRM*. Chichester: John Wiley and Sons Ltd.
A useful chapter which provides a wide range of perspectives on understanding the nature of absence from work. Johns considers process and decision models, the withdrawal model, demographic models, the medical model, the stress model, social and cultural models, the conflict model, the deviance model and the economic model. An awareness of such a range of perspectives is useful as it provides a context against which to understand any one approach to absence.

Robson, F. (2006) 'How to manage absence effectively', *People Management*, Vol. 12, No. 17, pp. 44–5.
This is a brief and well-focused summary of how to improve absence management.

Silcox, S. (2005) 'Absence essentials: the why and wherefores of sick notes', *IRS Employment Review*, No. 850, pp. 18–21.
This interesting article explains the current sickness certification system and explores the role of the GP in this. The GP perspective is outlined and the tensions between this and the government's proposed welfare reforms aimed at reducing long-term absence from work and the numbers receiving invalidity benefit.

REFERENCES

Barham, C. and Leonard, J. (2002) 'Trends and sources of data on sickness absence', *Labour Market Trends*, April. London: ONS, pp. 177–85.

Bevan, S. (2002) 'Counting the cost of absence', *IRS Employment Review*, No. 739, pp. 46–7.

CBI/AXA (2005) *Who Cares Wins: Absence and labour turnover 2005*. London: CBI/AXA.

CBI/AXA (2006) *Absence Minded: Absence and labour turnover in 2006. The lost billions: Addressing the cost of absence*. London: CBI.

CIPD (2005) *Absence Management: A survey of policy and practice*. London: CIPD.

CIPD (2006) *Employee Absence 2006*. London: CIPD.

CIPD (2009) *Absence Management Survey Report*. London: CIPD.

Dunn, C. and Wilkinson, A. (2002) 'Wish you were here: managing absence', *Personnel Review*, Vol. 31, No. 2, pp. 228–46.

HSE (2002a) *Initiative Evaluation Report: Back in work*, HSE Research Report No. 441. London: HSE.

HSE (2002b) *Interventions to Control Stress at Work in Hospital Staff*, HSE Contract Research Paper No. 435. London: HSE.

HSE (2002c) *Survey of the Use of Occupational Health Support*, HSE Research Report No. 445. London: HSE.

Huczynski, A.A. and Fitzpatrick, M.J. (1989) *Managing Employee Absence for a Competitive Edge*. London: Pitman.

IDS (2001) *Absence Management*, No. 702, January. London: IDS.

IDS (2005a) *Absence Management*, No. 810, November. London: IDS.

IDS (2005b) 'Brakes', *Absence Management*, No. 801, November. London: IDS.

IRS (2002a) 'Tackling long-term absence in local government (1): Bracknell Forest Borough Council', *IRS Employment Review*, No. 762, 21 October, pp. 42–6.

IRS (2002b) 'Tackling long-term absence (2): London Borough of Brent', *IRS Employment Review*, No. 763, 11 November, pp. 44–6.

James, P., Cunningham, I. and Dibben, P. (2002) 'Absence management and the issues of job retention and return to work', *Human Resource Management Journal*, Vol. 12, No. 2, pp. 82–94.

Lokke, A., Eskildsen, J. and Jensen, T. (2007) 'Absenteeism in the Nordic countries', *Employee Relations*, Vol. 29, No. 1, pp. 16–29.

McFadzean, M. (2003) 'Managing absence', paper presented at the CIPD National Conference, Harrogate, 22–24 October.

Neal, L.F. and Robertson, A. (1968) *The Manager's Guide to Industrial Relations*. London: George Allen and Unwin.

Nicholson, N. (1977) 'Absence behaviour and attendance motivation: a conceptual synthesis', *Journal of Management Studies*, Vol. 14, pp. 231–52.

People Management (2002) 'Flexible working cuts sickness absence', Vol. 8, No. 1, p. 13.

Rhodes, S. and Steers, R. (1990) *Managing Employee Absenteeism*. Reading: Addison Wesley.

Roberts, Z. (2003) 'Get well sooner', *People Management*, Vol. 9, No. 7, pp. 10–11.

Silcox, S. (2005a) 'Making progress towards an absence-recording standard', *IRS Employment Review*, No. 820, pp. 18–19.

Silcox, S. (2005b) 'Absence essentials: using focus groups in stress management', *IRS Employment Review*, No. 832, pp. 21–4.

Silcox, S. (2005c) 'Absence Essentials: Maintaining Contact', *IRS Employment Review*, No. 818, pp. 23–4.

Silcox, S. (2005d) 'Attendance incentives are on the HR agenda once again', *IRS Employment Review*, No. 832, pp. 18–20.

Silcox, S. (2005e) 'Exeter City Council wants its employees to "Be Active 4 Life"', *IRS Employment Review*, No. 836, pp. 19–21.

Silcox, S. (2005f) 'Corporation of London tackles long-term absence', *IRS Employment Review*, No. 834, pp. 19–21.

Silcox, S. (2005g) 'Absence essentials: phased return to work', *IRS Employment Review*, No. 828, pp. 18–21.

Silcox, S. (2006) 'The CBI and EEF agree that absence is falling', *IRS Employment Review*, No. 850, pp. 22–3.

Smethurst, S. (2006) 'Sporting chance', *People Management*, Vol. 12, No. 13, pp. 32–4.

TUC (2005) *Countering an Urban Legend: Sicknote Britain?* London: TUC.

An extensive range of additional materials, including multiple choice questions, answers to questions and links to useful websites can be found on the Human Resource Management companion website at **www.pearsoned.co.uk/torrington**.

Part 3 CASE STUDY PROBLEM

Bakersfield University

Bakersfield (new) University is in a process of change in order to promote more effective service delivery to its customers within tight budget constraints. Teaching staff have increasingly taken on higher teaching hours as the staff to student ratio has increased from 1:18 to 1:28 over the past 12 years. The decrease in staff numbers has been managed through the non-replacement of leavers and a limited level of early retirement. In addition to taking on increased teaching loads staff have been exhorted to engage themselves in commercial work and in research to a much greater extent and to complete PhDs. The staff have increasingly felt under pressure, but have on the whole been dedicated workers. Those staff who were most seriously disillusioned by the changes taking place were generally those opting for early retirement, although this process also meant that much expertise was suddenly lost to many departments.

The pressure of work seems set to increase and the goodwill and relatively high performance of staff are increasingly at risk. In the current circumstances departments have found it difficult to recognise the good work of staff by promotion, which had been the traditional approach. Many department heads have tried to deal with this by holding out the hope of future promotion and by recognition of a good job done. Some department heads were more effective in this than others.

The university as a whole has decided to introduce a performance management system (PMS) in order to enhance staff performance. Standard forms were produced for all departments to use and guidelines were produced relating to the purpose and frequency of appraisal. All departments conformed in terms of carrying out the appraisals, but there were great differences in how this was handled in different departments. Those heads who had experience of successful systems elsewhere, or who were enthusiastic about this change, carried out the appraisals in a more thorough and committed way, and did try to integrate them into the running of the department and link them to departmental goals. Other heads failed to do this, and some were positively against the system as they saw it as impinging on academic freedom, and in any case had never seen themselves as true managers.

The reaction of staff was mixed, often depending on their past employment experiences and length of time employed by the university. In general, staff were resistant and sceptical. The culture of the university had been easygoing with staff able to 'do their own thing', and relied on to focus on work that was important for the university and to organise themselves in a conscientious manner. Those who had come to the university from industry had been attracted by the opportunity to control the nature and content of their own work. The new system was perceived as wresting control away from the individual and as an indication that they were not trusted.

Managers have the impression that short-term sickness absence has substantially increased, possibly as a result of work intensification and stress but also possibly as a result of declining staff morale. Historically, however, there have been no formal systems for monitoring absence and no procedures for dealing with it. The PMS addresses performance issues but not conduct issues such as sickness absence. There is growing dissatisfaction among staff at the impact of sporadic absence on their workloads and a cynicism as to the value of attempting to manage performance against a backdrop of poor attendance from a proportion of staff.

Required

1 Explain how a performance management system sits within a high performance work system aimed at enhancing individual and organisational performance. To what extent is the PMS likely to succeed given the wider context?

2 What role do you think leadership has to play in the successful implementation of this scheme?

3 What would you recommend to the university in terms of its approach to monitoring and managing staff absence?

DEVELOPMENT

Having set up appropriate methods of organisation and systems to ensure performance, we now have to consider in more detail the ways in which the organisation itself can be developed and how people acquire skill, knowledge and effectiveness in their capacity to perform.

In our fast-changing world, organisations need to be both proactive and responsive to change, and our first chapter in this Part focuses on how such change can be most effectively implemented taking account of the natural difficulties which people experience when change is thrust upon them. We move into the second chapter by taking two allied approaches to developing the organisation: knowledge management and organisational learning. Both approaches focus on the value of sharing information and how such learning can be embedded within the organisation so that it remains even when people leave.

A key feature of development is the national framework within which vocational skills can be acquired. Here the individual employer relies on, and attempts to influence, the provision of the education and training system and the arrangements of professional and other bodies, which specify the appropriate standards for vocational competence.

Individuals are developed further within the business, especially in management development, where the skills and knowledge needed tend to be much more specific to the organisation within which they are employed where the methods of development are geared to the ongoing processes of the business.

ORGANISATIONAL CHANGE AND DEVELOPMENT

THE OBJECTIVES OF THIS CHAPTER ARE TO:

1. Review the nature of change, the traditional model of planned change, and the limitations of this model
2. Explain how organisations may be designed to be more responsive to change
3. Explore the employee experience of change and the impact this may have on the success of change
4. Examine the nature of change when the organisation is conceptualised as a human living system
5. Explore the nature of organisational development (OD) as a specific approach to change in organisations
6. Describe the evolution of OD and consider its future

We are all now familiar with the mantra that change is a constant in our world and that its pace is ever increasing. For example Worrall and Cooper (2006) in their survey found that 90 per cent of managers were affected by change (97 per cent in the public sector), compared with 83 per cent five years earlier. In addition over half the managers were affected by three or more forms of change compared with 45 per cent five years earlier. Inevitably therefore leaders find themselves leading, promoting, encouraging and stimulating change as a key part of their role, with a belief that they can 'manage' change.

However, all change, no matter how small, presents a challenge for everyone in the organisation. For leaders there is the challenge of making the required changes happen, and for everyone else there is the challenge of coping with changes over which they often have no control and for which they have potentially no desire. Such changes invariably involve them in engaging in new activities, behaviours and thinking, and the even more difficult task of letting go and unlearning old activities, behaviours and thinking.

It is therefore unsurprising that there is a large body of evidence cataloguing the difficulties with and failure of many change programmes; for example compare Soltani and colleagues (2007: 153):

> very few change programmes produce an improvement in bottom-line, exceed the company's cost of capital, or even improve service delivery

with Beer and Nohria (2000: 133) recognising that the consequences of such programmes

> exert a heavy toll both human and economic.

In this chapter we explore the ways in which organisations approach change; explore some of the reasons why change may be unsuccessful; and review current approaches to improving that success rate. In the final part of the chapter we consider OD as a specific approach to change which may bring added benefits to the change process.

THE NATURE OF CHANGE AND THE ROLE OF PLANNED CHANGE

There are many reasons why a business has to change, such as competitor behaviour, customer expectations, development of technology and communications, or a need to maximise shareholder value (*see*, for example, Greenhalgh 2001). Sometimes change is an initiative to seize an advantage and make something happen (proactive); on other occasions it is an attempt to catch up with what is already happening (reactive). Other distinctions are made, for example whether the push for change comes externally or internally. The change may be revolutionary, sudden and dramatic, or it may be evolutionary and incremental. However, underlying all of this is the fundamental reason for change, which is organisational survival and competitiveness in the complex and global world which we have created. Beer and Nohria (2000: 133) put it well when they say that 'most traditional organizations have accepted, in theory at least, that they must change or die' and that newer types of enterprises need to manage the changes associated with rapid growth.

Table 15.1 Aspects of change

Structure, size and shape	Formal and informal systems Processes and procedures
Culture, values and beliefs	People and behaviours at all levels

The nature of change has also been hotly debated and the emphasis has increasingly been on transformational change. It is sometimes suggested that transformational change is equivalent to revolutionary change, but we suggest that evolutionary change can equally be transformational. Change may involve movements in organisational shape, size, structure which are technically termed 'hard' aspects, and which are very visible and perhaps more straightforward to implement. Change may also involve 'softer' aspects such as rewards, values, beliefs, systems, procedures, roles, responsibilities, culture, tasks and behaviour which are potentially more difficult to manage. In Table 15.1 we have summarised the different aspects of the organisation which change might affect.

While transformational change may involve all of the aspects shown in Table 15.1 it is generally agreed that transformational change is more than this and involves fundamentally new ways of understanding what the organisation is for and is doing. Beckhard (1992), for example, suggested that transformational change may involve the organisation's shape, structure or nature, but more than this requires a re-examination of the organisation's mission and a vision of a different future state of the organisation. As Binney and Williams (2005) suggest transformational change is about the change in mental models of what the organisation is about, sometimes referred to as change in the organisational paradigm.

ACTIVITY 15.1

Think of a major change which you have experienced at work, university, school or in any other organisation. (You may even consider your family to be an organisation.)

Consider all of the different aspects of that change and then draw a diagram similar to Table 15.1 and allocate the different aspects of the change to each box.

There has been a long-running school of thought which proposes that leaders can plan and manage change given the right processes and tools to use, and there is a variety of models in the literature, and used by consultants, with most focusing on such stages as:

- identify the need for change
- define our current state
- envisage the future desired state
- identify the gap
- diagnose capacity for change including barriers and how they can be overcome
- plan actions and behaviours needed to close the gap

- implement required actions
- manage the transition
- constantly reinforce changes, sustain momentum and measure progress

For more details on such processes *see*, for example, Hayes (2007) and Walton (1999). Such models make this top-down change process sound very straightforward with a logical approach to what needs to happen, and may well involve a good degree of training to prepare people for what will happen and what they will need to do. However, as we highlighted in our introduction to this chapter, change is often both painful and unsuccessful.

In beginning to understand the great difficulties of achieving change it is helpful to address the limitations of the planned change model. On a practical level we have little time for such lengthy processes in our world of constant change and there is little opportunity to reinforce and embed a change as another change follows closely on its heels and indeed may be happening at the same time. Organisations need to become more responsive to the need for change as well as proactive where possible. Case 15.1 on this book's companion website, **www.pearsoned.co.uk/torrington**, focuses on readiness for change.

A second difficulty with the planned approach to change is its underlying assumptions. It can be seen as allied to the metaphor of the organisation as a machine which emphasises rationality and ignores emotion (*see*, for example, Lewis *at al*. 2008; Morgan 2006). The machine develops a problem: the owners of the machine work out how to fix it: they put the plan into action and repair the machine. It is based on a scientific logical approach to problem solving in organisations, which may be appropriate for some problems, but is often inappropriate as it neglects the important fact that the organisational machine is made up of human beings who have a will of their own. Binney and Williams (2005) suggest that this approach deals inadequately with the unintended consequences of change, its messiness, the gap in perceptions between leaders and followers, the fact that visions often do not inspire. They also point out that it is based on the assumption that change is something which is done to organisations (and hence the people that make them up), rather like the assumption that leadership is done to followers rather than with them (Goffee and Jones 2006). The machine metaphor also focuses change on the observable, in other words behaviour, and does not allow for employee thinking processes, and fails to consider the employee experience of change and employees' potential contribution to change.

In the next three sections we address the above limitations of the planned change model.

HOW CAN ORGANISATIONS BE RESPONSIVE TO CHANGE?

On a very practical level one way of trying to enable organisations to be more responsive to change is to **design** them so that they can change more easily, and Lawler and Worley (2009) suggest that given the increasing pace of change organisations need to anticipate change and constantly reconfigure and hence require a built-in capacity to change continuously. To do this they suggest that organisations need to design themselves so that they can 'adjust their strategic intents, structures and human deployments as a matter of routine' (p. 28), and need to develop the ability to think creatively about the future to achieve sustained success.

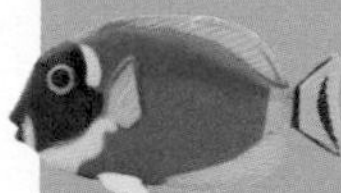

WINDOW ON PRACTICE

Built-to-change

Lawler and Warley (2009) use the example of Capital One Financial Services to demonstrate a built-to-change approach.

1. **Strategising:** At Capital One change is a continuous forward-looking activity rather than an annual or biannual one and there is a 'test and learn' approach to drive growth. To do this Capital One identifies services, products and other elements that will, under a range of conditions, create high performance. These become strategic imperatives where capabilities must be developed.
2. **Structure:** The organisation is designed flexibly, ensuring that no one is more than one or two steps away from the external environment to ensure connection with the marketplace, regulators and so on.
3. **Information production and sharing:** Capital One employs processes to share internal and external information such as financial performance, market conditions, competitor performance on the basis that people are more likely to accept change if they understand what needs to happen for the business to succeed.
4. **Job design:** New entrants to Capital One are rotated round the business so that they can contribute in any area. This ensures flexibility and responsiveness to changing demands.
5. **Selecting the right people:** Capital One selects employees who enjoy change, are quick to learn and actively seek professional growth.
6. **Employment contract based on employee willingness to accept change:** Employees are expected to learn new skills and deliver high performance. Capital One cannot promise to always offer the training and support that employees need and if an individual's skills are outdated that person may no longer have a place in the organisation if the skills are readily available in the external labour market.
7. **Performance management and development:** This is a flexible, dynamic and interactive process with goals regarding performance and the development experiences that individuals will need to contribute to the business in the future. Appraisals focus on both performance achievement and the acquisition and application of skills and knowledge required for the future.
8. **Leadership:** Lawler and Worley propose that given the complexity of change today, leadership needs to shift from a small group of people at the top of the organisation to all levels where managers are urged to grasp leadership opportunities immediately they arise.

Source: Adapted from E. Lawler and C. Worley (2009) 'The rebirth of change', *People Management*, Vol. 15, No. 3, 29 January, pp. 28–30.

ACTIVITY 15.2

How would you assess the advantages and disadvantages of working for the type of organisation described in the Window on practice?

This approach goes some way to address the needs of organisations in a constantly changing environment, but it does not address other fundamental problems with the planned change model.

ADDRESSING THE EMPLOYEE EXPERIENCE OF CHANGE

There has been increasing recognition of the value of understanding the employee experience of HRM, with Boselie *et al.* (2005) suggesting that this is central to HRM research and practice, and yet that there remains a 'dearth of evidence on employee reactions to change' (Conway and Monks 2008: 73). Reactions are likely to be affected by the context of the change, for example whether the company is shrinking and fighting for survival or is expanding. The planned change model pays insufficient attention to employee perceptions of and reactions to change.

When our jobs and their context change significantly the psychological contract can be damaged and unable to support the employee. Particularly where change involves mergers and acquisitions it is possible that employees end up doing a job for which they did not apply, in a company for which they do not want to work, so it is not surprising that employees are likely to experience a breach of the psychological contract (CIPD 2009a) as the deal for which employees signed up appears to have been broken. When the psychological contract is breached employees may display behavioural symptoms such as holding back information, may make more errors or leave the organisation; and may express feelings such as frustration, anger and distrust (*see*, for example, Robinson and Morrison 2000).

While the planned change model inevitably focuses on employee behaviour, as this is an essential part of the change being successful, it neglects other types of employee responses such as the emotions referred to above. If behaviour does not change in the required manner there is a tendency for change agents and leaders to ascribe this to the fact that the planned change model was not applied rigorously enough (Lewis *et al.* 2008). Within this view there is an assumption that employee resistance to change is a characteristic of the individual psyche that, ultimately, has to be overcome, rather than that resistance stems from legitimate reasons and is partly a result of the way that change is conceived and led in the organisation. Case 15.2 focuses on employee reaction to change and the different perspectives at different management levels at this book's companion website, **www.pearsoned.co.uk/torrington**.

Oreg (2006), for example, suggests that individuals react to change in three ways: affective (emotions), cognitive and behavioural. We would also add physical reactions, drawing on evidence from Worrall and Cooper (2006). Employee response to change is typically couched in terms of 'resistance' to change, a most unhelpful word, suggesting

WINDOW ON PRACTICE

It depends on your perspective

How many times have you heard it said that the old system was more efficient than the new one? As a change is implemented it is almost inevitable that efficiency suffers as new procedures are being learned, flaws in new procedures are identified and fixed, and sometimes old and new systems are run in parallel. So lack of efficiency is often a temporary matter. But not always. For example the centralisation of administrative officers and systems in an organisation (usually associated with a reduction in staff numbers) may well permanently, or for a period of years, result in records being more difficult to access and amend, lengthier and more time-consuming processes, loss of accuracy of data and a loss of local knowledge. No matter how great the goodwill of all parties the new system is less efficient than the old, and the frustrated and demoralised administrative staff and their contacts may feel they could have contributed to designing a more efficient system. Organisational leaders may however be very satisfied with the change as savings have been made, budgets are looking healthier and the share price has gone up.

Table 15.2 Individual response to change

Behavioural responses	Cognitive responses
Emotional responses	Physical responses

an illegitimate reaction, and hence we use the term response, a neutral word, implying that this can be understood and developed. Table 15.2 shows the combination of individual responses to change.

As human beings our reactions to change are a mix of all four areas, which are bound up together and difficult to separate. A cognitive response to change may be to re-evaluate the advantages and disadvantages of working for a current employer and the advantages and disadvantages of seeking and gaining alternative employment. When an organisation moves geographically to another part of town, say from the centre to a redevelopment area employees may decide that this has detrimental consequences for their journey, costs, lunchtime shopping and eating; and if they have marketable skills they may seek alternative employment in the town centre. So a cognitive assessment results in the behaviour of leaving the organisation.

In an example focusing on cognitive and emotional responses, Jones *et al.* (2004) comment that in a restructuring/downsizing environment involving the removal or amalgamation of work units employees may lose their role identity. In other words they are unclear of where they fit in the new structure, cease to feel confident and may construe this loss of role identity as a threat to their self-esteem and work validation. The Window on practice below presents an alternative example of role identity being under threat.

WINDOW ON PRACTICE

Resisting change in an Australian credit union

Cutcher (2009) explains how the credit union Coast implemented changes affecting front-line staff in its branches in rural communities in New South Wales, and how staff resisted such changes.

In the context of the deregulation of financial services with the loss of special provisions for credit unions, including tax advantages, management introduced a new sales strategy emulating that employed by the large retail banks. This shift from service to sales appeared to be accepted in the northern and central regions of the union which were more urban areas but resisted in the southern, poorer, rural region branches, labelled as problem branches by the General Manager.

Coast's new strategy places a requirement on members to be profitable customers, with front-line staff focusing on increasing sales of new financial products in competition with each other. Employee performance was measured by level of sales against sales performance targets which had an influence on pay increases. Overall 25 per cent of Coast's employees left when the new strategy was introduced, and remaining employees reported higher levels of stress.

Management blamed the problems in the southern region on the intransigence of staff but failed to recognise the contradictions within the new sales strategy and the complexity of the employee response to the changes.

Front-line staff continued to refer to members, rather than customers two years after management changed the language. They also continued to refer to themselves as Member Service Officers rather than Sales Consultants (their new job title). Staff disliked the idea of targeting individuals in the queue and the competition to get to them first, knowing there was a possible sale of an insurance policy to be had. They cared more about knowing the people who used the union, whom they had known over many years, and who were satisfied with the service they got. They enjoyed being welcoming and friendly and valued going out of their way to help people. This was the basis of their work identity and they refused to accept the new discourse of 'enterprise'.

Staff explained that they did not want to compete against each other as they were all local women who had grown up together. Some described the branch as like a family – including staff and members. They did not want targets coming between them and entered the daily sales figures to show that the sales were shared equally between themselves irrespective of who had actually made the sales. They saw their work as a team effort, and were concerned to ensure that branch performance was good.

Their resistance to change was based on protecting their friendships both within the union and with members of their community. Managers had failed to take account of this.

Source: Adapted from L. Cutcher (2009) 'Resisting change from within and without the organisation', *Journal of Organisational Change Management*, Vol. 22, No. 3, pp. 275–89.

In trying to understand employees' emotional reactions to change, managers have used models from other parts of the social sciences. An example is the Kubler-Ross change curve (1997) which tracks the stages an individual generally experiences when coping with loss, a model that was developed in the context of bereavement. This model suggests that individuals move through the stages of shock; denial; fear; anger; bargaining; depression; understanding and acceptance before moving on. While the theoretical base for this is weak, it does have an intuitive appeal. Eriksson (2004) highlights the legitimate role of emotion, finding that change programmes resulted in employees exhibiting signs of depression and experiencing feelings of failure. He also draws our attention to the work of Kanter (1983) who identifies change as exhilarating when done by us and disturbing when done to us.

Emotions have a powerful impact on our behaviour, and are very personal to the individual and we should not assume that emotions can be managed in line with organisational strategy. Individuals themselves have enough trouble managing their emotions, but it is known that suppressing them is not a healthy approach. In times of change it is important therefore for individuals to accept and address their emotions, and for change leaders to recognise that such emotions may be negative, and to be prepared to try and understand them and accept them, responding where possible, rather than trying to manipulate them. The role of emotions helps to explain why change leaders have such different perceptions about the success of change compared with employees. Loss of choice and uncertainty for employees can trigger a wide variety of emotional responses.

Research by Les Worrall and Cary Cooper (2006) provides us with a managerial/employee perspective on change, rather than that of the leader(s) at the top of the organisation. In their study managers felt that changes were a result of cost reductions and created work intensification and increased pressure to perform. This had negatively affected their morale (61 per cent), sense of job security (56 per cent), motivation (51 per cent), sense of employee well-being (48 per cent) and loyalty (47 per cent). Managers felt they were subject to greater top-down control, and greater scrutiny, and felt overloaded, having insufficient time and resources to do their job to the standard they felt appropriate.

Change can cause a wide range of physical reactions and Worrall and Cooper (2006) found that absence levels were significantly higher in those organisations with cost-cutting programmes, and larger proportions of managers reported insomnia, persistent headaches, appetite problems, muscular tension, constant tiredness and other symptoms, and the researchers suggest that such levels of change are literally making managers ill. Such problems interestingly did not apply to the same extent to directors, who felt much more positively about the changes taking place, reporting lower levels of stressors.

Recognising the different feelings, physical reactions and perceptions that employees may have is the first step in helping change become more successful. There is a range of measures that may help. Communication is the first in helping to address the uncertainty associated with change.

WINDOW ON PRACTICE

Merging First Choice and Tui Travel

Jacky Simmonds, Tui Travel's HR Director explains the challenge of merging two very different companies. To their credit they carried out a survey to see how staff were feeling. Whilst they had put a big effort into communications, they found from the survey that even more communication was required, and Simmonds comments that she was surprised how much emotion the merger stirred up, even with senior staff, and recognised how difficult some people find it to cope with uncertainty. 'People want to be updated even if there isn't anything specific to say' says Simmonds.

Source: H. Syedain (2009) 'A smooth landing', *People Management*, 29 March, pp. 18–22.

ACTIVITY 15.3

Consider a change which you instigated either at work or in your personal life. Then consider a change that was forced upon you in your work or personal life.

For each of these situations identify the emotions that you experienced and how you dealt with them.

Other measures that may help change leaders include involving different levels of employee in shaping some of the details of the change and allowing them some feelings of control. Discussing and, where possible, addressing concerns of staff and monitoring levels of engagement may also keep change leaders in touch with employees, as was done when BBC Scotland moved from the West End of Glasgow to Pacific Quay on the Clyde (Phillips 2008).

In helping employees through change and recognising their needs Conway and Monks (2008) distinguish between management-centred and employee-centred HR practices and argue that employee-centred HR practices might be more important than sophisticated management-centred high performance work system (HPWS) practices in encouraging employee commitment to change (*see* Chapter 4 for further details). In their research they found that basic HR practices such as communication, sufficient staffing and appropriate reward were important influences and explain how each is particularly relevant in a period of change.

They also suggest that a positive employment relationship is an important factor measured by the industrial relations climate or the psychological contract. Iverson (1996) demonstrates, for example, that more favourable industrial relations (IR) climates were associated with greater acceptance of change.

Understanding the employee perceptions of and reactions to change takes us further towards a different approach to change whereby employees are viewed as human beings rather than cogs in a machine, and this is a step towards dealing with change in an alternative manner.

RECONCEPTUALISING CHANGE

In response to concerns about the leadership of change, Binney and Williams (2005), among others suggest alternative ways in which change can be led by reconceptualising change, based on the metaphor of the organisation as a living system rather than a machine. They suggest that this perspective helps us see organisations as adaptive (as behaviour and thinking shift of their own accord in response to the pressure of events); as self-organising (to achieve an equilibrium); as interdependent with their environment (interacting in complex ways); and as dynamic.

They propose that this perspective suggests change is natural, if painful, and that the challenge is to release the potential for change rather than drive it. In addition they identify the need for some stability as well as change. They suggest that this perspective encourages the view that managers cannot control change, and that the problem with a vision for the future is that it denigrates the present and the past of the organisation. A good example of this is the town of Crewe. Much effort and money is being put into regenerating and developing the town, but while there are newcomers who feel this is an excellent change programme, there are many people who were brought up in the town who feel that the changes are unnecessary and are spoiling things. The living organism approach also suggests that trying to copy excellence elsewhere is a fruitless task, as is a change consultant or chief executive telling people to change; changes, they suggest, emerge and the key is seeing the new pattern, drawing attention to it and re-inforcing it. An acceptance that the future is unknowable and unpredictable is important, as is the need for leaders to recognise that they are also part of the problem, and to acknowledge that people are not rational and that feelings and emotion are legitimate. They characterise this approach to change as a learning approach rather than a leading approach, but recognise that both perspectives add value in a change situation; in order to reflect this they propose the concept of 'leaning into the future'. Figure 15.1 summarises their thinking.

If you look back to the characteristics of empowering leadership in Chapter 13 you will be able to see the commonality between this and the learning approach to change suggested by Binney and Williams (2005).

This combination of approaches also reflects 'top-down and bottom-up' approaches to change and you will find a good example of this in the recommended reading at the end of the chapter.

ACTIVITY 15.4

Explore the similarities and differences between the empowering approach to leadership and the learning approach to change.

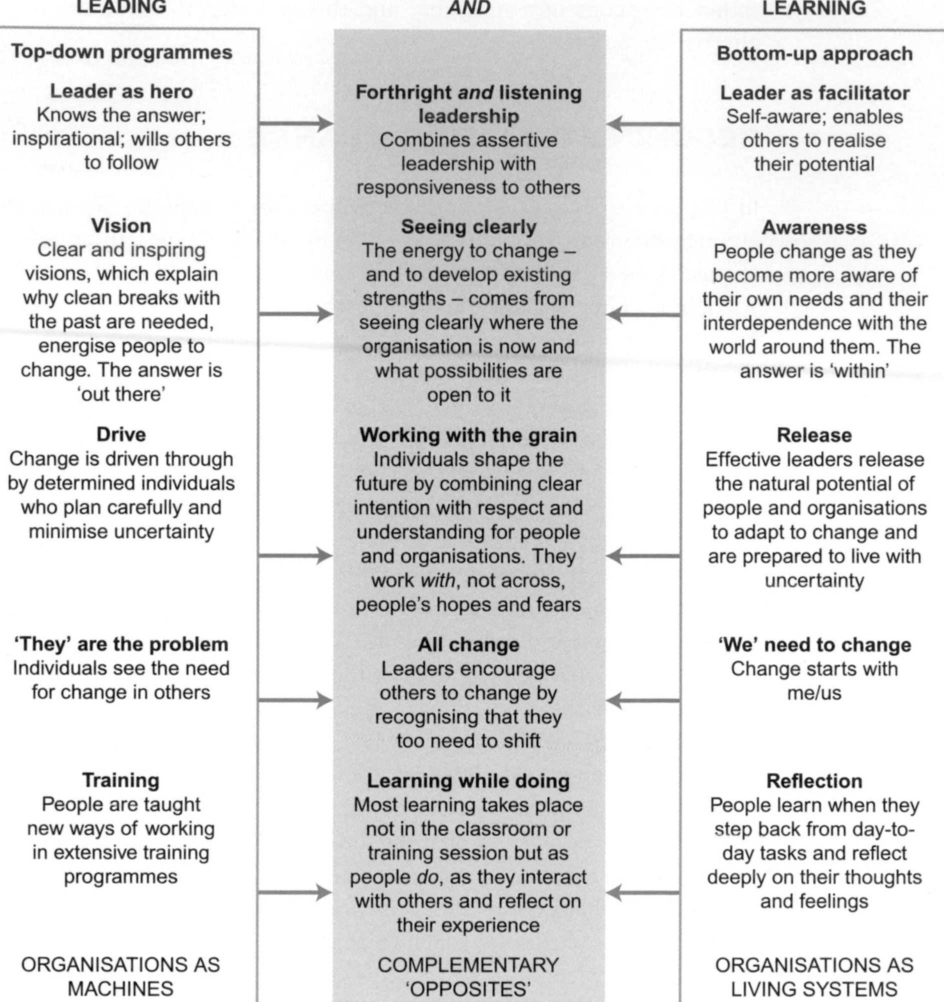

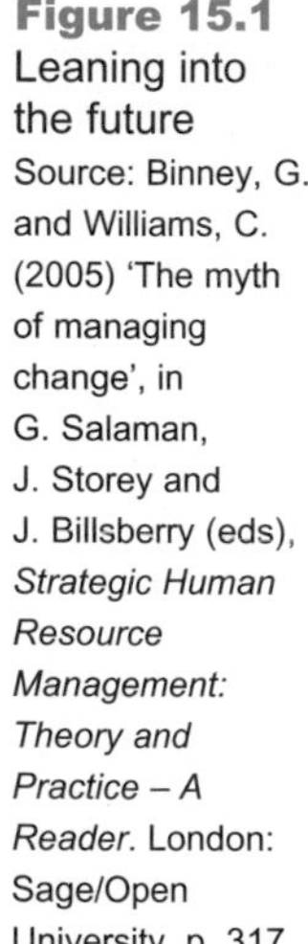
Figure 15.1 Leaning into the future
Source: Binney, G. and Williams, C. (2005) 'The myth of managing change', in G. Salaman, J. Storey and J. Billsberry (eds), *Strategic Human Resource Management: Theory and Practice – A Reader*. London: Sage/Open University, p. 317.

WINDOW ON PRACTICE

Leadership and change

Hope (2006) explains how Lady Marie Stubbs turned round an inner London school after its previous Head, Philip Lawrence, was murdered. Stubbs set out to make the children feel valued, first by physically transforming the building and second by welcoming them back to the school individually. Another way she approached this was to break down the division between teachers and pupils. For example, instead of locking the pupils out and the staff in at break times, she opened the school and created an atrium that students could use, with staff presence, and played music that the pupils would relate to. In the same vein she secured the part-time use of games pitches at Harrow Public School. She consulted the pupils on changes and gave them responsibility, such as handling reception for school visitors, focused on their aspirations and believed in them.

Edwards (2006) explains how Greg Dyke led the BBC. While having a vision for the corporation Dyke constantly asked staff how he could improve, and really listened to their views. He worked on the basis that he wanted to demonstrate to staff that he cared about them, as people work better if they are valued than if they are afraid. He was not afraid to be himself, and to admit mistakes and say sorry where this was appropriate. He made an effort to look at things from the point of view of the staff, and considered their interests – persuading them that the changes were in their best interests rather than just telling them what to do. He made a great effort to be accessible to staff and when he left thousands of staff across the country staged protests.

Sources: Hope, K. (2006) 'Lessons Learnt', *People Management*, Vol. 12, No. 6, 23 March, pp. 30–1.
Edwards, C. (2006) 'On being Gregarious', *People Management*, Vol. 12, No. 8, 20 April, pp. 32–4.

ACTIVITY 15.5

Identify the similarities and differences in the approaches of Stubbs and Dyke.

How would you describe their approach to leadership and their approach to change?

ORGANISATIONAL DEVELOPMENT AS A SPECIFIC APPROACH TO CHANGE

Organisational development (OD) is a specific approach to change, also based on the concept of the organisation as a living system, which we have discussed above. However, it is not only this systemic approach which distinguishes OD but more importantly its legacy of humanistic values (*see*, for example, Garrow *et al.* 2009). These humanistic values, derived primarily from the work of Carl Rogers (1961), underpin the work of an OD specialist. Humanistic values comprise:

- a respect for and the valuing of individuality
- a belief that people are basically 'good' and do the best they can in the circumstances in which they find themselves
- a belief that every individual is a set of potentials that can be realised
- a belief that individuals have the capacity to strive for growth, dignity and self-determination in being all that they can (akin to achieving Maslow's self-actualisation)

There is also some resonance here with McGregor's theory 'y' of motivation which has a similar positive view of workers wanting to do their best, being trustworthy, reliable and responsible, and that as long as managers treat them in this way, then this is what they are able to be. From an OD point of view individuals need to be given the environment and opportunity in the workplace which facilitates their striving to be themselves and realise their potential. Allied with humanistic values OD work aims to make the organisation a better workplace for the benefit of both employees and the wider public that the organisation serves.

Alongside this respect for humanity, and with equal weight, OD specialists also focus on the efficient and effective running of the organisation. Such effectiveness is often expressed in terms of the alignment of the organisation with its environment so that it is responsive to it and interacts effectively with it. It is not surprising therefore that much current OD work is expressed strategically, as the organisation needs to review its mission and values and implement strategic interventions so that it is successful in a constantly changing world. Such interventions may include, for example, organisational learning; knowledge management and organisational design (*see* Yaeger and Sorensen 2006 for a fuller list). In Chapter 16 we focus on knowledge management and organisational learning.

Internal alignment is also considered key so that all parts of the organisation interact effectively together. This may involve teambuilding and working on interpersonal and inter-group conflict. OD employs a systemic approach where work on any part of the organisation (such as a particular department) is never isolated but encompasses the impact of this on the rest of the organisation and its relationship with the environment.

WINDOW ON PRACTICE

School parking system

A high school asked parents not to park in the road near the front of the school when picking up their children. The school explained that this was causing hold-ups in the road for residents and other passing traffic and was a danger. The willing group of parents realised the next best place to wait was near the side entrance to the school which led into the next-door leisure centre car park. They therefore waited in the leisure centre car park, resulting in serious car park chaos for users of the leisure centre who found it difficult to get either in or out of the car park, causing them to be late for leisure centre sessions they had booked. The school's best efforts at reducing chaos in one area resulted in the unanticipated consequence of chaos developing in another area! The school had neglected to consider the whole car parking system and just looked at one aspect of it in isolation.

ACTIVITY 15.6

1. If you work, or have worked, in an organisation, think of two or three organisational changes and identify both the intended and unintended impacts of these on different parts of the organisational system.
2. Alternatively think of two or three changes in school, university, sports teams, family or other membership groups to which you belong. Identify both the intended and unintended consequences of this on different parts of the whole system.

A key part of the OD approach is that in order to solve organisational problems and improve the organisation data need to be collected which enable members of the organisation to understand the nature of the problem or current state and upon which solutions may be built. Given OD's humanistic approach it is unsurprising that members of the organisation collect this information for and from themselves with the guidance of the OD specialist. This is the first step of the whole OD process which moves from data collection to diagnosis to action to evaluation, very much as in action research.

Finally OD specialists emphasise a processual approach where the focus of investigation and diagnosis is on the process of what is happening rather than on the content. For example in a meeting we could summarise the content of what is discussed and agreed but from a processual approach we would be more interested in how the meeting was controlled, how different members contributed, how decisions were made and so on.

OD work is based on a broad base of behavioural science knowledge including social science, psychology and therapeutic psychology, and uses an eclectic mix of tools and techniques, for example CIPD (2009b: 4) refers to it as a 'scavenger discipline'. OD practice is contextual (Garrow *et al.* 2009), meaning that how it is carried out depends very much on the context, so it is difficult to paint a clear picture of what is as it is played out in many different ways in different organisations.

Definitions of OD are many and varied and depend on the perspective of the author, but we suggest the following one identifying what OD work aims to achieve:

> a pragmatic improvement of organisational capabilities – enhancing intra-organisational efficiency and performance, including those capabilities relating to individual health and psychological well-being at work. (King and Anderson 2002)

So OD has twin foci: a humanistic approach to enabling people to become all that they can within the organisation and a business imperative to help the organisation become effective and successful in its environment. The aim is sometimes expressed as achieving the best fit between organisational and individual goals. This is no mean task!

THE EVOLUTION AND FUTURE OF OD

OD has been used in organisations for over 50 years, and just like HRM it has evolved. It reached some level of popularity in and around the 1960s and early 1970s but this tailed off and it is only recently that OD has regained a high profile, perhaps because of a stronger business focus. Interestingly Marshak and Grant (2008) make some helpful comparisons between classical earlier OD and newer approaches since the 1980s onwards. They characterise classical OD as having a positivist perspective, assuming that there is one objective reality, that the one truth can be uncovered using rational processes, that collecting data and using objective problem solving leads to change which can be planned and managed with the emphasis on changing behaviour. In contrast to this, newer approaches are based on a post-modernist perspective, where truth emerges and there are many socially constructed realities (in that we all perceive our world differently – *see* Chapter 18 on Learning and Development). In these approaches creating new mindsets, possibly through negotiation, can lead to change which is continuous.

The contrast between these two approaches is very much in line with the traditional planned view of change and the alternative approach, characterised by Binney and Williams's (2005) learning approach to change. Some of the newer approaches to OD include Appreciative Inquiry (AI), which put simply includes the use of conversation to highlight, reinforce and encourage the spread of the positive aspects of what people currently do, rather than focusing on the negative ones. An excellent text on this growing approach is Lewis *et al.* (2008).

A key challenge for OD going into the future is whether the more traditional humanistic values of OD are still relevant or whether more weight should be given to pragmatic business considerations (Marshak and Grant 2008). For example David Stephenson, Group Head of OD at Royal Mail, explained that the recession enabled OD specialists to engage with changes that would not have been possible otherwise, but he warned that both HR and OD professionals may be pressured by short-term demands to 'collude and command' (*People Management* 2009: 11) and that both sets of specialists are facing a challenge in 'keeping true to their values' (*People Management* 2009: 11).

OD is not a discipline but a field of practice and hence does not have an organisational home (*see*, for example, Garrow *et al.* 2009) when OD specialists are employed in-house. Indeed it does not have a professional and regulatory body unless the OD specialist is a member of the British Psychological Society (BPS: OD division). There have been moves of late to combine OD more closely with HRM and the latest set of ten professional standards from the CIPD, operational from 2010, have a whole standard devoted to OD. Job advertisements increasingly combine an HR and OD job, for example in the *People Management* 2009 editions the following were found: 'Assistant Director of Human Resources and Organisational Development', 'HR/OD Business Partner' and 'Head of Human Resources and Organisational Development'. Indeed OD has been termed a 'strategic **HR tool**' (*HR Magazine* 2007). Similar combinations with learning and development functions were also found, for example 'Learning and Organisational Development Manager'and 'Assistant Director: Workforce and organizational development' where perhaps a greater fit is to be found.

One of the challenges with this potential coupling is that it is advised that an OD specialist should not remain in an organisation for more than five years in order to maintain sufficient distance from an organisation and the ability to challenge in that organisation. HR is derived from different roots, for example human capital theory, behaviourism and performance engineering (*see*, for example, Dunn 2006) and this in itself may form a pressure to dilute the humanistic values characteristic of OD.

SUMMARY PROPOSITIONS

15.1 Change is constantly increasing and leaders use the planned change model in an attempt to manage change, but it has limitations

15.2 It may be possible to design organisations to be more responsive to change

15.3 It is important to take the employee experience into account and consider all four forms of response: behavioural; emotional; cognitive; physical

15.4 Communication and involvement are important aspects of successful change management as are basic aspects of HRM such as sufficient staffing and appropriate reward

15.5 An alternative approach to change is based on reconceptualising the organisation as a human living system rather than a machine

15.6 OD is a specific approach to change and the key characteristics of OD are that it is based on humanistic values, aiming to get the best fit between both individual and organisational goals, and has a systemic and processual approach

15.7 OD has received more attention of late and recent trends in OD encompass social constructivist principles and Appreciative Inquiry (AI). OD is increasingly paired with HRM.

GENERAL DISCUSSION TOPICS

1 'Change has to be planned and dictated from the top otherwise the organisation would be out of control.' Discuss reasons for agreeing or disagreeing with this statement.

2 'Organisation Development loses its unique contribution to the organisation if its humanistic values base is diluted; and this unique contribution is too important to lose.' Discuss reasons for agreeing or disagreeing with this statement.

FURTHER READING

Paton, S. and Boddy, D. (2007) 'Stuck in the middle: a case study investigating the gap between top-down and bottom-up change', *Journal of General Management*, Vol. 32, No. 4, pp. 39–51.

This is a very revealing and fascinating ethnographic case study exploring the differing roles of those at the top and those at the bottom of the organisation in implementing the complexity of change. In this case corporate top management set the direction for change and encouraged individual businesses to implement this in a way appropriate to their situation. Real change did take place on the shop floor in one business unit but these changes were marginalised by local senior management and there appeared to be a disconnect between them and corporate top management.

Self, D. and Schrader, M. (2009) 'Enhancing the success of organizational change: matching readiness strategies with sources of resistance', *Leadership and Organization Development Journal*, Vol. 30, No. 2, pp. 167–82.
Coming from the planned change perspective this article summarises the resistance to change and the readiness to change literatures leading to recommendations for reducing resistance by specific readiness to change strategies.

REFERENCES

Beckhard, R. (1992) 'A model for the executive management of organizational change', in G. Salaman (ed.), *Human Resource Strategies*. London: Sage.

Beer, M. and Nohria, N. (2000) 'Cracking the code of change', *Harvard Business Review*, Vol. 78, May–June, pp. 133–41.

Binney, G. and Williams, C. (2005) 'The myth of managing change', in G. Salaman, J. Storey and J. Billsberry (eds), *Strategic Human Resource Management: Theory and practice. A reader*. London: Sage.

Boselie, P., Dietz, G. and Boon, C. (2005) 'Commonalities and contradictions in HRM and performance research', *Human Resource Management Journal*, Vol. 15, No. 3, pp. 67–73.

CIPD (2009a) *The Impact of Mergers and Acquisitions*. London: CIPD.

CIPD (2009b) *Organisation Development Factsheet*. London: CIPD.

Conway, E. and Monks, K. (2008) 'HR practices and commitment to change: an employee-level analysis', *Human Resource Management Journal*, Vol. 18, No. 1, pp. 72–89.

Cutcher, L. (2009) 'Resisting change from within and without the organisation', *Journal of Organisational Change Management*, Vol. 22, No. 3, pp. 275–89.

Edwards, C. (2006) 'On being gregarious', *People Management*, Vol. 12, No. 8, pp. 32–4.

Eriksson, C. (2004) 'The effects of change programmes on employee emotions', *Personnel Review*, Vol. 33, No. 1, pp. 110–26.

Garrow, V., Varney, S. and Lloyd, C. (2009) *Fish or Bird? Perspectives on organisational development*. Brighton: Institute of Employment Studies.

Goffee, R. and Jones, G. (2006) 'The Lizard Kings', *People Management*, Vol. 12, No. 2, pp. 32–4.

Greenhalgh, L. (2001) 'Managers face up to the new era', *Mastering Management*, Series 23. London: Financial Times.

Hayes, J. (2007) *The Theory and Practice of Change Management*, 2nd edn. Basingstoke: Palgrave Macmillan.

Hope, K. (2006) 'Lessons learnt', *People Management*, Vol. 12, No. 6, pp. 30–1.

HR Magazine (2007) 'Organization development: A strategic HR tool', *HR Magazine*, Vol. 52, No. 9, pp. 1–9.

Iverson, R. (1996) 'Employee acceptance of organisational change: the role of organisational commitment', *International Journal of Human Resource Management*, Vol. 14, No. 1, pp. 122–49.

Jones, L., Watson, B., Gardener, J. and Gallois, C. (2004) 'Organisational communication: where do we think we are going?', *Journal of Communication*, Vol. 54, No. 4, pp. 722–50.

Kanter, R.M. (1983) *The Change Masters*. New York: Simon and Schuster.

King, N. and Anderson, N. (2002) *Managing Innovation and Change: A critical guide for organizations*. London: Thompson.

Kubler-Ross, E. (1997) *On Death and Dying*. Washington DC: Touchstone.

Lawler, E. and Worley, C. (2009) 'The rebirth of change', *People Management*, Vol. 15, No. 3, pp. 28–30.

Lewis, S., Passmore, J. and Cantore, S. (2008) *Appreciative Inquiry for Change Management: Using AI to facilitate organisational development*. London: Kogan Page.

Marshak, R. and Grant, D. (2008) 'Organisational discourse and new organisational development practices', *British Journal of Management*, Vol. 19, pp. S7–17.

Morgan, G. (2006) *Images of Organisation*. Thousand Oaks: Sage Publications.

Oreg, S. (2006) 'Personality, context and resistance to organisational change', *European Journal of Work and Organizational Psychology*, Vol. 15, No. 1, pp. 73–101.

Ortenblad, A. (2001) 'On differences between organisational learning and learning organisation', *The Learning Organisation*, Vol. 8, No. 3, pp. 125–33.

People Management (2009) 'Recession benefits ODs who stay true to their values', *People Management*, 8 October, p. 11.

Phillips, L. (2008) 'Programme for change', *People Management*, Vol. 14, No. 9, pp. 18–23.

Robinson, S. and Morrison, E. (2000) 'The development of psychological contract breach and violations: a longitudinal study', *Journal of Organizational Behaviour*, Vol. 21, August, pp. 525–46.

Rogers, C. (1961) *On Becoming a Person: A therapist's view of psychotherapy*. London: Constable.

Senge, P. (1990) *The Fifth Discipline: The art and practice of the learning organisation*. London: Century Business, Random House.

Sloman, M. (1999) 'Seize the day', *People Management*, Vol. 5, No. 10, p. 31.

Soltani, E., Lai, P. and Mahmoudi, V. (2007) 'Managing change initiatives: Fantasy or reality? The case of public sector organisations', *Total Quality Management*, Vol. 18, No. 1–2, pp. 153–79.

Syedain, H. (2009) 'A smooth landing', *People Management*, 29 March, pp. 18–22.

Walton, J. (1999) *Strategic Human Resource Development*. Harlow: Financial Times/Prentice Hall.

Worrall, L. and Cooper, C. (2006) 'Short changed', *People Management*, Vol. 12, No. 13, pp. 36–8.

Yaeger, T. and Sorensen, P. (2006) 'Strategic organization development: Past to present', *Organization Development Journal*, Vol. 24, No. 4, pp. 10–17.

KNOWLEDGE MANAGEMENT AND ORGANISATIONAL LEARNING

THE OBJECTIVES OF THIS CHAPTER ARE TO:

1 Explain the importance, concept and practice of knowledge management

2 Explore the potential problems of knowledge management

3 Identify roles in knowledge management and the potential impact on HRM

4 Explore the concepts of organisational learning and learning organisations

5 Examine some models of learning organisations and learning capabilities

6 Explore the difficulties of learning organisations and organisational learning

Towards the end of the previous chapter we identified two strategic approaches to organisational improvement where the OD specialist may make a valuable contribution: knowledge management and organisational learning/learning organisations, and we look at these in more detail in this chapter. Both areas reflect the resource-based view of the firm and have been identified as key to competitive advantage and sustainable organisational performance (*see*, for example, Miller 2010).

These two areas are sometimes focused on separately and each has individual journals: *The Learning Organization* and *Journal of Knowledge Management*. However, some of the same researchers investigate both areas, others link the two areas explicitly together (*see*, for example, Easterby-Smith and Lyles 2005), and conferences and research span both areas. Knowledge management and learning organisations have much in common and Jain and Mutula (2008) have likened the learning organisation to a knowledge-intensive organisation. Similarities include the importance of teamwork, communities of practice, a learning/sharing climate and the important base of trust, and similar dilemmas are addressed, such as how to embed individual knowledge and learning into organisational systems and processes. Conceptualising how they fit together is a challenge and the learning organisation has been identified as a central element of achieving knowledge management (Lundvall and Nielson 2007) or a perspective on knowledge management (Scarbrough and Carter 2000).

It could be said that knowledge management is portrayed as a more practical 'down to earth' area of management while the learning organisation is portrayed as idealistic, visionary and an aspiration. In this chapter we look at each separately while accepting there are significant overlaps.

KNOWLEDGE MANAGEMENT

Knowledge and its perceived value

Knowledge is increasingly viewed as a critical organisational resource which provides competitive advantage and Ajit Kambil (2009: 66), Global Director of Deloitte Research, says that knowledge management is strategically important as:

> In a knowledge economy it would seem that knowledge is the most important asset for competitive advantage.

As the speed of change gets faster organisations increasingly need innovations, new ideas and new ways of doing things to keep ahead of the competition, and they constantly need to know what their competitors and customers are doing. Increasing organisational knowledge is seen to underpin this. In addition knowledge-based organisations, such as consultancies and finance companies, are growing, and the growth of knowledge work and the increasing number of knowledge workers has been well reported. Examples of knowledge workers are research and development staff, legal, IT, accounting and other professionals. But, although knowledge workers remain a minority of the workers in the UK, it would be a mistake to see knowledge as relevant only to such a narrow range of staff, and we take the view in this chapter that knowledge is important for everyone in the organisation.

There are many different perspectives in the literature on what constitutes knowledge, and for an academic debate about the nature of knowledge *see* Tsoukas and Vladimirou (2001). At a simple level we can say that data are raw facts, that analysis and contextualisation of raw data so that they become something meaningful produce information, and that knowledge is more than information in that it has been reflected on and processed to the extent that it can be applied and is with the person who needs to apply it. Explicit knowledge, sometimes referred to as operational knowledge, or the 'know what' type of knowledge, can be codified and stored for others to access. Examples here might be competitors' price changes, new competitor products, customer buying patterns and changes in employment legislation.

However, most knowledge is more complex than this, it is something which resides in a person's head and we are often unaware of what we know until we come to use it. This is usually referred to as tacit knowledge, or the 'know how' type of knowledge. This is made up of our accumulated experiences about how things are done, how problems can be solved, what works, what doesn't and in what contexts and under what conditions. An example of this might be a firefighter who during a fire would be able to work out when a backdraught would be likely to occur and could then make sure the immediate area is clear of people. Working this out involves a series of decision processes about the current conditions of the fire and comparing this with previous experiences when backdraughts have occurred. This is usually done intuitively. For anyone else to use this knowledge it needs to be made explicit, which is recognised by many as difficult, and by some as unachievable. Knowledge management initiatives may cover either or both types of knowledge.

WINDOW ON PRACTICE

We have just cited changing employment legislation as an example of explicit knowledge which could easily be written down and shared. But an experienced lawyer would bring deeper and more detailed tacit knowledge to enhance this. For example, from past experiences and case law he or she may have some feel for the way new regulations will be interpreted, or the stance that different judges may take on such regulations.

Knowledge in itself is not enough as it has to be accessed, applied appropriately and used to enhance the organisation's ability to achieve its objectives. Thus for knowledge to be of value it needs to be turned into action. Given this, it is not surprising that attention has been focused on how to generate knowledge, how to share knowledge and how to reuse it – in other words knowledge management.

ACTIVITY 16.1

Think of an activity in which you are skilled, where you will have a high level of tacit knowledge. You could even think of riding a bike or crossing a busy road.

Try to write down all the comparisons and decisions that you make when applying your knowledge to the task in hand.

Managing knowledge

Knowledge management has been variously defined and the term is ambiguous. In this chapter we define knowledge management as a range of strategies, tools and techniques focusing on the generation, communication, integration and exploitation of knowledge.

Our understanding of what knowledge is will have implications for the way we try to manage it. Early approaches to knowledge management focused on IT systems as a means of codifying an individual's knowledge, storing it and making it available to others in the organisation. This somewhat simplistic approach was based on the concept that knowledge is an abstract objective truth which can be easily recorded and manipulated, separately from the person who created the knowledge. The resultant activity led to a proliferation of organisational databases, search programmes, Yellow Pages type directories, intranets and extranets. An example of an extranet is provided by Hunter *et al.* (2002) in the context of a legal firm which offered professional knowledge in this format to valued clients as part of the service that they paid for. While this may be useful for the explicit knowledge referred to above, and is the focus of much research work in the area, this type of use of the technology has very limited value.

The alternative perspective is that knowledge is personal and socially constructed. In other words, knowledge is an ongoing interpretation of the external world, as suggested by Blackler (2000: 61):

> knowledge to be . . . pragmatic, partial, tentative and always open to revision – it is no more, and no less, than a collective interpretation.

This perspective suggests that codifying knowledge and using IT systems to store and share it is inadequate. Instead attention needs to be focused on 'communities of interest' or 'communities of practice' – in other words the way in which individuals with a common interest network to share knowledge and spark off new ideas. A second focus is on the way that knowledge becomes embedded into systems, processes and culture within the organisation. This perspective requires that individuals need to be willing to share their knowledge and, since knowledge is power, there can be no assumptions that individuals will comply. To this end encouraging and perhaps facilitating various types of networking would be more appropriate. For this to work there needs to be an organisational culture in which people are able to trust their colleagues, as sharing knowledge may involve admitting to failures and what has been learned from them and giving bad news. A culture of mutual trust and confidence is not easy to establish and maintain, often taking a long time to become reliable. Project write-ups and reports may also be used in trying to make tacit knowledge explicit, especially when individuals holding the knowledge may leave the organisation. An example of this is a Department Head in a university who was aware that a valued member of staff teaching a very specialist area was about to retire and instigated a project to document that person's teaching content and methods so that this particular knowledge would not be lost to the university.

WINDOW ON PRACTICE

Knowledge sharing across organisational boundaries

Dana and his colleagues (2005) investigated knowledge management practices in high-technology knowledge-intensive companies in the Silicon Valley (USA), Singapore, The Netherlands and Israel. To do this they used the Knowledge Practices Survey Instrument (KPSI) and found no statistical differences between the four regions, suggesting that such firms have similar approaches.

Key current practices were found to be:

- a propensity for experimentation
- collective sharing of knowledge
- collective decision making

The four areas where practice falls to a greater extent behind perceived importance are:

- flow of knowledge within the organisation
- openness and trust
- learning processes
- tacit knowledge transfer

In follow-up interviews employees saw a discrepancy between what top management was promoting and actual practice.

Source: Summarised from Dana, L., Korot, L. and Tovstiga, G. (2005) 'A cross-national comparison of knowledge management practices', *International Journal of Manpower*, Vol. 26, No. 1, pp. 10–22.

The advent of Web 2.0 has enabled technology to be used in a social and sociable way, combining IT and communities of interest, and such technologies have been identified as a panacea for the challenges associated with the management of knowledge (Razmerita *et al.* 2009). Web 1.0 focused on one-way data generation and publication, while Web 2.0 is interactive and democratic, enabling everyone to contribute who wishes as in social/professional networking sites such as Facebook and LinkedIn. Other forms of social networking include blogs, social bookmarks, online collaboration/discussion forums and wiki formats. These technologies are open and allow the externalisation of individual knowledge which is either self initiated (such as a blog or a wiki) or responsive to questions from others (such as LinkedIn Answers). By such means individual knowledge is shared and collaboratively built upon. You will find an article in the Further reading section below which gives more details of Web 2.0.

WINDOW ON PRACTICE

Using Web 2.0 for knowledge management

The law firm Allen & Overy

Allen & Overy was attracted to using technology for knowledge development and sharing and decided to develop social business networking across its practice and have a number of networking communities. One is the 'HR exchange' for its 80 HR staff based in London and worldwide. Instead of passing on information via group or individual emails HR staff are now encouraged to share information and experience using social networking technology. The site contains information on HR procedures and standard letter templates, but in addition there are discussion spaces where all HR staff can contribute on current projects and which encourage advice and knowledge sharing on HR practices.

Another site is for all staff, worldwide, who are parents and so far there are 250 members. Some content is generated by the firm such as information on the availability of relevant training programmes (e.g. a seminar on parenting), and regular news feeds of items that busy parents might otherwise miss. However, much is contributed by members of the site, such as suggestions for school holiday activities and recommended websites for buying school clothes. In addition there are discussion forums and a monthly 'Ask the expert' series.

The biomedical and pharmaceutical company Pfizer

Pfizer has developed 'Pfizerpedia' which is similar to Wikipedia and is open to all employees. The company says it is fast becoming a key resource for research and development staff seeking knowledge relevant to their jobs, and enables employees to share and access knowledge more quickly than before. Pfizer suggests that this is helping to break down 'silo protectionism' and avoids bureaucratic approval processes.

Source: Sloman, M. and Martin, G. (2008) 'Social climbers', *People Management*, Vol. 14, No. 23, 13 November, pp. 32–4.

Nonaka and Takeuchi (1995) model the ways that organisational knowledge can be created: via socialisation (sharing tacit knowledge); externalisation (making tacit knowledge explicit); combination (transforming explicit knowledge into further explicit knowledge) and internalisation (turning explicit knowledge into tacit knowledge). Some practical examples are given in Table 16.1, but bear in mind that some activities will develop knowledge in more than one way.

Table 16.1

Socialisation	Brainstorming, informal meetings, conversations, coaching, mentoring, interacting with customers, on-the-job training, observation, secondments, job rotation, social networking
Externalisation	Databases, exchange of best practices, building models, after-action and project reviews, master classes, wikis, collaboration and co-creation tools, organisational development activities, videos and podcasts
Combination	Conferences, publications and electronic libraries
Internalisation	Feedback from customers, facilitation of activities, and development counselling and coaching

Source: Developed and adapted from: Kermally, S. (2002) *Effective Knowledge Management*. Chichester: John Wiley.

WINDOW ON PRACTICE

Advantages of wikis

On the basis of case study research Grace (2009) identifies a range of benefits of using wikis which are sites where any individual can update the knowledge base, as with Wikipedia:

- a bottom-up informal approach
- time saving (e.g. collaboration without travelling)
- ease of use (similar to everyday tools they use)
- a central repository for information (helps information sharing and gaps can be easily identified)
- users attribute their contributions and changes can be tracked thus avoiding ill-intentioned editing/misinformation
- attribution may improve engagement as users may feel that their reputation is enhanced by their contributions
- allows collaboration between organisations
- solves information overload by emails (publication of a draft on wiki makes it clear which is the up-to-date draft with the facility to identify who has accessed it and what they have done to it)
- building a trusting culture (users choose to collaborate and the process is informal giving a voice to employees and encouraging ownership of what is produced)

Source: Grace, T. (2009) *Journal of Knowledge Management*, Vol. 13, No. 4, pp. 64–74.

Factors identified as encouraging knowledge management are an organisation which engenders trust and openness; a knowledge-centric culture; defined roles and responsibilities in knowledge management; supportive organisational structures such as team, cross-functional and network structures; support through the performance management system (such as targets about sharing knowledge and team/organisational rewards); leadership which supports, promotes and acts as role models for knowledge management; building on informal practices which already exist; and the use of OD practices to support knowledge management.

WINDOW ON PRACTICE

Knowledge management and the older worker

One key knowledge management challenge is the retention of older workers and facilitating the transfer of knowledge from such employees before they retire, as once such knowledge is lost it can never be fully recovered. This in particular applies to the public sector where job tenure tends to be longer, resulting in a greater knowledge loss at retirement. In addition to general methods of encouraging knowledge sharing the following could be used to focus on older workers:

- Draw up a demographic profile of the workforce, focusing on age and length of service, identifying those employees likely to retire within the next five years.
- Identify those employees whose retirement represents a significant knowledge loss and consider their potential successors and how knowledge can be transferred to these.
- Consider using policies of flexible working to allow a better work/life balance and phased retirement to encourage older workers to remain longer with the organisation.
- Consider structuring jobs around older workers in the years before retirement to increase motivation and encourage knowledge sharing, for example emphasising coaching and mentoring roles and highlighting these as vital for the organistion.
- Use a coaching style of management with older workers to encourage their continued self-development and continue to support appropriate career growth increasing motivation and commitment.
- Reinforce the value of older employees, focusing on respect and appreciation, ensuring that they are not seen as superfluous when they have passed their knowledge on.
- Ensure that older staff are incorporated into multi-generational teams and reward cross-generational knowledge transfer.

Sources: Adapted from a number of sources but in particular Calo, T. (2008) 'Talent management in an era of the aging workforce: The critical role of knowledge transfer', *Public Personnel Management*, Vol. 37, No. 4, Winter, pp. 403–16; and Slagter, F. (2007) 'Knowledge management among the older workforce', *Journal of Knowledge Management*, Vol. 11, No. 4, pp. 82–96.

ACTIVITY 16.2

Interview three or four people about practices in their organisation for retaining and sharing the knowledge of older workers. If you are employed use your own organisation also.

- What practices does the organisation explicitly recommend, if any?
- What practices do older workers actually experience?
- How do older workers feel about the knowledge they have acquired over their period of employment?
- To what extent is knowledge lost when older workers retire?

It has been suggested that organisations need to make all their knowledge management activities explicit in order to justify the investment made and demonstrate the organisation's commitment to knowledge. Strategies for making knowledge management explicit are the subject of Case 16.1 at this book's companion website, **www.pearsoned.co.uk/torrington**.

Roles in knowledge management

Evans (2003) notes that there is still much confusion about the responsibility for and accountabilities in knowledge management, and Lank (2002) suggests three organisational roles intended to promote knowledge management. The first are the **knowledge architects** who have strategic roles that focus on which knowledge is critical, how it can be shared and how collaborative working is rewarded. Second are the **knowledge facilitators** such as librarians, writers of customer case studies, information service providers, web masters and learning facilitators of post-event reviews, all of whom aid the flow of knowledge. And third are the **knowledge aware**. This term refers to all employees, who have a responsibility to share their own expertise and knowledge, participate in post-event reviews and are prepared to collaborate. Recent thinking focuses more on the knowledge-aware group and Wain (2009) suggests that as employees are in control of how they contribute their knowledge it might be more useful to stop trying to 'manage' knowledge, but instead focus on 'liberating' it. In order that knowledge is shared rapidly Kambil (2009: 68) suggests that traditional knowledge management needs to be obliterated and:

> everyone should be empowered and offered the tools to easily collaborate and own the creation, classification, dissemination, management and monetization of knowledge within and outside their companies.

Line managers also have a role to play and MacNeil (2003) identifies the line manager's contribution as creating a positive learning climate, encouraging open exchange, reinforcing that making mistakes is acceptable and that it is helpful to share errors. She does, however, note that there are questions about the extent to which line managers have the skills to facilitate knowledge management.

With this broader understanding of knowledge as outlined above, it is clear that knowledge management is inevitably bound up with human resource management in overcoming barriers and in proactively supporting knowledge management. HR professionals may, for example, utilise facilitation skills in supporting knowledge management, or they may align human resource activities with knowledge management needs.

Knowledge management and human resource management

MacNeil (2003) goes on to suggest that there has been a lack of research on the links between HRM and knowledge management, yet Lengnick-Hall and Lengnick-Hall (2003: 90) suggest that knowledge facilitator is a key HR role in:

> developing the motivation, competencies, value orientation, and knowledge of the firm's strategic intent to use knowledge to enhance organisational capabilities.

In more detail they recommend that HR managers need to design organisational structures and processes that promote knowledge diffusion, contribute to designing user-friendly systems for contributing to and accessing knowledge and training people in their use, develop a knowledge-centric culture, provide mechanisms for people to share knowledge – for example allowing teams to work together for long enough to develop knowledge together and then move people around the organisation to cross-fertilise.

Scarbrough and Carter (2000) asked their sample of researchers in the knowledge management area what implications their work had for HRM, and found that the biggest impacts were seen to be on culture change and training and development but smaller impacts on recruitment and selection and rewards and appraisal. The impact on HRM will to some extent be determined by the strategic approach of the organisation to knowledge management. Two broad strategies have been identified, one focusing on exploiting/sharing knowledge and the other on explorative/creating knowledge/innovation. Alternative labels are 'codification of knowledge' versus 'personalisation'. Edvardsson (2008) provides examples showing how each approach impacts on recruitment/selection, training and development, performance management and reward and recognition. For example explorative companies emphasise graduate intakes and provide mentoring and work with an experienced practitioner in order to encourage the development of analytical and creative skills to be applied to business problems. Exploitative companies, on the other hand, are more likely to recruit undergraduates and train them in groups to be implementers of existing knowledge.

At a more conceptual strategic level Scarbrough and Carter identify five different perspectives in the work on knowledge management and draw out the implications that each has for HRM:

- **Best practice perspective.** Encouraging employees to share knowledge and cooperate with knowledge management initiatives. If commitment is required in order that individuals are prepared to share their knowledge and remain with the organisation then 'best practice' HRM will be important to generate that commitment. (*See* Chapter 3 for a reminder of this approach.)

- **Knowledge work perspective.** Managing knowledge work and knowledge workers. Such workers may have distinctive needs in terms of motivation, job challenge, autonomy, careers and so on. HR policies will need to address these. For further depth on this issue *see* Beaumont and Hunter (2002).
- **Congruence perspective.** Increasing performance by aligning HRM and knowledge management practices. For a reminder of this *see* the fit model of HR strategy in Chapter 3.
- **Human and social capital perspective.** This involves the development of human and social resources in the organisation. This both underpins the success of knowledge management initiatives and mobilises longer-term capabilities. This perspective is based on the resource-based view of the firm that we explored in Chapter 3.
- **Learning perspective.** This perspective incorporates two different approaches. First is the notion of communities of learning, discussed above, which draws attention to the way tacit knowledge is developed and shared in practitioner groups. Second, there is organisational learning which focuses on how learning can be embedded in organisational routines and processes to improve organisational performance.

It is on this last perspective that we will now focus after reviewing the difficulties with knowledge management.

Potential problems with knowledge management

The barriers to knowledge management have been variously identified as the culture of the organisation, the risk of admitting to failure, lack of incentive to change, resistance to ideas and learning from other contexts, internal competition and individual reward practices. McCall and colleagues (2008) found problems with dependence on knowledge management systems compared with reference to traditional reference manuals and this work is listed below in the Further reading section. Some specific examples of the problems with knowledge management are detailed in the Window on practice below.

WINDOW ON PRACTICE

The dark side of successful knowledge management initiatives

Chua (2009) investigated four different organisations and found some successful outcomes from knowledge management practices, but in each he also found a dark side:

- **The competency trap**: Being overconfident about initial successes in knowledge management and discounting new experiences on this basis and therefore becoming unable to cope with a changing context. One organisation, H-bank, used a knowledge management pilot study which worked well but applied this unthinkingly to other sites where the context was different. They first used a word and text search tool for use within a call centre as a pilot project which worked very well, but when they used this in other departments it was not helpful as concept search was of more value.

- **Diminished problem solving ability:** InfoSys found that there was little use of their central digital repository of knowledge, and to motivate employees to use it they implemented a reward system. Thereafter postings surged on the new system and searches took much longer because of information overload. In E-Telco a knowledge based system for engineers resulted in a few engineers contributing their knowledge while the majority depended on this source to help solve their problems. In the long run while engineers became more adept at searching for solutions their problem solving ability was diminished.
- **Dogmatism and social alienation:** At M-College the community of practice mutated from a healthy knowledge producing group into one that monopolised the creation and transfer of knowledge. The group created an impermeable boundary between it and other staff members and the leadership of the group became entrenched, with an inner circle protecting their roles of influence and giving new members little opportunity to contribute ideas. The group only engaged with the rest of the college in a limited way.
- **Opportunistic behaviours and ethically questionable practices:** In S-Welfare knowledge management was measured by targets and became a numbers game limiting the development of other initiatives. Measurement in this case was not neutral and became the end game rather than the means of increasing knowledge.

Source: Chua, A. (2009) 'The dark side of successful knowledge management initiatives', *Journal of Knowledge Management*, Vol. 13, No. 4, pp. 32–40.

ORGANISATIONAL LEARNING AND LEARNING ORGANISATIONS

The interest in organisational learning and learning organisations has been stimulated by the need to be competitive, as learning is considered to be the only way of obtaining and keeping a competitive edge and getting ahead of the competition. While the concept of organisational learning has a long history, the concept of the learning organisation dates back in the literature to the late 1980s. It was conceived partly as a reaction to sluggish bureaucratic organisations not fulfilling their potential and frustrating the development efforts of individuals (Pedler *et al*. 1989). Proponents suggested a variety of models and definitions of a learning organisation (*see* for example, Senge 1990; Garvin 1993; Garratt 1990) and Pedler *et al*. (1989) defined the learning organisation, which they identified as a 'dream' rather than a description of current practice, as:

> an organisation which facilitates the learning of all its members and continually transforms itself.

The models were normative in that they prescribed what should be done and all are based on the idea that by

> implementing systems, processes and mechanisms designed to promote learning, organisations will become more effective, anticipating and pre-empting the competitive environment. (Shipton 2006: 239)

The study of *organisational learning* is based on the detached observation of individual and collective learning processes in the organisation. The approach is critical and academic, and the focus is the nature and processes of learning unlike the learning organisation literature, much of which comes from the research consultants and organisations that are involved in the process. In other words the data come from an action learning perspective and are produced by interested parties, giving, inevitably, a positive spin to what is produced. This is not to say that the learning organisation perspective is devoid of theory. The study of learning organisations often focuses on organisational learning mechanisms, and these can be seen as a way of making the concept of organisational learning more concrete, and thus linking the two perspectives by identifying organisational learning structures, mechanisms and procedures that allow organisations to learn. The terms are often used loosely and while the emphasis has moved away from *becoming* a learning organisation, the models developed remain useful in terms of the ideas they express.

Organisational and individual learning

Although some pragmatic definitions of learning organisations centre on more and more individual learning, learning support and self-development, organisational learning is more than just the sum of individual learning in the organisation. It is only when an individual's learning has an impact on and interrelates with others that organisation members learn together and gradually begin to change the way things are done.

WINDOW ON PRACTICE

The difference between individual and organisational learning

Brian learns from the last research project team he ran that it would be much more effective if a member of the marketing department were fully involved at an early stage. Therefore he includes a marketing specialist from the outset on the next project team and finds that this reduces the time needed for the project team and results in less hassle towards the end of the project. Brian and the organisation have gained from this learning, but if only Brian learns this lesson the learning will be lost when he leaves the organisation. If, however, Brian discusses the idea with colleagues, or if there is heated debate at the beginning of the project team due to resistance to marketing specialists being included, and/or if there is some appraisal at the end of the project, there is some chance that others may learn from being involved in this experience. Others may feel that marketing specialists should be involved from the outset, may request that this happens, may apply it to other teams, and the new practice may become the way that the organisation operates. In this second scenario, if Brian leaves the organisation, he may take his learning with him, but the organisation also retains the learning as it has become embedded in the way that the organisation operates.

In this way mutual behaviour change is achieved which increases the collective competence, rather than just individual competence. Argyris and Schön (1978) see such learning as a change in the 'theory in use' (that is, the understanding, whether conscious or unconscious, that determines what we actually *do*) rather than merely a change in the 'espoused' theory (what we *say* we do). In other words the often unspoken rules of the organisation have changed. The question of how individual learning feeds into organisational learning and transformation, and how this is greater than the sum of individual learning, is only beginning to be addressed. Viewing the organisation as a process rather than an entity may offer some help here. Another perspective is that of viewing the organisation as a living organism, which we discussed in the previous chapter, and which is the subject of Case 16.2 on this book's companion website, **www.pearsoned.co.uk/torrington**.

Argyris and Schön (1978) describe different levels, or loops, of organisational learning, which others have developed. These levels are:

- **Level 1: Single loop learning.** Learning about *how* we can do better, thus improving what we are currently doing. This is seen as learning at the operational level, or at the level of rules.
- **Level 2: Double loop learning.** A more fundamental level, which is concerned with '*why*' questions in relation to what we are doing rather than with doing the same things better, that is, questioning whether we should be *doing different things*. This level is described as developing knowledge and understanding due to insights, and can result in strategic changes and renewal.
- **Level 3: Triple loop learning.** This level of learning is the hardest of all to achieve as it is focused on the purpose or principles of the organisation, challenging whether these are appropriate, and is sometimes described as learning at the level of will or being.

All these levels of organisational learning are connected, as shown in Figure 16.1.

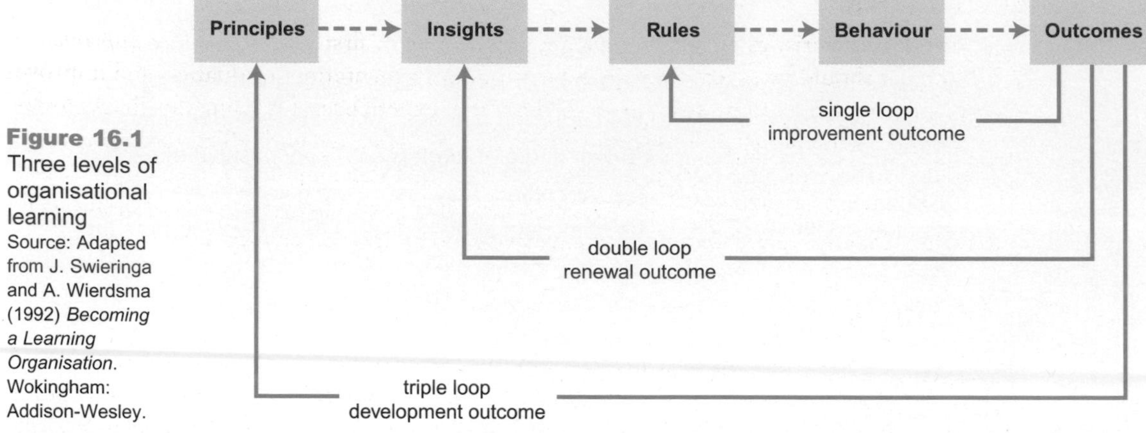

Figure 16.1 Three levels of organisational learning
Source: Adapted from J. Swieringa and A. Wierdsma (1992) *Becoming a Learning Organisation*. Wokingham: Addison-Wesley.

WINDOW ON PRACTICE

Organisational learning in multinational companies (MNCs)

In a survey of the MNCs in Ireland, McDonnell and his colleagues found that over half had an organisational learning policy with almost 90 per cent claiming this to be a global policy. The mechanisms used to facilitate organisational learning internationally varied and the most widely used are listed below:

informal international networks (76%)

international project groups (69%)

expatriate assignments (59%)

international formal secondments (50%)

secondments to external organisations internationally (22%)

The researchers found that many organisations used several mechanisms aimed at developing learning between operations and over 60 per cent used more than three methods.

Source: McDonnell, A., Gunnigle, P. and Lavelle, J. (2008) 'Research Topic: Organisational Learning', *People Management*, Vol. 14, No. 22, 30 October, p. 44.

What are the characteristics of learning organisations?

There are many different approaches to describing the characteristics of a learning organisation, and we shall briefly consider two of these and then look at a model of organisational learning capability based on learning organisational characteristics.

Pedler *et al.*'s model of the learning company

This model (Pedler *et al.* 1989) identifies 11 characteristics of a learning company grouped into five themes:

1. Strategy

Two characteristics within this theme are suggested, first that a *learning approach to strategy* should be taken. Strategy formation, implementation, evaluation and improvement are deliberately structured as learning experiences by using feedback loops. Second, *participative policy making* infers that this is shared with all in the organisation, and even further, that suppliers, customers and the total community have some involvement. The aim of the policy is to 'delight customers', and the differences of opinion and values that are revealed in the participative process are seen as productive tensions.

2. Looking in

Four characteristics are suggested within this theme – the first being *informating* which involves using technology to empower and inform employees, and to ensure information is made widely available. They note that such information should be used to provide understanding about what is going on in the company, and so stimulate learning, rather than being used to reward, punish or control. Second, there is *formative accounting and control* which involves designing accounting, budgeting and reporting systems to assist learning. Third, there is *internal exchange* which involves all internal units seeing themselves as customers and suppliers of each other. Fourth, they identify *reward flexibility*, which implies that the question of why some receive more money than others is a debate to be brought out into the open. They recommend that alternatives are discussed and tried out, but recognise that this is the most difficult of the 11 characteristics to put into practice.

3. Structures

Enabling structures suggest that roles are loosely structured in line with the needs of internal customers and suppliers, and in a way that allows for personal growth and experimentation. Internal boundaries can be flexible. For example, project groups and transient structures help to break down barriers between units, provide mechanisms for spreading new ideas and encourage the idea of change.

4. Looking out

Boundary workers as environmental scanners implies that part of the role of all workers in contact with suppliers, customers and neighbours of the organisation should be to participate in data collection. A second feature in this theme is *inter-company learning*, which entails joining with customers, suppliers and possibly competitors in training experiences, research and development and job exchanges. They also suggest that benchmarking can be used to learn from other companies.

5. Learning opportunities

First, a *learning climate* is important, that is, one that encourages experimentation and learning from experience, questioning current ideas, attitudes and actions and trying out new ideas. Mistakes are allowed because not all new ideas will work. There is a focus on continuous improvement, and the involvement of customers, suppliers and neighbours in experimentation is suggested. A learning climate suggests that feedback from others is continually requested, is made available and is acted upon. Second, *self-development opportunities for all* requires resources and facilities for self-development for employees at all levels in the organisation, and coaching, mentoring, peer support, counselling, feedback and so on must be available to support individuals in their learning.

ACTIVITY 16.3

How do the 11 dimensions identified by Pedler *et al.* (1989) compare to what happens in your organisation, or any organisation with which you are familiar?

Apart from 'reward flexibility', which of the 11 would be the most difficult for your organisation to pursue? What are the barriers, and how might they be overcome?

Senge's Fifth Discipline

Peter Senge (1990) takes a slightly different perspective. In his book about the art and practice of a learning organisation he identified five vital dimensions in building organisations which can learn, and he refers to these as disciplines.

1 **Systems thinking.** This is an understanding of the interrelatedness between things, seeing the whole rather than just a part and concentrating on processes. In terms of organisational actions it suggests that connections need to be constantly made and that there must be consideration of the implications that every action has elsewhere in the organisation.
2 **Personal mastery.** This underlines the need for continuous development and individual self-development.
3 **Mental models.** This is about the need to expose the 'theories in use' in the organisation. These can block change and the adoption of new ideas, and can only be confronted, challenged and changed if they are brought to the surface rather than remaining unconscious.
4 **Shared visions.** This is expressing the need for a common purpose or vision which can inspire members of the organisation and break down barriers and mistrust. Senge argues that such a vision plus an accurate view of the present state results in a creative tension which is helpful for learning and change.
5 **Team learning.** Teams are seen as important in that they are microcosms of the organisation, and the place where different views and perspectives come together, which Senge sees as a productive process.

Senge acknowledges that he presents a very positive vision of what organisations can do, and recognises that without the appropriate leadership this will not happen. He goes on to identify three critical leadership roles: designer, teacher and steward. As designer the leader needs to engage employees at all levels in designing the vision, core purpose and values of the organisation: design processes for strategic thinking and effective learning processes. As teacher the leader needs to help all organisation members gain more insight into the organisational reality, to coach, guide and facilitate, and help others bring their theories into use. As steward the leader needs to demonstrate a sense of

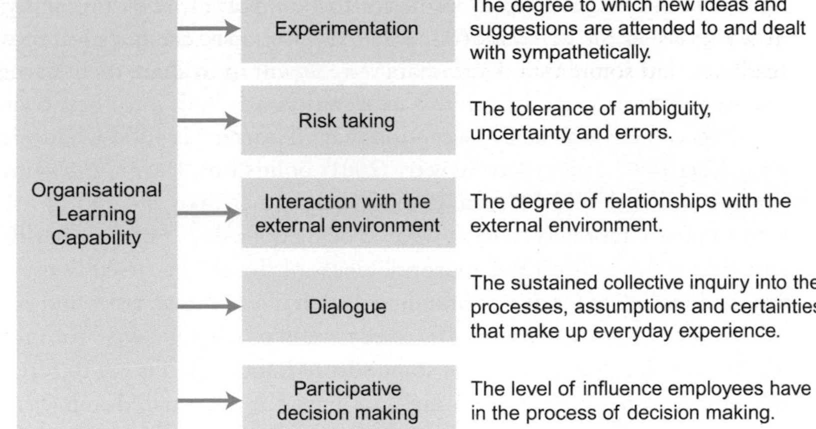

Figure 16.2 A model of organisational learning capability
Source: Chivas *et al.* (2007: 227).

personal commitment to the organisation's mission and take responsibility for the impact of leadership on others.

Chiva *et al.* model of organisational learning capability

While these models are ideals they do offer sound principles for the encouragement of organisational learning, and Chiva and colleagues (2007) have produced a useful model of organisational learning capability, as shown in Figure 16.2. The model was produced on the basis that prescriptive learning organisation models incorporate the factors facilitating organisational learning, and that a measurement instrument could be devised to assess the organisational learning capability of the workforce, rather than trying to assess the holistic nature of the organisation. This approach to the concept of the learning organisation is more practical and realistic.

Critique

The concept of the learning organisation was initially promoted with evangelistic fervour and little critique. As Marshall and Smith (2009) point out, the problems with collective learning have been glossed over as the learning organisation prescription is 'based on an idealization of real organizational life' (p. 16). These early ideals are now recognised as naive and problems have also focused on confusion over the concept and a lack of tangible practices to implement. The politics of the organisation are neglected, as is the desire of some to hold on to knowledge as it represents power. There has also been a lack of attention to emotion, ethics and human irrationality. Harris (2002), for example, demonstrates how the potential for learning in her retail bank case studies was constrained by the overwhelming desire to maintain continuity in the organisation. Other qualitative work concentrating on employee perceptions has found that some employees exclude themselves from being part of a learning organisation, apparently feeling no need to develop further (Dymock and McCarthy 2006).

In particular, Senge (1990) and others have high expectations of the leaders of organisations. To what extent are these expectations realistic, and how might they be achieved? The literature of learning organisations has a clear unitarist perspective – the question of whether employees desire to be involved in or united by a vision of the organisation needs to be addressed. Harris also raised the question of willing participation when she found that contractors were unwilling to share their learning when leaving the organisation, even though this expectation was built into their contracts.

Further, there is a basic assumption that all learning is good whatever is being learned (Hawkins 1994) and yet as Stewart (2001) points out, learning is neither objective nor neutral and it should be seen as the means rather than the end in itself. For example learning to be more efficient at what is being done does not necessarily make one more effective; it depends on the appropriateness of the activity itself. Tosey (2008) points to the shadow side of learning reminding us that it is perilous, risky and emotional; and has subversive potential. He warns us to be careful of what we wish for in treating the quest for the learning organisation as some sort of holy grail. Trying to force the characteristics of a learning organisation may not have the anticipated impact as we are dealing with a political and value-laden organisational system where there may be unexpected consequences of our actions as we demonstrated in the school car parking example in Chapter 15.

This takes us back to the idea of the organisation as a living system and on this basis Ng (2009) argues that people can be seen as self-organising in developing their learning processes to get things done, suggesting that there is limited value in forcing people to come together in, say, dialogue groups if they are uninterested. In the same vein Tosey (2008) suggests that learning comes from a changed context rather than attempts to impose the characteristics of a learning organisation to change behaviour. He suggests that as learning is a response to changing contexts then the 'learning organisation' could be seen as moments when new patterns emerge, and hence is transient and evolutionary.

WINDOW ON PRACTICE

Intention and impact of measures to improve organisational learning

Caemmerer and Wilson (2008) report their research into a UK-based economic development agency with a head office and branches, where national customer feedback mechanisms were introduced to enhance organisational learning. The researchers interviewed middle managers, who explained that the information provided by this national process was less helpful than local customer feedback gained at branch level. The problem with the national feedback was that middle managers were not involved in its design, found it distant, irrelevant and superficial and that it resulted in additional internal bureaucracy to gather and analyse additional data. They interpreted the national feedback system as 'imposed by senior management to track organisational objectives . . . providing little knowledge about how service operations can be improved at branch level'.

Source: Caemmerer, B. and Wilson, A. (2008) 'Customer feedback mechanisms and organisational learning in service operations', *International Journal of Operations and Production Management*, Vol. 30, No. 3, pp. 288–311.

It is not surprising therefore that there is a lack of evidence linking learning organisation strategies with financial performance (*see*, for example, Sonsino 2002).

WINDOW ON PRACTICE

Is organisational learning capability related to performance outcomes?

Increasing investigation of this relationship has only produced contradictory findings. For example Bhatnagar and Sharma (2005), in an Indian context, found organisational learning capability to be related to the firm's profit, but not its turnover, and Bhatnagar (2006) in a different study found that the relationship was with financial turnover rather than profit. Prieto and Revilla (2006), in a Spanish context, found organisational learning capability to be related to measures of non-financial performance (including measures of job satisfaction) and not directly related to financial performance, although non-financial performance was related to financial performance. In the USA Kiedrowski (2006) carried out a study with a control group and found that although an organisational learning intervention over five years showed a positive relationship with improved job satisfaction in one large department of a bank, the control departments (with no intervention) showed similar improvements in job satisfaction.

Part of the difficulty here may be that almost all these studies used different methods of measuring organisational learning capability.

Given the above it is not surprising that Sun and Scott (2003) suggest that attention needs to refocus on organisational learning in order to understand how individual learning can be transformed into collective learning. Popper and Lipshitz (2000) have identified four conditions under which organisational learning is likely to be productive. These are in situations where there is:

1 **Valid information** – that is, complete, undistorted and verifiable information.
2 **Transparency** – where individuals are prepared to hold themselves open to inspection in order to receive valid feedback. This reduces self-deception, and helps to resist pressures to distort information.
3 **Issues orientation rather than a personal orientation** – that is, where information is judged on its merits and relevance to the issue at hand, rather than on the status or attributes of the individual who provides the information.
4 **Accountability** – that is, 'holding oneself responsible for one's own actions and their consequences and for learning from these consequences'.

SUMMARY PROPOSITIONS

16.1 Knowledge management and organisational learning/learning organisations have much in common and are increasingly combined although they have different roots and are presented differently.

16.2 Knowledge management is key to our knowledge economy and the aim of knowledge management is to encourage the generation, integration, sharing and re-use of knowledge. Social networking and wikis are of growing importance as knowledge management tools.

16.3 Problematic aspects include encouraging employees to share knowledge, information overload, overdependence on existing knowledge and the possible reduction in problem-solving ability.

16.4 Organisational learning is greater than the sum of individual learning within the organisation and can be understood on three levels: single loop learning (understanding how we can do better the things we are doing); double loop learning (questioning why we are doing what we are doing and asking 'should we be doing different things?'); and triple loop learning (learning about the principles of the organisation, questioning its purpose).

16.5 Models of the learning organisation propose a structure, processes and systems intended to enhance organisation learning.

16.6 Problematic aspects include the idealistic nature of the learning organisation, the need to take account of politics and context and the unknown impact of implementing changes to improve learning. Fundamentally we cannot assume that all learning is 'good'.

GENERAL DISCUSSION TOPICS

1 'Knowledge management is nothing other than learning organisation strategies presented in a more user-friendly way.' To what extent would you support this statement, and why?

2 'Learning organisations are dreams which can never come true.' Discuss why you agree or disagree with this statement.

3 To what extent will Web 2.0 technology increase the willingness of workers to engage with knowledge management initiatives?

FURTHER READING

Levy, M. (2009) 'Web 2.0 implications on knowledge management', *Journal of Knowledge Management*, Vol. 13, No. 1, pp. 120–34.

A useful summary of the nature of Web 2.0 with examples of social networking facilities. The author connects the features of Web 2.0 with knowledge management and demonstrates how the principles of each match well.

Collinson, C. (2006) 'Avoiding the typical barriers to effective KM', *Knowledge Management Review*, Vol. 4, No. 4, pp. 16–19.
And in the same issue:
Kishore, K., Singh, M. and Sidu, G. (2006) 'Identifying and overcoming barriers to sharing', pp. 6–7.
Both of these articles provide practical examples of what gets in the way of effective knowledge management.

McCall, H., Arnold, V. and Sutton, S. (2008) 'Use of knowledge management systems and the impact on the acquisition of explicit knowledge', *Journal of Information Systems*, Vol. 22, No. 2, pp. 77–101.
An interesting comparison of the impact and use of a knowledge management system and traditional handbooks and manuals.

REFERENCES

Argyris, C. and Schön, D.A. (1978) *Organisational Learning*. Reading: Addison-Wesley.

Argyris, C. and Schön, D.A. (1996) *Organisation Learning II: Theory, method and practice*. Reading: Addison-Wesley.

Beaumont, P. and Hunter, L. (2002) *Managing Knowledge Workers: Research Report*. London: CIPD.

Bhatnagar, J. (2006) 'Measuring organizational learning capability in Indian Managers and establishing firm performance linkage: An empirical analysis', *The Learning Organisation*, Vol. 13, No. 5, pp. 416–33.

Bhatnagar, J. and Sharma, A. (2005) 'The Indian perspective of strategic HR roles and organizational learning capability', *International Journal of Human Resource Management*, Vol. 16, No. 9, pp. 1711–39.

Blackler, F. (2000) 'Collective wisdom', *People Management*, Vol. 6, No. 13, p. 61.

Caemmerer, B. and Wilson, A. (2008) 'Customer feedback mechanisms and organisational learning in service operations', *International Journal of Operations and Production Management*, Vol. 30, No. 3, pp. 288–311.

Calo, T. (2008) 'Talent management in an era of the aging workforce: The critical role of knowledge transfer', *Public Personnel Management*, Vol. 37, No. 4, pp. 403–16.

Chiva, R., Alegre, J. and Lapiedra, R. (2007) 'Measuring organisational learning capability among the workforce', *International Journal of Manpower*, Vol. 28, No. 3/4, pp. 224–42.

Chua, A. (2009) 'The dark side of successful knowledge management initiatives', *Journal of Knowledge Management*, Vol. 13, No. 4, pp. 32–40.

Dana, L., Korot, L. and Tovstiga, G. (2005) 'A cross-national comparison of knowledge management practices', *International Journal of Manpower*, Vol. 26, No. 1, pp. 10–22.

Dymock, D. and McCarthy, C. (2006) 'Towards a learning organization? Employee perceptions', *The Learning Organization*, Vol. 13, No. 5, pp. 525–36.

Easterby-Smith, M. and Lyles, M. (eds) (2005) *The Blackwell Handbook of Organisational Learning and Knowledge Management*. Oxford: Blackwell.

Edvardsson, I. (2008) 'HRM and Knowledge Management', *Employee Relations*, Vol. 30, No. 5, pp. 553–61.

Evans, C. (2003) *Managing for Knowledge: HR's strategic role*. Oxford: Butterworth Heinemann.

Garratt, B. (1990) *Creating a Learning Organisation*. Hemel Hempstead: Director Books.

Garvin, D. (1993) 'Building a learning organisation', *Harvard Business Review*, Vol. 71, No. 4, pp. 78–92.

Grace, T. (2009) 'Wikis as a knowledge management tool', *Journal of Knowledge Management*, Vol. 13, No. 4, pp. 64–74.

Harris, L. (2002) 'The learning organization: myth or reality? Examples from the UK retail banking industry', *The Learning Organisation*, Vol. 9, No. 2, pp. 78–88.

Hawkins, P. (1994) 'Organisational learning: Taking stock and facing the challenge', *Management Learning*, Vol. 25, No. 1, pp. 71–82.

Hunter, L., Beaumont, P. and Lee, M. (2002) 'Knowledge management practice in Scottish law firms', *Human Resource Management Journal*, Vol. 12, No. 2, pp. 4–21.

Jain, P. and Mutula, S. (2008) 'Libraries as learning organisations: implications for knowledge management', *Library Hi Tech News*, No. 8, pp. 10–14.

Kambil, A. (2009) 'Strategy crossroads: obliterate knowledge management – everyone is a knowledge manager', *Journal of Business Strategy*, Vol. 30, No. 6, pp. 66–8.

Kermally, S. (2002) *Effective Knowledge Management*. Chichester: John Wiley.

Kiedrowski, P. (2006) 'Quantitative assessment of a Senge learning organisation intervention', *The Learning Organisation*, Vol. 13, No. 4, pp. 369–83.

Lank, E. (2002) 'Head to head', *People Management*, Vol. 8, No. 4, pp. 46–9.

Lengnick-Hall, M. and Lengnick-Hall, C. (2003) *Human Resource Management in the Knowledge Economy*. San Francisco: Berrett-Koehler Inc.

Lundvall, B. and Nielsen, P. (2007) 'Knowledge management and innovation performance', *International Journal of Manpower*, Vol. 28, No. 3/4, pp. 207–23.

McCall, H., Arnold, V. and Sutton, S. (2008) 'Use of knowledge management systems and the impact on the acquisition of explicit knowledge', *Journal of Information Systems*, Vol. 22, No. 2, pp. 77–101.

McDonnell, A., Gunnigle, P. and Lavelle, J. (2008) 'Research topic: organisational learning', *People Management*, Vol. 14, No. 22, p. 44.

MacNeil, C. (2003) 'Line managers: facilitators of knowledge sharing in teams', *Employee Relations*, Vol. 25, No. 3, pp. 294–307.

Marshall, J. and Smith, S. (2009) 'Learning organisations and organisational learning: what have we learned?', *Management Services*, Autumn, pp. 14–19.

Miller, J. (2010) 'Take a long view', *People Management*, 28 January, pp. 20–2.

Ng, P. (2009) 'Examining the use of new science metaphors in the learning organistaion', *The Learning Organization*, Vol. 16, No. 2, pp. 168–80.

Nonaka, I. and Takeuchi, H. (1995) *The Knowledge-Creating Company: How Japanese companies create the dynamics of innovation*. Oxford: Oxford University Press.

Pedler, M., Boydell, T. and Burgoyne, J. (1989) 'Towards the learning company', *Management Education and Development*, Vol. 20, Pt 1.

Pedler, M., Burgoyne, J. and Boydell, T. (1991) *The Learning Company*. Maidenhead: McGraw-Hill.

Popper, M. and Lipshitz, R. (2000) 'Organisational learning', *Management Learning*, Vol. 31, No. 2, pp. 181–96.

Prieto, I. and Revilla, E. (2006) 'Learning capability and business performance: a non-financial and financial assessement', *The Learning Organisation*, Vol. 13, No. 2, pp. 166–85.

Razmerita, L., Kirchner, K. and Sudzina, F. (2009) 'Personal knowledge management: the role of Web 2.0 tools for managing knowledge at individual and organizational levels', *Online Information Review*, Vol. 33, No. 6, pp. 1021–39.

Scarbrough, H. and Carter, C. (2000) *Investigating Knowledge Management: Research Report*. London: CIPD.

Senge, P. (1990) *The Fifth Discipline: The art and practice of the learning organisation*. London: Century Business, Random House.

Shipton, H. (2006) 'Cohesion or confusion: towards a typology for organisational learning research', *International Journal of Management Review*, Vol. 8, No. 4, pp. 233–52.

Slagter, F. (2007) 'Knowledge management among the older workforce', *Journal of Knowledge Management*, Vol. 11, No. 4, pp. 82–96.

Sloman, M. and Martin, G. (2008) 'Social climbers', *People Management*, Vol. 14, No. 23, pp. 32–4.

Sonsino, S. (2002) 'How convincing is the evidence that learning organizations generate better financial returns?', *People Management*, Vol. 8, No. 12, p. 65.

Stewart, D. (2001) 'Reinterpreting the learning organisation', *The Learning Organisation*, Vol. 8, No. 4, pp. 141–52.

Sun, Y. and Scott, J. (2003) 'Explore the divide: organisational learning and learning organisation', *The Learning Organisation*, Vol. 10, No. 4, pp. 202–15.

Swieringa, J. and Wierdsma, A. (1992) *Becoming a Learning Organisation*. Wokingham: Addison-Wesley.

Tosey, P. (2008) 'Once upon a time . . . Tales of organizational learning', *The Learning Organisation*, Vol. 15, No. 6, pp. 454–62.

Tsoukas, H. and Vladimirou, E. (2001) 'What is organisational knowledge?', *Journal of Management Studies*, Vol. 38, No. 7, pp. 973–93.

Wain, D. (2009) 'Freedom of thought', *People Management*, 26 March, p. 15.

CHAPTER 17

THE CONTEXT OF EMPLOYEE LEARNING AND DEVELOPMENT

THE OBJECTIVES OF THIS CHAPTER ARE TO:

1 Review the national UK picture of skills, training and development

2 Explore the national training framework: outline the recommendations in the Leitch Report 2006 and examine progress to date

3 Outline key national bodies and initiatives designed to support improved training and skills

4 Identify the NVQ framework and explain characteristics of NVQs including their strengths and weaknesses

> A labyrinth, a maze and even a dog's breakfast. All three terms have been used by employers to describe the UK's skills landscape as it stands now, more than two years after Lord Leitch's review identified the reforms and simplifications necessary to secure the nation's economic competitiveness. A recent count identified a bewildering array of more than 3,000 government-funded training support schemes and 2,000 delivery agencies, costing more than £2.5 billion a year. (Phillips 2009a: 21)

Development, training and skills are at the heart of government policy as they impact on business and economic performance, unemployment levels, employability and social inclusion. Yet, at the time of the *Leitch Review* (2006) the UK ranked twentieth out of 30 OECD countries in terms of its intermediate skills base. Successive governments have constantly changed and developed the national framework to encourage skills development and training by employers and reduce the skills gap between what employers need and what employees can offer. The skills gap however remains at large. In spite of the downturn with fewer vacancies and more job-seekers the CIPD (2009a) reported that 81 per cent of respondents to its 2009 Recruitment, Retention and Turnover Survey said they were still experiencing recruitment difficulties, the majority being due to a lack of specialist skills.

WINDOW ON PRACTICE

UK skills gaps

- 'the labour market lacked the skills needed to expand in renewable technologies and as a result the UK could fail to reach its legally binding energy targets' (Matthew Lockwood, senior research fellow at the Institute for Public Policy Research, reported by Phillips 2009c).
- 'projected shortages of security staff for the London 2012 Olympics . . . there would be a shortage unless recruits are prepared now. Staff can work on an event such as the Olympics only if they have the right qualifications and experience' (Churchard 2009).
- A shortage of IT skills has been identified for many years, but between 2004 and 2007 computer science graduates had consistently higher unemployment rates. 'Not all employers of IT professionals are looking for pure technical skills. Around 45 per cent of new IT professionals are recruited from other disciplines. These trends reflect the underlying skills shifts taking place in IT. For example there is a growing demand among employers for business-focused, multi-disciplined technology professionals who understand how to use the technology to meet business goals' (representative of e-skills, the technology sector skills council, reported by Smedley 2009).

Sources: Phillips, L. (2009c) 'UK skills gap casts doubt over future of green jobs', *People Management*, 23 April, p. 8. Churchard, C. (2009) 'Olympic struggle to get staff', *People Management*, 10 September, p. 11. Smedley, T. (2009) 'To a lesser degree', *People Management*, 10 September, pp. 24–9.

While there seems to be general agreement that training and development is a good thing it is difficult to demonstrate a causal link between training and development and organisational and economic performance, partly because such terms are difficult to define precisely, and partly because the payoff from development may not be seen in the short term. However there is a clear employee demand for training and qualifications and unions are beginning to engage in bargaining for development.

A Green Paper produced by the Department for Education and Employment (1998) stated that 'investment in human capital will be the foundation of success in the 21st century'. Nationally the emphasis on qualifications is increasing and Case 17.1 on this book's companion website, **www.pearsoned.co.uk/torrington**, focuses on the development of directors from this perspective.

THE NATIONAL PICTURE AND STRATEGY

Employee development has traditionally been seen as a cost rather than an investment in the UK, although this is certainly changing in some organisations. For over 30 years it has been demonstrated that UK organisations give little support to training and development compared with our European partners. This lack of investment in training and development has been identified as a major factor in Britain's economic performance, and it has been argued that without such investment we will be trapped in a low-wage, low-skills economy (Rainbird 1994; Keep and Mayhew 1999), with the emphasis on competing on price rather than quality. Our national training framework is voluntarist, with the government's role limited to *encouraging* training rather than intervening, as in many other countries.

WINDOW ON PRACTICE

Access to training: an international comparison with the USA

Finegold and his co-researchers (Finegold *et al.* 2005) investigated the access to training of temporary workers. They found that less than 25 per cent of these workers took part in training and that educated and experienced individuals were more likely to be offered training. Lower-skilled individuals were, however, more likely to accept training when offered it. For temporary office staff, formal training was associated with significant wage growth in the following year. However there was no such association for blue-collar workers. On-job skill development was associated with greater wage growth for both office and blue-collar temporary staff.

Source: Finegold, D., Levenson, A. and Van Buren, M. (2005) 'Access to training and its impact on temporary workers', *Human Resource Management Journal*, Vol. 15, No. 2, pp. 66–85.

Alternatively it has been argued that it is not a lack of investment in training that is the problem but the way such investment is distributed: who it is spent on and the content of the training. Training spend is unevenly distributed and people at the lower end of the hierarchy miss out on training. For example Westwood (2001: 19) reports that:

Access to workforce development is unequal with managers and professionals or those with a degree up to five times more likely to receive work based training than people with no qualification and/or unskilled jobs.

Hoque (2008) labels this very aptly as the 'training apartheid' and the WERS survey found that professionals, associated professionals, managers and those with most qualifications receive most training rather than low-skilled workers (Kersley *et al.* 2006). Thomson (2001) explains that broader development is concentrated on those at the beginning of their careers and those in more senior and specialist posts, rather than part-timers and those with fewer qualifications to begin with. In the aerospace and pharmaceuticals businesses, defined as high-skills sectors, Lloyd (2002) found a conflict of interests between employees' desire for training and development and managerial short-term aims, lack of accreditation of skills, structured development focused on key employees, access to training being dependent on individual initiative, senior managers viewing training as a minor issue to be dealt with by lower-level managers and insufficient resources. She suggests that there was under-investment and lack of support for flexibility and employability. Westwood (2001) concludes that while we do not do as much training as in Europe, we do spend a lot of money on training that does not last very long and on the people who may not need it. In terms of training content there is evidence to suggest that much training is related to induction and particularly health and safety, as demonstrated in the WERS survey, and it has been argued that this does nothing to drive the development of a knowledge-based economy (*see*, for example, Westwood 2001). Employees in small organisations are at a disadvantage in terms of access to training and evidence from the WERS survey suggests that the highest levels of training are in the public sector and larger organisations, particularly those employing high levels of professional employees.

ACTIVITY 17.1

1 In your own organisation how is training/development shared out between employees?

2 Is there an explicit rationale for this? And if so what is it?

3 How would you explain the spread of training?

4 If you are not currently in employment choose five consecutive editions of *People Management* and analyse all articles and news items identifying the type of training/development being discussed and those for whom the training is provided.

The solution to this problem may be increasing state intervention, as many view voluntarism as having a limited effect (*see*, for example, Sloman 2001). It is argued that potential intervention would not mean a return to the levy system, where employers were forced to make an annual payment relative to profits which they could recoup by providing evidence that the equivalent money had been spent of training. But, for example, statutory rights for paid study leave and employer tax credits, and funding mechanisms to create a demand-led system, could be introduced.

A demand-led approach is currently receiving much attention, but there are subtle differences in how this is interpreted. The *Leitch Review* (Leitch 2006) provides a useful starting point in differentiating between a supply-led and a demand-led training system. He characterises the supply-driven approach as being based on ineffectively articulated collective employer views of training needed and a central system of provision planned by the government to meet these needs, and predict future needs. He suggests that employers and individuals find it difficult to articulate their needs partly because they are asked to provide input to a profusion of bodies, and because this approach results in too little investment by employers, too little responsibility being taken by individuals for their own training and a qualifications system divorced from the needs of the workplace. In contrast he suggests a demand-led system is about directly responding to demand rather than planning supply. To achieve this suppliers (such as colleges of further education) only receive funding as they attract customers (rather than being given block funding in advance, based on estimated demand), driving them to respond flexibly and immediately to employer demand, thus providing training provision which is more relevant, reflects the needs of customer and is likely to produce higher completion rates and better value for money.

However, there are current problems relating to demand-led and employer-led training in terms of the mismatch between employer needs and training provision. Keep (2006), for example, suggests that colleges offer longer-term accredited courses as these attach Learning and Skills Council (LSC) funding in response to government targets, while employers may be seeking short uncertificated courses. Such a mismatch is addressed in the recommendations of the *Leitch Review*. If demand-led mechanisms are effective, training supply should be much more reactive to the real needs of employers; however, the limitations of this approach are that such a reactive approach focuses on current and short-term needs at the expense of anticipating and preparing for future needs, and does not address the structure of jobs in this country.

There is, however, a subtly different school of thought in relation to the supply/demand debate which suggests the problem lies with the demand side of the equation rather than the supply side. In other words the problem is not with government initiatives and measures to encourage training, development and learning but with the way that skills are used and jobs are constructed, and hence the employer demand for training, development and learning. For example Stevens (2002: 44) is concerned with 'whether the UK can generate enough jobs for people who have learnt and can learn' and Lloyd (2002) suggests that the country cannot solve its problems just by developing skills, as it is critical to change the structure of jobs:

> All this suggests that we still have a situation in which the majority of organizations are using a reactive strategy: training only in response to the immediate short-term demands of the business, rather than being considered a strategic issue. (Ashton 2003: 23)

This implies that training and development needs to be considered at a strategic level in the business, but also, and perhaps more challenging, that employers need to change their business strategies to focus on quality rather than cost.

NATIONAL TRAINING FRAMEWORK

The UK training framework is complex and based on a number of reports and papers, and comprises implementing bodies and a range of specific initiatives. The framework constantly evolves, sometimes dramatically but most often in smaller changes as, for example, individual initiatives or bodies are introduced, changed or abandoned. Harrison (2009) provides a useful table listing many of the reports, bodies and initiatives. We have chosen to discuss just some key government initiatives/bodies, rather than attempting to be comprehensive, highlighting any consequences of the *Leitch Review* 2006 which we discuss first.

The *Leitch Review*

The latest government review of the national training framework was undertaken by Lord Leitch in 2006. The purpose of the review was to identify the UK's optimal skills mix for 2020 to maximise economic growth, productivity and social justice, to set out how responsibilities should be balanced for achieving that skills profile and to consider the policy framework required to support it. He proposed improved mechanisms and structures to encourage the extent and nature of employer training and development in order to narrow the skills gap, achieve a set of 2020 skills targets, and improve British industrial performance.

WINDOW ON PRACTICE

Vision, principles and recommendations of the *Leitch Review*

Vision for 2020

- The vision is for the UK to become a world leader in skills by 2020 with reference to the top quartile of the 31 leading industrial countries that make up the OECD. This will require the almost doubling of skills attainment, and the targets include:
- 95 per cent of adults to achieve basic literacy and numeracy (compared with 85 per cent for literacy and 79 per cent for numeracy in 2005);
- more than 90 per cent of adults to achieve NVQ/NVQ equivalent level 2 (compared with 69 per cent in 2005);
- moving the balance of intermediate skills from level 2 to level 3 (this will mean a further 1.9 million level 3 completions and increase the number of apprentices to 500,000 per year);
- more than 40 per cent of adults to achieve level 4 (compared with 29 per cent in 2005).

Principles

Leitch proposed that delivery of the vision should be underpinned by the following principles:

→

- Shared responsibility for skill development between employers, the individual and the government.
- The focus should be on economically valuable skills which should where possible be portable so as to encourage labour mobility.
- Skills should be demand led, meeting the needs of employers and individuals rather than being centrally planned.
- The framework must adapt and respond to future market needs as they arise.
- Existing structures to be built upon (rather than swept away), and improved through simplification and rationalisation, as continuity is important.

Main recommendations

- Progress is best measured by increased adult skill attainment at all levels, with the government increasing the share of gross domestic product (GDP) allocated to education and skills, together with additional investment by employers and individuals.
- Train to Gain and Individual Learner Accounts should be the route for all public funding for vocational skills by 2010 (the date for this has since been delayed).
- Employer voice to be strengthened, and employers' ability to better articulate skill needs to be improved via a new Commission for Employment and Skills to channel views, as well as rationalising existing bodies.
- A voluntary employer 'pledge' to be launched reflecting a commitment to train all eligible employees to level 2, with a statutory entitlement to be introduced if progress is insufficient by 2010.
- Increase employer involvement in level 3 and 4 qualifications in the workplace, increasing apprenticeships, extending Train to Gain to higher levels, and improving engagement between employers and universities.
- Increase people's aspirations and awareness of skills, via sustained awareness programmes and a new universal adult careers service.
- Create a new integrated employment and skills service, based on existing structures, to include basic skills programmes for the unemployed and a network of employer-led Employment and Skills Boards.

Source: Summarised from Leitch, S. (2006) *The Leitch Review of Skills: Prosperity for all in the global economy – world-class skills.*

Progress since the *Leitch Review* recommendations

The economic downturn has dictated that effort has been redirected from upskilling to reskilling so that those made unemployed can move into other sectors. In addition there is evidence that training is being used as an alternative to redundancy as in Honda (Phillips 2009a). While the Learning and Skills Council (LSC) reported that over 10,000 employers had signed up to the Skills Pledge, as at November 2008 (Phillips 2009b), in the 2009 *Learning and Development Survey* (CIPD 2009b) only 19 per cent of respondents reported having made the pledge.

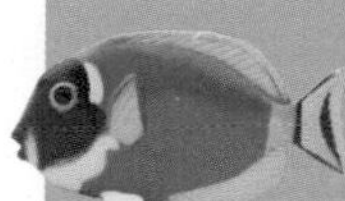

WINDOW ON PRACTICE

The Nissan Skills Pledge

We will develop and expand the contributions of all staff by strongly emphasising training and by the expansion of everyone's capabilities.

This means that it is part of our drive to improve our business that every eligible employee shall be:

- actively encouraged and supported to gain the basic skills they need to help our business succeed;
- actively encouraged and supported to achieve at least their first full level 2 qualification . . . , including skills for life;
- actively encouraged and supported to achieve appropriate higher-level skills.

Source: IDS (2009) 'Training strategies: Nissan', IDS HR Study No. 896, June, pp. 10–15.

Progress on the Leitch recommendations was reviewed in depth by the Innovation, Universities, Science and Skills (IUSS) Committee (now the Science and Technology Committee) in 2009, and they expressed a range of concerns (IUSS 2009). First they questioned whether a demand-led system was appropriate, especially in a downturn, as it assumed that employers could predict which skills they required. They suggested that the targets were too ambitious and that targets based on qualifications only are problematic, suggesting that the focus should be on the skills themselves. The review raises the difficulty that while employers need soft skills and bite-sized chunks of training which can be built upon, qualifications do not generally meet either of these needs. They identified a further problem with the targets in that an individual can only be included in the figures of people meeting the targets if they are achieving a qualification of a higher level than they already have. This excludes many people who may achieve a qualification at the same level that they already have but in another area, for example when moving to a job in another sector. There has been some relaxation of this rule for small and medium-sized enterprises (SMEs) and some sectors, and there is pressure for this relaxation to be applied more generally. A further problem that the IUSS identified with targets is that they are based on OECD comparisons, and this being so may help the UK up the OECD league table but may not reflect what the UK economy needs and so may not have an effect on performance. In addition the targets are national and therefore do not reflect local or sectoral needs.

UK Commission for Education and Skills (UKCES)

This is the new independent strategic skills body set up after Leitch in 2008 and its purpose is outlined on its website:

> The UK Commission aims to raise UK prosperity and opportunity by improving employment and skills. Its ambition is to benefit individuals, employers, government and society by providing independent advice to the highest levels of the UK Government and Devolved Administrations on how improved employment and skills systems can help the UK become a world class leader in productivity, in employment and in having a fair and inclusive society. **www.ukces.org.uk** (2009)

In practice this means that UKCES advises the government on skills policy and monitors progress towards the 2020 targets. The body is charged with simplifying government funded training as it is generally agreed that there are too many brokers and providers. The UKCES remit is to reform structures and make it simpler for employers to get funding. At the time of writing it is running a campaign called 'Now is the time to invest in skills' to encourage employers to invest now in the skills they will need for the upturn, and has devised a website **www.talentplan.org.uk** to enable employers to get access to funding more easily.

Learning and Skills Councils

LSCs are responsible for planning and funding all post-16 education and training, except for the university sector. While there are plans to disband the LSC and to redistribute its work to the Skills Funding Agency and the UKCES, the IUSS Committee (2009) recommends that the LSC remains in operation for now.

Sector Skills Councils (SSCs) and the SSDA

The SSCs have to apply to be licensed by the UKCES before they can operate, and are funded and supported by this body. SSCs are employer-led independent organisations and are designed to build a skills system that is driven by employer demand. Twenty-five have been licensed at the time of writing, covering around 90 per cent of the workforce. SSCs aim to reduce skills gaps and shortages; improve productivity and performance; increase opportunities to develop skills and productivity; and improve the learning supply through National Occupational Standards, apprenticeships, and Further Education (FE) and higher education (HE). The Sector Skills Development Agency (SSDA) is responsible for funding, supporting and monitoring the network of SSCs.

Train to Gain

Train to Gain is accessed through the LSCs, which via a broker, who is part of Business Link, offer advice to employers on their skills needs and match this up with appropriate provision from training providers and the FE sector. The aim is for advice to be flexible and tailored to the business, and that solutions be negotiated in a similar manner between the employer and the provider. Train to Gain is targeted on smaller employers and low-skill sectors of the economy. Brokers are charged with proactively contacting 'hard to reach' employers and to focus on the attainment of level 2 qualifications and basic numeracy and literacy, but also to go beyond this in terms of level.

Some elements of provision under Train to Gain will be state funded, including some wages costs for employers with fewer than 50 staff. Since January 2009 organisations employing 250 people or less have been able to apply for funding for shorter courses in areas critical to their business, and the CBI is keen that this flexibility is available to all employers. The approach is demand led as training providers do not receive any funding until an employee begins training.

By May 2009 127,000 employers had used Train to Gain, and in a recent LSC survey 76 per cent of employers using the scheme reported that their employees gained useful job-related skills; however, in a CBI survey 42 per cent of employers found no impact on job performance (Carrington 2009). In the 2009 Learning and Development Survey (CIPD 2009b) 31 per cent of respondents had used Train to Gain and a further 23 per cent were considering doing so.

National Apprenticeship Service

This new service is taking over apprenticeships as the LSC is abolished in 2010. It is designed to reduce bureaucracy, while providing government funding and a national vacancy matching service. The government is campaigning to encourage employers to increase apprenticeships and 35,000 new apprenticeship places were created in early 2009. However, in the CIPD Skills Survey (CIPD 2009c) only 7 per cent of respondents knew of this new body while 76 per cent felt there were clear business benefits to apprenticeships and 78 per cent supported the government campaign to increase apprenticeships. Case 17.2 on this book's companion website at **www.pearsoned.co.uk/torrington** focuses on apprenticeships.

WINDOW ON PRACTICE

Apprenticeships

Apprentices work for an employer alongside a skilled member of staff while engaging in an appropriate college course for one or two days a week. Apprentices work towards NVQ level 2 and advanced apprentices towards level 3. Schemes vary by sector and employer but can take from one to four years and are partly funded by the government. They are therefore a long-term training commitment and most often used by larger employers, the most well known being BT and British Gas. Apprenticeships appear very popular with young people and Alan Johnson from British Gas reports that only approximately 11 per cent of applications get through the online values test and fewer get as far as the assessment centre.

Sources: Smedley, T. (2008) 'Learning from the past', *People Management*, Vol. 14, No. 15, 24 July, pp. 18–22. Phillips, L. and Churchyard, C. (2009) 'Training grants under the strain as take-up soars', *People Management*, 4 June, p. 7.

Investors in People (IiP)

The IiP standard is developed and promoted by Investors in People UK, a public body representing employers, training organisations and unions. Compared with many government initiatives IiP has had a long-lasting impact since being introduced in 1991, although since then there have been several major revisions. More recent versions are increasingly less prescriptive and have more emphasis on outcomes rather than the process by which the business achieves IiP recognition. In addition they have attempted to simplify the framework and make it more user friendly. There are now three principles: plan, do and review, and there are ten criteria in total set against the three principles in the latest framework applied from January 2006 and developed further in 2009. There are 39 outcome-based evidence requirements in the plan-do-review cycle which are intended to give a full picture of how the business is managing its people and where improvements can be made. The current approach is more flexible, providing more opportunities to build on existing organisational processes; assessment no longer requires huge amounts of paperwork, as assessors now take on the responsibility of collecting mainly verbal evidence by interviewing a range of employees in relation to the standard.

Following the 2009 consultation with customers IiP launched three levels of recognition (bronze, silver and gold) beyond the standard, depending on the number of evidence-based requirements the organisation has met, and a new way of working with the framework, focusing more fully on the needs and priorities of the client in what IiP terms a 'choice based' approach.

While major revisions to the standard have generally been received as improvements the process of moving from an existing to a revised standard may be challenging and problematic for organisations and advisers/assessors alike (*see*, for example, Collins and Smith 2004) and as the standard is constantly evolving research results inevitably relate to previous versions.

A commitment to IiP requires significant time and effort, and the benefits from gaining recognition of IiP status have been debated. Some studies have found an increase in commitment to HR development, a belief in the value of the process and perceived performance gains (*see*, for example, Alberga *et al.* 1997) and are more likely to achieve organisational goals (Bourne 2008). Hoque (2008), reporting on the 2004 WERS survey data, found that training incidence and duration are higher in workplaces with the IiP standard and employees were more likely to agree with the statement 'Managers here encourage people to develop their skills'. However, they found no evidence to suggest greater equality in the distribution of development opportunities and in fact IiP workplaces demonstrated less equality than non-IiP workplaces. In addition they found that those workplaces with the standard were no better than others in respect of 'training apartheid' where the unskilled and those with no academic qualifications are provided with fewer training opportunities.

There is considerable evidence that the standard is sought for its 'stamp of approval' rather than because of a genuine commitment to improving training (Ram 2000); and Down and Smith (1998) also argue convincingly that it is those organisations that have most to gain from pursuing the standard that are least likely to attempt to do this. There is a tendency in the IiP process to focus on formal qualifications, such as NVQs, and for the significance of informal development to be neglected.

ACTIVITY 17.2

Using an IiP accredited organisation with which you, or someone you know, is familiar, consider the following:

1 How did the process of gaining accreditation impact on employees and managers?
2 What type of changes were experienced as a result of IiP accreditation?
3 Analyse the overall benefits and disadvantages of IiP accreditation.

NVQ FRAMEWORK AND COMPETENCES

The NVQ framework

The NVQ framework attempts to simplify UK qualifications by putting in place nine levels of NVQ (0–8) reflecting increased difficulty from zero being basic numeracy and literacy to 8 being high-level specialist skills. An NVQ framework has been put in place for all occupational areas, and an individual may gain the award by completing an NVQ directly and gaining a national qualification. Alternatively all other qualifications can now be expressed as NVQ equivalents so that it is clear for employers and individuals what the value of every qualification is. Even higher education is expressed in terms of the framework with first year degree being level 4 and PhD being 8.

Characteristics and benefits of NVQs

NVQs are described in terms of standards, and are directed at developing the ability of trainees to perform specific tasks directly related to the job they hold or for which they are preparing, expressed in terms of performance outcomes. It is a reaction against the confetti-scattering approach to training and is seen as a good thing in its own right, concerned with the general education of people. The design of the standards themselves was initially somewhat complex, but revisions have tried to simplify this.

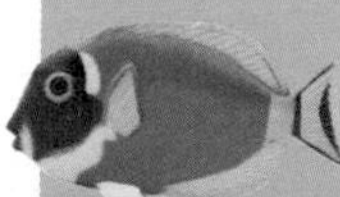

WINDOW ON PRACTICE

Example: Management and Leadership Standards 2008

This new revision of the standards divides them into six key areas:

A Managing self and personal skills (3 units)

B Providing direction (12 units)

C Facilitating change (6 units)

D Working with people (17 units)

E Using resources (17 units)

F Achieving results (19 units)

Different combinations of units are relevant for different awards.

Inside one unit, for example **D7 'Provide Learning Opportunities for Colleagues'**, you will find:

List of relevant skills: for example coaching, mentoring, providing feedback

Outcomes of effective performance: for example 'give colleagues fair and regular feedback on their work performance, discussing and agreeing how they can improve'

Behaviour which underpins effective performance: for example 'You recognise the achievements and success of others'

Knowledge and understanding

General: for example 'How/where to identify and obtain information on different learning activities'

Industry sector specific: for example 'working culture and practices in the industry/sector'

Context specific: for example 'the current knowledge, skills and understanding of colleagues'

The standards to be achieved are determined by designated standards-setting bodies some of which are SSCs, which involve or consult employers, practitioners and professional bodies, so that vocational standards are decided by those in charge of the workplace instead of by those in charge of the classroom. The standards-setting body for the management and leadership standards is the Management Standards Organisation (**www.management-standards.org.uk**).

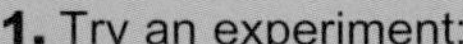

ACTIVITY 17.3

1. Try an experiment:

- On the Internet search and locate the full set of health and social care standards and identify the name of the standards setting body.
- On the Internet search and locate the full set of management and leadership standards from the standards setting body **without** typing in **www.management-standards.org.uk**.

(a) How easy was it to complete these tasks?

(b) What difficulties did you experience with these tasks?

(c) What recommendations would you make for improving access to the standards?

2. Go to **www.management-standards.org.uk** and compile the units relevant to a level 4 NVQ in management and leadership and map this against the 2004 level 4 standards.

(a) How easy was this?

(b) What problems did you encounter?

(c) What recommendations would you make for improving clarity?

There is an emphasis on being able to do rather than to know and the standards are designed so that the vast majority of work can be done 'on the job' with maybe small inputs from educational providers. This introduces greater flexibility into the learning process, so that career aspirants are not restrained by the elitist exclusiveness of either educational institutions or professional associations, and there are no artificial barriers to training, such that it is available only to people who have certain previous qualifications. Flexibility is further supported as candidates can stop and start their work towards the standard as it suits their personal or work needs, and they can complete the elements in any order. This means that standards can be worked on in line with business demands.

The focus on what people can do, rather than on the process and time of learning, means that the qualification is awarded when candidates can demonstrate competence, however long or short a period it takes them to achieve the standard. Flexibility in assessment is partly achieved by the portfolio principle, as candidates accumulate evidence of their competence from their regular, day-to-day working and submit it for assessment to a qualified assessor as appropriate.

The standards have strong support from some quarters, but there have been fewer reports of the benefits of pursuing the standards. Winterton and Winterton (1999) report that organisations adopting the management standards have been able to identify gaps in competence, identify competence development targets, develop a coherent structure for training and development and identify clearer criteria for HR planning and career progression. In our own studies, again in relation to the management standards, it was found that participants developed self-confidence in their managerial role, became better organised and were motivated to focus on improvement and that following the standards was a rite of passage for those who were new to the managerial world.

Case 17.3 on the companion website **www.pearsoned.co.uk/torrington** focuses on vocational qualifications.

Problematic aspects of NVQs

NVQs have had a rough ride since the concept was introduced, coming under some heavy criticism and not being extensively taken up. Revisions of the standards have aimed to address problems, but this has not always been achieved satisfactorily. However, research on the use of the standards inevitably relates to earlier versions, and there is a time lag before the impact of improvements can be investigated. In spite of problems and reservations they have become embedded in the national training framework of the UK.

One of the most common reservations about NVQs is the laborious nature of assessment, with candidates heavily engaged in a 'paper chase' to gather evidence of their competence, and this seemed to take over from the importance of the learning process and what was being learned. It is also very difficult to ensure a satisfactory quality of assessment, where so much depends on a large number of individual assessors.

NVQs have developed an entire vocabulary to bring the concept into action, and this causes difficulties (*see*, for example, Priddley and Williams 2000). The standards have been simplified from their original conception, however the framework remains complex.

Many standards now have both mandatory and optional units at each level so that the qualification itself gives only a partial indication of areas of competence. In relation to the management standards in particular there is a criticism that the standards are reductionist. In other words, because the standards try to spell out the detail of what management entails, the complexity of management gets lost as it is difficult to specify this in the structure and language of the standards.

It has also been argued that following the standards rubber-stamps the level of competence already achieved, rather than stimulating further development.

ACTIVITY 17.4

Interview at least three people who have followed the NVQ standards. They may be employees of your organisation, but this is not essential, so friends and family can be included. Ask your interviewees:

1 What were the most positive aspects of following the standards, and why?

2 What were the problematic aspects of following the standards, and why?

3 How might these negative aspects be overcome?

SUMMARY PROPOSITIONS

17.1 There is currently a voluntarist approach to training and development in the UK, which means that employers make their own choices about the extent to which they train. The government attempts to influence what organisations do by a range of supply-side initiatives.

17.2 The *Leitch Review* 2006 is the latest in a long line of initiatives to improve the UK skills base; there are, however, already concerns about the premises on which it is based.

17.3 The national bodies and schemes to deliver skills in the UK continue to change: at the moment they include UKCES, the LSC, SSCs, Train to Gain, the National Apprenticeship Service and IiP.

17.4 National Vocational Qualifications form a structure to integrate all UK qualifications and in this sense they have become embedded in the UK training framework, in spite of concerns about their design.

GENERAL DISCUSSION TOPICS

1 Both the UK as a whole and organisations themselves would benefit if the government adopted an interventionist approach to training.
- Do you agree or disagree? Why?
- How might this intervention be shaped?

2 'The Leitch targets may be unrealistic, but what is more important to the British economy is that they are aspirational and stretching.' Discuss the case for and against this statement.

FURTHER READING

Harrison, R. (2009) *Learning and Development*. London: CIPD.
Chapter 2, 'The National Framework for workforce development', is an excellent overview of the government's vision for national vocational education and training, and its implementation. The chapter explains the development of the current approach and also addresses emerging concerns.

Smith, A. and Collins, L. (2007) 'How does IIP deliver the lifelong learning agenda to SMEs?', *Education and Training*, Vol. 49, No. 8/9, pp. 720–31.
This paper based on a case study demonstrates the difficulties in matching IiP requirements with the individual requirements of SMEs. Business Link Advisers, acting as consultants to SMEs, find themselves in a difficult position trying to hit government set targets for IiP and delivering a useful consultancy service at the same time which might not lead to IiP recognition.

Wright, P. and Geroy, G. (2001) 'Changing the mindset: the training myth and the need for world-class performance', *International Journal of Human Resource Management*, Vol. 12, No. 4, pp. 586–600.
An interesting article which challenges the link between training and productivity. The article argues that training is used instead of addressing the problems of poor management, job design and physical aspects of the job. The authors argue that training is often not applied, due to cultural barriers and the fact that it is too narrowly focused on current jobs. They suggest that training should be more broadly based on developing capability and that the training function needs to reinvent itself and have a broader-based approach rather than concentrating on skills development.

REFERENCES

Alberga, T., Tyson, S. and Parsons, D. (1997) 'An evaluation of the Investors in People standard', *Human Resource Management Journal*, Vol. 7, No. 2, pp. 47–60.

Ashton, D. (2003) 'Training trends: past, present and future', in A. Booth and D. Snower (eds), *Reflections: New Developments in Training*. London: CIPD.

Bourne, A. (2008) *The Impact of Investors in People Standard on People Management Practices and Firm Performance*. Cranfield: Cranfield University.

Carrington, L. (2009) 'Keep on running', *PM Guide to Surviving the Downturn*, 7 May, pp. 4–7.

Churchyard, C. (2009) 'Olympic struggle to get staff', *People Management*, 10 September, p. 11.

CIPD (2009a) *Recruitment, Retention and Turnover Survey*. London: CIPD.

CIPD (2009b) *Learning and Development Survey*. London: CIPD.

CIPD (2009c) *Skills Survey*. London: CIPD.

Collins, L. and Smith, A. (2004) 'Understanding the new Investors in People standard: lessons from experience', *Personnel Review*, Vol. 33, No. 5, pp. 583–604.

Department for Education and Employment (1998) *The LEARNING Age: a renaissance for a new Britain*, Green Paper, Cm. 3790. London: HMSO.

Department for Education and Employment (2007) *Vocational Qualifications in the UK 2005/06*, Statistical Bulletin No. 05/07. London: HMSO.

Down, S. and Smith, D. (1998) 'It pays to be nice to people: Investors in People – the search for measurable benefits', *Personnel Review*, Vol. 27, No. 2, pp. 143–55.

Finegold, D., Levenson, A. and Van Buren, M. (2005) 'Access to training and its impact on temporary workers', *Human Resource Management Journal*, Vol. 15, No. 2, pp. 66–85.

Grugulis, I. (2003) 'The contribution of National Vocational Qualifications to the growth of skills in the UK', *British Journal of Industrial* Relations, Vol. 41, No. 3, pp. 457–75.

Harrison, R. (2009) *Learning and Development*. London: CIPD.

Hoque, K. (2008) 'The impact of Investors in People on employer-provided training, the equality of training provision and the "training apartheid" phenomenon', *Industrial Relations Journal*, Vol. 39, No. 1, pp. 43–62.

IDS (2009) *Training Strategies: Nissan*, IDS HR Study No. 896, June, pp. 10–15.

Innovation, Universities, Science and Skills Committee (2009) *Re-skilling for recovery: After Leitch, implementing skills and training policies – government response to the First Report from the Committee*, Session 2008–09.

Keep, E. (2006) 'Live and Learn', *People Management*, Vol. 12, No. 15, 27 July, p. 7.

Keep, E. and Mayhew, K. (1999) 'The assessment: knowledge, skills and competitiveness', *Oxford Review of Economic Policy*, Vol. 15, No. 1, pp. 1–15.

Kersley, B., Alpin, C., Forth, J., Bryson, A., Bewley, H., Dix, G. and Oxenbridge, S. (2006) *Inside the Workplace: Findings from the 2004 Workplace Employment Relations Survey*. Abingdon: Routledge.

Leitch S. (2006) *Leitch Review of Skills: Prosperity for all in the global economy – final report*. London: HMSO, December.

Lloyd, C. (2002) 'Training and development deficiencies in "high-skill" sectors', *Human Resource Management Journal*, Vol. 12, No. 2, pp. 64–81.

Phillips, L. (2009a) 'The skills maze', *People Management*, 7 May, pp. 21–4.

Phillips, L. (2009b) 'Support for people out of work rises to top of skills agenda', *People Management*, Vol. 15, No. 3, p. 10.

Phillips, L. (2009c) 'UK skills gap casts doubt over future of green jobs', *People Management*, 23 April, p. 8.

Phillips, L. and Churchyard, C. (2009) 'Training grants under the strain as take-up soars', *People Management*, 4 June, p. 7.

Priddley, L. and Williams, S. (2000) 'Cognitive styles: enhancing the developmental component in National Vocational Qualifications', *Personnel Review*, Vol. 29, Issue 2.

Rainbird, H. (1994) 'Continuing training', in K. Sisson (ed.), *Personnel Management in Britain*. Oxford: Blackwell.

Ram, M. (2000) 'Investors in People in small firms: case study evidence from the businesses services sector', *Personnel Review*, Vol. 29, No. 1.

Sloman, M. (2001) 'Sharing the power of learning', in CIPD (ed.), *The Future of Learning for Work*. London: CIPD.

Smedley, T. (2008) 'Learning from the past', *People Management*, Vol. 14, No. 15, pp. 18–22.

Smedley, T. (2009) 'To a lesser degree', *People Management*, 10 September, pp. 24–9.

Stevens, J. (2002) 'Balancing act', *People Management*, Vol. 8, No. 25, p. 44.

Stewart, J. and Hamblin, B. (1992) 'Competence-based qualifications: the case for established methodologies', *Journal of European Industrial Training*, Vol. 16, No. 10, pp. 91–6.

Thomson, A. (2001) 'Too much apple pie', *People Management*, Vol. 7, No. 9, p. 49.

Westwood, A. (2001) 'Drawing a line: who is going to train our workforce?', in CIPD (ed.), *The Future of Learning for Work*. London: CIPD.

Winterton, J. and Winterton, R. (1999) *Developing Managerial Competence*. London: Routledge.

LEARNING AND DEVELOPMENT

THE OBJECTIVES OF THIS CHAPTER ARE TO:

1 Explore four perspectives on the nature of learning and consider the implications that each has for development provision and support

2 Explain the role of behavioural competencies in learning and development

3 Review some of the practical characteristics of learning and development

4 Explain the various methods of addressing learning and development needs

5 Investigate the nature of evaluation in this context

There has been a considerable shift in the way that individual development is understood and characterised. We have moved from identifying training needs to identifying learning needs, the implication being that development is owned by the learner with the need rather than by the trainer seeking to satisfy that need. This also has implications for who identifies the needs and the way that those needs are met. Current thinking suggests that needs are best developed by a partnership between the individual and the organisation, and that the methods of meeting these needs are not limited only to formal courses, but to a wide range of on-the-job development methods and distance/e-learning approaches. While a partnership approach is considered ideal the phrase 'self-development' is an important one in our development lexicon, indicating the growing emphasis on individuals having ownership of and taking responsibility for their own development. There has also been a shift in the type of skills that are the focus of development activity from an interest in technical skills to the development of personal skills, self-management and attitudes. Lastly, while the focus on development for the current job remains high, there is greater pressure for development which is also future oriented. These shifts reflect the changes that we have already discussed in terms of global competition, fast and continuous change and the need for individuals to develop their employability in an increasingly uncertain world.

THE NATURE OF LEARNING

For the purpose of this text we consider the result of learning to be changed or new behaviour resulting from new or reinterpreted knowledge that has been derived from an external or internal experience. There are broadly four theoretical approaches or perspectives to understanding the nature of learning, and the training and development that organisations carry out reflect the explicit or implicit acceptance of one or more perspectives. We will look at each perspective, in the evolutionary order in which they became important. There is no right or wrong theory – each has strengths and weaknesses.

The **behaviourist** perspective is the earliest which, reflecting the label, concentrates on changes in observable behaviour. Experiments with animals formed the foundation of this theory, for example the work of Skinner, Watson and Pavlov. Researchers sought to associate rewards with certain behaviours in order to increase the display of that behaviour. The relevance of this for organisations today may be seen for example in telesales training where employees are taught to follow a script and calls are listened to, to ensure that the script is followed. Reward or punishment follows depending on behaviour. Trainers are not interested in what is going on in the heads of employees, they merely want them to follow the routine to be learned. This approach has also been used for a range of interpersonal skills training. One American company, for example plays video sequences to trainees portraying the 'correct' way to carry out, say, a return to work interview. Trainees then practise copying what they have seen and are given cue cards to use when carrying out that particular interpersonal event. The problems with the perspective are that it is overtly manipulative, simplistic and limited. It may produce only temporary changes in behaviour and increase cynicism.

Cognitive approaches are based on an information-processing perspective and are more concerned with what goes on in the learner's head. This is a more technical perspective and maps out the stages of learning, such as: expectancy to learn (motivation); attention and perception required; experience is coded (meaning is derived); meaning is stored in long-term memory; meaning is retrieved when needed; learning is applied; feedback is received (which may supply reinforcement). The strengths of this perspective are that it stresses the importance of learner motivation and individual needs, it recognises that the individual has some control over what is learned and it identifies feedback as an important aspect of learning. The weaknesses are that it assumes learning is neutral and unproblematic and it is a purely rational approach that ignores emotion. From this perspective useful development activities would be seen as formal courses offering models and ideas with lots of back-up paperwork. Activities to improve learning motivation are also important, for example helping employees to recognise their own development needs and providing rewards for skills development. Mechanisms for providing feedback to employees are also key.

The third perspective is based on **social learning theory**, in other words learning is a social activity and this is based on our needs as humans to fit in with others. In organisations this happens to some extent naturally as we learn to fit in with things such as dress codes, behaviour in meetings and so on. Fitting in means that we can be accepted as successful in the organisation, but it is not necessary that we internalise and believe in these codes. Organisations often use role models, mentors and peer support, and 'buddies', to intensify our natural will to fit in. The disadvantages of this perspective are that it ignores the role of choice for the individual and it is based, to some extent, on a masquerade.

The **constructivist** perspective is a development of the information-processing perspective, but does not regard learning as a neutral process: it is our perception of our experiences that counts; there is no 'objective' view. This perspective accepts that in our dealings with the world we create 'meaning structures' in our heads and these are based on our past experiences and personality. New information and potential learning need to fit with these meaning structures in some way, which means that a similar new experience will be understood differently by different people. We tend to pay attention to things which fit with our meaning structures and ignore or avoid things that do not fit. As humans we are also capable of constructing and reconstructing our meaning structures without any new experiences. These meaning structures are mainly unconscious and therefore we are not aware of the structures which constrain our learning. We are generally unaware of how valid our meaning sets are, and they are deeply held and difficult to change. Making these structures explicit enables us to challenge them and to start to change them. This perspective recognises that learning is a very personal and potentially threatening process. We develop mechanisms to protect ourselves from this threat, and thus protect ourselves from learning. The implication of this is that learning support needs to encourage introspection and reflection, and providing the perspectives of others (for example as in 360-degree feedback, outdoor courses or relocations) may assist in this process.

PRACTICAL CHARACTERISTICS OF LEARNING AND DEVELOPMENT

Learning from experience

A significant amount of work has been done which helps us understand how managers, and others, learn from their experiences. Kolb *et al.* (1984) argue that it is useful to combine the characteristics of learning, which is usually regarded as passive, with those

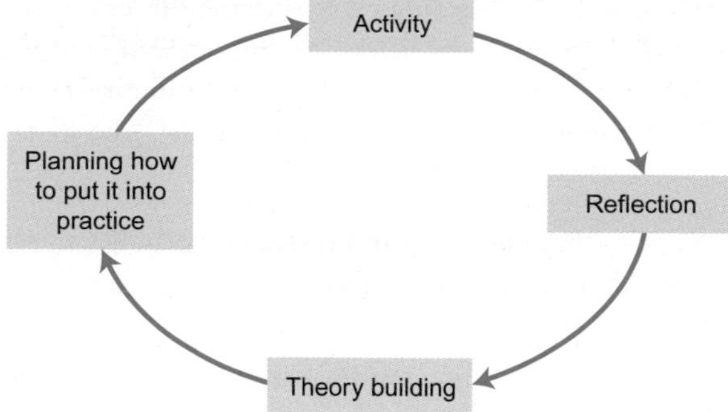

Figure 18.1 The learning cycle

of problem solving, which is usually regarded as active. From this combination Kolb *et al.* developed a four-stage learning cycle, which was further developed by Honey and Mumford (1989).

The four stages, based on the work of both groups of researchers, are shown in Figure 18.1.

WINDOW ON PRACTICE

Gwen is a management trainer in a large organisation running a number of in-house management courses. She has just moved into this position from her role as section leader in the research department; the move was seen as a career development activity in order to strengthen her managerial skills.

Gwen is working with her manager to learn from her experiences. Here is an extract from her learning diary based on the learning cycle:

Activity – I've had a go at running three sessions on my own now, doing the input and handling the questions.

Reflection – I find the input much easier than handling questions. When I'm asked a question and answer it I have the feeling that they're not convinced by my reply and I feel awkward that we seem to finish the session hanging in mid-air. I would like to be able to encourage more open discussion.

Theory building – If I give an answer to a question it closes off debate by the fact that I have 'pronounced' what is 'right'. If I want them to discuss I have to avoid giving my views at first.

Planning practice – When I am asked a question rather than answering it I will say to the group: 'What does anyone think about that?' or 'What do you think?' (to the individual who asked) or 'What are the possibilities here?' I will keep encouraging them to respond to each other and reinforce where necessary, or help them change tack by asking another question.

Each of these four stages of the learning cycle is critical to effective learning, but few people are strong at each stage and it is helpful to understand where our strengths and weaknesses lie. Honey and Mumford designed a questionnaire to achieve this which identified individuals' learning styles as 'activist', 'reflector', 'theorist' and 'pragmatist', and explain that:

- **Activists** learn best from 'having a go', and trying something out without necessarily preparing. They would be enthusiastic about role-play exercises and keen to take risks in the real environment.
- **Reflectors** are much better at listening and observing. They are effective at reflecting on their own and others' experiences and good at analysing what happened and why.
- **Theorists'** strengths are in building a concept or a theory on the basis of their analysis. They are good at integrating different pieces of information, and building models of the way things operate. They may choose to start their learning by reading around a topic.
- **Pragmatists** are keen to use whatever they learn and will always work out how they can apply it in a real situation. They will plan how to put it into practice. They will value information/ideas they are given only if they can see how to relate them to practical tasks they need to do.

Understanding how individuals learn from experience underpins all learning, but is particularly relevant in encouraging self-development activities. Understanding our strengths and weaknesses enables us to choose learning activities which suit our style, and gives us the opportunity to decide to strengthen a particularly weak learning stage of our learning cycle. While Honey and Mumford adopt this dual approach, Kolb firmly maintains that learners *must* become deeply competent at all stages of the cycle. There has been considerable attention to the issue of matching and mismatching styles with development activities and the matching and mismatching of trainer learning style with learner learning style.

ACTIVITY 18.1

1. If you have not already done so obtain the Honey and Mumford questionnaire and work out your learning style(s).
2. Select your weakest style and try to identify two different learning activities which fit with this style, but that you would normally avoid.
3. Seek opportunities for trying out these learning activities. If you practise these activities on a regular basis this should help you strengthen the style you are working on.
4. Log your experiences and in particular what you have learned about these 'new' learning activities.

Table 18.1 Planned and emergent learning

Learner type	Planned learning score	Emergent learning score
Sage	High	High
Warrior	High	Low
Adventurer	Low	High
Sleeper	Low	Low

Source: Adapted from D. Megginson (1994) 'Planned and emergent learning: A framework and a method', *Executive Development*, Vol. 7, No. 6, pp. 29–32.

Planned and emergent learning

From a different, but compatible, perspective, David Megginson characterises learners by the extent to which they plan the direction of their learning and implement this (planned learning), and the extent to which they are able to learn from opportunistic learning experiences (emergent learning). Megginson (1994) suggests that strengths and weaknesses in these two areas will influence the way individuals react to self-development. These two characteristics are not mutually exclusive, and Megginson combines them to identify four learning types, as shown in Table 18.1.

Warriors are those who are strong at planning what they want to learn and how, but are less strong at learning from experiences they had not anticipated. They have a clear focus on what they want to learn and pursue this persistently. On the other hand Adventurers respond to and learn from opportunities that come along unexpectedly, they are curious and flexible. However, they tend not to plan and create opportunities for themselves. Sages are strong on both characteristics, and Sleepers display little of either characteristic at present. To be most effective in self-development activities learners need to make maximum use of both planned and emergent learning. For a further explanation of this model also *see* Megginson and Whitaker (1996/2007).

ACTIVITY 18.2

Consider your development over the past year: do you feel that your strengths are in planning your learning or in learning opportunistically?

Choose your weaker approach, and identify how you could strengthen this.

Identifying learning and training needs

The 'systematic training cycle' was developed to help organisations move away from ad hoc non-evaluated training, and replace it with an orderly sequence of training activities, but this approach has been less prominent of late. Harrison (2009) contests that such a cycle is not necessarily the most appropriate to use as it falls far short of the messy world of practice, and does not focus adequately on learning. In spite of this the cycle does retain some value, and we describe an adaptation of such a model to make it more applicable to today's environment. The model is set within an external environment and

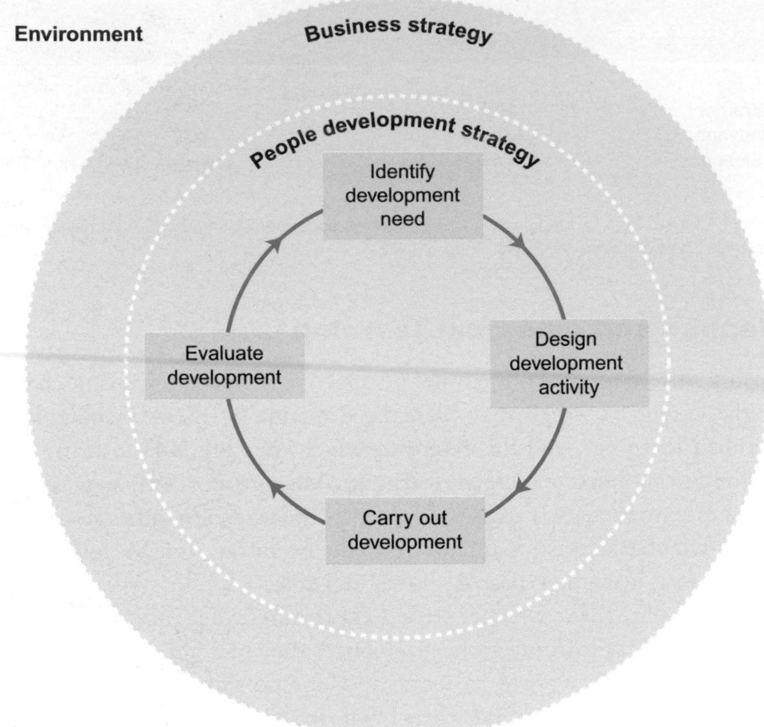

Figure 18.2 A systematic model of learning and training

within an organisation strategy and an HR development strategy. Even if some of these elements are not made explicit, they will exist implicitly. Note that the boundary lines are dotted, not continuous. This indicates that the boundaries are permeable and overlapping. The internal part of the model reflects a systematic approach to learning and to training. Learning needs may be identified by the individual, by the organisation or in partnership, and this applies to each of the following steps in the circle. This dual involvement is probably the biggest change from traditional models where the steps were owned by the organisation, usually the trainers, and the individual was considered to be the subject of the exercise rather than a participant in it, or the owner of it. The model that we offer does not exclude this approach where appropriate, but is intended to be viewed in a more flexible way. The model is shown in Figure 18.2.

There are various approaches to analysing needs, the two most traditional being a problem-centred approach and matching the individual's competency profile with that for the job that person is filling. The problem-centred approach focuses on any performance problems or difficulties, and explores whether these are due to a lack of skills and, if so, which. The profile comparison approach takes a much broader view and is perhaps most useful when an individual, or group of individuals, are new to a job. This latter approach is also useful because strategic priorities change and new skills are required of employees, as the nature of their job changes, even though they are still officially in the same role with the same job title. We discuss competencies in the following section. When a gap has been identified, by whatever method, the development required needs to be phrased in terms of a learning objective, before the next stage of the cycle, planning and designing the development, can be undertaken. For example, when a gap or need has been identified around team leadership, appropriate learning objectives may be that learners, by the end of the development, will be able 'to ask appropriate questions at the outset of a team activity to ascertain relevant skills and experience, and to check understanding of the task' or 'to review a team activity by involving all members in that review'.

ACTIVITY 18.3

Write learning objectives for the following individuals who are experiencing problems in their performance:

1. Tina, who always dominates meetings, and neglects the contribution of others.
2. Brian, who has never carried out a selection interview before, and is very unsure of how to go about this.
3. Mark, who feels he has lots of contributions to make at meetings, but never actually says anything.
4. Sara, who can never get to meetings on time.

The planning and design of learning will be influenced by the learning objectives and also by the HR development strategy, which for example may contain a vision of who should be involved in training and development activities, and the emphasis on approaches such as self-development and e-learning. Once planning and design have been specified the course, or coaching or e-learning activity, can commence, and should be subject to ongoing monitoring and evaluated at an appropriate time in the future to assess how behaviour and performance have changed.

BEHAVIOURAL COMPETENCIES

Characteristics of behavioural competencies

Boyatzis (2008) in a development of his previous work defines a competency as an ability or capability expressed in a range of related behaviours attached to 'intent'. He uses the example of a range of listening and questioning behaviours which may be attached to the underlying intent of genuinely being interested in the other person's views. This competency might be described as 'understanding the other person'. But he does warn us that there may be other intents for such behaviours! Boyatzis maintains his position that a competency is: 'an underlying characteristic of a person which results in effective and/or superior performance in a job' (Boyatzis 1982: 21), and in 2008 identifies three major groups of competencies relating to emotional intelligence; social intelligence; and cognitive intelligence.

Boyatzis originally developed a common competency framework for managers but subsequently tailor-made competency frameworks have come thick and fast from the training and development specialists, and most large companies have produced such a framework. Most frameworks have clusters of competencies, like the Boyatzis model, and to each of the competencies within the cluster a list of behavioural indicators is usually attached. Some frameworks include level definitions encapsulating the simplicity or sophistication of the way that the competency is displayed while others include positive and negative behaviours in relation to a competency, as shown in the following two Windows on practice.

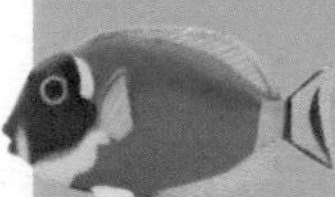

WINDOW ON PRACTICE

An example of behavioural skills with level definitions from Connexions

Working with others

The ability to work constructively within a group/team environment

Level definitions	Examples of actions demonstrated at each level
Stage Three – Contributes to organisational success by defining, planning and implementing strategies for the future and building strategic relationships and alliances – Manages and allocates available resources, including financial, capital and people to best meet current and future requirements (2 of 4)	– Is able to recognise opportunities for organisation-wide networking – Develops and maintains strategic partnerships and alliances – Understands the strategic implications of working within different cultures (3 of 4)
Stage Two – Able to transfer knowledge – Challenges procedures – Develops best practice – Provides leadership to others (4 of 6)	– Builds confidence in others to take further responsibility – Provides constructive feedback to others on performance and impact on others – Maximises networking opportunities (3 of 7)
Stage One – Uses information to improve systems – Regularly acts on own initiative – Takes responsibility for own actions and decisions	– Understands team goals and objectives and works proactively for team success – Shares knowledge, skills and experience openly and honestly – Volunteers to work in projects or sub-committees – Helps others to achieve goals (4 of 10)
Foundation stage – Takes responsibility for own actions and decisions – Understands fundamental principles and applications – Refers to others for guidance – Follows procedures and processes	– Responsive, open and friendly in manner – Considers and relates well to all kinds of people – Personally enthusiastic, positive and approachable – Owns up to responsibility, even if mistakes happen – resilient (4 of 9)

Source: Connexions Cheshire and Warrington, but a national framework.

WINDOW ON PRACTICE

A sample competency from the Police Force

Respect for Race and Diversity – A

Behaviour category

Considers and shows respect for the opinions, circumstances and feelings of colleagues and members of the public, no matter what their race, religion, position, background, circumstances, status or appearance.

Understands other people's views and takes them into account. Is tactful and diplomatic when dealing with people, treating them with dignity and respect at all times. Understands and is sensitive to social, cultural and racial differences.

Positive indicators

- Sees issues from other people's viewpoints
- Is polite and patient when dealing with people, treating them with respect and dignity
- Shows understanding and sensitivity to people's problems, vulnerabilities and needs
- Makes people feel valued by listening to and supporting their needs and interests
- Understands what offends and adapts own actions accordingly
- Respects confidentiality wherever appropriate

(this is a selection from a full list of 13)

Negative indicators

- Does not consider other people's feelings
- Does not encourage people to talk about personal issues
- Makes situations worse with inappropriate remarks, language or behaviour
- Is thoughtless and tactless when dealing with people
- Is dismissive and impatient with people
- Does not respect confidentiality
- Uses humour inappropriately

(this is a selection from a full list of 11)

Source: Police (Cheshire Constabulary). However, these are national competencies.

Case 18.1 on this book's companion website at **www.pearsoned.co.uk/torrington** concentrates on Goleman's emotional intelligence competencies which we discussed in Chapter 13 on leadership.

Advantages of behavioural competencies

Behavioural competencies are often seen as a means of expressing what is valued by the organisation as well as what characteristics have been seen to result in superior performance. In addition they are seen to provide a critical mechanism for the integration of human resource practices which is considered essential to a strategic approach to HR. Thus, once a competency framework has been researched and designed it can be used in recruitment, selection, training, performance management and reward (*see*, for example, IDS 2008). In this way employees are given consistent messages about what is valued and what is expected of them, and as not all competencies are equally developable it gives good direction as to which competencies need to be selected for in new employees. Westminster City Council, for example, has introduced a competency framework (CIPD 2006) which Tony Reynolds, Organisation Development Manager, describes as 'a golden thread running through the people management process' (p. 12); he also says that 'they are the behaviours we want to recruit, develop, manage and reward' (p. 12). However, in practice this link is often weak; for example Abraham and his colleagues (2001) found organisations willing to identify a set of managerial competencies that described a successful manager, but did not place a corresponding emphasis on including these competencies in their performance appraisal. A further advantage of competency frameworks is that, as they can be expressed as behaviours, they are more easily measurable, and thus can be used explicitly in all HR processes. This means, for example, that in a development centre, assessors can be trained in how to observe a long list of behaviours. In the centre itself each assessor can then check the behaviours of the candidates under observation to record how many times that particular behaviour is displayed.

Problematic aspects of behavioural competencies

Criticisms of the approach have been focused around the complex process required to research the appropriate competencies for the organisation, and perhaps more importantly, the fact that such competencies, due to the research process itself, will be inevitably backward looking rather than future oriented. Hayes *et al.* (2000) also note that a competency framework may not include every aspect that is critical to superior performance, and also that while one set of competencies may result in high performance this does not necessarily mean that such performance may not be achieved via a different set of competencies. Whiddett and Kandola (2000) similarly argue that processes *solely* based on competencies are flawed and that a wider perspective needs to be taken. Without the wider perspective the scope for encouraging and using diversity may be diminished. In terms of performance management they also highlight that changes in behaviour may be due to factors other than competencies, and this, of course, has implications for development. We also need to remember that a person's behaviour is not necessarily consistent, and may be affected by the environment and the situation, and Boyatzis (2009) does suggest that it is important to identify the 'tipping point' which identifies how often the relevant behaviours need to be displayed. Salaman and Taylor (2002) suggest that there are five inherent weaknesses where organisations limit themselves to a behavioural competency approach for managers including: marginalisation of the cultural, social and organisational context, the fact that such frameworks emphasise a narrow set of behaviours and attitudes with a lack of emphasis on the long-term processes of management development, and that competencies are founded on the questionable assumption that managers behave rationally and are achievement driven.

ACTIVITY 18.4

Research the use of behavioural competencies in your own organisation (if they are used), or one with which you are familiar.

1 What are the advantages of their use?
2 What are the disadvantages?
3 Compare views, if you can, from members of the HR function, line managers elsewhere, and other professionals.

METHODS OF LEARNING AND DEVELOPMENT

Off-job methods: education and training courses

Educational courses undertaken during a career are frequently done on a part-time basis leading to a diploma or master's degree with a management or business label, and/or qualification for a professional body. It is considered that such courses provide value for both the employer and the participant – and MBA study is a popular route. For advantages of such a course for the employee *see*, for example, Baruch and Leeming (2001). An alternative approach to qualification is the NVQ route which we discussed in the previous chapter, which is more closely tied to on-job experiences and not concerned with 'education'.

In addition there are consultancy courses. Varying from a half-day to several weeks in length, they are run by consultants or professional bodies for all comers. They have the advantage that they bring together people from varying occupational backgrounds and are not, therefore, as introspective as in-house courses and are popular for topical issues. They are, however, often relatively expensive and superficial, despite their value as sources of industrial folklore, by which we mean the swapping of experiences among course members.

The most valuable courses of this type are those that concentrate on specific skills or knowledge, such as developing time management, interviewing or disciplinary skills, or being introduced to a new national initiative. This short-course approach is probably the only way for individuals to come to terms with some new development, such as a change in legislation, because they need not only to find an interpretation of the development, but also to share views and reactions with fellow employees to ensure that their own feelings are not idiosyncratic or perverse.

In-house courses are often similar in nature to consultancy courses, and are sometimes run with the benefit of some external expertise. In-house courses can be particularly useful if the training needs to relate to specific organisational procedures and structures, or if it is geared to encouraging employees to work more effectively together in the organisational environment. The drawbacks of in-house courses are that they suffer from a lack of breadth of content, and there is no possibility of learning from people in other organisations.

Alternatively, there are outdoor-type courses (sometimes known as Outward Bound, after the organisation that pioneered them). Outdoor courses attempt to develop skills involved in working with and through others, and aim to increase self-awareness and self-confidence through a variety of experiences, including outdoor physical challenges. Courses like these continue to be increasingly used, and their differential value is assumed to hinge on their separation from the political, organisational environment. A natural, challenging and different environment is assumed to encourage individuals to forsake political strategising, act as their raw selves and be more open to new ideas, but the idea of providing a de-politicised environment is perhaps a naive hope rather than a reality. Learning experiences based on drama are increasingly popular; in these participants are engaged in improvisation through role play and exercises. For a fascinating insight into the variety of forms this may take *see* Monks *et al.* (2001). There are other forms of simulation and experiential learning in addition to role play, such as games and computer simulations, virtual worlds, and mock-up worlds which take place away from the job as shown in the Window on practice.

WINDOW ON PRACTICE

Fake station offers real training

London Underground has designed a mock tube station called West Ashfield, as reported by Stevens (2010) which is used to prepare staff for real-life situations before they go out into the field. It is being used to train drivers, gate operators and apprentices and also to provide retraining when staff are moved to new areas.

The station will also be used by police, fire and ambulance services who will be trained alongside London Underground staff in preparation for emergency situations such as mass evacuations, and people falling under trains.

Previously this training would have been done on a Sunday and required the closing of a real tube station. London Underground recognises the importance of hands-on experience in developing staff confidence and with simulation it can expose staff to the pressures they will experience in the real workplace.

Virtual building sites

Based on experiences in the Netherlands a new construction training centre has been opened in Coventry designed to use computer technology to create virtual construction sites with the aim of improving the people management skills of site workers. Participants use a control stick to 'work' on a 12-metre high panoramic screen. Actors are used to present scenarios for the trainees to deal with and supervisors can observe via cameras. Balfour Beatty is intending to use the site for management, people and communication skills, particularly for site managers, and the company's training manager believes that it will provide higher-value training as it is specific and highly relevant to their day-to-day work.

Sources: Stevens, M. (2010) 'Fake Station offers real training', *People Management*, 28 January, p. 12. Phillips, L. (2009b) '"Virtual building sites" at new training centre', *People Management*, 4 June, p. 10.

One of the major concerns with these different types of off-job courses and activities is the difficulty of ensuring transfer of learning back to the workplace. As part of their research on the contribution of off-job courses to managers Longenecker and Ariss (2002) asked managers what helped them retain what they had learned and transfer it to the workplace. Developing goals/plans for implementing new skills was most frequently identified. In addition managers said that it helped to review materials immediately after the programme; be actively involved in the learning itself; make a report to peers/superiors on what they had learned; review material and development plans with their mentor/manager; and include development goals in performance reviews. It is generally agreed that a supportive climate helps transfer (for example line manager interest and involvement) and Nielsen (2009) found that collaborative activities on return to the workplace aided trainees in transferring their course-based learning to the workplace. Santos and Stewart (2003), for example, found that transfer was more likely if reward such as promotion or pay was attached to developmental behaviour change, and also where there was a helpful management climate in terms of pre- and post-course briefings and activities.

WINDOW ON PRACTICE

Experiential activities

Brockett (2006) explains how EDF Energy aims to improve customer service via experiential course activities for engineers, dispatch and call-centre workers. During the course participants play the roles of guests at a sixtieth birthday party. Cake, music and decorations accompany this. Half-way through the party there is a surprise power cut represented by a blackout and audio recording of family members becoming distressed and stumbling about in the dark. The aim was to let course members experience what their customers experience when they have a power cut so that they can better understand the effect that it has on people's lives. Performance improvements followed in terms of repair times, accuracy of estimated repair times and increase in commendations letters from the public. This suggests that an experience, especially in the shoes of the customer, can have a powerful impact on employee perceptions and behaviours.

Phillips (2006) provides an example of BUPA care staff in a retirement home. As part of a 'Personal Best' programme aimed at improving customer service staff took the role of residents so as to see life through their customers' eyes. So, for example, they were fed puréed food and were hoisted in a mechanical sling from a chair into a bed. As a result staff behaviour towards residents has changed, for example explaining the hoisting procedure to residents and doing it more slowly.

Sources: Brockett, J. (2006) 'Energy firm gets party vibe', *People Management*, Vol. 12, No. 10, 18 May, p. 12; Phillips, L. (2006) 'BUPA Stars', *People Management*, Vol. 12, No. 22, 9 November, pp. 30–2.

Learning on the job

Manager coaching and other internal and external coaching

The line manager's role in learning and development has increased with the devolution of HR tasks. Coaching is an informal approach to individual development based on a close relationship between the individual and one other person, either internal or external to the organisation. The coach is often the immediate manager, who is experienced in the task, but there is increasing use of external coaches, especially for more senior managers, or specially trained internal coaches, and 'coaching' has become very much a professional occupation with its own code of ethical practice. We will look at this in more detail, but first we explore the coaching role of the line manager.

The manager as coach helps trainees to develop by giving them the opportunity to perform an increasing range of tasks, and by helping them to learn from their experiences. Managers work to improve the trainee's performance by asking searching questions, actively listening, discussion, exhortation, encouragement, understanding, counselling and providing information and honest feedback. The manager coach is usually in a position to create development opportunities for the trainee when this is appropriate. For example, a line manager can delegate attendance at a meeting, or allow a trainee to deputise, where this is appropriate to the individual's development needs. Alternatively a line manager can create the opportunity for a trainee to join a working party or can arrange a brief secondment to another department. Coaches can share 'inside' information with the individual being coached to help him or her understand the political context in which the individual is working. For example, they are able to explain who will have most influence on a decision that will be made, or future plans for restructuring within a department.

Skilled coaches can adapt their style to suit the individual they are coaching, from highly directive at one end of the scale to non-directive at the other. The needed style may change over time, as the trainee gains more confidence and experience. IDS (2009) found that a good coach is one who had a genuine interest in the coachees; believes that everyone is capable of more and focuses on potential rather than past performance; knows that the coach does not have all the answers; believes a person's past is no indication of his or her future; understands that an open, supportive and mutual relationship is required for effective coaching; understands that results may be short or long term and believes they should build awareness, responsibility and self-belief. A variety of barriers to coaching have been identified including performance pressures and a feeling that the role was not valued, but Anderson (2009) found that time pressures, lack of confidence to deal with difficult people and organisational culture were key. IDS (2006a) suggests that in view of the emphasis in coaching on honest self-reflection, there will be barriers in organisations where the culture is not one of openness and honesty. They also point out that coaching has been seen as a remedial tool but that it probably has more to offer as a development opportunity for turning good performers into excellent ones.

There has been an increasing trend to broaden the concept of coaching in terms of both content and who carries out the coaching. Many organisations are now providing or arranging intensive training for designated internal coaches who operate broadly in the organisation, just in a coaching role. This is quite different from the basic training line managers are likely to receive. External executive coaching is often provided by consultancies and specialist coaching organisations. IDS (2009) provides an excellent range of case studies demonstrating the different ways in which organisations are using coaching. Various forms of coaching may include career coaching, performance coaching, skills coaching, business coaching and life coaching. Given the increasing professionalisation of coaching it is not surprising that the quality of the coaching experience is receiving attention. Supervision of practice is increasingly being used in a way that is similar to supervision for counsellors, which involves regular meetings with a more experienced practitioner to explore their client relationships and reflect on practice. A CIPD study carried out by the Bath Consultancy Group (Arney 2006) found that nearly half the coaches received regular supervision, and that supervision was a fast growing practice. There are as yet no industry guidelines on required supervision but Mahony (2009) suggests that one hour's supervision to between 8 and 15 hours' coaching practice is a typical ratio. Such individual supervision is carried out with a mind to client confidentiality; however there is also a growing trend for group supervision of coaches and also for organisations wanting to collect common themes discussed in coaching sessions as these can be used to inform organisational thinking (Arney 2006). Both these approaches put client confidentiality at greater risk.

WINDOW ON PRACTICE

Group supervision at PricewaterhouseCoopers

Group supervision has been used for internal coaches for some time and involves sessions of three hours every month led by an external facilitator with experience of coaching supervision and a background in psychology or psychotherapy.

Coaches present a case, with the emphasis on the work of the coach and the coaching relationship rather than the individual client. In order to protect confidentiality real names are not disclosed. It is an opportunity for an individual coach to get reactions from others about their own practice, and also to reflect on approaches that others take. So the aim is to encourage constant learning and reflection, through making one's work open to scrutiny.

Source: Summarised from E. Arney (2006) 'Insider's Guide', *People Management*, Vol. 12, No. 23, 23 November, pp. 40–2.

Coaching at the Medical Research Council (MRC) and Unilever

Hall (2006) reports on the arrangement that external coaching company 'Laughing Phoenix' has made with the Medical Research Council (MRC) which involves coaching the 30 most senior HR professionals. One of the conditions of the agreement was that the company would feed back recurring themes to the MRC so that they could align coaching with the wider business picture. Unilever has contacted internal coaches regularly to 'harvest some of the intelligence they had gathered from their clients', again keen to pick up recurring themes, helping the organisation know which areas to tackle and help the coaches understand the context of their work.

Source: Hall, L. (2006) 'Inside Job', *People Management*, Vol. 12, No. 16, 10 August, pp. 34–6.

The emphasis on coaching is underlined by the CIPD journal, *Coaching at Work*, and the development of the institute's coaching standards; more than two-thirds of the organisations responding to the CIPD *Learning and Development Survey* used coaching in their organisations (CIPD 2009). Concerns for quality are being addressed, for example by a kitemarking scheme for coaching and mentoring qualifications, launched by the European Coaching and Mentoring Council (*see* **www.emccouncil.org**), and the British Psychological Society now has a specialist interest group focused on coaching. Web case 18.2 is on coaching at this book's companion website, **www.pearsoned.co.uk/torrington**.

Mentoring

Mentoring offers a wide range of advantages for the development of the mentee or protégé, coaching as described above being just one of the possible benefits of the relationship. The mentor may occasionally be the individual's immediate manager, but usually it is a more senior manager in the same or a different function. Kram (1983) identifies two broad functions of mentoring, the first of which is the career function, including those aspects of the relationship that primarily enhance career advancement, such as exposure and visibility and sponsorship. The second is the psychosocial function, which includes those aspects of the relationship that primarily enhance a sense of competence, clarity of identity and effectiveness in the managerial role. Mentoring for women managers currently has a high profile (*see*, for example, Ehrich 2008 and Maxwell 2009). More generally Fowler and O'Gorman (2005), on the basis of research with both mentors and mentees, describe eight individual mentoring functions which are: personal and emotional guidance; coaching; advocacy; career development facilitation; role modelling; strategies and systems advice; learning facilitation; and friendship. There is evidence that mentoring does benefit both parties, and Broadbridge (1999) suggests that mentors can gain through recognition from peers, increased job satisfaction, rejuvenation, admiration and self-satisfaction. Indeed reciprocity is expected in a mentoring relationship and there is evidence both mentor and mentee can make claims on each other (Oglensky 2008). The drawbacks to mentoring that were revealed in Broadbridge's research include the risk of over-reliance, the danger of picking up bad habits, the fact that the protégé may be alienated from other sources of expertise and the sense of loss experienced when a mentor leaves. In addition, the difficulty of dealing with conflicting views in such an unequal relationship was identified. Perceived benefits, however, considerably outweighed any drawbacks. There is a danger of assuming that mentoring is unquestionably good and Oglensky (2008) notes that mentoring can be a source of stress, conflict and dysfunction.

Managers are also seen as responsible for developing talent, and while a mentor/protégé relationship might not naturally occur, mentorship may be encouraged or formalised. For example, there are systems where all new graduates are attached to a mentor as soon as they join the organisation. The difficulties of establishing a formal programme include the potential mismatch of individuals, unreal expectations on both sides and the time and effort involved.

WINDOW ON PRACTICE

Reverse mentoring

Dell, the computer company, has begun a new mentoring programme where male senior executives are mentored by female middle managers with the aims of giving the male bosses an insight into the challenges that women face in the organisation and also of helping more women gain senior jobs.

Source: Phillips, L. (2009b) 'Dell to roll out "reverse mentoring"', *People Management*, 22 October, p. 12.

Mentoring at Fifteen

Liam Black, Director of Fifteen (Jamie Oliver's project to turn disadvantaged youngsters into cooks), initiated a structured programme to turn six members of staff into qualified mentors able to support the more vulnerable youngsters to aid retention. The staff are from different companies run by Oliver and are not directly working with the youngsters. The six are working towards a Certificate in Workplace Mentoring from the Oxford School of Coaching and Mentoring (accredited by Oxford Brookes University), which is suitably tailored to their work-based needs. The programme is a six-month blended learning package and the mentors will work with the youngsters setting goals, developing coping strategies and building their often non-existent self-esteem.

Cottee, P. (2006) 'Oliver's Army', *People Management*, Vol. 12, No. 19, 28 September, pp. 44–5.

Web case 18.3 is on mentoring at this book's companion website, **www.pearsoned.co.uk/torrington**.

Peer relationships

Although mentor-protégé relationships have been shown to be related to high levels of career success, not all developing individuals have access to such a relationship, and even formal schemes are often reserved for specific groups such as new graduate entrants. Supportive peer relationships at work are potentially more widely available to the individual and offer a number of benefits for the development of both parties. The benefits that are available depend on the nature of the peer relationship, and Kram and Isabella (1985) have identified three groups of peer relationships, which are differentiated by their primary development functions. These can be expressed on a continuum from 'information peer', based primarily on information sharing, through 'collegial peer', based on career strategising, giving job-related feedback and friendship, to 'special peer', based on emotional support, personal feedback, friendship and confirmation. Most of us benefit from one or a number of peer relationships at work but often we do not readily appreciate their contribution towards our development. Peer relationships most often develop on an informal basis and provide mutual support. Some organisations, however, formally appoint an existing employee to provide such support to a new member of staff through their first 12–18 months in the organisation. These relationships may, of course, continue beyond the initial period. The name for the appointed employee will vary from organisation to organisation, and sometimes the word 'buddy', 'coach' or 'mentor' is used – which can be confusing! The skills and qualities sought in peer providers are likely to include accessibility, empathy, organisational experience and proven task skills.

ACTIVITY 18.5

Consider each significant peer relationship that you have at work. Where does each fit on the continuum of relationships described above, and what contributions does it make towards your development?

If you are in full-time education consider the contribution that each of your relationships (whether at university, home or work) has to your development.

Self-development

Natural learning is learning that takes place on the job and results from an individual's everyday experience of the tasks to be undertaken. Natural learning is even more difficult to investigate than coaching, mentoring or peer relationships, and yet the way in which we learn from everyday experiences, and our level of awareness of this, is very important for our development. To some extent self-development may be seen as a conscious effort to gain the most from natural learning in a job, and to use the learning cycle as a framework. Self-development can be focused in specific skills development, but often extends to attitude development and personal growth.

ACTIVITY 18.6

The video *Groundhog Day* can be viewed as a journey of self-development. Watch the video and answer the following questions:

- How did Phil's attitudes change and how was this reflected in his behaviour?
- What do you think Phil learned?
- How did he learn it?
- Why is personal development so difficult?

The emphasis in self-development is that each individual is responsible for, and can plan, his or her own development, although he or she may need to seek help when working on some issues. Self-development involves individuals in analysing their strengths, weaknesses and the way in which they learn, primarily by means of questionnaires and feedback from others. This analysis may initially begin on a self-development course, or with the help of a facilitator, but would then be continued by the individual back on the job. From this analysis individuals, perhaps with some help at first, plan their development goals and the way in which they will achieve them, primarily through development opportunities within the job. When individuals consciously work on self-development they use the learning cycle in a more explicit way than in natural learning. They are also in a better position to seek appropriate opportunities and help, in their learning, from their manager.

Many of the activities included in self-development are based on observation, collecting further feedback about the way they operate, experimenting with different approaches and in particular reviewing what has happened, why and what they have learned. Self-development, however, is not a quick fix as it requires a long-term approach and careful planning and, attention needs to be paid to how the self-development process is to be supported. Extensive induction into the process is important as is an explanation of the theoretical underpinning, appropriate skill development, preparation for peer feedback, and further support in tracking progress.

Self-development groups

Typically, in self-development groups a group of individuals are involved in a series of meetings where they jointly discuss their personal development, organisational issues and/or individual work problems. Groups may begin operating with a leader who is a process expert, not a content expert, and who therefore acts as a facilitator rather than, but not to the complete exclusion of, a source of information. The group itself is the primary source of information and may operate without outside help as its members' process skills develop. The content and timings of the meetings can be very flexible, although meetings will require a significant level of energy and commitment if they are to operate well. It is important that the members understand what everyone hopes to get out of the group, the role of the facilitator (if there is one), the processes and rules that the group will operate by and how they agree to interact.

Learning logs

Learning logs are a mechanism for learning retrospectively as they encourage a disciplined approach to learning from opportunistic events. The log may be focused around one particular activity and is usually designed to encourage the writer to explain what happened, how he or she has reflected on this, what conclusions he or she has made and what future learning actions he or she wishes to make. Alternatively logs can be used in the form of a daily or weekly diary.

ACTIVITY 18.7

Identify a management skills area that you need to develop. (You may find it particularly helpful to choose an interpersonal area, for example, assertiveness, influencing others, presentation, being more sociable, contributing to meetings, helping others.)

Keep a learning diary over the next few weeks, logging anything that is relevant to your development area. Use the framework which Gwen used in a previous example (see Window on practice box at the beginning of this chapter).

At the end of the period review what you have learned in your development area and also what you have learned about the learning cycle.

Learning contracts

There is increasing use of learning contracts, sometimes used within more formalised self-development groups; on other management courses; as part of a mentoring or coaching relationship; or in working towards a competency-based qualification. These contracts are a formal commitment by the learner to work towards a specified learning goal, with an identification of how the goal might be achieved. They thus promote a proactive approach to learning. Boak (1991) has produced a very helpful guide to the use of such contracts and suggests that they should include:

- an overall development goal
- specific objectives in terms of skills and knowledge
- activities to be undertaken
- resources required
- a method of assessment of learning

The value that individuals gain from learning contracts is dependent on their choosing to participate, their identification of the relevant goal and the importance and value they ascribe to achieving it. Only with commitment will a learning contract be effective, because ultimately it is down to the individual learner manager to make it happen.

WINDOW ON PRACTICE

David wanted to improve his influencing skills and has sent the following draft learning contract to his manager for discussion:

Goal

To improve my influencing skills with both peers and more senior managers.

Specific objectives

- To prepare for influencing situations.
- To try to understand better the perspective of the other.
- To identify the interpersonal skills required – probably active listening, reflecting, summarising, stating my needs, collaboration (but maybe more).
- To be able to identify that I have had more influence in decisions made.

Activities

- Watch a recommended DVD on influencing skills.
- Re-read my notes from the interpersonal skills course I attended.
- Watch how others in my department go about influencing.
- Ask other people (supportive ones) how they go about it.

- Identify possible influencing situations in advance, and plan for what I want and what might happen.
- Reflect back on what happened, and work out how to do better next time.
- Ask for feedback.

Resources

- DVD.
- Notes.
- The support of others.

Assessment

- I could ask for feedback from colleagues and my manager.
- My own assessment may be helpful.
- Make a log over time of decisions made and my originally preferred outcome.

E-learning and blended learning

E-learning can be defined as 'learning that is delivered, enabled or mediated by electronic technology' (Sloman and Rolph 2003: 1), and by 2009 (CIPD 2009) 42 per cent of organisations reported expanding their use of e-learning, but there remained 26 per cent of organisations where e-learning was not used at all. E-learning covers a wide variety of approaches from using CD-roms to use of the company intranet and the Internet. More sophisticated approaches do not confine e-learning to interactive learning at a distance. Increasingly, synchronous learning is used where all participants log on at the same time, with a tutor or facilitator being available online. Individuals can progress through material alone or network with others to complete a task and use chatrooms and have a dialogue with the tutor. Videoconferencing can also be used to bring participants together at the same time. For example, some MBAs have been delivered via videoconferencing rather than classroom-based teaching. Web 2.0 interactive technology has also widened the possibilities, as we demonstrated in Chapter 16.

The advantages of e-learning are that:

- Learning can often take place at a convenient time, for example when the job is less busy meaning that it is less disruptive
- Learning does not usually have to be planned in and can be used opportunistically as time becomes available
- Learning does not have to take place during working hours
- E-learning can be cost effective when delivering a unit to a large number of employees
- Modules or units can be completed when topics are relevant to job demands, rather than according to schedule determined by others

- When a learning need is identified development via e-learning can take place immediately rather than waiting for a slot on a course
- Large numbers of employees can all be trained at the same time, for example where there is a new product launch, rather than waiting for a slot on a course
- E-learning means that the training delivered is always consistent and not dependent on tutor or manager skills
- Learners can take as long as they need to progress rather than being constrained by a timetable that applies to all
- The material produced for e-learning is sustainable and easy to update and can be customised
- E-learning can encompass virtual reality in training, for example preparing employees to deal with dangerous situations where it would be inappropriate to rely solely on learning on the job

Hammond (2001), for example, describes the case of Cisio which is constantly launching new IT-based products. The company has moved from 90 per cent classroom-based training for its sales representative to 80 per cent online training so that the large numbers of representatives can experience training immediately the product is launched. Channel 4 (Cooper 2001) has a strategy to replace much of its classroom teaching activity with interactive learning, and the London Emergency Services are using virtual reality training to prepare employees for emergency events, as in the London Underground example (Stevens 2010) on page 404 of this chapter.

Progress however has been modest despite high expectations. One of the reasons for this is that while organisations are often enthusiastic there has been much evidence of employees being unwilling to use e-learning. E-learning can be a solitary activity and is often very dependent on individual self-discipline, and there are some learners who will simply find that an interactive computer-based learning unit does not compare with the conviviality and action associated with attending a course. Thus motivation dwindles unless there is other support to encourage learners to complete the units they need. Computer literacy is another barrier for many employees. At one level this may be basic computer skills, but more sophisticated packages involving synchronous learning and joint learner tasks, bulletin boards and group/tutor dialogues can also be very difficult for many employees who have good everyday computer skills and they will need time to learn how particular packages work and how to use the facilities. If the right preparation and support are not made available employees can easily be put off by one difficult experience in which they found they could not keep up with the rest of the synchronous learning group. In some organisations access to the appropriate equipment was a problem for those employees who did not have a personal computer on their desks. There is evidence that some initial concerns were perhaps unfounded. For example in the Indian banking sector Mittal (2008) found that older age did not compromise the effectiveness of e-learning and nor did a lower job level.

There was much initial euphoria about what e-learning could contribute but increasingly it has been recognised that motivating learners is critical and most organisations now have much more realistic expectations of what e-learning can achieve, and often have to improve and re-launch e-learning solutions before they bed in. The support provided may well be critical, as may the way that such methods are introduced and used.

WINDOW ON PRACTICE

A different slant on e-learning

Virtual Reality has been around for many years in the gaming world but it is only recently that learning and development professionals have begun to grasp the potential that this technology has to offer.

For example 'Second Life'™ produced by Linden, is a site that can be used just for fun, but also for learning and development. In this 'second life' world an individual creates a virtual persona, called an avatar, and engages with other avatars, involving themselves in making and selling things, education, discussion groups and so on as in the real world.

Organisations that use it as a vehicle for people development may have a custom version of the world built for them, sometimes creating their office, store or campus so that learners experience a virtual world which mirrors their real one.

Virtual worlds can be used to give individuals experience of trying out new skills, learning new ideas and making mistakes. There is the potential for individuals to 'meet' and engage with others in ways that would be difficult in the real world. One way that the virtual worlds can be used for people development is for there to be a 'scripted' approach. This means that some of the avatars are controlled to create situations which can then be discussed afterwards. 'Open access' (that is not scripted) learning may also be used, for example for team exercises where teams address a challenge and are given feedback, just as on an 'outdoor' team training event.

Sources: **www.secondlife.com**; CIPD (2008) 'Virtual worlds and learning: using Second Life at Duke Corporate Education', CIPD case study from **www.cipd.co.uk**; Syedain, H. (2008) 'Out of this world', *People Management*, Vol. 14, No. 8, 17 April, pp. 20–3.

The difficulties experienced with e-learning have focused some organisations on understanding where e-learning fits with other approaches to learning and using it in ways that provide the most value. For example e-learning can be very effectively used before a face-to-face course to do pre-work so that for example all attendees are starting from a roughly similar knowledge base. In this case those employees who have the knowledge base already can be exempt, while e-learning enables the others to get up to speed before the course begins. Similarly e-learning can be used effectively for course briefings and general preparation, such as the completion and analysis of pre-course questionnaires and other pre-work which saves time at the beginning of the event itself.

At the end of a course e-learning can be used for refreshers, for self-checking of understanding and planning how to apply the learning gained on the course. Similarly e-learning can be used in combination with manager coaching. This has led to the term 'blended learning' which is often used to indicate the blending of e-learning with face-to-face learning experiences, while others use it more broadly to indicate 'a range of ways that e-learning can be delivered when combined with multiple additional routes that support and facilitate learning' (Sloman and Rolph 2003: 6).

Blended learning is increasingly used to indicate a blend of any approaches to learning, and there is evidence that learning and training now involve a much wider range of activities (CIPD 2006); for example Pickard (2006) reports on the blended learning approach at the Department for Work and Pensions which integrates self-managed learning, coaching and e-learning.

In conclusion, e-learning has a critical role to play but it would be dangerous to see it as the answer to all learning needs and the future of learning and development at work. Its value is best exploited where it is the most appropriate approach to meeting key development needs, such as preparing for dangerous tasks by using virtual reality, and where it can be combined with other learning activities to ensure a more complete learning experience and where it particularly suits the learning style of the individual learner.

WINDOW ON PRACTICE

Julie Scumming at AXA

Clarke (2006) recounts a very inventive learning experience at AXA, highly job based and involving a variety of activities. The exercise started with a Christmas card from a fictitious employee Julie Scumming. Posters followed announcing her arrival and then her fictitious husband entered the offices, shouting. After this there were diary entries on the intranet from both Julie and her boss which staff began to follow, and picked up the story that Julie was a devout Christian who felt she was being discriminated against and bullied by her boss and peers. Dummy tabloid articles were circulated, a stand-up row in the canteen was performed by actors. Sticky notes were put on computers saying not to get 'stuck like Julie', and an advent calendar counted down the days to the main event which was a tribunal hearing for managers. When the tribunal panel retired to consider their verdict actors acted out scenes which had led up to the tribunal. Meanwhile employees could log on to discussion forums to express their views about the case, and there was a poll about the anticipated results. Involvement in all of this was voluntary but many staff participated. The objective was to raise awareness about discrimination issues. Responses to questionnaires after the event demonstrated that managers were more aware of religious discrimination issues.

Source: Clarke, E. (2006) 'Julie Diligent', *People Management*, Vol. 12, No. 14, 13 July, pp. 32–43.

EVALUATION OF TRAINING AND DEVELOPMENT

One of the most nebulous and unsatisfactory aspects of the training job is evaluating its effectiveness, yet it is becoming more necessary to demonstrate value for money. While Campbell (2006) estimates that employer, public and individual spend on workforce training and development in the UK nears £30 billion each year, Phelps (2002) suggests there is no satisfactory return on investment calculation to prove its value, and that we remain unsure whether training breeds success or success breeds training. Evaluation is straightforward when the output of the training is clear to see, such as reducing the number of dispatch errors in a warehouse or increasing someone's typing speed. It is more difficult to evaluate the success of a management training course or a programme of social skills development, but the fact that it is difficult is not enough to prevent it being done. Cunningham (2007), however, suggests that there is a danger that trainers and developers become too focused on trying to prove return on investment, and he works with an organisation where the focus of evaluation is for the trainees to present to their sponsors/managers their assessment of value that they and the organisation have gained from their learning.

A familiar method of evaluation is the post-course questionnaire, which course members complete on the final day by answering vague questions that require them to assess aspects of the course using only such general terms as 'good', 'very good' or 'outstanding'. The drawbacks with such questionnaires are, first, that there is a powerful halo effect, as the course will have been, at the very least, a welcome break from routine and there will probably have been some attractive fringe benefits such as staying in a comfortable hotel and enjoying rich food. Second, the questionnaire tends to evaluate the course and not the learning, so that the person attending the course is assessing the quality of the tutors and the visual aids, instead of being directed to examine what has been learned.

Hamblin (1974), in a much-quoted work, identified five levels of evaluation: (1) evaluating the training, as in the post-course questionnaire above; (2) evaluating the learning, in terms of how the trainee now behaves; (3) evaluating changes in job performance; (4) evaluating changes in organisation performance; and (5) evaluating changes in the wider contribution that the organisation now makes. Perhaps the most well-referenced approach to evaluation is Kirkpatrick (1959) who suggested four levels of evaluation, somewhat similar to Hamblin: (1) reaction level; (2) learning level (have the learning objectives been met?); (3) behaviour (how has the individual's behaviour changed after returning to the job?); and (4) results and impact on the bottom line (what is the impact of training on performance?).

Measuring performance effectiveness after a learning intervention involves identifying changes in behaviour, knowledge, skills and attitudes and it is important that the criteria for evaluation are built into development activities from the very beginning, and not tagged on at the end. Lingham and his co-researchers (2006) provide a good example of how this can be done in practice. They describe an action research project where evaluation was built in from the outset and involved collaboration between organisational leaders, trainers, participants and evaluators. A four-phase approach was used:

- Phase 1: Design of training programme (organisational leaders, trainers and evaluators agree design and methods to obtain feedback from participants after the initial runs of the training programme).
- Phase 2: Launch and evaluation of initial programme (training conducted and agreed methods used to collect participants' views).
- Phase 3: Feedback and design of evaluation instrument (organisational leaders, trainers and evaluators meet to review feedback and field notes and adapt the training programme where necessary. A survey instrument designed for evaluation of future iterations of the programme).
- Phase 4: Ongoing training and evaluation (training programme conducted with new design/content, evaluation survey used and results fed back into Phase 3.

(adapted from Lingham *et al.* 2006)

SUMMARY PROPOSITIONS

18.1 There are four perspectives on learning: behaviourist, cognitive, social and constructivist. Each has different implications for the approach taken to training and development.

18.2 The emphasis has moved from training to learning, with individuals taking ownership of their own learning needs. To be effective learners we need to understand the nature of learning and our own strengths and weaknesses.

18.3 Behavioural competencies are useful for identifying learning needs and assessing learning progress.

18.4 The emphasis on formal development programmes is declining in favour of greater interest in approaches to on-the-job development, such as coaching, mentoring, peer relationships and self-development.

18.5 There has been an upsurge of interest in e-learning. However, the extent to which employees take advantage of such opportunities will be affected by the context and the support available. E-learning is increasingly being blended with other forms of learning.

18.6 Evaluation of development is critical but difficult. It is most effective when built into the design of the development activity rather than tagged on at the end.

GENERAL DISCUSSION TOPICS

1 If learning is an individual process, why is so much training done in groups? What are the implications of moving towards more individualised learning?

2 Discuss the view that the role of the trainer/facilitator is critically important in the effectiveness of a training programme.

FURTHER READING

CIPD (2009) *E-learning Progress and Prospect: A CIPD factsheet*. London: CIPD.
A useful summary of types of e-learning, measures of take-up to date and guidance on implementation.

Neilsen, A. and Norrekit, H. (2009) 'A discourse analysis of the disciplinary power of management coaching', *Society and Business Review*, Vol. 4, No. 3, pp. 202–14.
This is a fascinating and thought-provoking review of the literature on coaching from the point of view of control. The article finds that there are two approaches to coaching: employee coaching which seems to involve action control and direct monitoring; and executive coaching which appears to involve the control of the spirit as well as results and achievements and the authors argue that this acts as a constraint of the individual's self-realisation project. They conclude that coaching can be a stronger disciplining technique than control by targets/numbers.

Passmore, J. (ed.) (2006) *Excellence in Coaching: The industry guide*. London: Kogan Page.
A combination of contributions from both academics and practitioners provides expertise in a range of areas relevant to coaching.

Slotte, V. and Herbert, A. (2008) 'Engaging workers in simulation-based e-learning', *Journal of Workplace Learning*, Vol. 20, No. 3, pp. 165–80.
This is a lovely example of how simulation-based e-learning and face-to-face methods can be combined. The authors explain how this approach was used in a bookstore to develop customer service skills. The simulation package presented scenarios of different types of difficult customer and staff initially worked with a live coach to facilitate their discussions of how to approach each situation, and offer concepts where appropriate. They found this thought provoking and their discussions continued after the end of the one-day initial programme. Later they continued to use the simulation programme with virtual coaching from 'Esko' who gave continuous feedback. Some said they preferred this mechanical feedback to their responses to different scenarios in that it felt safer to try out alternatives and make mistakes.

REFERENCES

Abraham, S., Karns, L., Shaw, K. and Mena, M. (2001) 'Managerial competencies and the managerial appraisal process', *Journal of Management Development*, Vol. 20, No. 10, pp. 842–52.

Anderson, V. (2009) 'Research: line manager as coach', *People Management*, 21 May, p. 42.

Arney, E. (2006) 'Insider's Guide', *People Management*, Vol. 12, No. 23, pp. 40–2.

Baruch, Y. and Leeming, A. (2001) 'The added value of MBA studies: graduates' perceptions', *Personnel Review*, Vol. 30, No. 5, pp. 589–601.

Boak, G. (1991) *Developing Managerial Competencies. The management learning contract approach*. London: Pitman.

Boyatzis, R. (1982) *The Competent Manager*. New York: John Wiley.

Boyatzis, R. (2008) 'Guest Editorial: competencies in the 21st century', *Journal of Management Development*, Vol. 27, No. 1, pp. 5–12.

Boyatzis, R. (2009) 'Guest editorial: competencies as a behavioural approach to emotional intelligence', *Journal of Management Development*, Vol. 28, No. 9, pp. 749–70.

Broadbridge, A. (1999) 'Mentoring in retailing: a tool for success?', *Personnel Review*, Vol. 28, No. 4.

Brockett, J. (2006) 'Energy firm gets party vibe', *People Management*, Vol. 12, No. 10, p. 12.

Campbell, M. (2006) 'Demonstrating the value of learning, training and development', in *Latest Trends in Learning, Training and Development: Reflections on the 2006 Learning and Development Survey*. London: CIPD.

Carroll, S. and Gillen, D. (2001) 'Exploring the teaching function of the managerial role', *Journal of Management Development*, Vol. 21, No. 5, pp. 330–42.

CIPD (2006) *Learning and Development: Annual Survey 2006*. London: CIPD.

CIPD (2008) 'Virtual worlds and learning: using Second Life™ at Duke Corporate Education', CIPD case study from **www.cipd.co.uk**.

CIPD (2009) *Learning and Development Annual Survey, 2009*. London: CIPD.

Clarke, E. (2006) 'Julie diligent', *People Management*, Vol. 12, No. 14, 13 July, pp. 32–43.

Cooper, C. (2001) 'Connect four', *People Management*, February.

Cottee, P. (2006) 'Oliver's army', *People Management*, Vol. 12, No. 19, 28 September, pp. 44–5.

Cunningham, I. (2007) 'Viewpoint: sorting out evaluation of learning and development: making it easier for ourselves', *Development and Learning in Organisations*, Vol. 21, No. 5, pp. 4–6.

Ehrich, L. (2008) 'Mentoring and women managers: another look at the field', *Gender in Management: An International Journal*, Vol. 23, No. 7, pp. 469–83.

Fowler, J. and O'Gorman, J. (2005) 'Mentoring functions: a contemporary view of the perceptions of mentees and mentors', *British Journal of Management*, Vol. 16, pp. 51–7.

Hall, L. (2006) 'Inside job', *People Management*, Vol. 12, No. 16, pp. 34–6.

Hamblin, A.C. (1974) *Evaluation and Control of Training*. Maidenhead: McGraw-Hill.

Hammond, D. (2001) 'Reality bytes', *People Management*, January.

Harrison, R. (2009) *Learning and Development*, 5th edn. London: CIPD.

Hayes, J., Rose-Quirie, A. and Allinson, C. (2000) 'Senior managers' perceptions of the competencies they require for effective performance: implications for training and development', *Personnel Review*, Vol. 29, No. 1, pp. 92–105.

Honey, P. and Mumford, A. (1989) *A Manual of Learning Opportunities*. Maidenhead: Peter Honey.

IDS (2006a) *Coaching in the Workplace*. HR Studies No. 831, October. London: IDS.

IDS (2006b) *E-Learning*. HR Studies No. 818. London: IDS.

IDS (2008) *Competency Frameworks*. HR Study No. 865, March. London: IDS.

IDS (2009) *Coaching and Mentoring*. HR Study No. 897, July. London: IDS.

Kirkpatrick, D. (1959) 'Techniques for evaluating training programs', *Journal of the American Society of Training Directors*, Vol. 13, pp. 3–26.

Kolb, D.A., Rubin, I.M. and McIntyre, J.M. (1984) *Organization Psychology*, 4th edn. Englewood Cliffs: Prentice-Hall.

Kram, K.E. (1983) 'Phases of the mentor relationship', *Academy of Management Journal*, Vol. 26, No. 4, pp. 608–25.

Kram, K.E. and Isabella, L.A. (1985) 'Mentoring alternatives: the role of peer relationships in career development', *Academy of Management Journal*, Vol. 28, No. 1, pp. 110–32.

Lingham, T., Richley, B. and Rezania, D. (2006) 'An evaluation system for training programs: a case study using a four-phase approach', *Career Development International*, Vol. 11, No. 4, pp. 334–51.

Longenecker, C. and Ariss, S. (2002) 'Creating competitive advantage through effective management education', *Personnel Review*, Vol. 21, No. 9, pp. 640–54.

Mahony, D. (2009) 'Coaches need supervision too', *People Management*, 24 September, p. 33.

Maxwell, G. (2009) 'Mentoring for enhancing females' career development: the bank job', *Equal Opportunities International*, Vol. 28, No. 7, pp. 561–76.

Megginson, D. (1994) 'Planned and emergent learning: a framework and a method', *Executive Development*, Vol. 7, No. 6, pp. 29–32.

Megginson, D. and Whitaker, V. (1996/2007) *Cultivating Self-development*. London: IPD.

Mittal, M. (2008) 'Evaluating perceptions on effectiveness of e-learning programs in Indian banks: identifying areas for improvement', *Development and Learning in Organisations*, Vol. 22, No. 2, pp. 12–14.

Monks, K., Barker, P. and Mhanachain, A. (2001) 'Drama as an opportunity for learning and development', *Personnel Review*, Vol. 20, No. 5, pp. 414–23.

Nielsen, K. (2009) 'A collaborative perspective on learning transfer', *Journal of Workplace Learning*, Vol. 21, No. 1, pp. 58–70.

Oglensky, B. (2008) 'The ambivalent dynamics of loyalty in mentorship', *Development and Learning in Organisations*, Vol. 61, No. 3, pp. 419–49.

Phelps, M. (2002) 'Blind faith', *People Management*, Vol. 8, No. 9, p. 51.

Phillips, L. (2006) 'BUPA stars', *People Management*, Vol. 12, No. 22, pp. 30–2.

Phillips, L. (2009a) '"Virtual building sites" at new training centre', *People Management*, 29 January, p. 10.

Phillips, L. (2009b) 'Dell to roll out "reverse mentoring"', *People Management*, 22 October, p. 12.

Pickard, J. (2006) 'Suits ewe', *People Management*, Vol. 12, No. 12, pp. 36–7.

Prickett, R. (1997) 'Screen savers', *People Management*, 26 June, pp. 36–8.

Salaman, G. and Taylor, S. (2002) 'Competency's consequences: changing the character of managerial work', paper presented at the ESRC Critical Management Studies Seminar: Managerial Work. Cambridge: The Judge Institute of Management.

Santos, A. and Stewart, M. (2003) 'Employee perceptions and their influence on training effectiveness', *Human Resource Management Journal*, Vol. 13, No. 1, pp. 27–45.

Sloman, M. and Rolph, J. (2003) *E-learning: The learning curve – The change agenda*. London: CIPD.

Smethurst, S. (2006) 'Staying power', *People Management*, Vol. 12, No. 7, pp. 34–6.

Stevens, M. (2010) 'Fake station offers real training', *People Management*, 28 January, p. 12.

Syedain, H. (2008) 'Out of this world', *People Management*, Vol. 14, No. 8, pp. 20–3.

Whiddett, S. and Kandola, B. (2000) 'Fit for the job?', *People Management*, 25 May, pp. 30–4.

Part 4 CASE STUDY PROBLEM

Micropower

Micropower is a rapidly growing computer software firm, specialising in tailor-made solutions for business. Increasingly, training for other businesses in their own and other software packages has occupied the time of the consultants. Micropower sees this as a profitable route for the future and such training is now actively sold to clients. Consultants both sell and carry out the training. As an interim measure, to cope with increasing demand, the firm is now recruiting some specialist trainers, but the selling of the training is considered to be an integral part of the consultant's role.

Micropower has just issued a mission statement which accentuates 'the supply of and support for sophisticated computer solutions', based on a real understanding of business needs. The firm considers that it needs to be flexible in achieving this and has decided that multiskilling is the way forward.

All consultants need to sell solutions and training at all levels, and be excellent analysts, designers and trainers. Some 200 consultants are now employed; most have a degree in IT and most joined the firm initially because of their wish to specialise in the technical aspects of software development, and they spent some years almost entirely in an office-based position before moving into a customer contact role. A smaller proportion were keen to concentrate on systems analysis, and were involved in customer contact from the start.

In addition there are 300 software designers and programmers who are primarily office based and rarely have any customer contact. It is from this group that new consultants are appointed. Programmers are promoted to two levels of designer and those in the top level of designer may then, if their performance level is high enough, be promoted to consultant. There is some discontent among designers that promotion means having to move into a customer contact role, and there are a growing number who seek more challenge, higher pay and status, but who wish to avoid customer contact. Another repercussion of the promotion framework is that around a quarter of the current consultants are not happy in their role. They are consultants because they valued promotion more than doing work that they enjoyed. Some have found the intense customer contact very stressful, feel they lack the appropriate skills, are not particularly comfortable with their training role and are unhappy about the increasing need to 'sell'.

Required

1 What immediate steps could Micropower take to help the consultants, particularly those who feel very unhappy, perform well and feel more comfortable in their new roles?

2. In the longer term how can Micropower reconcile its declared aim of multiskilling with a career structure which meets both organisational and employee needs?
3. What other aspects of human resource strategy would support and integrate with the development strategy of multiskilling?
4. Micropower wishes to develop a competency profile for the consultant role. How would you recommend that the firm progress this, and how might the profile be used in the widest possible manner in the organisation?

EMPLOYEE RELATIONS

Surveys of the activities and priorities of HR specialists carried out in the 1970s and early 1980s invariably found employee relations to be the activity on which they spent most of their time and which were central to the human resource function. Twenty-five years on, the situation has wholly changed. Nowadays surveys of HR managers always show that employee relations issues are well down their lists of current and perceived future priorities. The emphasis is overwhelmingly on recruitment, staff retention, organisational restructuring, development and absence management, along with the HR implications associated with the introduction of new technologies and particularly legislation. The main reason appears to be a widespread perception that employee relations in UK organisations are in a reasonably healthy state. The 2004 Workplace Employment Relations (WER) Survey found that 93 per cent of HR managers believed their own organisations' employment relations climate to be either 'good' or 'very good', while only 1 per cent saw it as being poor (Kersley *et al.* 2006: 277), suggesting that the pressures placed on many workforces to become more efficient and flexible are not in the main leading to overt forms of conflict. Employee relations is not therefore seen as an organisational problem. Interestingly the WER Survey also found that a majority of employees were positive about the employee relations climate in their own organisations, although theirs was a less enthusiastic endorsement (16 per cent characterised the climate as being 'poor' or 'very poor'). Employee relations activities may not be as significant to HR practitioners as they once were, but they remain important. A poor employee relations climate can easily develop, while a good one is not created or maintained automatically; ongoing action on the part of managers is required.

The past 30 years have thus witnessed a sea change in the UK employee relations scene. Most of the once well-established norms in British industry have been abandoned or have withered away as the nature of the work that we do and the types of workplace in which we are employed have evolved. To an extent, cultural change has accompanied this structural change too, creating a world of work in which employees attitudes towards their employers and employer attitudes towards their employees have developed in new directions. Ongoing change of one kind or another has affected and continues to affect most areas of HRM activity, but it is in the field of employee relations that the most profound transformations have occurred.

That said, it is important to appreciate that change in this field proceeds at a different pace in different places. There remain many workplaces, particularly in the public sector and in the former public sector corporations, in which more traditional models of employee relations continue to operate despite attempts by successive governments to change them. What we now have, therefore, is a far greater variety of approaches in place across the different industrial sectors than was the case in past decades.

Overt conflict between labour and management representing different *sides* with fundamentally different interests persist, but usually alongside a newer rhetoric that reflects aspirations towards greater partnership and employee involvement in decision making. In these organisations trade union membership remains high, while terms and conditions of employment continue to be established through formal collective bargaining mechanisms. Negotiations are, however, increasingly carried out at local rather than industry level with individual employers and not with employers' associations as was once common.

This model of employee relations no longer exists in most private sector organisations where there is little effective collective employee consciousness on the part of employees and where trade unions are irrelevant (if they have any serious presence at all). Here too the rhetoric of partnership and voice is common, but the extent to which there is any meaningful employee involvement in important decision making can be very limited indeed.

Profound though these changes in employee relations may be, it remains the case that all jobs have the potential to be alienating, making the job holder indifferent or hostile both to the job and to management. Employee relations activity continues to be largely concerned with preventing or alleviating that type of alienation. In doing so, however, managers are increasingly required to take account of regulation. Indeed, so great has been the growth of employment law that we now have a situation in which employment rights are protected through the law and the employment tribunal system to a much greater extent than they are by trade unions.

Regulation is one, but by no means the only, reason behind the growth of interest in equality and diversity issues. The same is true of health, safety and welfare. The law has plenty to say about these areas of HR practice, but there is also a compelling business case linking the presence of a healthy and diverse workforce to positive business outcomes. The law also determines the framework and broad approaches employers take when dealing with disciplinary matters and handling formal grievances lodged by their staff. There remains, however, plenty of scope to manage these difficult matters in different ways.

EMPLOYEE VOICE

THE OBJECTIVES OF THIS CHAPTER ARE TO:

1. Introduce the main methods used by employers to involve employees in decision making
2. Assess the extent of information sharing and its purpose
3. Set out the case for formal and informal consultation with employees and their representatives
4. Explore situations in which co-determination occurs in UK and overseas organisations

It is quite possible to run a successful organisation without involving employees in management activities to any meaningful extent, but the chances of sustained success are higher when employees have a 'voice', that is they are involved in and can influence what happens in the organisation. Objectives are more effectively and efficiently achieved if employees have some say in decision making, especially as it affects their own areas of work. This is for two principal reasons:

1 Ultimately it is for managers to make decisions and to be held accountable. Such decisions can be tough to make, but the chances that they will make the right decision are enhanced if they listen to the views of others and allow their own ideas to be subjected to a degree of scrutiny and constructive criticism. Moreover, involvement allows managers to tap into the ideas and suggestions of staff. The best new ideas often originate from people lower down organisational hierarchies because they are closest to the operational coalface and often to customers.

2 Employees like having a voice. They appreciate having their opinions listened to and acted upon, particularly in matters that directly concern their day-to-day activities. The chances of their being positively satisfied with their work are thus greatly improved if they are genuinely able to be involved. The knock-on effects include lower staff turnover, lower levels of absence, the ability to attract more recruits and higher levels of performance. The effective management of change is especially enhanced by employee involvement because people are always happier to support what they helped to create.

Employee voice comes in many different forms. It can be formal or informal, direct or indirect, one-off or sustained over time, central to an organisation's core business or relatively peripheral. In recent years the number and extent of voice mechanisms have increased. This is partly due to the requirements of the law and partly because they have a part to play in many of the more common, contemporary HRM initiatives we have discussed elsewhere in this book – becoming an 'employer of choice', 360-degree appraisal, employee engagement and knowledge management programmes.

Our aim in this chapter is to discuss the major forms employee voice takes, to explore the difficulties that can be experienced in the implementation of initiatives and to evaluate their contribution to the achievement of an organisation's objectives.

TERMINOLOGY

A variety of labels are used to describe employee voice. While some writers have sought to make distinctions between them, there is no generally accepted usage. Hence you will read about 'involvement', 'employee participation', 'industrial democracy' and 'empowerment'. Each of these terms differs subtly and suggests a different perspective, Urwin *et al.* (2007), for example, suggest that voice mechanisms are associated with trade union representation whereas HR practices tend to give rise to employee involvement. All terms are used to a greater or lesser extent to describe a situation in which employees are given, gain or develop a degree of *influence* over what happens in an organisation. The extent and nature of that influence, however, varies considerably.

Marchington and Wilkinson (2005) helpfully distinguish between the major categories of voice with their 'escalator' model (Figure 19.1). The focus here is on the extent of influence.

At the bottom of the escalator are organisations where there is no voice at all, managers taking all decisions without taking any meaningful account of what employees

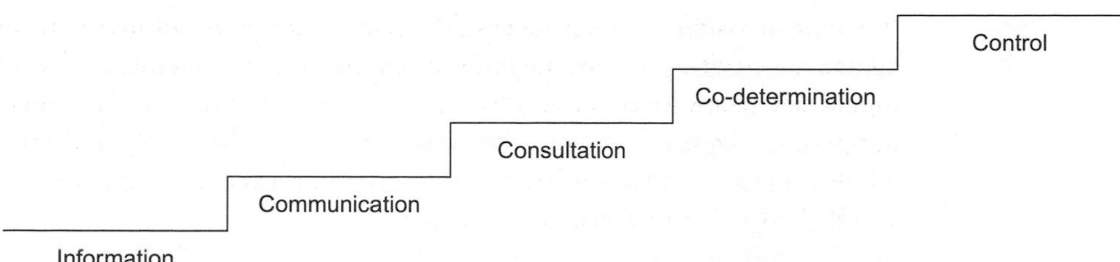

Figure 19.1 The escalator of participation
Source: Marchington, M. and Wilkinson, A., 'Direct participation and involvement', in S. Bach (ed.) *Managing Human Resources: Personnel Management in Transition*, 4th edn (Oxford: Blackwell, 2005), p. 401, Fig. 15.1.

might think. By contrast, at the top of the escalator are organisations or parts of organisations which are controlled by employees rather than by a distinct group of managers. Employee control is very rare in the UK at the level of the organisation, although there are one or two examples of companies which are communally owned and run by staff in a partnership arrangement. We outline in the Window on practice below proposals to develop co-determination in the public sector. A substantial degree of control is much more often exercised, however, by employees at the level of an individual department or team within a larger organisation.

WINDOW ON PRACTICE

Public-sector workers would be able to form co-operatives to take over the running of their organisations, under plans outlined by the Conservatives. Promising a 'power-shift to public-sector workers', then Shadow Chancellor George Osborne said that staff at underperforming schools, hospitals and job centres would be given the power to club together to take over the management of their employer as a not-for-profit social enterprise.

'This is as big a transfer of power to working people since the sale of council house homes in the 1980s,' said Osborne. 'We are saying to public sector workers: "if you want to, and only if you want to, you can create employee-led co-operatives and you can run state services, paid for by the taxpayer".' He added: 'This is a power shift to public sector workers so that they take control of their own working environment and they get away from these top-down bureaucracies which have made life a misery for so many people in the public sector.'

The policy builds on a Tory announcement last year to create 'partnership models' in the NHS, which would give health workers more of a say in the way services are run. The principle was compared at the time to the model at the retailer John Lewis, which is owned by its employees who are called 'partners'. Osborne said the plans were aimed at giving public-sector employees a stake in their employer and therefore increasing their effectiveness.

Source: *People Management* (2010) 'Tories outline plans for public-sector workers' co-operatives', 15 February, available at **http://www.peoplemanagement.co.uk/pm/articles/2010/02/tories-outline-plans-for-public-sector-workers-co-operatives.htm.**

Between 'no involvement' and 'employee control', there are three further stages, each in turn representing a deepening of the extent of involvement. The first is 'communication', signalling a very limited degree of involvement. At this stage employer and employees simply exchange information. Managers disclose defined classes of information, ensuring that employees are aware of the decisions they are taking, the economic situation and their objectives. Employees are also given an opportunity to respond, to voice concerns or put their own ideas forward. But decision making remains exclusively in the management realm. The next step up the escalator is 'consultation'. Here information is exchanged, often through formalised channels. Decision making is still the responsibility of managers, but full and proper consideration is given to the views expressed by staff (or their elected representatives) before key decisions are taken. Finally, a further step up the escalator takes us to co-determination or joint decision making. This is relatively rare in a formal sense in the UK, although it happens informally all the time. But it is very common indeed in Northern European countries where the law requires the agreement of a works council before significant decisions affecting employment can be taken.

At each of these stages voice initiatives can be either direct or indirect in nature. The term 'direct' relates to situations in which managers enter into a dialogue with, consult with or co-determine decisions with employees as individuals. People thus have a direct input in some shape or form. By contrast, the term 'indirect' refers to a situation in which employers take account of employee views through the filter of a representative institution. This may be a trade union, or it may be another kind of body such as a works council, a working party or a consultative committee. Either way, indirect involvement is restricted to representatives of the workforce as a collective group.

Academic research into employee involvement often encompasses payment arrangements such as profit sharing and employee share ownership schemes which are referred to as types of 'financial participation'. These help to develop a community of interest between employers and their staff and can lead to situations in which individual employees cast votes at annual general meetings. We will discuss them in Chapter 24. The remainder of this chapter will focus on the major information-sharing, consultation and co-determination initiatives.

INFORMATION SHARING

According to the 2004 Workplace Employment Relations Survey formal systems of communication between managers and employees are present in the vast majority of UK organisations (Kersley *et al.* 2006: 135). In many cases, however, the communication is carried out at the local level (e.g. line managers meeting with employees individually), there being no formal mechanisms provided for more senior managers to communicate directly with their staff or vice versa. Moreover, where a degree of formality is reported it can be limited simply to the posting of important data on noticeboards or ad hoc circulation of information by e-mail. As a result, a substantial minority of UK employees are reported to believe that they are not kept informed about what their companies are doing (45 per cent) or are not even given sufficient information to do their jobs effectively (35 per cent) (ORC International 2004, cited by IRS 2005a).

The extent to which the disclosure of information by managers can be regarded as a form of employee involvement is debatable. After all, merely being told about an organisation's plans or its financial results does not in any way give employees influence.

Nonetheless it can help to make employees feel a sense of involvement or at least of inclusion in the circle of those 'in the know'. It also enables employees, either individually or collectively, to exercise informal influence locally, simply because they are in a position to develop and articulate credible alternative approaches to those their immediate line managers would otherwise impose. Alternatively they are in a position to help improve or refine their strategies. It is often rightly stated that 'knowledge is power' and it therefore follows that spreading relevant knowledge beyond the ranks of management to employees is an empowering activity. This is why managers may hold back information from their staff. Except in a crisis situation in which there is a need to promote calm and keep everyone focused on their jobs, often no damage would be done to the organisation by disclosing the information and labelling it 'confidential'. Refusing to disclose it serves to enhance managers' own sense of personal authority and power.

However reluctant line managers may be to share information to which they are privy, there is substantial evidence to back up the view that regular, extensive information sharing has positive outcomes for organisations. This occurs because it improves levels of commitment among staff (*see* Peccei *et al.* 2005) and because in a practical sense it helps everyone to clarify what their role is in the wider organisation. It thus enhances communication and coordination across divisions. It also helps to prevent false understanding developing among staff thanks to the inevitable 'rumour mills' that operate in all organisations and can make employees view change initiatives with less cynicism than otherwise might be the case (Brown and Creagan 2008).

Two-way communication, by contrast, especially when it takes the form of a formal exercise, clearly falls into the category of employee involvement. Staff are being asked to respond to a suggested new approach, asked their opinion, being invited to make suggestions for improvements or given an opportunity to point out flaws in current systems or management thinking. Provided the exercise is not merely cosmetic, and that the views of staff are given serious consideration, influence is gained. Trust in management is, however, vital if staff are to become involved in two-way communication (Tae-Yeol Kim *et al.* 2009). The following are some of the most common methods of information sharing.

Team briefing

Team briefing is an initiative that attempts to do a number of different things simultaneously. It provides authoritative information at regular intervals, so that people know what is going on, the information is geared to achievement of production targets and other features of organisational objectives, it is delivered face to face to provide scope for questions and clarification, and it emphasises the role of supervisors and line managers as the source of information:

> Team briefings are often used to cascade information or managerial messages throughout the organisation. The teams are usually based round a common production or service area, rather than an occupation, and usually comprise between four and fifteen people. The leader of the team is usually the manager or supervisor of the section and should be trained in the principles and skills of how to brief. The meetings last for no more than 30 minutes, and time should be left for questions from employees. Meetings should be held at least monthly or on a regular pre-arranged basis. (Holden 1997: 624)

With goodwill and managerial discipline, team briefing can be a valuable contributor to employee involvement, as it deals in that precious commodity, information. Traditionally, there has perhaps been a managerial view that people doing the work are not interested in anything other than the immediate and short term and that the manager's status partly rests on knowing what others do not know. For this reason all the managers and supervisors in the communications chain have to be committed to making it a success, as well as having the training that Holden refers to above.

Team briefing gets easier once it is established as a regular event. The first briefing will probably go very well and the second will be even better. It is important that management enthusiasm and commitment do not flag just as the employees are getting used to the process.

During economic recessions there is a boost to the team briefing process because so many managements have so much bad news to convey. When you are losing money and profitability, there is a great incentive to explain to the workforce exactly how grim the situation is, so that they do not look for big pay rises. Whatever the economic climate, team briefing continues to be used widely and was found to operate in a majority of organisations featured in the 2004 WER Survey. (Kersley *et al.* 2006: 135)

Sometimes, instead of cascading information down a management hierarchy, senior managers in larger organisations like to brief larger groups of employees about significant developments directly. Roadshows or 'interactive executive sessions' of this kind are common and are seen by managers as being almost as effective a means of passing information to employees as more conventional forms of team-briefing. (IRS 2005a: 11)

Quality circles

Originating in Japanese firms, quality circles comprise small groups of employees (10–15 maximum) who meet regularly to generate ideas aimed at improving the quality of products and services and of organisational productivity. They can also be used as problem-solving groups and as a means by which employee opinion is transmitted to senior management. Some quality circles consist of staff who work together within a team or organisational function, others are cross-functional and focus on interdepartmental issues.

These sorts of practice have several objectives, such as to increase the stock of ideas within an organisation, to encourage co-operative relations at work, and to legitimise change. These practices are predicated on the assumption that employees are recognised as a (if not the) major source of competitive advantage for organisations, a source whose ideas have been ignored in the past or who have been told that 'they are not paid to think'. (Marchington 2001: 235)

Not only, therefore, are quality circles a potential source of useful ideas for improving systems and saving costs. They also give people a welcome opportunity to contribute their thoughts and experience. A generally positive impact on employee attitudes should thus result.

News sheets

Another common form of employee involvement occurs through the regular publication of in-house journals or news sheets either in paper or electronic form. On one level they simply provide a means by which information concerning finances, policy and proposed change can be transmitted by managers to employees. This is a limited form of employee involvement which does little more than improve the extent to which employees are informed about what is going on elsewhere in their organisations. This will engender a perception of greater involvement and belonging, but does not directly involve employees in any type of decision making. For that to occur the news sheet must be interactive in some way. It may, for example, be used as a means by which employees are consulted about new initiatives, or may provide a forum through which complaints and ideas are voiced.

Attitude surveys

Regular surveys of employee opinion are very useful from a management point of view, particularly where there are no unions present to convey to management an honest picture of morale and commitment in the organisation. Indeed, in their study of workplace bullying, Pate and Beaumont (2010) suggest that attitude surveys are one of the leading employee voice mechanisms. In order to be effective (that is, honest), responses must be anonymous, individuals stating only which department they work in so that interdepartmental comparisons can be made. It also makes sense to ask the same questions in the same format each time a survey is carried out, so that changes in attitude and/or responses to initiatives can be tracked over time.

The major problems with attitude surveys are associated with situations in which they reveal serious problems which are then not properly addressed. This can easily lead to cynicism and even anger on the part of the workforce. The result is a poorer employee relations climate than would have been the case had no survey taken place. It is counterproductive to involve employees if their contribution is subsequently ignored, yet this appears to happen in many of the organisations where regular surveys are conducted. IRS (2005b) found that the main reasons employers in their sample gave for carrying out employee surveys were to 'take the pulse of the organisation' and to 'demonstrate commitment to employee views'. Only a minority subsequently used the information gathered to shape decision making, even in the HR arena.

Suggestion schemes

A common system of formal bottom-up communication employed by organisations involves encouraging staff to make suggestions about how practices and processes could be improved to make them more effective, efficient or safe. Employees are often best placed to observe in detail what happens operationally on the front-line because they have the greatest level of interaction on a day-to-day basis with customers, equipment and organisational procedures. Many organisations go to great lengths to encourage suggestions from employees, as we illustrate in the Window on practice that follows.

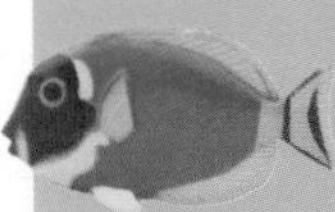

WINDOW ON PRACTICE

Tube Lines staff are pitching business ideas to a panel of bosses in the style of the BBC2 television programme *Dragons' Den*. The firm, responsible for the infrastructure of three London Underground lines, rewards workers whose schemes save the company money with £1,000 worth of retail vouchers. Runners-up get £500 and £200 in vouchers.

The Change Challenge Cup, which takes place every three months, is designed to encourage employees to improve the way the business operates. The 15-strong panel of judges, chaired by chief executive Terry Morgan, is made up of the firm's Change Council, which monitors the organisation's improvements.

The first competition was won jointly by two employees. One developed a new way to clean iron filings from the trackside train position detectors, which has the potential to save the company £1.3m a year in avoided train delays.

The other winning suggestion was to fit a metal platform across the track to the tunnel wall, allowing workers to cross safely. Morgan said: 'Tube Lines can only continue to move forward if employees are encouraged to come up with better ways of working.'

Source: Adapted from *People Management* (2008) 'Tube lines launches "dragons' den" scheme', 21 August, p. 14.

Managers often only become aware of problems when their employees report them, and without such reports can have no opportunities for improving things. So it makes sense to encourage staff to put forward suggestions; and having a formal scheme enhances the chances that they will do so. IDS (2005a) describes several types of scheme and draws together from these examples some good practice points. IDS argues that employees should be recognised financially or otherwise when they make a suggestion which is taken up, that systems for submitting ideas should be as uncomplicated as possible, that feedback should be given to all who submit ideas, that past suggestions should be revisited periodically and that schemes must be regularly publicised to remind staff of their existence. IDS also found that organisations are increasingly benefiting from schemes which operate electronically. Suggestions are submitted via e-mail or a form placed on an intranet and filed systematically by an evaluator. Feedback is then given electronically and the successes of the whole scheme publicised regularly through e-mail bulletins sent to all staff.

ACTIVITY 19.1

Despite plenty of evidence that demonstrates how beneficial two-way information sharing can be for organisations, only a minority of non-union employers operate formal systems. Why do you think this is? What are the likely consequences? What arguments would you use to persuade a team of managers of the need to listen to the views of staff and to take them seriously?

CONSULTATION

After information sharing, the next step up the 'employee involvement escalator' is consultation. Here employees are asked either directly or through representatives to express views which management take into account when making decisions. Such processes fall short of negotiation or co-determination because there is no ultimate expectation of agreement if the views of staff and management diverge. In some organisations regular meetings are held to enable consultation to take place about a wide range of issues. In others consultation exercises take place irregularly and focus on specific areas such as organisational restructuring or policy changes. Consultation is generally regarded as a hallmark of good management and UK employers have legal obligations to consult with employees (we outline these in Chapter 20). An employer who fails to consult properly, particularly at times of significant change, is likely to be perceived as being unduly autocratic. The result will be dissatisfaction, low levels of motivation, higher staff turnover and poorer levels of customer service. Moreover, consultation has important advantages as a means by which good ideas are brought forward and weak ones challenged.

In workplaces where unions are recognised it is usual for consultation to take place over a range of issues through permanent consultative institutions. The joint consultative committee (JCC) is the most common form, being a forum in which managers and staff representatives meet on a regular basis. In more traditional unionised organisations JCCs are kept distinct from negotiating forums – despite the fact that the membership is often the same. A clear divide is thus established between areas which are to be the subject of negotiation (typically terms and conditions of employment) and matters which are the subject of consultation such as health and safety or training. In recent years as partnership agreements have become more common (*see* Chapter 20), there has been a shift from negotiation towards consultation, the aim being to downplay the adversarial nature of the union–employer relationship and to widen the range of topics about which both sides can engage constructively.

JCCs are found in only 14 per cent of UK workplaces employing over ten people, but they are present in a majority of those employing over 200 (Kersey *et al*. 2006: 126–7). It is unusual for the very largest workplaces not to have some form of consultative forum which meets periodically, although in some multi-site corporations formal consultation with employee representatives is restricted to the corporate level and does not take place in individual workplaces. JCCs are four times as common in union workplaces than in those where unions are not recognised (Kersley *et al*. 2006: 127), suggesting that they are mostly still used in parallel with collective bargaining machinery. However, some researchers (e.g. Marchington 1989 and Kelly 1998) have argued that they are used in some workplaces as a substitute for collective bargaining or as a means of discouraging the development of a union presence. Managers in such workplaces believe that unions are less likely to gain support and request recognition if the employer keeps the staff informed of issues that affect them and consults with them before taking decisions. Consultative forums in non-union firms also provide a means whereby managers can put their case effectively without the presence of organised opposition.

From a management perspective, the great danger is that people come to believe that management is not genuinely interested in hearing their views or in taking them on board. Rose (2001: 391) refers to this approach as 'pseudo-consultation' in which managers are really doing little more than informing employees about decisions that have already been taken. Cynicism results because there is perceived to be an attempt on the part of managers to use consultative forums merely as a means of legitimising their decisions. They can say that consultation has taken place, when in truth it has not. Pseudo-consultation typically involves assembling employees in large groups with senior managers present. The management message is then put across strongly and a short time is given for others to respond. In such situations employees have no time to give proper consideration to the proposals and are likely to feel too intimidated to articulate criticisms. The result is often worse in terms of employee morale and engagement with the changes than would have been the case had no consultation been attempted.

Even where managers genuinely intend to undertake meaningful consultation, they can very easily create an impression that it is no more than a 'pseudo' exercise. It is therefore important to avoid the approaches outlined in the above paragraph. Employees should be informed of a range of possible ways forward (not just the one favoured by management) and invited to consider them in small groups. The results of their deliberations can then be fed back to senior managers and given proper consideration. In this way the appearance of pseudo-consultation, as well as the reality, can be avoided.

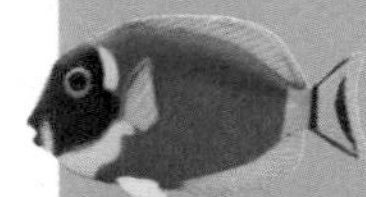

WINDOW ON PRACTICE

IRS (2006) describe how a marketing company called BI increased its profitability and halved its staff turnover, in part by introducing a range of employee involvement initiatives. The early years had seen company revenues decline markedly, leading to a pay freeze and staff turnover of 60 per cent.

In 2004, following the appointment of a new chief executive and HR director, a wide range of measures were introduced to tackle these problems. Improving employee involvement was a priority, to signal very clearly the adoption of a new management style, to promote a positive culture and to encourage staff to identify problems and possible solutions. The initiatives included the following:

- weekly e-mail bulletins to staff from senior managers explaining major developments;
- annual letters to staff from the managing director thanking them and setting out key achievements;
- quarterly company meetings at which all staff are briefed about financial matters and strategy;
- an intranet site updated daily with fresh information about the company's activities;
- monthly meetings at which the HR director talks in confidence to ten randomly selected employees about their concerns;
- regular meetings of a 'people forum' at which representatives from each team are consulted about developments.

As a result of these involvement activities many changes were made to operational processes and also to HR practices. Hours of work were made more flexible, and staff discouraged from working more hours than was necessary. A scheme was also introduced to allow people to trade some of their salary for additional holiday.

CO-DETERMINATION

In the UK, important decision making in organisations is nearly always the preserve of managers. Decisions in the employment area are often taken after extensive and genuine consultation, or after negotiation with union representatives, but anything approaching serious co-determination with employees is very rare indeed. Nevertheless, it must be pointed out that at the level of the individual team, a degree of informal co-determination is common. Indeed, in recent years it has become more common as organisations have tended to de-layer, reducing the number of managers and levels of hierarchy. Increasingly employees and team leaders have found themselves 'empowered' to take decisions for themselves that once they would have had to refer to a manager. It is important not to overestimate the significance of this trend, as any discretion that is given operates within tightly defined boundaries. What gets done is still determined by managers, but there is greater flexibility about when and how exactly it gets done.

The limitations are well illustrated by the following findings from the 2004 Workplace Employment Relations Survey (Kersley *et al.* 2006: 89–90):

- 72 per cent of workplaces employ people to work in 'formally designated teams';
- 83 per cent of these teams are given responsibility for products or services;
- in 61 per cent of these teams members jointly decide how work is done;
- in 66 per cent of these teams tasks are rotated among members;
- in only 6 per cent of these teams are team members able to choose their own leader.

Elsewhere in Europe the extent of co-determination at the level of the team and of individual empowerment varies from country to country. In southern European nations such as France, Italy and Spain managers at the local level tend to guard their autonomy more tightly than typical British line managers. Co-determination at the local level over day-to-day workplace activities is thus rarer than in the UK. In northern Europe, by contrast, a far greater degree of team-based autonomy is common. The best-known examples of teams assuming responsibility and decision-making authority are in the Scandinavian countries. The approach involves organising a workforce into small groups of about a dozen members, who are mutually supportive and who operate with minimal supervision. Managers set performance targets (often after consultation) and allocate tasks, but it is for the team itself to decide exactly how these are to be achieved. The team organises its own activities, appoints its own leaders and works out for itself how to overcome problems. Teamworking can thus be characterised as a form of worker control, even though it operates within heavily prescribed limits. Managers refrain from giving day-to-day supervision, but are on hand to give advice or more direct assistance where necessary. Disciplining staff, for example, is a task carried out by managers and not by team members. Teamworking is often associated with situations in which several regionally based teams compete with each other to meet or exceed performance targets. Team-based remuneration then accounts for a proportion of the total pay received.

While practice varies at the local team level across Europe, at the level of the organisation co-determination is a great deal more established and widespread in most countries than is the case in the UK. It occurs through two distinct mechanisms:

1. through the legal empowerment of works councils or enterprise committees;
2. by reserving places on executive boards for worker directors.

Both approaches are famously used in Germany, where co-determination over employment matters is standard practice in organisations of any size. In the UK most of the activities described in this book are the preserve of managers, while in Germany they are decided jointly between managers and workforce representatives. German managers cannot impose any decision relating to changing workplace rules, disciplinary procedures, working hours, holidays, bonus payments, overtime arrangements, health and safety matters, training or selection methods without first securing the agreement of their organisation's works council. Moreover, their autonomy to make decisions about any changes relating to the nature of the work their employees do or the physical environment in which it is performed is subject to them first consulting with the works council and taking its objections and suggestions into account. In addition the law requires that managers share a great deal of financial and planning information with works councils that goes well beyond the employment sphere (Budd 2004: 129). Seats are also reserved on the supervisory boards of German companies for workforce representatives. In companies employing more than 500 people, a third of the seats are reserved. Where over 2,000 are employed, half the seats are taken by worker representatives. Such national variations are likely to be the cause of some difficulty for multinational corporations operating in a number of companies. A recent study by Marginson *et al.* (2009) showed that such employers are engaging in significant innovations in representation and voice arrangements in order to address these variations.

You will find further information and discussion exercises about variations in the way employee relations is managed internationally on this book's companion website, **www.pearsoned.co.uk/torrington**.

ACTIVITY 19.2

In many European companies works councils or enterprise committees tend to be dominated by trade unions, even where a majority of the staff are not members. Why do you think this is? What do you think are the major advantages and disadvantages of trade union representatives also acting as works council members or worker directors?

SUMMARY PROPOSITIONS

19.1 Genuine employee voice serves to increase commitment and to improve decision making in organisations.

19.2 Information sharing is common in the UK. Team briefing, news sheets and suggestion schemes are the most common mechanisms adopted.

19.3 The use of formal consultation processes is common in larger UK organisations. Joint Consultative Committees are found in most unionised workplaces.

19.4 Co-determination at the level of the organisation or workplace is rare in the UK, but common in many other EU countries.

19.5 Co-determination at the level of teams is increasing in the UK, but is limited in the extent to which it empowers employees.

GENERAL DISCUSSION TOPICS

1 Why do you think employers in the UK are more reluctant to involve employee representatives in strategic decision making than is the case in a country such as Germany?

2 How far do you agree with the view that information sharing barely constitutes employee involvement at all?

3 In what ways would you like to see increased or decreased employee involvement in your organisation, and why?

FURTHER READING

Benson, J. and Brown, M. (2010) 'Employee voice: does union membership matter?', *Human Resource Management Journal*, Vol. 20, No. 1, pp. 80–99.
In this article, the authors explore the relationship between trade union membership and employee perceptions of voice. Their findings are counterintuitive, that trade union membership has a significantly negative impact upon employee perceptions of voice, and they set about explaining why this might be the case.

Dundon, T. *et al.* (2005) 'The management of voice in non-union organisations: managers' perspectives', *Employee Relations*, Vol. 27, No. 3, pp. 307–19.
In this article Tony Dundon and his colleagues explore the views of managers about the role played by consultative fora in seven non-union organisations. They conclude that commentators have often been too hasty to dismiss these practices as inconsequential or ineffective.

Storey, J. (ed.) (2005) *Adding Value through Information and Consultation*. Basingstoke: Palgrave Macmillan/Open University.
Harley, B., Hyman, J. and Thompson, P. (2005) *Participation and Democracy at Work: Essays in honour of Harvie Ramsay*. Basingstoke: Palgrave Macmillan.
Two books of articles by leading academic researchers which between them cover every aspect of informing, consulting and involving employees.

REFERENCES

Benson, J. and Brown, M. (2010) 'Employee voice: does union membership matter?', *Human Resource Management Journal*, Vol. 20, No. 1, pp. 80–99.

Brown, M. and Creagan, C. (2008) 'Organizational change cynicism: the role of employee involvement', *Human Resource Management*, Vol. 47, No. 4, pp. 667–86.

Budd, J. (2004) *Employment with a Human Face*. Ithaca: Cornell University Press.

Dundon, T., Wilkinson, A., Marchington, M. and Ackers, P. (2005) 'The management of voice in non-union organisations: managers' perspectives', *Employee Relations*, Vol. 27, No. 3, pp. 307–19.

Harley, B., Hyman, J. and Thompson, P. (2005) *Participation and Democracy at Work: Essays in honour of Harvie Ramsay*. Basingstoke: Palgrave Macmillan.

Holden, L. (1997) 'Employee involvement', in I. Beardwell and L. Holden (eds), *Human Resource Management*, 2nd edn. London: Pitman.

IDS (2005a) *Suggestion Schemes*, IDS Study No. 812. London: IDS.

IDS (2005b) *Information and Consultation Arrangements*, IDS Study No. 790. London: IDS.

IRS (2005a) 'Dialogue or monologue: is the message getting through?', *IRS Employment Review* No. 834, October. London: IRS.

IRS (2005b) 'More questions than answers? Employee surveys revealed', *IRS Employment Review* No. 820, March. London: IRS.

IRS (2006) 'BI bounces back with culture of employee engagement', *IRS Employment Review* No. 839. January. London: IRS.

Kelly, J. (1998) *Rethinking Industrial Relations: Mobilization, collectivism and long waves*. London: Routledge.

Kersley, B., Alpin, C., Forth, J., Bryson, A., Bewley, H., Dix, G. and Oxenbridge, S. (2006) *Inside the Workplace: Findings from the 2004 Workplace Employment Relations Survey*. Abingdon: Routledge.

Kim, Tae-Yeol, Rosen, B. and Lee, Deog-Ro (2009) 'South Korean managerial reactions to voicing discontent: the effects of employee attitude and employee communication styles', *Journal of Organizational Behavior*, Vol. 30, pp. 1001–18.

Marchington, M. (1989) 'Joint consultation in practice', in K. Sisson (ed.), *Personnel Management in Britain*. Oxford: Blackwell.

Marchington, M. (2001) 'Employee involvement at work', in J. Storey (ed.), *Human Resource Management: A critical text*, 2nd edn. London: Thomson Learning.

Marchington, M. and Wilkinson, A. (2005) 'Direct participation and involvement', in S. Bach (ed.), *Managing Human Resources: Personnel Management in Transition*, 4th edn. Oxford: Blackwell.

Marginson, P., Edwards, P., Edwards, T., Ferner, A. and Tregaskis, O. (2009) 'Employee representation and consultative voice in multinational companies operating in Britain', *British Journal of Industrial Relations*, online early view August 2009.

Pate, J. and Beaumont, P. (2010) 'Bullying and harassment: a case of success?', *Employee Relations*, Vol. 32, No. 2, pp. 171–83.

Peccei, R., Bewley, H., Gospel, G. and Willman, P. (2005) 'Is it good to talk? Information disclosure and organisational performance in the UK', *British Journal of Industrial Relations*, Vol. 43, No. 1, pp. 11–39.

People Management (2008) 'Tube lines launches "dragons' den" scheme', 21 August, p. 14.

People Management (2010) 'Tories outline plans for public-sector workers' co-operatives', 15 February, available at **http://www.peoplemanagement.co.uk/pm/articles/2010/02/tories-outline-plans-for-public-sector-workers-co-operatives.htm.**

Rose, E. (2001) *Employee Relations*. London: Financial Times/Prentice Hall.

Storey, J. (ed.) (2005) *Adding Value through Information and Consultation*. Basingstoke: Palgrave Macmillan/Open University.

Urwin, P., Murphy, R. and Michielsens, E. (2007) 'Employee voice regimes and the characteristics of conflict: an analysis of the 2003 survey of employment tribunal applications', *Human Resource Management Journal*, Vol. 17, No. 2, pp. 178–97.

An extensive range of additional materials, including multiple choice questions, answers to questions and links to useful websites can be found on the Human Resource Management companion website at **www.pearsoned.co.uk/torrington**.

THE LEGAL FRAMEWORK OF WORK

THE OBJECTIVES OF THIS CHAPTER ARE TO:

1. Demonstrate the great extent to which the regulation of workplaces and labour markets has increased in recent decades
2. Introduce the contract of employment and its significance in the regulation of employment
3. Explain and illustrate the major principles of discrimination law and the defences that employers can deploy when accused of unlawful actions in this area
4. Summarise the major principles underpinning the criminal and civil law aspects of health and safety regulation
5. Set out the major family-friendly employment rights that have been introduced in recent years
6. Introduce the law regulating working time and the National Minimum Wage
7. Debate the extent to which employment law is best characterised as a benefit or a burden from the point of view of employing organisations

A REGULATORY REVOLUTION

As was pointed out in Chapter 2, one of the most important contemporary developments which has shaped HR practice in organisations has been the seemingly relentless increase, year on year, of new employment regulation. Forty years ago it was commonly and correctly stated that UK workplaces and labour markets were among the most lightly regulated in the industrial world. It was a long-standing tradition for the state to make a virtue of not intervening in the relationship between employers and employees except when it was absolutely necessary to do so. As a result, with the exception of basic health and safety entitlements, laws preventing the exploitation of child workers and the basic principle that the terms of all contracts of employment were legally enforceable, there was hardly any such thing as 'employment law' in the UK. Since then the position has wholly reversed. Though still less tightly regulated than some European countries, the UK now has one of the most highly regulated labour markets in the world. As far as the regulation of work is concerned, the past 40 years can truly be characterised as a revolutionary period.

Today a wide range of legally imposed restrictions severely limit employers' freedom to manage people and run their organisations as they please. Regulation plays a role in almost every area of HRM from recruitment and selection, through arrangements for paying people, managing working time, determining rights to leave from work, ensuring a decent level of health and safety, dealing with trade unions, managing retirements and dismissals. One aim is to provide some re-balancing of the power relationship between employers and employees, helping to restrict the extent to which managers can abuse their power by exploiting their employees unfairly or acting in an unjustly arbitrary manner towards them. Another is to promote good practice in people management via flexible working and partnership with unions and other employee representatives. We covered dismissal law thoroughly in Chapter 10. Our purpose here is to introduce the other major areas of UK employment law, principally contracts of employment, discrimination law, family-friendly and health and safety regulation, and the law relating to pay and working time.

The regulatory revolution began properly in the early 1970s with the introduction of unfair dismissal law and of specialised labour law courts called Industrial Tribunals (now renamed 'Employment Tribunals') to hear cases brought by aggrieved individuals. These developments were followed by the establishment of the right for women to take a period of paid maternity leave following the birth of a child and to return to their jobs afterwards, a right not to be discriminated against on grounds of sex, marital status, race, ethnicity or national origin, and a right for men and women to be paid 'equal pay for equal work'. Health and safety law was consolidated and extended so that the same principles and the same type of inspection regime now apply in all workplaces. The 1980s saw the introduction of further measures, for the most part with a European origin. Extensive rights for workers whose organisations passed from one owner or 'controlling body' to another were introduced, while the extent of health and safety law and equal pay law were substantially extended. The Conservative Thatcher and Major governments (1979–1997) expressed their dislike of the Continental approach to employment regulation which they saw as placing an unnecessary and counterproductive 'burden on business' and as a disincentive to job creation, but they did not repeal the new individual employment rights established by their predecessors in any fundamental way. Indeed, 1995 saw a substantial augmentation of employment rights with the passing of the Disability Discrimination Act. Earlier a variety of measures were introduced which remain on the statute book aimed at reducing the number of strikes and restricting the rights of employers to take account of someone's trade union membership or non-membership when making recruitment decisions.

After 1997 however, following the election of the Blair Labour government, the pace at which new law was introduced sped up very considerably. This was partly because the government believed it was the right thing to do and that it had been elected on that platform, but also importantly as a result of the introduction of a wide range of significant new employment rights at the European level. For example, we have seen major extensions of discrimination law into new areas. As a result it is now unlawful to discriminate on grounds of sexual orientation, religion or belief, age or because someone is employed on either a fixed-term or a part-time contract. We have also seen a very substantial extension of family-friendly employment rights, so that most women are now entitled to a year's maternity leave, fathers can take periods of paid paternity leave, while parents of young children and adult carers have gained the right to request flexible working. Other major new employment rights have included the National Minimum Wage, the Working Time Regulations, compulsory trade union recognition where a majority of a workforce vote for it, a degree of protection for 'whistleblowers', a raft of new data protection rights, a ban on smoking in public places (including workplaces), collective consultation rights, regulations concerning the employer's right to intercept e-mails and phone calls and a right for all to be accompanied by a union official or work colleague at serious disciplinary and grievance meetings. Moreover, further extensions are planned for the future, most notably in the area of maternity and paternity rights.

It is important to appreciate that in most instances the passing of new Acts of Parliament or of sets of regulations issued under these Acts is very often the start of a process of law making rather than the end. This is because statutes typically lack detail on how principles should be applied in different circumstances. It often takes a further five to ten years for sufficient numbers of test cases to be brought before the courts in order that definitive judgments can be made about precise points of interpretation. It is only when cases on points of principle are appealed to the higher courts that binding precedents are established. Hence, at the time of writing (spring 2010), it is impossible with real certainty to give definitive advice about many important aspects of age discrimination law, despite its having been introduced in 2006. What exactly is and is not lawful, for example, in the wording of recruitment advertisements has yet to be established. In a year or two the higher courts will get the opportunity to make rulings about whether it is generally lawful to advertise for a 'youthful' or an 'experienced' person, but as yet they have not done so.

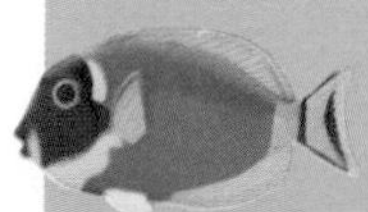

WINDOW ON PRACTICE

In 2006 Helen Green, an assistant company secretary employed in London won her case in the High Court. She had suffered two nervous breakdowns which were due, it was found, to her having been bullied at work by five colleagues. Over a period of four years Ms Green claimed to have been verbally abused, ignored and denigrated by them to such an extent that she became seriously ill, at one point being placed on

'suicide watch' in hospital. On her return to work following the first breakdown, she found that little had changed and she suffered a relapse a few months later. Her employment was subsequently terminated when it became clear that she was unlikely to be able to return to work in the foreseeable future. Having found in favour of Ms Green, the High Court ordered her former employers, Deutsche Bank, to pay her compensation of £35,000 for pain and suffering, £25,000 for disadvantage in the labour market, £128,000 for lost earnings and a massive £640,000 for loss of future earnings and pension. In addition to this total of £828,000 damages, the bank was ordered to pay Ms Green's legal costs, taking its total payout to around £1.5 million – and that is before taking its own costs into account.

The day after the ruling and on subsequent days the newspapers covered the story in some depth. This was partly because of the size of the award (sizeable indeed for a woman who was earning £45,000 a year prior to her breakdown), partly because Ms Green is a good-looking young woman whose photograph editors were keen to publish, and partly because the nature of the 'bullying and harassment' that she had suffered appeared to many to have amounted to no more than the kind of banter and political game-playing that goes on regularly in the majority of larger UK organisations.

Many opinion articles and letters appeared in the papers. Some supported Ms Green, arguing that it was about time employers were required to take bullying of the kind she had suffered more seriously. Many, however, were critical, in one case accusing her of acting like a 'gold-digging cry-baby' who had seriously put back the cause of women seeking careers in the financial services industry. The net result was a great deal of negative publicity for Deutsche Bank, particularly when it later emerged in newspaper interviews that the bank had sought both to undermine Ms Green's case by suggesting that her breakdowns were due to unfortunate circumstances in her earlier life (she had been sexually abused by her adoptive father) and had tried unsuccessfully to find evidence to demonstrate that her mother had suffered from a serious mental illness.

Yet in many respects it can be plausibly argued that Deutsche Bank was unlucky in this case. The bank had after all kept Helen Green's job open for her and had paid her a full salary for over two years before dismissing her. It had promoted her twice before her breakdown, had provided a counselling service and had sent her on a stress-management training programme. Moreover, some of the specific incidents that had led to Ms Green's breakdowns do appear on the face of it to be childish in nature and unlikely to offend most people to anything like the same extent. They included removing her name from a circulation list, hiding her post, blowing raspberries at her and, on one occasion, a colleague 'crossing her arms in a very dramatic way and staring at Ms Green'.

Whatever the rights and wrongs of the ruling in this case, it demonstrates clearly how employers can easily find themselves on the wrong side of the law in their dealings with employees and how the results can be costly in terms of compensation, staff time and lost reputation.

Sources: BBC 2006, Tait 2006, Guest 2006 and *The Times* 2006.

THE CONTRACT OF EMPLOYMENT

Although a great deal is written about 'psychological contracts' and 'contracts for performance', the association between employer and employee remains at base a legal relationship governed by 'a contract of employment'. Whatever expectations employers and employees have of one another when the employment begins, the basic terms and conditions will be agreed and understood at the start and may, if necessary, be enforced in a court. In law the existence of such a contract confers on both parties important obligations as well as giving the employee access to significant legal rights which are not available to people who work under different contractual arrangements.

Employment contracts are very varied, and in recent years all industrialised countries have seen a trend away from what are usually described as being 'traditional' arrangements in which employees are employed on an open-ended basis for 38 hours or so over a five-day standard 'working week' towards a variety of different alternative types of contract. In some industrial sectors we have seen a move away from employment altogether as people have chosen, or been required, to switch to self-employment or agency working. However, as far as the law is concerned over 80 per cent of people who work in the UK are employees. This means that they have a contract of employment with their employer, with the duties and privileges that that implies. As far as the law is concerned they are working under 'a contract of service'. This derives from the old notion of a master and servant relationship and indicates that the employee (or servant) has obligations to the employer or master and vice versa. In contrast, those who are self-employed or subcontractors have greater autonomy, but no one standing between them and legal accountability for their actions. The law makes an important distinction between the two groups, employees having access to a wider range of legal rights than non-employees. While some areas of employment law apply to all workers, others apply only to employees. Non-employees are deemed to be working under 'a contract for services' rather than 'a contract of service'. In 2010 the main statutory rights that applied to each were those shown in Table 20.1.

Table 20.1 Access to statutory employment rights

Employment rights which apply to all workers	Employment rights which apply only to employees
Equal pay for equal work	Right to a statement of terms and conditions of employment
Non-discrimination on grounds of sex, race, religious belief, sexual orientation, age and disability	Right to an itemised pay statement
Right not to have unauthorised deductions from pay	Statutory Sick Pay
Basic health and safety rights	Time off for public duties
Minimum wage	Nine months' maternity pay
Working time regulations	Trade union rights
Data protection rights	Minimum notice periods
Time off to care for dependants	Fixed-term employment regulations
Part-time workers regulations	Parental leave (after one year's service)
Twelve months' maternity leave	Unfair dismissal rights (after one year's service)

In addition to the statutory rights conferred by Acts of Parliament, a range of common law duties are owed by employers to employees and vice versa which do not apply in the case of other forms of relationship. The major obligations are as follows:

Owed by employers to employees:

- a general duty of care
- a duty to pay agreed wages
- a duty to provide work
- a duty not to treat employees in an arbitrary or vindictive manner
- a duty to provide support to employees
- a duty to provide safe systems of work

Owed by employees to employers:

- a duty to cooperate
- a duty to obey reasonable/lawful instructions
- a duty to exercise reasonable care and skill
- a duty to act in good faith

Owed by employers to employees and vice versa:

- to maintain a relationship of mutual trust and confidence

Owed by employees and ex-employees:

- duty of fidelity

A contract of employment, contrary to common perception, need not exist in written form. It is much more satisfactory for both parties if there is documentary evidence of what terms and conditions have been offered and accepted, but a contract of employment exists whether agreed verbally on the telephone or sealed with no more than a handshake. Where there is any doubt about whether someone is an employee or not, the courts look at the evidence presented to them concerning the reality of the existing relationship between the two parties. If they consider, on balance, that it is governed by a 'contract of service' rather than a 'contract for services', they will consider the worker to be an employee and entitled to the full range of rights outlined above.

WINDOW ON PRACTICE

A case heard in the House of Lords (now reinvented as The Supreme Court) illustrates the importance of employee status. Mrs Carmichael and a colleague were employed as tour guides at a power station run by National Power PLC. They started working for the company on a casual basis in 1989, undertaking about four hours' work each week as and when they were needed. By 1995 they each were working around 25 hours a week, so they decided to ask for written particulars of their terms and conditions of employment. The company refused on the grounds that they were casual workers and not employees. The women won their case in the lower courts, but the company decided to appeal right up to the House of Lords. At this stage the women lost their case on the grounds that there was no mutuality of obligation. They could, and indeed had, turned down requests to work without suffering any disciplinary action. They were therefore not employees and not entitled to the rights associated with full employment status.

An employment contract comes into existence when an unambiguous offer of employment is made and is unconditionally accepted. Once it is agreed neither side can alter the terms and conditions which govern their relationship without the agreement of the other. An employer cannot therefore unilaterally cut employees' pay, lengthen their hours of work, reduce their holiday entitlement, change their place of work or move them to another kind of work. To do so the employer either has to secure the employees' agreement (maybe by offering some kind of sweetener payment) or has to ensure that the right to make adjustments to terms and conditions is written into the contract by means of flexibility clauses. Where an employer forces changes through without securing the agreement of employees directly, or in many cases through negotiation with union representatives, legal action may follow. An employee may simply bring a claim for breach of contract and ask that the original contract be honoured. In such circumstances compensation may or may not be appropriate. Alternatively, where the employer's breach is serious or where it is one of the implied duties listed above that has not been honoured, employees are entitled to resign and claim constructive dismissal in an Employment Tribunal, in which case their situation is treated as if they had actually been dismissed (*see* Chapter 10). Table 20.2 provides a checklist for preparing a contract of employment.

Table 20.2 Checklist for preparing a contract of employment

1. Name of employer; name of employee.
2. Date on which employment began.
3. Job title.
4. Rate of pay, period and method of payment.
5. Normal hours of work and related conditions, such as meal-breaks.
6. Arrangements for holidays and holiday pay, including means whereby both can be calculated precisely.
7. Terms and conditions relating to sickness, injury and sick pay.
8. Terms and conditions of pension arrangements.
9. Length of notice due to and from employee.
10. Disciplinary rules and procedure.
11. Arrangements for handling employee grievances.
12. (Where applicable) Conditions of employment relating to trade union membership.

ACTIVITY 20.1

Substantial and growing numbers of people in the UK work under atypical sets of terms and conditions, for example on casual or agency contracts. As a rule such staff are classed as 'workers' rather than 'employees' because they are not deemed to be working under 'contracts of service'. As a result they are denied many important employment rights (*see* Table 20.1).

What do you think are the main arguments for and against extending full employment rights to these groups? Where do you stand in this debate and why?

DISCRIMINATION LAW

Most anti-discrimination law is now covered by European treaties or directives and thus applies in all member states of the EU. Central to the achievement of this harmonisation was the issuing in 2000 of the Equal Treatment Framework Directive which required the governments of all the member states to introduce new laws and, where necessary, to amend their existing laws in order to ensure that it complied with the core principles set out in the directive. As a result, across the EU there is now regulation to deter discrimination at work on the following grounds:

- sex
- race, ethnicity and national origin
- sexual orientation
- religion or belief
- age
- disability

In each case the details differ somewhat, but the same broad principles apply. Below we illustrate these by describing sex discrimination law at some length, going on briefly to explain how and why some of the other fields of discrimination law employ slightly different approaches.

Sex discrimination law

In the UK, extensive law in the area of sex discrimination has been on the statute books since the passing in 1975 of the Sex Discrimination Act. This has been amended on several occasions since then and has been interpreted in different ways as a result of new case law, but the core tenets have always remained the same. As matters stand there are four separate headings under which a case can be brought: direct sex discrimination, indirect sex discrimination, sexual harassment and victimisation.

Direct discrimination

Direct discrimination is straightforward. It occurs simply when an employer treats someone unfavourably and when sex or marital status is an important factor in this decision. In judging claims the courts use the 'but for' test, asking whether the woman would have received the same treatment as a man (or vice versa) but for her sex. Examples of direct sex discrimination include advertising for a man to do a job which could equally well be done by a woman, failing to promote a woman because she is pregnant or dismissing a married woman rather than her single colleague because she is known to have a working husband.

If an employer is found to have discriminated *directly* on grounds of sex or marital status, except in one type of situation, there is no defence. The courts cannot, therefore, take into account any mitigating circumstances or make a judgment based on the view that the employer acted reasonably. Once it has been established that direct discrimination has occurred, proceedings end with a victory for the claimant.

The one exception operates in the area of recruitment, where it is possible to argue that certain jobs have to be reserved for either women or men. For this to be acceptable the employer must convince a court that it is a job for which there is a 'genuine occupational qualification'. The main headings under which such claims are made are as follows:

- authenticity (e.g. acting or modelling jobs);
- decency (e.g. lavatory or changing room attendants);
- personal services (e.g. a counsellor engaged to work in a rape crisis centre).

Direct discrimination on grounds of pregnancy or maternity is assumed automatically to constitute unlawful sex discrimination. This means that there is no defence of reasonableness whatever the individual circumstances. It is thus unlawful to turn down a job application from a well-qualified woman who is eight months pregnant, irrespective of her intentions as regards the taking of maternity leave.

Indirect discrimination

Indirect discrimination is harder to grasp, not least because it can quite easily occur unintentionally. It occurs when a 'provision, criterion or practice' is set or operated which has the effect, in practice, of disadvantaging a significantly larger proportion of one sex than the other. In other words, if substantially fewer women than men can comply with the condition, even if it is applied in exactly the same way to both men and women, it is potentially unlawful. A straightforward example is a job advertisement which specifies that applicants should be taller than 5 feet 10 inches. This is indirectly discriminatory because a substantially smaller proportion of women are able to comply than men.

Indirect discrimination differs from direct discrimination in that there is a defence that an employer can deploy. An employer can objectively justify the condition or requirement they have set 'on grounds other than sex', in which case it may be lawful. An example might be a job for which a key requirement is the ability to lift heavy loads. It is reasonable in such circumstances for the employer to restrict recruitment to people who are physically able to comply, for example by including a test of strength in selection procedures. The fact that more men than women will be able to do so does not make the practice unlawful, provided the lifting requirement is wholly genuine. In judging cases of this kind the tribunal has to decide whether or not the provision, criterion or practice constitutes 'a proportionate means of achieving a legitimate aim'. If the tribunal decides it does, the employer wins, if not the employee wins. It is not sufficient for the employer to show that the practice was convenient or administratively desirable – that does not amount to objective justification – to form the basis of an acceptable defence it must be shown to be genuinely necessary for the achievement of a legitimate business objective.

WINDOW ON PRACTICE

The Equality and Human Rights Commission

Employer actions in the area of discrimination are policed to some extent by the Equality and Human Rights Commission (ERCH) which is required to keep the legislation under review, to conduct formal investigations into employer actions where it has reason to suspect there has been a contravention of the law, to issue codes of practice and to provide legal assistance to employees who consider themselves to be victims of unfair discrimination. On occasions the EHRC itself represents employees before employment tribunals. It also brings its own test cases in a bid to push back the frontiers of the law.

The EHRC began operating in 2007, replacing three well-established commissions – the Equal Opportunities Commission, the Commission for Racial Equality and the Disability Rights Commission. However, its remit extends much further than those of the commissions it replaced to encompass fields covered by the Human Rights Act 1998 as well as discrimination law.

Sexual harassment

Sexual harassment is defined as unwanted conduct of a sexual nature or based on sex, which affects the dignity of men and women at work. It can be physical or verbal in nature, leading *either* to material detriment (i.e. it affects promotion, pay, access to training, etc.) *or* to the creation of an intimidating or humiliating work environment.

Although the law applies equally to men and women, the vast majority of cases are brought by women. The employer's liability in harassment cases arises from the application of the doctrine of **vicarious liability**, under which employers are held responsible for the commitment of civil wrongs by employees when they are at work. In judging cases the courts focus on the reaction of the victim and do not apply any general definitions of what types of conduct do and do not amount to unlawful harassment. Hence conduct which may not offend one person in the slightest can be found to constitute sexual harassment when directed at someone else who is deeply offended.

For an employer the only valid defences relate to the notion of vicarious liability. An employer can, for example, claim ignorance of the incident of which the victim is complaining or can claim that vicarious liability does not apply because it occurred away from the workplace and outside office hours. Finally the employer can defend itself by showing that all reasonable steps were taken to prevent the harassment from occurring or continuing. In order to succeed here, the employer needs to produce evidence to show that initial complaints were promptly acted upon and that appropriate action, such as disciplining the perpetrators or moving them to other work, was taken.

In the field of sex discrimination the term '**victimisation**' means the same as it does in other areas of employment law. An employer victimises workers if it disadvantages them in any way simply because they have sought to exercise their legal rights or have assisted others in doing so. An employee would thus bring a claim of victimisation to a tribunal if he or she had been overlooked for promotion having recently successfully settled an equal pay claim. Importantly, victimisation covers situations in which someone threatens to bring an action or plans to do so even if no case is ultimately brought.

Positive sex discrimination

Positive sex discrimination involves directly or indirectly discriminating in favour of women in situations where they are under-represented – usually at senior levels in an organisation or in occupational groups which are male dominated. Such practices are unlawful under UK law when they involve actively discriminating against men who are better qualified to fill the positions concerned. However, it is lawful to take positive action aimed at encouraging and supporting women provided it stops short of actually discriminating in their favour. It is thus acceptable to include an equal opportunities statement in a job advertisement as a means of indicating that the organisation welcomes applications from women. Similarly employers can design and offer training courses tailored specifically for women. As long as men are not prevented from participating, such action is lawful.

ACTIVITY 20.2

The only situation in UK law when positive discrimination can occur lawfully is in the selection of parliamentary candidates. Here it is lawful for political parties to draw up 'all women shortlists' to help ensure that a reasonable number of female candidates are elected to represent safe seats. Many commentators, however, argue that unless employers are permitted generally to discriminate positively in favour of minority or under-represented groups a truly equal society will never be created (*see* Fredman 2002). The problem, it is argued, is that discrimination law aims to promote 'equality of opportunity' rather than 'equality of outcome', and this is not sufficient to bring about radical social change. Some go as far as to argue that employers should be required to discriminate positively in certain circumstances.

What is your view about positive discrimination? Should the law be changed or should it remain as it is? Justify your answer.

Other fields of discrimination law

These same core principles apply across the other fields of discrimination law covered by the EU's Equal Treatment Framework Directive too, although the types of situation differ. There are, however, some significant differences in the case of age discrimination and disability discrimination law:

- In age discrimination law it is permissible to discriminate directly if the act is objectively justified. In such cases the same defence that applies in cases of indirect discrimination must be complied with if the employer is to be able to show that it has acted lawfully, namely that the act of discrimination amounted to 'a proportionate means of achieving a legitimate aim'.

- In age discrimination law (at least as of 2010) it is lawful for employers to retire staff mandatorily at the age of 65 or at a later age provided they comply with a statutory procedure. This involves writing to employees as they approach the set retirement age and offering them the opportunity to request an opportunity to work beyond that date.
- In disability discrimination law it is not possible to bring a claim of 'indirect discrimination' as defined above. The Disability Discrimination Act 1995 is solely concerned with direct discrimination, harassment and victimisation. This means that an individual has no basis for claiming that an organisation's policies or practices favour able-bodied people in general terms more than disabled people.
- Positive discrimination in favour of disabled people is entirely lawful. This is simply because there is no protection provided in discrimination law for able-bodied people.
- Disability discrimination law permits employers to discriminate against a disabled person, a job applicant or an existing employee who becomes seriously ill, provided they have first genuinely considered whether any 'reasonable adjustments' could be made to enable that person to work or continue working. This typically involves adjusting working practices to accommodate someone's particular needs or making alterations to premises.

WINDOW ON PRACTICE

Religion or belief

Under European Union law it is a requirement that all member states have in place regulations to deter employers from discriminating against their staff on grounds of 'religion or belief'. In 2003 when this law was introduced, the UK government was keen to ensure that members of extreme political organisations could not use it to defend themselves when an employer objected to their views by, for example, refusing to promote them or even dismissing them. The UK law was thus phrased in terms of discrimination on grounds of 'any religion or similar philosophical belief'. This formulation soon proved to be unsatisfactory and hard to justify because it excluded people who did not have any religious belief and who were found, quite lawfully, to have been excluded from work in religious organisations and faith schools on these grounds. The wording was thus altered in 2006 to 'any religious or philosophical belief', the aim being to include people with deeply held beliefs about 'life, the universe and everything', whether or not they were religious in character. The new wording still sought to exclude instances in which people are discriminated against because of their political opinions or stance on an issue, but exactly who and what beliefs met the definition remained unclear.

In 2009 the issue became further confused when the Employment Appeals Tribunal (EAT) gave judgment in the case of *Grainger PLC* v. *Nicholson*. Here the claimant, Mr Nicholson alleged that he had been made redundant from his post as Head of

Sustainability at Grainger, in part, because of his belief in climate change – a point of view he expressed and acted on while at work with some passion. The tribunal ruled that such a belief did fall within the new definition and found in his favour.

In the process the EAT set out a list of criteria which tribunals will now have to use when determining whether or not 'a philosophical belief' is or is not covered by the regulations. These are as follows:

- it must be a belief and not merely an opinion or viewpoint based on current information
- the belief must be genuinely held
- the belief must concern a weighty and substantial aspect of human behaviour
- the belief must have a 'certain level of cogency, seriousness, cohesion and importance'
- the belief must be 'worthy of respect in a democratic society, not incompatible with human dignity and not in conflict with the fundamental rights of other.'

The aim here is presumably to steer a careful path so that beliefs that are racist, unpleasant or perverse cannot be protected, while 'allowing through' other deeply held and sincere beliefs. The trouble is that it leaves many questions unanswered, hence creating less clarity than was there before. In short, how can an employer now know whether it is acting lawfully when faced with decisions in this field? A great deal is now left to the subjective opinion of tribunal members.

Remedies

Victorious claimants in discrimination cases are awarded damages of two kinds. First they can claim from the employer compensation for any financial losses they have sustained as a result of the unlawful discrimination they have suffered. This may be very limited, but where someone has resigned or been dismissed there can be extensive sums awarded to compensate for lost earnings and potential future losses. The second category is 'injury to feelings'. The sums awarded here range from £500 for one-off incidents that cause very limited distress (e.g. being turned down for a job at the shortlisting stage when the individual had little expectation of being successful at interview) up to £30,000 where someone has, for example, been subjected to a lengthy campaign of racial harassment.

EQUAL PAY LAW

The Equal Pay Act 1970 was the first legislation promoting equality at work between men and women. It came into force in December 1975 and was subsequently amended by the Equal Pay (Amendment) Regulations 1983. The Act is solely concerned with eliminating unjustifiable differences between the treatment of men and the treatment of women in terms of their rates of pay and other conditions of employment. It is thus the vehicle that is used to bring a case to tribunal when there is inequality between a man's contract of employment and that of a woman. In practice the majority of cases are brought by women and concern discriminatory rates of payment, although there have been some important cases brought by men focusing on aspects of pension provision. The Act, as amended in 1983, specifies three types of claim that can be brought. These effectively define the circumstances in which pay and other conditions between men and women should be equal:

1 **Like work:** where a woman and a man are doing work which is the same or broadly similar – for example where a woman assembly worker sits next to a male assembly worker, carrying out the same range of duties.
2 **Work rated as equivalent:** where a man and a woman are carrying out work which, while of a different nature, has been rated as equivalent under a job evaluation scheme.
3 **Work of equal value:** where a man and a woman are performing different tasks but where it can be shown that the two jobs are equal in terms of their demands, for example in terms of skill, effort and type of decision making.

Unlike sex discrimination law where the 'but for test' permits the use of hypothetical comparators, in order to bring a case under the Equal Pay Act the claimant must be able to point to a comparator of the opposite gender with whom he or she wishes to be compared. The comparator must be employed by the same employer and at an establishment covered by the same terms and conditions. When an equal value claim is brought which an employment tribunal considers to be well founded, an 'independent expert' may be appointed to carry out a job evaluation exercise in order to establish whether or not the two jobs being compared are equal in terms of the demands they make.

Employers can employ two defences when faced with a claim under the Equal Pay Act. First, they can seek to show that a job evaluation exercise has been carried out which indicates that the two jobs are not like, rated as equivalent or of equal value. To succeed the job evaluation scheme in use must be both analytical and free of sex bias. Second, the employer can claim that the difference in pay is justified by 'a genuine material factor not of sex'. For this to succeed, the employer has to convince the court that there is a good business reason for the unequal treatment and that there has thus been no sex discrimination. Examples of genuine material factors that have proved acceptable to the courts are as follows:

- different qualifications (e.g. where a man has a degree and a woman does not);
- performance (e.g. where a man is paid a higher rate than a woman because he works faster or has received a higher appraisal rating);
- seniority (where the man is paid more because he has been employed for several years longer than the woman);
- regional allowances (where a man is paid a London weighting, taking his pay to a higher rate than that of a woman performing the same job in the Manchester branch).

The courts have ruled that differences in pay explained by the fact that the man and woman concerned are in separate bargaining groups, by the fact that they asked for different salaries on appointment or because of an administrative error are not acceptable genuine material factor defences. It is possible to argue that a difference in pay is explained by market forces, but evidence has to be produced to satisfy the court that going rates for the types of work concerned are genuinely different and that it is therefore genuinely necessary to pay the comparator at a higher rate.

When a claimant wins an equal pay claim he or she is entitled to have their pay equalised with that of their chosen comparator and is also paid compensatory back-pay for a period of up to six years.

WINDOW ON PRACTICE

The Equality Bill

At the time of writing (February 2010) a major new piece of employment legislation is making its way through Parliament. However, because Parliament is about to be dissolved in preparation for a general election and because it is not clear what government will emerge after that election, it is by no means certain that the Equality Bill will ever become the Equality Act 2010. Moreover, if passed, it is not clear whether parts of it will ever be implemented in practice. If the Act does become law, the plan is to introduce it in phases during 2010 and 2011. Some of the key provisions are as follows:

- There will be a single, standard 'equality duty' on public sector employers to promote equality across all the protected grounds, and also when making strategic decisions to address 'socio-economic disadvantage'.
- Discrimination against people on grounds of gender reassignment and pregnancy/maternity will explicitly be added to the existing list of 'protected characteristics' (i.e. sex, race, disability, etc.).
- The principle of indirect discrimination, long established in the fields of sex and race discrimination, will be extended to cover disability discrimination.
- The statutory definition of a 'disability' is being amended so that while there will be a need to show that someone is unable to carry out 'normal day-to-day activities', the eight specific functions listed in the law need no longer be affected in order for a case to be brought.
  - mobility
  - manual dexterity
  - physical coordination
  - continence
  - ability to lift, carry or move everyday objects
  - speech, hearing or eyesight
  - memory/ability to concentrate, learn or understand
  - perception of the risk of physical danger
- Contractual 'pay secrecy' clauses will be made unenforceable in a bid to make it easier for colleagues to find out how their pay compares to that of their colleagues.
- The Bill envisages permitting positive discrimination in circumstances where two equally qualified candidates apply for the same position.

HEALTH AND SAFETY LAW

Health and safety law can be neatly divided into two halves, representing its criminal and civil spheres. The first is based in statute and is policed both by the Health and Safety Executive and by local authority inspectorates. The second relies on the common law and allows individuals who have suffered injury as a result of their work to seek damages against their employers. The former is intended to be preventative, while the latter aims to compensate individuals who become ill as a result of their work.

Criminal law

Health and safety inspectors potentially wield a great deal of power, but their approach is to give advice and to issue warnings except where they judge that there is a high risk of personal injury. They visit premises without giving notice beforehand in order to inspect equipment and make sure that the appropriate monitoring procedures are in place. They have a general right to enter premises, to collect whatever information they require and to remove samples or pieces of equipment for analysis. Where they are unhappy with what they find, inspectors issue **improvement notices** setting out recommended improvements and requiring these to be put in place by a set date. In the case of more serious lapses, where substantial risk to health is identified, the inspectors issue **prohibition notices** which prevent employers from using particular pieces of equipment until better safety arrangements are established. Breach of one of these statutory notices is a criminal offence, as is giving false information to an inspector. Over a thousand prosecutions are brought each year for non-compliance with a Health and Safety Executive Order, leading to fines of up to £20,000.

Prosecutions are also brought after injuries have been sustained where it can be shown that management knew of risks and had not acted to deal with them. Where fatalities result and an employer is found guilty of committing corporate manslaughter, fines of several hundred thousand pounds are levied. Moreover, in some cases custodial sentences have been given to controlling directors held to have been individually liable.

The Health and Safety at Work etc. Act 1974 is the source of most health and safety law in the UK, under which more detailed sets of regulations are periodically issued. Its main purposes are:

- to secure the health, safety and welfare of people at work;
- to protect the public from risks arising from workplace activities;
- to control the use and storage of dangerous substances;
- to control potentially dangerous environmental emissions.

The Act places all employers under a general duty 'to ensure, as far as is reasonably practicable, the health, safety and welfare at work' of all workers. In addition there are specific requirements to maintain plant and equipment, to provide safe systems of working, to provide a safe and healthy working environment, to consult with trade union safety representatives, to maintain an accident reporting book and to post on a notice board a copy of the main provisions contained in the 1974 Act.

Since 1974 numerous sets of regulations have been issued, many of a very specialised nature, to add to the more general principles established in the Health and Safety at Work Act. The most significant have been the following, most of which originate at the European level:

- The First Aid Regulations 1981 place employers under a general duty to provide adequate first aid equipment and facilities.
- The Control of Substances Hazardous to Health (COSHH) Regulations 1988 concern the safe storage and usage of potentially dangerous substances.
- The Management of Health and Safety at Work Regulations 1992 place a variety of duties on employers. Examples include regulations on the safe lifting of heavy loads, the prolonged use of video display units (VDUs) and the particular health and safety needs of pregnant workers.
- The Health and Safety (Consultation with Employees) Regulations 1996 require employers to consult collectively with their employees about health and safety matters irrespective of whether a trade union is recognised.
- The Health Act 2006 bans smoking in public spaces, including most workplaces and company vehicles in England. Equivalent legislation has been passed by the Scottish parliament and the Welsh and Northern Irish assemblies.

ACTIVITY 20.3

Devise a health and safety policy for your organisation. Include information about:

- General policy on health and safety.
- Specific hazards and how they are to be dealt with.
- Management responsibility for safety.
- How the policy is to be implemented.

Or:

Obtain the Health and Safety Policy from any organisation and assess the policy in the light of these four points.

Civil law

While distinct in origin and nature from the criminal sanctions, civil cases relating to health and safety are often brought alongside criminal proceedings in connection with the same incident. When someone is seriously injured or suffers ill health as a direct result of his or her work the health and safety authorities will bring a criminal prosecution, while the injured party will sue for damages in the civil courts. Most claims are brought under the law of negligence, the injured party alleging that the employer acted negligently in allowing him or her to become injured.

In such cases the courts have to be satisfied that the employer failed to act reasonably and that the injury or illness was sustained 'during the course of employment'. Central here, as in the criminal law, are the notions of foreseeability and risk assessment. Cases often hinge on what the employer knew at the time the injury was sustained and whether or not reasonable precautions in the form of training or the provision of equipment had been taken. Employers can thus defend themselves effectively by satisfying the court that little else could have been done by any reasonable employer to prevent the accident from occurring. Importantly the principle of vicarious liability applies in this field, so employers are legally liable for negligence if one employee causes another to become injured.

In recent years, as is demonstrated by the *Green* v. *Deutsche Bank* case described at the start of this chapter, people suffering from psychiatric injuries brought about from undue workplace stress have successfully brought claims. In practice, however, as was the case with Helen Green, large sums by way of damages are only won where employees suffer two serious breakdowns both of which are work-related. Otherwise it is very difficult to satisfy a court that the risk of injury was genuinely 'reasonably foreseeable' and hence that the employer is liable.

Working time

Some of the most significant recent developments in the field of health and safety law have derived from the Working Time Regulations 1998, an example of law that was introduced into the UK rather reluctantly in order to meet European treaty obligations. The basic 'headline' entitlements are as follows:

- a limit of 48 hours per week
- 28 days' paid leave each year
- 20 minutes' rest in any period of work lasting six hours or more
- 11 hours' rest in any one 24-hour period
- 24 hours' rest in any seven-day period
- night workers limited to eight hours' work in any one 24-hour period
- free health checks for night workers
- special regulations restricting working time of young workers (i.e. those aged 16–18 years)

On the surface these requirements look clear-cut and straightforward, but this is not the case. The regulations are complex, running to more than 100 pages in length. What is more, parts of them do not apply in some situations, meaning that many workers in the UK are, in practice, either unprotected or only partially protected:

- The regulations allow for considerable flexibility because they allow employers to average time worked over a 17-week reference period.
- Anyone can if they wish formally 'opt out' of the 48-hour week restriction by signing or writing a written declaration. Employers in the UK are lawfully able to make the signing of such an opt-out a requirement of employment. Staff are permitted at any time to 'opt' back in by informing their employer in writing and giving notice and cannot be victimised for exercising this right.
- Workforce agreements can be established which allow an employer to vary the working time regulations in various ways. Where the majority of the workforce assent to a proposal in a vote, by signing up directly or via a trade union agreement a workplace can adapt its interpretation of the working time regulations to suit their needs.

The existence of opt-outs has long been a controversial aspect of the UK regulations. Such arrangements are not used in other EU countries and they are criticised for giving UK companies an unfair competitive advantage in European markets. To date the UK government has successfully resisted attempts to abolish opt-out arrangements, but they may well not survive in the long term in their current form. Further controversy surrounds some rulings of the European Court of Justice (ECJ) in relation to working time issues. A prominent example is the case of *Stringer* v. *HM Revenue and Customs* (2009). Here the ECJ overturned judgments in the UK courts in deciding that workers continue to accrue their paid holiday entitlement while they are absent due to a long-term sickness and that pay in lieu of untaken holiday entitlement is payable when a worker who has been absent due to long-term sickness is dismissed. The UK courts found against the employee in this case on the grounds that holiday is 'leave' and that you cannot take 'leave' from work if you have not been at work during the time that that holiday accrues. The ECJ took a different view, judging that annual leave entitlement should be treated like any other part of the remuneration package and is a right irrespective of whether a worker is fit enough to work or not. The Stringer judgment has had the effect of raising costs for UK employers quite considerably because it means that workers recovering from illness can delay their return to work for several weeks while they take accrued holiday or can return to work and then go off again on holiday very soon. Moreover, it means that if employees fall sick just before they are due to take annual leave they must be permitted to postpone that leave until they are able to take it when they are fit. It also follows that people who fall sick while on leave can reclaim those days and take them as leave at a further date.

ACTIVITY 20.4

What is your view of the opt-out arrangement maintained by the UK? Should employers be able to make it a condition of employment that new starters sign such an agreement? Aside from the cost implications, what other disadvantages might follow from an employer perspective were opt-outs to be outlawed?

FAMILY-FRIENDLY EMPLOYMENT LAW

In recent years a significant contribution to the development of workplaces which offer a better work-life balance has been made via the introduction of new and enhanced employment rights which require employers to take account of the needs of people with family responsibilities. These are straightforward but have been highly significant both for employers who have to find ways of accommodating them and for the many employees who have benefited considerably. The key rights are as follows:

- The right for pregnant employees to take reasonable time off work to attend antenatal medical appointments without losing any pay.
- The right for a mother to take time off before, during and after her baby is born. Most employed women are entitled to take six months' 'ordinary maternity leave' followed by a further six months' 'additional maternity leave'.
- The right to statutory maternity pay (SMP) for a period of nine months while maternity leave is being taken. SMP is paid at the 'higher rate' for the first six weeks (90 per cent of salary) and thereafter at the 'lower rate' (£124.88 per week in 2010).

- A right for both parents of a child to take up to 13 weeks' unpaid leave during the first five years of the child's life or during the five years following the adoption of a child. This right currently only extends to employees who have completed a year's continuous service with their employer.
- A right for fathers of new babies to take two weeks' paid paternity leave within the first 56 days of the birth.
- A right for parents and carers to take reasonable amounts of time off during working hours for urgent family reasons, employers being informed of the intention to take the leave 'as soon as is reasonably practicable'.
- A right for parents of children aged up to 18 and carers of sick adults to request flexible working. The procedure requires the parent or carer to write formally to his or her employer asking for a one-off change in terms and conditions, together with an explanation as to how the request could be accommodated in practice. The employer can turn the request down, but only when one of eight specific business reasons applies.
- Equivalent rights for parents of adopted children, one being able to claim maternity rights, the other paternity rights.

Further substantial extension of rights in this area is planned for 2011 and 2012. Proposals include the extension of paid maternity leave to 12 months and the introduction of an arrangement whereby a mother can swap a portion of her maternity leave with the baby's father. She will be able to return to work, leaving her husband or partner to claim extended paternity leave until the couple has taken a full year's leave between them.

THE NATIONAL MINIMUM WAGE

Since 1999 most workers in the UK have been entitled in law to be paid a minimum hourly rate for the work that they do. The rate of the National Minimum Wage (NMW) is not linked to any formula, but is set by the Secretary of State for Business, Enterprise and Regulatory Reform after consultation with a body of experts and representatives from industry called the Low Pay Commission. The aim is always to set the highest rate possible that will not appreciably have an adverse impact on employment levels. In practice the level of the NMW is increased in October each year, and in recent years the increases have been well in excess of the prevailing rate of inflation. In early 2010 it stood at £5.80 an hour.

Not everyone, however, is entitled to the full amount. There are some groups who are excluded altogether, such as people engaged in family work (au pairs, nannies, etc.), people working in sheltered work schemes run for homeless persons, apprentices, barristers, pupils and students undertaking periods of work experience as part of a course of higher education. Other groups are only entitled to a lower 'development rate' which is set at around 80 per cent of the full rate (£4.83 an hour in 2010). This applies to people who are aged 18–22 and those over that age who are in the first six months of a new job during which at least 26 days are being spent training to achieve a National Vocational Qualification (NVQ) or Scottish Vocational Qualification (SVQ). Finally, there is a lower 'youth rate' for 16–17-year-olds which is around 60 per cent of the full adult rate (£3.57 an hour in 2010).

In practice it can be very difficult for employers to establish that they are in fact paying staff at or above the National Minimum Wage. One reason is the complexity of the regulations on what payments and payments in kind can and cannot be included as part of someone's salary for NMW purposes. For example, the regulations state that overtime and on-call payments must not be included and thus, in effect, must be paid in addition to the NMW. On the other hand, employers are entitled to include in their calculations a sum to compensate for live-in accommodation, meaning that live-in staff may be paid slightly less than the NMW because they enjoy this type of benefit. Staff meals, however, cannot be included, nor can tips. There are also quite complicated rules about times when people are and are not deemed to be working for the purposes of the payment of the NMW, while further complexity arises in situations where people are paid entirely on a piecework basis and do not therefore receive an hourly rate (e.g. where people are paid for the amount of work they do, not the amount of time spent doing it).

The government has appointed a team of inspectors to investigate incidents of willful refusal to pay the NMW. They have the right to inspect records of hours worked and wages paid so as to establish whether or not the NMW has been and is being paid. Where an employer knowingly refuses to comply with the NMW regulations, it can be charged with a criminal offence and fined. Until 2007 the maximum fine was £5,000. Since then it has been calculated according to the following formula:

> Twice the rate of the minimum wage at the time of the charge multiplied by the number of employees who have been paid below the level of the NMW multiplied by the number of working days they have not been paid the NMW.

In addition, of course, workers who are found not to have been paid the NMW are entitled to receive their full entitlement in the future and to receive back pay too by way of compensation.

ACTIVITY 20.5

When the National Minimum Wage was introduced some groups representing employers argued that it would have a negative impact on both the level of unemployment and the level of inflation. Why do you think there is a danger of these effects when minimum wages are introduced? Why do you think they have not occurred in practice in the UK as a result of the National Minimum Wage?

Deductions from wages

All employees in the UK are entitled in law to receive an itemised pay statement which sets out the gross rate of pay for the month or week and any deductions that have been made. The Employment Rights Act 1996 sets out what deductions can lawfully be made, the implication being that other types of deduction are unlawful and can lead to action in the employment tribunals. The list of permissible deductions includes those authorised by legislation such as tax and national insurance contributions and those authorised in the contract of employment such as trade union subscriptions or pension fund contributions. Sometimes courts issue 'attachment orders' requiring an employer to pay a fine or a debt on behalf of an employee and to make an equivalent deduction from the pay package, and from time to time mistakes are made in salary administration resulting in overpayments to employees that need to be recovered. In both these situations deductions are lawful. Importantly, however, it is unlawful for an employer to levy any kind of fine on an employee as a punishment when a disciplinary offence has been committed or where an individual's performance in the job is unsatisfactory. In such circumstances along with any others in which underpayments of agreed wages are made, aggrieved employees have the right to take their case to an employment tribunal and to argue that they should be reimbursed.

IS EMPLOYMENT LAW A BENEFIT OR A BURDEN FOR BUSINESSES?

It is common for managers and owners of small businesses, as well as the journalists, politicians and employers' associations who support their interests, to argue that the extent of employment regulation is now so great as to be having a substantial, negative impact. At base this argument concerns economic competitiveness, it being said that regulation both adds unnecessary costs and stifles the capacity of organisations to act flexibly and opportunistically. The result is reduced international competitiveness because so many rival organisations are based in countries which have far less regulation to contend with. It follows, according to its critics, that employment law acts as a disincentive to job creation and also provides an incentive for UK-based organisations to 'export jobs' by relocating aspects of their operations overseas or by subcontracting them to overseas-based suppliers.

There is no question that employment regulation adds to employers' costs, not least by taking up a good deal of management time. A recent survey carried out by the Chartered Institute of Personnel and Development found that two-thirds of HR managers in the UK spend over 20 per cent of their time 'dealing with employment law issues', a further 25 per cent spending over 40 per cent of their time in this way (CIPD 2002). In addition to the costs of time spent making sure that an organisation is complying there are further direct costs associated with the introduction of new measures. Every time Statutory Sick Pay, Statutory Maternity Pay, the National Minimum Wage or minimum redundancy payments are increased, some employers' costs rise considerably. The same has been true of recent extensions to the length of maternity leave and amount of paid holiday to which staff are entitled. A research study undertaken by the Confederation of British Industry estimated that the costs to employers in the UK associated with the implementation of the National Minimum Wage and the Working Time Regulations when they were introduced was over £10 billion (CBI 2000: 9). To these can be added the costs associated with defending cases in the employment tribunal. In recent years, as the scope of employment law has widened, unsurprisingly the number of claims being brought has increased too, as has the complexity of many of these claims. In the year to 31 March 2009 there were 151,028 claims lodged with employment tribunals in the UK (ETS 2009). This compares with 91,913 in 1998/99 and just 29,304 in 1986/87

(Taylor and Emir 2009: 6). Finally, to this additional cost burden we can plausibly add lost opportunity costs. Although it is impossible to quantify these at all accurately, it is reasonable to ask what benefits could accrue if managers were free to devote the time they spend dealing with employment law matters on value-adding activities instead?

A further argument contends that the effect of employment law, even if it is not the intention of legislators, is to harm the career interests of those groups who are afforded the most legal protection (e.g. ethnic minorities, disabled people and mothers with dependent children). This occurs because it makes organisations less likely to employ them. There is less evidence to back this argument up, but some surveys carried out among owners and managers running small businesses suggest that there is a real practical impact. The Institute of Directors, for example, reported that 45 per cent of its members believe recent extensions to maternity rights have created 'a disincentive to hiring women of prime child-bearing age' (Lea 2001: 56), while economists based in the USA such as Richard Epstein (2002: 8) have long argued that in practice 'equal opportunity', when imposed by government 'leads to less opportunity'. Lord Alan Sugar, one of the country's best-known employers, recently said that many employers in practice simply bin CVs that are sent to them by women of childbearing age. In his view it should be the responsibility of the state and not employers to bear the costs associated with the employment of mothers with young children (*Daily Telegraph* 2008).

The main arguments in favour of employment law relate to social justice and the need to reduce the extent to which people suffer unreasonably at the hands of prejudiced, negligent or bullying managers abusing the power their position gives them. It is necessary to protect employees via the law, just as it is necessary to protect other vulnerable groups from injustice. Such arguments are strong, straightforward and accepted by most, although disagreements will always persist about where the balance should lie between protecting the interests of employees and protecting those of employers. However, there are also influential economic arguments in favour of extensive employment protection legislation. The implication here is that regulation of the employment relationship does not just benefit employees, but that organisations and the economy generally have also stood to gain from its extension in recent decades.

There are a number of distinct strands that make up the economic argument in favour of employment law. The first has been used on many occasions by ministers introducing new legislation in the face of business opposition. It was very effectively articulated in the government White Paper entitled 'Fairness at Work' (DTI 1998) where it is simply argued that the most productive workplaces, particularly in the service sector which now accounts for the vast majority of UK jobs, are those in which people are managed effectively and fairly. In requiring managers to treat their staff with dignity, fairness and in an equitable manner, employment regulation helps to raise employment standards. In turn this has positive benefits for businesses in terms of higher levels of motivation and productivity, lower levels of staff turnover and a healthy, high-trust employee relations climate. Employment law, it is argued, should hold no fears whatever for good employers. All it aims to do is to bring all employment practice up to that same broad standard.

The second strand of the argument relates directly to the issue of growing skills shortages among some key professional groups. The starting point here is the view that the inability of many employers to recruit and retain people with the skills and experience that they need constitutes a significant national economic problem which holds back economic growth (*see* Frogner 2003). It follows that the amelioration of skills shortages should properly be a significant public policy objective. Improving employment standards by forcing employers to treat their employees well helps to achieve this because it makes work more attractive than it otherwise would be. It follows that more people with a choice about whether to work or not choose to do so in a world of regulated employment than would do so if the employment relationships were unregulated. The result is a higher economic participation rate as women with young children, people with long-term ill health issues and those who could afford to retire if they wanted to put their skills, at least for part of the time, at the disposal of the economy. High standards also help to attract into the country highly skilled migrant workers from overseas who might otherwise choose to work elsewhere.

The final, third strand of the argument concerns the UK economy's competitive position internationally. It is argued that highly developed economies such as the UK's cannot sustain themselves in the face of competition from developing and newly industrialised countries by competing on the basis of cost. There is no future for such a business strategy because wage levels in China, India and elsewhere are invariably much lower than in the UK and, as a result, the goods and services that they produce will always be far cheaper. It follows that the UK needs clearly to position itself as a high wage, knowledge-based economy which produces innovative hi-tech goods and provides upmarket services. In order to achieve this organisations need to be encouraged to work in partnership with their employees and, particularly, to invest in their training. There is little economic incentive for employers to devote resources to extensive employee development programmes in environments characterised by high staff turnover and low-trust employment relationships. Government thus needs to intervene to push employers in this direction and employment law is one of several public policy tools that are used to achieve this. The long-term aim is thus to help sustain economic growth in a rapidly changing and highly competitive business environment.

The most persuasive conclusion to reach is that employment regulation is both a burden and a benefit to UK employers, although it is of less benefit to and a much greater burden for smaller businesses without the expertise and resources to ensure that they are managing within its requirements. It is a burden because it adds substantial costs and because it limits the freedom managers have to run their businesses as they might otherwise wish. However, it is also a benefit because it helps to raise employment standards throughout the country, making work more attractive to skilled migrants and to people who have skills and experience that they might otherwise choose not to make use of in the employment context. In the process it contributes to reduced staff turnover, helps to encourage later retirement, helps to create the conditions in which superior individual performance is more likely and, crucially, in which low-trust, adversarial industrial relations are less likely to emerge.

ACTIVITY 20.6

Where do you stand in this debate about employment legislation? Does it serve to underpin economic prosperity or reduce international competitiveness? What further measures would you welcome and which would you oppose?

SUMMARY PROPOSITIONS

20.1 In the space of a single generation UK workplaces have gone from being among the least regulated in the world to being among the most highly regulated.

20.2 At base the employment relationship is contractual. A legally binding agreement is formed when an employee starts working for an employer. Neither side can lawfully breach that contract and cause the other some kind of detriment without risking legal action and the requirement to pay some compensation.

20.3 Discrimination law has grown rapidly in recent years, extending to new grounds such as age, sexual orientation and religion or belief. Equal pay law requires men and women to be paid the same wage for doing work which is the same or which can be shown to be of equal value unless the employer can justify a difference on grounds other than sex.

20.4 The legal framework for health and safety includes both the criminal and civil law. The former is policed by health and safety inspectors; the latter provides a vehicle for those who suffer illness or injury as a result of their work to claim damages.

20.5 Family-friendly employment law has been very much extended in recent years and will be further extended in the future. It aims to help people better combine their work and domestic responsibilities.

20.6 Two major recent additions to employment regulation have been the National Minimum Wage and the Working Time Regulations. Both have had, and continue to have, a major impact on HR practice in organisations.

20.7 Employment regulation increases the cost burden for employers and reduces their freedom of action, but in helping to ensure that reasonably high minimum standards are maintained in employee relations it also brings economic advantages to organisations.

GENERAL DISCUSSION TOPICS

1 How far do you think that UK discrimination law is effective in achieving its aims? What could be done to make it more effective?

2 To what extent do you agree with the view that employment regulation now imposes so many restrictions and costs on employers as to make businesses based in European countries uncompetitive internationally?

FURTHER READING

Davies, A.C.L. (2009) *Perspectives on Labour Law*, 2nd edn. Cambridge: Cambridge University Press.

An excellent book which analyses UK employment regulation in the round, explaining its purpose and debating its strengths and weaknesses from a variety of perspectives.

Fredman, S. (2002) *Discrimination Law*. Oxford: Oxford University Press.
Sandra Fredman has written extensively on discrimination law. The key debates are discussed concisely and effectively in this book.

There are several good textbooks on employment law. Those aimed primarily at management students rather than lawyers include those authored by Janice Nairns (2007), David Lewis and Malcolm Sargeant (2009), Brian Willey (2009) and Stephen Taylor and Astra Emir (2009). (For details *see* References.)

REFERENCES

BBC (2006) 'Bullied City worker wins £800,000', BBC News website, 1 August.

Chartered Institute of Personnel and Development (2002) *Employment Law: Survey Report*. London: CIPD.

Confederation of British Industry (2000) *Cutting through Red Tape: The impact of employment legislation*. London: CBI.

Daily Telegraph (2008) 'Sir Alan Sugar: our children need enterprise', 2 February.

Davies, A.C.L. (2009) *Perspectives on Labour Law*, 2nd edn. Cambridge: Cambridge University Press.

Department for Trade and Industry (1998) *Fairness at Work. Government White Paper*. London: HMSO.

Employment Tribunal Service (2009). *Annual Report 2008–9*. London: ETS.

Epstein, R. (2002) *Equal Opportunity or More Opportunity? The good thing about discrimination*. London: Civitas.

Fredman, S. (2002) *Discrimination Law*. Oxford: Oxford University Press.

Frogner, M.L. (2003) 'Skills shortages', *Labour Market Trends*, January. London: ONS.

Guest, K. (2006) 'Why I deserve every penny of the £800,000, by the bullied City exec', *The Independent*, 6 August.

Lea, R. (2001) *The Work–Life Balance and All That: The re-regulation of the labour market*. London: Institute of Directors.

Lewis, D. and Sargeant, M. (2009) *Essentials of Employment Law*, 10th edn. London: CIPD.

Nairns, J. (2007) *Employment Law for Business Students*, 3rd edn. London: Longman.

Tait, N. (2006) 'Courts take bullying by the horns', *Financial Times*, 6 August.

Taylor, S. and Emir, A. (2009) *Employment Law: An introduction*, 2nd edn. Oxford: Oxford University Press.

The Times (2006) Letters page, 8 August.

Willey, B. (2009) *Employment Law in Context*, 3rd edn. London: FT/Prentice Hall.

LEGAL CASES

Grainger PLC & others v. *Nicholson* (2010) IRLR 4

Green v. *Deutsche Bank* (2006) EWHC 1898

Stringer and others v. *HM Revenue and Customs* (2009) IRLR 214

EQUAL OPPORTUNITIES AND DIVERSITY

THE OBJECTIVES OF THIS CHAPTER ARE TO:

1. Review the current employment experiences of the members of some socially defined minority groups
2. Analyse the differing approaches to achieving equality for those groups, in particular contrasting the more traditional equal opportunities approach with the management of diversity approach
3. Explore the implications which managing diversity has for organisations

In today's times of globalisation and demographic change, the workforce is becoming increasingly diverse and it is more than ever important for organisations to develop equal opportunity and diversity strategies to attract and retain talent to improve workforce performance and so retain and promote their competitive position. Legislation, voluntary codes of practice and equality initiatives have resulted in some progress towards equality of treatment for minority groups, but there remains inescapable evidence of continuing discrimination. More recent approaches under the banner of management of diversity include the economic and business case for equality, the valuing and managing of diversity in organisations, culture change and the mainstreaming of equality initiatives. Such approaches are partly a response to the insufficient progress made from the equal opportunities route, yet there is only limited evidence that they have made a difference. While diversity approaches offer some useful perspectives and practices, the underlying concepts also raise some issues and concerns. We consider issues relating to both equality of opportunity and diversity management in this chapter.

HOW 'EQUAL' IS THE WORKFORCE?

The workforce in the UK and internationally has changed radically in the past 50 years, becoming more diverse in terms of gender, age, race and ethnicity, sexual orientation and political and religious beliefs, to name just some of the criteria in terms of which employees may differ. Diversity can also extend beyond social category to include informational diversity (differences in terms of education, tenure and functional background) and value diversity (which includes differences in personality and attitudes) (CIPD 2003). We have therefore been necessarily selective in the groups we have chosen to discuss here and include: women, racial/ethnic minorities, people who are disabled, older people and individuals who are lesbian, gay, bisexual or transsexual. We present evidence of the equality of opportunity available to these diverse employee groups.

Women

If **participation** in the labour force is an indication of decreasing discrimination then recent figures are encouraging. From 1971 to 2008 the female participation rate in employment increased from 56 per cent to 70 per cent, compared with the male participation rate which is slowly falling, and now at 78 per cent (ONS 2009, based on the December 2008 Labour Force Survey). Indeed, this same survey suggests that women have been less adversely affected by the economic downturn than men, possibly as a result of working more often in the public sector or in part-time jobs. As we note in Chapter 4, however, part-time employment is often low paid, low skilled and insecure so the over-representation of women in this type of employment hardly creates equality of opportunity.

Some of the more obvious signs of discrimination, such as in recruitment advertising, may have disappeared, and there is some evidence to suggest that women are beginning to enter some previously male-dominated occupations, for example, women have now been ordained as priests in the Church of England. Similarly men are beginning to enter some previously female-only occupations, such as midwifery. However, there remains a high degree of subtle discrimination, for example in access to training and support for development and promotion, and not-so-subtle discrimination, as in the continued

gender segregation in terms of both type and level of work. Care work is, for example, largely dominated by women (Carroll *et al.* 2009) and the EOC (now the Equality and Human Rights Commission (2007)) reports that only 10 per cent of FTSE directors, only 20 per cent of MPs and 26 per cent of top civil servants are women.

Pay differentials between men and women have narrowed very little except for an upwards increase in women's pay when the Equal Pay Act 1970 came into force in 1975. According to the *Annual Survey of Hours and Earnings* (2009 available on the Office for National Statistics website), the average weekly rate for full-time women is £510 as against £643 for full-time men, some 21 per cent lower. IDS (2004) identifies a range of unintentional consequences of pay systems which prove to be a barrier to achieving equal pay, and these are shown in Table 21.1.

Table 21.1 Barriers to the achievement of gender-based equal pay

Starting pay is frequently individually negotiated	As men usually have higher previous earnings this means they can negotiate a higher starting rate
Length of service	Men generally have longer service and fewer career breaks, and while this may result in greater experience early in a career it is less of a performance-influencing factor as general length of service increases
Broadbanding	There is a lack of transparency in such systems and there is a lack of structured progression, managers are likely to have high levels of discretion and may be unaware of biases
Lack of equal access to bonus payments	There is evidence that appraisal ratings and assessments discriminate unfairly against minority groups
Market allowances not evenly distributed	Such allowances are more likely to be given to men
Different pay structures and negotiating bodies	As some jobs are done primarily by women and some primarily by men, direct comparisons are harder to make
Job evaluation	Such schemes often perpetuate old values and may be subject to managerial manipulation

Source: Based primarily on material in IDS (2004) 'Employers move on equal pay', *IDS Report*, No. 897, January, pp. 10–18.

Racial and ethnic groups

Labour market participation of racial and ethnic minority groups is typically lower than for other groups in both the UK and elsewhere. In the UK, for example, the (then) Commission for Racial Equality (2006) reported that the gap in employment between whites and racial and ethnic minority groups was 15.4 per cent in spring 2005. This picture of **comparative level of unemployment** has barely changed over the past 18 years. In the Netherlands, there is also recent evidence of ethnic minority groups being marginalised, stigmatised and discriminated against in the labour market (der Laan Bouma-Doff 2008). There is also segregation in the UK across occupations, with ethnic minority male employees being disproportionately employed in sectors such as hotel and catering and manufacturing industry. Ethnic minorities further tend to be under-represented at senior levels of organisations, a recent study by Cook and Glass (2009) even suggesting that the appointment of ethnic minorities to senior positions in organisations can adversely affect share price. Racial discrimination may also happen less blatantly.

Rana (2003) reports on a project designed to understand why ethnic minority managers are under-represented in senior levels of local government. The researchers found that in 360-degree feedback results the line managers' assessments of ethnic minority employees were less favourable for each individual than all other assessments, which were generally similar. This discrepancy did not occur when considering the ratings of white employees.

WINDOW ON PRACTICE

Work with recruiters helps BT to become more diverse

Working with recruitment agencies to make requirements clear has been the key to creating a racially diverse workforce at BT. BT is top of the Race for Opportunity index, which uses survey data to benchmark the most race-friendly employers in the country. The research looked at the policies and practices used by organisations in attraction and recruitment, talent progression, measurement of diversity, and engaging with customers, suppliers and the wider community.

Becky Mason, people and policy manager, BT Group, highlighted work with suppliers as a key factor in the firm's success. 'The work we have been doing with recruitment agencies – our suppliers of people – is crucial. We demonstrate our policies to them and ask them to tell us what their policy is. It's quite clear, stating the standards that we expect, that we expect to be sent a diverse mix of candidates and for agencies to set in place statistical monitoring of their processes to ensure that is the case.' BT reviews its preferred suppliers every two to three years and HR works with procurement colleagues to ensure that diversity is a factor in these decisions, added Mason.

BT currently has 10.8 per cent Black Minority Ethnic (BME) staff, which is in excess of the proportion in the population overall of around 8 per cent. Mason also pointed out that, with three people from a BME background on BT's board, there was no doubt that minorities were able to progress in the organisation.

'If initiatives such as BT's encouraging of its suppliers to sign up to minimum standards on race diversity were to become common practice, I am confident that the UK could make real progress on tackling the gross under-representation of ethnic minorities,' said Sandra Kerr, national campaign director for Race for Opportunity.

Source: Brockett, J. (2009) 'Work with recruiters helps BT to become more diverse', BBC Radio 4, PM Online, 19 June.

People with a disability

Woodhams and Danieli (2000) point out that people who have a disability face common barriers to full integration into society and yet are a very varied group in that impairments can vary in severity, stability and type. Based on the Labour Force Survey in spring 2005 there are 6.9 million people in the UK who have a current long-term health problem or disability which has a substantial adverse impact on their day-to-day activities and affects the work they can do (ONS 2005). People with a disability are more likely to be unemployed than their able-bodied counterparts, and once unemployed they are likely to remain so for a longer period (Meager and Hill 2005). Choice of job is often restricted for people with a disability, and where they do find work it is likely to be in low-paid, less attractive jobs. Disability discrimination legislation may have improved the lot of the disabled worker in the past decade, however. Woodhams and Corby (2007), for example, conducted a longitudinal analysis from the period 1995–2003 which suggests that the percentage of disabled people in employment doubled in the period from 1.2 per cent to 2.4 per cent.

Age

Demographic changes, legislation and labour shortages have led to an increased recognition of the need for equality in respect of age. Riach (2009) suggests that the labour market participation of older workers has risen since the turn of the millennium. However, the CIPD (2005a) reports that age discrimination remains a significant problem, with 59 per cent of respondents reporting that they had been disadvantaged at work due to age, although the number of people, aged 55 and over, who thought they had been passed over for promotion due to age had halved since 1995. And the Department for Work and Pensions (DWP 2006) reports that employment rates continue to fall for the over 50s, a trend that is perhaps not surprising given decades of policies to encourage the early retirement of this age group (Loretto and White 2006).

Evidence suggests that age biases are deeply ingrained (Riach 2009). For example, line managers have negative perceptions of older workers, seeing them as less able to cope with change, training or technology and less interested in their careers, more likely to be sick and to cost more money to employ. There are also, however, some positive stereotypes depicting older workers as more loyal and conscientious, having better interpersonal skills, more efficient and that their experience counteracts any age-related factors lowering productivity. Older workers also have lower turnover rates which saves the organisation money.

On the basis of their research Snape and Redman (2003) argue that discrimination for being too young is at least as common as that for being too old. Both forms of discrimination adversely affected commitment to the organisation, and hence, it could be argued, performance.

Sexuality

Lesbian, gay and bisexual discrimination is the most difficult to identify due to the fact that group membership may not be revealed, usually due to the anticipation of discrimination. It is therefore difficult to quantify the extent to which these groups experience active discrimination. The Business and Human Rights Resource Centre

(**http://www.business-humanrights.org**) suggests that despite policy rhetoric, homophobia and discrimination are still common in certain sectors, for example, financial services. Stonewall (2010) adopts a Workplace Equality Index analysing the policies or organisations which support lesbian, gay and bi-sexual employees. Each year, it makes awards to the best 100 employers in the UK, IBM having won the award for the past two years. While this represents great progress in eradicating discrimination for these groups of employees, there is still a distance to go in achieving equality. Many of the top 100 employers in the Workplace Equality Index are large firms, smaller firms perhaps being slower to respond with formal policies on sexual orientation. Research by Day and Greene (2008), however, suggests that small firms may have advantages in promoting inclusiveness in terms of a positive work climate.

In summary

Discrimination and inequality remain in the workplace and are particularly evident for certain groups. We now turn to the theoretical debate which underpins different organisational approaches to tackling such discrimination and inequality.

ACTIVITY 21.1

Talk to people you know across a range of socially defined groups – gender, race, disability and older workers for example. What are their experiences of discrimination in the workplace? To what extent do you think equality for these groups is apparent?

DIFFERENT APPROACHES TO EQUALITY

There has been a continuing debate concerning the action that should be taken to alleviate the disadvantages that minority groups encounter. One approach, generally referred to as equal opportunities or a liberal approach, supports legislative action (Chapter 20). A second approach, managing diversity, argues that legislation will not be effective and that a fundamental change to the attitudes and preconceptions held about these groups is required. The initial emphasis on legislative action was adopted in the hope that this would eventually affect attitudes. A third, more extreme, radical approach, which enjoys less support, comes from those who advocate legislation to promote positive or reverse discrimination to compensate for a history of discrimination against specified groups and to redress the balance more immediately. In the UK, legislation provides for positive action, such as special support and encouragement, for disadvantaged groups, but not positive or reverse discrimination (discriminating in their favour), except for disability legislation. The labels 'equal opportunities' and 'management of diversity' are used inconsistently, and to complicate this there are different perspectives on the meaning of managing diversity, so we shall draw out the key differences which typify each of these approaches, and offer some critique of their conceptual foundations and effectiveness.

The equal opportunities approach

The equal opportunities approach seeks to influence behaviour through legislation so that discrimination is prevented. It has been characterised by a moral and ethical stance promoting the rights of *all* members of society. This liberal approach concentrates on the equality of opportunity rather than the equality of outcome found in more radical approaches. The approach is based on the understanding that some individuals are discriminated against, for example in the selection process, due to irrelevant criteria. These irrelevant criteria arise from assumptions based on the stereotypical characteristics attributed to them as members of a socially defined group, for example that women will not be prepared to work away from home due to family commitments or that a person with a disability will have more time off sick. The equal opportunities approach therefore seeks to formalise procedures so that relevant, job-based criteria are used (using job descriptions and person specifications) and discrimination is based on fair criteria, i.e. the ability to do the job.

The rationale, therefore, is to provide a 'level playing field' on which all can compete on equal terms. Differences between socially defined groups are glossed over, and the approach is generally regarded as one of 'sameness'. Positive action, not positive discrimination, is allowable in order that some may reach the level at which they can compete equally. For example, an organisation may advertise its vacancies in publications which target particular under-represented ethnic groups. Once it has generated a pool of applicants, however, it must not then use ethnic origin as a selection criterion.

Equal opportunities approaches stress disadvantaged groups, and the need, for example, to set targets for those groups to ensure that their representation in the workplace reflects their representation in wider society. Targets are needed in occupations where they are under-represented, such as firefighters, police officers and in the armed forces, where small numbers of ethnic minorities are employed (*see* IDS 2006 for an air force example) or senior management roles where there are small numbers of women. These targets are not enforceable by legislation, as in the United States, but organisations have been encouraged to commit themselves voluntarily to improvement goals, and to support this commitment by putting in place measures to support disadvantaged groups such as special training courses and flexible employment policies.

Problems with the equal opportunities approach

There is an assumption in the equal opportunities approach that equality of outcome will be achieved if fair procedures are used and monitored. In other words, if this is done it will enable any minority groups to achieve a fair share of what employment has to offer. Once such minority groups become full participating members in employment, the old stereotypical attitudes on which discrimination against particular social groups is based will gradually change, as the stereotypes will be shown to be unhelpful.

The assumption that fair procedures or procedural justice will lead to fair outcomes has not been borne out in practice, as we have shown. The focus of equal opportunities is on formal processes and yet it is it not possible to formalise everything in the organisation. In addition there has been criticism of the assumption that once members of minority groups have demonstrated their ability to perform in the organisation this will change attitudes and beliefs in the organisation. Further, there can be a general lack of support within organisations, partly because equality objectives are not linked to business objectives (Shapiro and Austin 1996) and partly because equal opportunities has often been viewed as the concern of the HR function (Kirton and Greene 2003). A focus on disadvantaged groups may also alienate the large sections of the workforce not identified as such, for example, flexible working for those with children which creates a burden for those without (Atkinson and Hall 2009). There is also, during the difficult economic times which prevail at the time of writing (spring 2010), a concern that legislation promoting the rights of, for example, parents will undermine competitiveness by increasing employers' costs base.

In summary the equal opportunities approach is considered simplistic and to be attempting to treat the symptoms rather than the causes of unfair discrimination.

The management of diversity approach

The management of diversity approach concentrates on individuals rather than groups, and includes the improvement of opportunities for *all* individuals and not just those in minority groups. Hence managing diversity involves everyone and benefits everyone, which is an attractive message to employers and employees alike. Thus separate groups are not singled out for specific treatment:

> The basic concept of managing diversity accepts that the workforce consists of a diverse population of people consisting of visible and non-visible differences . . . and is founded on the premise that harnessing these differences will create a productive environment in which everyone feels valued, where all talents are fully utilized and in which organizational goals are met. (Kandola and Fullerton 1998: 4)

The CIPD (2005b: 2) suggests the central theme of diversity as:

> valuing everyone as individuals – as employees, customers, clients and extending diversity beyond what is legislated about to looking at what's positively valued.

So the focus is on valuing difference rather than finding a way of coping fairly with it. Whereas the equal opportunities approach minimised difference, the managing diversity approach treats difference as a positive asset.

WINDOW ON PRACTICE

'At Zurich Financial Services we believe that managing diversity is about valuing people as individuals. The scope of this definition includes age, colour, disability, ethnicity, economic status, family/marital status, nationality, religious beliefs, sexual orientation, spent convictions, part-time working, political opinion/affiliation and gender reassignment. It also embraces the range of individual skills, educational qualifications, work experience and background, languages and other relevant attributes and experiences that differentiate us; all differences can result in varying experiences, values, and ways of thinking, behaving, communicating and working.'

Source: CIPD (2005b) *Managing Diversity: Linking Theory and Practice to business performance*. London: CIPD.

This brings us to a further difference between the equal opportunities approach and the managing diversity approach which is that the managing diversity approach is based on the economic and business case for recognising and valuing difference, rather than the moral case for treating people equally. Rather than being purely a cost, equal treatment offers benefits and advantages for the employer if it invests in ensuring that everyone in the organisation is valued and given the opportunities to develop his or her potential and make a maximum contribution. The practical arguments supporting the equalisation of employment opportunities are thus highlighted. CIPD (2006a) suggests that business benefits can be summed up in three broad statements: that diversity enhances customer relations and market share; that it enhances employee relations and reduces labour costs; and that it improves workforce quality and performance in terms of diverse skills, creativity, problem solving and flexibility.

For example, a company that discriminates, directly or indirectly, against older or disabled people, women, ethnic minorities or people with different sexual orientations will be curtailing the potential of available talent, and employers are not well known for their complaints about the surplus of talent. The financial benefits of retaining staff who might otherwise leave due to lack of career development or due to the desire to combine a career with family are stressed, as is the image of the organisation as a 'good' employer and hence its attractiveness to all members of society as its customers. A relationship between a positive diversity climate and job satisfaction and commitment to the organisation has also been found (Hicks-Clarke and Iles 2000). Although the impact on performance is more difficult to assess, it is reasonable to assume that more satisfied and committed employees will lead to reduced absence and turnover levels. In addition, the value of different employee perspectives and different types of contribution is seen as providing added value to the organisation, particularly when organisational members increasingly reflect the diverse customer base of the organisation. This provides a way in which organisations can better understand, and therefore meet, their customer needs. The business case argument is likely to have more support from managers as it is less likely to threaten the bottom line. We outline in the Window on practice below the London 2012's business case approach to diversity.

WINDOW ON PRACTICE

London 2012 puts diversity at its heart

The London 2012 games will be the first Olympics to be organised with diversity and inclusion as one of its central goals, Stephen Frost, head of diversity and inclusion at LOCOG, the organising committee for the Games, said that unlike previous Olympiads, the capital's diversity was central to the 2012 brand and would help inspire young people from all communities to take up sport.

'It might surprise some people that we are a private-sector company, funded by private-sector sponsors. Therefore, we aren't bound by public-sector duties and motivated by compliance – we are doing this because we really believe it will benefit our games,' Frost said. The LOCOG workforce is constantly expanding – it started with

just 150 people and will swell to around 200,000 during the games once temporary workers come on board. This demand for talent makes it essential to engage local communities. The organisation has a prominent diversity board to provide leadership on the issue and every manager making hiring decisions is directly responsible for ensuring the diversity of their team, said Frost. External efforts to recruit a more diverse range of people have included recruitment evenings aimed at specific communities, blogs by BME (black and minority ethnic) staff detailing their experiences and job adverts being read out along with the call to prayer in London mosques. With the Paralympic games an important part of the package, there is also an emphasis on hiring disabled workers. LOCOG has launched Access Now – a scheme that guarantees disabled people an interview if they meet basic criteria. The organisation also operates a talent pool, so that unsuccessful disabled candidates can be kept in mind for other posts as they arise, said Frost.

Source: Brockett, J. (2009) 'London 2012 puts diversity at its heart', BBC Radio 4, PM Online, 19 November.

Managing diversity highlights the importance of culture in two ways. First, organisational culture is one determinant of the way that organisations manage diversity and treat individuals from different groups. Equal opportunity approaches tended to concentrate on behaviour and, to a small extent, attitudes, whereas management of diversity approaches recognise a need to go beneath this. So changing the culture to one which treats people as individuals and supports them in developing their potential is critical, although the difficulties of culture change make this a very demanding task.

Second, depending on the approach to the management of diversity, the culture of different groups within the organisation comes into play. For example, recognising that men and women present different cultures at work, and that this diversity needs to be managed, is key to promoting a positive environment of equal opportunity, which goes beyond merely fulfilling the demands of the statutory codes. Women may be more collectivist than men, for example, who tend to be more individualistic. These cultural differences may mean, for example, that men and women need managing and developing in different ways. Attending to the organisation's culture suggests a move away from seeing the individual as the problem, and requiring that the individual needs to change because he or she does not fit the culture. Rather, it is the organisation that needs to change so that traditional assumptions of how jobs are constructed and how they should be carried out are questioned, and looked at afresh.

Finally, managing diversity is considered to be a more integrated approach to implementing equality. Whereas equal opportunities approaches were driven by the HR function, managing diversity is seen to be the responsibility of all managers. And, as there are business reasons for managing diversity it is argued that equality should not be dealt with as a separate issue, as with equal opportunities approaches, but integrated strategically into every aspect of what the organisation does; this is often called mainstreaming.

Table 21.2 summarises the key differences between equal opportunities and managing diversity.

Table 21.2 Major differences between 'equal opportunities' approaches and 'management of diversity' approaches

Aspect	Equal opportunities	Managing diversity
Purpose	Reduce discrimination	Utilise employee potential to maximum advantage
Approach	Operational	Strategic
Case argued	Moral and ethical	Business case – improve profitability
Whose responsibility	HR/personnel department	All managers
Focuses on	Groups	Individuals
Perspective	Dealing with different needs of different groups	Integrated
Benefits for employees	Opportunities improved for disadvantaged groups, primarily through setting targets	Opportunities improved for all employees
Focus on management activity	Recruitment	Managing
Remedies	Changing systems and practices	Changing the culture
Monitoring success	Changed processes	Business outcomes

Case study 21.2 on this book's companion website at **www.pearsoned.co.uk/torrington** considers in more detail the differences between the equal opportunities and managing diversity approaches.

Problems with the managing diversity approach

While many saw the management of diversity approach as revitalising the equal opportunities agenda, and as a strategy for making more progress on the equality front, this progress has been slow to materialise. In reality, there remains the question of the extent to which approaches have really changed in organisations. Redefining equal opportunities in the terms of its 'business case' may just be a way of making it more palatable in today's climate. Indeed, only a small number of organisations are ever quoted as management of diversity exemplars (Kirton and Greene 2003) and the workforces of those that are so described are not necessarily more diverse than those of other organisations.

Apart from this there are some fundamental problems with the diversity management approach. The first of these is its complexity, as there are differing interpretations, which we have so far ignored, and which focus on the prominence of groups or individuals. Miller (1996) highlights two different approaches to the management of diversity. The first is where individual differences are identified and celebrated, and where prejudices are exposed and challenged via training. The second, more orthodox, approach is where the organisation seeks to develop the capacity of all. This debate between group and individual identity is a fundamental issue:

> Can people's achievements be explained by their individual talents or are they better explained as an outcome of their gender, ethnicity, class and age? Can anything meaningful be said about the collective experience of all women or are any generalisations undermined by other cross-cutting ideas? (Liff 1997: 11)

The most common approach to the management of diversity is based on individual contribution, as we have explained above, rather than on group identity. The *individualism* approach is based on dissolving random differences, not those that accrue due to membership of a particular social group. The advantage of this approach is that it is inclusive and involves all members of the organisation. An alternative emphasis in the management of diversity is that of *valuing differences* based on the membership of different social groups. Following this approach would mean recognising and highlighting differences, and being prepared to give special training to groups who may be disadvantaged and lack self-confidence, so that all in the organisation feel comfortable. This could, however, lead to reinforcement of group-based stereotypes and indeed, problems which can result from a more diverse workforce, for example, increased conflict.

A significant criticism of managing diversity is its basis in the 'business case'. The business case is unreliable because it will only work in certain contexts (Atkinson and Hall 2009). For example, where skills are easily available there is less pressure on the organisation to promote and encourage the employment of minority groups. Not every employee interacts with customers so if image and customer contact are part of the business case this will apply only to some jobs and not to others. Also some groups may be excluded. For example, there is no systematic evidence to suggest that disabled customers are attracted by an organisation which employs disabled people. UK managers are also driven by short-term budgets and the economic benefits of equality may only be reaped in the longer term. The CIPD (2006a) argues that the evidence of performance improvements resulting from diversities is weak, which may mean that the business case is in fact potentially detrimental to equality (Kirton and Greene 2003).

In terms of implementation of a diversity approach there are also difficulties. Foster and Harris (2005) in their research in the retail sector found that it was a concept that lacked clarity for line managers in terms both of what it is and of how to implement it within anti-discrimination laws, and some were concerned that it may lead to feelings of unfairness and claims of unequal treatment. There are also concerns about whether diversity management, which originated in the USA, will travel effectively to other countries where the context is different, especially in terms of the demographics and the history of equality initiatives. Indeed, some raise concerns about whether diversity can be managed at all:

> the belief that diversity management is do-able rests on a fantasy that it is possible to imagine a clean slate on which memories of privilege and subordination leave no mark. (Lorbiecki and Jack 2000: 528)

Diversity management is clearly a complex concept.

Equal opportunities or managing diversity?

Are equal opportunities and managing diversity completely different things? If so, is one approach preferable to the other? For the sake of clarity, earlier in this chapter we characterised a distinct approach to managing diversity which suggests that it is different from equal opportunities. However, as we have seen, managing diversity covers a range of approaches and emphases, some closer to equal opportunities, some very different.

Much of the management of diversity approach suggests that it is superior to and not compatible with the equal opportunities approach. There is, however, increasing support for equal opportunities and managing diversity to be viewed as mutually supportive and for this combination to be seen as important. Dickens (2006) suggests that social justice and economic efficiency are increasingly being presented as complementary, although there is so far a lack of guidance about how this can be done in practice. To see equal opportunities and management of diversity as *alternatives* threatens to sever the link between them and may therefore be detrimental to organisational objectives. Legislation on equality may support diversity approaches in preventing discrimination which arises from market forces (Dickens 2006) and be of value in setting minimum standards (Woodhams and Lupton 2006).

IMPLICATIONS FOR ORGANISATIONS

Equal opportunities and managing diversity: strategies, policies and plans

Kersley *et al.* (2006) found that 73 per cent of organisations in the Workplace Employee Relations (WER) Survey had equal opportunities or diversity policies or a statement, up from 64 per cent in 1998. The public sector was more likely to have such policies (97 per cent, a level unchanged from the last survey) and larger organisations were more likely to have policies than smaller ones, which means that 88 per cent of the labour force are in organisations where such a policy exists. In addition the existence of a policy was more likely in organisations where there was union recognition. Organisations were more likely to have a policy if they had an employment relations specialist (even allowing for size), a finding confirmed by Woodhams and Lupton (2006) who found that the existence of an HR specialist in small firms increased the likelihood of a policy existing. It would be a mistake, however, to assume that all policies cover all potentially disadvantaged groups: the CIPD (2006b) found that while 93 per cent of organisations which responded to its survey did have a diversity policy, the disadvantaged groups covered by these were very variable, and many did not cover all the groups for whom there is legislative protection. Similarly, policies may not cover all organisational activity. Woodhams and Corby (2007) suggest, for example, that many organisations have policies in place which cover the recruitment but not the promotion or career progression of those with disabilities.

In the WER Survey the existence of a policy was positively associated with the existence of processes aimed at preventing discrimination such as job evaluation and monitoring of recruitment, selection, promotion and pay. However, these activities were still only carried out by a minority of such organisations. Despite the prevalence of policies there is always the concern that having a policy is more about projecting the right image than about reflecting how the organisation operates. For example, Hoque and Noon (1999) found that having an equal opportunities statement made no difference to the treatment of speculative applications from individuals who were either white or from an ethnic minority group and that 'companies with ethnic minority statements were more likely to discriminate *against* the ethnic minority applicant'. Creegan *et al.* (2003) investigated the implementation of a race equality action plan and found a stark difference between paper and practice. Line managers who were responsible for implementing the plan were operating in a devolved HR environment and so had to pay for advice, training and support from HR. The consequence of this was that in order to protect their budgets they were reluctant to seek help. Employees felt that there was no ownership of the strategy or the plan within the organisation by senior or middle managers. Further, Kirton and Healey's (2009) study of the use of competencies to promote equality and diversity in the selection of judges suggests that, while competencies can give an impression of fairness, they are nevertheless interpreted by human actors. This gives rise to the continuing exercise of bias and prejudice.

ACTIVITY 21.2

Consider the equal opportunities and diversity policies in your own organisation, or another with which you are familiar.

1. To what extent does practice match policy?
2. Explore the reasons for the achievement of a match or mismatch.

A process for managing diversity

Ross and Schneider (1992) advocate a strategic approach to managing diversity that is based on their conception of the difference between seeking equal opportunity and managing diversity. Their process involves the following steps:

1. Diagnosis of the current situation in terms of statistics, policy and culture, and looking at both issues and causes.
2. Setting aims which involve the business case for equal opportunities, identifying the critical role of commitment from the top of the organisation, and a vision of what the organisation would look like if it successfully managed diversity.
3. Spreading the ownership. This is a critical stage in which awareness needs to be raised, via a process of encouraging people to question their attitudes and preconceptions. Awareness needs to be raised in all employees at all levels, especially managers, and it needs to be clear that diversity is not something owned by the personnel function.
4. Policy development comes after awareness raising as it enables a contribution to be made from all in the organisation – new systems need to be changed via involvement and not through imposition on the unwilling.
5. Managing the transition needs to involve a range of training initiatives. Positive action programmes, specifically designed for minority groups, may be used to help them understand the culture of the organisation and acquire essential skills; policy implementation programmes, particularly focusing on selection, appraisal, development and coaching; further awareness training and training to identify cultural diversity and manage different cultures and across different cultures.
6. Managing the programme to sustain momentum. This involves a champion, not necessarily from the HR function, but someone who continues in his or her previous organisation role in addition. The continued involvement of senior managers is

important, together with trade unions. Harnessing initiatives that come up through departments and organising support networks for disadvantaged groups are key at this stage. Ross and Schneider also recommend measuring achievements in terms of business benefit – better relationships with customers, improvements in productivity and profitability, for example – which need to be communicated to all employees.

Ellis and Sonnenfield (1994) make the point that training for diversity needs to be far more than a one-day event. They recommend a series of workshops which allow time for individuals to think, check their assumptions and reassess between training sessions. Key issues that need tackling in arranging training are ensuring that the facilitator has the appropriate skills; carefully considering participant mix; deciding whether the training should be voluntary or mandatory; being prepared to cope with any backlash from previously advantaged groups who now feel threatened; and being prepared for the fact that the training may reinforce stereotypes. They argue that training has enormous potential benefits, but that there are risks involved.

While the ideal may be for organisations to work on all aspects of diversity in an integrated manner, the reality is often that organisations will target specific issues or groups at different times. Case 21.2 on this book's companion website, **www.pearsoned.co.uk/torrington**, is focused on improving diversity practice for people with disabilities.

WINDOW ON PRACTICE

Arriva: dramatic results on diversity

Arriva embarked on a diversity programme in 2003 and claims that it has stimulated a change in workforce profile and reduced employee turnover. This is a key outcome as one of the drivers behind the programme was to become an employer of choice in response to predicted demographic and legislative changes, recruitment challenges, and a need to reflect the broader community in order to stay ahead in business. The company was aware for example that it was a traditional white male environment, with bus driving, for example, being seen as a man's job. Arriva began by setting up a diversity committee made up of senior leaders from across the business to review progress and measures of success. In addition a Diversity Best Practice Forum was set up with responsibility for delivering the diversity agenda. Diversity behaviours and leadership competencies were included in management and individuals at all levels have objectives linked to diversity.

Training was a key part of the company's approach to diversity and was accomplished in two phases. The first was innovative, and a drama-based training organisation started off the programme, called Managing and Valuing Difference. They prepared by researching what actually happened in the business and identified current key issues relating to diversity. Scenarios were then acted out and participants were encouraged to be involved by interactive exercises and discussions. The aim was to create an understanding in the workforce of diversity and the business case for it, to help people appreciate the differences in others and to create a situation where people

felt able to challenge unacceptable behaviour. The second part of the training involved Arriva staff who volunteered to be trained as facilitators and the use of video scenarios. This second part of the training addressed 'Valuing and welcoming difference'.

In addition it was decided to extend flexible working and to strengthen the role of minority groups. For example there was a women's networking event attended by the chief executive with a view to encouraging, developing and retaining women in senior management. A recruitment monitoring process was also introduced to help decide how to allocate resources on diversity. For example in one part of the business it might be to target under-represented groups and produce a tailored approach to recruitment advertising, while in another it might be to have greater involvement in the local community. Open days have been held to encourage the recruitment of women bus drivers where existing women drivers also attend to share their views. Two-part application forms are used so that any personal data is separate from the application form and cannot bias shortlisting, and the use of male and female mentors has proved successful.

Source: Adapted from Wolff, C. (2007) 'Arriva; dramatic results on diversity', *Equal Opportunities Review*, No. 160, January, pp. 5–11.

ACTIVITY 21.3

Prepare a strategy for managing diversity which would be appropriate for your organisation, or one with which you are familiar.

SUMMARY PROPOSITIONS

21.1 The essence of much HR work is to discriminate between individuals. The essence of equality is to avoid unfair discrimination. Unfair discrimination often results from people being treated on the basis of limited and prejudiced understanding of the groups to which they belong rather than on the basis of an assessment of them as individuals. People are not always aware when they are discriminating unfairly.

21.2 Legislation can have only a limited effect in achieving equality, and does not change attitudes, beliefs and cultures and structures. Organisations and their cultures, processes and structures are founded on the needs of the majority group and individuals from other groups are expected to adapt to this norm. This explains why progress towards equality of opportunity has been very slow.

21.3 Equal opportunities approaches highlight the moral argument for equal treatment, whereas managing diversity highlights the business case.

21.4 Actual changes in practice relating to equalising opportunity are taking place very slowly, and only long-term organisational transformation is likely to support equality.

21.5 Equal opportunities approaches and the management of diversity are best viewed, not as alternatives, but as complementary approaches which need to be interrelated.

GENERAL DISCUSSION TOPICS

1 Discuss Liff's (1997) question:
'Can people's achievements be explained by their individual talents or are they better explained as an outcome of their gender, ethnicity, class and age? Can anything meaningful be said about the collective experience of all women or are any generalisations undermined by other cross-cutting ideas?' (p. 11)

2 Thinking about Cook and Glass's (2009) findings that the appointment of racial/ethnic minorities to top management positions can have a negative impact on share price:

- Why do you think that this is the case?
- How could organisations try to address this?

FURTHER READING

Cook, A. and Glass, C. (2009) 'Between a rock and a hard place: managing diversity in a shareholder society', *Human Resource Management Journal*, Vol. 19, No. 4, pp. 393–412.
This is a fascinating study examining whether the appointment of racial/ethnic minorities to top management positions has a different impact on share price than the appointment of Caucasians to equivalent positions. The findings suggest that market reaction to the appointment of racial/ethnic minorities in corporate leadership positions is significant and negative, while the market's reaction to the appointment of Caucasians is significant and positive. The authors suggest, however, that the negative market reaction to the appointment of racial/ethnic minorities can be mitigated by the explicit incorporation of diversity into organisation strategy.

Fagan, C., Rubery, J., Grimshaw, D., Smith, M., Hebson, G. and Figueiredo, H. (2005) 'Gender mainstreaming in the enlarged European Union: recent developments in the European employment strategy and social inclusion process', *Industrial Relations Journal*, Vol. 36, No. 6, pp. 568–91.
Provides some excellent data comparing progress in the UK with that in other members of the EU in relation to employment rates and gender gaps.

Phillips, T. (2007) *Fairness and Freedom: Final Report of the Equalities Review*. London: HMSO.
Specifically the section on employment, Chapter 3, which discusses the idea of employment penalties.

WEB LINKS

http://www.business-humanrights.org

www.equalityhumanrights.com

www.direct.gov.uk/.../RightsAndObligations/DisabilityRights/

REFERENCES

Annual Survey of Hours and Earnings (2009) **http://www.statistics.gov.uk/downloads/theme_labour/ASHE-2009/2009_age.pdf**. Accessed 23 February 2010.

Atkinson, C. and Hall, L. (2009) 'The role of gender in varying forms of flexible working', *Gender, Work and Organisation*, Vol. 16, No. 6, pp. 650–66.

Carroll, M., Smith, M. and Oliver, G. (2009) 'Recruitment and retention in front-line services: the case of childcare', *Human Resource Management Journal*, Vol. 19, pp. 59–74.

CIPD (2003) 'Diversity: stacking up the evidence', *Executive Briefing*. London: CIPD.

CIPD (2005a) *Tackling Age Discrimination in the Workplace: Creating a new age for all*. London: CIPD.

CIPD (2005b) *Managing Diversity: Linking theory and practice to business performance*. London: CIPD.

CIPD (2006a) *Managing Diversity: Measuring success*. London: CIPD.

CIPD (2006b) *Diversity in Business: How much progress have employers made? First findings*. London: CIPD.

Cook, A. and Glass, C. (2009) 'Between a rock and a hard place: managing diversity in a shareholder society', *Human Resource Management Journal*, Vol. 19, No. 4, pp. 393–412.

CRE (2006) *Employment and Ethnicity, Factfile 1*. Manchester: CRE.

Creegan, C., Colgan, F., Charlesworth, R. and Robinson, G. (2003) 'Race equality policies at work: employee perceptions of the "implementation gap" in a UK local authority', *Work, Employment and Society*, Vol. 17, No. 4, pp. 617–40.

Day, N. and Greene, P. (2008) 'A case for sexual orientation diversity management in small and large organizations', *Human Resource Management*, Vol. 47, No. 3, pp. 637–54.

Department for Work and Pensions (2006) *Opportunity for All*, available at **www.dwp.gov.uk/publications/policy-publications/opportunity-for-all/indicators/table-of-indicators/people-of-working-age/indicator-19/**

der Laan Bouma-Doff, W. (2008) 'Concentrating on participation: ethnic concentration and labour market participation of four ethnic groups', *Journal of Applied Social Science Studies*, Vol. 128, No. 1, pp. 153–73.

Dickens, L. (2006) 'Re-regulation for gender equality: from "either/or" to "both"', *Industrial Relations Journal*, Vol. 37, No. 4, pp. 299–309.

Ellis, C. and Sonnenfield, J.A. (1994) 'Diverse approaches to managing diversity', *Human Resource Management*, Vol. 33, No. 1, Spring, pp. 79–109.

Equal Opportunities Commission (2007) *Sex and power: who runs Britain?* Manchester: EOC.

Foster, C. and Harris, L. (2005) 'Easy to say, difficult to do: diversity in retail management', *Human Resource Management Journal*, Vol. 15, No. 3, pp. 4–17.

Hicks-Clarke, D. and Iles, P. (2000) 'Climate for diversity and its effects on career and organizational attitudes and perceptions', *Personnel Review*, Vol. 29, No. 3, pp. 324–45.

Hoque, K. and Noon, M. (1999) 'Racial discrimination in speculative applications: new optimism six years on?', *Human Resource Management Journal*, Vol. 9, No. 3, pp. 71–82.

IDS (2004) *Employers Move on Equal Pay*, IDS Report, No. 897. London: IDS.

IDS (2006) *Promoting Race Equality*, IDS HR Studies No. 825. London: IDS.

Kandola, R., Fullerton, J. and Mulroney, C. (1996) *1996 Pearn Kandola Survey of Diversity Practice: Summary Report*. Oxford: Pearn Kandola.

Kersley, B., Alpin, C., Forth, J., Bryson, A., Bewley, H., Dix, G. and Oxenbridge, S. (2006) *Inside the Workplace: Findings from the 2004 Workplace Employment Relations Survey*. London: Routledge.

Kirton, G. and Greene, A. (2003) *The Dynamics of Managing Diversity: A critical approach*. Oxford: Butterworth Heinemann.

Kirton, G. and Healey, G. (2009) 'Using competency-based assessment centres to select judges: implications for diversity and equality', *Human Resource Management Journal*, Vol. 19, No. 3, pp. 302–18.

Liff, S. (1997) 'Two routes to managing diversity: individual differences or social group characteristics?', *Employee Relations*, Vol. 19, No. 1, pp. 11–26.

Lorbiecki, A. and Jack, G. (2000) 'Critical turns in the evolution of diversity management', *British Journal of Management*, Vol. 11, pp. S17–S31.

Loretto, W. and White, P. (2006) 'Employer practices, policies and attitudes towards older workers', *Human Resource Management Journal*, Vol. 16, No. 3, pp. 313–30.

Meager, N. and Hill, D. (2005) 'The Labour Market Participation and Employment of Disabled People in the UK', Work Research Institute, Norway. Available at **http://www.employment-studies.co.uk/pdflibrary/wp1.pdf.** Accessed 24 February 2010.

Miller, D. (1996) 'Equality management: towards a materialist approach', *Gender, Work and Organisation*, Vol. 3, No. 4, pp. 202–14.

ONS (2005) *Labour Force Survey December 2005*. London: HMSO.

ONS (2009) *Labour Force Survey December 2009*. London: HMSO. Available at **http://www.statistics.gov.uk/cci/nugget.asp?id=2145**. Accessed 23 February 2010.

Rana, E. (2003) 'Council appraisals discriminate', *People Management*, Vol. 9, No. 2, p. 11.

Riach, K. (2009) 'Managing difference: understanding age diversity in practice', *Human Resource Management Journal*, Vol. 19, No. 3, pp. 319–35.

Ross, R. and Schneider, R. (1992) *From Equality to Diversity: A business case for equal opportunities*. London: Pitman.

Shapiro, G. and Austin, S. (1996) 'Equality drives total quality', Occasional Paper. Brighton: Brighton Business School.

Snape, E. and Redman, T. (2003) 'Too old or too young? The impact of perceived age discrimination', *Human Resource Management Journal*, Vol. 13, No. 1, pp. 78–89.

Stonewall (2010) *Workplace Equality Index*. London: Stonewall.

Wolff, C. (2007) 'Arriva: dramatic results on diversity', *Equal Opportunities Review*, No. 160, January, pp. 5–11.

Woodhams, C. and Corby, S. (2007) 'Then and now: disability legislation and employers' practices in the UK', *British Journal of Industrial Relations*, Vol. 45, No. 3, pp. 556–80.

Woodhams, C. and Danieli, A. (2000) 'Disability and diversity: a difference too far?', *Personnel Review*, Vol. 29, No. 3.

Woodhams, C. and Lupton, B. (2006) 'Gender-based equal opportunities policy and practice in small firms: the impact of HR professionals', *Human Resource Management Journal*, Vol. 16, No. 1, pp. 74–97.

An extensive range of additional materials, including multiple choice questions, answers to questions and links to useful websites can be found on the Human Resource Management companion website at **www.pearsoned.co.uk/torrington.**

DISCIPLINE AND GRIEVANCE

THE OBJECTIVES OF THIS CHAPTER ARE TO:

1 Examine the nature and explain the place of grievance and discipline in the employment contract

2 Review the Milgram experiments with obedience and use them to explain our response to authority

3 Explain the framework of organisational justice in the business

4 Explain grievance and discipline procedures

Consider these two press reports:

In February 2010 Jacqueline Cartner, a Chief Petty Officer in the Royal Navy, complained to an Employment Tribunal that she had been passed over for promotion to Warrant Officer despite having carried out the role in an acting capacity. Now CPO Cartner, a married mother of two, could be in line for a payout equivalent to 10 years' pay. (*Daily Telegraph*, 3 February 2010)

Michael Mitchell, 58, Director General of Railways at the Department of Transport, appeared at Peterborough Magistrates' Court, accused of attacking and swearing at Peter Etherington as he served vegetables to diners on a GNER King's Cross to Newcastle service. (*The Times*, 7 July 2006)

Both of these cases indicate the importance of managements taking employee grievances seriously, otherwise there will be recourse to the courts, where the costs will be substantial and the publicity grievous.

In 2009 there was a change in British legal requirements about formal grievances to give employees the right to take a grievance directly to a tribunal without necessarily going through internal procedures. Between 2004 and 2009 it was not possible to take a case unless it had already been through the employer's internal arrangements, but research by Mordsley and Aylott (2006) to analyse recent EAT decisions concluded that:

- there is no requirement to comply with any internal procedures
- employees do not have to ask for a meeting to discuss the complaint

The employee must still advise the employer of the complaint, but does not need to set out the full basis of it until invited to a meeting with the employer. This is a further reason for employers to take complaints seriously and to ensure that their internal procedures are effective and fully respected.

We use the words grievance and discipline as technical terms to describe the breakdown of mutual confidence between employer and employee, or between managers and managed. When someone starts working at an organisation there are mutual expectations that form the basis of the forthcoming working relationship. We explained in the opening chapter of this book how the maintenance of those mutual expectations is the central purpose of human resource management. Apart from what is written in the contract of employment, both parties will have expectations of what is to come. Employees are likely to expect, for instance, a congenial working situation with like-minded colleagues, opportunities to use existing skills and to acquire others, work that does not offend their personal value system, acceptable leadership and management from those more senior and opportunities to grow and mature. Employers will have expectations such as willing participation in the team, conscientious and imaginative use of existing skills and an ability to acquire others, compliance with reasonable instructions without quibbles, acceptance of instructions from those placed in authority and a willingness to be flexible and accept change.

That working relationship is sometimes going to go wrong. If the employee is dissatisfied, then there is potentially a grievance. If the employer is dissatisfied, there is the potential for a disciplinary situation. The two complementary processes are intended to find ways of avoiding the ultimate sanction of the employee quitting or being dismissed, but at the same time preparing the ground for those sanctions if all else fails.

Usually, the authority to be exercised in a business is impersonalised by the use of roles in order to make it more effective. If a colleague mentions to you that you have overspent your budget, your reaction might be proud bravado unless you knew that the colleague had a role such as company accountant, internal auditor or financial director. Everyone in a business has a role. Most people have several roles each conferring some authority. The canteen assistant who tells you that the steak and kidney pudding is off is more believable than the managing director conveying the same message. Normally in hospitals people wearing white coats and a stethoscope are seen as being more authoritative than people in white coats without a stethoscope.

Dependence on role is not always welcome to those in managerial positions, who are fond of using phrases like, 'I know how to get the best out of people' or 'I have a loyal staff'. This may partly be due to their perception of their role being to persuade the reluctant and command the respect of the unwilling by the use of personal leadership qualities, and it is indisputable that some managers are more effective with some groups of staff than with others, as we saw in Chapter 13, but there is more to it than personal skill: we are predisposed to obey those who outrank us in any hierarchy.

THE MILGRAM EXPERIMENTS WITH OBEDIENCE

Obedience is the reaction expected of people by those in authority positions, who prescribe actions which, but for that authority, might not necessarily have been carried out. Stanley Milgram (1974) conducted a classic and controversial series of experiments to investigate obedience to authority and highlighted the significance of obedience and the power of authority in our everyday lives. His work remains a standard explanation of how we all behave.

Subjects were led to believe that a study of memory and learning was being carried out which involved giving progressively more severe electric shocks to a learner who gave incorrect answers to factual questions. If the learner gave the correct answer the reward was a further question; if the answer was incorrect there was the punishment of a mild electric shock. Each shock was more severe than the previous one. The 'learner' was not actually receiving shocks, but was a member of the experimental team simulating progressively greater distress, as the shocks were supposedly made stronger. Eighteen different experiments were conducted with over 1,000 subjects, with the circumstances between experiments varying. No matter how the variables were altered the subjects showed an astonishing compliance with authority even when delivering 'shocks' of 450 volts. Up to 65 per cent of subjects continued to obey throughout the experiment in the presence of a clear authority figure and as many as 20 per cent continued to obey when the authority figure was absent. One might think that people no longer behave so submissively in the twenty-first century, but an interesting copy of the experiment was carried out in 2009 (Nick and Eltchaninoff 2010), in which volunteers were also asked to inflict electric shocks to a screaming victim. The key difference was that the volunteers were told they were piloting a new reality TV show. Almost all of the 80 participants continued to the end.

Milgram (1974: 123) was dismayed by his results:

> With numbing regularity good people were seen to knuckle under to the demands of authority and perform actions that were callous and severe. Men who are in everyday life responsible and decent were seduced by the trappings of authority, by the control of their perceptions, and by the uncritical acceptance of the experimenter's definition of the situation into performing harsh acts.

Our interest in Milgram's work is simply to demonstrate that we all have a predilection to obey instructions from authority figures, even if we do not want to. He points out that the act of entering a hierarchical system (such as any employing organisation) makes people see themselves acting as agents for carrying out the wishes of someone else, and this results in these people being in a different state, described as the agentic state. This is the opposite to the state of autonomy when individuals see themselves as acting on their own. Milgram then sets out the factors that lay the groundwork for obedience to authority.

1. **Family.** Parental regulation inculcates a respect for adult authority. Parental injunctions form the basis for moral imperatives, as commands to children have a dual function. 'Don't tell lies' is a moral injunction carrying a further implicit instruction: 'And obey me!' It is the implicit demand for obedience that remains the only consistent element across a range of explicit instructions.
2. **Institutional setting.** Children emerge from the family into an institutional system of authority: the school. Here they learn how to function in an organisation. They are regulated by teachers, but can see that the head teacher, the school governors and central government regulate the teachers themselves. Throughout this period they are in a subordinate position. When, as adults, they go to work they may find that a certain level of dissent is allowable, but the overall situation is one in which they are to do a job prescribed by someone else.
3. **Rewards.** Compliance with authority is generally rewarded, while disobedience is frequently punished. Most significantly, promotion within the hierarchy not only rewards the individual but also ensures the continuity of the hierarchy.
4. **Perception of authority.** Authority is normatively supported: there is a shared expectation among people that certain institutions do, ordinarily, have a socially controlling figure. Also, the authority of the controlling figure is limited to the situation. The usher in a cinema wields authority, which vanishes on leaving the premises. Where authority is expected it does not have to be asserted, merely presented.
5. **Entry into the authority system.** Having perceived an authority figure, an individual must then define that figure as relevant to the subject. The individual not only takes the voluntary step of deciding which authority system to join (at least in most of employment), but also defines which authority is relevant to which event. The firefighter may expect instant obedience when calling for everybody to evacuate the building, but not if asking employees to use a different accounting system.

6 The overarching ideology. The legitimacy of the social situation relates to a justifying ideology. Science and education formed the background to the experiments Milgram conducted and therefore provided a justification for actions carried out in their name. Most employment is in realms of activity regarded as legitimate, justified by the values and needs of society. This is vital if individuals are to provide willing obedience, as it enables them to see their behaviour as serving a desirable end.

Managers are positioned in an organisational hierarchy in such a way that others will be predisposed, as Milgram demonstrates, to follow their instructions. As the American Benjamin Franklin said in the eighteenth century, 'those who seek to command must first learn to obey'. Managers put in place a series of frameworks to explain how they will exact obedience: they use *discipline*. Because individual employees feel their relative weakness in the hierarchy, they seek complementary frameworks to challenge the otherwise unfettered use of managerial disciplinary power: they may join trade unions, but they will always need channels to present their *grievances*.

In later work Milgram (1992) made an important distinction between obedience and conformity, which several experimental psychologists had studied, most notably Asch (1951) and Abrams *et al.* (1990). Conformity and obedience both involve abandoning personal judgement as a result of external pressure. The external pressure to conform is the need to be accepted by one's peers and the resultant behaviour is to wear similar clothes, to adopt similar attitudes and adopt similar behaviour. The external pressure to obey comes from a hierarchy of which one is a member, but in which certain others have more status and power than oneself.

> There are at least three important differences . . . First, in conformity there is no explicit requirement to act in a certain way, whereas in obedience we are ordered or instructed to do something. Second, those who influence us when we conform are our peers (or equals) and people's behaviours become more alike because they are affected by example. In obedience, there is . . . somebody in higher authority influencing behaviour. Third, conformity has to do with the psychological need for acceptance by others. Obedience, by contrast, has to do with the social power and status of an authority figure in a hierarchical situation. (Gross and McIlveen 1998: 508)

In this chapter we are concerned only with grievance and discipline within business organisations, but it is worth pointing out that managers are the focal points for the grievances of people outside the business as well, but those grievances are called complaints. You may complain *about* poor service, shoddy workmanship or rudeness from an employee, but you complain *to* a manager.

HR managers make one of their most significant contributions to business effectiveness by the way they facilitate and administer grievance and disciplinary issues. First, they devise and negotiate the procedural framework of organisational justice on which both discipline and grievance depend. Second, they are much involved in the interviews and problem-solving discussions that eventually produce solutions to the difficulties that have been encountered. Third, they maintain the viability of the whole process which forms an integral part of their work: they monitor to make sure that grievances are not overlooked and so that any general trend can be perceived, and they oversee the disciplinary machinery to ensure that it is not being bypassed or unfairly manipulated.

Grievance and discipline handling is one of the roles in HRM that few other people want to take over. Ambitious line managers may want to select their own staff without HR intervention or by using the services of consultants. They may try to brush their HR colleagues aside and deal directly with trade union officials or organise their own management development, but grievance and discipline is too hot a potato.

The requirements of the law relating to grievance handling and the legal framework in place to avoid unfair dismissal combine to make this an area where HR people must be both knowledgeable and effective. That combination provides a valuable platform for influencing other aspects of management. The HR manager who is not skilled in grievance and discipline is seldom in a strong organisational position.

Everything we have said so far presupposes both hierarchy and the use of procedures. You may say that we have already demonstrated that hierarchy is in decline and that there is a preference for more flexible, personal ways of working than procedure offers. Why rely on Milgram's research, which is now nearly 40 years old? Surely we have moved on since then? Our response is simply that hierarchical relationships continue, although deference is in decline. We still seek out the person 'in authority' when we have a grievance and managers readily refer problems they cannot resolve to someone else with a more appropriate role. Procedures may be rigid and mechanical, but they are reliable and we use them even if we do not like them.

WHAT DO WE MEAN BY DISCIPLINE?

Discipline is regulation of human activity to produce a controlled performance. It ranges from the guard's control of a rabble to the accomplishment of lone individuals producing spectacular performance through self-discipline in the control of their own talents and resources.

In *managerial* discipline everything depends on the leader from start to finish. There is a group of people who are answerable to someone who directs what they should all do. Only through individual direction can that group of people produce a worthwhile performance, like the person leading the community singing in the pantomime or the conductor of an orchestra. Everything depends on the leader.

Team discipline is where the quality of the performance depends on the mutual dependence of all, and that mutual dependence derives from a commitment by each member to the total enterprise: the failure of one would be the downfall of all. This is usually found in relatively small working groups, like a dance troupe or an autonomous working group in a factory.

Self-discipline is like that of the juggler or the skilled artisan, where a solo performer is absolutely dependent on training, expertise and self-control. One of the few noted UK researchers working in the field of discipline concludes that self-discipline has recently become much more significant, as demonstrated in the title of his work, 'Discipline: towards trust and self-discipline' (Edwards 2000).

Discipline is, therefore, not only negative, producing punishment or prevention. It can also be a valuable quality for the individual who is subject to it, although the form of discipline depends not only on the individual employee but also on the task and the way it is organised. The development of self-discipline is easier in some jobs than others and many of the job redesign initiatives of recent years have been directed at providing scope for job holders to exercise self-discipline and find a degree of autonomy from

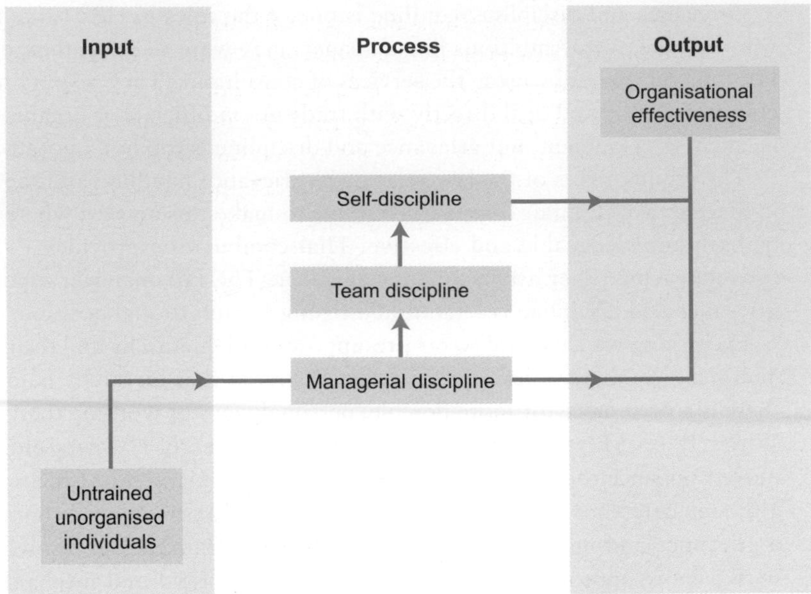

Figure 22.1 Three forms of discipline

managerial discipline. Figure 22.1 shows how the three forms are connected in a sequence or hierarchy, with employees finding one of three ways to make their contribution to organisational effectiveness. However, even the most accomplished solo performer has at some time been dependent on others for training and advice, and every team has its coach.

ACTIVITY 22.1

Note three examples of managerial discipline, team discipline and self-discipline from your own experience.

Managers are not dealing with discipline only when rebuking latecomers or threatening to dismiss saboteurs. As well as dealing with the unruly and reluctant, they are developing the coordinated discipline of the working team, engendering that *esprit de corps* which makes the whole greater than the sum of the parts. They are training the new recruit who must not let down the rest of the team, puzzling over the reasons why A is fitting in well while B is still struggling. Managers are also providing people with the equipment to develop the self-discipline that will give them autonomy, responsibility and the capacity to maximise their powers. The independence and autonomy that self-discipline produces also bring the greatest degree of personal satisfaction, and often the largest pay packet. Furthermore the movement between the three forms represents a declining degree of managerial involvement. If you are a leader of community singing, nothing can happen without your being present and the quality of the singing depends on your performance each time. If you train jugglers, the time and effort you invest pays off a thousand times, while you sit back and watch the show.

In employment there has long been an instinctive tendency to put discipline together with punishment, however limited this notion may be. The legislation on unfair dismissal is to most managers the logical final point of disciplinary procedures, yet it covers dismissal on the grounds of capability and ill health as well as more obvious forms of indiscipline. Because of this general feeling that disciplinary procedures imply disobedience, there is an emerging trend to have separate procedures to cover capability, so as to avoid the stigma, but being unsatisfactory in any way is difficult for many people to cope with. No matter how hard one tries, the prefix 'in-' causes problems. To be indisciplined is unwelcome (and does not actually appear in the dictionary): to be incapable is even worse.

WHAT DO WE MEAN BY GRIEVANCE?

We can distinguish between the terms dissatisfaction, complaint and grievance as follows:

- **Dissatisfaction.** Anything that disturbs an employee, whether or not the unrest is expressed in words.
- **Complaint.** A spoken or written dissatisfaction brought to the attention of a manager or other responsible person.
- **Grievance.** A complaint that has been formally presented to an appropriate management representative or to a union official.

This provides a useful categorisation by separating out grievance as a formal, relatively drastic step, compared with simply complaining. It is much more important for management to know about dissatisfaction. Although nothing is being expressed, the feeling of hurt following failure to get a pay rise or the frustration about shortage of materials can quickly influence performance.

Much dissatisfaction never turns into complaint, as something happens to make it unnecessary. Dissatisfaction evaporates with a night's sleep, after a cup of coffee with a colleague, or when the cause of the dissatisfaction is in some other way removed. The few dissatisfactions that do produce complaint are also most likely to resolve themselves at that stage. The person hearing the complaint explains things in a way that the dissatisfied employee had not previously appreciated, or takes action to get at the root of the problem.

Grievances are rare since few employees will openly question their superior's judgement, whatever their private opinion may be, and fewer still will risk being stigmatised as a troublemaker. Also, many people do not initiate grievances because they believe that nothing will be done as a result of their attempt. Tribunal hearings since the introduction of the 2004 regulations, already referred to, have often found great difficulty in deciding when a complaint becomes a grievance.

HR managers have to encourage the proper use of procedures to discover sources of dissatisfaction. Managers in the middle may not reveal the complaints they are hearing, for fear of showing themselves in a poor light. Employees who feel insecure, for any reason, are not likely to risk going into procedure, yet the dissatisfaction lying beneath a repressed grievance can produce all manner of unsatisfactory work behaviours from apathy to arson. Individual dissatisfaction can lead to the loss of a potentially valuable employee; collective dissatisfaction can lead to industrial action.

In dealing with complaints it is important to determine what lies behind the complaint as well as the complaint being expressed; not only verifying the facts, which are the *manifest* content of the complaint, but also determining the feelings behind the facts: the *latent* content. An employee who complains of the supervisor being a bully may actually be expressing something rather different, such as the employee's attitude to any authority figure, not simply the supervisor who was the subject of the complaint.

ACTIVITY 22.2

Think of an example from your own experience of dissatisfaction causing inefficiency that was not remedied because there was no complaint. Why was there no complaint?

THE FRAMEWORK OF ORGANISATIONAL JUSTICE

The organisation requires a framework of justice to surround the employment relationship so that managers and supervisors, as well as other employees, know where they stand when dissatisfaction develops. An illustration of this is in Figure 22.2.

Organisation culture and management style

The culture of an organisation affects the behaviour of people within it and develops norms that are hard to alter and which provide a pattern of conformity. If, for instance, everyone is in the habit of arriving ten minutes late, a 'new broom' manager will have

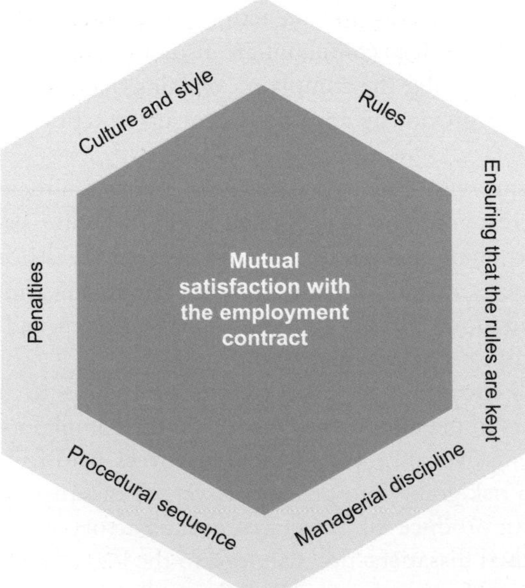

Figure 22.2 The framework of organisational justice

a struggle to change the habit. Equally, if everyone is in the habit of arriving punctually, then a new recruit who often arrives late will come under strong social pressure to conform, without need for recourse to management action. Culture also affects the freedom and candour with which people discuss dissatisfactions with their managers without allowing them to fester.

The style of managers in handling grievances and discipline reflects their beliefs. The manager who sees discipline narrowly as being punishment, and who regards grievances as examples of subordinates getting above themselves, will behave in a relatively autocratic way, being curt in disciplinary situations and dismissive of complaints. The manager who sees disciplinary problems as obstacles to achievement that do not necessarily imply incompetence or ill will by the employee will seek out the cause of the problem. That problem may then be revealed as one requiring firm, punitive action by the manager, or it may be revealed as a matter requiring management remedy of a different kind. The manager who listens out for complaints and grievances, gets to the bottom of the problems and finds solutions will run little risk of rumbling discontent from people obsessed by trivial problems. Among the selected HR skills in Part 8 we have a section on dealing with bullying, a specific type of problem that is not often complained about early. This is a good example of how a manager needs to pay close attention to rumour and gossip, as this is where indications of bullying first come to light.

Rules

Every workplace has rules; the difficulty is to have rules that people will honour. Some rules come from legislation, such as the tachograph requirement for HGV drivers, but most are tailored to meet the particular requirements of the organisation in which they apply. For example, rules about personal cleanliness are essential in a food factory but less stringent in a garage.

Rules should be clear and readily understood; the number should be sufficient to cover all obvious and usual disciplinary matters. To ensure general compliance it is helpful if rules are jointly determined, but it is more common for management to formulate the rules and for employee representatives eventually to concur with them. Employees should have ready access to the rules through the employee handbook and noticeboard, and the HR manager will always try to ensure that the rules are known as well as published.

Rules can be roughly grouped into various types:

1. **Negligence** is failure to do the job properly and is different from incompetence because of the assumption that the employee can do the job properly, but has not.
2. **Unreliability** is failure to attend work as required, such as being late or absent.
3. **Insubordination** is refusal to obey an instruction, or showing deliberate disrespect to someone in a position of authority. It is not to be confused with the use of bad language. Some of the most entertaining cases in employment tribunals have involved weighty consideration of whether or not colourful language was intended to be insubordinate.
4. **Interfering with the rights of others** covers a range of behaviours that are socially unacceptable. Fighting is clearly identifiable, but harassment or intimidation may be more difficult to establish.

5 **Theft** is another clear-cut aspect of behaviour that is unacceptable when it is from another employee. Theft from the organisation should be covered by very explicit rules, as stealing company property is regarded by many offenders as one of the perks of the job. How often have you taken home a box of paper clips or a felt tip pen without any thought that you were stealing from the employer?

6 **Safety offences** are those aspects of behaviour that can cause a hazard.

The value of rules is that they provide guidelines on what people should do, as the majority will comply. It is extremely difficult to apply rules that do not command general acceptance.

WINDOW ON PRACTICE

In a recent discussion with a group of senior managers, employees identified the following as legitimately taken at will:

- paper clips, pencils, disposable pens, spiral pads, local telephone calls, plain paper, computer CDs, adhesive tape, overalls and simple uniforms.

Among the more problematic were:

- **Redundant or shop-soiled stock.** One DIY store insisted that the store manager should personally supervise the scrapping of items that were slightly damaged, to ensure that other items were not slightly damaged on purpose.
- **Surplus materials.** One electricity supplier had some difficulty in eradicating the practice of surplus cable and pipe being regarded as a legitimate perequisite of fitters at the end of installation jobs, as they suspected their engineers were using the surplus for private work. Twelve months later the level of material requisition had declined by 14 per cent.

Ensuring that the rules are kept

It is not sufficient just to have rules; they are only effective if they are observed. How do we make sure that employees stick to the rules?

1 **Information** is needed so that everyone knows what the rules are. Written particulars may suffice in an employment tribunal hearing, but most people conform to the behaviour of their colleagues, so informal methods of communication are just as important as formal statements.

2 **Induction** can make the rules coherent and reinforce their understanding. Rules can be explained, perhaps with examples, so that people not only know the rules but also understand why they should be obeyed.

3 **Placement or relocation** can avoid the risk of rules being broken, by placing a new recruit with a working team that has high standards of compliance. If there are the signs of disciplinary problems in the offing, then a quick relocation can put the problem employee in a new situation where offences are less likely.

4 **Training** increases awareness of the rules, improving self-confidence and self-discipline. There will be new working procedures or new equipment from time to time, and again training will reduce the risk of safety offences, negligence or unreliability.

5 **Reviewing the rules periodically** ensures that they are up to date, and also ensures that their observance is a live issue. If, for instance, there is a monthly staff council meeting, it could be appropriate to have a rules review every 12 months. The simple fact of the rules being discussed keeps up the general level of awareness of what they are.

6 **Penalties** make the framework of organisational justice firmer if there is an understanding of what penalties can be imposed, by whom and for what. It is not feasible to have a fixed scale, but neither is it wise for penalties to depend on individual managerial whim. This area has been partially codified by the legislation on dismissal, but the following are some typical forms of penalty:

   (a) **Rebuke.** The simple 'Don't do that' or 'Smoking is not allowed in here' or 'If you're late again, you will be in trouble' is all that is needed in most situations, as someone has forgotten one of the rules, had not realised it was to be taken seriously, or was perhaps testing the resolution of the management. Too frequently, managers are reluctant to risk defiance and tend to wait until they have a good case for more serious action rather than deploy their own, then-and-there authority.

   (b) **Caution.** Slightly more serious and formal is the caution, which is then recorded. This is not triggering the procedure for dismissal, it is just making a note of a rule being broken and an offence being pointed out.

   (c) **Warnings.** When managers begin to issue warnings, great care is required because unfair dismissal legislation has made the system of warnings an integral part of disciplinary practice, which must be followed if the employer is to succeed in defending a possible claim of unfair dismissal at tribunal. For the employer to show procedural fairness there should normally be a formal oral warning, or a written warning, specifying the nature of the offence and the likely outcome if the offence is repeated. It should also be made clear that this is the first, formal stage in the procedure. Further misconduct could then warrant a final written warning containing a statement that further repetition would lead to a penalty such as suspension or dismissal. All written warnings should be dated, signed and kept on record for an agreed period. The means of appeal against the disciplinary action should also be pointed out.

   (d) **Disciplinary transfer or demotion.** This is moving the employee to less attractive work, possibly carrying a lower salary. The seriousness of this is that it is public, as the employee's colleagues know the reason. A form of disciplinary transfer is found on assembly lines, where there are some jobs that are more attractive and carry higher status than others. Rule breakers may be 'pushed down the line' until their contempt is purged and they are able to move back up.

   (e) **Suspension.** This tactic has the benefit of being serious and is not as long lasting as demotion. The employer has a contractual obligation to provide pay, but not to provide work, so it is easy to suspend someone from duty with pay either as a punishment or while an alleged offence is being investigated. If the contract of employment permits, it may also be possible to suspend the employee for a short period without pay.

The important general comment about penalties is that they should be appropriate in the circumstances. Where someone is, for instance, persistently late or absent, suspension would be a strange penalty. Also penalties must be within the law. An employee cannot be demoted or transferred at managerial whim, and unpaid suspension can only be imposed if the contract of employment allows it.

Procedural sequence

This is the clear, unvarying logic of procedure, which should be well known and trusted. Procedure makes clear, for example, who does and who does not have the power to dismiss. The dissatisfied employee, who is wondering whether or not to turn a complaint into a formal grievance, knows who will hear the grievance and where an appeal could be lodged. This security of procedure, where step B always follows step A, is needed by managers as well as by employees, as it provides them with their authority as well as limiting the scope of their actions.

Managerial discipline

This preserves general respect for the justice framework by managers exercising self-discipline in how they work within it. With very good intentions some senior managers maintain an 'open door' policy with the message: 'My door is always open . . . call in any time you feel I can help you'. This has many advantages and is often necessary, but it has danger for matters of discipline and grievance if it encourages people to bypass middle managers. There is also the danger that employees come to see the settlement of their grievances as being dependent on the personal goodwill of an individual rather than on the business logic or their human and employment rights.

Managers must be consistent in handling discipline and grievance issues. Whatever the rules are, they will be generally supported only as long as they deserve support. If they are enforced inconsistently they will soon lose any moral authority, and will be obeyed only because of employees' fear of penalties. Equally, the manager who handles grievances quickly and consistently will enjoy the support of a committed group of employees.

The other need for managerial discipline is to test the validity of the discipline assumption. Is it a case for disciplinary action or for some other remedy? There is little purpose in suspending someone for negligence when the real problem is lack of training. Many disciplinary problems disappear under analysis, and it is sensible to carry out the analysis before making a possibly unjustified allegation of indiscipline.

GRIEVANCE PROCEDURE

Managers who believe that it introduces unnecessary rigidity into the working relationship often resent the formality of the grievance procedure: 'I see my people all the time. We work side by side and they can raise with me any issue they want, at any time they want . . .'. The problem is that many people will not raise issues that could be regarded as contentious with the immediate superior, in just the same way that managers frequently shirk the rebuke as a form of disciplinary penalty. Formality in procedure provides a structure within which individuals can reasonably air their grievances and avoids the likelihood of managers dodging the issue when it is difficult. It avoids the risk of inconsistent ad hoc decisions, and the employee knows at the outset that the matter will be heard and where it will be heard. The key features of grievance procedure are fairness, facilities for representation, procedural steps and promptness.

1 **Fairness** is needed, to be just, but also to keep the procedure viable. If employees develop the belief that the procedure is only a sham, then its value will be lost and other means will be sought to deal with grievances. Fairness is best supported by the obvious even-handedness of the ways in which grievances are handled, but it will be greatly enhanced if the appeal stage is either to a joint body or to independent arbitration, as the management is relinquishing the chance to be judge of its own cause.
2 **Representation** can help the individual employee who lacks the confidence or experience to take on the management single-handedly. A representative, such as a union official, has the advantage of having dealt with a range of employee problems and may be able to advise the aggrieved person whether the claim is worth pursuing. There is always the risk that the presence of the representative may produce a defensive management attitude that is affected by a number of other issues on which the manager and union official may be at loggerheads. Therefore the managers involved in hearing the grievance have to cast the representative in the correct role for the occasion.
3 **Procedural steps** are best limited to three. There is no value in having more just because there are more levels in the management hierarchy. This will only lengthen the time taken to deal with matters and will soon bring the procedure into disrepute. The reason for advocating three steps is that three types of management activity are involved in settling grievances. Nevertheless, it is quite common for there to be more than three steps where there is a steep hierarchy, within which there may be further, more senior, people to whom the matter could be referred. The reason for there being more steps has nothing to do with how to process grievances but is purely a function of the organisation structure.
   - The first step is the *preliminary*, when the grievance is lodged with the immediate superior of the person with the complaint. In the normal working week most managers will have a variety of queries from members of their departments, some of which could become grievances, depending on the manager's reaction. Mostly the manager will either satisfy the employee or the employee will decide not to pursue the matter. Sometimes, however, a person will want to take the issue further. This is the preliminary step in procedure, but it is a tangible step as the manager has the opportunity to review any decisions made that have caused the dissatisfaction, possibly enabling the dissatisfied employee to withdraw the grievance. In our experience it is rare for matters to be taken any further unless the subject of the grievance is something on which company policy is being tested.
   - The *hearing* gives the complainant the opportunity to state the grievance to a more senior manager, who is able to take a broader view of the matter than the immediate superior and who may be able both to see the issue more dispassionately and to perceive solutions that the more limited perspective of the immediate superior obscured. It is important for the management that the hearing should finalise the matter whenever possible, so that recourse to appeal is not automatic. The hearing should not be seen by the employees as no more than an irritating milestone on the way to the real decision makers. This is why ideally procedural steps should be limited to three.

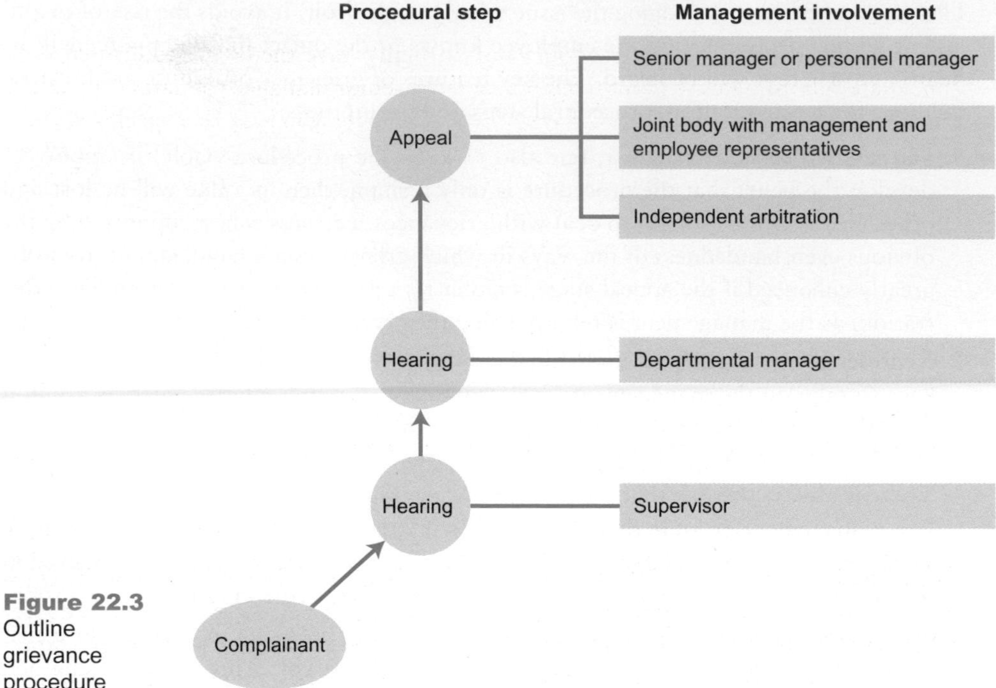

Figure 22.3 Outline grievance procedure

- If there is an *appeal*, this will usually be to a designated more senior manager, and the outcome will be either a confirmation or a modification of the decision at the hearing. This three-step approach has now been incorporated in legislation on dismissal, which requires dismissal to be preceded by these steps, although they are called letter, meeting and appeal.

4 **Promptness** avoids the bitterness and frustration that comes from delay. When an employee 'goes into procedure', the action is not taken lightly and is in anticipation of a swift resolution. Furthermore, the manager whose decision is being questioned will have a difficult time until the matter is resolved. The most familiar device to speed things up is to incorporate time limits between the steps, specifying that the hearing should take place no later than, say, four working days after the preliminary notice and that the appeal should be no more than five working days after the hearing. This gives time for reflection and initiative by the manager or the complainant between the stages, but does not leave time for the matter to be forgotten.

Where the organisation has a collective disputes procedure as well as one for individual grievances, there needs to be an explicit link between the two so that individual matters can be pursued with collective support if there is not a satisfactory outcome. An outline grievance procedure is in Figure 22.3.

DISCIPLINARY PROCEDURE

Procedures for discipline are very similar to those for grievance and depend equally on fairness, promptness and representation. There are some additional features.

Authorisation of penalties

The law requires that managers should not normally have the power to dismiss their immediate subordinates without reference to more senior managers. Whatever penalties are to be imposed, they should only be imposed by people who have that specific authority delegated to them. Usually this means that the more serious penalties can only be imposed by more senior people, but there are many organisations where such decisions are delegated to the HR department.

Investigation

The procedure should also ensure that disciplinary action is not taken until it has been established that there is a problem that justifies the action. The possibility of suspension on full pay is one way of allowing time for the investigation of dubious allegations, but the stigma attached to such suspensions should not be forgotten.

Information and explanation

If disciplinary action is possible, the person to be disciplined should be told of the complaint, so that an explanation can be made, or the matter denied, before any penalties are decided. If an employee is to be penalised, then the reasons for the decision should be explained to make sure that cause and effect are appreciated. The purpose of penalties is to prevent a recurrence. An outline disciplinary procedure is in Figure 22.4.

ARE GRIEVANCE AND DISCIPLINE PROCESSES EQUITABLE?

For grievance and discipline processes to work they must command support, and they will only command support if they are seen as equitable, truly just and fair. At first it may seem that concern for the individual employee is paramount, but the individual cannot be isolated from the rest of the workforce. Fairness should therefore be linked to the interests that all workers have in common in the business, and to the managers who must also perceive the system as equitable if they are to abide by its outcomes.

Procedures have a potential to be fair in that they are certain. The conduct of employee relations becomes less haphazard and irrational: people 'know where they stand'. The existence of a rule cannot be denied and opportunities for one party to manipulate and change a rule are reduced. Procedures also have the advantage that they can be communicated. Formalising a procedure that previously existed only in custom and practice clarifies the ambiguities and inconsistencies within it and compels each party to recognise the role and responsibility of the other. By providing pre-established avenues for responses to various contingencies, procedures make it possible for the response to be less random and so more fair. The impersonal nature of procedures offers the possibility of removing hostility from the workplace, since an artificial social situation is created in which the ritual displays of aggression towards management are not seen as personal attacks on managers.

The achievement of equity may not match the potential. Procedures cannot, for instance, impart equity to situations that are basically unfair. Thus attempting to cope with an anomalous pay system through a grievance procedure may be alleviating

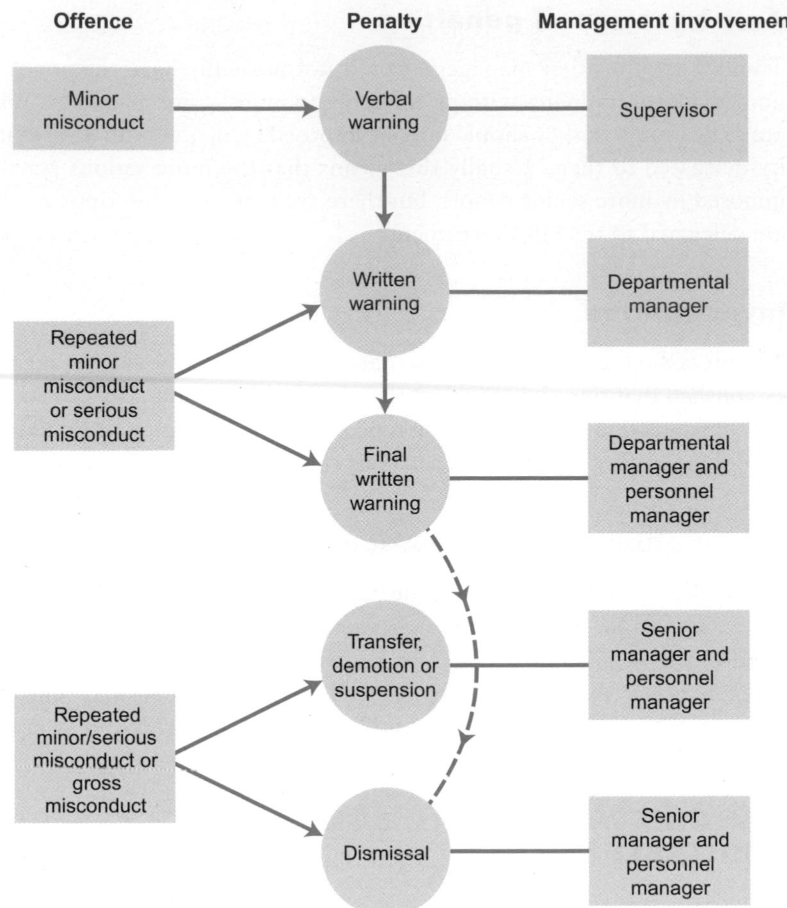

Figure 22.4 Outline disciplinary procedure

symptoms rather than treating causes. It is also impossible through a grievance procedure to overcome accepted norms of inequity in a company, such as greater punctuality being required of manual employees than of white-collar employees.

A further feature of procedural equity is its degree of similarity to the judicial process. All procedures adopt certain legalistic mechanisms, such as the right of individuals to be represented and to hear the case against them, but some aspects of legalism, such as burdens of proof and strict adherence to precedent, may cause the application of standard remedies rather than the consideration of individual circumstances.

There is a nice irony in the fact that equity is best achieved when procedures are not used. Procedure is there in the background and expresses principles for fair and effective management of situations. All the time that the principles are followed and the framework for organisational justice is observed, procedure is not invoked. The advantage of this is that individuals, whether employees or managers, are not named and shamed so that matters are much easier to deal with. Only when the matter is dealt with badly does the procedural step come closer.

The existence of the procedure becomes the incentive rather than the means for action to be taken: it is not an excuse for inaction. It is accepted that some employment situations require naming and shaming first, with possible remedial action following. In most sports there is on-the-spot penalising of players for breaking the rules.

WINDOW ON PRACTICE

The 'red-hot stove' rule of discipline offers the touching of a red hot stove as an analogy for effective disciplinary action:

1. The burn is immediate. There is no question of cause and effect.
2. You had warning. If the stove was red-hot, you knew what would happen if you touched it.
3. The discipline is consistent. Everyone who touches the stove is burned.
4. The discipline is impersonal. People are burned not because of who they are, but because they touch the stove.

ACTIVITY 22.3

Think of an attempt at disciplinary action that went wrong. Which of the features of the red-hot stove rule were missing?

Notions of fairness are not 'givens' of the situation; they are socially constructed and there will never be more than a degree of consensus on what constitutes fairness. Despite this, the procedural approach can exploit standards of certainty and consistency, which are widely accepted as elements of justice. The extent to which a procedure can do this will depend on the suitability of its structure to local circumstances, the commitment of those who operate it and the way in which it reconciles legalistic and bargaining elements.

SUMMARY PROPOSITIONS

22.1 The authority of managers to exercise discipline in relation to others in the organisation is underpinned by a general predilection of people to obey commands from those holding higher rank in the hierarchy of which they are members.

22.2 The exercise of that discipline is limited by the procedural structures for grievance and discipline.

22.3 Grievance and discipline handling are two areas of human resource management that few other people want to take over, and provide HR managers with some of their most significant contributions to business effectiveness.

22.4 Discipline can be understood as being managerial, team or self-discipline, and the three types are connected hierarchically.

22.5 Dissatisfaction, complaint and grievance form another hierarchy. Unresolved employee dissatisfaction can lead to the loss of potentially valuable employees. In extreme cases it can lead to industrial action.

22.6 Grievance and disciplinary processes both require a framework of organisational justice.

22.7 The procedural framework of disciplinary and grievance processes is one of the keys to their being equitable.

22.8 Effective management of both discipline and grievance is achieved by following the principles of the procedures without necessarily invoking them in practice.

GENERAL DISCUSSION TOPICS

1 Do you think Milgram's experiments would have had a different outcome if the subjects had included women as well as men?

2 What examples can individual members of the group cite of self-discipline, team discipline and managerial discipline?

3 'The trouble with grievance procedures is that they encourage people to waste a lot of time with petty grumbles. Life at work is rarely straightforward and people should just accept the rough with the smooth.'

What do you think of that opinion?

FURTHER READING

ACAS (2009) *Disciplinary and Grievance Procedures*. Code of Practice 1. London: Advisory, Conciliation and Advisory Service.

BIS (2009) *Avoiding and Resolving Discipline and Grievance Issues at Work*. London: Department for Business Innovation and Skills.

CIPD (2009) *Discipline and Grievances at Work*. London: Chartered Institute of Personnel and Development.

Each of these sets out the current legal situation in Britain about these two central issues, taking slightly different perspectives.

Taylor, S. and Emir, A. (2006) *Employment Law*. Oxford: Oxford University Press, chapters 13 and 14.

This standard text is a comprehensive account of UK employment law and the chapters suggested deal with the background to the material in this chapter.

REFERENCES

Abrams, D., Wetherell, M., Cochrane, S., Hogg, M.A. and Turner, J.C. (1990) 'Knowing what to think by knowing who you are: self-categorization and norm formation', *British Journal of Social Psychology*, Vol. 29, pp. 97–119.

Advisory, Conciliation and Arbitration Service (2000) *Code of Practice on Disciplinary Practice and Grievance Procedures at Work*. London: HMSO.

Asch, S.E. (1951) 'Effect of group pressure upon the modification and distortion of judgements', in H. Guetzkow (ed.), *Groups, Leadership and Men*. Pittsburgh: Carnegie Press.

Edwards, P. (2000) 'Discipline: towards trust and self-discipline', in S. Bach and K. Sisson (eds), *Personnel Management*, 3rd edn. Oxford: Blackwell.

Gross, R. and McIlveen, R. (1998) *Psychology: A new introduction*. London: Hodder & Stoughton.

Nick, C. and Eltchaninoff, M. (2010) *L'Experience Extreme*. Paris: Don Quichotte.

Milgram, S. (1974) *Obedience to Authority*. London: Tavistock.

Milgram, S. (1992) *The Individual in a Social World*, 2nd edn. New York: Harper & Row.

Mordsley, B. and Aylott, C. (2006) 'A grievance by any other name', *People Management*, 13 July, p. 19.

An extensive range of additional materials, including exercises, a case study, multiple choice questions, answers to questions and links to useful websites can be found on the Human Resource Management companion website at **www.pearsoned.co.uk/torrington**.

Part 5 CASE STUDY PROBLEM

Industrial disputes at British Airways

British Airways (BA) was formed in 1974 when the government of the day nationalised four separate airlines to create a single, government-owned corporation. BA was the UK's designated flag-carrying airline. Like Lufthansa, Air France and Air Italia and numerous others, this put it in a privileged position vis-à-vis independent airlines. At that time the number of routes flown internationally was determined in government negotiations and the national carriers had first pick as to which routes they wanted to operate.

The corporation was privatised in February 1987 and immediately expanded both organically, by operating more routes and acquiring more aircraft, and by taking over other airlines. Fast growth was accompanied by high ratings for the quality of its service, and by 1990 it was recognised as the world's most popular and most profitable airline. BA continued to thrive commercially in the 1990s when de-regulation opened up more routes and required airlines to compete for them among themselves. The company acquired a 20 per cent interest in Qantas, set up subsidiaries based in other countries and launched Go – a low-cost airline that flew short-haul routes.

This considerable success was achieved partly as a result of two initiatives:

1 In order to maintain its market leadership the airline embarked on a programme of staff training to develop commitment to customer service. As a result, in the early 1990s the quality of service to the customer improved markedly, so that British Airways was able to maintain its premier position despite ever-increasing competition.
2 Following privatisation BA underwent a series of reorganisations in order to become more efficient. There was a drastic reduction in staff numbers from 60,000 to 38,000, achieved by a combination of voluntary severance and natural wastage. (Hopfl 1993: 117)

Throughout this period, however, employee relations were problematic at BA. In 1996 a strike by pilots was narrowly averted, but the summer of 1997 saw a 72-hour strike by cabin staff begin. It was an official stoppage called by the Transport and General Workers Union following protracted negotiations and a ballot among its members working for the airline. According to British Airways only 142 cabin crew formally joined the strike, but 1,500 (compared with a normal daily average of 120) reported sick – a novel strategy! The number that reported for work as usual was 834.

Another interesting feature of the dispute was reported by *The Times*:

> During the past few years, BA, like many companies in Britain, has appointed middle and senior managers who fear for their jobs. To get on, they believe, they must show they are tough. I have heard these 'performance managers' brusquely warning vacillating staff that if they follow their union and refuse to work, they will 'face the consequences'. This has irked the cabin crew far more than the dispute over pay and conditions. They no longer feel part of a team and believe they are being bullied. (Elliott 1997: 41)

The management reaction to the strike was to announce that all strikers would forfeit travel perks and promotion prospects for three years. Film was also taken of strikers on picket lines. Although the threats were later withdrawn and the filming was stopped, damage was done to the level of trust that had previously existed between management and unions. As usual, the dispute moved on to talks to find a resolution, but BA had lost many flights and its reputation was as severely dented as its financial position. The share price dropped from 763p to 583p before recovering to 635p, and there were varying reports about how many millions of pounds the dispute was costing.

In 1999 BA's financial position started to deteriorate seriously, as profits fell by 84 per cent. The response was a further round of cost cutting and reduced staffing. An operating loss was reported for the first time in 2002 following the terrorist attack on the World Trade Center in New York which had badly affected full-service airlines, especially those with transatlantic services like BA.

Competition from low-cost airlines and anxiety about the war in Iraq added to the pressure, so cost cutting had to slice even deeper. One method introduced was Automated Time Recording (ATR) that kept a tighter control on hours worked. Many check-in and engineering staff were alarmed at this innovation, fearing that it might lead to a reduction in flexibility about working hours, which was a major attraction for many who relied on this to fit in with their domestic arrangements. They were also angered by senior managers using terms such as 'feather-bedding' and making comments about high absenteeism in the summer. On 18 July 2003, on one of the busiest weekends of the year, BA's operations at Heathrow were paralysed by a wildcat strike by check-in and other ground staff. It cost the airline another £100 million.

Two years later, in August 2005, British Airways was again badly hit by industrial action of a different nature. A dispute over restructuring plans at Gate Gourmet, the catering supplier to British Airways at Heathrow airport, resulted in unofficial strike action in August 2005 and the dismissal of hundreds of workers involved. BA ground staff at Heathrow took 'sympathy' action, which was also not authorised by the trade union concerned. This resulted in the cancellation of more than 700 flights at one of the busiest times of the year. Around 1,000 baggage handlers and loading staff at Heathrow refused to work to express their support for the sacked Gate Gourmet workers. Both groups belonged to the same union and had been colleagues until the meals business was outsourced by BA in 1997. The walkout by BA staff led to the cancellation of hundreds of flights and stranded 100,000 passengers. The disruption was estimated to have cost the company up to £40 million.

A persistently poor employment relations climate was also, in large part, responsible for much of the debacle that followed the opening of Terminal 5 at Heathrow airport in March 2008 (*see* Chapter 1). This time it was not a strike that hit BA's reputation, but chaos at check-in desks in the first few days after the terminal opened. Thousands of bags were lost and over 300 flights cancelled. All manner of problems were behind the mess, but staff showed little enthusiasm for helping to put things right due to the low trust relationships that had been established between them and their managers (Done and Willman 2008). The total cost to the company was estimated at around £150 million.

There was further deterioration in BA's financial position in 2009, another operating loss being announced in March. The company was finding it increasingly difficult to compete with lower-cost rivals which operated flights with fewer people, on lower pay and who were employed on more flexible contracts. Management therefore brought forward proposals to reduce the number of cabin crew on BA flights and to reform working practices. Many staff would see their pay reduced and there would be further redundancies, but the future of the airline should be secured by a return to profitability.

The unions objected to the proposals which would have a serious adverse effect on pay and working conditions. They also believed that health and safety would be compromised and expressed anger at the way that managers were, in their view, simply seeking to impose changes without seriously negotiating them with union officials. In December 2009 a strike ballot was organised by the Unite trade union which represented most of the airline's cabin crew. This resulted in over 90 per cent voting in favour of strike action. Dates for strikes were then announced. The union decided to maximise disruption by organising these over the Christmas period. Had these strikes gone ahead at that time, the blow to BA's already poor reputation among business travellers and holiday-makers would have been enormous, but in the event they did not go ahead.

The cancellation of the Christmas strike did not occur thanks to successful negotiation between management and unions. Instead it followed a highly controversial High Court ruling in which ballot irregularities were cited as being sufficient in law for an interlocutory injunction to be granted suspending the strike. The union was angered by the ruling because the irregularities, while serious, could not have affected the outcome of the ballot which had been so overwhelmingly in favour of the strike.

In March 2010 a new ballot was held among Unite members. Again the vote in favour of taking industrial action was overwhelming and again a series of strikes were announced. This time management's response was to organise the training of a casual workforce to man some flights. Employees who went on strike were also threatened with the removal for ever of all discretionary travel benefits, including the discounts on BA flights which many relied on in order to fly to London from elsewhere in the UK in order to join their crews.

Required

1 Do you think it is inevitable that the pressures of international competition drive companies into a situation where unilateral managerial decision making must prevail and there is simply no time for the consultation and compromise that is involved in union negotiation?

2 How accurate do you regard Harvey Elliott's views to be as a general comment on recent and current management practice?

3 Why do you think trade union membership among cabin crew at BA remains so high when it is low in many other airlines and almost non-existent across much of the service sector in the UK?

References

Done, K. and Willman, J. (2008) 'Goodwill of staff is often in short supply', *Financial Times*, 5 April.

Elliott, H. (1997) 'BA is Plunging towards disaster', *The Times*, 10 July.

Hopfl, H. (1993) 'Culture and commitment: British Airways', in D. Gowler, K. Legge and C. Clegg (eds), *Case Studies in Organizational Behaviour and Human Resource Management*, 2nd edn. London: Paul Chapman Publishing, pp. 117–25.

REWARD

A variety of different terms are used to describe the rewards that are given by an employer in return for the work carried out by workers. In previous editions of this book we have used the term 'payment', but this is often nowadays seen as being too narrow in scope because many of the rewards that people take from their work do not take a monetary form. 'Compensation' is a term widely used in the American literature, yet the idea of compensation is that it involves making amends for something that has caused loss or injury. Do we want to suggest that work necessarily causes loss or injury? 'Remuneration' is a more straightforward word which means exactly the same as payment but has five more letters and is misspelled (as renumeration) more often than most words in the human resource manager's lexicon. 'Reward' is not a perfect term to use because it suggests a special payment for a special act, but it is the best available for describing the whole range of elements which combine to make work 'rewarding' and worthwhile rather than 'unrewarding' and thankless.

Reward is clearly central to the employment relationship. While there are plenty of people who enjoy working and who claim that they would not stop working even if they were to win a big cash prize in a lottery, most of us work in large part because it is our only means of earning the money we need to sustain us and our families in the style to which we are accustomed. How much we are paid and in what form is therefore an issue which matters hugely to us. These questions are also central ones for the human resource management function because money spent on salaries, benefits and other forms of reward typically accounts for well over half an organisation's total costs. For commercial organisations it is thus a major determinant of both profitability and competitive advantage. In the public sector the cost of rewarding staff is determined by and, in turn helps determine, the level of taxes that we pay.

For these reasons, to a greater extent than is the case in other areas of HR practice, the management of reward is heavily constrained by the financial position of the organisation. The aim is to design competitive reward packages which serve to attract, retain and motivate staff, while at the same time keeping a lid on the costs so as to ensure the organisation's commercial and financial viability. This is not an easy task, and it is made harder because of the great significance that employees themselves attach to their pay, and particularly to the level of pay they receive vis-à-vis other people. Getting it wrong has major, negative consequences, because it can demotivate in quite serious ways, leading to the departure of good performers, higher absence levels, less effort and the deterioration of the organisation's employee relations climate. Over time, of course, these too serve to reduce an organisation's effectiveness and damage its financial performance.

As markets for goods and services become more competitive and global, the extent to which employers are able to use payment systems as a means of achieving their HR objectives is increasingly constrained. Profit margins are tighter than they used to be in most industries making it less possible than it once was to tackle skills shortages or to raise the quality of job applications simply by increasing the salaries on offer. The need to restrain labour costs is particularly significant in the public sector as governments have cut their expenditure in the aftermath of the recession in order to reduce public debt. As a result employers are having to think more creatively and more broadly about the rewards that they offer, looking for ways of motivating and retaining valued staff, without increasing their pay bills. For these reasons the concept of 'total reward' has become attractive and significant in recent years. This involves thinking about the reward package in a very broad sense, not only the aspects that involve payment, but a range of other elements too. Organisations may be increasingly constrained in terms of how much more they can pay someone, but there is a good deal less constraint when it comes to providing them with career development opportunities, flexible working patterns or even a stimulating and pleasant working environment.

The other major contemporary development in this field of HR practice is the increasing prominence in many organisations of well-articulated reward strategies. Over time managers are taking a less reactive approach to the management of their payment systems. Increasingly they are thinking about how the approaches they use to reward staff can be designed so as to achieve specific longer-term objectives. If increasing the level of skills in the organisation is a priority, the response is thus to make salary progression or bonus payments conditional on the attainment of new or increased skills. By contrast, where the overriding aim is to increase productivity, payment systems are developed which reward people or teams for the quantity of their output. Reward strategies are thus about encouraging a confluence of interest between employees and the organisation.

This approach has often been described as 'the new pay' by researchers working in the field of reward management (*see* Druker and White 2009), and this is an appropriate label because it is only over the past two or three decades that reward management has attained a strategic dimension in many organisations. Change started in the private sector during the 1980s, later becoming prevalent in many public sector organisations too. It is associated with the decline in trade union influence we introduced in Part 5, and in particular with the breaking down of the national collective bargaining system. In the recent past managers in many organisations were thus restricted to deciding who should be employed on which grade, how they should progress up the grade hierarchy, what should be paid by way of an annual increment and how much overtime they worked. This system of multi-employer bargaining declined steeply during the 1980s and 1990s, so that by 2004 only 36 per cent of public sector employees and just 1 per cent of those employed in the private sector had their pay determined by such arrangements (Kersley *et al*. 2006: 184).

As a result, unlike other areas of HRM, there have been relatively few years in which new approaches to the management of pay have been tried out, established and subsequently evaluated. This means that it is only relatively recently that HR managers have had the opportunity to manipulate reward systems in their organisations so as to seek to achieve defined organisational objectives. Previously all employers in an industry paid the same amounts to the same grades of staff in the same way, effectively taking reward out of the competitive equation. This is manifestly no longer the case in the private sector and is rarer as each year passes in the public sector. We are thus living through a most interesting time as far as reward management is concerned. New approaches are being developed, tested, implemented and reviewed all the time. Where they do not work as well as expected, employers are developing different approaches. There is as yet no consensus about what constitutes 'good practice', while managers, consultants, academic researchers, politicians and other commentators maintain vigorous debates about the merits and de-merits of different systems.

In this part of the book we explore the major elements that make up the reward package, including an introduction to 'total reward' thinking. In Chapter 23 we will look at how salaries are determined and at how organisations go about deciding how much each employee should be paid in comparison to others. In Chapter 24 our focus is on incentives and bonus payments of one kind or another and in Chapter 25 on pensions and benefits.

REFERENCES

Druker, J. and White, G. (2009) 'Introduction', in G. White and J. Druker (eds), *Reward Management: A critical text*, 2nd edn. London: Routledge.

Kersley, B., Alpin, C., Forth, J., Bryson, A., Bewley, H., Dix, G. and Oxenbridge, S. (2006) *Inside the Workplace: Findings from the 2004 Workplace Employment Relations Survey*. Abingdon: Routledge.

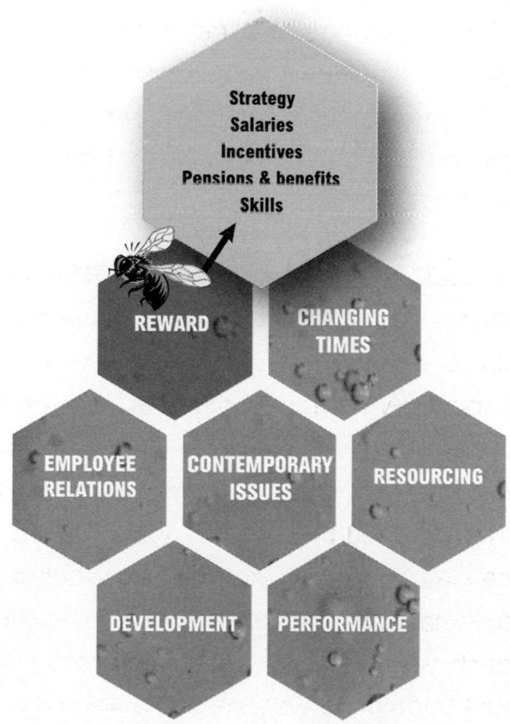

CHAPTER 23

SETTING PAY

THE OBJECTIVES OF THIS CHAPTER ARE TO:

1. Set out the different elements that can make up a reward package
2. Assess the objectives managers have when determining reward systems
3. Consider the main employee objectives from a reward package
4. Evaluate the alternative methods of setting base pay rates
5. Explore major current developments in the management of salary progression systems
6. Explain the concept of 'Total Reward' and the reasons for its increasing prominence

INTRODUCING REWARD MANAGEMENT

It is helpful to think about reward management in terms of two key decisions:

1 How much should we pay each person in our organisation?

2 How should the payment package be made up?

These are among the most important decisions HR managers have to take because they have such significant outcomes. On the one hand they are a major determinant of organisational profitability vis-à-vis competitors and may help determine whether an organisation thrives or even survives. They also help determine the standard of living that individual employees are able to enjoy, the choices they are able to make about how they and their families live their lives, when they can retire and how many hours a week they are obliged to work. Importantly they also play a large part in determining whether employees are motivated at work and prepared to demonstrate discretionary effort. When poor decisions about pay are made the result is demotivation, higher levels of absence, reduced productivity and an increased chance that an adversarial, low-trust employee relations climate will develop. Finally, of course, these decisions are crucial to an organisation's ability to recruit and retain effective staff in competitive labour markets. Organisations are obliged to compete with one another for good staff as well as for customers, and as Charles Cotton points out in a recent CIPD survey of reward practices, 'respondents report that employees are becoming just as discerning as their customers in what they want from their employer' (CIPD 2007: 33). The tighter the labour market becomes, the harder it is to recruit and retain the best-qualified people, and the more pressure there is placed on employers to develop rewards packages that suit employees as much as they suit their own needs.

For these reasons great care must be taken when answering the two core questions set out above, and it makes sense to think about how they should be answered in strategic terms. This leads us to asking and looking for answers to a range of further questions:

- What are we seeking to achieve in designing or re-designing our payment systems?
- What are our competitors doing?
- How do we wish to position ourselves as an employer so as to compete effectively in the labour market?
- What constraints do we face when designing our reward systems?
- How can we avoid demotivating employees when making decisions about how much and in what way we pay them?
- To what extent should employees or their representatives be involved in helping to determine who is paid how much and in what form?

According to Armstrong and Brown (2009: 34) there are four key components in a written reward strategy. First of all there needs to be a statement of intentions setting out, in general terms, what the reward strategy of the organisation is seeking to achieve and which reward initiatives have been chosen in order to achieve these core objectives. Second, these ideas are expanded through a more detailed 'rationale' which explains the objectives in greater depth and shows how the various elements that form the organisation's reward policy support the achievement of those objectives. In effect this amounts to a statement of the business case that underpins the strategy. To that end the rationale should include costings, a statement of the benefits that will accrue and an indication of the means that will be used to evaluate its success. The third element is an explanation of the guiding principles or values that have been used in developing the initiatives and will be used to adapt them in the future. Typically this will include statements which deal with ethical issues or which reiterate a commitment to core principles such as equality between men and women, fair dealing or rewarding exceptional individual performance. The final component is an implementation plan, setting out exactly what initiatives are being brought forward and when, who has responsibility for their introduction and what their cost will be.

ACTIVITY 23.1

Consider the following list of jobs and job holders. In each case think about how much you think each currently receives annually in basic pay (i.e. excluding benefits, overtime, bonuses, etc.) and about how much you think each *should* be paid. Make a list of the key criteria you are using in making your decisions.

Primary school head teacher

The Prime Minister

Private soldier

Chief Executive of British Telecom

Newly qualified junior doctor

Experienced firefighter

Lollipop lady/man

Wayne Rooney

You can find information about what these people are actually paid on the companion website for this book – **www.pearsoned.co.uk/torrington**.

Employer objectives

Reward strategies and the initiatives developed as part of those strategies should be judged according to their ability to meet certain core objectives.

Attracting staff

The reward package on offer must be sufficiently attractive vis-à-vis that of an organisation's labour market competitors to ensure that it is able to secure the services of the staff it needs. The more attractive the package, the more applications will be received from potential employees and the more choice the organisation will have when filling its vacancies. Attractive packages thus allow the appointment of high-calibre people and often mean that organisations are able to fill vacancies more quickly than is the case with a reward offering which is either unattractive or poorly communicated. However, what is 'attractive' in one labour market will be less attractive in others because people vary in what they are looking for. There is thus a need to establish what the target market values most and to tailor the offering accordingly.

Retaining staff

The costs associated with recruiting and developing people, as well as the growing significance of specialist organisational knowledge in creating value and maintaining competitive advantage, mean that retaining effective performers is a central aim of reward strategy in many organisations, particularly those competing in knowledge-intensive industries where highly qualified people are in short supply. This requires a package which is attractive enough to prevent people from becoming dissatisfied and looking elsewhere for career development opportunities. It may also involve the development of policies which reward seniority so as to provide an incentive for staff to stay when they might otherwise consider applying for alternative work.

Motivating staff

Aside from helping to ensure that effective performers are recruited and retained, in more general terms it is necessary that the reward package they are given serves to motivate positively and does not demotivate. The question of the extent to which money ever can positively motivate has long been debated by occupational psychologists, many of whom accept that the power of monetary reward to motivate is very limited, at least over the longer term. What is not in doubt, however, is the very considerable power of poorly designed or implemented reward practices to demotivate, particularly when staff perceive them to be inequitable in some shape or form. Ultimately the aim must be to reward people in such a way as to create the conditions in which they are prepared to work hard to help achieve their employer's objectives and, if possible, to demonstrate discretionary effort. Employers who want their workforces to be positively engaged with their work, to participate in continuous improvement programmes and to work beyond contract when required must have in place a reward package which does not demotivate and which, as far as is possible, motivates positively.

Driving change

Pay can be used specifically as one of a range of tools underpinning change management processes. The approach used is to tie higher base pay, bonuses or promotion to the development of new behaviours, attitudes or skills gained by employees. Pay works far more effectively than simple exhortation because it provides a material incentive to those whose natural inclination is to resist change. It also sends out a powerful message to employees indicating the seriousness of the employer's intentions as regards proposed or ongoing changes. The use of pay in this way is sometimes criticised because it serves to enhance management control in a very conspicuous way. Sociologists in particular tend to be uneasy about the capacity of payment systems to reinforce the position of powerful groups in organisations and in society generally at the expense of those who are relatively powerless. Examples are the use by employers of individualised reward packages which undermine the power of trade unions to organise and resist effectively, and systems which have the effect of increasing the pay of predominantly male groups vis-à-vis those which are predominantly female.

Corporate reputation

Aside from the aim of developing and maintaining a reputation as a good employer in the labour market, organisations are increasingly concerned to establish a positive corporate reputation more generally. For some the notion of 'prestige' is something they aim for as part of a business strategy that seeks to produce high-quality, high-value added or innovative goods or services. For others the maintenance of an ethical reputation is important in order to attract and retain a strong customer base. Either way delivery is significantly linked in part to the organisation's reputation as an employer. Paying poorly or having in place policies which are perceived as operating unfairly serve to undermine any reputation gained for being either a prestigious organisation or one which acts ethically and in a socially responsible manner.

Affordability

The above objectives are all desirable for organisations and form the basis of their reward strategies. But in this field of HR activity there is a major restriction in the shape of affordability which serves to limit what can be done at any time. The extent to which a particular objective is affordable also varies over time and tends to be unpredictable as so much depends on the current financial performance of the organisation. If money were no object organisations would develop 'ideal' reward packages which paid above market rates to ensure that the best people were recruited and retained and which linked pay both to individual and collective achievement so as to maximise effort and performance. But the real world is not like this, except some would argue when it comes to developing pay packages for senior executives, so tough choices inevitably have to be made when devising reward strategies. Organisational objectives have to be prioritised and decisions made about how limited resources are best deployed so as to maximise the positive impact of reward management interventions on the organisation's performance.

When considering affordability it is important to remember that pay can be as much an investment in human capital as a cost to the business. Paying people poorly has a strong tendency to result in decreased effort, and hence a need to employ more people overall, not least to take account of high absence levels. By contrast paying well, if it results in the attraction, retention and motivation of strong performers who are willing to demonstrate discretionary effort, can mean that productivity increases and that fewer people in total are required. It is thus wise to remember the remark of Henry Ford, one of the most successful businessmen in history, that doubling his workers wages was 'one of the finest cost-cutting moves I ever made' (Bryson and Forth 2008: 499).

Employee objectives

You might think that employees only have one objective as far as reward is concerned, namely to maximise the amount that they earn. Indeed some theorists further argue that employees are primarily interested in maximising the amount they earn while also minimising the effort they put in to achieve these earnings. This was one of the assumptions about worker behaviour that underlay scientific management thinking in the early twentieth century (*see* Steers *et al.* 1996: 25–8). In fact for most employees aims are more diverse and more subtle, particularly when the full range of elements that make up a total reward package are taken into consideration.

Purchasing power

The absolute level of weekly or monthly earnings determines the standard of living of the recipient, and will therefore be the most important consideration for most employees. How much can I buy? Employees are rarely satisfied about their purchasing power, and the annual pay adjustment will do little more than reduce dissatisfaction, even if it exceeds the current level of inflation. Enhanced satisfaction only occurs when a pay rise is given which surpasses expectations. It is important to remember, however, that surveys of employee satisfaction invariably show that while a good majority of employees are dissatisfied with the level of their pay, most are satisfied or very satisfied with other aspects of their jobs (*see* Kersley *et al.* 2005: 33).

Fairness

Elliott Jacques (1962) averred that every employee had a strong feeling about the level of payment that was fair for the job. In most cases this is a rough, personalised evaluation of what is appropriate, bearing in mind the going market rate and their personal contribution vis-à-vis that of fellow employees. The employee who feels underpaid is likely to demonstrate the conventional symptoms of withdrawal from the job: looking for another, carelessness, disgruntlement, lateness, absence and the like. Perhaps the worst manifestation of this is among those who feel the unfairness but who cannot take a clean step of moving elsewhere. They then not only feel dissatisfied with their pay level, but also feel another unfairness too: being trapped in a situation they resent. Those who feel they are overpaid (as some do) may simply feel guilty, or may seek to justify their existence in some way by trying to look busy. That is not necessarily productive.

Rights

A different aspect of relative income is that concerned with the rights of the employee to a particular share of the company's profits or the nation's wealth. The employee is here thinking about whether the division of earnings is providing fair shares of the Gross National Product. The focus is often on the notion of need – the idea that someone has a right to a greater share because they or their families are suffering unjustly. These are features of many trade union arguments and part of the general preoccupation with the rights of the individual.

Recognition

Most people have an objective for their payment arrangements, that their personal contribution is recognised. This is partly seeking reassurance, but also a way in which people can mould their behaviour and their career thinking to produce progress and satisfaction. It is doubtful if financial recognition has a significant and sustained impact on performance, but providing a range of other forms of recognition while the pay packet is transmitting a different message is certainly counterproductive.

Composition

How is the pay package made up? The growing complexity and sophistication of payment arrangements raises all sorts of questions about pay composition. Is £800 pay for 60 hours' work better than £600 for 40 hours' work? The arithmetical answer that the rate per hour for the 40-hour arrangement is marginally better than that for 60 hours is only part of the answer. The other aspects will relate to the individuals, their circumstances and the conventions of their working group and reference groups. Another question about composition might be: is £450 per week plus a pension better than £500 per week without? Such questions do not produce universally applicable answers because different groups of employees tend to have different priorities. For example, younger staff tend to be more interested in maximising cash earnings than older colleagues who tend to be more interested in indirect forms of payment such as pension arrangements. Those in mid-career who have mortgages to pay off are likely to be interested in overtime rates and in systems which allow them to trade holiday entitlement or other benefits for cash. For second-income earners in a family cash is often less significant than flexible working arrangements, childcare vouchers or crèche facilities.

ACTIVITY 23.2

Which of the above objectives do you consider to be most important to you? How far do you think priorities in this area change with age?

THE ELEMENTS OF PAYMENT

The payment of any individual employee will be made up of one or more elements from those shown in Table 23.1. Fixed elements are those that make up the regular weekly or monthly payment to the individual, and which do not vary other than in exceptional circumstances. Variable elements can be varied by either the employee or the employer.

Table 23.1 The potential elements of payment

Bonus	Profit allocation		**Variable elements**
	Discretionary sum		• Irregular
Incentive	Group calculation basis		• Variable amount
	Individual calculation basis		• Usually discretionary
Overtime payment			
Premia	Occasional		
	Contractual		
Benefits	Fringe benefits		**Fixed elements**
	Payments in kind	Other	• Regular
		Accommodation	• Rarely variable
		Car	• Usually contractual
	Benefit schemes	Other	
		Pension	
		Sick pay	
Plussage	'Fudge' payments		
	Special additions		
Basic rate of payment			**Basic**

Basic rate

The irreducible minimum rate of pay is the basic. In most cases this is the standard rate also, not having any additions made to it. In other cases it is a basis on which earnings are built by the addition of one or more of the other elements in payment. Some groups of employees, such as factory workers, typically have little more than half of their earnings in basic, while primary and secondary school teachers have virtually all their pay in this form. In the UK a majority of employees receive no additional payments at all beyond their basic pay.

Plussage

Sometimes the basic has an addition to recognise an aspect of working conditions or employee capability. Payments for educational qualifications and for supervisory responsibilities are quite common. There is also an infinite range of what are sometimes called 'fudge' payments, whereby there is an addition to the basic as a start-up allowance, mask money, dirt money, and so forth.

Benefits

Extras to the working conditions that have a cash value are categorised as benefits and can be of great variety. The most common are company cars, subsidised meals, childcare vouchers, private health insurance and occupational pensions. Many employers make arrangements with other organisations for staff to access services at substantial discounts or offer their own goods and services to staff on discounted terms.

Premia

Where employees work at inconvenient times – or on shifts or permanently at night – they receive a premium payment as compensation for the inconvenience. This is for inconvenience rather than additional hours of work. Sometimes this is built into the basic rate or is a regular feature of the contract of employment so that the payment is unvarying. In other situations shift working is occasional and short lived, making the premium a variable element of payment.

Overtime

It is customary for employees working more hours than are normal for the working week to be paid for those hours at an enhanced rate, usually between 10 and 50 per cent more than the normal rate according to how many hours are involved. Seldom can this element be regarded as fixed. No matter how regularly overtime is worked, there is always the opportunity for the employer to withhold the provision of overtime or for the employee to decline the extra hours. Overtime is earned by around 20 per cent of the UK workforce (National Statistics 2009: 12). It is particularly associated with less well paid manual work. Where overtime is paid it can account for a major portion of an individual's gross pay.

Incentive

Incentive is here described as an element of payment linked to the working performance of an individual or working group, as a result of prior arrangement. This includes payment-by-results schemes that reward people for the quantity of their output (e.g. sales commission) as well as other forms of performance-based payment. The distinguishing feature is that the employee knows what has to be done to earn the payment, though he or she may feel very dependent on other people, or on external circumstances, to receive it. Incentives are paid to 44 per cent of employees in the private sector, compared with only 19 per cent in the public sector (Kersley *et al.* 2006: 190).

Bonus

A different type of variable payment is the gratuitous payment by the employer that is not directly earned by the employee: a bonus. The essential difference between this and an incentive is that the employee has no entitlement to the payment as a result of a contract of employment and cannot be assured of receiving it in return for a specific performance. The most common example of this is the Christmas bonus. Bonuses often take the form of profit-sharing schemes which seek to link individual pay levels to the performance of the organisation as a whole.

ACTIVITY 23.3

If your employer offered you a 'remuneration package', which could be made up from any of the items in Table 23.1 provided that the total cost was no more than £*X*, what proportion of each item would you choose and why? Does your answer suggest ideas for further development of salary policies?

SETTING BASE PAY

One of the most important decisions in the development of reward strategies concerns the mechanism or mechanisms that will be used to determine the basic rate of pay for different jobs in the organisation. In practice employers enjoy rather less freedom when making this decision than is the case when deciding how the total package should be made up. There are two main reasons for this:

1. The law imposes restrictions directly through the operation of the National Minimum Wage (£5.80 an hour in 2010) and indirectly through the operation of equal pay law (*see* Chapter 21). Moreover, in many countries incomes policies are operated as tools of inflation control. These restrict the amount of additional pay that people can receive in any one year while remaining in the same job. While formal incomes policies were abandoned in the UK after the 1970s, similar thinking continues to underpin government decision making in the area of public sector pay.
2. There is a limit on how much any employer can afford to pay if it is to remain competitive in its industry. On the other hand there is a limit below which it becomes impossible to attract or retain people with the required skills and experience. Hence as Gerhart (2009: 225) points out, product and labour market pressures effectively set a ceiling and a floor to overall pay levels for any one job or individual.

It is possible, notwithstanding the above restrictions, to identify four principal mechanisms for the determination of base pay. They are not entirely incompatible, although one tends to be used as the main approach in most organisations.

External market comparisons

In making external market comparisons the focus is on the need to recruit and retain staff, a rate being set which is broadly equivalent to 'the going rate' for the job in question. The focus is thus on **external relativities**. Research suggests that this is always a major contributing factor when organisations set pay rates, but that it increases in significance higher up the income scale. Some employers consciously pay over the market rate in order to secure the services of the most talented employees. Others 'follow the market', by paying below the going rate while using other mechanisms such as flexibility, job security or longer-term incentives to ensure effective recruitment and retention. In either case the decision is based on an assessment of what rate needs to be paid to compete for staff in different types of labour market. Going rates are more significant for some than for others. Accountants and craftworkers, for instance, tend to identify with an external employee grouping. Their assessment of pay levels is thus greatly influenced by the going rate in the trade or the district. A similar situation exists with jobs that are clearly understood and where skills are readily transferable, particularly if the employee is to work with a standard piece of equipment. Driving heavy goods vehicles is an obvious example, as the vehicles are common from one employer to another, the roads are the same, and only the loads vary. Other examples are secretaries, switchboard operators and computer operators. Jobs that are less sensitive to the labour market are those that are organisationally specific, such as much semi-skilled work in manufacturing, general clerical work and nearly all middle-management positions.

There are several possible sources of intelligence about market rates for different job types at any one time. A great deal of information can be found in published journals such as the pay bulletins issued by Incomes Data Services (IDS) and Industrial Relations Services (IRS), focusing on the hard-to-recruit groups such as computer staff. More detailed information can be gained by joining one of the major salary survey projects operated by firms of consultants or by paying for access to their datasets. Information on specific types of job, including international packages for expatriate workers, is collected by specialised consultants and can be obtained on payment of the appropriate fee. In addition there are more informal approaches such as looking at pay rates included in recruitment advertisements in papers, at job centres and on web-based job-board sites. New staff, notably HR people, often bring with them a knowledge of pay rates for types of job in competitor organisations and can be a useful source of information. Finally, it is possible to join or set up salary clubs. These consist of groups of employers, often based in the same locality, who agree to share salary information for mutual benefit.

Internal labour market mechanisms

Just as there is a labour market of which the company is a part, so there is a labour market within the organisation which also needs to be managed so as to ensure effective performance. According to Doeringer and Piore (1970) there are two kinds of internal labour market: the enterprise and the craft. The enterprise market is so called because the individual enterprise defines the boundaries of the market itself. Such will be the market encompassing manual workers engaged in production processes, for whom the predominant pattern of employment is one in which jobs are formally or informally ranked, with the jobs accorded the highest pay or prestige usually being filled by promotion from within and those at the bottom of the hierarchy usually being filled only from outside the enterprise. It is, therefore, those at the bottom that are most sensitive to the external labour market. Doeringer and Piore point out that there is a close parallel with managerial jobs, the main ports of entry being from management trainees or supervisors, and the number of appointments from outside gradually reducing as jobs become more senior. This modus operandi is one of the main causes of the problems that redundant executives face.

Recent American research has stressed the importance of this kind of internal labour market in determining pay rates. Here the focus is on **internal differentials** rather than external relativities. An interesting metaphor used is that of the sports tournament in which an organisation's pay structure is likened to the prize distribution in a knock-out competition such as is found, for example, at the Wimbledon Tennis Championships. Here the prize money is highest for the winner, somewhat lower for the runner-up, lower again for the semi-final losers and so on down the rounds. The aim, from the point of view of the tournament organisers, is to attract the best players to compete in the first round, then subsequently to give players in later rounds an incentive to play at their peak. According to Lazear (1995: 26–33), the level of base pay for each level in an organisation's hierarchy should be set according to similar principles. The level of pay for any particular job is thus set at a level which maximises performance lower down the hierarchy among employees competing for promotion. The actual performance of the individual receiving the pay is less important. The second type of internal labour market identified by Doeringer and Piore is the craft market, where barriers to entry are relatively high – typically involving the attainment of a formal qualification. However, once workers are established in the market, seniority and hierarchy become unimportant as jobs and duties are shared among the individuals concerned. Such arrangements are usually determined by custom and practice, but are difficult to break down because of the vested interests of those who have successfully completed their period of apprenticeship. Certain pay rates are expected by those who have achieved the required qualification and it is accepted by everyone that this is a fair basis for rewarding people.

Job evaluation

Job evaluation involves the establishment of a system which is used to measure the size and significance of all jobs in an organisation. It results in each job being scored with a number of points, establishing in effect a hierarchy of all the jobs in the organisation ranging from those which require the most knowledge and experience and which carry a great deal of responsibility to those which require least knowledge and experience and require the job-holder to carry relatively low levels of responsibility. Each job is then assimilated to an appropriate grade and payment distributed accordingly. The focus is thus on the relative worth of jobs within an organisation and on comparisons between these rather than on external relativities and comparisons with rates being paid by other employers. Fairness and objectivity are the core principles, an organisation's wage budget being divided among employees on the basis of an assessment of the nature and size of the job each is employed to carry out.

Usage of job evaluation has increased in recent years. It is currently used by around a third of organisations in the UK, and by a higher proportion still in larger organisations (CIPD 2009: 13). It is a well-established technique, having been developed in all its most common forms by the 1920s. It later received a series of boosts. First, various types of incomes policy between 1965 and 1974 either encouraged the introduction of job evaluation or specifically permitted expenditure above the prevailing norm by companies wishing to introduce it. In the 1980s the use of job evaluation became the hinge of most equal pay cases. More recently organisations have found it useful as part of moves towards single-status contractual arrangements and resolving pay issues following organisational mergers. Much of the recent growth has been in the public sector, local authorities and the NHS being examples of major employers establishing new schemes, but the surveys suggest that job evaluation is very widely used in the private sector as well. Moreover, few organisations abandon it, once introduced. The maxim that 'job evaluation is the one management tool that refuses to go out of fashion' thus continues to hold true.

Despite its popularity it is often misunderstood, so the following points have to be made:

- Job evaluation is concerned with the job and not the performance of the individual job-holder. Individual merit is not assessed.
- The technique is systematic rather than scientific. It depends on the judgement of people with experience, requiring them to decide in a planned and systematic way, but it does not produce results that are infallible.
- Job evaluation does not eliminate collective bargaining where trade unions are recognised. It determines the differential gaps between incomes; it does not determine pay levels or annual pay rises.
- Only a structure of pay rates is produced. Other elements of earnings, such as premia and incentives, are not determined by the method.

There are many methods of job evaluation in use and they are summarised by Armstrong and Murlis (2007: 129–64). Where a non-analytical or 'whole job' scheme is used a panel of assessors examines each job as a whole, in terms of its difficulty or value to the business, to determine which should be ranked more highly than others. No attempt is made to break each job down into its constituent parts. By contrast, an analytical scheme requires each element or factor of the job to be assessed. Since 1988 it has been the practice of courts only to accept the results of analytical schemes in equal pay cases. The most widely used analytical schemes are based on points-rating systems, under which each job is examined in terms of factors such as skill, effort and responsibility. Each factor is given a weighting indicating its value relative to the others and for each factor there are varying degrees. A score is then given depending on how demanding the job is in terms of each factor, with the overall points value determining the relative worth of each job – and hence its grade in the organisation's pay structure.

In recent years there has been a great growth in the use of highly sophisticated computer-assisted job evaluation systems marketed by leading firms of consultants which award scores to each job on the basis of information gathered from job analysis questionnaires.

The points values eventually derived for each job can be plotted on a graph or simply listed from the highest to the lowest to indicate the ranking. Then – and only then – are points ratings matched with cash amounts, as decisions are made on which points ranges equate with various pay grades. This process is illustrated in Figure 23.1, each

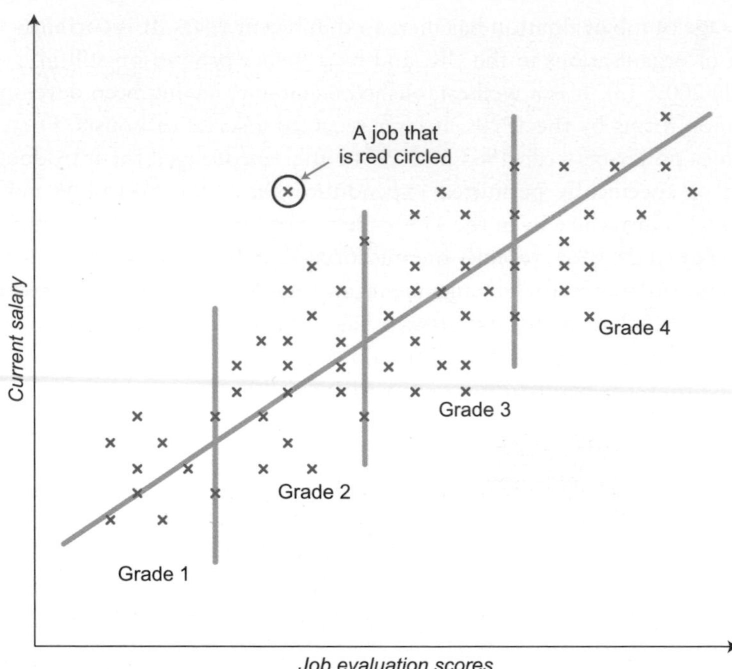

Figure 23.1
Job evaluation analysis

cross representing a job. The most common approach involves using a graph on which one axis represents the *current* salary for each job evaluated and the other the number of *job evaluation points* awarded. A line of best fit is then drawn and each job assigned to a grade. Salary-modelling software is widely available to help with this process.

It is virtually inevitable that some jobs will be found to be paid incorrectly after job evaluation has been completed. If the evaluation says that the pay rate should be higher then the rate duly rises, either immediately or step by step, to the new level. The only problem is finding the money, and introducing job evaluation always costs money. More difficult is the situation where evaluation shows the employee to be overpaid. It is not feasible to reduce the pay of the job-holder without breaching the contract of employment. There have been two approaches. The first is buying out. The overpaid employee is offered a large lump sum in consideration of the fact of henceforth being paid at the new, lower rate. The second device used is that of the personal rate or red-circling, so called because the job is circled in red on the job evaluation chart. The outcome is that current job-holders continue to be paid at the present level, but their successors are paid at the lower job-evaluated rate.

WINDOW ON PRACTICE

In 2002 three local careers services serving the West Midlands merged to form the Coventry, Solihull and Warwickshire Partnership (CSWP). It is a not-for-profit organisation which is independent, but each of its three constituent parts was once part of a local authority. Following the merger it became apparent that it was very unsatisfactory to continue employing staff on three completely different sets of terms and conditions. Not only were holiday entitlements and mileage allowances different, but the merger also brought about a situation in which people doing essentially the same job were paid different amounts because the grading systems used by each of the three legacy organisations differed considerably.

It was therefore decided to draw up a new set of terms and conditions that would apply to everyone (i.e. a single-status arrangement) and a new payment system consisting of 18 grades and 66 spinal column points (i.e. steps) on to which all existing staff would be assimilated. The system was devised by the Hay Group using its job evaluation system, the hope of managers being that subcontracting the work to an independent consultancy would make the results more acceptable to employees.

However, officials of UNISON (the recognised trade union at CWSP) were unhappy about some of the details and refused to recommend acceptance of the new package of terms and conditions when their members were balloted about it in 2003. As a result it was soundly rejected in the vote, despite the fact that the majority of staff would benefit financially from their regrading and that those who did not would have their pay red-circled indefinitely. A general pay rise of 3.5 per cent was also associated with acceptance of the deal. A subsequent analysis of the reasons established that a lack of communication by managers with employees about the implications of moves to single-status was responsible, along with a dislike among staff for the pressure they had been put under to accept the whole deal as a condition for receiving the 3.5 per cent rise.

Over the following two years negotiations with UNISON continued, resulting in some concessions being made on the details of the new pay structure. Moreover, senior managers took care to consult more effectively with staff, staging roadshows at which they explained the implications for staff and gave everyone an opportunity to express their views. A further ballot was held and this time the new deal was accepted.

Source: IRS 2006.

Collective bargaining

The fourth approach involves determining pay rates through collective negotiations with trade unions or other employee representatives. Forty years ago this was the dominant method used for determining pay in the UK, negotiations commonly occurring at industry level. The going rates for each job group were thus set nationally and were adhered to by all companies operating in the sector concerned. Recent decades have seen a steady erosion of these arrangements, collective bargaining being decentralised to company or plant level in the manufacturing sector, where it survives at all. Meanwhile the rise of service sector organisations with lower union membership levels has ensured that collective bargaining arrangements now cover only a minority of UK workers. According to Kersley *et al.* (2006: 180) only 40 per cent now have any of their terms and conditions determined in this way, collective bargaining over any kind of issue continuing in only 27 per cent of workplaces. The experience of many other countries is similar, but there remain regions such as Eastern Europe and Scandinavia where collective bargaining remains the major determinant of pay rates. Where separate clusters of employees within the same organisation are placed in different bargaining groups and represented by different unions, **internal relativities** become an issue for resolution during bargaining.

In carrying out negotiations the staff and management sides make reference to external labour market rates, established internal pay determination mechanisms and the size of jobs. However, a host of other factors come into the equation too as each side deploys its best arguments. Union representatives, for example, make reference to employee need when house prices are rising and affordable accommodation is hard to find. Both sides refer to the balance sheet, employers arguing that profit margins are too tight to afford substantial rises, while union counterparts seek to gain a share of any increased profits for employees. However good the case made, what makes collective bargaining different from the other approaches is the presence of industrial muscle. Strong unions which have the support of the majority of employees, as is the case in many public sector organisations, are able to ensure that their case is heard and taken into account. They can thus 'secure' a better pay deal for their members than market rates would allow.

ACTIVITY 23.4

Which of the four mechanisms outlined above do you think is usually most efficient for setting the following?

- Base pay
- Annual cost of living increases
- Executive remuneration packages
- Bonus schemes

THE IMPORTANCE OF EQUITY

Whatever methods are used to determine pay levels and to decide what elements make up the individual pay package, employers must ensure that they are perceived by employees to operate equitably. It has long been established that perceived inequity in payment matters can be highly damaging to an organisation. Classic studies undertaken by J.S. Adams (1963) found that a key determinant of satisfaction at work is the extent to which employees judge pay levels and pay increases to be distributed fairly. These led to the development by Adams and others of **equity theory** which holds that we are very concerned that rewards or 'outputs' equate to our 'inputs' (defined as skill, effort, experience, qualifications, etc.) and that these are fair when compared with the rewards being given to others. Where we believe that we are not being fairly rewarded we show signs of 'dissonance' or dissatisfaction which leads to absence, voluntary turnover, on-job shirking and low-trust employee relations. It is therefore important that an employer not only treats employees equitably in payment matters but is *seen* to do so too.

While it is difficult to gain general agreement about who should be paid what level of salary in an organisation, it is possible to employ certain clear principles when making decisions in the pay field. Those that are most important are the following:

- a standard approach for the determination of pay (basic rates and incentives) across the organisation;
- as little subjective or arbitrary decision making as is feasible;
- maximum communication and employee involvement in establishing pay determination mechanisms;
- clarity in pay determination matters so that everyone knows what the rules are and how they will be applied.

These are the foundations of procedural fairness or 'fair dealing'. In establishing pay rates it is not always possible to distribute rewards fairly to everyone's satisfaction, but it should always be possible to do so using procedures which operate equitably. You will find further information and discussion exercises about the way people perceive their pay and talk about it on this book's companion website **www.pearsoned.co.uk/torrington.**

WINDOW ON PRACTICE

Countries vary considerably in terms of how much different groups are paid, some being a good deal more equal than others in terms of how organisations pay people at different levels and how far income is subsequently redistributed via taxation and state benefits.

International statistics on inequality are published each year by the United Nations in its Human Development Reports. The level of equality in a society is measured using the gini coefficient, an internationally accepted measurement tool. It operates on a scale of 0–100. Were a country to be reported as having a gini coefficient of 100 it would mean that all the wealth was in the hands of a single individual (i.e. as unequal as it is possible to be). By contrast, a gini coefficient of 0 would indicate a society in which all wealth was distributed wholly equally between everyone. The reported figures for 2009 show that the most unequal country in the world (or at least the most unequal country that reports its figures to the UN) was Namibia with a gini coefficient of 74.3. Other African countries also report very high levels of inequality as do most countries in South America. Among the Western industrialised countries the most unequal is the USA (gini coefficient of 40.8), the UK following closely behind with a figure of 36. By contrast some northern European countries are a great deal more equal. The gini coefficient in Sweden in 2009 was just 25, Denmark being even more equal with a figure of 24.7. Japan and Germany also come right at the top of the equality table.

While wealth varies across international borders for many reasons, the level of pay plays a major part. The same patterns are reflected in the figures on pay equity in industrialised countries published regularly by the OECD (Organisation for Economic

Cooperation and Development). One measure that OECD uses is the difference between the gross male full-time average earnings of the top and bottom deciles in a population.

According to the most recent OECD statistics, dating from 2006, the difference in the USA is 5.5, meaning that the top 10 per cent earned 5.5 times more than the bottom 10 per cent. In the UK the difference in 2006 was 3.7, in Germany it was 3.3 and in France 3.1. Here too the lowest figures are reported in Scandinavian countries: in Sweden and Denmark it was 2.4, and in Finland only 2.1.

While the precise figures for each country fluctuate from year to year, the overall pattern across most of the world during the past 30 years has been towards greater inequality as measured by both these indices.

Sources: OECD Employment Database, available at **www.oecd.org/document/21/0,3343,en_2649_33927_40917154_1_1_1_1,00.html**, and United Nations (2009) *Human Development Report*.

SALARY PROGRESSION

Most organisations of any size have in place some form of grading structure which is used as the basis for determining the basic rate of pay for each job. The traditional approach involves developing a salary structure of groups, ladders and steps, whereby different groups or 'families' of jobs in an organisation are identified, each having a separate pay scale. Increasingly the term 'job family' is being replaced by 'career framework' (IDS 2006: 2), but the principle is the same. It is illustrated in Figure 23.2.

The first element of the structure is the broad groupings of salaries, each group or job family being administered according to the same set of rules. The questions in making decisions about this are to do with the logical grouping of job-holders, according to their common interests, performance criteria, qualifications and, perhaps, bargaining arrangements and trade union membership. Massey (2000: 144) suggests the following as a typical seven-way division of jobs into distinct families:

1. Executives
2. Management
3. Professional
4. Technical
5. Administrative
6. Skilled manual
7. Manual

The broad salary ranges are then set against each group, to encompass either the maximum and minimum of the various people who will then be in the group or – in the rare circumstance of starting from scratch – the ideal maximum and minimum levels. Some commentators place importance on the relationship of the maximum to the minimum of a ladder, described as the span, and the relationship between the bottom rung of adjacent ladders, referred to as the differential. A span of 50 per cent above the minimum or 20 per cent on either side of the midpoint is common.

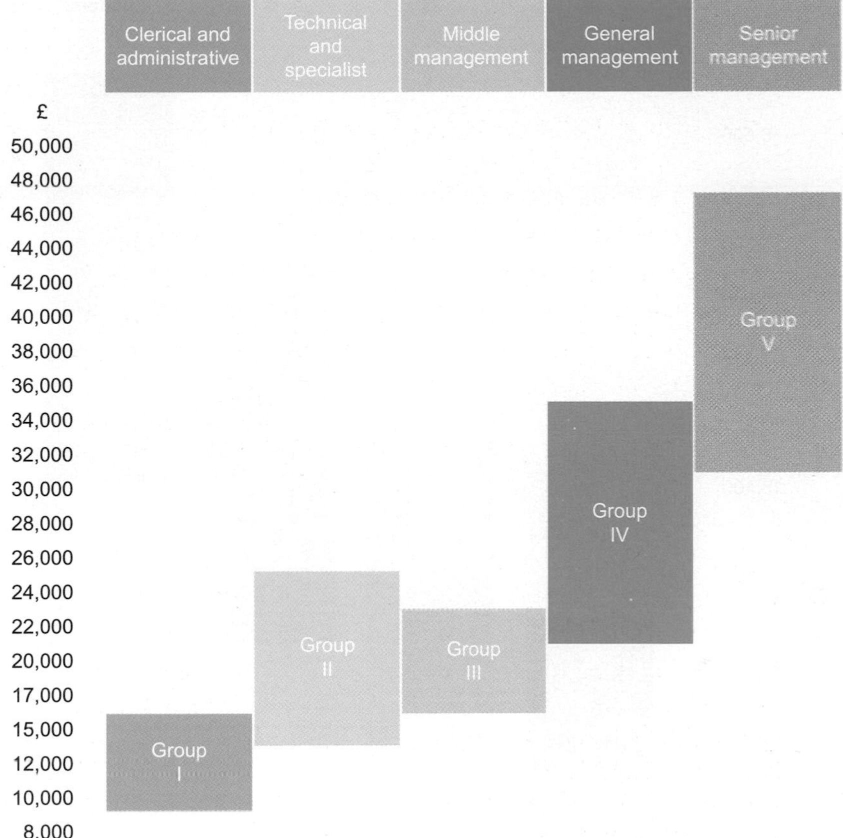

Figure 23.2 Typical salary groups

Salary groups will not stack neatly one on top of another in a salary hierarchy. There will be considerable overlap, recognising that there is an element of salary growth as a result of experience as well as status and responsibility. Because employees are assumed to be career oriented, salary arrangements are based on that assumption, so each salary group has several ladders within it and each ladder has a number of steps (often referred to as 'scales' and 'points'). In the traditional model increments are simply awarded annually until an individual reaches the top of the ladder, at which point progression stops unless that person is promoted into a more highly graded job. New starters enter employment with the organisation at the lowest rung on the ladder in the grade for that job.

The number of ladders will vary from organisation to organisation depending on particular circumstances, but for many large organisations offering a potential long-term career path it would be usual for there to be five or six separate ladders or grades for each job family. IDS (2006: 30) gives the following example of the approach used at Zarlink Semiconductors. Here there are six ladders for each job family, descriptors being used to indicate broadly which jobs are graded at which level:

1 entry
2 developing
3 working
4 senior (team leader)

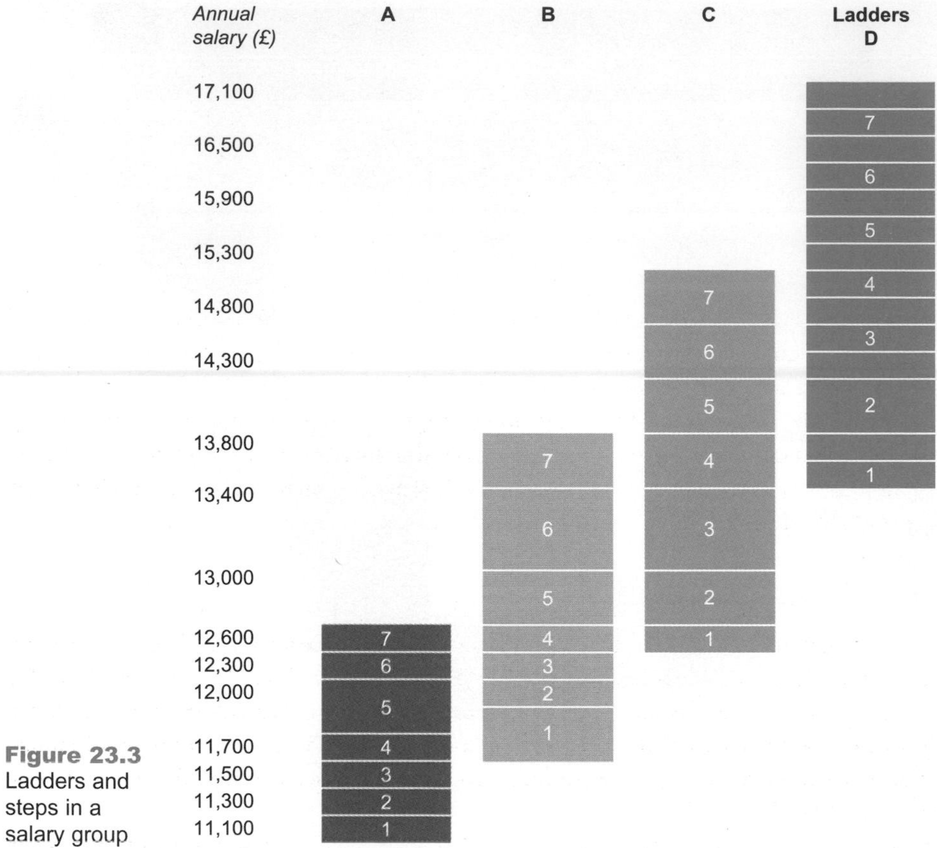

Figure 23.3 Ladders and steps in a salary group

5 specialist (manager)

6 principal (director)

As with groups there is considerable overlap, the top rung of one ladder being rather higher than the bottom rung of the next. Taking a typical general employee group as an example, we could envisage four ladders, as shown in Figure 23.3. The size of the differential between steps varies from £200 to £600 according to the level of the salary, and the overlapping could be used in a number of ways according to the differing requirements. Steps 6 and 7 on each ladder would probably be only for those who had reached their particular ceiling and were unlikely to be promoted further, while steps 4 and 5 could be for those who are on their way up and have made sufficient progress up one ladder to contemplate seeking a position with a salary taken from the next higher ladder.

It is generally believed that fixed incremental payment schemes are self regulating, so that introducing incremental payment schemes does not mean that within a few years everyone is at the maximum. The assumption is that just as some move up, others retire or resign and are replaced by new recruits at the bottom of the ladder. However, this will clearly not be the case when staff turnover is low, nor will it be the case in very tight labour markets where it is necessary to appoint external candidates to points on the scales which reflect their market worth rather than simply starting them at the base of the grade as would typically occur in the case of an internal promotion.

ACTIVITY 23.5

If incremental scales cease to be self financing through lack of labour market movement, what advantage is there to the employer in keeping them?

Contemporary trends

Above we have described a traditional approach to salary progression as a means of introducing the topic, an approach in which quite complex salary scales are set for each job grouping in an organisation and in which progression up scales is determined by seniority. While elements of this traditional approach remain in place across many organisations, particularly in the public sector and in larger private sector corporations, in recent years there have been some major developments which can be seen as challenges to the traditional model.

Single pay spines

A key development has been a strong tendency to do away with multiple pay spines for different job families and to replace them with one single pay ladder and set of grades covering a whole organisation. Where this has proved too difficult to achieve, some organisations have settled for a rationalisation process where by a number of spines have been assimilated and a much simpler structure introduced consisting of just two or three distinct ladders.

Interest in the development of single pay structures has increased in recent years for a number of reasons. It has accompanied a more general preference among employers for taking an organisation-wide approach to a whole range of HR initiatives. New technologies often demand a more flexible workforce, leading to a blurring of the organisational distinction between groups of workers. Harmonisation of the terms and conditions of employment follows, so that all employees work the same number of hours, are given the same training opportunities and enjoy the same entitlement to occupational pensions, sick pay and annual leave. Such practices have also been conspicuously imported into British subsidiaries of overseas companies, which typically have longer experience of single-status employment practices. Moreover, substantial increases in the occurrence and frequency of corporate mergers and acquisitions means that payment systems can become overwhelmingly complex when previously separate organisations are brought together for the first time. The result is a tendency to simplify as a means of achieving a workable harmonised salary system. Interest has also arisen following recent judgments in which courts have awarded equal pay to employees who have sought to compare their jobs with those of other individuals in wholly different job families. As a result, employers who continue to operate different mechanisms for determining the pay of different groups of employees have had difficulty in defending their practices when faced with equal value claims.

The argument against such a system is that it applies a common set of assumptions that may be inappropriate for certain groups. In general management, for instance, it will probably be an assumption that all members of the group will be interested in promotion and job change; this will be encouraged by the salary arrangements, which will encourage job-holders to look for opportunities to move around. In contrast, the research chemist will be expected to stick at one type of job for a longer period, and movement into other fields of the company's affairs, such as personnel or marketing, will often be discouraged. For this reason it will be more appropriate for the research chemist to be in a salary group with a relatively small number of ladders, each having a large number of steps; while a general management colleague will be more logically set in a context of more ladders, each with fewer steps.

There are other reasons too for sticking with or moving towards a structure composed of a number of different distinct job families. Key is the flexibility it gives employers to respond efficiently to developments in specific labour markets. As a result, when one group of staff become harder to recruit and retain because demand for their skills increases pay rates can be adjusted upwards without the need to incur the costs associated with a general pay rise for all employees.

Moreover, in practice it is very difficult to develop a single pay structure which is acceptable to all parties in an organisation. The more diverse the skills, values or union affiliation of the employees, the more difficult is such a single job family. The factors used to compare job with job always tend to favour one grouping at the expense of another; one job at the expense of another. The wider the diversity of jobs that are brought within the purview of a single scheme, the wider will be the potential dissatisfaction, with the result that the payment arrangement is one that at best is tolerated because it is the least offensive rather than being accepted as satisfactory.

ACTIVITY 23.6

In what type of situations do you think a single, integrated pay structure would be appropriate? Where would such a pay structure be inappropriate? What are the most likely management problems in each case?

WINDOW ON PRACTICE

Over the past ten years the National Health Service, like many public sector organisations, has been moving towards a single streamlined pay structure for all its staff except doctors and dentists. It started by securing agreement with its many trade unions to pilot a scheme in 12 NHS Trusts. The new pay scales that resulted formed part of a wider package of measures being introduced by the government under the heading 'Agenda for change'.

The new pay structure radically simplified established NHS pay practices. Instead of each professional group negotiating its own grading structure, the Agenda for change approach created a standard pay scale which covers everyone. Six hundred and fifty different pay grades were replaced with just 16 pay bands (two spines each with eight grades) along with harmonised terms and conditions which apply across the whole NHS.

All existing jobs were allocated to one of the eight new bands using a job evaluation scheme which takes account of five factors:

- the level of responsibility held by the job-holder
- the extent of knowledge, training and experience needed to do the job
- the extent to which the job-holder has freedom to act independently
- the level and type of skills deployed by the job-holder
- the nature of the working environment and amount of effort required to carry out the job.

The number of incremental steps varies from band to band. Band 1 (mainly for lower-skilled ancillary and clerical roles) contains four steps, while Band 7 (specialist nurses and section managers) contains nine. Progression is mainly based on seniority, so after each completed year of service, the employee is awarded one increment and climbs a step. But two steps in each band (the second from the bottom and one higher up the scale) can only be attained if the job-holder also satisfies a competency-based assessment.

Sources: IDS (2003) 'Pay modernisation in the NHS', *IDS Report* 884, July. London: IDS; and Department of Health website (**www.doh.gov.uk/agendaforchange**).

Performance-based progression

Another significant recent development has been a move away from automatic incremental progression up a salary ladder towards systems which make progression conditional on the achievement of performance-based objectives. As is pointed out by Thompson (2009: 132), traditional approaches have relied on the assumption that age and seniority are 'as good proxy measures for performance improvement as any', each individual being rewarded annually with an incremental pay rise as well as any general cost-of-living rise until they reach the ceiling for their particular grade. Rewarding seniority in this way also serves as a very effective employee retention device and also may serve to attract would-be employees to an organisation because it gives new starters the opportunity to look forward, in a highly predictable way, to steady salary progression over a number of years. This is why seniority-based progression systems remain widely used in the public sector.

However, there are of course also significant disadvantages, the most obvious being the strong tendency to end up with a situation in which poor performers are paid considerably more than colleagues doing the same job to an excellent standard. This is particularly the case when pay spines are long, as they are in many public sector organisations, requiring new entrants to wait ten or more years before they progress incrementally to the top of the pay spine relevant to their grade. In such systems very effective performers with three or four years' service in their roles are often paid much less than more senior colleagues who have reached the top of the spine but are far weaker in terms of their performance. This leads to real and perceived unfairness which in turn can reduce the amount of effort people are prepared to put in. The problem is ameliorated in situations where the good performers can be promoted into higher-graded jobs, but this is not always a possibility, leaving a situation in which pay bears no relation to performance, in which there are few incentives to improve individual performance and in which an organisation is effectively spending a great deal of money rewarding 'the wrong people'.

The solution to this problem is one that has been increasingly adopted across the private sector in recent years. This has involved doing away with automatic seniority-based progression and instead making progression contingent on individual performance. Such approaches have proliferated in recent years (*see* Palmer 2009: 64–5 and Thompson 2009: 132–5) and represent one of the most significant trends in contemporary reward management practice. The new systems, however, are not without their problems. As we will demonstrate in Chapter 24, performance-based payment systems are splendid in theory, but often very difficult indeed to make work well in practice. Basing incremental progression on length of service may lead to unfairness, but such approaches have the advantage in that they do not require managers to make decisions about whether or not any individual deserves an incremental rise this year on the basis of his or her performance. There is thus less potential for individuals to feel aggrieved, to perceive that their manager has treated them unfairly, to think that others are being shown undue favouritism or to react negatively or even destructively when not rewarded with an increment they believe they have earned.

Despite these problems, there remain good reasons for moving towards performance-based salary progression. First, of course, such systems allow managers to exercise a far greater degree of cost control. Once progression ceases to be automatic, it inevitably becomes possible to reduce the amount of money spent on pay increases in a particular year simply by restricting them to proven high performers. A potential knock-on effect will be a situation in which the organisation is more attractive as a potential employer to good performers because they are confident that their efforts will be rewarded. Similarly, better performers are more likely to stay, while weaker colleagues leave, over time increasing the general level of performance across the organisation. There is also a third reason for shifting away from seniority-based progression, and this may well explain some of the more recent moves in this direction. We refer here to the as yet uncertain role that age discrimination law may have over time on an organisation's capacity to maintain a salary progression system which is entirely seniority based. The traditional model clearly operates in such a way as to favour older over younger employees. Where pay ladders have just a few steps, perhaps rewarding people automatically with annual increments only during their first five years in a role, it is not difficult to justify the continuation of a scheme on the grounds that it genuinely rewards relevant experience. However, systems which stretch over a longer timescale (10 or 15 years) are far harder to justify in business terms and may well, over time, be challenged successfully in the courts by younger employees.

Broadbanding

Attention has increasingly been given in recent years to the introduction of 'broadbanding' as a way of retaining the positive features of traditional pay scales while reducing some of the less desirable effects (*see* Armstrong and Brown 2009 and CIPD 2007). One of these less desirable effects is the built-in incentive to focus on being promoted rather than on performing well in the current job. This can lead to individuals playing damaging political games in a bid to weaken the position of colleagues or even undermine their own supervisors. Inflexibility can also occur when individuals refuse to undertake duties or types of work associated with higher grades. Moreover, in making internal equity the main determinant of pay rates within an organisation, rigid salary structures prevent managers from offering higher salaries to new employees. This tends to hinder effective competition in some labour markets.

Broadbanding essentially involves retaining some form of grading system while greatly reducing the numbers of grades or salary bands. The process typically results in the replacement of a structure consisting of ten or a dozen distinct grades with one consisting of only three or four. Pay variation within grades is then based on individual performance, skill or external market value rather than on the nature and size of the job. The great advantage of such approaches is their ability to reduce hierarchical thinking. Differences in pay levels still exist between colleagues but they are no longer seen as being due solely to the fact that one employee is graded more highly than another. This can reduce feelings of inequity provided the new criteria are reasonably open and objective. As a result, teamwork is encouraged as is a focus on improving individual performance in order to secure higher pay.

In theory, therefore, broadbanded structures increase the extent to which managers have discretion over the setting of internal differentials, introduce more flexibility and permit organisations to reward performance or skills acquisition as well as job size. Their attraction is that they achieve this while retaining a skeleton grading system which gives order to the structure and helps justify differentials. Time will tell how acceptable such approaches are to the courts when it comes to judging equal value claims.

WINDOW ON PRACTICE

The Britannia is the UK's second largest mutual building society. It employs approximately 4,000 staff – 1,500 in its branches and 2,500 in its head office. Until 2002 the society operated a traditional hierarchical grading system consisting of 16 separate grades. Once employees were paid at the top of the scale for their particular grade, the only way they could earn more was to apply for promotion. Excellence and experience in their current job could not be further rewarded. This approach was seen by managers to be too rigid and inflexible to enable the society to meet its staffing objectives satisfactorily. In particular it was believed to be providing a disincentive to enhanced individual performance and effective employee development.

The decision was thus taken to move to a far simpler, broadbanded system. Instead of 16 grades there are now just six bands into which all employees have been assimilated. Instead of 670 quite tightly defined job descriptions, there are now 38 more flexibly written role profiles. For each band a midpoint is identified which is set broadly at the market rate for the majority of jobs that are covered by the relevant role profiles. Where individual employees sit within the broad bands depends on their performance. The best performers are paid above the midpoint, the poorer performers below it. Annual pay rises thus reflect market rates (aiding effective recruitment and retention), but also reward individual effort.

Source: Dennis 2005.

TOTAL REWARD

So far in this chapter we have focused on transactional or tangible rewards, by which we mean those which are financial in nature, and this will remain our focus in Chapters 24 and 25. However, it is important to remember that employees also value the intangible (or relational) rewards which they gain from coming to work, to all of which we have made extensive reference in earlier chapters. These include opportunities to develop their careers and more generally as a human being, to enjoy the social life which is associated with working in communal settings, to earn recognition from managers and colleagues for a job well done and for the effort expended, and more generally to gain a sense of personal achievement. Increasingly the opportunity to work flexibly so as to achieve a better 'work-life balance' is discussed in this context too. The trend towards viewing reward policies and practices as extending well beyond the realms of payment has led to widespread interest in the concept of 'total reward' which involves managers viewing the way that they reward employees in the round, taking equal account of both the tangible and intangible ingredients that together help to make work and jobs 'rewarding' in the widest sense of the word. The idea is effectively illustrated in graphical form by Armstrong and Brown (2009: 25) in their model adapted from work by the Towers Perrin reward consultancy (*see* Figure 23.4). Here four distinct categories of rewards are identified, the implication being that each has equal potential significance as a source of reward from the employee perspective.

The change in perspective away from a narrow focus on payment towards a broader focus on 'total reward' has come about largely because of developments in the commercial environment. Every year, organisations operating in the private sector are facing greater competitive pressure in their product markets leading them to search for ways of reducing their costs while retaining or improving the levels of quality they achieve. In the public sector competitive forces increasingly play a role too, but here pressure to keep costs down come primarily from tax payers seeking good value for their money. The trouble is that these pressures are being faced simultaneously with tighter labour

	Transactional
Base pay Contingent pay Bonuses Incentives Shares Profit sharing **Individual**	Pensions Holidays Healthcare Other perks Flexibility
	Communal
Learning and development Training Career development **Relational**	Leadership Organisational values Voice Recognition Achievement Job design Work-life balance

Figure 23.4 Categories of reward

market conditions, making it difficult for employers to recruit, retain and motivate the staff they need without substantially increasing pay levels. There are a variety of responses to this conundrum that organisations are embracing. One involves employing fewer, but more highly paid people to carry out existing work more efficiently. Another involves keeping a lid on payment levels while simultaneously looking for other ways of rewarding staff effectively. It is this latter approach which has led managers to think about the 'total reward' package that they offer.

As a rule managing the tangible components (i.e. the financial ones) is relatively unproblematic provided basic principles are adhered to and the correct technical decisions are made. While they enable organisations to secure a degree of competitive advantage in their labour markets, these tangible parts of a total reward package are readily imitated by competitors. It is much harder, in practice, to replicate intangible rewards. Over the longer term it is thus in the interests of organisations to improve the perceived value of the intangible elements, but that is a great deal harder both to achieve and to evaluate. Moreover, several important intangible rewards are 'intrinsically' rather than 'extrinsically' motivating, and by definition cannot be directly provided by managers. These are terms used by psychologists to distinguish between sources of positive motivation which are external to individuals and *given* to them by their employer, such as money or praise, and those which are internally generated. An example of intrinsic motivation is people putting a great deal of effort into a project at work simply because they find it interesting or enjoyable. The result may be very considerable satisfaction on the part of the employees concerned, but this has not resulted directly from any management action. All managers can do is try to create and sustain a culture in which individual employees can achieve intrinsic motivation and hence experience work which is rewarding.

ACTIVITY 23.7

How far do you agree with the proposition that managers should think in terms of 'total reward' as a means of recruiting, retaining and motivating their staff? Are praise and career development as important as pay? Would you trade some of your pay for greater recognition and development opportunities?

WINDOW ON PRACTICE

Total reward at the Crown Prosecution Service

In 2006 the Crown Prosecution Service (CPS) launched a new reward system which was heavily influenced by the 'total reward' concept. Until 1996 when responsibility for reward management was devolved, the CPS's 8,500 staff were paid on standard terms and conditions which were negotiated nationally for civil servants working across all government departments. After devolution incremental changes were introduced that

aimed to meet the particular needs of the CPS, culminating in this major overhaul. Labelled 'Invest', the new approach aims to underpin the Service's evolving agenda.

The first priority for the CPS is to successfully manage a major programme of expansion. New responsibilities taken over from the police require that the CPS employs 300 new lawyers and 500 new administrators. 'Invest' is designed to increase the attractiveness of a career within the CPS and to help retain staff more effectively. A explicit objective of the service is to make itself 'an employer of choice' for lawyers and people seeking a career in public administration. A second aim is substantially to improve performance. The CPS has as its central corporate objective a mission to become recognised as 'a world-class prosecution authority'. This requires cultural change and the acquisition by staff of a range of new skills and attributes.

The new strategy aims to meet these objectives in a number of ways. First, a job evaluation system has been introduced to ensure that each job is fairly graded according to the skills its holders require and the responsibilities they shoulder. Secondly, a new performance appraisal system has come into effect to strengthen links between pay and individual effort and contribution. The existing civil service benefits package has been enhanced with new elements such as childcare services and a counselling service, the whole package being promoted with greater coherence at the recruitment stage. A major element is enhanced training and development opportunities for staff, allowing easier career progression within the service. Employees are sponsored to attain professional qualifications, while e-learning packages have also been developed to support career development. Finally flexible working initiatives have been developed, including a great deal more home-working, which aim to meet the needs both of the service and its employees. In the future it is intended to introduce long-service awards and to recognise individual achievements with formal letters of recognition from senior managers.

Source: Suff 2006.

SUMMARY PROPOSITIONS

23.1 Until relatively recently many employers in the UK were greatly restricted in their capacity to design reward strategies which met their priorities by the prevailing system of multi-employer or industry-level collective bargaining. The experimentation that followed the disintegration of this system has led to both successful and unsuccessful outcomes.

23.2 In payment matters employees are principally concerned with purchasing power, fairness and recognition of effort and skills. Employers are concerned with recruitment, retention, motivation and minimising the wage budget. Employers are restricted in pay matters by the law and the realities of their product markets.

23.3 The main elements of payment are basic rate, plussage, benefits, premia, overtime, incentives and bonus.

23.4 There are four main alternative methods of setting base pay rates: external labour market comparisons, internal labour market mechanisms, job evaluation and collective bargaining.

23.5 Procedural equity is essential to the design of successful payment systems.

23.6 Traditional salary structures assign each job to a grade in which there are a number of incremental steps.

23.7 Recent years have seen moves towards single pay spines covering all jobs in an organisation and towards progression based on performance rather than seniority. Another recent development is a move towards broadbanded structures which reduce the number of grades in each salary scale to allow managers greater flexibility in setting pay levels for individual employees.

23.8 Simultaneous competition in product and labour markets has led employers increasingly to think in terms of 'total reward' when developing reward strategies. This involves incorporating all management initiatives which may have the effect of adding value to the experience of working in an organisation.

GENERAL DISCUSSION TOPICS

1 Can payment ever be truly fair?

2 Do you think it is possible to identify 'best practice' in payment policy? What elements would you consider should make up any such package?

3 'Job evaluation does not produce equitable payment: it merely produces a ramshackle method of justifying the status quo.' Do you agree with this statement?

4 What do you think would be the major organisational problems associated with a move from a narrow to a broadbanded payment structure?

FURTHER READING

The Chartered Institute of Personnel and Development (CIPD) carries out a big annual survey of reward management policy and practice which is published in February each year. It can be downloaded from the Institute's website. In addition CIPD publishes the results of other research projects that focus on reward. Two recent examples are the report of a symposium held in 2005 at which academics and practitioners who specialise in reward matters met to discuss developments in the field (Armstrong *et al.* 2005) and a series of papers by John Purcell and Sue Hutchison (2006–7) summarising their research on the role played by line managers in the implementation of reward initiatives.

Reward management continues to be an area of HRM practice which is heavily researched. Good summaries of the most important recent contributions are the following:

Kessler, I. (2005) 'Remuneration systems', in S. Bach (ed.), *Managing Human Resources: Personnel management in transition*, 4th edn. Oxford: Blackwell.

Guthrie, J. (2007) 'Remuneration: Pay effects at work', in P. Boxall, J. Purcell and P. Wright (eds), *The Oxford Handbook of Human Resource Management*. Oxford: Oxford University Press.

Gerhart, B. (2009b) 'Compensation', in A. Wilkinson, N. Bacon, T. Redman and S. Snell (eds), *The Sage Handbook of Human Resource Management*. London: Sage.

White, G. and Druker, J. (eds) (2009) *Reward Management: A critical text*, 2nd edn. London: Routledge.

REFERENCES

Adams, J.S. (1963) 'Towards an understanding of inequity', *Journal of Abnormal and Social Psychology*, Vol. 67, pp. 422–36.

Armstrong, M. and Brown, D. (2009) *Strategic Reward: Implementing more effective reward management*. London: Kogan Page.

Armstrong, M. and Murlis, H. (2007) *Reward Management: A handbook of remuneration strategy and practice*. London: Kogan Page.

Armstrong, M., Thompson, P., Brown, D. and Cotton, C. (2005) *Reward Management: Report on a one-day conference held on 13th July 2005, organised jointly by e-reward and the Chartered Institute of Personnel and Development*. London: CIPD.

Bryson, A. and Forth, J. (2008) 'The theory and practice of pay setting', in P. Blyton, N. Bacon, J. Fiorito and E. Heery (eds), *The Sage Handbook of Industrial Relations*. London: Sage.

CIPD (2007) *Reward Management: Annual Survey Report 2007*. London: CIPD.

CIPD (2009) *Reward Management: Annual Survey Report 2009*. London: CIPD.

Dennis, S. (2005) 'Rejecting pay hierarchy: broadbanding at Britannia', *IRS Employment Review*, No. 828, 29 July.

Doeringer, P.B. and Piore, M.J. (1970) *Internal Labour Markets and Manpower Analysis*. Washington DC: Office of Manpower Research, US Department of Labor.

Druker, J. and White, G. (2009) 'Introduction', in G. White and J. Druker (eds), *Reward Management: A critical text*, 2nd edn. London: Routledge.

Gerhart, B. (2009a) 'Compensation', in J. Storey, P. Wright and D. Ulrich (eds), *The Routledge Companion to Strategic Human Resource Management*. London: Routledge.

Gerhart, B. (2009b) 'Compensation', in A. Wilkinson, N. Bacon, T. Redman and S. Snell (eds), *The Sage Handbook of Human Resource Management*. London: Sage.

IDS (2003) *Pay Modernisation in the NHS. IDS Report*, No. 884, July. London: IDS.

IDS (2006) *Job Families. IDS Study*, No. 814, January. London: IDS.

IRS (2006) 'Three into one does go: harmonisation at CSWP', *IRS Employment Review*, No. 842, pp. 31–5.

Jacques, E. (1962) 'Objective measures for pay differentials', *Harvard Business Review*, January–February, pp. 133–7.

Kersley, B., Forth, J., Bryson, A., Bewley, H., Dix, G. and Oxenbridge, S. (2005) *Inside the Workplace: First findings from the 2004 Workplace Employment Relations Survey*. London: DTI.

Kersley, B., Alpin, C., Forth, J., Bryson, A., Bewley, H., Dix, G. and Oxenbridge, S. (2006) *Inside the Workplace: Findings from the 2004 Workplace Employment Relations Survey*. Abingdon: Routledge.

Kessler, I. (2001) 'Reward system choices', in J. Storey (ed.), *Human Resource Management: A critical text*, 2nd edn. London: Thomson Learning.

Kessler, I. (2005) 'Remuneration Systems', in S. Bach (ed.) *Managing Human Resources: Personnel Management in Transition*, 4th edn. Oxford: Blackwell.

Lazear, E.P. (1995) *Personnel Economics*. Boston: Massachusetts Institute of Technology.

Massey, C. (2000) 'Strategic reward systems: pay systems and structures', in R. Thorpe and G. Homan (eds), *Strategic Reward Systems*. London: Financial Times/Prentice Hall.

National Statistics (2009) *2009 Annual Survey of Hours and Earnings*. London: National Statistics.

Palmer, S. (2009) 'Paying for progression: ever onwards and upwards?', in S. Corby, S. Palmer and E. Lindop (eds), *Rethinking Reward*. Basingstoke: Palgrave.

Purcell, J. and Hutchinson, S. (2006–7) *Rewarding Work: The vital role of line managers*. London: CIPD.

Steers, R.M., Porter, L.W. and Bigley, G.M. (1996) *Motivation and Leadership at Work*, 6th edn. Singapore: McGraw-Hill.

Suff, R. (2006) 'Investing in excellence at the Crown Prosecution Service', *IRS Employment Review*, No. 841, 17 February, pp. 24–7.

Thompson, M. (2009) 'Salary progression systems', in G. White and J. Druker (eds), *Reward Management: A critical text*, 2nd edn. London: Routledge.

United Nations (2009) *Human Development Report*. New York: United Nations.

An extensive range of additional materials, including multiple choice questions, answers to questions and links to useful websites can be found on the Human Resource Management companion website at **www.pearsoned.co.uk/torrington**.

INCENTIVES

THE OBJECTIVES OF THIS CHAPTER ARE TO:

1. Set out the major choices faced by employers contemplating setting up or reviewing incentive payment schemes
2. Explore the question of how many people are paid different types of incentive in the UK
3. Outline the main forms of payment by results (PBR) schemes and discuss their advantages and disadvantages
4. Debate the merits of individual performance-related pay (PRP)
5. Introduce skills-based pay and discuss its major advantages and disadvantages
6. Outline the major forms of profit-sharing schemes that operate, including those sponsored by the government

Incentive payments remain one of the ideas that fascinate managers as they search for the magic formula. Somewhere there is a method of linking payment to performance so effectively that their movements will coincide, enabling the manager to leave the workers on automatic pilot, as it were, while attending to more important matters such as strategic planning or going to lunch. This conviction has sustained a continuing search for this elusive formula, which has been hunted with all the fervour of those trying to find the Holy Grail or the crock of gold at the end of the rainbow.

In recent years incentives of all kinds have been the source of much debate among HR professionals, consultants, trade unionists and academic writers. While particular attention has been given to the pros and cons of individual performance-related reward systems, much has also been written in support of and against the use of team-based incentives and those which reward the acquisition of defined skills. Profit sharing and employee share ownership have been the subject of significant government initiatives and have thus also become topics about which a great deal is written.

BASIC CHOICES

While incentive payment systems are common in the UK, there are millions of employees who do not receive this kind of reward and many employers who use them only in a limited way (often in the remuneration of senior managers). It is thus perfectly possible, and some would argue desirable, to recruit, retain and motivate a workforce by paying a simple, fixed rate of pay for each job in the organisation. There is other equipment in the HR manager's toolkit which can be used to reward effort and maintain good levels of job satisfaction. The most fundamental question is therefore whether or not to use an incentive payment system at all. In the opinion of Sisson and Storey (2000: 123–4) many organisations in the UK have introduced schemes for 'ideological reasons' as a means of impressing stockmarket analysts, reinforcing management control or undermining established collective bargaining machinery. These, they suggest, are poor reasons which have generally met with little long-term success. Incentive schemes should only be used where they are appropriate to the needs of the business and where they can clearly contribute to the achievement of organisational objectives.

There is a long tradition in the academic literature of hostility to incentive schemes in general and those which focus on the individual in particular. In 1966, Frederick Herzberg argued that pay was a 'hygiene factor' rather than a 'motivator'. He claimed that its capacity to motivate positively was limited, while it can very easily demotivate when managed poorly. It follows that there is little to be gained and a great deal to lose from the introduction of incentive schemes. Others (for example, Thompson 2000) have focused on the way that incentives are perceived by employees as tools of management control which reduce their autonomy and discretion. This, it is argued, causes resentment and leads to dissatisfaction and industrial conflict. A third source of criticism is the considerable additional costs which invariably mount up when organisations introduce incentive schemes. Cox (2006: 1493) labels these 'costly side-effects' and shows that they are both considerable and largely unanticipated at the time a new scheme is introduced.

A different school of thought argues in favour of incentives on the grounds that they reward effort and behaviours which the organisation wishes to encourage (Gerhart 2009: 226). As a result they not only are a fair basis for rewarding people, but also can enhance organisational effectiveness and productivity. Advocates of **expectancy theory** hold this position with their belief that individual employees will alter their behaviour (e.g. by working harder or prioritising their actions differently) if they believe that in so doing they will be rewarded with something they value. Hence, where additional pay is a valued reward, employees will seek it and will work to secure it. A positive outcome for both employer and employee is achievable provided the incentive is paid in return for a form of employee behaviour which genuinely contributes to the achievement of organisational objectives.

In addition, many reward specialists point to a significant **sorting effect** which leads employees who are willing and able to perform to a higher standard to be attracted to jobs in which their superior relative contribution will be properly rewarded. At the same time, it is argued, existing employees who perform relatively poorly are more likely to seek alternative employment than colleagues who perform well and are rewarded for doing so. Hence, over time, the quality of employees rises as a result of the presence of incentive schemes. Conversely, of course, it can be plausibly argued that employers who fail to recognise superior individual contribution in their payment systems are more likely to lose higher-performing people because they perceive themselves to be being inadequately rewarded for their skills and efforts.

The research evidence is patchy on the question of how far incentives actually lead to performance improvements at the organisational level. Some studies suggest a correlation between superior performance and some types of incentive scheme (e.g. Huselid 1995, Lazear 2000, Piekkola 2005, Gielen *et al.* 2006, Cadsby *et al.* 2007 and Gerhart and Trevor 2008), while others (e.g. Pearce *et al.* 1985, Thompson 1992, Makinson 2000 and Marsden 2004) have found no significant evidence of any link. In any case, as Corby *et al.* (2005: 5–6) point out, there are very few published studies which focus on performance or productivity levels before and after the introduction of a new scheme. What we have are correlation studies which link superior organisational performance to the presence of incentive schemes, but no proof of any causal relationship. Much seems to depend on the circumstances. Incentives are not universally applicable, but can play a role in enhancing individual effort or performance where the conditions and scheme design are right. Problems occur when the wrong system is imposed, on the wrong people, in the wrong circumstances or for the wrong reasons.

Where an incentive scheme is used, the next choice relates to the way the scheme is to operate. There are two basic approaches that can be used: bonus payments and incremental progression. In the case of the former, the employee is rewarded with a single payment (possibly made in stages) at the end of a payment period. In the case of profit sharing it will often be an annual payment, while sales commission is usually paid monthly. Whatever the timing, the key principle is that the pay is variable. Good performance in one period is rewarded, but the same individual could earn rather less in the next if his or her performance deteriorates. Some writers refer to such systems as putting 'pay at risk', because earnings vary from period to period depending on how much incentive is earned. The alternative approach involves making incremental progression dependent on the individual's contribution (*see* Chapter 23). The reward takes the form of a general pay rise over and above any cost of living increment being paid in a particular year. The incentive payment thus becomes consolidated into overall earnings and is not variable or 'at risk' after it has been earned.

ACTIVITY 24.1

What in your view are the main advantages and disadvantages of these alternative approaches from a management perspective? Would you be more motivated by the prospect of a pay rise or a one-off bonus payment?

Another basic choice concerns the extent of the incentive. In practice this is a decision of rather greater importance than the type of incentive scheme to be used, although it is given rather less coverage in the literature. There is the world of difference, in terms of cost and employee perception, between a scheme which rewards people with 3 per cent or 4 per cent of salary and one which pays a sum equivalent to 25 per cent. Studies undertaken in the USA, reported by Bartol and Durham (2000: 14), suggest that the minimum level of bonus or pay rise 'necessary to elicit positive perceptual and attitudinal responses' is between 5 per cent and 7 per cent of salary. Piekkola (2005), in her studies of links between incentives and firm performance in Finland, found that a positive impact on productivity only began to kick in once the incentive exceeded 3.6 per cent of salary. Lesser payments are thus unlikely to provide meaningful incentives and will have only a peripheral impact. According to Hendry *et al.* (2000: 54) this has been a major problem for schemes introduced in the public sector where incentives have tended to be worth a maximum of only 2 per cent or 3 per cent of salary.

The final choice concerns the level at which the incentive will be paid. Some schemes reward individuals for individual performance, others reward a group of employees or team for their collective performance. Finally there are schemes which share incentive payments out among all employees in the organisation or within individual business units. Team-based incentives have tended to get a better press in recent years than individual incentives, a major problem with the latter being their tendency to undermine teamworking in situations where it is an important contributor to competitive advantage (*see* Pfeffer 1998: 218–20 and Gerhart 2009: 232), but the different forms of incentive are by no means mutually exclusive. It is possible, for example, to reward a salesperson with three types of incentive, one from each level. The basic pay would thus be enhanced with commission calculated individually, with a performance-based payment made to all in his/her sales team to reflect excellent customer feedback, and finally with a profit-related bonus paid to all employees in the organisation. Indeed, the more recent research suggests that employers are increasingly mixing different types of incentive scheme so as to enable them to help meet a range of distinct organisational objectives. It is not at all uncommon, as a result, for more senior employees to have an opportunity to earn additional income from three or four different types of bonus, some individual, some group based, some leading to a pay rise, others resulting in a one-off bonus payment. The schemes themselves also appear to be becoming increasingly sophisticated and administratively complex (IDS 2005: 7; CIPD 2007: 15).

WINDOW ON PRACTICE

Peter and Patrick are sales consultants for a financial services company and both had business targets for a six-month period. Peter met his target comfortably and received the predetermined bonus of £6,000 for reaching on-target earnings. Patrick failed to reach his target because his sales manager boss left the company and poached two of Patrick's prime customers just before they signed agreements with Patrick, whose bonus was therefore £2,000 instead of £6,250.

Joanne was a sales consultant for the same company as Peter and Patrick. Before the sales manager left, he made over to her several promising clients with whom he had done considerable preparatory work and who were not willing to be 'poached' by his new employer. All of these signed agreements and one of them decided to increase the value of the deal tenfold without any reference to Joanne until after that decision was made, and without knowing that she was now the appropriate contact. Her bonus for the period was £23,400.

Henry is a production manager in a light engineering company with performance pay related to a formula combining output with value added. Bonus payments were made monthly in anticipation of what they should be. One of Henry's initiatives was to increase the gearing of the payment by results scheme in the factory. Through peculiarities of company accounting his bonus payments were 'justified' according to the formula, but later it was calculated that the production costs had risen by an amount that cancelled out the value-added benefits. Also 30 per cent of the year's output had to be recalled due to a design fault.

Patrick had his bonus made up to £6,250. Joanne had her bonus reduced to £8,000, but took legal advice and had the amount cut restored, whereupon Peter and Patrick both threatened to resign until mollified by ex gratia payments of £2,000 each. Peter resigned three months later. Henry was dismissed.

THE EXTENT TO WHICH INCENTIVES ARE PAID

There is conflicting evidence about how widespread incentive payments are in the UK and about whether or not they are becoming more or less common. Until 2005, each year the government's New Earnings Survey (published by the Office for National Statistics (ONS)) selected a sample of over 100,000 employees from across the country and asked their employers to fill in a form outlining their earnings in the previous tax year. One of the questions asked about incentive payments 'such as piecework, commission, profit sharing, productivity and other incentives/bonuses'. The survey results persistently showed that only around 15–20 per cent of employees were receiving such payments, most of which was accounted for by traditional piecework or payment-by-results systems operated in manufacturing organisations. The incidence of individual incentives paid to non-manual workers was low. Only around 10 per cent were recorded as receiving such payments in 2003 (ONS 2003). The New Earnings Survey has now been superseded by the Annual Survey of Hours and Earnings (ASHE) which no longer includes a general question about incentive payments. Instead it simply records the amount of earnings that are comprised of 'bonuses and commissions' in each payment period (i.e. each week or month). As a result, data about annual bonuses and pay rises that are linked to performance criteria are not captured.

In any event, other surveys have long painted a rather different picture. The authors analysing the 2004 Workplace Employment Relations Survey (Kersley *et al.* 2006: 190–1) concluded that around 40 of the workplaces in their sample operated either a payment by results or a merit pay incentive scheme, while 21 per cent operated some form of share-ownership scheme. Around 30 per cent paid profit-related bonuses to at least some employees. Even allowing for a strong degree of overlap between schemes as a result of employers operating different payment systems simultaneously, these figures suggest that incentive payments form at least some part of some people's reward packages in a majority of UK workplaces. The 2004 Employment Relations Survey also found evidence of substantial growth in the incidence of individual performance-related payment systems since the previous survey conducted in 1998. The CIPD's annual survey of reward practice covers a much smaller sample of employers, but it too suggests both high usage of incentives in the UK and considerably increased usage of incentives over recent years. In 2009 CIPD reported that 70 per cent of its respondents used 'cash-based/incentive plans'. Sixty-one per cent used individual-based schemes, 23 per cent used team-based schemes, while 56 per cent used schemes that 'are driven by business results'. While such approaches are used by a sizeable minority of employers in the public and voluntary sectors, it is in the private sector that activity is focused.

It is not easy to reconcile the diverse results produced by these surveys. One possibility is that the different results may reflect the different samples used. The ONS New Earnings Survey covered workplaces of all sizes, including the very smallest, while the others tend to focus on somewhat larger employers. It could therefore be the case that incentive schemes are largely used in bigger firms with more sophisticated management practices. Another possibility is that a high proportion of the schemes in operation reward employees with performance-based incremental payments (that is, a pay rise) rather than a one-off annual or monthly bonus. These would not have been picked up by the New Earnings Survey, which asked specifically about the amount of incentive payment received in the previous tax year. A further possibility is that many of the schemes in operation only apply to senior managers and not to the generality of staff. Either way, there is clear evidence of growth in the extent to which employers make use of incentive payment systems. Morever this is very much an international trend and one which is associated with all industrial sectors (Marginson 2009: 103; IRS 2009).

ACTIVITY 24.2

What other factors might account for the different results picked up by these surveys? How could a survey be designed which would give definitive information about the extent of incentive payments in the UK?

PAYMENT BY RESULTS SCHEMES

Historically, the most widely used incentive schemes have been those which reward employees according to the number of items or units of work they produce or the time they take to produce them. This approach is associated with F.W. Taylor and the phase in the development of personnel management described in Chapter 1 under the heading 'Humane bureaucracy'. Little attention has been paid to the operation of piecework schemes in recent years and there is some evidence to show that they are in decline, both in terms of the proportion of total pay which is determined according to PBR principles and in terms of the number of employees paid in this way (Bryson and Forth 2008: 499). However, PBR is still widely used in some shape or form by employers of manual workers, and it is apparent that new schemes are commonly introduced in manufacturing organisations (Cox 2006).

Individual time saving

It is rare for a scheme to be based on the purest form of piecework, a payment of X pence per piece produced, as this provides no security against external influences which depress output such as machine failure or delays in the delivery of raw materials. The most common type of scheme in use, therefore, is one where the incentive is paid for time saved in performing a specified operation. A standard time is derived for a work sequence and the employee receives an additional payment for the time saved in completing a number of such operations. If it is not possible to work due to shortage of materials or for some other reason, the time involved is not counted when the final total of time saved is calculated.

Standard times are derived by the twin techniques of method study and work measurement, which are the skills of the work study engineer. By study of the operation, the work study engineer decides what is the most efficient way to carry it out and then times an operator actually doing the job over a period, so as to measure the 'standard time'. Work-measured schemes of this kind have, however, been subject to a great deal of criticism and are only effective where people are employed on short-cycle manual operations with the volume of output varying between individuals depending on their skill or application.

The main difficulty, from the employee's point of view, is the fluctuation in earnings that occurs as a consequence of a varying level of demand for the product. If the fluctuations are considerable then the employees will be encouraged to try to stabilise them, either by pressing for the guaranteed element to be increased, or by storing output in the good times to prevent the worst effects of the bad, or by social control of high-performing individuals to share out the benefits of the scheme as equally as possible.

Measured daywork

To some people the idea of measured daywork provides the answer to the shortcomings of individual incentive schemes. Instead of employees receiving a variable payment in accordance with the output achieved, they are paid a fixed sum as long as they maintain a predetermined and agreed level of working. Employees thus have far less discretion over the amount of effort they expend. Theoretically, this deals with the key problem of other schemes by providing for both stable earnings and stable output instead of 'as much as you can, if you can'.

The advantage of measured daywork over time-saving schemes, from the management point of view, is the greater level of management control that is exercised. The principal disadvantage is the tendency for the agreed level of working to become a readily achievable norm which can only be increased after negotiation with workforce representatives.

Group and plant-wide incentives

Sometimes the principles of individual time saving are applied to group rather than individual output to improve group performance and to promote the development of teamworking. Where jobs are interdependent, group incentives can be appropriate, but they may also put great pressure on the group members, aggravating any interpersonal animosity that exists and increasing the likelihood of stoppages for industrial action. Group schemes can also severely reduce the level of management control by allowing the production group to determine output according to the financial needs of individual group members.

A variant on the group incentive is the plant-wide bonus scheme, under which all employees in a plant or other organisation share in a pool bonus that is linked to the level of output, the value added by the employees collectively or some similar formula. The attraction of these methods lies in the fact that the benefit to the management of the organisation is 'real' because the measurement is made at the end of the process, rather than, as is more usual, at different points within the process, whereby wages and labour costs can go up while output and profitability both come down. Theoretically, employees are also more likely to identify with the organisation as a whole, they will cooperate more readily with the management and each other, and there is even an element of workers' control. The difficulties lie in the fact that there is no tangible link between individual effort and individual reward, so that those who are working effectively can have their efforts nullified by others working less effectively or by misfortunes elsewhere.

Commission

The payment of commission on sales is a widespread practice about which surprisingly little is known as these schemes have not come under the same close scrutiny as incentive schemes for manual employees. They suffer from most of the same drawbacks as manual incentives, except that they are linked to business won rather than to output achieved.

ACTIVITY 24.3

A problem with sales commission is its tendency to reward the quantity of goods sold without having regard to the quality of service provided by sales staff. In which circumstances might this have negative consequences? How could a commission-based incentive scheme be adapted to incorporate measures of quality as well as quantity?

DISADVANTAGES OF PBR SCHEMES

The whole concept of payment by results was set up to cope with a stable and predictable situation, within the boundaries of the workplace. External demands from customers were irritations for others – such as sales representatives – to worry about. The factory was the arena, the juxtaposed parties were the management on the one hand and the people doing the work on the other, and the deal was output in exchange for cash. The dramatic changes of the past 20 years, which have swept away stability, dismantled the organisational boundary and enthroned the customer as arbiter of almost everything have also made PBR almost obsolete.

According to the ONS New Earnings Survey the proportion of manual workers receiving PBR payments steadily declined between 1983 and 2003, and there is every reason to believe that this decline has continued in the years since (Bryson and Forth 2008: 499). This trend can be explained, in part, by changing technologies and changes in working practices. A payment system that puts the greatest emphasis on the number of items produced or on the time taken to produce them is inappropriate in industries where product quality is of greater significance than product quantity. Similarly a manufacturing company operating a just-in-time system will rely too heavily on overall plant performance to benefit from a payment scheme that primarily rewards individual effort.

In addition to the problem of fluctuating earnings, described above, there are a number of further inherent disadvantages which explain the decline of PBR-based remuneration arrangements.

Operational inefficiencies

For incentives to work to the mutual satisfaction of both parties, there has to be a smooth operational flow, with materials, job cards, equipment and storage space all readily available exactly when they are needed, and an insatiable demand for the output. Seldom can these conditions be guaranteed and when they do exist they seldom last without snags. Raw materials run out, job cards are not available, tools are faulty, the stores are full, customer demand is fluctuating or there is trouble with the computer. As soon as this sort of thing happens the incentive-paid worker has an incentive either to fiddle the scheme or to negotiate its alteration for protection against operational vagaries.

Quality of work

The stimulus to increase volume of output can adversely affect the quality of output, as there is an incentive to do things as quickly as possible. If the payment scheme is organised so that only output meeting quality standards is paid for, there may still be the tendency to produce expensive scrap. Operatives filling jars with marmalade may break the jars if they work too hurriedly. This means that the jar is lost and the marmalade as well, for fear of glass splinters.

Renewed emphasis on quality and customer satisfaction mean that employers increasingly need to reward individuals with the most highly developed skills or those who are most readily adaptable to the operation of new methods and technologies. PBR, with its emphasis on the quantity of items produced or sold, may be judged inappropriate for organisations competing in markets in which the quality of production is of greater significance than previously.

The quality of working life

There is also a danger that PBR schemes may demotivate the workforce and so impair the quality of working life for individual employees. In our industrial consciousness PBR is associated with the worst aspects of rationalised work: routine, tight control, hyper-specialisation and mechanistic practices. The worker is characterised as an adjunct to the machine, or as an alternative to a machine. Although this may not necessarily be the case, it is usually so, and generally expected. Payment by results in this way reinforces the mechanical element in the control of working relationships by failing to reward employee initiative, skills acquisition or flexibility. There is also evidence to suggest that achieving high levels of productivity by requiring individuals to undertake the same repetitive tasks again and again during the working day increases stress levels and can make some employees susceptible to repetitive strain injuries.

The selective nature of the incentive

Seldom do incentive arrangements cover all employees. Typically, groups of employees are working on a payment basis which permits their earnings to be geared to their output, while their performance depends on the before or after processes of employees not so rewarded, such as craftsmen making tools and fixtures, labourers bringing materials in and out, fork-lift truck drivers, storekeepers and so forth.

The conventional way round the problem is to pay the 'others' a bonus linked to the incentive earned by those receiving it. The reasoning for this is that those who expect to earn more (such as the craftspeople) have a favourable differential guaranteed as well as an interest in high levels of output, while that same interest in sustaining output is generated in the other employees (such as the labourers and the storekeepers) without whom the incentive earners cannot maintain their output levels. The drawbacks are obvious. The labour costs are increased by making additional payments to employees on a non-discriminating basis, so that the storekeeper who is a hindrance to output will still derive benefit from the efforts of others, and the employees whose efforts are directly rewarded by incentives feel that the fruits of their labour are being shared by those whose labours are not so directly controlled.

Obscurity of payment arrangements

Because of these difficulties, incentive schemes are constantly modified or refined in an attempt to circumvent fiddling or to get a fresh stimulus to output, or in response to employee demands for some other type of change. This leads to a situation in which the employees find it hard to understand what behaviour by them leads to particular results in payment terms. This same obscurity is often found in the latest fashion in PRP. In an unpublished study comparing performance management in two blue-chip companies, less than half the people in management posts claimed to understand how the payments were calculated. Many of those actually misunderstood their schemes!

PERFORMANCE-RELATED PAY

Arguments about the advantages and disadvantages of individual PRP have been some of the most hotly contested in recent decades. The topic has formed the basis of numerous research studies and remains one which attracts much controversy, as was shown in recent debates about the introduction of PRP for teachers working in state schools. The main reason is the apparent contrast between the theoretical attractiveness of such systems – at least from a management perspective – and their supposed tendency to disappoint when operated in practice. While there are many different types of scheme available, all involve the award of a pay rise or bonus payment to individual employees following a formal assessment of their performance over a defined period (normally the previous year). Two distinct varieties of scheme can be identified.

1 **Merit-based systems** simply involve the immediate supervisor undertaking an appraisal of each subordinate's work performance during the previous year. This will typically be done following a formal appraisal interview and often requires the completion of standard documentation drawn up by an HR department. A proportion of future remuneration is then linked to a score derived from the supervisor's assessment. Some systems require supervisors to award a percentage mark against different criteria, while others oblige them to assess individual performance as 'excellent', 'good', 'satisfactory' or 'inadequate'. Merit-based systems are generally regarded as unsatisfactory because they allow considerable scope for assessors to make subjective judgements or to allow personal prejudice to colour their assessments. There is also a tendency to give undue weight to recent events at the expense of achievements taking place early in the appraisal period.

2 **Goal-based systems** are more objective, but are not appropriate for all kinds of job. They are, however, particularly well suited for the assessment of managerial work. Here the supervisor and subordinate meet at the start of the appraisal period and agree between them a list of objectives which the appraisee will seek to meet during the coming months. Examples would be the completion of particular projects, the establishment of new initiatives, undertaking a course of training or making substantial progress towards the solving of a problem. Many employers nowadays seek to link individual objectives directly to defined organisational goals for the year as a means of reinforcing their significance and ensuring that all are pulling in the same direction. At the end of the year the employee is assessed on the basis of which objectives have or have not been met. A score is then derived and a bonus payment or pay rise awarded. Where performance in a job can meaningfully be assessed in this way, such systems are recommended because they are reasonably objective and straightforward to score. Where the nature of the job involves the consistent achievement of a defined level of performance, and cannot usefully be assessed in terms of the achievement of specific objectives, the goal-based approach has less to offer. It may still be possible to assess part of the job in this way, but there will also have to be a merit-based element if the appraisal is to reflect all of a person's activity during the appraisal period.

ACTIVITY 24.4

Make a list of five jobs that you consider would be best rewarded by a merit-based system and five more that are best rewarded via the goal-based approach.

The attractions of PRP

It is not difficult to see why PRP has attracted the interest of managers, consultants and government ministers. Its theoretical attractions are considerable and include the following:

- attracting and retaining good performers;
- improving individual and corporate performance;
- clarifying job roles and duties;
- improving communication;
- improving motivation;
- reinforcing management control;
- identifying developmental objectives;
- reinforcing the individual employment relationship at the expense of the collective;
- rewarding individuals without needing to promote them.

In short, PRP aims to provide a flexible and cost-effective means of distributing rewards fairly between the good and poorer performers while also contributing towards improved organisation performance. Moreover, it is based on principles to which most people, employees as well as managers, seem to adhere (Brown and Armstrong 2000: 11–13). Most of us are very happy to see individuals rewarded for superior performance and/or effort and would like payment decisions to be based on such criteria. The problems arise when attempts are made to put the principles into practice. A system which is fair and objective in theory can easily fail to achieve these objectives when implemented.

Critiques of PRP

Performance-related pay attracted a great amount of criticism from academic researchers in the 1980s and 1990s during a period when its virtues were frequently asserted by HR managers and consultants. The attacks came from several quarters. Occupational psychologists tended to question the ability of PRP to motivate positively (e.g. Kohn 1993), while sociologists saw it as a means of reinforcing management control at the expense of worker autonomy (e.g. Hendry *et al.* 2000). A further source of criticism has come from those who suspect that PRP is used as a means of perpetuating gender inequality in payment matters (e.g. Rubery 1995). However, the most colourful and damning criticisms have come from management thinkers such as W. Edwards Deming who advocate Total Quality Management approaches and for whom PRP represents exactly the wrong kind of initiative to introduce. The whole basis of their philosophy is the substitution of 'leadership' for 'supervision', removing organisational hierarchies and managing people with as little direction and control as possible. They see PRP as having the opposite effect. It reinforces the hierarchy, enhances the power of supervisors and strengthens management control. For many critics, including those cited above, PRP has fundamental flaws which cannot be overcome. Kohn, for example, argues that incentives can only succeed in securing temporary compliance. Their use cannot change underlying attitudes, while the attempt to do so ultimately damages the long-term health of an organisation by undermining relationships and encouraging employees to focus on short-term aims: Managers who insist that the job will not get done properly without rewards have failed to offer a convincing argument for behavioural manipulation. Promising a reward to someone who appears unmotivated is a bit like offering salt water to someone who is thirsty. Bribes in the workplace simply cannot work (Kohn 1993: 60).

A second stream of criticism is more moderate, arguing that PRP can have a role to play in organisations, but that its positive effects are limited. Moreover, they say, while not fundamentally flawed, PRP is very difficult to implement effectively in practice. As a result, systems fail as often as they succeed. The arguments are summarised well by Gomez-Mejia and Balkin (1992: 249–55), Cannell and Wood (1992: 66–101), Pfeffer (1998: 203–4), Purcell (2000) and more recently by Armstrong and Brown (2009: 47–9) and Gerhart (2009) The major points made by these authors are as follows:

- Employees paid by PRP, especially where the incentive is substantial, tend to develop a narrow focus to their work. They concentrate on those aspects which they believe will initiate payments, while neglecting other parts of their jobs.
- PRP, because of its individual nature, tends to undermine teamworking. People focus on their own objectives at the expense of cooperation with colleagues.
- PRP, because it involves managers rating employees according to their perceptions of performance, can lead to a situation in which a good proportion of staff are demotivated when they receive their rating.
- Employees are rarely in a position wholly to determine the outcomes of their own performance. Factors outside their control play an important role, leading to a situation in which the achievement or non-achievement of objectives is partially a matter of chance.
- Even the most experienced managers find it difficult to undertake fair and objective appraisals of their employees' performance. Subjective judgements are often taken into account leading to perceptions of bias. Some managers deliberately manipulate ratings for political reasons, allowing their judgement to be coloured by the effect they perceive the outcome will have on particular employees. Low ratings are thus avoided, as are very high ratings, where it is perceived that these will lead to disharmony or deterioration of personal relationships.
- In organisations subject to swift and profound change, objectives set for the coming year may become obsolete after a few months. Employees then find themselves with an incentive to meet goals which are no longer priorities for the organisation.
- PRP systems tend to discourage creative thinking, the challenging of established ways of doing things and a questioning attitude among employees.
- Budgetary constraints often lead managers to reduce ratings, creating a situation in which excellent individual performance is not properly rewarded.
- It is difficult to ensure that all line managers take a uniform approach to the rating of their subordinates. Some tend to be more generously disposed in general than others, leading to inconsistency and perceptions of unfairness.
- When the results of performance appraisal meetings have an impact on pay levels, employees tend to downplay their weaknesses. As a result development needs are not discussed or addressed.

- PRP systems invariably increase the paybill. This occurs because managers fear demotivating their staff by awarding low or zero rises in the first years of a system's operation. Poorer performers are thus rewarded as well as better performers.
- PRP systems can be too successful, leading people to take unecessary risks or to act recklessly in order to secure higher rewards.

WINDOW ON PRACTICE

One of the fundamental problems associated with PRP derives from the so-called 'Lake Wobegon Effect' (Guthrie 2007: 350). The label derives from the words the great American humourist Garrison Keillor uses each week on his radio show when completing his monologue about the goings on in his fictional, but archetypal, small rural town:

> And that's the news from Lake Wobegon where all the women are strong, all the men are good looking, and all the children are above average.

Just as it is not mathematically possible for all children to be 'above average', nor is it possible for all employees to be so. Yet whenever people are asked to rate their own performance they have a very strong tendency to rate themselves as being 'above average'. The inevitable consequence is a situation in which most employee ratings of their own performance are considerably higher than those of their managers. The result is disappointment when manager ratings are revealed, and a tendency for most people to be demotivated.

Using PRP effectively

Despite the problems described above it is possible to implement PRP successfully, as is shown by the experience of case study companies quoted by Brown and Armstrong (2000), IRS (2005a, 2005b) and IDS (2005). It will only work, however, if it is used in appropriate circumstances and if it is implemented properly. Part of the problem with PRP has been a tendency in the HR press to portray it as universally applicable and as a panacea capable of improving performance dramatically. In fact it is neither, but is one of a range of tools that have a useful if limited role to play in some situations. Gomez-Mejia and Balkin (1992) specify the following favourable conditions:

- Where individual performance can be objectively and meaningfully measured.
- Where individuals are in a position to control the outcomes of their work.
- Where close teamworking or cooperation with others is not central to successful job performance.
- Where there is an individualistic organisational culture.

A consensus now appears to be emerging in support of the view that PRP does not generally work as well in the public sector as it does in the private sector (OECD 2005;

Prentice *et al.* 2007). Only a minority of public sector workers appear to be motivated positively by PRP, while some groups find that it actively undermines their motivation simply because they are not primarily motivated by pay. Introducing PRP thus cuts across the established professional culture and is not compatible with their perceptions of 'the public sector ethos'. By contrast PRP does seem to fit better with cultures in some of the growing private sector industries. Armstrong and Brown (2009) focus particularly on knowledge-intensive work and on customer service, finding in both cases that the circumstances are often, if not always, suited to individualised rewards such as PRP.

Brown and Armstrong (2000) also point to the importance of careful implementation and lengthy preparation prior to the installation of a scheme. Moreover, they argue that PRP should not be looked at or judged in isolation from other forms of reward, both extrinsic and intrinsic. Success or failure can hinge on what else is being done to maximise motivation, to develop people and to improve their job security.

Ultimately PRP has one great advantage which no amount of criticism can remove: it helps ensure that organisational priorities become individual priorities. Managers can signal the importance of a particular objective by including it in a subordinate's goals for the coming year. If the possibility of additional payment is then tied to its achievement, the chances that the objective concerned will be met increases significantly. Organisational performance is improved as a result. Where the achievement of such specific objectives forms a relatively minor part of someone's job, PRP can form a relatively minor part of their pay packet. Other rewards can then be used to recognise other kinds of achievement.

WINDOW ON PRACTICE

Many job descriptions for supervisory positions include reference to responsibility for ensuring that the appropriate health and safety at work regulations are adhered to. Few supervisors, however, left to themselves would see this aspect of their work as a priority. In one organisation known to the authors it was decided to try to raise the profile of health and safety issues by including objectives in this field into managers' annual performance targets. It therefore became clear that the level of PRP in the following year would, in part, be determined by the extent to which the health and safety objectives had been met. The result was the swift establishment of departmental health and safety committees and schemes whereby staff could bring safety hazards to the attention of supervisors.

SKILLS-BASED PAY

A further kind of incentive payment scheme is one which seeks to reward employees for the skills or competencies which they acquire. It is well established in the United States and became fashionable in the UK during the 1990s and early 2000s. Since then interest has waned, most recent texts on reward management paying it relatively little attention. It is most useful as a means of rewarding technical staff, but there is no reason why the principle should not be extended to any group of employees for whom the acquisition of additional skills might benefit the organisation. There are several potential benefits for an employer introducing a skills-based pay scheme. Its most obvious effect is to encourage multiskilling and flexibility, enabling the organisation to respond more effectively and speedily to the needs of customers. A multiskilled workforce may also be slimmer and less expensive. In addition it is argued that, in rewarding skills acquisition, a company will attract and retain staff more effectively than its competitors in the labour market. The operation of a skills-based reward system is proof that the sponsoring employer is genuinely committed to employee development.

Most skills-based payment systems reward employees with additional increments to their base pay once they have completed defined skill modules. A number of such schemes are described in detail in a study published by Incomes Data Services (1992). Typical is the scheme operated by Venture Pressings Ltd where staff are employed on four basic grades, each divided into ten increments. Employees progress up the scale by acquiring specific skills and demonstrating proficiency in them to the satisfaction of internal assessors. New starters are also assessed and begin their employment on the incremental point most appropriate to the level of skills they can demonstrate. In many industries it is now possible to link payment for skills acquisition directly to the attainment of National Vocational Qualifications (NVQs) for which both the setting of standards and the assessment of individual competence are carried out externally.

A skills-based pay system will only be cost effective if it results in productivity increases which are sufficient to cover the considerable costs associated with its introduction and maintenance. A business can invest a great deal of resources both in training its workforce to attain new skills, and in rewarding them once those skills have been acquired, only to find that the cost of the scheme outweighs the benefit gained in terms of increased flexibility and efficiency. Furthermore, in assisting employees to become more highly qualified and in many cases to gain NVQs, an employer may actually find it harder to retain its staff in relatively competitive labour markets.

The other major potential disadvantage is associated with skills obsolescence. Where a business operates in a fast-moving environment and needs to adapt its technology regularly, a skills-based payment system can leave the organisation paying enhanced salaries for skills which are no longer significant or are not required at all. Employers seeking to introduce skills-based systems of payment therefore need to consider the implications very carefully and must ensure that they only reward the acquisition of those skills which will clearly contribute to increased productivity over the long term.

ACTIVITY 24.5

A number of commentators praise skills-based pay as a system which avoids some of the pitfalls associated with PRP schemes. Look back at the list of practical problems with PRP schemes above and consider which do and which do not apply to skills-based incentive systems.

PROFIT SHARING

There are a number of different ways in which companies are able to link remuneration to profit levels. In recent decades governments all over the world have sought to encourage such schemes and have actively promoted their establishment with advantageous tax arrangements. The European Union has been particularly interested in promoting schemes of this type. Underlying government support is the belief that linking pay to profits increases the employee's commitment to his or her company by deepening the level of mutual interest. As a result, it is argued that such schemes act as an incentive encouraging employees to work harder and with greater flexibility in pursuit of higher levels of take-home pay. Other potential advantages for employers and governments described by Pendleton (2009) are better cost flexibility, changed attitudes on the part of employees and the discouragement of union membership.

Cash-based schemes

The traditional and most common profit-sharing arrangement is simply to pay employees a cash bonus, calculated as a proportion of annual profits, on which the employee incurs both an income tax and a national insurance liability. Some organisations pay discretionary profit bonuses on this basis, while others allocate a fixed proportion of profits to employees as a matter of policy. **Gainsharing** is a variation on cash-based profit sharing which is widely used in the USA and which can be used in non-profit-making organisations as well as those operating in the commercial sector. Here the bonus relates to costs saved rather than profit generated in a defined period. So if a workforce successfully achieves the same level of output at lower overall cost, the gain is shared between employer and employees.

Between 1987 and 2000 the government operated an approved profit-related pay scheme which became increasingly popular. By 1996 there were over 14,000 schemes in operation, covering 3.7 million employees. The attraction was the ability profit-related pay schemes gave employers to award pay rises to all employees, while recouping the cost through tax concessions. The scheme was phased out and has now been replaced by the Share Incentive Plan (*see* below).

Share-based schemes

There are several methods of profit sharing which involve employees being awarded shares rather than cash. Here too there are government-sponsored schemes in operation which involve favourable tax treatment. There are several distinct schemes available for employers to use some of which are more tax efficient than others. Traditionally senior managers have been paid, in part, through share-based reward systems, but companies are increasingly seeing an advantage in extending these arrangements to a greater proportion of their staff. The purpose is to increase commitment by giving employees a significant financial stake in the future of the business for which they work, at the same time helping to align employees' interests with those of shareholders. The result should be improved staff retention and higher levels of individual performance, but it is difficult to prove that such outcomes result in practice from the introduction of these schemes. For most ordinary employees the level of reward is too low and the extent to which their actions impact on a firm's performance too indirect, for there to be a clear-cut incentive effect. Cohen (2006) and IDS (2007) provide concise and clear guides to the whole range of systems. The two most common are the following:

1. **Savings-Related Share Option** schemes permit companies to grant share options to directors and employees in a tax-effective manner. This means that they are given the opportunity to buy shares in their own companies at a future date, but at the current price. The hope is that the value will have increased in the meantime, allowing the purchaser to cash in a tidy profit. This particular government-sponsored scheme requires participants to put between £5 and £250 of their monthly pay aside and then to use the proceeds of the accumulated fund, after three, five or seven years, to buy shares at a discount of 20 per cent of the price they were when the plan started. The scheme is popularly known as 'save as you earn' or 'sharesave'.
2. **Inland Revenue Approved Share Incentive Plans** (previously called All-Employee Share Schemes) allow employees to obtain shares in their own companies while avoiding tax and national insurance contributions. Employers can give such shares to employees to a maximum value of £3,000 per year. Some can be given in recognition of individual or team performance, making it possible to award some employees more shares than others. Where employees subsequently hold these shares for three years or more, there is no tax liability when they are sold. In addition, under the scheme, employees can buy up to a further £1,500 worth of shares out of pre-tax income and subsequently avoid a proportion of the tax owed when they are sold. Companies are also allowed to give 'free' matching shares for each share purchased by an employee under the scheme. Employers as well as employees gain tax advantages from operating these schemes. Deductions in corporation tax can be made equivalent to the amount of salary used by employees to purchase shares, as well as monies used in establishing and operating the scheme.

Disadvantages of profit-related schemes

The obvious disadvantage of the schemes described above from the employee's point of view is the risk that pay levels may decline if the company fails to meet its expected profit levels. If no profit is made it cannot be shared. Share values can go down as well as up. Companies are not permitted to make guarantees about meeting payments and will have their schemes revoked by the Inland Revenue if they do so. In any event it is likely that profit-based incentives will vary in magnitude from year to year.

For these reasons it is questionable to assert that profit-sharing schemes do in fact act as incentives. Unlike PRP awards they do not relate specifically to the actions of the individual employee. Annual profit levels are clearly influenced by a whole range of factors which are both internal and external to the company. An employee may well develop a community of interest with the company management, shareholders and other employees but it is unlikely seriously to affect the nature of his or her work. Furthermore, both poor and good performers are rewarded equally in profit-related schemes. The incentive effect will therefore be very slight in most cases and will be restricted to a general increase in employee commitment.

SUMMARY PROPOSITIONS

24.1 Incentive schemes should be used where they are appropriate to the needs of the business and where they can clearly contribute to the achievement of organisational objectives.

24.2 The extent to which different types of incentive arrangement are used in the UK is unclear. There is evidence of growth in recent years, but the majority of employees are not covered by such schemes.

24.3 Methods of payment by results include individual time saving, group incentives, measured daywork, plant-wide schemes, productivity schemes and commission.

24.4 Performance-related pay systems are either merit based or goal based. They have been the subject of notable debate in recent years, many researchers finding a mismatch between their theoretical attractions and practical outcomes.

24.5 Skills-based pay involves linking incentives to the achievement of defined competencies or qualifications. It rewards what people bring to the job rather than the results of their efforts.

24.6 Profit sharing has been promoted by governments for many years. The Share Incentive Plan is the latest attempt to encourage employees to hold shares in their own companies.

GENERAL DISCUSSION TOPICS

1 What are the relative advantages of: (a) a system of straight salary that is the same each month, and (b) a system of salary with an individual performance-related addition so that the total payment each month varies?

2 In what circumstances might it be appropriate to base individual payment on team performance?

3 What do you think about Peter, Patrick, Joanne and Henry in the Window on practice box early in this chapter?

FURTHER READING

Brown, D. and Armstrong, M. (2000) *Paying or Contribution: Real performance-related pay strategies*. London: Kogan Page.

Kohn, A. (1993) 'Why incentive plans cannot work', *Harvard Business Review*, September–October, pp. 54–63.

The debate about the merits of individual performance-related pay is so polarised that it is rare to find a balanced account that sets out the views of those who are for and those who are against. It is best to read the partisan accounts. Kohn's (1993) article contains an eloquent and damning critique of such schemes, while Brown and Armstrong (2000) paint a more positive picture.

Incomes Data Services: various publications.
Industrial Relations Services: various publications.
Information about trends in the design of incentive payment schemes is regularly provided in the IDS and IRS publications. They also commonly feature case studies which show exactly how the various schemes operate in practice as well as regular surveys of current practice that can be used for benchmarking processes.

Gerhart, B. (2009) is a very good, comprehensive summary of academic research on incentives of all kinds, reviewing the major studies and reaching sound, balanced conclusions.

REFERENCES

Armstrong, M. and Brown, D. (2009) *Strategic Reward: Implementing more effective reward management*. London: Kogan Page.

Bartol, K.M. and Durham, C.C. (2000) 'Incentives: Theory and Practice', in C. Cooper and E. Locke (eds), *Industrial and Organizational Psychology*. Oxford: Blackwell.

Brown, D. and Armstrong, M. (2000) *Paying for Contribution: Real performance-related pay strategies*. London: Kogan Page.

Bryson, A. and Forth, J. (2008) 'The theory and practice of pay setting', in P. Blyton, N. Bacon, J. Fiorito and E. Heery (eds), *The Sage Handbook of Industrial Relations*. London: Sage.

Cadsby, C., Song, F. and Tapon, F. (2007) 'Sorting and incentive effects of pay-for-performance: an experimental investigation', *Academy of Management Journal*, Vol. 37, pp. 554–79.

Cannell, M. and Wood, S. (1992) *Incentive Pay: Impact and evolution*. London: IPM.

CIPD (2007) *Reward Management: Annual Survey Report 2007*. London: CIPD.

CIPD (2009) *Reward Management: Annual Survey Report 2009*. London: CIPD.

Cohen, S. (2006) *Employee Share Plans: Supporting business performance*. London: CIPD.

Corby, S., White, G. and Stanworth, C. (2005) 'No news is good news? Evaluating new pay systems', *Human Resource Management Journal*, Vol. 15, No. 1, pp. 4–24.

Cox, A. (2006) 'The outcomes of variable pay systems: tales of multiple costs and unforeseen consequences', *International Journal of Human Resource Management*, Vol. 16, No. 8, pp. 1475–97.

Gerhart, B. (2009) 'Compensation', in J. Storey, P. Wright and D. Ulrich (eds), *The Routledge Companion to Strategic Human Resource Management*. London: Routledge.

Gerhart, B. and Trevor, C. (2008) 'Merit pay', in A. Varma, P. Budhwar and A. DeNisi (eds), *Performance Management Systems: A global perspective*. London: Routledge.

Gielen, A.C., Kerkhofs, M.J.M. and Van Ours, J.C. (2006) *Performance-related Pay and Labor Productivity*. IZA Discussion Paper 2211. Berlin: Institute for the Study of Labor (IZA).

Gomez-Mejia, L. and Balkin, D. (1992) *Compensation, Organizational Strategy and Firm Performance*. Cincinnati: South Western Publishing.

Guthrie, J. (2007) 'Remuneration: Pay effects at work', in P. Boxall, J. Purcell and P. Wright (eds), *The Oxford Handbook of Human Resource Management*. Oxford: Oxford University Press.

Hendry, C., Woodward, S., Bradley, P. and Perkins, S. (2000) 'Performance and rewards: cleaning out the stables', *Human Resource Management Journal*, Vol. 10, No. 3, pp. 46–62.

Herzberg, F. (1966) *Work and the Nature of Man*. Cleveland: World Publishing.

Huselid, M. (1995) 'The impact of HRM practices on turnover, productivity and corporate performance', *Academy of Management Journal*, Vol. 38, No. 3, pp. 635–72.

IDS (1992) *Skills-based pay*, IDS Study No. 500. London: IDS.

IDS (2005) *Bonus Schemes*. IDS Study No. 794. London: Incomes Data Services.

IDS (2007) *Share Incentive Plans*. IDS Study No. 840. London: Incomes Data Services.

IRS (2005a) 'Pay 4 Performance at Yorkshire Water', *IRS Employment Review*, No. 833, pp. 31–5.

IRS (2005b) 'Performing flexible reward at Severn Trent Water', *IRS Employment Review*, No. 834, pp. 30–3.

IRS (2009) 'Charity employers are turning to performance-related pay', *IRS Employment Review*, No. 914, January.

Kersley, B., Alpin, C., Forth, J., Bryson, A., Bewley, H., Dix, G. and Oxenbridge, S. (2006) *Inside the Workplace: Findings from the 2004 Workplace Employment Relations Survey*. Abingdon: Routledge.

Kohn, A. (1993) 'Why incentive plans cannot work', *Harvard Business Review*, September–October, pp. 54–63.

Lazear, E.P. (2000) 'Performance pay and productivity', *American Economic Review*, Vol. 90, No. 5, pp. 1346–61.

Makinson, J. (2000) *Incentives for Change*. London: HMSO.

Marginson, P. (2009) 'Performance pay and collective bargaining: a complex relationship', in S. Corby, S. Palmer and E. Lindop (eds), *Rethinking Reward*. Basingstoke: Palgrave.

Marsden, D. (2004) 'The role of performance-related pay in renegotiating the "effort bargain": the case of the British public service', *Industrial and Labor Relations Review*, Vol. 57, No. 3, pp. 350–70.

OECD (2005) *Performance-related Pay Policies for Government Employees*. Paris: OECD.

Office for National Statistics (2003) *New Earnings Survey*. London: HMSO.

Office for National Statistics (2009) *Annual Survey of Hours and Earnings*. London: ONS.

Pearce, J.L., Stevenson, W.B. and Perry, J.L. (1985) 'Managerial compensation based on organizational performance: a time series analysis of the effects of merit pay', *Academy of Management Journal*, Vol. 28, pp. 261–78.

Pendleton, A. (2009) 'Employee share ownership in Europe', in S. Corby, S. Palmer and E. Lindop (eds), *Rethinking Reward*. Basingstoke: Palgrave.

Pfeffer, J. (1998) *The Human Equation: Building profits by putting people first*. Boston: Harvard Business School Press.

Piekkola, H. (2005) 'Performance-related pay and firm performance in Finland', *International Journal of Manpower*, Vol. 7, No. 8, pp. 619–35.

Prentice, G., Burgess, S. and Propper, C. (2007) *Performance Pay in the Public Sector: A review of the issues and evidence*. London: Office of Manpower Economics.

Purcell, J. (2000) 'Pay per view', *People Management*, 3 February, pp. 41–3.

Rubery, J. (1995) 'Performance-related pay and the prospects for gender pay equity', *Journal of Management Studies*, Vol. 32, No. 5, pp. 637–54.

Sisson, K. and Storey, J. (2000) *The Realities of Human Resource Management*. Buckingham: Open University Press.

Thompson, M. (1992) *Pay and Performance: The employer experience*. Institute of Manpower Studies Report 218. London: IMS.

Thompson, M. (2000) 'Salary progression systems', in G. White and J. Druker (eds), *Reward Management: A critical text*. London: Routledge.

An extensive range of additional materials, including multiple choice questions, answers to questions and links to useful websites can be found on the Human Resource Management companion website at **www.pearsoned.co.uk/torrington**.

PENSIONS AND BENEFITS

THE OBJECTIVES OF THIS CHAPTER ARE TO:

1. Introduce the different types of pension scheme provided by the state, by employers and by financial services organisations
2. Explain the causes and significance of current trends in the provision of occupational pensions
3. Outline the roles played by HR professionals in the field of occupational pensions
4. Distinguish between statutory sick pay (SSP) and occupational sick pay (OSP)
5. Assess developments in the provision of company cars by UK employers
6. Explore the potential of flexible benefits systems in the UK context

Employee benefits commonly used to be known as 'fringe benefits', suggesting a peripheral role in the typical pay packet. The substantial growth in the value of most benefits packages over the past 20 or 30 years means that the title 'fringe' is no longer appropriate. An increasing proportion of individual remuneration is made up of additional perks, allowances and entitlements which are mostly paid in kind rather than cash. The total value of benefits 'paid' by employers to employees commonly represents between 20 per cent and 50 per cent of an organisation's salary budget, depending on what is included. Pensions alone can easily account for 20 per cent, to which must be added the costs of providing some or all of the following: company cars, sick pay, meals, live-in accommodation, parking facilities, private health insurance, crèche facilities, mobile phones, Christmas parties, staff discounts, relocation expenses and any holiday or maternity allowances paid in excess of the required statutory minima. Wright (2009a: 184) shows that these extra elements of pay are distributed unevenly between members of staff. Those earning at the top of the scale (especially directors and senior managers) tend to gain rather more than average employees, 30 per cent or 50 per cent of their take-home pay being accounted for by benefits of various kinds.

This is an area of HRM policy in which practice varies considerably from country to country. In the USA, for example, there is no legal entitlement to paid holiday and it is usual for people to take just two weeks leave in a year. Yet the extent and generosity of employer-provided private health insurance and pensions is as good as it is anywhere in the world. By contrast, in France holiday entitlements and redundancy payments are very generous, but pensions are rarely provided for most employees at all. In the UK statutory paid maternity leave and associated rights are the most generous in the world, have become increasingly generous in recent years and are still exceeded by many employers. Occupational pensions are in decline in the UK, but still cover many more employees than is the case in most European countries. Generally speaking, however, everywhere in the world the long-term trend is towards the provision of a wider range of benefits, and for this element of the total pay package to increase as a proportion of the whole.

Despite these developments, there remains doubt about the extent to which employees value the benefits provided to them by their employers or appreciate the extent of the costs involved in their provision. Surveys of both employers and employees regularly demonstrate that staff have little understanding of the value of the benefits they receive and that there is thus little by way of any positive motivational effect generated by their presence (*see* Accor 2008; Thomson Online 2007). This does not mean, of course, that employers can easily stop offering benefits. While the full cost may not be appreciated by employees, they are generally in favour of the benefits and would resent their removal. Poor publicity would also inevitably follow the withdrawal of rewards such as pensions which are generally seen as being the hallmark of a good employer. The alternative courses of action involve communicating the true value of benefits to employees more effectively and providing them with a degree of choice as to which benefits they wish to receive. The latter approach, involving the provision of 'flexible' or 'cafeteria' benefits, has become very common in the USA and has received a great deal of attention in the UK too. You will find further information and discussion exercises about the objectives of benefits strategies on this book's companion website at **www.pearsoned.co.uk/torrington**.

PENSIONS

The role of employers in providing pensions has moved up the public policy agenda for several reasons in recent years, but underlying all of them are the long-term demographic trends which have called into question the ability of the established UK pension system to provide an adequate income to older people after they retire. First and foremost, people are living increasingly longer and thus require a bigger pension to provide them with an income during their years of retirement. In 1950 men aged 65 in the UK could expect to live for a further 12 years on average, and women for a further 15. The figures are now over 19 years for men and 22 for women, and with rapid developments in medical science there is every reason to expect life expectancy rates to accelerate further in the coming 50 years. It is likely, according to many projections, that over half of the people born in the 1980s will live into their 90s and beyond. Second, fewer children are being born, birth rates in the UK having been at below replacement rates since the late 1960s (Pemberton *et al.* 2006: 4). These trends are soon going to lead to a steady increase in the **dependency ratio**, by which is meant the proportion of retired people vis-à-vis working people in the economy. At present in the UK 27 per cent of the adult population is aged over 65. By 2050 according to the Government Actuary, the proportion will be 48 per cent (Turner 2004: 4). Demographic trends are thus leading us steadily towards a situation in which the funding of adequate pensions using established approaches is going to become harder and harder to achieve. The trend for more young people to stay at school until the age of 18 and for many more to go on to university makes the problem more acute because it further reduces the proportion of the population which is economically active.

The UK is by no means unique in facing this long-term problem. Indeed, in many other industrialised countries the situation is worse because fertility rates are lower still and there is a tradition of greater reliance on the state to provide pension income than has hitherto been the case in the UK. Everywhere it is increasingly being realised that action needs to be taken now in order to avoid a future scenario in which either the elderly live in unacceptable poverty or taxation has to be increased to economically unsustainable levels in order to fund a decent level of state pension.

In the UK the situation has been made worse over the past 15 years by some most unwelcome trends in the occupational pensions sector. Until the 1990s the UK could boast that it had one of the most extensive and well-funded systems of occupational pension provision in the world. Well over half of the workforce were members of reasonably generous, well-funded occupational pension schemes provided for them by their employers, while millions of retired employees drew a substantial income from the schemes which supplemented their state pensions. This system was likened by commentators who drew international comparisons to the goose that laid the golden egg. It meant that the UK had a great deal less to worry about from population ageing than other countries because so much more of our pension income was sourced privately through both individual savings and these huge long-established occupational pension funds. Unfortunately, the goose has now stopped laying the golden eggs and the long-established system is in terminal decline. Employers are less likely to offer membership of occupational schemes than they were, and where they still do, it is on a less satisfactory financial basis when seen from the perspective of most employees. A combination of factors is responsible, but the core problem is the hugely increased costs that are now associated with the provision of good pensions for staff. This is due to taxation changes, to increased life expectancy and to the need to keep topping up pension funds whenever the stock market suffers falls of the kinds it has in recent years.

The government has responded to this situation in a way that most commentators have welcomed, although some argue that the plans that have been put in place do not go far enough. In 2002 Adair Turner (now Lord Turner), a former Director General of the Confederation of British Industry (CBI) was appointed by the Department for Work and Pensions to lead an extensive review of future pension provision in the UK. The Turner Commission has since produced three substantial reports setting out its findings and recommendations. The government accepted the vast majority of these and brought forward legislation in the form of the Pensions Act 2007 to encourage later retirement and significantly greater levels of saving into pension funds. It also makes important changes to the established state pension system which are aimed particularly at improving the position of women. At the same time other steps have been taken by the government to ease the pressures on the pension system caused by demographic trends. The equalisation of state pension ages between men and women is such a step, as in many respects is the recent substantial growth in immigration. Other measures include new incentives for people who are not working (e.g. single parents and early retirees) to re-enter the workforce.

ACTIVITY 25.1

The UK has always been unusual in having such a substantial occupational pensions sector. There is a similar system in the Netherlands and in the Republic of Ireland, but in most EU countries most employers see no reason why they should be involved in the provision of pensions. Why do you think these differences persist? What arguments would you advance to persuade a company based in an EU country of the need to offer occupational pensions to employees in a new UK subsidiary?

State schemes

The state runs two schemes: a basic scheme and the State Second Pension (S2P) scheme. Every employee is obliged to contribute a standard amount to the basic scheme, which currently provides an old age pension at the age of 65 for men and 60 for women. By 2020 the pensionable age for both men and women will be 65 and in the ten years prior to this date there will be a gradual phasing in of the new pensionable age for women. The Pensions Act 2007 pushes back the state pension age for men and women once equalisation has been achieved. It will increase to 66 from 2016, to 67 from 2034 and to 68 from 2044, but changes may in fact come in considerably earlier than this. The Act also states that from 2012 annual uprating of the basic state pension will be determined in line with growth in the average earnings of UK workers 'subject to affordability and the fiscal position'. At present the level of the pension goes up each year in line with prices.

Individuals earning above a 'low earnings threshold' determined by the government (£13,900 a year in 2010) makes payments towards S2P through their national insurance contributions. At present both contributions and the final pension are earnings related, but this position is planned to change over the coming decades. At the same time that the level of the basic state pension becomes earnings related, a flat rate for S2P will be phased in. It is anticipated that this process will be completed for people retiring after 2030.

The state pension schemes are organised on a pay-as-you-go basis. This means that there is no state pension fund as such, and the money that is paid to today's pensioners comes from today's taxes and national insurance contributions. The money that will be paid to today's contributors, when they become pensioners, will come not from the investment of their and their employers' contributions, but from the contributions of the workforce and their employers in the future. This is why there is growing concern about the ability of future governments to be able to fund state pensions for many more retired people, beyond a basic subsistence level.

Occupational schemes

The UK has had, for many years, one of the most extensive and effective systems of occupational pension provision in the world. According to the most recent government statistics, there are around 96,000 separate schemes in operation with combined assets worth approximately £800 billion. Just under ten million people are members of occupational pension schemes, while around eight million pensioners draw an income from their funds (Government Actuary 2006: 19). Although there has been some reduction recently in the proportion of the workforce covered by occupational pensions, they remain by far the most significant employee benefit in terms of their cost to employers.

Occupational schemes provide an additional retirement pension on top of the state pension, providing better and wider-ranging benefits than the state schemes and a great deal more flexibility. They are most often found in large organisations and the public sector, but some smaller organisations also run such schemes. Men and women have equal access to occupational schemes and, since 1990, have had to be treated equally in respect of all scheme rules. Yet, in spite of this, men and women continue to fare differently in terms of pensions benefits due to the typical pattern of women's employment being different from male patterns and women's longer average life expectancy. A higher proportion of managerial and professional workers have occupational pensions than other groups, unskilled workers being the least likely to be in schemes. It is no longer lawful for an employer to exclude part-time or temporary workers.

With the exception of one or two in the public sector, occupational schemes do not pay their pensioners in the pay-as-you-go manner operated by the state, but create a pension fund, which is managed separately from the business. The advantage of this is that should the organisation become bankrupt, the pension fund cannot be seized to pay debtors because it is not part of the company. The money in the pension fund is invested and held in trust for the employees of the company at the time of their retirement. However, where a company becomes insolvent at a time when its pension fund is in deficit, employees can lose all or part of their pensions. This has happened in one or two high-profile cases recently, leading the government to establish a central fund to provide a measure of compensation to those whose pensions are reduced as a result of their employer's insolvency.

Larger organisations traditionally administer their own pension funds through an investment or fund manager. The manager will plan how to invest the money in the fund to get the best return and to ensure that the money that is needed to pay pensions and other benefits will be available when required. An actuary can provide mortality tables and other statistical information in order to assist planning and must be hired regularly to carry out a formal actuarial assessment of the scheme's assets and liabilities. Smaller organisations tend to appoint an insurance company or a bank to administer their pension funds, and so use their expertise. Pension funds can be invested in a variety of different ways, and are often worth more than the market value of their sponsoring companies. As a result they have come to dominate investment on the stock market.

During the 1990s as the worth of stocks and shares increased, the typical pension fund found itself in surplus. It thus had more assets than it needed to pay its liabilities. As a result benefit levels were increased and many employers were able to enjoy lengthy 'contribution holidays', meaning that they did not have to put any money into their funds. In more recent years this position has changed radically as stock markets have fallen, life expectancy has risen, the amount of taxation levied on the funds has been increased and costly new regulations have been imposed. Many of the FTSE 100 companies (i.e. the largest in the country) have pension funds in deficit, the combined shortfall in 2009 amounting to £96 billion (Fletcher 2009). Occupational funds take three main forms.

Defined benefit schemes

Defined benefit schemes dominated in the final decades of the twentieth century, but the number of people with access to them has declined hugely in the past 10 years. Virtually all the public sector schemes still take this form, but 77 per cent of the private sector schemes have now been closed to new members (National Association of Pension Funds 2009). They remain operational only for the purposes of paying pensions to retired members and for the benefit of employees who joined before their closure. Here contributions are made into a single organisation-wide fund which is invested on behalf of members by a fund manager. Retired employees then draw a pension from the fund calculated according to a defined formula. Most defined benefit schemes take the final salary form, in which the value of the pension is determined by the level of salary being received by each individual at the time of retirement. In the private sector it is common for this to be calculated on a 'sixtieths' basis, whereby the retiree is paid an annual pension equivalent to 1/60th (1.67 per cent) of their final salary multiplied by the number of years' pensionable service they have completed. In the public sector it is usual for the figure to be based on 'eightieths', with a tax-free lump sum being paid in addition at the time of retirement. In either case the size of pension is heavily related to the length of scheme membership, the maximum pension payable equalling two-thirds of final salary. Examples of final salary calculations are given in Table 25.1.

Another form of defined benefit scheme bases the pension calculation on the average salary earned over a period of 5, 10 or 20 years prior to retirement rather than on pay in the final year. Unless most of someone's pensionable service has been spent earning close to the final salary level, such schemes are less generous than the final salary variety in terms of the amount of pension paid. High levels of inflation also reduce the value of pensions calculated on an average salary basis. The government has signalled that it wishes over time to convert some of the public sector schemes from the final salary to an average salary formula, while also removing the right enjoyed by many public sector workers to retire on a full pension at the age of 60. Such proposals have been met with

Table 25.1 Final salary schemes – examples of various contribution periods with a 1/60th and a 1/80th scheme

Sixtieths scheme	
Final salary	= £24,000
Contributions for 5 years	= 1/60 × 24,000 × 5
Pension	= £2,000 per year
Final salary	= £24,000
Contributions for 25 years	= 1/60 × 24,000 × 25
Pension	= £10,000 per year
Final salary	= £24,000
Contributions for 40 years	= 1/60 × 24,000 × 40
Pension	= £16,000 per year
Eightieths scheme	
Final salary	= £24,000
Contributions for 25 years	= 1/80 × 24,000 × 25
Pension	= £7,500 per year
Lump sum	= 3/80 × 24,000 × 25 = £22,500

strong resistance from the workers concerned and have led to instances of industrial action. However, in the future it is likely that further attempts will be made to move in this direction because the cost to the taxpayer of funding existing schemes is substantial and hard to justify when workers in the private sector are seeing the value of their occupational pensions fall and their retirement ages increase.

Most defined benefit schemes are contributory. This means that monies are paid into the fund on a regular basis by both the employer and the employee. In the case of employees the contribution is fixed as a percentage of salary (typically five per cent), a sum which is subject to tax relief. Employers, by contrast, are obliged only to pay in sufficient funds to ensure that the scheme remains solvent. When the pension fund is in surplus, as many were in the 1980s and 1990s, employers can take 'contribution holidays'. By contrast, when the fund is in deficit, the employer has to contribute whatever is necessary to ensure that assets are sufficient to meet possible liabilities. This means that the amount of employer contribution can vary considerably, year on year, in an unpredictable fashion. In 2009 contribution rates for employers were averaging over 20 per cent of salary (ACA 2009). However, employers, like employees, gain from tax relief on contributions paid.

In some industries, as well as parts of the public sector, it has been traditional for occupational pensions to be non-contributory. In such schemes the employee makes no contribution at all, but nonetheless draws a pension calculated according to the final salary. Civil servants benefit from this kind of arrangement, as do many employees in the banking and finance sectors. Defined benefit schemes also typically offer extra benefits such as ill-health pensions for those forced to retire early and death-in-service benefits for widows and widowers.

Defined contribution schemes

Defined contribution schemes (also known as money purchase schemes) are organised in a totally different way from defined benefit arrangements. There are no promises about what the final level of pension will be. Instead employees and employers both contribute a fixed percentage of current salary to these schemes, usually five per cent to eight per cent on a monthly basis. The pension benefits received are then entirely dependent on the money that has been contributed and the way that it has been invested. Where investments perform well, a good level of pension can be gained. Where investments are disappointing, the result is a low level of pension. Further uncertainty derives from the way that money purchase schemes result in the payment of a single lump sum to the employee when he/she retires. This is then used to buy an annuity from an insurance company from which a weekly or monthly income is paid for life. Annuity rates vary considerably from year to year, and there is also considerable variation between the deals offered by different providers. In essence this means that the risk associated with pension investments is carried by the employee in a defined contribution arrangement, rather than by the employer as in a final salary scheme. For this reason defined contribution schemes are generally less satisfactory than defined benefit schemes when seen from an employee's perspective. Investments have to perform unusually well while inflation remains low for a money purchase scheme to give an equivalent level of benefit. However, despite these drawbacks, money purchase schemes are more flexible and more easily transferable than defined benefit arrangements. For people changing jobs frequently or working on a self-employed basis for periods of time, particularly during the early years of a career, they can thus be a more attractive option.

In recent years there has been a strong trend away from defined benefit schemes and towards defined contribution provision. The majority of newly established schemes take the defined contribution form, while many organisations now offer only a money purchase scheme to new employees (Dobson and Horsfield 2009). The trend has coincided with a period in which long contribution holidays have come to an end and in which the amount of regulation to which defined benefit schemes are subject has increased substantially. Employers have thus taken the opportunity to reduce their own liabilities and to move to a form of provision which is more predictable financially from their point of view, but which is likely to pay a far lower level of pension to their employees when they retire.

Hybrid schemes

Hybrid schemes too are becoming more common, although as yet they represent a small minority of UK pension funds. These, in various different ways, combine elements of the defined benefit and defined contribution forms of provision. The most common form is the 'money purchase underpin' which is basically a final salary arrangement, but one which calculates pensions and transfer values on a money purchase basis where these are higher. Such schemes seek to combine the best aspects of both main types of scheme. They offer a generous, secure and predictable pension, but also incorporate the flexibility associated with defined contribution schemes.

In the USA some organisations have moved towards the provision of cash-balance pension plans which work on a final salary basis, but pay out a single lump sum at retirement rather than a monthly pension (Field *et al.* 2009: 185). The employee uses the money to purchase an annuity, so the level of pension received varies considerably depending on market rates at the time of retirement. Such schemes make the financial commitment more predictable from the employer perspective, but tend to result in lower pensions than a conventional final salary arrangement.

ACTIVITY 25.2

Which of these three types of occupational pension scheme would you find most attractive at the current stage in your career? Under what circumstances might you change your preference?

Group personal pensions

Since the 1980s there has been substantial growth in the market for personal pensions. Self-employed people have always used these, but increasingly as employers have withdrawn from occupational pensions, employees have had to start up personal pensions too. More general attention has been focused on this area due to increasing job mobility and the perceived greater portability of personal pensions. A personal pension is arranged, usually through an insurance company, and the individual pays regular amounts into his/her own 'pension fund' in the same way as with a company fund. The employer may also make a contribution to the fund, but at present very few employers have chosen to do so.

An alternative arrangement is a Group Personal Pension plan (GPP) set up by an employer instead of an occupational pension scheme. From a legal and taxation perspective a GPP is no different from any individual personal pension arrangement, but charges are lower because the employer is able to arrange a bulk discount. The scheme is administered by an insurance company, the employer making contributions as well as the employee. Pensions are calculated on the same basis as an occupational money purchase scheme, but tend to be less extensive because employees are responsible for paying some of the administrative charges. From an employee perspective a GPP is inferior to an occupational pension scheme, but is better than a situation in which no employer provision is made at all. Such arrangements are mainly entered into by small firms, but one or two big companies have also set them up in place of conventional occupational pensions. A key difference is that a GPP is contract based rather than trust based. This means that unlike an occupational pension there is no board of trustees appointed to oversee the running of the scheme; instead a contract is signed with an external provider.

Stakeholder pensions

A new form of government-sponsored pension arrangement, the stakeholder pension, was established in 2001. These are aimed primarily at the five million or so middle income earners (that is, those earning in the £15,000 to £25,000 a year range) who do not have access to an occupational scheme. The aim is to reduce the number of people in future decades who are reliant on state pensions for their retirement income. A stakeholder pension scheme can be operated by an employer, a financial services company or a trade union. They operate along money purchase lines and are regulated by established authorities. Charges are kept low because providers are obliged to follow minimum standards set by the government. Employers are not obliged to make contributions to a stakeholder pension, but must provide access to one through their payroll. If employees join a scheme, for example one provided by their trade union, the employer is therefore obliged to make deductions via the payroll out of pre-tax income. Views vary on whether or not the stakeholder scheme can be hailed as a success. Supporters point to the fact that over 1.4 million plans have now been set up, while critics stress that 80 per cent of these are 'designation only' which means that no money has actually been invested in them. Moreover, because many of the schemes which are being used are set up by employers to replace existing money purchase plans, it would seem that relatively few of the five million target group are actually benefiting in practice.

WINDOW ON PRACTICE

The Pensions Act 2007 includes very significant measures aimed at forcing both employees and employers to contribute to pension funds. Central is the concept of 'Personal Accounts' which will, once established, effectively make occupational pension provision of some kind available to all employees. The Act therefore substantially extends the principles underlying stakeholder pensions.

From 2012 employers who do not provide a superior occupational pension or GPP will be required to pay a contribution of three per cent of all employees' earnings between £5000 and £33,000 a year into a personal account. Employees will pay a contribution of four per cent, a further one per cent being paid in as a result of tax relief. Employees will be permitted to opt out, but they will be automatically enrolled by their employer either into an occupational scheme or the new personal accounts scheme. The latter will be commercially provided but will operate within strict government regulations.

OCCUPATIONAL PENSIONS AND HRM

While occupational pension schemes are governed by a board of trustees which includes member representatives, in most organisations the pensions manager and pensions department are part of the HR function. It is thus important that HR professionals are familiar with the types of scheme offered and the main operating rules so that they can give accurate and timely advice to staff and to potential recruits. They also need to be familiar with the regulatory environment for occupational pensions, which has changed considerably in recent years. Apart from new legislation outlawing discrimination on grounds of sex or against part-time and temporary staff, several other important regulatory changes have been made and new regulatory bodies established. The Pensions Act 1995 sets out in detail what information must be disclosed to scheme members on request and what must be sent to them automatically each year. The Act also requires all occupational funds to meet a defined minimum funding level so that they are always able to meet their liabilities in the event of the employing company being wound up. Moreover, strict restrictions are now placed on 'self-investment', making sure that fund assets cannot be invested in property or other business ventures controlled by the sponsoring organisation.

The Social Security Act 1985 put in place a series of measures to protect 'early leavers', ensuring that people who switch employers during their careers do not suffer substantial loss in the value of their pensions. Early leavers now have one of three options in making their pension arrangements when they begin work for a new employer. One option is to claim back the contributions that the individual has made into the former employer's pension scheme. Deductions are made in accordance with tax laws, and of course the employer's contribution is lost, but a substantial sum can be reinvested in the new employer's scheme or in a personal pension. Another alternative involves opting for a preserved pension. With a final salary scheme, if there were no inflation, and if the individual progressed very little up the career ladder, a preserved pension from an old employer plus a pension from the recent employer would equate well with the pension this person would have received had he/she been with the new employer for the whole period. However, if these conditions are not met, which in recent times they have not been, individuals who have had more than one employer lose out in the pension stakes. Past employers are required to revalue preserved pensions in line with inflation (to a maximum of five per cent), but the value of such a pension remains linked to the level of salary at the date of leaving.

The third option is usually preferable, but is only open to people who have completed two years' membership of a scheme. This involves the transfer of the pension from the old employer's fund into that of the new employer. The process is straightforward in the case of a money purchase scheme, because the worth of each person's pension is readily calculated. It is simply the value of the employee's contributions, plus those of the employer, together with funds accrued as a result of their investment. The process is more complicated in the case of a final salary scheme, the transfer value being calculated according to standard actuarial conventions which take account of the employee's age, length of pensionable service, level of salary at the time of leaving and the current interest rate. All things being equal, 'early leavers' still fare worse than 'stayers' in terms of final pensions, but the difference is a great deal less than used to be the case.

Apart from giving advice and taking overall responsibility for pensions issues, HR managers are concerned with determining their organisations' pension policy. Is an occupational pension to be offered? If so, what form should it take? What level of contribution is the employer going to make? It is quite possible to make a judgement in favour of generous occupational provision simply on paternalistic grounds. Many organisations have thus decided that they will offer pensions because it is in the interests of their staff that they should. Occupational schemes represent a convenient and tax-advantageous method of providing an income in old age; it therefore makes sense to include a pension in the total pay and benefits package. The problems with such a commitment, particularly in the case of defined benefit schemes, are the cost and the fact that the long-term financial consequences are unpredictable. This, combined with the fact that many employees do not seem to appreciate the value of an occupational pension, is one of the reasons that many employers have been questioning their commitment to final salary schemes and to pension provision in general.

Research suggests that interest in and understanding of occupational pensions varies considerably from person to person (Taylor 2009). Older people, professional workers and those working in the financial services sector usually have a clearer perception of their value than other groups of staff. For these groups pensions are important, and their labour market behaviour will be affected as a result. A firm which does not offer a good pension will thus find it harder to recruit and retain them than one which does. By contrast, a firm which largely employs younger people, and/or workers in lower-skilled occupations, may find that it makes more sense to offer additional pay in place of an occupational scheme. You will find further information and discussion exercises about the HR perspective on occupational pensions on this book's companion website **www.pearsoned.co.uk/torrington.**

ACTIVITY 25.3

It has been argued that by making occupational pensions readily transferable, by increasing the complexity of the regulatory regime and by increasing taxation levied on pension funds, successive governments have provided a major disincentive to employers considering the establishment of a scheme. To what extent do you agree with this point of view?

SICK PAY

As with pension schemes, the provision of sick pay is seen as the mark of a good employer. Sick pay is an important issue due to the need for control and administration of absence. Research suggests that sickness absence represents around four per cent of working time (CBI 2008), although there are large differences between sectors and job types. The HR manager and the HR department have a variety of roles to play in relation to sick pay, particularly in relation to the administration of Statutory sick pay.

Statutory sick pay (SSP)

Statutory sick pay is a state benefit that has been in existence for several decades. It provides a basic income (£79.15 per week in 2010) to employees who are incapable of going to their normal place of work as a result of illness. SSP, however, is not claimed from a benefit office; it is administered by employers and paid through the payroll according to regulations set out in statute.

Employers are required to take full financial responsibility for SSP for the first four weeks of absence, after which they can claim back a portion of the costs from the state through reduced employer national insurance contributions. However, the method of calculation used ensures that smaller employers are able to claim back a very considerably higher proportion of the costs than larger employers who usually have to fund it all themselves. Most employees are entitled to state sickness benefit; however, there are some exceptions: employees who fall sick outside the EU, employees who are sick during an industrial dispute, employees over pensionable age and part-timers whose earnings are below the lower earnings limit (£95 per week in 2010). These groups, as well as self-employed people, are obliged to claim state incapacity benefit instead from the Benefits Agency. SSP is built around the concepts of qualifying days, waiting days, certification, linked periods, transfer to the Department for Work and Pensions (DWP) and record periods.

- **Qualifying days** are those days on which the employee would normally have worked, except for the fact that he or she was sick. For many Monday-to-Friday employees this is very straightforward. However, it is more complex to administer for those on some form of rotating week or shift system. Sick pay is only payable for qualifying days.

- **Waiting days** have to pass before the employee is entitled to receive sick pay – at present the number of days is three. These three days must be qualifying days, and on the fourth qualifying day the employee is entitled to sickness benefit, should he or she still be away from work due to sickness.
- **Certification** from a doctor is required after seven days of sickness absence. Prior to this the employee provides self-certification. This involves notifying the employer of absence due to sickness by the first day on which benefit is due – that is, immediately following the three waiting days.
- **Linked periods** of illness mean that the three waiting days do not apply. If the employee has had a period of incapacity from work (PIW) within the previous eight weeks, then the two periods are linked and treated as just one period for SSP purposes, and so the three waiting days do not have to pass again.

The employer does not have to administer SSP for every employee indefinitely. Where the employee has been absent due to sickness for a continuous or linked period of 28 weeks the responsibility for payment passes from the employer to the state. A continuous period of 28 weeks' sickness is clearly identifiable. It is not so clear when linked periods are involved. An employee who was sick for five days, back at work for four weeks, sick for one day, at work for seven weeks and then sick for two days would have a linked period of incapacity of eight days. Alternatively, an employee who was sick for four days, back at work for ten weeks and then sick for five days would have a period of incapacity this time of five days. The DWP requires employers to keep SSP records for three years so that these can be inspected.

Occupational sick pay

There is no obligation on employers to pay employees for days of absence due to sickness beyond what is required under the state's SSP scheme. However, most employers choose to do so via a benefit known as occupational sick pay (OSP). The most common approach is to continue paying the full salary for a set period of time, but other schemes involve reducing the pay rate for days taken off as a result of illness. In either case a sum in excess of the statutory minimum is paid, the portion accounted for by SSP being reclaimed from the state where possible. Paying the full salary is straightforward for those staff who receive a basic salary with no additions. It is more difficult to define for those whose pay is supplemented by shift allowances or productivity bonuses.

Occupational sick pay arrangements tend to be most generous in unionised environments and in the public sector, although professional and managerial employees are usually well covered in most organisations. The common public sector approach involves paying full pay for the first six months of an illness, once three years' service have been completed, before moving the employee on to half-pay for a further six months. Thereafter OSP ceases. At the other end of the scale are employers who pay no OSP at all. They take the view that occupational sick pay will be abused and so pay only what is due under the state scheme. Another approach involves paying a predetermined flat rate in addition to money provided via SSP.

Occupational sick pay schemes also vary according to the period of service required. Some employers provide sick pay for sickness absence from the first day of employment.

Others require a qualifying period to be served. For some this is a nominal period of four weeks, but the period may be three or six months, or a year or more. There is a major difference here between OSP and SSP. With SSP pay is available immediately after employment has begun.

COMPANY CARS

A form of employee benefit which is a great deal more common in the UK than in other countries is the company car, but they are a good deal less common than they used to be. In 2000 84 per cent of companies offered a car to at least some of their staff. By 2009 the proportion had fallen to 49 per cent (CIPD 2009). Managers from overseas often take some persuading that cars are necessary to attract and retain high-calibre managers, but the received wisdom is that they are. Their importance to employees is demonstrated by the comparative lack of take-up of cash alternatives where these are offered (Smith 2000a: 161). After pensions, they are the second most significant employee benefit in cost terms, and are provided for some employees by over 90 per cent of large and medium-sized companies.

There are a number of sound reasons underlying the provision of company cars. First, for some there is a need as part of their jobs to travel very widely and regularly. Not everyone can be assumed to own a reliable car, so it is sometimes necessary to provide one simply to enable an employee to carry out his/her day-to-day job duties. In the case of sales representatives and senior managers the impression created when travelling on company business can be important. It is therefore often considered necessary to provide them with upmarket and up-to-date models to ensure that clients and potential clients are suitably impressed. A case can also be made on cost efficiency grounds for people who drive a great number of business miles each year. The cost of paying them a reasonable mileage allowance to drive their own cars is often greater than the cost of providing them with a company vehicle; it costs £9,000 a year to reimburse someone who has travelled 30,000 miles at 30p per mile.

However, most possessors of company cars do not fit either of the above categories. Their car entitlements simply come as an expected part of the pay package for middle and senior managers. As such, they signify the achievement of a certain level of status. Indeed, in many companies the cars offered become steadily more imposing as people climb up the corporate hierarchy. Being upgraded to a more impressive car thus signifies in a very manifest way the company's approval. Downgrading, of course, has the opposite effect.

One of the reasons that company cars are so significant in the UK is historical. Until 1994 they were a highly tax-efficient benefit. It was a good deal cheaper to drive a company car than to purchase one's own out of taxed income, so it made sense for people to be 'paid' in part with a car. This is now far from being the case. The current tax regime introduced in 2002 encourages employers to lease or purchase cars which are environmentally friendly. Formerly company cars were simply taxed according to the number of miles driven on company business, the annual tax paid by the driver being equivalent to a percentage of the car's list price. The more business miles clocked up, the less tax was paid. In addition there were substantial discounts for people who drove older cars. Since 2002 the tax paid depends on carbon emissions or engine size and there are no reductions for people who drive a great number of miles or use an older vehicle.

So there is a substantial incentive for people who drive a great deal as part of their jobs to use smaller cars or larger ones with low carbon emissions. Most employers offer cash alternatives equal to the tax payable on the car, but many of those eligible choose not to take these up despite the fact that there are no longer any obvious tax advantages associated with driving a company car. This is partly because company cars tend to be more expensive than individuals could justify spending from their own income, but mainly because of the substantial savings that still accrue in terms of insurance, maintenance and repair costs. The tax changes have, however, led to a preference for 'trading down'. This means that, where a choice is given, employees are increasingly opting for a smaller car and more cash in their pay packets.

According to IDS (2006: 6–7) employers are increasingly distinguishing between 'status drivers', for whom a car comes as part of a senior employee's standard remuneration package, and 'need drivers'. The latter group comprise people who are required to drive as part of their job. They may not therefore be highly paid, and may well if offered a cash alternative prefer to purchase an inexpensive or second-hand car which is fine for their personal purposes, but which is inappropriate in terms of the image it presents of their organisation when on company business. For this reason a majority of companies are now either abandoning cash alternatives for 'need drivers' or are stipulating that the money must be used to purchase an 'appropriate' car which is 'fit for purpose'.

A major policy choice faced by employers in the provision of cars is whether to buy or lease their fleet. There are advantages and disadvantages associated with both approaches, much depending on the nature of the deal that is struck with a leasing company. Where the company is reputable and where the agreement provides for insurance, maintenance and repair of vehicles, the financial case for leasing is strong.

ACTIVITY 25.4

Assume that you have been offered a new job which comes with either the use of a new company car or a cash allowance. The salary is £35,000 per year. The car is worth £15,000, giving you an annual tax bill of £5,250. This is also the amount being offered by way of an annual cash allowance. Which option would you choose and why?

LONDON ALLOWANCES

Most larger employers pay a standard, organisation-wide allowance or salary weighting to employees working in central London. In some cases such allowances are also paid to employees working in the region around London. The purpose is to attract and retain staff who are obliged to live and commute in the capital where the cost of property, transport and parking is so much higher than it is elsewhere in the country. The typical level of allowance is between £2,500 and £4,500 a year, the highest sums being paid by the finance houses of the City and the lowest by the retailers. Recent years have seen considerable increases in the London weighting supplements paid to public sector workers. In the private sector the level of allowances has tended to rise more slowly than wage inflation generally and allowances have often been frozen for a number of years. This has occurred either because employers are increasingly moving towards the development of wholly separate London-based salary scales, or because moves towards broadbanding (*see* Chapter 23) allow higher wages to be paid to London-based staff without the need for a separate supplementary payment. Over time, therefore, the flat-rate allowance has thus become a less significant part of the total pay packet. Instead employers are tending to target resources on the groups who are hardest to recruit. In tight labour markets this means that there is now a greater differential between pay rates in and out of London than was the case ten years ago.

A more general trend, mainly in the private sector, is a move away from national pay scales and regional weightings altogether. Instead systems which allow organisations to pay different levels of salary to people doing the same or similar work in different regions of the country are being introduced (see IRS 2006). Increasingly, salaries are determined with reference to what other local employers are paying, rather than to what other employees of the same organisation but based elsewhere in the UK are paid. While this may well seem deeply unfair to those who receive lower pay as a result, it can be seen as a fair approach because it means that pay reflects the variable cost of living in different parts of the country. Data from the government's Annual Survey of Hours and Earnings on what major groups of employees are being paid are now freely available from the Office of National Statistics website. The survey breaks wages down by occupation for each local authority area, allowing employers to establish very easily whether they are paying below, at or above 'the going rate' in specific locations.

FLEXIBLE BENEFITS

Flexible benefits or 'cafeteria plans' have proliferated in the United States over recent years where they are specifically recognised in the tax regime. By contrast, take-up of the idea in the UK has tended to be slow (Wright 2009b: 207). However, several high-profile organisations have now moved towards greater flexibility and there is unquestionably a great deal more interest in the approach developing among UK employers more generally. This has been driven by skills shortages and by initiatives in the work-life balance arena.

The case for flexible benefits from an HRM perspective is strong, but the systems themselves can prove to be very costly to operate. The approach involves giving individual employees a choice about exactly how their pay packet is made up. The overall value of the package is set by the employer, but it is for employees to choose for themselves what balance they wish to strike between cash and the different kinds of benefit. Those who have children, for example, can opt for benefits that are of value to them such as childcare vouchers, access to a company crèche or additional holidays. A young person in his or her first job might well prefer to forgo most benefits in return for higher take-home pay, while an older person may wish to purchase additional years of pensionable service in exchange for cash or perhaps a car.

There are a number of good reasons for considering such an approach. First, it helps ensure that employees are only provided with benefits of which they are aware and which they appreciate. Resources that would otherwise be wasted by providing unwanted benefits are thus saved. The employer gets maximum value per pound spent, while at the same time employees are allowed to tailor their own 'perfect' benefits mix. The result should be improved staff retention and a better motivated workforce.

WINDOW ON PRACTICE

In 1998 a large-scale merger took place between two of the world's largest professional services firms – Price Waterhouse and Coopers & Lybrand. The merged firm, called PricewaterhouseCoopers, employs 150,000 people in 150 different countries. While the two organisations were culturally similar, they had rather different traditions in the provision of benefits. Rather than continue with people employed on different sets of terms and conditions, partners decided to harmonise everyone as soon as was possible. This process was made a great deal easier and less contentious by the decision to develop a new flexible benefits scheme called 'Choices'. It allows employees to trade cash for additional holiday, a choice of car, childcare vouchers, retail vouchers, insurance of various kinds and a pension. No one was required to alter their existing benefits package as a result of the merger unless they wished to.

Source: O. Franks and D. Thompson (2000) 'Rights and rites of passage', *People Management*, 17 February.

Flexible benefits plans take many different forms, the main distinction being between those that are 'fully flexible' and those that allow a degree of flexibility within prescribed limits. The former allow employees a free hand to make up their own package and to change it at regular intervals. Under such a regime employees could theoretically swap all benefits for cash, or could double their holiday entitlement in exchange for a pay cut. A degree of restriction is more common, a compulsory core of benefits being compulsory, with flexibility beyond that. Under such a scheme everyone might be required to take four weeks' holiday and invest in a minimal pension, but be allowed freedom to determine whether or not they wished to benefit from private health insurance, gym membership, discounts on company products, etc. Typical plans also permit some choice of the make and model of car.

A third approach is administratively simpler but is more restrictive in terms of employee choice. This involves 'prepackaging' a number of separate benefits menus designed to suit different groups of employees (rather like a pre-set banquet menu in a Chinese restaurant). Employees must then opt for one package from a choice of five or six, each having the same overall cash value. One is typically tailored to meet the needs of older staff, another is for those with young families, a third for new graduates and so on.

A number of disadvantages with flexible benefits systems can be identified which may well explain their relatively slow development in the UK. These are summarised by Smith (2000b: 381–2) as follows:

> Objections include difficult administration; problems connected with handling individual employee choices; the requirement for complex costing and records; difficulty in getting employees to make effective choices; employees making mistakes (for example leaving themselves with inadequate pension cover); employees' circumstances changing over time leaving [their] package inappropriate and giving the employer the costly headache of re-designing the package; and finally the possible hiring of expensive specialist or consultant skills and financial counselling to support the move to flexibility.

Uncertainty about the future tax position may also be a deterrent, especially where changes have the potential to throw a whole system out of kilter (as happened in 1997 when the Chancellor of the Exchequer substantially extended taxation on pension fund investments).

SUMMARY PROPOSITIONS

25.1 Between 20 per cent and 50 per cent of the typical employer's pay bill is spent on the provision of supplementary benefits. Evidence suggests that most employees do not appreciate the true financial value of such benefits.

25.2 Occupational pensions are a tax-efficient means of providing funds for retirement in excess of what is provided by state and personal pension schemes.

25.3 Occupational pensions take one of three forms: defined benefit, defined contribution and hybrid. Employers can choose as an alternative to set up a group personal pension or to provide a stakeholder pension under the government's scheme. In recent years employers have been closing their defined benefit schemes and offering defined contribution schemes and group personal pensions instead.

25.4 Employers are required to facilitate the payment of statutory sick pay to employees who are away from work as a result of an illness. Most pay occupational sick pay in addition either as a result of moral obligation or in order to attract, retain and motivate their workforces.

25.5 Company cars are commonly provided by UK employers for senior staff. The tax regime aims to discourage demand for larger cars which are not environmentally friendly.

25.6 In theory flexible benefits plans have a great deal to offer employees. It is likely that their use will grow more widespread in the next few years.

GENERAL DISCUSSION TOPICS

1 Why do you think so few people seem to have an appreciation of the value of their occupational pensions and other benefits? What could be done to raise awareness of the costs involved in their provision?

2 Draw up three flexible benefits packages; one aimed at new graduates, one at employees in their thirties, and one for those aged over 50.

FURTHER READING

Taylor, S. (2009) 'Occupational pensions', in G. White and J. Druker (eds), *Reward Management: A critical text*. London: Routledge.

Wright, A. (2009a) 'Benefits', in G. White and J. Druker (eds), *Reward Management: A critical text*. London: Routledge.

Field, S., Olsen, C. and Williams, R. (2009) 'The pensions revolution', in S. Corby, S. Palmer and E. Lindop (eds), *Rethinking Reward*. Basingstoke: Palgrave.

Wright, A. (2009b) 'Flexible benefits', in S. Corby, S. Palmer and E. Lindop (eds), *Rethinking Reward*. Basingstoke: Palgrave.

Between them, these four chapters in two recently published edited books cover the issues raised in this chapter very effectively. All review the most recent research and explain contemporary trends in a clear and concise manner.

Government Research Studies.

The Department for Work and Pensions is the government department with responsibility for pensions policy and regulatory issues. It publishes dozens of high quality research reports on its website each year. Recent studies looking at occupational pensions issues, including the 2012 reforms, are Research Reports 535, 547, 579, 592, 608 and 617.

The Turner Report (2004) contains several chapters looking at the background to pension provision over the next few decades, including demographic and funding issues.

Incomes Data Services.

IDS regularly publishes issues of its HR Studies that are focused on employee benefits. The approach is practical, case studies being provided to illustrate the approaches that employers are currently choosing to take. Two excellent recent editions are Study 856 on Employee Benefits and Study 811 on Flexible Benefits.

REFERENCES

ACA (2009) *Twilight or a New Dawn for Defined Benefit Schemes?* London: Association of Consulting Actuaries.

Accor (2008) *Reward to Engage: Rewards, benefits and employee engagement in today's organisations*. London: Accor Services.

CBI (2008) *CBI/AXA Absence Survey 2008*. London: Confederation of British Industry.

CIPD (2009) *Reward Management: Annual Survey Report 2009*. London: CIPD.

Dobson, C. and Horsfield, S. (2009) *Defined Contribution Pension Provision*, Research Report 608. London: Department for Work and Pensions.

Field, S., Olsen, C. and Williams, R. (2009) 'The pensions revolution', in S. Corby, S. Palmer and E. Lindop (eds), *Rethinking Reward*. Basingstoke: Palgrave.

Fletcher, A. (2009) 'Survey reveals record £96 billion deficit for FTSE 100 pension schemes', *Risk Magazine*, 5 August.

Franks, O. and Thompson, D. (2000) 'Rights and rites of passage', *People Management*, 17 February.

Government Actuary (2006) *Occupational Pension Schemes: Thirteenth Survey*. London: The Government Actuary's Department.

IDS (2006) *Company Cars and Business Travel*, IDS Study 817. London: IDS.

IRS (2006) 'Spotlight on the regions', *IRS Employment Review*, No. 856, 6 October.

NAPF (1992) *Seventeenth Annual Survey of Occupational Pension Funds*. London: National Association of Pension Funds.

NAPF (2009) *Annual Survey of Occupational Pension Funds 2009*. London: National Association of Pension Funds.

Pemberton, H., Thane, P. and Whiteside, N. (2006) *Britain's Pension Crisis: History and policy*. Oxford: The British Academy.

Smith, I. (2000a) 'Benefits', in G. White and J. Druker (eds), *Reward Management: A critical text*. London: Routledge.

Smith, I. (2000b) 'Flexible plans for pay and benefits', in R. Thorpe and G. Homan (eds), *Strategic Reward Systems*. London: Financial Times/Prentice Hall.

Taylor, S. (2009) 'Occupational Pensions', in G. White and J. Druker (eds), *Reward Management: A critical text*. London: Routledge.

Thomson Online (2007) Employee Rewards Watch 2007, available at **www.thomsons.com**.

Turner, A. (2004) *Pensions: Challenges and Choices. The First Report of the Pensions Commission*. London: HMSO.

Wright, A. (2009a) 'Benefits', in G. White and J. Druker (eds), *Reward Management: A critical text*. London: Routledge.

Wright, A. (2009b) 'Flexible benefits: shaping the way ahead?', in S. Corby, S. Palmer and E. Lindop (eds), *Rethinking Reward*. Basingstoke: Palgrave.

An extensive range of additional materials, including multiple choice questions, answers to questions and links to useful websites can be found on the Human Resource Management companion website at **www.pearsoned.co.uk/torrington**.

Part 6 CASE STUDY PROBLEM

Daphne Jones has recently been appointed as personnel manager of the Cavendish Hall Hotel, a 200-bedroom, four-star country house hotel located in rolling hills a few miles south of a major northern industrial conurbation. The hotel provides a wide range of conference and banqueting facilities and is a popular wedding location. Despite poor reviews from guests concerning the cost of drinks and the quality of the food on offer, the hotel is financially successful, having recently recorded increased annual profits.

Soon after her appointment Daphne decides that it is necessary and desirable to introduce a new payment system which links reward to individual effort and competence. She is concerned that the present system of paying everyone in a job role the same rate irrespective of their individual performance is unfair and tends to demotivate the best performers. She therefore decides to take a different approach when determining this year's annual pay rises.

1. Each member of staff will receive a one per cent salary increase irrespective of performance to take account of the increased cost of living.
2. Each line manager will be required to score their staff based on their individual performance over the past year. There are four options:
   - excellent
   - good
   - satisfactory
   - unsatisfactory
3. Staff scored as 'excellent' will receive a four per cent pay rise (three per cent plus the one per cent cost of living increase), those marked as 'good' will receive three per cent and those as 'satisfactory' two per cent. People who are marked as 'unsatisfactory' will simply receive the one per cent cost of living increase.

The hotel has not hitherto operated any kind of formal performance management system. There are no annual appraisals or development reviews. Managers vary greatly in the extent to which they communicate with their staff at all, let alone discuss their individual performance. For many employees the only indicator they have that they are doing a good job is the amount they receive from guests in the form of tips. As a result, when the new scheme is announced in a series of staff meetings, there is enormous excitement. There is massive anticipation among staff in the days and weeks running up to the announcement of the pay awards.

At the last minute, however, there are hitches and as a result the announcement is delayed for a week. This occurs because Daphne finds herself disagreeing profoundly with the scores awarded by two of her managers:

- George Clapham, the head porter, has awarded all his staff excellent ratings. When Daphne questions him about this he replies that he thinks all his lads are wonderful, that they have all worked very hard over the last year and that they all deserve the full four per cent. Surely, Daphne argues, he cannot give Graham Dudd an excellent rating? Not only has he been absent most of the past year, but he is regularly found away from his post chatting up chambermaids in the staff room? George argues that Graham means well and is very much liked by his colleagues. Daphne insists he is downgraded to 'satisfactory'.
- Henry Oldham-Down, the head chef, has awarded two of his senior staff excellent ratings, but has rated all the commis-chefs and kitchen porters as 'unsatisfactory'. When questioned about this, Henry says that they are all 'crap' and a waste of space as far as he is concerned and that giving them the one per cent cost of living rise is much more than they deserve. Daphne lists some names of kitchen staff who she thinks do a good job. After each name is mentioned Henry just says 'crap'. Daphne insists that one or two of the staff are upgraded to 'satisfactory'.

The following week letters are sent to all staff telling them how they have been rated by their managers and what the implications are for their pay. At the end of the letter is a sentence that asks staff who are unhappy with their pay rises to see Daphne Jones.

The following day a long line of disappointed staff forms outside Daphne's office. There is a perceivable drop in morale and this leads to reduced effort. In the coming weeks absence rates increase and guest complaints rise. There are particular problems in the kitchen, leading several guests to write very strongly worded letters of complaint.

Daphne is not surprised that poor performers are disappointed, but she finds it hard to understand why so many strong performers who have been rated 'good' are so negative about the whole exercise. What is more, she finds herself under fire from the Finance Director of the company which owns the hotel. He says that the pay bill is now too high and that it will have to be cut back next year.

The General Manager of Cavendish Hall thinks that the problems with the scheme have mainly been caused by different managers rating people according to different criteria. Next year, he says, we will use a forced ranking system. This will mean that each line manager will be asked to rank their staff in order of performance. The top 25 per cent will then receive the excellent rating and highest pay rise. Those in the second quartile will be scored as 'good' and those in the third and fourth quartiles as 'satisfactory' and 'unsatisfactory' respectively. This system also means that a budget can be set and that it will be adhered to in practice.

Required

1. What was wrong with the design of the payment system?
2. What was wrong with the way it was introduced?
3. What do you think of the new 'forced ranking system' that is planned for next year?
4. What alternative type of system would you argue should be introduced and why?

PART 7

CONTEMPORARY ISSUES

As we come to the close of the book, we have a different sort of Part. In Part 7 we are not considering activities in a specific functional grouping, but issues that tend to influence all functional areas. We start with the growing interest in talent management which focuses on all aspects of HR in pursuit of attracting, retaining and developing talented people, however defined, so that their potential is realised and they can make their maximum contribution to the business.

The ethical dimension of management in general and HR management in particular has aroused great interest recently, although the bulk of the small literature is yet to produce many really useful insights.

The nature of the HR function is undergoing some changes and those engaged in the area need to be aware of these and how changes may move forward. The effectiveness of the HR function is frequently questioned so all HR people need to consider how valuable their contribution is and how it can be effectively measured, especially by the proper deployment of information technology and by measuring changes in human capital.

Finally we consider the importance of health and well-being at work in terms of both an ethical approach to employment but also as a means of encouraging higher performance.

CHAPTER 26

TALENT MANAGEMENT

THE OBJECTIVES OF THIS CHAPTER ARE TO:

1 Clarify various definitions of talent and talent management

2 Explore talent management activities

3 Examine strategic talent management

4 Explain how organisations evaluate the practice of talent management

5 Consider barriers to talent management

6 Critique talent management

During the 2008/9 economic downturn organisations in the UK have fought to protect and keep their talented employees. Some even saw it as an opportunity to pick up talent from competitors. This is very different from the previous downturn when many organisations let go of their talented employees and consequently did not have the talent resources to take advantage of the upturn when it came. We may conclude that organisations recognise the value of managing talent in driving competitive advantage and long-term success, and are attracted by its active and positive focus. This is supported by Krinks and Strack (2008) who, in an international HR survey, found that managing talent was identified as the most important HR challenge in nine of the 17 countries surveyed including the UK, the USA, Singapore, Australia and Japan.

As the West is experiencing the retirement of the baby boomer generation and developing countries continue to grow in spite of the world downturn there is a shortage of talent and inevitable competition for talent as we saw in Chapter 7. In addition to these two drivers Yapp (2009) in her research found that organisations used talent management to secure a long-term leadership pipeline and to drive business transformation.

WHAT IS TALENT?

Definitions of talent are varied, and different organisations will use a definition appropriate to their needs. Michaels *et al.* (2001), employees of McKinsey, who coined the term 'war for talent', initially identified talent as a small number of individuals with high potential to reach the top jobs in the organisation. This is an elitist definition which focuses on a few employees. For example Bacardi-Martini focus attention on the top 20 per cent of the workforce who are the rising stars (Maynardleigh Associates 2009).

However, this approach may miss those who are most critical to business success and Boudreau (Chubb and Phillips 2008) stresses the importance of linking talent to the organisation's strategy, maintaining that it is necessary to identify the talent in the organisation that when improved would be pivotal to the organisation's achievements. This gives room for a slightly different way of identifying which talent to focus on and Snell (Pickard 2007) uses Ryanair as an example, arguing that its value is created by turnaround speed and therefore the most valuable, but not the highest paid or trained, jobs are ground staff. These jobs are critical to the competitive advantage of the organisation.

Both the above perspectives are selective, and an alternative view is that *all* employees possess latent talent. This inclusive approach is about enabling everyone in the organisation to be their best by unlocking the talent that they have. This is exemplified by Stuart-Kotze and Dunn (2008: 2) who say:

> There is no shortage of talented people. There is a shortage of people who know how to identify, develop, recruit and retain talent.

In a survey by Maynardleigh Associates (2009) half the respondent companies including Bourne Leisure and BSkyB adopted the view that talent is about everyone realising their full potential. They also found that during the recession Britannia has also moved from an elitist approach concentrating on the top 100 employees to focusing on the whole

5,000 employees in the workforce. It is interesting that McKinsey have now adopted a more inclusive definition of talent (Guthridge and Lawson 2008), reflecting the human capital debate and the need for all to perform well not just a few.

WINDOW ON PRACTICE

Nando's approach to talent management

UK Learning and Development Manager, Marcelo Borges says 'Let's assume that everyone who works for us is talented, and let them grow and develop in their own environment'. The firm argues that its ability to fill jobs internally is proof that this approach to talent management is working. Almost half the manager jobs are filled internally, as are around two thirds of area managers and regional directors, and management retention is 22 per cent, which is approximately double the sector average.

Source: Evans, J. (2007) 'Talent strategy feeds growth at Nando's', *People Management*, Vol. 13, No. 9, 3 May, p. 16.

ACTIVITY 26.1

- How does your organisation define talent? (If you are a full-time student read one or two relevant cases in *People Management* and interpret these as 'your organisation'.)
- Is this definition explicit or implicit?
- What are the advantages and disadvantages of the approach taken?
- Provide evidence to support your conclusions.

In this chapter we recognise that the two approaches above are not mutually exclusive and many organisations will adopt a balance between the two. We have therefore included topics and examples which may apply to either the inclusive or exclusive approach or indeed both.

TALENT MANAGEMENT ACTIVITIES

The CIPD provides a practical guide to talent management and suggests that is:

> the systematic attraction, identification, development, engagement, retention and deployment of those individuals with high potential who are of particular value to the organization. (CIPD 2009)

This highlights one of the greatest challenges in talent management which is the coordination of a wide range of activities, often requiring specialist expertise, which is normally dealt with by separate individuals and even by separate departments in different places. Territory issues may make this more complex, for example between recruitment and development.

The total range of activities that organisations and academics have included in talent management extends to the list of all activities which comprise HRM and as Garrow and Hirsh (2008) point out this is not very helpful in narrowing down what talent management is about. In this section therefore we have been selective and focused on those activities which we consider to be most critical.

Recruitment and retention

To enhance recruitment and retention organisations need to make themselves attractive to talent, and current thinking focuses on employer branding which involves setting out a proposition to potential employees, as we discussed in Chapter 7. This is a means of marketing the organisation to employees and potential employees in the same way that organisations market their brand to customers. Different propositions may be required for different types of employee as expectations and desires will be different for different groups. The proposition needs to be real and experienced once employees have joined the organisation, otherwise they will be more likely to leave, their expectations not having been met. Web case 26.1 on this book's companion website at **www.pearsoned.co.uk/torrington** focuses on employer branding in attracting talent. Retention allows the organisation to grow or develop the talent it has recruited; this not only means that talent is available when required, it also makes the organisation attractive to new talent. Organisations that focus on recruiting talent, but not on retaining it, are likely to have much higher levels of staff turnover as talented employees leave to work for competitors.

WINDOW ON PRACTICE

Kellogg's

Phillips (2009) explains how Kellogg's launched a Europe-wide employer brand programme to help attract and keep talent during the recession, feeling that its current website did not do it justice in terms of explaining the culture and benefits of working for Kellogg's. The aim of this programme was to make Kellogg's famous for its employment story in the same way that it is for its products. Kellogg's wanted to pass on its key selling points as an employer which are that there are a variety of flexible work options; there are 'summer hours'; generous training and development; and a culture based on relationships not hierarchy.

All managers are provided with a toolkit which gives them advice on how to bring the brand to life when communicating with staff.

Source: Adapted from Phillips, L. (2009) 'Kellogg's starts the hunt for European talent', *People Management*, Vol. 14, No. 3, 12 March, p. 10.

Equally important is attracting talent back to the organisation. Cappelli (2008), for example, explains how Deloitte keeps in touch with former employees when they are working for another employer and UBS aims to attract back talented people who have been on a career break as shown in the Window on practice below.

WINDOW ON PRACTICE

UBS attracts talent back

Aware that career breaks may mean losing talent for ever, UBS instigated a 'career comeback scheme'. This is aimed at professionals with a minimum of 5 years' experience and a break of between 18 months and seven years. This pool was mainly women and they were offered an updating programme in law, marketing and technology and were provided with coaching and a personal action plan. In the US they found that 40 per cent of this talent pool was employed in the business within two months.

Source: Phillips, L. (2008b) 'UBS helps latent talent make a career comeback', *People Management*, Vol. 14, No. 3, 7 February, p. 13.

Identification and placement of talent

The recruitment and selection process is one way to identify and then buy in talent. For current employees there are other options such as the assessment of current performance and potential. Assessment and development centres are commonly used to identify talent by means of psychometric tests, interviews, role play, business games and direct experiences of work tasks at higher or different grades. We have discussed these centres in some detail in Chapter 8, and when used internally they usually assess candidates against a set of competencies required or desired at higher job grades.

When competencies were first used they provided a much needed method of describing employee behaviour in order to match an employee to the demands of a job. However, only assessing sets of competencies can be problematic. For example Goffe and Jones (Chubb and Phillips 2008) warn against assessing people against a rigid set of competencies as this provides a limited view of employees and minimises diversity within the organisation; and Cunningham (2007b) suggests that organisations go astray when they expect a total talent package from one individual, insisting that this person displays talent across a wide range of competencies in order to justify being labelled as talented. He goes on to suggest that people may have an enormous talent in one area but be weak in others so jobs need to be designed around their talents to maximise them.

It is also important to remember that some may not display talent in their current junior role but they might in a higher-level role, or a different role. Alternatively an individual may display talent in a current role, such as a professional or technical role, but may not in a managerial role if he/she is promoted. In addition talent needs to be identified in terms of the future needs of the organisation rather than solely of current needs. So a clear distinction needs to be made between current performance and potential future performance in a different role.

Cunningham (2007a) identifies two strategic approaches to talent management, first aligning roles with people (in other words fitting talented people to current job roles) and second aligning people with roles (in other words designing jobs to fit the talented people in the organisation). He suggests that both these strategies are critical and there needs to be a dynamic interaction between these two approaches.

ACTIVITY 26.2

How might an organisation project what type of talent needs it is likely to have in the future? Competencies are only one way of expressing talent. Use your creativity skills to propose two or three other approaches.

Managing talent and supporting engagement

Employers not only need to understand what people's capabilities are; they also need to give them scope to use them. Charles Handy suggests that organisations should take more risks and allow talented people more power to make decisions. The way that talented people are managed will not only affect their performance but also determine whether they wish to stay with the organisation.

Talented people generally want to display their talents and give of their best but can be alienated by lack of empowerment within their job and by formal organisational procedures and processes. Managers need to engage talented employees by providing appropriate scope and decision-making capacity and manage them lightly on a day-to-day basis, and you may wish to refer back to Chapter 4 on organisation design and flexibility at this point. Managers also need to be prepared to manage talented employees' careers in a joint and flexible manner. As high flyers move through an organisation quickly there is evidence that they experience difficulties and therefore support needs to be available to them.

Goffee and Jones (2009), for example, recognise that while talented people may add most value to the organisation, they are often the hardest to manage. Some of their recommendations for those who manage bright people are that they should: recognise their knowledge accepting their independence and difference; try and align the goals of the individual with those of the organisation; win resources for them but allow them space to get on with things alone; encourage them to achieve external recognition; protect them from administrative matters which they may see as a distraction and provide as few rules as possible.

In a similar vein Powell and Lubitsh (2007) propose that talented people know their worth to the organisation and have their own views on the direction of their career. They will often fail to respond to traditional management approaches and may respond unpredictably, not valuing hierarchy and avoiding being controlled.

Developing talent

If managers fail to provide expected development for the talented they are likely to leave and the result may be that the organisation is forced into buying in talent on a constant basis, as the organisation has not developed a talent pool ready for succession. However, if development is provided but is only focused on the talented few there may be many of the remaining employees who feel disillusioned and disengaged. Cunningham (2007b) suggests that it is wise for an organisation to provide development activities for all rather than the few who are early on identified as having potential as talented individuals may emerge even though they may not fit the standard profile.

Promotion and succession planning

Organisations can choose to buy in talent or grow talent internally and the appropriate balance between the two will be different for different organisations. A major strength of growing talent is the building of talent pipelines, which is a key aspect of the CIPD's Shaping the Future research, so that a depth of talent is available if a key employee leaves unexpectedly. This is important as it avoids long gaps between an employee leaving and a new recruit beginning, thus protecting service and production levels. Such a pipeline may involve both company-suggested lateral and upwards moves and applications for promotions from those on the talent track. Building flexible pools of talent ready to fill a wide range of roles within the business is different from older approaches to succession planning where specific individuals were groomed and developed to fill a specific, or at best a very narrow range of roles when they became available in the future.

WINDOW ON PRACTICE

China's talent management challenge

China has so far made minimal progress in building locally sourced talent according to Brenda Wilson (2008). She points out the shortage of entrepreneurial management talent in the current leadership generation and the following one, as such managers have grown up during the Cultural Revolution, when skills such as hard work, tenacity and perseverance enabled success rather than strategic, innovation and entrepreneurial skills.

China has used expatriates for key leadership positions and although this practice appears to be reducing, Wilson suggests that China has not achieved the best balance between growing and buying in talent. Building a leadership pipeline is a long-term investment, and using expatriates to fill gaps is a useful short-term ploy but creates a long-term problem. She suggests that such use of expatriates creates a perceived 'glass ceiling' for locally born Chinese. While expatriates command very high salaries and benefits, the process of transitioning (i.e. moving from having a role

filled by an expatriate to appointing a local person) is difficult, especially when the local person in that position will be paid much less that the outgoing expatriate. This creates feelings of inequity and frustration. The timescale for these moves is slow as many expatriates say that they do not have the time to develop their successors, and the growing complexity of the business environment means that developing the necessary skills is a long-term process. Wilson suggests that a strategy based only on buying in talent is unsustainable in the long term, but knowing where to start on development schemes seems to be a key barrier. Companies often have an appropriate strategy to develop local talent but implementation is weak. Wilson provides an example of a more proactive employer, Estee Lauder (in conjunction with Mercer), whose strategy for local managers starts with an assessment against region-specific leadership behaviours, plus a 12-month development programme with personal feedback, experiential learning modules, a year-long business case supported by the all-important long-term commitment of the senior leadership.

Source: Wilson, B. (2008) 'Hidden dragons', *People Management*, Vol. 14, No. 6, 7 August, pp. 18–23.

ACTIVITY 26.3

- In your own organisation what is the balance between growing and buying in talent? (If you are a student choose a case organisation from *People Management* magazine or elsewhere.)
- How well does this balance work? Provide evidence for your conclusion.
- What might be the disadvantages of an over-reliance on growing talent?

Before responding to this activity you might find it helpful to read the article by Angela Hills (2009) in *Industrial and Commercial Training* as detailed in the references at the end of the chapter.

Valuing employees' perspective and meeting their needs

It is not only the high-potential few who seek development opportunities and career progression. While an organisation may focus on them it would be a mistake to ignore career support for all employees. For example Vodafone launched 'career deal' for its workforce to improve engagement and perceptions of career development. This involves a toolkit for employees where they can work through the questions: Where am I now?; Where do I want to be? and How do I get there? (Scott 2007).

WINDOW ON PRACTICE

R&SA intranet aids career planning

R&SA are using a new intranet site to encourage staff to plan their careers. The site enables people to assess their strengths and weaknesses, their motivations and to set development goals. This site was produced in response to employee desire to understand the career opportunities available to them. It also provides thumbnails of how various people from across the business reached their current role and has encouraged more career discussions with managers and inspired leaders to become more involved in career development. Users of the site are alerted to international vacancies so that staff see them even if they are not proactively looking for a new role.

Source: Chubb, L. (2008) 'R&SA intranet aids career planning', *People Management*, Vol. 14, No. 4, 21 February, p. 10.

Job role design and flexibility can also be important in retaining talent. We noted before that for the high-potential few designing jobs which make the most of their strengths and contribution is worth consideration. In addition flexible working may retain older people who are talented but who may not wish to continue to work full time as the only alternative to retiring. Offering part-time and flexible hours is a way to hold on to the knowledge of talented people. At the other end of the spectrum many younger employees, 'generation Y', often expect a better balance between work and home life. As Jenny Watson, Chairwoman of the EOC (now the Equality and Human Rights Commission), says:

> Failing to rethink about the way we've traditionally organized work is a chronic waste of talent. (Phillips 2007)

Flexible working may also help attract talent back after career breaks. It is important to engage people in discussions about their careers as their views may be surprisingly different from what senior managers may suppose. For example work-life balance, the meaningfulness of a job, the interest in a job, travel opportunities, speed of promotion will all be valued differently by different individuals. Web case 26.2 on this book's companion website at **www.pearsoned.co.uk/torrington** focuses on the use of flexibility to retain talent.

STRATEGIC TALENT MANAGEMENT

Having considered the activities that are central to talent management it is important to say that a fundamental of talent management is that is a strategic and integrated approach rather than just a set of practices. In this respect talent management in organisations often falls short. Such a strategic approach, similar to the strategic criteria we discussed in Chapter 3, requires that:

- the approach needs to be embedded in the organisation and therefore requires senior management sponsorship rather than being led by the HR department;
- talent management activities need to be integrated with each other and consistent;
- the approach needs to support the strategic objectives for the organisation. Garrow and Hirsh (2008) suggest three questions that need to be answered in terms of focus on strategic objectives. The first is which job roles need to be managed in this way (e.g. senior leadership; IT specialists; airport ground staff; or all roles?). The second is where does the talent come from for these roles (e.g. from outside the organisation or is there potential to be developed within, the classic buy-in or grow balance?). The third is what are the development outcomes required for individuals who have the potential to fill the specified job roles?);
- the approach to talent management needs to fit more generally with the organisation, its values and other activities. Garrow and Hirsh (2008) say there needs to be a fit with culture, the psychological contract in the organisation, other HR policies and practices and the skills of the managers who will be implementing talent management; and Powell and Lubitsh (2007) suggest talent activities need to be congruent with the aspirations of the organisation, its underlying systems and processes and core beliefs and warn that a mismatch will cause confusion and cynicism.

Strategic talent management is most often expressed as a system incorporating a structured approach to job development and planned moves. Powell and Lubitsh (2007) suggest that this works for some, but they suggest that such a traditional approach may not be suitable for all talented people and that a more flexible approach may be required. A traditional approach focusing on integrating talent management activity is exemplified by the Civil Service example in the Window on practice below.

WINDOW ON PRACTICE

'Early talent' in the Civil Service

Allen (2008) spoke to Claire Wilson of the Department for Work and Pensions (DWP) who explains how there were three separate talent management programmes running but these were all aimed at niches and not linked together. 'Early talent' was devised to be open to all rather than being selective and for senior people; it was seen as an opportunity to link up with the senior programmes. The intention was to apply this approach across other government departments and produce a deeper talent pool, which involved creating consistent tools and frameworks. 'Early talent' is targeted at people who are identified as having the capability to rise rapidly by two civil service grades and falls into three stages:

- Stage 1: Any employee can use the STEP (Seeing Talent Emerge and Progress) website and use an online simulation tool introducing them to the challenges of a senior manager role. This is to help candidates decide if they are capable of carrying out such a role.

- Stage 2: If candidates decide they have the potential to carry out a senior role they progress to the first assessed test – the Situational Judgement test – designed to look at thinking and personal styles.
- Stage 3: Candidates who pass Stage 2 then carry out capability-based assessments linked to the skills required in a given role.

After taking part in the last assessment candidates are provided with personal feedback, and all are encouraged to view this process as career development rather than a guarantee of promotion for those who pass, given the limited number of promotions available.

There is then an ongoing development programme with candidates working in small groups and action learning sets supported by a facilitator. There are also skills workshops and master classes and a business-critical project to carry out.

Source: Adapted from Allen, A. (2008) 'Bright and Early', *People Management*, Vol. 14, No. 7, 3 April, pp. 30–2.

A more flexible approach generally focuses on talent pools and their development rather than specific jobs and job moves. For example Google adopts a more flexible approach as in the Window on practice below.

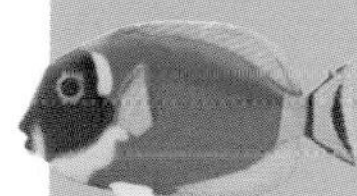

WINDOW ON PRACTICE

Talent at Google

Brockett (2008) reports that Google uses rigorous recruitment and selection methods and has a very low attrition rate but there are no specific 'talent programmes'. Google's argument for this approach is that it does not want to label people. It feels that people are attracted to work at Google because of the brand. While the company is not hierarchical and there is little room for promotion it broadens jobs to allow people to develop and expand their skills, encouraging self-managing teams and autonomy. So Google seems to focus on the appropriate management style for engaging clever people rather than a formal talent system. However there is a career development system which emphasises internal moves rather than external recruitment, with a desire to tip the balance towards internal moves. Google promotes training and development, job shadowing with Europe/Asia Pacific and allows people time to innovate in their jobs. Meeting other employee needs the company provides flexible working, free food, an on-site gym, sofas, and many offices have crèches.

Source: Adapted from Brockett, J. (2008) 'Finders Keepers', *People Management*, Vol. 14, No. 9, 18 September, pp. 28–34.

HOW ORGANISATIONS EVALUATE TALENT MANAGEMENT

Measuring the outcomes of HR practices has a long history and has always been beset by difficulties and talent management is no different. Internal HR measures are often used as these are easier to collect (such as internal promotions and retention rates) and these can be of great value if there is an identified problem around these issues. Linkerman (2007) warns against measuring processes and activities rather than outcomes. For example an organisation may measure the numbers of people who have a development plan, but this does not tell us whether the development plan is actually used, whether intended development has been achieved or whether this has impacted on the individual's performance. At the other end of the scale there are external measures such as profit, share price and sales. As with any case of measurement there is the hurdle of proving that the results obtained, such as increased retention or a higher share price, are indeed caused by the talent management activity that has been undertaken.

In the Cranfield School of Management study (Parry and Tyson 2007) of over 600 UK organisations only 15 per cent systematically measured the return on investment (ROI) for talent management. They found that the most common measures were cost per individual (58 per cent); overall cost of talent management (53 per cent) and the individual cost of talent management techniques (33 per cent). In addition costs of talent management were measured against retention (43 per cent); other career progression (40 per cent); and productivity. Yapp (2009) in her research with an unspecified number of global organisations found that the measures used were internal HR measures such as retention, engagement, promotion, succession and diversity.

Both of these studies revealed little in terms of external measures such as business performance, revenue, margins and shareholder value.

WINDOW ON PRACTICE

Maynardleigh Associates (2009) found that only one company of the 20 they researched calculated return on investment (ROI) of talent management activities in a formal way. This company used a comparative approach and calculated the value of graduate trainees by identifying the profit on revenue-generating projects they were involved in multiplied by the number of graduates. They did a similar calculation with a non-graduate control group. The graduate group contributed more revenue and they found that for every £1 of money spent on talent management (with the graduates) they received multiple returns in respect of extra sales.

Yapp (2009) describes a similar approach which she calls a micro ROI approach in npower. This company invested heavily in identifying and developing leaders and future leaders who could successfully drive culture change in the organisation by inspiring, promoting pride in the company, providing opportunities for personal growth and helping employees understand their role in the company. The leadership project was evaluated in terms of sales revenue and employee perceptions. In the first division to experience this initiative sales were up by 54 per cent and productivity almost 5 per cent and customer service complaints down by 14 per cent. Employees' pride in working for npower increased by 14 points, and their willingness to recommend npower as an employer increased by 11 points. Staff retention also increased by 33 per cent. Comparison figure with other divisions are however not provided.

Source: Maynardleigh Associates (2009) *Talent Management at the Crossroads: How 20 of the UK's best employers are rising to meet the challenge of turbulent times*. London: Maynardleigh Associates; Yapp, M. (2009) 'Measuring the ROI of talent management', *Strategic HR Review*, Vol. 8, No. 4, pp. 5–10.

Yapp (2009) makes the point that if talent mangement is already accepted or if talent management is clearly satisfying the organisation's strategic priorities measurement may not be necessary; and that for others internal HR measures may be of more relevance in the short term. For example at Standard Chartered Bank (Syedain 2007) there is a concern for attrition so that a lot of talent management is about staff engagement, personal development and career planning. The measures regularly taken are rates of attrition, internal v. external recruitment, promotion rates and whether people are achieving their personal development plans.

Other measures may include internal employee opinion, and external customer or competitor opinion.

BARRIERS TO TALENT MANAGEMENT

Successful talent management requires the leadership of the chief executive officer of an organisation, as only the CEO can insist that managers take on the responsible for finding potential, tracking and developing it. Only the CEO can make them accountable for this via performance management and the objectives they are set. So if the CEO and senior managers leave talent to the HR Department then it is doomed to failure, as the proper HR role is facilitating talent management not leading it.

It is important that HR supports a talent management model that incorporates the role of line managers, as it is these managers who need to action talent management. However, while Tim Miller (Phillips 2008a), Director of People, Property and Assurance at Standard Chartered Bank says that the responsibility for talent management lies firmly with the line, the Hewlett UK Talent Survey found that 84 per cent of managers do not have the time to do it (*People Management* 2008). Sixty per cent of the 240 respondents to this survey also thought that managers did not have adequate skills, although 88 per cent thought talent management a top strategic priority. The main problem identified was that talent strategies were not filtering down to managers and their decisions did not reflect talent management strategies (55 per cent).

Similarly in China (Wilson 2008), 76 per cent of respondents to a Mercer survey did have a strategy in place that defined how to assess, develop and retain current and future leaders but the problem seemed to be translating this into practice, having the skills and knowledge of where to start being the biggest barrier.

In general there appears to be a problem of isolated initiatives, carried out in an ad hoc manner rather than having an integrated system. Thus the final barrier is lack of a strategic approach.

CRITIQUE OF TALENT MANAGEMENT

One of the greatest problems with talent management is that it is very difficult to pin down precisely what it is, as we have hinted throughout the chapter.

ACTIVITY 26.4

Go back over the chapter and identify areas of confusion or lack of clarity in the way that talent management is interpreted by organisations and academics.

At a fundamental level Lewis and Heckman (2006: 139) note:

> a disturbing lack of clarity regarding the definition, scope and overall goals of talent management.

They go on to identify three different perspectives on what talent management really is. The first is that talent management is just a new term for human resource management in that it covers standard human resource activities but doing them more quickly, although they recognise that talent management implies a more integrated and systematic approach. Second, they suggest it can be viewed as workforce planning in that it models or anticipates the flow of people through the organisation matched against jobs and tackles issues such as supply, demand, progression and retention. The third conception focuses on the word talent, rather than on management as do the first two. Here there is an assumption that talent is an undeniable good and the emphasis is on differential treatment for those with high potential or talent, with pools of talent being managed but not being matched against specific jobs. However, as we have seen, this is complicated by the idea that all individuals have some talent to offer and therefore differential treatment may not be appropriate.

Powell and Lubitsh (2007) found five different interpretations of talent management in their research. The first is the process perspective where talent management should include all processes needed to get the best out of people. The second is the cultural perspective where talent management is more of a mindset than a set of activities. Third, they found the competitive perspective where talent management is about identifying talented people and meeting their needs so that competitors cannot pick them up. Fourth, they found a developmental perspective which focuses on accelerated development paths; and lastly they found the HR planning perspective where talented people are matched to the right jobs at the right time doing the right thing.

Picking up on the cultural perspective Hughes and Rog (2008: 746) treat talent management as

> an organizational mindset or culture in which employees are truly valued; a source of competitive advantage; an effectively integrated and enterprise-wide set of sophisticated, technology enabled evidence-based HRM policies and practices.

However, this is more of an aspiration than a reality and is dependent on an inclusive definition of talent, an integrated system of practices and evidence that it works, which brings us to the next two problems in talent management.

Problem number two is the lack of integration in talent management and the prevalence of ad hoc practices. This demonstrates the gap between rhetoric and reality in talent management, and Powell and Lubitsh (2007) found in their research that different conceptions of talent management existed within the same organisation and these did not sit comfortably together, creating contradiction and dissonance.

The third problem is that as yet the evidence base for talent management is weak. Organisations measure talent management in very limited ways, often focusing on internal HRM measures. There is not an adequate research base demonstrating whether talent management is worthwhile.

The last problem with talent management is that if the 'high potential' definition is adopted this cuts across equal opportunities, values and actions, creating contradictions. Pfeffer (2001) suggests that there are unintended negative consequences of an exclusive focus on those identified as having high potential. For example there is increased emphasis on individual performance and hence employee competition which damages teamwork; and there may be the glorification of outsiders with talent, which may make other employees feel undervalued and may result in higher staff turnover. Focusing development opportunities on the talented few also means that there are fewer opportunities for the many and they are therefore likely to do less well, creating a self-fulfilling prophecy. He also suggests that constantly buying in new talent is unhelpful in the development of organisational culture, and that it results in a lack of emphasis on systemic, process and cultural issues that get in the way of performance.

SUMMARY PROPOSITIONS

26.1 Talent is sometimes defined exclusively as possessed by the high-potential few and sometimes inclusively as something that everyone has that can be developed and maximised.

26.2 Talent management activities include recruitment and retention; identification and placement; managing talent and supporting engagement; development; promotion and succession planning; taking account of the employee's perspective and more.

26.3 The key to talent management is that it is an integrated approach that fits with organisational rather than ad hoc activities. A traditional approach will be structured and planful whereas some organisations use a more flexible approach, creating a talent pool.

26.3 Few organisations formally evaluate talent management and those who do use internal HR measures to a greater extent than external outcomes.

26.4 There are a number of barriers to talent management, the lack of skills and time of line managers being a key one.

26.5 Talent management can be criticised as lacking a clear definition, being an aspiration rather than a reality, lacking a clear evidence base and potentially cutting across equal opportunities.

GENERAL DISCUSSION TOPICS

1 'Talent management programmes targeted on the high potential few are very divisive. Recognising the different talents of each employee and enabling everyone in the organisation to do their best is a much healthier approach and more likely to result in employee engagement and the long-term success of the organisation.' Discuss the value and limitations of this perspective.

2 'Talent management is nothing more than a euphemism for HRM.' Discuss the arguments for and against this proposition.

FURTHER READING

Chuai, X., Preece, D. and Iles, P. (2008) 'Is talent management just "old wine in new bottles"?: the case of multinational companies in Beijing', *Management Research News*, Vol. 31, No. 12, pp. 901–11.
This interesting paper looks at the similarities and differences between HRM and talent management. The authors use the literature and case studies of multinational companies in Beijing and conclude that there is an overall difference. They also challenge the claim that talent management is yet another way for HRM specialists to gain legitimacy, credibility and status.

Uren, L. and Samuel, J. (2007) 'From talent compliance to talent commitment: moving beyond the hype of talent management to realizing the benefits', *Strategic HR Review*, Vol. 6, No. 3, pp. 32–5.
The authors draw on their research in 57 organisations to identify the key implementation challenges in talent management. They highlight the best practices for creating a culture of talent management commitment rather than merely compliance.

Tansley, C., Turner, P., Foster, C., Harris, L., Sempok, A., Stewart, J. and Williams, H. (2007) *Talent Strategy, Management and Measurement*. London: CIPD.
A very useful report from Nottingham Trent Business School authors which looks in more detail at the nature of talent and provides good models on strategic linkages. Some useful case studies are also included.

REFERENCES

Allen, A. (2008) 'Bright and Early', *People Management*, Vol. 14, No. 7, 3 April, pp. 30–2.

Brockett, J. (2008) 'Finders keepers', *People Management*, Vol. 14, No. 9, 18 September, pp. 28–34.

Cappelli, P. (2008) 'Talent management for the 21st century', *Harvard Business Review*, March, pp. 74–81.

Chubb, L. and Phillips, L. (2008) 'A global approach to talent: the best of the world congress', *People Management*, Vol. 14, No. 9, pp. 12–13.

CIPD (2009) *The War On Talent: Talent management under threat in uncertain times*, Part 1. London: CIPD.

Cunningham, I. (2007a) 'Viewpoint: talent management – making it real', *Development and Learning in Organisations*, Vol. 21, No. 2, pp. 4–6.

Cunningham, I. (2007b) 'Disentangling false assumptions about talent management: the need to recognize difference', *Development and Learning in Organisations*, Vol. 21, No. 4, pp. 4–5.

Evans, J. (2007) 'Talent strategy feeds growth at Nando's', *People Management*, Vol. 13, No. 9, 3 May, p. 16.

Garrow, V. and Hirsh, W. (2008) 'Talent management: issues of focus and fit', *Public Personnel Management*, Vol. 37, No. 4, Winter, pp. 389–402.

Goffee, R. and Jones, G. (2009) *Clever: Leading your smartest and most creative people*. Boston: Harvard Business School Press.

Guthridge, M. and Lawson, E. (2008) 'Divide and survive', *People Management*, Vol, 14, No. 19, 18 September, pp. 40–4.

Hills, A. (2009) 'Succession planning: or smart talent management?', *Industrial and Commercial Training*, Vol. 41, No. 1, pp. 3–38.

Hughes, J. and Rog, E. (2008) 'Talent management: a strategy for improving employee recruitment, retention and engagement within hospitality organizations', *International Journal of Contemporary Hospitality*, Vol. 20, No. 7, pp. 743–57.

Krinks, P. and Strack, R. (2008) 'The talent crunch', *People Management*, Vol. 14, No. 3, pp. 30–1.

Lewis, R. and Heckman, R. (2006) 'Talent management: a critical review', *Human Resources Management Review*, Vol. 16, pp. 139–54.

Linkerman, A. (2007) 'How to measure the success of talent management', *People Management*, Vol. 13, No. 4, pp. 46–7.

Maynardleigh Associates (2009) *Talent Management at the Crossroads: How 20 of the UK's best employers are rising to meet the challenge of turbulent times*. London: Maynardleigh Associates.

Michaels, E., Handfield-Jones, H. and Axelrod, B. (2001) *The War for Talent*. Boston: Harvard Business School Press.

Parry, E. and Tyson, S. (2007) *UK Talent Report*. London: Capital Consulting and Cranfield School of Management.

People Management (2008) '"Managers don't have time to develop talent"', Vol. 14, No. 17, 21 August, p. 10.

Pfeffer, J. (2001) 'Fighting the war for talent is hazardous to your organisation's health', *Organizational Dynamics*, Vol. 29, No. 4, pp. 248–59.

Phillips, L. (2007) 'Work flexibly or waste talent', *People Management*, Vol. 13, No. 3, p. 14.

Phillips, L. (2008a) 'Talent Management up to managers not HR', *People Management*, Vol. 14, No. 5, p. 10.

Phillips, L. (2008b) 'UBS helps latent talent make a career comeback', *People Management*, Vol. 14, No. 3, p. 13.

Phillips, L. (2009) 'Kellogg's starts the hunt for European talent', *People Management*, Vol. 14, No. 3, p. 10.

Pickard, J. (2007) 'Go with the flow', *People Management*, Vol. 13, No. 8, pp. 46–7.

Powell, M. and Lubitsh, G. (2007) 'Courage in the face of extraordinary talent: why talent management has become a leadership issue', *Strategic HR Review*, Vol. 6, No. 5, pp. 24–7.

Scott, A. (2007) 'Engagement rings at Vodaphone', *People Management*, Vol. 13, No. 7, p. 14.

Stuart-Kotze, R. and Dunn, C. (2008) *Who are Your Best People?* London: FT/Prentice Hall.

Syedain, H. (2007) 'A talent for numbers', *People Management*, Vol. 13, No. 12, pp. 36–8.

Wilson, B. (2008) 'Hidden dragons', *People Management*, Vol. 14, No. 6, pp. 18–23.

Yapp, M. (2009) 'Measuring the ROI of talent management', *Strategic HR Review*, Vol. 8, No. 4, pp. 5–10.

CHAPTER 27

ETHICS AND CORPORATE SOCIAL RESPONSIBILITY

THE OBJECTIVES OF THIS CHAPTER ARE TO:

1. Introduce the topic of ethics and corporate social responsibility
2. Consider the particular aspects of ethics that affect HRM
3. Review the variations of ethical practice across national boundaries
4. Suggest particular ethical questions facing HRM people in the future

WINDOW ON PRACTICE

In January 2004 the Treasury Select Committee of the British Parliament criticised chief executives of large insurance companies for taking big pay rises at a time when the profitability of their companies and the value of endowment policies were falling, both after a period during which endowment policies had been mis-sold. Between 1999 and 2002 the value of payouts from endowment policies had declined by an average of 25 per cent, the companies' share prices had declined by 50 per cent and the chief executives' remuneration had risen by amounts of between 45 per cent and 70 per cent to sums ranging up to £1.3 million. The chairman of the committee said, 'The industry is going downhill like a slalom skier . . . Why do you think you're worth so much?'

The committee chairman was demonstrating that committee members believed the chief executives were behaving unethically. Five years later British members of parliament were strongly criticised because many of them claimed expenses by means that were within the rules but seemed quite unreasonable by the country's electorate: their behaviour was regarded as unethical.

Source: Based on A. Senior (2004) 'MPs attack insurers over chiefs' pay', *The Times*, 28 January, p. 26.

This could be a starting point for the fourth general discussion topic at the end of this chapter.

THE ETHICAL DIMENSION

In September 2009 Helen Goddard, an English music teacher in a girls' school, was jailed for engaging one of her pupils in a sexual relationship that had begun when the girl was under 15. Two days later an anonymous letter to a national newspaper included the comment that the writer had had a similar relationship as a teacher with a pupil, but had no feelings of guilt, 'It may have been unethical, but it was not wrong.' That makes a nice distinction that echoes the attitude of the members of parliament in the above Window on practice. It implies that rule-breaking is wrong, but unethical behaviour is a matter of personal choice and nothing to do with anyone else. So what do we mean by ethics and what are the ethical dimensions of HRM?

In Western thought the major set of ideas are those set out by Aristotle 2,300 years ago, that virtues, such as generosity, charity and justice impel people possessing them to act in a way that benefits them and their surrounding society. This benign concept remains dominant, perhaps because of its common-sense attractiveness and its reflection in the Judaeo-Christian tradition. In 1781 the German philosopher Immanuel Kant published his *Critique of Pure Reason* setting out a more ruthlessly rational view that it was the rational thinking human mind that saw a duty to respect other rational beings. The third Western approach was developed by Jeremy Bentham and extended by John Stuart Mill, whose 1861 book *Utilitarianism* defined ethical behaviour as that which produces the greatest good for the greatest number. Whichever explanation one adopts it is relatively simple to see that every member of a business will seek to behave, and to carry out their duties, in a way which they individually regard as ethical although they may find their personal ethics conflict with aspects of law or company policy.

In a very large hospital or clinic nurses or surgeons who are ethically opposed to abortion will not be obliged to participate in such procedures. If they wished to be employed in a small clinic that specialised in abortion, their employer would be completely justified in discriminating against them by not offering them employment if their view was made clear at the recruitment stage. If their ethical position was concealed at interview, there would be fair grounds for their dismissal. This demonstrates that law out-scores ethics in employment matters. In several Western countries this has been demonstrated in attitudes to aspects of dress with, for instance, schoolgirls in France not being allowed to wear the burka and some British employers not permitting employees to incorporate religious insignia such as the cross into their clothing. In *Pickwick Papers* Charles Dickens produced the famous line, 'If the law supposes that,' said Mr Bumble, 'the law is a ass – an idiot.' Whatever one may think of a law, it remains the law until it is changed, no matter how offensive to one's personal views. Equally company official policy overrides anyone's personal ethical stance.

The argument of the last two paragraphs explains the position of the members of parliament who firmly believed that they had not done anything wrong because they had followed the rules and had had their expenses claims approved by the Fees Office, but can a business have ethical standards? How can HR people behave ethically in a way that all of its members accept and follow and which does more than simply comply with employment law?

Human resource management has always had an ethical dimension. The early days of personnel management were characterised by, and later scorned for, a preoccupation with employee welfare regardless of the development of the business. The odd thing is that practitioners have for so long been trying to bury this aspect, while academic commentators have grumbled that personnel practitioners fail to deliver on it. Forty years ago it was possible to write a chapter in a book on personnel management with the title 'The Social Role of Personnel' (Torrington 1968: 147–60) and generate a series of reviews that all vehemently disagreed with the implicit proposition that there actually was a social role for the personnel manager in the business. In 1977 Peter Anthony reminded his readers of an earlier statement by Michael Fogarty at an IPM conference, 'the business of business is business' before adding his own comment, 'it is the business of the industrial relations specialist to make sure that the business can get done'.

Since then there has been some increase of interest in ethics, but now it is not a vain attempt of the nice personnel people to act as the conscience of the company. Instead, it is a much more general management interest. Kenneth Blanchard is an American academic and consultant of considerable reputation, including being the author of the best-selling book, *The One-Minute Manager*. He teamed up with Norman Vincent Peale, who had written in 1952 *The Power of Positive Thinking*, which had sold no fewer than 20 million copies. Together they produced a slim, popular book about ethics in management which they described as follows:

> ethical behaviour is related to self-esteem. We both believe that people who feel good about themselves have what it takes to withstand outside pressure and to do what is right rather than do what is merely expedient, popular or lucrative. We believe that a strong code of morality in any business is the first step toward its success. We believe that ethical managers are winning managers. (Blanchard and Peale 1988: 7)

Aristotle would have been proud of them! It is interesting that the idea is 'sold' as a means to an end rather than as an end in itself, and it sounds almost as 'expedient, popular or lucrative' as the alternative that they are disparaging. We will return to the general management interest in business ethics later in the chapter, but we can get Blanchard and Peale in clearer perspective if we consider some definitions.

Any dictionary will indicate that ethics can be both singular and plural. In the singular it relates to:

> the moral value of human conduct and the principles that ought to govern that conduct.

The plural form describes:

> a social, religious or civil code of behaviour considered to be correct, especially that of a particular group or profession.

In the business context we can therefore understand ethics as a part of the culture of the individual business corporation that sets norms of behaviour by which people in the business will abide because the norms have some moral authority, as well as being convenient. It is also a set of guidelines followed by people in a particular group or profession because it makes practical sense in enabling them to do their jobs. Barristers will not represent two different clients if there is likely to be a conflict of interest between the clients. Doctors will generally refrain from sexual relationships with their patients. In both cases there are sound practical reasons, quite apart from any moral dimension. The medical profession is, however, an interesting point of comparison because the importance of ethics is so obvious, public discussion of medical ethics is regular, academic examination of medical ethics is widespread and there is a history that goes back at least 2,400 years to the Greek 'Father of medicine' Hippocrates. Among the contemporary attempts to formulate a universal code of ethics, the most widely reported is described by Gillon (2003) as having four principles, their longevity being demonstrated by three of them being given a definition in Latin as well as in English:

- Beneficence – a practitioner should act in the best interest of the patient. (*Salus aegroti suprema lex.*)
- Non-maleficence – 'first, do no harm' (*primum non nocere*).
- Autonomy – the patient has the right to refuse or choose their treatment. (*Voluntas aegroti suprema lex.*)

- Justice – concerns the distribution of scarce health resources, and the decision of who gets what treatment.

Gillon explains how this affects the individual practitioner:

> The best moral strategy for justice that I have found for myself as a health care worker is first to distinguish whether it is I or an organisation, profession, or society itself that has to make a decision. For example, 'how should I respond to a particular patient who wants an abortion?' is distinct from, 'what is this hospital's organisational view on abortion?' and 'what is the medical profession's collective view on abortion?' and 'what is society's view as expressed in law and practice?'
>
> Firstly, for decisions that I must take myself I must try to exclude decisions that have no moral basis or justification. Neither pursuit of my own self interest – for example, accepting bribes from patients, hospitals, or drug manufacturers – nor action that discriminates against patients on the basis of personal preference or prejudice can provide a just or morally acceptable basis for allocating scarce health care resources or for any other category of justice. Moreover, it is not my role as a doctor to punish patients; withholding antibiotics from smokers who do not give up smoking or refusing to refer heavy drinkers with liver damage induced by alcohol for specialist assessment on the grounds that they are at fault is not a just or morally acceptable basis for rationing my medical resources. (Gillon 2003: 267)

Although these comments are directed at medical practitioners or healthcare workers, it is an interesting intellectual exercise to substitute the word 'employee' for 'patient' to see how helpful and practical they might be for HR people. It is interesting that a book by four American academics (Wicks *et al.* 2010: 10) writing for a business readership enlarges the Hippocratic principles, without any reference to their origin, into a Standards of Conduct Decision Guide:

> Beneficence – People should provide help to others.
>
> Non-maleficence – People should avoid doing harm to others, especially intentional and direct harm.
>
> Autonomy – People should be free to make their own choices, particularly when they relate to their own welfare and life projects.
>
> Justice – People ought to give others what they are due and operate with a sense of fair play.
>
> Responsibility – People have certain expectations of themselves, and feel certain obligations to themselves, which they expect in return from others.

This discussion and the examples demonstrate four aspects of ethics for managers:

1. Ethics are about behaviour which stems from personal conviction.
2. If personal conviction conflicts with law or specific company policy, then law prevails.

3 Managerial interest in ethics relates to the extent to which they can emphasise, extend or transcend desirable behaviours within the general framework of company policy.

4 Some ethical standards may be determined by a professional body of which an employee is a member, and with which the employee will feel obliged to comply, even if such compliance leads to behaviours in conflict with company policy and practice.

EARLY MANAGEMENT CONCERN WITH ETHICS

The early management concern with ethics was led by philanthropic industrialists in the nineteenth century, such as the Quaker pioneers Cadbury, Lever, Salt and Rowntree. An American contemporary was Andrew Carnegie, who was born in Scotland but made a considerable fortune after emigrating to the United States and devoted the last years of his life to giving most of it away. In 1900 he wrote a book called *The Gospel of Wealth*, which set out a statement of corporate social responsibility that was quite as paternalist as that of his British counterparts. He believed that corporate social responsibility had two principles, charity and stewardship. The more fortunate in society had an obligation to aid the less fortunate (charity) and those with wealth should see themselves as owning that wealth in trust for the rest of society by using it for purposes which were socially legitimate (stewardship).

Carnegie was very influential, largely because he dispensed charity on such a massive scale, but the paternalism gradually drew more and more criticism and the involvement in social responsibility waned. It was more or less destroyed altogether by Milton Friedman, who argued that those in business were not qualified to decide on the relative urgency of social needs. He contended that managers who devoted corporate resources to pursue personal interpretations of social need might be misguided in their selection and would unfairly 'tax' their shareholders, employees and customers:

> There is one and only one social responsibility of business: to use its resources and energy in activities designed to increase its profits as long as it stays within the rules of the game, engaging in open and free competition, without deception and fraud. (Friedman 1963: 163)

A rather more intemperate view was recently expressed by James Murdoch of News International:

> There is an inescapable conclusion that we must reach if we are to have a better society. The only reliable, durable, and perpetual guarantor of independence is profit. (Murdoch 2009)

RENEWED INTEREST IN BUSINESS ETHICS

The 1980s saw the return of interest in business ethics, although to many people it remains an incongruous concept:

> Many persons educated in the humanities (with their aristocratic traditions) and the social sciences (with their quantifying, collectivist traditions) are uncritically anti-capitalist. They think of business as vulgar, philistine, and morally suspect . . . Three accusations come up.
>
> (a) In pursuit of profits, won't businesses act immorally whenever necessary?
> (b) Aren't executive salaries out of line? Isn't dramatic inequality wrong?
> (c) Isn't it wrong to subject workers and middle managers in their mature years to so much insecurity? Isn't it wrong to let people go abruptly and without a parachute? (Novak 1996: 7–8)

That was an American perspective, but it would be echoed by many people in Europe. There is also the more general feeling that any commercially driven activity has dominant motivations that are inevitably opposed to social considerations. Another version of the same view, echoing Friedman, is that those in management positions should not make moral judgements as they have no authority to do so. Instead they should respond to public opinion as expressed by customers' purchasing decisions, demonstrations by pressure groups or trade unions or by government legislation.

WINDOW ON PRACTICE

One relatively recent form of control on management decision making is whistle-blowing, which describes the practice of an employee metaphorically blowing a whistle to attract attention from the outside to some ethical malpractice within the business. Originally this was done by lone individuals taking great risks with their employment, but the method has now altered through the establishment of a charity, Public Concern at Work, which gives free legal advice to potential whistle-blowers. Its director claims that most issues are now settled within the business:

> 90 per cent of clients who follow our advice report a successful outcome. This has much to do with our policy that, if raised responsibly within the organisation, concerns about malpractice will be addressed properly by those in charge. (Dehn 1997)

A further development of Dehn's work is in Borrie and Dehn (2002).

An alternative point of view sees business practice as a product of its past:

> Wealth or value creation is in essence a moral act. The individual entrepreneurs who first organised production systematically were steeped in largely Nonconformist religious convictions that blocked most customary routes to advancement in British society of the eighteenth and early nineteenth centuries [who] . . . shared a belief that their works on this earth would justify them, that the Kingdom of Heaven was to be built by them, here and now. (Hampden-Turner and Trompenaars 1993: 3)

These authors then argue that the moral values that drive wealth creation are rooted in the national and organisational cultures of the wealth-creating corporations, although that is frequently forgotten because of the prominence given to the 'value-empty' discipline of economics, of which Milton Friedman was the supreme example:

> The qualities of work performed by these corporations depend as much on the durable values of their work cultures as they once depended on the values of their founders. In our survey of 15,000 executives we found that culture of origin is the most important determinant of values. In any culture, a deep structure of beliefs is the invisible hand that regulates economic activity. (Friedman 1963: 4)

The need for ethical guidelines

The logic supporting the need for ethical guidelines is that actions in business are the result of decisions by human beings, and human beings tend to seek justification for their actions beyond the rule of value for money. Frequently this takes the form of grotesque rationalisation. The various Mafia families apparently have a very robust code of conduct, based on strong family cohesion and a convenient interpretation of the Roman Catholic faith. This 'justification' enables them to peddle drugs, launder money, run large-scale prostitution and extortion operations, to say nothing of killing people, without a sense of guilt. Osama bin Laden apparently is motivated by a personal interpretation of Islam that legitimises terrorism.

Fortunately most people do not resort to such extreme behaviour, but will still seek to justify to themselves actions they take that can have unpleasant consequences for other people. The person who is totally rational in decision making is a rare creature in business life. In Chapter 22 there was an account of Milgram's work, which showed people acting in a most extreme way when they were put in an 'agentic state', whereby the responsibility lay somewhere else, absolving individuals of any guilt or responsibility associated with their actions. Recent concern about responsibility for fatal accidents has created great interest in the concept of corporate manslaughter. Who is responsible for a train crash, the train driver or those in overall charge of the business who did not arrange for suitable training, supervision or other facilities?

Moral justification

Sometimes the moral justification comes from a value system that is independent of the business itself and where individual opinions can be sharply divided. Some doctors and nurses are happy to work in abortion clinics, while others refuse, as some people are passionately committed to the woman's right to choose and others are equally passionately pro-life. Some people are enraged about the destruction of green land to build motorways, while others are enthusiastic. Other actions and decisions are more generally supported by the external value system. Few would disagree that people at work should be honest and that claims about a product or service should be accurate. Most would also agree with the general proposition of equal opportunity for all, although there may be sharp disagreement about what exactly that means in practice.

Ethical principles

Some standards of ethics derive from voluntary agreement by members of a particular industry, such as editors of national newspapers, or statutory 'watchdogs' such as those monitoring the activities of privatised public utilities. The problem of pensions and similar financial services being mis-sold produced the Personal Investment Authority, which was dissolved in 2009 with its powers being transferred to the Financial Services Authority with swingeing powers intended to prevent a repetition of that sort of problem. Then there are the ethical standards that are generated within a particular business. The Royal Dutch/Shell Group of Companies relies largely for its international effectiveness on the values shared by all its companies and employees. No new joint venture will be developed unless the partner company accepts them.

> The business principles are a set of beliefs which say what the Shell group stands for and covers in general terms its responsibilities to its principal stakeholders, its shareholders, employees, customers and society. They are concerned with economic principles, business integrity, political activities, the environment, the community and availability of information. (Haddock and South 1994: 226)

These principles were first set out in 1976 and were not imposed from the top, but were a codification of already accepted behaviour. The principles are revised from time to time and one of the challenging tasks for the central HR function was to introduce a code of practice relating to drugs and alcohol, which took considerable discussion and consultation before agreement could be reached:

> At the heart of our Business Principles are three core values: honesty; integrity and respect for people. Consistently behaving with integrity requires clear and simple requirements (like our zero tolerance for bribes and fraud); effective procedures to check and reward compliance, and a company culture that does not tolerate dishonest or illegal practices. (Royal Dutch Shell 2009)

Individuals encounter moral dilemmas frequently in their working lives and are likely to find them very difficult. In carrying out research a few years ago about performance appraisal practice in a large building society, it was possible to see the rise in sickness absence at the time of the annual appraisal discussion, and this was most marked among appraisers: those who had to pass on bad news. We saw in Chapter 22 that few managers wish to take over responsibility for grievance and discipline from HR people, and making the decision to dismiss someone for almost any reason other than gross misconduct is a most unpopular management task because it seems that the interests of the business are being considered at the expense of the interests of individual employees. At times like this managers are very anxious to find some justifying framework for their actions.

ACTIVITY 27.1

Eric was deaf, mute and suffered from cerebral palsy. He had been unemployable all his adult life, but in his late twenties he started to follow round the local authority refuse collectors emptying dustbins. As the lorry reached the end of a street, Eric would go ahead of it and drag dustbins out from behind the houses to the front. His handicap made it a very slow and painful process, but it was something he could do and he worked until he dropped with exhaustion. This completely unofficial arrangement was accepted by the refuse collectors as they were able to complete their rounds more quickly and they were on an incentive payment arrangement and Eric's participation enabled them to complete their rounds in slightly less time. At the end of the week they had a collection and gave Eric a few pounds. This transformed his life, as he had a purpose and had some mates.

1. Do you feel that Eric was being exploited by the refuse collectors? Local authority officials heard about what Eric was doing and said it had to stop.
2. Why do you think they made this decision? Do you agree with it? A personnel manager in the neighbourhood heard about Eric and arranged for him to be taught to operate a sewing machine. He was then employed in the personnel manager's factory to maintain and repair all the overalls: a straightforward job carried out skilfully and conscientiously.
3. Do you feel that Eric was being exploited by the personnel manager?
4. As Eric was able to draw invalidity benefit, do you feel that the job should have been offered first to someone who was able-bodied? In the following three years investigations twice demonstrated that the overalls could be repaired more cheaply by subcontracting the work to another company, but that decision was not taken. Eric carried on as an employee.
5. Why do you think they did not make that decision? Do you agree with it?

Fisher and Lovell (2009: 139–45) provide an interesting evaluation framework for an individual manager or business to assess the ethical validity of a particular course of action.

Codes of ethics

By the early 1990s one-third of leading British companies had a written code of ethics, which was nearly double the number in 1987. The key issue with ethical codes is the extent to which they are supported by the people to whom they apply. They are not rules that can be enforced by penalties for non-compliance. It is necessary that they are understood, appreciated and willingly honoured by the great majority of those who are affected. There will then be considerable social pressure on the few who do not wish to comply. Imposing ethics is very tricky. While examining equal opportunities some years ago, researchers found an interesting situation in an American computer company with a rapidly growing British subsidiary. The company had a high-profile commitment to 'positive action to seek out and employ members of disadvantaged groups'. This was reinforced in the annual appraisal system for managers, who had to indicate what they had done in the past 12 months to implement a 'programme of employment and development for minorities'. The company annual report made a claim that this initiative was advancing at all international locations. In Britain, however, it was found in practice that:

> Without exception, all managers to whom we spoke ignored that part of their appraisal . . . They put a line through the offending clause and wrote 'not applicable in the UK' . . . despite the corporate objective of 'citizenship', applicable in the UK, requiring recruitment officers to seek out the disadvantaged in the community . . . Suggestions by the researchers that such an active recruitment policy was an obligation on the part of management . . . invoked the reaction, 'we're not a welfare organisation'.
> (Torrington *et al.* 1982: 23)

ETHICS AND HUMAN RESOURCE MANAGEMENT

Some academics have criticised HR managers for management failures in the employment field and derided them as powerless because of their inability to carry out 'simple' tasks such as introducing genuine equality of opportunity and humanising the workplace. Forty years ago Flanders criticised them, and their managerial colleagues, for getting the balance wrong between who did what in management:

> Confusion over the role of personnel management can produce a compromise that gets the worst of all worlds. In major areas of industrial relations policy – such as employment, negotiations, communications and training – line management may shed all the details of administration, while retaining ultimate authority and an illusion of responsibility. (Flanders 1964: 254)

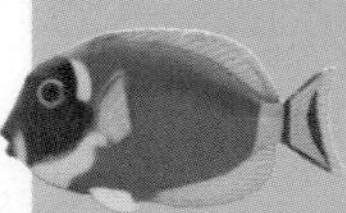

WINDOW ON PRACTICE

One of the most telling caricatures of the HR manager comes from a Tyneside shop floor:

> Joe, an old labourer, is trudging through the shipyard carrying a heavy load on his shoulders. It is a filthy, wet day and the sole of his shoe is flapping open. The personnel manager, passing at the time, stops him, saying 'Hey Joe, you can't go round with your shoe in that state on a wet day like this' and reaching into his back pocket takes out a bundle of bank notes. Joe beams in anticipation. 'Here' says the personnel manager, slipping the elastic band off the bundle of notes, 'put this round your shoe, it will help keep the wet out'. (Murray 1972: 279)

The most vigorous denunciation of personnel people for not putting the world to rights has been from Tim Hart (1993) with his onslaught on HRM, which had three points of criticism:

1. HRM is amoral and anti-social because it has moved away from the principles of the famous social philanthropists who realised that the standard economic paradigm of labour utility needed to be tempered with social and religious values. HRM ignores the pluralistic nature of work organisations and personnel managers have abandoned their welfare origins.
2. Personnel managers, aided and abetted by the Institute of Personnel Management, have lost their claim to independent professional standing, as HRM is a managerial rather than professional approach, producing a purely reactive response to situations.
3. HRM is ecologically destructive because it consolidates an exploitative relationship between people at work which is then reproduced in our approach to relationships in the wider society and with our environment.

Other management specialists do not receive these criticisms, either because their activities are more limited in their social implications or because their academic commentators are more interested in the technical than the social aspects of what they are doing.

HR interest in ethics

HR people have long held a strong interest in ethics, although it was usually caricatured as welfare. Some of the academic critics argue that personnel managers should remain aloof from the management hurly-burly so that 'professional values will be paramount and prevail over other interests' (Hart 1993: 30). The problem with that simplistic argument is that HR people do not have a separate professional existence from the management of which they are a part. HRM is a management activity or it is nothing. The company doctor and the company legal adviser are bound by codes of professional ethics different from those of managers, but they are employed for their specialist, technical expertise and they are members of long-established, powerful professional groupings with their own normal places of work. When they leave their surgeries or their courtrooms to align themselves with managers in companies, they are in a specialised role. They can maintain a non-managerial, professional detachment, giving advice that is highly regarded, even when it is highly unpopular. Furthermore they advise; they do not decide. For instance, any dismissal on the grounds of ill health is a management decision and not a medical decision, no matter how explicit and uncompromising the medical advice may be.

HR specialists do not have separate places and conventions of work which they leave in order to advise managements. They are employed in no other capacity than to participate closely in the management process of the business. They do not even have the limited degree of independence that company accountants have, as their activities are not subject to external audit, and it is ludicrous to expect of them a fully fledged independent, professional stance, although there is a move in that direction since the professional body became chartered. The chartered personnel practitioner can only retain that particular cachet after regular reassessment of professional competence.

The change in general management orientation during the 1980s and 1990s towards the idea of leaner and fitter, flexible organisations, downsizing, delayering, outplacement and all the other ideas that eventually lead to fewer people in jobs and fewer still with any sort of employment security have usually been implemented by personnel people. HR and personnel managers cannot behave like Banquo's ghost and be silently disapproving of their colleagues' actions. What they can do is to argue vigorously in favour of what they see as the best combination of efficiency and justice, but they can only argue vigorously if they are present when decisions are made. If they are not generally 'on side', they do not participate in the decision making and they probably do not keep their jobs. Either they are a part of management, valued by their colleagues, despite their funny ideas, or they are powerless. There are no ivory towers for them to occupy, and no more employment security for them than for any other member of the business.

In the different era of the 1970s Legge (1978) propounded her formulation of the conformist and the deviant innovator as alternative strategies for the personnel manager to pursue. The conventions of employment security then, especially those of managers, were such that personnel specialists could perhaps pursue a deviant path with impunity. Now it is more difficult:

> The 'deviant innovator' bolt hole based on a plea to consider the merits of social values and to ponder the value of an independent 'professional stance' appeared to be offering a less secure refuge. (Storey 1992: 275)

They can still take such an approach, if they are valued by their managerial colleagues for the wholeness of their contribution, and if they accept the fact that they will often lose the argument: they cannot do it by masquerading as an unrepresentative shop steward. They have no monopoly of either wisdom or righteousness, and other members of the management team are just as likely as they are to be concerned about social values.

HR managers have not abandoned their interest in welfare; they have moved away from an approach to welfare that was trivial, anachronistic and paternalist. In the HR vocabulary the term 'welfare' is code for middle-class do-gooders placing flowers in the works canteen. HR managers increasingly shun the traditional approach to welfare not for its softness, but because it is ineffectual. It steers clear of the work that people are doing and concentrates on the surroundings in which the work is carried out. It does not satisfy the HR obsession with getting progress in the employment of people, and it certainly does not do enough to satisfy the people who are employed. In many undertakings HR specialists are taking their management colleagues along with them in an enthusiastic and convinced attempt to give jobs more meaning and to humanise the workplace. Their reasoning is that the business can only maintain its competitive edge if the people who work there are committed to its success, and that commitment is volitional: you need hearts and minds as well as hands and muscle. Investment in training and the dismantling of elaborate, alienating organisation structures do more for employee well-being than paternalistic welfare programmes ever did.

ETHICS ACROSS NATIONAL BOUNDARIES

The international dimension of the social responsibility question has still to be developed. Logging operations in South America are ravaging the rainforests, which are essential to life continuing on the planet. Error, or neglect, in the management of manufacturing processes can produce a tragedy like that of Chernobyl in Ukraine or the various discharges of crude oil that have occurred all over the world. We have already referred to the concern about values in Shell, yet this business suffered serious difficulties about its plans for the disposal of the Brent Spar oil rig. Since the first formal warning by the American Surgeon General about the risks of smoking, tobacco consumption has been falling in Western countries, so the tobacco companies have increased their marketing in less developed countries, which is widely regarded as a most dubious practice.

Ethical standards vary. Becker and Fritzsche (1987) carried out a study of different ethical perceptions between American, French and German executives. Thirty-nine per cent of the Americans said that paying money for business favours was unethical. Only 12 per cent of the French and none of the Germans agreed. In the United States Japanese companies have been accused of avoiding the employment of ethnic minority groups by the careful location of their factories (Cole and Deskins 1988: 17–19). On the other hand, Japanese standards on employee health and safety are as high as those anywhere in the world (Wokutch 1990). In South East Asia the contrast in prosperity between countries such as Malaysia and Singapore on the one hand and Indonesia and the Philippines on the other means that there are ethical questions about the employment of illegal immigrants that are superficially similar to those applying to Cubans and Mexicans in the United States, but which do not occur in other parts of the world. There are very low wages and long working hours in China; and in Europe, Britain initially refused to accept the social chapter of the Maastricht Treaty harmonising employment conditions across the European Union.

The various high-profile cases over the past decade of offering inducements to individuals in order to obtain business has led the British government to introduce the Bribery Act of 2010. This makes it an offence (a) to offer or pay a bribe, (b) to request or receive a bribe, (c) to bribe a foreign public service official and there is also (d) a corporate offence of failing to prevent a bribe being offered or paid on behalf of the business.

The most remarkable recent case in the area of ethics has been the long-running saga of the American company Enron, an energy company employing 21,000 people and with revenues of $111 billion in 2000. *Fortune* magazine named Enron 'America's Most Innovative Company' for six consecutive years. At the end of 2001 it was revealed that Enron's reported financial condition was sustained mostly by institutionalised, systematic, and creatively planned accounting fraud. After a long and complex trial the directors of the company paid large sums in compensation. The scandal also caused the dissolution of the Arthur Andersen accounting firm.

The differences in ethical standards between countries will be one of the key HR issues to be addressed in the future. There will gradually be a growing together of national practice on working hours, but it will take much longer for rates of pay to harmonise. One can visualise common standards on health and safety developing much more quickly than equality of opportunity between the sexes and across ethnic divisions.

It seems that games are played between governments and multinational companies. Among the most recent examples is the long-running saga of General Motors/Opel/Vauxhall. General Motors is an American business that also owns Opel, with plants in Belgium and Germany, and Vauxhall, with plants in Britain. By 2008 General Motors was in serious financial difficulties and the sale of Opel and Vauxhall seemed its best hope for survival. British and German governments were immediately concerned about the likely implications for their two economies and attempted to influence the sale process in their favour by offering financial inducements. For some months the sale was to be made to a Canadian company, which duly received similar blandishments. In autumn 2009 General Motors suddenly announced that its financial situation had improved so the sale was off. So British and German officials had to dust off some of their earlier files and start all over again. In both countries the issue of jobs was of crucial importance, but General Motors still needed to save money. One account of this long process is in Arnott 2009, who explains:

> The company needs to cut between a fifth and a quarter of the capacity of its loss-making Vauxhall/Opel business. But until there is unanimous agreement, and GM has raised the necessary funding in the form of loans or loan guarantees, the company will give no indications of where the expected 10,000 job cuts will fall or which countries might face factory closures.

SOME CURRENT AND DEVELOPING ETHICAL DILEMMAS

We conclude this chapter by suggesting some of the less obvious ethical dilemmas for those in management positions. Issues such as the environment and equalising opportunity are extensively discussed, but there are others that receive less attention.

Life in the business

What sort of quality does working life have and what sort of quality will it have in the future? Twenty years ago a team of experts were employed by the British government in a Quality of Working Life Unit. Their task was to suggest ways in which that quality could be improved, mainly through job redesign initiatives. Since then the general belief is that quality of working life has declined, partly through overwork and partly through fear of losing employment. At the beginning of the twenty-first century workplace stress is one of the most common causes of absence and the place of work is an arena where newspapers would have us believe that harassment, poor supervision and bullying are rife. In this edition of our book we include for the first time a skills section on dealing with bullying.

> Few people go off to work these days with a song in their hearts . . . many people dread each day because they have to work in places where they feel abused and powerless. What is happening to us? Why are talented, productive people being thwarted and sabotaged? Why do we treat each other so badly? Why are tyrannical bosses tolerated? Does the bottom line really justify the hurt and frustration we experience? (Wright and Smye 1996: 3)

We now lack the comfortable feelings of security that the employing organisation used to provide. Whether people really are more or less secure in their jobs is debatable, but there is no doubt that they feel less secure. Furthermore, delayering and downsizing to become leaner and fitter has mainly affected people in middle-range posts, who used to be the most secure and who valued their security most highly.

As the gradual shift in organisation from entity to process continues we shall have to find ways that make work less stressful and more satisfying, despite the absence of certain of its traditionally most attractive features: security and community.

Information technology and the workplace

We have plenty of predictions of what the computer, the Internet and the microprocessor can do and what will in due course logically happen: manufacturing will progressively be taken over by robots, there will be rapid transfer and manipulation of data, the paperless office, people working from home instead of coming into a centre, and so forth: the golden age of the post-industrial society and the World Wide Web. The ethical dilemma is to wonder what will be done to make up for what the computer will take from us: the conviviality and communal feeling of organisational life.

Managers have long had the opportunity to spend more of their time, and make more of their decisions, by rational planning and operational research methods than in fact they do. The strange thing is that there continues to be a preference among managers in general and HR managers in particular to spend their time talking with people and to make their decisions as a result of discussion and shrewd judgement. Will managers now begin to eschew face-to-face discussion in favour of face-to-terminal decision making, or will they continue to confer and keep busy while others feed to them an ever-increasing flow of processed information requiring interpretation, evaluation and further discussion? Research findings suggest that managers work in the way that they do at least partly because they like it that way. Nobody saw it more clearly than one of the management greats, Henry Mintzberg:

> The manager actually seems to prefer brevity and interruption in his work. Superficiality is an occupational hazard of the manager's job. Very current information (gossip, hearsay, speculation) is favoured; routine reports are not. The manager clearly favours the . . . verbal media, spending most of his time in verbal contact. (Mintzberg 1973: 51–2)

The date and male gender of that quotation may be significant. Most of the studies of managerial work have been of men and of men and women working in a male-dominated culture. It may be that the increasing proportion of managerial jobs done by women will alter the stereotype. The women authors of *Corporate Abuse* are quite clear about the need to care for souls:

> Studies of work flow suggest there is five times more opportunity to experience joy in the workplace on a daily basis than in the home environment if it is a workplace that is in tune with the needs of the soul . . . Once we have a community of fully nurtured souls, the possibility of creativity is limitless. Everyone in the workforce will be tapped into his or her own power source as well as being part of a larger community of effort and partnership. (Wright and Smye 1996: 248–9)

This rings strangely in management ears, but maybe this is the way to rediscover the sense of community that employing organisations used to provide.

How great will the influence of the computer on HRM work actually become? How will we make up for what the computer takes away? If there is a general tendency for people to work at home, taking their laptop with them, how popular will that turn out to be? It is over a century since the household ceased to be the central productive unit and the men, and later the women, began to spend a large part of their waking hours at a different social centre: the factory, shop or office – the organisational entity. To be housebound has become a blight.

WINDOW ON PRACTICE

Jeremy is a newspaper journalist who works from home. Having a young family he needed more space for an office, so he had a 'posh shed' erected in his garden, with heating and light, to accommodate him at work. After a few months this ideal environment became not so ideal and Jeremy now spends most mornings with his laptop and his mobile phone in a local café.

We have dismantled, or allowed to wither, all the social mechanisms that supported self-sufficiency, and developed instead the social institution of the workplace as the arena for many of our human needs, such as affiliation, interaction, teamworking and competition. It really seems most unlikely that the move away from working in the household will be reversed. In every country of the world roads and railways are jammed with people at the beginning and end of the day going to work or returning, despite the tendency for the organisational entity to decline.

The World Wide Web may not turn everyone into a homeworker, but it is still having a significant impact. There is the slightly isolating nature of the work that computerisation produces. The individual employee is not one of many in a crowded workshop, but one of a few scattered around a mass of busy machines. The clerical employee spends more time gazing at a computer terminal and less talking to colleagues. What employee behaviour will this engender and what attitudes will be associated with that behaviour?

WINDOW ON PRACTICE

Susan is not a high-flier, but an extremely competent and conscientious PA/secretary who is happy to work part time so as to maintain an active family role. She explains what she has progressively 'lost':

> When I started I worked for one boss. He was a bit of a pain at times, but I got very involved, partly because he was so disorganised. He relied on me and I could follow all the ups and downs of his office politics. There was good camaraderie with other secretaries, who really ran the place. Not at all PC, but interesting and worthwhile. Nowadays there is more concentration on just doing the basic job of setting out letters and endless hours staring at that bloody screen. I feel more and more isolated.

As more people become able to use the computer there is a net loss of jobs. This has been seen in its most dramatic form in the publishing of newspapers, where typesetting has been eliminated through journalists typing their copy directly at a computer terminal.

The central ethical dilemma seems to be that we are allowing information technology gradually to take away the social institution of the organisation on which we have become so dependent. How will this scenario unfold?

ACTIVITY 27.2

What difference has the computer made to your working life so far? What further effect do you expect it to have in the next five years? How readily would you be (or are you) a homeworker?

Employment

If employing organisations are not to provide the security of a job for life, how will people find employment, both as a way of earning their livelihood and as a means of finding their place in society? There has been much brave talk of people managing their own careers and concentrating on ensuring their continuing employability. Charles Handy enunciated his concept of portfolio living, whereby people put together a portfolio of different activities so that they could control their own lives without becoming dependent on a single employer. This is fine for the able, well educated and independently minded, but human society has not evolved to the point where that description fits everyone; it probably fits only a minority.

There have always been large proportions of any society who were dependent. The golden age of Ancient Greece was based on slavery, as was the earlier Pharoanic period in Egypt. The lord of the manor had his tenants, mass production required masses of people and countries have always required large numbers for their armies. Not only were there dependent people, but society depended on them. We are now moving into this strange new world where there seems to be no place for that large proportion of the population.

It is unrealistic to expect every middle-aged redundant unskilled operative or every school-leaver without GCSEs to develop their own flexible employability. They need someone or something to provide them with the opportunity to work. Current economic wisdom is that jobs can only come through the activity of the market. This is one of the common political debating points: where are the jobs going to come from? Surely, however, it is one of the salient questions for human resource management. If HR managers have social responsibility, how will they improve job prospects in the economy?

Self-improvement

For a long time we have lived with inflation that was, in many ways, the engine of growth. Not only did we spend in order to avoid higher prices next month, but we always felt we were making progress when our take-home pay kept going up. Rationally we knew that we were not necessarily doing better at all, but it vaguely felt as if we were. Recently the level of inflation in most Western countries has been so firmly controlled that we no longer have that spurious feeling of making progress, as cost-of-living adjustments either do not exist or seem so small.

Without the mirage of progress provided by inflation, people need to have a more genuine sense of being able to do better. We have already considered the advantages and drawbacks of relating pay to performance, which is the main way in which it has been possible recently to see an improvement in one's material circumstances, but this really pays off only for a minority.

Delayering has taken out another yardstick of progress, as the scope for promotion is much reduced. This may reduce costs and may replace the phoney improvement of promotion by the possibility of real improvement through finding new opportunities, but we should remember that the business that is 'lean and mean' feels very mean indeed to the people who are inside it.

A nice HR challenge is to develop novel aspects of corporate culture that will recognise achievement and give a sense of progress for all those who seek it, without generating envy:

> Conspicuous privilege, ostentation, and other forms of behaviour, even when not necessarily wrong, typically provoke envy. Unusually large salaries or bonuses, even if justified by competition in a free and open market, may offer demagogues fertile ground on which to scatter the seeds of envy. It is wise to take precautions against these eventualities. (Novak 1996: 144)

Personal (note: not personnel) management

One ethical challenge in HRM is to ensure that the processes of management are seen to be carried out by people who can be seen, talked to, argued with and persuaded.

While it is clearly important for managers to avoid an over-preoccupation with procedural trivia, which reinforce the status quo and inhibit change, management is not all about strategy, and HRM has only a modest strategic element. It is the operational or technical aspects that require the skill and confer the status. Is there anything harder for a manager to do well than carry out a successful appraisal interview? Are there many more important jobs to be done than explaining strategy, or making the absolutely right appointment of someone to a key role? This is operational management for HR specialists, yet so often we find that they have retreated to the strategy bunker to think great thoughts and discuss the shape of the world with like-minded people consuming endless cups of coffee, while the appraisal and the selection and the communication are left to 'the line'.

There used to be a management approach known as MBWA, or management by walking about. This exhorted managers to get out of their offices and walk about to see what was going on and to be available. We have already referred in this chapter to the apparent preference among managers for spending their time in face-to-face discussion rather than in solitary activities. The trouble is that more and more of their contacts are with other managers rather than with people in the front line.

We suggest that it is important to maintain the work of HR as largely 'a contact sport', dealing face to face with people in all sorts of jobs in all parts of the business, so that, although the business employs the HR managers, they are agents of that employing business with whom employees can reason and debate.

Future HR managers will need a shrewd strategic sense and a set of operational managerial skills. They will also need an ethical sense and be able to set management action in its context, understanding the implications for the enterprise, for each person and for the community at large. Many aspects of management work can be developed into a science: successful HRM is an art.

Corporate social responsibility

As was set out in Chapter 2, there has recently developed an interest in corporate social responsibility or CSR. This is an interest in a wide range of matters where some companies wish to review their activities and includes topics like climate change, pollution, charitable contributions, customer care and others that are only narrowly the province of HR and therefore lie outside the scope of this book, although Maureen Stapley (2010) describes an interesting broad-based approach at Mondial Assistance that has generated the useful by-product of short-term absence declining from 2007 to 2009 from 3.76 days to 3.2 while staff turnover fell from 22.68 per cent to 6.4 per cent. She offers the obvious reservation:

> While these decreases were driven by a number of factors within the business, our team of executive directors . . . firmly believe that the commitment and focus on CSR were a very strong contributing factor. (Stapley 2010: 55)

However, Chapter 28 shows that there are signs of HR pushing for HR to absorb CSR. This, of course, is at the same time that environmental issues are currently the most fashionable aspect of ethical concern. What special expertise in environmental matters is vested in HR is unclear. Nottingham Business School and the ESCP Europe Business School are among those which have recently developed MBA electives in environment and sustainability.

Reviewing the development of CSR Stefan Stern (2004) made the following comment:

> CSR is bound to fail in companies where it is adopted simply for reasons of public relations . . . It may be successful in changing attitudes to your company in the short term, but if your activities are morally dubious they will eventually be exposed. CSR, if it is to mean anything, cannot be a bolted-on attitude or a departmental annexe . . . It is not about 'putting something back' – it is about how you make your money in the first place. (. . . In any case, if you really feel the need to 'put something back', doesn't that suggest you have taken too much already?) (Stern 2004: 35)

SUMMARY PROPOSITIONS

27.1 In the business context, ethics are part of the corporate culture that sets norms of behaviour by which people in the business will abide because they have some moral authority as well as being convenient.

27.2 Ethical standards in different national cultures vary, making international standards difficult.

27.3 Ethical codes are only valid if they are appreciated and willingly implemented by the great majority of those to whom they apply.

27.4 Personnel management has always had a strong ethical dimension, although personnel managers and the practice of HRM are regularly criticised for failure in social responsibility.

27.5 The CIPD has a code for its members, setting standards of conduct in accuracy, confidentiality, counselling, developing others, equal opportunities, fair dealing and self-development.

27.6 Among current and developing ethical dilemmas are the quality of life in the business, information technology in the workplace, employment, self-improvement and personal management.

GENERAL DISCUSSION TOPICS

1 The chapter opens by explaining that personnel managers for years played down their ethical/welfare role. Why do you think this was?

2 To what extent do you regard Tim Hart's (1993) criticisms as valid?

3 What examples can members of the group produce that would put you in the position of feeling that the demands of your job were in conflict with what you regarded as being right? How would you deal with this and how do the Milgram experiments on obedience, described in Chapter 22, explain, or fail to explain, your actions?

4 Most people agree that differences in rates of pay according to value or effort are justified, but that some differences are 'obscene'. What criteria would you suggest for setting pay differentials within a business that both are seen as fair and are effective in being able to attract and retain appropriate people from the labour market?

FURTHER READING

Fisher, C. and Lovell, A. (2009) *Business Ethics and Values*, 3rd edn. Harlow: Prentice Hall.
This is a fairly weighty textbook providing an integrated discussion of ethical issues for managers in general. There are sections of particular interest to HRM people, including some careful treatments of international comparisons and ethical diferences.

People Management (2003), 10 July.
This issue of the journal is dedicated to examining corporate social responsibility.

Wicks, A.C., Freeman, R.E., Werhane, P.H. and Martin, K.E. (2010) *Business Ethics: A managerial approach*. Boston: Prentice Hall.
An American text which takes an unashamedly managerial approach to the topic and sometimes to blur difficult issues, but still a useful text to provide a distinctly different approach to Fisher and Lovell.

Redman, T. and Wilkinson, A. (2001) *Contemporary Human Resource Management*. Harlow: Prentice Hall.
There is an excellent chapter on employment ethics by Peter Ackers in this volume.

REFERENCES

Arnott, S. (2009) 'GM foresees fewer job cuts', *Busines Week*, 18 November.

Becker, H. and Fritzsche, D.J. (1987) 'A comparison of the ethical behavior of American, French and German managers', *Columbia Journal of World Business*, Winter, pp. 87–95.

Blanchard, K. and Peale, N.V. (1988) *The Power of Ethical Management*. London: Heinemann.

Borrie, G. and Dehn, G. (2002) *Whistleblowing: The new perspective*. London: Public Concern at Work.

Cole, R.E. and Deskins, D.R. (1988) 'Racial factors in site location and employment patterns of Japanese auto firms in America', *California Management Review*, Autumn, p. 11.

Dehn, G. (1997) 'Blow the whistle, save a life', *The Times*, 8 April.

Fisher, C. and Lovell, A. (2009) *Business Ethics and Values*, 3rd edn. Harlow: Prentice Hall.

Flanders, A. (1964) *The Fawley Productivity Agreements*. London: Faber & Faber.

Friedman, M. (1963) *Capitalism and Freedom*. Chicago: University of Chicago Press.

Gillon, R. (2003) 'Four scenarios', *Journal of Medical Ethics*, Vol. 29, pp. 267–8.

Haddock, C. and South, B. (1994) 'How Shell's organisation and HR practices help it to be both global and local', in D.P. Torrington (ed.), *International Human Resource Management*. Hemel Hempstead: Prentice Hall International.

Hampden-Turner, C. and Trompenaars, F. (1993) *The Seven Cultures of Capitalism*. New York: Doubleday.

Hart, T.J. (1993) 'Human resource management: time to exorcize the militant tendency', *Employee Relations*, Vol. 15, No. 3, pp. 29–36.

Institute of Personnel and Development (1996) *Code of Professional Conduct*. London: IPD.

Legge, K. (1978) *Power, Innovation and Problem-solving in Personnel Management*. Maidenhead: McGraw-Hill.

Mintzberg, H. (1973) *The Nature of Managerial Work*. London: Harper & Row.

Murdoch, J. (2009) 'The MacTaggart Lecture', Edinburgh International Television Festival, 29 August.

Murray, J. (1972) 'The role of the shop steward in industry', in D.P. Torrington (ed.), *Handbook of Industrial Relations*. Epping: Gower.

Novak, M. (1996) *Business as a Calling: Work and the examined life*. New York: Free Press.

Royal Dutch Shell (2009) *Business Principles*, available at **www.shell.com/business principles**.

Senior, A. (2004) 'MPs attack insurers over chiefs' pay', *The Times*, 28 January, p. 26.

Stern, S. (2004) 'The perils of CSR', *Royal Society of Arts Journal*, January.

Stapley, M. (2010) 'How HR made a difference at work', *People Management*, February, p. 55.

Storey, J. (1992) *Developments in the Management of Human Resources*. Oxford: Blackwell.

Torrington, D.P. (1968) *Successful Personnel Management*. London: Staples Press.

Torrington, D.P., Hitner, T.J. and Knights, D. (1982) *Management and the Multi-racial Workforce*. Aldershot: Gower.

Wicks, A.C., Freeman, R.E., Werhane, P.H. and Martin, K.E. (2010) *Business Ethics: A managerial approach*. Boston: Prentice Hall.

Wokutch, R.E. (1990) 'Corporate social responsibility, Japanese style', *Academy of Management Executive*, May, pp. 56–72.

Wright, L. and Smye, M. (1996) *Corporate Abuse*. New York: Macmillan.

An extensive range of additional materials, including multiple choice questions, answers to questions and links to useful websites can be found on the Human Resource Management companion website at **www.pearsoned.co.uk/torrington**.

CHAPTER 28

THE CHANGING HR FUNCTION

THE OBJECTIVES OF THIS CHAPTER ARE TO:

1. Identify and explain current models relating to the roles and structure of the HR function
2. Explore the extent to which the HR function operates strategically
3. Examine the extent of shared services and outsourcing and the benefits and drawbacks of these approaches
4. Explore the role of line managers in HRM
5. Debate and critique the current developments in HR roles and structures

The personnel/HR function has developed considerably since its earliest welfare role, through a range of different incarnations. There is a long history of the specialist function analysing its role in the organisation and promoting the way in which such roles need to develop in order for the function to gain greater power and credibility. Much emphasis has been placed therefore on a strategic role. If HR is strategic to business success (Boxall and Purcell 2003) then HR needs to be a strategic player and:

> the case for HR being a strategic partner is becoming stronger, as it rests on the reality that human capital and how it is organized are increasingly pivotal to organizational effectiveness. (Lawler and Boudreau 2009: 15)

In the first decade of the twenty-first century there has been a great deal of attention on how HR roles and structures are changing and much opinion of how they should change in the future.

ANALYSIS OF HR ROLES AND STRUCTURES

One earlier well-known example of the analysis of HR roles is by Tyson and Fell (1985) who identified three roles using a construction management metaphor: architect, clerk of works and contract negotiator, but perhaps the most frequently quoted is Storey's (1992) four roles (handmaiden, regulator, changemaker and adviser) which he identified at the threshold of the move from personnel management to HRM. Both of these typologies were based on the analysis of empirical data.

In 1997 Ulrich proposed an HR role set which has had a significant influence on the way in which HR has subsequently been structured in the UK, and elsewhere. On the basis of work with leading-edge organisations in the USA he proposed four HR roles, using the metaphors of **employee champion**; **administrative expert**; **change agent**; and **strategic partner**. He further identified the summary role of **business partner**, explaining that HR fulfils this role if the four roles above are all effectively achieved.

One of the fundamental features of Ulrich's approach is his view that HR effectiveness can only be achieved if all business needs relating to HR are met, and therefore all roles are fulfilled. Thus, Ulrich argues that HR must deliver on both an administrative level and a strategic level and he still maintains this stance (*see* Crabb 2008). This view has been echoed elsewhere, with comments that operational HR excellence is an essential precursor for the involvement of HR professionals at a strategic level (e.g. Caldwell 2003; CIPD 2006). This is a clear change of thinking from the earlier views which exhorted HR to move from administration to strategy, as in the characterisation of HRM as being in opposition to traditional personnel management (*see*, for example, Storey 1992). It has been argued that Ulrich's model has been the biggest reconception of the HR function since the personnel versus HRM debate and a cursory glance at the advertisements in *People Management* at the time reflects the attraction of the 'Business Partner' role. However, while making the case for strength from the combining of roles, Ulrich does acknowledge the paradox created by trying to fulfil all roles, such as representing employee needs at the same time as implementing a management agenda.

On the basis of further research Ulrich and Brockbank (2005a, 2005b) provided a view of the way in which HR roles had evolved since 1997, and this new analysis focuses on what an HR professional has to do to create value. In the new synthesis of roles, most of the roles have new titles. These are: Employee advocate; Human capital developer; Strategic partner; Functional expert and the compound role of Leader. However, the roles reported in 2005 can be linked back to the earlier model, as shown in Table 28.1.

Roles in Ulrich and Brockbank (2005b)	Explanation of 2005 role	Equivalent role in Ulrich (1997)
Employee advocate	Caring for, listening to, understanding and responding to employee needs, covering issues such as grievances, the impact of strategy on employees, equality, diversity, health and safety, discipline. All of these are played out in a context of the realities of the firm and the performance standards required of individuals.	Employee champion
Human capital developer	Based on the premise that people are a critical asset of the organisation and thus need to be developed proactively with a focus on maximising their potential and contribution in the future. Such human capital developers would be located in Centres of HR Expertise, and often act as coaches working on behaviour and attitudes.	Employee champion
Strategic partner	Multiple dimensions including business expert, change agent, knowledge manager and consultant. Aligning HR with business strategy is key, alongside transformation and cultural change.	Combination of Strategic partner and Change agent
Functional expert	Application of the HR body of knowledge through HR practices. There are two categories of HR practices, those for which HR has direct responsibility (such as recruitment) and those for which responsibility is indirect (such as communications). Some practices are delivered through administrative efficiency and others through policies and interventions.	An expansion of Administrative expert
Leader	Leading the HR function, establishing the function's agenda within the firm and acting as a role model demonstrating the importance of HR in the way they lead their own function. Also contributing to the leadership of the organisation. This role requires that the functions of the four roles above are met.	Similar to the Business partner role in that it requires the functioning of all other roles, but goes beyond this.

Table 28.1 Comparison of HR roles in the Ulrich and Brockbank (2005b) model and the Ulrich (1997) model

We can make some interesting observations about how roles have evolved, in Ulrich's view, over the period. For example the Employee advocate role is now a single clear role rather than being combined with people development as in the old Employee champion role. This reflects the recent imperative to explore and understand the employee voice and employee well-being and a recognition that these are important for the individual and the organisation and were underrepresented in earlier thinking and practice in HRM.

The Human capital developer role reflects increasing attention on the management and development of human capital and the role of HR in this. It is resonant of role titles, both academic and professional, with 'human capital' in the title and in other analyses of HR roles such as the 'human capital steward' in Lengnick-Hall and Lengnick-Hall's analysis, 2003. We discuss the concept of human capital in more detail in Chapters 3 and 29.

While one of the key and differentiating features of the 1997 roles was the prominence of the Administrative expert role, in that it was of equal value to other roles, it is interesting to see that administration has now been subsumed in a role reflecting functional expertise.

Note that while these new roles were published some time ago, much of the debate in academia and professional journals still relates to both the original 1997 roles and the new roles. This is due partly to publishing time-lags, but also reflects the gradual process by which organisations absorb and implement new ideas.

ACTIVITY 28.1

Using a sample (say, between 3 and 6) of the most recent issues of *People Management* analyse the job advertisements in order to answer the following questions:

1. How do the job titles quoted compare with the roles identified by Ulrich (1997) and Ulrich and Brockbank (2005b)?
2. Select those advertisements containing job titles much as 'Strategic partner' or 'Business partner' or 'HR partner' (or equivalents). What are the key objectives, job content and competencies required in each of these roles? What types of variation are there between the job titles and within each job title?
3. What other strategic roles are represented in advertisements?
4. Using a similar sample of magazine issues from 2005 for comparison, how have job titles and objectives/content changed overall?

In addition to a new analysis of HR roles recommendations for a different structure for the HR function have also emerged from Ulrich's work, much of which is suggested in the 1997 text. Initially he proposed a three-legged structure comprising:

- **strategic/business roles**;
- **shared service centres/outsourcing/intranet support**; and
- **centres of HR expertise**

There is evidence that in some large organisations (*see*, for example, Robinson 2006) this structure has replaced the integrated model where one HR team carried out this full range of roles. However, research by the CIPD (2007) found low levels of implementation of the full model (although there is insufficient information on firm size to assess the impact this has in their sample) and the authors comment that it is not as prevalent in its pure form as much of the publicity surrounding the model suggests. They also report some difficulties with the business partner role such as getting drawn into the wrong (operational) activities; tensions between corporate and business levels; failure to be strategic and difficulties finding the right staff. Partly in response to this, and after further work with organisations, Ulrich and his colleagues (2008, 2009) have developed and expanded the model to better reflect the complexity of modern organisations.

The current model has five elements rather than the original three, and which are explained as distinct but overlapping:

- **Corporate HR**: being concerned with corporation-wide integration and initiatives, working with top management.
- **Centres of expertise**: providing specialist support to the service centres, providing expert advice and being involved in the design of HR policy and activities.
- **Embedded HR**: those who focus on the strategic needs of the business unit rather than the corporation, working with the leadership team and sometimes line managers and having a wide range of role titles such as including 'business partner' and 'HR generalist'.
- **Operational executors**: who are based within the business unit dealing with operational HR issues and occasionally administrative work that cannot be dealt with by service centres, enabling 'embedded HR' to focus on strategic issues.
- **Service centres/e-HR**: focusing on administrative and routine issues.

Thus there are now two clear strategic/business partner roles, 'corporate HR' and 'embedded HR', and Ulrich and Brockbank (2009) additionally point out that HR specialists in the centres of expertise can operate as business partners, as can some of those involved with service centres when they build or manage the systems.

The emphasis in this recent work is on the importance of the HR structure matching the structure of the larger business, for example in the extent to which it is decentralised, giving much greater priority to context than the previous model. They also suggest that the five-element model fits most closely with an organisation comprised of allied/diversified businesses rather than a single business of a holding company comprising of vastly different businesses. Ulrich and his colleagues (2009) suggest that for the transformation of the HR function all five elements need to be reviewed.

HR STRATEGIC ROLE

There is much evidence that the strategic or business partner role is the one which has been most attractive to organisations, with these job titles used very heavily initially, although a greater variety of titles is now emerging. HR needs to be credible to offer a strategic contribution and it has been suggested that such credibility needs to come from being involved in a wider range of business agendas, and there is some evidence of this happening.

WINDOW ON PRACTICE

Broader business involvement for HR professionals

Robinson (2006) reports on the first stage of a CIPD-sponsored research project which aims to explore the changing face of the HR function. One part of this first stage was to convene a panel of academics and senior HR professionals from the Royal Bank of Scotland, Dell, PwC, Centrica, Standard Chartered Bank, Barclays and Diesel. HR professionals agreed that HR needs to be involved in a wider range of business agendas, such as branding, ethics, risk management and corporate social responsibility (CSR) as well as change, and that these would be central to the HR of the future, as would involvement in creating 'employer of choice' status and selling the customer brand.

Source: Summarised from V. Robinson (2006) 'Three legs good?', *People Management*, Vol. 12, No. 21, 26 October, pp. 62–4.

It is worth bearing in mind however that the term business partner is often used as a synonym for strategic partner, and used interchangeably (Francis and Keegan 2006; Robinson 2006), although this is not what Ulrich was originally suggesting. We have already noted that most recently Ulrich and Brockbank (2009) suggest that the business partner role can be played in four of the five elements in their structural model (the operational executor being excluded), but Hennessy (2009: 24) points out that:

> in practice, organisations usually refer to the roles embedded within the business – including operational executors – as HR business partners.

For example Pickard (2004), suggesting that business partners are emerging as the dominant model, explains how in Vauxhall 'partners are working with the business, developing close relationships with line managers and helping to solve issues'. In other organisations partners are roles of a more strategic nature, providing consultancy to senior managers and becoming involved in the wide range of business issues, as above, and in the Prudential example quoted by Pickard in the same article. So, different organisations are interpreting the role in a variety of ways.

In a local government context Griffiths (2005) reports an Employers' Organisation survey which found that 68 per cent of senior HR managers had a strategic partner role as their primary role; however, the survey report suggests reasons for this high figure, one of which is that there are varied interpretations of that role. Furthermore Truss *et al.* (2002) identify ambivalence over the precise meaning of the word 'strategic'. Lawler and Boudreau (2009: 18) put it well when they say:

> It is one thing to say that HR should be a strategic partner; it is quite another to define what it looks like and what it takes to make it happen.

The focus on HR's strategic involvement was a fundamental part of the move towards HRM from personnel management. However, prescriptive literature appears to display similar levels of exhortation for the function to become more strategic, and research suggests that while some progress may have been made there remains a wide gap between rhetoric and reality. Indeed, Lawler and Boudreau (2009), looking at trends in their surveys from 1998 to 2007 found no increase in HR's role in strategy.

In addition to the lack of clarity about the nature of the strategic role, another problem with assessing the extent of strategic involvement is that many surveys on the HR roles are completed by HR specialists alone, and it has often been demonstrated that others in the organisation will not necessarily share the view of the HR specialist on this, and other topics. In a survey which included an assessment of the HR strategic role in India Bhatnagar and Sharma (2005) found that line managers and HR managers differed significantly in their assessment of HR's strategic partner role, with HR managers having a much more positive view of their involvement in this capacity.

Caldwell's (2004) interviewees were mostly optimistic about the growing links between HR policy and business strategy, but this rarely was sufficient for them to be defined as a 'business partner', even though 16 of the 24 respondents were represented in the boardroom. The general view was that HR people are at the implementation end of strategy. We must therefore question the extent to which changes in role titles actually reflect changes in roles carried out.

The extent to which the HR function becomes involved in both organisational and human resource strategy development is dependent on a range of factors, the most often quoted being the presence of an HR Director and this has previously been used as a proxy for strategic involvement. Sparkes (2001) identifies a key role for the HR director as promoting the connection between organisational strategy, culture and people strategy. He maintains that being an HR director means that 'we can almost guarantee that a human element is built into everything strategic from the start' (p. 45).

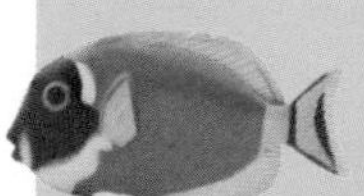

WINDOW ON PRACTICE

Johnson (2008) reports on an increasing phenomenon reflecting the task remit of senior HR people. Increasingly she reports that HR Directorships are combined with other areas and quotes examples as Director of HR and Strategic Change; Director of People and Policy; HR and Customer Services; HR and Property; and Director of HR and Communications. She acknowledges that these roles appear more often in the public sector and to an extent are a response to the need for leaner, more efficient organisations. However, in previous years when Directorships were combined she reminds us that it was usually Finance who took the lead role, for example Director of Finance and HR, whereas now HR are taking the lead.

While this might appear positive news for the function she reports the concerns expressed by Reilly (2008) (Director of HR Research at the Institute for Employment Studies) that this might be a backwards step in HR becoming responsible for 'lots of odd bits'.

Source: Summarised from Johnson, R. (2008) 'More than word play', *People Management*, Vol. 14, No. 14, 10 July, pp. 20–3.

There is some historical evidence over the long term to suggest that HR board membership has increased. However, we found, as did Truss *et al.* (2002), that Directoral HR roles can come and go depending on the context and there is evidence that HR do not have an automatic right to be on the board, and that the function has to earn its place.

The focus on assessing trends in HR Directorships has weakened more recently with the emphasis moving to strategic contributions in a variety of different HR roles, as we have previously seen, the competencies for strategic capability being a key theme.

It is suggested that HR managers need to use business and financial language; describe the rationale for HR activities in terms of added value; use strategic thinking, act as a business manager first and an HR manager second; appoint line managers into the HR function; concentrate on priorities as defined by the business; understand the business they work in, display business acumen, use relationship building and networking skills, and offer well-developed change-management skills that can be used immediately. Sheehan (2005) argues that the business expertise and credibility of the senior HR specialist can either support or prevent strategic HR integration and Truss (2009) found that tenure and reputation effectiveness were important enablers.

Vicky Wright (President of the CIPD) (2006) considers that HR will never get to the strategy table unless it delivers at a basic operational level, which is reminiscent of Ulrich's stance, and on similar lines Lawler and Boudreau (2009) demonstrate that metrics skills are an important precursor to strategic involvement, while not being as key as strategic judgement skills. We look at HR metrics in more detail in Chapter 29.

Other factors influencing the role of the HR function in strategic concerns include the overall philosophy of the organisation towards the value of its people, its culture (*see*, for example, Hennessy 2009; Truss 2009), the mindset of the chief executive, and the working relationship between the chief executive and the most senior HR person.

Case 28.1 on this book's companion website at **www.pearsoned.co.uk/torrington** focuses on the potentially difficult strategic role of the HR function.

HR SHARED SERVICES

Shared services refers to one element out of the five in Ulrich's latest model of the HR function, and service centre staff deal with transactional HR issues for both line managers and employees. They are usually remote call centres and replace local HR officer/administrative staff, with service centre staff having electronic access to personal employee details and HR policies and other information, and are sometimes referred to as partnership service centres or insourcing. Reasons for introducing them revolve around costs savings, the creation of more effective HR services for line managers and employees, and enabling embedded HR/business partners to focus on strategic rather than transactional issues.

WINDOW ON PRACTICE

Strategic reasons for HR shared Service Centres in the Netherlands

Farndale and his colleagues contacted all the companies in the Netherlands using HR shared services and found that the four most common reasons for their introduction were:

52 per cent Improve professionalisation – customer orientation

48 per cent Reorganisation of the HR function to be more customer focused

32 per cent Improve quality, flow and management of work processes

32 per cent Cost savings

Source: Summarised from Farndale, E., Paauwe, J. and Hoeksema, L. (2009) 'In-sourcing HR: shared service centres in the Netherlands', *International Journal of Human Resource Management*, Vol. 20, No. 3, pp. 544–61.

Service centres may be shared across all geographical locations of a business; and some provide services shared with other functions such as IT and finance. HR service centres may provide for transactional needs on an even wider basis, such as across a number of different businesses in a corporation where the businesses have sufficient in common. Alternatively in the public sector the most frequent form of shared services is a centre which serves two or more public bodies, such as local councils. Lastly a shared service centre may be an independent unit jointly owned by the organisation and an external supplier, for example as Rotherham Borough Council entered into a strategic partnership with BT to create RBT (Rotherham Brought Together) with a plan to take on work from other clients once the service has bedded in (IDS 2003).

In almost every case this form of HR delivery is supported by e-HR, a self-service intranet (*see* Chapter 29 for more details), so that line managers and employees can update records, or get information to solve their query online, and only if this approach fails do they ring the service centre. In addition in most cases shared services are usually accompanied by a push to devolve operational HR tasks to line managers.

The centre typically has front office staff who deal with phone calls and back office staff who are involved with a variety of other transactional work such as sending out interview invitations, preparing contracts and so on. However, work is sometimes structured by specialist function, for example training or recruitment, or client group. A more recent innovation is allocating staff on an employee life-cycle basis where a new starter will always be dealt with by the same member of service centre staff wherever they move in the organisation (Pickard 2009b). There is usually a system of escalation whereby queries can be fed up to the next level or tier if the original call centre operator cannot resolve them, so for example there would be access to a functional specialist for non-routine or complex queries.

WINDOW ON PRACTICE

HR Shared Service Centre at Capgemini

Capgemini have split their HR department into three divisions: HR business partners; HR specialists; and an HR Service Centre covering enquiries and transactions. The Service Centre is based in two locations: Nairn, Scotland (28 employees) and Kolkata, India (50) with the aim of engendering a 'one team' approach. The Service Centre covers:

payroll administration

an HR helpdesk

recruitment services for graduates and junior staff

management of recruitment offers

processing employment references

processing joiners, leavers and transfers

training administration

sickness absence administration and monitoring

non-sickness absence administration and different forms of leave

The UK service centre went live in 2006 and the Indian centre in 2008, and the aim is to offshore as much work to the Indian centre as possible.

The service centre is supported by an HR intranet for both employees and line managers. The centre operates according to standards, such as a job offer should be turned around in 24 hours; and is subject to a monthly service review. Future plans include expanding the scope of work undertaken by the service centre and offering its facilities to other companies.

Source: IDS (2009) 'Centralising HR Service Provision', HR Study 888, February. London: IDS.

Shared services are a form of centralisation which avoids duplication but which can also be responsive to local needs. Benefits are expected from efficiency savings and lower transaction costs, a more consistent HR approach across the whole of a company and an HR service which is more customer focused and more responsive to business needs. In addition there are potentially increased opportunities for shared learning. One of the advantages of such centres is the metrics that can be derived to assess their performance. Examples are call waiting time, call count, call length, time taken to resolve queries, accuracy and satisfaction measures from users.

WINDOW ON PRACTICE

MoD shares HR operations

The Ministry of Defence (MoD) set up a dedicated in-house agency called the People, Pay and Pensions Agency (PPPA) in 2006 to act as a shared services operation dealing with transactional HR issues. There are shared service centres, in Manchester and Bath, and they cover payroll, absence management, discipline services, health and welfare. This covers 800,000 non-military staff and 200,000 managers. It was expected to save £283 million in its first ten years.

The move was intended to support attempts to devolve more HR responsibility to line managers, and to enable the professional HR function to concentrate more on strategic issues. The strategic HR team is made up of Business Partners and a core strategic team focusing on such areas as talent management. In parallel with these changes the overall HR function is being reduced.

Sources: Adapted from R. Manocha (2006) 'MoD shares HR operations', *People Management*, Vol. 12, No. 5, 9 March, p. 10; and J. Pickard (2009b) 'Calling in the shots', *People Management*, 2 July, pp. 20–3.

The problems with the service centre structure are that local knowledge and business solutions may be lost in the changeover, many low-level administrative roles are created with little potential for career development and there may be an obsession with measurement at the expense of service delivery. Associated e-HR can induce feelings of remoteness, dehumanisation and lack of customer friendliness and anecdotal evidence suggests that in some organisations line managers have difficulty getting through to the centre and eventually give up, and in a survey Reilly (2008) found gaps in service provision and difficulties in defining and communicating the boundary with other parts of HR. He also found that customers did not like standardised services and having various different contact points. Higher staff turnover was also found as employees saw these HR jobs as dull, and cost savings were not always sustained.

WINDOW ON PRACTICE

HR Shared Service in the Scottish Government

This approach has now improved the efficiency of HR delivery but there were initial set up problems. Firstly that the decision to use shared services had not been well communicated and managers and employees were confused and suspicious. HR lost credibility with their customers and the morale of HR staff was very low resulting in the loss of many experienced staff. To solve these problems they focused on the needs of their customers, recognising the differences between their priorities and those of HR and redesigned the system.

Source: Griffiths, J. (2008) 'Shared services works for Scottish Government', *People Management*, Vol. 14, No. 4, 21 February, p. 13.

OUTSOURCING HR

Outsourcing is an alternative approach to shared services but typically involves the same delivery channels: e-HR and a service centre. HR administration, for example pensions, payroll and recruitment, has typically been outsourced. But more specialist aspects have been subject to outsourcing too, such as training and legal work. The definition of outsourcing is somewhat elastic and there is a lack of consensus about a clear definition as Woodall (2009) points out, but she separates out traditional subcontracting of low-skilled tasks from outsourcing business processes where an external provider owns, manages and administers them. Outsourcing the whole of HR (sometimes called end-to-end outsourcing) is also a very different proposition from outsourcing differentiated activities, which has been happening in an ad hoc manner for a much longer time.

The key drivers for outsourcing HR are frequently quoted as reducing costs and improving service delivery. Outsourcing appears to encourage the measurement of the value of HR, which comes about through the need for service-level agreements and key performance indicators with a greater focus on customer satisfaction. Sometimes current HR inefficiencies drive the move to outsourcing. Most of the publicity surrounding HR outsourcing focuses on larger global companies but outsourcing is a slightly different proposition for smaller organisations.

WINDOW ON PRACTICE

Outsourcing in a smaller organisation: Dartford Borough Council

In a deal believed to be the first of its kind Dartford Borough Council has outsourced its entire HR and payroll function. The authority has 400 staff and was originally supported by five members of HR and one member of payroll. The new five year contract with Northgate means that there are no internal HR employees, but one member of Northgate will be on site and others can be contacted remotely. A major driver was dissatisfaction with the current HR service and it is estimated that the Council will save £50,000 a year. When asked whether the Council would miss out on the strategic element of HR, Brooks, Head of Finance and Resources who will handle the outsourced relationship countered that the contract will enable the council to gain strategic expertise from Northgate.

Source: Brockett, J. (2008) 'Dartford Council outsources HR in ground-breaking deal', *People Management*, Vol. 14, No. 5, 6 March, p. 10.

Cooke *et al.* (2005) in the USA identify a wide range of benefits from outsourcing such as allowing a firm to concentrate on its core business; gaining from the specialist supplier's economies of scale and learning from them; shifting the burden of risk and enabling greater numerical flexibility; and the ability to keep costs down due to competitive tendering processes. Outsourcing has also been introduced as a vehicle for effecting changes that would be hard to implement internally. For example in large organisations outsourcing has been used to bring different parts of the organisation together to reduce costs, apply common standards and share best practice, and to provide access to innovative IT solutions. A further advantage that is claimed is that the internal HR function can now concentrate on driving the direction of HR rather than carry out more mundane tasks.

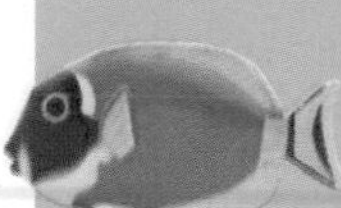

WINDOW ON PRACTICE

BP and Hewitt renew HR outsourcing deal

There was speculation as to whether BP would renew their outsourcing contract with Hewitt, but when they did they expanded it to cover worldwide operations rather than just the UK and US as previously. However most aspects of recruitment have been taken back in-house, and highly complex ex-pat administration was handed back as early as 2006. BP was the first company to secure a major outsourcing contract in 1998 but has experienced problems reflected in the reduction of the scope of the contract.

Source: Pickard, J. (2009a) 'BP and Hewitt renew outsourcing deal', *People Management*, Vol. 15, No. 4, 12 February, p. 10.

However, time is needed to select and develop a relationship and trust with a service provider, and fit with the service provider is important. There is evidence to suggest that the HR function is not the key mover in outsourcing (Woodall 2009) and the CIPD (2009) found that the involvement of HR professionals in the outsourcing process was limited, while considered important, and that decisions were generally made by senior executives in the organisation. Outsourcing providers are more likely to find themselves negotiating with the purchasing department, which is more likely to be concentrating solely on cost, rather than the HR function (*see*, for example, Brockett 2006).

There has been increasing attention to end-to-end outsourcing with strategic functions being included – which is usually the part that is kept in-house. Such deals are reported as growing in North America (Klass 2008); however, in the UK a CIPD survey (2007) found that only 4 per cent of those organisations that used service centres outsourced the whole of the function, and outsourcing discrete processes in a tactical way remains most evident (Reilly 2008). There is also evidence that big outsourcing contracts are being replaced by smaller deals although some are focused on less typical areas such as staff surveys and mediation (Syedain 2009), thus resembling traditional subcontracting.

It will be some time before the full impact of such major long-term outsourcing relationships can be assessed. However, a range of problems is beginning to come through and many large contracts continue to be renegotiated due to problems such as suppliers bidding at too low a price and not being able to fulfil the deal, not knowing which processes need to stay in-house and lack of clarification of roles.

ACTIVITY 28.2

We noted that outsourcing the whole of the HR function is a different proposition from outsourcing some specific aspects. In the context of your own organisation, or one with which you are familiar:

1 If you were to outsource some specific aspects of HR, what would they be and why would you choose them?
Or
What aspects of HR are already outsourced, how effective has this proved to be and why?

2 If you were to outsource the whole HR function what reactions would you anticipate from employees and line managers, why do you think they would react like this and what could be done to support them through this change?
Or
If your organisation has already outsourced the entire HR function how effective has this proved to be and why?

WINDOW ON PRACTICE

BT and Accenture: Managing a global multi-process outsourcing contract

Julie Clapham, HR Transformation Director for BT characterises outsourcing as an evolutionary journey as BT continues to renegotiate its second contract with Accenture, three years into it. She suggests that too little attention is paid in advance to the details of what needs to be done and who will do what; and more effort should be made to decide which processes to outsource and which need to stay in-house as they are culture-dependent. She also suggests that the time needed for negotiating and managing the contract is much greater than anticipated, and that there are huge hidden costs with ongoing commitment, such as developing retained HR staff to adapt to the changes.

Source: Pickard, J. (2009), 'Taught in the Act', *People Management Guide*, Vol. 14, No. 6, 20 March, pp. 8–10.

Main (2006) suggests the lack of success of some outsourcing experiences is due to the fact that outsourcing is seen as a way to get rid of a problem (such as cost and inadequate computer systems) and the view that once activities are outsourced management responsibility for them ends. Overall problems include the potential loss of skill, knowledge and capacity, limiting the development of a distinctive HR contribution; short-term disruption and discontinuity and potentially a longer-term reduction in the quality of services, damaging HR's relationship with the line. The loss of HR employee morale and motivation, partly due to more limited career prospects, has also been identified, and damage to long-term competitiveness. In addition Woodall (2009) found that rather than cost savings there were sometimes increases in costs. Some organisations have even brought HR back in-house but as Reilly (2008) points out this is very often difficult due to the lack of infrastructure, resources and knowledge.

WINDOW ON PRACTICE

LV= brings HR back in-house

LV= was formerly Liverpool Victoria and is a mutual insurance company employing around 4,000 staff.

In this growing company Dave Smith, HR Director of LV= was given the opportunity to redesign the HR function and one of the first things he did was to bring the outsourced HR function back in-house. The Chief Executive saw HR strategy as integral to the growth of and change in the company so there was support from the top. Smith stated that the savings made by bringing HR back in-house were estimated to be £3 million over the past year.

Source: *People Management* (2009) 'In-house HR saves £3m for insurance group', *People Management*, 24 September, p. 10.

John Hofmeister, director of HR at the Royal Dutch/Shell group, attacks outsourcing as leading to the corrosion of HR departments, and he argues that only high levels of internal HR staffing can lead to and maintain high levels of HR practices (*People Management* 2002). In a slightly different vein Gratton (2003) argues that outsourcing combined with other trends such as devolution fragments the HR function, and she identifies a growing alienation between diffrent providers (outsourcing agencies, line managers and remaining specialists in the HR function). One of the major challenges is for the HR function to manage an outsourcing contract (*see*, for example, Main 2006 for advice) and pull together the separate outsourced and segmented elements (CIPD 2006).

Case 28.2 on this book's companion website, **www.pearsoned.co,uk/torrington** focuses on HR outsourcing.

THE ROLE OF LINE MANAGERS IN HR

For some time there has been an emphasis on the devolution of HR management by integrating HR activities with day-to-day line management. We use the word devolution here to mean the reallocation of HR tasks to managers outside the HR function, focusing on the line taking ownership of HR activities, enabling HR specialists to act as consultant, coach, facilitator and strategic partner, which has been identified as a key plank of HRM, being different from a traditional personnel management approach (*see*, for example, Storey 1992). Such devolution of operational day-to-day HR tasks has been described by Hope-Hailey *et al.* (2005) as devolving the employee champion role.

The advantages of this approach to restructuring HR activities have been identified as allowing HR specialists to focus on strategic rather than operational concerns, and a strengthening of the relationship between the employee and his or her manager, resulting in a more positive management approach to employee performance. The importance of the role of the line manager in delivering HR is well documented, especially by Hutchinson and Purcell (2004: ix), as in their research they found that first-line manager behaviour is:

> the most important factor explaining the variation in both job satisfaction and job discretion, or the choice that people have over how they do their jobs. It is also one of the most important factors in developing organizational commitment.

Hutchinson and Purcell suggest that line managers bring HR policies to life, and in the extract quoted above show how line managers have a direct impact on employee performance.

However, the difficulties of devolving HR activities to first-line managers have also been consistently highlighted, and Purcell and Hutchinson (2007) identify a gap between what is formally required in the HR policy and what line managers actually deliver. In our research, we found that implementation was difficult, sometimes being described as a game of tennis where although there was a deliberate policy to devolve HR activities, and managers were encouraged to take them on, these often bounced straight back to HR specialists (Hall and Torrington 1998). The idea that line managers need to take on more day-to-day HR activities has been countered by line managers' lack of skills and interest in this. For example Hope-Hailey *et al.* (2005) on the basis of their research found that line managers neither were motivated nor had the ability to take on people management responsibilities. Interestingly McConville (2006) in the context of the NHS, the Armed Forces and the Fire Services, found that middle managers wanted to be proactive in HR, were committed to it, and exceeded their job requirements to carry out HR activities, but their already substantial workload created the greatest barrier. Caldwell (2004) found that managers resisted taking full ownership of HR and conversely HR professionals wanted to retain control over HR policy. His interviewees were generally reluctant to take devolution 'too far', as ultimately too much devolution may result in the HR role itself being devalued, and we found that HR specialists were keen to hand over the responsibility for day-to-day HR activities, but were less keen to hand over authority for them and the associated budgets. Devolution has also been identified as problematic due the lack of consistency of HR decisions and lack of integration resulting in more difficulties in implementing HR strategy.

Maxwell and Watson (2007), on the basis of their investigation into line manager and HR manager perspectives of line management involvement in HR in Hilton Hotels, propose three types of line manager buy-in which are key to their active involvement in HR activities. These are:

- a conceptual understanding of the reasons for their involvement;
- the ability to implement these activities effectively through a clear HR role and having sufficient capability; and
- belief that their involvement in HR is valuable.

Interestingly the authors also found a general lack of shared understanding between line managers and HR specialists about the role of line managers in HR, and some indications that the more similar the perceptions of HR and line managers, the better the hotel performance, whereas the more divergent their perceptions, the weaker the hotel performance.

CRITIQUE OF THE DEVELOPMENT OF HR ROLES AND STRUCTURES

The evidence suggests that while it is difficult successfully to change HR roles, as they are socially constructed and depend on the expectations of other members of the role set (*see*, for example, Truss *et al.* 2002), there have been changes in the overall level of line manager involvement in HR, in the use of outsourcing and shared service centres and in the emphasis on strategic roles.

WINDOW ON PRACTICE

Reality of HR: strategy or administration?

Brewster and Less (2006) conducted research in 60 international non-governmental organisations (NGOs), many small, but including some large ones such as the Roman Catholic Church. They found HRM issues were neglected and not regarded as strategic, and that the emphasis was on campaigning programmes, rather than on enhancing the employee experience and performance. Where HR specialists did exist they were rarely represented at senior levels. Yet internally there was dissatisfaction with HR, particularly among fieldworkers. HR managers felt their role was purely administrative and reactive, and that they lacked involvement in strategic planning and had no presence on trustee boards. Line managers lacked the skills to promote employee commitment via concern for employee capability and work-life balance.

Source: Summarised from C. Brewster and S. Less (2006) 'The success of NGOs hinges on their people – but HR is neglected in the sector', *People Management*, Vol. 12, No. 6, 23 March, p. 44.

One interpretation of these developments is that the HR function is finally gaining prized strategic involvement giving it credibility and power in organisations. However, not only do we need to separate the rhetoric from real changes, but these developments in the function are not without their problems. As Hope-Hailey *et al.* (2005) suggest on the basis of their investigation into the banking industry, the HR function may be able to become more strategic, but the employee experience may deteriorate. The concentration on strategic roles appears to have gone hand in hand with the abandonment of the role of employee champion. There is considerable evidence to suggest that the employee champion role is still equated with tea and sympathy, and that concern for employee well-being is seen as a signal that the HR function is being dragged back to its old welfare role (*see*, for example, Francis and Keegan 2006; Beckett 2005; and Pickard 2005), with consequent loss of status and credibility. In an interview one senior CIPD adviser stated that 'nobody wants to be an employee champion. They all think it's ideologically unsound' (Francis and Keegan 2006).

In case studies of the HR function in large local authorities Harris (2006) found increasing use of self-service and outsourcing, which appeared to undermine the role of employee champion. She suggests that as the HR function becomes distanced from the workforce and line managers, the consequent loss of knowledge of operational issues means that the function is less able to act as an employee advocate. She found that employees were less likely to see HR as a form of support and advice and suggests they are more likely to approach the union or use legal redress, making the employment relationship more adversarial. She proposes that this loss of touch hinders rather than enables a strategic role, and that lack of opportunity to build relationships and trust with both the line and employees may have a negative impact on promoting employee commitment (Harris 2007).

Along the same lines Francis and Keegan (2005) in their research, which involved interviews with key CIPD staff, HR practitioners, HR course leaders, students and union representatives, found the employee champion role was disintegrating in almost all of the organisations they looked at. They found growth of the business partner role and the parallel restructuring of the HR function which appeared to downgrade the employee-facing role, a reduction in the number of HR specialists and the devolution of face-to-face HR to line managers. They identified a loss of employee trust and confidence and a cost to employee well-being. Respondents believed employees were losing out because line managers did not have time to prioritise HR issues, or their training, and often HR advisers were geographically distant, and so employees were more likely to turn to the union for advice.

The unions are already aware of this trend and Harry Donaldson (Regional Secretary of GMB Scotland) commented that unions were worried about HR shifting its focus away from the workforce and away from 'traditional HR' which was associated with welfare and trust. Given that line managers do not always have the necessary skills, he suggested that the chasm thus created between HR and the workforce would be filled by the unions (*People Management* 2005).

Not only do these developments have potential consequences for employees, they also have consequences for HR practitioners. Francis and Keegan (2006) found that HR practitioners do not consider employee champion roles as career-enhancing moves, and in 2005 Francis and Keegan reported that HR professionals were further concerned that the 'people' element of the job was diminishing. They suggested the people element is a key reason why many enter the profession, and that changes are resulting in disenchanted HR professionals. In addition they found evidence of an increasing split between strategic and non-strategic HR roles. Not only does this split hinder strategic parts of the role and therefore the fulfilment of the HR role overall, but HR professionals perceive that people are parachuted into the top HR jobs from outside the profession (Francis and Keegan 2006), a development which clearly limits career progression for HR professionals.

In terms of the HR function as a whole devolution (to line managers) and decentralisation (from the centre to specific business units) create problems for consistency and integration. Caldwell (2003) also suggests that the decentralisation of HRM to the business unit level has resulted in HRM being under more pressures associated with costs, value and delivery and suggests that this has been the driver for the fragmentation or balkanisation of HR into specialist subtasks with some parts outsourced externally or to the line. Caldwell suggests that the main risk here is de-professionalisation of the function, and that decentralisation may cause the HR contribution to constantly shift, thereby diminishing the clarity of its role or function. He suggests that the function remains dogged by ambiguity and conflict.

There is however a view that Ulrich's work has been misinterpreted and that by roles he meant tasks to be achieved rather than discrete jobs. In spite of this the current focus on Ulrich's roles and structures appears to be based on the assumption that what is good for the organisation is good for the employee. Francis and Keegan (2006) put this well when they say that current models, like earlier ones, are premised upon the assumption of mutuality of interests between all stakeholders – employees, managers, consultants and HR professionals. And Hope-Hailey *et al*. (2005) suggest Ulrich's conception of roles is at best unitarist or at worst naive. The emerging consensus appears to be that there is too much emphasis on models and not enough on skills, people and delivery in context, and that there is a need for the HR function to be agile and flexible in response to the needs of the organisation and consequently for the less rigid application of models (*see*, for example, CIPD 2006).

SUMMARY PROPOSITIONS

28.1 For many years categorisations of the HR role have been proposed. These include Tyson and Fell (1985); and Storey (1992). The most recent proposal is from Ulrich and Brockbank (2005a) who identify these roles: employee advocate; human capital developer; strategic partner; functional expert; and leader, with a compound role.

28.2 There is some evidence of larger organisations employing Ulrich's recommended three-legged HR department structure. However, problems experienced have resulted in a new five-element model: corporate strategic HR; embedded HR, the strategic/business partner group within the business; operational executors within the business; an administrative/transactional group, usually comprising shared services, e-HR and/or outsourcing; and a centre of functional expertise group.

28.3 The strategic partner role has been most attractive to organisations. The extent to which HR specialists are involved in HR strategy is influenced by the environment of the business, its culture, the perspective of the chief executive, HR board membership and the qualities, characteristics and working relationships of the most senior HR specialist.

28.4 While there have been some early problems with outsourcing, this continues to be pursued by many organisations, and often involves cost savings and staff reductions.

28.5 Devolution of HR activities to line managers enables HR professionals to focus on strategic issues. But line managers often do not have the required motivation, skills or time to carry out HR activities effectively.

28.6 There are concerns that the focus on the business partner role has been at the expense of the employee champion/advocate role, with the consequence that employee well-being is compromised.

28.7 The current trends in HR roles and structure are fragmenting the HR function, resulting in a lack of integration and consistency, and difficulties in effective strategic HR.

GENERAL DISCUSSION TOPICS

1 Does it really matter whether the most senior HR person is on the board of directors, or are personal work relationships, political alliances and personal track records more important?

2 'Outsourcing may be an effective solution in the medium term, but it brings short-term disruption and long-term damage to organisational capability and success.' To what extent do you agree or disagree with this statement?

3 Debate the following comment: 'There has always been a debate about the extent to which day-to-day HR activities should be shared between the professional function and the line. In essence nothing has really changed.'

FURTHER READING

Caldwell, R. (2008) 'HR Business partner competency models: re-contextualising effectiveness', *Human Resource Management Journal*, Vol. 18, No. 3, pp. 275–94.
Based on survey and interview evidence Caldwell provides a useful insight into the value of competency models, finding them to be weak at predicting performance in business partner roles. He also highlights the importance of contextual factors such as the degree of change within the HR function, patterns of centralisation/decentralisation, the consistency of the implementation of business partnering and overall levels in the reduction of transactional HR work.

Delmotte, J. and Sels, L. (2008) 'HR Outsourcing: threat or opportunity?', *Personnel Review*, Vol. 37, No. 5, pp. 543–63.
This article reports research in the Belgian context which provides some interesting data on a key debate: whether outsourcing is a means of cost cutting and reducing the numbers in HR or whether it is an instrument for creating more time for HR to play a more strategic role.

Ulrich, D. and Allen, J. (2009) 'Grow your own', *People Management*, 3 December, pp. 32–4.
An insightful summary of the recent five-element model of HR structures. This is an informative yet quick read if you do not have time for the full book or the lengthier academic articles.

Reilly, P. and Williams, T. (2006) *Strategic HR: Building the capability to deliver*. London: Gower.

It is refreshing to find a book on the HR role which is set in a UK rather than a US context. The purpose of the book is not to sell an approach but to enable practitioners to work through the reasons for adopting a particular approach and how this might be pursued. The authors draw on experiences of the HR role in the UK and how it is evolving, and provide a sound critique of the challenges and barriers to be overcome. They emphasise the development of capability rather than purely focusing on structures and processes.

REFERENCES

Beckett, H. (2005) 'Perfect partners', *People Management*, Vol. 11, 1 April, pp. 16–23.

Bhatnagar, J. and Sharma, A. (2005) 'The Indian perspective of strategic HR roles and organizational learning capability', *The International Journal of Human Resource Management*, Vol. 16, No. 9, pp. 1711–39.

Boxall, P. and Purcell, J. (2003) *Strategy and Human Resource Management*. Basingstoke: Palgrave Macmillan.

Brewster, C. and Less, S. (2006) 'The success of NGOs hinges on their people: but HR is neglected in the sector', *People Management*, Vol. 12, No. 6, p. 44.

Brockett, J. (2006) 'London bodies plan shared services', *People Management*, Vol. 12, No. 11, p. 10.

Brockett, J. (2008) 'Dartford Council outsources HR in ground-breaking deal', *People Management*, Vol. 14, No. 5, p. 10.

Caldwell, R. (2003) 'The changing roles of personnel managers: old ambiguities, new uncertainties', *Journal of Management Studies*, Vol. 40, No. 4, pp. 983–1004.

Caldwell, R. (2004) 'Rhetoric, facts and self-fulfilling prophecies: exploring practitioners' perceptions of progress in implementing HRM', *Journal of Management Studies*, Vol. 35, No. 3, pp. 196–215.

CIPD (2006) *The HR Function: A report on an event to discuss the changing shape of the HR function*. London: CIPD.

CIPD (2007) *The Changing HR Function*. London: CIPD.

CIPD (2009) *HR Outsourcing and the HR Function: Threat or opportunity?* London: CIPD.

Cooke, F., Shen, J. and McBride, A. (2005) 'Outsourcing HR as a competitive strategy? A literature review and an assessment of implications', *Human Resource Management*, Vol. 44, No. 4, pp. 413–32.

Crabb, S. (2008) 'Don't drop transactional role, Ulrich warns HE', *People Management*, Vol. 14, No. 7, p. 10.

Farndale, E., Paauwe, J. and Hoeksema, L. (2009) 'In-sourcing HR: shared service centres in the Netherlands', *International Journal of Human Resource Management*, Vol. 20, No. 3, pp. 544–61.

Francis, H. and Keegan, A. (2005) 'Slippery slope', *People Management*, Vol. 11, No. 13, pp. 26–31.

Francis, H. and Keegan, A. (2006) 'The changing face of HRM: in search of balance', *Human Resource Management Journal*, Vol. 16, No. 3, pp. 231–49.

Gratton, L. (2003) 'The Humpty Dumpty effect', *People Management*, Vol. 9, No. 9, p. 18.

Griffiths, J. (2005) 'Local heroes?', *People Management*, Vol. 11, No. 5, pp. 12–13.

Griffiths, J. (2008) 'Shared services works for Scottish Government', *People Management*, Vol. 14, No. 4, p. 13.

Guest, D. and King, Z. (2001) 'Personnel's paradox', *People Management*, Vol. 17, No. 19, pp. 24–9.

Hall, L. and Torrington, D. (1998) *The Human Resource Function: The dynamics of change and development*. London: Financial Times/Pitman Publishing.

Harris, L. (2006) 'Have council changes eroded HR's role as employee champion?', *People Management*, Vol. 12, No. 21, p. 72.

Harris, L. (2007) 'The changing nature of the HR function in UK local government and its role as "employee champion"', *Employee Relations*, Vol. 30, No. 1, pp. 34–47.

Hennessy, J. (2009) 'Take your partners and advance', *People Management*, Vol. 15, No. 3, pp. 24–7.

Hope-Hailey, V., Farndale, E. and Truss, C. (2005) 'The HR department's role in organizational performance', *Human Resource Management Journal*, Vol. 15, No. 3, pp. 49–66.

Hutchinson, S. and Purcell, J. (2004) *Bringing Policies to Life: The vital role of front-line managers in people management. Executive Briefing*. London: CIPD.

IDS (2003) *Outsourcing HR Administration*, IDS Study Plus. London: IDS.

IDS (2009) *Centralising HR Service Provision*, HR Study 888, February. London: IDS.

Johnson, R. (2008) 'More than word play', *People Management*, Vol. 14, No. 14, pp. 20–3.

Klass, B. (2008) 'Outsourcing and the HR Function: an examination of trends and developments within North American Firms', *International Journal of Human Resource Management*, Vol. 19, No. 8, pp. 1500–14.

Lawler, E. and Boudreau, J. (2009) 'The strategic partner role', *People and Strategy*, Vol. 32, No. 1, pp. 15–22.

Lengnick-Hall, M. and Lengnick-Hall, C. (2003) *Human Resource Management in the Knowledge Economy*. San Francisco: Berrett-Koehler Inc.

McConville, T. (2006) 'Devolved RM responsibilities, middle-managers and role dissonance', *Personnel Review*, Vol. 35, No. 6, pp. 637–53.

Main, C. (2006) 'How to manage an outsourcing contract', *People Management*, Vol. 12, No. 13, pp. 44–5.

Manocha, R. (2006) 'MoD Shares HR operations', *People Management*, Vol. 12, No. 5, p. 10.

Maxwell, G. and Watson, S. (2007) 'Perspectives on line managers in human resource management: Hilton International's UK Hotels', *International Journal of Human Resource Management*, Vol. 17, No. 6, pp. 1152–70.

People Management (2002) 'HR departments are corroded by the extent of outsourcing', Vol. 8, No. 20, p. 10.

People Management (2005) 'Address people needs, not just business needs, advises GMB', Vol. 11, No. 6, p. 10.

People Management (2009) 'In-house HR saves £3m for insurance group', *People Management*, 24 September, p. 10.

Pickard, J. (2004) 'One step beyond', *People Management*, Vol. 10, No. 13, pp. 26–31.

Pickard, J. (2005) 'Part, not partner', *People Management*, Vol. 11, No. 21, pp. 48–50.

Pickard, J. (2009a) 'BP and Hewitt renew outsourcing deal', *People Management*, Vol. 15, No. 4, p. 10.

Pickard, J. (2009b) 'Calling in the shots', *People Management*, 2 July, pp. 20–3.

Pickard, J. (2009c) 'Taught in the act', *People Management Guide*, Vol. 14, No. 6, pp. 8–10.

Purcell, J. and Hutchinson, S. (2007) 'Front-line managers as agents in the HRM-performance causal chain: theory, analysis and evidence', *Human Resource Management Journal*, Vol. 17, No. 1, pp. 3–20.

Reilly, P. (2008) 'Should you branch out?', *People Management*, Vol. 14, No. 6, pp. 16–17.

Rippin, S. and Dawson, G. (2001) 'How to outsource the HR function', *People Management*, Vol. 7, No. 19, pp. 42–3.

Robinson, V. (2006) 'Three legs good?', *People Management*, Vol. 12, No. 21, pp. 62–4.

Sheehan, C. (2005) 'A model for HRM strategic integration', *Personnel Review*, Vol. 32, No. 2, pp. 192–209.

Sparkes, J. (2001) 'Job's a good 'un', *People Management*, Vol. 7, No. 20, pp. 44–7.

Storey, J. (1992) *Developments in the Management of Human Resources*. Oxford: Blackwell.

Syedain, H. (2009) 'Out of the ordinary', *People Management*, 5 November, pp. 20–2.

Truss, C., Gratton, L., Hope-Hailey, V., Stiles, P. and Zaleska, J. (2002) 'Paying the piper: choice and constraint in changing HR functional roles', *Human Resource Management Journal*, Vol. 12, No. 2, pp. 39–63.

Truss, C. (2009) 'Changing HR functional forms in the UK public sector', *International Journal of Human Resource Management*, Vol. 20, No. 4, pp. 717–37.

Tyson, S. (1995) *Human Resource Strategy*. London: Pitman.

Tyson, S. and Fell, A. (1985) *Evaluating the Personnel Function*. London: Hutchinson.

Ulrich, D. (1997) *Human Resource Champions: The next agenda for adding value and delivering results*. Boston: Harvard Business School Press.

Ulrich, D. and Brockbank, W. (2005a) 'Role call', *People Management*, Vol. 11, No. 13, pp. 24–8.

Ulrich, D. and Brockbank, W. (2005b) *The HR Value Proposition*. Boston: Harvard Business School Press.

Ulrich, D. and Brockbank, W. (2009) 'The HR business-partner model: past learnings and future challenges', *People and Strategy*, Vol. 32, No. 2, pp. 5–7.

Ulrich, D., Younger, J. and Brockbank, W. (2008) 'The twenty-first-century HR Organisation', *Human Resource Management*, Vol. 47, No. 4, pp. 829–50.

Ulrich, D., Allen, J., Brockbank, W., Younger, J. and Nyman, M. (2009) *HR Transformation*. Maidenhead: McGraw-Hill.

Woodall, J. (2009) 'Making the decision to outsource human resources', *Personnel Review*, Vol. 38, No. 3, pp. 236–52.

Wright, V. (2006) 'Shaping up for strategy', *People Management*, Vol. 12, No. 21, p. 7.

CHAPTER 29

INFORMATION TECHNOLOGY AND HUMAN CAPITAL MEASUREMENT

THE OBJECTIVES OF THIS CHAPTER ARE TO:

1 Explore the contribution of information technology to the effective and efficient provision of HR

2 Identify a variety of approaches to measuring HR and human capital

3 Explain a range of simple measures which are frequently used

4 Explore the use of scorecards and other strategic frameworks in measuring human capital

5 Identify types of human capital reporting and the role of these

Technology is being used increasingly and in a variety of ways to support HR activities and, arguably, to give HR professionals more time for more strategic matters. Some of this extra time is being redirected to a range of human capital evaluation activities that are also supported by a more advanced use of technology. We have already explored some of the research which shows how different HR activities affect the bottom line, and how critical intangible assets are to a firm's value. This focus is growing in importance. Traditional accountancy measures are inadequate to reflect the value of people to the organisation. Measures are needed to demonstrate how people are an asset adding value to the business rather than just a cost. Measurement of HR has become increasingly important but many HR specialists resist the concept and methods of measurement and progress is challenging.

THE CONTRIBUTION OF TECHNOLOGY TO EFFECTIVE AND EFFICIENT HR PROVISION

There is a wide range of ways in which technology can contribute to the HR function and we have discussed many of these so far in this text, for example the use of technology to enhance recruitment and selection activities and to widen the range of learning experiences, and a broad summary of the potential uses of technology to support HR activities is given in Table 29.1.

In this section therefore we will focus on technology as a means of providing and manipulating HR information, via HRMS (human resource management systems) and technology as a means of delivering HR as in e-HR which we touched upon in

Table 29.1 Potential uses of technology to support HR activities

Activity	Examples
People development and performance management	E-learning Online appraisal systems such as 360° feedback Training needs analysis Career management and succession planning
Resource management	Online recruitment and selection Induction packages HR planning and forecasting Time and attendance
Employee relations and communications	Intranet Shared service centres Organisational development (OD) approaches Team development
HR information and accounting	Intranet Employee and manager self-service HR metrics/human capital
Retention and reward	Payroll Total reward statements Employee self-service in creation of flexible rewards packages Reward modelling and pay reviews Pensions and benefits administration

Source: Adapted from CIPD (2007a) *Technology in HR: How to get the most out of technology in people management*. London: CIPD.

Chapter 28. In the latter part of this chapter we will see how such systems also have the potential to provide a major input into Human Capital Measurement (HCM).

HRMS/HRIS

HRISs (Human Resource Information Systems), in one form or another, have been around for over three decades. Early systems were basic administrative tools containing employee data, with operational, management, analysis, modelling, and interactive facilities gradually being exploited over time. There continues to be an emphasis on administrative purposes and the development of such systems for analytical ends and exploitation has been painfully slow and patchy, although the renaming of such systems as Human Resource *Management* Systems, as evidenced in IDS's 2008 Study, reflects the progress that some organisations have made. Depending on the system introduced or updated, benefits are expected in terms of quality of service, speed, accuracy, cost and flexibility. One of the key attractions of technology for the HR function is that it can reduce time on administrative chores to free this up for more strategic activities. However, the introduction and enhancement of HRMS is usually accompanied by staff cuts, and Gardener and her colleagues (2003) found that although the technology did free up time in one sense it also created a need to spend time on IT support and training.

In terms of the contribution that technology makes to the HR function, Zuboff (1988) makes a very useful distinction between automating current activities, so that they are done more efficiently and require fewer staff, and informating. This latter is explained as supplying new forms of information which requires new ways of thinking, for example by carrying out activities in a different way, carrying out new activities, integrating data across the whole organisation, making access to the data available to different users, rather than replicating current activities and ways of doing things. The tendency to automate rather than informate severely restricts the potential of any HRMS.

If we link this view of the potential of technology with the HR capability model of Reddington *et al.* (2005), the variable contribution of HRMSs to HRM becomes clearer. Reddington *et al.* suggest that three primary drivers promote HR capability:

- 'operational' (i.e. improving cost effectiveness by reducing the costs of its services and headcount);
- 'rational' (i.e. improving its services to employees and line managers who are increasingly demanding); and
- 'transformational' (i.e. addressing the key strategic drivers of the organisation).

Automating in Zuboff's terms clearly addresses the operational driver, and we have seen evidence of this in reducing HR headcounts, and automating may also make some contribution to the rational driver. Informating, however, is essential to progress the transformational driver and also to satisfactorily progress the rational driver, and this is essential for HRMSs to make a significant contribution to HCM. So if technology is to make a real contribution to the HR function we need to go beyond automating. The evidence for this is patchy but increasing and there are some good examples of new approaches which we have quoted in previous chapters.

In the CIPD survey on *People Management and Technology* (CIPD 2005), which is the latest published at the time of writing, just over three-quarters of the respondents reported use of an HRIS, and just over half of these had a single integrated HR system, but few (16 per cent) were integrated with other IT systems in the wider organisation, which is important for informating. The three key functions of an HRIS were reported as absence management, training and reward, and these are also the three most likely to be run as an integrated system within HR. Analysis showed that the greater the proportion of functions that are integrated as part of the HRIS, the more likely that the system would be used to aid human capital reporting, comply with supply-chain partner requirements, improve profitability, reduce headcount and deliver against economic criteria. Interestingly, respondents said that if they were to introduce their system again almost three-quarters would seek greater integration and more clarity with providers; slightly fewer respondents said they would arrange more training.

Initial users of HRMSs were HR staff themselves, but there has been considerable development over the past 10 to 15 years. Gainey and Klaas (2008) identify three other user groups: line managers; employees; and applicants to the organisation, and 46 per cent of respondents to the CIPD survey identified line managers elsewhere in the business as intended users of the system, with 32 per cent including employees. This suggests that some progress is being made in this respect towards informating.

Tansley and colleagues (2001) provide an excellent insight into an organisation trying to develop an HRIS intended to encourage transformational change in the organisation and going beyond automating. This system is shown in the Window on practice below.

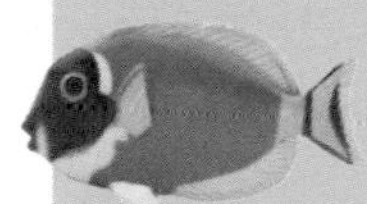

WINDOW ON PRACTICE

Developing an integrated HRIS: a cautionary tale

Tansley and her colleagues (2001) report on an engineering company that was developing an HRIS as part of a business-wide Enterprise Resource Planning System (ERS). This approach meant not only that all HR information would be integrated but that it would also be integrated with other IT systems in the business. This new system was considered to be one of the most important changes in the organisation and an opportunity to break with the past and move to an HRM style of people management. It was to be designed to allow access beyond the HR function, i.e. to other line managers and employees and beyond the organisation, e.g. to any outsourced functions, such as payroll. While the HR project team (designing the HR part of the ERS) were aware that success depended on changing attitudes and the culture of the business, line managers were unfortunately excluded from the planning process. The first stage of work for the project planning team was to map HR processes, but difficulties arose as owners of some of the processes felt their previous work was ignored. There was also an attempt to find a standard 'one best way' to carry out different processes, and this caused problems with different parts of the business, who wanted to tailor things to meet their own needs. A further problem was that each HR process was mapped separately, thereby missing the potential of seeing and doing things differently, and preventing adoption of a more strategic approach. While the HR project manager saw the process as an opportunity to think anew and do things differently others did not want to think so radically and preferred to keep things the same (especially those who were the process owners). Many had difficulties with the idea of devolving HR to line managers and there was a view that senior HR managers were gradually distancing themselves from the project as it was seen to be political suicide to give HR away. Training on the system was confusing as improved versions were constantly being produced. In retrospect, many said they had not understood the full potential of the system.

The researchers concluded that the company had used IT to reproduce, extend and improve on current HR processes by automating HR data, and that it was thus able to add some value at an operational level and reduce headcount. However, the opportunity of informating and reconfiguring the nature of HR work and roles was missed.

Source: C. Tansley, S. Newell and H. Williams (2001) 'Effecting HRM-style practices through an integrated human resource information system. An e-greenfield site?', *Personnel Review*, Vol. 30, No. 3, pp. 351–70.

e-HR

One of the difficulties with e-HR is that it can be defined in a wide range of ways. It can include HR and corporate intranets containing static information, interactive HR and corporate intranets, email-based initiatives and the Internet. The emphasis here is on interactive intranets, and our definition of e-HR is 'using computer-based technologies to put HR activities in the hands of "customers"' (Gainey and Klaas 2008: 51), with such systems sometimes being referred to as self-service HR for line managers and employees. Facilities can be wide ranging and are summarised in Table 29.2.

Clearly some of the above items are password protected as confidential information is involved, and employees and their line managers may have different levels of access. Such systems are often introduced along with HR service centres, the intention being that the system should be the first port of call, before the service centre. In this way the pressure on service centres, using a version of these systems themselves, should be reduced in the long run.

As with other initiatives, much of the drive for such systems has come from the need to reduce the time the HR function spends on administrative tasks to allow it to focus on more strategic matters (Gainey and Klaas 2008; CIPD 2005). IRS (2003) found that improvement in communications (73 per cent) was most frequently cited as the specific reason for introducing e-HR whereas only 37 per cent said they were looking specifically for cost savings. Some organisations cite empowering employees as a reason for introduction. In terms of impact of the system Gainey and Klaas (2008) found improvements in delivery of HR (e.g. time and accuracy); improved communications; cost reduction; HR strategic involvement; and employee involvement.

Some of these applications will clearly require changes in the organisational culture. There are also issues about the access to computers and the computer literacy of some staff. Some companies have introduced kiosks where computers can be used by a range of staff, but there are issues about the extent to which staff will prefer to use their coffee breaks booking holidays on the computer. The CIPD found that access to such self-service systems was limited as only 64 per cent of organisations reported that all employees have access to this, and only 32 per cent said that all employees have been trained to use the system.

Type of facility	Examples
Information and communication	HR policies and procedures Online employee handbooks Induction information Benefits information Available training courses News/newsletters
Downloading of forms	Expenses claim forms Overtime forms Application forms Training request
Interrogation of recorded data	Provision of personal information to employee or line manager such as absence or leave taken to date Pension forecasts
Queries via email to be answered by an HR specialist	Training requests Requests for advice
Uploading information	Change of address and personal details Attendance data Submitting forms such as expenses Choosing flexible benefits from a menu Responding to a staff survey
Managing HR processes	Performance management uses with ongoing recording of performance and development goals, progress and outcomes by employee and manager, maybe including salary review

Table 29.2
e-HR facilities

In addition, such systems may offer cost saving advantages, but can pose special problems of their own inducing feelings of remoteness, dehumanisation and lack of customer friendliness. In addition there are concerns about the loss of the personal touch and security of information (Trapp 2001). *People Management* (2006) reports on a study by Roffey Park Institute which investigated line manager perceptions of e-HR. The two negative aspects reported most frequently were that line managers felt they had insufficient training on the system, and that employees were penalised when they did not keep their records up to date. Managers also felt that they spent too much time on HR administration and that online help available was of poor quality. There is evidence from Voermans and van Veldhoven (2007) that the availability of greater support is likely to lead to a more favourable response from line managers and Alleyne and colleagues (2007) found that line manager satisfaction with such systems was influenced by level of communication and training.

ACTIVITY 29.1

We referred to the 'loss of the personal touch' in the introduction to this discussion of these alternative means of providing HR services.

How important is 'the personal touch' to the employees of today and why do you think this is so?

Web case 29.1 on this book's companion website, **www.pearsoned.co.uk/torrington**, focuses on the use of technology in HR.

MEASURING HR AND HUMAN CAPITAL

Some of the research referred to in previous chapters has a very clear focus on identifying and measuring a range of best practices in terms of workforce organisation and management (such as self-managing teams, high training spend, reduced status differentials) and relating these to impact on productivity and profitability. This is a very specific approach to 'proving' that HR practices affect bottom-line performance. In this chapter we later focus on this type of measurement in the context of specific organisations, but we begin by taking a wider perspective and will review a broader and simpler range of measures which are used to demonstrate how the HR function and HR capital contribute to the organisation.

HR measures are sometimes talked about in the context of measuring the contribution of the HR function. An example of such measures might be the staffing costs of the HR function, recruitment speed, training delivery, management satisfaction with HR advice and services, and so on. The Window on practice provides one of many approaches to such measurement.

WINDOW ON PRACTICE

HR survey: What do managers need from the function?

Cathy Cooper (2001) reports on how Fidelity International redesigned its annual manager survey so that it became a meaningful tool in helping the company to improve people management. The original survey which had been used for five years tended to be a 'popularity contest for HR'. The first stage in redesign was to investigate what the survey should focus on. To this end an external consultant was employed to hold focus group sessions with HR staff to establish the strengths and weaknesses of the department. The survey manager then held one-to-one interviews with managers to establish their concerns. The interview data were then used to frame topics for the survey. The approach taken in the survey was to ask how well all managers, including HR, managed their people rather than how well or badly HR was doing. The survey was designed to take ten minutes to complete and respondents were asked to identify the extent to which they agreed or disagreed with a number of statements. Respondents were invited to make any additional comments they wished. Some questions were retained, however, to get specific information on HR's performance. The survey was delivered by the company intranet to make responding easy. Of the 500 managers they invited to participate they received completed questionnaires from over half.

The results of the survey were used to develop 12 broad goals for the HR function with which individual objectives will be aligned. Senior managers have been involved in deciding how the goals could best be met, and then HR directors and their teams in different locations will develop a project action plan.

Source: Summarised from C. Cooper (2001) 'Win by a canvass', *People Management*, Vol. 7, No. 2, 25 January, pp. 42–4.

Such factors are clearly the responsibility of the people in the HR function and are under their control. They are designed to show how the HR function adds value to the organisation and can provide a way of capturing how that value is improved over time. Most HR measures, however, are within the control partly of members of the HR function, and partly of others in the organisation, particularly where HR is devolved to line managers. For example absence and employee turnover are typical measures in many organisations. But to what extent are absence levels, for example, the result of the absence policy (and HR may or may not have designed this alone)? Other factors that may have an effect are: the way the policy is implemented by line managers, the influence of other policies (such as work-life balance), the influence of the way that work is structured and commitment to peers (as for example in self-managing teams). The list could go on. It could be argued that the HR function has an ultimate responsibility for all of this. In reality, however, this is not a tenable view. There is also a very great emphasis on partnership in HR, requiring many activities to be business driven and owned rather than HR driven and owned. Thus many HR measures represent aspects of human capital in the organisation on which the HR function has some influence.

ACTIVITY 29.2

Employee turnover is frequently measured in organisations. Identify which aspects of the organisation have an influence on this and who in the organisation would be seen as having a responsibility for these aspects.

We move on now from the specific contribution of the HR function to discuss human capital measurement (HCM), which has attracted considerable attention, with some organisations setting up dedicated roles and units to undertake HCM, either within or attached to the HR function. We identified broadly above the ultimate purpose of measurement in that it identifies the contribution of people to the performance of the organisation and enables the organisation to improve this contribution. This contribution is as we have noted previously very difficult to disentangle from other factors in the situation and is also difficult to measure quantitatively. As we showed in the earlier part of this chapter many HRMSs continue to focus on administration rather than analysis and evaluation, thereby possibly limiting what the organisation can achieve in this area. We have discussed previously the nature of human capital and the resource-based view (in Chapter 3) and human capital and knowledge management (in Chapter 16) and it may be useful to read or re-read these sections before moving on.

There is no single measure or set of measures that represent the value of human capital in the organisation (*see*, for example, Robinson 2009; Kingsmill 2003). This is largely because every context is different and, as Elias and Scarborough (2004) discovered, different organisations are driven by different things in their human capital measurement. They found that approaches differed in two significant ways. One major area of difference concerned whether the whole or part of the workforce was covered in human capital reporting; the other concerned whether a strategic, holistic and aggregate (such as balanced scorecard) approach was taken or whether individual aspects were reported. Interestingly they found that most organisations in their sample reported on individual aspects. The CIPD (2009) identifies three different levels of sophistication of human capital data: basic, intermediate and higher, which we explain below.

At a **basic level** actions include the collection of basic data (*see* the examples discussed above) and the use of existing data to communicate to managers essential departmental information on such matters as absence, accidents, turnover and so on. In addition trends and patterns in the data are identified and causes investigated. The outcome of this exercise is to provide measures of efficiency and effectiveness so that identified problems can be tackled, for example to reduce absence or accidents or to improve the diversity profile. These basic measures represent the 'individual' measures that Elias and Scarborough (2004) found to be most common.

At an **intermediate level** the CIPD (2009) suggests that actions involve designing data collection for specific human capital needs, such as designing an employee attitude survey to measure satisfaction, and then using these data to inform the development of people policies and procedures. In addition correlations are investigated, say, between levels of satisfaction and potential antecedents such as levels of training, flexible working, line manager coaching, and so on. The final action is to communicate to line managers which processes influence desired outcomes such as satisfaction, and therefore highlight the value of these processes. The outcome at this level is to provide measures of processes in order to aid the design of the most appropriate HR model for the context, and to communicate to managers why the processes are important and what they can achieve, as well as how to implement them.

At the **higher level** the CIPD suggests that actions include the identification of key performance indicators in relation to business strategy and the collection of qualitative and quantitative data specifically to measure these, and to feed these data into a model such as the balanced scorecard. Managers are then provided with a range of indicators on a range of measures which they can use to monitor the progress of their department. The resulting data can be used to inform decisions and communicate human capital measures to a range of audiences. The outcome at this level is to identify the drivers of the business, to provide better informed internal decision making and to report externally on progress in relation to strategy.

We focus on simple basic measures initially and then move to the higher-level ones.

Frequently used basic measures

IRS (2002) divides measures into hard and soft measures, with training days, for example, being a hard (objective) measure and employee satisfaction, for example, being a soft measure. In its survey IRS found that employers most frequently calculated absence rates, employee turnover and expenditure on training. Other popular measures were employee relations indicators (such as number of grievances and tribunal cases), training days, cost to fill vacancies, time to fill vacancies, HR costs as a proportion of profit or total costs and time spent communicating with staff. Very few of the organisations surveyed measured productivity. In terms of soft measures, they found that the most popular measures were employee satisfaction, followed by line manager satisfaction, senior manager satisfaction and customer satisfaction. Employee satisfaction was considered to be the most effective soft measure.

Such measures are frequently collected in an ad hoc manner, are not integrated or tied in with business strategy and may not result in action being taken. The CIPD Factsheet

(2009) on human capital provides a very useful framework in which to understand the different areas of human capital that may be evaluated. The CIPD suggests that the data collected fall under five broad headings: performance data; demographic data; recruitment and retention data; training and development data; and opinion data. In the following section we give some examples of the more popular and simple measures using the categorisation proposed by the CIPD (2009).

Performance data – specific example: absence analysis and costing

The CIPD suggests that performance data may include performance management data, productivity and profitability data, customer satisfaction and loyalty data. Absence and attendance clearly come into this category. For aggregate analysis the **absence rate** is the number of days of absence, that is, when attendance would have been expected, of all employees. The **absence percentage rate** is this figure divided by the total number of actual working days for all employees over the year, multiplied by 100. This simple percentage figure is the one most often used and enables the organisation's absence level to be compared with national figures, or those of other organisations in the same sector.

The **absence frequency rate** is the number of spells of absence over the period, usually a year. Comparing this and the absence percentage rate gives critical information about the type of absence problem that the organisation is experiencing.

Absence data, as well as enabling external comparisons, can be analysed by department, work group, occupation, grade and so on. In this way the analysis will throw up problem areas, and additional analysis can be undertaken to try to identify the causes of differing levels of absence in different parts of the organisation. The data may be supplemented by information from questionnaires or interviews with employees or line managers.

The purpose of producing this information is to understand the causes and extent of absence in order to manage it effectively. So, for example, such analysis may result in a new absence policy, employee communications about the impact of absence, appropriate training for line managers, changes to specific groups of jobs and the introduction of a new type of attendance system such as flexitime. The information provides a base for future monitoring. Absence data can be analysed further to provide benchmarks of 'high', 'medium' and 'low' absence levels in the organisation, and can be used to set improvement targets. This analysis can also be used to trigger specific management actions when an employee reaches different benchmark levels. For example, a trigger may be the number of days or number of spells per year or, as in the Bradford factor (*see* Figure 14.2 on p. 315 for the formula), a combination of both.

The costing of absence needs to have a wider focus than just the pay of the absent individual. Other costs include:

- line manager costs in finding a temporary replacement or rescheduling work;
- the actual costs of the temporary employee;
- costs of showing a temporary employee what to do;
- costs associated with a slower work rate or more errors from a temporary employee;
- costs of contracts not completed on time.

These costs can be calculated and provide the potential for productivity improvement.

Performance data – specific example: relating the workforce to organisational performance

Various analytical methods relate the contribution of the workforce to organisational performance. This analysis can be used to control headcount, and to measure organisational effectiveness and compare it with that of similar organisations. The information can also be used to communicate to employees what their contribution is to the business. Turnover per employee and profit per employee can be calculated in order to monitor performance and to demonstrate to each employee the importance of cost consciousness. If an employee of an organisation employing 3,000 employees realises that profit per employee is only £900 this means far more to that individual than expressing profit as £2.7 million. Cost consciousness suddenly becomes important as the fragile and marginal nature of profits is demonstrated. A further calculation expresses the cost of employees in relation to the total costs of production. To work this out, turnover less profit (that is, the cost of production) is compared with employee costs (salary plus on-costs). The percentage of production costs accounted for by employees will vary markedly according to the nature of the business. For example, in some pharmaceutical businesses people costs will account for 70 per cent of all production costs (due to a heavy emphasis on research and development) whereas in a less people-intensive business, as found in other parts of the manufacturing sector, people costs may only account for around 15 per cent. Changes in the percentage of people costs over time would need to be investigated. People costs are a good way of communicating to employees just how important they are to the success of the business.

Demographic data – specific example: equal opportunities analysis

The CIPD defines these as data on the composition of the workforce, and these may include equal opportunities analysis which aims to provide an organisational profile of, most frequently, ethnic origin, gender, age and disability. The resulting percentages from this can be compared with national and local community figures to give an initial idea of how representative the organisation is. Further analyses break these figures down to compare them by department, job category and grade. It is in this type of analysis that startling differences are likely to be found, for example as shown in Figure 29.1.

The information gleaned can be used to:

- question the extent and spread of disadvantaged groups in the organisation;
- identify specific barriers to a more representative spread;
- formulate appropriate policy and action plans;
- set targets to be achieved and to monitor year on year compared with these base figures.

Other analyses can be carried out to show promotion, internal moves and secondment figures for disadvantaged groups compared with advantaged groups, for example white males. Further mention is made of these and the recruitment system in the following section.

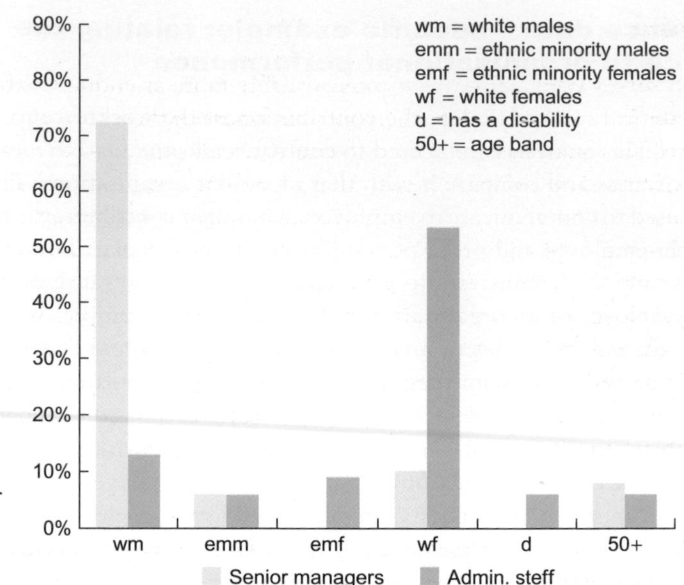

Figure 29.1 Breakdown of senior manager staff group and administrative staff group

ACTIVITY 29.3

1. What basic metrics does your HR function calculate?
2. What is the purpose of each one?
3. How are the results translated into action?
4. To what extent are these measures related to business strategy?
5. To what extent are these measures integrated?

Recruitment and retention data – specific example: turnover analysis and costing

We cover this aspect in Chapter 9 on Staff retention.

Training and development data

Typical training and development data include annual training days per employee, training spend per employee, existence of personal development plans for what percentage of the workforce and for which job roles, and the elapsed time between an employee joining an organisation and being involved in an induction programme. Other measures may cover the number of accredited or trained coaches and mentors, or the competencies/skills of staff as judged by a variety of measures.

Opinion data

While opinion survey data are not new, considerably more attention has been given to such data of late. For example in the National Heath Service there is an annual employee opinion survey which focuses on employee views of hours worked, appraisal, training, teamwork, injuries, harassment, work-life balance, job satisfaction, work pressure, intention to leave, quality of leadership, and positive feelings within the organisation, as well as other issues. Hospital Trusts are able to compare their ratings against the national picture and can also break down their data by job type.

Basic measures can be benchmarked externally against other similar organisations which would allow a meaningful comparison, such as competitors. They can also be benchmarked internally by comparing departments, different locations and so on. IRS (2002) found that around one-third of the organisations it surveys regularly carried out external benchmarking and the same percentage regularly carried out internal benchmarking.

While the measures described above can clearly add value, much of this work is done in an ad hoc manner and lacks strategic integration. We turn now to the higher, strategic end of the spectrum of HCM.

Strategic frameworks and scorecards for HCM

Higher-level approaches are more representative of human capital management, which the Accounting for People Task force defined as 'an approach to people management that treats it as a high level strategic issue rather than an operational matter "to be left to the HR people" and seeks systematically to analyse, measure and evaluate how people policies and practices contribute to value creation' (Kingsmill 2003: 5). The emphasis is not just on measurement, but on using this measurement approach as a management tool for effecting change and improvement. Such an approach addresses the problem often found in measurement, namely that the wrong things are measured (*see*, for example, Chartered Management Institute 2006, quoted in IRS 2006; Gratton 2004).

Through the use of a strategic framework or model the organisation can identify what drives the performance of employees in relation to the organisation's strategy. These drivers can then be expressed as a range of measures with indicators, and targets can be set at about the levels that need to be achieved. These targets are often cascaded down to employee level, and form the base for the 'hard' metrics approach to performance management as opposed to the 'soft' good management approach to performance management which we discussed in Chapter 12.

There are a variety of models that can be used and Matthewman and Matignon (2005) identify six such frameworks: the human resource benchmarking model; the balanced scorecard; the human capital monitor; the human capital index; the engagement model; and the organisational performance model. We look at Kaplan and Norton's Balanced Scorecard, the Human Resource Scorecard and Mayo's Human Capital Monitor in more detail below, and the Window on practice shows the CAA's tailormade balanced scorecard approach.

Considerable attention has been given to the use of scorecards, such as the balanced scorecard (Kaplan and Norton 1992) and, later, the HR scorecard (Becker *et al.* 2001), in linking people, strategy and performance. These are perhaps the best-known scorecards, but many different scorecards have been developed over the past decade or so.

'To achieve our vision/mission/strategic goals, how will we be able to sustain our ability to change and improve?'

What are the critical success factors?	What are the critical measurements?

Figure 29.2 Kaplan and Norton's approach using the 'learning and growth' quadrant of the balanced scorecard
Source: Adapted from Kaplan and Norton (1992).

Such scorecards utilise a range of measures of HR which are viewed as critical to the success of the business strategy, and which move the process of measurement on from an ad hoc to a strategic and integrated approach. Kaplan and Norton widened the perspective on the measurement of business performance by measuring more than financial performance. Their premise is that other factors which lead to financial performance need to be measured to give a more rounded view of how well the organisation is performing. This means that measures of business performance are based on measures of strategy implementation in a range of areas. Kaplan and Norton identify three other areas for measurement in addition to financial measures: customer measures, internal business process measures and learning and growth measures. Figure 29.2 provides an example of Norton and Kaplan's approach.

In each of these areas critical elements need to be identified and then measures devised to identify current levels and to measure progress. Some organisations implementing this scorecard have developed the learning and growth area to include a wider range of HR measures.

WINDOW ON PRACTICE

Civil Aviation Authority's (CAA) approach to human capital measurement (HCM)

As 60 per cent of the CAA's costs are people costs they began an HCM process hoping that it would allow them to quantify the value of its staff and explore the relationship between staff performance and business outcomes. The CAA also anticipated that it would help in quantifying its objectives of continuous improvement, improved efficiency and cost effectiveness. They developed a balanced scorecard approach to measuring human capital based on what constituted the 'bottom line', being a not-for-profit organisation. This bottom line comprised:

External customer perception of CAA's performance

Achievement of objectives

Assessment of staff expertise

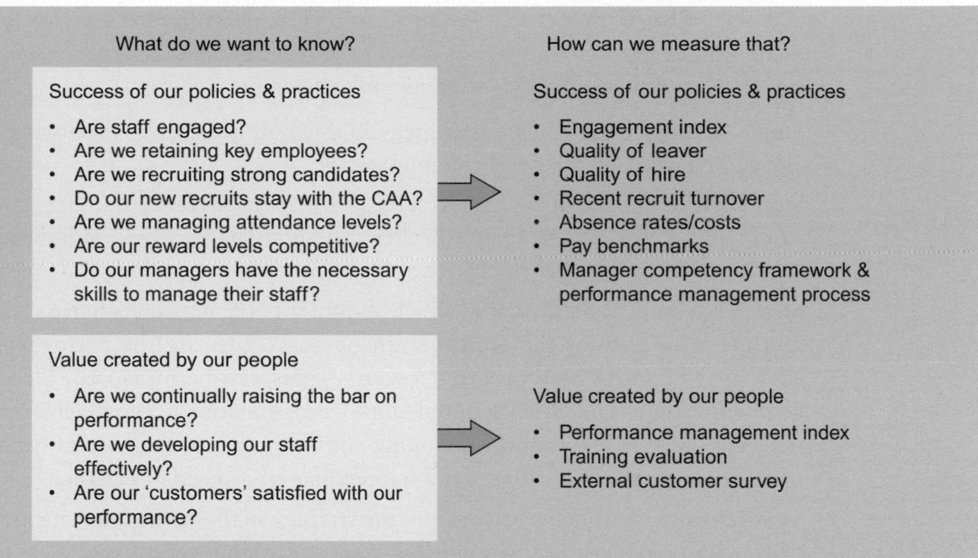

Figure 29.3 How the CAA defined measures to answer their human capital questions
Source: Robinson, D. (2009) 'Human capital measurement: an approach that works', *Strategic HR Review*, Vol. 8, No. 6, pp. 5–11, Figure 1.

In order to measure the value of their people, policies and practices they asked themselves what they wanted to know about each of these in relation to the defined 'bottom line'. Having decided the questions they then worked out where that information might be found and how it could be measured. The questions and measures are shown in Figure 29.3.

They then ordered their measures in a four-level hierarchy and worked up the hierarchy starting with the basic measures at the base:

Level 4: Performance Measures: Link between input/output data and measures of CAA strategic performance

Level 3: Outcome Measures: e.g. absence rates and costs, engagement data

Level 2: Operational data: e.g. number of training days

Level 1: Workforce data: e.g. headcount, demographics, equal opportunities data

The fourth level, not surprisingly, was the hardest to define and measure and the CAA are looking at correlations between input measures such as absence, turnover, training and length of service and outputs such as employee engagement.

Source: Summarised from Robinson, D. (2009) 'Human capital measurement: an approach that works', *Strategic HR Review*, Vol. 8, No. 6, pp. 5–11.

Becker *et al.* (2001: 4) argue that it is important to have a 'measurement system [that] convincingly showcases HR's impact on business performance', otherwise, they argue, the HR function cannot show how it adds value and risks being outsourced. The system they suggest focuses on 'HR architecture', and by this they mean the 'sum of the HR function, the broader HR system, and the resulting employee behaviours' (Becker *et al.*

2001: 1). This is therefore a broad view of HR measurement, as we discussed at the beginning of this chapter. Becker and his colleagues have designed a seven-step process to clarify and measure HR's strategic influence:

Step 1. Clearly define business strategy in a way that involves discussing how the strategy can be implemented and communicated.

Step 2. Develop a business case for HR as a strategic asset explaining how and why HR can facilitate business strategy – Becker and his colleagues suggest how current research relating HR to firm performance can be useful here.

Step 3. Create a strategy map – which should involve managers across the organisation, and needs to address the critical strategic goals, identify the performance drivers for each goal, identify how progress towards goals can be measured, identify barriers to goal achievement, identify required employee behaviour for goal achievement, question whether the HR function is developing employee competencies and behaviours needed to meet the goals, and if this is not happening, what needs to change.

Step 4. Identify HR deliverables from the strategy map – which may include performance drivers and enablers; for example low turnover, high levels of specific competencies and so on may be needed to reduce product development time.

Step 5. Align HR architecture with the deliverables in step 4. Policies can be developed to result in these deliverables – for example policies encouraging low turnover may be supported by family-friendly and work-life balance policies, diversity policies, career development opportunities and so on.

Step 6. Design a strategic HR measurement system. This requires that valid measures of HR deliverables are developed. For example in specifying low turnover it would be important to identify which particular staff groups this applies to, whether voluntary turnover only is to be calculated, whether internal job moves are included and so on.

Step 7. Implement management by measurement – Becker and his colleagues suggest that once the measurement system has been developed this can then become a powerful management tool.

In designing measures Becker and his colleagues suggest that HR efficiency as well as deliverables need to be measured. Efficiency measures tend to be cost measures, for example cost per new hire, or HR cost per employee. They suggest that these are both lagging indicators. Leading indicators can also be measured. These are defined as measures of 'high-performance work system' and HR system alignment. The high-performance work system appears to be defined in terms of best-practice-type measures, for example hours of training received each year by each employee, or percentage of the workforce regularly undergoing annual appraisal. HR system alignment indicates the extent to which the high-performance work system is tailored to business strategy via supporting each HR deliverable. Useful lists of HR deliverables and efficiency measures can be found in Ulrich (1997).

An alternative framework for monitoring, measuring and managing human capital is the 'human capital monitor' and this has been developed in the UK by Andrew Mayo (2001). The human capital monitor is designed to connect the intrinsic value of the human capital in the organisation with the working environment. It includes processes and systems which impact on employees' behaviour together with the value that is created by people. As with the previous models discussed this is not specifically designed for the HR function to monitor itself. The model adds together the value of people as

THE HUMAN CAPITAL MONITOR

People as assets		People motivation and commitment		People contribution to added value
Human asset worth = Employment costs × Individual asset multiplier (IAM)/1000 IAM = a function of • capability • potential • contribution • values alignment *Maximising human capital* • Acquisition – How successful • Retention are we? • Growth – What drives success?	+	Measures – How successful are we? **The work environment that drives success** • Leadership • Practical support • The work group • Learning and development • Rewards and recognition	=	The value added to each stakeholder • Financial • Non-financial • Current • Future

Figure 29.4 Mayo's human capital monitor

Source: Adapted from A. Mayo (2001) *The human value of the enterprise: Valuing people as assets – monitoring, measuring and managing*. London: Nicholas Brealey, p. 65.

assets (box 1) and the motivation and commitment (box 2) to produce the people contribution to added value (box 3). The model is shown in Figure 29.4.

The first box in the model, people as assets, provides a method of balancing people costs with a measure of the value that they contribute. Mayo argues that calculating the value of people is important for four reasons. First, resourcing decisions should be about more than just cost; second, it is important to understand relative values of individuals and teams; third, it helps make informed investment decisions, showing the relative benefits of investing in people as opposed to other assets; and finally, it enables the company to monitor whether its talent is increasing or decreasing. To demonstrate the types of measures that Mayo suggests, we use the example of capability, where the following measures are provided: personal behaviour; business and professional know-how; network of contacts; qualifications and experience; attitudes and values. In terms of maximising human capital we will look at potential. Here Mayo suggests that success in acquisition could be measured by total human asset worth, average IAM (individual asset multiplier) of new recruits and the increase in strategically important core capabilities. The drivers for acquisition of potential include employer brand and acceptance rates, among others.

We turn now to the second box concerning motivation and commitment. Here Mayo suggests such measures as absence levels, satisfaction surveys, attrition rates and reasons for leaving, among others. He suggests five influencing factors as listed in the model, and for the work group, for example, he proposes two measures: team assessments of working practices and a team stability index.

In the final box, people contribution to added value, Mayo suggests that the focus should be on wealth creation, which is a much broader concept than profit, as some of the wealth created can be reinvested in the business. To this end he compares a conventional income statement with a value-added financial statement, which goes beyond seeing people as just costs. In assessing current value Mayo suggests that work needs to be analysed into work which creates value and non-value added work (such as re-doing work, duplication, computer downtime, cross-charging and so on), and that the percentage of each type of work needs to be a focus. He argues that building future value is dependent on innovation and that measures of this need to be derived.

Case 29.2 on this book's companion website, **www.pearsoned.co.uk/torrington**, focuses on human capital.

HUMAN CAPITAL REPORTING

Elias and Scarborough (2004) liken internal and external human capital reporting (HCR) to management accounting and financial accounting, in that the first is internal and aimed at managing the organisation in an increasingly better way whereas the second is for external consumption. Currently there is minimal external reporting of human capital but a greater extent of internal reporting, which we suggest is a necessary precursor. The CIPD (2007b) suggests that there are two principal reasons for encouraging the evaluation and reporting of human capital; first, to educate and influence analysts to use these data in their assessments of companies; and second, to influence companies to adopt better people management practices which are more informed.

The British government's White Paper, *Modernising Company Law* (Department of Trade and Industry 2002), suggested that the largest 1,000 companies should publish an annual operating and financial review (OFR), and experts believed this would need to include a review of the ways that employees are managed. However, this planned requirement was scrapped and a simpler version is now required which meets the minimum demands of the EU Accounts and Modernisation Directive (EAMD). The legal requirement (in force since April 2005) now is a report entitled the 'Business Review' which forms part of the Director's Report. The Business Review requires 'a balanced and comprehensive analysis of the business', and that human capital management issues should be included 'where material'. The scrapping of the OFR raised fears that human capital reporting would have less priority in the business; however, the Business Review does apply in some form to all organisations except small firms. The profile of 'sustainability reporting', of which human capital is one aspect, is increasing as demonstrated by the Association of Chartered Certified Accountants (*see* CIPD/ACCA 2009) who now make awards for sustainability reporting (as well as others including climate change issues; bribery and corruption; and stakeholder engagement).

Matthewman and Matignon (2005) state that human capital reporting needs to be tailored to the goals, needs and character of each organisation. However, the variety of internal and voluntary external reporting appears to be one of the factors that seem to hold back some form of mandatory external reporting. While the Kingsmill Report (2003) declared that there could be no single approach to HCM others have not given up on this, and there is evidence to suggest that lack of comparability, consistency or predictability of presentation of workforce statistics means that investors take little notice of them while thinking they would be valuable if delivered on a dependable basis (Scott-Jackson *et al.* 2006). However, such an approach would diminish the importance of context. A further problem is the mistrust of company-produced figures and the CIPD (2007b) suggests that such information collected by an independent body would be more attractive to investors and analysis. Alongside this some organisations may fear that human capital information is too sensitive to reveal to competitors and there may be concerns from unions and employees.

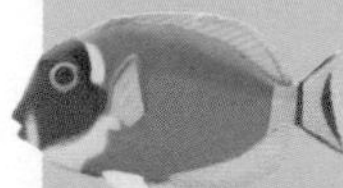

WINDOW ON PRACTICE

The ACCA Human Capital Reporting awards 2009

Forty organisations submitted their reports to the awarding body and each was assessed against the criteria below:

1. Strategic Intent

Strategy	Description of the link between HCM and business strategy and evidence of employee input into development of business direction
Materiality	Identification of material HCM issues for inclusion in strategy, and evidence of execution of strategy
Vision	Disclosure of organisational vision and values and how they are disseminated
Engagement	Evidence of robust employee engagement on future business direction, strategic planning and decision making

2. Governance and Assurance

Governance	Evidence of robust governance structures in place to management HCM performance, including board committees, individual board member responsibility and remuneration linkages to HCM performance indicators
Assurance	HCM information is assured using the AA1000AS and/or ISAE3000 standards

3. Policy and performance

Performance	Systematic reporting on material HCM areas, including KPI data and narrative information and SMART targets
Policy	Description of any policies and management systems in place to manage key HCM performance areas

The assessment resulted in a percentage score. Vodafone came closest to the criteria scoring 87 per cent with the Co-op group not far behind at 77 per cent. However, it was noted that the average score was 49 per cent so there is some way to go, even for organisations really making an effort. The judges said there were only a few exemplar organisations who 'wove metrics and evidence throughout their reports, proving the integral role of people in driving both sustainability and organisation performance' (p. 7).

Source: Adapted from CIPD/ACCA (2009) *Human Capital Management: An analysis of disclosure in UK Reports*. London: ACCA, pp. 5–7.

SUMMARY PROPOSITIONS

29.1 Technology has an important role in freeing up HR professionals to work on more strategic issues. However, most HRISs automate existing processes rather than informating. HRISs contribute to human capital management, and more sophisticated systems which facilitate informating have the potential to make a much greater contribution.

29.2 Ad hoc measures of human capital are likely to include absence and turnover analysis and equal opportunities monitoring, but these measures are frequently not strategically integrated and do not necessarily lead to action.

29.3 Strategic frameworks enable a more sophisticated approach to human capital measurement and management. For example Kaplan and Norton's balanced scorecard, Becker *et al.*'s HR scorecard and Mayo's human capital monitor have all been used as a framework. Such frameworks integrate measures and relate them to organisational strategy.

29.4 Human capital reporting can be both internal and external, but most organisations focus on the former rather than the latter.

GENERAL DISCUSSION TOPICS

1. 'Quantitative measures mean nothing. The way that questions are asked, the subjective understanding of what the question means, biased response patterns, and the way that data are analysed and presented, all mean that statistics can be made to say whatever the author of them wishes.' To what extent do you agree or disagree with this statement, and why?

2. 'HCM is too complex and resource intensive for any but the largest of organisations.' What factors support this statement, and how could you argue against it?

FURTHER READING

Baron, A. and Armstrong, M. (2007) *Human Capital Management*. London: Kogan Page.
A useful text covering all aspects of human capital management including concepts, processes, data, applications, reporting, and the HR skills needed for this area of work.

Parry, E., Tyson, S., Selbie, D. and Leighton, R. (2007) *HR and Technology: Impact and advantages*. London: CIPD.
A helpful text summarising the various use of technology in HRM; planning for an e-HR system; and achieving stakeholder buy-in. The authors also outline the impact of HR technology on the efficiency of HR activities and processes; employee engagement and communication and the role and skills of HR and other managers.

IDS (2008) *The Role of Technology in HR*, IDS Studies Update No. 867, April. London: IDS.
Some very useful company case studies of technology use in HR including AstraZeneca, HJ Heinz and Norwich Union.

Likierman, A. (2005) 'How to measure the performance of HR', *People Management*, Vol. 11, No. 16, pp. 64–5.
Sound and punchy advice on measuring HR.

Stuff, P. (2006) 'Benchmarking the benchmarks', *IRS Employment Review*, No. 853, pp. 22–4.
Reviews a variety of levels of benchmarking, from basic hard data, to benchmarking processes, to strategic benchmarking. In addition it looks at different benchmarking approaches, including internal; competitive; functional; and generic. A useful summary article with company examples.

WEB LINKS

www.saratogapwc.co.uk (the website of Saratoga, the human capital metrics business of PricewaterhouseCoopers).

www.accountingforpeople.gov.uk (the website of the Task Force on Human Capital).

www.cipd.co.uk (the website of the Chartered Institute of Personnel and Development – useful for interactive tools on technology in HR and human capital management together with a wide range of relevant reports).

REFERENCES

Alleyne, C., Kakabadse, A. and Kakabadse, N. (2007) 'Using the HR intranet: an exploratory analysis of its impact on managerial satisfaction with the HR function', *Personnel Review*, Vol. 36, No. 2, pp. 295–310.

Becker, B., Huselid, M. and Ulrich, D. (2001) *The HR Scorecard: Linking people, strategy and performance*. Boston: Harvard Business School Press.

CIPD (2005) *People Management and Technology: Progress and potential*. London: CIPD.

CIPD (2006) *HR and Technology: Beyond delivery, a change agenda*. London: CIPD.

CIPD (2007a) *Technology in HR: How to get the most out of technology in people management*. London: CIPD.

CIPD (2007b) *Research Insight: Investors' views of human capital*. London: CIPD.

CIPD (2009) *Human Capital Factsheet*. London: CIPD.

CIPD/ACCA (2009) *Human Capital Management: An analysis of disclosure in UK Reports*. London: ACCA.

Cooper, C. (2001) 'Win by a canvass', *People Management*, Vol. 7, No. 2, pp. 42–4.

Department of Trade and Industry (2002) *Modernising Company Law*. Cm. 5553-I. London: HMSO.

Elias, J. and Scarborough, H. (2004) 'Evaluating human capital: an exploratory study of management practice', *Human Resource Management Journal*, Vol. 14, No. 4, pp. 21–40.

Gainey, T. and Klaas, B. (2008) 'The use and impact of e-HR: a survey of HR professionals', *People and Strategy*, Vol. 31, No. 3, pp. 50–5.

Gardener, S., Lepak, D. and Bartol, K. (2003) 'Virtual HR: the impact of information technology on the human resource professional', *Journal of Vocational Behaviour*, Vol. 63, pp. 159–79.

Gratton, L. (2004) 'Means to an end', *People Management*, Vol. 10, p. 20.

Hall, L. and Torrington, D.P. (1998) *The Human Resource Function: The dynamics of change and development*. London: Financial Times/Pitman Publishing.

IDS (2008) *The Role of Technology in HR*, IDS Studies Update No. 867, April. London: IDS.

IRS (2002) 'Measure for measure', *IRS Employment Review*, No. 754, June, pp. 8–13.

IRS (2003) 'HR goes strategic', *IRS Employment Review*, No. 733, 4 April, pp. 9–14.

IRS (2006) 'Human capital reporting: rising from the ashes', *IRS Employment Review*, 18 August, p. 8.

Kaplan, R. and Norton, D. (1992) 'The balanced scorecard: measures that drive performance', *Harvard Business Review*, January–February, pp. 71–9.

Kingsmill, D. (2003) *Accounting for People Report*. London: Task Force on Human Capital.

Matthewman, J. and Matignon, F. (2005) *Human Capital Reporting: An internal perspective, a guide*. London: CIPD.

Mayo, A. (2001) *The Human Value of the Enterprise: Valuing people as assets – monitoring, measuring and managing*. London: Nicholas Brealey.

People Management (2006) 'e-HR can alienate managers', Vol. 12, No. 4, 23 February, p. 16.

Reddington, M., Withers, M. and Williamson, M. (2005) *Transforming HR: Creating value through people*. Oxford: Elsevier Butterworth-Heinemann.

Robinson, D. (2009) 'Human capital measurement: an approach that works', *Strategic HR Review*, Vol. 8, No. 6, pp. 5–11.

Scott-Jackson, W., Cook, P. and Tajer, R. (2006) *Measures of Workforce Capability for Future Performance*. London: Chartered Management Institute.

Tansley, C., Newell, S. and Williams, H. (2001) 'Effecting HRM-style practices through an integrated human resource information system: an e-greenfield site?', *Personnel Review*, Vol. 30, No. 3, pp. 351–70.

Trapp, R. (2001) 'Of mice and men', *People Management*, Vol. 7, No. 13, pp. 24–32.

Ulrich, D. (1997) 'Measuring human resources: an overview of practice and a prescription for results', *Human Resource Management*, Vol. 36, pp. 303–20.

Voermans, M. and van Veldhoven, M. (2007) 'Attitude towards e-HRM: an empirical study at Phillips', *Personnel Review*, Vol. 36, No. 6, pp. 887–902.

Zuboff, S. (1988) *In the Age of the SMART Machine*. New York: Basic Books.

CHAPTER 30

HEALTH AND WELL-BEING

THE OBJECTIVES OF THIS CHAPTER ARE TO:

1. Discuss the nature of health and well-being in an organisational context
2. Outline the range of initiatives that sit within a health and well-being agenda
3. Explore the impact of health and well-being initiatives on individuals and organisations
4. Examine criticisms of health and well-being initiatives

THE NATURE OF HEALTH AND WELL-BEING

The links between employee health and performance were identified long ago. Indeed, the origins of personnel management lie with social reformers such as the Cadbury family who, in the late nineteenth century began to provide housing, healthcare and education to their workforces. Welfare officers, the early incarnation of today's human resources officers, were appointed to oversee the well-being of the workforce. While altruism played a part in this paternalistic approach towards employees, there was also a strong business case underpinning these practices. Healthy and well-educated workforces are more productive than those struggling in poor accommodation and with insufficient access to education and healthcare. The impact of this focus on well-being on workers' lives was substantial, as can be seen in Cadbury's museum in Bourneville which documents these early attempts at improving employee health and well-being.

As we explain in Chapter 1, however, the development of personnel management into human resource management has had many stages and, since those early days, there has been little enthusiasm to associate the function with what came to be viewed as a 'tea and sympathy role'. Certainly the supposed evolution of personnel into human resource management in the 1980s, and its preoccupation with the strategic aspects of business, left little room for considerations of employee health. In recent years, however, health and well-being have again become central to the HR agenda. Indeed, CIPD has demonstrated significant interest in health and well-being, suggesting that attempts to promote this focus upon:

> creating an environment to promote a state of contentment which allows an employee to flourish and achieve their full potential for the benefit of themselves and their organisation. (CIPD 2007: 4)

While some might argue that contentment is not the desired state for employees, it is one of a range of states within well-being which organisations seek to promote. Thus health and well-being goes beyond the typically narrower concerns of absence management to include a holistic approach to employees which seeks to promote physical, mental, emotional and social health (Wilson *et al*. 2004). While a widely agreed definition is lacking, there is a general consensus that health and well-being create 'contented' employees who perform well and are productive: a sound business case clearly underlies attempts to ameliorate the lot of employees.

The re-emergence of health and well-being in HR's agenda can perhaps be explained by the changes to the employment relationship which have been widely reported since the mid-1980s. Changes to the psychological contract have given rise to far less job security for employees, organisational restructuring has led in many sectors to work intensification and the negative consequences for employee morale have been widely reported. Alongside this, there has been an explosion in stress-related illness and absence. A need to re-focus on employee well-being to prevent detriment to organisations became apparent. A further impetus has derived from the increasing interest in corporate social responsibility within firms. Employers have a responsibility to create healthy workplaces for reasons beyond performance, bearing a responsibility to society to ensure employees are well treated and healthy. See, for example, IBM's website where information on its wellness programme is presented in its corporate social responsibility section, **www.ibm.com/ibm/responsibility/employee_well_being_management.shtml.** Promoting the work environment as a source of better health and improving health in the workplace act as means to reduce social inequality through employment.

These developments have coincided with a prominent government interest in health and well-being, aimed at reducing sickness absence and tackling developing social phenomena such as obesity. There are many government agencies with remits to improve public health and national productivity offering employers advice, for example:

> a healthier, more engaged workforce makes good business sense. A motivated, healthy workforce is more likely to perform well. Employers and employees benefit through improved morale, reduced absenteeism, increased retention and improved productivity. (Department of Health 2004)

There are thus seen to be strong links between health and individual/organisational performance and ultimately national performance. The emphasis within government programmes has been upon proactive employee support, good employment practice to reduce prospects of ill health and injury and effective return to work and rehabilitation strategies. As with many other areas of the employment relationship, the government has to a large extent eschewed regulation and exhorted employers to action based upon the business case, developing a range of policies to support this. For example, a ten-year strategy to improve occupational health, 'Securing Health Together', was implemented in 2000 by a range of government agencies, as was a 'Health, Work and Well-being' strategy in 2005.

As we noted above, health and well-being agendas seek to deal holistically with employees and encompass a wide range of issues. This breadth is evident in the Management Standards on workplace stress introduced by the Health and Safety Executive (HSE) in 2004. The HSE estimates the costs to society of work-related stress to be around £4 billion each year, while 13.5 million working days were lost to stress in 2007/08 (HSE 2009). Indeed, stress-related conditions are now one of the two most common causes of sickness absence (Department of Health 2004). The HSE's (2004) Management Standards outline six key areas in which employers and employees should work together in order to reduce stress and improve well-being. We outline these in the Window on practice below.

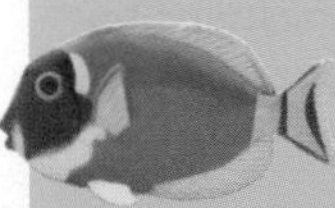

WINDOW ON PRACTICE

HSE's management standards on managing stress in the workplace

Demands – includes workload, work patterns and the work environment.

Control – how much say a person has in the way they do their work.

Support – includes the encouragement, sponsorship and resources provided by the organisation, line management and colleagues.

Role – whether people understand their role within the organisation and whether the organisation ensures that they do not have conflicting roles.

Change – how organisational change (large or small) is managed and communicated in the organisation.

Relationships – promoting positive working to avoid conflict and dealing with unacceptable behaviour.

Source: HSE 2004.

The role of HR practitioners across these six areas is evident in, for example, designing involvement policies that devolve control to employees and ensuring that roles are clearly designed and meet employees' social and psychological needs (*see* Chapter 4). While this breadth is reflected in academic literature on health and well-being, the conception of health and well-being by HR practitioners tends to be much more narrowly drawn. As a recent CIPD survey demonstrates (Table 30.1), the focus is on initiatives which deal mainly with physical and mental health. As we note later in the chapter, this narrow focus draws a great deal of criticism.

ACTIVITY 30.1

Look at a health and well-being policy on a corporate website – this might be IBM's (*see* above) or another one you can find. To what extent do you think these policies set out to address the corporate social responsibilities of organisations?

INITIATIVES WITHIN A HEALTH AND WELL-BEING AGENDA

While there is not a great deal of academic literature on the types of initiatives presented in Table 30.1, entering 'employee health and wellbeing' into an Internet search engine returns a plethora of consultancies offering advice on the subject (*see*, for example,

Table 30.1 Organisational well-being initiatives

	Organisations (%)					
	Total	**Manufacturing and production**	**Private services**	**Non-profit organisations**	**Public services**	**Ireland**
Advice on healthy eating	25	29	18	15	40	43
Healthy menu in employee canteen	25	28	20	17	37	40
Healthy snacks in vending machines	13	21	10	1	11	22
In-house gym	12	7	9	8	27	9
Subsidised gym membership	28	21	30	25	43	28
Exercise classes provided on work premises	9	4	6	7	25	13
Support to stop smoking	34	40	21	31	57	34
Regular health checks	28	40	18	17	30	42
Private health insurance	60	71	77	31	12	76
Personalised healthy living programmes for employees	2	2	2	1	5	5
Employee assistance programme	32	25	32	47	40	42
Access to counselling service	55	49	46	62	87	52
Stress risk assessment	25	23	20	29	44	13
Access to physiotherapy	21	26	12	17	29	15
Massage	9	4	10	10	12	12

Source: From *What's Happening with Wellbeing at Work?*, CIPD (2007), Table 2. With the permission of the publisher, the Chartered Institute of Personnel and Development, London (www.cipd.co.uk).

http://www.pearnkandola.com/well-being and **www.workandwellbeing.com**), alongside a large number of organisations outlining such policies and suggesting that employee health and well-being are important to their success. This is so across both the public and private sectors. Wiltshire County Council, for example, has introduced a range of awards for its business partners, which include promoting physical health, healthy eating and innovative walking routes. It is an international, not just a British phenomenon. IBM, for example, outlines a range of initiatives across its international subsidiaries (**www.ibm.com/ibm/responsibility/employees_global_wellness.shtml**).

Table 30.1 presents a range of widely adopted health and well-being initiatives. These initiatives are widely adopted, particularly in the public sector where the government encourages its agencies to lead by example and be 'model employers'. As can be seen, there is a significant, and narrow, focus on physical and mental health, the latter dealing particularly with workplace stress. To this end, 55 per cent of organisations, 87 per cent in the public sector, offer counselling services, 32 per cent offer employee assistance programmes and a quarter offer stress risk assessments. Even more notable, however, is the number of practices which relate to physical health. A key concern here is obesity which, with its links to illnesses such as cancer and heart disease, has emerged as one of the most significant threats to health in modern times. While its causes are complex, diet and exercise are thought to be two major contributory factors and government policy has sought to encourage both individuals and employers to adopt healthier lifestyles. This is clearly reflected in organisational policy which is

focused upon healthy eating, mechanisms to promote physical exercise such as gym membership, health checks and support with giving up smoking. Indeed such is the emphasis on promoting physical health that it has even found its way into building design, as we outline in the Window on practice below.

WINDOW ON PRACTICE

Get fit while you work

The Broadgate Centre in the City of London was redesigned with fitness in mind. It is one example of a new generation of 'fit' office buildings being designed by architects to encourage employees to become healthier by making them walk while they are at work. The design policy is for fitter people and a fitter environment. Meeting rooms, canteens and car parks are being put at appreciable distance from desks so workers have to expend energy getting to them.

Source: Department of Health 2004.

The range of practices adopted by organisations in attempts to promote employee health and well-being is vast, and many are not captured in Table 30.1. Our own experiences, and those of colleagues and other contacts, suggest that it is common for employers to offer free fruit, various forms of massage, free cholesterol tests, cycle to work schemes, dance and yoga classes, meditation – the list is seemingly endless! This is certainly the message in a recent article on health and well-being schemes in British universities, demonstrated in the Window on practice.

WINDOW ON PRACTICE

Well-being in British universities

Examples of health and well-being initiatives in British universities are presented on a website, **www.wellbeing.ac.uk**. The emphasis on physical and mental health is again apparent in a range of initiatives focusing on stress, counselling and physical activity. City University, for example, offers health and stress checks and 'body MOTs', while Birmingham City University includes among its initiatives information on alcohol abuse, workshops on relaxation techniques, healthy eating and t'ai chi.

Source: Adapted from Newman, R. (2010) 'Get happy and get on with it', *Times Higher Education*, 21–27 January, pp. 32–6.

For information and inspiration, readers should visit the Investors in People website which offers a database of suggestions for health and well-being initiatives.

ACTIVITY 30.2

What health and well-being initiatives are offered by your employer or an organisation on **www.wellbeing.ac.uk**?

What is your opinion on the usefulness of these initiatives? How likely are they to improve employee health and well-being?

Case 30.1 on this book's companion website, **www.pearsoned.co.uk/torrington** explores health and well-being initiatives further.

THE IMPACT OF HEALTH AND WELL-BEING INITIATIVES ON INDIVIDUALS AND ORGANISATIONS

Health and well-being initiatives are not cheap: one university spent £50,000 on a programme to encourage staff to keep fit, and this level of expenditure is not unusual. Clearly employers expect that there will be substantial returns on this investment, often in the form of improved employee attendance (*see* Chapter 14 which discusses the cost of employee absence). But returns are expected to go significantly beyond reduced sickness absence, as we outline in Table 30.2. Indeed, one survey suggests that there is a return of £4.17 for every £1 spent on employee well-being (Newman 2010).

Crush (2009) reports on Royal Mail's health and well-being initiatives. While he recognises that the contribution can be hard to assess, he cites a recent international survey which suggests that well-being is one of the prime drivers of employee engagement. We summarise part of his work in the Window on practice which describes Royal Mail's health and well-being policy and practices and their outcomes and considers the wider implications of health and well-being for economic performance.

Table 30.2 Benefits of health and well-being initiatives

Recruitment	Many organisations promote their health and well-being policies in order to attract applicants for vacancies that they advertise. An example of this can be seen on the website of the Australian law firm, Lavan Legal, **www.lavanlegal.com.au/go/careers/employee-well-being-policy**.
Improved performance	Through more productive employees and better service via a reduced dependence on replacement employees.
Competitive advantage	GlaxoSmithKline suggests that investing in health and well-being will help to build competitive advantage through employees: **http://www.gsk.com/investors/reps03/EHS03/GSKehs-11.htm**.
Positive employee attitudes	Employees will be more engaged, committed and contented. As we discuss in Chapter 11, such positive employee attitudes have been demonstrated to be performance enhancing.
Retention	Fewer employees will be lost due to ill health and intention to quit employment is likely to be reduced as a result of positive employee attitudes.

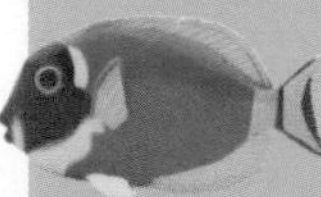

WINDOW ON PRACTICE

Royal Mail Group's health and well-being 'blueprint' could provide a £1.45 billion boost to UK's struggling sectors: Innovative measures help the organisation cut absence by 25 per cent and save £227 million in three years.

Health and well-being initiatives introduced by Royal Mail Group could hold the key to reducing the impact of absence across the UK's worst performing sectors and deliver savings of £1.45 billion a year, a study by the London School of Economics revealed. In its 'Value of Rude Health' report – the result of a unique, year-long study – the London School of Economics also calculated that the value of Royal Mail Group's approach to tackling absence could bring more than 94,000 people absent through illness or injury back into work more quickly.

The study revealed that Royal Mail Group's health and well-being activities have:

- Slashed absence by 25 per cent between 2004 and 2007
- Brought 3,600 employees absent through illness or injury back into work
- Saved more than £227 million in terms of direct costs (wages and benefits)

Royal Mail Group's success in cutting absence by a quarter has been achieved through:

- Health screening for employees and occupational support services including physiotherapy and occupational therapy
- Health clinics in more than 90 Royal Mail Group sites to help people return to work and prevent them getting ill
- Fitness centres run by trained instructors in larger sites
- Health promotion campaigns targeting smoking and back pain
- Increased support and training for managers to improve the effectiveness of absence to attendance policies

And the business is continuing its activities to improve the health and well-being of its people through two new initiatives – an online health check-in and assessment service and the recruitment of health trainers to help fellow workers improve their health through advice and practical support.

David Marsden, a Professor in the Centre for Economic Performance at London School of Economics and author of the report, commented: 'Our study suggests that the 13 sectors of the economy least effective at addressing employees' health and wellbeing could benefit significantly from Royal Mail Group's "blueprint". Following the organisation's example in bringing high rates of absence in specific sites to average levels would deliver huge financial gains and provide a boost to the performance of a range of companies and organisations.'

These include:

- Bringing more than 94,000 workers absent through illness or injury back in to work
- Adding an extra 21 million days worked by UK employees a year
- Annual cost savings of £1.45 billion to the UK economy

At a time when absence is an increasing priority for employers, the London School of Economic's 'Value of Rude Health' report has created one of the most compelling investment cases to date for health and well-being policies. One of the UK's largest employers, Royal Mail Group, has invested £46 million over three years in approaches that address the biological, social and psychological causes of absence, delivering a return on investment of five to one.

Source: Adapted from **www.news.royalmailgroup.com/articlea.asp?id=2213&brand=royal_mail_group.**

ACTIVITY 30.3

The Royal Mail has attempted to clearly identify the benefits that have accrued from its health and well-being initiatives. How easy is this to do? What are the experiences of an organisation with which you are familiar in identifying such benefits?

Case 30.2 on this book's companion website, **www.pearsoned.co.uk/torrington**, explores the impact of health and well-being initiatives further.

CRITICISMS OF HEALTH AND WELL-BEING INITIATIVES

There are a variety of criticisms of health and well-being initiatives, ranging from questions of definition to challenges to HR's conception of the issue. While health and well-being programmes have grown in popularity in recent years, there is a suggestion that they contain little new, rather that they are a re-branding of absence management programmes. Even where they are seen to contain practices of merit, it is argued that lack of resources or senior management buy-in can lead them to be largely ineffective. It is also suggested that such initiatives are beyond the financial means of many smaller firms which form the majority of organisations.

A further concern is the extent to which organisations have the right to interfere in employees' lives. While employers may have a responsibility to tackle work-related stress, there is an argument that an employee's weight and fitness levels are nobody's business but their own. Indeed, many employees have expressed concern about information obtained by employers as part of these programmes being put to inappropriate use, in for example, redundancy or promotion selection decisions. When Walmart launched its wellness campaign in 2005, requiring employees to volunteer information on weight and take steps to reduce this if appropriate, there were accusations of heavyhandedness and even fascism from employees and their representatives.

The major criticism of health and well-being initiatives as conceived by the HR community, however, is their narrow focus on concerns such as fitness and healthy eating. As we noted earlier, academic treatments of health and well-being take a much wider view on what it constitutes and academic publications on the subject rarely concern the kinds of initiatives outlined earlier. Rather, they consider issues such as job design and the extent to which workers have autonomy and experience job satisfaction (Holman 2002). It has been suggested that these narrow approaches are a facade to conceal the fact that the employer is seeking to get more out of employees for less:

> Overall, 'wellness' is a sham. It is aimed at distracting attention from more stressful work, more bullying and the weakness of unions which means that workers have less 'voice' at work. (Newman 2010: 36)

Table 30.3 outlines both organisational and individual aspects of health and well-being from this broader perspective. It is evident from this that physical health is a relatively small part of overall individual well-being and that organisational responsibilities are significant and draw on much wider aspects of HR practice than providing healthy food in canteens or free gym membership.

Holman's (2002) work on employee well-being in call centres, the findings of which are outlined in the Window on practice below, reinforces the point that organisations have broad responsibilities in supporting health and well-being. He suggests, for example, that autonomy and limited but supportive supervision are the fundamentals of health and well-being.

Table 30.3 Organisational and individual well-being in context

ORGANISATIONAL WELL-BEING	INDIVIDUAL WELL-BEING
Values-based working environment and management style	Maintaining a healthy body by making healthy choices about diet, exercise and leisure
Open communication and dialogue	Developing an attitude of mind that enables the employee to have self-confidence, self-respect and to be emotionally resilient
Teamworking and cooperation	Having a sense of purpose, feelings of fulfilment and meaning
Clarity and unity of purpose	Possessing an active mind that is alert, open to new experiences, curious and creative
Flexibility, discretion and support for reasonable risk taking	Having a network of relationships that are supportive and nurturing
A balance between work and personal life	
The ability to negotiate workload and work pace without fear of reprisals or punishment	
Being fairly compensated in terms of salary and benefits	

Source: Adapted from CIPD (2007).

WINDOW ON PRACTICE

Employee well-being in call centres

Call centres are often perceived to have a negative impact on employee well-being, mainly attributed to four factors: job design, performance monitoring, HR practices and team leader support. This article reports on a survey of 557 customer service representatives that examined the relationship of these factors to four measures of well-being: anxiety, depression and intrinsic and extrinsic job satisfaction. One distinctive feature of this article is its focus on anxiety and depression, two major dimensions of well-being not addressed in call centre research to date. Results demonstrated that the factors most highly associated with well-being were high control over work methods and procedures, a low level of monitoring and a supportive team leader. Evidence also indicates that the level of well-being in some call centres is similar to that in other comparable forms of work.

Source: Adapted from Holman, D. (2002) 'Employee Wellbeing in Call Centres', *Human Resource Management Journal*, Vol. 12, No. 4, pp. 35–50.

Our argument thus far has been that current HR initiatives are too narrowly drawn and there is growing weight to this argument. A recent article in the UK higher education press makes the point strongly that there is more to health and well-being than massage and free fruit (Newman 2010). It may also be that this is becoming apparent to HR practitioners. In the Window on practice below, we draw from two speeches by senior HR professionals, both of whom suggest that a narrow focus on physical and mental health is unhelpful and that the HR perspective on health and well-being needs to be widened. A greater focus is needed on the fundamentals of the workplace that may lead to poor health, rather than presenting solutions to problems that have already emerged.

WINDOW ON PRACTICE

What drives employee wellbeing?

'What HR professionals need to decide is whether health and wellbeing is about providing lettuce for lunch or about far less obvious but potentially more effective things,' says David Batman, group medical officer, Nestlé UK. 'Simply giving staff more autonomy in their jobs will reduce the level of stress they suffer. This impacts blood pressure and heart conditions. To me, just giving people the opportunity to do their job will have a far more significant impact on the health of a company's employees than persuading them to give up smoking and eating more healthily in the staff canteen.'

'Old-style wellbeing is like walking downstream of a river, rescuing employees who are flailing around in the water, needing saving,' says Margaret Samuel, chief medical officer at EDF Energy. 'What we need to do is turn around and walk upstream to find out why so many of these employees are ending up in the water in the first place; we need to find the source of the emergency.'

Source: Crush, P. (2009) 'Health and wellbeing: the science of employee wellbeing', *Human Resources*, 1 July. Available at www.hrmagazine.co.uk/.../Health-wellbeing-science-employee-wellbeing/.

ACTIVITY 30.4

What are the key causes of reduced productivity and/or commitment in an organisation with which you are familiar? To what extent do you think that these issues will be improved or resolved by the initiatives outlined in Table 30.1?

SUMMARY PROPOSITIONS

30.1 The links between health and well-being and employee performance were identified long ago, although there was little emphasis on them from an HR perspective for much of the twentieth century.

30.2 The past decade has seen a substantial increase in interest in employee health and well-being from both an organisational and a governmental perspective. This has been driven by social, economic and political changes.

30.3 Initiatives within a health and well-being policy have typically focused narrowly on employees' physical and mental health. This focus has attracted a great deal of criticism.

30.4 It is suggested that health and well-being initiatives have a range of positive outcomes including improvements in recruitment, performance, engagement and retention, more positive employee attitudes and enhanced competitive advantage.

30.5 There are many criticisms of HR's narrow approach to health and well-being. These include assertions that such approaches differ little from traditional absence management, are likely to lack management buy-in and are financially beyond the reach of the many smaller firms in the economy.

30.6 Other concerns surround the argument that an employee's health is no concern of the employer and, most fundamentally, that health and well-being initiatives often tackle the symptoms of poor employment practice. Better job design and more worker autonomy would be much more effective in improving the lot of the employee.

30.7 There is some evidence that HR practitioners are beginning to recognise the need for wider conceptions of health and well-being.

GENERAL DISCUSSION TOPICS

1 The positive outcomes from health and well-being initiatives justify their significant cost. Discuss this statement.

2 An organisation does not have the right to concern itself with the weight and fitness levels of its employees. To what extent do you think this is true?

3 Evaluate the suggestion that organisations would obtain more significant benefits from designing jobs well than from providing access to free fruit and low-cost gym membership.

FURTHER READING

CIPD (2007) *What's Happening with Wellbeing at Work?* London: CIPD.
This report presents detailed information on a range of health and well-being initiatives. It provides case study evidence that workplaces which invest in the well-being of their employees have high workplace standards and also help those people to improve their own well-being.

Danna, K. and Griffin, R. (1999) 'Health and well-being in the workplace: a review and synthesis of the literature', *Journal of Management*, Vol. 25, No. 3, pp. 357–84.
This article presents a comprehensive review of the literature that serves to define health and well-being. It then discusses the primary factors associated with health and well-being, the consequences of low levels of health and well-being and common methods for improving health and well-being in the workplace.

Marsden, D. and Moriconi, S. (2008) 'The value of rude health', London School of Economics, available at **ftp://ftp.royalmail.com/Downloads/public/ctf/rmg/Value_of_rude_health_report_FINAL_280408.pdf.**
This report reflects the interest of businesses and government interest in health and well-being. It explores the Royal Mail's comprehensive approach to managing health and well-being and demonstrates that it benefits both people and business. Its effects on business performance – from employee morale to productivity and other indicators of business performance – are clearly laid out in this report.

WEB LINKS

www.gsk.com/investors/reps03/EHS03/GSKehs-11.htm (website of GlaxoSmithKline).

www.ibm.com/ibm/responsibility/employee_well_being_management.shtml (IBM website, section on corporate social responsibility).

www.ibm.com/ibm/responsibility/employees_global_wellness.shtml (IBM website, section on international wellness initiatives).

www.investorsinpeople.co.uk (website of Investors in People).

www.lavanlegal.com.au/go/careers/employee-well-being-policy (website of Australian law firm Lavan Legal: employee well-being).

www.pearnkandola.com/well-being (website of Pearn and Kanolola).

www.news.royalmailgroup.com/articlea.asp?id=2213&brand=royal_mail_group (website of Royal Mail Group).

www.wellbeing.ac.uk (website of Wellbeing funded by the HEFCE and the Scottish Funding Council to investigate and promote well-being in higher education, accessed 3 June 2010).

www.wiltshire.gov.uk/healthandsocialcare/2010healthandwellbeingawards/2010healthandwell beingawardscategories.htm (website of Wiltshire County Council, accessed 25 January 2010).

www.workandwellbeing.com (website of Work and Well-Being Ltd, a consultancy, accessed 3 June 2010).

REFERENCES

ACAS (2009) *Bullying and Harassment at Work: Guidance for employees*. London: ACAS. Available at: **www.acas.org.uk/index.aspx?articleid=797** (accessed 23 January 2010).

CIPD (2007) *What's Happening with Wellbeing at Work?* London: CIPD.

Ball, M. (2009) 'The dark side of girl power: female bullying at work', *People Management*, 30 October. Available at **www.peoplemanagement.co.uk/pm/articles/2009/10/the-dark-side-of-girl-power-female-bullying-at-work.htm**.

Crush, P. (2009) 'Health and wellbeing: the science of employee wellbeing', *Human Resources*, 1 July. Available at **www.hrmagazine.co.uk/.../Health-wellbeing-science-employee-wellbeing/**.

Danna, K. and Griffin, R. (1999) 'Health and well-being in the workplace: a review and synthesis of the literature', *Journal of Management*, Vol. 25, No. 3, pp. 357–84.

Department of Health (2004) *Choosing Health: Making healthy choices easier*. Cm 6374. London: HMSO. Online version also available at: **www.dh.gov.uk/dr_consum_dh/groups/dh_digitalassets/@dh/@en/documents/digitalasset/dh_4120792.pdf** (accessed 23 January 2010).

Health and Safety Executive (2004) *Management Standards for Work-related Stress*. London: HSE.

Health and Safety Executive (2009) *How to Tackle Work-related Stress: A guide for employers on making the Management Standards work*. London: HSE. Online version also available at: **www.hse.gov.uk/pubns/indg430.pdf** (accessed 23 January 2010).

Holman, D. (2002) 'Employee wellbeing in call centres', *Human Resource Management Journal*, Vol. 12, No. 4, pp. 35–50.

Marsden, D. and Moriconi, S. (2008) 'The value of rude health'. London: London School of Economics. Available at: **ftp://ftp.royalmail.com/Downloads/public/ctf/rmg/Value_of_rude_health_report_FINAL_280408.pdf** (accessed 25 January 2010).

Newman, A. (2010) 'Get happy and get on with it', *Times Higher Education*, 21–27 January, pp. 32–6.

Vartia, M. (2001) 'Consequences of workplace bullying with respect to the well-being of its targets and the observers of bullying', *Scandinavian Journal of Work and Environmental Health*, Vol. 27, No. 1, pp. 63–9.

Wilson, M., Dejoy, D., Vandenberg, R., Richardson, H. and McGrath, A. (2004) 'Work characteristics and employee health and well-being: test of a model of a healthy work organisation', *Journal of Occupational and Organizational Psychology*, Vol. 77, No. 4, pp. 565–88.

Part 7 CASE STUDY PROBLEM

Offshoring to India

Since 2000 dozens of large corporations based in the UK, the USA and Canada have transferred parts of their operations to cities such as Bangalore and Mumbai in India. In the main the activities that are 'offshored' are those carried out in call centres, such as customer enquiries, telemarketing and back-office administration. Most of the larger finance companies either have made such a move or are actively considering doing so. The same is true of many e-businesses, mail-order retailers and other service sector companies. Rail and airline enquiries may well soon be answered down the phone from India, while some larger legal firms rely on secretarial services based in India to type up dictated letters. Offshoring has clearly become a major business trend.

The potential advantages are very evident. The salary that has to be paid to a call-centre worker in India is around 20 per cent of the figure required to secure the services of someone in the UK. This means that call centres in India operate at around 40 per cent of their cost in the UK once international telephone charges have been taken into account. Setting up a 850-seat centre in India costs about £20 million, but can easily yield annual savings of £15 million once it is established. Savings of that kind are just too significant to pass up in highly competitive industries that must cut costs wherever possible if they are to survive and grow.

Moreover, by Indian standards, these are well-paid jobs which attract highly educated people, including graduates, who perform more effectively and more quickly than the typical UK call-centre worker. Employers report that as well as having lower salary expectations, Indian employees are more adaptable to change and more responsive to management demands than their UK counterparts. Their level of spoken English is generally very high too. It is thus argued that costs are saved and quality is increased when an organisation offshores its operations to India.

Offshoring has been criticised vigorously by trade unions representing the British workers whose jobs are put at risk by the offshoring trend. They argue that it is no more than a 'corporate fashion' which cannot be justified over the longer term. They point to the very high levels of staff turnover that are found in many Indian call-centre operations and to persistent power maintenance problems. Over the long term, the critics argue, shortages of appropriately qualified staff will emerge as the Indian economy develops its own high-tech industrial sector. Cost savings will thus reduce substantially within ten years. Critics also point to well-publicised instances of poor-quality services being provided by some Indian operations.

It appears that in order to be successful, a great deal of effort must be put into training Indian staff to adopt western personas, particularly in the telesales operations. They have to make 200 calls to the UK or the USA on each shift that they work, and these yield more sales if the operator poses as someone called Jack or Cathy and is able to chat about the weather in the UK or the latest television programmes.

Required

1 Companies transferring their call-centre operations to India can either outsource to one of the established India-based providers (which typically operate 10,000-seat centres), or set up their own bespoke operation via a subsidiary company. What are the major advantages and disadvantages of each of these options from the perspective of the corporation?

2 Critics of offshoring often claim that the practice is unethical, when seen from the perspective of both UK and Indian employees. To what extent do you agree with this view and why? What steps might be taken by a company that aims to be a champion of corporate social responsibility to ensure that it acted ethically when offshoring?

3 A great deal of customer demand for call-centre services is concentrated in the evenings and at weekends, and this is also the prime time for selling goods and services to UK and US-based consumers via cold calling. What implications does this have for the achievement of a work-life balance for Indian call-centre workers?

4 Some companies have already outsourced parts of their HR function to India – mainly basic back-office tasks such as payroll administration, the maintenance of databases and intranet systems, generation of standard letters and sets of documentation and benefits administration. How much further do you think this process could be taken? To what extent would it be feasible to offshore some of the advisory functions carried out by HR specialists as well as the basic administrative tasks?

Sources: Crabb, S. (2003) 'East India companies', *People Management*, 20 February, pp. 28–32; and articles downloaded from the BBC News website (**www.bbc.co.uk**).

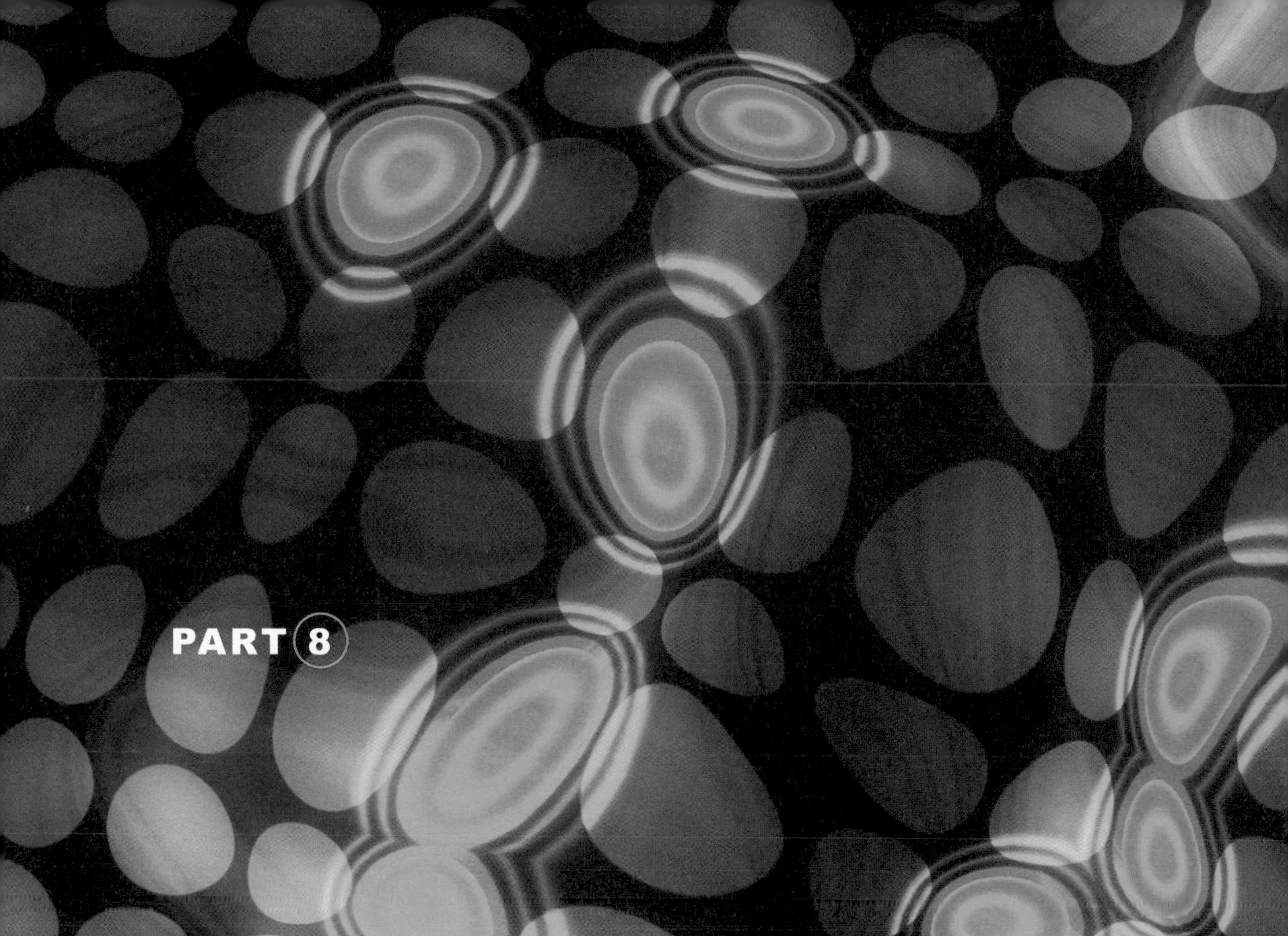

SELECTED HR SKILLS

Introduction

Most of the skills in management are generic in that they are equally important to all those in managerial roles, no matter what their specialism, but here we consider the skills which are the essence of HRM, even though some of them are important to other managers as well.

In previous editions of this book we have limited our treatment to skills in face-to-face situations, as they are central to so many HR activities, such as selection, appraisal, training, grievance and discipline. The most successful self-help book ever published, Dale Carnegie's *How to Win Friends and Influence People*, sold 16 million copies over 70 years. The ability to influence people is an ambition of most human beings and is fundamental to HR management. Professor Tom Lupton was the second Director of Manchester Business School and a distinguished industrial relations academic. When addressing a national conference of the Institute of Personnel Management he stressed the importance of personnel people being involved in strategy because, 'otherwise all you have left is selling it to the lads'. Yet 'selling it to the lads' is a prime example of a rare and vital skill: not working out what to do, but getting people to share that understanding and then make it happen.

For this edition we have broadened our range to include other aspects of communication: report writing, presentation at tribunals and dealing with bullying.

We also have for the first time four areas of quite different types of skill. There are some simple statistical techniques applicable to measurement in a number of aspects of HR. Then we suggest the elements of designing procedures, designing questionnaires and how to use consultancy services, so that you receive and use the service you need rather than what the consultant will provide if not given the necessary steer and carefully managed.

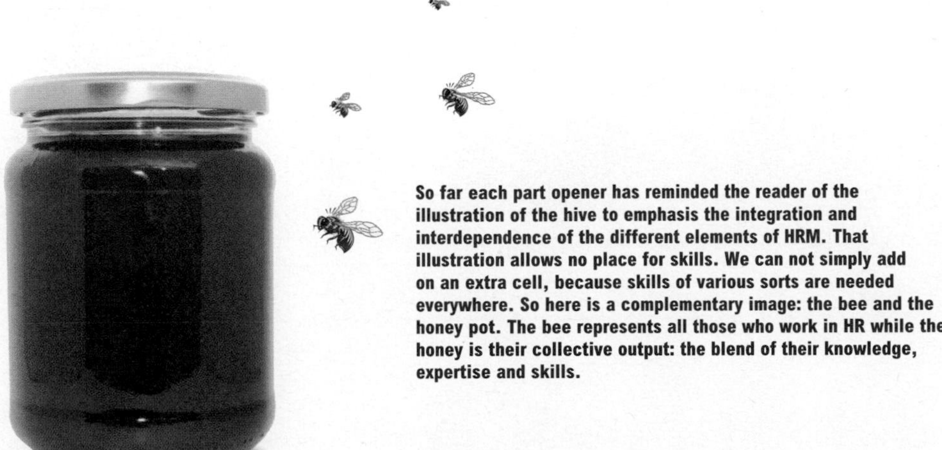

So far each part opener has reminded the reader of the illustration of the hive to emphasis the integration and interdependence of the different elements of HRM. That illustration allows no place for skills. We can not simply add on an extra cell, because skills of various sorts are needed everywhere. So here is a complementary image: the bee and the honey pot. The bee represents all those who work in HR while the honey is their collective output: the blend of their knowledge, expertise and skills.

SKILLS SET 1:

Face-to-face and other communications skills

- I The selection interview
- II The appraisal interview
- III Coaching
- IV Presentation
- V Mediation
- VI The disciplinary or grievance interview
- VII Report writing
- VIII Presentation at tribunal
- IX Dealing with bullying and harassment at work

The core expertise of HR specialists is skill in interaction and handling of face-to-face situations effectively, which is essential throughout human resource management. As well as being articulate and receptive in any face-to-face situation, HR specialists need to develop specific skills for different situations.

The recruiter has to be effective in the highly specialised interaction of the selection interview, where the task is to find out relevant information about an applicant on which to base a judgement as to whether or not that person would match the skills, experience and attitudes required in the job to be filled. That information will only come from an applicant who has confidence in the interviewer's integrity and who volunteers the information, responding willingly and helpfully to the questions that are posed.

The industrial relations manager, in contrast, needs to be an effective negotiator, explaining a position that those on the other side of the table may not appreciate and who have themselves a position which the industrial relations manager may not appreciate. Common ground has to be established, differences clarified and possibilities for reconciling those differences explored.

Both interactions have things in common, but they require different skills.

Our objectives in this introduction to communication skills are to:

1 Explain what makes for effectiveness in interaction
2 Explain the different types of interaction
3 Review the fundamental skills of (a) setting the tone, (b) listening, (c) questioning and (d) feedback

EFFECTIVENESS IN INTERACTION

We all reveal our feelings by what we do as well as in what we say. Someone blushing is obviously embarrassed and someone crying is clearly distressed, but there are a host of other signs or *tells* that indicate what a person is feeling. The person who is able to read these signals has a great advantage in interactions. The term 'tell' comes from the study of poker players, who are as anxious to conceal their own hand as they are to guess what is in someone else's. It is an interesting feature of human behaviour that we all lie when we think it will help us socially. As H.G. Wells said a century ago:

> The social contract is . . . a vast conspiracy of human beings to lie and humbug themselves and one another for the general good. Lies are the mortar that bind the savage individual man into the social masonry. (*Love and Mr Lewisham* 1900)

Effective face-to-face people are likely to have some basic qualities. *Poise* enables a person to be at ease in a wide variety of social situations, often enjoying them, and able to talk with different types of people in a relaxed and self-confident way. This self-confidence comes partly from the feedback of willing responses constantly provided by other people.

Another element of poise is knowing what you are talking about; we demonstrate our poise much more in situations with which we are familiar than we do in strange circumstances. There is less fear of what the other may say and less apprehension about appearing naive. Questions, and even criticism, are easier to deal with and are often wanted, so stimulating the interchange.

Poise is often associated with maturity, due to a person having succeeded in developing a rounded view of themselves without feeling too much anxiety about the possible adverse opinions of others. The process of acquiring poise can be accelerated by the experience of meeting a variety of people from differing backgrounds.

A necessary feature of poise is the quality of being *responsive* to the needs, feelings and level of understanding in other people. This prevents poise from becoming too egocentric. The teacher, for instance, will be looking for signs of misunderstanding in the student so that the message can be restated or clarified, and the market research interviewer will be looking for signals that the question has been accurately construed, or that it needs elaboration. Responsiveness can also include offering rewards, like friendliness, warmth, sympathy and helpfulness as features of general style or as part of a relationship with other participants. These not only sustain the relationship, but also may be held back as a means of trying to get one's own way.

Certain general problems impair effectiveness. They mostly concern the way that people tend to hear what they expect to hear rather than what they are being told.

The *frame of reference* is the standpoint from which a person views an issue, and understanding of the issue will be shaped by that perspective rather than any abstract 'reality'. It is a set of basic assumptions or standards that frame our behaviour. These are developed through childhood conditioning, through social background, education and through our affiliations. Differences in the frames of reference held by participants in interactions present inescapable problems. Can Israelis and Arabs ever really understand each other? How can those who manage and direct ever appreciate the point of view of those who are managed and directed?

The frame of reference on any particular matter is largely determined by opinions developed within a group with which we identify, as few of us alter our opinions alone. We both follow and help to shape opinion in our group, and most of us are in a number of such reference groups. Because of this, complexities arise: some people can be vociferously anti-union as citizens and voters in general elections, yet support a union of which they are members at their workplace.

The *stereotype* is the standardised expectation we have of those who have certain dominant characteristics: typical stereotypes are that all Scots are mean, all shop stewards are disruptive, women are more caring than men and that men are more aggressive than women. The behaviour of some people in a category makes us expect all those in that category to behave in the same way. The outstanding example in Western countries at the moment is a general attitude towards all Muslims that is shaped by the actions of Islamic extremists.This is obviously invalid, but is a tendency to which we are prone. We have to listen to what people are actually saying to us rather than hearing what we think a person of that type *would say*.

Making use of stereotypes is necessary at the start of working relationships; it is not feasible to deal with every individual we meet as being a void until we have collected enough information to know how to treat them, so we always try to find a pigeon-hole in which to put someone. We begin conversations with a working stereotype, so that, for example, we stop someone in the street to ask directions only after we have selected a person who looks intelligent and sympathetic. If we are giving directions to a stranger we begin our explanation having made an assessment of their ability to understand quickly, or their need for a more detailed, painstaking explanation. The stereotype becomes a handicap only when we remain insensitive to new information enabling us to develop a fuller, more rational appraisal of the individual with whom we are interacting.

Being aware of the dangers of stereotyping others, and trying to exercise self-discipline, can reduce the degree to which you misunderstand other people, but you still have the problem that your respondents will put *you* into a stereotype and hear what you say in accordance with whatever their predetermined notion may be.

Cognitive dissonance is the difficulty we all have in coping with behaviour that is not consistent with our beliefs. Such behaviour will make us uncomfortable and we will try to cope with the dissonance in various ways in order to reduce the discomfort. Either we persuade ourselves that we believe in what we are doing, or we avoid the necessary behaviour. We all interpret or decode words that we hear in order to make sense of them. If we decode the words we hear in a way that does not match what we believe, then we tend to reinterpret them in a way that we can believe.

DIFFERENT TYPES OF INTERACTION

Meetings are needed to make decisions, to overcome misunderstanding and to develop ideas. Interviews are used for selection, discipline, appraisal, counselling, problem solving and grievance handling. Managers 'put things across' in selling, persuasion, presentation and negotiation.

It is helpful to group interactions into four broad types: enquiry, exposition, joint problem solving and conflict resolution.

Enquiry is that group of situations where the HR specialist needs to find things out from someone else, with the selection interview being the classic example. What needs to be found out may be factual information, attitudes, feelings, levels of understanding or misunderstanding. The main skill is in types of questioning.

Exposition is almost the direct opposite. Instead of finding things out, the HR person is trying to convey information, to develop in the other person a level of knowledge and understanding, acceptance of an argument or agreement with a proposition. Although some questioning is often an integral part of exposition, the main skill is in clear articulation, fluency, good organisation of material and effective illustration. You may think, for instance, that the above explanation of cognitive dissonance could have been improved with an illustration. So, sorry for the oversight, try this: a medication was recently developed enabling small children to be protected against measles, mumps and rubella by a single injection rather than three. A spurious piece of research was published apparently demonstrating an increased risk of autism among children immunised in this way rather than with separate injections. Few people read the article publishing the findings, but rumours spread and large numbers of parents *believed* the rumours rather than rational explanation and authoritative rebuttals, they refused the single injection for their children and the incidence of infections rose.

Joint problem solving involves developing an exchange in which both parties work together to unravel a problem or understand a situation which neither fully understands beforehand. It is not one person transferring an 'answer' to another, but both trying to understand together something which they can only partly understand alone. The skills involve some questioning and explanation, but also careful listening and feedback.

Joint problem solving assumes that both parties trust each other and see a common interest in helping the other. *Conflict resolution* begins without that mutual confidence, as the parties have interests that inevitably conflict and they are not likely to trust each other fully. The skills here are, first, those of presentation and then of listening, questioning and feedback.

FUNDAMENTAL SKILLS IN SETTING THE TONE

Any interaction begins by someone setting the tone of what is to follow. A shop assistant who says, 'Can I help you', or the strangely common, 'Are you all right *there*?' is trying to set a tone of knowledgeable helpfulness to a customer that might eventually result in a sale. It is the inclusion of the apparently superfluous 'there' that is puzzling. Of course you are there; where else would you be? Presumably the reason is to make the question less blunt, avoiding the implication that you are not all right. The HR specialist will set the tone of a selection interview, for instance, by explaining what is to happen and providing other contextual information that will enable the candidate to engage in the process constructively. There will also be a process of conveying more subtle messages to say, 'I'm in charge; I know what I'm doing; you can trust me'. In other interactions the way of setting the tone is different, but some features are common:

- Speak first.
- Smile, looking confident and relaxed (much easier said than done).
- Have brief, harmless exchanges that enable the parties to speak to each other without the answers mattering (weather, travel problems, etc.), but always react appropriately to answers.
- Explain your understanding of what is to happen.
- Check that that is understood and accepted.

FUNDAMENTAL SKILLS IN LISTENING

Tone of voice

Different feelings express themselves in different voice characteristics. Possible meanings for various characteristics are tabulated below.

Characteristic	Probable meaning
Monotone voice	Boredom
Slow speed, low pitch	Depression
High voice, emphasis	Enthusiasm
Ascending tone	Astonishment
Abrupt speech	Defensiveness
Terse speed, loud tone	Anger
High pitch, drawn-out speech	Disbelief

Giving attention

Inclining the body towards the other person is a signal of attentiveness, so our posture should be inclined forward and facing the other squarely with an open posture: folded arms can be inhibiting.

Eye contact is crucial to good listening, but is a subtle art:

> Effective eye contact expresses interest and a desire to listen. It involves focusing one's eyes softly on the speaker and occasionally shifting the gaze from his face to other parts of the body, to a gesturing hand, for example, and then back to the face and then to eye contact once again. Poor eye contact occurs when a listener repeatedly looks away from the speaker, stares at him constantly or blankly, or looks away as soon as the speaker looks at the listener. (Bolton 1987: 36)

The distinction between 'focusing one's eyes softly' and staring is vital, though difficult to describe, and competence in eye contact is never easy to establish. It is one of the most intimate ways of relating to a person and many managers fear that the relationship may become too close.

We also show *physical responses* in our attentiveness. First we have to avoid distracting the other person by physical behaviour that is unrelated to what is being said; fiddling with a pen, playing with car keys, scrutinising our fingernails, wringing our hands, brushing specks of dust off our sleeves are a few typical behaviours that indicate inattention. Skilled listeners not only suppress these, they also develop minor gestures and posture variants that are directly responsive to what the other is saying.

Being silent helps you to listen by providing space for incoming messages, but it also provides opportunities to observe the other person and to think about what is being said. Most people are uncomfortable with silence and try to fill it with inconsequential chat, but this interferes with listening. Silence still has to be attentive and the longer the silence, the harder it is to be attentive.

FUNDAMENTAL SKILLS IN QUESTIONING

Closed questions seek precise, terse information and are useful when you want clear, straightforward data. Most encounters feature closed questioning at some point.

Open-ended questions avoid terse replies by inviting respondents to develop their opinions without the interviewer prescribing what the answer should be. The question does little more than introduce a topic to talk about. The main purpose of such questions is to obtain the type of deeper information that the closed question misses, as the shape of the answer is not predetermined by the questioner. You are informed not simply by the content of the answers, but by what is selected and emphasised.

Indirect questions take an oblique approach on a difficult matter. A blunt 'Did you like that job?' almost suggests you didn't, or at least raises the suspicion that the interviewer thinks you didn't; it is a bit like the shop assistant avoiding being too blunt. Put indirectly as 'What gave you the most satisfaction in that job?' it has the merit of concentrating on the work rather than the person.

The *probe* is a form of questioning to obtain information that the respondent is trying to conceal. When the questioner becomes aware that the respondent is doing so he or she has to make an important, and perhaps difficult, decision: whether to respect the candidate's unwillingness and let the matter rest, or to persist with the enquiry. Reluctance is quite common in selection interviews where a candidate may wish to gloss over an aspect of the recent employment history. The most common sequence for the probe takes the following form: (a) direct questions, replacing the more comfortable open-ended approach ('What were you doing in the first six months of 2009?'). Careful phrasing may avoid a defensive reply, but those skilled at avoiding unwelcome enquiries may still deflect the question, leading to (b) supplementaries, which reiterate the first question with different phrasing ('Yes, I understand about that period. It's the first part of 2009 that I'm trying to get clear: after you came back from Belgium and before you started with Amalgamated Widgets'). Eventually this should produce the information the questioner needs. (c) Closing. If the information has been wrenched out like a bad tooth and the interviewer looks horrified or sits in stunned silence, then the candidate will feel badly put down. The interviewer needs to make the divulged secret less awful than the candidate had feared, so that the interview can proceed with reasonable confidence ('Yes, well you must be glad to have that behind you'). It may be that the interviewer will feel able to develop the probe by developing the answer by a further question such as 'And how did that make you feel?' or 'And how did you react to that? It must have been a terrible blow.' It is only reasonable to do this if the resultant exchange adds something useful to the questioner's understanding of the client: simple nosiness is not appropriate.

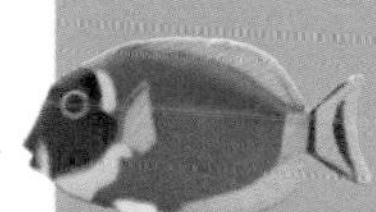

WINDOW ON (MAL)PRACTICE

One dubious version of the probe is to offer an exaggerated explanation for something being avoided. In the imaginary situation described above the selector might do this:

> *Selector*: Yes, I understand about that period. It's the first part of 2006 that I'm trying to get clear: after you came back from Belgium and before you started with Amalgamated Widgets. You weren't in prison or anything, were you?
>
> *Candidate*: Oh no. I had a nervous breakdown.

The explanation offered by the selector is so appalling that the candidate rushes to offer a less appalling explanation. This is not recommended, but it is interesting to know about. It might happen to you one day.

Some common lines of questioning should be avoided because they can produce an effect that is different from what is intended.

Leading questions ('Would you agree with me that . . . ?') will not necessarily produce an answer that is informative, but an answer in line with the lead that has been given.

Multiple questions give the candidate too many inputs at one time ('Could you tell me something of what you did at university, not just the degree, but the social and sporting side as well, and why you chose to backpack your way round the world? You didn't travel on your own, did you?'). This sort of questioning is sometimes adopted by interviewers who are trying very hard to efface themselves and let the respondent get on with the talking. However helpful the interviewer intends to be, the effect is that the candidate will usually forget the later parts of the question, feel disconcerted and ask, 'What was the last part of the question?' By this time the interviewer has also forgotten, so they are both embarrassed.

Taboo questions are those that do not respect the reasonable personal privacy of the other person. Some questions have to be avoided, especially in selection interviews, as they could be interpreted as biased. It is potentially discriminatory, for instance, to ask women how many children they have and what their husbands do for a living. Questions about religion or place of birth should also be avoided. Some questions may do no more than satisfy the idle curiosity of the questioner. If there is no point in asking them, they should not be put.

FUNDAMENTAL SKILLS IN FEEDBACK

As well as listening, it is necessary to provide feedback to demonstrate that you have received and understood what you are being told.

In *reflection*, the listener picks up and re-states the content of what has just been said. In a difficult situation the listener picks out the emotional overtones of a statement and 'reflects' them back to the respondent without any attempt to evaluate them. The interviewer expresses neither approval nor disapproval, neither sympathy nor condemnation.

At a more prosaic level, there is *summary and re-run* to show you are listening and providing the opportunity for any misunderstanding to be pointed out. In appraisal, for instance, the respondent will produce lots of information in an interview and you will be selecting that which is to be retained and understood. From time to time you interject a summary sentence or two with an interrogative inflection. This shows that you are listening, gives the respondent the chance to correct any false impressions and reinforces the key points that are being retained. It is also a useful way of making progress, as the interjection is easily followed by another open-ended question – 'Now perhaps we can turn to . . .'.

The standard method in both reflection and summary is *paraphrasing*, by which the listener states the essence of what has been said. This is done concisely, giving the speaker a chance to review what has been said and, perhaps, to correct it.

We all respond positively when a listener shows *interest* in what is being said. If it is possible also to agree with what is being said, the reinforcement of the respondent will be greater.

The most common form of *affirmation* in feedback is the head nod, and many public speakers look for head nods (not to be confused with nodding off) as a way of judging the supportive mood of the audience. Other ways of affirming involve the use of the eyes. These are too subtle and individual to describe, but we each have a repertoire of signals to indicate such reactions as encouragement, surprise and understanding. When the eyes are part of a smile, there will be stronger reward to the talker. There are also words and phrases: 'Really?', 'Go on . . .', 'Yes . . .', 'Of course . . .', 'My word . . .', 'You were saying . . .'.

Interaction contains a variety of noises that are ways of feeding back to the other party. They are impossible to reproduce in words but are usually variations of a theme of 'Mmm . . .' and they form a part of the exchanges that is inarticulate yet meaningful, keeping things going without interrupting.

SUMMARY PROPOSITIONS

1.1 Face-to-face skills are a fundamentally important aspect of all managerial work.

1.2 Effectiveness in interaction is aided by poise and being responsive to others, as well as by understanding the effects of the frame of reference, stereotyping and cognitive dissonance.

1.3 The basic types of interaction can be categorised as enquiry, exposition, joint problem solving and conflict resolution.

1.4 Listening skills include tone of voice, giving attention, eye contact, physical responses and being silent.

1.5 The main types of question are closed, open ended, indirect and the probe. Inappropriate questions are leading, multiple and taboo.

1.6 Methods of feedback include reflection, summary and re-run, paraphrasing, showing interest, affirmation and using appropriate noises.

GENERAL DISCUSSION TOPICS

1 What are the advantages of face-to-face conversation compared with a combination of e-mail, fax, text messages and telephone calls? To what extent is videoconferencing adequate as an alternative to meeting face to face?

2 If a central part of HRM is getting things done by other people, what is the difference between telling them what to do and asking them to do things? In what sort of situations would each approach be appropriate?

FURTHER READING

Argyle, M. (1994) *The Psychology of Interpersonal Behaviour*. Harmondsworth, Middlesex: Penguin Books.
This classic was first published in 1967 and remains the ideal introduction to understanding the dynamics of interpersonal skills.

Caro, M. (1994) *The Body Language of Poker*. Secaucus: Carol Publishing Group.
An analysis of the ways in which poker players try to conceal their reactions to different stages of play, especially as cards are dealt.

Collett, P. (2003) *The Book of Tells*. London: Doubleday.
A comprehensive explanation of non-verbal behaviours that reveal a person's true feelings. The author is a social psychologist who has combined research at the Oxford University Department of Experimental Psychology with acting as resident psychologist for the television programme *Big Brother*.

Glass, L. (1992) *He Says, She Says*. London: Piatkus.
This shows the differences in communication behaviour between men and women, which lead to such extensive misunderstanding of motives. The author explains differences in body language, voice tone, speech patterns and even choice of words.

REFERENCE

Bolton, R. (1987) *People Skills*. Brookvale, New South Wales: Simon & Schuster.

I. THE SELECTION INTERVIEW

Central to all HRM is the selection interview, in which the interviewer is trying to obtain information from an applicant in order to form a judgement about that person for a particular job or position in an organisation, working with a particular group of working colleagues. At the same time the people being interviewed are presenting information to influence that decision and collecting information that will help them decide whether they want the job or not. This fact of *exchange* has led personnel/HR texts to describe the interview as 'a two-way conversation with a purpose'. This comfortable axiom, like many axioms, is largely accurate but misses an important element, that the interviewer is in charge, setting the agenda, controlling the development, deciding when to close and making the key judgement: yes or no. Even if candidates soon decide not to take your lousy job, even if it is offered, they would still like to have the confidence-boosting offer which they can have the ego boost of refusing. The candidate needs the interviewer to set the agenda and to lead the interview, otherwise he or she is at sea and tends towards making an egocentric pitch that does more for his or her self-esteem than for his/her job prospects.

A second important point about the selection interview is that the approach and skills used are similar to those needed in other working situations in which your purpose is to obtain information face to face from someone else: assessing the merit of a computer system that is being sold to you, assessing the situation when trying to mediate between two colleagues, dealing with the facts of a disciplinary situation, and so on.

Varieties of selection interview

Practice in selection interviewing varies. At one extreme is, for instance, is the selection of glamour models for a photo-shoot, where physique and appearance are dispassionately assessed and spoken words are mainly shared between the assessors unless it is a brusque instruction to the model to adopt different positions. At the opposite extreme we hear of people being telephoned by complete strangers and being offered handsome contracts to work in Hollywood studios.

There is a range of employee participation in the employment process which correlates with the type of work. There are working situations where the amount of discussion between the parties is limited to perfunctory exchanges about trade union membership, hours of work and rates of pay: labourers on building sites and extras on film sets being two examples. As interviews move up the organisational hierarchy there is growing equilibrium, with the interviewer becoming more courteous and responsive to questions from the applicant, who will probably be described as a 'candidate' or someone who 'might be interested in the position'. For the most senior positions it is less likely that people will be invited to respond to vacancies advertised in the press, although equality legislation is leading to more senior positions being openly advertised. It is more likely that individuals will be approached, either directly or through consultants, and there will be an elaborate ritual in which each party tries to persuade the other to declare an interest first.

The purpose of the selection interview

The interview is a controlled conversation with a purpose. There are more exchanges in a shorter period related to a specific purpose than in an ordinary conversation. In the selection interview the purposes are:

- to collect information in order to predict how well the applicants would perform in the job for which they have applied, by measuring them against predetermined criteria;
- to provide candidates with full details of the job and organisation to facilitate their decision making;
- to conduct the interview in such a way that candidates feel that they have been given a fair hearing.

Handling this most crucial of encounters is a key skill for personnel and other managers as the interview has a number of important advantages which cannot be provided by any other means. It cannot be bettered as a means of exchanging information and meeting the human and ritual aspects of the employment process.

Human and ritual aspects

An interview can be used to assess matters that cannot be approached in any other way, such as the potential compatibility of two people who will have to work together. Both parties need to meet before the contract begins, to 'tune in' to each other and begin the process of induction. The interview is valuable in that way to both potential employee and potential employer. It gives interviewees the feeling that they matter, as another person is devoting time to them and they are not being considered by a computer. Also, giving applicants a chance to ask questions underlines their decision-making role, making them feel less helpless in the hands of the all-powerful interviewer. Selection interviewing has important ritual elements, as the applicant is seeking either to enter, or to rise within, a social system. This means that they defer to the interviewer more than they would in other situations.

At the same time those who are already inside and above display their superiority and security, even unconsciously, in contrast with the behaviour of someone so obviously anxious to share the same privileged position. Reason tells us that this is inappropriate at the beginning of the twenty-first century as the books are full of advice to interviewers not to brandish their social superiority, but to put applicants at their ease and to reduce the status differentials. This, however, still acknowledges their superiority as they are the ones who take the initiative; applicants are not expected to help the interviewer relax and feel less apprehensive. Also the reality of the situation is usually that of applicant anxious to get in and selector choosing among several. Status differentials cannot simply be set aside. The selection interview is at least partly an initiation rite, not as elaborate as entry to commissioned rank in the armed forces, nor as whimsical as finding one's way into the Brownie ring, but still a process of going through hoops and being found worthy in a process where other people make all the rules.

ACTIVITY I.1

For a selection interview in which you recently participated, either as selector or as applicant, consider the following:

1. What were the ritual features?
2. Were any useful ritual features missing?
3. Could ritual have been, in any way, *helpfully* reduced?

Interview strategy

The approach to selection interviewing varies considerably from the amiable chat in a bar to the highly organised, multi-person panel.

By far the most common is the approach which has been described as *frank and friendly*. Here the interviewer is concerned to establish and maintain rapport. This is done in the belief that if interviewees do not feel threatened, and are relaxed, they will be more forthcoming in the information that they offer. It is straightforward for both interviewer and interviewee and has the potential advantage that the interviewees will leave with a favourable impression of the business.

A variation is the *problem-solving approach*. The interviewer presents the candidate with a hypothetical problem and evaluates the answer. The questions asked are derived from the job description. Candidates are required to imagine themselves as the job holder and describe what they would do in a variety of hypothetical situations. This method is most applicable to testing elementary knowledge, such as the colour coding of wires in electric cables or maximum dosages of specified drugs. It is less effective for testing understanding and ability.

There is no guarantee that the candidate would actually behave in the way suggested. The quick thinker will score at the expense of those who can take action more effectively than they can answer riddles.

Similar to the problem-solving strategy is the biographical method. The focus is on the candidate's past behaviour and performance, which is a more reliable way of predicting future performance than asking interviewees what they would do in a certain situation. Candidates are asked to describe the background to a situation and explain what they did and why; what their options were; how they decided what to do; and the anticipated and real results of their action. The success of this method depends on in-depth job analysis, and preferably competency analysis, in order to frame the best questions. Bearing in mind the importance of structure in selection interviewing, the biographical approach is an excellent method.

In the *stress approach* the interviewer becomes aggressive, disparages the candidates, puts them on the defensive or disconcerts them by strange behaviour. The advantage of the method is that it may demonstrate a necessary strength or a disqualifying weakness that would not be apparent through other methods. The disadvantages are that evaluating the behaviour under stress is problematic, and those who are not selected will think badly of the employer. The likely value of stress interviewing is so limited that it is hardly worth mentioning, except that it has spurious appeal to many managers, who are attracted by the idea of injecting at least some stress into the interview 'to see what they are made of', or 'to put them on their mettle'. Most candidates feel that the procedures are stressful enough, without adding to them.

Number of interviews and interviewers

There are two broad traditions governing the number of interviewers. One says that effective, frank discussion can only take place on a one-to-one basis, so candidates meet one interviewer, or several interviewers, one at a time. The other tradition is that fair play must be demonstrated and nepotism prevented so the interview must be carried out, and the decision made, by a panel of interviewers. Within this dichotomy there are various options.

The individual interview

The individual interview gives the greatest chance of establishing rapport, developing mutual trust and is the most efficient deployment of time in the face-to-face encounter, as each participant has to compete with only one other speaker. It is usually also the most satisfactory method for the candidate, who has to tune in to only one other person instead of needing constantly to adjust to different interviewers. The candidate can more readily ask questions, as it is difficult to ask a panel of six people to explain the workings of the pension scheme, and it is the least formal type of interview. The disadvantages lie in the reliance the organisation places on the judgement of one of its representatives, although this can be mitigated by a series of individual interviews, and the ritual element is largely missing. Candidates may not feel they have been 'done' properly. A sole interview with the line manager is very popular in the selection of people for manual work, being used in a third of all interviews. It is less popular for administrative and management posts.

Sequential interviews

Sequential interviews are a series of individual interviews. The series most often consists of just two interviews for blue- and white-collar staff, but more than two for managerial staff. The most frequent combination is an interview with the line manager and one with a representative of the HR department. For managerial posts this will be extended to interviews with other departmental managers, top managers and significant prospective colleagues. Sequential interviews can give the employer a broader picture of the candidate and they also allow the applicant to have contact with a greater number of potential colleagues. However, for the advantages of sequential interviews to be realised there is a need for effective organisation and for all interviews to be held on the same day. It is important that all interviewers meet beforehand to agree on the requirements of the post and to decide how each will contribute to the overall theme. Immediately after the interviews candidates can be jointly evaluated at a further meeting. One disadvantage is the organisation and time that it takes from both the employer's and the candidate's point of view. It requires considerable commitment from the candidate who may have to keep repeating similar information and whose performance may deteriorate throughout the course of the interviews due to fatigue.

Panel interviews

The panel interview method has the specious appeal of sharing judgement and may appear to be a way of saving time in interviewing as all panel members are operating at once. It is also possible to legitimise a quick decision, always popular with candidates, and there can be no doubt about the ritual requirements being satisfied. Panel interviews reduce the likelihood of personal bias in interviewing, particularly in guarding against possible infringements of legal requirements.

WINDOW ON (MAL)PRACTICE

We have said above that panel interviews reduce the likelihood of personal bias. Perhaps we should have written 'reduce but do not eliminate personal bias', as indicated by the situation following a panel interview to select a senior manager for a public corporation. After the interview and after the decision had been made, the HR manager was tidying up the papers in the room and found a scrap of paper on which a member of the panel had scribbled, 'looks like a good screw'. The HR manager decided that this was not a case of a panel member relieving boredom by examining the structure of the table round which the members had been sitting.

They can also ensure the candidate is acceptable to the whole organisation, and allow the candidate to get a good feel for the business and its culture. The drawbacks lie in the tribunal nature of the panel. They are not having a conversation with the candidates; they are sitting in judgement upon them and assessing the evidence they are able to present in response to the panel's requests. There is little prospect of building rapport and developing discussion, and there is likely to be as much interplay between members of the panel as there is between the panel and the candidate.

Panel interviews tend towards over-rigidity and give ironic point to the phrase, 'it is only a formality'. They are ritualistically superb, but dubious as a useful preliminary to employment. However, the benefits of the panel interview can be increased, and the disadvantages reduced, if the interviewers are properly trained and the interview well organised, thoroughly planned and made part of a structured selection process.

ACTIVITY I.2

In your organisation how many interviews and interviewers are used? How effective is this approach and why? In what ways could the approach be improved?

The selection interview sequence

Preparation

We assume that the preliminaries of job analysis, recruitment and shortlisting are complete and the interview is now to take place. The first step is for the interviewers to brief themselves by checking the job description or similar details of the post to be filled, a candidate specification or statement of required competencies and the application forms or curricula vitae of the candidates.

If there are several people to be interviewed the interview timetable needs greater planning than it usually receives. The time required for each interview can be determined beforehand only approximately. A rigid timetable will weigh heavily on both parties, who will feel frustrated if the interview is closed arbitrarily at a predetermined time. If an interview that has 'finished' is drawn out to complete its allotted timespan it becomes increasingly artificial and exasperating. However, the disadvantages of keeping people waiting are considerable and underrated.

Most candidates will have competing calls on their time, as they will have taken time off to attend and have earmarked the anticipated interview time to fit in a busy schedule. Some may have other interviews to go to. An open-ended waiting period can be worrying, enervating and a poor preliminary to an interview. If the dentist keeps you waiting you may get distressed, but when the waiting is over you are simply a passive participant and the dentist does not have the success of the operation jeopardised. The interview candidate has, in a real sense, to perform when the period of waiting is over and the success of the interaction could well be jeopardised.

The most satisfactory timetable is the one that guarantees a break after all but the most voluble candidates. If candidates are asked to attend at hourly intervals, for example, this would be consistent with interviews lasting between 40 and 60 minutes. This would mean that each interview began at the scheduled time and that the interviewers had the opportunity to review and update their notes in the intervals. The whole plan can still go wrong if one or more candidates fail to turn up.

Reception

Candidates arrive on the premises of their prospective employer on the lookout for every scrap of evidence they can obtain about the business and its people. A candidate is likely to meet at least one and possibly two people before meeting the interviewer. First will be the commissionaire or receptionist. There is frequently also an emissary from the HR department to shepherd them from the front door to the waiting-room. Both are valuable sources of information, and interviewers may wish to prime such people so that they can see their role in the employment process and can be cheerful, informative and helpful.

The candidate will most want to meet the interviewer, the unknown but powerful figure on whom so much depends. Interviewers easily forget that they know much more about the candidates than the candidates know about them, because the candidates have provided a personal profile in the application form.

Interviewers do not reciprocate. To bridge this gap it can be useful for interviewers to introduce themselves to the candidate in the waiting-room, so that contact is made quickly, unexpectedly and on neutral territory. This makes the opening of the interview itself rather easier.

Candidates wait to be interviewed. Although there are snags about extended, open-ended waiting periods, some time is inevitable and necessary to enable candidates to compose themselves. It is a useful time to deal with travelling expenses and provide some relevant background reading about the employing organisation.

Setting

The setting for an interview has to be right for the ritual and right from the point of view of enabling a full and frank exchange of information. It is difficult to combine the two. Many of the interview horror stories relate to the setting in which it took place. A candidate for a senior local authority post was interviewed on a stage while the panel of 17 sat in the front row of the stalls, and a candidate for a headteacher post came in to meet the interview panel and actually moved the chair on which he was to sit. He only moved it two or three inches because the sun was in his eyes, but there was an audible frisson and sharp intake of breath from the members of the panel.

Remaining with our model of the individual interviewer, here are some simple suggestions about the setting:

- The room should be suitable for a private conversation.
- If the interview takes place across a desk, as is common, the interviewer may wish to reduce the extent to which the desk acts as a barrier, inhibiting free flow of communication.
- All visitors and telephone calls should be avoided, as they do not simply interrupt: they intrude and impede the likelihood of frankness.
- It should be clear to the candidates where they are to sit.

Interview structure

There are several important reasons why the employment interview should be structured, making use of the application or CV:

- The candidate expects the proceedings to be decided and controlled by the interviewer and will anticipate a structure within which to operate.
- It helps the interviewer to make sure that they cover all relevant areas and avoid irrelevancies.
- It looks professional.
- Structure can be used to guide the interview and ensure that it makes sense.
- It assists the interviewer in using the time available in the most effective way.
- The application form can be used as a memory aid by the interviewer when making notes directly after the interview or during it.
- It makes it easier to compare candidates.

The interview

There are several different ways to structure the interview. We recommend the form set out in Table I.1. This divides activities and objectives into three interview stages: opening, middle and closing. While there are few, if any, alternative satisfactory ways

Table I.1 Interview structure: a recommended pattern

Stage	Objectives	Activities
Opening	To put the candidate at ease, develop rapport and set the scene	Greet candidate by name Introduce yourself Explain interview purpose Outline how purpose will be achieved Obtain candidate's assent to outline
Middle	To collect and provide information	Ask questions within a structure that makes sense to the candidate, such as biographical areas of the application form, or competencies identified for the job Listen Answer questions Summarise interview
Closing	To close the interview and confirm future action	Check candidate has no more questions Indicate what happens next and when

for conducting the beginning and the end of the interview, the middle can be approached from a number of different angles, depending on the circumstances.

The interviewer needs to work systematically through the structure that has been planned, but not too rigidly. Interviewers should abandon their own route whenever the candidate chooses one that seems more promising.

The opening of the interview is the time for mutual preliminary assessment and tuning in to each other. A useful feature of this phase is for the interviewer to sketch out the plan or procedure for the interview and how it fits into the total employment decision process. The application form may provide an easy, non-controversial topic for these opening behaviours.

One objective is for the two parties to exchange words so that they can feel reasonably comfortable with each other. Interviewers who can do this can then further develop a relationship in which candidates trust the interviewer's ability and motives so that they speak openly and fully. The interviewer's effectiveness will greatly depend on being skilled at this process.

We are working on the assumption that candidates will behave in a reasonably genuine way, provided the interviewer can convince them that the process is fair. Some candidates do not and such people have been labelled as 'white collar psychopaths', although it has to be said that they are rare. They are very good at presenting themselves as being exactly what the interviewer is looking for. Not only are they manufacturing the truth about their experience, the trait (or psychopathic tendency) that drives them causes them to wreak havoc once they are appointed. A New York psychologist cites the example of 'Ron' who was appointed to a sales post in a pharmaceuticals company:

> Ron fiddled his sales figures, charged call girls to the company and nearly succeeded in using his charm to get his new boss fired when he was questioned about his behaviour. Psychopaths are motivated by three things: thrill-seeking, game-playing and hurting people. Once inside the organization they build networks of influence that make it very difficult to get rid of them and can help them join the management fast track.
> (Paul Babiak, quoted in *Financial Times*, 12 January 2004)

For the middle of the interview the biographical approach is the simplest. It works on the basis that candidates at the time of the interview are the product of everything in their lives that has gone before. To understand the candidate the interviewer must understand the past and will talk to the candidate about the episodes of his or her earlier life, education and previous employment.

The advantage of this is that the objectives are clear to both interviewer and interviewee, there is no deviousness or 'magic'. Furthermore, the development can be logical and so aid the candidate's recall of events. Candidates who reply to enquiries about their choice of A level subjects will be subconsciously triggering their recollection of contemporaneous events, such as the university course they took, which are likely to come next in the interview. The biographical approach is the simplest for the inexperienced interviewer to use as discussion can develop from the information provided by the candidate on the application form. Some version of sequential categories, such as employment, education and training, seems the most generally useful, but it will need the addition of at least two other categories: the work offered and the organisational context in which it is to be done. The middle of the interview can be structured by systematically working through items of the job description or the person specification. Increasingly, where competencies have been identified for the job, these are used as the basis of the structure.

In the preparatory stage of briefing, the interviewer will also prepare notes on two elements to incorporate in their plan: key issues and checkpoints. Key issues will be the two or three main issues that stand out from the application form for clarification or elaboration. This might be the nature of the responsibilities carried in a particular earlier post, the content of a training course, the reaction to a period of employment in a significant industry or whatever else strikes the interviewer as being productive of useful additional evidence. Checkpoints are matters of detail that require further information: grades in an examination, dates of an appointment, rates of pay, and so forth.

At the close of the interview the explanation of the next step needs especial attention. The result of the interview is of great importance to the candidates and they will await the outcome with anxiety. Even if they do not want the position they will probably hope to have it offered. This may strengthen their hand in dealings with another prospective employer, or with their present employer, and will certainly be a boost to their morale. The great merit of convention in the public sector is that the chosen candidate is usually told before the contenders disperse: the great demerit is that they are asked to say yes or no to the offer at once.

In the private sector it is unusual for an employment offer to be made at the time of the interview, so there is a delay during which the candidates will chafe. Their frustration will be greater if the delay is longer than expected and they may start to tell themselves that they are not going to receive an offer, in which case they will also start convincing themselves that they did not want the job either! It is important for the interviewer to say as precisely as possible when the decision will be made, but ensuring that the candidates hear earlier rather than later than they expect, if there is to be any deviation.

The interviewer will need to call into play certain key aspects of method.

1 Some data can be collected by simple observation of the candidate. Notes can be made about dress, appearance, voice, height and weight, if these are going to be

relevant (and not unlawfully discriminatory), and the interviewer can also gauge the candidate's mood and the appropriate response to it by the non-verbal cues that are provided.

2 The remainder of the evidence will come from listening to what is said, so the interviewer has to be very attentive throughout; not only listening to the answers to questions, but also listening for changes in inflection and pace, nuances and overtones that provide clues on what to pursue further. The amount of time that the two spend talking is important, as an imbalance in one direction or the other will mean that either the candidate or the interviewer is not having enough opportunity to hear information. Being silent and deliberately leaving verbal lulls in face-to-face situations provide the opportunity for the other person to say more, perhaps more than was initially intended. Silence still has to be attentive and the longer the silence, the harder it is to be attentive.

3 In order to have something to hear, the interviewer will have to direct the candidate. This, of course, is done by questioning, encouraging and enabling the candidate to talk, so that the interviewer can learn. The art of doing this depends on the personality and style of the interviewer who will develop a personal technique through a sensitive awareness of what is taking place in the interviews.

The selection interviewer needs to distinguish between different types of question. In our introduction to face-to-face and communication skills we explained the difference in nature and usage of various questioning methods.

4 The best place for the interviewer to make notes is on the application form or CV. In this way they can be joined to information that the candidate has already provided and the peculiar shorthand that interviewers use when making notes during interviews can be deciphered by reference to the form and the data that the note is embellishing. It also means that the review of evidence after the interview has as much information as possible available on one piece of paper. An alternative is to record notes on the interview plan where the structure is based on job description, person specification or competencies. Interviewers are strangely inhibited about note taking, feeling that it in some way impairs the smoothness of the interaction. This apprehension seems ill founded as candidates are looking for a serious, businesslike discussion, no matter how informal, and note taking offers no barrier, provided that it is done carefully in the form of jottings during the discussion, rather than pointedly writing down particular comments by the candidate which make the interviewer seem like a police officer taking a statement.

5 Data exchange marks a change of gear in the interview. Establishing rapport is necessarily rather rambling and aimless, but data exchange is purposeful, with the interviewer controlling both the direction and the pace of the exchanges. Candidates will be responsive throughout to the interviewer's control, and the better the rapport the more responsive they will be. Skilled interviewers close off areas of discussion and open fresh ones. They head off irrelevant reminiscences and probe where matters have been glossed over. They never abandon control. Even when the time has come for the candidates to raise all their queries, they will do this at the behest of the interviewer and will constantly look for a renewal of the mandate to enquire by using conversational prefixes such as, 'Can I ask you another question?', 'If it's not taking up your time, perhaps I could ask . . . ?', 'I seem to be asking a lot of questions, but there was just one thing . . .'

6 Closing the interview can be as skilful as opening it. Most of the suggestions so far have been to encourage a response, but it is easy to nod and smile your way into a situation of such cosy relaxation that the respondent talks on and on . . . and on. A surprising number of interviewers have great difficulty closing. These methods can help:

- *Braking* slows the rate of talking by the candidate by working through a series of steps. You will seldom need to go beyond the first two or three, but five are described in case you have to deal with a really tough case. (a) One or two closed questions to clarify specific points may stem the tide. (b) The facial expression changes with the brow furrowed to indicate mild disagreement, lack of understanding or professional anxiety. The reassuring nods stop and the generally encouraging, supportive behaviours of reward are withdrawn. (c) Abstraction is when the eyes glaze over, showing that they belong to a person whose attention has now shifted away from the respondent and towards lunch. (d) To look at one's watch during a conversation is a very strong signal indeed, as it clearly indicates that time is running out. Other, milder ways of looking away are: looking for your glasses, looking at your notes or looking at the aircraft making a noise outside the window. A rather brutal variant is to allow your attention to be caught by something the respondent is wearing, a lapel badge, a tie, a ring or piece of jewellery, maybe. Putting on your glasses to see it more clearly is really going too far! (e) If all else fails, you simply have to interrupt.
- *Closing* requires the interview to end smoothly. Future action is either clarified or confirmed. Also, candidates take a collection of attitudes away with them, and these can be influenced by the way the interview is closed. There is a simple procedure. (a) First signal, verbal plus papers. The interviewer uses a phrase to indicate that the interview is nearing its end ('Well now, I think we have covered the ground, don't you? There isn't anything more I need to ask you. There's nothing further you want from me?'). In this way you signal the impending close at the same time as obtaining the candidate's confirmation. There is additional emphasis provided by some paper play. A small collection of notes can be gathered together and stacked neatly, or a notebook can be closed. (b) Second signal, the interviewer confirms what will happen next ('There are still one or two people to see, but we will write to you no later than the end of the week'). (c) The final signal is to stand up: the decisive act to make the close. By standing up the interviewer forces the candidate to stand as well and there remain only the odds and ends of handshakes and parting smiles.

Practical exercise in selection interviewing

For this exercise you need a cooperative, interested relative, or a very close friend, who would welcome interview practice.

1 Follow the sequence suggested in Table I.1 to give your partner practice in being interviewed for a job, and giving yourself practice in interviewing and note taking.

2 After the interview, discuss your mutual feelings about the process around questions such as:

Selector Did you ever feel you were being misled? When? Why?
Did you feel the interview got out of your control? When? Why?

How could you have avoided the problem?
How was your note taking?
What, if anything, made you bored or cross?
What did you find most difficult?
How comprehensive are the data you have collected?

Candidate Were you put at your ease?
Were you at any time inhibited by the selector?
Did you ever mislead the selector? When? How?
Did the selector ever fail to follow up important points? When? Which?
Were you in any way disconcerted by the note taking?
Has the selector got a comprehensive set of data about you, so that you could feel any decision made about you would be soundly based?
What did you think of the interview experience?

3 Now swap roles.

SUMMARY PROPOSITIONS

I.1 Despite criticisms and shortcomings, the selection interview remains a central feature of the recruitment and selection process.

I.2 Typical interview strategies are frank and friendly, problem solving, biographical and stress.

I.3 Aspects of interview preparation are timetabling, reception and deciding the right setting.

I.4 Features of the interview itself are the opening for preliminary mutual assessment; data gathering, involving a logical sequence, key issues and checkpoints; and the closure, which prepares candidates for the next step in the process.

GENERAL DISCUSSION TOPICS

1 This analysis of the selection interview assumes that the candidate is seeking to become an employee. How would the interview be different if the candidate was being interviewed with a view to becoming a freelance consultant doing work for the organisation rather than being an employee in it?

2 'HR are constantly wanting to "involve me" in their recruitment and selection of staff. I'm too busy to spend time doing that. I want HR to do their job properly and send the people through to me when everything is sorted out and a new recruit is ready to start.' How do you react to that comment from an operations manager in an airline?

FURTHER READING

Anderson, N. and Shackleton, V. (1993) *Successful Selection Interviewing*. Oxford: Blackwell.
Newell, S. and Shackleton, V. (2000) 'Recruitment and Selection', in S. Bach and K. Sisson (eds), *Personnel Management: A comprehensive guide to theory and practice*. Oxford: Blackwell.
Both of these books provide full treatment of the selection interview in all its forms.

Brewster, C. and Tyson, S. (eds) (1991) *International Comparisons in Human Resource Management*. London: Pitman.
Lawler, J.J., Zaidi, M.A. and Atriyanandana, V. (1989) 'Human resources strategies in South East Asia: the case of Thailand', in A. Nedd, G.R. Ferris and K.M. Rowland (eds), *Research in*

Personnel and Human Resources Management, Supplement 1. Greenwich: JAI Press, pp. 201–23.
Tan, K.H. (1995) *Planning, Recruiting and Selecting Human Resources*. Shah Alam, Malaysia: Federal Publications.
Each of these works provides research findings on interview validity.

McDaniel, M.A., Whetzel, D.A., Schmidt, F.L. and Maurer, S.D. (1994) 'The validity of the employment interviews', *Journal of Applied Psychology*, Vol. 79, No. 19, pp. 599–616.
Smith, M. (2002) 'Personnel selection research', *International Journal of Organizational and Occupational Psychology*.
Williamson, L.G. *et al.* (1996) 'Employment interview on trial: linking interview structure with litigation outcomes', *Journal of Applied Psychology*, Vol. 82, No. 6, pp. 900–12.
Selection interviewing varies considerably across different cultures. This skill unit and most of the available literature is rooted in Anglo-American practice. Some insights into practice in other situations can be found in the three works given above.

WEB LINKS

Apart from material on the companion website for this book **www.pearsoned.co.uk/torrington**, plenty of material from consultants can be reached.

www.thedevco.com (the Development Company).

www.bps.org.uk (British Psychological Society).

www.opp.co.uk (Oxford Psychologists Press).

www.shlgroup.com/uk (Saville and Holdsworth, test developer/supplier).

www.psl.net (test developer).

www.intest.com is the website of the International Test Commission which has provided guidelines on computer-based and Internet-delivered testing.

REFERENCE

Babiak, P. (2004) quoted in Butcher, S., 'When the ideal applicant is too good to be true', *Financial Times*, 12 January, p. 12.

II. THE APPRAISAL INTERVIEW

Throughout the first years of the twenty-first century the British government ran various programmes within its civil service departments to manage performance by setting specific targets by which senior civil servants' performance would be judged and rewarded. This is a common enough feature of employment outside the Civil Service, however varied its effectiveness, but novel in government service. In the middle of 2006 a survey by the Prime Minister's Delivery Unit cast doubt on the impact of this policy. The survey assessed four of the largest Departments of State: Education and Science, Constitutional Affairs, Home Office, Work and Pensions. On a four-point scale, with 4 at the top, they all scored 2 for managing performance and even less well for providing value for money. In a foreword to the document the Prime Minister said the departments needed to transform the way they deliver services to meet growing public expectations and that government ministers could not 'micro-manage' services. Most people would probably say, 'Thank God for that!', but it is a common cry in business circles as well, with senior managers confidently inhabiting the sunlit uplands of strategy formulation and therefore being far to busy to 'micro-manage' performance. Although the Prime Minister's claim that ministers could not micro-manage civil servants was welcomed, some people continued to grumble that they had grown a different pattern of micro-managing by setting lots of targets, which were not always mutually compatible and usually linked to some form of individual bonus. Oh dear!

This part of the skills package is unequivocally about a crucial act of micro-management: appraising performance *face to face*. It is linked to Chapter 12, where performance management is thoroughly discussed. We open with an examination of the performance appraisal process, with particular reference to the appraisal interview. We have seen how effective performance may be that of the organisation as a complete entity, that of a managed team within that framework or that of an individual person. We have also seen the place of leadership and motivation in producing a situation where effective performance is likely. Face-to-face appraisal is crucial within the whole complex process of achieving an effective focused performance. It may be undertaken in conversations with our colleagues, our bosses and perhaps our customers or clients, both by assessing how things are going and by providing a basis for future development. We move forward in our understanding of how we are doing and how we are going to be where we need to be. Usually it is an erratic sequence of a word here, an observation there, a complaint, an argument, an explanation of why something failed or was brilliantly successful. As we build up our understanding of who we are, where we want to be, what we want to do and how we can make progress towards whatever our goals may be, we piece together the products of dozens of such inputs. There are occasional landmark conversations, which crystallise our thinking. These are most likely to be appraisal interviews, and they are landmarks because of their relative formality and their official nature and because they are dedicated solely to bringing our personal performance up to an even higher level than it is already.

Our objectives in this skill unit are:

1. To explain the purpose and nature of the appraisal interview
2. To suggest a model sequence for conducting appraisal interviews

The appraisal interview

The novelist, the textbook writer, the popular vocalist, the newspaper editor, the sculptor or painter, the athlete or the owner of a corner shop all have in common the fact that their performance is measurable in an absolute way by numbers. When Beyoncé releases an album, she can see the effectiveness of her performance in the irrefutable logic of the numbers sold. When Usain Bolt runs a race the effectiveness of that performance is measured in the time taken. The measure of both performances can then be compared with that of competitors. There are no mitigating circumstances. The writer may feel that the publisher should have done a better job (not often!) or that the reviewers were incompetent (usually), but that has no weight compared with the inescapable fact of the numbers. The shop owner may grumble about local authority planners or about unfair competition from the local hypermarket, but that explanation will not stop customers from drifting away.

Few working people have that same absolute measure for their own personal performance, which is all part of a more general, corporate endeavour. Individual effectiveness is rarely measurable by a market indicator, as so many other members of the corporate body contribute to the effectiveness or ineffectiveness of any individual's activity. The inexorable logic of the marketplace or other external arena has to be replaced by internal measures, mediated by managerial judgement. This is tricky.

Appraising performance is not a precise measurement but a subjective assessment. It has a long history of being damned for its ineffectiveness at the same time as being anxiously sought by people wanting to know how they are doing. It is difficult to do, it is frequently done badly with quite serious results, but on the rare occasions when it is done well it can be invaluable for the business, and literally life transforming for the appraisee. It is probably the most demanding and skilful activity for any manager to undertake and is dreaded by both appraisers and appraisees. Recent research about appraising the performance of British schoolteachers found that the appraisal itself was often accompanied by long periods of sickness absence due to stress. To a great extent this centred on the difficulty of appropriate criteria, particularly where

> headteachers link capability to personal qualities such as 'open-minded and prepared to adapt and take on new skills' or 'attitude' or where generalised descriptions such as 'unable to do the job properly' or 'not meeting standards' are offered. Measurement is also inevitably imprecise when it is subjective, making the judgement difficult to substantiate and prone to challenge. This leads to the risk that the yardsticks of acceptable performance chosen are those that can best be justified rather than those that are most important. (Torrington *et al.* 2003)

If appraisal is so difficult to get right, why does it survive? Why do we persist with something that was described over 15 years ago as an idea whose time had *gone* (Fletcher 1993)?

The reason is simple: we all seek approval and confirmation that we are doing the right thing, we could all do better, and many of us yearn to advise or direct what other people should do.

There are appraisal schemes in all areas of employment. Once installed, schemes are frequently modified or abandoned, and there is widespread management frustration about their operation. Despite the problems, the potential advantages of appraisal are so great that organisations continue to introduce them and appraisal can produce stunning results. Here is an extract from a CIPD examination answer:

> I have had [an] annual appraisal for three years. Each time it has been a searching discussion of my objectives and my results. Each interview has set me new challenges and opened up fresh opportunities. Appraisal has given me a sense of achievement and purpose that I had never previously experienced in my working life. (from an insurance company)

In Chapter 12 we considered the place of the interview in the overall performance management process with the comment:

> What is appraised varies and might cover personality, behaviour or job performance, with the measures being either quantitative or qualitative. Qualitative appraisal is often an unstructured narrative on the general performance of the appraisee, although some guidance might be given on the areas about which the appraiser should comment. The problem with qualitative appraisals is that they may leave important areas unappraised, and that they are not suitable for comparison purposes.

It is this tendency for qualitative appraisal to be unstructured, avoiding awkwardness and being unsuitable for comparison that we have to try and reduce. There are two difficulties: the first is the potential lack of the *systematic* reporting that is looked for in attempts at management control of, and information about, the process; the second is that qualitative appraisal interviewing is not easy and requires a high level of *mutual trust* between appraiser and appraisee. How many appraisees are appraised by a paragon in whom they can trust?

Frances Storr described an approach to performance appraisal that sought to take out almost all the formality; it included the appraisees choosing their own appraisers and usually the feedback is face to face, with virtually no form filling:

> its purpose is stated clearly: to improve performance and enable people to learn and grow. We emphasise that appraisal is as much about celebrating people's achievements, as it is about helping them to identify areas in which they can improve. Within that framework it is up to individuals to decide how they will carry out their own 360 degree appraisal. In more than 90 per cent of cases, feedback is given face to face, with people talking to their appraisers as a group. Any written material . . . belongs to the appraisee, with the result that the appraisal has become a dialogue rather than a survey.
> (Storr 2000: 39)

ACTIVITY II.1

A managerial approach to appraisal is to *control* performance. Those being appraised are interested in *developing* their performance. Can the benefits of both approaches be achieved in a single scheme?

Who does the appraisal?

Individuals are appraised by a variety of people, including their immediate superior, their superior's superior, a member of the HR department, themselves, their peers or their subordinates. Sometimes, assessment centres are used to carry out the appraisal.

There are, however, many problems for those carrying out the appraisal. For example:

- **Prejudice**: the appraiser may actually be prejudiced against the appraisee, or be anxious not to be prejudiced; either could distort the appraiser's judgement.

- **Insufficient knowledge of the appraisee**: appraisers often carry out appraisals because of their position in the hierarchy rather than because they have a good understanding of what the appraisee is doing.
- **The 'halo effect'**: the general likeability (or the opposite) of an appraisee can influence the assessment of the work that the appraisee is doing.
- **The problem of context**: the difficulty of distinguishing the work of appraisees from the context in which they work, especially when there is an element of comparison with other appraisees.

Problems for both the appraiser and the appraisee include:

- **The paperwork**: documentation soon gets very cumbersome in the attempts made by scheme designers to ensure consistent reporting.
- **The formality**: although appraisers are likely to try to avoid stiff formality, both participants in the interview realise that the encounter is relatively formal, with much hanging on it.

ACTIVITY II.2

Think of jobs where it is difficult to disentangle the performance of the individual from the context of the work. How would you focus on the individual's performance in these situations?

Other common problems, which often cause appraisal schemes to fail, are:

- **Outcomes are ignored**: follow-up action for management to take, although agreed in the interview, does not happen.
- **Everyone is 'just above average'**: most appraisees are looking for reassurance that all is well, and the easiest way for appraisers to deal with this is by stating or inferring that the appraisee is doing at least as well as most others, and better than a good many. It is much harder to deal with the situation of presenting someone with the opinion that they are average; who wants to be average?
- **Appraising the wrong features**: sometimes issues other than real work are evaluated, such as time-keeping, looking busy and being pleasant, because they are easier to see.

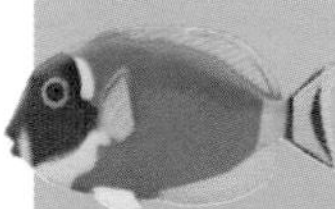

WINDOW ON PRACTICE

The worldwide recession of 2008 onwards was centred on the banking and finance industries, where there was great criticism of the system of bonuses adopted, especially in the entrepreneurial or deal-making areas. Bonuses were criticised first for being disproportionate to the skill and time involved in achieving them and second for being concentrated on short-term gains despite possible long-term problems – like those that triggered the recession.

The appraisal interview style

The different styles of appraisal interview were succinctly described 50 years ago by the American psychologist Norman Maier (1958). His threefold classification remains the most widely adopted means of identifying the way to tackle the interview. The *problem-solving* style can be summarised as an opening in which the appraiser encourages appraisees to review their performance, evaluate it and identify any problems. The appraiser then takes a more active role by sharing in reviewing the problems that the appraisee has first identified and discussing jointly possible solutions. Any evaluation comes as a result of the discussion rather than being a unilateral judgement by the appraiser.

This is certainly the most effective style provided that both the appraiser and appraisee have the skill and ability to handle it, but it is not the only style. Maier's alternatives included, first, *tell and sell*, where the appraiser acts as judge, using the interview to tell the appraisee the result of the appraisal and how to improve. This 'ski instructor' approach can be appropriate with appraisees who have little experience and who lack the self-confidence to analyse their own performance. *Tell and listen*, the second alternative, still casts the appraiser in the role of judge, passing on the outcome of an appraisal that has already been completed and listening to reactions. Both of these approaches could sometimes change the assessment, as well as enabling the two people to have a reasonably frank exchange.

It is tempting to identify the problem-solving approach as 'the best', because it appears to be the most civilised and searching, but not all appraisal situations call for this style, not all appraisees are ready for it and not all appraisers normally behave in this way.

The appraisal interview sequence

Certain aspects of the appraisal interview are the same as those of the selection interview. The appraiser determines the framework of the encounter, there is a need to open in a way that develops mutual confidence as far as possible and there is the use of closed and open-ended questions, reflection and summarising. It is also a difficult meeting for the two parties to handle.

The appraiser has to have a degree of confidence and personal authority that few managers have in their relationship with all those whom they have to appraise. The most contentious aspect of many appraisal schemes is the lack of choice that appraisees have in deciding who the appraiser should be.

For the appraisee there are concerns about career progress, job security, the ongoing working relationship with the appraiser and the basic anxieties relating to self-esteem and dealing with criticism.

The fundamental difference between selection and appraisal that every appraiser has to remember is that the objective is to reach an understanding that will have some impact on the future performance of the appraisee: it is not simply to formulate a judgement by collecting information, as in selection. A medical metaphor may help. A surgeon carrying out hip replacements will select patients for surgery on the basis of enquiring about their symptoms and careful consideration of the evidence. The surgeon asks the questions, makes the decision and implements that decision. A physician examining a patient who is overweight and short of breath may rapidly make the decision that the patient needs to lose weight and take more exercise. It is, however, not the physician but the patient who has to implement that decision. The physician can help with diet sheets, regular check-ups and terrifying advice; the real challenge is how to get the patient to respond.

The easy part of appraisal is sorting out the facts. Actually bringing about a change in performance is the difficult bit. The interview, like the discussion in the physician's consulting rooms, is crucial in bringing about a change of attitude, fresh understanding and commitment to action.

Preparation

The appraiser should brief the appraisee on the form of the interview, possibly asking for a self-appraisal form to be completed in advance. To some extent this is establishing rapport and makes the opening of the eventual interview easier.

Asking for the self-appraisal form to be completed will only be appropriate if the scheme requires this. As we have seen, self-appraisal gives the appraisee some initiative, ensures that the discussion will be about matters which the appraisee can handle and on 'real stuff'.

The appraiser has to collect and review all the available evidence on the appraisee's performance, including reports, records or other material regarding the period under review. Most important will be the previous appraisal and its outcomes.

Most of the points made about preparing for the selection interview apply to appraisal as well, especially the setting. Several research studies (e.g. Anderson and Barnett 1987) have shown the extremely positive response of appraisees who felt that the appraiser had taken time and trouble to ensure that the setting and supportive nature of the discussion was considerate of the appraisee's needs.

Interview structure

A recommended structure for a performance appraisal interview is shown in Table II.1. Alternative frameworks can be found in Anderson (1993: 112–13) and Dainow (1988).

Rapport is unusual because it attempts to smooth the interaction between two people who probably have an easy social relationship, but now find themselves ill at ease. This is not the sort of conversation they are used to having together, so they have to find new ground-rules. The appraisal interview itself may be easier to introduce and handle if, as generally recommended, there are mini-reviews throughout the year. This should ensure that there are no surprises, and the two people concerned get used to having performance-focused meetings, however informal. This type of review happens in some companies, but some appraisers find it difficult. There is still the problem of appraisee reaction to the tentative presentation of things they are not doing properly. A minority will misconstrue comments to focus on the good at the expense of the not so good, while a different minority will do the exact opposite: demoralised collapse at facing a suspended sentence. The majority will react sensibly and most appraisees will have the simple guts to face up to issues that are problematic.

The opening of the interview itself still needs care. The mood needs to be light, but not trivial, as the appraisee has to be encouraged towards candour rather than gamesmanship and the appraiser needs to concentrate on the basis of feedback, which we considered in introducing face-to-face skills.

Table II.1 Structure for a performance appraisal interview

1 Purpose and rapport	Agree purpose with appraisee Agree structure for meeting Check that pre-work is done
2 Factual review	Review of known facts about performance in previous period. Appraiser reinforcement.
3 Appraisee views	Appraisee asked to comment on performance over the last year. What has gone well and what has gone less well; what could be improved; what they liked; what they disliked; possible new objectives.
4 Appraiser views	Appraiser adds own perspective, asks questions and disagrees, as appropriate, with what appraisee has said.
5 Problem solving	Discussion of any differences and how they can be resolved.
6 Objective setting	Agreeing what action should be taken, and by whom.

ACTIVITY II.3

What do you think of the following openings to appraisal interviews heard recently?

(a) 'Well, here we are again. I'm sure you don't like this business any more than I do, so let's get on with it.'

(b) 'Now, there's nothing to worry about. It's quite painless and could be useful. So just relax and let me put a few questions to you.'

(c) 'I will be straight with you if you will be straight with me. All right?'

(d) 'Right. Let battle commence!'

Factual review is reviewing aspects of the previous year's work that are unproblematic. The appraiser begins by reviewing the main facts about the performance, without expressing opinions about them but merely summarising them as a mutual reminder, perhaps reviewing previous objectives set and including the outcome of the previous appraisal. This will help to key in any later discussion by confirming such matters as how long the appraisee has been in the job, any personnel changes in the period, turnover figures, training undertaken, and so forth.

The appraiser will still be doing most, but not all, of the talking, and can isolate those aspects of performance that have been disclosed which are clearly satisfactory, mention them and comment favourably. This will develop rapport and provide the basic reassurance that the appraisee needs in order to avoid being defensive. The favourable aspects of performance will to some extent be *discovered* by the factual review process. It is important that 'the facts speak for themselves' rather than appraiser judgement being offered. Not, for instance:

> Well, I think you are getting on very well. I'm very pleased with how things are going generally.

That sort of comment made at this stage would have the appraisee waiting for 'but . . .' as the defences have not yet been dismantled. A different approach might be:

> Those figures look very good. How do they compare with . . . ? That's X per cent up on the quarter and Y per cent on the year . . . That's one of the best results in the group. You must be pleased with that . . . How on earth did you do it?

This has the advantage of the evidence, including that collected throughout the year as we suggested earlier, being there before the eyes of both parties, with the appraiser pointing out and emphasising. It is also specific rather than general, precise rather than vague. This type of approach invariably raises the question from appraisers about what to do in a situation of poor performance. Appraising stars is easy; what about the duds? The answer is that all appraisees have some aspects of their performance on which favourable comment can be made, and the appraisal process actually identifies strengths that might have been previously obscured by the general impression of someone who is not very good – the opposite of the halo effect. The appraiser may discover something on which to build, having previously thought the case was hopeless. If there is not some feature of the performance that can be isolated in this way, then the appraiser probably has a management or disciplinary problem that should have been tackled earlier. If the system is one in which appraisees complete a self-report beforehand, then much of the factual review could be centred on this.

The appraiser then asks for the *appraisee's views* on things that are not as good as they might be in the performance, areas of possible improvement and how these might be addressed. These will only be offered by the appraisee if there has been effective positive reinforcement in the previous stages of the interview. People can only acknowledge shortcomings about performance when they are reasonably sure of their ground. Now the appraisee is examining areas of dissatisfaction by the process of discussing them with the appraiser, with whom it is worth having the discussion, because of the appraiser's expertise, information and 'helicopter view'. There are three likely results of debating these matters:

- some will be talked out as baseless;
- some will be shown to be less worrying than they seemed when viewed only from the single perspective of the appraisee, and ways of dealing with them become apparent;
- some will be confirmed as matters needing attention.

This stage in the interview is fraught with difficulties for the manager, and is one of the reasons why an alternative style is sometimes preferred. Some people prefer to be told on the basis that the appraiser is the one whose judgement matters and they do not like having to make the running, perhaps exposing themselves to criticism before they have been able to work out what the appraiser's position is.

This is particularly likely in the high power distance cultures that are discussed in Chapter 6. Many countries do not aspire to the particular type of social sophistication which Western nations regard as the height of cool.

These, however, are problems to be recognised and overcome: they are not reasons for not bothering to try.

Appraiser views can now be used in adding to the list of areas for improvement. In many instances there will be no additions to make, but usually there are improvement needs that the appraisee cannot, or will not, see. If they are put at this point in the interview, there is the best chance that they will be understood, accepted and acted upon. It is not possible to guarantee success. Demoralised collapse or bitter resentment is always a possibility, but this is the time to try, as the appraisee has developed a basis of reassurance and has come to terms with some shortcomings that he or she had not already recognised.

The appraiser has to judge whether any further issues can be raised and if so, how many. None of us can cope with confronting all our shortcomings, all at the same time, and the appraiser's underlying management responsibility is to ensure that the appraisee is not made less competent by the appraisal interview. There is also a fundamental moral responsibility not to use a position of organisational power to damage the self-esteem and adjustment of another human being.

Problem solving is the process of talking out the areas for improvement that have been identified, so that the appraisee can cope with them. Underlying causes are uncovered through further discussion. Gradually huge problems come into clearer and less forbidding perspective, perhaps through being analysed and broken up into different components. Possibilities for action, by both appraiser and appraisee, become clear.

These central stages of the interview, factual exchange, appraisee views, appraiser views and problem solving, need to move in that sequence. Some may be brief, but none should be omitted and the sequence should not alter.

The final stage of the encounter is to agree what is to be done: *objective setting*. Actions need to be agreed and nailed down, so that they actually take place. One of the biggest causes of appraisal failure is with action not being taken, so the objectives set must be not only mutually acceptable, but also deliverable. It is likely that some action will be needed from the appraiser as well as some from the appraisee.

Making appraisal interviewing work

Appraisers need training in how to appraise and how to conduct appraisal interviews. Appraisees will also need some training if they have any significant involvement in the process. An excellent performance appraisal system is of no use at all if managers do not know how to use the system to best effect.

In all appraisal situations where the style is problem solving or tell and listen, rather than tell and sell, the interview must be given appropriate salience in the whole process: it must fit and other features must fit with it. If the outcome of the overall appraisal is pre-determined then tell and sell is better. This can often be the emphasis where appraisal is directly linked to pay rather than to development or improvement.

SUMMARY PROPOSITIONS

II.1 Performance appraisal has a poor track record, but it has considerable potential, when done well.

II.2 Among the problems of appraisal are prejudice, insufficient knowledge by the appraiser of the appraisee, the halo effect, the problem of context, the paperwork, the ignoring of outcomes, appraising the wrong features and the tendency for everyone to be appraised as just above average.

II.3 Three approaches to the appraisal interview are problem solving, tell and sell and tell and listen.

II.4 Features of the interview itself are the opening for preliminary mutual assessment; factual review; appraisee views on performance; appraiser views, to add perspective; problem solving; and objective setting.

II.5 Appraisers must follow up on interviews, making sure that all agreed action (especially that by the management) takes place.

II.6 Training in appraisal is essential for appraisers and for appraisees.

GENERAL DISCUSSION TOPICS

1 'What right does he have to ask me questions about my motivation and objectives? I come here to do a job of work and then go home. What I want to do with my life is my business.' How would you react to that comment by someone who had just emerged from an appraisal interview?

2 In what situations have you seen outstanding individuals depress the performance of a team where the other people were demoralised by the dominance of that individual? How do you cope with this?

FURTHER READING

Fletcher, C. (1999) *Appraisal: routes to improved performance*. London: CIPD.

Lowry, D. (2002) 'Performance management', in J. Leopold (ed.), *Human Resources in Organisations*. London: Prentice Hall.

The appraisal interview has not been the subject of much research in recent years, but the above reviews provide practical suggestions.

Redman, T. and McElwee, G. (1993) 'Upward appraisal of lecturers: lessons from industry', *Education and Training*, Vol. 35, No. 2, pp. 20–5.

Redman, T., Snape, E., Thompson, D. and Kaching Yan, F. (2000) 'Performance appraisal in the National Health Service', *Human Resource Management Journal*, Vol. 10, No. 1, pp. 1–16.

Torrington, D.P., Earnshaw, J.M., Marchington, L. and Ritchie, M.D. (2003) *Tackling Underperformance in Teachers*. London: Routledge Falmer.

Recent studies of appraisal in specific professional contexts include the above, Redman and McElwee (1993) on further education and Redman *et al.* (2000) on the National Health Service.

WEB LINKS

The book's companion website **www.pearsoned.co.uk/torrington** contains practical exercises in appraisal interviewing. General information about aspects of performance can be found at:

www.hrmguide.co.uk/hrm/chap10

www.som.cranfield.ac.uk (the Performance Management Association)

Trade unions, some employers and most public bodies provide information about the performance management arrangement on their websites. An example of general interest is at:

www.governyourschool.co.uk

Consultancy firms provide information about their particular approach. A selection of interesting sites (without any assessment of the value of their products) is:

www.hrwigwam.co.uk

www.targetimprovement.co.uk

www.openview.hp.com/solutions

www.hse.gov.uk (the Health and Safety Executive)

www.statistics.gov.uk (the Office for National Statistics site)

www.cbi.org.uk (the Confederation of British Industry)

www.leadersdirect.com (an American site of the Self Renewal Group)

www.apse.org.uk (Association for Public Service Excellence)

www.performance-appraisals.org (an American business site)

www.employment-studies.co.uk (the Institute of Employment Studies site)

www.acas.org.uk (Advisory, Conciliation and Arbitration Service)

REFERENCES

Anderson, G.C. (1993) *Managing Performance Appraisal Systems*. Oxford: Blackwell.

Anderson, G.C. and Barnett, J.G. (1987) 'The characteristics of effective appraisal interviews', *Personnel Review*, Vol. 16, No. 4, pp. 18–25.

Dainow, S. (1988) 'Goal-oriented appraisal', *Training Officer*, January, pp. 6–8.

Fletcher, C. (1993) 'Appraisal: an idea whose time has gone?', *Personnel Management*, Vol. 25, No. 9, pp. 34–8.

Goodge, P. and Watts, P. (2000) 'How to Manage 360 degree feedback', *People Management*, February, pp. 50–2.

Maier, N.R.F. (1958) *The Appraisal Interview: Objectives, methods and skills*. New York: John Wiley.

Storr, F. (2000) 'This is not a circular', *People Management*, May, pp. 38–40.

Torrington, D.P., Earnshaw, J.M., Marchington, L. and Ritchie, M.D. (2003) *Tackling Underperformance in Teachers*. London: Routledge Falmer.

III. COACHING

Although this section is about coaching, we need to remember the frequent close connection with mentoring, which has been explained in Chapter 18.

Coaching is not teaching people how to do things, but helping them to do even better things that they have already learned. Janice Caplan has described it this way:

> Coaching is about enhancing and developing the performance of an individual . . . Coaching . . . is a way of learning that is highly personal, flexible and individualized. (Caplan 2003: ix)

Coaching is as important for the competent, proficient or expert as it is for the advanced beginner, and it is important for novices, even though they are still acquiring the basics. The more expert a person becomes, the more important a coach becomes to hone performance, to take a broad view of the context in which the learner's career is developing and how it may proceed. Although coaching is a skill, it is not simply an encounter that has to be managed, like most of the skills described in this skills package, it is a skill in managing a relationship.

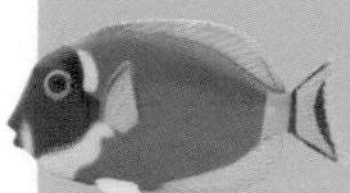

WINDOW ON PRACTICE

In 2005 the British sporting public was hungry for success in tennis. Wimbledon annually stages the world's greatest tennis tournament and winning is the greatest achievement in a player's career, yet it was over 70 years since a British man had won the title. A young Scot, Andy Murray, suddenly emerged as the great hope of British tennis. He was young, skilled and with a great competitive temperament, who had been coached by his mother, but he needed a different coach to take him forward to international success. He needed someone with international experience as well as personal authority, who could take the already-acquired skill of this fiery young man and develop it, and him, to greater international achievement. Brad Gilbert was an experienced coach. He took on the coaching of Andy Murray, whose accomplishments soon began to increase. Brad Gilbert was not personally as good a player as Andy Murray, but had a breadth of international experience and expertise that provided exactly the right complement to Andy's youth, talent and temperament *at that time*. The two would soon part as Andy Murray would seek other mentors and assistance to achieve his ambition, but Brad Gilbert had built on what Mrs Murray had earlier achieved before others took over.

Coaching is a part of the job of every manager, but it is an approach being used increasingly in business circles to bring on the effectiveness of people at all levels. As long ago as 1994 Clutterbuck and Wynne (1994: 156) made a comment combining mentoring and coaching:

> They represent an increasing trend towards helping the individual take charge of his or her own learning: the primary driver . . . becomes the employee; the coach or mentor is available to give guidance, insight and encouragement.

Currently there is great enthusiasm for coaching to be seen as a central feature of the managerial role so that every manager is expected to act as a coach to those for whom the manager has direct line responsibility. Coaching takes the place of supervision and instruction to the extent that the manager concentrates on developing the skills and capacities of the individual members of his or her team, enabling them to perform rather than directing their performance. This is a nice distinction that takes account of changes in the types of jobs that people have and the moves towards flexible rather than hierarchical organisation structures. The reality is rarely so clear cut, as managers have to combine coaching with direction. Not all managers like the coaching role. As was pointed out in Chapter 18, Carroll and Gillen (2001) identified various barriers to line manager acceptance of a teaching or coaching role, including lack of interpersonal competence, lack of time, performance pressures, a feeling that the teaching role was not valued and should be done by the HR department. The article also provides material on what makes an effective coach.

Other members of the business may be involved in coaching on particular aspects of the learner's work. Janice Caplan identifies a coaching style of management as having three elements: role model, interim and directive

> to enable, encourage and facilitate so that staff have a stronger sense of control over their own work and their own time, and so that they identify their own options and solutions to problems . . . The manager also needs to act as a role model of the desired . . . behaviours. Nonetheless, there may be times when the manager will still need to be more directive. (Caplan 2003: 20)

Before considering the appropriate qualities of a coach, we note the important concept of the career anchor, identified by Edgar H. Schein, one of the founding fathers of organisational psychology during his 30 years as Sloan Fellows Professor of Management at Massachusetts Institute of Technology. The Career Anchor is something that is so important to a person's self-confidence that it will be abandoned only reluctantly, and then only if it can be replaced by something else equally rewarding. Schein described career anchors as much broader than motivation, and as including the following:

- self-perceived talents and abilities;
- self-perceived motives and needs;
- self-perceived attitudes and values.

Our perception of ourselves in these areas comes from direct experiences of work, from successes, from self-diagnosis and from feedback. The conclusions that we draw both drive and constrain future career development. Career anchors can identify a source of personal stability in the person which has determined past choices and will probably determine future choices.

The problematic aspect of career anchors is the accuracy of the individual's self-perceptions, and the question of what happens in mid-career to those who feel their attitudes and values are changing. Schein acknowledges that career anchors are learned rather than reflecting latent abilities and are the sorts of things that people are reluctant to abandon. Not only do we all need to identify and understand what our anchors are in order to make sure we are doing the right thing, we also need to appreciate that there are things that we shall continue to need even if we make a career change.

Among the anchors most widely found are technical/functional competence, managerial competence and security. Those who are confident of their technical competence in their job and enjoy those aspects of their duties will move to a job with a lower technical component very reluctantly. For those anchored to managerial competence the exercising of managerial responsibility is an end in itself, and technical/functional jobs just a way of getting there. They are likely to possess three key competences: analytical competence to solve problems characterised by incomplete information in areas of uncertainty; interpersonal competence to influence and control; and emotional resilience, with the ability to be stimulated rather than paralysed by crises. They will readily move away from technical specialisation if they can maintain, or enhance their managerial role. Security and stability is an anchor for those who seek this above all else.

All coaches need to identify these anchors for individuals they are coaching. If a coach can spot the anchors correctly, he or she has a very good chance of establishing trust, especially if the person being coached has never really worked out what his or her anchors are, nor heard of the concept. If a coach guesses the anchors wrongly, or has strong views on what they should be, then coaching becomes very difficult (Schein 1990, 2004).

Anchors can move, and certainly change over time. The person who is technically anchored at 30 may be managerially anchored at 40 and security/stability anchored at 50, but that is a stereotypical assumption only. Coaches have to work out the anchors for each individual at the time when the coaching conversation takes place, not yesterday or last year.

The qualities of the coach

Coaching is usually a one-to-one activity, for which the coach needs various qualities.

1 **Trust.** As the coach will often need to deal with what are usually very private aspects of someone's life, it is first necessary that the learner has absolute trust in the coach's integrity and commitment to the coaching. The interpersonal chemistry has to be completely correct between the two of them. They will probably argue, may have flaming rows and not speak to each other for days. Learners will, for instance, usually be highly skilled performers with a shrewd knowledge of their job and a fair understanding of what they can and cannot do. A coach may need to challenge some part of that self-confidence, which the learner will then be anxious about, because that seems to be removing one of the things that the learner has previously relied on – a career anchor – and there will be a disagreement. It will not be easy for a learner to abandon something that has previously been an anchor, but it will probably not happen unless there is a grounded belief in the coach's trustworthiness.

2 **Respect.** Closely allied to trust and the next requirement of expertise is *mutual* respect. The learner needs to feel that the coach is worthy of respect because he or she is trustworthy, is expert in the job of the learner, is proficient at the job of coaching, has a great deal of broader experience, is good at explaining things and explaining the right things. These 'things' have to be strong enough to overwhelm other possible thoughts about the coach, such as 'has-been', 'past-it', 'couldn't hack it at the sharp end', 'the job is not like it was in his day'. Coaches are nearly always older than learners, so there may be a temptation for ambitious learners to have such thoughts. Equally the coach must have respect for the learner: no condescension or patronising behaviour, but a real respect for the learner's skill, accomplishments and ambitions.

3 **Job expertise.** The coach needs to *know how* to do the learner's job at least as well as the learner; this is not the same as *being able* to do the job as well as the learner. The person training the novice usually has to be expert at actually doing the job of the learner; the coach enhancing the skill of someone who is proficient does not need that particular level of ability, as long as there is the understanding. It is often

important that the coach is *not* as practically skilled; otherwise coaching may become 'watch me; do this' instead of 'listen to what I say and then work out how to do better'.

4 **Listening.** Coaches have to be very sensitive and conscientious listeners. The coaching relationship has many similarities with performance appraisal, in that the coach can only work to improve what the learner is able to acknowledge and understand. There will be a lot of explanation and even simple instruction, but the starting point will usually be in the learner's head. The learner will ask questions, express frustrations or describe a problem that the coach may believe to be the wrong problem. All the time the coach listens with close attention and works on understanding the questions, what lies behind the frustrations and why the wrong problem has been identified – and what makes the coach so sure it is the wrong problem anyway?

Schoolteachers sometimes say that gifted teachers are able to develop children's understanding almost entirely by getting them to ask the right questions. Coaches who can do this with adults are on the way to being outstanding, although the method has to be rather more subtle and not manipulative. We have already identified some of the basic skills required in this type of listening, especially reflection and reflecting and summarising.

5 **Evaluating.** The coach listens to the learner, listens to what other people say and can probably study aspects of the learner's performance, so that there is a collection of information to process. The coach needs to be able to evaluate all of these data dispassionately but effectively, having the advantage of a degree of objectivity which the learner cannot hope to have, and assembling it in a way that will make a constructive contribution to the coaching process.

6 **Challenging.** However true it may be that talking a problem through should enable a learner to solve whatever the career block may be, it is also true that few of us can do this with everything. We always tend to construe a situation in a way that puts us in the right. There will be times when the coach simply has to confront the learner with a different interpretation of what is going on and challenge the learner to accept the validity of criticism. Some coaches who are not the direct line manager say that it is not their role to do that, and that challenging should be left to the manager, but that is just shirking the responsibility. A coach cannot just do the nice, agreeing things with lots of understanding smiles and sympathetic nods of support. The coach is in a privileged position, being trusted by the learner to provide help, including guidance on what is wrong, however reluctant they may be to hear it.

7 **Practical help.** A part of the coaching relationship will be for the coach to provide straightforward practical suggestions: 'Have you thought of . . . ?', 'Have you spoken to . . . ?', 'Would it help if I went through it with you . . . ?', 'No, that simply won't work'.

It might well be thought that all of these great qualities are to be found in any competent manager, so that the learner automatically has the line manager as coach. However, not all managers have all these qualities particularly well developed, and there are advantages in the coach being outside the line. The act of talking with a 'supportive outsider' can be a help to managers in unravelling and evaluating the mixed messages they are hearing in the workplace, where custom and practice are lagging behind policy, which – in turn – appears to be out of line with organisational culture. However, a line manager may well be suspicious of supportive outsiders who appear to be giving messages that contradict what the manager is saying. After all, coaching is not quite the same as counselling, where an outsider has a better justification.

The solution to this dilemma seems to be to acknowledge that all managers need to adopt a coaching mode of working with individual members of their department, but that other supportive *insiders* could be called upon to act as individual mentors, where there is a good working relationship or prior familiarity between prospective coach and prospective learner. Clutterbuck and Gover (2004) suggest there are seven stages in the coaching process:

1 Identify the need
2 Gather evidence
3 Motivate and set targets
4 Plan how to achieve
5 Create opportunities to practise
6 Observe and give feedback
7 Support through the setbacks

A further twist is that there are two different ways of focusing on coaching: pre-coaching and post-coaching. Pre-coaching is the main emphasis as you are preparing someone for the event they are about to handle – so lines of questioning may be, 'What difficulties do you anticipate?', 'How will you handle that?' 'What will you do if . . . ?'. All of these look forward. Post-coaching is equally valuable, but has a different nature after the event has happened. There is less intense focus, less adrenaline; much more reflective and analytical. It could include questions like 'How did it go?' 'What happened that you didn't expect?', 'What can you learn from this experience?', and so on. The first focus is on motivation: the second is on learning and embedding the lessons learned.

SUMMARY PROPOSITIONS

III.1 Coaching is a way in which one person (the coach) enhances the working performance of another (the protégé) regardless of the level of job skill that the two have and regardless of the hierarchical relationship between them.

III.2 The career anchor is something that it is absolutely essential for the protégé to maintain if he or she is to be able to retain self-confidence and the ability to develop. These vary greatly between individuals and a coach has to understand what anchors each protégé.

III.3 Essential qualities in a coaching relationship are for there to be mutual trust and respect between the parties.

III.4 Required qualities of a coach are: expertise in the job of the protégé, skilled listening, skill in evaluating information, an ability to challenge and a willingness to provide practical help.

III.5 Coaching takes place that is pre-, looking forward and motivating, or post-, looking back to embed lessons learned.

GENERAL DISCUSSION TOPICS

1 How would you rank (from 1 to 3) the relative importance of the coach being (a) expert in the protégé's job, (b) older than the protégé and (c) the direct line manager.

2 What are the career anchors held by members of your group? What anchors have changed?

FURTHER READING

Schein, E.H. (1990) *Career Anchors*. San Diego: University Associates.
Schein, E.H. (2004) *Organizational Culture and Leadership*, 3rd edn. New York: John Wiley.
The 1990 book by Ed Schein is now not easy to obtain, although it contains the most thorough explanation of the career anchor concept. The 2004 third edition of his classic text contains a perfectly adequate treatment of the topic.

Hawkins, P. and Schwenk, G. (2006) *Coaching Supervision: Maximising the potential of coaching, a change agenda*. London: CIPD.
Jarvis, J. and Lane, D. (2006) *The Case for Coaching: Making evidence-based decisions on coaching*. London: CIPD.
Both these publications include solid research evidence to produce a thorough assessment of current practice, including examples of good practice and guidelines for managers.

WEB LINKS

On this book's website **www.pearsoned.co.uk/torrington** there is supplementary material on handling group discussion as a form of learning. This is the usual method for social skills training and attitude development.

Another useful website is: **www.emccouncil.org** (the site for the European Coaching and Mentoring Council who have recently launched a kitemarking scheme for coaching and mentoring qualifications).

REFERENCES

Caplan, J. (2003) *Coaching for the Future*. London: CIPD.

Carroll, S. and Gillen, D. (2001) 'Exploring the teaching function of the managerial role', *Journal of Management Development*, Vol. 21, No. 5, pp. 330–42.

Clutterbuck, D. and Wynne, B. (1994) 'Mentoring and coaching', in Mumford, A. (ed.), *Handbook of Management Development*, 4th edn. Epping: Gower Press.

Clutterbuck, D. and Gover, S. (2004) *The Effective Coach Manual*. Burnham: Clutterbuck Associates.

Schein, E.H. (1990) *Career Anchors*. San Diego: University Associates.

Schein, E.H. (2004) *Organizational Culture and Leadership*, 3rd edn. New York: John Wiley.

IV. PRESENTATION

The skill of presentation is required to inform and explain. HR people constantly have to make presentations on such matters as explaining a change of policy, clarifying details of a new trade union agreement or setting out the implications of a change of employment legislation. There may be presentations on career prospects in the business at careers conventions, pitching to a senior management group for an improvement in the budget, 'selling' the advantages of a new performance-related pay scheme, or explaining to a small group of job applicants the details of the post for which they have applied.

Objectives

As with almost every aspect of management, the starting point is the objective. What are you aiming to achieve? What do you want the listeners to do, to think or to feel? Note that the question is not 'What do you want to say?' The objective is in the response of the listeners. That starting point begins the whole process with a focus on results and payoff, turning attention away from ego. It also determines tone. If your objective is to inform, you will emphasise facts. If you aim to persuade, you will try to appeal to emotion as well as to reason.

The material

What is to be said or, more accurately, what should members of the audience go away having understood and remembered?

> Organise your material with an introduction that previews, a body that develops, and a conclusion that reviews. When you organize the body of your presentation, start by sorting out the theme. The theme is a planning device that holds together the various ideas you want to discuss. If the theme of your presentation is informative, then the body should provide facts. If the theme is persuasive, the body should develop persuasive arguments. (Fandt 1994: 159)

In the introduction the speaker establishes rapport with the audience. Apart from gaining their attention, the speaker will include here an answer to the unspoken questions: Is it going to be worth our while listening? Is this person worth listening to? The person who is worth listening to is someone who looks at the audience and looks friendly, knowledgeable and, above all, enthusiastic. A useful format for the introduction is to explain what the members of the audience will know or be able to do at the end. It is also helpful to sketch out the framework of what is to come, so that people can follow it more readily. But stick to what you promise. If you say there are going to be five points, the audience will listen for five to make sure that they have not missed one.

Having secured the attention of the listeners, you now have them waiting not just for what you say next, but with a framework in their heads of what they will hear, so they will be able to locate their understanding within that framework. The main body of the presentation is the message that is to be conveyed, the development of the argument and the build-up of what it is that the audience should go away having understood and remembered.

The main body needs to be effectively organised. This will not only help members of the audience to maintain attention, but also discipline the speaker to avoid rambling, distracting irrelevance or forgetting. The most common methods are:

- *Chronological sequence*, dealing with issues by taking the audience through a series of events. A presentation to an employment tribunal often follows this pattern.
- *Known to unknown, or simple to complex*. The speaker starts with a brief review of what the audience already know or can easily understand and then develops to what they do not yet know or cannot yet understand. The logic of this method is to ground the audience in something they can handle so that they can make sense of the unfamiliar. This is the standard method of organising teaching sessions.

- ***Problem to solution*** is almost the exact opposite of simple to complex. A problem is presented and a solution follows. The understanding of the audience is again grounded, but this time grounded in an anxiety that the speaker is about to relieve.
- ***Comparison*** is a method of organisation which compares one account with another. Selling usually follows this path, as the new is compared with the old.

Whatever the method of organisation for the material, the main body will always contain a number of key thoughts or ideas. This is what the speaker is trying to plant in the minds of the audience: not just facts, which are inert, but the ideas which facts may well illustrate and clarify. The idea that inflation is dangerously high is only illustrated by the fact that it is at a particular figure in a particular month.

The ideas in a presentation can be helpfully linked together by a device that will help audience members to remember them and to grasp their interdependence. One method is to enshrine the ideas in a story. If the story is recalled, the thoughts are recalled with it, as they are integral to the structure. Another method is to use key words to identify the points that are being made, especially if they have an alliterative or mnemonic feature, such as 'People Produce Prosperity'. In a lecture it is common to provide a framework for ideas by using a drawing or system model to show the interconnection of points.

Facts, by giving impact, keep together the framework of ideas that the speaker has assembled. They clarify and give dimension to what is being said. The danger is to use too many, so that the audience are overwhelmed by facts and figures which begin to bemuse them. If the presentation is to be accompanied by a hand-out, facts may be usefully contained in that, so that they can be referred to later, without the audience having to remember them.

Humour is the most dangerous of all aids to the speaker. If the audience laugh at a funny story, the speaker will be encouraged and may feel under less tension, but how tempting to try again and end up 'playing for laughs'. Laughter is a most seductive human reaction, but too many laughs are even more dangerous than too many facts. What will the audience remember, the joke, or what the joke was intended to illustrate? Attempted humour is also dangerous for the ineffective comedian. If you tell what you think is a funny story and no one laughs, you have made a fool of yourself (at least in your own eyes) and risk floundering.

Very few people speak effectively without notes. Although there is a tendency to marvel at those who can, relying solely on memory risks missing something out, getting a fact wrong or drying up completely. Notes follow the pattern of organisation you have established, providing discipline and limiting the tendency to ramble. It is both irritating and unhelpful for members of an audience to cope with a speaker who wanders off down a blind alley. When an amusing anecdote pops up in your brain, it can be almost irresistible to share it.

There are two basic kinds of notes: headlines or a script. Headlines are probably the most common, with main points underlined and facts listed beneath. Sometimes there will also be a marginal note about an anecdote or other type of illustration. The alternative, the script, enables the speaker to try out the exact wording, phrases and pauses to achieve the greatest effect. The script will benefit from some marking or arrangement that will help you to find your place again as your eyes constantly flick from the page to the audience and back again. This can be underlining or using a highlighter. When using a script it is important not to make the reading too obvious. Head down, with no eye contact and little light and shade is a sure-fire way of turning off the attention of the audience. Public figures increasingly use electronic prompters which project the script progressively through the presentation on to a glass screen some way in front of the speaker. By this means the script can be spoken with little break in eye contact with the audience. This will be too ambitious for most HR people, but the important thing is that the words should be *spoken* rather than *read*.

There are many variations of these basic methods of organising the material, so that one approach is to use varying line length, while another is to use rows of dots to indicate pause or emphasis. Some people like to have their notes on small cards, so that they are unobtrusive, but this is difficult if the notes are more than headlines. Standard A4 paper should present no problem, if the notes are not stapled, are well laid out and can be handled discreetly. Never forget to number the pages or cards, as the next time you speak they may slip off your lap moments before you are due to begin, and they do not land on the floor in the same order that they were on your lap.

Most presentations benefit from using visual aids. You may use a model, a sample or even a person ('Here is our trainee of the month'), but mostly you will use visual images. Blackboards still exist and white boards are fairly common. Flip charts and overhead projector acetates are widely used. The most rapidly growing type of visual image in presentation is that from a computer, projected on a screen, usually using a PowerPoint package. PowerPoint is so good that it can be dangerous. One problem is its relative sophistication technically. It has to be operated by someone who knows what he or she is doing and has confidence in being able to manage the computer rather than being managed by it. Every reader will have had experience of a presenter being baffled by a technical glitch that held up the presentation and knocked the presenter's confidence sideways. If the computer is being managed by someone other than the presenter, there is the potential difficulty of presenter and operator not always being coordinated.

WINDOW ON PRACTICE

In 2006 a newly appointed vice chancellor of a British university was giving his first major address to a large audience, using a PowerPoint presentation which he controlled with a remote, although technical staff at the side of the hall had overall control. At one point he went back to a previous page, then went forward to the wrong page without realising it. Technical staff corrected the mistake at the same time as he noticed it. He then corrected it without realising they had spotted it. Confusion and uncertainty persisted for several minutes. At the subsequent lunch the muddle was discussed more extensively than the content of the address.

The rationale for visual aids is that we remember what we see for longer than we remember what we are told, and we can sometimes understand what we see better than we can understand what we hear. Too much displayed material can obscure rather than illuminate what is being said. Television news provides a good example of how much can be used. The dominant theme is always the talking head with frequently intercut pieces of film. Very seldom do words appear on the screen and then usually as extracts from a speech or report, where a short sentence or passage is regarded as being especially meaningful. The other situation in which words and numbers appear is when facts are needed to illustrate an idea, so that ideas such as football scores or a change in the value of the US dollar almost always have the figures shown on the screen to clarify and illustrate. Seldom, however, will more than two or three numbers be displayed at the same time. Speakers need to remember the size of what they are displaying as well as its complexity. Material has to be big enough for people to read and simple enough for them to follow. Material also has to be timed to coincide with what is being said.

PowerPoint is a most seductive toy for the presenter. The box of tricks is enormous and too many people give a show, with clever figures dancing across the screen as well as other distractions. We must always remember what the purpose of the presentation is; clever or spectacular forms of display can become what people remember rather than the message that is to be conveyed. Television news is again an illustration. Between programmes there may be all manner of clever visual entertainment in brief clips. Once the news report begins there are no such fancy tricks.

SUMMARY PROPOSITIONS

IV.1 Presentation is the main method used to convey information and understanding to a group of listeners.

IV.2 Alternative methods of constructing a presentation are (a) chronological sequence, (b) known to unknown or simple to complex, (c) problem to solution, (d) comparison.

IV.3 A presentation is spoken, not read. Visual aids illustrate but do not distract.

GENERAL DISCUSSION TOPICS

1. There is an old saying, 'What I hear I forget, what I see I can understand and what I do I know.' What is the relevance of this to presentation?

2. Why do students attend lectures where information is presented to them, rather than reading that information presented in a book?

FURTHER READING

Fandt, P.M. (1994) *Management Skills: Practice and experience*. St Paul: West Publishing.

Quinn, R.E. (1988) *Beyond Rational Management: Mastering the paradoxes and competing demands of high performance*. San Francisco: Jossey-Bass.

Quinn, R.E., Faerman, S.R., Thompson, M.P. and McGrath, M.R. (2002) *Becoming a Master Manager*. New York: John Wiley.

Material on management skills is everywhere, but in this context the above works are especially helpful.

Yate, M. and Sander, P. (2003) *The Ultimate Business Presentations Book*. London: Kogan Page.

Presentation is also preached very widely. This excellent recent import from the United States covers the ground very thoroughly and readably.

WEB LINKS

On the book's companion website, **www.pearsoned.co.uk/torrington**, there is supplementary material on handling group discussion as a form of learning. This is the usual method for social skills training and attitude development. There is also material on job instruction.

Other useful websites are:

www.lsc.gov.uk (Learning and Skills Council).

www.mmu.ac.uk/academic/studserv/learningsupport/studyskills/presentations (Manchester Metropolitan University).

www.spokenwordltd.com/coaching (Spoken Word Ltd, providing teaching and coaching in spoken word skills).

REFERENCE

Fandt, P.M. (1994) *Management Skills: Practice and experience.* St Paul: West Publishing.

V. MEDIATION

Mediation is resolving a disagreement, a misunderstanding or the breakdown of a relationship between two parties with the assistance of a third: the third party being cast in the role of honest broker. In some instances it is a straight alternative to negotiation in industrial relations. The parties are sufficiently estranged that they will not be able to resolve their difficulties on their own, so a mediator is asked to chair joint meetings, partly to clarify the differences and partly to suggest ways forward. This is slightly different from arbitration, which is where the arbitrator proposes a solution rather than a way for the parties to move forward to find their own.

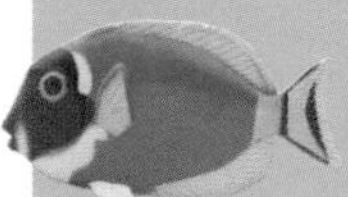

WINDOW ON PRACTICE

In the late summer of 2009 there was a series of short strikes in British Royal Mail which seriously disrupted postal services. This was the culmination of a long-running dispute between management and unions about modernisation. Matters had reached a stalemate. Negotiations had made no progress, one party wanted to try arbitration but the other didn't and neither party was willing to concede to the other. Eventually 'a way forward' was reached after mediation by Brendan Barber, General Secretary of the Trade Union Congress. A final settlement was reached several months later.

A type of situation which is similar in process, but different in nature, is disagreement and relationship breakdown between individuals, most dramatically seen in divorce but also to be found in employment situations. If colleagues need to work closely together but have a row or begin to suspect the others' motives, then mediation may be helpful.

WINDOW ON PRACTICE

Since the head designer had left suddenly, Barry had been asked to stand in pending a permanent appointment being made. Interviews were held among internal applicants, including Barry, who was surprised and bitterly disappointed when Julia was appointed head designer. As Barry put it to the HR Manager, '. . . a relative newcomer of 28 with less experience and far too big for her boots.' When Julia had been offered the job she had said, 'Barry won't like it, but it really would be a good idea if he moved on. He's good at the detail, but very old-fashioned.' The Divisional Director believed Barry was essential to the smooth running of the department and asked the HR Manager to mediate. The HR Manager followed the general plan described below.

The format outlined here will sound more formal and rigid than that in most situations in normal working life. Often mediation will occur spontaneously or the need will come at a very difficult time when two people have just had a flaming row and the mediator is inadvertently thrust into a mediator role. Sometimes it will be more like the Barry/Julia situation, but we are setting it out in this way to illustrate a pattern which seems to be appropriate, despite the need to modify it to suit for specific situations.

Mediator briefing

The mediator will need to find out as much as possible about the problem beforehand, e.g. Who has said what? To whom? What are the real points of contention? Such information will mainly be hearsay.

Introductory remarks

The mediator will wait until both parties are present and then make introductions. The physical setting will be controlled so that no party feels threatened. The mediator will then give an opening statement. This outlines the role of the participants and demonstrates the mediator's neutrality. Some mediators will make comments about what they see as the issue and confirm the case data if briefs have been pre-submitted. Next, the mediator will define protocol and set the time frame for the process. There will be a review of the mediation guidelines and the mediator will briefly recap what it is that he or she has heard as the issues.

The opening statement during the introductory remarks will set out the ground rules for the mediation. These ground rules are what help the mediation move along smoothly. The mediator will usually ask that if lawyers are present, they can confer, but the clients should speak for themselves. Parties should not interrupt each other; the mediator will give each party the opportunity to fully share their side of the story.

Statement of the problem by the parties

After the opening statement, the mediator will give each side the opportunity to tell their story uninterrupted. Most often, the person who requested the mediation session will go first. The statement is not necessarily a recital of the facts, but it is to give the parties an opportunity to frame issues in their own minds, and to give the mediator more information on the emotional state of each party. If there are lawyers present who make the initial statement, the mediator will then ask the client to also make a statement. The rationale behind the statement of the problem is not a search for the truth; it is just a way to help solve the problem.

Information gathering

The mediator will ask the parties open-ended questions to get to the emotional undercurrents. The mediator may repeat back key ideas to the parties, and will summarise often. This helps the mediator build rapport between the parties, especially when a facilitative style is used.

Problem identification

This might also be part of other segments. The mediator tries to find common goals between the parties. The mediator will figure out which issues are going to be able to settle or those that will settle first.

Bargaining and generating options/reaching an agreement

Methods for developing options may include group processes, discussion groups or subgroups, developing hypothetical plausible scenarios, or a mediator's proposal where the mediator puts a proposal on the table and the parties take turns modifying it. However, the most commonly used method is the caucus.

Once the participants are committed to achieving a negotiated settlement, the mediator will propose a brainstorming session to explore potential solutions. This can lead to a final agreement, which diffuses the conflict and provides a new basis for future relations.

The mediator may decide to hold private sessions with both parties in order to move the negotiations along. This caucus session will be confidential. The caucus provides a safe environment in which to brainstorm and reveal underlying fears. The goal of the session is to find some common ground by exploring lots of options, and to bring about possible solutions for the parties to think about. Parties can also entertain alternative solutions to their problems without committing themselves to offer the solutions as concessions.

VI. THE DISCIPLINARY OR GRIEVANCE INTERVIEW

If the appraisal interview is the hardest aspect of management for any manager to undertake, disciplinary interviewing is certainly the least popular: talking to people when things have gone wrong and have to be sorted out. At some point this involves a meeting between a dissatisfied manager and an employee who is seen as the cause of that dissatisfaction, or between a dissatisfied employee and a manager representing the employing organisation that is seen as the cause of the employee's dissatisfaction.

Procedures, as described in Chapter 22, can do no more than force meetings to take place: it is the meetings themselves that produce answers.

The concepts of discipline and grievance

Many present-day views of discipline are connected with the idea of punishment: a disciplinarian is one seen as an enforcer of rules, a hard taskmaster or martinet. Disciplinary procedures in employment are usually drawn up to provide a preliminary to dismissal, so that any eventual dismissal will not be viewed as unfair by a tribunal. This background makes a problem-solving approach to discipline difficult for a manager, as there is always the sanction in the background making the employee cautious or apprehensive. There will always be a fear that a manager in a disciplinary interview is looking for a justification to punish rather than looking for a more constructive solution. Our approach is based on the more accurate notion of discipline of the manager attempting to modify the working behaviour of a subordinate, but regarding punishment as a last resort.

The idea of grievance similarly has problems of definition and ethos. In Chapter 22 we used the convenient scale of dissatisfaction–complaint–grievance as an explanation, but that is just a convenient technical classification. The general sense of the word is closer to the dictionary definitions which use phrases such as 'a real or imaginary wrong causing resentment' or 'a feeling of injustice, of having been unfairly treated'. This is absolutely right for harassment or bullying, which we deal with later in this skills package, but notions of resentment and injustice seem too heavy for situations where the basic problem is that the maintenance crew have fallen down on the job or the central heating is not working properly. Where we have unresolved problems about our jobs (even when we are deeply worried by them) we are often reluctant to construe our feelings as 'having a grievance'. We just want to get more information, or an opportunity for training, or a chance to talk to someone a bit more senior. Very few people indeed want to be seen to be grumbling. Customers are generally reluctant to grumble about the service they receive, because it is too much trouble, because no one would listen, or just because they do not want to make a fuss; yet they can simply walk away. Compared with customers, employees are much less inclined to complain, or even to point out problems, for fear of being categorised as a nuisance.

Despite the difficulties, our aim here is to formulate an approach to the interview that achieves an adjustment in attitude, with the changed attitude being confirmed by subsequent experience. Either the manager believes that the employee's subsequent working behaviour will be satisfactory, or the employee believes that his or her subsequent experience in employment will be satisfactory. The conflict of interest between the parties is resolved and the interview only succeeds when there is that confirmation.

ACTIVITY VI.1

What grievance or disciplinary incidents can you recall where the situation was not clear-cut and where an interview with a manager produced a resolution to the problem that was effective, although quite different from what had been anticipated by the manager at the beginning of the interview?

The nature of grievance and disciplinary interviewing

Many grievance or discipline interviews are simple: giving information, explaining work requirements and delivering rebukes, but from time to time every manager will need to use a problem-solving approach, involving sympathy, perception, empathy and the essential further feature that some managers provide only with reluctance: time. The method will be analytical and constructive; not only for the interviews built into the grievance and discipline procedure, but also for interviews that avoid recourse to the rigid formality of procedure. Such interviews are one of the means towards self-discipline and autonomy of employees, reducing the need for supervision. The sequence we advocate has discipline and grievance intertwined for much of the process but diverging in the interview itself (*see* Figure VI.1).

As mentioned in Chapter 22, grievance may be expressed only in manifest form, requiring interviewing to understand its latent content in order that appropriate action is taken to remove the underlying dissatisfaction. Discipline problems will have underlying reasons for the unsatisfactory behaviour which need to be discovered before solutions to the problems can be found.

The discipline and grievance sequence

Preparation

First, check the procedural position to ensure that the impending interview is appropriate. In a grievance situation, for instance, is the employee pre-empting the procedure by taking the matter to the wrong person or to the wrong point in the procedure? This is most common when the first-line supervisor is being bypassed, either because the employee or the representative feels that it would be a waste of time, or perhaps because the supervisor is unsure of the appropriate action and is conniving at the side-stepping of the procedure. It is also possible that the supervisor knows what to do but is shirking the responsibility or the potential unpopularity of what has to be done.

In disciplinary matters even more care is needed about the procedural step, as the likelihood of penalties may already have been set up by warnings, thus reducing the scope for doing anything else in the impending interview apart from imposing a further penalty. In most cases we believe that interviews will precede procedure, so the parties to the interview are less constrained by procedural rules. Then the manager will be at pains to explain that the interview is informal and without procedural implications. Alternatively the interview may be one where the likelihood of a move into procedure is so remote that the manager will be at pains to avoid any such reference, for fear of the complainant taking fright.

Who will be there? Here there are similar procedural considerations. In procedure there is the likelihood of employee representation; out of procedure that is less likely, even though the employee may feel anxious and threatened without it. If the manager is accompanied in the interview, the employee may feel even more insecure, and it is doubtful how much can be achieved informally unless the employee feels reasonably secure and able to speak frankly.

What are the facts that the interviewer needs to know? In grievance it will be the subject of the grievance and how it has arisen. This type of information will have been filtered through the management hierarchy and perhaps modified in the process, so it needs careful consideration and any additional background information collected.

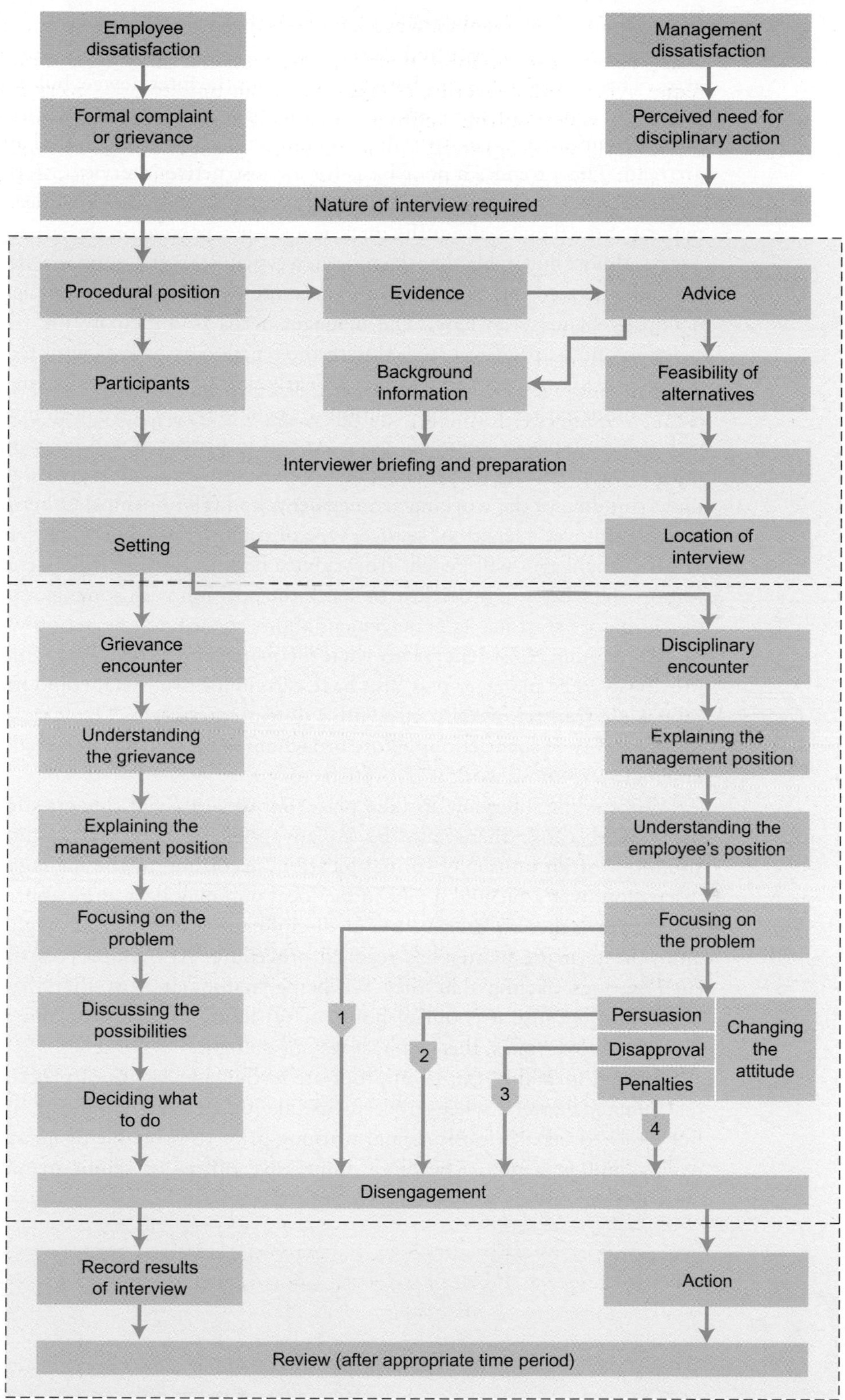

Figure VI.1
The grievance and disciplinary interviews

Disciplinary interviews always start at the behest of the management so the manager will again collect evidence and consider how it may have been interpreted by intermediaries. This will include some basic details about the interviewee, but mainly information about the aspects of the working performance that are unsatisfactory and why. Too often this information exists only in opinions that have been offered and prejudices that are held. This provides a poor basis for a constructive interview, so the manager needs to ferret out details, with as much factual corroboration as possible, and should try to make a shrewd guess about the interviewee's perspective on the situation.

It is almost inevitable that the interviewee will start the interview defensively, expecting to be blamed for something and therefore ready to refute any allegations, probably deflecting blame elsewhere. The manager needs to anticipate the respondent's initial reaction and be prepared to deal with the reaction as well as with facts that have been collected. Unless the interview is at an early, informal stage, the manager also needs to know about earlier warnings, cautions or penalties that have been invoked.

For both types of interview more general information will be required, not just the facts of the particular grievance or disciplinary situation, but knowledge to give a general understanding of the working arrangements and relationships. Other relevant data may be the employee's length of service, type of training, previous experience, and so forth.

Most managers will benefit from advice before starting. It is particularly important for anyone who is in procedure to check the position with someone such as a personnel officer before starting, as management ability to sustain any action will largely depend on maintaining consistency with what the management has done with other employees previously. The manager may also have certain ideas of what could be done in terms of retraining, transfer or assistance with a domestic problem. The manager needs to verify the feasibility of such actions before broaching them with an aggrieved employee or with an employee whose work is not satisfactory.

Where is the interview to take place? However trivial this question may seem it is included, because there may be an advantage in choosing an unusually informal situation, or an unusually formal location, according to the manager's assessment. A discussion over a pie and a pint in the local pub may be a more appropriate setting for some approaches to grievance and disciplinary problems, although they are seldom appropriate if the matter has reached procedure. Also employees frequently mistrust such settings, feeling that they are being manipulated or that the discussion 'does not count' because it is out of hours or off limits. If, however, one is trying to avoid procedural overtones, this can be a way of doing it.

Unusual formality can be appropriate in the later stages of procedure, especially in disciplinary matters, when proceedings take on a strongly judicial air. An employee is not likely to take seriously a final warning prior to probable dismissal if it is delivered over a pint in a pub. The large, impressive offices of senior managers can provide appropriate settings for the final stages of procedure.

ACTIVITY VI.2

What incidents have you experienced or heard about where the location of the interview was clearly unsuitable for the nature of the encounter?

The grievance interview

The first step in the grievance interview is for the manager to be clear about what the grievance is; a simple way of doing this is to state the *subject* of the grievance and get confirmation from the employee that it is correct. This is important because the manager will probably have a different perspective on the affair from the employee, particularly if it has got beyond the preliminary stage. A supervisor may report to a superior that Mr X has a grievance and 'will not take instructions from me', but when the interview begins Mr X may state his grievance as being that he is unwilling to work on Saturday mornings. In other situations it might be the other way round, with the supervisor reporting that Mr X will not work Saturday mornings and Mr X saying in the interview that he finds the style of his supervisor objectionable. Even where there is no such confusion, an opening statement and confirmation of the subject demonstrate that the two parties are talking about the same thing.

Having clarified or confirmed the subject of the grievance, the manager will then invite the employee to state the case, explaining the nature and reasons for the dissatisfaction. This enables the employee to explain why he or she is aggrieved, citing examples, providing further information and saying not just 'what' but also 'why'. Seldom will this be done well. The presentation of a case is not an easy task for the inexperienced, and few aggrieved employees are experienced at making a case of this type. Furthermore, there is the inhibition of questioning the wisdom of those in power and some apprehension about the outcome. Because of this the manager will need to ask questions in order to fill in the gaps that have been left by the employee and to clarify some points that were obscure in the first telling. It is generally better to have an episode of questioning after the case has been made, rather than to interrupt on each point that is difficult. Interruptions make a poorly argued case even more difficult to sustain. There may, however, be disguised pleas for assistance that provide good opportunities for questioning to clarify: 'I'm not very good with words, but do you see what I'm getting at?', 'Do you see what I mean?' or 'Am I making myself clear?' Among the communication ploys that the manager will need at this stage could be the method of *reflection* that was mentioned briefly in our introduction to face-to-face skills.

After all the necessary clarification has been obtained the manager restates the employee's grievance, and gives an outline of the case that has been presented, and will ask the employee to agree with the summary or to correct it. By this means the manager is confirming and demonstrating an understanding of what the grievance is about and why it has been brought. This is not agreeing with it or dismissing it; all that has happened is that the grievance is now understood.

This phase of the interview can be summarised in sequential terms, as follows:

Manager	Employee
1 States subject of grievance	
	2 Agrees with statement
	3 States case
4 Questions for clarification	
5 Restates grievance	
	6 Agrees or corrects

The grievance is now understood

The next phase is to set out the management position on the grievance. This is not the action *to be taken* but the action that *has been taken*, with the reasons for the action. This may include an explanation of company policy, safety rules, previous grievances, supervisory problems, administrative methods and anything else which is needed to make clear why the management position has been what it has been. The manager will then invite the employee to question and comment on the management position to ensure that it is understood and the justifications for it are understood, even if they are not accepted. The objective is to ensure that the parties to the discussion see and understand each other's point of view.

The management position is now understood

Setting out the two opposed positions will have revealed a deal of common ground. The parties will agree on some things, though disagreeing on others. In the third phase of the interview the manager and employee sort through what they have discussed and identify the points of disagreement. The points on which they agree can be ignored, as the need now is to find the outer limits.

Points of disagreement are now in focus

As a preliminary to taking action in the matter under discussion, various possibilities can be put up for consideration. It is logical that the employee's suggestions are put first. Probably this has already been done either explicitly or implicitly in the development of the case. If, however, specific suggestions are invited at this stage they may be different ones, as the aggrieved employee now understands the management position and is seeing the whole matter clearly following the focusing that has just taken place. Then the manager can put forward alternatives or modifications, and such alternatives may include, or be limited to, the suggestion that the grievance is mischievous and unfounded so that no action should be taken. Nevertheless, in most cases there will be some scope for accommodation even if it is quite different from the employee's expectation. Once the alternative suggestions for action are set out, there is time for the advantages and disadvantages of both sets to be discussed.

Alternatives have now been considered

The action is to be taken by the manager alone; it is not a joint decision even though the manager will look for a decision that all parties find acceptable. In bringing a grievance the employee is challenging a management decision and that decision will now be confirmed or it will be modified, but it remains a management decision.

Before making the decision the manager may deploy a range of behaviours to ensure that the decision is correct. There may be an adjournment for a while to seek further advice or to give the employee time to reflect further, but the manager has to decide and then explain the decision to the employee, not simply deciding and announcing, but supporting the decision with explanation and justification in the same way that the employee developed the case for the grievance at the beginning. There may be employee questions, the employee may want time to think, but eventually the management decision will have to be accepted, unless there is some further procedural step available.

Management action is now clear and understood.

The disciplinary interview

Discipline arises from management dissatisfaction rather than employee dissatisfaction with the employment contract, so the opening move is a statement of why such dissatisfaction exists, dealing with the *facts* of the situation rather than managerial feelings of outrage about them. This shows that the manager sees the interview as a way of dealing with a problem of the working situation and not (at least not yet) as a way of dealing with a malicious or indolent employee. If an employee has been persistently late for a week, it would be unwise for a manager to open the disciplinary interview by saying, 'Your lateness this week has been deplorable' as the reason might turn out to be that the employee has a seriously ill child needing constant attendance through the night. Then the manager would be embarrassed and the potential for a constructive settlement of the matter would be jeopardised. An opening factual statement of the problem, 'You have been at least twenty minutes late each day this week . . .', does not prejudge the reasons and is reasonably precise about the scale of the problem. It also circumscribes management dissatisfaction by implying that there is no other cause for dissatisfaction; if there is, it should be mentioned.

Now the manager asks the employee to say what the reasons for the problem are, perhaps also asking for comments on the seriousness of the problem itself, which the employee may regard as trivial but the manager regards as serious. If there is such dissonance it needs to be drawn out. Getting the employee's reaction is usually straightforward, but the manager needs to be prepared for one of two other types of reaction. Either there may be a need to probe because the employee is reluctant to open up, or there may be angry defiance. Disciplinary situations are at least disconcerting for employees and frequently very worrying, surrounded by feelings of hostility and mistrust, so that it is to be expected that some ill feeling will be pent up and waiting for the opportunity to be vented.

First possible move to disengagement

If the employee sees something of the management view of the problem and if the manager understands the reasons for the problem, the next step is to seek a solution. A disciplinary problem is as likely to be solved by management action as by employee action. If the problem is lateness, one solution would be for the employee to catch an earlier bus, but another might be for the management to alter the working shift to which the employee is assigned. If the employee is disobeying orders, one solution would be to start obeying them, but another might be for the employee to be moved to a different job where orders are received from someone else. Some managers regard such thinking as unreasonable, on the grounds that the contract of employment places obligations on individual employees that they should meet despite personal inconvenience. However, the point is not how people *should* behave, but how they do. Can the contract of employment be enforced on an unwilling employee? Not if one is seeking such attitudes as enthusiasm and cooperation, or behaviour such as diligence and carefulness. The disenchanted employee can always meet the bare letter rather than the spirit of the contract.

The most realistic view is that many disciplinary problems require some action from both parties, some require action by the employee only and a small proportion require management action only. The problem-solving session may quickly produce the possibility for further action and open up the possibility of closing the interview.

This simple, logical approach outlined so far may not be enough, due to the unwillingness of employees to respond to disciplinary expectations. They may not want to be punctual or to do as they are instructed, or whatever the particular problem is. There is now a test of the power behind management authority. Three further steps can be taken, one after the other, although there will be occasions when it is necessary to move directly to the third.

Second possible move to disengagement: persuasion

A first strategy is to demonstrate to employees that they will not achieve what they want, if their behaviour does not change:

> You won't keep your earnings up if you don't meet targets.
>
> It will be difficult to get your appointment confirmed when the probationary period is over if. . . .

By such means employees may see the advantages of changing their attitude and behaviour. If they are convinced, there is a strong incentive for them to alter, because they believe it to be in their own interests.

Third possible move to disengagement: disapproval

Another strategy is to suggest that continuing the behaviour will displease those whose goodwill the employee wishes to keep:

> The Management Development Panel are rather disappointed. . . .
>
> Some of the other people in the department feel that you are not pulling your weight.

A manager using this method needs to be sure that what is said is both true and relevant. Also the manager may be seen as shirking the issue, so it may be appropriate to use a version of 'I think this is deplorable and expect you to do better'.

We asked for a restraint from judgement in the early stages of the interview, until the nature of the problem is clear. The time for judgement has now come, with the proper deployment of the rebuke or the caution.

Fourth possible move to disengagement: penalties

When all else fails or is clearly inappropriate, as with serious offences about which there is no doubt, penalties have to be invoked. In rare circumstances there may be the possibility of a fine, but usually the first penalty will be a formal warning as a preliminary to possible dismissal. In situations that are sufficiently grave, summary dismissal is both appropriate and possible within the legal framework.

Disengagement

We have indicated possible moves to disengagement at four different points in the disciplinary interview. Now we come to a stage that is common to both grievance and disciplinary encounters from the point of view of describing the process, although the nature of disengagement will obviously differ. The manager now needs to think of the working situation that will follow. In a grievance situation can the employee now accept the decision that has been made? Are there faces to be saved or reputations to be restored? What administrative action is to be taken? In closing a disciplinary interview, the manager will aim for the flavour of disengagement to be as positive as possible so that all concerned put the disciplinary problem behind them. Where the outcome of the interview is to impose or confirm a dismissal, then the manager will be exclusively concerned with the fairness and accuracy with which it is done, so that the possibility of tribunal hearings is reduced, if not prevented. It can never be appropriate to close an interview of either type leaving the employee humbled and demoralised.

WINDOW ON PRACTICE

The American Eric Harvey reduced what he calls 'positive discipline' to three simple steps:

1 Warn the employee orally.

2 Warn the employee in writing.

3 If steps 1 and 2 fail to resolve the problem, give the employee a day off, with pay (Harvey 1987).

A similar, very positive, approach was outlined in a seminal paper by Huberman in 1967.

SUMMARY PROPOSITIONS

VI.1 Grievance and disciplinary interviews are central to the process of sorting things out when there is a management/employee problem, but most managers dislike such interviews intensely.

VI.2 Grievance and disciplinary interviews are one of the means whereby people at work achieve self-discipline and autonomy, reducing the need for supervision and reducing the need for recourse to the formality of procedure.

VI.3 The steps in conducting a grievance interview are first to understand the nature of the grievance, to explain the management position, to focus on the problem, to discuss possibilities and then to decide what to do.

VI.4 The disciplinary interview starts the other way around, first explaining the management position, then understanding the employee's position and focusing on the problem. If that does not produce a satisfactory result, the manager may have to move through three more steps: persuasion, showing disapproval or invoking penalties.

GENERAL DISCUSSION TOPICS

1 Do individual grievance and disciplinary procedures weaken trade union organisation in a workplace by enabling the management to deal with employees individually rather than having to face the potential strength of collective action and representation?

2 In 1791 Edmund Burke, a British statesman, said, 'He that wrestles with us strengthens our nerves, and sharpens our skill. Our antagonist is our helper.' Do trade union officials help HR managers by strengthening their nerves and sharpening their skill?

3 How would your boss establish a gap between your actual performance and what is expected of you?

4 Are those lowest in the organisational hierarchy accused of poor performance because it is easier to establish a gap that is clearly the responsibility of the person being accused?

FURTHER READING

Edwards, P.K. (2000) 'Discipline: towards trust and self-discipline?', in S. Bach and K. Sisson (eds), *Personnel Management: A comprehensive guide to theory and practice*. Oxford: Blackwell, pp. 317–37.
Redman, T. and Wilkinson, A. (2006) *Contemporary Human Resource Management*. Harlow: Pearson Education, pp. 177–92.
Hook, C.M., Rollinson, D.J., Foot, M. and Handley, J. (1996) 'Supervisor and manager styles in handling discipline and grievance', *Personnel Review*, Vol. 25, No. 3, pp. 20–34.
These studies provide further background and discussion of the place of interviewing in employment relations processes.

Borg, J. (2004) *Persuasion: The art of influencing people*. Harlow: Pearson Education.
This is a rather different book, popular in style but with solid content on this particular aspect of discipline and grievance handling.

WEB LINKS

www.thefreelibrary.com/undertaking+a+disciplinary+interview ('Undertaking a Disciplinary Interview', Check List 109).

www.entrepreneur.com/tradejournals/article/100509019.

REFERENCES

Harvey, E.L. (1987) 'Discipline versus punishment', *Management Review*, March, pp. 25–9.
Huberman, J.C. (1967) 'Discipline without punishment', *Harvard Business Review*, May, pp. 62–8.

VII. REPORT WRITING

Reports are written for both reading and action by the reader. What the writer wants to say is not as important as what the reader needs to know and then do. Action by the reader is the constant objective of the writer. Reports should be as brief as possible, but proposed action has to be thoroughly justified.

Content of report

Often the report has an appended *Executive Summary*. Most of the readers do not really want to read your report at all; what they want is a quick summary of the main points. This may annoy you as you have spent sleepless hours perfecting your arguments and analysing your data, but the executive summary may lead the reader to refer to your main report for further explanation of recommendations or for the justification of a puzzling conclusion. It is, of course, a summary of the report that you have already written, not the other way round. You do not write some brief notes in summary and then expand them with more information for the full report. The summary requires thorough analysis and succinct explanation, with clear references to the relevant sections and page numbers of the full report.

In order to help the cohesiveness and readability of the report, there may be *appendices*. These remove detailed data from the report which are illustrative of points made in the report, but not essential to understanding. Reference to the extra information in an appendix may help to convince a reader of an argument that is presented in the report with enough evidence to convince most readers, but not enough to persuade the sceptical.

Some reports may require a note of *sources*, if some of the readers may need to refer to published material which you have relied on. You may not need full bibliographical details, but always sufficient information for the reader to locate the material you have used.

Writing procedure

Before the writing begins you need to *assemble and organise your material*. Chucking a pile of papers on the back seat of your car may be a form of assembling, but certainly not organising. A simple method is to divide the pile into several piles of different categories like raw data, interview responses, external comparisons, suggestions, implications and probably not needed. Leaving out the 'probably not needed' for the time being, the next stage is to review the content of each pile for three reasons. First, you are recalling everything and beginning to see where you want to go. Second, you are probably moving some more material to that which is probably not needed. Third, as you begin to see where you want to go, you see what material you need to add: checks on the Internet, visits to the library, telephone calls, finding *and marking* pages where you may need to refer to that book on the shelf behind you. If you now have a clear idea of what you want to achieve with your report, and can see the logical way of getting there, you can proceed to the next stage. If not you may find the technique of mind-mapping helpful (Buzan 2009).

Structure

You now need an outline, or *framework*, to give a logical sequence to the writing and avoid risks of duplication, as well as to ensure that you present material early in the report that will be needed to justify points made later. Ways of doing this vary. One popular writer of fiction, Harold Robbins, worked with just a diagram above his typewriter showing how each of his characters was connected. An equally popular writer of much better fiction, John Grisham, works out a comprehensive and detailed structure for each book before he starts writing. You have to employ the method that works for you. The framework comes from analysing the message that is to be sent in terms of the action expected and then subdividing the components of that message to be logically grouped. The framework may be modified during the writing until the writer is convinced that it is satisfactory.

As you are not writing popular fiction you are likely to need a structure that has the following features:

Terms of reference

Who commissioned the report

Who has written it

Sources/methods used

A list of acronyms

Executive summary at front (as well as normal summary at end)

Contents list

Recommendations

Date

This is not necessarily the order in which they should appear, as you will want to draw the reader into the body of the report as soon as possible.

The logical grouping of the material takes the form of *sections*, each dealing with a distinct aspect of the report material. This arrangement emphasises the logic of the way the material is grouped, but it is a part also of the communication to the reader, because the sections have titles, like headlines in a newspaper, which sum up what the section contains. Titles should not tease or muddle the reader. 'Which way now?', for example, is an unhelpful title as it poses a question without giving any clue to the answer.

The *paragraph* is a unit of thought in the writing, dealing with a single topic or idea, and good paragraphing will ensure the material is read. Paragraphing also reassures the reader that there will be breathing spaces from time to time rather than a long solid block of text to be ploughed through.

The appropriate length of paragraph varies with the material being written. Textbooks usually average 100–200 words, popular novels 60–75 and popular newspapers 30–40. Short paragraphs are easier for the reader, but reports will sometimes require detailed argument involving greater length. It is wise to keep the average under 120, if possible.

The *sentence* is the bit of writing between full stops, which makes sense and usually has a subject and a verb. The main difficulties in writing sentences are that either they are too long or they set up expectations that are not realised. Writing sentences that are too long comes through adding extra clauses and qualifications. Setting up expectations that are not realised comes from inferring what is to come in the sentence, but then changing tack or emphasis without returning to the original thought.

Punctuation is important in making your meaning clear. Journalist Lynne Truss demonstrated this with a best-selling book in 2004 entitled *Eats Shoots and Leaves.*

Written like that it accurately describes the eating habits of a giant panda. Inserting a single comma changes it to describe a gangster eating dinner in a restaurant, executing a gangland rival at a nearby table and leaving before the police arrive. There are great subtleties of punctuation that can be deployed by pedants, but the basics are simple.

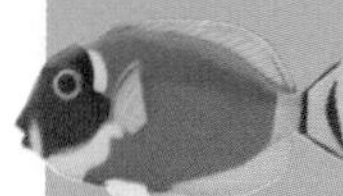

PUNCTUATION

A comma makes a logical division within a sentence:

1 to separate the subject from descriptive words or phrases, 'Charles, Prince of Wales, plays polo.'

2 to separate clauses, 'if he scores, the crowd will cheer.'

3 to separate items on a list, 'her parents, husband and children came to watch.'

A semi colon links two sentences so closely related that a full stop would make too great a break: 'he didn't score; Jones did.'

A colon separates an announcement from what is announced, 'the order of play is as follows:'

An apostrophe indicates either a possessive, 'the team's performance' or a missing syllable in abbreviations, 'it's time for tea'. There is so much uncertainty about the apostrophe that one often sees the quite unnecessary and misleading use of an apostrophe in a simple plural. On the side of a delivery van, 'Laptops and PC's'; In a newspaper, 'The 1960's were the best time ever for popular music.'

Inverted commas can be quite confusing. Basically they are to identify in a sentence something that is being quoted, as in the above examples. They are sometimes used to highlight the use of a phrase which you know is not quite right, but which you are too idle to express properly: the fans are 'not best pleased' with the manager's performance.

Emphasis can be shown in various ways, by means of *italics*, <u>underlining</u>, **emboldening**, CAPITAL LETTERS or !!!!!!! The important thing is to use your chosen style for emphasis consistently and sparingly. Using styles for emphasis is quite different from using styles to differentiate headings, marking stages in the development of your argument and signalling what is coming next. In this text headings they are given different weights, with Emboldened Capitals being for the biggest sections, followed perhaps by italics for sections within a bigger section and so on. For simple emphasis the best method is in the choice of words. In popular media there is a tendency to rely on extravagant language; in a reality TV programme a singer is described by successive judges as 'fantastic', 'absolutely fantastic' and 'truly amazing'. Much more effective are words and phrases which provide emphasis by describing what has happened accurately and meaningfully.

The following box provides a useful checklist for writers of reports.

A CHECKLIST FOR REPORT WRITERS

I Before writing

a What action do you expect from this report?

b Who will read it?

c How short can it be?

2 Outline

a What precisely is the topic of the report?

b How many components are there?

c How can those best be grouped?

d How are the components brought into sections?

e Do the titles inform the reader?

Will the report, as outlined produce the action specified in la above?

3 Writing the report

a Is the average paragraph length less than 100 words?

b Have you used more words than are needed?

c Have you used words that are precise and concrete rather than words that are vague and abstract?

d Have you any superfluous adverbs, adjectives and roundabout phrases?

e Have you shown the source of any facts quoted?

f Are any of the sentences too long?

4 Revising the report

a Will the report, as written, produce the action specified in la above?

b Is anything missing?

c Are all calculations accurate?

d Are the recommendations clear and justified?

e Is the choice between alternatives clear?

f Is any part of the report likely to cause offence to anyone? If so, can that be avoided?

g What objections do you expect to the recommendations, and how will you deal with them?

h Can any of the possible objections be prevented by rewriting part of the report?

5 Final presentation

a Is the typing perfect and without spelling mistakes?

b Are all the pages numbered?

c Are abbreviations and symbols used consistently throughout?

d Does the general appearance of the report encourage the reader to read it?

e Is there a single page summary of proposals?

f Is the report being distributed to all the appropriate people?

g If the report is confidential, is that indicated on the report and ensured by the method of distribution?

SUMMARY PROPOSITIONS

VII.1 Reports are written to be read and acted upon, not to show how clever the writer is.

VII.2 A short executive summary is often added to the main report, both to summarise the main points and to guide the reader to particular sections for fuller explanation and evidence.

VII.3 Appendices are often used to remove detailed evidence or illustration from the main report, while retaining it for reference by those who need it. One appendix might be necessary to give details of sources used.

VII.4 Any report is planned with a framework, within which are sections so that the argument and recommendations can be written logically and appropriately for the reader.

VII.5 Punctuation can alter the meaning of a phrase or sentence.

VII.6 Some of the problems to be aware of in report writing are cant or cliché, inappropriate jargon, *non sequitors,* syllepsis and tautology.

FURTHER READING

Eats, Shoots and Leaves by Lynne Truss was first published in 2003. Although she has received some criticism, it is a popular and helpful book available in various editions. The original English edition as well as a special edition for Indian readers are published by Profile Books in London. Gotham Books of New York publish an American edition.

For German readers there is a similar book: Bastian Sick, *Der Dativ ist dem Genitiv sein Tod* (Cologne: Kiepenhauer and Witsch).

So far we have said little about writing style. The classic guide is Burchfield, R.W. (2004) *Fowler's Modern English Usage*, revised 3rd edn (Oxford: Oxford University Press). This is an updated version of the original 1926 book by Henry Watson Fowler. Oxford University Press re-published the original in 2009, with an introduction and notes by David Crystal. A more compact guide is *The Elements of Style* by two Americans, William Strunk and E.B. White. It was first published in 1959 but a fourth edition (2000) is obtainable in the UK from Allyn and Bacon (a Pearson Education company).

The technique of mind mapping may be helpful in organising your thinking before planning your report. See **www.ThinkBuzan.com/MindMaps**.

REFERENCE

Buzan, T. (2009) *How to Remember Anything you Want*. London: BBC.

VIII. PRESENTATION AT TRIBUNAL

When Employment Tribunals were first established in the 1970s (then called Industrial Tribunals) the intention was that they should resemble traditional courts in terms of their function and power, but that they should be a great deal more informal in their style of operation. In particular it was envisaged that the parties should represent themselves, professional lawyers only being present in unusually difficult cases. Over the years things have changed. As the amount of employment law has grown and become more complex, both claimants and respondents have tended increasingly to brief lawyers to advocate their cases and to undertake a proportion of the preparatory work. Employment law has become a major source of earnings for some solicitors and barristers, firms of specialist consultants also being established to carry out this line of work. The rise of no-win-no-fee agreements has opened up the possibility of affordable, professional representation to employees and former employees as well as the employers with whom they are in dispute.

It nonetheless remains the case that anyone is permitted to represent anyone else in the Employment Tribunal and it is common for claimants either to represent themselves or to be represented by a trade union official, and for respondents to be represented in the tribunal by an HR manager. Employment judges are very used to managing such situations by taking a more active role than they do when the parties are professionally represented. They are also well practised in the art of providing balanced chairmanship when one party is represented by a confident, knowledgeable lawyer and the other is not and requires some help in presenting their case effectively. Representing your organisation in the tribunal can be challenging and daunting, even where a case is relatively straightforward. But if you prepare thoroughly there is no reason why you cannot do a very effective job and save a lot of money that would otherwise be spent on legal fees.

The key to being an effective representative is unquestionably very thorough preparation. It is essential that the person advocating the case is absolutely on top of all the facts of the case and, more importantly still, fully understands the relevant law and how it is applied by the courts. You need to have a clear understanding of the strengths and weaknesses of your case, what points you need to persuade the panel to accept, precisely what you are trying to prove and how you can do so in practice. This level of preparation is necessary not only in the tribunal room once a hearing has commenced, but also in the weeks and months beforehand as documents are collated, witness statements prepared and negotiations for a possible out-of-court settlement undertaken.

Settlements

A good majority of cases lodged at a tribunal office are settled prior to a formal hearing, often quite late in the day. The number varies from year to year, but the last statistics issued by the tribunal service (Employment Tribunal and EAT Statistics (GB) 1 April 2008 to 31 March 2009) stated that 65 per cent of claims were either 'withdrawn' (that could be because they are settled or because the claimant decided not to fight on with a weak case) or settled via ACAS. It is not at all unusual for the parties to settle cases 'on the steps of the courtroom' a few minutes before a hearing is due to start. Sometimes the parties even agree the terms of a settlement after a hearing has commenced and may well be urged in that direction by the judge.

In the months leading up to the hearing the parties or their representatives are often, though not always, contacted by an ACAS conciliation officer, whose role is to explore the possibility of an agreement and to facilitate the drawing up of a full and final, legally binding settlement. Conciliation officers are always keen to advocate a settlement and this is very helpful if your side's case has significant weaknesses and could well be lost if a full hearing goes ahead. However, when your case is strong and you are genuinely confident of a likely, ultimate victory on the key points, it is important to resist the blandishments of ACAS and to reject any suggested settlement which is more generous to your opponent than the tribunal is likely to be. In such circumstances you should be resolute when talking to the conciliation officer, stressing the strengths of your case and turning down any suggested offer politely but firmly.

When negotiating a settlement either through the services of ACAS or directly with the claimant's representative it is vital to be fully aware of what a tribunal would award by way of compensation were your side to lose the case. It is helpful to calculate a worst case scenario and also to work out the most likely outcome. This will enable you to negotiate credibly by demonstrating to the claimant that you are not going to pay them off with an over-inflated sum simply in order to dispose of the matter quickly. Paying a large sum is often tempting and can be justified as a means of reducing the costs which your organisation will have to shoulder if it goes ahead and fights the case in the tribunal room. But it sends out a bad message to other would-be litigants. An employer which is known to settle at pretty well any price to avoid tribunal hearings will inevitably attract speculative claims in the future.

Preparing for the hearing

The best advice is to start by preparing your closing statement. This is the statement that the representative of each side makes at the end of proceedings after all the evidence has been presented. It is your opportunity to set out your case clearly, to remind the panel of the main facts of the case as you see them and to explain how you think the law should be applied to the facts when the ruling is made. Representatives also use closing statements to draw the panel's attention to any case law that is relevant to the case and helpful to their arguments. Lawyers extemporise their closing statements and take considerable pride in their ability to do so well, often without recourse to even a few notes. This is not advisable for an inexperienced representative. It is much better to read out a carefully prepared closing statement, even if it is one that has to be adjusted to take account of unexpected developments during the hearing.

Writing a comprehensive, legally credible and clear closing statement is thus an essential stage in the preparation of a successful case. Take plenty of time to get it right and produce several drafts if necessary. Having completed it, you can then use it as your guide when preparing everything else. You need to be able to prove every fact in your closing statement and to be sure of your interpretation of each point of law you make.

Facts are proved either with reference to documents in the bundle which is presented to the panel at the start of proceedings or with reference to the evidence given by witnesses as a hearing proceeds. So you need to make sure, as far as you can, that each fact in the statement is provable with reference to one, the other or both. Points of law are made with reference to the wording of statutes and to published reports of previous cases dealing with the same legal principles. Tribunals are bound to follow precedents on points of law which have already been determined in the appeal courts, so you need to be aware of these and in a position to present copies of case reports to the panel when you start reading out your closing statement.

Your closing statement guides you when thinking about which documents you need to include in the bundle and also when taking statements from your witnesses. At the hearing your witnesses will take it in turn to enter the witness box (actually they just sit behind a table in most tribunal rooms), take their oath and read out their witness statements. This evidence will constitute the core of your case, so it is important that all points on which you want to rely are included in the statements and that they are structured clearly.

The final stage is to prepare your cross-examinations and examinations-in-chief. A week or two before the hearing you will exchange witness statements with your opponents. This needs to happen at the same time (or at least on the same day) so as to ensure that neither side can adjust their statements having had sight of the other's. At the hearing after your opponent's witnesses have read out their statements you will have the opportunity to question them about their evidence. This is known as cross-examination. Your aim is to push them into admitting points that weaken their case and to confirm agreed facts that serve to strengthen yours. A good cross-examination is courteous in style, but persistent. Don't give up a line of questioning if you don't get quite the answers you are hoping for. Instead try another way of asking the same question or putting the same points. By the same token though, it is important to know when to stop a line of questioning that is having the effect of strengthening your opponents' case or weakening yours. If you get into a hole when cross-examining, stop digging! Sometimes it is necessary to accuse a witness of failing to tell the whole truth or to have lied when giving evidence. This is not easy to do, but is often a necessary feature of an effective cross-examination. The key is to do this in a relatively polite way, avoiding aggression. A good approach involves asking the question with a degree of apparent regret, as in:

> I'm afraid I have to put it to you that that statement is untrue.

Or to ask directly about a conflict in the evidence that has been presented, as in:

> You stated in evidence that you were not formally warned about your poor performance before you were dismissed. Yet the letter sent to you on 1st April clearly contains a formal warning. Your witness statement was inaccurate, wasn't it?

The stage in proceedings known as examination-in-chief is your opportunity to put questions to your own witnesses after they have read out their witness statements. No new evidence can be presented at this stage, but witnesses can be asked to expand on points or to clarify exactly what they meant by words used in their statement. The most important task, however, is to give your witnesses an opportunity to comment on something, or to contradict, a point which has been made in the claimants' witness statement or in that of one of the other witnesses appearing to support the claimant's case.

Remedies

As the respondent employer's representative you will always be anticipating that you are going to win your case on all points and that there will be no need for the tribunal to address the question of the remedy. However well prepared you are, and however strong your case, you can never be sure that you are going to win. Litigation always carries some risks. So you will need to prepare for the possibility that the tribunal will find against you and turn its attention at the end of the hearing to determining appropriate compensation. Sometimes claimants are not looking for compensation, wanting reinstatement for example, or a straightforward declaration that they have been treated unlawfully. Either way you need to be in a position to argue that the remedy the claimant is seeking is overly generous or inappropriate. Here too you will be guided by published precedents and by guidance set out in statutes.

Prior to the hearing the claimant will usually have sent you a copy of the 'Schedule of Loss'. This document sets out what is being sought by the claimant in terms of compensation. In practice, it is rare for victorious claimants to receive every penny they are seeking by way of compensation, but this can only happen if you as the respondents' representative argue strongly that a lower sum is appropriate. Here too, thorough preparation is necessary. You may, for example, in an unfair dismissal case be able to argue that the claimant was in part responsible for his or her own dismissal and that compensation should be reduced to take account of that. Alternatively you could argue that the claimant has not mitigated his or her losses adequately by seeking alternative employment and that compensation should be reduced on that account. In a redundancy case you can argue that while the matter was handled unlawfully in terms of procedure, the chances are that the claimant would have been selected and dismissed had a lawful procedure been followed. This should be reflected in the compensation. In discrimination cases there is usually an opportunity to argue that what is being sought by way of damages for 'injury to feelings' is too high and out of line with awards in similar cases decided in the past.

FURTHER READING

Aside from thoroughly familiarising yourself with the facts of the case and the relevant law, there are a number of good sources of information which are helpful when preparing a case for the first time:

- The Legal Action Group (LAG) publishes a number of very user-friendly guides aimed at non-lawyers presenting cases in the Employment Tribunal, such as Jeremy McMullen, Rebecca Tuck and Betsan Criddle (2004) *Employment Tribunal Procedure: A user's guide to tribunals and appeals* (London: Legal Aid Group) and Naomi Cunningham and Michael Reed (2009) *Employment Tribunal Claims: Tactics and precedents* (London: Legal Aid Group).
- The Law Society publish a practical guide by Isobel Manley and Elaine Heslop (2008) *Employment Tribunals* along with a series of books about the major areas of employment law which

put a particular focus on tribunal issues such as compensation and key precedents. Incomes Data Services also publish an excellent practical guide to *Employment Tribunal Practice and Procedure*.

- Each year Oxford University Press publishes a new edition of *Blackstone's Employment Law Practice*. This is a vast book edited by a team of leading lawyers who specialise in the field. It includes a detailed guide to the employment tribunal system, different types of hearings and all manner of procedural issues. It also contains copies of all the major employment statutes.

REFERENCES

Brown, D., Forshaw, S., Korn, A. and Palca, J. (2010) *Blackstone's Employment Law Practice 2010*, 5th edn. Oxford: Oxford University Press.

Cunningham, N. and Reed, M. (2009) *Employment Tribunal Claims: Tactics and precedents*. London: Legal Action Group.

IDS (2006) *Employment Tribunal Practice and Procedure*, 2nd edn. London: IDS.

Manley, I. and Heslop, E. (2004) *Employment Tribunals: A practical guide*. London: The Law Society.

McMullen, J., Tuck, R. and Criddle, B. (2004) *Employment Tribunal Procedure: A user's guide to tribunals and appeals*. London: Legal Action Group.

IX. DEALING WITH BULLYING AND HARASSMENT AT WORK

The objectives of this skills section are to:

1 Define bullying and harassment and outline some examples of behaviour that could be considered to be bullying

2 Explain the elements that an employer should include in a bullying and harassment policy

3 Consider the employee perspectives on and reactions to bullying and harassment

4 Outline the skills required to deal with bullying and harassment

Defining bullying and harassment

Bullying and harassment is increasingly common in the modern workplace and research suggests that around 20 per cent of employees have experienced it in one form or another (Pate and Beaumont 2010). The consequences can be serious: it has been demonstrated to have a negative impact on employee well-being (Vartia 2001), there are potential legal consequences and one estimate puts the associated costs at around £2 billion a year (Tehrani 2005). Clearly it is an important issue. In this chapter, we first define what constitutes bullying and harassment, demonstrating that a wide range of behaviours can be classified under this heading. We then consider both employer and employee perspectives on bullying and harassment and the skills required to deal with these issues.

ACAS (2009a, 2009b) gives the following definitions of harassment and bullying. The terms are used interchangeably by many people, although some definitions may include bullying as a form of harassment.

> Harassment, in general terms, is unwanted conduct affecting the dignity of men and women in the workplace. It may be related to age, sex, race, disability, religion, sexual orientation, nationality or any personal characteristic of the individual, and may be persistent or an isolated incident. The key is that the actions or comments are viewed as demeaning and unacceptable to the recipient. (ACAS 2009a: 2)

> Bullying may be characterised as offensive, intimidating, malicious or insulting behaviour, an abuse or misuse of power through means intended to undermine, humiliate, denigrate or injure the recipient. (ACAS 2009b: 2)

These are broad definitions intended as guidance to both managers and employees as to the types of conduct that are unwelcome in the workplace. In practice, examples of what constitute bullying are actions such as gossip, unwelcome jokes, exclusion from social or work groups or items such as posters and graffiti. Managers misusing power, setting impossible deadlines or blocking promotions may also be classed as bullying employees. Tehrani (2005) presents very detailed examples of bullying behaviours in the workplace that the reader may find useful in establishing what can be classed as bullying. We list a couple of examples in the excerpts in the Window on practice below. D'Cruz and Noronha (2010) also present a fascinating study of bullying in Indian call centres from an employee perspective, demonstrating that bullying and harassment is an issue that has relevance internationally.

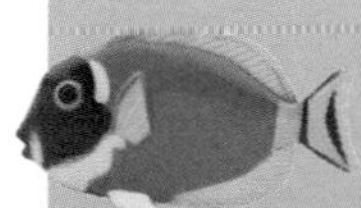

WINDOW ON PRACTICE

A secretary joined a media organisation to work for a senior manager. Within a few days, she found that he was behaving very badly towards her. He would criticise her work, pointing out errors in front of visitors. He would become angry whenever he was kept waiting. The secretary then found out that he had behaved in the same way with all his secretaries and that no one stayed with him long.

Two research scientists had been working on a project and when one of the researchers made a breakthrough, he wrote a paper that failed to recognise the work undertaken by his colleague. From that time, the two men would not work together and continually undermined each other. The situation got so bad that they were moved to different locations.

Source: Excerpts from Tehrani (2005).

While the legal definitions of these terms are more precise than the definitions and examples given in Chapter 20, it can be seen that the parameters of bullying and harassment in the workplace are broadly drawn. Additionally, it is the individual's **perception** of being bullied that is the defining factor in establishing whether bullying has taken place. One employee may, for example, take exception to a joke that another finds inoffensive. This can make dealing with bullying and harassment complex and the CIPD (2007) has, therefore, devised useful self-assessment checklists for assessing and analysing organisational culture to determine whether it is likely to support or suppress bullying. Bullying and harassment may be hard to identify but employers have a legal and moral duty to tackle it. We consider in the following section the means through which employers can do this.

Policies to deal with bullying and harassment

In order to deal effectively with bullying and harassment, employers must have appropriate policies and procedures and ensure that they are enacted. Over 80 per cent of employers in a recent survey suggest that they now have a policy as a mechanism for tackling these issues (Tehrani 2005). This is likely to be easier for large employers with appropriate resources than for small firms. ACAS (2009a), however, presents a detailed guide to employers on the subject and a helpful checklist (p. 6) on what should be included in a policy to deal with bullying and harassment. In the box below, we present a similar checklist on the topic from CIPD (2009).

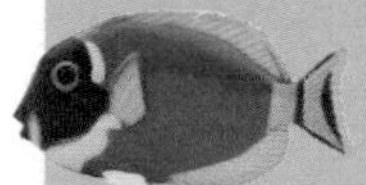

CHECKLIST FOR A POLICY ON BULLYING AND HARASSMENT

- Give examples of what constitutes harassment, bullying and intimidating behaviour including cyber-bullying, work-related events and harassment by third parties.
- Explain the damaging effects and why it will not be tolerated.
- State that it will be treated as a disciplinary offence.
- Clarify the legal implications and outline the costs associated with personal liability.
- Describe how to get help and make a complaint, formally and informally.
- Promise that allegations will be treated speedily, seriously and confidentially and that you prevent victimisation.
- Clarify the accountability of all managers, and the role of union or employee representatives.
- Require supervisors/managers to implement policy and ensure it is understood.
- Emphasise that every employee carries responsibility for his or her behaviour.

Source: Adapted from CIPD (2009) *Factsheet: Harassment and bullying at work.*

It is important that a policy in some way covers all these steps and also that it is supported, and seen to be supported by senior management who act in accordance with the policy. It is advisable to deal with issues informally where possible, to prevent the escalation of the situation. If this fails, or if the matter is serious, it will be necessary to deal with a complaint formally. Some organisations have procedures specific to the bullying and harassment policy but many organisations simply rely on their usual grievance procedures. We outline these in detail in Chapter 22. Depending on the outcome of the investigation, disciplinary action may be taken against the perpetrator of the bullying and we also cover these procedures in Chapter 22.

Where policies are robustly drawn and effectively implemented, they can have great effect, as we outline in the Window on practice below.

WINDOW ON PRACTICE

Pate and Beaumont (2010) present a case study which outlines the actions taken by one public sector organisation to tackle bullying and harassment. In response to attitude surveys which identified bullying as an increasing problem, a new CEO launched a Dignity at Work policy which adopted a two-pronged approach to problem. First, reported cases of bullying and harassment were vigorously pursued and this led to the dismissal of a number of employees, some of whom were at a senior level. Second, compulsory training for all employees was rolled out. A further attitude survey demonstrated that there was a significant reduction in employee perceptions of bullying and harassment in the organisation. Indeed, those perceiving bullying to be problematic declined from a half to a quarter of employees in a three-year period. Trust in senior management overall, however, was not enhanced. Tackling bullying is not, it seems, a panacea for all ills.

Source: Adapted from Pate, J. and Beaumont, P. (2010) 'Bullying and harassment: a case of success?', *Employee Relations*, Vol. 32, No. 2, pp. 171–83.

Employee perspectives on bullying and harassment

The role of the organisation is critical in influencing employees' responses to bullying and harassment. It is, as noted above, important to have an effective policy but there is a danger that this may not be communicated to or believed by employees who may avoid the issue or resign rather than tackle it (D'Cruz and Noronha 2010). In the Window on practice below we illustrate how difficult it can be for employees to assimilate the fact that they are being bullied.

WINDOW ON PRACTICE

It never struck me what was happening. Work pressures are so high and TLs [team leaders] are also caught up with them – they yell and scream abuse to get the work done. So how can one dream that this is harassment. It is only after repeatedly experiencing it and carefully observing that it was only me who was getting the worst, the most frequent, the lousiest treatment from him that I realized what was happening. It just took me off guard because I was a top performer, always at the top of the team . . . so there is no reason for this. Merit, objectivity . . . these are all jargons used to describe the organization – they are so empty. But at that time, they deceived me well.

Source: Excerpt from: D'Cruz, P. and Noronha, E. (2010) 'The exit coping response to work place bullying', *Employee Relations*, Vol. 32, No. 2, pp. 102–20.

Vartia (2001), however, notes that it is not only the targets of bullying and harassment who suffer but bystanders and that it is the problem of the entire work unit, not just the person targeted. The CIPD (2009) and ACAS (2009b) advocate certain actions for the organisation to ensure that bullying and harassment policies are implemented and taken seriously. For example, employees should be introduced to policies at induction and made aware of their rights and personal responsibilities. There should then be continuous communication of and training in policies and employees should have a point of contact to whom they can turn for advice and information. Many organisations appoint 'champions' as a source of advice for employees with concerns about bullying. Employees should also be made aware of the mechanisms for taking a complaint forward.

While much of the focus is, rightly, on those who suffer bullying and harassment, the impact on those instigating it should not be overlooked. At the time of writing, spring 2010, there has been a high-profile example of a senior public figure found guilty of bullying. The case involved a Metropolitan Police Commander, convicted and ultimately jailed for serious offences of this nature. Although one may consider the individual involved to be the author of his own misfortune in engaging in this behaviour, a working environment that refuses to condone such behaviour protects all parties, not just the victims of it.

ACTIVITY IX.1

Look at an organisation's policy on bullying and harassment, for example, the University of Bradford's (2007) policy (**www.brad.ac.uk/admin/equalopp/policies/HarassmentandBullyingPolicy07.pdf**) or one from an organisation with which you are familiar.

1 What are key aspects of the policy?

2 To what extent do you think it is likely to be successful in tackling bullying and harassment?

Tackling bullying and harassment

As we suggest above, many organisations tackle bullying and harassment using their grievance policies and we discuss the skills appropriate to this above. In brief, the key aspects of dealing with bullying and harassment are:

- To address the issue as quickly as possible. It is often advised that grievances are best resolved informally, but this may not be appropriate for allegations of bullying and harassment. Where the allegations are of a serious or sensitive nature, the formal procedure should be instigated without delay.
- To provide a confidential and supportive environment for both the person who feel bullied and the person accused of bullying. The allegations may or may not be substantiated and both need to be dealt with fairly during the course of the investigations.
- The face-to-face and communication skills we deal with throughout this section are vital in what can be sensitive investigations and discussions.
- An open, transparent and fair investigation is essential, as are appropriate feedback mechanisms once the investigation is complete.
- Both parties are likely to need support once the process is completed, unless the outcome leads to dismissal. The provision of counselling can be invaluable in maintaining positive employment relations.

SUMMARY PROPOSITIONS

IX.1 Bullying and harassment are common and problematic for both employers and employees.

IX.2 Employers need to decide how to respond to these issues and are advised to do so using policies and procedures which require senior management support.

IX.3 Employee responses to bullying and harassment often include avoidance and resignation. They need to clearly understand the policy and how to use it if it is to be successful in reducing bullying and harassment.

IX.4 Dealing with allegations of bullying and harassment can be very sensitive and a wide range of skills must be deployed.

GENERAL DISCUSSION TOPICS

1 To what extent do you believe that setting challenging deadlines can be considered to be bullying?

2 'A robust policy on bullying and harassment will be effective in reducing employee perceptions that these issues take place within an organisation.' Discuss this statement.

3 What actions can be taken to prevent employees resigning as a result of bullying and harassment?

FURTHER READING

ACAS (2009a) *Bullying and Harassment at Work: A guide for employers and managers*, available at **www.acas.org.uk/index.aspx?articleid=797** (accessed 6 February 2010).

ACAS (2009b) *Guidance for Employees: Bullying and harassment at work*, available at **www.acas.org.uk/index.aspx?articleid=794** (accessed 6 February 2010).
ACAS has produced these two comprehensive and user-friendly guides to explain both employer and employee responsibilities on how to deal with bullying and harassment. The employer guide offers advice on how to establish policies and procedures and the employee guide advises employees on how to manage a workplace situation in which they are being bullied.

CIPD (2007) *Tool: Tackling bullying at work – a good practice framework*. London: CIPD
The CIPD present a tool that employers can adopt in analysing their workplace culture and establishing an action plan to eradicate workplace bullying.

WEB LINKS

www.nationalbullyinghelpline.co.uk/ (the UK national bullying helpline).

www.acas.org.uk (ACAS, Advisory Conciliation and Arbitration Service).

www.CIPD.co.uk (Chartered Institute of Personnel and Development).

REFERENCES

ACAS (2009a) *Bullying and Harassment at Work: A guide for employers and managers*, available at **www.acas.org.uk/index.aspx?articleid=797** (accessed 6 February 2010).

ACAS (2009b) *Guidance for Employees: Bullying and harassment at work*, available at **www.acas.org.uk/index.aspx?articleid=794** (accessed 6 February 2010).

CIPD (2007) *Tool: Tackling bullying at work – a good practice framework*. London: CIPD.

CIPD (2009) *Factsheet: Harassment and bullying at work*, available at **www.cipd.co.uk/subjects/dvsequl/harassmt/harrass.htm?IsSrchRes=1** (accessed 6 February 2010).

D'Cruz, P. and Noronha, E. (2010) 'The exit coping response to work place bullying', *Employee Relations*, Vol. 32, No. 2, pp. 102–20.

Pate, J. and Beaumont, P. (2010) 'Bullying and harassment: a case of success?', *Employee Relations*, Vol. 32, No. 2, pp. 171–83.

Tehrani, N. (2005) *Bullying at Work: Beyond policies to a culture of respect*. London: CIPD.

University of Bradford (2007) *Personal Harassment and Bullying Policy and Procedures*, available at **www.brad.ac.uk/admin/equalopp/policies/HarassmentandBullyingPolicy07.pdf** (accessed 6 February 2010).

Vartia, M. (2001) 'Consequences of workplace bullying with respect to the well-being of its targets and the observers of bullying', *Scandinavian Journal of Work and Environmental Health*, Vol. 27, No. 1, pp. 63–9.

SKILLS SET 2:

Skills for analysis and decision making

X Using and interpreting statistics

XI Designing procedures

XII Designing questionnaires

XIII Using consultants

Now we have a short group of skills that are quite disparate. Using statistical techniques is an almost universal practice in management, even if it is quickly calculating a percentage on the back of an envelope. A number of our earlier chapters include statistics and refer to specific measures, but we introduce here a range of techniques that have wide applicability for data analysis and as an aid to decision making.

Designing procedures aids decision making in a quite different way, by working out logical sequences of actions to be taken by people to reach a specified objective. These can be as varied as running down a manufacturing plant before the Christmas break, authorising travel expenses, dealing with grievances and so forth. Careful thought and planning can produce a template leading to effective action.

We are all familiar with questionnaires, and equally familiar with the frustration of trying to answer questions that don't make sense. It is all a matter of skilful design that will not only elicit the constructive participation of the questionnaire recipient, but also make possible accurate analysis of the answers.

Perhaps you had never thought of using consultants as being a skill. Surely you are simply paying them to use *their skills* on your behalf? Not at all. The skill with which you specify what needs to be done, and then identifying the people capable of doing it, will enable the consultants to use their skills on your behalf in the way you need. Without this even the most conscientious consultants will do what they think you need, and that will be what they find easiest to do. It may be just right, but that would be simple luck rather than good judgement; it is also rare.

X. USING AND INTERPRETING STATISTICS

The objective of this section is to help you interpret the meaning and value of statistics when they are presented in a report or article, and to guide you in choosing the appropriate statistics to use when presenting numerical data. We focus on basic statistics with most relevance for business and human resource management, and we have been very selective.

This section concentrates on descriptive statistics which are used to organise and summarise data in order to communicate them more clearly. They are used when we have data for the whole population we are aiming to describe, for example, all employees within an organisation. Some government statistics also cover the whole of the relevant population, such as unemployment statistics and of course, the census, so these are descriptive statistics.

Descriptive statistics can also be used to describe the findings of a sample, for example a sample survey sent to HRM managers, each responding on behalf of a different multi-national company (MNC), but it must be remembered that the results apply to the sample only. If we wish to say something about the total population from which the sample is drawn (i.e. all MNCs) we would need to use 'inferential statistics', which are more complex.

Our constant message throughout this section is one of caution. Statistics are factual pieces of information, but remember that they are designed to give the message that the producer of the statistics wants to put across. As someone once said, possibly Benjamin Disraeli, there are:

Lies, damned lies, and statistics. (**www.en.wikipedia.org/wiki/Lies,_damned_lies,_and_statistics**, 24 September 2010)

Frequency distributions

These distributions are often used in business generally and in HRM. For example we could break down the workforce by gender, or by highest qualification, or days of absence. Figure X.1 shows how the workforce may be broken down by highest NVQ equivalent qualification displayed as a bar chart, and in table form it would look like Table X.1.

For another example of a bar chart see Figure 5.6 in Chapter 5 on Workforce Planning. If you wanted to present ages or salaries in a bar chart or frequency table it would be sensible to divide them into groups or bands as otherwise the figure or table would be far too big and fairly meaningless. Frequencies are often displayed as pie charts using the relevant percentages or frequencies, which are excellent for visual presentation. The category which is most popular is the **mode**, and in this case it is the NVQ Level 3. The mode is the **most frequently occurring**, or most numerous category. Frequency tables and the mode are particularly useful for categorical measures. Another

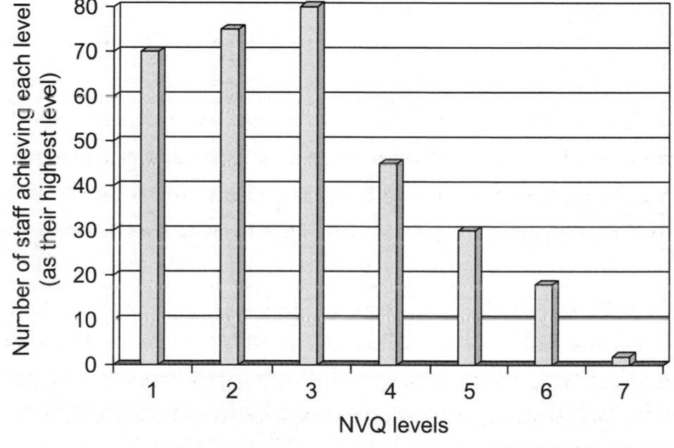

Figure X.1 A bar chart of qualification levels

Table X.1 Frequency table of qualification levels

NVQ level	Number of employees who have this as their highest qualification	Percentage of employees who have this as their highest qualification
1	70	22
2	75	23
3	80	25
4	45	14
5	30	9
6	18	6
7	2	1

Employee total number = 320.

example of the use of these measures is in an analysis of stated reasons for leaving an organisation.

WINDOW ON PRACTICE

Some simple definitions

A categorical (sometimes called discrete) measure is just that, a category: such as gender, highest qualification, job type, reason for leaving. These measures are usually labelled by means of a word.

Some measures are ordinal measures such as in the NVQ example in that they are ranked numerically in order of difficulty; however, the rankings are not necessarily evenly spaced, and do not have a true zero. Therefore the numbers do not have any arithmetic relationship: so we cannot say that NVQ4 is twice as hard as NVQ2 or an NVQ1 plus an NVQ5 adds up to an NVQ6.

Continuous numeric measures, which have a true zero, such as length of service, salary and age all have arithmetic properties so a person with four years' service has twice as much service as a person with two years' service.

Measures of central tendency

If you have done no statistics before you may find the idea of 'central tendency' somewhat impenetrable but it is fairly straightforward if you think of the word 'average', and apply this to, say, the average annual salary in your organisation. It involves adding up the salaries of everyone in the organisation and dividing by the number of people receiving a salary. Actually 'average' is not a statistical term, and the correct statistical term for what we have just described is the **arithmetic mean**. This is a useful measure of central tendency but it has limitations. For example let us consider EntrepreneurCo, which employs ten people including the owner manager (who earns £80,000 p.a. – the accountant has not been very creative). A full list of all the salaries is:

£80,000 (owner manager)	£14,000
£29,000	£13,000
£17,000	£13,000
£15,000	£13,000
£14,000	£13,000

The mean salary would be £22,100 calculated by adding all salaries together and dividing by 10 (number of employees). However, there is no indication here that eight employees earned less than the mean and only two employees earn above the mean, or that one of the salaries is at least £50,000 more than any other salary.

WINDOW ON PRACTICE

The clipped mean

Sometimes the clipped, or cropped mean is used to remove the effects of outliers, such as the £80,000 in the example above. This would be done by removing the top 5 per cent and the bottom 5 per cent of all salaries.

The same mean salary figure could have been reached in Co-operativeCo, round the corner, where the salary list looks very different, and is based solely on length of service:

£22,850	£22,100
£22,850	£21,600
£22,600	£21,600
£22,600	£21,600
£22,100	£21,000

Someone comparing the wages paid in these two organisations on the basis of mean salary only would have no idea how different they were.

WINDOW ON PRACTICE

Some more about different types of measures

The mean can only be calculated for continuous measures like salary, age and years of post-qualification experience. If we try and work out a mean for discrete measures the answer just does not make sense. For example we cannot find an average for gender of racial groups or area of functional expertise.

Using the example above you either have an NVQ3 or an NVQ2 not an NVQ2.85, which would be the mean if we calculated it! The mean is not appropriate as we are dealing with ordinal data with no evidence that the NVQ levels are equally spaced and no true zero.

However, if we worked out the mean age of the workforce in our company it might work out at 32.25 years. This makes sense because age moves continuously, and a specific person could be 32.25 years old. This works because we are dealing with continuous numeric data with a true zero.

If on the other hand we took another measure of central tendency, the **median**, this would be £13,500, in EntrepreneurCo, a very different figure from the mean, as this represents the mid-point after everyone has been ranked according to their salary. The mid-point means that there are equal numbers of people above this salary and below it in the ranking. In EntrepreneurCo there is an even number of employees so the median is calculated by taking the middle two measures which are £14,000 and £13,000, and taking the mid-point of these, which is £13,500.

This figure does distinguish the two organisations, as in Co-operativeCo the median salary would be £ 22,100 (again based on taking the two middle salary points, which in this case turn out to be exactly the same). However, while the median may differentiate EntrepreneurCo from Co-operativeCo it is also a limited measure unless the end points of the range are disclosed. Tony Smith on completing his degree, and keen to pay off his student loan as fast as possible, might, on the basis of mean salaries, have no idea which was the best place to apply for a job, however, Tony gets more information from the median which suggests that he might receive a better starting salary from Co-operativeCo. However, even this information is insufficient, as it doesn't tell Tony anything about the range of salaries. We know that they are tightly bunched in Co-operativeCo but salaries in another company could be spread more widely and still have the same median. We look at spread in the following section.

All this goes to show that it is unwise to take statistics at face value, and organisations can use statistics very cleverly and selectively in order to support their message. In looking at a statistic three key questions to ask are:

1 What exactly can this statistic tell me?
2 What is it unable to tell me?
3 What more information do I need?

ACTIVITY X.1

Gather some organisational HR statistics and look carefully at the information you are given. Absence statistics could be a good one to look at here or turnover statistics. Ask yourself the above three questions. When you have answered them check out your understanding with someone else, preferably the person who produced the statistics.

Measures of dispersion

Dispersion explains how the measures are spread out, and there are two well used measures of spread which can be used in addition to the mean and the median, and which give us more information. The **range** is determined from the highest and the lowest points. So in EntrepreneurCo salaries go from £80,000 down to £13,000, giving a range of 67,000; while in Co-operativeCo it is from £22,850 down to £21,000, giving a range of 1,850. The range is useful and simple to identify, but its limitation is that it is very affected by 'outliers', measures at the extremes which are disconnected to the majority of measures. The owner manager's salary of £80,000 is an outlier at EntrepreneurCo. As another example we might say the age range in our organisation is from 18 to 66, but while there are many employees between 18 and 51 there is only one employee older than 51 and that person is 66. So while the range is a useful piece of information it only gives us limited knowledge about spread.

WINDOW ON PRACTICE

The interquartile range

As the range can be very affected by outliers, sometimes the interquartile range is used to counteract this effect. This uses the same principle as the median: if you remember that the median is the point at which half the results are above this point and half below. Imagine the results being divided into quarters rather than just halves. So the top point of the interquartile range is where one quarter of the results are above this point and three-quarters are below it. And the bottom point of the interquartile range is where three-quarters of the results are above this point and one quarter below it. Subtracting the lower point from the higher point gives the interquartile range.

The other well used measure of spread is the **standard deviation** and this statistic expresses the average deviation from the mean. In other words having worked out the mean we now work out how much each measure, such as salary in the above example, differs from that mean, and then average all those differences. If everyone in an organisation earned exactly the same amount of money the standard deviation would be zero. It would not matter what that actual salary is, it could be £20,000 or £50,000 – as long as everyone earns the same and there is no spread, the standard deviation is zero. The larger the standard deviation the larger the spread it represents, and we would expect that the standard deviation for EntrepreneurCo would be greater than that for Co-operativeCo.

WINDOW ON PRACTICE

Let us compare the standard deviation at EntrepreneurCo and Co-operativeCo.

The standard deviation from the mean at EntrepreneurCo is £20,934

The standard deviation from the mean at Co-operativeCo is 631

So you can see that they are quite different.

The standard deviation is affected by outliers just like the mean and the range, and so it is useful to accompany this statistic with the median and with the mean. In some calculations there is a method for removing outliers and it is worth asking if this has been done when you are given a standard deviation.

Describing relationships or association

There are many times when we would like to see how measures within our organisation are connected, and these often focus on performance measures of some kind or other.

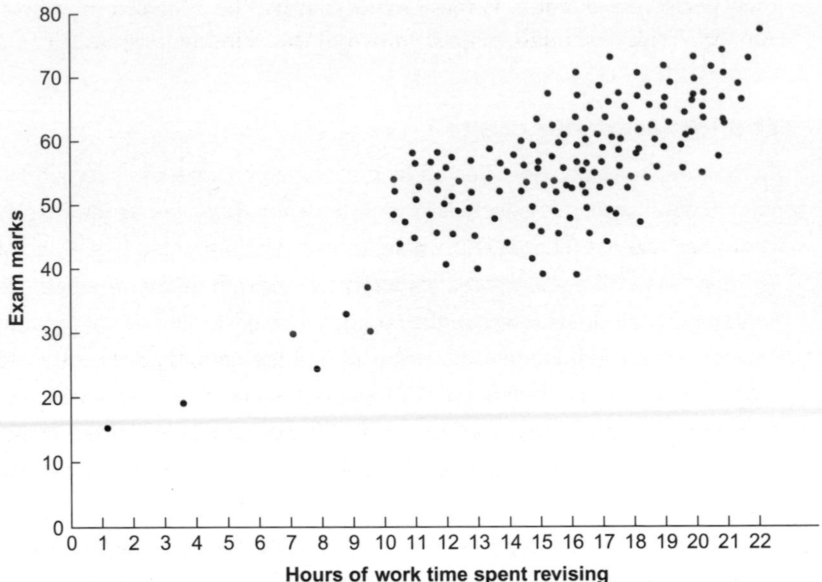

Figure X.2 A scatterplot: Plotting revision time against test scores

We might like to find out how days of absence are related to age, or how absence is related to length of service. One way we can look at relationships is to do this visually in a scatter plot, and a further method is to use a statistical technique called correlation.

Scatterplots

These are fairly simple to draw up and just require that for every person we have the two measures that we are investigating. For example what is the relationship between the amount of work time devoted to test revision and the scores of trainees in the test? So we draw a plot with test scores on the vertical axis and hours of work time devoted to revision on the horizontal axis, and then plot each individual on that according to their score and the time they were allowed for revision by their manager. In the example in Figure X.2 we can see how a greater number of work hours devoted to revising appears to be associated with higher test scores, which is generally what we would expect.

Correlation

Correlation is a more sophisticated approach and is often applied when relating the selection scores of individuals to eventual performance levels in the organisation. The selection processes are generally intended to give us sufficient information to enable us to predict who we think will perform best in our organisation. In our example we are going to relate the results that candidates achieved at an assessment centre to their performance two years later to see whether there is any relationship between them. To do this we need to rank the candidates who have been successful at the assessment centre and then rank their performance in two years' time. So, for example, we may be appointing 50 graduates to the company all of whom have been through the assessment centre, and we rank these from 1 to 50 according to their overall score at the centre. Two years later we look at the performance of each individual and again rank them from 1 to 50. Each individual will now have a rank from the assessment centre and a rank for their performance and it is these ranks that will be analysed in the correlation, and the sorts of results we might get are shown in the Window on practice.

WINDOW ON PRACTICE

There are different statistics that can be used for correlation based on the nature of the data, but the results of a correlation are always between 1 and −1 and are expressed as a correlation co-efficient (r).

In our example if the assessment centre ranks perfectly matched the performance ranks, this would mean that Joe who was ranked sixth in the assessment centre would also be ranked sixth for performance, and Penny who was ranked forty-ninth in the assessment centre would also be ranked forty-ninth for performance, and so on for each graduate.

In this case of perfect correlation r = 1. If there were such an assessment tool it would be very popular!

If the relationship was completely random (imagine the scatterplot with dots all over the place and no pattern whatsoever) then r = 0. The assessment tool results do not appear to be able to relate to performance.

Somewhere nearer the middle, which is where most assessment tools are, would be something like r = 0.3 in which case the tool shows some relationship with performance but not a great deal. Occasionally higher associations have been found but they do not generally exceed r = 0.7.

If the relationship between assessment centre ranking and performance ranking produces a negative correlation, for example r = −0.6 then there is some evidence that higher assessment centre scores are related to lower performance scores and vice versa.

The statistic to use here would be a Spearman correlation co-efficient as this is the appropriate one for ranked data.

One of the reasons that the results from selection tools do not appear to be highly related to performance measures may be that the performance measures are not well thought through. They could of course be anything, from scores on performance assessment reports to days of absence, level of promotion, assessment of potential and so on.

When any statistics are presented it is always wise to ask how the measures have been developed, before being impressed by the statistics that are produced.

Treating statistics with caution

We have indicated throughout this section how easy it is to misinterpret statistics and how important it is to question them. So here are a series of questions to ask when presented with statistics:

1. If you are given as statistic which you have not met before, ask 'What can this statistic tell me and what can it not tell?' This should prevent you from making any assumptions.
2. Ask for the number of people that percentages are based on, as percentages can sound impressive, but mean nothing if you do not know the numbers they are representing.

WINDOW ON PRACTICE

One of the authors was listening to student presentations on the psychological contract. One particular group contrasted the psychological contract in two organisations by comparing their answers to a range of questions. They produced wonderful histograms and pie charts and there were some impressive differences in the percentages. The students never mentioned how many responses the percentages were based on. When asked at the end of the presentation it turned out that there were 20 responses from one organisation and six from the other! The students explained that all six were from one department and that had they gone to another department they think the answers to the questions might have been quite different!

3. Also ask how the sample was chosen, as responses from employees in one department do not represent the organisation as a whole. Responses from managers do not represent responses from employees.
4. If you are presented with a measure which is ambiguous, such as 'Performance' ask how that measure has been compiled.
5. Survey results purport to reflect the responses of all members of the organisation, as the survey, for example an employee engagement survey, has been sent to all employees. In this case it is important to ask about response rate. Did all employees reply? If not, what percentage of employees did reply? Also what patterns are there in relation to responses and non-responses?
6. When presented with the results of a questionnaire always ask for a copy of the questionnaire as the way in which questions are asked can prompt different sorts of responses.
7. Ask yourself what further data you require to understand fully the information you are looking at.

ACTIVITY X.3

Have a look at the results of an organisational survey, for example an employee engagement survey or something similar. Go through the above seven questions. Check out your interpretation with someone else, preferably the compiler of the survey.

XI. DESIGNING PROCEDURES

Procedures can be of two types: administrative action or mutual control.

Procedures for administrative action

Procedures get things done. Splendid ideas and bold decisions will be of little value without precise and efficient procedures to translate intention into action. Among the many types of administrative procedure designed by HR people are:

Signing on new employee	Health and safety routines
Terminating an employee's contract	Induction
Filling a vacancy	Authorising expenses
Running appraisal	Pay increases
Running courses	Implementing new legal obligations
Accidents/illness	

There are four main benefits of such procedures. First, they reduce the need for decisions in the future. When the solution to a problem has been worked out once, the procedure provides a model for dealing with the same problem when it recurs. The procedure is a recipe, and the necessary action can be taken more quickly and by more people in an identical way than if it had to be worked out afresh.

Second, procedures produce consistency of action. If things are always done in the same way, those who are involved become practised in their dealings. Retail outlets develop similar procedures for dealing with customers, so that a customer will frequently need to ask only one question: 'Do you serve yourself or does someone serve you?' before being able to move smoothly through the purchasing routine. Employees also become accustomed to procedural drills and are able to work together swiftly and harmoniously as long as methods are unaltered.

Third, procedures provide a form of control for management. Managers know that the system will keep things working correctly and smoothly, so that they can turn their attention to future challenges and current problems without being distracted by constant requests for guidance and information. Whenever there is a man-made disaster, like the abuse and death of a child who should have been cared for, or a train crash, or an industrial accident, the appropriate authorities some time later announce that 'procedures have been reviewed'. It sounds hollow, but is usually the correct response.

Finally, there is the benefit of freedom from supervision. Learner drivers are under constant supervision during their first lesson, but as they learn the procedures of driving, supervision becomes less overbearing. The good administrative procedure gives staff members information and authority, so that they know what to do and how to do it, with scope to interpret the rules in unexpected situations. In this way, the benefits of management control are accompanied by the advantages of individual autonomy.

The biggest problem with procedures is that they are dull, so that few managers like to invest the time needed to get them right. Other problems can be that procedures inhibit change by providing a secure and familiar routine that people are reluctant to abandon. There is sometimes a problem of duplication, where one department has a procedure for its own stage in a process which is repeated by the next department in sequence. In producing a standard way of doing things, procedure may be interpreted as the only way of doing things and bring problems of rigidity. When procedural rigidity confronts managerial enthusiasm or employee discontent, enthusiasm undermines by 'cutting through the red tape' and discontent overcomes rigidity by 'short-circuiting the system'. The procedure will then collapse or become obsolete.

Procedures are developed by applying logic to common sense and understanding. Here is a **checklist** of principles:

1 What are *all* the objectives you want to achieve?

2 Are any of these not really needed because there is already a satisfactory method, or because procedure is not the right answer to the problem?

3 What are the starting and finishing points of the procedure?

4 What are the interim steps to be? They should be:

a as few as possible

b as simple as possible

c clear and logical

d as complete as possible

5 Pilot the procedure in circumstances that are as realistic as possible.

6 Modify the procedure in the light of the pilot. Re-test.

7 Implement and monitor for effectiveness.

A simple way of moving forward from the checklist is the **flowchart**, a method originally developed by Frank Gilbreth in the early twentieth century to represent a process, showing the steps as boxes of various kinds, with their sequence being shown by connecting arrows. This was first used in industrial engineering and later in writing computer programs, but the method is equally valid for working out administrative procedures.

The chart is sketched out using symbols for each part of the process, either a box or an arrow. A box is an event or something being done. Arrows show what is called 'flow of control' in computer science. Figure XI.1 shows a skeleton simplified procedure for buying a house. Most readers will regard this as ridiculously over-simplified, but it is merely to illustrate the method.

This simple sketch is a basis for various developments:

1 Spotting omissions.

2 Working out ways to consolidate or take out steps that are not essential.

3 Identifying activities which are shown as being sequential, but could be carried out in parallel to save time.

4 Reviewing the logic of the flow to find other improvements and begin the process of understanding how the introduction of the procedure can be communicated to those who have to operate it.

Figure XI.2 shows how the procedure might be changed, first by identifying actions that do not have to proceed in sequence, but can be done in parallel. (In HR procedures this is often a great way of expediting progress, which is often missed in procedure development.) Second, the figure also shows two more activities being added.

When the procedure appears to be perfect, you have two more steps to take: writing it out and testing it. You ***write it out*** because it has to be understood, used and believed

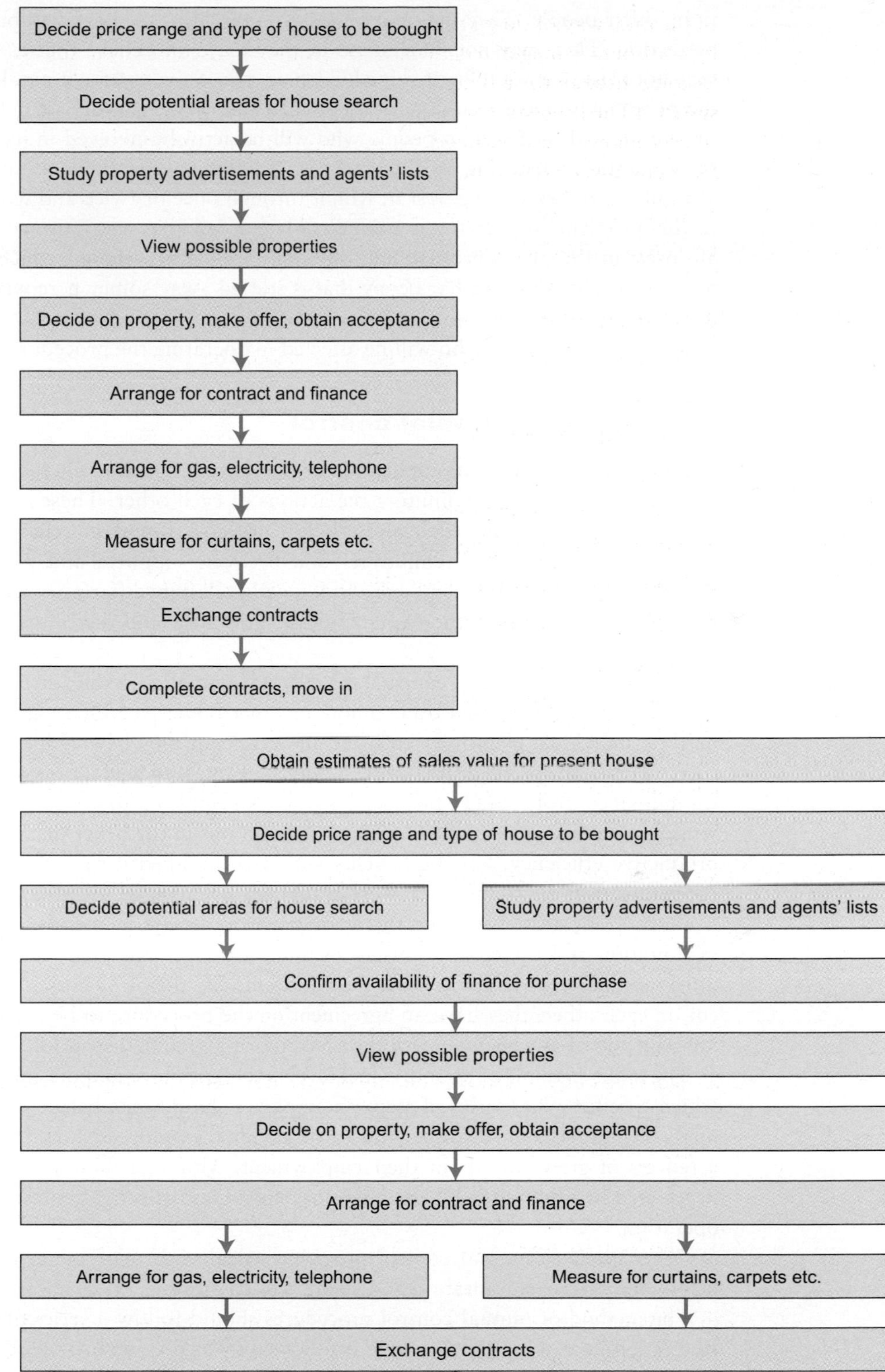

Figure XI.1 Simple procedure for buying house

Figure XI.2 Modified procedure for buying a house

in by other people. They may not be keen on the idea, so flaws will be found in your perfection. They may not understand it, they may not believe that it will work, they may not trust you not to have some hidden agenda. So you write it out, keeping in mind the people who have to use it, as they will either make it work or help it to fail. Go through it with one or two people who will be actively involved in its use, answering their questions, listening to their suggestions and asking them to spot flaws. After re-thinking and re-writing, ***test it***. Run it through once or twice and work on whatever further problems appear. If it is going to fail, let it fail in its test. Turn your write-up into an insert in the procedure manual, especially its online version, which is more likely to be up to date than the hard copy that is stuffed away somewhere with lots of coffee stains on the cover.

Then ***train*** everyone who will be affected in operating the procedure.

Procedures for mutual control

We now look at a different application of the procedural idea, whereby two parties use procedure as a device for limiting the actions of each other. These are most common between employers and trade unions, but are also found in relationships between employers and individual employees and between suppliers and purchasers and in various other ways in which people work together despite differing objectives. The main example in this book is the explanation of grievance and disciplinary procedures in Chapter 22.

Procedures for mutual control are created mainly to avoid disputes between an employer and a recognised trade union, or other bodies representing employees; alternatively individual employees enshrine an agreement they have made about the action each will take in specified situations. A typical example of a situation where a procedure for mutual control could be beneficial is where an employer desires to change an existing working practice. The employer might try to do this in the belief that it would improve productive efficiency, but the benefits would be nullified if the employees refused to cooperate, or if the cooperation were grudgingly given, and only after protracted industrial action. In such a situation the union needs to protect its members against possible exploitation and therefore wants to examine management proposals before they are introduced in order either to resist them or to modify them. As both parties are dependent on each other, they have an agreement on the procedure to be followed before the introduction of any change, with the objective of avoiding disruption.

The main example at an individual level is the grievance and disciplinary procedure, which specifies what series of steps an employer should take before attempting to dismiss an employee, and also specifies how individual employees should set about seeking a redress of grievance about their employment. Although these procedures are often negotiated by union officials, they do not depend on collective representation for their operation.

Other types of mutual control procedures deal with matters such as redundancy, health and safety, consultation and changes to pay rates.

The method of mutual control procedures should follow a series of specified steps: step A is followed by step B, which is followed by step C, and so on. The steps usually involve the matter being considered by a fresh mind at each stage, e.g. supervisor—plant manager—general manager. It is important that the steps are few enough to prevent procrastination, but also sufficient to provide genuinely different opportunities for resolving the difficulty. The method should then link the steps to times, so that each should be completed within a given period. The third general feature of such procedures relates to preserving the status quo. There will usually be a provision stating that no threatened action, like dismissal, lock-out, redundancy or strike, will take place until the procedure is exhausted.

And finally, procedures are the link between *policy* (what we would like to happen) and *practice* (what does happen). Procedure is never a substitute for poor policy and never the right answer for an organisational problem requiring a policy decision.

SUMMARY PROPOSITIONS

XI.1 Administrative procedures (a) reduce the need for decisions in the future, (b) produce consistency of action, (c) provide a form of management control over what is going on, and (d) enable people to work free from close supervision.

XI.2 The main problem is that they are dull.

XI.3 Designing procedures requires (a) objectives, (b) a check that all objectives are needed and do not duplicate pre-existing arrangements, (c) that they have a clear and correct start and finish point, and (d) interim steps that are full, simple, clear and complete.

XI.4 A standard method is to use a flowchart.

XI.5 After working out the flowchart it should be written out as a procedure. This procedure should be used as a basis for consultation (to seek to improve it), for testing and training before implementation.

FURTHER READING

For a general understanding of flowcharting, *see* a sound article in Wikipedia, **www.wikipedia.org**. There is also coverage of an associated method, Critical Path Method, which is useful for finding the most efficient route through a maze of different, interdependent activities.

ACTIVITY XI.1

Use the checklist shown, together with the flowcharting steps, to do one or more of the following:

1 Getting ready to go on holiday.

2 Organising a stag or hen party.

3 Find someone else in your organisation who has to implement a policy decision and work out how you would put appropriate procedures in place. Then compare the other person's procedure plan and compare it with your own.

What have you learned about designing procedures?

XII. DESIGNING QUESTIONNAIRES

In HR questionnaires are used in different ways, perhaps most often being used to test attitudes among employees towards some draft policy initiative, although some organisations use them instead of exit interviews to establish reasons for leaving. Other examples are post-course assessments, views on aspects of current working practice, checking understanding of a new payment scheme, or testing the value of a house newspaper.

It is a method of finding out, but very different from the finding out that is deployed in the selection interview that we have already considered: it is much more like the finding out that is used in application forms. The source of information, however, is not a sole individual where there is the need to shape the enquiry to the respondent as the interview proceeds. The questionnaire is intended to produce aggregate information from a group of people. Precise questions have to be prepared in advance with great care so that all respondents will understand them in the same way and provide an inflexible pattern of focused responses. In other words the questionnaire must be designed to elicit responses that are answers to exactly the question presented and not to a similar but different question that the questionnaire has not asked.

ACTIVITY XII.1

For which of the following would an attitude survey be an appropriate method of finding out the information required:

1 the sales prospects of a new line in cutlery;

2 the most popular dates for a company close-down at Christmas;

3 suggestions for improving company management;

4 the value of team briefing in a company;

5 identifying prospective volunteers for voluntary redundancy?

One of the preconditions for accurate responses is that the respondent should feel confident in the neutrality of the inquiry and in the anonymity of the respondent, so that answers will be truthful and informative, rather than answers that sound right but may be misleading. We discovered one survey in XYZ Ltd, a light engineering company, where every sixth question was, 'Is XYZ a great place to work?', so it was hardly neutral.

Preparing a questionnaire

In deciding what the survey is to discover, we begin by considering what this form of inquiry can discover. There are two basic requirements:

1 Respondents must have sufficient common vocabulary for it to be possible to formulate questions which will have the same meaning to all respondents.

2 The questions must be unambiguous, so that all respondents understand what information is sought.

Careful pilot investigations, development and pre-testing will provide a final schedule of questions that meets these requirements. For the inquiry to be successful the respondents must, therefore, be a population with sufficient in common to fulfil the expectations. Also, the information sought must be of the type that can be reduced to precise units of response to standard questions. Here is a checklist:

1 What will be the reaction of respondents to the subject of the survey? Responses to questions about payment arrangements are likely to be more guarded than responses on the (slightly) less sensitive topic of catering facilities.

2 How can the subject be presented to respondents to achieve a high degree of useful responses? In-company investigations are less likely to have problems with response rate than those conducted among the public at large, as the respondents are almost a captive population, but the requirement of anonymity makes it possible that you will get some blank or spoiled responses if the initial reaction to the survey is not positive. The presentation of the questionnaire needs not only to make clear its subject and purpose, but also to explain what is expected from the respondent and what will be done with the aggregated information being collected.

3 What is the best order in which to introduce topics? The early questions need to be easy for respondents to understand and reply to accurately, as well as getting them 'on the wavelength' of the inquiry before proceeding to more complex questions.

4 What wording of questions will produce precise data? Spend as much time as possible on writing them out, improving them and trying them out on people. Here you need to take into account vocabulary and semantics; you need to use words that are unequivocal, where the meaning is not likely to 'drift' with the respondent. Another consideration is the distinction between questions to obtain facts and questions to seek opinion. There is more on this topic later.

5 How long will the questionnaire take to complete? The need to know has to be balanced with the ability and willingness of the respondent to reply. Some respondents will have difficulty in maintaining concentration and others will have much more to say than the questionnaire provides for. It is not much use if the questionnaire is completed fully only by the conscientious and enthusiastic. Some people will be fed up after 10–15 minutes, others will still be happily answering after 30.

6 What is the best layout of the survey forms? To some extent this depends on the make-up of the respondent population, but the layout must be clear and easy to follow, with a short explanatory introduction answering the questions, What is it for? Why me? Is it in my interests to respond? How long will it take? What do I have to do? Each section of the form needs to have a short introduction indicating what the respondent is to expect, using phrases such as, 'Now we turn to . . . ', 'Now we have a slightly different type of question . . . '.

Types of question

When describing different types of question in our introduction to face-to-face situations, we made a distinction between closed and open-ended questions. There is a similar distinction in a questionnaire. There will be some *closed questions*, which ask for specific, factual information, like length of service. If the need of the questionnaire is for a precise number of years, it is best done with a box in which the four digits of a year can be written, but if a more general distribution will suffice, there could be a set of choices with a box to tick. For example:

How long have you been with the company? Please tick the appropriate box:

Less than one year ....

1–5 years ....

6–10 years ....

More than 10 years ....

The latter question has the advantage of being easier and more anonymous, and it probably gives you the sort of general indication that you need.

Opinion-seeking questions are harder. Face to face you can ask a question like, 'What do you think about . . .', and gradually shape and focus answers to clarify what the person means. In a questionnaire you have only one chance, so one method is the *forced choice* approach, by asking respondents to pick which one of several statements most closely reflects their personal opinion. For example:

1 I understand the new pay arrangements and believe they represent a good way forward.

2 I don't yet fully understand the new pay arrangements, but they seem all right.

3 I don't understand the new pay arrangements and do not see the need to change.

4 I understand the new pay arrangements, but think they need improvement.

5 I understand the new pay arrangements and don't like them at all.

6 I will go along with whatever is suggested.

A different type of forced choice question is where the respondent is asked to rank a series of statements by writing a digit between 1 and 5, 1 and 9 or whatever number of statements is presented, with 1 being closest to the respondent's personal view and so on. There is a need to point out that each digit is used only once.

An alternative type of question is one that asks, 'To what extent do you agree with . . . ?', with a scale of 1–5, 1–7, 1–10, or even 1–3 being provided for the respondent to tick the appropriate box. The end points of such a scale may be labelled 'Disagree completely' or 'Agree completely' or other more appropriate wording.

Some questions may be of the simple Yes or No variety. They are closed because there are only two options, but the options must be precise and clear-cut.

Questions such as these save the respondent from needing to find a suitable form of words to express an opinion and make the process easy. The difficulty is to find a range of statements that reflects reliably the attitudes that are likely to prevail among the people completing the questionnaire. Devising these statements in fact begins the process of classifying the answers.

Another method of seeking opinions is simply to ask respondents to put in writing their opinion on a question, but this is difficult. Some will not have an opinion at all, some will have a vague idea only, some people write clearly and succinctly while others express themselves poorly on paper. Classifying the answers is a nightmare. A modification is to provide after a forced choice question a box in which the respondent may add further comments. By now you have forced a focus on their thinking, so you may get some additional useful ideas – but don't count on it, and don't be seduced into thinking that one interesting statement is representative of all respondents.

Data analysis

When all the forms are complete and gathered together, analysis of the data begins. This is basically counting the numbers in each category in each section and making sense of those numbers. This will first be done by compiling simple totals of answers, e.g. those saying 'Yes' and those saying 'No' or whatever the question asked. There may then be a stage of collating the numbers for different groups and perhaps deploying some of the statistical interpretations, such as moving averages or the standard deviation, described earlier in this skills package. Whatever is done is for the sole purpose of answering the classic question, 'So what?' Analysis is not just for fun, nor to show how clever you are, but to provide a justification for some form of action to be taken, abandoned or changed.

Report writing

Having processed all the numbers, you now need to write a report to show what the facts mean and how they are related. The information has to be understood and then explained in the report by means of a theory which makes sense of the data. The final, and crucial, stage of the report is producing some conclusions about future action which the interpretation of the facts illuminates.

FURTHER READING

Wilson, N. and Maclean, S. (1994) *Questionnaire Design: A Practical Introduction*. Newtonabbey: University of Ulster.

WEB LINKS

Galloway, Alison, *Questionnaire Design and Analysis*, available at **www.tardis.ed.ac.uk**.

Guide to the Design of Questionnaires, available at **http://iss.eeds.ac.uk**.

Questionnaire Design, available at **www.statpac.com/surveys/questionnaire-design**.

XIII. USING CONSULTANTS

Arnold Weinstock was a leading industrialist in the 1980s and is reported to have said:

> Consultants are invariably a waste of money. There has been the occasional instance when a useful idea has come up, but the input we have received has usually been banal and unoriginal, wrapped up in impressive sounding but irrelevant rhetoric. (Caulkin 1997)

The amount of money spent by the UK government and its agencies has recently been increasing at a rapid rate, and this has been widely criticised by political opponents and by media correspondents expressing great scepticism about the value for money that has been achieved. Unflattering views of consultants persist, whether justified or unjustified, but the problem can be as much with those who employ them as with the consultancies themselves. Too often the reason for calling in consultants is inappropriate or not properly thought through. Some of the reasons are these (although they are rarely expressed this way):

> I really don't know how to handle this, so I'll give the job to a consultant.

> We're short-staffed since we had our budget cut, so I'll farm it out.

> This is going to be really unpopular, so I'll bring in consultants; they can take the blame.

> The MD plays golf with X and thinks he would be really useful to us in a consultancy role. I wonder how long it will be before he gets my job.

> I think I will bring in a consultant to do some of this difficult stuff. If they mess things up it will prove that they upstairs should never have introduced this crazy idea in the first place – as I told them.

Consultants can rarely produce useful results if the project is simply parcelled up and given to them to get on with, particularly if it is given to them with the grudging or negative attitude expressed above. They may undertake jobs that others do not have the time or skill to do, but their input must always be monitored closely and built in to the rest of the work that has to be done so that the benefits of their work can be maximised and used in the future, after the consultants have left. We suggest the following approach to using consultants in HR work.

Describe the problem. What is the issue about which you are thinking of obtaining outside assistance? This is not as obvious as it might seem. If, for example, the Marketing Director leaves abruptly, the immediate 'problem' presents itself as being to find a replacement, but worrying away at that issue might suggest that the real problem is to find out why the Marketing Director left so abruptly, especially if the current deputy would not fancy the promotion. You might then re-shape your description of the problem as: 'work out why the position of Marketing Director is untenable'. Be honest. If your motivation is like one of the last three examples quoted above, you are heading for trouble. You must be able to present a consultant with a clear and realistic brief, otherwise you may prove Lord Weinstock right.

Work out how to do it without using consultants. Consultants are expensive and they take time because they have to find out exactly how your business works, the structure, the ethos and the personalities of the key players, as well as its policies and products. Time and expense could both be saved if you could find an easier way of dealing effectively with your problem. Perhaps a recently retired senior executive from the organisation would come and spend a few days wandering round and chatting to people to give you a different perspective on the issue, or to show that you are dead right. Have one or two people to lunch to talk it over: people from your local CIPD branch or from a nearby business school, provided that you know them and have confidence in them. Talk to the Marketing Director's deputy to find out what makes the obvious promotion unattractive. You now already have the answers to the first questions that a consultant would ask and can work out how to tackle the problem without turning to a consultant. If you can convince yourself that it is a sound answer, and if you can sell it to your key colleagues and organisational superiors, then the job is done. If you are unsure, or cannot get backing, then move to the next step.

Approach consultants. Provided that you have identified and understood the problem accurately, and provided that you can describe it clearly to someone who has never been inside your business, then you can brief one or more outside suppliers of expertise and invite them to bid for the business. Don't start until you can pass all the tests in that sentence!

You need to keep control of the project at this stage. Beware of the suggestion that they will come and carry out a preliminary study at your expense before they formulate their approach. Any consultancy will want to work within the framework of their own expertise, but also of their own *experience*. You may not necessarily need some well-practised approach that has worked elsewhere, but in situations that are markedly different from your own. Successful experience elsewhere is invaluable but is limited in value if the organisational context or the business situation is dissimilar. Even large and well-regarded consultancies can be unsuitable. Their breadth of experience in all sorts of different situations may gradually generate an excellent standard product, which they may be reluctant to adapt, or even abandon, if they encounter the unfamiliar.

You have to produce a brief that will be the basis of your dealings with them. You should have the basis after going through the steps suggested above, but the brief needs to be re-worked so as to make unequivocal sense to an outsider and to form a framework from which they cannot deviate.

WINDOW ON DUBIOUS PRACTICE

There is a legend about a very long-established firm of consultants, based in the United States (it will remain anonymous for obvious reasons), that had a practice of responding to a call for help from a company by flying in a team of three to carry out a free preliminary investigation that would take up to five days. The story goes that their mission was to locate a possible crisis in the business and to estimate what the company would be able to pay to solve the problem. The team would then prepare to leave before reporting to the chief executive that the 'real' problem was both different and more serious than they 'had been led to believe'. They would finalise their conversation in one of two ways. If they had decided that the business would be able to pay a significant amount, then they would offer to brief other colleagues about the crisis when they returned who could prepare a fully-costed proposal for the chief executive's consideration. If they had decided that the company was in a bad way, they would simply leave with apologies.

Like all apocryphal stories there is probably a great deal of exaggeration in this legend and the practice is extremely rare nowadays, but it is wise to be wary. One of the people who told a version of how he might have been misled by such a report explained that there had been a problem that the consultants had spotted and that he had missed, but it certainly was not a crisis; he solved it quite easily and quickly, so he had no regrets.

Decide between alternatives. You now have to decide whether to continue with the consultants or to pursue your own rough-cut strategy. If the consultants can produce the most desirable outcome, can you afford it? Have you the resources to implement your own plan? How much time do you have?

Own the solution. If you do decide to continue with the consultants, your objective must be to control the next phase and to follow implementation closely, creating a situation in which local ownership of the solution is achieved as quickly as possible. Only when the new arrangements are working well and owned by your own people will the implantation be complete.

SUMMARY PROPOSITIONS

XIII.1 Using consultants can often fail because there is insufficient clarity in briefing them and a reluctance to work closely with them on the project.

XIII.2 Suggested steps in approaching consultants are (a) describe the problem, (b) work out how to solve the problem without consultants, (c) approach consultants, (d) decide between the alternatives and (e) own the solution.

GENERAL DISCUSSION TOPICS

1 Earlier we quoted, 'This is going to be really unpopular, so I'll bring in consultants; they can take the blame.' Is this a manager avoiding unfairly and unrealistically a proper responsibility,

or is it a sensible way of dealing with a problem on the grounds that management is weakened by making itself unpopular?

2 What aspects of HR work do you think are most suitable for using consultants?

FURTHER READING

Two books of general interest on the subject from a US perspective are:

Lewis, H. (2008) *Choosing and Using Consultants and Advisers*. London: Kogan Page.

Zahn, D. (2004) *The Quintessential Guide to Using Consultants*. New York: HRD Press Inc.

WEB LINKS

Finding and Using Consultants, available at **www.cim.co.uk**.

Using Consultants in Your Business, available at **www.yoursmallbusiness.co.uk**.

REFERENCE

Caulkin, S. (1997) 'The great consultancy cop-out', *Management Today*, February, pp. 32–8.

Part 8 CASE STUDY PROBLEM AND EXERCISES

Refer back to the case study that closed Part 1. You are now six months into the job and things are going well. Charles has now left in order to take a job as a lecturer in a Further Education College in charge of a group of apprentices. Henry is changing his view of women and is now working very well after you had a long discussion with him about his understanding of Catherine's employee-involvement proposals. He is working on a modification to that plan, which he believes will deliver what the members of the board will encourage and of which he thinks he can get shop floor acceptance. He is due to discuss it with you next week. Susan has calmed down and clearly has a lot to offer.

Exercise 1

Time has passed since you wrote your notes on the Part 1 Case Study, it may be days, weeks, months or even years. Review those notes and answer these questions:

(a) How would you change what you wrote then in the light of what you know now?

(b) To what extent are your changes due to external circumstances that you could not then have anticipated, such as economic, legal or social developments?

(c) To what extent are the changes due to changes in the particular situation of the organisation in which you originally located them?

(d) To what extent are they due to what you know now about HRM that you did not know then?

(e) To what extent are they due to you being a different person to what you were then?

Exercise 2

You need to replace Charles.

(a) Referring back to Chapter 8 and to Skill II above, how would you rate, from 1 to 7, the following in their importance in identifying the most appropriate candidate – and why:

Experience	Qualifications	Aptitude testing
Personality testing	Trainability testing	General intelligence testing
Competencies		

(b) Assume you have 50 applications, of which you decide 20 are worth interviewing. What statistical analysis, if any, would you use at any further stage in the selection process?

(c) Who should interview the candidates, and how (e.g. you, Henry and Susan individually; you and a Board member together; you, Henry, Susan and a Board member together; or some other arrangement)?

(d) In the light of your answer to (a) above what other means of assessment would you use when the candidates come for interview, and why?

Exercise 3

Henry was not making his full contribution because of a poor relationship with Catherine, based on his attitude towards working with women. It is now apparent to you that there are other long-serving employees who share this attitude. Referring to Chapters 12, 13, 21 and Skills II and III above, what sort of initiatives will you consider to deal with this problem?

Exercise 4

Surf the Internet for news stories about cases of alleged bullying at work. Which of the methods in Skill IX above would you regard as especially appropriate to forestall such incidents?

Exercise 5

Think of a situation in your experience where a number of people are working together in one place. It might be a workplace where you have been employed, a sports team or a course of which you have been a member, a voluntary body you have joined, or anything similar.

(a) Identify a topic on which you would like to canvas opinion among the people involved, preferably one that is not too simple!

(b) Prepare a questionnaire for use, following recommendations in Skill XII above.

(c) What methods will you use to analyse your data?

EITHER

(d) Explain your answers to questions (a) to (c) above to a small group of friends or fellow students and discuss their criticisms, OR

(e) Test and then administer the questionnaire, analysing the results.

(f) What have you learned from this exercise?

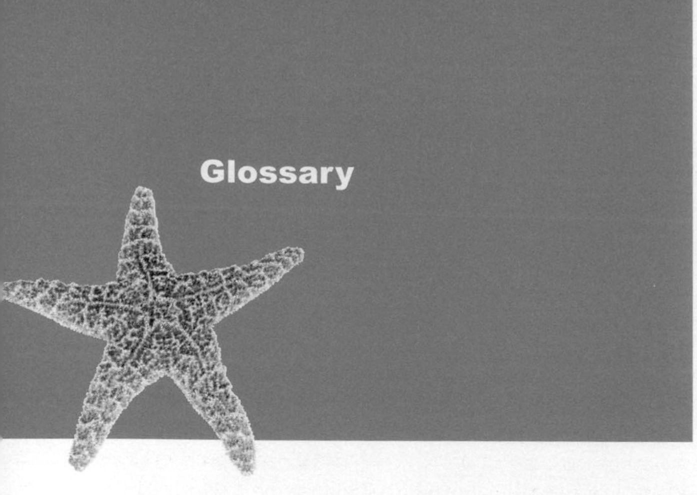

Glossary

The terms in this glossary have been taken selectively from the text. Rather than repeating definitions we have already given, we have chosen terms which are neologisms that may not appear in a dictionary, or are invented words, like outsourcing, which do not yet appear in a dictionary. We also include terms, like bureaucracy, which require more interpretation than we have provided in the text.

Absence/Attendance. Until quite recently attendance at work was universally accepted as a duty and absence had to be justified by external verification, such as by a medical note or a call to undertake jury service. Without such independent evidence, some sort of punishment was usual. As social attitudes have changed and rights to time off have increased, so the managerial emphasis has changed, requiring managers to manage attendance, by paying attention to reasons for avoidable absence. This has a degree of altruistic concern for employee well-being, where some aspect of the work required from employees is a contributory cause of, for instance, an inability to return to work. There is also an emphasis on trying to minimise disruption to working patterns and persuading people not to be unreasonable. Stress has become a major absence factor since it has become more socially acceptable. Usually it is a perfectly valid feature of a person's working or personal life and can perhaps be alleviated by managerial initiatives. In some other situations it is manipulated by people who place their own interpretation on a right to sick leave. A recent visit to an engineering drawing office in March was surprising as more than half the staff were missing. The drawing office manager explained that the absentees were 'getting in their sick leave' before the end of the leave year. A management attempt to make allowance for understandable sickness absence had been mismanaged in allowing it to become gradually accepted as an additional leave entitlement. In a different, current situation a schoolteacher has recently shown such unwillingness to implement new professional requirements that there is a risk of the school implementing capability procedure with the response, 'if they do that I will simply go off with stress'.

Benchmarking. Originally a benchmark was a mark on a work bench that could be used to measure off a standard size. This idea of comparative measurement is used in HRM to describe the process of checking some aspect of work in one's own business against an external standard, like the average number of days lost through absence across the working population as a whole, or in a particular industry, by age, occupation, gender and so forth. It is slightly different from 'yardstick', which is literally a measuring stick a yard long. This is sometimes used as a rough and ready measure for some aspect of management effectiveness, but it lacks the dimension of external comparison.

Best fit/Fit. In many fields of human endeavour there is an aim to find and implement the one best way, or the right way, of doing things. An alternative is to work out the best way of doing things in this or that situation. There is no single approach or method that is always right.

Bottom line. A term derived from accountancy, where it is the final total in a profit and loss statement or other financial document. In management generally it is used as the ultimate criterion or most important factor: financial viability.

Brand. A term taken from marketing to describe a company or product name that is very distinctive and powerful. Examples are Coca-Cola, Microsoft, Rolls-Royce or Virgin. It was illustrated by the retail director of a fashion chain who said, 'If I buy a ready meal from X and I don't like it, I take it back. If I buy it from Marks & Spencer, either I haven't followed the instructions or there is something wrong with my cooker.' To HR people the company brand can be very important in matters of commitment and recruitment.

Bureaucracy. This has become almost a term of abuse, describing rigidity, lack of responsiveness by staff, lack of willingness to take responsibility and too much emphasis on the rules. It is, however, a time-honoured method of making any large organisation work. In contemporary business usage it describes a type of centralised social order that makes things happen by having guidelines of policy, procedure and precedent to empower role holders to do their jobs, conferring appropriate authority for action as well as limiting the scope for individual whim or prejudice. It is therefore both more acceptable and more practical as a method of organisation for any large undertaking than relying on the autocratic alternative of everything being decided by a small number of people at the centre, while everyone else waits and grumbles. Human resource managers are occasionally derided by some of their colleagues in other functions for their apparent preoccupation with the 'rules' of procedure and employment law. These colleagues are, of course, wrong, but bureaucracy has a serious inherent flaw in that it always grows, requiring frequent pruning and review.

Career. The idea of a career involving moving from job to job is relatively recent. For most people a career was an occupation, like nursing or teaching or carpentry or bricklaying. It was only in bureaucracies that people looked for a promotional ladder. In most of the long-standing professions a career was a lifetime of doing the same job, although perhaps introducing a change of emphasis. A clergyman was a clergyman, even though a few might become deans or bishops. A writer was a writer, although there might be moves from writing poetry to writing novels. An architect is an architect, a dentist is a dentist, a driver is a driver. In some areas the idea of moving 'up' has been created artificially by inventing new pay grades and titles. Until the 1970s British nursing had three levels: nurse, sister and matron. In order to provide a career structure, new jobs were introduced: nursing officer, senior nursing officer and principal nursing officer. The flattening of hierarchies is changing the emphasis. There is now a greater number of sideways, cross-functional moves than vertical moves, thus the increasing trend for careers to involve changes in occupation.

Casual work is work where someone is employed on a temporary and probably irregular basis without any obligation on either party to further employment when a spell is complete.

Change/Initiatives are often regarded as invariably desirable, particularly by consultants trying to sell you something. Although constantly advocated in HRM, they have to be balanced against other issues such as stability and security. Furthermore few changes in HR practice can be made quickly and easily. The ideas are usually easy or obvious. Getting them accepted and making them work requires a great deal of hard work, which means that changes have to be worth the trouble and not just some transitory idea that will have been overtaken by something else in six months' time. 'Initiative fatigue' is a term used to describe the experience of some people who have scarcely got used to one new initiative before another is imposed that contradicts the first.

Clocking on (or in) is a term still in common usage, although the practice is not now widespread. In the heyday of large-scale production businesses, manual employees registered their arrival for work by operating an automatic time-recording machine, usually by punching a hole in a personal card. Sometimes they clocked out as well as on. This gave a reliable record of hours worked and enabled pay calculations to be made. Although initially seen as a way to be fair, it eventually became a symbol of close, overbearing control – 'The tyranny of clocking on'. It has become less common although variants are used by, for example, security staff who clock their arrival at various parts of the premises at regular times during the night, or by managers of motorway service stations to demonstrate that they have recently checked the cleanliness of the toilets. A refinement and extension of clocking is the tachograph in road-haulage vehicles.

Coach/Mentor/Protégé. A coach is someone who gives specialised training and guidance as well as general support and encouragement. This may be to an individual, like a tennis player, or to a team, as in cricket. A mentor gives the same sort of service to an individual in what is often a very close personal relationship, requiring from the protégé a high degree of trust in the integrity and goodwill of the mentor. A protégé is someone who is guided by a mentor, acknowledging a need for that person's greater standing and expertise. Tiger Woods is the world's most successful golfer, but still needs a coach: he is not the coach's protégé. One of the most ghastly bits of management jargon is the word 'mentee', presumably invented by someone who could not cope with three syllables, as an alternative to protégé.

Commitment is widely used in contemporary HR to describe the quality of being dedicated to the cause, and various methods are used (*see* Chapter 9, for example) to develop this quality among the members of the workforce in their dedication to the cause of company success. Some may be committed to a career or to the employment security that is associated with the success of the business, while others are committed to the success of their career perhaps at the expense of the business, and others have no commitment at all. In these circumstances the value of the brand may be important.

Competitive advantage. Any business has to be competitive, no matter how much many of its members may not like the idea. A school has to be seen by parents to be at least as good as other schools, otherwise parents will remove their children and the pupils will not have self-respect. Commercial organisations seek competitive advantage for more immediate reasons of survival, but schools, hospitals, charities and churches will all decline and may close if they do not meet the current needs and expectations of their 'clients', although they will quite rightly cavil at the terms 'customers' or 'clients'.

Contingency is a word much used in sociology and organisation theory. Apart from its normal usage of describing a possible future event that cannot be predicted with certainty, in management it is used to differentiate from the absolute. Solutions to problems are seldom invariably right: it depends on the particular circumstances of the event.

Contract/Consideration. In this book the use of material about contract is mainly about legal agreements, although there is also the reference to psychological contracts. The fundamental principle of a legal contract is that there must be consideration. A contract is a spoken or written agreement that is intended to be enforceable at law, but the offer of agreement by one party only becomes legally enforceable when there is consideration from the other party, that is an undertaking of some sort, to do something or to stop doing something or to abandon a claim. An offer of employment, for instance, is not legally binding on the employer making the offer until and unless the prospective employee accepts the offer and agrees to provide the work (consideration) that the employer is offering. This same sense of reciprocity is equally fundamental to the psychological contract: there must be an agreed exchange. Contracting out (from a pension scheme, for instance) involves withdrawing from an agreement and thereby relinquishing the benefits that would otherwise have been received.

Culture/Organisational culture. In management circles interest in culture is an attempt to grasp the realities of collective life in a department or organisation that cannot be easily seen and described with such identifiers as job titles, departments and organisation charts. It is an aspect of the hard/soft distinction. Recently it has been especially important in explaining the differences in management practice in various countries, but organisational culture refers to the beliefs, conventions and general patterns of behaviour that characterise a particular organisation.

Delayering is a method of downsizing that reduces the number of people in a hierarchy by removing a tier in the organisational structure.

Demographics describes statistical data relating to the age and gender structure of the population. This is an important element in understanding the labour market.

Diversity is subtly different from equality and refers principally to the value to management of making the most of employees from two distinct groups, women and those from ethnic minorities, rather than assuming that core employees are white and male. Although these two groups have been the main focus of debate and action, greater attention has recently been paid to other groups, such as those who are potentially discriminated against on the grounds of age or disability.

Downsizing describes an approach to increasing organisational efficiency by reducing the number of people employed in the business and therefore reducing the costs associated with their employment. The main methods are delayering and outplacement/outsourcing.

Employee relations/Industrial relations are not simply different terms for the same activities; they denote a significant change of emphasis. Concern with industrial relations developed when the emphasis was on collective relationships within an industry, such as engineering, agriculture or teaching. Each business within the ambit of that industry observed the terms and conditions agreed between employers' representatives and unions, which bound every employer. Employee relations have little regard for industry criteria and focus on collective arrangements within an individual business.

Employee voice is a term that has only come into use during the twenty-first century, largely as a result of the globalisation issue that was discussed in Chapter 6. At a time when trade union membership is not as widespread in European countries as it was, and is unknown in many other countries, employee voice refers to a wide variety of processes and structures which enable people to contribute to decision making in the place where they work and perhaps to influence decision making in other places that affect the place where they work.

Environment. We typically think nowadays of the physical environment in which we live and the environmental issues that are of concern: pollution, greenhouse gases, GM crops, vulnerable species and so forth. In HRM it is more likely to refer to the social, political and legal environment of the business.

Flexibility is something managers try hard to achieve and trade unions and the legal system try to limit. The flexible workforce makes managerial life easier by giving more scope to managers to manipulate the labour supply, as do flexible hours arrangements. Flexibility agreements with unions reduce rigidity in work practices. All these practices reduce the problems of bureaucracy but the advantages for employees may be more mixed. Flexible hours are probably the most attractive, but there are always disadvantages for employees with flexibility initiatives that at least slightly erode their personal security.

Globalisation/Internationalisation are both terms coined recently to describe two slightly different aspects of modern business. Many companies work internationally, importing materials and resources and exporting products and services. If their business expands they may appoint agents in overseas countries to represent their interests, or they may establish overseas subsidiaries. The company remains, with a distinctive national head office and branding. Globalisation represents a distinctive further step as the company operates major businesses in different countries and regions. Its national identity is submerged beneath its global identity and branding. As these businesses grow larger and therefore more powerful, some commentators and pressure groups grow very concerned that their commercial interests can destabilise and harm the economies of individual countries, especially smaller countries in the developing world.

Grievance/Discipline. Everyone who is employed has a contract in two parts. The first part is the wage/work bargain. One party to the contract pays money and provides benefits to the other party, who provides work in exchange. The second part of the contract is the psychological contract, referred to throughout this book, where what is exchanged between the two parties is a less tangible – but no less important – form of satisfaction. Both parts of the contract are maintained through the mutual satisfaction of the parties. When something happens to reduce the level of satisfaction of either party HRM uses the terms 'grievance' or 'discipline' to describe the processes whereby satisfaction may be restored.

Hard/Soft. Hard data are precise and can be accurately measured by numbers and statistical calculation. Soft data are less precise but may be more important in planning. They include judgement, assessment and informed guesswork.

Hierarchy is the system of organisation which ranks all the people according to their status or authority. This is used for all manner of purposes, ranging from the trivial, like who has the biggest office and who is allowed to travel first class, to the identification of who is empowered to do what, as the hierarchical system includes titles or labels to make sense of the jobs that people do. In Britain the growth of hierarchy received a boost when an early management theorist, E.F.L. Brech, advanced his theory of the span of control, saying that no manager should supervise directly the work of four or five subordinates *whose work interlocks*. Many people accepted the theory but conveniently forgot the last three words.

Human capital. Economists, rather reluctantly, conceded that any economic analysis of an organisation or an economy needed to include the concept of a value or cost assigned to skills, knowledge or experience of the population. It has proved a more acceptable and useful concept than the sterile accountancy technique of human asset accounting. Its main value to HR practitioners is the idea that human capital requires investment.

The Human Relations School. A school of thought that developed in the 1930s as a reaction against the perceived mechanical thinking of Scientific Management. It aimed to develop high productivity by concentrating on the well-being of the individual worker and the surrounding social relationships in the workplace, with an emphasis on adapting the task to the worker rather than adapting the worker to the task.

Marketplace/Labour market. The importance of both these concepts (taken from Economics) in HRM is to emphasise that people management can never be entirely inward in focus. The business has to operate in a context in which there is a market for its products or service, and the business has to survive in that market no matter how inconvenient it may be for the people inside the business. Equally there is an external market for labour and skills, which cannot be ignored. Even employees totally loyal to the business will be aware of prevailing conditions elsewhere, not only how much people are paid but also conditions of work, hours and fringe benefits.

Matrix is a term that has recently come into popular currency because of film and television programmes using it in a very specialised way. In management it has long been used to describe a particular form of organisation in which levels of specialisation, accountability and responsibility are set out in vertical columns crossed by horizontal lines, with points of intersection identifying individual people who have a line of communication in one direction (line management) as well as a distinct accountability to someone else. An office manager, for instance, might be responsible for most things to the immediate superior, but accountable to the HR manager for health and safety issues. 'The line' is often mentioned in this book and refers to the vertical line of accountability.

Meta-analysis is an analysis with combines a number of existing analyses already carried out by others into one summary analysis. 'Meta' is a scientific term indicating a change in condition, such as in metamorphosis. In social sciences it denotes something beyond, of a higher-order kind.

Mission/Aims/Objectives/Targets. These are all terms used quite loosely in management jargon and are in a rough hierarchy from the broad to the specific. Mission comes from religion and is used in a business to describe what the organisation is for, what its purpose is. It is fashionably set out in a mission statement and is typically vague and general, but can be useful in developing commitment. Aims and objectives describe the more specific purposes of individual functions, departments, teams or individuals within the mission framework. Targets are very specific and usually short term as stages on the way for teams and individuals to achieve longer-term objectives.

Occupational health. Many businesses describe their medical departments as 'Occupational Health' departments, regardless of the skills possessed by the people who work in them, but it is worth bearing in mind that occupational medicine is a defined specialism, not general practice in an occupational setting. Both doctors and nurses can acquire qualifications in occupational medicine, but they are most likely to be needed in a business with specific hazards, like radiation or toxic materials.

Organisation. Few words have attracted so much attention in so many different areas of human enquiry, fascinating administrators, anthropologists, archaeologists, biologists, economists, military strategists, political activists and theorists, psychologists, sociologists, trade unionists and many more. This plethora of perspectives can be confusing or even bewildering when trying to define a management perspective that comes within the purview of this book, especially for those whose education has included a thorough grounding in such widely taught subjects as economics, psychology or sociology. Basically our interest in two meanings of the word, organisation as an arena in which human activity takes place (an **entity**) and organisation as a way of getting things done in such an arena (a **process**). To most academics the first is of much greater interest than the second: to most managers the second is of more interest than the first.

HR managers need to understand first the contexts within which their organisation or entity operates. There is the political context which provides a legal and broad administrative framework of benefits and limitations. The social context includes the availability of prospective employees, the educational situation and the prevailing ethical standards that govern attitudes and behaviour. Every organisational entity exists within a market, or series of markets. If there is not sufficient demand for the products and services that are offered, the entity will eventually wither and die. This is not only true of commercial activities. In 1780 Robert Raikes started a Sunday School for the children of chimney sweeps in the appropriately named Sooty Alley in the centre of Gloucester. This was the first time that education of any type apart from the memorising of catechisms had been provided for working class children and adults. Sunday schools spread rapidly, so that four years later there were nearly 2,000 pupils in Manchester and Salford and in Leeds. They continued to flourish for a century until their function was taken over by the secular authorities. Sunday Schools steadily declined as centres for general education until the middle of the twentieth century before they finally relinquished that function.

Organisation behaviour, organisation development, organisational psychology all focus on the micro entity of the individual business or businesses. Organisational psychology, for instance, is a branch of psychology that studies the interaction between working people and their employing organisational entity and the resultant behaviour of those people.

Outplacement/Outsourcing. There is a small difference between these two terms. Outplacement describes taking a complete activity and shifting it to a supplier, while outsourcing describes looking outside the business for human resources.

Peers is an equivocal term in Britain because it has two meanings. One is to describe members of the aristocracy: earls, baronets, dukes, marquesses and viscounts. In this book, and in more general usage, it describes people of the same age, status, ability or qualification as oneself. A peer group is therefore a group of one's equals, not one's superiors.

Performance. Everyone wants effective performance. The individual wants the satisfaction of achievement and results, managers want individuals to be effectively coordinated and productive, customers want a good product and good service at the right price, governments want efficient businesses in a growing economy. Achieving performance is complicated. It is not simply paying people lots of money, although not paying people enough money may well inhibit performance. It is not simply being nice to people and releasing them from supervision, as without supervision they may do the wrong things. Achieving effective performance also varies according to the work done. A symphony orchestra requires members of great expertise at different instruments, yet all must work to an identical score under the strict leadership of the conductor, with very little scope for individual flair. The jazz quartet is more loosely coordinated, with many individual riffs. Those working for a courier firm or in the operating theatre of a hospital can only perform well by following a tight schedule arranged by someone else. Those working in an advertising agency have a much looser rein in order to encourage their creativity.

Portfolio is a collection of items that represent a person's work. Very familiar for people whose work can best be demonstrated by examples, like painters or cartoonists, it is also now much used by all classes of worker to demonstrate their skills and accomplishments, thereby justifying a qualification to practise.

Reactive/Proactive. This distinction is important in HRM because there is a natural emphasis in people matters to await developments and deal with them (reactive). Many HR people report that they spend much of their time putting right problems created by the impetuosity or thoughtlessness of their colleagues in other functions. There is also a need, however, to create opportunities for growth and change and to think ahead of issues so that problems can be averted. A well-rounded HR/personnel function is able to maintain a balance between both types of approach, vigorously and calmly sorting out problems or disasters but also taking matters forward in a creative way when the problems are all under control.

Recruitment/Selection. Recruitment is the process whereby a business seeks applicants either generally or for particular vacancies. Potential applicants are interested but there is no mutual obligation. Selection is the process whereby not only does the employer choose between two or more interested applicants, but applicants also select, deciding how much further they wish to pursue their original enquiry. The end of the process is a legally binding agreement.

Resourcing. This term has only recently come into common usage and means simply providing the needed resources. For HR people this is providing the human resources that are needed, although some pedantic academics (like at least one of your authors) dislike the term 'employee resourcing' as it is the employing organisation that is being provided with resources; not the employees. Also employees are not the only source of human resources for the business. Consultants or subcontractors are alternative sources.

Ritual is a series of actions or a type of behaviour that is invariably followed, in accordance with a convention. Developed originally to help people feel secure in the mysteries of religious practices, rituals are widespread in contemporary society (the ritual of going to the pub on Friday after work, the ritual of the pre-match huddle, the ritual of Prime Minister's Question Time). All provide the benefit of enabling people to feel comfortable and accepted in a social situation, and are therefore important in many employment situations where there is a felt need to conform to existing conventions. The selection interview is the most obvious. Other examples are the 'leaving do', collections before a marriage, negotiations, and the office party.

Scenario. A method of envisaging the future is to bring together various bits of evidence, both hard and soft, and fit them together in a way that describes a reliable version of the future in *X* years' time.

Scientific management. The first modern theory of management, formulated by F.W. Taylor and using the principles of industrial engineering to raise productivity by adapting the worker to the machine or the process. It relied heavily on adjusting the worker's earnings to the level of individual output. The basic ideas remain in place and are at the root of many payment systems, but most management academics and commentators throughout the last three-quarters of the twentieth century disparaged and deplored the 'mechanistic and inhuman' practices spawned by scientific management.

Sex/Gender. The word sex is pretty clear in its meaning as describing either a range of interesting activities, or to describe the biological distinction between male and female. Until recently gender was a grammatical term to distinguish between classes of noun or pronoun in some languages, loosely based on natural distinctions of sex: masculine, feminine or neuter. It is now also used to refer to social and cultural differences between the sexes.

Statutory rights. Rights of the individual citizen or citizens that derive explictly from a statute or Act of Parliament.

Stress presents managers with two problems. An employee may be absent from work suffering from stress, but this is a condition that is easy to fake and not easy to diagnose. How does a manager detect malingering and take appropriate action? More significantly, a manager may exacerbate or cause stress in someone. How can this be avoided and what remedies are available to employees? A further complication is that stress is not necessarily undesirable. Any football fan will suffer periods of intense stress when the wrong team is winning a match, but this only makes sweeter the euphoria when the right team wins. Stress can be stimulating as well as harmful and some jobs are best done and most enjoyed where there is frequent stress followed by achievement (journalists' deadlines and surgical crises being two examples).

Tells. 'I love you' is a statement by one person to another that is normally accompanied by certain actions and behaviours that demonstrate to the recipient how sincere the feeling is. Sometimes, however, we say things that we do not believe, or of which we are unsure. Then the listener may try to guess what we really mean, not just what the words say. We give clues to our uncertainty or our truthfulness by what we do, especially what we cannot help doing. These are tells. Blushing shows we are embarrassed, many people put their hands to their mouths when they feel guilty. HR managers need to learn what tells to look for in situations like selection, where not all candidates are strictly accurate in what they say, or in appraisal, where people may be very guarded in what they say.

Tribunal in this book refers almost exclusively to the three-person panel that makes up the employment tribunal that decides matters of employment law, although it can be any sort of body used to settle disputes. It is not always made up of three people, but it is normal to have an odd number to avoid deadlock.

Unitarist/Pluralist. For HRM these terms come from industrial relations analysis. A unitarist thinker believes that all authority and all responsibility are centred in one place or person, so that senior management can, and must, decide on all key issues, while other people involved simply have to accept the consequences. The pluralist says that is both unacceptable and impractical. Employees have a legitimate interest in the business that cannot be disregarded; the local community is another important stakeholder.

Index